Teacher's Edition

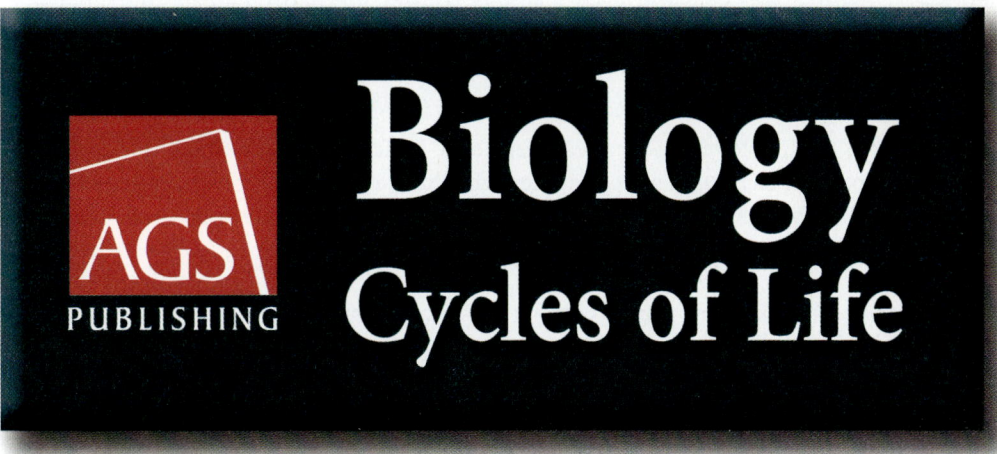

by
Helen M. Parke
and
Patrick Enderle

AGS Publishing
Circle Pines, Minnesota 55014-1796
800-328-2560
www.agsnet.com

About the Authors

Helen M. Parke, Ph.D., is a former secondary and university biology teacher. With 30 years of teaching experience, Dr. Parke has taught science methods courses for undergraduate and graduate level secondary science majors. She has directed centers for science, mathematics, and technology education and is currently Research and Development Manager for Cisco Learning Institute. Dr. Parke designs e-learning professional development for K–12 teachers of mathematics and science.

Patrick Enderle, M.S., received his master's degree in Molecular Biology/Biotechnology from East Carolina University. He has taught biology at the high school, community college, and university levels. He is currently teaching at East Carolina University in Greenville, North Carolina.

Photo credits for this textbook can be found on page 666.

The publisher wishes to thank the following educators for their helpful comments during the review process for *Biology: Cycles of Life.* Their assistance has been invaluable.

Pamela J. Graham, Special Education Teacher/Intervention Specialist, Euclid High School, Euclid, OH; **Debora J. Hartzell,** Lead Teacher for Special Ed, Columbia High School and Lakeside High School, Dekalb County, GA; **Debby Houston,** Research Associate, Florida State University, Tallahassee, FL; **Pamela A. Kazee,** Director, Student Support Services, NE, Clark County School District, Las Vegas, NV; **Denise M. King,** Instructional Coordinator, Leary School of Virginia, Alexandria, VA; **Johnny McCarty,** Special Education Teacher, Science, Flour Bluff High School, Corpus Christi, TX; **Katherine Pasquale,** Euclid High School, Euclid, OH; **Dr. Craig L. Sanders,** Teacher, Richmond Hill High School, East Meadow, NY; **Ann Marie Strozynski,** Director of Secondary Education, Hamtramck, MI; **Susan Sztain;** Teacher, Desert Sands Charter High School, Lanc, CA; **Michelle Villegas,** Biology Teacher, Flour Bluff High School, Corpus Christi, TX

Publisher's Project Staff

Vice President of Curriculum and Publisher: Sari Follansbee, Ed.D.; Director of Curriculum Development: Teri Mathews; Managing Editor: Julie Maas; Editors: Judy Monroe, Jan Jessup; Assistant Editor: Sarah Brandel; Development Assistant: Bev Johnson; Director of Creative Services: Nancy Condon; Senior Designers: Tony Perleberg, Diane McCarty; Production Artist: Mike Vineski; Purchasing Agent: Carol Nelson; Product Manager–Curriculum: Brian Holl

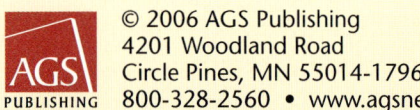

© 2006 AGS Publishing
4201 Woodland Road
Circle Pines, MN 55014-1796
800-328-2560 • www.agsnet.com

All rights reserved, including translation. No part of this publication may be reproduced or transmitted in any form or by any means without written permission from the publisher.

AGS Publishing is a trademark and trade name of American Guidance Service, Inc.

Printed in the United States of America
ISBN 0-7854-3973-0
Product Number 94182
A 0 9 8 7 6 5 4 3 2 1

Contents

Overview

Biology: Cycles of Life Overview T5
AGS Publishing Science Textbooks T6
Skill Track Online T7
Biology: Cycles of Life Student Text Highlights T8
Biology: Cycles of Life Teacher's Edition Highlights T10
Support for Students Learning English T12
Learning Styles T14
Teacher's Resource Library Highlights T15
Synopsis of Scientific Research Base T16
Skills Chart T20
National Science Education Standards Correlation T22

Lesson Plans

How to Use This Book: A Study Guide x
Safety Rules and Symbols xix
Chapter 1 Biology: Investigating the Cycles of Life 1
Chapter 2 Basic Chemistry 30
Chapter 3 Chemistry at the Cellular Level 68
Chapter 4 Cells: The Basic Units of Life 102
Chapter 5 A Journey into the Eukaryotic Cell 132
Chapter 6 ATP and Energy Cycles 168
Chapter 7 Cellular Respiration in Energy Cycles 194
Chapter 8 Photosynthesis in Energy Cycles 222
Chapter 9 The Life Cycles of Cells and Reproduction 246
Chapter 10 Inheritance Patterns in Life Cycles 276
Chapter 11 Genetic Information Cycles 304
Chapter 12 Human Body Systems 342
Chapter 13 Evolution and Natural Selection 386
Chapter 14 Speciation and Punctuated Equilibrium 426
Chapter 15 Phylogenies and Classifying Diversity 456
Chapter 16 Behavioral Biology 504
Chapter 17 Populations and Communities 534
Chapter 18 Ecosystems 564
Chapter 19 Human Impact and Technology 590
Appendix A: The Periodic Table of Elements 618
Appendix B: Body Systems 620
Appendix C: Measurement Conversion Factors 624
Appendix D: Geologic Time Scale 626
Appendix E: World Map 627
Appendix F: Alternative Energy Sources 628
Appendix G: Plant Kingdom 634
Glossary 635
Index 653
Photo and Illustration Credits 666

Contents, continued

Teacher's Resources

Midterm and Final Mastery Tests................................667
Discovery Investigation Answer Key...............................670
Teacher's Resource Library Answer Key............................675
    Workbook Activities..675
    Alternative Workbook Activities.............................684
    Lab Manual...690
    Graphic Organizer..702
    Community Connection.......................................706
    Self-Study Guide...706
    Mastery Tests..706
Scoring Rubic for Chapter Mastery Tests..........................717
Scoring Rubic for Midterm and Final Mastery Tests................719
Materials List for Biology: Cycles of Life Lab Manual............720
Some Suppliers of Science Education Materials....................723

Biology: Cycles of Life

Biology: Cycles of Life is designed to help students and young adults learn about the biological sciences. The textbook discusses cycles of life; basic chemistry; cell growth, development, and reproduction; human body systems; genetics and inheritance patterns; classification and organization; behavioral biology; ecosystems; and more. Written to meet national standards, it offers students who read below grade level the opportunity to sharpen their abilities to interpret data, formulate hypotheses, observe and record information, analyze data, and draw conclusions. Throughout the text, the use of simple sentence structure and assistance with difficult vocabulary work together to enhance comprehension.

Short, concise lessons hold students' interest. Clearly stated objectives presented at the beginning of each lesson focus on what students will learn in the lesson. Illustrations and photos enhance students' understanding of the content. Lesson Reviews and Chapter Reviews include open-ended questions to encourage students to use critical-thinking skills. Express Labs quickly draw students into chapter content. Hands-on Investigations and Biology in Your Life activities lead students to apply the skills they are learning to everyday life. Discovery Investigations encourage higher level thinking as students design parts of an experiment. Full-color photographs and illustrations add interest and appeal as students learn key biology concepts.

Biology: Cycles of Life **T5**

AGS Publishing Science Textbooks

Enhance your science program with AGS Publishing textbooks—an easy, effective way to teach students the practical skills they need. Each AGS Publishing textbook meets your science curriculum needs. These exciting, full-color books use student-friendly text and real-world examples to show students the relevance of science in their daily lives. Each provides comprehensive coverage of skills and concepts. The short, concise lessons will motivate even your most reluctant students. With readabilities of all the texts at or below fourth-grade reading level, your students can concentrate on learning the content. AGS Publishing is committed to making learning accessible to all students.

For more information on AGS Publishing worktexts and textbooks:
call **800-328-2560**, visit our Web site at **www.agsnet.com**,
or e-mail AGS Publishing at **agsmail@agsnet.com**

Skill Track Online

Skill Track Online monitors student progress and helps schools meet the demands of adequate yearly progress (AYP). Students using AGS Publishing curriculum access online multiple-choice assessments to see how well they understand the content of each textbook lesson and chapter. Skill Track Online is a tool available anytime through the Internet. With timely and ongoing feedback from individual student and class reports, teachers can make informed instructional decisions. Administrators can use the reports to support teacher effectiveness and parents can keep up to date on what their students are learning.

Simple to use, Skill Track Online is secure and confidential. Students enter through two paths—lesson by lesson, or at the end of a chapter. Either way, mastery is assessed by a variety of multiple-choice items; parallel forms are available for chapter assessments. Hundreds of items cover the content and skills in each textbook. Students may retake any assessment as often as necessary and scores are reported for each attempt. Accordingly, teachers can identify areas in need of reinforcement and practice for individual learners as well as the class.

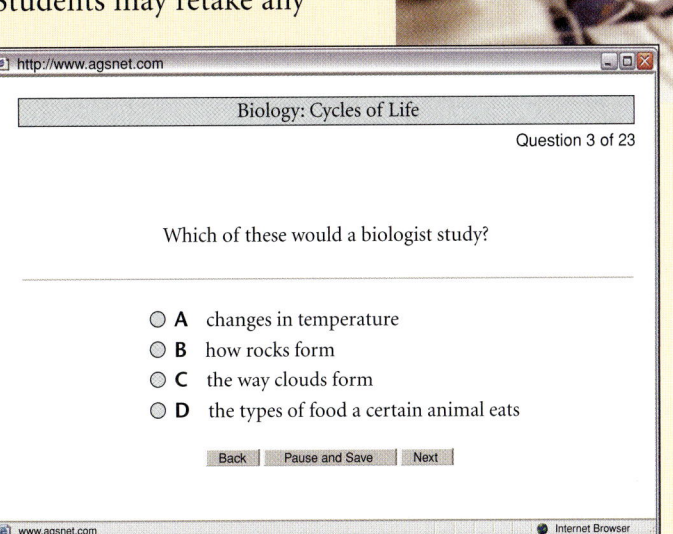

For more information about Skill Track Online:
call 800-328-2560 or visit our Web site at www.agsnet.com/SkillTrack/

Student Text Highlights

◆ Each lesson is clearly labeled to help students focus on the skill or concept to be learned.

◆ Vocabulary terms are bold-faced and then defined in the margin at the top of the page and in the glossary.

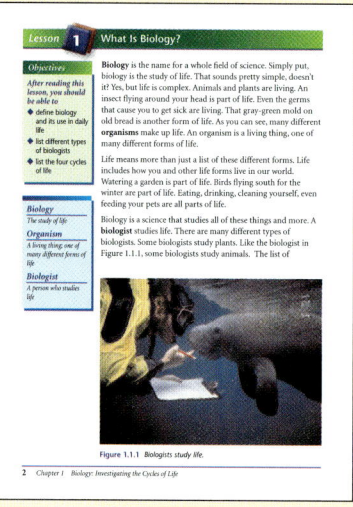

Biology
The study of life

Organism
A living thing; one of many different forms of life

Biologist
A person who studies life

Some brands of toothpaste contain baking soda. This substance neutralizes the acids produced by the bacteria on teeth that cause tooth decay.

◆ Goals for Learning at the beginning of each chapter identify learner outcomes.

Goals for Learning

◆ To understand that biology is the study of life
◆ To describe energy and understand what happens in an energy cycle
◆ To describe what happens in a growth cycle
◆ To explain what happens during an evolutionary cycle
◆ To explain what an ecological cycle is
◆ To tell why scientists use the scientific method

Math Tip

To find the isotope number, add the number of protons and neutrons together. Only the number of neutrons changes between different isotopes.

◆ Many features reinforce and extend student learning beyond the lesson content.

Science Myth

Myth: For best performance, athletes should always have sports drinks during a workout.

Fact: During most exercise, plain water is the best choice to replace lost fluids. Sports drinks may help during long workouts.

Link to Health

The cells in the human body require a large amount of water to stay healthy. Drinks containing alcohol or caffeine cause the body to dehydrate. Alcohol and caffeine block the body cells from reabsorbing water.

Technology and Society

Engineers use the power of enzymes to clean up polluted soils and streams. They create huge containers of enzymes called bioreactors. These bioreactors are specially mixed to clean up the chemicals in a polluted area. The chemicals are then added to the bioreactor and digested by the enzymes. This process models the way enzymes in your body digest food.

◆ Technology and Society helps students make connections between biology and technology and society.

Achievements in Science

Discovering Photosynthesis

In 1771, English chemist Joseph Priestley was the first scientist to study photosynthesis. Priestley burned a candle in a sealed, glass jar until the candle went out. He opened the jar, put in a small plant, and sealed the jar again. After several days, he lit a candle in the jar. The candle burned. Priestley thought the plant had released a substance that supported burning.

That substance was oxygen. In 1779, Dutch physician Jan Ingenhousz showed that a plant produces oxygen only when exposed to light. Experiments in the early 1800s by Nicholas de Saussure from France showed that plants absorb carbon dioxide from the air. By the mid-1800s, scientists had learned that plants store light energy from the sun as chemical energy.

◆ Achievements in Science offers information about historic science-related events, achievements, or discoveries.

BIOLOGY IN THE WORLD

Worldwide Photosynthesis

Where do you think most of the world's photosynthesis takes place? You may think it occurs in tropical rain forests. Or maybe you think it occurs in the vast evergreen forests in northern regions. These would be good guesses, but they are not correct. Most photosynthesis occurs in the oceans.

The upper layers of the oceans are home to microscopic organisms called plankton. Some plankton, such as bacteria and algae, carry out photosynthesis. These plankton are called phytoplankton. Although tiny, phytoplankton are very important. Phytoplankton performs more than 40 percent of the photosynthesis that takes place on the earth. They provide food, directly or indirectly, for all other marine animals.

Like plants on land, phytoplankton use carbon dioxide and release oxygen. Carbon dioxide and oxygen are reused in global cycles. Each cycle involves many living things, including humans. For example, the burning of coal, oil, and gasoline releases carbon dioxide. About one-half of this human-produced carbon dioxide goes into the atmosphere.

Scientists do not know how much of the remaining carbon dioxide is taken up by phytoplankton. They are not sure how much carbon dioxide is dissolved in ocean water. They also do not know how much of the earth's oxygen is produced by phytoplankton. Scientists who study the oceans have found that global changes in temperature influence phytoplankton growth. Many scientists think the world is becoming warmer. This could increase the numbers of phytoplankton.

1. Where does most of the earth's photosynthesis take place?
2. Why do phytoplankton live in the upper layers of the ocean?
3. How do phytoplankton affect the amount of oxygen on the earth?

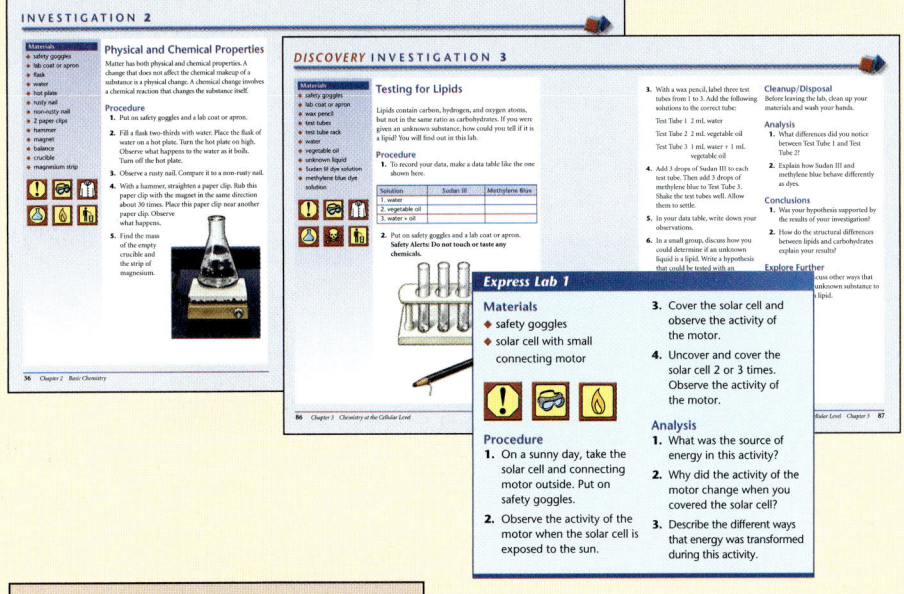
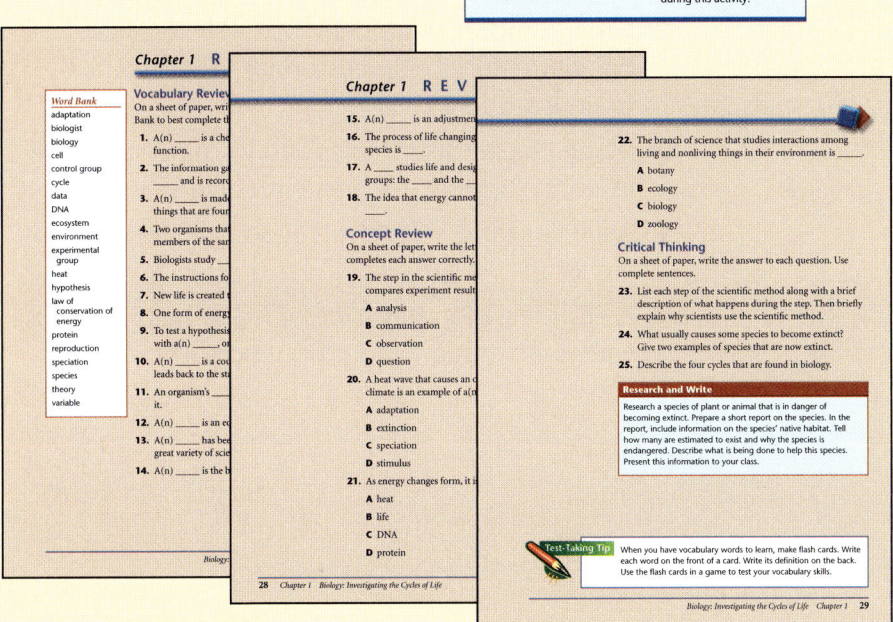

- **Biology in Your Life** helps students relate chapter content to everyday life.

- **Science at Work** provides examples of some science careers.

- **Investigation and Discovery Investigation** activities give students hands-on practice with chapter concepts. Students use critical-thinking skills to complete each investigation. Discovery Investigations are less-structured activities that encourage more student involvement.

- **Lesson Review** questions allow students to check their understanding of key concepts presented in the text.

- **Summaries** at the end of each chapter highlight main ideas for students.

- **Chapter Reviews** allow students and teachers to check for skill mastery. These cover the objectives in the Goals for Learning at the beginning of each chapter.

- **Test-Taking Tips** at the end of each Chapter Review help reduce test anxiety and improve test scores.

Biology: Cycles of Life **T9**

Teacher's Edition Highlights

The comprehensive, wraparound Teacher's Edition provides instructional strategies at point of use. Everything from preparation guidelines to teaching tips and strategies are included in an easy-to-use format. Activities are featured at point of use for teacher convenience.

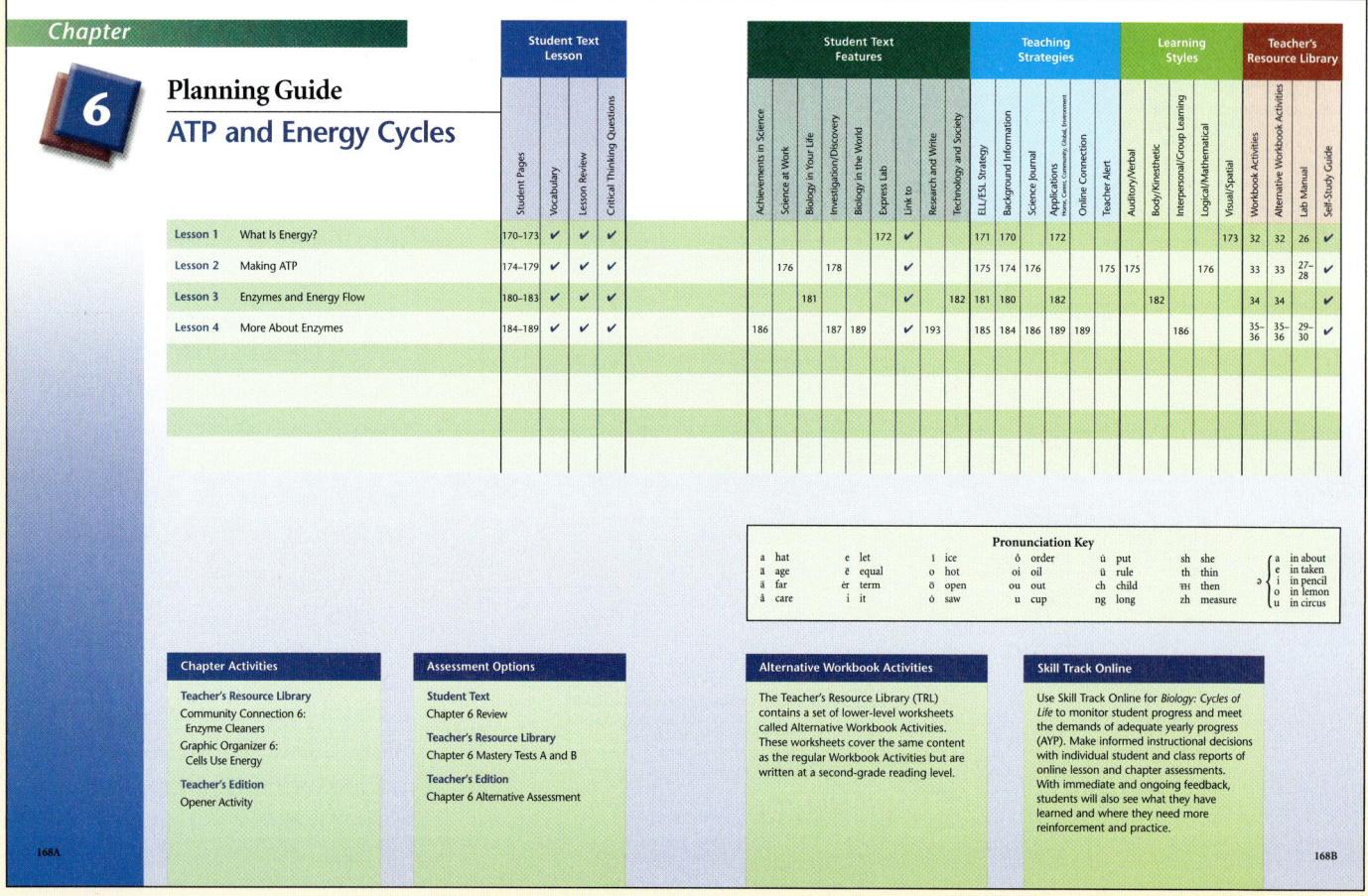

Chapter Planning Guides

- The Planning Guide saves valuable preparation time by organizing all materials for each chapter.
- A complete listing of lessons allows you to preview each chapter quickly.
- Assessment options are highlighted for easy reference. Options include:
    - Lesson Reviews
    - Chapter Reviews
    - Chapter Mastery Tests, Forms A and B
    - Alternative Assessment
    - Midterm and Final Tests
- Page numbers of Student Text and Teacher's Edition features help customize lesson plans to your students.
- Many teaching strategies and learning styles are listed to support students with diverse needs.
- Activities for the Teacher's Resource Library are listed.
- A Pronunciation Key is provided to help teachers work with students to pronounce difficult words correctly.

T10 Biology: Cycles of Life

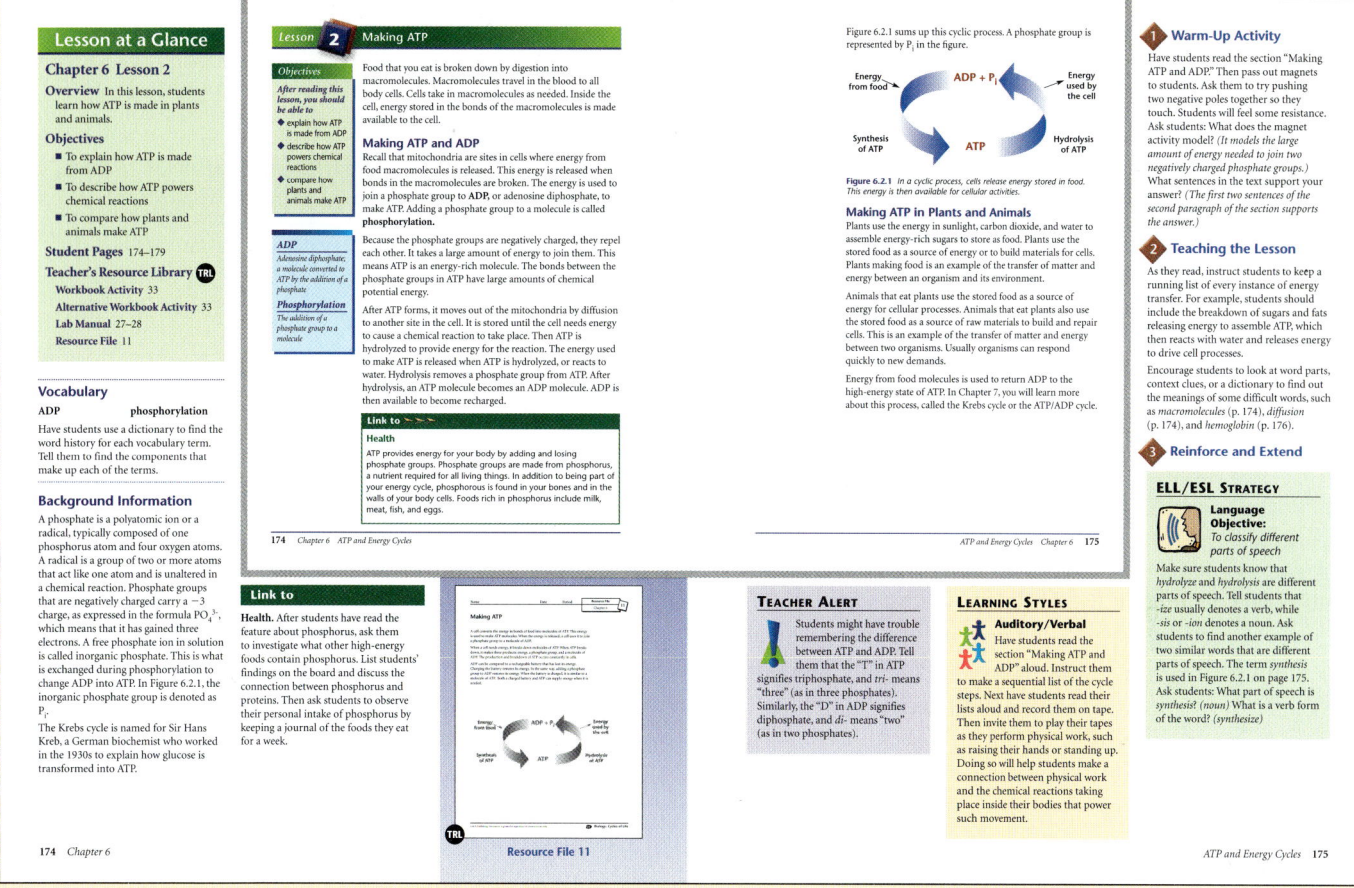

Lessons

- Quick overviews of chapters and lessons save planning time.
- Lesson objectives are listed for easy reference.
- Page references are provided for convenience.
- Easy-to-follow lesson plans in three steps save time: Warm-Up Activity, Teaching the Lesson, and Reinforce and Extend.
- Teacher Alerts highlight content that may need further explanation.
- Science Journal activities give students an opportunity to write about science.
- Applications: Five areas of application—At Home, Career Connection, Global Connection, In the Community, and In the Environment—help students relate science to the world outside the classroom. Applications motivate students and make learning relevant.
- A Portfolio Assessment, which appears at the end of each lesson, lists items the student has completed for that lesson.
- Online Connections list relevant Web sites.
- Learning Styles provide teaching strategies to help meet the needs of students with diverse ways of learning. Modalities include Auditory/Verbal, Visual/Spatial, Body/Kinesthetic, Logical/Mathematical, and Interpersonal/Group Learning. Additional teaching activities are provided for ELL students.
- Answers are provided in the Teacher's Edition for all reviews in the Student Text. Answers to the Teacher's Resource Library, Student Workbook, and Lab Manual are provided at the back of this Teacher's Edition and on the TRL CD-ROM.
- Worksheet, Workbook, Lab Manual, and Test pages from the Teacher's Resource Library are shown at point of use in reduced form.

Biology: Cycles of Life **T11**

Support for Students Learning English

Increasing numbers of students learning English are among the students in most schools and classrooms. The purpose of the ELL/ESL Strategy feature in this Teacher's Edition is to incorporate the language and content needs of English Language Learners in a regular and explicit manner.

ELL/ESL Strategy activities promote English language acquisition in the context of content area learning. Students should not be separated or isolated for these activities and interaction with English-speaking peers is always encouraged.

The ELL/ESL Strategy helps the teacher scaffold the content and presentation in relation to students' language and skill proficiency. Each activity suggests to the teacher some ideas about how to adjust the presentation of content to meet the varying needs of diverse learners, including students learning English. *Scaffolding* refers to structuring the introduction of vocabulary, concepts, and skills by providing additional supports or modifications based on students' needs. Ideally, these supports become less necessary as students' language proficiency increases and their knowledge and skill level becomes more developed.

ELL/ESL Strategy

Language Objective: *To summarize vocabulary terms in this lesson*

Have students learning English make a graphic organizer that summarizes the information presented about the four macromolecules on pages 72–73. Students may want to make a chart, a concept map, or a word web. After students have completed their graphic organizer, have them review the organizer orally, filling in any definitions of terms used in the organizer that they can.

Each activity includes a language objective and strategy related to *listening, speaking, reading,* or *writing.* The language objective and activity relate to one or more content objectives listed in the Teacher's Edition under Lesson at a Glance. Some examples of language objectives include: reading for meaning, understanding different styles or purposes of writing, identifying and practicing common grammar structures, learning vocabulary specific to the content area, preparing and giving a group presentation, speaking in front of a group, or discussing an assigned topic as a small group.

Strategies That Support English Learners

- Identify and build on prior knowledge or experience; start with what's familiar and elaborate to include new content and new connections, personal associations, cultural context
- Use visuals and graphic organizers—illustrations, photos, charts, posters, graphs, maps, tables, webs, flow charts, timelines, diagrams
- Use hands-on artifacts (realia) or manipulatives
- Provide *comprehensible input*—paraphrase content, give additional examples, elaborate on student background knowledge and responses; be aware of rate of speech, syntax, and language structure and adjust accordingly
- Begin with lower-level, fact recall questions and move to questions that require higher-order critical-thinking skills (application, hypothesis, prediction, analysis, synthesis, evaluation)
- Teach vocabulary—pronunciations, key words or phrases, multiple meanings, idioms/expressions, academic or content language
- Have students create word banks or word walls for content (academic) vocabulary
- Teach and model specific reading and writing strategies—advance organizers, main idea, meaning from context, preview, predict, make inferences, summarize, guided reading
- Support communication with gestures and body language
- Teach and practice functional language skills—negotiate meaning, ask for clarification, confirm information, argue persuasively
- Teach and practice study skills—structured note-taking, outlining, use of reference materials
- Use cooperative learning, peer tutoring, or other small group learning strategies
- Plan opportunities for student interaction—create a skit and act it out, drama, role play, storytelling
- Practice self-monitoring and self-evaluation—students reflect on their own comprehension or activity with self-checks

How Do AGS Publishing Textbooks Support Students Learning English?

AGS Publishing is committed to helping all students succeed. For this reason, AGS Publishing textbooks and teaching materials incorporate research-based design elements and instructional methodologies configured to allow diverse students greater access to subject area content. Content access is facilitated by controlled reading level, coherent text, and vocabulary development. Effective instructional design is accomplished by applying research to lesson construction, learning activities, and assessments.

AGS Publishing materials feature key elements that support the needs of students learning English in sheltered and immersion settings.

Key Elements	AGS Publishing Features
Lesson Preparation	◆ Content- and language-specific objectives
Building Background	◆ Warm-Up Activity ◆ Explicit vocabulary instruction and practice with multiple exposures to new words ◆ Background information; building on prior knowledge and experience
Comprehensible Input	◆ Controlled reading level in student text (Grades 3–4) ◆ Highlighted vocabulary terms with definitions ◆ Student glossary with pronunciations ◆ Clean graphic and visual support ◆ Content links to examples ◆ Sidebar notes to highlight and clarify content ◆ Audio text recordings (selected titles) ◆ Alternative Activity pages (Grade 2 reading level)
Lesson Delivery	◆ Teaching the Lesson/3-Step Teaching Plan ◆ Short, skill- or content-specific lessons ◆ Orderly presentation of content with structural cues
Strategies	◆ ELL/ESL Strategy activities ◆ Learning Styles activities ◆ Writing prompts in student text ◆ Teaching Strategies Transparencies provide additional graphic organizers ◆ Study skills: Self-Study Guides, Chapter Outlines
Interaction	◆ Vocabulary-building activities ◆ Language-based ELL/ESL Strategy activities ◆ Learning Styles activities ◆ Reinforce and Extend activities
Practice/Application	◆ Skill practice or concept application in student text ◆ Reinforce and Extend activities ◆ Career, home, and community applications ◆ Student Workbook ◆ Multiple TRL activity pages
Review and Assessment	◆ Lesson reviews, chapter reviews, unit reviews ◆ Skill Track monitors student progress ◆ Chapter, Unit, Midterm, and Final Mastery Tests

For more information on these key elements, see Echevarria, J., Vogt, M., & Short, D. (2004). *Making content comprehensible for English language learners: The SIOP model* (2nd ed.). Boston, MA: Allyn & Bacon.

Learning Styles

Differentiated instruction allows teachers to address the needs of diverse learners and the variety of ways students process and learn information. The Learning Styles activities in this Teacher's Edition provide additional teaching strategies to help students understand lesson content by teaching or expanding upon the content in a different way. The activities are designed to help teachers capitalize on students' individual strengths and learning styles.

The Learning Styles activities highlight individual learning styles and are classified based on Howard Gardner's theory of multiple intelligences: Auditory/Verbal, Body/Kinesthetic, Interpersonal/Group Learning, Logical/Mathematical, and Visual/Spatial. In addition, the various writing activities suggested in the Student Text are appropriate for students who fit Gardner's description of Verbal/Linguistic intelligence.

Following are examples of activities featured in the *Biology: Cycles of Life* Teacher's Edition:

Body/Kinesthetic
Students learn from activities that include physical movement, manipulatives, or other tactile experiences.

> **LEARNING STYLES**
>
>  **Body/Kinesthetic**
> Have students act out the reaction to the following stimuli: someone tickles your nose with a feather; you accidentally touch a hot object; a mouse sees a cat; and a pet sees its food being prepared. Ask volunteers to supply additional reactions and stimuli.

Auditory/Verbal
Students learn by listening to text read aloud or from an audiorecording, and from other listening or speaking activities. Musical activities related to the content may help auditory learners.

> **LEARNING STYLES**
>
> **Auditory/Verbal**
> Have students work in small groups to write lyrics about the Calvin-Benson cycle, using the tune of a familiar song. Be sure students include descriptions of the four main steps of the Calvin-Benson cycle. Students may wish to use tunes from current popular music or from an old folk song such as *She'll Be Coming Around the Mountain*.

Interpersonal/Group Learning
Students learn from working with at least one other person or in a cooperative learning group on activities that involve a process and an end product.

> **LEARNING STYLES**
>
>  **Interpersonal/Group Learning**
> Have students work in small groups to make models of the DNA molecule. Provide students with scissors, glue, and different colored sheets of construction paper. Before students begin, decide which colors will represent each of the four different bases. Display the completed models around the classroom.

Logical/Mathematical
Students learn by using logical/mathematical thinking and problem solving in relation to the lesson content.

> **LEARNING STYLES**
>
>  **Logical/Mathematical**
> As students are introduced to more complex chemical formulas involving radicals and subscripts, they may be more likely to mistake the number of atoms in these compounds. Instruct students to create tables like Tables 2.3.3 and 2.3.4 if they get confused. For practice, write the following formulas on the board:
>
> $C_6H_{12}O_6$ (glucose: 6 carbon atoms, 12 hydrogen atoms, 6 oxygen atoms)
>
> $Fe_3(PO_4)_2$ (iron phosphate: 3 iron atoms, 2 potassium atoms, 8 oxygen atoms)

Visual/Spatial
Students learn by viewing or creating illustrations, graphics, patterns, or additional visual demonstrations beyond what is in the text.

> **LEARNING STYLES**
>
>  **Visual/Spatial**
> Have students make a poster that depicts different examples of foods that contain saturated fats and unsaturated fats. Students can cut out photographs from magazines, use labels from foods, or make their own drawings of the foods. Encourage students to be creative but accurate in their presentation of the material.

Synopsis of the Scientific Research Base, continued

Instructional Design: Lesson Structure and Learner Support Strategies

Research-Based Principles

Instruction that includes the components of effective instruction, utilizes effective strategies and interventions to facilitate student learning, and aligns with standards improves learning for all students, especially diverse learners and students who are struggling.

Elements of effective instruction:

Step 1: Introduce the lesson and prepare students to learn
Step 2: Provide instruction and guided practice
Step 3: Provide opportunities for applied practice and generalization

Organizational tools:
Advance organizers
Graphic organizers

Instructional process techniques:
Cooperative learning
Student self-monitoring and questioning
Real-life examples
Mnemonics

AGS Publishing Textbooks

Step 1: Introduce the lesson and prepare students to learn

In the Student Edition:
◆ "How to Use This Book" feature explicitly teaches text organization
◆ Chapter and lesson previews with graphic and visual organizers
◆ Goals for Learning
◆ Sidebar notes review skills and important facts and information

In the Teacher's Edition:
◆ Lesson objectives
◆ Explicit *3-Step Teaching Plan* begins with "Warm-Up Activity" to inform students of objectives, connect to previous learning and background knowledge, review skills, and motivate students to engage in learning

Step 2: Provide instruction and guided practice

In the Student Edition:
◆ Short, manageable lessons break content and skills into smaller, step-by-step, part-by-part pieces
◆ Systematic presentation of lesson concepts and skills
◆ Chapter and lesson headings presented as questions or statements
◆ Graphic organizers arrange content visually—charts, graphs, tables, diagrams, bulleted lists, arrows, graphics, mnemonics, illustrations, and captions
◆ Models or examples link directly to the explanation of the concept
◆ Multiple opportunities for direct practice throughout

In the Teacher's Edition:
◆ *3-Step Teaching Plan* for each lesson includes "Teaching the Lesson" with direct instruction, and helps teachers present and clarify lesson skills and concepts through guided practice and modeling of important ideas
◆ Supplemental strategies and activities, including hands-on modeling, transparencies, graphic organizers, visual aids, learning styles

Step 3: Provide opportunities for applied practice and generalization

In the Student Edition:
◆ Each skill or concept lesson is followed by direct practice or review questions
◆ Multiple exercises throughout
◆ Generalization and application activities in sidebars and lessons link content to real-life applications
◆ Chapter reviews and summaries highlight major points

References

Allsopp, D. H. (1990). Using modeling, manipulatives, and mnemonics with eighth-grade math students. *Teaching Exceptional Children, 31*(2), 74–81.

Chambliss, M. J. (1994). Evaluating the quality of textbooks for diverse learners. *Remedial and Special Education, 15*(5), 348–362.

Ciborowski, J. (1992). *Textbooks and the students who can't read them: A guide to teaching content*. Cambridge, MA: Brookline.

Cole, R. W. (Ed.). (1995). *Educating everybody's children: Diverse teaching strategies for diverse learners*. Alexandria, VA: Association for Supervision and Curriculum Development.

Curtis, M. E. (2002, May 20). Adolescent reading: A synthesis of research. Paper presented at the Practice Models for Adolescent Literacy Success Conference, U.S. Department of Education. Washington, DC: National Institute of Child Health and Human Development. Retrieved September 15, 2003, from http://216.26.160.105/conf/nichd/synthesis.asp

Dickson, S. V., Simmons, D. C., & Kameenui, E. J. (1995). *Text organization: Curricular and instructional implications for diverse learners* (Technical Report No. 18). National Center to Improve the Tools of Educators. Eugene, OR: University of Oregon. Retrieved January 26, 2000, from http://idea.uoregon.edu/~ncite/documents/techrep/tech18.html

Dixon, R. C., Carnine, D. W., Lee, D., Wallin, J., & Chard, D. (1998). *Review of high quality experimental mathematics research: Report to the California State Board of Education*. Sacramento, CA: California State Board of Education.

Jarrett, D. (1999). *The inclusive classroom: Mathematics and science instruction for students with learning disabilities—It's just good teaching*. Portland, OR: Northwest Regional Educational Laboratory.

Johnson, D. W., Johnson, R. T., & Stanne, M. B. (2000, May). *Cooperative learning methods: A meta-analysis*. Minneapolis: The Cooperative Learning Center, University of Minnesota. Retrieved October 29, 2003, from http://www.co-operation.org/pages/cl-methods.html

Kameenui, E. J., & Simmons, D. C. (1990). *Designing instructional strategies*. Columbus, OH: Merrill Publishing Company.

Lovitt, T. C., & Horton, S. V. (1994). Strategies for adapting science textbooks for youth with learning disabilities. *Remedial and Special Education, 15*(2), 105–116.

Marzano, R. J. (1998). *A theory-based meta-analysis of research on instruction*. Aurora, CO: Mid-Continent Research for Education and Learning. Retrieved October 1, 2003, from http://www.mcrel.org/topics/productDetail/asp?productID=83

Marzano, R. J., Pickering, D. J., & Pollock, J. E. (2001). *Classroom instruction that works: Research-based strategies for increasing student achievement*. Alexandria, VA: Association for Supervision and Curriculum Development.

Miller, S. P., & Mercer, C. D. (1993). Mnemonics: Enhancing the math performance of students with learning difficulties. *Intervention in School and Clinic, 29*(2), 78–82.

Montague, M. (1997). Cognitive strategy instruction in mathematics for students with learning disabilities. *Journal of Learning Disabilities, 30*(2), 164–177.

Reiser, R. A., & Dick, W. (1996). *Instructional planning: A guide for teachers* (2nd ed.). Boston: Allyn and Bacon.

Roderick, M., & Camburn, E. (1999). Risk and recovery from course failure in the early years of high school. *American Educational Research Journal, 36*(2), 303–343.

Steele, M. (2002). Strategies for helping students who have learning disabilities in mathematics. *Mathematics Teaching in the Middle School, 8*(3), 140–143.

Swanson, H. L. (2000). What instruction works for students with learning disabilities? Summarizing the results from a meta-analysis of intervention studies. In R. Gersten, E. P. Schiller, & S. Vaughn (Eds.), *Contemporary special education research: Syntheses of the knowledge base on critical instructional issues* (pp. 1–30). Mahwah, NJ: Lawrence Erlbaum Associates, Inc.

Tyree, R. B., Fiore, T. A., & Cook, R. A. (1994). Instructional materials for diverse learners: Features and considerations for textbook design. *Remedial and Special Education, 15*(6), 363–377.

Vaughn, S., Gersten, R., & Chard, D. J. (2000). The underlying message in LD intervention research: Findings from research syntheses. *Exceptional Children, 67*(1), 99–114.

Teacher's Resource Library Highlights

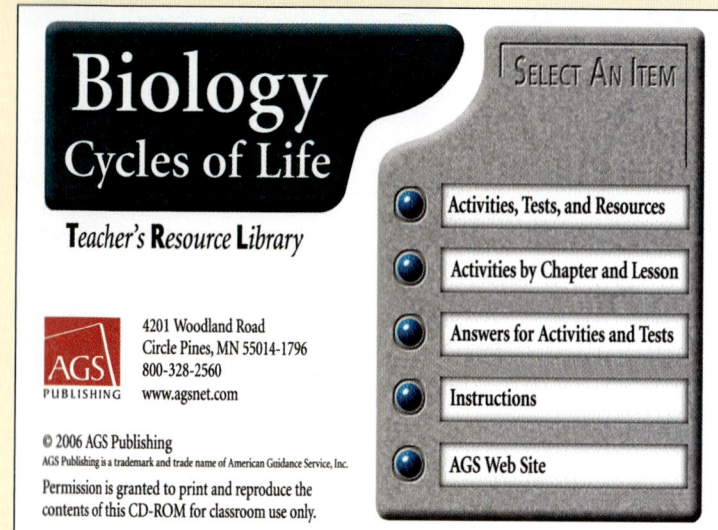

TRL All of the activities you'll need to reinforce and extend the text are conveniently located on the AGS Publishing Teacher's Resource Library (TRL) CD-ROM. All of the reproducible activities pictured in the Teacher's Edition are ready to select, view, and print. You can also preview other materials by linking directly to the AGS Publishing Web site.

Workbook Activities
Workbook Activities are available to reinforce and extend skills from each lesson of the textbook. A bound workbook format is also available.

Alternative Activities
These activities cover the same content as the Workbook Activities but are written at a second-grade reading level.

Lab Manual
These activities build critical-thinking and teamwork skills. A bound format is also available.

Community Connection
Relevant activities help students extend their knowledge to the real world and reinforce concepts covered in class.

Graphic Organizer
These activities help students organize information about important chapter concepts.

Resource File
These reference sheets with lesson content are tools for student study as well as teaching aids.

Self-Study Guide
An assignment guide provides teachers with the flexibility for individualized instruction or independent study.

Mastery Tests
Chapter, Midterm, and Final Mastery Tests are convenient assessment options. Critical-thinking items are included.

Answer Key
All answers to reproducible activities are included in the TRL and in the Teacher's Edition.

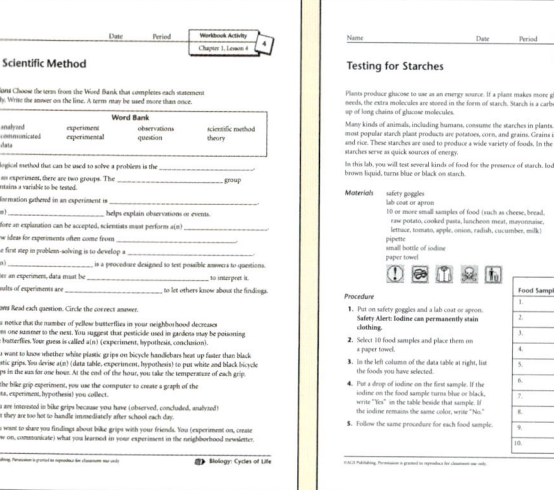

Workbook Activities   **Lab Manual**

Community Connections   **Mastery Tests**

Synopsis of the Scientific Research Base

Research-Based Principles	AGS Publishing Textbooks	References
Standards Alignment Subject area instruction needs to be based on skills, concepts, and processes represented by common standards for that subject area.	◆ Textbook content and skills aligned with national standards and state grade-level or course-specific content standards, where available	Matlock, L., Fielder, K., & Walsh, D. (2001). Building the foundation for standards-based instruction for all students. *Teaching Exceptional Children, 33*(5), 68–72. Miller, S. P., & Mercer, C. D. (1997). Educational aspects of mathematics disabilities. *Journal of Learning Disabilities, 30*(1), 47–56. Reys, R., Reys, B., Lapan, R., Holliday, G. & Wasman, D. (2003). Assessing the impact of standards-based middle grades mathematics curriculum materials on student achievement. *Journal of Research in Mathematics Education, 34*(1), 74–95.
Readability Many students struggle to learn from core content-area textbooks that are written too high above their reading level. Students need access to textbooks written at a level they can read and understand, where the reading level is within the students' range of comprehension.	◆ Grade 4.0 or lower readability using the Spache formula ◆ Controlled vocabulary matched to student reading ability and use of synonyms to replace non-essential difficult words above grade 4 ◆ Simple sentence structures ◆ Limited sentence length	Allington, R. L. (2002). You can't learn much from books you can't read. *Educational Leadership, 60*(3), 16–19. Chall, J. S., & Conard, S. S. (1991). *Should textbooks challenge students? The case for easier or harder textbooks.* New York: Teachers College Press. *Readability calculations.* (2000). Dallas: Micro Power & Light Company.
Language Complexity and Sequence Students struggling with vocabulary and text comprehension need textbooks with accessible language.	◆ Simple, direct language using an active voice ◆ Clear organization to facilitate understanding ◆ Explicit language signals to show sequence of and links between concepts and ideas	Anderson, T. H., & Armbruster, B. B. (1984). Readable texts, or selecting a textbook is not like buying a pair of shoes. In R. C. Anderson, J. Osborne, & R. J. Tierney (Eds.), *Learning to read in American schools* (pp. 151–162). Hillsdale, NJ: Lawrence Erlbaum Associates, Inc. Curtis, M. E. (2002, May 20). *Adolescent reading: A synthesis of research.* Paper presented at the Practice Models for Adolescent Literacy Success Conference, U.S. Department of Education. Washington, DC: National Institute of Child Health and Human Development. Retrieved September 15, 2003, from http://216.26.160.105/conf/nichd/synthesis.asp McAlpine, L., & Weston, C. (1994). The attributes of instructional materials. *Performance Improvement Quarterly, 7*(1), 19–30. Seidenberg, P. L. (1989). Relating text-processing research to reading and writing instruction for learning disabled students. *Learning Disabilities Focus, 5*(1), 4–12.
Vocabulary Use and Development Students need content-related vocabulary instruction in the context of readable and meaningful text.	◆ New vocabulary boldfaced on first occurrence, used in context, and defined in a sidebar ◆ Glossary with pronunciation, definition, and relevant graphic illustrations for all vocabulary words ◆ Direct vocabulary instruction introduced in the Teacher's Edition and reinforced in context throughout ◆ Multiple exposures to new vocabulary in text and practice exercises	Ciborowski, J. (1992). *Textbooks and the students who can't read them: A guide to teaching content.* Cambridge, MA: Brookline. Kameenui, E. J., & Simmons, D. C. (1990). *Designing instructional strategies.* Columbus, OH: Merrill Publishing Company. Marzano, R. J. (1998). *A theory-based meta-analysis of research on instruction.* Aurora, CO: Mid-Continent Research for Education and Learning. Retrieved October 1, 2003, from http://www.mcrel.org/topics/productDetail/asp?productID=83 McAlpine, L., & Weston, C. (1994). The attributes of instructional materials. *Performance Improvement Quarterly, 7*(1), 19–30. National Reading Panel. (2000). *Teaching children to read: An evidence-based assessment of the scientific research literature on reading and its implications for reading instruction.* Reports of the subgroups. Washington, DC: National Institute of Child Health and Human Development. Taylor, S. E., Frackenpohl, H., White, C. E., Nieroroda, B. W., Browning, C. L., & Birsner, E. P. (1989). *EDL core vocabularies in reading, mathematics, science, and social studies.* Austin, TX: Steck-Vaughn.

Research-Based Principles	AGS Publishing Textbooks	References
Text Organization: Presentation and Structure Students need an uncluttered page layout, with easy-to-read print, that clearly directs the reader to main ideas, important information, examples, and comprehensive practice and review. Reading comprehension is improved by structural features in the text that make it easier for learners to access the content.	*Print characteristics and page layout:* ◆ Serif font for body copy; sans serif font for boxed features, examples ◆ Maximum line length of 5" for ease of reading ◆ Unjustified (ragged) right margins ◆ Major/minor column page design presents primary instructional information in the major column and support content in the sidebar or in a box *Presentation characteristics:* ◆ Lesson introductions, summaries ◆ Explicit lesson titles, headings, and subheadings label and organize main ideas ◆ Signals alert readers to important information, content connections, illustrations, graphics ◆ Cues (e.g., boldface type) highlight important information *Text structure:* ◆ Lesson heads in question or statement format guide comprehension ◆ Text written to explicitly link facts and concepts within and across lessons; text cohesiveness ◆ Each skill or concept linked to direct practice and review	Armbruster, B. B., & Anderson, T. H. (1988). On selecting "considerate" content area textbooks. *Remedial and Special Education, 9*(1), 47–52. Beck, I. L., McKeown, M. G., & Grommoll, E. W. (1989). Learning from social studies texts. *Cognition and Instruction, 6*(2), 99–158. Chambliss, M. J. (1994). Evaluating the quality of textbooks for diverse learners. *Remedial and Special Education, 15*(5), 348–362. Ciborowski, J. (1992). *Textbooks and the students who can't read them: A guide to teaching content.* Cambridge, MA: Brookline. Dickson, S. V., Simmons, D. C., & Kameenui, E. J. (1995). *Text organization and its relation to reading comprehension: A synthesis of the research* (Technical Report No. 17) and *Text organization: Curricular and instructional implications for diverse learners* (Technical Report No. 18). National Center to Improve the Tools of Educators. Eugene, OR: University of Oregon. Retrieved January 26, 2000, from http://idea.uoregon.edu/~ncite/documents/techrep/tech17.html and http://idea.uoregon.edu/~ncite/documents/techrep/tech18.html Dickson, S. V., Simmons, D. C., & Kameenui, E. J. (1998). Text organization: Research bases and Text organization: Instructional curricular basics and implications. In D. C. Simmons & E. J. Kameenui (Eds.), *What reading research tells us about children with diverse learning needs: Bases and basics* (pp. 239–278; 279–294). Mahwah, NJ: Lawrence Erlbaum Associates, Inc. Mansfield, J. S., Legge, G. E., & Bane, M. C. (1996). Psychophysics of reading. XV: Font effects in normal and low vision. *Investigative Ophthalmology and Vision Science, 37*, 1492–1501. McAlpine, L., & Weston, C. (1994). The attributes of instructional materials. *Performance Improvement Quarterly, 7*(1), 19–30. McNamara, D. S., Kintsche, E., Songer, N. B., & Kintsche, W. (1996). good texts always better? Interactions of text coherence, background knowledge, and levels of understanding in learning from text. *Cognition and Instruction, 14*(1), 1–43. Tyree, R. B., Fiore, T. A., & Cook, R. A. (1994). Instructional mat diverse learners: Features and considerations for textbook de *Remedial and Special Education, 15*(6), 363–377.
Differentiated Instruction and Learning Styles Student learning is more successful when tasks are aligned with academic skill levels and developmental stage, and adjustments are made to allow students multiple means to engage and express their learning strengths and styles at appropriate levels of challenge and support. Differentiated instruction allows teachers to organize instruction to adjust for diverse learning needs within a classroom. Learning activities that capitalize on students' learning styles can structure planning for individual differences based on multiple intelligences theory.	◆ Multiple features, including Learning Styles activities, help teachers match assignments to students' abilities and interests ◆ Variety of media to select from—print, audio, visual, software ◆ Step-by-step, part-by-part basic content and skill-level lessons in the Student and Teacher's Editions ◆ Alternative Activities written at a Grade 2 (Spache) readability in the Teacher's Resource Library ◆ Variety of review materials, activities, sidebars, and alternative readings ◆ Multiple assessments—lesson or chapter reviews, end-of-chapter tests, cumulative midterm/final mastery tests, alternative assessment items *Learning Styles activities include:* ◆ Auditory/Verbal ◆ Body/Kinesthetic ◆ Interpersonal/Group Learning ◆ Logical/Mathematical ◆ Visual/Spatial *ELL/ESL Strategies provide support for students who are learning English and lesson content concurrently.*	Allington, R. L. (2002). You can't learn much from books you *Educational Leadership, 60*(3), 16–19. Carnine, D. (1994). Introduction to the mini-series: Diverse l and prevailing, emerging, and research-based educational and their tools. *School Research Review, 23*(3), 341–350. Forsten, C., Grant, J., & Hollas, B. (2003). *Differentiating text Strategies to improve student comprehension and motivatic* Peterborough, NH: Crystal Springs Books. Gardner, H. (1983). *Frames of mind: The theory of multiple i* New York: Harper and Row. Gersten, R., & Baker, S. (2000). The professional knowledge instructional practices that support cognitive growth for language learners. In R. Gersten, E. P. Schiller, & S. Vaugh *Contemporary special education research: Syntheses of the base on critical instructional issues* (pp. 31–80). Mahwa Lawrence Erlbaum Associates, Inc. Hall, T. (2002, June). *Effective classroom practices report: D instruction.* Wakefield, NJ: National Center on Accessi Curriculum. Retrieved September 29, 2003, from http org/cac/indexn.cfm?i=2876 Lazear, D. (1999). *Eight ways of knowing: Teaching for m intelligences* (3rd ed.). Arlington Heights, IL: Skylight Publishing. Orlich, D. C., Harder, R. J., Callahan, R. C., & Gibson, *Teaching strategies: A guide to better instruction* (6th e Houghton Mifflin Company. Roderick, M. & Camburn, E. (1999). Risk and recover failure in the early years of high school. *American E Research Journal, 36*(2), 303–343. Tomlinson, C. A. (1999). *The differentiated classroom: needs of all learners.* Alexandria, VA: Association fo Curriculum Development.

Research-Based Principles	AGS Publishing Textbooks	References

Instructional Design: Lesson Structure and Learner Support Strategies, *continued from previous page*

In the Teacher's Edition:
- *3-Step Teaching Lesson Plan* concludes with "Reinforce and Extend" to reinforce, reteach, and extend lesson skills and concepts
- Unit or chapter projects link and apply unit or chapter concepts
- Multiple supplemental/alternative activities for individual and group learning and problem solving
- Career, home, and community application exercises

In the Teacher's Resource Library:
- Multiple exercises in Student Workbook and reproducibles offer applications, content extensions, additional practice, and alternative activities at a lower (Grade 2 Spache) readability

Skill Track Online:
- Monitors student learning and guides teacher feedback to student

Ongoing Assessment and Tracking Student Progress

Textbooks can incorporate features to facilitate and support assessment of learning, allowing teachers to monitor student progress and provide information on mastery level and the need for instructional changes.

Assessment should measure student progress on learning goals over the course of a lesson, chapter, or content-area textbook.

Students and teachers need timely and ongoing feedback so instruction can focus on specific skill development.

- Test-taking tips and strategies for students who benefit from explicit strategy instruction
- Lesson and chapter reviews check student understanding of content
- Workbook and reproducible lesson activities (Teacher's Resource Library) offer additional monitoring of student progress
- Discussion questions allow teachers to monitor student progress toward lesson objectives
- Self-Study Guides (Teacher's Resource Library) allow teacher and student to track individual assignments and progress
- Chapter assessment activities and curriculum-based assessment items correlate to chapter Goals for Learning:
  - Chapter reviews
  - End-of-chapter tests
  - Cumulative Midterm and final mastery tests
  - Alternative chapter assessments
  - Skill Track Online assesses and tracks individual student performance by lesson and chapter

Deshler, D. D., Ellis, E. S., & Lenz, B. K. (1996). *Teaching adolescents with learning disabilities: Strategies and methods* (2nd ed.). Denver, CO: Love Publishing Company.

Jarrett, D. (1999). *The inclusive classroom: Mathematics and science instruction for students with learning disabilities—It's just good teaching.* Portland, OR: Northwest Regional Educational Laboratory.

Reiser, R. A., & Dick, W. (1996). *Instructional planning: A guide for teachers* (2nd ed.). Boston: Allyn and Bacon.

Tyree, R. B., Fiore, T. A., & Cook, R. A. (1994). Instructional materials for diverse learners: Features and considerations for textbook design. *Remedial and Special Education, 15*(6), 363–377.

For more information on the scientific research base for AGS Publishing Textbooks, please go to www.agsnet.com or call Customer Service at 800-328-2560 to request a research report.

Biology: Cycles of Life

Biology: Cycles of Life Skills Chart

Science Content	1	2	3	4	5	6	7	8	9	10	11	12	13	14	15	16	17	18	19
Behavior of Organisms								✓				✓	✓			✓	✓		
Biological Evolution	✓				✓				✓	✓	✓		✓	✓	✓	✓			
The Cell	✓	✓	✓	✓	✓	✓	✓	✓	✓	✓	✓	✓			✓				
Diversity and Adaptations of Organisms	✓	✓											✓	✓	✓	✓	✓	✓	✓
Ecosystems	✓																✓	✓	✓
Energy Cycles	✓	✓															✓		
History and Nature of Science	✓	✓	✓	✓	✓	✓	✓	✓	✓	✓	✓	✓	✓	✓	✓	✓	✓	✓	✓
Human Biology									✓	✓	✓								
Inquiry and Investigation	✓	✓	✓	✓	✓	✓	✓	✓	✓	✓	✓	✓	✓	✓	✓	✓	✓	✓	✓
Interdependence of Organisms	✓	✓	✓			✓	✓							✓		✓	✓	✓	✓
Matter, Energy, and Organization of Living Systems	✓	✓	✓		✓	✓	✓					✓			✓		✓	✓	
Molecular Basis of Heredity			✓		✓	✓			✓		✓	✓		✓		✓			
Population	✓															✓	✓	✓	✓
Reproduction and Heredity									✓	✓	✓					✓			
Science and Technology	✓	✓	✓	✓	✓	✓	✓	✓	✓	✓	✓	✓	✓	✓	✓	✓	✓	✓	✓
Science in Personal and Social Perspectives	✓	✓	✓	✓	✓	✓	✓	✓	✓	✓	✓	✓	✓	✓	✓	✓	✓	✓	✓

Process Skills	1	2	3	4	5	6	7	8	9	10	11	12	13	14	15	16	17	18	19
Communicating	✓	✓	✓	✓	✓	✓	✓	✓	✓	✓	✓	✓	✓	✓	✓	✓	✓	✓	✓
Collecting Information	✓	✓	✓	✓	✓	✓	✓	✓	✓	✓	✓	✓	✓	✓	✓	✓	✓	✓	✓
Creating Charts, Graphs, Tables, or Diagrams	✓	✓	✓	✓	✓	✓	✓	✓	✓	✓	✓	✓	✓	✓	✓	✓	✓	✓	✓
Describing	✓	✓	✓	✓	✓	✓	✓	✓	✓	✓	✓	✓	✓	✓	✓	✓	✓	✓	✓
Designing Experiments	✓	✓	✓	✓	✓	✓	✓	✓	✓	✓	✓	✓	✓	✓	✓	✓	✓	✓	✓
Following Written Directions	✓	✓	✓	✓	✓	✓	✓	✓	✓	✓	✓	✓	✓	✓	✓	✓	✓	✓	✓
Formulating a Hypothesis	✓	✓	✓	✓	✓	✓	✓	✓	✓	✓	✓	✓	✓	✓	✓	✓	✓	✓	✓
Indentifying and/or Controlling Variables	✓	✓	✓	✓	✓	✓	✓	✓	✓	✓	✓	✓	✓	✓	✓	✓	✓	✓	✓
Making and/or Using Models									✓	✓	✓	✓		✓			✓		
Measuring	✓	✓	✓	✓		✓	✓	✓	✓		✓	✓		✓	✓				✓
Observing	✓	✓	✓	✓	✓	✓	✓	✓	✓	✓	✓	✓	✓	✓	✓	✓	✓	✓	✓
Performing Experiments	✓	✓	✓	✓	✓	✓	✓	✓	✓	✓	✓	✓	✓	✓	✓	✓	✓	✓	✓

CHAPTER

Process Skills, continued	1	2	3	4	5	6	7	8	9	10	11	12	13	14	15	16	17	18	19
Recording Data	✓	✓	✓	✓	✓	✓	✓	✓	✓	✓	✓	✓	✓	✓	✓	✓	✓	✓	✓
Researching and Writing About Science	✓	✓	✓	✓	✓	✓	✓	✓	✓	✓	✓	✓	✓	✓	✓	✓	✓	✓	✓
Using Science Lab Equipment	✓	✓	✓	✓	✓	✓	✓	✓	✓	✓	✓	✓	✓	✓	✓	✓	✓	✓	✓

Thinking Skills	1	2	3	4	5	6	7	8	9	10	11	12	13	14	15	16	17	18	19
Analyzing Data	✓	✓	✓	✓	✓	✓	✓	✓	✓	✓	✓	✓	✓	✓	✓	✓	✓	✓	✓
Applying Information	✓	✓	✓	✓	✓	✓	✓	✓	✓	✓	✓	✓	✓	✓	✓	✓	✓	✓	✓
Classifying and Categorizing	✓	✓	✓	✓	✓	✓	✓	✓	✓	✓	✓	✓	✓	✓	✓	✓	✓	✓	✓
Comparing and Contrasting	✓	✓	✓	✓	✓	✓	✓	✓	✓	✓	✓	✓	✓	✓	✓	✓	✓	✓	✓
Drawing Conclusions	✓	✓	✓	✓	✓	✓	✓	✓	✓	✓	✓	✓	✓	✓	✓	✓	✓	✓	✓
Explaining Ideas and Concepts	✓	✓	✓	✓	✓	✓	✓	✓	✓	✓	✓	✓	✓	✓	✓	✓	✓	✓	✓
Formulating Questions	✓	✓	✓	✓	✓	✓	✓	✓	✓	✓	✓	✓	✓	✓	✓	✓	✓	✓	✓
Identifying and Solving Problems	✓	✓	✓	✓	✓	✓	✓	✓	✓	✓	✓	✓	✓	✓	✓	✓	✓	✓	✓
Identifying Similarities and Differences	✓	✓	✓	✓	✓	✓	✓	✓	✓	✓	✓	✓	✓	✓	✓	✓	✓	✓	✓
Interpreting Data	✓	✓	✓	✓	✓	✓	✓	✓	✓	✓	✓	✓	✓	✓	✓	✓	✓	✓	✓
Interpreting Visuals	✓	✓	✓	✓	✓	✓	✓	✓	✓	✓	✓	✓	✓	✓	✓	✓	✓	✓	✓
Learning Science Vocabulary	✓	✓	✓	✓	✓	✓	✓	✓	✓	✓	✓	✓	✓	✓	✓	✓	✓	✓	✓
Making Decisions	✓	✓	✓	✓	✓	✓	✓	✓	✓	✓	✓	✓	✓	✓	✓	✓	✓	✓	✓
Making Inferences	✓	✓	✓	✓	✓	✓	✓	✓	✓	✓	✓	✓	✓	✓	✓	✓	✓	✓	✓
Organizing Information	✓	✓	✓	✓	✓	✓	✓	✓	✓	✓	✓	✓	✓	✓	✓	✓	✓	✓	✓
Predicting Outcomes	✓	✓	✓	✓	✓	✓	✓	✓	✓	✓	✓	✓	✓	✓	✓	✓	✓	✓	✓
Recalling Facts	✓	✓	✓	✓	✓	✓	✓	✓	✓	✓	✓	✓	✓	✓	✓	✓	✓	✓	✓
Recognizing Cause and Effect	✓	✓	✓	✓	✓	✓	✓	✓	✓	✓	✓	✓	✓	✓	✓	✓	✓	✓	✓
Recognizing Main Ideas	✓	✓	✓	✓	✓	✓	✓	✓	✓	✓	✓	✓	✓	✓	✓	✓	✓	✓	✓
Recognizing Patterns	✓	✓	✓	✓	✓	✓	✓	✓	✓	✓	✓	✓	✓	✓	✓	✓	✓	✓	✓
Recognizing Relationships	✓	✓	✓	✓	✓	✓	✓	✓	✓	✓	✓	✓	✓	✓	✓	✓	✓	✓	✓
Understanding Concepts	✓	✓	✓	✓	✓	✓	✓	✓	✓	✓	✓	✓	✓	✓	✓	✓	✓	✓	✓

Biology: Cycles of Life

National Science Education Standards Correlation

STANDARD A Science as Inquiry

As a result of activities in grades 9–12, all students should develop:

Biology: Cycles of Life

- Abilities necessary to do scientific inquiry

  Page xiii; Pages xix–xxi; **Ch. 1:** Pages 15–16, 17–27; **Ch. 2:** Pages 33, 36–37, 40, 57–58; **Ch. 3:** Pages 74, 75–76, 86–87; **Ch. 4:** Pages 106–107, 109–110, 121–122, 128; **Ch. 5:** Pages 135, 157–158, 161–162; **Ch. 6:** Pages 172, 178–179, 187–188; **Ch. 7:** Pages 198, 206–207, 212–213; **Ch. 8:** Pages 226, 228–229, 236–237; **Ch. 9:** Pages 250, 254–255, 269–270; **Ch. 10:** Pages 283, 290–291, 297–298; **Ch. 11:** Pages 308, 314–315, 330–331; **Ch. 12:** Pages 346, 357–358, 379–380; **Ch. 13:** Pages 393, 402–403, 407, 414–415; **Ch. 14:** Pages 433, 438–439, 445–446; **Ch. 15:** Pages 460, 462–463, 495–496; **Ch. 16:** Pages 509, 511–512, 527–528; **Ch. 17:** Pages 544, 546–547, 553–554; **Ch. 18:** Pages 570, 571–572, 578–579; **Ch. 19:** Pages 597, 599–600, 607–610, 611–612, 614; Pages 624–625

- Understandings about scientific inquiry

  Pages xii–xiii; Pages xix–xxi; **Ch. 1:** Pages 7, 15–16, 17–27; **Ch. 2:** Pages 33, 36–37, 40, 41, 57–58; **Ch. 3:** Pages 74, 75–76, 81, 86–87; **Ch. 4:** Pages 106–107, 109–110, 115, 121–122, 125, 128; **Ch. 5:** Pages 135, 143, 151, 157–158, 161–162; **Ch. 6:** Pages 172, 178–179, 182, 187–188; **Ch. 7:** Pages 198, 206–207, 208, 212–213; **Ch. 8:** Pages 226, 228–229, 231, 236–237; **Ch. 9:** Pages 250, 253, 254–255, 269–270; **Ch. 10:** Pages 283, 287, 290–291, 297–298; **Ch. 11:** Pages 308, 314–315, 328, 330–331; **Ch. 12:** Pages 346, 357–358, 370, 379–380; **Ch. 13:** Pages 393, 402–403, 404, 407, 414–415; **Ch. 14:** Pages 433, 437, 438–439, 445–446; **Ch. 15:** Pages 460, 462–463, 484, 495–496; **Ch. 16:** Pages 509, 511–512, 522, 527–528; **Ch. 17:** Pages 538, 544, 546–547, 553–554; **Ch. 18:** Pages 570, 571–572, 578–579, 581; **Ch. 19:** Pages 597, 599–600, 607–610, 611–612, 614

STANDARD C Life Science

As a result of activities in grades 9–12, all students should develop an understanding of:

Biology: Cycles of Life

- The Cell

  Ch. 1: Pages 7–9; **Ch. 2:** Pages 32–33; **Ch. 3:** Pages 70–79, 82, 84–96, 98; **Ch. 4:** Pages 102–131; **Ch. 5:** Pages 132–167; **Ch. 6:** Pages 168–177, 180–188, 190–193; **Ch. 7:** Pages 194–209, 211, 214–221; **Ch. 8:** Pages 222–229, 231–245; **Ch. 9:** Pages 246–265, 267, 271–275; **Ch. 10:** Pages 279, 284, 286, 288, 291–294, 299–300; **Ch. 11:** Pages 306, 312, 316–336, 338–341; **Ch. 12:** Pages 344–345, 350, 353–356, 364, 367, 370, 372–378, 381–383; **Ch. 15:** Pages 457 461, 464–468, 472–474, 478, 479–481, 487, 500

- Molecular basis of heredity

  Ch. 3: Pages 94–96, 98–99; **Ch. 5:** Pages 142–145; **Ch. 6:** Page 170; **Ch. 9:** Pages 247–251, 254–259, 269–272; **Ch. 10:** Pages 276–303; **Ch. 11:** Pages 304–341; **Ch. 13:** Pages 402, 404–405, 416, 422; **Ch. 16:** Page 507

- Biological evolution

  Ch. 1: Pages 10–11; **Ch. 5:** Pages 142–145; **Ch. 9:** Pages 267, 272; **Ch. 10:** Pages 282, 296; **Ch. 11:** Pages 319–327, 330; **Ch. 13:** Pages 386–425; **Ch. 14:** Pages 426–455; **Ch. 15:** Pages 456–503; **Ch. 16:** Pages 507–510, 513–526; **Ch. 17:** Pages 534–542, 548–563; Page 626

- Interdependence of organisms

  Ch. 1: Pages 2–14, 26; **Ch. 2:** Pages 30–67; **Ch. 3:** Pages 68–76; **Ch. 4:** Pages 116–117; **Ch. 6:** Pages 168–193; **Ch. 7:** Pages 194–221; **Ch. 8:** Pages 222–245; **Ch. 13:** Pages 416–420; **Ch. 15:** Pages 458–494; **Ch. 16:** Pages 507–510, 520–526; **Ch. 17:** Pages 534–563; **Ch. 18:** Pages 564–589; **Ch. 19:** Pages 590–617; Pages 628–633

- Matter, energy, and organization in living systems

  Ch. 1: Pages 5–16, 26–27; **Ch. 2:** Pages 30–37, 48–58, 64; **Ch. 3:** Pages 68–101; **Ch. 4:** Pages 104–115, 121–128; **Ch. 5:** Pages 134–137, 146–149; **Ch. 6:** Pages 168–193; **Ch. 7:** Pages 194–221; **Ch. 8:** Pages 222–245; **Ch. 12:** Pages 342–385; **Ch. 15:** Pages 458–503; **Ch. 17:** Pages 534–563; **Ch. 18:** Pages 565–589; Pages 628–631

STANDARD C Life Science, continued

◆ Behavior of organisms

Ch. 8: Pages 225–245; Ch. 12: Pages 362–366, 367–371, 382; Ch. 13: Pages 410–411, 413; Ch. 16: Pages 504–533; Ch. 17: Pages 548–552, 559; Page 620

STANDARD E Science and Technology

As a result of activities in grades 9–12, all students should develop:

Biology: Cycles of Life

◆ Abilities of technological design

Pages xvi–xxi; Ch. 1: Pages 17–21, 23–24, 26; Ch. 2: Pages 57–58; Ch. 3: Pages 86–87; Ch. 4: Pages 121–122; Ch. 5: Pages 161–162; Ch. 6: Pages 187–188; Ch. 7: Pages 212–213; Ch. 8: Pages 236–237; Ch. 9: Pages 269–270; Ch. 10: Pages 297–298; Ch. 11: Pages 330–331; Ch. 12: Pages 379–380; Ch. 13: Pages 414–415; Ch. 14: Pages 445–446; Ch. 15: Pages 495–496; Ch. 16: Pages 527–528; Ch. 17: Pages 553–554; Ch. 18: Pages 578–579; Ch. 19: Pages 608–609, 611–612

◆ Understandings about science and technology

Pages xii–xiii; Ch. 1: Pages 7, 13, 21, 25, 29; Ch. 2: Pages 40, 41, 52, 63, 67; Ch. 3: Pages 81, 84, 89, 91, 97, 101; Ch. 4: Pages 115, 118, 125, 127, 131; Ch. 5: Pages 140, 143, 148, 151, 163, 167; Ch. 6: Pages 181, 182, 186, 189, 193; Ch. 7: Pages 205, 208, 215, 217, 221; Ch. 8: Pages 227, 231, 239, 241, 245; Ch. 9: Pages 253, 267, 268, 271, 275; Ch. 10: Pages 287, 288, 289, 296, 299, 303; Ch. 11: Pages 307, 328, 334, 336, 337, 341; Ch. 12: Pages 356, 365, 370, 381, 385; Ch. 13: Pages 404, 409, 412, 421, 425; Ch. 14: Pages 432, 436, 437, 451, 455; Ch. 15: Pages 466, 470, 484, 499, 503; Ch. 16: Pages 518, 522, 525, 529, 533; Ch. 17: Pages 538, 542, 557, 558, 559, 563; Ch. 18: Pages 567, 576, 581, 583, 585, 589; Ch. 19: Pages 591, 598, 603, 605–614, 617; Pages 628–633

STANDARD F Science in Personal and Social Perspectives

As a result of activities in grades 9–12, all students should develop an understanding of:

Biology: Cycles of Life

◆ Personal and community health

Ch. 1: Pages 7–16, 18, 21, 25; Ch. 2: Pages 40, 51, 54, 63; Ch. 3: Pages 78–93, 97; Ch. 4: Pages 104–106, 115–116, 120, 125–128; Ch. 5: Pages 140, 143, 151, 152; Ch. 6: Pages 170–174, 181–182, 185–186, 189, 193; Ch. 7: Pages 208, 210, 215, 217; Ch. 9: Pages 250, 252–255, 260–268, 272; Ch. 10: Pages 282, 286–289, 293–296; Ch. 11: Pages 310, 318–324, 327–339; Ch. 12: Pages 342–385; Ch. 13: Pages 404–406, 411, 412, 418; Ch. 14: Pages 447–450, 452; Ch. 15: Pages 460, 464, 468–469; Ch. 16: Pages 524, 525, 527–529; Ch. 17: Pages 541–545, 548–558, 560, 563; Ch. 18: Pages 565–589; Ch. 19: Pages 592, 594–614

◆ Population growth

Ch. 1: Pages 7–8; Ch. 16: Pages 497–498; Ch. 17: Pages 538–563; Ch. 18: Pages 565–589; Ch. 19: Pages 592–617

◆ Natural resources

Ch. 1: Page 5; Ch. 2: Page 59; Ch. 5: Page 146; Ch. 6: Pages 175, 182; Ch. 7: Page 204; Ch. 8: Pages 223–226, 230, 238, 239, 241; Ch. 15: Pages 465, 470; Ch. 17: Pages 541–545, 555–563; Ch. 18: Pages 564–589; Ch. 19: Pages 591, 602–605, 611–615; Pages 628–633

◆ Environmental quality

Ch. 1: Pages 1–29; Ch. 2: Pages 41, 51; Ch. 5: Pages 148, 150; Ch. 6: Pages 182, 189; Ch. 9: Pages 267, 268; Ch. 10: Page 285; Ch. 11: Pages 318, 319; Ch. 15: Page 470; Ch. 16: Pages 497–498; Ch. 17: Pages 538–563; Ch. 18: Pages 564–579, 583–584; Ch. 19: Pages 590–617; Pages 628–633

National Science Education Standards Correlation, continued

STANDARD F Science in Personal and Social Perspectives, continued

- Natural and human-induced hazards

    Ch. 1: Page 13; Ch. 2: Pages 40, 51; Ch. 5: Pages 148, 150; Ch. 6: Pages 182, 189; Ch. 9: Page 268; Ch. 10: Page 285; Ch. 11: Pages 318, 319; Ch. 12: Page 346; Ch. 13: Pages 404, 406; Ch. 14: Pages 447–450; Ch. 15: Page 475; Ch. 17: Pages 555, 556; Ch. 18: Pages 583, 584; Ch. 19: Pages 590–617; Pages 628, 631

- Science and technology in local, national, and global challenges

    Pages xii–xiii; Ch. 1: Pages 7, 13, 21, 25, 29; Ch. 2: Pages 40, 41, 52, 63, 67; Ch. 3: Pages 81, 84, 89, 91, 97, 101; Ch. 4: Pages 115, 118, 125, 127, 131; Ch. 5: Pages 140, 143, 148, 151, 163, 167; Ch. 6: Pages 181, 182, 186, 189, 193; Ch. 7: Pages 205, 208, 215, 217, 221; Ch. 8: Pages 227, 231, 239, 241, 245; Ch. 9: Pages 253, 267, 268, 271, 275; Ch. 10: Pages 287, 288, 289, 296, 299, 303; Ch. 11: Pages 307, 328, 334, 336, 337, 341; Ch. 12: Pages 356, 365, 370, 381, 385; Ch. 13: Pages 404, 409, 412, 421, 425; Ch. 14: Pages 432, 436, 437, 451, 455; Ch. 15: Pages 466, 470, 484, 499, 503; Ch. 16: Pages 518, 522, 525, 529, 533; Ch. 17: Pages 538, 542, 557, 558, 559, 563; Ch. 18: Pages 567, 576, 581, 583, 585, 589; Ch. 19: Pages 591, 598, 603, 605–614, 617; Pages 628–633

STANDARD G History and Nature of Science

As a result of activities in grades 9–12, all students should develop an understanding of:

Biology: Cycles of Life

- Science as a human endeavor

    Ch. 1: Pages 11, 13, 21, 25; Ch. 2: Pages 35, 41, 52; Ch. 3: Pages 81, 89, 91; Ch. 4: Pages 118, 124, 125; Ch. 5: Pages 140, 148, 150; Ch. 6: Pages 176, 181, 186; Ch. 7: Pages 205, 210, 215; Ch. 8: Pages 227, 239, 240; Ch. 9: Pages 261, 267, 268; Ch. 10: Pages 278–282, 288, 294, 296, 300, 303; Ch. 11: Pages 307–308, 310, 313, 318, 334, 336; Ch. 12: Pages 356, 365, 373; Ch. 13: Pages 389–390, 393, 399–400, 408–409, 412, 418, 422; Ch. 14: Pages 428–429, 432, 434–435, 436, 441, 442; Ch. 15: Pages 466, 470, 474; Ch. 16: Pages 515, 517, 518, 524, 525; Ch. 17: Pages 542, 551, 557; Ch. 18: Pages 576, 583, 584; Ch. 19: Pages 591, 593, 598, 605–614

- Nature of scientific knowledge

    Page xiii; Pages xix–xxi; Ch. 1: Pages 15–16, 17–27; Ch. 2: Pages 33, 36–37, 40, 57–58; Ch. 3: Pages 74, 75–76, 86–87; Ch. 4: Pages 106–107, 109–110, 121–122, 128; Ch. 5: Pages 135, 157–158, 161–162; Ch. 6: Pages 172, 178–179, 187–188; Ch. 7: Pages 198, 206–207, 212–213; Ch. 8: Pages 226, 228–229, 236–237; Ch. 9: Pages 250, 254–255, 269–270; Ch. 10: Pages 283, 290–291, 297–298; Ch. 11: Pages 308, 314–315, 330–331; Ch. 12: Pages 346, 357–358, 379–380; Ch. 13: Pages 393, 402–403, 407, 414–415; Ch. 14: Pages 433, 438–439, 445–446; Ch. 15: Pages 460, 462–463, 495–496; Ch. 16: Pages 509, 511–512, 527–528; Ch. 17: Pages 543, 544, 546–547, 553–554; Ch. 18: Pages 570, 571–572, 578–579; Ch. 19: Pages 597, 599–600, 603–604, 607–610, 611–612, 614; Pages 624–625

- Historical perspectives

    Pages xii–xiii; Ch. 1: Pages 7, 20–22; Ch. 2: Pages 32, 39–41, 47, 52, 54, 64; Ch. 3: Pages 79–81, 83, 89–92; Ch. 4: Pages 115, 118, 125; Ch. 5: Pages 143, 146, 148, 151–152; Ch. 6: Pages 174, 181–182, 185, 186; Ch. 7: Pages 205, 208; Ch. 8: Pages 231, 239; Ch. 9: Pages 252, 253, 268; Ch. 10: Pages 282, 287, 293, 296; Ch. 11: Pages 328, 334; Ch. 12: Pages 365, 370; Ch. 13: Pages 395, 397, 398, 388–401, 404–409, 418–419, 422, 433, 442–443; Ch. 14: Pages 436, 437, 440; Ch. 15: Pages 460, 466, 484; Ch. 16: Pages 518, 522; Ch. 17: Pages 538, 542; Ch. 18: Pages 576, 581; Ch. 19: Pages 605–614, 591; Pages 626, 628–633

Teacher's Resource Library Highlights

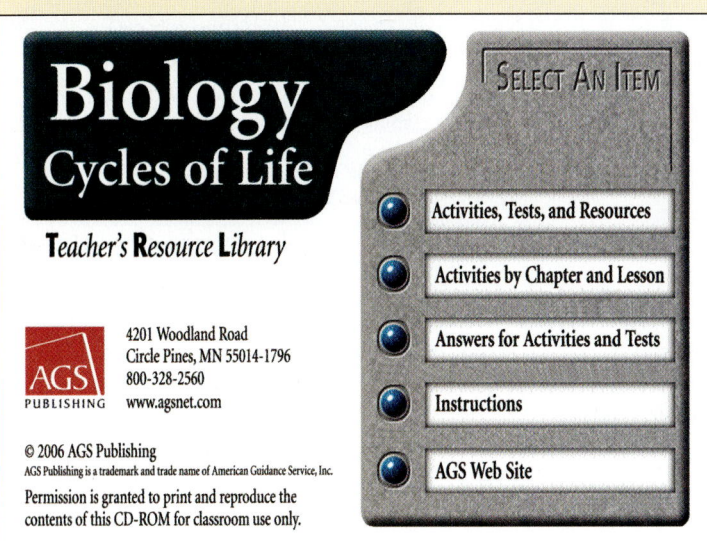

TRL All of the activities you'll need to reinforce and extend the text are conveniently located on the AGS Publishing Teacher's Resource Library (TRL) CD-ROM. All of the reproducible activities pictured in the Teacher's Edition are ready to select, view, and print. You can also preview other materials by linking directly to the AGS Publishing Web site.

Workbook Activities
Workbook Activities are available to reinforce and extend skills from each lesson of the textbook. A bound workbook format is also available.

Alternative Activities
These activities cover the same content as the Workbook Activities but are written at a second-grade reading level.

Lab Manual
These activities build critical-thinking and teamwork skills. A bound format is also available.

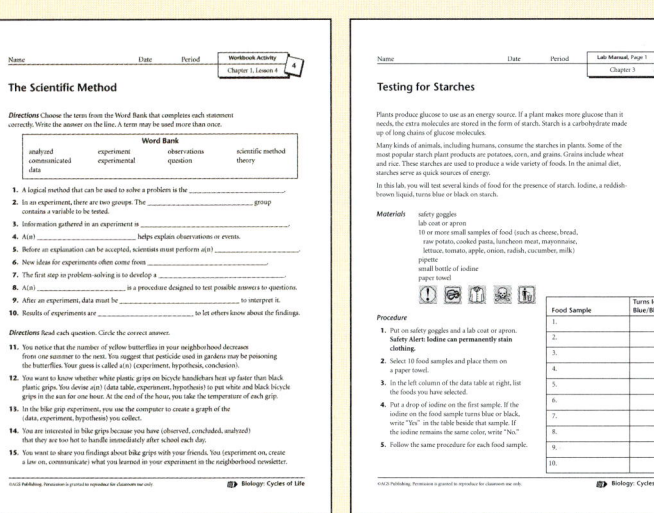

Workbook Activities   **Lab Manual**

Community Connection
Relevant activities help students extend their knowledge to the real world and reinforce concepts covered in class.

Graphic Organizer
These activities help students organize information about important chapter concepts.

Resource File
These reference sheets with lesson content are tools for student study as well as teaching aids.

Self-Study Guide
An assignment guide provides teachers with the flexibility for individualized instruction or independent study.

Mastery Tests
Chapter, Midterm, and Final Mastery Tests are convenient assessment options. Critical-thinking items are included.

Answer Key
All answers to reproducible activities are included in the TRL and in the Teacher's Edition.

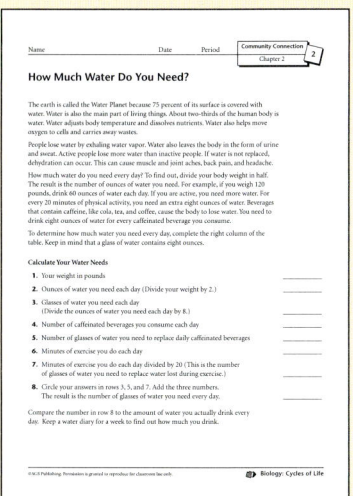

Community Connections   **Mastery Tests**

Biology: Cycles of Life   **T15**

Synopsis of the Scientific Research Base

Research-Based Principles	AGS Publishing Textbooks	References
Standards Alignment Subject area instruction needs to be based on skills, concepts, and processes represented by common standards for that subject area.	◆ Textbook content and skills aligned with national standards and state grade-level or course-specific content standards, where available	Matlock, L., Fielder, K., & Walsh, D. (2001). Building the foundation for standards-based instruction for all students. *Teaching Exceptional Children, 33*(5), 68–72. Miller, S. P., & Mercer, C. D. (1997). Educational aspects of mathematics disabilities. *Journal of Learning Disabilities, 30*(1), 47–56. Reys, R., Reys, B., Lapan, R., Holliday, G. & Wasman, D. (2003). Assessing the impact of standards-based middle grades mathematics curriculum materials on student achievement. *Journal of Research in Mathematics Education, 34*(1), 74–95.
Readability Many students struggle to learn from core content-area textbooks that are written too high above their reading level. Students need access to textbooks written at a level they can read and understand, where the reading level is within the students' range of comprehension.	◆ Grade 4.0 or lower readability using the Spache formula ◆ Controlled vocabulary matched to student reading ability and use of synonyms to replace non-essential difficult words above grade 4 ◆ Simple sentence structures ◆ Limited sentence length	Allington, R. L. (2002). You can't learn much from books you can't read. *Educational Leadership, 60*(3), 16–19. Chall, J. S., & Conard, S. S. (1991). *Should textbooks challenge students? The case for easier or harder textbooks.* New York: Teachers College Press. *Readability calculations.* (2000). Dallas: Micro Power & Light Company.
Language Complexity and Sequence Students struggling with vocabulary and text comprehension need textbooks with accessible language.	◆ Simple, direct language using an active voice ◆ Clear organization to facilitate understanding ◆ Explicit language signals to show sequence of and links between concepts and ideas	Anderson, T. H., & Armbruster, B. B. (1984). Readable texts, or selecting a textbook is not like buying a pair of shoes. In R. C. Anderson, J. Osborne, & R. J. Tierney (Eds.), *Learning to read in American schools* (pp. 151–162). Hillsdale, NJ: Lawrence Erlbaum Associates, Inc. Curtis, M. E. (2002, May 20). *Adolescent reading: A synthesis of research.* Paper presented at the Practice Models for Adolescent Literacy Success Conference, U.S. Department of Education. Washington, DC: National Institute of Child Health and Human Development. Retrieved September 15, 2003, from http://216.26.160.105/conf/nichd/synthesis.asp McAlpine, L., & Weston, C. (1994). The attributes of instructional materials. *Performance Improvement Quarterly, 7*(1), 19–30. Seidenberg, P. L. (1989). Relating text-processing research to reading and writing instruction for learning disabled students. *Learning Disabilities Focus, 5*(1), 4–12.
Vocabulary Use and Development Students need content-related vocabulary instruction in the context of readable and meaningful text.	◆ New vocabulary boldfaced on first occurrence, used in context, and defined in a sidebar ◆ Glossary with pronunciation, definition, and relevant graphic illustrations for all vocabulary words ◆ Direct vocabulary instruction introduced in the Teacher's Edition and reinforced in context throughout ◆ Multiple exposures to new vocabulary in text and practice exercises	Ciborowski, J. (1992). *Textbooks and the students who can't read them: A guide to teaching content.* Cambridge, MA: Brookline. Kameenui, E. J., & Simmons, D. C. (1990). *Designing instructional strategies.* Columbus, OH: Merrill Publishing Company. Marzano, R. J. (1998). *A theory-based meta-analysis of research on instruction.* Aurora, CO: Mid-Continent Research for Education and Learning. Retrieved October 1, 2003, from http://www.mcrel.org/topics/productDetail/asp/productID=83 McAlpine, L., & Weston, C. (1994). The attributes of instructional materials. *Performance Improvement Quarterly, 7*(1), 19–30. National Reading Panel. (2000). *Teaching children to read: An evidence-based assessment of the scientific research literature on reading and its implications for reading instruction.* Reports of the subgroups. Washington, DC: National Institute of Child Health and Human Development. Taylor, S. E., Frackenpohl, H., White, C. E., Nieroroda, B. W., Browning, C. L., & Birsner, E. P. (1989). *EDL core vocabularies in reading, mathematics, science, and social studies.* Austin, TX: Steck-Vaughn.

Research-Based Principles	AGS Publishing Textbooks	References
Text Organization: Presentation and Structure		
Students need an uncluttered page layout, with easy-to-read print, that clearly directs the reader to main ideas, important information, examples, and comprehensive practice and review. Reading comprehension is improved by structural features in the text that make it easier for learners to access the content.	*Print characteristics and page layout:* ♦ Serif font for body copy; sans serif font for boxed features, examples ♦ Maximum line length of 5" for ease of reading ♦ Unjustified (ragged) right margins ♦ Major/minor column page design presents primary instructional information in the major column and support content in the sidebar or in a box *Presentation characteristics:* ♦ Lesson introductions, summaries ♦ Explicit lesson titles, headings, and subheadings label and organize main ideas ♦ Signals alert readers to important information, content connections, illustrations, graphics ♦ Cues (e.g., boldface type) highlight important information *Text structure:* ♦ Lesson heads in question or statement format guide comprehension ♦ Text written to explicitly link facts and concepts within and across lessons; text cohesiveness ♦ Each skill or concept linked to direct practice and review	Armbruster, B. B., & Anderson, T. H. (1988). On selecting "considerate" content area textbooks. *Remedial and Special Education, 9*(1), 47–52. Beck, I. L., McKeown, M. G., & Grommoll, E. W. (1989). Learning from social studies texts. *Cognition and Instruction, 6*(2), 99–158. Chambliss, M. J. (1994). Evaluating the quality of textbooks for diverse learners. *Remedial and Special Education, 15*(5), 348–362. Ciborowski, J. (1992). *Textbooks and the students who can't read them: A guide to teaching content.* Cambridge, MA: Brookline. Dickson, S. V., Simmons, D. C., & Kameenui, E. J. (1995). *Text organization and its relation to reading comprehension: A synthesis of the research* (Technical Report No. 17) and *Text organization: Curricular and instructional implications for diverse learners* (Technical Report No. 18). National Center to Improve the Tools of Educators. Eugene, OR: University of Oregon. Retrieved January 26, 2000, from http://idea.uoregon.edu/~ncite/documents/techrep/tech17.html and http://idea.uoregon.edu/~ncite/documents/techrep/tech18.html Dickson, S. V., Simmons, D. C., & Kameenui, E. J. (1998). Text organization: Research bases *and* Text organization: Instructional and curricular basics and implications. In D. C. Simmons & E. J. Kameenui (Eds.), *What reading research tells us about children with diverse learning needs: Bases and basics* (pp. 239–278; 279–294). Mahwah, NJ: Lawrence Erlbaum Associates, Inc. Mansfield, J. S., Legge, G. E., & Bane, M. C. (1996). Psychophysics of reading. XV: Font effects in normal and low vision. *Investigative Ophthalmology and Vision Science, 37*, 1492–1501. McAlpine, L., & Weston, C. (1994). The attributes of instructional materials. *Performance Improvement Quarterly, 7*(1), 19–30. McNamara, D. S., Kintsche, E., Songer, N. B., & Kintsche, W. (1996). Are good texts always better? Interactions of text coherence, background knowledge, and levels of understanding in learning from text. *Cognition and Instruction, 14*(1), 1–43. Tyree, R. B., Fiore, T. A., & Cook, R. A. (1994). Instructional materials for diverse learners: Features and considerations for textbook design. *Remedial and Special Education, 15*(6), 363–377.
Differentiated Instruction and Learning Styles		
Student learning is more successful when tasks are aligned with academic skill levels and developmental stage, and adjustments are made to allow students multiple means to engage and express their learning strengths and styles at appropriate levels of challenge and support. Differentiated instruction allows teachers to organize instruction to adjust for diverse learning needs within a classroom. Learning activities that capitalize on students' learning styles can structure planning for individual differences based on multiple intelligences theory.	♦ Multiple features, including Learning Styles activities, help teachers match assignments to students' abilities and interests ♦ Variety of media to select from—print, audio, visual, software ♦ Step-by-step, part-by-part basic content and skill-level lessons in the Student and Teacher's Editions ♦ Alternative Activities written at a Grade 2 (Spache) readability in the Teacher's Resource Library ♦ Variety of review materials, activities, sidebars, and alternative readings ♦ Multiple assessments—lesson or chapter reviews, end-of-chapter tests, cumulative midterm/final mastery tests, alternative assessment items *Learning Styles activities include:* ♦ Auditory/Verbal ♦ Body/Kinesthetic ♦ Interpersonal/Group Learning ♦ Logical/Mathematical ♦ Visual/Spatial *ELL/ESL Strategies provide support for students who are learning English and lesson content concurrently.*	Allington, R. L. (2002). You can't learn much from books you can't read. *Educational Leadership, 60*(3), 16–19. Carnine, D. (1994). Introduction to the mini-series: Diverse learners and prevailing, emerging, and research-based educational approaches and their tools. *School Psychology Review, 23*(3), 341–350. Forsten, C., Grant, J., & Hollas, B. (2003). *Differentiating textbooks: Strategies to improve student comprehension and motivation.* Peterborough, NH: Crystal Springs Books. Gardner, H. (1983). *Frames of mind: The theory of multiple intelligences.* New York: Harper and Row. Gersten, R., & Baker, S. (2000). The professional knowledge base on instructional practices that support cognitive growth for English-language learners. In R. Gersten, E. P. Schiller, & S. Vaughn (Eds.), *Contemporary special education research: Syntheses of the knowledge base on critical instructional issues* (pp. 31–80). Mahwah, NJ: Lawrence Erlbaum Associates, Inc. Hall, T. (2002, June). *Effective classroom practices report: Differentiated instruction.* Wakefield, NJ: National Center on Accessing the General Curriculum. Retrieved September 29, 2003, from http://www.cast.org/cac/index.cfm?i=2876 Lazear, D. (1999). *Eight ways of knowing: Teaching for multiple intelligences* (3rd ed.). Arlington Heights, IL: Skylight Training and Publishing. Orlich, D. C., Harder, R. J., Callahan, R. C., & Gibson, H. W. (2001). *Teaching strategies: A guide to better instruction* (6th ed.). Boston: Houghton Mifflin Company. Roderick, M. & Camburn, E. (1999). Risk and recovery from course failure in the early years of high school. *American Educational Research Journal, 36*(2), 303–343. Tomlinson, C. A. (1999). *The differentiated classroom: Responding to the needs of all learners.* Alexandria, VA: Association for Supervision and Curriculum Development.

Synopsis of the Scientific Research Base, continued

Research-Based Principles	AGS Publishing Textbooks	References

Instructional Design: Lesson Structure and Learner Support Strategies

Instruction that includes the components of effective instruction, utilizes effective strategies and interventions to facilitate student learning, and aligns with standards improves learning for all students, especially diverse learners and students who are struggling.

Elements of effective instruction:

Step 1: Introduce the lesson and prepare students to learn
Step 2: Provide instruction and guided practice
Step 3: Provide opportunities for applied practice and generalization

Organizational tools:
Advance organizers
Graphic organizers

Instructional process techniques:
Cooperative learning
Student self-monitoring and questioning
Real-life examples
Mnemonics

Step 1: Introduce the lesson and prepare students to learn

In the Student Edition:
- "How to Use This Book" feature explicitly teaches text organization
- Chapter and lesson previews with graphic and visual organizers
- Goals for Learning
- Sidebar notes review skills and important facts and information

In the Teacher's Edition:
- Lesson objectives
- Explicit *3-Step Teaching Plan* begins with "Warm-Up Activity" to inform students of objectives, connect to previous learning and background knowledge, review skills, and motivate students to engage in learning

Step 2: Provide instruction and guided practice

In the Student Edition:
- Short, manageable lessons break content and skills into smaller, step-by-step, part-by-part pieces
- Systematic presentation of lesson concepts and skills
- Chapter and lesson headings presented as questions or statements
- Graphic organizers arrange content visually—charts, graphs, tables, diagrams, bulleted lists, arrows, graphics, mnemonics, illustrations, and captions
- Models or examples link directly to the explanation of the concept
- Multiple opportunities for direct practice throughout

In the Teacher's Edition:
- *3-Step Teaching Plan* for each lesson includes "Teaching the Lesson" with direct instruction, and helps teachers present and clarify lesson skills and concepts through guided practice and modeling of important ideas
- Supplemental strategies and activities, including hands-on modeling, transparencies, graphic organizers, visual aids, learning styles

Step 3: Provide opportunities for applied practice and generalization

In the Student Edition:
- Each skill or concept lesson is followed by direct practice or review questions
- Multiple exercises throughout
- Generalization and application activities in sidebars and lessons link content to real-life applications
- Chapter reviews and summaries highlight major points

Allsopp, D. H. (1990). Using modeling, manipulatives, and mnemonics with eighth-grade math students. *Teaching Exceptional Children, 31*(2), 74–81.

Chambliss, M. J. (1994). Evaluating the quality of textbooks for diverse learners. *Remedial and Special Education, 15*(5), 348–362.

Ciborowski, J. (1992). *Textbooks and the students who can't read them: A guide to teaching content.* Cambridge, MA: Brookline.

Cole, R. W. (Ed.). (1995). *Educating everybody's children: Diverse teaching strategies for diverse learners.* Alexandria, VA: Association for Supervision and Curriculum Development.

Curtis, M. E. (2002, May 20). *Adolescent reading: A synthesis of research.* Paper presented at the Practice Models for Adolescent Literacy Success Conference, U.S. Department of Education. Washington, DC: National Institute of Child Health and Human Development. Retrieved September 15, 2003, from http://216.26.160.105/conf/nichd/synthesis.asp

Dickson, S. V., Simmons, D. C., & Kameenui, E. J. (1995). *Text organization: Curricular and instructional implications for diverse learners* (Technical Report No. 18). National Center to Improve the Tools of Educators. Eugene, OR: University of Oregon. Retrieved January 26, 2000, from http://idea.uoregon.edu/~ncite/documents/techrep/tech18.html

Dixon, R. C., Carnine, D. W., Lee, D., Wallin, J., & Chard, D. (1998). *Review of high quality experimental mathematics research: Report to the California State Board of Education.* Sacramento, CA: California State Board of Education.

Jarrett, D. (1999). *The inclusive classroom: Mathematics and science instruction for students with learning disabilities—It's just good teaching.* Portland, OR: Northwest Regional Educational Laboratory.

Johnson, D. W., Johnson, R. T., & Stanne, M. B. (2000, May). *Cooperative learning methods: A meta-analysis.* Minneapolis: The Cooperative Learning Center, University of Minnesota. Retrieved October 29, 2003, from http://www.cooplearn.org/pages/cl-methods.html

Kameenui, E. J., & Simmons, D. C. (1990). *Designing instructional strategies.* Columbus, OH: Merrill Publishing Company.

Lovitt, T. C., & Horton, S. V. (1994). Strategies for adapting science textbooks for youth with learning disabilities. *Remedial and Special Education, 15*(2), 105–116.

Marzano, R. J. (1998). *A theory-based meta-analysis of research on instruction.* Aurora, CO: Mid-Continent Research for Education and Learning. Retrieved October 1, 2003, from http://www.mcrel.org/topics/productDetail/asp?productID=83

Marzano, R. J., Pickering, D. J., & Pollock, J. E. (2001). *Classroom instruction that works: Research-based strategies for increasing student achievement.* Alexandria, VA: Association for Supervision and Curriculum Development.

Miller, S. P., & Mercer, C. D. (1993). Mnemonics: Enhancing the math performance of students with learning difficulties. *Intervention in School and Clinic, 29*(2), 78–82.

Montague, M. (1997). Cognitive strategy instruction in mathematics for students with learning disabilities. *Journal of Learning Disabilities, 30*(2), 164–177.

Reiser, R. A., & Dick, W. (1996). *Instructional planning: A guide for teachers* (2nd ed.). Boston: Allyn and Bacon.

Roderick, M., & Camburn, E. (1999). Risk and recovery from course failure in the early years of high school. *American Educational Research Journal, 36*(2), 303–343.

Steele, M. (2002). Strategies for helping students who have learning disabilities in mathematics. *Mathematics Teaching in the Middle School, 8*(3), 140–143.

Swanson, H. L. (2000). What instruction works for students with learning disabilities? Summarizing the results from a meta-analysis of intervention studies. In R. Gersten, E. P. Schiller, & S. Vaughn (Eds.), *Contemporary special education research: Syntheses of the knowledge base on critical instructional issues* (pp. 1–30). Mahwah, NJ: Lawrence Erlbaum Associates, Inc.

Tyree, R. B., Fiore, T. A., & Cook, R. A. (1994). Instructional materials for diverse learners: Features and considerations for textbook design. *Remedial and Special Education, 15*(6), 363–377.

Vaughn, S., Gersten, R., & Chard, D. J. (2000). The underlying message in LD intervention research: Findings from research syntheses. *Exceptional Children, 67*(1), 99–114.

Research-Based Principles	AGS Publishing Textbooks	References

Instructional Design: Lesson Structure and Learner Support Strategies, *continued from previous page*

In the Teacher's Edition:
- *3-Step Teaching Lesson Plan* concludes with "Reinforce and Extend" to reinforce, reteach, and extend lesson skills and concepts
- Unit or chapter projects link and apply unit or chapter concepts
- Multiple supplemental/alternative activities for individual and group learning and problem solving
- Career, home, and community application exercises

In the Teacher's Resource Library:
- Multiple exercises in Student Workbook and reproducibles offer applications, content extensions, additional practice, and alternative activities at a lower (Grade 2 Spache) readability

Skill Track Online:
- Monitors student learning and guides teacher feedback to student

Ongoing Assessment and Tracking Student Progress

Textbooks can incorporate features to facilitate and support assessment of learning, allowing teachers to monitor student progress and provide information on mastery level and the need for instructional changes.

Assessment should measure student progress on learning goals over the course of a lesson, chapter, or content-area textbook.

Students and teachers need timely and ongoing feedback so instruction can focus on specific skill development.

- Test-taking tips and strategies for students who benefit from explicit strategy instruction
- Lesson and chapter reviews check student understanding of content
- Workbook and reproducible lesson activities (Teacher's Resource Library) offer additional monitoring of student progress
- Discussion questions allow teachers to monitor student progress toward lesson objectives
- Self-Study Guides (Teacher's Resource Library) allow teacher and student to track individual assignments and progress
- Chapter assessment activities and curriculum-based assessment items correlate to chapter Goals for Learning:
  - Chapter reviews
  - End-of-chapter tests
  - Cumulative Midterm and final mastery tests
  - Alternative chapter assessments
  - Skill Track Online assesses and tracks individual student performance by lesson and chapter

Deshler, D. D., Ellis, E. S., & Lenz, B. K. (1996). *Teaching adolescents with learning disabilities: Strategies and methods* (2nd ed.). Denver, CO: Love Publishing Company.

Jarrett, D. (1999). *The inclusive classroom: Mathematics and science instruction for students with learning disabilities—It's just good teaching*. Portland, OR: Northwest Regional Educational Laboratory.

Reiser, R. A., & Dick, W. (1996). *Instructional planning: A guide for teachers* (2nd ed.). Boston: Allyn and Bacon.

Tyree, R. B., Fiore, T. A., & Cook, R. A. (1994). Instructional materials for diverse learners: Features and considerations for textbook design. *Remedial and Special Education, 15*(6), 363–377.

For more information on the scientific research base for AGS Publishing Textbooks, please go to **www.agsnet.com** or call Customer Service at 800-328-2560 to request a research report.

Biology: Cycles of Life Skills Chart

Science Content	1	2	3	4	5	6	7	8	9	10	11	12	13	14	15	16	17	18	19
Behavior of Organisms								✓				✓	✓			✓	✓		
Biological Evolution	✓				✓				✓	✓	✓		✓	✓	✓	✓	✓		
The Cell	✓	✓	✓	✓	✓	✓	✓	✓	✓	✓	✓	✓			✓				
Diversity and Adaptations of Organisms	✓	✓										✓	✓	✓	✓	✓	✓	✓	✓
Ecosystems	✓																✓	✓	✓
Energy Cycles	✓	✓															✓		
History and Nature of Science	✓	✓	✓	✓	✓	✓	✓	✓	✓	✓	✓	✓	✓	✓	✓	✓	✓	✓	✓
Human Biology									✓	✓	✓								
Inquiry and Investigation	✓	✓	✓	✓	✓	✓	✓		✓	✓	✓	✓	✓	✓	✓	✓	✓	✓	✓
Interdependence of Organisms	✓	✓	✓			✓	✓						✓		✓	✓	✓	✓	✓
Matter, Energy, and Organization of Living Systems	✓	✓	✓		✓	✓	✓						✓			✓		✓	
Molecular Basis of Heredity			✓		✓	✓			✓		✓	✓		✓		✓			
Population	✓															✓	✓	✓	✓
Reproduction and Heredity									✓	✓	✓					✓			
Science and Technology	✓	✓	✓	✓	✓	✓	✓	✓	✓	✓	✓	✓	✓	✓	✓	✓	✓	✓	✓
Science in Personal and Social Perspectives	✓	✓	✓	✓	✓	✓	✓	✓	✓	✓	✓	✓	✓	✓	✓	✓	✓	✓	✓

Process Skills	1	2	3	4	5	6	7	8	9	10	11	12	13	14	15	16	17	18	19
Communicating	✓	✓	✓	✓	✓	✓	✓	✓	✓	✓	✓	✓	✓	✓	✓	✓	✓	✓	✓
Collecting Information	✓	✓	✓	✓	✓	✓	✓	✓	✓	✓	✓	✓	✓	✓	✓	✓	✓	✓	✓
Creating Charts, Graphs, Tables, or Diagrams	✓	✓	✓	✓	✓	✓	✓	✓	✓	✓	✓	✓	✓	✓	✓	✓	✓	✓	✓
Describing	✓	✓	✓	✓	✓	✓	✓	✓	✓	✓	✓	✓	✓	✓	✓	✓	✓	✓	✓
Designing Experiments	✓	✓	✓	✓	✓	✓	✓		✓	✓	✓	✓	✓	✓	✓	✓	✓	✓	✓
Following Written Directions	✓	✓	✓	✓	✓	✓	✓	✓	✓	✓	✓	✓	✓	✓	✓	✓	✓	✓	✓
Formulating a Hypothesis	✓	✓	✓	✓	✓	✓	✓	✓	✓	✓	✓	✓	✓	✓	✓	✓	✓	✓	✓
Indentifying and/or Controlling Variables	✓	✓	✓	✓	✓	✓	✓	✓	✓	✓	✓	✓	✓	✓	✓	✓	✓	✓	✓
Making and/or Using Models									✓	✓	✓	✓		✓			✓		
Measuring	✓	✓	✓	✓		✓	✓	✓				✓	✓		✓		✓		✓
Observing	✓	✓	✓	✓	✓	✓	✓	✓	✓	✓	✓	✓	✓	✓	✓	✓	✓	✓	✓
Performing Experiments	✓	✓	✓	✓	✓	✓	✓	✓	✓	✓	✓	✓	✓	✓	✓	✓	✓	✓	✓

CHAPTER

Process Skills, continued	1	2	3	4	5	6	7	8	9	10	11	12	13	14	15	16	17	18	19
Recording Data	✓	✓	✓	✓	✓	✓	✓	✓	✓	✓	✓	✓	✓	✓	✓	✓	✓	✓	✓
Researching and Writing About Science	✓	✓	✓	✓	✓	✓	✓	✓	✓	✓	✓	✓	✓	✓	✓	✓	✓	✓	✓
Using Science Lab Equipment	✓	✓	✓	✓	✓	✓	✓	✓	✓	✓	✓	✓	✓	✓	✓	✓	✓	✓	✓

Thinking Skills	1	2	3	4	5	6	7	8	9	10	11	12	13	14	15	16	17	18	19
Analyzing Data	✓	✓	✓	✓	✓	✓	✓	✓	✓	✓	✓	✓	✓	✓	✓	✓	✓	✓	✓
Applying Information	✓	✓	✓	✓	✓	✓	✓	✓	✓	✓	✓	✓	✓	✓	✓	✓	✓	✓	✓
Classifying and Categorizing	✓	✓	✓	✓	✓	✓	✓	✓	✓	✓	✓	✓	✓	✓	✓	✓	✓	✓	✓
Comparing and Contrasting	✓	✓	✓	✓	✓	✓	✓	✓	✓	✓	✓	✓	✓	✓	✓	✓	✓	✓	✓
Drawing Conclusions	✓	✓	✓	✓	✓	✓	✓	✓	✓	✓	✓	✓	✓	✓	✓	✓	✓	✓	✓
Explaining Ideas and Concepts	✓	✓	✓	✓	✓	✓	✓	✓	✓	✓	✓	✓	✓	✓	✓	✓	✓	✓	✓
Formulating Questions	✓	✓	✓	✓	✓	✓	✓	✓	✓	✓	✓	✓	✓	✓	✓	✓	✓	✓	✓
Identifying and Solving Problems	✓	✓	✓	✓	✓	✓	✓	✓	✓	✓	✓	✓	✓	✓	✓	✓	✓	✓	✓
Identifying Similarities and Differences	✓	✓	✓	✓	✓	✓	✓	✓	✓	✓	✓	✓	✓	✓	✓	✓	✓	✓	✓
Interpreting Data	✓	✓	✓	✓	✓	✓	✓	✓	✓	✓	✓	✓	✓	✓	✓	✓	✓	✓	✓
Interpreting Visuals	✓	✓	✓	✓	✓	✓	✓	✓	✓	✓	✓	✓	✓	✓	✓	✓	✓	✓	✓
Learning Science Vocabulary	✓	✓	✓	✓	✓	✓	✓	✓	✓	✓	✓	✓	✓	✓	✓	✓	✓	✓	✓
Making Decisions	✓	✓	✓	✓	✓	✓	✓	✓	✓	✓	✓	✓	✓	✓	✓	✓	✓	✓	✓
Making Inferences	✓	✓	✓	✓	✓	✓	✓	✓	✓	✓	✓	✓	✓	✓	✓	✓	✓	✓	✓
Organizing Information	✓	✓	✓	✓	✓	✓	✓	✓	✓	✓	✓	✓	✓	✓	✓	✓	✓	✓	✓
Predicting Outcomes	✓	✓	✓	✓	✓	✓	✓	✓	✓	✓	✓	✓	✓	✓	✓	✓	✓	✓	✓
Recalling Facts	✓	✓	✓	✓	✓	✓	✓	✓	✓	✓	✓	✓	✓	✓	✓	✓	✓	✓	✓
Recognizing Cause and Effect	✓	✓	✓	✓	✓	✓	✓	✓	✓	✓	✓	✓	✓	✓	✓	✓	✓	✓	✓
Recognizing Main Ideas	✓	✓	✓	✓	✓	✓	✓	✓	✓	✓	✓	✓	✓	✓	✓	✓	✓	✓	✓
Recognizing Patterns	✓	✓	✓	✓	✓	✓	✓	✓	✓	✓	✓	✓	✓	✓	✓	✓	✓	✓	✓
Recognizing Relationships	✓	✓	✓	✓	✓	✓	✓	✓	✓	✓	✓	✓	✓	✓	✓	✓	✓	✓	✓
Understanding Concepts	✓	✓	✓	✓	✓	✓	✓	✓	✓	✓	✓	✓	✓	✓	✓	✓	✓	✓	✓

National Science Education Standards Correlation

STANDARD A Science as Inquiry

As a result of activities in grades 9–12, all students should develop:

Biology: Cycles of Life

- Abilities necessary to do scientific inquiry

  Page xiii; Pages xix–xxi; **Ch. 1:** Pages 15–16, 17–27; **Ch. 2:** Pages 33, 36–37, 40, 57–58; **Ch. 3:** Pages 74, 75–76, 86–87; **Ch. 4:** Pages 106–107, 109–110, 121–122, 128; **Ch. 5:** Pages 135, 157–158, 161–162; **Ch. 6:** Pages 172, 178–179, 187–188; **Ch. 7:** Pages 198, 206–207, 212–213; **Ch. 8:** Pages 226, 228–229, 236–237; **Ch. 9:** Pages 250, 254–255, 269–270; **Ch. 10:** Pages 283, 290–291, 297–298; **Ch. 11:** Pages 308, 314–315, 330–331; **Ch. 12:** Pages 346, 357–358, 379–380; **Ch. 13:** Pages 393, 402–403, 407, 414–415; **Ch. 14:** Pages 433, 438–439, 445–446; **Ch. 15:** Pages 460, 462–463, 495–496; **Ch. 16:** Pages 509, 511–512, 527–528; **Ch. 17:** Pages 544, 546–547, 553–554; **Ch. 18:** Pages 570, 571–572, 578–579; **Ch. 19:** Pages 597, 599–600, 607–610, 611–612, 614; Pages 624–625

- Understandings about scientific inquiry

  Pages xii–xiii; Pages xix–xxi; **Ch. 1:** Pages 7, 15–16, 17–27; **Ch. 2:** Pages 33, 36–37, 40, 41, 57–58; **Ch. 3:** Pages 74, 75–76, 81, 86–87; **Ch. 4:** Pages 106–107, 109–110, 115, 121–122, 125, 128; **Ch. 5:** Pages 135, 143, 151, 157–158, 161–162; **Ch. 6:** Pages 172, 178–179, 182, 187–188; **Ch. 7:** Pages 198, 206–207, 208, 212–213; **Ch. 8:** Pages 226, 228–229, 231, 236–237; **Ch. 9:** Pages 250, 253, 254–255, 269–270; **Ch. 10:** Pages 283, 287, 290–291, 297–298; **Ch. 11:** Pages 308, 314–315, 328, 330–331; **Ch. 12:** Pages 346, 357–358, 370, 379–380; **Ch. 13:** Pages 393, 402–403, 404, 407, 414–415; **Ch. 14:** Pages 433, 437, 438–439, 445–446; **Ch. 15:** Pages 460, 462–463, 484, 495–496; **Ch. 16:** Pages 509, 511–512, 522, 527–528; **Ch. 17:** Pages 538, 544, 546–547, 553–554; **Ch. 18:** Pages 570, 571–572, 578–579, 581; **Ch. 19:** Pages 597, 599–600, 607–610, 611–612, 614

STANDARD C Life Science

As a result of activities in grades 9–12, all students should develop an understanding of:

Biology: Cycles of Life

- The Cell

  Ch. 1: Pages 7–9; **Ch. 2:** Pages 32–33; **Ch. 3:** Pages 70–79, 82, 84–96, 98; **Ch. 4:** Pages 102–131; **Ch. 5:** Pages 132–167; **Ch. 6:** Pages 168–177, 180–188, 190–193; **Ch. 7:** Pages 194–209, 211, 214–221; **Ch. 8:** Pages 222–229, 231–245; **Ch. 9:** Pages 246–265, 267, 271–275; **Ch. 10:** Pages 279, 284, 286, 288, 291–294, 299–300; **Ch. 11:** Pages 306, 312, 316–336, 338–341; **Ch. 12:** Pages 344–345, 350, 353–356, 364, 367, 370, 372–378, 381–383; **Ch. 15:** Pages 457–461, 464–468, 472–474, 478, 479–481, 487, 500

- Molecular basis of heredity

  Ch. 3: Pages 94–96, 98–99; **Ch. 5:** Pages 142–145; **Ch. 6:** Page 170; **Ch. 9:** Pages 247–251, 254–259, 269–272; **Ch. 10:** Pages 276–303; **Ch. 11:** Pages 304–341; **Ch. 13:** Pages 402, 404–405, 416, 422; **Ch. 16:** Page 507

- Biological evolution

  Ch. 1: Pages 10–11; **Ch. 5:** Pages 142–145; **Ch. 9:** Pages 267, 272; **Ch. 10:** Pages 282, 296; **Ch. 11:** Pages 319–327, 330; **Ch. 13:** Pages 386–425; **Ch. 14:** Pages 426–455; **Ch. 15:** Pages 456–503; **Ch. 16:** Pages 507–510, 513–526; **Ch. 17:** Pages 534–542, 548–563; Page 626

- Interdependence of organisms

  Ch. 1: Pages 2–14, 26; **Ch. 2:** Pages 30–67; **Ch. 3:** Pages 68–76; **Ch. 4:** Pages 116–117; **Ch. 6:** Pages 168–193; **Ch. 7:** Pages 194–221; **Ch. 8:** Pages 222–245; **Ch. 13:** Pages 416–420; **Ch. 15:** Pages 458–494; **Ch. 16:** Pages 507–510, 520–526; **Ch. 17:** Pages 534–563; **Ch. 18:** Pages 564–589; **Ch. 19:** Pages 590–617; Pages 628–633

- Matter, energy, and organization in living systems

  Ch. 1: Pages 5–16, 26–27; **Ch. 2:** Pages 30–37, 48–58, 64; **Ch. 3:** Pages 68–101; **Ch. 4:** Pages 104–115, 121–128; **Ch. 5:** Pages 134–137, 146–149; **Ch. 6:** Pages 168–193; **Ch. 7:** Pages 194–221; **Ch. 8:** Pages 222–245; **Ch. 12:** Pages 342–385; **Ch. 15:** Pages 458–503; **Ch. 17:** Pages 534–563; **Ch. 18:** Pages 565–589; Pages 628–631

STANDARD C   Life Science, continued

◆ Behavior of organisms

Ch. 8: Pages 225–245; Ch. 12: Pages 362–366, 367–371, 382; Ch. 13: Pages 410–411, 413; Ch. 16: Pages 504–533; Ch. 17: Pages 548–552, 559; Page 620

STANDARD E   Science and Technology

As a result of activities in grades 9–12, all students should develop:

Biology: Cycles of Life

◆ Abilities of technological design

Pages xvi–xxi; Ch. 1: Pages 17–21, 23–24, 26; Ch. 2: Pages 57–58; Ch. 3: Pages 86–87; Ch. 4: Pages 121–122; Ch. 5: Pages 161–162; Ch. 6: Pages 187–188; Ch. 7: Pages 212–213; Ch. 8: Pages 236–237; Ch. 9: Pages 269–270; Ch. 10: Pages 297–298; Ch. 11: Pages 330–331; Ch. 12: Pages 379–380; Ch. 13: Pages 414–415; Ch. 14: Pages 445–446; Ch. 15: Pages 495–496; Ch. 16: Pages 527–528; Ch. 17: Pages 553–554; Ch. 18: Pages 578–579; Ch. 19: Pages 608–609, 611–612

◆ Understandings about science and technology

Pages xii–xiii; Ch. 1: Pages 7, 13, 21, 25, 29; Ch. 2: Pages 40, 41, 52, 63, 67; Ch. 3: Pages 81, 84, 89, 91, 97, 101; Ch. 4: Pages 115, 118, 125, 127, 131; Ch. 5: Pages 140, 143, 148, 151, 163, 167; Ch. 6: Pages 181, 182, 186, 189, 193; Ch. 7: Pages 205, 208, 215, 217, 221; Ch. 8: Pages 227, 231, 239, 241, 245; Ch. 9: Pages 253, 267, 268, 271, 275; Ch. 10: Pages 287, 288, 289, 296, 299, 303; Ch. 11: Pages 307, 328, 334, 336, 337, 341; Ch. 12: Pages 356, 365, 370, 381, 385; Ch. 13: Pages 404, 409, 412, 421, 425; Ch. 14: Pages 432, 436, 437, 451, 455; Ch. 15: Pages 466, 470, 484, 499, 503; Ch. 16: Pages 518, 522, 525, 529, 533; Ch. 17: Pages 538, 542, 557, 558, 559, 563; Ch. 18: Pages 567, 576, 581, 583, 585, 589; Ch. 19: Pages 591, 598, 603, 605–614, 617; Pages 628–633

STANDARD F   Science in Personal and Social Perspectives

As a result of activities in grades 9–12, all students should develop an understanding of:

Biology: Cycles of Life

◆ Personal and community health

Ch. 1: Pages 7–16, 18, 21, 25; Ch. 2: Pages 40, 51, 54, 63; Ch. 3: Pages 78–93, 97; Ch. 4: Pages 104–106, 115–116, 120, 125–128; Ch. 5: Pages 140, 143, 151, 152; Ch. 6: Pages 170–174, 181–182, 185–186, 189, 193; Ch. 7: Pages 208, 210, 215, 217; Ch. 9: Pages 250, 252–255, 260–268, 272; Ch. 10: Pages 282, 286–289, 293–296; Ch. 11: Pages 310, 318–324, 327–339; Ch. 12: Pages 342–385; Ch. 13: Pages 404–406, 411, 412, 418; Ch. 14: Pages 447–450, 452; Ch. 15: Pages 460, 464, 468–469; Ch. 16: Pages 524, 525, 527–529; Ch. 17: Pages 541–545, 548–558, 560, 563; Ch. 18: Pages 565–589; Ch. 19: Pages 592, 594–614

◆ Population growth

Ch. 1: Pages 7–8; Ch. 16: Pages 497–498; Ch. 17: Pages 538–563; Ch. 18: Pages 565–589; Ch. 19: Pages 592–617

◆ Natural resources

Ch. 1: Page 5; Ch. 2: Page 59; Ch. 5: Page 146; Ch. 6: Pages 175, 182; Ch. 7: Page 204; Ch. 8: Pages 223–226, 230, 238, 239, 241; Ch. 15: Pages 465, 470; Ch. 17: Pages 541–545, 555–563; Ch. 18: Pages 564–589; Ch. 19: Pages 591, 602–605, 611–615; Pages 628–633

◆ Environmental quality

Ch. 1: Pages 1–29; Ch. 2: Pages 41, 51; Ch. 5: Pages 148, 150; Ch. 6: Pages 182, 189; Ch. 9: Pages 267, 268; Ch. 10: Page 285; Ch. 11: Pages 318, 319; Ch. 15: Page 470; Ch. 16: Pages 497–498; Ch. 17: Pages 538–563; Ch. 18: Pages 564–579, 583–584; Ch. 19: Pages 590–617; Pages 628–633

National Science Education Standards Correlation, continued

STANDARD F Science in Personal and Social Perspectives, continued

- Natural and human-induced hazards

  Ch. 1: Page 13; Ch. 2: Pages 40, 51; Ch. 5: Pages 148, 150; Ch. 6: Pages 182, 189; Ch. 9: Page 268; Ch. 10: Page 285; Ch. 11: Pages 318, 319; Ch. 12: Page 346; Ch. 13: Pages 404, 406; Ch. 14: Pages 447–450; Ch. 15: Page 475; Ch. 17: Pages 555, 556; Ch. 18: Pages 583, 584; Ch. 19: Pages 590–617; Pages 628, 631

- Science and technology in local, national, and global challenges

  Pages xii–xiii; Ch. 1: Pages 7, 13, 21, 25, 29; Ch. 2: Pages 40, 41, 52, 63, 67; Ch. 3: Pages 81, 84, 89, 91, 97, 101; Ch. 4: Pages 115, 118, 125, 127, 131; Ch. 5: Pages 140, 143, 148, 151, 163, 167; Ch. 6: Pages 181, 182, 186, 189, 193; Ch. 7: Pages 205, 208, 215, 217, 221; Ch. 8: Pages 227, 231, 239, 241, 245; Ch. 9: Pages 253, 267, 268, 271, 275; Ch. 10: Pages 287, 288, 289, 296, 299, 303; Ch. 11: Pages 307, 328, 334, 336, 337, 341; Ch. 12: Pages 356, 365, 370, 381, 385; Ch. 13: Pages 404, 409, 412, 421, 425; Ch. 14: Pages 432, 436, 437, 451, 455; Ch. 15: Pages 466, 470, 484, 499, 503; Ch. 16: Pages 518, 522, 525, 529, 533; Ch. 17: Pages 538, 542, 557, 558, 559, 563; Ch. 18: Pages 567, 576, 581, 583, 585, 589; Ch. 19: Pages 591, 598, 603, 605–614, 617; Pages 628–633

STANDARD G History and Nature of Science

As a result of activities in grades 9–12, all students should develop an understanding of:

Biology: Cycles of Life

- Science as a human endeavor

  Ch. 1: Pages 11, 13, 21, 25; Ch. 2: Pages 35, 41, 52; Ch. 3: Pages 81, 89, 91; Ch. 4: Pages 118, 124, 125; Ch. 5: Pages 140, 148, 150; Ch. 6: Pages 176, 181, 186; Ch. 7: Pages 205, 210, 215; Ch. 8: Pages 227, 239, 240; Ch. 9: Pages 261, 267, 268; Ch. 10: Pages 278–282, 288, 294, 296, 300, 303; Ch. 11: Pages 307–308, 310, 313, 318, 334, 336; Ch. 12: Pages 356, 365, 373; Ch. 13: Pages 389–390, 393, 399–400, 408–409, 412, 418, 422; Ch. 14: Pages 428–429, 432, 434–435, 436, 441, 442; Ch. 15: Pages 466, 470, 474; Ch. 16: Pages 515, 517, 518, 524, 525; Ch. 17: Pages 542, 551, 557; Ch. 18: Pages 576, 583, 584; Ch. 19: Pages 591, 593, 598, 605–614

- Nature of scientific knowledge

  Page xiii; Pages xix–xxi; Ch. 1: Pages 15–16, 17–27; Ch. 2: Pages 33, 36–37, 40, 57–58; Ch. 3: Pages 74, 75–76, 86–87; Ch. 4: Pages 106–107, 109–110, 121–122, 128; Ch. 5: Pages 135, 157–158, 161–162; Ch. 6: Pages 172, 178–179, 187–188; Ch. 7: Pages 198, 206–207, 212–213; Ch. 8: Pages 226, 228–229, 236–237; Ch. 9: Pages 250, 254–255, 269–270; Ch. 10: Pages 283, 290–291, 297–298; Ch. 11: Pages 308, 314–315, 330–331; Ch. 12: Pages 346, 357–358, 379–380; Ch. 13: Pages 393, 402–403, 407, 414–415; Ch. 14: Pages 433, 438–439, 445–446; Ch. 15: Pages 460, 462–463, 495–496; Ch. 16: Pages 509, 511–512, 527–528; Ch. 17: Pages 543, 544, 546–547, 553–554; Ch. 18: Pages 570, 571–572, 578–579; Ch. 19: Pages 597, 599–600, 603–604, 607–610, 611–612, 614; Pages 624–625

- Historical perspectives

  Pages xii–xiii; Ch. 1: Pages 7, 20–22; Ch. 2: Pages 32, 39–41, 47, 52, 54, 64; Ch. 3: Pages 79–81, 83, 89–92; Ch. 4: Pages 115, 118, 125; Ch. 5: Pages 143, 146, 148, 151–152; Ch. 6: Pages 174, 181–182, 185, 186; Ch. 7: Pages 205, 208; Ch. 8: Pages 231, 239; Ch. 9: Pages 252, 253, 268; Ch. 10: Pages 282, 287, 293, 296; Ch. 11: Pages 328, 334; Ch. 12: Pages 365, 370; Ch. 13: Pages 395, 397, 398, 388–401, 404–409, 418–419, 422, 433, 442–443; Ch. 14: Pages 436, 437, 440; Ch. 15: Pages 460, 466, 484; Ch. 16: Pages 518, 522; Ch. 17: Pages 538, 542; Ch. 18: Pages 576, 581; Ch. 19: Pages 605–614, 591; Pages 626, 628–633

by
Helen M. Parke
and
Patrick Enderle

AGS Publishing
Circle Pines, Minnesota 55014-1796
800-328-2560

About the Authors

Helen M. Parke, Ph.D., is a former secondary and university biology teacher. With 30 years of teaching experience, Dr. Parke has taught science methods courses for undergraduate and graduate level secondary science majors. She has directed centers for science, mathematics, and technology education and is currently Research and Development Manager for Cisco Learning Institute. Dr. Parke designs e-learning professional development for K–12 teachers of mathematics and science.

Patrick Enderle, M.S., received his master's degree in Molecular Biology/Biotechnology from East Carolina University. He has taught biology at the high school, community college, and university levels. He is currently teaching at East Carolina University in Greenville, North Carolina.

Photo credits for this textbook can be found on page 666.

The publisher wishes to thank the following educators for their helpful comments during the review process for *Biology: Cycles of Life*. Their assistance has been invaluable.

Pamela J. Graham, Special Education Teacher/Intervention Specialist, Euclid High School, Euclid, OH; **Debora J. Hartzell,** Lead Teacher for Special Ed, Columbia High School and Lakeside High School, Dekalb County, GA; **Debby Houston,** Research Associate, Florida State University, Tallahassee, FL; **Pamela A. Kazee,** Director, Student Support Services, NE, Clark County School District, Las Vegas, NV; **Denise M. King,** Instructional Coordinator, Leary School of Virginia, Alexandria, VA; **Johnny McCarty,** Special Education Teacher, Science, Flour Bluff High School, Corpus Christi, TX; **Katherine Pasquale,** Euclid High School, Euclid, OH; **Dr. Craig L. Sanders,** Teacher, Richmond Hill High School, East Meadow, NY; **Ann Marie Strozynski,** Director of Secondary Education, Hamtramck, MI; **Susan Sztain,** Teacher, Desert Sands Charter High School, Lanc, CA; **Michelle Villegas,** Biology Teacher, Flour Bluff High School, Corpus Christi, TX

Publisher's Project Staff

Vice President of Curriculum and Publisher: Sari Follansbee, Ed.D.; Director of Curriculum Development: Teri Mathews; Managing Editor: Julie Maas; Editors: Judy Monroe, Jan Jessup; Assistant Editor: Sarah Brandel; Development Assistant: Bev Johnson; Director of Creative Services: Nancy Condon; Senior Designers: Tony Perleberg, Diane McCarty; Production Artist: Mike Vineski; Purchasing Agent: Carol Nelson; Product Manager–Curriculum: Brian Holl

© 2006 AGS Publishing
4201 Woodland Road
Circle Pines, MN 55014-1796
800-328-2560 • www.agsnet.com

All rights reserved, including translation. No part of this publication may be reproduced or transmitted in any form or by any means without written permission from the publisher.

AGS Publishing is a trademark and trade name of American Guidance Service, Inc.

Printed in the United States of America
ISBN 0-7854-3972-2
Product Number 94180
A 0 9 8 7 6 5 4 3 2 1

Contents

How to Use This Book: A Study Guide x
Safety Rules and Symbols xix

Chapter 1   **Biology: Investigating the Cycles of Life** 1
- Lesson 1   What Is Biology? 2
- Lesson 2   Energy and Growth Cycles 5
- Lesson 3   Evolutionary and Ecological Cycles 10
- ◆ Investigation 1 15
- Lesson 4   The Scientific Method 17
- ◆ Discovery Investigation 1 23
- ◆ Biology in the World 25
- ◆ Chapter 1 Summary 26
- ◆ Chapter 1 Review 27
- ◆ Test-Taking Tip 29

Chapter 2   **Basic Chemistry** 30
- Lesson 1   Matter, Energy, and Chemical Processes of Life ... 32
- ◆ Investigation 2 36
- Lesson 2   Atoms and Molecules 38
- Lesson 3   Chemical Formulas 42
- Lesson 4   Bonding Patterns 48
- Lesson 5   Properties of Water 53
- ◆ Discovery Investigation 2 57
- Lesson 6   Acids, Bases, and pH 59
- ◆ Biology in the World 63
- ◆ Chapter 2 Summary 64
- ◆ Chapter 2 Review 65
- ◆ Test-Taking Tip 67

Chapter 3   **Chemistry at the Cellular Level** 68
- Lesson 1   What Are Organic Molecules? 70
- ◆ Investigation 3 75
- Lesson 2   Carbohydrates 77
- Lesson 3   Lipids 82
- ◆ Discovery Investigation 3 86
- Lesson 4   Proteins 88
- Lesson 5   Nucleic Acids 94
- ◆ Biology in the World 97
- ◆ Chapter 3 Summary 98
- ◆ Chapter 3 Review 99
- ◆ Test-Taking Tip 101

Chapter 4 — Cells: The Basic Units of Life 102
- Lesson 1 What Is a Cell? 104
- ◆ Investigation 4 109
- Lesson 2 Cellular Structure and Function 111
- Lesson 3 What Kind of Cell Is It? 116
- ◆ Discovery Investigation 4 121
- Lesson 4 After the Cell 123
- ◆ Biology in the World 127
- ◆ Chapter 4 Summary 128
- ◆ Chapter 4 Review 129
- ◆ Test-Taking Tip 131

Chapter 5 — A Journey into the Eukaryotic Cell 132
- Lesson 1 What Are Cell Membranes? 134
- Lesson 2 What Do Membranes Do? 138
- Lesson 3 Information Organelles 142
- Lesson 4 Energy Organelles 146
- Lesson 5 The Endomembrane System 150
- Lesson 6 The Cytoskeleton 154
- ◆ Investigation 5 157
- Lesson 7 Plant Cells 159
- ◆ Discovery Investigation 5 161
- ◆ Biology in the World 163
- ◆ Chapter 5 Summary 164
- ◆ Chapter 5 Review 165
- ◆ Test-Taking Tip 167

Chapter 6 — ATP and Energy Cycles 168
- Lesson 1 What Is Energy? 170
- Lesson 2 Making ATP 174
- ◆ Investigation 6 178
- Lesson 3 Enzymes and Energy Flow 180
- Lesson 4 More About Enzymes 184
- ◆ Discovery Investigation 6 187
- ◆ Biology in the World 189
- ◆ Chapter 6 Summary 190
- ◆ Chapter 6 Review 191
- ◆ Test-Taking Tip 193

Chapter 7 Cellular Respiration in Energy Cycles 194
- Lesson 1 What Is Cellular Respiration? 196
- Lesson 2 The Stages of Cellular Respiration 200
- ◆ Investigation 7 206
- Lesson 3 Fermentation 208
- ◆ Discovery Investigation 7 212
- Lesson 4 Controlling Cellular Respiration............ 214
- ◆ Biology in the World............................... 217
- ◆ Chapter 7 Summary 218
- ◆ Chapter 7 Review 219
- ◆ Test-Taking Tip 221

Chapter 8 Photosynthesis in Energy Cycles 222
- Lesson 1 What Is Photosynthesis? 224
- ◆ Investigation 8 228
- Lesson 2 The Light Reaction......................... 230
- ◆ Discovery Investigation 8 236
- Lesson 3 The Dark Reaction: The Calvin-Benson Cycle... 238
- ◆ Biology in the World............................... 241
- ◆ Chapter 8 Summary 242
- ◆ Chapter 8 Review 243
- ◆ Test-Taking Tip 245

Chapter 9 The Life Cycles of Cells and Reproduction ... 246
- Lesson 1 The Cell Cycle and Mitosis 248
- Lesson 2 What Is Cancer? 252
- ◆ Investigation 9 254
- Lesson 3 Meiosis: The Life Cycle of Sex Cells 256
- Lesson 4 The Human Reproductive System 260
- Lesson 5 Human Development....................... 265
- ◆ Discovery Investigation 9 269
- ◆ Biology in the World............................... 271
- ◆ Chapter 9 Summary 272
- ◆ Chapter 9 Review 273
- ◆ Test-Taking Tip 275

Chapter 10 — Inheritance Patterns in Life Cycles 276
- Lesson 1 What Did Mendel Discover? 278
- Lesson 2 Different Ways Alleles Cooperate 284
- ◆ Investigation 10 290
- Lesson 3 The Importance of Sex Chromosomes 292
- ◆ Discovery Investigation 10 297
- ◆ Biology in the World 299
- ◆ Chapter 10 Summary 300
- ◆ Chapter 10 Review 301
- ◆ Test-Taking Tip 303

Chapter 11 — Genetic Information Cycles 304
- Lesson 1 How Are Molecules of Life Involved in Heredity? 306
- Lesson 2 DNA Replication 310
- ◆ Investigation 11 314
- Lesson 3 The Path of Genetic Information 316
- Lesson 4 What Are Viruses? 321
- Lesson 5 Using the Path of Genetic Information 325
- ◆ Discovery Investigation 11 330
- Lesson 6 Natural Defenses Against Disease 332
- ◆ Biology in the World 337
- ◆ Chapter 11 Summary 338
- ◆ Chapter 11 Review 339
- ◆ Test-Taking Tip 341

Chapter 12 — Human Body Systems 342
- Lesson 1 The Digestive System 344
- Lesson 2 The Respiratory System 348
- Lesson 3 The Circulatory System 352
- ◆ Investigation 12 357
- Lesson 4 The Excretory System 359
- Lesson 5 The Nervous System 362
- Lesson 6 The Sensory System 367
- Lesson 7 The Endocrine System 372
- Lesson 8 The Skeletal and Muscular System 375
- ◆ Discovery Investigation 12 379
- ◆ Biology in the World 381
- ◆ Chapter 12 Summary 382
- ◆ Chapter 12 Review 383
- ◆ Test-Taking Tip 385

Chapter 13 Evolution and Natural Selection 386
- Lesson 1 What Is Biological Evolution? 388
- Lesson 2 Evidence of Evolution 392
- Lesson 3 Rates of Evolutionary Change 397
- ◆ Investigation 13 402
- Lesson 4 Processes in Evolution 404
- Lesson 5 Natural Selection 410
- ◆ Discovery Investigation 13 414
- Lesson 6 Microevolution and Macroevolution 416
- ◆ Biology in the World 421
- ◆ Chapter 13 Summary 422
- ◆ Chapter 13 Review 423
- ◆ Test-Taking Tip 425

Chapter 14 Speciation and Punctuated Equilibrium 426
- Lesson 1 What Is Speciation? 428
- Lesson 2 Classifying Species 434
- ◆ Investigation 14 438
- Lesson 3 Conditions for Speciation to Occur 440
- ◆ Discovery Investigation 14 445
- Lesson 4 Conditions That Affect Species Survival .. 447
- ◆ Biology in the World 451
- ◆ Chapter 14 Summary 452
- ◆ Chapter 14 Review 453
- ◆ Test-Taking Tip 455

Chapter 15 Phylogenies and Classifying Diversity 456
- Lesson 1 How Do Scientists Classify Living Things? 458
- ◆ Investigation 15 462
- Lesson 2 The Kingdom Protista 464
- Lesson 3 The Kingdom Fungi 468
- Lesson 4 The Kingdom Plantae 472
- Lesson 5 The Kingdom Animalia 479
- Lesson 6 Invertebrates 482
- Lesson 7 Vertebrates 489
- ◆ Discovery Investigation 15 495
- Lesson 8 Humans 497
- ◆ Biology in the World 499
- ◆ Chapter 15 Summary 500
- ◆ Chapter 15 Review 501
- ◆ Test-Taking Tip 503

Chapter 16	**Behavioral Biology** **504**

Lesson 1 What Is Behavioral Biology? 506
◆ Investigation 16 511
Lesson 2 Types of Behavior 513
Lesson 3 Forms of Communication 520
◆ Discovery Investigation 16 527
◆ Biology in the World 529
◆ Chapter 16 Summary 530
◆ Chapter 16 Review 531
◆ Test-Taking Tip 533

Chapter 17	**Populations and Communities** **534**

Lesson 1 Understanding Populations
and Communities 536
Lesson 2 Populations and Their Activities 541
◆ Investigation 17 546
Lesson 3 Relationships in Communities 548
◆ Discovery Investigation 17 553
Lesson 4 How Do Communities Start and Survive? 555
◆ Biology in the World 559
◆ Chapter 17 Summary 560
◆ Chapter 17 Review 561
◆ Test-Taking Tip 563

Chapter 18	**Ecosystems** **564**

Lesson 1 How Does Energy Flow Through Ecosystems? . . 566
◆ Investigation 18 571
Lesson 2 The Cycling of Chemicals in an Ecosystem 573
◆ Discovery Investigation 18 578
Lesson 3 Biomes 580
◆ Biology in the World 585
◆ Chapter 18 Summary 586
◆ Chapter 18 Review 587
◆ Test-Taking Tip 589

Chapter 19   Human Impact and Technology 590
    Lesson 1   What Impact Do Humans Have
                   on Ecosystems? 592
    ◆ Investigation 19 599
    Lesson 2   Conservation Biology 601
    Lesson 3   Science and Technology 607
    ◆ Discovery Investigation 19 611
    ◆ Biology in the World 613
    ◆ Chapter 19 Summary 614
    ◆ Chapter 19 Review 615
    ◆ Test-Taking Tip 617

Appendix A: The Periodic Table of Elements 618

Appendix B: Body Systems 620

Appendix C: Measurement Conversion Factors 624

Appendix D: Geologic Time Scale 626

Appendix E: World Map 627

Appendix F: Alternative Energy Sources 628

Appendix G: Plant Kingdom 634

Glossary 635

Index 653

Photo and Illustration Credits 666

Using This Section

How to Use This Book: A Study Guide

Overview This section may be used to introduce the study of biological science, to preview the book's features, and to review effective study skills.

Objectives
- To introduce the study of biological science
- To preview the student textbook
- To review study skills

Student Pages x–xviii

Teacher's Resource Library
How to Use This Book 1–3

Introduction to the Book
Have volunteers read aloud the three paragraphs of the introduction. Discuss with students why studying science and developing scientific skills are important.

How to Study
Read aloud each bulleted statement, pausing to discuss with students why the suggestion is a part of good study habits. Distribute copies of the How to Use This Book 1, "Study Habits Survey," to students. Read the directions together and then have students complete the survey. After they have scored their surveys, ask them to make a list of the study habits they plan to improve. After three or four weeks, have students complete the survey again to see if they have improved their study habits. Encourage them to keep and review the survey every month or so.

To help students organize their time and work in an easy-to-read format, have them fill out How to Use This Book 2, "Weekly Schedule." Encourage them to keep the schedule in a notebook or folder where they can refer to it easily. Suggest that they review the schedule periodically and update it as necessary.

Give students an opportunity to become familiar with the textbook features and the chapter and lesson organization and structure of *Biology: Cycles of Life*.

How to Use This Book: A Study Guide

Welcome to *Biology: Cycles of Life*. Science touches our lives every day, no matter where we are—at home, at school, or at work. This book covers the biological sciences. It also focuses on science skills that scientists use. These skills include asking questions, making predictions, designing experiments or procedures, collecting and organizing information, calculating data, making decisions, drawing conclusions, and exploring more options. You probably already use these skills every day. You ask questions to find answers. You gather information and organize it. You use that information to make all sorts of decisions. In this book, you will have opportunities to use and practice all of these skills.

As you read this book, notice how each lesson is organized. Information is presented in a straightforward manner. Tables, illustrations, and photos help clarify concepts. Read the information carefully. If you have trouble with a lesson, try reading it again.

It is important that you understand how to use this book before you start to read it. It is also important to know how to be successful in this course. Information in this first section of the book can help you achieve these things.

How to Study
These tips can help you study more effectively.
- Plan a regular time to study.
- Choose a desk or table in a quiet place where you will not be distracted. Find a spot that has good lighting.
- Gather all the books, pencils, paper, and other equipment you will need to complete your assignments.
- Decide on a goal. For example: "I will finish reading and taking notes on Chapter 1, Lesson 1, by 8:00."
- Take a five- to ten-minute break every hour to stay alert.
- If you start to feel sleepy, take a break and get some fresh air.

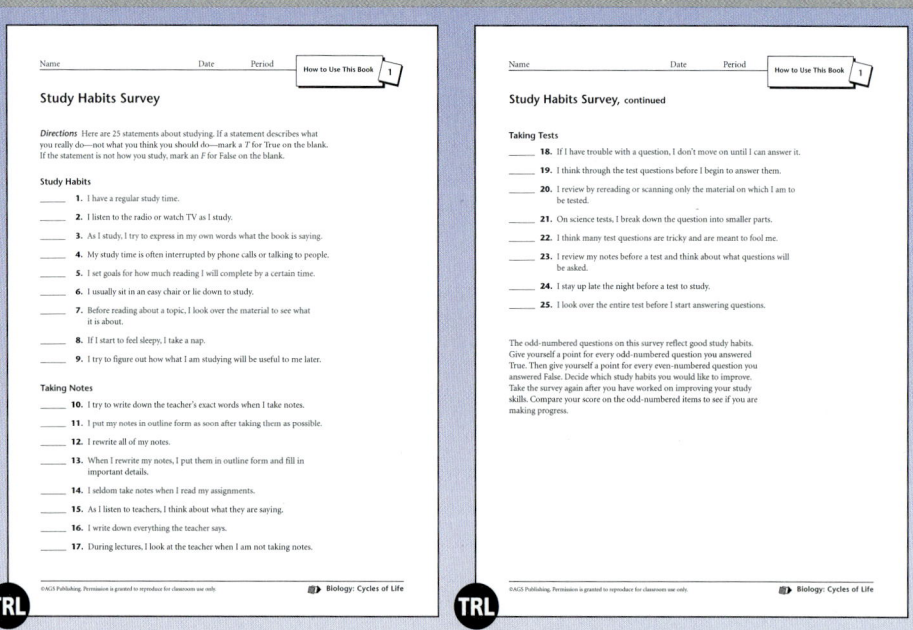

How to Use This Book 1, pages 1 and 2

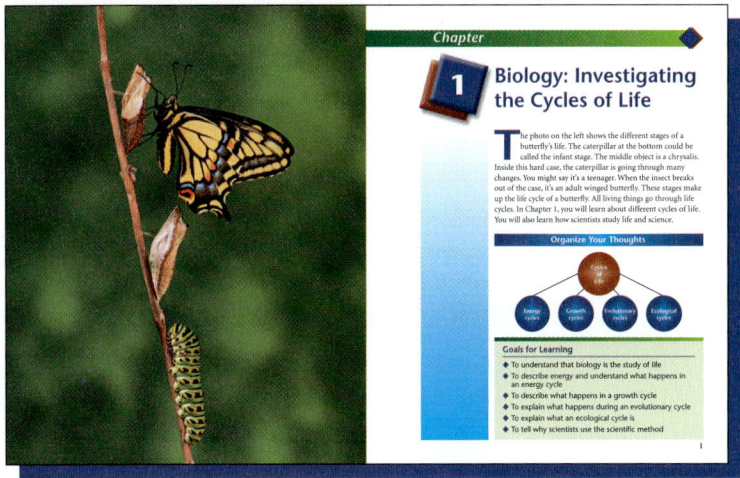

Before Beginning Each Chapter

- Read the chapter title and study the photograph. What does the photo tell you about the chapter title?
- Read the opening paragraphs.
- Study the Goals for Learning. The Chapter Review and tests will ask questions related to these goals.
- Look at the Chapter Review. The questions cover the most important information in the chapter.

Note These Features

Notes
Points of interest or additional information that relate to the lesson

Science Myth
Common science misconceptions followed by the correct information

How to Use This Book: A Study Guide

List the following text features on the board: Table of Contents, Chapter Opener, Lesson, Lesson Review, Investigation, Discovery Investigation, Biology in the World, Chapter Summary, Chapter Review, Appendix A: The Periodic Table of Elements, Appendix B: Body Systems, Appendix C: Measurement Conversion Factors, Appendix D: Geologic Time Scale, Appendix E: World Map, Appendix F: Alternative Energy Sources, Appendix G: Plant Kingdom, Glossary, Index.

Remind students that they can use the Table of Contents to help identify and locate major features in the text. They can also use the Index to identify specific topics and the text pages on which they are discussed.

Before Beginning Each Chapter

Chapter Openers organize information in easy-to-read formats. When students begin their study of Chapter 1, you may wish to have them read aloud and follow each of the bulleted suggestions under "Before Beginning Each Chapter." Actually trying the suggestions will help students recognize how useful the suggestions are when previewing a chapter.

At the beginning of other chapters, refer students to page xi and encourage them to follow the suggestions. You may wish to continue to do this as a class each time or allow students to work independently.

In addition to these bulleted suggestions, the Teacher's Edition text for each Chapter Opener offers teaching suggestions for introducing the chapter. The text also includes a list of Teacher's Resource Library materials for the chapter.

Note These Features

Use the information on pages xi–xiii to identify features included in each chapter. As a class, locate examples of these features in Chapter 1. Read the examples and discuss their purpose.

Notes in the margins extend the information presented in the text. For example, the note on page 20 of Chapter 1 presents an interesting fact about the scientific method.

Have students look at the Science Myth on page 21 in Chapter 1. Ask a volunteer to read the "Myth" and another volunteer to read the "Fact."

How to Use This Book: A Study Guide

Tell the students that each chapter has features that relate biology to their life and to the world around them. Have a volunteer read the title of the Biology in Your Life on page 13. Ask students: How does this topic relate to your life?

Each Achievements in Science feature describes a significant historical event. After reading them, tell students to ask themselves: Why was this event so significant?

Discuss each Science at Work feature as students come upon them. Ask students: Can you picture yourself in this career? Why?

Point out to students that throughout this book they will have opportunities to practice the chapter concepts. Explain to them that the Investigation, Discovery Investigation, and Express Lab features have experiments related to chapter material. In addition, the Teacher's Edition has answers to any questions that appear in the Student Edition for this feature.

Ask a volunteer to read the Technology and Society feature in Chapter 1 on page 7. Explain to students that this feature is unique, because it connects biology to technology and society. Tell them that they will have opportunities to do further research on the interesting topics discussed in this feature.

Have a volunteer read the title of the Biology in the World on page 25. Ask students: How does this topic relate to the world around you? Emphasize how biological sciences are an important part of life.

Biology in Your Life
Examples of science in real life with connections to the environment, technology, and consumer choices

Achievements in Science
Historical scientific discoveries, events, and achievements

Science at Work
Careers in science

Investigation
Experiments that give practice with chapter concepts

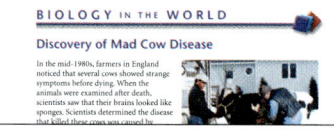

Discovery Investigation
Experiments with student input to give practice with chapter concepts

Technology and Society
Examples of science in real life with connections to biology, technology, and society

Biology in the World
Examples of real-life problems or issues and solutions affecting the United States or the world

Math Tip
Short math reminders or tips connected to a lesson

Express Lab
Short experiments that give practice with chapter concepts

Link to
A fact that connects biology to another subject area such as chemistry, environmental science, physics, earth science, social studies, language arts, math, health, home and career, arts, and cultures

Research and Write
Research a topic or question, then write about it

Before Beginning Each Lesson

Read the lesson title and restate it in the form of a question.

For example, write:
What are evolutionary cycles?

Look over the entire lesson, noting the following:
◆ bold words
◆ text organization
◆ notes in the margins
◆ photos and illustrations
◆ lesson review questions

Explain to students how disciplines are all interrelated. This book will provide them with tips and facts that connect biology to other disciplines.

The Math Tip feature provides a tip or reminder about a math skill that relates to the lesson. Have students find a Math Tip in their book. Ask a volunteer to explain how the tip is related to the text.

Emphasize how the Link to features have lots of fascinating information. For example, have students look at page 3 in Chapter 1. Ask a volunteer to read the Link to feature about extreme climates. Explain to students that this feature discusses life forms, which makes it related to biology, and it also discusses Earth features found deep in the ocean, which makes it related to earth science.

Tell students that they will also have an opportunity to do research on their own when there is a Research and Write feature. Explain to students that this feature provides information on a topic that they can further research. Have students look at page 29 in Chapter 1. Ask students: Where would you look first to find more information about an endangered species?

Please note that all of these features have teaching suggestions in the Teacher's Edition text.

Before Beginning Each Lesson

With students, read through the information in "Before Beginning Each Lesson." Then assign each of the three lessons in Chapter 1 to a small group of students. Have them restate the lesson title in the form of a statement or a question. Then have them make a list of the bold words in their lesson. Explain to students that these words are important to the content in their lesson. Have groups note any subheads in their lesson. Then have them list any special features.

Encourage them to pay attention to any illustrations in their lesson. Explain that these visuals will help them understand the lesson content.

After their survey of the lesson, have each group report to the class on their findings. Then have each group turn to the Lesson Review for their lesson. Explain that the review provides an opportunity to determine how well they have understood the lesson content.

As You Read the Lesson

Read aloud the statements in the section "As You Read the Lesson." Have students preview lessons in Chapter 1 and note lesson titles and subheads. Remind students as they study each lesson to follow this study approach.

Using the Bold Words

Read aloud the information about how to use bold words. Make sure students understand what the term *bold* means. Explain to students that the words in bold are important vocabulary terms. Then ask them to look at the boxed words in Chapter 1. Have a volunteer read the boxed term *biology* and then find and read the sentence in the text in which that word appears in bold type. Have another volunteer read the definition of the word in the box.

Point out that boxed words may appear on other pages in a lesson besides the first page. Explain that vocabulary terms appear in a box on the same page that they are used in the text. Have volunteers find and read the sentences in Lesson 2 of Chapter 1 in which the vocabulary terms for that lesson are used. Have students turn to the Glossary at the back of the book and read the definitions of these same vocabulary terms.

Word Study Tips

Have a volunteer read aloud the information for "Word Study Tips." You may wish to demonstrate how to make a vocabulary card by filling out an index card for the term *biology* and its definition (page 2).

Distribute copies of How to Use This Book 3, "Word Study," to students. Suggest that as they read, students write unfamiliar words, their page numbers, and their definitions in the sheet. Point out that having such a list will be very useful for reviewing vocabulary before taking a test. Point out that students can use words they listed on How to Use This Book 3 to make their vocabulary card file.

As You Read the Lesson

◆ Read the lesson title.
◆ Read the subheads and paragraphs that follow.
◆ Before moving on to the next lesson, see if you understand the concepts you read. If you do not understand the concepts, reread the lesson. If you are still unsure, ask for help.
◆ Practice what you have learned by completing the Lesson Review.

Bold type
Words seen for the first time will appear in bold type

Glossary
Words listed in this column are also found in the glossary

Using the Bold Words

Knowing the meaning of all the boxed vocabulary words in the left column will help you understand what you read.

These words are in **bold type** the first time they appear in the text. They are often defined in the paragraph.

Biology is the study of life.

All of the words in the left column are also defined in the **glossary.**

Biology (bī ol´ a jē) The study of life (p. 2)

Word Study Tips

◆ Start a vocabulary file with index cards to use for review.
◆ Write one term on the front of each card. Write the chapter number, lesson number, and definition on the back.
◆ You can use these cards as flash cards by yourself or with a study partner to test your knowledge.

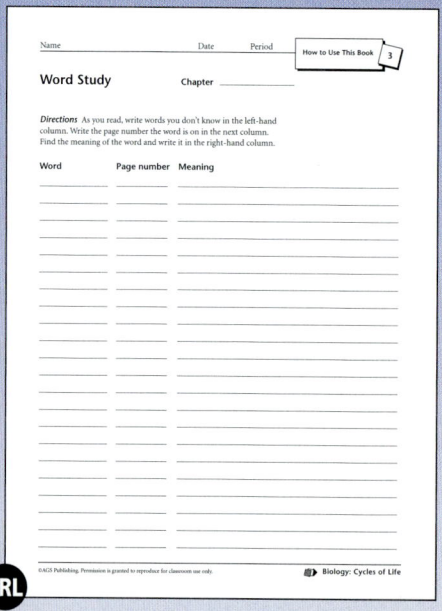

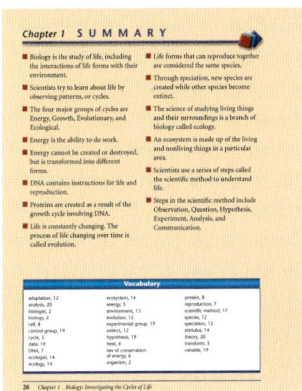

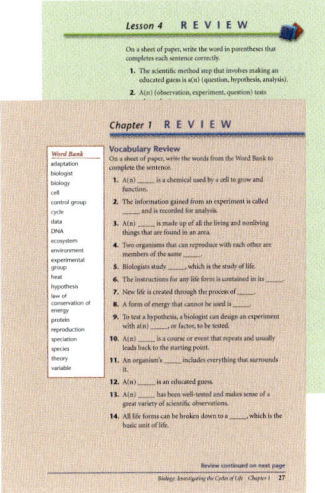

Using the Summaries

◆ Read each Chapter Summary to be sure you understand the chapter's main ideas.

◆ Make up a sample test of items you think may be on the test. You may want to do this with a classmate and share your questions.

◆ Read the vocabulary words in the Vocabulary box.

◆ Review your notes and test yourself on vocabulary words and key ideas.

◆ Practice writing about some of the main ideas from the chapter.

Using the Reviews

◆ Answer the questions in the Lesson Reviews.

◆ In the Chapter Reviews, answer the questions about vocabulary under the Vocabulary Review. Study the words and definitions. Say them aloud to help you remember them.

◆ Answer the questions under the Concept Review and Critical Thinking sections of the Chapter Reviews.

◆ Review the Test-Taking Tips.

Preparing for Tests

◆ Complete the Lesson Reviews and Chapter Reviews.

◆ Complete the Investigations and Discovery Investigations.

◆ Review your answers to Lesson Reviews, Investigations, Discovery Investigations, and Chapter Reviews.

◆ Test yourself on vocabulary words and key ideas.

◆ Use graphic organizers as study tools.

How to Use This Book: A Study Guide

Using the Summaries

Have students turn to page 26 and examine the Chapter 1 Summary. Emphasize that Chapter Summaries identify the main ideas of the chapter. Suggest that students can use the summary to focus their study of the chapter content. They might write each main idea in a notebook and add a few details that reinforce it. These notes will make a useful study tool.

Using the Reviews

Have students turn to page 4 and examine the Lesson 1 Review for Chapter 1. Explain that Lesson Reviews provide opportunities for students to focus on important content and skills developed in the lesson.

Then have students view pages 27–29. Point out that the Chapter Review is intended to help them focus on and review the key terms, content information, and skills presented in the chapter before they are tested on the material. Suggest that they complete the review after they have studied their notes, vocabulary lists, and worksheets.

Preparing for Tests

Encourage students to offer their opinions about tests and their ideas on test-taking strategies. Ask students: What do you do to study for a test? List their comments on the board. Then ask a volunteer to read the set of bulleted statements under "Preparing for Tests." Add these suggestions to the list on the board if they are not already there.

Discuss why each suggestion can help students when they are taking a test. Lead students to recognize that these suggestions, along with the Test-Taking Tips in their textbooks, can help them improve their test-taking skills.

Have students find a Test-Taking Tip in the Chapter Reviews. Remind them that Chapter Reviews can be found at the end of each chapter. Ask several volunteers to read aloud the tips they find in the Chapter Reviews. Discuss how using the tips can help students study and take tests more effectively.

How to Use This Book: A Study Guide

Using Graphic Organizers

Explain to students that graphic organizers provide ways of visually organizing information to make it easier to understand and remember. Tell students that they can use a variety of organizers to record information for a variety of purposes. Encourage them to create graphic organizers to help them understand a concept in the text, compare several things, visualize how information is related, summarize information, and study for a test.

Concept Maps

Concept maps help organize information such as main ideas and related details. Encourage students to look at the Organize Your Thoughts chart at the beginning of each chapter. Discuss how these graphic organizers provide a preview of the chapter content. Another type of concept map shown on page xvii provides more information about how the information is related. Encourage students to take this concept map and write sentences from it. Place an example on the board. *(Compounds can be either ionic or molecular.)*

Using Graphic Organizers

Graphic organizers are visual representations of information. Concept maps, flowcharts, circle diagrams, Venn diagrams, column charts, and graphs are some examples of graphic organizers. You can use graphic organizers to organize information, connect related ideas, or understand steps in a process. You can use them to classify or compare things, summarize complex topics, and communicate information. You can also use them to study for tests.

As you read this book, practice making your own graphic organizers. You will find that graphic organizers are helpful tools for learning biology and any other subject.

Concept Maps

A concept map consists of a main concept or idea and related concepts. Each concept—usually one or two words or a short phrase—is written in a circle or box. The organization of concepts in the map shows how they are related.

In the concept map below, Organic Molecules is the main concept. It appears at the top of the map. Carbohydrates, Lipids, Proteins, and Nucleic Acids are all concepts related to Organic Molecules. Each of these related concepts appears in a box below Organic Molecules. Each one is connected to Organic Molecules with a straight line to show they are related. The main concept is the most general. The other concepts are more specific. You will find a concept map at the beginning of each chapter of the book. This simple concept map identifies the main concepts discussed in the chapter and shows how they are connected.

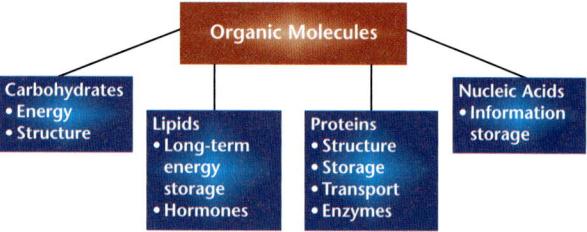

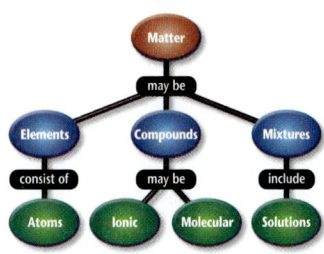

The graphic organizer at the left is another example of a concept map. To create this concept map, write the main concept. Draw a circle around it. Next, identify important ideas related to the main concept. Choose a word or a short phrase for each idea. Arrange these under or around the main concept. Draw a circle or box around each idea. Then add lines to link related ideas and concepts. The lines should not cross. You can label the lines to tell why the circles are linked.

Flowcharts

You can use a flowchart to diagram the steps in a process or procedure. The flowchart at the left shows the process of mitosis. Notice it is a vertical chart. Flowcharts can be vertical or horizontal. To make a flowchart, identify the steps to include. Write each step in the correct order, either in a vertical column or in a horizontal row. Draw a box around each step. Connect the boxes with arrows to show direction. You can label the arrows to tell what must happen to get from one step to the next.

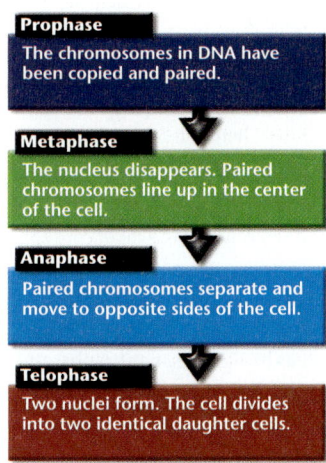

Column Charts

You can use a chart or a table to record information and organize it into groups or categories for easy reference. A chart can be a table, a graph, or a diagram. A table is data systematically arranged in rows and columns. To create a column chart, determine the number of items, groups, or categories you want to use. Decide on the number of columns and rows. Draw a chart with that number of columns and rows. Write a heading at the top of each column. Fill in the chart and a title.

Flowcharts

Tell students that flowcharts can help them visually see the order and the amount of steps in a particular process or procedure. Have students look at the flowchart on this page. Ask volunteers to describe how this flowchart helps them understand the process of mitosis.

Column Charts

Explain to students that charts can contain lists of information that include every detail that is known about the category. The information might show similarities and/or differences between each of the headings. Explain to students that it is best to include the same type of details in each column. For example, the first detail in each column of the "Four Biomes" is related to climate. This type of organization provides an easy reference tool.

Venn Diagrams

Show students how a Venn diagram is useful for comparing and contrasting information. Draw a Venn diagram on the board. Explain how to use the diagram to compare and contrast two items, such as a ball and a globe. Discuss how the diagram clearly shows the similarities and differences between the two items.

Circle Diagrams

Make sure students understand the difference between a circle diagram and a flowchart. Draw the water cycle on the board (*evaporation, condensation, precipitation, accumulation*). Tell students that a circle diagram is the best way to show this process, because the water cycle is continuous.

Graphs

Take the data in the circle graph and create a line graph and a bar graph on the board. Discuss with students how each type of graph provides a different visual representation of the same data. As you draw the graphs, remind students that the horizontal line is called the *x*-axis and the vertical line is called the *y*-axis.

Encourage students to refer back to the pages in this section, "How to Use This Book," as often as they wish while using this textbook.

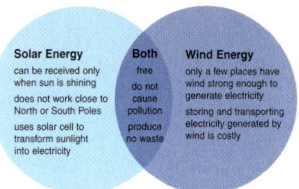

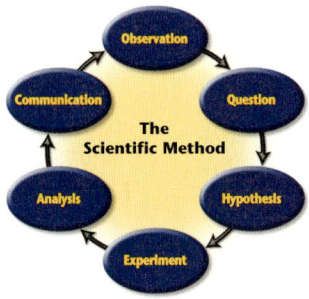

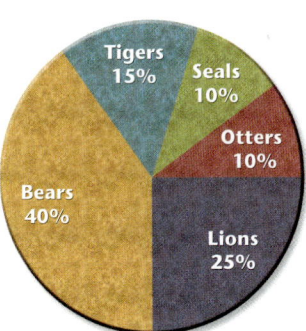

Venn Diagrams

A Venn diagram can help you compare and contrast two objects or processes. To create a Venn diagram, draw two circles of equal size that partially overlap. The circles represent the two things you want to compare. List the characteristics of one in the left circle. List the characteristics of the other in the right circle. List the characteristics both have in common in the area where the two circles intersect.

Circle Diagrams

A circle diagram shows a cycle that repeats. A circle diagram is similar to a flowchart except the last step is connected to the first step. To make a circle diagram, first identify the steps in the process or procedure. Then write the steps in a circle instead of a line. Use arrows to connect the steps. The circle diagram at the left shows the scientific method.

Graphs

You can use a graph to make comparisons and identify patterns among data. Graphs come in many forms such as line graphs, bar graphs, and circle graphs. To create a line or bar graph, draw two perpendicular axes. Label each axis to represent one variable. Add data. Each point or bar indicates a set of values for the two variables. Connect the points or compare the bars to see how the two variables relate. A circle graph shows the size of parts in a whole. To make one, draw a circle. Draw pie-shaped sections of the circle in proportion to the parts. For example, if lions make up one-quarter of a whole population, their section is one-quarter of the circle. Label each section and write its percentage of the whole.

Safety Rules and Symbols

In this book, you will learn about biology through investigations and labs. During these activities, it is important to follow safety rules, procedures, and your teacher's directions. You can avoid accidents by following directions and handling materials carefully. Read and follow the safety rules below, and learn the safety symbols. To alert you to possible dangers, safety symbols will appear with each investigation or lab. Reread the rules below often and review what the symbols mean.

General Safety
- Read each Express Lab, Investigation, and Discovery Investigation before doing it. Review the materials list and follow the safety symbols and safety alerts.
- Ask questions if you do not understand something.
- Never perform an experiment, mix substances, or use equipment without permission.
- Keep your work area clean and free of clutter.
- Be aware of other students working near you.
- Do not play or run during a lab activity. Take your lab work seriously.
- Know where fire extinguishers, fire alarms, first aid kits, fire blankets, and the nearest telephone are located. Be familiar with the emergency exits and evacuation route from your room.
- Keep your hands away from your face.
- Immediately report all accidents to your teacher, including injuries, broken equipment, and spills.

Flame/Heat Safety
- Clear your work space of materials that could burn or melt.
- Before using a burner, know how to operate the burner and gas outlet.
- Be aware of all open flames. Never reach across a flame.
- Never leave a flame or operating hot plate unattended.
- Do not heat a liquid in a closed container.
- When heating a substance in a test tube or flask, point the container away from yourself and others.
- Do not touch hot glassware or the surface of an operating hot plate or lightbulb.
- In the event of a fire, tell your teacher and leave the room immediately.
- If your clothes catch on fire, stop, drop to the floor, and roll.

Safety Rules and Symbols

Please make sure all students read the safety rules before performing an investigation or a lab. Ask them to become familiar with the symbols explained below. Answer any questions that students might have. For additional information, the Council of State Science Supervisors (CSSS) has put together a set of commonly asked questions regarding inquiry instruction. These can be downloaded as a PDF file at http://csss.enc.org/media/scisafe.pdf.

General Safety

Have a volunteer read aloud each item listed under "General Safety." Tell students that in addition to these bulleted points, they should not bring food or beverages into any lab setting. Remind them that it is important to wash their hands after each investigation or lab. Also, make sure that each student is familiar with the location of emergency exits and fire extinguishers.

Flame/Heat Safety

Encourage students to read each of the points about flame and heat safety. Discuss any questions that individuals have. Pick a day to practice what to do in the event of a fire. Have a volunteer demonstrate how to stop, drop, and roll if their clothes catch fire.

Electrical Safety

Explain to students that electricity can be very dangerous. Read aloud as a class each of the bulleted points. Encourage students to memorize the first point. Be sure that you know the location of circuit breakers for the laboratory and how to turn off the power to all the outlets. Also, make sure that all high-powered equipment has plugs with three prongs. This will ensure that the equipment is grounded. Always avoid using extension cords.

Chemical Safety

After students read everything under "Chemical Safety," ask them if they have any questions. Explain to students that different chemicals have different instructions for handling. When you receive a Material Safety Data Sheet, be sure to share the handling information with students. This data should be kept on file, because it also will provide information about cleanup and disposal.

Eye Protection

Have students look at the symbol for "Eye Protection." Tell them to look through several chapters and find this symbol. Explain that they will often be required to wear safety goggles while performing an experiment. If there are not enough safety goggles for every student, then pair or group students together for an experiment. Explain to students that they will need to wash the goggles after each person has used them. Encourage students to tell you if anything gets in their eye or on their face.

Animal Safety

Using animals in a lab can provide students with a greater understanding and appreciation of the complexity and connectivity of all animals. Please consider the safety of both the students and the animals. Follow all local, state, and national laws governing the humane treatment of animals. A list of precautions can be found within the CSSS file at http://csss.enc.org/media/scisafe.pdf.

Also, remember to be sensitive to any concerns expressed by students.

Electrical Safety
- Never use electrical equipment near water, on wet surfaces, or with wet hands or clothing.
- Alert your teacher to any frayed or damaged cords or plugs.
- Before plugging in equipment, be sure the power control is in the "off" position.
- Do not place electrical cords in walkways or let cords hang over table edges.
- Electricity flowing in wire causes the wire to become hot. Use caution.
- Turn off and unplug electrical equipment when you are finished using it.

Chemical Safety
- Check labels on containers to be sure you are using the right substance.
- Do not directly smell any substance. If you are instructed to smell a substance, gently fan your hand over the substance, waving its vapors toward you.
- When handling substances that give off gases or vapors, work in a fume hood or well-ventilated area.
- Do not taste any substance. Never eat, drink, or chew gum in your work area.
- Do not return unused chemicals to their original containers.
- Avoid skin contact with chemicals. Some chemicals can irritate or harm skin.
- If a chemical spills on your clothing or skin, rinse the area immediately with plenty of water. Tell your teacher.
- When diluting an acid or base with water, always add the acid or base to the water. Do not add water to the acid or base.
- Wash your hands after working with chemicals.

Eye Protection
- Wear safety goggles at all times or as directed by your teacher.
- If a chemical gets in your eyes or on your face, use an eyewash station or flush your eyes and face with running water immediately. Tell your teacher.

Animal Safety
- Do not touch or approach an animal without your teacher's permission.
- Handle and care for animals only as your teacher directs.
- If you are bitten, stung, or scratched by an animal, tell your teacher.
- Do not expose animals to loud noises, overcrowding, or other stresses.
- Wash your hands after touching an animal.

Hand Safety
- Wear protective gloves when working with chemicals or solutions. Wear gloves for handling preserved specimens and plants.
- Do not touch an object that could be hot.
- Use tongs or utensils to hold a container over a heat source.
- Wash your hands when you are finished with a lab activity.

Plant Safety
- Do not place any part of a plant in your mouth. Do not rub plant parts or liquids on your skin.
- Wear gloves when handling plants or as directed by your teacher.
- Wash your hands after handling any part of a plant.

Glassware Safety
- Check glassware for cracks or chips before use. Give broken glassware to your teacher; do not use it.
- Keep glassware away from the edge of a work surface.
- If glassware breaks, tell your teacher. Dispose of glass according to your teacher's directions.

Clothing Protection
- Wear a lab coat or apron at all times or as directed by your teacher.
- Tie back long hair, remove dangling jewelry, and secure loose-fitting clothing.
- Do not wear open-toed shoes, sandals, or canvas shoes in the lab.

Sharp Object Safety
- Take care when using scissors, pins, scalpels, or pointed tools or blades.
- Cut objects on a suitable work surface. Cut away from yourself and others.
- If you cut yourself, notify your teacher.

Cleanup/Waste Disposal
- If a chemical spills, alert your teacher and ask for clean up instructions.
- Follow your teacher's directions to dispose and clean up substances.
- Turn off burners, water faucets, electrical equipment, and gas outlets.
- Clean equipment if needed and return it to its proper location.
- Clean your work area and work surface.
- Wash your hands when you are finished.

Hand Safety

Tell students that gloves will provide protection from a number of substances. Ask a volunteer to find a lab in the text that has the "Hand Safety" symbol. Have students discuss why this particular lab has this symbol.

Plant Safety

Tell students that they need to be careful when handling plants both inside and outside of the lab setting. Emphasize the need for students to wash their hands after handling plants.

Glassware Safety

Have a volunteer read aloud the bulleted points under "Glassware Safety." Ask students to notify you of any broken glass during a lab. Make sure that all the pieces are cleaned up immediately. Provide students with a thick container such as a cardboard box for disposing of the broken glass.

Clothing Protection

After students read the safety points regarding clothing, explain to them why these are important. Ask that they remember to dress appropriately for labs. This includes remembering proper footwear. Have students discuss other types of clothing or accessories that might be inappropriate to wear during a lab.

Sharp Object Safety

Ask students to look at the symbol for "Sharp Object Safety." Tell students that even though the symbol is of scissors, the safety message if for any sharp object. Have students look through several chapters until they find this symbol. Ask them to find out what sharp object is being used in the lab they found. Then list all the objects on the board.

Cleanup/Waste Disposal

Explain to students that these steps are just as important as all the others mentioned in the "Safety Rules and Symbols" section. Have a volunteer read each of these bulleted items. Make sure students know the proper place to throw away each substance.

Chapter 1

Planning Guide
Biology: Investigating the Cycles of Life

	Student Pages	Vocabulary	Lesson Review	Critical-Thinking Questions
Lesson 1 What Is Biology?	2–4	✔	✔	✔
Lesson 2 Energy and Growth Cycles	5–9	✔	✔	✔
Lesson 3 Evolutionary and Ecological Cycles	10–16	✔	✔	✔
Lesson 4 The Scientific Method	17–25	✔	✔	✔

(Student Text Lesson)

Chapter Activities

Teacher's Resource Library
Community Connection 1:
 Biology Is Part of Everyone's Life
Graphic Organizer 1:
 Cycles of Life

Teacher's Edition
Opener Activity

Assessment Options

Student Text
Chapter 1 Review

Teacher's Resource Library
Chapter 1 Mastery Tests A and B

Teacher's Edition
Chapter 1 Alternative Assessment

Student Text Features									Teaching Strategies						Learning Styles					Teacher's Resource Library			
Achievements in Science	Science at Work	Biology in Your Life	Investigation/Discovery	Biology in the World	Express Lab	Link to	Research and Write	Technology and Society	ELL/ESL Strategy	Background Information	Science Journal	Applications (Home, Career, Community, Global, Environment)	Online Connection	Teacher Alert	Auditory/Verbal	Body/Kinesthetic	Interpersonal/Group Learning	Logical/Mathematical	Visual/Spatial	Workbook Activities	Alternative Workbook Activities	Lab Manual	Self-Study Guide
						✔			3	2		4			3					1	1	1	✔
					5			7	6	5	8			7					6	2	2	1–2	✔
	11	13	15			✔			12	10		12				12				3	3	3	✔
21			23	25		✔	29		19	17	19	19, 21	25	20				19	20	4–5	4–5	4–5	✔

Pronunciation Key

a	hat	e	let	ī	ice	ô	order	ủ	put	sh	she
ā	age	ē	equal	o	hot	oi	oil	ü	rule	th	thin
ä	far	ėr	term	ō	open	ou	out	ch	child	ŦH	then
â	care	i	it	ȯ	saw	u	cup	ng	long	zh	measure

ə { a in about, e in taken, i in pencil, o in lemon, u in circus }

Alternative Workbook Activities

The Teacher's Resource Library (TRL) contains a set of lower-level worksheets called Alternative Workbook Activities. These worksheets cover the same content as the regular Workbook Activities but are written at a second-grade reading level.

Skill Track Online

Use Skill Track Online for *Biology: Cycles of Life* to monitor student progress and meet the demands of adequate yearly progress (AYP). Make informed instructional decisions with individual student and class reports of online lesson and chapter assessments. With immediate and ongoing feedback, students will also see what they have learned and where they need more reinforcement and practice.

Chapter at a Glance

Chapter 1: Biology: Investigating the Cycles of Life
pages 1–29

Lessons

1. What Is Biology?
   pages 2–4

2. Energy and Growth Cycles
   pages 5–9

3. Evolutionary and Ecological Cycles
   pages 10–16

   Investigation 1 pages 15–16

4. The Scientific Method
   pages 17–25

   Discovery Investigation 1
   pages 23–24

   Biology in the World page 25

Chapter 1 Summary page 26

Chapter 1 Review pages 27–29

Audio CD

Skill Track Online
for Biology: Cycles of Life

Teacher's Resource Library TRL

  Workbook Activities 1–5

  Alternative Workbook Activities
  1–5

  Lab Manual 1–5

  Community Connection 1

  Graphic Organizer 1

  Resource File 1–2

  Chapter 1 Self-Study Guide

  Chapter 1 Mastery Tests A and B

(Answer Keys for the Teacher's Resource Library begin on page 675 of the Teacher's Edition. The Materials List for the Lab Manual activities begins on page 720.)

Opener Activity

Display an assortment of photographs showing some of the variety of life on Earth. Include photographs of viruses, bacteria, common plants and animals, and unusual marine plants and animals. As the chapter progresses, have students revisit the photographs and describe what biologists might study about each organism.

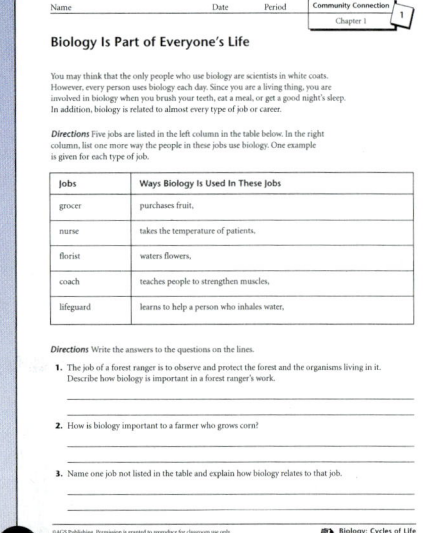

Community Connection 1

Chapter 1

Biology: Investigating the Cycles of Life

The photo on the left shows the different stages of a butterfly's life. The caterpillar at the bottom could be called the infant stage. The middle object is a chrysalis. Inside this hard case, the caterpillar is going through many changes. You might say it's a teenager. When the insect breaks out of the case, it's an adult winged butterfly. These stages make up the life cycle of a butterfly. All living things go through life cycles. In Chapter 1, you will learn about different cycles of life. You will also learn how scientists study life and science.

Organize Your Thoughts

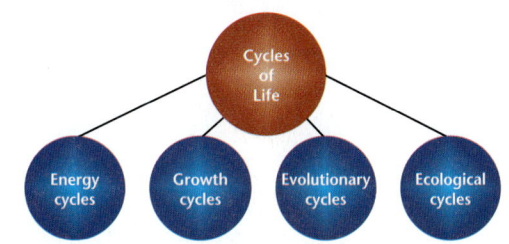

Goals for Learning

- ◆ To understand that biology is the study of life
- ◆ To describe energy and understand what happens in an energy cycle
- ◆ To describe what happens in a growth cycle
- ◆ To explain what happens during an evolutionary cycle
- ◆ To explain what an ecological cycle is
- ◆ To tell why scientists use the scientific method

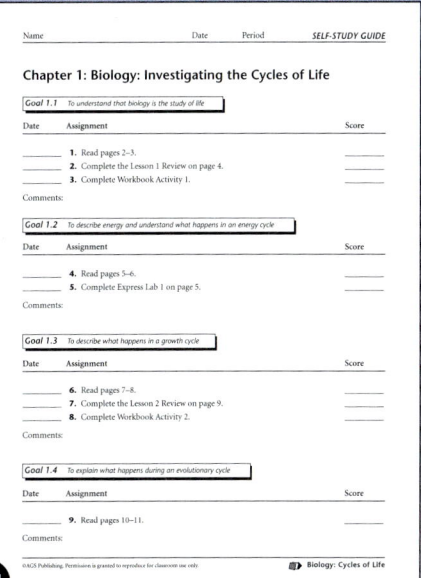

Chapter 1 Self-Study Guide

Introducing the Chapter

Use the opening paragraph to introduce the idea of cycles. Have students draw on a sheet of paper a diagram of the life cycle of a butterfly. Explain to students that all living things go through a life cycle. Ask students to draw on another sheet of paper the life cycle of a human.

Have students read the Goals for Learning. For each goal, have students write what they know and what they would like to learn. As they learn more about each goal, have them write what they learned.

Notes and Math Tips

Ask volunteers to read the notes and math tips that appear in the margins throughout the chapter. Then discuss them with the class.

TEACHER'S RESOURCE

The AGS Publishing Teaching Strategies in Science Transparencies may be used with this chapter. The transparencies add an interactive dimension to expand and enhance the *Biology: Cycles of Life* program content.

CAREER INTEREST INVENTORY

The AGS Publishing Harrington-O'Shea Career Decision-Making System-Revised (CDM) may be used with this chapter. Students can use the CDM to explore their interests and identify careers. The CDM defines career areas that are indicated by students' responses on the inventory.

Biology: Investigating the Cycles of Life

Lesson at a Glance

Chapter 1 Lesson 1

Overview In this lesson, students learn about the four cycles of life. Students also will learn how biologists use the scientific method.

Objectives

- To define *biology* and its use in daily life
- To list different types of biologists
- To list the four cycles of life

Student Pages 2–4

Teacher's Resource Library TRL

Workbook Activity 1
Alternative Workbook Activity 1
Resource File 1

Vocabulary

biologist	cycle
biology	organism

Have students look up the vocabulary terms in a dictionary and write the definitions. Have students find the meaning of the prefixes and roots of *biology* and *biologist*. Have students use all of the words in written sentences.

Background Information

The study of biology is a very broad discipline. Some biologists study the behavior and characteristics of large land animals. Other biologists specialize in the study of marine life from the whale to the diatom. Still others study organisms that cannot be seen with the unaided eye. These microbiologists study viruses and bacteria that cause diseases and those that decompose dead organisms. The study of biology encompasses a vast diversity of life on Earth.

 Warm-Up Activity

To introduce the concept of a cycle, show students the cycle of weekdays. Explain that the week begins on Sunday and ends on Saturday, then starts over. Cycles in biology work in a similar way.

2 Chapter 1

Lesson 1 What Is Biology?

Objectives

After reading this lesson, you should be able to
- define biology and its use in daily life
- list different types of biologists
- list the four cycles of life

Biology
The study of life

Organism
A living thing; one of many different forms of life

Biologist
A person who studies life

Biology is the name for a whole field of science. Simply put, biology is the study of life. That sounds pretty simple, doesn't it? Yes, but life is complex. Animals and plants are living. An insect flying around your head is part of life. Even the germs that cause you to get sick are living. That gray-green mold on old bread is another form of life. As you can see, many different **organisms** make up life. An organism is a living thing, one of many different forms of life.

Life means more than just a list of these different forms. Life includes how you and other life forms live in our world. Watering a garden is part of life. Birds flying south for the winter are part of life. Eating, drinking, cleaning yourself, even feeding your pets are all parts of life.

Biology is a science that studies all of these things and more. A **biologist** studies life. There are many different types of biologists. Some biologists study plants. Like the biologist in Figure 1.1.1, some biologists study animals. The list of biologists and what they do is long.

Figure 1.1.1 *Biologists study life.*

2 Chapter 1 Biology: Investigating the Cycles of Life

Cycle
A course or series of events or operations that repeats

Link to >>>
Earth Science
You might think about life as being present only in places where people live. However, some form of life exists in nearly every place on Earth. Scientists have discovered microscopic life at deep-sea vents on the bottom of the ocean and within thick layers of ice at the poles. They have even found life in the intense heat of rocket boosters!

There are many different ways to study life. How do biologists decide how to study life? They observe the world around them and find something they do not understand. When they find something they do not understand, they ask questions about it. Using different methods, they try to answer those questions. As biologists answer more and more questions, they notice patterns.

One pattern seen in different parts of life is a **cycle**. Saying life runs in cycles means that many of life's activities repeat themselves. It also means that many actions start at one point. These actions go through different steps to return to that same point. Upon returning to that point, they then begin the cycle all over again.

These cycles come in many different forms. Many overlap. This means parts of one cycle may be the starting point for other cycles. It may take a long time for some cycles to get back to the starting point. It may take others less than a second.

To better understand biology, we will look at some cycles that make life work. There are four major groups of cycles. Each cycle is made up of many different individual cycles. The four cycles are Energy, Growth, Evolutionary, and Ecological. As seen in Figure 1.1.2, all of these cycles work together.

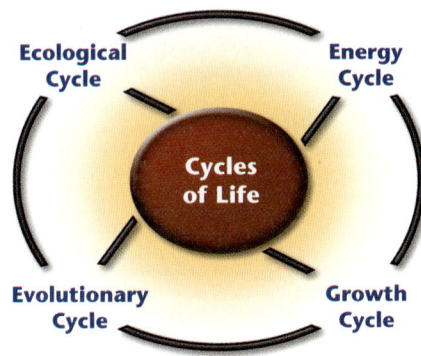

Figure 1.1.2 *Life cycles work together.*

2 Teaching the Lesson

As students read the lesson, have them write down the main ideas from each paragraph. Also have them write down any questions they may have about the material.

Write the following terms on the board: *biology, organism, biologist,* and *cycle.* Ask students to give a definition of each term in their own words. Correct any misconceptions that students may have about the meaning of each term.

Have students brainstorm about other cycles, such as months in a year, phases of the moon, and hours in a day.

3 Reinforce and Extend

LEARNING STYLES

Auditory/Verbal
Have small groups of students discuss what the word *life* means. Then have each group explain its definition to the class.

ELL/ESL STRATEGY

Language Objective:
To define the word cycle

To fully understand the word *cycle,* students who are learning English will benefit from an illustration of the "motion" of a cycle. Draw a circular diagram on the board, showing the word *egg* as the starting point. Draw an arc to the words *baby bird*. Then draw an arc to the words *adult bird*. Close the circle by drawing an arc back to the egg. Emphasize that the changes are moving in a circle, which is the way a cycle moves.

Link to

Earth Science. Have students read the feature about life found in extreme locations. Ask students: Why do you think life found in deep-sea vents is unusual? *(Sunlight does not reach these areas, and photosynthesis cannot occur.)*

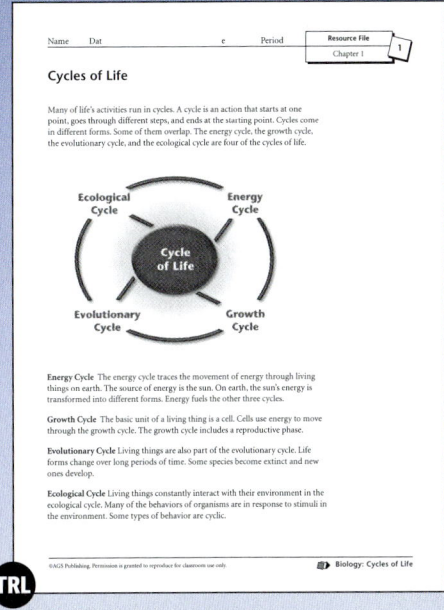

Resource File 1

Lesson 1 Review Answers

1. life **2.** cycles **3.** organisms **4.** C **5.** B
6. A **7.** A cycle is a pattern that repeats.
8. Answers will vary. Responses may include a variety of life forms, such as plants, animals, fungi, and microorganisms. **9.** A scientist begins by observing and asking questions. The scientist then tries to answer the questions and recognize patterns. A scientist would study a spider by first observing its behavior and then questioning why certain patterns of behavior appear.
10. The cycle begins again.

Portfolio Assessment

Sample items include:
- Questions and comments on Goals for Learning
- List of main ideas from each paragraph
- Lesson 1 Review answers

IN THE COMMUNITY

Have students list places they have been within the last week where they would be able to study biology in real life. Ask them to specify the life forms that they would find in those places.

LAB ACTIVITIES

Chapter 1 has Investigation and Discovery Investigation lab activities. Two additional lab activities for Chapter 1 appear in the Biology: Cycles of Life Lab Manual and on the Teacher's Resource Library CD-ROM.

4 Chapter 1

Lesson 1   REVIEW

On a sheet of paper, write the word that completes each sentence correctly.

1. Biology is the study of _____.
2. The activities of life run in patterns, or _____.
3. Life is made up of different _____, or forms of life.

On a sheet of paper, write the letter of the answer that completes each sentence correctly.

4. The first step a biologist takes when deciding how to study life is to _____.
   - **A** do an experiment   **C** make an observation
   - **B** write a paper   **D** make a hypothesis
5. A biologist studies _____.
   - **A** soil   **C** weather
   - **B** life   **D** rocks
6. Energy, growth, evolutionary, and ecological describe different types of _____.
   - **A** cycles   **C** experiments
   - **B** organisms   **D** life

Critical Thinking
On a sheet of paper, answer the following questions. Use complete sentences.

7. What is a cycle?
8. List three different examples of life.
9. How might a scientist begin to study the behavior of a spider?
10. What happens when a cycle returns to its starting point?

4   Chapter 1   Biology: Investigating the Cycles of Life

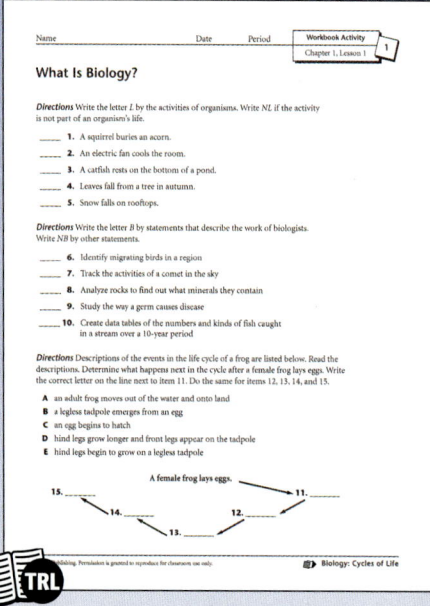

Workbook Activity 1

Lesson 2 Energy and Growth Cycles

Objectives

After reading this lesson, you should be able to
- define energy and give examples
- state the law of conservation of energy
- define reproduction
- name different parts of life that can reproduce
- connect energy and growth cycles

Energy
The ability to do work; found in many different forms

Transform
To change form or makeup

Energy Cycles

Energy is the ability to do work. Think about how you use energy. You use energy to walk, talk, sing, and even eat. You need energy to do anything. Energy is found in many different forms. Energy allows life to do what it is supposed to do. Where does energy come from? The sun serves as the main source of energy for our planet. How does sunlight give you energy to play a game, even when you are inside? The energy from the sun changes into different forms.

Energy can **transform**, or change form, into different types, depending on how it is used. What happens when the energy runs out? Energy never runs out. It just changes completely into other forms.

Express Lab 1

Materials
- safety goggles
- solar cell with small connecting motor

Procedure
1. On a sunny day, take the solar cell and connecting motor outside. Put on safety goggles.
2. Observe the activity of the motor when the solar cell is exposed to the sun.
3. Cover the solar cell and observe the activity of the motor.
4. Uncover and cover the solar cell 2 or 3 times. Observe the activity of the motor.

Analysis
1. What was the source of energy in this activity?
2. Why did the activity of the motor change when you covered the solar cell?
3. Describe the different ways that energy was transformed during this activity.

Biology: Investigating the Cycles of Life Chapter 1 5

Lesson at a Glance

Chapter 1 Lesson 2

Overview In this lesson, students learn about the energy cycle, the law of conservation of energy, and growth cycles.

Objectives
- To define *energy* and give examples
- To state the law of conservation of energy
- To define *reproduction*
- To name different parts of life that can reproduce
- To connect energy and growth cycles

Student Pages 5–9

Teacher's Resource Library
Workbook Activity 2
Alternative Workbook Activity 2
Lab Manual 1–2

Vocabulary

cell	law of conservation of energy
DNA	protein
energy	reproduction
heat	transform

Have students work in pairs. Have one student read the definition of a vocabulary term and the other student supply the term. Repeat until all of the terms have been used. Have students exchange roles.

Background Information

Energy is a fundamental need for all life. The sun supplies a constant supply of energy that is used by all organisms. Green plants directly use energy from the sun. They use photosynthesis to convert sunlight into a form of chemical energy that other organisms can use. Organisms that eat green plants provide energy for other organisms higher up on the food chain or food web.

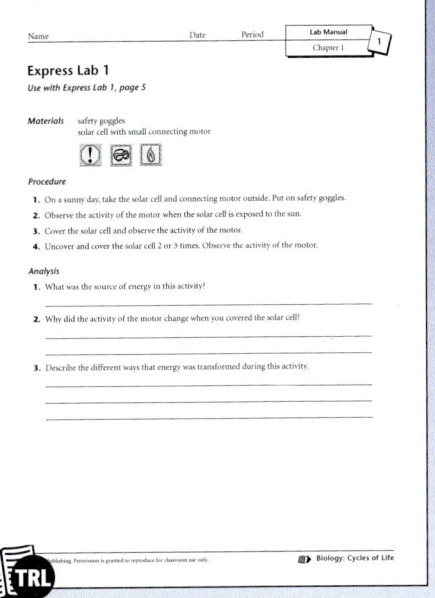

Lab Manual 1

1 Warm-Up Activity

Show students a solar-powered calculator. Show them that if you cover the sensor, the calculator will turn off. Explain that the calculator uses a solar cell to generate electricity. Energy from the sun is converted to electrical energy by the solar cell. Have students complete the Express Lab.

Express Lab Answers

1. the sun **2.** The source of energy, the sun, was blocked. **3.** Solar energy from the sun was transformed into electrical energy in the solar cells. The electrical energy was transformed into mechanical energy of the motor.

Biology: Investigating the Cycles of Life 5

2 Teaching the Lesson

Before the class reads the lesson, light a candle. Tell students that a burning candle is part of an energy cycle. The chemical bonds in the candle wax are broken and release thermal energy and light. The chemical energy is not destroyed. It is converted to thermal energy and light.

Tell students that the human body is similar to the burning candle. The energy in the food that people eat is used by the body to undergo body processes such as growth and reproduction.

To reinforce the idea of energy cycles, have students rub their hands together very quickly for a minute. The kinetic energy in their hands is converted to thermal energy. The air around their hands is heated up slightly by the thermal energy from their hands.

3 Reinforce and Extend

ELL/ESL Strategy

Language Objective: *To describe an energy cycle*

Have students work in small groups to make a poster showing an energy cycle. Have them label each part of the cycle. Then have each group present its poster to the class.

Learning Styles

Visual/Spatial

Have students study Figure 1.2.1 and identify the energy source for each organism found in the photograph. *(All green plants get their energy from the sun. The animal gets its energy from green plants, products of green plants such as nuts or berries, or other living things such as insects or other small animals. The energy source for the insects and other small animals can also be traced back to the sun.)*

Law of conservation of energy
Energy cannot be created or destroyed

Heat
A form of energy resulting from the motion of particles in matter

A law in science states that energy cannot be created or destroyed. This is called the **law of conservation of energy.** Each time energy changes form, some of it is given off as **heat.** Heat is a form of energy. That means that during any energy transformation, all the energy will not be able to be used in the new form.

So how does energy cycle? Overall, the energy in the universe cycles through different forms. On Earth, energy gets cycled through life in different forms. Figure 1.2.1 shows that different organisms have their own cycles they run through to do work.

We will look at some of the different forms of energy and their cycles in the next sections. Understanding how energy cycles through life lets us see how life operates.

Figure 1.2.1 *Every life form needs energy to do work.*

6 Chapter 1 Biology: Investigating the Cycles of Life

Reproduction
The process of making new life

DNA
Deoxyribonucleic acid; a chemical in an organism that contains the instructions for life

Cell
The basic unit of life

Growth Cycles

If you use energy to do work, what kind of work are you doing? That answer depends on what part of life you study. A major job of all forms of life is to grow. Growth is found at many different levels.

One of the biggest parts of growth is the making of new life through **reproduction.** Reproduction occurs in many ways from **DNA.** The letters DNA stand for deoxyribonucleic acid, a chemical in an organism that contains the instructions for life. Different cycles are involved in growing. Each cycle ties into the next.

All of these cycles use energy from different energy cycles to run. By growing, the smallest units of life, called **cells,** are able to carry out their job. As cells grow, so do organisms. As organisms grow, they can reproduce and start the cycles all over again in new organisms. One cycle that all life runs is that of life and death.

Technology and Society

Genetic disorders can cause different kinds of diseases in humans. When a person has a genetic disorder, it means that an important section of his or her DNA does not work properly. Scientists are learning how to insert healthy DNA into human cells to cure a disease. This technique is called gene therapy. The hope is that when cells with healthy DNA are added to a person's body, they will begin to produce new cells that work properly. In time, the new cells would correct the damage and heal the person. Doctors are using gene therapy to help patients with many diseases, including cancer and cystic fibrosis.

TEACHER ALERT

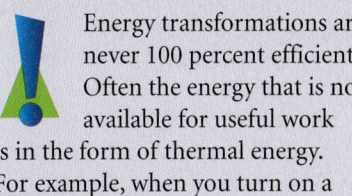

Energy transformations are never 100 percent efficient. Often the energy that is not available for useful work is in the form of thermal energy. For example, when you turn on a flashlight, some of the chemical energy transforms to light. That is the energy transformation that is useful. Some of the chemical energy is transformed into thermal energy as the flashlight bulb gets hot. This energy is not available for useful work.

PRONUNCIATION GUIDE

Use the pronunciation shown here to help students pronounce difficult words in the lesson. Refer to the pronunciation key on the Chapter Planning Guide for the sounds of the symbols.

deoxyribonucleic (dē ok´sə rī´bō nü klē´ik)

genetic (jə net´ik)

gene (jēn)

Technology and Society

Have students read the feature about genetic disorders and gene therapy. Tell students that there are two types of gene therapy: somatic-cell therapy and germ-line therapy. In somatic-cell therapy, doctors attempt to fix malfunctions in body cells such as blood cells and skin cells. In germ-line therapy, doctors attempt to alter sperm and egg cells in an attempt to prevent genetic diseases in children. Have students research to find more information about gene therapy.

SCIENCE JOURNAL

Have students write a paragraph in their journal discussing specific characteristics they have inherited that make them a unique individual. Students may include characteristics such as eye color, hair color, face shape, height, and skin color.

Protein
A chemical used by cells to grow and work

Some growth cycles not only help in reproduction, but also in doing work. The instructions found in DNA are turned into action through different cycles. The products of these cycles, such as **proteins,** water, and heat, help a cell to grow and work. These products run their own cycles. As a cell ages, it begins to reproduce itself through different methods.

When DNA and cells reproduce, random events occur that help bring about each organism's uniqueness. You can see in Figure 1.2.2 that each individual has his or her own special group of qualities. This uniqueness in organisms is important for life to continue.

Figure 1.2.2 *Every individual has special qualities.*

8 *Chapter 1   Biology: Investigating the Cycles of Life*

Lesson 2 REVIEW

On a sheet of paper, write the letter of the answer that completes each sentence correctly.

1. When energy changes form, some energy is _____.
   - A lost
   - B gained
   - C given off as heat
   - D added as heat

2. A chemical called _____ contains the instructions for life.
   - A protein
   - B DNA
   - C cell
   - D atom

3. The process of making new life is called _____.
   - A reproduction
   - B DNA
   - C heat
   - D growth cycle

On a sheet of paper, write the word that completes each sentence correctly.

4. The main source of energy for our planet comes from the _____.

5. The smallest unit of life is the _____.

6. The idea that energy cannot be created or destroyed is the law of _____ of energy.

Critical Thinking

On a sheet of paper, answer the following questions. Use complete sentences.

7. Give two examples of how you used energy today.

8. How are energy cycles and growth cycles related?

9. Explain why the sentence, "Rubbing your hands together creates energy," is an incorrect statement.

10. Why is it important to get enough protein in your diet?

Biology: Investigating the Cycles of Life Chapter 1   9

Lesson 2 Review Answers

1. C **2.** B **3.** A **4.** sun **5.** cell **6.** conservation **7.** Answers will vary. Examples may include any actions performed by students. **8.** The cycles of life require the transformation of energy. **9.** It is incorrect because energy cannot be created or destroyed. **10.** Proteins help your cells grow and work correctly.

Portfolio Assessment

Sample items include:
- Answers to Express Lab
- Research findings about gene therapy from Technology and Society
- Lesson 2 Review answers

Lab Manual 2, pages 1–2

Workbook Activity 2

Biology: Investigating the Cycles of Life   9

Lesson at a Glance

Chapter 1 Lesson 3

Overview In this lesson, students learn about evolutionary and ecological cycles.

Objectives
- To define *evolution*
- To tell how species change
- To define *ecosystem*
- To list examples of behavior changes

Student Pages 10–16

Teacher's Resource Library
Workbook Activity 3
Alternative Workbook Activity 3
Lab Manual 3

Vocabulary

adaptation	evolution
ecologist	extinct
ecology	speciation
ecosystem	species
environment	stimulus

Have students create crossword puzzles using the vocabulary terms. Have students exchange their puzzles and solve another student's puzzle.

Background Information

Some scientists believe that a huge meteorite may have struck Earth, causing the dinosaurs to become extinct. The meteorite may have created a huge dust cloud that blocked out the sun. This lowered the temperatures on Earth. The dinosaurs were not able to adapt to the changes on Earth quickly enough and died. Organisms that were able to survive the quick changes evolved over time.

Lesson 3 — Evolutionary and Ecological Cycles

Objectives
After reading this lesson, you should be able to
- define evolution
- tell how species change
- define ecosystem
- list examples of behavior changes

Evolution
The changes in a population over time

Species
A group of organisms that can reproduce with each other

Speciation
The process of making a new species

Extinct
When no members of a species are alive

Adaptation
An adjustment to environmental conditions

Evolutionary Cycles

Life must change to grow. Does this mean the way life is now is not the way it has always been? Think about it. Dinosaurs once existed on Earth, although we don't see these big lizards on the planet today. Scientists have discovered their bones. Dinosaurs are one of many examples that show biologists that life changes. The process of life changing over time is called **evolution.**

If life keeps changing, how does it cycle back to the beginning? The actions of evolution happen in cycles, but the products are different. Scientists group all organisms into **species.** Individuals in the same species can reproduce with each other. Life changes over time by creating new species, a process called **speciation.**

Speciation often happens in bursts. Usually, some event like an earthquake, flood, or other natural disaster causes some species to become **extinct.** Extinction means that species no longer exist. Extinction can make room for new species, and the evolutionary cycle continues. Many species will be created from the species that are left. As seen in Figures 1.3.1 and 1.3.2, new species have **adaptations,** or changes, that make them better able to live in new areas. As these new species grow, some are better able to live than others.

Figures 1.3.1 and 1.3.2 *Animals adapt to their environment.*

Environment
An organism's natural and man-made surroundings

Link to >>>
Environmental Science

Many advances in technology and the environment come from other organisms. Environmental engineers recently observed microscopic organisms called *bacteria* eating toxic waste on an abandoned industrial site in Michigan. They isolated and released the bacteria onto a test site filled with a poisonous chemical that was harming Lake Huron. The bacteria cleaned the poisons from the site in just a few weeks.

These species become the major species found in an area. Other species will become extinct or keep adapting to survive. At some point, another major event will happen to cause extinction. Speciation starts over again. Evolutionary cycles are some of the slowest to happen. Biologists who study evolution measure time in millions of years. Evolution is present in all areas of biology.

Biologists study life. Life must change, or evolve, to grow. Events that cause evolution are found in DNA, the cell, and the **environment.** The environment is an organism's natural and man-made surroundings. Through evolution, life has changed into many different forms. Scientists group these forms together based on what each form has in common.

Science at Work

Environmental Engineer

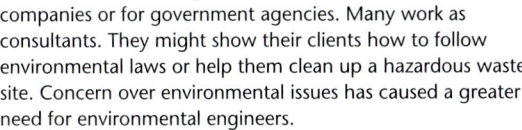

Environmental engineers use their knowledge of biology and chemistry to solve environmental problems. Environmental engineers work on a wide variety of projects. For example, they design water treatment systems and check levels of air pollution. They set up recycling programs, study the effects of acid rain, and protect wildlife.

Some environmental engineers work for manufacturing companies or for government agencies. Many work as consultants. They might show their clients how to follow environmental laws or help them clean up a hazardous waste site. Concern over environmental issues has caused a greater need for environmental engineers.

Environmental engineers have a degree from a four-year college. They also must pass a test to be licensed by the government.

---

1. Warm-Up Activity

Show students a photograph of two animals that live in different environments, such as a goldfish and a penguin or a whale and crab. Ask students to write down the characteristics of each animal. Then ask students why these characteristics also could be viewed as adaptations that these animals have made to their environments.

2. Teaching the Lesson

Before students read the lesson, have them write down what they know about evolution and ecosystems. As students read the lesson, have them write down the new information they learn.

Write the following words on the board: *rabbit, wolf,* and *lettuce.* Ask students: How do these organisms form an ecosystem? *(These organisms form an energy chain. The rabbit gets its energy from the lettuce, and the wolf gets its energy from the rabbit.)*

3. Reinforce and Extend

Science at Work

Ask volunteers to read the Science at Work feature.

Explain that environmental engineers work in laboratories and in the field. Their goal is to make the environment safe for all living things.

Have students research to find work projects in the local community that require environmental engineers.

Link to

Environmental Science. Have students read the feature on environmental cleanup.

Students may be surprised to learn that scientists are using bacteria to clean up oil spills. These bacteria ingest the toxic substances and turn them into harmless products.

LEARNING STYLES

Body/Kinesthetic
Have students act out the reaction to the following stimuli: someone tickles your nose with a feather; you accidentally touch a hot object; a mouse sees a cat; and a pet sees its food being prepared. Ask volunteers to supply additional reactions and stimuli.

IN THE ENVIRONMENT

Organisms that live in the wild react to many stimuli in order to survive. For example, bats use echolocation to fly and to find prey. Bats emit a high-frequency sound that bounces off objects. When the sound wave returns to the bat, the bat interprets the sound wave. The bat can tell where the object is and how fast it is moving. Have students research to find other stimuli that organisms use to stay alive.

ELL/ESL STRATEGY

Language Objective: *To summarize main ideas*

Divide the class into small groups. Assign half of the groups the Evolutionary Cycles section and half of the groups the Ecological Cycles section. Have each group prepare a presentation of the lesson content for another group. Encourage students to make visual aids, if needed, to present their material. Encourage students to ask questions if they do not understand the material.

Ecology
The study of interactions among living things and the nonliving things in their environment

Ecologist
A person who studies ecology

Ecosystem
All of the living and nonliving things found in any particular area

Stimulus
Anything to which an organism reacts

Ecological Cycles

You know that life uses energy to grow and change over time, or evolve. Scientists also look at life in the present. **Ecology** is the branch of biology that studies the relationships of living things with each other and their surroundings. This branch of science looks at how members of the same species and different species live together.

Ecologists look at how organisms act in their environments. The environment has its own cycles that keep everyday life going. **Ecosystems** are made up of all the living and nonliving things in a particular area. As an example, think about a frog in a lily pond. The frog and lilies are living things. The water and rocks are nonliving things. A biologist may want to study why this frog lives in this lily pond.

Ecologists also study the behavior of organisms, or how they respond to stimuli. A **stimulus** is anything to which an organism reacts. The light coming in your bedroom in the morning is a stimulus that causes you, an organism, to wake up.

Organisms' behaviors often occur in cycles. For example, birds fly south for the winter. Then they fly north in the spring. Chipmunks, woodchucks, box turtles, and toads go into hibernation in the winter. As spring approaches, they become active. The way a body receives and sends messages is a cycle. Some cycles happen in less than a second, like body messages. Other cycles take years to run a full course.

Biology in Your Life

The Environment

Have you traveled out of the country? If you have, you may have seen government agents searching luggage or vehicles for plants or animals. The movement of plants and animals across international borders is controlled to protect the wildlife that lives in various ecosystems.

Travelers are not allowed to bring plants and animals from one environment into another. Ecosystems build up a balance of life that keeps the population fairly stable. If a plant or animal is released into a new ecosystem, it often can upset this balance.

One example of a disrupted ecosystem is the problem of the African clawed frog in California. African clawed frogs are banned in California, but many people bring them into the state to keep as pets.

Some frogs have escaped into the wild. They have reproduced, creating a new population of wild African clawed frogs. These wild frogs are now causing problems by eating and destroying many of the plants and animals in the state.

African clawed frogs are not from, or native to, California. No animals eat them or compete with them for resources. Without competition or predators, the number of frogs has increased rapidly. State officials are looking for ways to control them.

1. Why are African clawed frogs spreading so rapidly in California?
2. What resources do plants or animals compete for?
3. See if you can identify a plant or animal in your local environment that is not native to the area. Find out if it is disrupting the ecosystem. Write a description that explains how it is disrupting the ecosystem.

Biology in Your Life

Have students read the Biology in Your Life feature.

Ask students: Why do animals that are introduced to new environments often harm those environments? *(There are no natural predators that keep the populations under control.)* What happens to the plants or animals that the new animals eat? *(Their numbers rapidly decrease because there are more animals that eat them than before.)*

Biology in Your Life Answers

1. No animals eat them or compete with them for resources. **2.** Sample answer: Animals compete for food, water, shelter, mates, and space. Plants compete for nutrients, water, space, and sunlight. **3.** Answers will vary. Most local environments include some exotic or introduced (nonnative) species. Some introduced plants that have caused local problems include water hyacinths and kudzu. Animals include starlings and aquatic species such as Eurasian ruffles, sea lampreys, and zebra mussels.

Lesson 3 Review Answers

1. speciation 2. ecosystem 3. extinct
4. adaptations 5. ecology 6. species
7. Sample answer: The polar bear's white color makes it harder for its prey to see the bear. Its thick fur and a lot of fat keep the bear warm. 8. The extinction of a species creates room for other species. 9. An ecosystem is all of the living and nonliving things found in an area. Examples will vary. Sample answer: A tree is an ecosystem made up of birds, squirrels, insects, nests, leaves for food and shelter, etc. 10. The water is the stimulus.

Portfolio Assessment

Sample items include:
- Student's list of local environmental projects that use environmental engineers from Science at Work
- Answers from Biology in Your Life
- Answers to Lesson 3 Review questions

Lesson 3   R E V I E W

Word Bank
ecosystem
extinct
speciation

On a sheet of paper, write the word from the Word Bank that completes each sentence correctly.

1. The process of creating new species is _____.
2. A(n) _____ is made of the living and nonliving things in an area.
3. When no members of a species are alive, the species is _____.

On a sheet of paper, write the word that completes each statement correctly.

4. Changes that make a species better able to live in new areas are _____.
5. The study of living things and their environment is called _____.
6. Two kinds of organisms that cannot reproduce with each other are separate _____.

Critical Thinking

On a sheet of paper, answer the following questions. Use complete sentences.

7. How is a polar bear adapted to living in cold polar areas?
8. How does extinction of a species cause more species to develop?
9. What is an ecosystem? Give an example.
10. You water a wilted plant. The plant becomes healthy. What is the stimulus?

Workbook Activity 3

INVESTIGATION 1

Materials
- safety goggles
- lab coat or apron
- houseplant
- insect in a jar
- mushroom in a plastic bag
- petri dish with bacteria culture
- plant seeds
- plant sprout
- rock
- flashlight

What Is Life?

Biologists study all kinds of life. Life takes on many diverse forms. All life runs through cycles of energy, growth, evolution, and ecology. In this lab you will examine some different forms of life and note their different cycles.

Procedure

1. To record your data, make a data table like the one shown here.

Sample	Energy Cycle	Growth Cycle	Evolutionary Cycle	Ecological Cycle	Living/Nonliving
1					
2					
3					
4					
5					
6					
7					
8					

2. Put on safety goggles and a lab coat or apron. **Safety Alert: Do not open containers or touch samples unless your teacher directs you to do so.**

3. Examine each sample. Use a flashlight if needed. Make a check mark in the Energy Cycle column if you think the sample is involved in an energy cycle.

4. Repeat Step 3 for each cycle. Place a check mark in the column if you think the sample is involved in that cycle.

5. In the final column, decide whether the sample is living or nonliving.

Safety Alert
- Make sure that students have read and understood all safety rules for working in the lab. Discuss the Safety Alerts with students.
- Be sure students wear safety goggles and a lab coat or apron.
- Make sure students do not open or touch the live bacteria culture.

- You may want to make a note on the bacterial culture that the bacteria is on an agar medium, which is made from plants (actually plantlike protists).

Continued on page 16

Investigation 1

Encourage students to read the investigation steps and formulate their own questions before beginning the investigation. Discuss with students the question in the title of this investigation. Encourage students to share their thoughts.

Objectives
- To make observations and reach conclusions about the nature of life and living things
- To organize observations and analytical thoughts into a table
- To infer information about life cycles from observing living things

Skills
Observing, classifying, organizing, recording data, analyzing data, drawing conclusions, creating a diagram

Background
Students may have misconceptions about what makes something living or nonliving. Some students will think about living things as animal or plant life, and think that all living things have obvious movement and feeding habits. Through guided observation, students should realize that all living things work within the four life cycles described in the chapter and process energy, grow and reproduce, evolve, and interact with their environment. In addition, students should realize after observing several different living things that organisms interact with one another and take a place in the living cycles of other organisms.

Time Frame
One class period

Procedure
- Organize the materials in a logical order. For example, put the seed next to the plant sprout and the houseplant so that a progression is obvious. It may be helpful to have an insect in a jar with plant material that the insect eats.
- Make sure the flashlight has batteries and operates so that students may observe that the (nonliving) flashlight does participate in an energy cycle.

Continued from page 15

Cleanup/Disposal
Instruct students in proper cleanup and disposal of materials.

Results
Students should make logical inferences about each organism's four cycles. They should note that the insect gets energy from a food source and also provides energy by becoming food for other organisms. The insect also occupies an ecological niche, reacts to stimuli, evolves, and reproduces. Students should realize that all living things do each of these things as well and note them accordingly.

Analysis Answers
1. Students should easily classify the plant, sprout, seeds, insect, bacteria, and mushroom as living. The rock and flashlight are nonliving.
2. The flashlight shows a cycle that is common with living samples. *(energy cycle)* The flashlight transforms energy. A rock may break apart into smaller rocks, but does not reproduce itself.

Conclusions Answers
1. Energy takes many forms. Energy is converted from the sun into sugars by plants. Plant material serves as an energy source for the insect, mushroom, and bacteria. Dead organisms ultimately serve as energy sources for the bacteria and mushroom.
2. The plant is part of the insect's cycle. The plant provides energy (food) for the insect. The seeds and sprout represent stages in the growth cycle of the plant's life.

Explore Further Answers
If students are having trouble getting started, encourage them to skim through the text. Various illustrations and photographs may prompt their thinking. Examples include birds flying south for the winter and returning in the spring, and a dinosaur species arising and then becoming extinct. Suggest that students use arrows in the diagram to help them visualize and communicate the cyclic nature of the processes involved.

Cleanup/Disposal
Follow your teacher's instructions for disposal of any samples.

Analysis
1. Which samples are living and which are nonliving?
2. Which nonliving samples show some cycles that are common with cycles of living samples? What are the cycles?

Conclusions
1. What forms does energy take while cycling between living things? Describe two examples.
2. Which living samples are a part of the cycles of other living samples?

Explore Further
Think of two or more organisms that are part of a cycle. Create a diagram showing the organisms in the cycle. Label your diagram with the cycle's name.

16 Chapter 1 Biology: Investigating the Cycles of Life

Assessment
Check students' data tables to be sure they correctly indicate whether each specimen is involved in the cycles listed in the data table. You might include the following items from this investigation in student portfolios:
- Data table
- Answers to Analysis and Conclusions questions
- Diagram from Explore Further

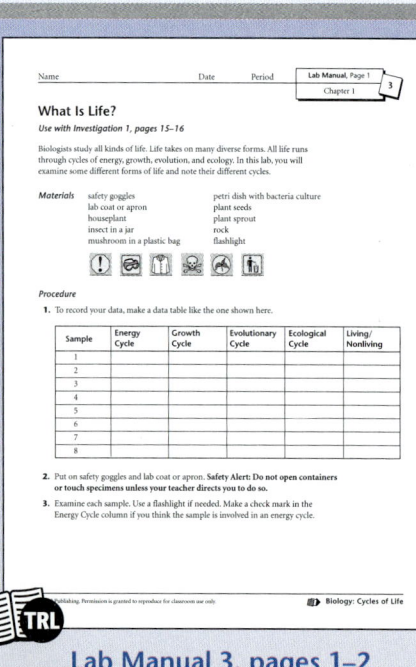

Lab Manual 3, pages 1–2

Lesson 4 The Scientific Method

Objectives

After reading this lesson, you should be able to
- understand why scientists use the scientific method
- define each step of the scientific method
- give examples of scientific theories

Specimen
A sample; an individual item or part considered typical of a group or whole

Scientific method
A series of steps used to test possible answers to scientific questions

You may wonder how biologists study all of these different forms of life. There are so many things to look at and understand. Science is a way of learning about the natural world. Scientific knowledge is described by physical, mathematical, and other models.

Scientists use scientific principles and knowledge to investigate living, physical, and designed systems. They ask questions and choose the ones they want to investigate. Different kinds of questions require different methods of scientific investigation. Some investigations involve observing and describing organisms, objects, or events. Others involve collecting **specimens,** or samples, and gathering information. Some require writing test procedures, running experiments, and making and using models.

Biologists have developed different ways to understand life. They use a logical process to explore the world and collect information. This process is called the **scientific method,** and it includes specific steps. Biologists follow these steps or variations of these steps to test possible answers to their questions.

All scientists use the scientific method. They may follow the steps in a different order. They may skip some steps, but they all follow this process. Scientists use the scientific method because scientific knowledge depends on facts that can be tested and retested by other scientists. Scientific explanations must be based on observations and experimental evidence.

Suppose one scientist researches a question and comes up with an answer that proves a fact. Using the scientific method, scientists from anywhere in the world should be able to find the same answer and prove the same fact. Scientists evaluate other scientists' findings. They examine and compare evidence. They communicate their results. If they don't come up with the same facts, they try to figure out why.

Biology: Investigating the Cycles of Life   Chapter 1   17

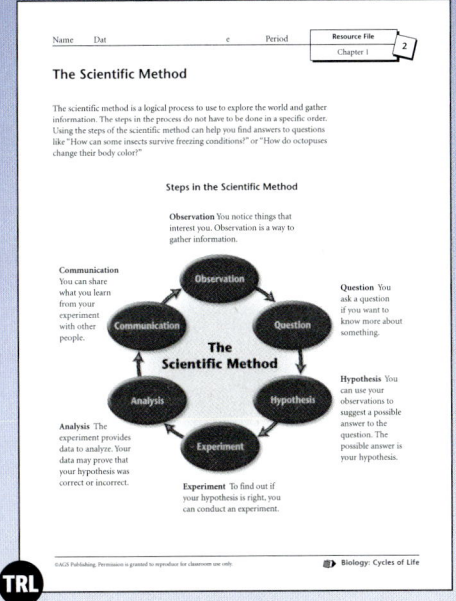
Resource File 2

Lesson at a Glance

Chapter 1 Lesson 4

Overview In this lesson, students learn what the scientific method is and why scientists use it.

Objectives
- To understand why scientists use the scientific method
- To define each step of the scientific method
- To give examples of scientific theories

Student Pages 17–25

Teacher's Resource Library TRL
Workbook Activities 4–5
Alternative Workbook Activities 4–5
Lab Manual 4–5
Resource File 2

Vocabulary

analysis   scientific method
control group   specimen
data   theory
experimental group   variable
hypothesis

Have students study the vocabulary terms. Then give students a matching test to see which terms require more study.

Background Information

Scientists use the scientific method to find answers to scientific questions because it is a logical and methodical way to work. Scientists develop hypotheses and then test them to see if they are correct. If the hypothesis is incorrect, a new one is devised. The cycle repeats over and over until satisfactory results are found.

1 Warm-Up Activity

Write the following on the board: *Which brand of fertilizer is best for a particular houseplant?* Have students brainstorm possible ways they could answer this question. Accept all reasonable responses.

Biology: Investigating the Cycles of Life   17

Teaching the Lesson

After students have read the lesson, write *Which brand of fertilizer is best for a particular houseplant?* on the board again. Guide students to use the scientific method to find an answer. Students should come up with ways to complete each part of the scientific method.

Have students turn back to Investigation 1. Have them identify the parts of the scientific method that are found in this investigation. For parts of the scientific method that are missing, have students brainstorm a way that part of the scientific method can be accomplished.

 ## Reinforce and Extend

Link to

Health. Have students read the feature about sickness.

Ask students why they often feel tired when they are sick. *(because the body is using much of its energy to combat the bacteria in the body)*

Doctors are becoming alarmed because some bacteria are no longer killed by certain antibiotics. These bacteria are becoming resistant to the antibiotics. Some doctors think that part of the problem is the over-prescribing of antibiotics. Ask students: How can doctors prevent bacteria from becoming resistant to antibiotics? *(Doctors should prescribe antibiotics only when they are needed. Doctors also should instruct patients on the proper use of antibiotics.)*

Link to ▶▶▶
Health

Sickness is often a battle between two life forms for resources. When you are infected with bacteria, you feel bad because a growing number of bacteria are feeding on the resources in your body. The bacteria are also releasing waste products poisonous to you. Your doctor may prescribe an antibiotic, which is a medicine that destroys the bacteria.

The scientific method requires scientists to use many skills. These skills include predicting, observing, organizing, classifying, modeling, measuring, inferring, analyzing, and communicating. The steps of the scientific method are:

1. Observation
2. Question
3. Hypothesis
4. Experiment
5. Analysis
6. Communication

Figure 1.4.1 shows the steps in the scientific method. Let's talk about each step.

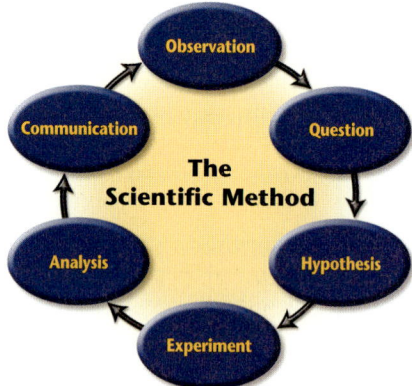

Figure 1.4.1 *The scientific method is a constant cycle scientists use to find answers to many questions.*

Observation. You perform this step without even being aware of it. Look around the classroom. Look at your classmates and all the objects in the room. This first step is simply looking at the world around you, watching life. Scientists also look at the world around them. While they are watching, or observing, they may see something they don't understand. If it interests them, they move to the next step of the scientific method.

18 Chapter 1 Biology: Investigating the Cycles of Life

Hypothesis
An educated guess; also the third step of the scientific method

Control group
The setup in an experiment that has no factor, or variable, changed

Experimental group
The same group as the control group, except for one factor, or variable, to be tested

Variable
The factor that is tested in an experiment

Question. You know what a question is. People ask each other questions every day. When scientists see something they do not understand, they ask a question and try to find the answer. The questions biologists try to answer deal with life and all its interactions. They work to find answers to questions like "Why do families look alike?" or "What type of fishes like to live in lakes?" Once biologists have questions, then they can begin looking for answers.

Hypothesis. A **hypothesis** is an educated guess. After asking a question, scientists guess at the answer. Scientists then test their answer to see if it is correct. Scientists usually make their guesses based on what they already know, then use experiments to see if they are right.

Experiment. An experiment is the procedure used to test whether a hypothesis is correct. Biologists perform many different kinds of experiments. The kind they perform depends on the question they are trying to answer. Biologists studying what kinds of fishes live in lakes do not want to perform experiments in a mountain cave. They want to look at lakes, maybe ones on mountains. They do not want to study the plants growing in lakes. They want to look at the kinds of fishes in lakes.

Scientists design experiments to test possible answers to the question. There are two separate groups in a science experiment: the **control group** and the **experimental group.** The control group is the setup in an experiment that has no variable, or factor, changed. The experimental group is the same as the control group, except for one factor to be tested. That factor is called the **variable.** Scientists control the conditions and variables of their experiments to get useful data.

As an example, say you want to see the effect of light on the sprouting of green bean seeds. Seeds grown in no light are the control group. Seeds grown with different amounts of light are the experimental group. The variable is the amount of light the seeds get every 24 hours. Seeds in the experimental group will get no light. Seeds in the experimental group will get four hours, eight hours, or twelve hours of light.

Biology: Investigating the Cycles of Life Chapter 1

ELL/ESL STRATEGY

Language Objective: *To explain the scientific method*

Divide students into small groups. Students should choose whether they want to write a skit or create a story. Have some students write a humorous skit that explains the scientific method. Have students perform the skit for the class. Have the other students write a story about the scientific method. Have students read the story to the class.

GLOBAL CONNECTION

The Internet is a valuable tool for biologists to communicate with one another about their scientific findings. Have students go to the Web site www.nbii.gov/datainfo/orgs and read about some of the professional organizations that are available to biologists. Have students find articles about a global issue and present the information to the class.

SCIENCE JOURNAL

Have students write a paragraph explaining why the Internet makes communication among scientists easy, quick, and efficient.

PRONUNCIATION GUIDE

Use the pronunciation shown here to help students pronounce difficult words in this lesson. Refer to the pronunciation key on the Chapter Planning Guide for the sounds of the symbols.

hypothesis (hī poth′ ə sis)
hypotheses (hī poth′ ə sēz)

LEARNING STYLES

Interpersonal/Group Learning

Have pairs of students discuss this question: Why is it important to observe and question before coming up with a hypothesis? Then discuss the question as a class.

TEACHER ALERT

Many students may think that scientists find answers to their questions on the first try. This usually is not true. Scientists often have to repeat the scientific method many times before they arrive at an acceptable answer.

LEARNING STYLES

Logical/Mathematical

Have students consider this question: What might result if a scientist concluded that her hypothesis was true before she began an experiment to test it? *(Sample answer: The scientist may not get reliable experiment results. She might do an experiment in a way that would make one outcome more likely than another. This could result in incorrect data. Or the scientist may misinterpret experiment results based on the idea that the hypothesis was true.)*

TEACHER ALERT

Some students may be confused by the terms *scientific law* and *theory*. A theory is a widely accepted idea that is based on knowledge gained from observations and investigations. A scientific law is a statement about what happens in nature that appears to be true. Scientific laws tell what will happen under certain conditions, but not why it will happen.

Data
Information collected from experiments

Analysis
Making sense of the results of an experiment; also the fifth step of the scientific method

You can use the scientific method to solve problems. The next time you have a question, use facts you know to answer it. If you do not know, research by reading or experimenting.

Scientists usually perform their experiments many times to be sure they get a similar answer every time. To keep track of all of the **data,** or information, they collect, scientists use different tools such as computers and calculators. Scientists often use special equipment specifically designed for their experiments. Math is also important in experiments. Scientists use math to gather data, analyze data, and to communicate results.

Analysis. After scientists get their results, they analyze them, or make sense of the experiment results. They compare the results to the hypothesis. Scientists need evidence before believing a hypothesis is correct. Scientists see if their results agree with their hypothesis. If the results don't agree, scientists may do more experiments or ask a different question. Sometimes the results answer the question but do not agree with the hypothesis. Remember that a hypothesis is a guess and can be wrong. Sometimes the results and hypothesis match. The answers scientists find often lead to more questions.

Communication. After scientists have checked their results and tested their hypothesis, they truthfully tell others their results. Other scientists may be interested in the same questions, so it is important for scientists to share their information. Scientists publish their methods and results in scientific publications. The Internet, a worldwide network of computers, helps scientists communicate. Scientists use the Internet to share their data and results. They also talk to each other and make the public aware of their findings.

Scientists check each other's work by repeating the same experiments. If the first results are accurate, then repeated experiments should give the same results. If the same experiments give different scientists the same results, then those results are considered true. This process is called peer review.

Biologists use the scientific method in some way to answer their questions about life. Sometimes they skip some steps or repeat steps. You can use these same steps in your daily life. This doesn't mean that every time you have a question, you have to run an experiment. It means you can solve different problems scientifically.

Theory
A well-tested explanation that makes sense of a great variety of scientific observations

Scientists judge a new theory by how well scientific data are explained by the new theory.

Science Myth

Myth: A theory is the same thing as a hypothesis.

Fact: A hypothesis is an educated guess that still must be tested. A theory has been well-tested over time and widely accepted by the scientific community. A scientific theory explains many observations and can be used to make predictions. A theory is logical, reasonable, and orderly.

When new evidence is discovered, scientific ideas and theories may change. A **theory** is a widely accepted idea that explains many different events. Some famous scientists, such as Nicolaus Copernicus and Charles Darwin, were ignored when they first presented their ideas. However, some scientists tested their research and experiments. The experiments always produced the same results. Over time, theories may change as scientists collect and analyze new evidence. For example, scientists once thought the earth was the center of the solar system. Research showed this was not true. We now know that the sun, not the earth, sits at the center of the solar system. In this case, a new theory fit observations better than the old theory.

Finding the answers to questions often leads to asking more questions. When new questions are asked, scientists use the scientific method again. This method is a constant cycle that scientists use to find the answers to many questions. Science is a vast body of changing and increasing knowledge.

Achievements in Science

Preventing Infectious Disease

One of the greatest achievements in science has been our understanding of infectious diseases. Before the 1860s, people didn't know much about disease. They didn't know why they got sick, how they got better, or how to keep from getting sick.

Beginning in the 1860s, scientists made many discoveries about disease. The French scientist Louis Pasteur discovered that many diseases were caused by tiny organisms called germs. In Germany, the scientist Robert Koch read about Pasteur's work. Koch began studying germs. Pasteur's and Koch's greatest tools were the microscope and the scientific method. Through many experiments, they concluded that germs cause infectious diseases—diseases that spread from one living thing to another. They also concluded that specific germs cause specific diseases.

Because of the work of Pasteur, Koch, and others, we know how to identify the cause of a disease. We also know how to prevent people and animals from getting some deadly infectious diseases.

Biology: Investigating the Cycles of Life Chapter 1 **21**

Pronunciation Guide

Use the pronunciation shown here to help students pronounce difficult words in this lesson. Refer to the pronunciation key on the Chapter Planning Guide for the sounds of the symbols.

Copernicus (kə pėr´nə kəs)

Pasteur (pa stėr´)

Koch (kŏk)

Science Myth

Have a volunteer read the first sentence of the Science Myth feature. Ask other volunteers to read the facts that follow. Ask volunteers to explain in their own words the difference between a theory and hypothesis.

Achievements in Science

Have students take turns reading aloud the Achievements in Science feature. Ask volunteers to explain why discovering that germs cause infectious disease was important in stopping the spread of disease. *(After scientists discovered why the disease was spreading, they could search for ways to stop the transmission.)*

Career Connection

Invite the school nurse to visit your class to describe why learning how germs are spread can help keep people from becoming sick.

At Home

Germs can be spread from one family member to another. This is especially true if one member of the family has a cold or flu. It is important to clean bathrooms and kitchens carefully to keep germs from spreading. Doorknobs and other items that are often touched also should be cleaned to prevent the spread of germs. Being especially careful when one member of the family is sick can keep other members from also becoming sick.

Lesson 4 Review Answers

1. hypothesis **2.** experiment
3. communicated **4.** Internet
5. hypotheses, data **6.** theory **7.** Answers will vary. Students might hypothesize that the grass didn't get enough sunlight, it didn't get enough water, or it didn't get enough air. **8.** A possible procedure is to place a clear glass tray and a nonclear tray on the grass. Water the grass the same for two weeks, lifting the trays to water the grass, then replacing the trays. See if the grass beneath the tray that blocks the sun turns yellow and if it returns to green after removing the trays for several days. **9.** An experiment must consistently get the same results in order to be valid. Doing an experiment over several times reinforces the validity of the results. **10.** New ideas are created or old ideas are changed when new evidence is discovered.

Portfolio Assessment

Sample items include:
- Answers to Lesson 4 Review

Lesson 4   R E V I E W

On a sheet of paper, write the word in parentheses that completes each sentence correctly.

1. A step in the scientific method that involves making an educated guess is a(n) (question, hypothesis, analysis).

2. A(n) (observation, experiment, question) tests a hypothesis.

3. The answer to a question must be (observed, communicated, hypothesized) to benefit society.

On a sheet of paper, write the word or words that complete each statement correctly.

4. Computers talk to each other through a worldwide system called the _____.

5. Scientists set up _____ to be tested during an experiment, and then record _____ as they conduct the experiment.

6. Many hypotheses that are supported by testing and accepted can be grouped together in a(n) _____.

Critical Thinking

On a sheet of paper, answer the following questions. Use complete sentences.

7. You set up a tent in the yard for two weeks. When you take down the tent, you notice the grass beneath it has turned yellow. You wonder why. Write a possible hypothesis to explain this observation.

8. Describe an experiment you could do to test your hypothesis for Question 7.

9. The results of an experiment support a scientist's hypothesis. Why is it important to repeat the experiment several times?

10. What happens to a theory or scientific knowledge when new evidence is discovered?

DISCOVERY INVESTIGATION 1

Materials
- safety goggles
- lab coat or apron
- 2 plastic cups
- 20 corn seeds
- water
- vinegar
- paper towels
- eyedropper

Using the Scientific Method

Scientists answer questions and solve problems in an orderly way. They use a series of steps called the scientific method. How can you use the scientific method to answer questions? You will find out in this lab.

Suppose you are watching a news report about acid rain. The report explains that acid rain is rain that has more acid in it than usual. The acid forms from certain kinds of air pollution. The report shows trees that have been damaged by acid rain. You wonder: How might acid rain affect the way a plant starts growing?

Procedure

1. In a small group, discuss the question in the second paragraph above. Then write a hypothesis about how acid rain might affect the way a plant starts growing. The hypothesis should be one that you could test with an experiment.

2. Write a procedure for your experiment. The experiment should take 8 days to complete. Use materials from the Materials list in your procedure. Number the steps. Include any Safety Alerts.

3. Be sure your experiment changes only one variable, or factor, at a time. Include a control group. Remember that a control is a setup for which you do not change any variables.

4. Draw a data table to record your data for 8 days.

5. Have your hypothesis, procedure, and Safety Alerts approved by your teacher. Then carry out your experiment.

SAFETY ALERT

- Make sure students wear safety goggles and a lab coat or apron.
- Monitor student proposals for any safety issues. This lab is a good opportunity to go over any safety concerns that will be followed throughout the course. Have students go over general lab safety issues and pick out the ones that apply to their investigation.

Discovery Investigation 1

This investigation is less structured than the first investigation in this chapter. It offers students more challenge and requires more teacher facilitation. Encourage students to read the investigation steps. Discuss questions they may have before beginning the investigation.

Objectives

- To become familiar with using the scientific method
- To develop a testable hypothesis
- To design an experiment to test a hypothesis

Skills

Communicating, observing, identifying and controlling variables, recording data, analyzing and interpreting data, describing, drawing conclusions

Background

Students may not know much about acid rain. The formation of acid rain occurs in a series of steps. Most acid rain begins when coal and oil are burned in power plants. The sulfur in the coal and oil combines with oxygen in the air, producing sulfur dioxide among other sulfur oxides. Sulfur dioxide reacts with water vapor in the air and makes tiny drops of sulfuric acid. This acid mixes with raindrops and falls to Earth as acid rain. The same process occurs in winter, producing acid snow. The acid rain or snow often falls a few hundred miles from the source power plants as the pollutants are carried by the winds.

The acidity of a substance is measured on the pH scale from 0 to 14. Distilled water is neutral and has a pH of 7. The pH of tap water is usually slightly higher. Numbers below 7 indicate varying degrees of acidity. Vinegar has a pH of 2.4–3.4. Acid rain often has a pH of 3.0, which is as acidic as vinegar.

Time Frame

30–45 minutes and 5 minutes per day for observations for the next 5–8 days

Continued on page 24

Continued from page 23

Procedure

- Have students work together in small groups to complete the activity.
- Have students document the procedure that they create, including the list of materials needed, the preparation required, and any information necessary for someone else to repeat their experiment. Have students record their results.

  Here is a possible procedure:
  1. Pack paper towels in both cups.
  2. Place half of the corn seeds between the paper towels and the inside of the cup so that you can see the kernels. Place the other half of the seeds in the other cup.
  3. Use the eyedropper to moisten the paper towels in one of the cups with water. Moisten the towels in the other cup with vinegar. Mark the cups "Water" and "Vinegar."
  4. Place both cups near a window where they will get plenty of sunlight.
  5. Observe the seeds each day for a week and record the results. Keep the paper towels moist. After 8 days, record how many seeds sprouted in each cup.

- Be sure students understand what a variable is (a part of an experiment that can change, such as the amount of sunlight a plant gets or the kinds of seeds used). Choose a sample procedure from one of the student groups and make a list of the variables. Explain that in an experiment, only one variable should change so that it is easy to tell whether or not that variable affected the results.

Cleanup/Disposal

Instruct students in proper cleanup and disposal of materials.

Results

Students should find that the fewest seeds that sprouted are those that were "watered" with vinegar.

Answers to Analysis, Conclusions, and Explore Further begin on page 670 of this Teacher's Edition.

24 *Chapter 1*

Cleanup/Disposal
Before leaving the lab, clean up your materials and wash your hands.

Analysis
1. What variable did you change in this experiment?
2. What changes did you see among the corn seeds after Day 4? What changes did you see after Day 8?

Conclusions
1. Was your hypothesis supported by the results of your investigation?
2. What problems did you have in performing the experiment? What part of the procedure would you change to be more successful?

3. If a hypothesis is not supported by data from an experiment, is that experiment a failure? Explain your answer.
4. How do you think acid rain affects the way plants start growing?

Explore Further
In your group, discuss other variables that might affect how a plant starts growing. Pick one variable your group would like to investigate. Using the scientific method, write a procedure to carry out your investigation.

24   Chapter 1   Biology: Investigating the Cycles of Life

Assessment

Check to see that students complete the data table. You might include the following items from this investigation in student portfolios:

- Hypothesis and experimental procedure
- Data table
- Answers to Analysis and Conclusions questions
- Student proposal for question to investigate in Explore Further

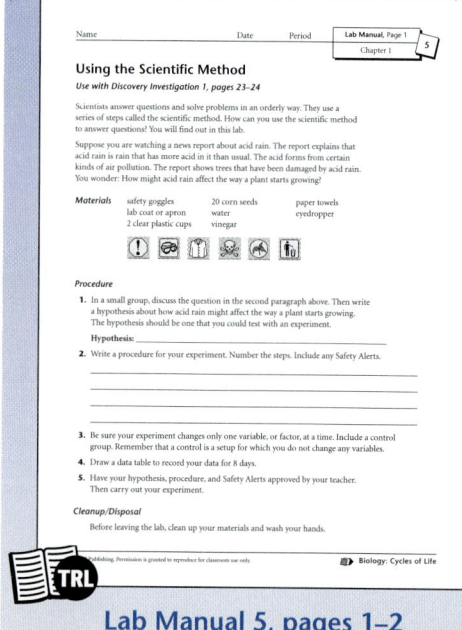

Lab Manual 5, pages 1–2

BIOLOGY IN THE WORLD

Discovery of Mad Cow Disease

In the mid-1980s, farmers in England noticed that several cows showed strange symptoms before dying. When the animals were examined after death, scientists saw that their brains looked like sponges. Scientists determined the disease that killed these cows was caused by a *prion*. Prions are proteins that cause disease by changing other proteins.

Prions are a fairly new idea in biology. When DNA was discovered, scientists assumed that DNA created proteins. Proteins are organic compounds that cells use to grow and work. Scientists also assumed that proteins could not be the cause of disease. They thought only bacteria and viruses caused diseases. *Bacteria* are the simplest single cells that carry out all basic life activities. Some bacteria cause disease. *Viruses* are nonliving particles that can cause disease. However, evidence now supports the theory that prions are proteins that cause disease. No DNA or other organism is involved.

The news became more startling in the 1990s when people in England suddenly started becoming sick with Creutzfeldt-Jakob disease. Creutzfeldt-Jakob disease is similar to mad cow disease but affects humans. Scientists examined the prions of infected humans and compared them to prions that cause mad cow disease. They hypothesized that the prions were the same. Testing of beef sold in grocery stores showed the presence of prions.

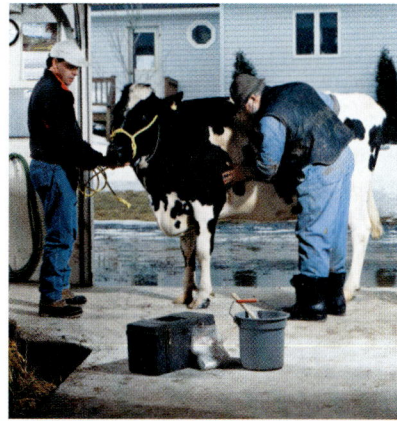

Given this information, many scientists now think that Creutzfeldt-Jakob disease is caused by mad cow prions. The prions are passed on to humans who eat infected beef. Today the United States government closely monitors any outbreak of mad cow disease. The government prevents cows raised near any outbreaks from being sold as beef.

1. What is the difference between mad cow disease and Creutzfeldt-Jakob disease?
2. Describe how these diseases are caused.
3. What evidence supported the hypothesis that Creutzfeldt-Jakob disease is connected to mad cow disease?

BIOLOGY IN THE WORLD

Have volunteers take turns reading the Biology in the World feature.

Ask a volunteer to describe what prions are. *(Prions are proteins that cause disease by changing other proteins.)*

Ask students what the prions appeared to do to the sick cows' brains. *(They caused their brains to look like sponges.)*

Ask students why it is important to keep possibly infected beef from being sold. *(People who eat infected beef can become sick.)*

Biology in the World Answers

1. Cruetzfeld-Jakob disease affects humans. Mad cow disease affects cows. **2.** Both diseases are caused by prions. Prions are proteins that cause other proteins to be changed. The changed proteins do not function properly. **3.** Scientists compared the prions that caused both diseases and found them to be similar.

PRONUNCIATION GUIDE

Use the pronunciation shown here to help students pronounce a difficult word in this lesson. Refer to the pronunciation key on the Chapter Planning Guide for the sounds of the symbols.

prion (prē´on)

ONLINE CONNECTION

For more information about genetic diseases, have students visit the National Institute of Health Web site at www.ncbi.nlm.nih.gov/books/. Have them search for books about genes and disease.

For more information about the African clawed frog, have students visit the Columbia University Web site at www.columbia.edu/itc/cerc/danoff-burg/invasion_bio/inv_spp_summ/xenopus_laevis.htm.

For more information about Louis Pasteur, have students visit the Massachusetts Institute of Technology Web site at web.mit.edu/invent/iow/pasteur.html.

Chapter 1 Summary

Have volunteers read aloud each summary item on page 26. Ask volunteers to explain the meaning of each item. Direct students' attention to the Vocabulary box on the bottom of page 26. Have them read and review each term and its definition.

Graphic Organizer

As students read Chapter 1, have them finish completing the chart on Graphic Organizer 1, Cycles of Life. Encourage students to read each lesson of the chapter and then have them fill in the portion of the chart that pertains to the lesson. When they have completed the chart, ask them to answer the questions.

Chapter 1 SUMMARY

- Biology is the study of life, including the interactions of life forms with their environment.
- Scientists try to learn about life by observing patterns, or cycles.
- The four major groups of cycles are energy, growth, evolutionary, and ecological cycles.
- Energy is the ability to do work.
- Energy cannot be created or destroyed, but is transformed into different forms.
- DNA contains instructions for life and reproduction.
- Proteins are created as a result of the growth cycle involving DNA.
- Life is constantly changing. The process of life changing over time is called evolution.
- Life forms that can reproduce together are considered the same species.
- Through speciation, new species are created while other species become extinct.
- The science of studying living things and their surroundings is a branch of biology called ecology.
- An ecosystem is made up of the living and nonliving things in a particular area.
- Scientists use a series of steps called the scientific method to understand life.
- The six steps in the scientific method include Observation, Question, Hypothesis, Experiment, Analysis, and Communication.

Vocabulary

adaptation, 10	ecosystem, 12	protein, 8
analysis, 20	energy, 5	reproduction, 7
biologist, 2	environment, 11	scientific method, 17
biology, 2	evolution, 10	speciation, 10
cell, 7	experimental group, 19	species, 10
control group, 19	extinct, 10	specimen, 17
cycle, 3	heat, 6	stimulus, 12
data, 20	hypothesis, 19	theory, 21
DNA, 7	law of conservation	transform, 5
ecologist, 12	of energy, 6	variable, 19
ecology, 12	organism, 2	

26 Chapter 1 Biology: Investigating the Cycles of Life

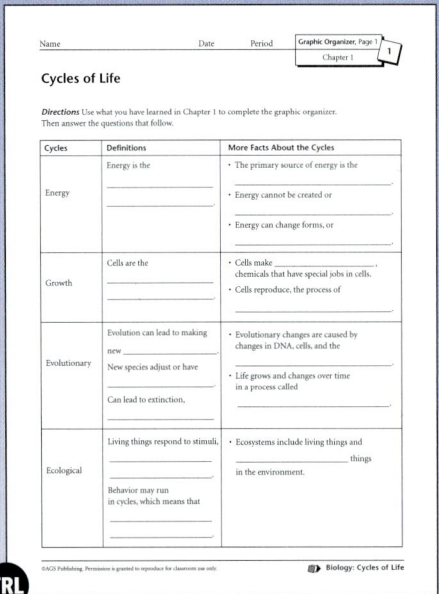

Graphic Organizer 1, pages 1–3

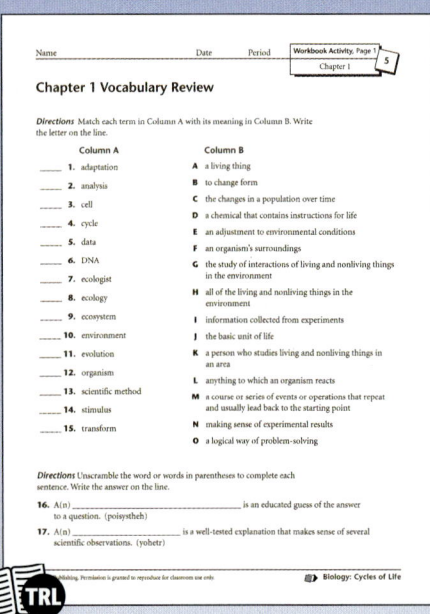

Workbook Activity 5, pages 1–2

Chapter 1 REVIEW

Word Bank
adaptation
biologist
biology
cell
control group
cycle
data
DNA
ecosystem
environment
experimental group
heat
hypothesis
law of conservation of energy
protein
reproduction
speciation
species
theory
variable

Vocabulary Review

On a sheet of paper, write the word or words from the Word Bank to best complete the sentence.

1. A(n) _____ is a chemical used by a cell to grow and function.
2. The information gained from an experiment is called _____ and is recorded for analysis.
3. A(n) _____ is made up of all the living and nonliving things that are found in an area.
4. Two organisms that can reproduce with each other are members of the same _____.
5. Biologists study _____, which is the study of life.
6. The instructions for any life form is contained in its _____.
7. New life is created through the process of _____.
8. One form of energy is _____.
9. To test a hypothesis, a biologist can design an experiment with a(n) _____, or factor.
10. A(n) _____ is a course or event that repeats and usually leads back to the starting point.
11. An organism's _____ includes everything that surrounds it.
12. A(n) _____ is an educated guess.
13. A(n) _____ has been well-tested and makes sense of a great variety of scientific observations.
14. A(n) _____ is the basic unit of life.

Review continued on next page

Chapter 1 Review

Use the Chapter Review to prepare students for tests and to reteach content from the chapter.

Chapter 1 Mastery Test

The Teacher's Resource Library includes two forms of the Chapter 1 Mastery Test. Each test addresses the chapter Goals for Learning. An optional third page of additional critical-thinking items is included for each test. The difficulty level of the two forms is equivalent.

Review Answers

Vocabulary Review

1. protein 2. data 3. ecosystem 4. species
5. biology 6. DNA 7. reproduction 8. heat
9. variable 10. cycle 11. environment
12. hypothesis 13. theory 14. cell

Review Answers

15. adaptation **16.** speciation **17.** biologist, control group, experimental group **18.** law of conservation of energy

Teacher Alert

In the Chapter Review, the Vocabulary Review activity includes a sample of the chapter's vocabulary terms. The activity will help determine students' understanding of key vocabulary terms and concepts presented in the chapter. Other vocabulary terms used in the chapter are listed below.

analysis	organism
ecologist	scientific method
ecology	specimen
energy	stimulus
evolution	transform
extinct	

Concept Review

19. A **20.** D **21.** A **22.** B

Chapter 1 REVIEW - continued

15. A(n) _____ is an adjustment to environmental conditions.

16. The process of life changing over time by creating new species is _____.

17. A _____ studies life and designs experiments with two groups: the _____ and the _____.

18. The idea that energy cannot be created or destroyed is the _____.

Concept Review

On a sheet of paper, write the letter of the answer that completes each answer correctly.

19. The step in the scientific method in which a scientist compares experiment results with a hypothesis is _____.

   A analysis

   B communication

   C observation

   D question

20. A heat wave that causes an organism to move to a cooler climate is an example of a(n) _____.

   A adaptation

   B extinction

   C speciation

   D stimulus

21. As energy changes form, it is often converted to _____.

   A heat

   B life

   C DNA

   D protein

28   Chapter 1   Biology: Investigating the Cycles of Life

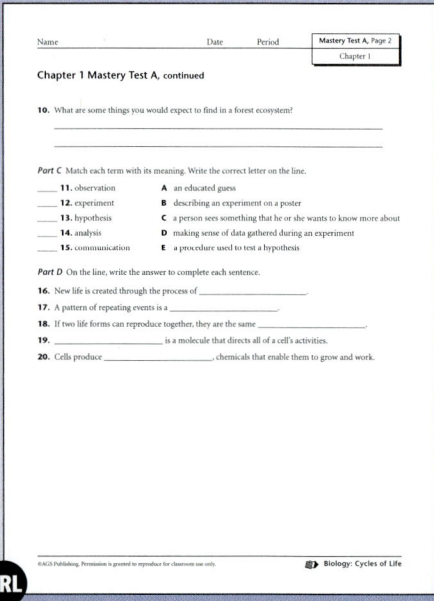

Chapter 1 Mastery Test A, pages 1–3

22. The branch of science that studies interactions among living and nonliving things in their environment is _____.

A botany

B ecology

C biology

D zoology

Critical Thinking

On a sheet of paper, write the answer to each question. Use complete sentences.

23. List each step of the scientific method along with a brief description of what happens during the step. Then briefly explain why scientists use the scientific method.

24. What usually causes some species to become extinct? Give two examples of species that are now extinct.

25. Describe the four cycles that are found in biology.

Research and Write

Research a species of plant or animal that is in danger of becoming extinct. Prepare a short report on the species. In the report, include information on the species' native habitat. Tell how many are estimated to exist and why the species is endangered. Describe what is being done to help this species. Present this information to your class.

Test-Taking Tip When you have vocabulary words to learn, make flash cards. Write each word on the front of a card. Write its definition on the back. Use the flash cards in a game to test your vocabulary skills.

Critical Thinking

23. Observation. Scientists look at the world around them to find something they don't understand. Question. Scientists ask questions and then try to find the answers. Hypothesis. Scientists guess at the answers to their questions. Experiment. Scientists follow an experiment, which is the test procedure to collect data to test whether the hypothesis is correct. Analysis. Scientists then make sense of the experiment results. Communication. Scientists communicate the results of their experiments and analysis. **24.** A natural disaster causes some species to become extinct. Examples of extinct species will vary, but some examples are the Lanai hookbill (bird), Tasmanian tiger (mammal), blackfin cisco (fish), and bigleaf scurfpea (plant). **25.** In energy cycles, energy cycles through different life forms. In growth cycles, organisms grow and reproduce again and again. In evolutionary cycles, species begin, change, and become extinct. In ecological cycles, the environment keeps everyday life going.

Research and Write

Students might look on the Internet for information about organizations that protect endangered species. These include the National Park Service at www.nationalparks.org. A helpful research keyword is *endangered*.

ALTERNATIVE ASSESSMENT

Alternative Assessment items correlate to the student Goals for Learning at the beginning of this chapter.

- Have students list the four cycles of life.
- Have students state the law of conservation of energy.
- Have students define *reproduction, evolution,* and *ecosystem*.
- Have students name different parts of life that can reproduce.
- Have students describe each step of the scientific method.
- Have students give an example of a scientific theory.

Chapter 2

Planning Guide
Basic Chemistry

	Student Pages	Vocabulary	Lesson Review	Critical-Thinking Questions
Lesson 1 Matter, Energy, and Chemical Processes of Life	32–37	✔	✔	✔
Lesson 2 Atoms and Molecules	38–41	✔	✔	✔
Lesson 3 Chemical Formulas	42–47	✔	✔	✔
Lesson 4 Bonding Patterns	48–52	✔	✔	✔
Lesson 5 Properties of Water	53–58	✔	✔	✔
Lesson 6 Acids, Bases, and pH	59–63	✔	✔	✔

(Student Text Lesson)

Chapter Activities

Teacher's Resource Library
Community Connection 2:
  How Much Water Do You Need?
Graphic Organizer 2:
  Matter, Energy, and Chemical Processes of Life

Teacher's Edition
Opener Activity

Assessment Options

Student Text
Chapter 2 Review

Teacher's Resource Library
Chapter 2 Mastery Tests A and B

Teacher's Edition
Chapter 2 Alternative Assessment

Student Text Features									Teaching Strategies						Learning Styles					Teacher's Resource Library			
Achievements in Science	Science at Work	Biology in Your Life	Investigation/Discovery	Biology in the World	Express Lab	Link to	Research and Write	Technology and Society	ELL/ESL Strategy	Background Information	Science Journal	Applications (Home, Career, Community, Global, Environment)	Online Connection	Teacher Alert	Auditory/Verbal	Body/Kinesthetic	Interpersonal/Group Learning	Logical/Mathematical	Visual/Spatial	Workbook Activities	Alternative Workbook Activities	Lab Manual	Self-Study Guide
	35		36		33				34	32		34					33			6	6	6–7	✓
		41				✓		40	40	38	40	40		39						7	7	8	✓
									45	42		43, 45		43, 46				44, 45	46	8	8		✓
52						✓			49	48		51		50, 51	51	51			50	9	9		✓
			57			✓			55	53		55			55					10	10	9	✓
				63		✓	67		61	59		60	63						61	11–12	11–12	10	✓

Pronunciation Key

a	hat	e	let	ī	ice	ô	order	ù	put	sh	she
ā	age	ē	equal	o	hot	oi	oil	ü	rule	th	thin
ä	far	ėr	term	ō	open	ou	out	ch	child	ŦH	then
â	care	i	it	ò	saw	u	cup	ng	long	zh	measure

ə { a in about / e in taken / i in pencil / o in lemon / u in circus }

Alternative Workbook Activities

The Teacher's Resource Library (TRL) contains a set of lower-level worksheets called Alternative Workbook Activities. These worksheets cover the same content as the regular Workbook Activities but are written at a second-grade reading level.

Skill Track Online

Use Skill Track Online for *Biology: Cycles of Life* to monitor student progress and meet the demands of adequate yearly progress (AYP). Make informed instructional decisions with individual student and class reports of online lesson and chapter assessments. With immediate and ongoing feedback, students will also see what they have learned and where they need more reinforcement and practice.

Chapter at a Glance

Chapter 2: Basic Chemistry
pages 30–67

Lessons

1. Matter, Energy, and Chemical Processes of Life pages 32–37

   Investigation 2 pages 36–37

2. Atoms and Molecules pages 38–41

3. Chemical Formulas pages 42–47

4. Bonding Patterns pages 48–52

5. Properties of Water pages 53–58

   Discovery Investigation 2 pages 57–58

6. Acids, Bases, and pH pages 59–63

   Biology in the World page 63

Chapter 2 Summary page 64

Chapter 2 Review pages 65–67

Audio CD

Skill Track Online for Biology: Cycles of Life

Teacher's Resource Library TRL

   Workbook Activities 6–12

   Alternative Workbook Activities 6–12

   Lab Manual 6–10

   Community Connection 2

   Graphic Organizer 2

   Resource File 3–4

   Chapter 2 Self-Study Guide

   Chapter 2 Mastery Tests A and B

(Answer Keys for the Teacher's Resource Library begin on page 675 of the Teacher's Edition. The Materials List for the Lab Manual activities begins on page 720.)

Opener Activity

To help students appreciate how important chemical processes are to life, display a small potted plant where students can see it. Ask students to think about how crops, such as corn, become harvestable food. Using the plant as a reference, explain that a chemical process called photosynthesis occurs in plants, whereby the elements in carbon dioxide and water are rearranged to form glucose and oxygen.

Community Connection 2

Chapter 2

Basic Chemistry

What makes the liquids in the photograph different colors? It's chemistry. You may be wondering what chemistry has to do with biology. Chemistry is the study of matter, and living things are made of matter. To understand the way living things work, you need to know something about chemistry. In Chapter 2, you will learn about the basic structure of matter. You will also learn about matter especially important to living things.

Organize Your Thoughts

Basic life processes depend on many chemical reactions.

Atoms
- Contain subatomic particles
- Form molecules

Elements
- Have the same kind of atom
- Form compounds

Goals for Learning

- ◆ To recognize that living things are made of matter
- ◆ To understand how elements can be recombined
- ◆ To recognize and understand chemical formulas
- ◆ To understand that recombining chemical elements results in storage and release of energy
- ◆ To describe water's unique properties
- ◆ To recognize that most chemical reactions are acid-base reactions

31

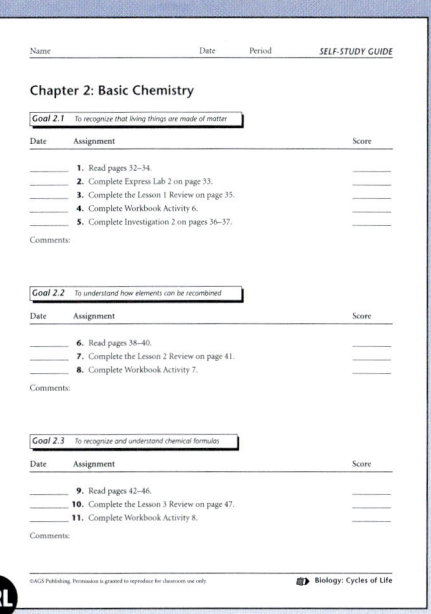

Chapter 2 Self-Study Guide

Introducing the Chapter

Students might look at the photograph on page 30 and get the idea that chemistry is something confined to a laboratory. However, chemistry is all around them, in everything they touch, see, and breathe.

All matter is made of basic chemical elements. *Chemistry* is defined in the text as the study of matter, but more specifically, it studies how atoms of elements combine and rearrange themselves. Chemistry is important to biology because living things use these elements for sustenance and life processes.

Elements are combined and rearranged through different chemical reactions. Energy is always either stored or released during chemical reactions. Chemical formulas tell what elements make up a substance and how many atoms of each element are present. The periodic table organizes elements according to their properties and the number of protons in one atom of the element. Appendix A shows the Periodic Table of Elements.

Notes and Math Tips

Ask volunteers to read the notes and math tips that appear in the margins throughout the chapter. Then discuss them with the class.

TEACHER'S RESOURCE

The AGS Publishing Teaching Strategies in Science Transparencies may be used with this chapter. The transparencies add an interactive dimension to expand and enhance the *Biology: Cycles of Life* program content.

CAREER INTEREST INVENTORY

The AGS Publishing Harrington-O'Shea Career Decision-Making System-Revised (CDM) may be used with this chapter. Students can use the CDM to explore their interests and identify careers. The CDM defines career areas that are indicated by students' responses on the inventory.

Lesson at a Glance

Chapter 2 Lesson 1

Overview In this lesson, students learn that living things are made of matter and that chemical processes are part of life.

Objectives

- To explain that all substances are made of matter
- To recognize that matter has physical and chemical properties
- To understand that living things are made of matter
- To explain how energy is released or stored during chemical processes

Student Pages 32–37

Teacher's Resource Library

Workbook Activity 6

Alternative Workbook Activity 6

Lab Manual 6–7

Vocabulary

atom	element
bacteria	mass
chemical bond	matter
chemical process	molecular
chemical property	molecule
chemical reaction	organization
chemistry	physical property
diversity	

Ask students to identify sentences in the text that demonstrate a relationship between some of the vocabulary terms. For example, "Chemical processes release and store energy in the bonds of molecules. Matter has physical properties. The chemical properties of matter do not change." To challenge students and build on their awareness of context, have them write sentences of their own relating two or more vocabulary terms.

Lesson 1 — Matter, Energy, and Chemical Processes of Life

Objectives

After reading this lesson, you should be able to

- explain that all substances are made of matter
- recognize that matter has physical and chemical properties
- understand that living things are made of matter
- explain how energy is released or stored during chemical processes

All living things are made up of **molecules.** A molecule is the smallest particle of a substance that has all the properties of the substance. Each molecule is made up of one or more **atoms.** An atom is the basic unit of **matter.** Matter is anything that has mass and takes up space. **Mass** is the amount of material an object has.

There is great **diversity** among living things, from small mice to large elephants. Whatever the size, living things can be studied at many levels of **organization.**

One level of organization is the **molecular** level. Studying biology at the molecular level requires an understanding of basic **chemistry.** Chemistry is the study of matter and how it changes. **Chemical processes** release and store energy in the bonds of molecules.

Similar activities occur in all cells at the molecular level. This is true for human cells, plant cells, or the cells of **bacteria.** Bacteria are the simplest single cells that carry out all basic life activities.

Molecule
The smallest particle of a substance that has all the properties of the substance

Atom
The basic unit of matter

Matter
Anything that has mass and takes up space

Mass
The amount of material an object has

Figure 2.1.1 What do these objects have in common?

32 Chapter 2 Basic Chemistry

Background Information

Microbiology is the field of biology that studies how microorganisms such as bacteria affect other living organisms. Bacteria and most protozoa belong to the organizational level of single-celled organisms. The importance of chemical processes in life can be observed in these microorganisms. Microbiologists have discovered bacteria that generate electricity, using sediments underwater. Bacteria also use chemical processes to decompose organic matter and treat sewage. Many antibiotics used to fight infection and disease are drugs that are chemically produced by certain bacteria.

32 Chapter 2

Diversity
Differing from one another

Organization
The arrangement of parts into a whole

Molecular
Related to molecules

Chemistry
The study of matter and how it changes

Chemical process
A rearrangement of atoms or molecules to produce one or more new substances with new properties

Bacteria
The simplest single cells that carry out all basic life activities

Physical property
A characteristic of a substance or an object that can be observed without changing the substance into a different substance

Scientists learn about cellular activities in humans by studying the cells of less complex organisms. We will begin our study of living things by learning about matter.

All substances are made of matter. Your desk, a plant, a bicycle, a water drop, and the air are all examples of matter. All matter has properties that are used to describe the matter. How would you describe the difference between your desk and a plant? Think about the differences between water and air.

Matter has **physical properties.** A physical property is a characteristic of a substance that can be observed without changing the substance into a different substance. Physical properties include density, color, boiling point, and freezing point. For example, as matter experiences a change in temperature or pressure, it may experience a phase change, or a physical change.

Express Lab 2

Materials
- safety goggles
- lab coat or apron
- 2 plastic cups
- plastic spoon
- baking soda
- water
- measuring cup
- vinegar

Procedure
1. Put on safety goggles and a lab coat or apron.
2. Put one level spoonful of baking soda into each plastic cup. **Safety Alert:** Do not taste or touch any chemicals.
3. Pour 1/4 cup of water into one cup.
4. Pour 1/4 cup of vinegar into the second cup.
5. Observe what happens in each cup.

Analysis
1. What happened in each cup?
2. In which cup is a chemical change happening?

Basic Chemistry   Chapter 2   33

1 Warm-Up Activity

Tell students that the amounts of vinegar and baking soda for the Express Lab are not as important as their respective chemical properties. Vinegar is about 95% water and 5% acetic acid ($C_2H_4O_2$). Baking soda is a base with the chemical formula $NaHCO_3$. Students will observe fizzing bubbles when they combine the vinegar and baking soda, which is evidence of the release of a new substance, carbon dioxide. Thus, a chemical change is happening in the cup containing vinegar and baking soda.

To connect the Express Lab to the larger chapter content, refer students to the final learning goal on page 31, which states that most chemical reactions are acid-base reactions.

Express Lab Answers

1. In the cup with water, the baking soda dissolved in the water. In the cup with vinegar, fizzing occurred. **2.** in the cup with vinegar

2 Teaching the Lesson

The text refers to physical changes as phase changes. Some students may be more familiar or comfortable with the synonymous phrase *changes of state*. There are three states of matter: solid, liquid, and gas. To reinforce the notion that boiling and freezing points of substances are physical properties, bring a covered pot of water to a boil. After the water starts boiling, remove the cover and show students the condensed water droplets on the surface. Explain that the water has boiled, changed states to become water vapor, then changed back to a liquid as water has condensed on the cover. Point out that the water on the cover is chemically identical to the water in the pot. The change is a physical change of state, and no different substances are formed.

Tell students there are several signs that scientists can look for to determine whether a chemical reaction is taking place. Some signs include (but are not limited to) the appearance of smoke or bubbles of gas, precipitates, a color change, or a change of odor or taste. The example in the text of a burning candle shows that the wick changes color, an odor is produced, and smoke is present.

3 Reinforce and Extend

LEARNING STYLES

Interpersonal/Group Learning
Divide students into groups and assign roles for the Express Lab. Have students discuss predictions for what will happen. Then have one student read the directions aloud, while others describe what they observe.

Basic Chemistry   33

IN THE ENVIRONMENT

Tell students that chemical processes are constantly at work in the environment. Photosynthesis is perhaps the most fundamental and important chemical process for life on Earth. Not only does it convert carbon dioxide into oxygen, but it also establishes the basis for food chains. Plants make glucose through the process, and glucose in turn provides energy to animals that eat plants. Another important chemical process is the reaction that occurs in the ozone layer. Ozone is a molecule of three oxygen atoms that is fundamental in partially protecting organisms from harmful ultraviolet rays from the sun. However, chlorofluorocarbons react with ozone and break it down, causing a thinner layer of ozone that is commonly referred to as the hole in the ozone layer.

ELL/ESL STRATEGY

Language Objective: *To understand the use of prepositions*

Tell students that prepositions are not literal in phrases such as *made up* and *carry out*. The meaning is the same if the reader omits *up* from the phrase, as is done on page 34: *Living things are made of matter*. Substitute *conduct* for *carry out* so that students do not imagine the act of carrying something out of a room.

Chemical property
A characteristic that describes how a substance changes into a different substance

Element
A substance that cannot be separated into other kinds of substances

Chemical reaction
A chemical change in which elements are combined or rearranged

Chemical bond
The force holding atoms together in a compound or molecule

A temperature change in water may result in solid ice changing to liquid water. Liquid water can then change to water vapor (gas). Salt dissolving in water is another example of a physical change.

Matter has **chemical properties.** A chemical property is a characteristic that describes how a substance changes into a different substance. For example, **elements** combine with each other in **chemical reactions.** An element is a substance that cannot be separated into other kinds of substances. A chemical reaction is a chemical change in which elements are combined or rearranged. The result is a chemically different substance. If you burn a piece of wood, a chemical change occurs. If you pour alcohol on a foam cup, a chemical change occurs. A different substance results.

Living things are made of matter. They need energy to live. You will learn more about energy and matter in this chapter. Energy is stored in the **chemical bonds** of matter. Energy is released or stored during chemical processes that occur in the cells of living things. The force holding atoms together in a compound is a chemical bond. You will learn more about compounds in the next lesson.

Some chemical reactions can take place in less than a second. Other chemical reactions take place over billions of years.

Figure 2.1.2 What chemical changes occur when a candle burns?

34   Chapter 2   Basic Chemistry

Lesson 1 REVIEW

Word Bank
element
molecular
chemical bonds

On a sheet of paper, write the word or words from the Word Bank that complete each sentence correctly.

1. Energy is stored and released in the _____ of molecules.
2. A(n) _____ is a substance that cannot be changed or separated into other kinds of substances.
3. All living things have similar activities at the _____ level.

Critical Thinking

On a sheet of paper, write the answers to the following questions. Use complete sentences.

4. What are three physical properties of a pencil?
5. What changes take place when you bake a cake? Describe the changes as physical or chemical. Explain how you know.

Science at Work

Food Chemist

When you eat some of your favorite foods, you probably have a food chemist to thank. Some foods contain natural or artificial flavors designed by a food chemist. Food chemists create new flavors and fine tune the flavors of other foods. The change of even a tiny amount of an ingredient can change the taste of a food.

Food chemists work closely with research and marketing experts to find popular flavors. They must complete a bachelor's or master's degree in chemistry to work in a food laboratory. Many successful food chemists complete a Ph.D.

Lesson 1 Review Answers

1. chemical bonds 2. element 3. molecular
4. Answers will vary but may include its phase (solid), its color, and its mass.
5. When a cake bakes, the batter changes into a new substance. The baked cake cannot be changed back into batter. The changes are chemical.

Portfolio Assessment

Sample items include:
- Express Lab answers
- Lesson 1 Review answers

Science at Work

Tell students that food chemists also work with preservatives and food additives to keep foods from spoiling. BHA and BHT are antioxidant compounds added to foods that have fats or oils. Oxygen reacts with BHA and BHT compounds, rather than with fats and oils, so the food does not spoil.

Have students conduct research to see what common foods contain BHA and BHT. Then ask them to find out the compounds' chemical formulas. If possible, bring in foods with nutrition labels that list BHA or BHT. *(BHA $[C_{11}H_{16}O_2]$ is found in butter, meats, and cereal. BHT $[C_{15}H_{24}O]$ is used to preserve color, odor, and taste of food. It is found in shortening and cereal.)*

LAB ACTIVITIES

Chapter 2 has Investigation and Discovery Investigation lab activities. Two additional lab activities for Chapter 2 appear in the Biology: Cycles of Life Lab Manual and on the Teacher's Resource Library CD-ROM.

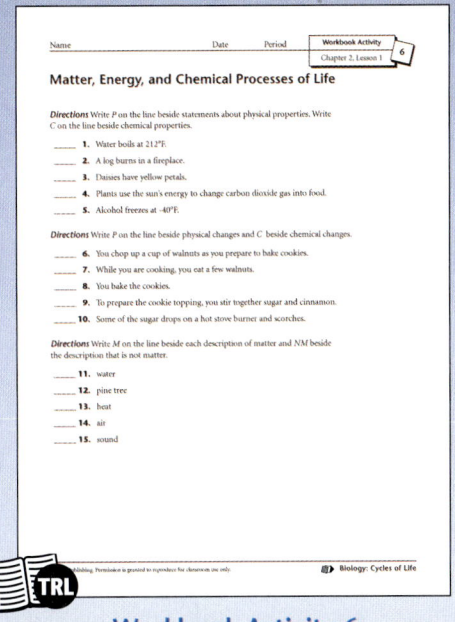

Workbook Activity 6

Investigation 2

Encourage students to read the investigation steps. Discuss questions they may have before beginning the investigation.

Objectives

- To observe physical and chemical changes
- To summarize observations

Skills

Measuring, using science lab equipment, observing, recording data, describing, inferring, analyzing data, drawing conclusions

Background

Emphasize to students that a chemical change affects the chemical composition of a substance. A change in the physical aspects of a substance that does not change the substance itself is not a chemical change, even if it affects the appearance or activity of the substance.

Time Frame

One class period

Procedure

- Have students work together in small groups.
- You can set up each substance as a station and have the groups move among the four stations.
- After students magnetize the paper clip, they can demagnetize it by hammering it several times. This should be done against a block of wood while holding the end of the paper clip with pliers. Demagnetizing the paper clip will show that this physical change can be reversed easily.

Cleanup/Disposal

Instruct students in proper cleanup and disposal of materials.

INVESTIGATION 2

Materials
- safety goggles
- lab coat or apron
- flask
- water
- hot plate
- rusty nail
- non-rusty nail
- 2 paper clips
- hammer
- magnet
- balance
- crucible
- magnesium strip

Physical and Chemical Properties

Matter has both physical and chemical properties. A change that does not affect the chemical makeup of a substance is a physical change. A chemical change involves a chemical reaction that changes the substance itself.

Procedure

1. Put on safety goggles and a lab coat or apron.
2. Fill a flask two-thirds with water. Place the flask of water on a hot plate. Turn the hot plate on high. Observe what happens to the water as it boils. Turn off the hot plate.
3. Observe a rusty nail. Compare it to a non-rusty nail.
4. With a hammer, straighten a paper clip. Rub this paper clip with the magnet in the same direction about 30 times. Place this paper clip near another paper clip. Observe what happens.
5. Find the mass of the empty crucible and the strip of magnesium.

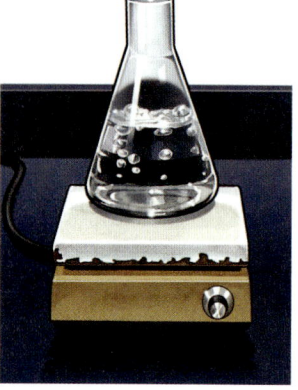

36   Chapter 2   Basic Chemistry

SAFETY ALERT

- Be sure students wear safety goggles throughout the procedure.
- Caution students to watch their fingers when using the hammer.
- If you do not want to burn the magnesium, burn any other substance (but possibly not mass it). Alternatively, for students' observations, produce a piece of wood and then a pile of ashes to show that it has been burned.
- Tell students not to touch the crucible while the magnesium burns.

6. Ask your teacher to ignite the magnesium strip. Let it burn inside the crucible. **Safety Alert: Do not handle or move the crucible while the magnesium burns.**

7. Observe the burnt magnesium. Find the mass of the magnesium ashes and crucible.

Cleanup/Disposal
Follow your teacher's instructions to dispose of the rusty nail and burnt magnesium.

Analysis
1. What happened to the water as it boiled? Was this a physical change or a chemical change?
2. What happened to the nail as it rusted? Was this a physical change or a chemical change?
3. What happened to the paper clip in Step 4? Was this a physical change or a chemical change?
4. Compare the mass of the magnesium strip to the magnesium ashes.
5. Did you watch a physical or chemical change in Step 6? Explain your answer.

Conclusions
1. Write a summary sentence for each of the four changes you observed. Explain what changes took place.
2. Why do you think there was a change in the mass of the magnesium after it burned? What happens to a substance when it burns?

Explore Further
Look for evidence of three physical and three chemical changes in the environment around you. Describe these changes in a list or a paragraph.

Basic Chemistry Chapter 2

Analysis Answers
1. The water changed state from liquid to gas. Energy from the hot plate caused the water molecules to move rapidly and change state. This is a physical change.
2. The nail rusts because it reacts chemically with oxygen and water. This is a chemical change.
3. In Step 4, a physical change took place. The iron is magnetized due to rearrangements of its molecules.
4. The mass of the ashes should be more than the mass of the strip.
5. When magnesium burns, it reacts chemically with oxygen. This is a chemical change.

Conclusions Answers
1. Students should summarize what they observed and label each activity as a chemical or physical change. They can present their data in a table like the one below or in short paragraphs.

Object	Observations
boiling water	physical change
rusty nail and non-rusty nail	chemical change
paper clips	physical change
mass of crucible and magnesium	physical change or chemical change
mass of crucible and magnesium ashes	chemical change

2. The magnesium reacted with the oxygen to create a new substance—magnesium oxide. The oxygen gas became solid and added mass to the magnesium. When something burns, a chemical change takes place because burning is a chemical reaction with oxygen.

Assessment
Check to see that students understand the difference between a physical change and a chemical change. You might include the following items from this investigation in student portfolios:

- Answers to Analysis and Conclusions questions
- Description from Explore Further

Explore Further Answers
Answers may vary. Some examples of chemical changes in daily life might be cooking food, using hair products, or eating.

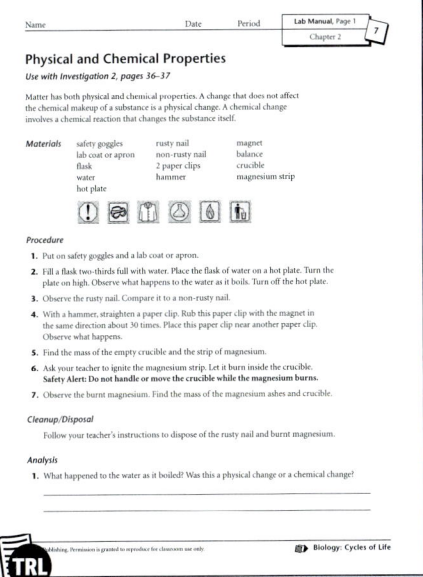

Lab Manual 7, pages 1–2

Lesson at a Glance

Chapter 2 Lesson 2

Overview In this lesson, students learn that matter is composed of elements, elements are composed of atoms, and atoms are composed of electrons, protons, and neutrons.

Objectives

- To explain that matter is composed of combinations of chemical elements
- To know that chemical elements are composed of atoms
- To know that atoms are composed of subatomic particles

Student Pages 38–41

Teacher's Resource Library

Workbook Activity 7
Alternative Workbook Activity 7
Lab Manual 8
Resource File 3

Vocabulary

atom mass	isotope
atomic number	neutron
compound	nucleus
electron	proton
electron cloud	radioactive
element	radioisotope
element symbol	subatomic particle

In the previous lesson, one of the vocabulary terms was *organization*. Ask students to consider organizational levels with respect to Lesson 2 vocabulary and arrange the new terms into graphic organizers such as flowcharts, webs, and tables. For example, write *subatomic particle* on the board and draw three lines under it. Ask students to come to the board and fill in the lines with the appropriate terms. (*electron, neutron, proton*)

You might make a list with students of the vocabulary terms that signify something on the periodic table: *symbol, atomic number, atomic mass*. Organizing terms into categories such as these will help students learn terms faster and recall these terms more easily on standardized tests.

38 Chapter 2

Lesson 2 Atoms and Molecules

Objectives

After reading this lesson, you should be able to

- explain that matter is composed of combinations of elements
- know that elements are composed of atoms
- know that atoms are composed of subatomic particles

Element symbol
One, two, or three letters that represent the name of an element

Compound
A substance that is formed when atoms of two or more elements join together

Elements and Compounds

Most matter is made up of combinations of elements. However, some matter has only one kind of atom. An element is matter that is made up of only one kind of atom. There are 92 elements that occur naturally. The remaining elements have been made in laboratory experiments. Look at the Periodic Table of Elements in Appendix A. Elements are arranged in a periodic table for easy reference. Each element is represented by a **symbol**. The symbol is one, two, or three letters that represent the name of an element. Examples of element symbols are C (carbon), O (oxygen), and Ca (calcium).

There are 25 elements essential to living things. In fact, four elements—oxygen, carbon, hydrogen, and nitrogen—make up 96.3 percent of a person's weight. These same elements make up the matter of most other living things. The other 21 elements are important for many reasons that you will study. The elements that make up the molecules of living things are combined and recombined in different ways.

Elements combine to form **compounds.** A compound is a substance that is formed when atoms of two or more elements join together. Two common examples of compounds are water and table salt. Table salt, NaCl, has equal parts of the elements sodium (Na) and chlorine (Cl). The table salt you use at home may include the trace element iodine as an added ingredient. The thyroid gland requires iodine to function properly.

Water, or H_2O, has two parts of the element hydrogen to one part of the element oxygen. Another example of a compound in living organisms is DNA. DNA carries the instructions to determine the characteristics of an organism. DNA contains the elements carbon, nitrogen, oxygen, hydrogen, and phosphorus.

38 Chapter 2 Basic Chemistry

Background Information

If you have a cross-section illustration of the human body available, show students where the thyroid gland is, or simply point out that it is at the base of the throat in front of and along either side of the windpipe. The thyroid gland requires iodine for chemical reactions that produce hormones.

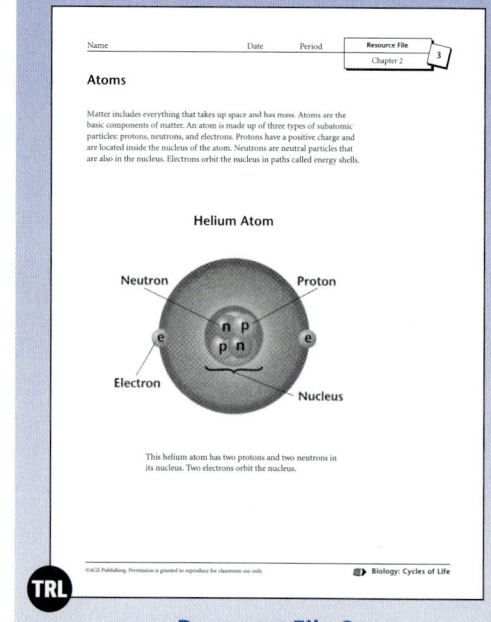

Resource File 3

Atoms and Molecules

Elements are made up of atoms. Remember that atoms are the basic units of matter. Atoms are composed of **subatomic particles.** An atom consists of a positively charged **nucleus** surrounded by a negatively charged cloud of **electrons.** Most of the mass of an atom is in the nucleus.

Look at the model of a helium atom in Figure 2.2.1. It shows the **protons** and **neutrons** in the nucleus. Protons are positively charged. Neutrons have no charge. The electrons orbit the nucleus. In real atoms, the **electron cloud** is much larger than the nucleus. Subatomic particles are too small to be seen. The relationship is like comparing the size of a football stadium (electron cloud) to the size of a pea (nucleus).

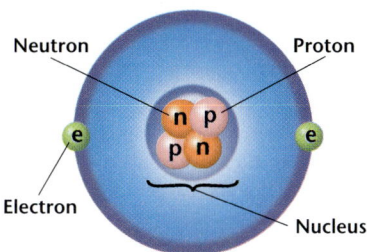

Figure 2.2.1 The Helium atom has two protons, two neutrons, and two electrons.

Look at the Periodic Table in Appendix A again. The **atomic number** appears above the symbol for each element. The atomic number of an atom is the number of protons in the atom. The atomic number identifies the element. For example, an atom with six protons is carbon. An atom with one proton is hydrogen. If the atom is neutral (neither negative nor positive), the number of protons equals the number of electrons.

Link to ▸▸▸

Physics

Physicists constantly search for smaller and smaller subatomic particles. Max Planck pioneered this branch of physics, which is called quantum physics. To honor his work, all subatomic particles are measured in Planck units.

Subatomic particle
A proton, neutron, electron, or other particle smaller than the atom

Nucleus
An atom's center; made of protons and neutrons

Electron
A tiny particle in an atom that moves around the nucleus; it has a negative electrical charge

Proton
A tiny particle in the nucleus of an atom; it has a positive electrical charge

Neutron
A tiny particle in the nucleus of an atom; it has the same mass as the proton and no electrical charge

Electron cloud
The space effectively occupied by electrons in an atom

Atomic number
The number of protons in the nucleus of an atom

3 Reinforce and Extend

ELL/ESL Strategy

Language Objective: To recognize common word parts

Students who are learning English will have an easier time learning vocabulary terms if they are able to break words into syllables and recognize common word parts. *Iso-* comes from the Greek root *isos*, which means "equal." The Greek word *topos* means "place," so *isotope* means "an equal place." Since isotopes have the same number of protons, they occupy the same position in the periodic table.

Science Journal

Instruct students to write a paragraph using at least three vocabulary terms from each of the first two lessons. Tell them that the purpose is to look for relationships and connections among the contents of each lesson. *(Sample answer: Chemistry is the study of structures that make up matter. Molecules are the smallest particles of a substance that have the same chemical and physical properties of the substance. Molecules are groups of two or more atoms. Atoms are made up of three types of subatomic particles: electrons, protons, and neutrons. Each element has its own atomic number, which is equal to the number of protons in its nucleus.)*

Technology and Society

Uranium is not the only element that breaks down to form radon. Radon can also seep into homes as thorium and radium decays. Radon is a leading cause of lung cancer, and its effects on public health are well documented. However, radon has some positive uses. In radiotherapy, small amounts can be used to treat some forms of cancer. Invite students to conduct further research about radon.

Atomic mass
The average mass of the atom of an element

Isotope
One of a group of atoms of an element with the same number of protons and electrons but different numbers of neutrons

Radioactive
The property of some elements (such as uranium) or isotopes (such as carbon-14) to give off energy as they change to another substance over time

Radioisotope
A radioactive isotope

Math Tip
To find the isotope number, add the number of protons and neutrons together. Only the number of neutrons changes between different isotopes.

The **atomic mass** appears below an element's symbol. The atomic mass of an atom is the total mass of the electrons, protons, and neutrons. It is the average mass of the atom of an element. Protons and neutrons are similar in size. Electrons have very little mass and are about $\frac{1}{1836}$ the mass of a proton.

Some elements have **isotopes** that differ only in the number of neutrons. Study Table 2.2.1. Carbon-12 has six protons and six neutrons. Its atomic mass is 12. Carbon-14 has an atomic mass of 14. It has six protons and eight neutrons. Isotopes of the same element have about the same chemical properties because the number of electrons is the same.

Table 2.2.1 Isotopes of Carbon			
	Carbon-12	Carbon-13	Carbon-14
Electrons	6	6	6
Protons	6	6	6
Neutrons	6	7	8

Many elements have multiple isotopes. Some isotopes may be **radioactive.** Radioactive isotopes are called **radioisotopes.** They can be detected because they emit radiation as they decay. For this reason they are also called tracers. Biologists and doctors use radioisotopes to trace the pathway of elements. For example, biologists can date fossils by measuring the ratios of different radioisotopes in the fossil. Doctors can follow chemical processes in the body by tracking the radiation emitted by tracers. However, uncontrolled exposure to radioactive isotopes can harm the molecules in cells. An example is radon gas.

Technology and Society

Radon is a radioactive gas. Inhaling high levels of radon gas over time can cause lung cancer. Radon has become a health problem as houses have become more energy efficient. Radon seeps into the house foundation from underground. It cannot escape easily because of insulation in the roof and tightly sealed window frames. People can buy detection kits to check radon levels in their homes and businesses.

40   Chapter 2   Basic Chemistry

Career Connection

Radiotherapy is the treatment of disease with radiation. Doctors increasingly rely on radioisotopes to treat disease and reduce pain. Iodine-131 is used to diagnose and treat thyroid cancer, and strontium-89 is helpful in easing the pain of patients who have bone and prostate cancer. The most widely used radioisotope in medicine is technetium-99m, due to its half-life of six hours. Half-life is the time required for half of the nuclei in a large sample of identical isotopes to undergo radioactive decay. The six-hour half-life of technetium-99m is long enough for doctors to examine and diagnose patients, but short enough to minimize the patient's radiation dose. Have students search the Internet for other radioisotopes that are used in medicine.

Lesson 2 REVIEW

On a sheet of paper, write the word that completes each sentence correctly.

1. Isotopes detected by their radiation are _____.
2. A letter that represents the name of an element is called a(n) _____.
3. Protons and neutrons are located in the _____ of an atom.

Critical Thinking

On a sheet of paper, write the answers to the following questions. Use complete sentences.

4. The isotope neon-22 has 10 protons. How many electrons and neutrons does it have?
5. Compare the masses of electrons, neutrons, and protons.

Biology in Your Life

Technology: The Search for the Perfect Plastic

Think about how many thin plastic containers you used recently. Did you have milk from a plastic jug? Did you carry a bottle of water with you? Before the early 1980s, most products were packaged in glass or heavy plastic. These materials were costly to make. They were rarely recycled and used large amounts of space in landfills.

Today, polyethylene terephthalate, or PET, is the most widely used plastic. PET bottles and packages are much thinner, lighter, and stronger than older plastics. PET bottles are less likely to break than glass bottles.

This new technology benefits communities. Since PET containers are made with less plastic, packaging that is thrown away is more easily compressed. It takes up less landfill space. PET is recyclable.

Recycled PET containers are used mainly as fibers and fleece materials for roofing, shoe insoles, and filters.

1. How are PET containers better for the environment than older plastic containers?
2. What other uses might there be for recycled plastics?
3. Name five PET containers you used recently.

Lesson 2 Review Answers

1. radioisotopes 2. element symbol 3. nucleus 4. It has 10 electrons and 12 neutrons. 5. Protons and neutrons are similar in mass. Electrons have much less mass than protons and neutrons have.

Portfolio Assessment

Sample items include:
- Lesson 2 Review answers
- Biology in Your Life answers
- Science Journal paragraph
- Career Connection research results

Biology in Your Life

Ask a volunteer to read the perfect plastics feature aloud. Bring in some samples of recyclable plastics, and pass them out to students. Help them find the recyclable code on the bottom or side of the package. Make a list on the board naming the type of container and its respective code. Most of the lighter plastic bottles have the number 1, which corresponds to PET plastics. The number 2 indicates HDPE (high-density polyethylene such as milk jugs and detergent bottles). PET and HDPE plastics are the most commonly recycled plastics.

Biology in Your Life Answers

1. They take up relatively little space in landfills and are very recyclable. 2. Other uses may include carpeting, down filling in jackets, playground equipment, woven rugs, ground covering, and decorative plastic plants. 3. Answers will vary. Sample answers: juice bottles, milk jugs, window cleaner bottles, detergent jugs, water bottles.

Pronunciation Guide

Use the pronunciation shown here to help students pronounce a difficult word in this lesson. Refer to the pronunciation key on the Chapter Planning Guide for the sounds of the symbols.

polyethylene terephthalate
   (pä′lē e′thə lēn′ ter′əf tha′lāt′)

Lesson at a Glance

Chapter 2 Lesson 3

Overview In this lesson, students learn about chemical formulas and compounds.

Objectives

- To explain how to write a chemical formula
- To interpret a chemical formula
- To tell how atoms combine to form compounds
- To give examples of binary compounds

Student Pages 42–47

Teacher's Resource Library

Workbook Activity 8

Alternative Workbook Activity 8

Vocabulary

binary compound   ion
chemical formula   ionic compound
empirical formula   radical

Have students make flash cards for the vocabulary terms in this lesson. Instruct students to write the term on one side of an index card and the definition and an example on the reverse side. After completing the lesson, have students add a sentence using each term.

Background Information

Explain to students that a positive ion has a positive charge because it has lost an electron. By losing an electron, it now has one more proton in the nucleus than electrons in the electron cloud, resulting in an overall positive charge. By contrast, a negative ion has gained an electron. Since there is now one more electron than the number of protons, the atom has a negative charge.

Lesson 3 Chemical Formulas

Objectives

After reading this lesson, you should be able to

- explain how to write a chemical formula
- interpret a chemical formula
- tell how atoms combine to form compounds
- give examples of binary compounds

Chemical formula
A set of symbols and subscripts that tell the kinds of atoms and how many of each kind are in a compound

Ion
An atom that has either a positive or a negative charge

Ionic compound
Two or more ions held next to each other by electrical attraction

Empirical formula
The simplest formula for a compound

Scientists use the symbols for elements to write **chemical formulas** for compounds. A chemical formula tells the kind of atoms and how many of each kind are present in the compound. Look at the formula for water: H_2O. Water is a molecule. The formula H_2O shows that each water molecule is made up of two hydrogen atoms bonded to one oxygen atom. The subscript 2 tells you two atoms of hydrogen are in the molecule. Notice there is no subscript after the O. If no subscript appears after the symbol of an element, the compound has only one atom of that element. The formula H_2O shows that one water molecule contains three atoms—two of hydrogen and one of oxygen. Table 2.3.1 shows the chemical formulas for two common chemical compounds.

Table 2.3.1 CH_4 (Methane) and CO_2 (Carbon Dioxide)			
Symbol	Element	Subscript	Number of Atoms
C H_4	carbon hydrogen	none 4	1 +4 5 total atoms
C O_2	carbon oxygen	none 2	1 +2 3 total atoms

Sometimes a compound is not a molecule. **Ions** can form compounds. An ion is an atom or particle that has either a positive or a negative charge. For example, table salt is NaCl. Both Na (sodium) and Cl (chlorine) form ions. NaCl is an **ionic compound.** An ionic compound has two or more ions held next to each other by electrical attraction. The sodium ion has a positive charge. The chloride ion has a negative charge.

Look at Figure 2.3.1. The formula for NaCl has one atom of sodium for every atom of chlorine. This formula is called an **empirical formula.** An empirical formula is the simplest formula for a compound. In comparison, a molecular formula is the same as or is a multiple of the empirical formula.

42   Chapter 2   Basic Chemistry

Radical *A group of two or more atoms that acts like one atom*

The molecular formula is based on the actual number of atoms of each type in the compound.

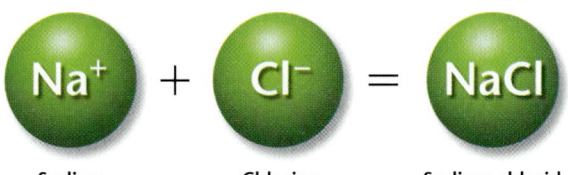

Sodium   Chlorine   Sodium chloride

Figure 2.3.1 *Table salt is an ionic compound.*

Compounds That Contain Radicals

The formulas for some compounds contain groups of two or more atoms that act as if they are one atom. These groups of atoms are called **radicals**. They form compounds by combining with other atoms. The atoms in a radical stay together during a chemical reaction.

The formula for household lye contains the negatively charged radical OH^-. Household lye is a strong chemical used to clean drains. The formula for household lye is NaOH. The OH^- radical contains one atom of oxygen and one atom of hydrogen. The chemical name for lye, NaOH, is sodium hydroxide. More examples of some common radicals are in Table 2.3.2.

Table 2.3.2 Some Common Radicals	
Radical	Name
SO_4	sulfate
ClO_3	chlorate
NO_3	nitrate
CO_3	carbonate
PO_4	phosphate

When a compound contains more than one radical, the radical is written in parentheses. A subscript outside the parentheses tells how many units of the radical are in one molecule of the compound.

Basic Chemistry Chapter 2

1 Warm-Up Activity

Write on the board the definition for *compound* as defined in Lesson 2. Distribute materials such as toothpicks and plastic-foam balls or balls of clay so students can model compounds as they read this lesson. Model a water molecule and explain that the toothpicks represent bonds and that the plastic-foam or clay balls represent atoms. Mark each atom with the appropriate symbol.

2 Teaching the Lesson

As you start the lesson, tell students that the term *radical* actually has two meanings in chemistry. The first, as described in the text, is a group of atoms that act as a single atom and remain together during a chemical reaction. The other meaning of *radical* refers to highly reactive atoms that have free, unpaired electrons.

3 Reinforce and Extend

IN THE ENVIRONMENT

Radicals (the type that are highly reactive because they have free, unpaired electrons) play an important role in processes in Earth's atmosphere. The hydroxyl radical (OH^-) is involved in the ozone formation cycle and reacts with greenhouse gases. When ozone, which is three atoms of oxygen, breaks down, a single oxygen atom can react with one molecule of water to form two hydroxyl radicals. Hydroxyl radicals also combine with carbon monoxide to create carbon dioxide.

TEACHER ALERT

Students may be confused by some symbols that have letters not in the element's name, such as potassium (K). The Latin equivalent for potassium is *kalium*, and that is where the symbol comes from. Make a table for students, listing elements that have seemingly unrelated symbols.

LEARNING STYLES

Logical/Mathematical

As students are introduced to more complex chemical formulas involving radicals and subscripts, they may be more likely to mistake the number of atoms in these compounds. Instruct students to create tables like Tables 2.3.3 and 2.3.4 if they get confused. For practice, write the following formulas on the board:

$C_6H_{12}O_6$ (glucose: 6 carbon atoms, 12 hydrogen atoms, 6 oxygen atoms)

$Fe_3(PO_4)_2$ (iron phosphate: 3 iron atoms, 2 potassium atoms, 8 oxygen atoms)

Look at Figure 2.3.2. In the formula $Ba(OH)_2$, one barium ion (Ba) combines with two OH^- radicals.

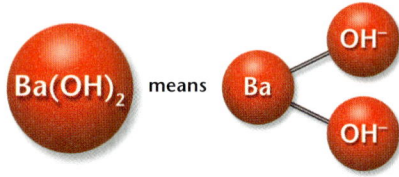

Figure 2.3.2 *One ion of barium bonds to two OH^- radicals in $Ba(OH)_2$.*

When formulas contain radicals with subscripts outside the parentheses, the subscripts multiply the number of atoms inside the parentheses as shown in Table 2.3.3. The compound $Ba(NO_3)_2$ is barium nitrate. The nitrate radical is made up of one nitrogen atom and three oxygen atoms. In barium nitrate, one barium ion combines with two nitrate radicals. Notice in Table 2.3.3 that the compound $Ba(NO_3)_2$ has a total of two nitrogen atoms and six oxygen atoms.

Table 2.3.3 $Al(OH)_3$ and $Ba(NO_3)_2$				
Symbol	Element	Subscript	Radical Subscript	Number of Atoms
Al	aluminum	none	not in a radical	1
O	oxygen	none	3	3 (3 x 1)
H	hydrogen	none	3	+3 (3 x 1)
				7 total atoms
Ba	barium	none	not in a radical	1
N	nitrogen	none	2	2 (2 x 1)
O_3	oxygen	3	2	+6 (2 x 3)
				9 total atoms

In more complex molecules, especially in organic substances, the configuration of the formula is important. Parentheses are often required. For example, nitroglycerin, $C_3H_5(NO_3)_3$, consists of three atoms of carbon, five atoms of hydrogen, and three nitrate radicals.

Binary compound
A compound that contains two elements

Study Table 2.3.4. It shows the chemical formula for $C_3H_5(NO_3)_3$.

Table 2.3.4 $C_3H_5(NO_3)_3$				
Symbol	Element	Subscript	Radical Subscript	Number of Atoms
C_3	carbon	3	not in a radical	3
H_5	hydrogen	5	not in a radical	5
N	nitrogen	none	3	3
O_3	oxygen	3	3	+9 (3 x 3)
				20 total atoms

An important element for healthy teeth is fluoride, which is a form of the trace element fluorine. Tooth decay is less frequent in societies that add fluoride to drinking water and to toothpaste. Fluoride prevents cavities by affecting the metabolism of bacteria that live in the plaque that coats teeth.

Naming Compounds

A compound that contains two elements is called a **binary compound.** The name of a binary compound is a combination of the names of the two elements that form the compound. The number of atoms in the compound is not considered when naming a compound. Use the following two rules to name compounds that contain two elements:

◆ The first name of a binary compound is the same as the name of the first element in the compound's formula.

◆ The second name of a binary compound is the name of the second element in the compound's formula with the ending changed to *–ide*. Table 2.3.5 shows how names of some elements are written when they are the second element in a formula.

Table 2.3.5 Naming Binary Compounds	
Element	The Second Element's Name in a Binary Compound
chlorine (Cl)	chlor**ide**
iodine (I)	iod**ide**
fluorine (Fl)	fluor**ide**
bromine (Br)	brom**ide**
oxygen (O)	ox**ide**
sulfur (S)	sulf**ide**

Basic Chemistry Chapter 2 45

ELL/ESL Strategy

Language Objective: *To learn summarizing skills*

Students who are learning English can be easily overwhelmed when reading dense material such as the content of this lesson. Help them concentrate on more important topics by stressing the importance of main ideas over details. Instruct English language learners to summarize each paragraph by writing down the main idea. After identifying the main idea, they can write down any relevant supporting details. Provide the following example from page 45:

Main idea: A binary compound has two elements.

Supporting details: (1) The first name of a compound is the first element in that compound. (2) The second name is the second element with the ending changed to *-ide.*

In the Community

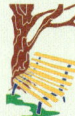

Ask a volunteer to read aloud the boxed feature about fluoride. Ask students if they knew that fluoride was added to drinking water. Then have students conduct research to seek out the contact information for their community's water-treatment facilities so they can find out what chemicals are added to the water they drink. If possible, arrange a field trip to the plant so students can see the tanks where water is treated and chemicals are added. If a field trip is not possible, ask an employee of the plant to come for a class visit to discuss the process of treating drinking water.

Learning Styles

Logical/Mathematical

Display a copy of the periodic table. Instruct students to locate each of the elements listed in Table 2.3.5. Ask students: What traits or patterns do you see? *(Sample answer: Chlorine, iodine, fluorine, and bromine are in the same vertical column, or "group," and therefore share characteristics and properties; oxygen and sulfur are also in the same group.)*

Basic Chemistry   45

TEACHER ALERT

Students may be more interested in learning about specific elements and compounds if they find out how these elements and compounds are used. Chlorine is used to treat drinking water and wastewater. Bromine can be used to disinfect water in pools. Bromine is also found in some pharmaceuticals, although its primary application is in brominated flame retardants to make electronics and appliances fire resistant. Iodine is a nutrient and disinfectant in medicine. Some campers put iodine tablets in their water to kill parasites such as giardia. Aluminum hydroxide is used to alleviate heartburn, acid reflux, indigestion, and ulcers.

LEARNING STYLES

Visual/Spatial

Students may wonder how scientists can know so much about atoms if they are small enough so that 250 million of them fit in an inch. Technology has enabled scientists to observe atoms like never before. A scanning tunneling microscope (STM) scans the surface of a material atom by atom. The technique was developed by Gerd Binning and Henrich Rohrer and earned them the 1986 Nobel Prize in Chemistry. A piece of the microscope called the stylus scans a surface. The tip of the stylus is a single electron. As the stylus scans, electrons move, or "tunnel," between the surface and the stylus. The stylus moves freely up and down to maintain a specified distance, creating a profile of the surface. A computer then generates a contour map, where each peak represents an individual atom. For further information about how STMs work, and for STM images, have students search the following Web site:

http://nobelprize.org/physics/educational/microscopes/scanning/index.html

---

If 250 million hydrogen atoms were placed side by side, the length would be about one inch. Molecules also tend to be small. Many more molecules are in a glass of water than there are glasses of water in the sea.

Look at the formula for a compound to help you determine the compound's name. In Figure 2.3.3, the formula BaO contains the symbols for the elements barium and oxygen. The first name of the compound is the name of the first element, barium. We change oxygen to oxide to form the second name of the compound. BaO is barium oxide.

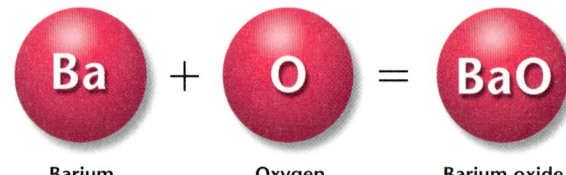

Barium   Oxygen   Barium oxide

Figure 2.3.3 *One ion of barium bonds to one ion of oxygen in BaO.*

Compounds with More Than Two Elements

A compound that contains more than two elements usually has a radical in its formula. The first name of the compound is the name of the first element in the formula. The second name of the compound varies according to the radical in the formula.

Look at the formula $Al(OH)_3$ in Figure 2.3.4. The first name of this compound is the name of the first element—aluminum. The second name identifies the OH radical—hydroxide. The name of the compound is aluminum hydroxide. You can find the names for some common radicals in Table 2.3.2 on page 43. The subscript numbers in a formula with radicals do not affect the name of the compound.

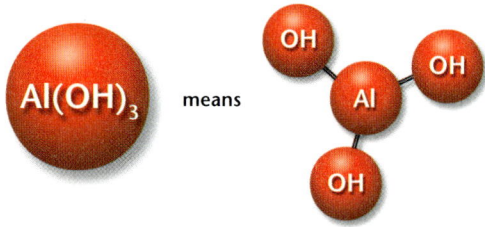

Figure 2.3.4 *One ion of aluminum bonds to three ions of oxygen in $Al(OH)_3$.*

Lesson 3 REVIEW

On a sheet of paper, write the letter of the answer that completes each sentence correctly.

1. The subscript in a chemical formula refers to the _____.
   - **A** atomic mass
   - **B** isotope number
   - **C** number of atoms
   - **D** radical state

2. The total number of atoms in a molecule of CH_3OH is _____.
   - **A** one
   - **B** three
   - **C** four
   - **D** six

3. A group of atoms, such as OH, is called a(n) _____.
   - **A** isotope
   - **B** radical
   - **C** ion
   - **D** binary compound

On a sheet of paper, write the word or words that complete each sentence correctly.

4. The compound $Al(NH_3)_2$ has _____ atoms of nitrogen.

5. When naming a compound with two elements, the ending of the second element is changed to _____.

6. The formula $CaCl_2$ represents the compound _____.

Critical Thinking

On a sheet of paper, write the answers to the following questions. Use complete sentences.

7. In the formula NO_3, what does the subscript 3 mean?

8. How do you name a compound with more than two elements?

9. What is the formula for potassium nitrate?

10. Describe how an ionic compound is formed.

Basic Chemistry Chapter 2 47

Lesson 3 Review Answers

1. C **2.** D **3.** B **4.** two **5.** *-ide* **6.** calcium chloride **7.** There are 3 atoms of oxygen in the molecule. **8.** The second name in the formula is the name of the radical. The first name is the name of the first element. **9.** KNO_3 **10.** An ionic compound is formed when a positively charged ion is electrically attracted to a negatively charged ion.

Portfolio Assessment

Sample items include:
- Vocabulary activity flash cards
- ELL/ESL Strategy summary paragraphs
- Lesson 3 Review answers

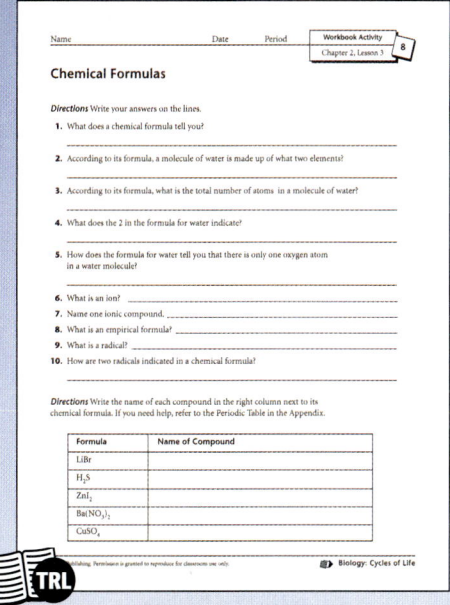

Workbook Activity 8

Basic Chemistry 47

Lesson at a Glance

Chapter 2 Lesson 4

Overview In this lesson, students learn about bonding patterns that hold elements together and how elements are rearranged when chemical reactions take place.

Objectives

- To explain that chemical elements combine and are held together by bonds that contain energy
- To know that when atoms share electrons, the bond between them is a covalent bond
- To explain how ions form chemical bonds
- To explain how electrons fill electron shells

Student Pages 48–52

Teacher's Resource Library TRL
Workbook Activity 9
Alternative Workbook Activity 9

Vocabulary

covalent bond	product
electron shell	reactant
ionic bond	

Write each vocabulary term on the board. As you teach the lesson, ask students to make flash cards. Instruct students to either define each term in their own words or write a sentence describing how some of the terms are related (such as *reactant* and *product*).

Background Information

Emphasize to students that each electron shell has a maximum number of electrons it can hold, and that the shells closer to the nucleus fill up with electrons before more-distant shells do. With this in mind, ask students to describe what they see in Figure 2.4.2. Oxygen has an atomic number of 8, so the oxygen atom has 8 electrons. The first shell is filled with the maximum number of 2 electrons, and the second shell is filled with the remaining 6 electrons. However, the second shell would be more stable with 8 electrons in it. Meanwhile, the hydrogen atoms have an atomic number of only 1, so their first electron shells do not have the maximum number of electrons and are one short. Since the oxygen atom needs two electrons to fill its second energy level, and since each hydrogen atom needs one more electron to fill its first energy level, they can all achieve stable outer electron shells by sharing two electrons with two covalent bonds.

Lesson 4: Bonding Patterns

Objectives

After reading this lesson, you should be able to

- explain that chemical elements combine and are held together by bonds that contain energy
- know that when atoms share electrons, the bond between them is a covalent bond
- explain how ions form chemical bonds
- explain how electrons fill electron shells

Electron shell
A specific energy level in which electrons orbit the nucleus

Chemical Bonds and Molecules

Combinations of atoms are held together by bonds that contain energy. Electrons are the subatomic particles that mainly determine how an atom behaves when it meets other atoms. Electron behavior determines chemical bonding. To understand this behavior, you need to understand that electrons have energy. All electrons have the same mass. However, electrons vary in the amount of energy they have.

The farther an electron is from the nucleus, the more energy it has. Electrons orbit the nucleus at nearly the speed of light. They orbit in specific energy levels called **electron shells.** Each shell accommodates a certain number of electrons. The number of electrons in an atom determines the number of electron shells in the atom. The shells fill with electrons in a regular pattern from the lowest energy level outward.

An atom has a tendency to fill its outer energy level. An atom becomes more stable when its outermost energy level is filled. An atom shares, lends, or borrows electrons to fill its outer energy level. Electrons in the outermost shell have the highest energy. When an electron absorbs energy, it can move up to a higher energy level.

Look at Figure 2.4.1, which is a model of the sodium atom. Sodium has 11 electrons. Only one electron is in the outer energy level. Sodium tends to lose one electron to another atom to become stable. By losing an electron, the outer level will have eight electrons. It will have the most electrons it can hold.

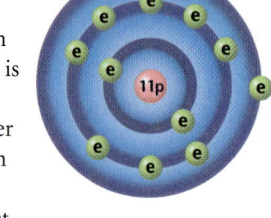

Figure 2.4.1 *The sodium atom has 11 electrons.*

The number of electrons in an atom's outermost shell determines the atom's chemical properties. Atoms whose outermost shells are not filled tend to interact with other atoms in chemical reactions.

48 Chapter 2 Basic Chemistry

Covalent bond
A bond resulting from the sharing of one or more pairs of electrons between two atoms

Atoms of elements on the right side of the periodic table tend to take electrons. Atoms of elements on the left side of the periodic table tend to give up electrons.

Remember that a chemical reaction is a chemical change in which atoms of elements are combined or rearranged. An atom's chemical properties are determined by the number of electrons it has and by how full or empty its outer electron shell is.

Atoms bond by adding, losing, or sharing electrons. An atom is stable when its outermost energy level is filled. This tendency dictates the kinds of chemical bonds atoms form with each other. When atoms transfer or share electrons, a chemical bond forms. Chemical bonds link atoms together. There are two types of bonds.

Covalent Bonds

One type of bond is a **covalent bond**. Two atoms that share one or more pairs of electrons form a covalent bond. Covalent bonds are shared pairs of electrons. Atoms held together by covalent bonds form molecules.

Look at Figure 2.4.2, which is a model of H_2O, or water. A water molecule is made up of two hydrogen atoms and one oxygen atom. An atom of hydrogen needs a second electron to become stable. This gives hydrogen two electrons in its outermost energy level. An atom of oxygen needs two more electrons to become stable with eight electrons. An atom of oxygen can share two electrons with two hydrogen atoms to become stable. The atoms share their electrons in a covalent bond. The composition of the atoms affects the shape and properties of the molecule.

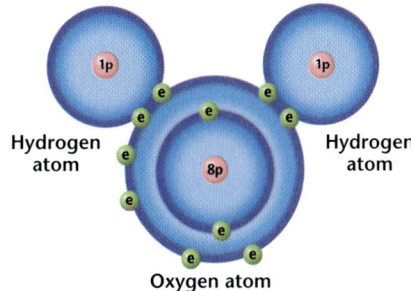

Figure 2.4.2 Water, or H_2O, is made of covalent bonds between two hydrogen atoms and one oxygen atom.

Basic Chemistry Chapter 2 49

 Warm-Up Activity

Pass out some magnets and some jigsaw puzzle pieces that fit together. Ask students to consider the title of the lesson (Bonding Patterns) and predict what the puzzle pieces and magnets are supposed to represent. Instruct students to put the puzzle pieces together and then arrange the magnets so they stick together. Refer to the vocabulary terms you wrote on the board, and ask the class which term is represented by the puzzle pieces and which one is represented by the magnets. Have students explain their answers. (*Sample answer: The puzzle pieces represent covalent bonding because the pieces that fit snugly into each other can be considered shared space and are like electrons that are shared between atoms. The magnets represent ionic bonding because ions are held together by the strong attraction of their opposite charges.*)

 Teaching the Lesson

As students read the lesson, have them construct an outline to organize the content into main ideas and supporting details.

◆ **Reinforce and Extend**

ELL/ESL Strategy

 **Language Objective:** *To build vocabulary*

English language learners may need help with some terms in this lesson. Ask them to look up challenging words in a dictionary and then provide synonyms that fit within the context. They can use a chart like the one below to organize their findings. If they need help getting started, provide the following examples:

Term	Synonym
orbit	revolve
accommodate	holds
stable	calm, not reactive

You should also make sure all students recognize that the terms *electron shell* and *energy level* are used interchangeably in chemistry texts.

Learning Styles

Logical/Mathematical
Some students may wonder how scientists theorize values for the maximum number of electrons at each energy level. Scientists actually calculate the values with the formula $2n^2$, where n is the number of the shell. At level O, that formula is 2×5^2, which is $2 \times 25 = 50$. At level Q, it is 2×7^2, which is $2 \times 49 = 98$. Have students write out the calculation for the first four energy levels. *(Level 1: $2 \times 1 = 2 \times 1 = 2$; Level 2: $2 \times 2^2 = 2 \times 4 = 8$; Level 3: $2 \times 3^2 = 2 \times 9 = 18$; Level 4: $2 \times 4^2 = 2 \times 16 = 32$)*

Teacher Alert

Point out to students that although electron shells beyond level 2 will hold more than 8 electrons, it is typical for them to hold only 8 because 8 electrons in the outer shell keeps the atom very stable. The chloride atom pictured in Figure 2.4.3 is an example.

Ionic bond
A type of bonding in which ions are held together by the strong attraction of their opposite charges

An atom has seven energy levels. They are named K, L, M, N, O, P, and Q. Scientists theorize that energy level O can hold 50 electrons, level P can hold 72, and level Q can hold 98.

Different molecules have different shapes depending on the atoms that make up the molecule.

Ionic Bonds

Ions with opposite charges attract and join together in an ionic bond. An **ionic bond** is a type of bonding in which ions are held together by the strong attraction of their opposite charges. An ion forms when an atom or molecule gains or loses one or more electrons. In an ionic bond, a complete transfer of electrons occurs between atoms. One atom gives up an electron to another atom. Look at Figure 2.4.3, which is a model for NaCl, or table salt.

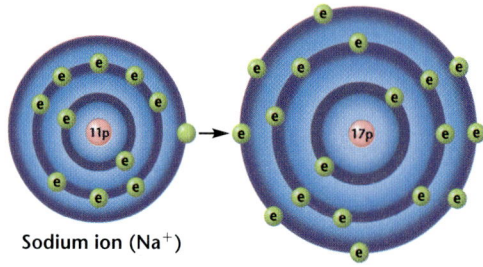

Sodium ion (Na$^+$)

Chloride ion (Cl$^-$)

Figure 2.4.3 *NaCl, or sodium chloride, is an example of an ionic bond.*

The sodium (Na) atom donates one of its 11 electrons to the chlorine (Cl) atom, which has 17 electrons. As a result, the Na atom and Cl atom each have a full outer electron shell. Also, the Na atom becomes positively charged and is written as Na$^+$. The chlorine atom gains an electron and becomes negatively charged. It is written as Cl$^-$. Both charged atoms are called ions. Since opposite charges attract, the two ions are held together by an electrical attraction called an ionic bond.

Look at Figure 2.4.3 again. Keep in mind that when sodium loses an electron, the number of protons in the nucleus remains the same. The Na$^+$ ion now has more positively charged protons than negatively charged electrons. An atom with equal numbers of electrons and protons has no charge. An atom with more protons than electrons is a positively (+) charged ion.

Sodium gives up an electron to chlorine to form the compound sodium chloride. The chlorine atom now has more electrons than protons. When an atom has more electrons than protons, it is a negatively (−) charged ion.

Chemical Reactions

In chemical reactions, atoms change patterns. Inside the cells of living organisms, molecules continually rearrange. The chemical bonds of molecules are breaking and new bonds are forming during chemical reactions. In all chemical reactions there are **reactants** and **products.** A reactant is a substance that is altered in a chemical reaction. A product is a substance that is formed in a chemical reaction. Reactants are rearranged to produce new products.

Remember that as matter is being rearranged, it is neither created nor destroyed. For example, two molecules of hydrogen gas can react with one molecule of oxygen gas to produce two molecules of water. Count the number of atoms on each side of the chemical reaction. You should find the same number of atoms on both sides of the equation.

$$\underset{\text{hydrogen plus oxygen}}{\underset{\text{Reactants}}{2H_2 + O_2}} \xrightarrow{\text{yields}} \underset{\text{water}}{\underset{\text{Products}}{2H_2O}}$$

Atoms share or transfer electrons in all chemical reactions. Because electrons carry and store energy, energy is also shared or transferred. The transfer of energy is important in the chemical processes in living things. For example, plants capture light energy, which is stored in electrons. Energy from electrons is stored in the molecules of an orange. By eating an orange, you access energy stored in the chemical bonds of molecules.

Reactant
A substance that is altered in a chemical reaction

Product
A substance that is formed in a chemical reaction

Link to >>>

Home and Career

Scientists have found that ionized particles in the air impact health. Negatively charged ions may help trap things like pollen that cause allergies. As a result, many home air conditioners and air filters have an ionizer that generates negatively charged ions.

LEARNING STYLES

Auditory/Verbal
Ask students to compare and contrast the two types of bonding that are discussed in this lesson.

Link to

Home and Career. Ask a volunteer to read aloud the Home and Career feature. Then tell students to conduct Internet research about ionizers. Have students go to the Environmental Protection Agency's Web site at www.epa.gov/iaq/pubs/hpguide.html#faq3.

The site casts doubt on the efficiency of ionizers in trapping particles and pollen. Moreover, an adverse effect of some ionizers is the production of ozone. Ozone is advantageous in the troposphere, where it blocks harmful radiation from the sun. But at the surface, it is a lung irritant. Instruct students to consult the owner's manual for any air conditioners in their home to see if they utilize ionizers.

LEARNING STYLES

Body/Kinesthetic
Divide students into groups of six. Tell them that they are going to model the atoms involved in the chemical reaction that produces water. Instruct four students in each group to write the symbol "H" on a sheet of paper, and two students to do the same with the symbol "O." Tell students to organize themselves into reactants. They should use metersticks or rulers to represent the bonds between them. *(There should be two molecules of two hydrogen atoms bonded together and one molecule of two oxygen atoms bonded together.)* Next, have students organize themselves into products. *(There should be two molecules of water; each should have one oxygen atom bonded to two hydrogen atoms.)*

TEACHER ALERT

Some students will be confused by the appearance of the numeral 2 in front of some of the molecules in the chemical equation on page 51. Explain to students that this is a coefficient, and it means that there are two of the molecule that follows it. On the reactant side of the equation, there are two molecules of two hydrogen atoms, and on the product side, there are two water molecules. Coefficients are used in chemical equations to ensure that there are the same number of atoms on each side of the equation.

Lesson 4 Review Answers

1. filled **2.** ion **3.** share **4.** Since matter is neither created nor destroyed, atoms of each element should be present in the same totals in the reactants and products. **5.** In a covalent bond, atoms are held together by one or more pairs of electrons. In an ionic bond, ions are held together by the attraction of their opposite charges.

Portfolio Assessment

Sample items include:
- Vocabulary activity flash cards
- Lesson 4 Review answers

Achievements in Science

Have volunteers read aloud the Achievements in Science feature. Have students write Dalton's four ideas about atoms on separate index card. Next have students go back through the chapter, find text that supports each idea, and summarize that text on the appropriate index card.

Remind the class that "philosophers" in ancient Greek were the scientific thinkers of their time. Then tell students to research either Dalton's biography, or the history of atomic discovery. Organize students into two groups (one for each topic) and instruct them to discuss their findings. Then ask students to give a brief presentation that summarizes their topic. Monitor groups' conversations to make sure students arrive at consensus through thoughtful inquiry and debate.

Lesson 4 REVIEW

On a sheet of paper, write the word that best completes each sentence.

1. An atom is most stable when its outermost shell is _____ with electrons.
2. An atom that gains or loses an electron becomes a(n) _____.
3. Atoms in covalent bonds _____ their electrons.

Critical Thinking

On a sheet of paper, write the answers to the following questions. Use complete sentences.

4. Why should the number of each kind of atom be equal on both sides of a chemical reaction?
5. Compare and contrast covalent bonds and ionic bonds.

Achievements in Science

Early Atomic Ideas

Over 2,500 years ago, the Greek philosopher Thales asked, "What is the nature of matter?" His question started a debate over what was the basic unit of matter. Democritus, another ancient Greek philosopher, said that all matter was made of particles too small to be seen. He called these particles "atoms."

In the early 1800s, British scientist John Dalton published four new ideas about atoms. He said: 1) every element is made of only one kind of atom; 2) every atom of the same element is alike and has the same weight; 3) atoms of different elements have different weights; and 4) atoms of different elements can bond together and form new substances.

Many scientists accepted Dalton's ideas. Later, scientists found that some of Dalton's ideas were not correct. Scientists revised his ideas as new discoveries were made. As scientists continue to make new discoveries, our modern theory of the atom may change.

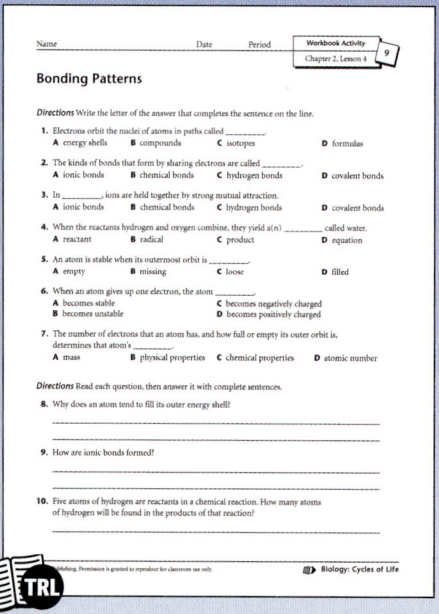

Workbook Activity 9

Lesson 5 — Properties of Water

Objectives

After reading this lesson, you should be able to
- explain why water molecules are polar
- list and describe each property of water

Organisms are made up of about 70 percent water. The cells in your body have between 70 percent to 95 percent water content. Water has a simple molecular structure.

Study Figure 2.5.1. The oxygen atom has six electrons in its outer shell. It needs two electrons to fill its outer shell. Each hydrogen atom has one electron. Each hydrogen atom needs one electron to fill its outer shell. To form a molecule of water, these atoms share electrons. They make covalent bonds. By sharing, the oxygen atom can have eight electrons in its outer shell. The hydrogen atoms can have two electrons.

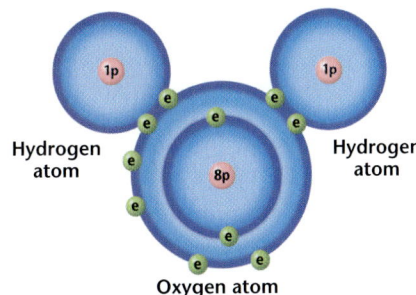

Figure 2.5.1 *Water has a simple molecular structure.*

Look at Figure 2.5.1 again. Notice that the 2 hydrogen atoms bond at an angle with the oxygen atom. This happens because the electrons of each covalent bond are not shared equally between the hydrogen and oxygen atoms. Since oxygen has 8 protons, it pulls electrons more strongly than the 2 hydrogen atoms. The hydrogen nucleus has only one proton. As a result, the oxygen end of the water molecule has a slight negative charge.

Lesson at a Glance

Chapter 2 Lesson 5

Overview In this lesson, students learn how important water is to chemistry.

Objectives
- To explain why water molecules are polar
- To list and describe each property of water

Student Pages 53–58

Teacher's Resource Library TRL
Workbook Activity 10
Alternative Workbook Activity 10
Lab Manual 9

Vocabulary

crystalline	hydrophobic
hydrogen bond	polar molecule
hydrophilic	solvent

Break each vocabulary term into individual word parts and write them in a random order on the board. Ask students to reassemble the words and write them on a sheet of paper. After students have written each term, have them define it. If students have trouble, have them work with a partner.

Background Information

How water moves against the direction of gravity in plants is actually still a topic of some debate. There are several theories, but the leading one is called the cohesion-tension theory. It is based on the fact that water molecules stick together because of hydrogen bonds. Transpiration is the evaporation of water from stomata (openings on the stem and leaves). As transpiration occurs, it creates a tension on water columns in the xylem, pulling one water molecule up in place of another through the entire length of the xylem.

As the text points out, water moderates temperatures by absorbing and releasing heat. This is why marine climates enjoy milder weather than continental climates farther inland do.

Continued on page 54

Continued from page 53

When it is warm, bodies of water absorb heat. When it is cold, they release heat. This explains why two cities at the same latitude can have such different climates if one is near an ocean and the other is not.

1 Warm-Up Activity

Photocopy and distribute the triboelectric series to pairs of students. The triboelectric series is a list of objects that lose electrons easily. (If you do not already have the list, you can find it at www.zoomwhales.com/physics/Staticelectricity.shtml.) When comparing two objects, the one higher on the list is the one that loses electrons.

Ask students to design an experiment to model a hydrogen bond. Have them write a procedure and if the objects are available, encourage students to test their procedures. Have students answer the following questions: Did you get the results you expected? How is this model different from the actual science of hydrogen bonding? *(Student procedures will vary, but ideally their procedures will involve rubbing two objects so that one attracts electrons to get a negative charge [to represent the oxygen atom in a water molecule], while the other object loses electrons to get a positive charge [to represent the hydrogen atoms]. The model is different because electrons are actually transferred. By contrast, in hydrogen bonding, bonding occurs because electrons have a slight attraction to the oxygen atom because it has more protons in its nucleus, making the hydrogen atoms slightly positive and more likely to bond with slightly negative atoms.)*

2 Teaching the Lesson

Point out to students that the second paragraph on page 53 is a good summary of the previous lesson's content regarding how electron shells function. Emphasize that the shared electrons between the oxygen atom and the hydrogen atoms are attracted more toward the oxygen atom's nucleus because it has a stronger positive charge than the hydrogen nuclei has. Ask students to describe this process with a partner. Have the partner take notes while the other student is talking. Then have students compare and contrast the notes, select what seems best, combine their notes into one description, and turn in a written paragraph for evaluation.

Polar molecule
A molecule with an uneven distribution of electron density

Hydrogen bond
A weak electrical attraction between the slight positive charge on a hydrogen atom and a slight negative charge on another atom

Link to ▶▶▶
Health

The cells in the human body require a large amount of water to stay healthy. Drinks containing alcohol or caffeine cause the body to dehydrate. Alcohol and caffeine block the body cells from reabsorbing water.

The end of the water molecule with the two hydrogen atoms has a slight positive charge. A molecule in which opposite ends have opposite electric charges is called a **polar molecule.**

Because of the unequal distribution of charges, water molecules readily form **hydrogen bonds** with each other. A hydrogen bond is a weak electrical attraction. Hydrogen bonds form between a slightly positive hydrogen atom in one molecule and a slightly negative atom in another molecule. Water molecules also form hydrogen bonds with other polar molecules such as sugars and proteins. Because of this, water dissolves these substances. The unique properties of water molecules give water the following characteristics.

Water has a large capacity to hold heat. The faster the molecules in a substance move, the greater the temperature of the substance. Water heats up slowly and holds heat much longer than other matter. As water gets hot, it absorbs and stores a large amount of heat. Some of that heat energy breaks down the hydrogen bond between water molecules. This speeds up the motion of water molecules.

As water cools, the water molecules slow down and form hydrogen bonds. A large amount of heat is released. However, the temperature drops only slightly. In other words, water moderates temperature by releasing heat in cold environments and absorbing heat in warm environments.

This property of water helps control human body temperature. When a person perspires, water evaporates from the surface of the skin. Perspiration draws heat from the skin to maintain a cooler interior temperature compared to the temperature of the external environment.

Water molecules stick together because of hydrogen bonds. These hydrogen bonds make water molecules near the surface of water stick together. These water molecules pull inward and create a strong surface tension. If you drop water onto a sheet of wax paper the water stays as a drop rather than spreading out flat. This property allows water to move from the roots of plants upward to other plant parts in an unbroken column.

Link to

Health. A person's health depends on many chemical processes. Have students read the feature on cells and how they require water to stay healthy. Tell students that alcohol and caffeine are diuretics, which means the body uses more water to process and expel them in urine, resulting in dehydration.

Solvent
A substance capable of dissolving one or more other substances

Hydrophilic
Water-loving; polar molecules are hydrophilic

Crystalline
A substance with a regularly repeating arrangement of its atoms

Hydrophobic
Water-hating; nonpolar molecules are hydrophobic

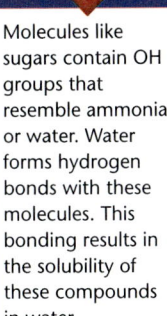

Molecules like sugars contain OH groups that resemble ammonia or water. Water forms hydrogen bonds with these molecules. This bonding results in the solubility of these compounds in water.

Figure 2.5.2 *By standing on water, this insect shows the surface tension of water.*

Water expands as it freezes. As water cools, the molecules move farther apart and eventually form ice. When a substance cools, it usually becomes denser. Ice floats in liquid water. Ice is less dense than its liquid form. Hydrogen bonds hold water molecules farther apart in solid form than in liquid form. Living things can live in liquid water below a frozen surface.

Water is an excellent solvent. A **solvent** is a substance that can dissolve one or more other substances. Water dissolves most biological substances. Because water is polar, it dissolves ionic substances such as table salt and polar molecules such as sugars.

Ions and polar molecules are **hydrophilic.** Hydrophilic means "water loving." For example, sodium chloride is often used in its **crystalline** form. When sodium chloride is added to water, it dissolves. This happens because Na^+ and Cl^- ions are attracted to the polar water molecules and break away from each other. The sodium ions are attracted to the negative end of the water molecule. The chloride ions are attracted to the positive end of the water molecule.

Nonpolar substances such as oils do not mix with water. Oils are **hydrophobic,** or "water hating." Oil and water separate from each other.

Basic Chemistry Chapter 2 55

3 Reinforce and Extend

ELL/ESL Strategy

Language Strategy: *To improve vocabulary skills and practice writing*

Pass a bar magnet around to students who are learning English so they can see the north and south poles. Ask them to write a sentence describing how a bar magnet is a model for a polar molecule. It would also be helpful to provide synonyms and antonyms for more challenging terms. For example, English language learners will probably be more familiar with *sweating* than *perspiration.* (*A bar magnet is a model for a polar molecule because both have two ends, or poles, with opposite charges.*)

Learning Styles

Auditory/Verbal
Lead a class discussion in which students talk about the different properties of water discussed in this lesson. Make a chart on the board of their responses. Refer back to the subject matter on chemical and physical properties in Lesson 1. Add another column to the chart and specify whether each property is a chemical or physical property. For example, water being a solvent is a chemical property. Water expanding and becoming less dense as it cools is a physical property.

At Home

Remind students that water dissolves both ionic substances and polar molecules because it is polar itself. Tell students to try adding sugar, salt, and vegetable oil to separate samples of water at home. Instruct them to get their parents' permission and supervision. They should use only small amounts of each substance and check each sample every 15 minutes. The salt and sugar will dissolve over time, but the oil will remain intact and float on the surface.

Basic Chemistry 55

Lesson 5 Review Answers

1. A **2.** B **3.** D **4.** polar **5.** two **6.** surface **7.** Oil is nonpolar. **8.** The heat from the sun must first break hydrogen bonds in the water before it starts to speed up the motion of the molecules and store heat. **9.** Hydrogen bonds cause water to expand as it freezes. Ice is less dense than water and floats on top. **10.** The polarity of water allows blood to dissolve and transport important biological substances, such as sugars.

Portfolio Assessment

Sample items include:
- Warm-Up Activity procedures
- Lesson 5 Review answers

Lesson 5 REVIEW

On a sheet of paper, write the letter of the answer that completes each sentence correctly.

1. A _____ bond forms when two atoms share one or more pairs of electrons.
   - **A** covalent
   - **B** electron
   - **C** hydrogen
   - **D** ionic

2. What is the chemical formula for water?
   - **A** HO
   - **B** H_2O
   - **C** HO_2
   - **D** H_2O_2

3. Water makes up about what percentage of most organisms?
   - **A** 10%
   - **B** 30%
   - **C** 50%
   - **D** 70%

On a sheet of paper, write the word that completes each sentence correctly.

4. Water can only dissolve _____ substances.
5. The oxygen atom needs _____ electrons to complete its outer shell.
6. Water beads on waxed cars due to _____ tension caused by hydrogen bonds.

Critical Thinking

On a sheet of paper, write the answers to the following questions. Use complete sentences.

7. Why do you think oil floats on top of water instead of mixing with it?
8. Why does it take the water in a swimming pool some time to heat up during a hot day?
9. How do hydrogen bonds make icebergs possible?
10. Why is water an important part of blood?

56 Chapter 2 Basic Chemistry

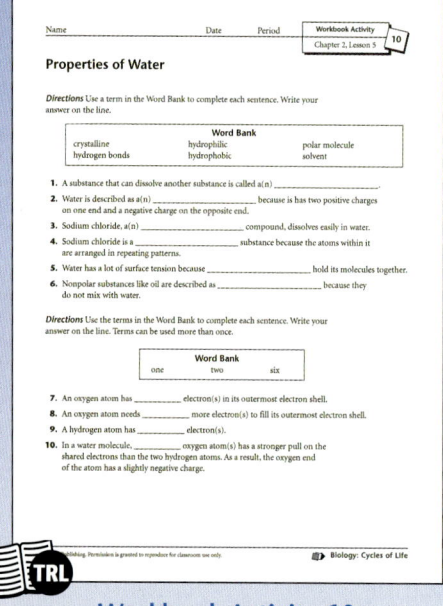

Workbook Activity 10

DISCOVERY INVESTIGATION 2

The Properties of Water

Materials
- safety goggles
- lab coat or apron
- clear plastic cups
- sand
- water
- sugar
- salt
- spoon
- thermometers
- heat lamp
- eyedropper
- pipette
- vegetable oil
- plastic water bottle
- freezer
- hot plate
- paper towels

Life on Earth owes much to the unique properties of water. These properties include water's ability to resist temperature change, creates surface tension, expand as it freezes, and dissolve certain substances. In this investigation, you will pick one property of water and then develop a procedure to test it.

Procedure

1. Choose one of the following properties of water:
   - It holds heat and resists temperature change.
   - Its molecules stick together, creating surface tension.
   - It expands as it changes from liquid to solid form.
   - It is an excellent solvent.

Basic Chemistry   Chapter 2   **57**

SAFETY ALERT

- Make sure that students have read and understood all safety rules for working in the lab. Discuss the Safety Alerts with students.
- Be sure students wear safety goggles and a lab coat or apron.
- If students use a hot plate, be sure they do not leave it unattended when it is on.

- A possible procedure that demonstrates the heat-holding ability of water could include placing sand in one plastic cup and water in another. Take the temperature of both. Heat under a heat lamp or in sunlight. Record the temperature at regular intervals to see how quickly the sand and water heat up. Remove the cups from the heat source and see how well each material retains the heat.
- Possible procedures to demonstrate surface tension could include observing water moving up a pipette or seeing how many water drops could fit on the head of a penny.

Continued on page 58

Discovery Investigation 2

This investigation is less structured than the first investigation in this chapter. It offers students more challenge and requires more teacher facilitation. Encourage students to read the investigation steps. Discuss questions they may have before beginning the investigation.

Objectives
- To formulate questions
- To develop a testable hypothesis about the properties of water
- To design an experiment that tests a specific property of water
- To observe evidence of the results of hydrogen bonds in water

Skills
Observing, using science lab equipment, identifying and controlling variables, designing an experiment, recording and interpreting data, communicating, analyzing data, drawing conclusions

Background
Encourage students to expand on the knowledge of water that they gained from the chapter. For example, students have learned that water is an important biological solvent that dissolves critical polar substances. Students may ask what kinds of substances are included in this category. Encourage them to consider possible candidates such as sugars and salts or other substances that could be tested.

Time Frame
One class period to develop the procedure; one class period to perform the experiment

Procedure
- Have students work together in small groups to complete the activity.
- Have students document the procedure they suggest, including the list of materials needed, the preparation and safety alerts required, and any information necessary for someone else to repeat their experiment. Have students record their results.

Continued from page 57

- A possible procedure to demonstrate the expansion of water could start with filling a water bottle completely with water. Do not cap it. Place it in the freezer. As the ice forms and expands, it will push out of the opening.
- To demonstrate water as a solvent, students could see which substances dissolve in water or what effect stirring or heating has on substances that dissolve in water.

Cleanup/Disposal

Instruct students in proper cleanup and disposal of materials.

Results

Check students' procedures for valid results criteria. They should think about the property they are testing and also consider what kind of data to record or observe. For example, if students have chosen to test the expansion of water while freezing, they should include measuring volumes as a part of their procedure.

Answers to Analysis, Conclusions, and Explore Further begin on page 670 of this Teacher's Edition.

Assessment

Check that students whose experiments did not support the hypothesis or were otherwise unsuccessful understand why this happened. Review the new procedure they write to correct the problem. You might include the following items from this investigation in student portfolios:

- Hypothesis and experimental procedure
- Data table
- Answers to Analysis and Conclusions questions
- Student procedure for Explore Further

2. Ask a question about the property you have chosen. For example, if you chose that water is an excellent solvent, you could question which substances it will or will not dissolve. Write a hypothesis.
3. Write a procedure that will demonstrate the property you chose. Include Safety Alerts.
4. Choose the materials you need from the materials listed on page 57. Or, create your own materials list. Include your materials list in your lab report.
5. Ask your teacher to approve your hypothesis, procedure, and Safety Alerts. Then obtain the materials you need and perform your procedure.

Cleanup/Disposal
Before you leave the lab, be sure your work area is clean.

Analysis
1. Present your data so that someone who did not see your experiment can evaluate it.
2. If your experiment did not support your hypothesis or was otherwise unsuccessful, evaluate your procedure for problems. Write a new procedure to correct these problems.

Conclusions
1. How did your data answer the question you asked in Step 2 about the property of water?
2. What makes this property important to life? What would be the consequences of losing this property?
3. What causes this property of water?

Explore Further
Choose another property of water from the list. Write a procedure to test it. Include the type of observations and data you would collect.

58 Chapter 2 Basic Chemistry

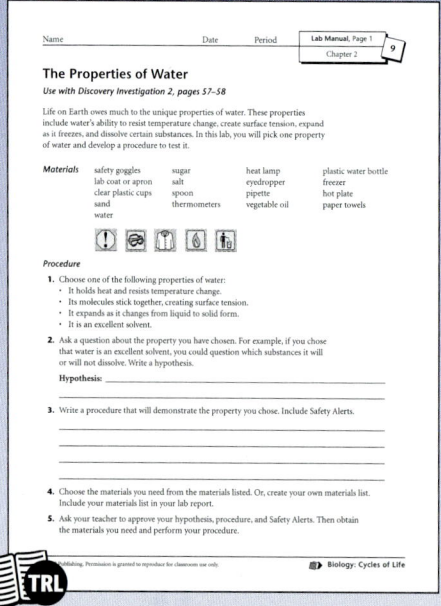

Lab Manual 9, pages 1–2

Lesson 6 Acids, Bases, and pH

Objectives

After reading this lesson, you should be able to
- understand the roles of acids and bases in the chemistry of living things
- identify acids and bases on a pH scale
- explain what buffers do

Acid
A substance that can donate a proton (H^+) or accept an electron pair

Base
A substance that can accept a proton (H^+), release OH^-, or donate an electron pair; an alkali

pH
A number that tells whether a substance is an acid or a base

Acid-Base Chemistry

Many important substances inside cells are **acids** or **bases**. An acid is a substance that can donate a proton (H^+) or accept an electron pair. A base is a substance that can accept a proton (H^+), release OH^-, or donate an electron pair. A base is also called an alkali.

Most of the water in living organisms is in the form of molecules. A small number of water molecules in living organisms dissociate, or break apart, into hydrogen ions (H^+) and hydroxide (OH^-) ions. The hydroxide ion is made up of an oxygen atom and hydrogen atom.

The concentration of H^+ ions indicate the acidity of a solution. It is measured as a **pH** value. The pH is a number that tells whether a substance is an acid or a base. The abbreviation pH stands for potential hydrogen. It is the measure of hydrogen ion concentration in a solution.

If a compound donates hydrogen ions to a solution, it is called an acid. A compound that accepts hydrogen ions is a base. A base decreases the concentration of H^+ in a solution. This increases the hydroxide ion (OH^-) concentration.

Chemical balances and temperature balances in living things are maintained by acid-base reactions. For example, when food is digested in the body, chemical reactions take place. Chemical reactions are involved when nutrients are transported across cell membranes. These are acid-base reactions.

Link to >>> Earth Science

Soil pH is an important part of plant health. When the soil becomes too acidic, plant roots cannot absorb nutrients. Farmers and gardeners often add lime, or calcium materials, to the soil. This raises the pH and keeps plants healthy.

Basic Chemistry   Chapter 2   59

Lesson at a Glance

Chapter 2 Lesson 6

Overview In this lesson, students learn about acids and bases.

Objectives

- To understand the roles of acids and bases in the chemistry of living things
- To identify acids and bases on a pH scale
- To explain what buffers do

Student Pages 59–63

Teacher's Resource Library
Workbook Activity 11–12
Alternative Workbook Activity 11–12
Lab Manual 10
Resource File 4

Vocabulary

acid   neutral solution
base   pH
buffer

Instruct students to make flash cards for the vocabulary terms introduced in this lesson. Have students include the term, a definition, and an example when applicable. Not only are flash cards advantageous because students can refer to them quickly, but they also get students to anticipate what information is on the other side of the card and to quiz themselves on new information.

Background Information

Students may be confused by the superscript plus and minus signs in the symbols for the hydrogen ion (proton) and hydroxide ion. Explain that these plus and minus signs represent the net charge of the ion. H^+ is the symbol for a hydrogen atom that has lost its electron, and therefore has a positive charge of one proton. That is why it is referred to as a proton; *proton* and *hydrogen ion* are both names for H^+. Likewise, OH^- is a hydroxide ion that has gained a negative charge of one electron. These charges are what cause the ions to react as acids and bases.

Link to

Earth Science. Earth science, biology, and chemistry are interrelated when it comes to the topic of soil pH. Read the soil pH feature aloud, and then provide these specifics to get students interested. Most plants thrive in soils with a pH between 6 and 7 because most nutrients are present in this range. Outside this range, however, important nutrients become less available for plants. The same is true for microorganisms that decompose organic matter and make soil fertile by redistributing nitrogen and other nutrients. A pH of 6.6 to 7.3 is favorable for such activity.

Basic Chemistry   59

1 Warm-Up Activity

Divide the class into groups of four. Get some high-accuracy pH paper and distribute four pieces to each group. Bring in samples of four substances listed in Table 2.6.2 and have students test the samples. (Use the milder substances, not lye or stomach acid.) Have students match their results with the color chart and record the pH of each substance. You can order pH paper and a color chart from a supplier of science education materials. Some are listed on page 699. Or you can do an Internet search for "pH paper." You could also use litmus paper, but the results are not as specific. Litmus paper turns red in the presence of an acid and blue in the presence of a base.

2 Teaching the Lesson

Ask students to make a three-column chart like Table 2.6.1. Instruct them to add a row for neutral solutions. As they read the lesson, have them write down definitions and examples of acids, bases, and neutrals. They can include characteristics with the definitions.

Ask students to keep an eye open for words that are variations of *acid* and *base*. For example, on page 60 the adjective forms of these terms (*acidic* and *basic*) appear.

Divide students into small groups and ask them to discuss Table 2.6.2. Monitor their discussions to see how well they describe the visual information that is presented in the table. Encourage them to make generalizations. For example, when looking at the table, substances become less acidic and more basic as you move from top to bottom on the vertical axis.

3 Reinforce and Extend

Science Myth

Instruct students to read the Science Myth feature so they understand the definition of an acid. Then ask students if they think only acids are dangerously reactive. Point out that strong bases can be corrosive just as strong acids. For example, strong solutions of sodium hydroxide can be harmful to the skin, even though it is used in manufacturing soap.

Neutral solution
A solution that has a pH of 7; it is neither an acid nor a base

Science Myth

Myth: All acids burn your skin.
Fact: The acids you see in action movies usually burn skin or disintegrate metal. However, the term *acid* refers to any solution with a pH below 7. Acids can be weak or strong.

Some brands of toothpaste contain baking soda. This substance neutralizes the acids produced by the bacteria on teeth that cause tooth decay.

Table 2.6.1 provides more information and examples of acids and bases.

Table 2.6.1 Differences Between Acids and Bases		
Solution	Definition	Example
Acid	A compound that breaks apart into H^+ ions and a negatively charged ion	Vinegar Lemon juice Amino acids Stomach acids
	Accepts an electron pair	Nucleic acids
	Donates a proton	
Base	A compound that breaks apart into OH^- ions and a positively charged ion	NaOH (sodium hydroxide) Baking soda
	Donates an electron pair	
	Accepts a proton	

pH Scale

The strength of an acid or base can be described by a pH scale. Table 2.6.2 on page 61 shows the pH of some common substances. A **neutral solution** has a pH of 7. It is neither an acid nor a base. In neutral solutions, the concentrations of H^+ and OH^- ions are equal. At lower pH values (below 7), a solution is acidic. At higher pH values (above 7), a solution is basic.

The pH scale usually shows a range in value from 0 (very acidic) to 14 (very basic). Each unit on the pH scale represents a tenfold change in the concentration of H^+ ions. For example, lemon juice has a pH of 2. It has 100 times more H^+ ions than an equal amount of tomato juice at pH 4.

60 Chapter 2 Basic Chemistry

GLOBAL CONNECTION

Search the Internet for the contact information of schools in other countries. Try to find teachers who would be willing to have their class conduct a soil pH test. Convey to them that you will conduct an identical pH soil test with your class so you can compare and contrast results. Agree on a procedure. Vary the procedure of the Warm-Up Activity and have each group bring in a cup of soil from one of the students' yards. Use distilled water to moisten the soil and then take the samples. (You could also do an Internet search to find test kits if you don't have pH paper.) Make sure students record their results, because they are going to compare them with students in another country.

Buffer
A solution that can receive moderate amounts of either acid or base without significant change in its pH

In most living cells, the pH is close to 7. A slight change in pH can harm the cell. Changes in the pH of blood are moderated at a safe level through the use of substances called **buffers.** A buffer is a solution that can receive moderate amounts of either acid or base without significantly changing its pH.

A buffer accepts excess H^+ ions when their levels rise. A buffer donates H^+ ions when their levels fall. In other words, a buffer can act like an acid or a base. For example, a change in the pH of a person's blood from 7.4 to 7.0 could cause a coma. Buffers in the person's body keep the pH at a safe level.

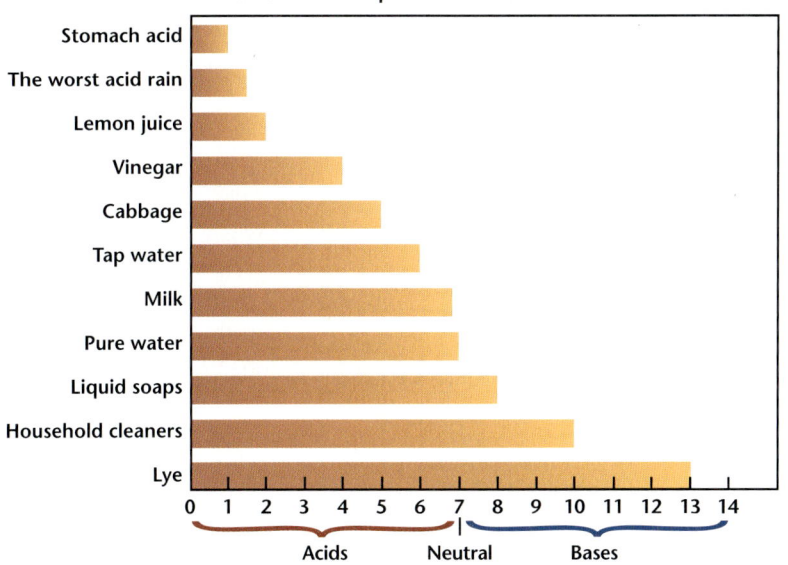

Table 2.6.2 The pH Scale of Some Common Substances

LEARNING STYLES

Visual/Spatial
Lead a discussion in which students compare and contrast the results they obtained in the Warm-Up Activity with the pH values in Table 2.6.2. Ask students to make a table that displays the pH values from their group's experiment.

ELL/ESL STRATEGY

Language Objective:
To learn vocabulary

English language learners may struggle with some terminology in this chapter. Provide descriptions or synonyms for words such as *concentration* and *membrane* (page 59), *tenfold* (page 60), and *coma* (page 61). Alternatively, you could ask students to define these terms in their own words by using context clues.

Lesson 6 Review Answers

1. A 2. B 3. C 4. 7 5. acid 6. basic 7. Water molecules break apart into hydrogen ions and hydroxide ions. 8. A buffer can accept or donate H ions to act as an acid or a base depending on the situation. 9. The digestion of food across cell membranes involves acid-base chemical reactions. 10. The protons in the acidic solution move to the basic solution. The result is a net neutral solution.

Portfolio Assessment

Sample items include:
- Vocabulary activity flash cards
- Global Connection results
- Teaching the Lesson charts
- Learning Styles Visual/Spatial tables
- Lesson 6 Review answers

Lesson 6   R E V I E W

On a sheet of paper, write the letter of the answer that completes each sentence correctly.

1. Which of the following is a base?
   - A baking soda
   - B lemon juice
   - C vinegar
   - D stomach acid

2. An acid is a(n) _____.
   - A neutron acceptor
   - B proton donor
   - C electron pair donor
   - D compound that breaks apart OH^- ions

3. Alkali is another word for _____.
   - A neutral
   - B acidic
   - C basic
   - D buffer

On a sheet of paper, write the word or words that complete each sentence correctly.

4. A pH of _____ is considered neutral.

5. Vinegar is a(n) _____ because its pH is about 3.5.

6. A solution with a higher concentration of OH^- ions than H^+ ions is _____.

Critical Thinking

On a sheet of paper, write the answers to the following questions. Use complete sentences.

7. What does it mean when we say that water molecules break apart?

8. How does a buffer work to keep pH from changing?

9. How do acids and bases play a role in your diet?

10. Describe the activity of protons when an acid and a base are mixed together.

62 Chapter 2 Basic Chemistry

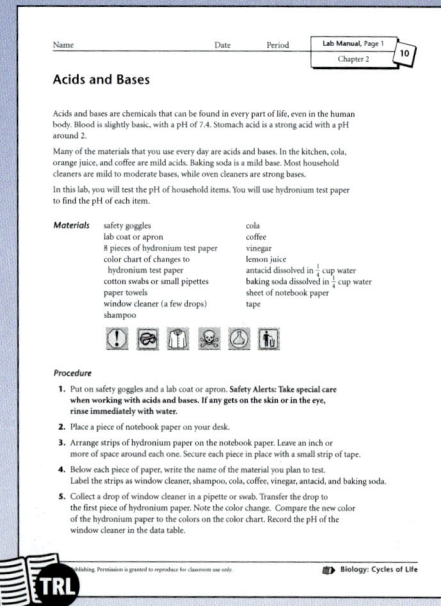

Workbook Activity 11   Lab Manual 10, pages 1–2

62 Chapter 2

BIOLOGY IN THE WORLD

Blood and pH

Your body works hard to keep itself stable. Your health depends on keeping a steady temperature, fluid balance, and pH.

The pH scale ranges from 0 to 14. Blood pH must stay within a narrow range. A healthy blood pH falls between 7.35 and 7.45. Blood that falls below 7.35 is too acidic and leads to a condition called *acidosis*. A person with acidosis becomes disoriented and could go into a coma.

A pH value above 7.45 means that blood is too basic and causes a condition called *alkalosis*. People with alkalosis may have muscle spasms and convulsions.

Doctors have discovered that sometimes problems with blood pH are linked to too much carbon dioxide or lactic acid in the blood. Carbon dioxide is removed when we breathe out. Problems with blood pH arise when a person has problems breathing or when the body cannot quickly remove waste in the form of lactic acid.

Your blood contains buffers that work as acids or bases to keep your pH in the normal range. Buffers are proteins or ions that can accept or donate protons depending on the pH of the blood.

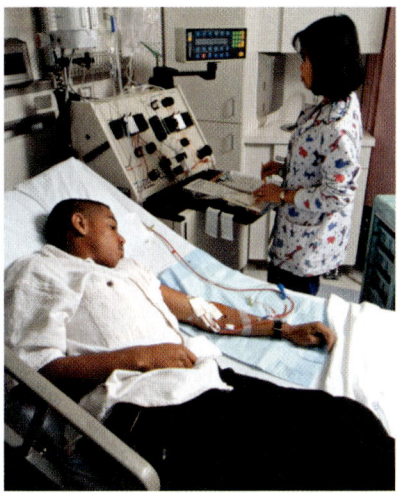

Your body also responds to changes in blood pH by controlling your breathing to keep carbon dioxide at a certain level. People with acidosis or alkalosis are usually treated with oxygen. They also are given artificial buffers to stabilize their blood pH.

1. What is the range of blood pH to maintain good health?
2. How are acidosis and alkalosis alike? How are they different?
3. How do buffers keep a person's blood pH in the normal range?

BIOLOGY IN THE WORLD

Read the blood and pH feature aloud. Point out to students that acidosis is a condition that results from blood that is too acidic (under 7.35). Alkalosis is the condition that results from blood that is too basic (over 7.45). If students have trouble keeping these terms straight, ask if they can think of any tricks to help them distinguish between them. *(Alkali is another name for* base, *and acidosis begins with the word* acid.*)* Emphasize that buffers are especially important in blood because blood has only a narrow range of allowable pH.

Biology in the World Answers

1. 7.35 to 7.45 **2.** Acidosis and alkalosis are both conditions resulting from unhealthy blood pH levels. Acidosis results from blood that is too acidic. Alkalosis results from blood that is too basic. **3.** Buffers act as acids or bases to keep the body pH in the normal range. They do this by accepting or donating protons depending on the pH of the blood.

ONLINE CONNECTION

If students are interested in learning more about a career in food chemistry, refer them to the career browser on the College Board's Web site. To access the career browser, have students go to www.collegeboard.com, click on *College Search*, then *Find a College*, and then the *Career Browser* under *Tools*. A menu of specific fields of study will appear. Under "Health and Assessment and Treating Occupations" is a Food Sciences and Nutrition item.

For a list of the seven different types of recyclable materials for the Biology in Your Life feature, have students go to www.eia.doe.gov/kids/energyfacts/saving/recycling/solidwaste/plastics.html.

Chapter 2 Summary

Have volunteers read aloud each summary item on page 64. Ask volunteers to explain the meaning of each item. Direct students' attention to the Vocabulary box on the bottom of page 64. Have them read and review each term and its definition.

Graphic Organizer

As students read Chapter 2, have them finish completing the concept map on Graphic Organizer 2: Matter, Energy, and Chemical Processes of Life. Encourage students to read each lesson of the chapter and then have them fill in the portion of the concept map that pertains to the lesson. When they have completed the concept map, ask them to answer the questions.

Chapter 2 SUMMARY

- All substances are made of matter that takes up space and has mass. Matter has physical and chemical properties.
- Matter can be broken down into elements. Two or more elements can combine to form a compound.
- The basic unit of matter is the atom. Atoms are made of a positively charged nucleus and a negatively charged cloud of electrons. The nucleus is made up of positively charged protons and neutral neutrons.
- Elements called isotopes differ in their number of neutrons.
- Compounds are represented by chemical formulas.
- Ionic compounds are two or more ions held together by an electrical attraction between their charges.
- Radicals are groups of atoms that behave as if they are one ion. Radicals stay together during chemical reactions.
- A compound of two elements is named by stating the name of the first element, then adding the name of the second element with the ending changed to –ide. The names of more complex compounds often use the names of radicals.
- Atoms share electrons in a covalent bond, like in water. Atoms form an ionic bond when one atom gives up an electron to another atom.
- The uneven distribution of electron density between oxygen and hydrogen atoms in a water molecule gives water polarity. Water has the ability to dissolve other polar substances, hold heat, create surface tension, and expand when it freezes.
- A solution can be measured by the concentration of H^+ ions, known as the pH. Solutions with a low pH are acidic. Solutions with a high pH are basic. A pH of 7 is neutral.

Vocabulary

acid, 59	chemistry, 33	hydrophobic, 55	pH, 59
atom, 32	compound, 38	ion, 42	physical property, 33
atomic mass, 40	covalent bond, 49	ionic bond, 50	polar molecule, 54
atomic number, 39	crystalline, 55	ionic compound, 42	product, 51
bacteria, 33	diversity, 33	isotope, 40	proton, 39
base, 59	electron, 39	mass, 32	radical, 43
binary compound, 45	electron cloud, 39	matter, 32	radioactive, 40
buffer, 61	electron shell, 48	molecular, 33	radioisotope, 40
chemical bond, 34	element, 34	molecule, 32	reactant, 51
chemical formula, 42	element symbol, 38	neutral solution, 60	solvent, 55
chemical process, 33	empirical formula, 42	neutron, 39	subatomic particle, 39
chemical property, 34	hydrogen bond, 54	nucleus, 39	
chemical reaction, 34	hydrophilic, 55	organization, 33	

64   Chapter 2   Basic Chemistry

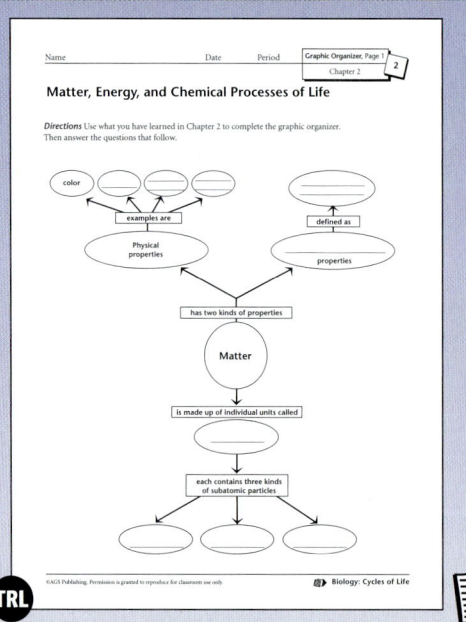

Graphic Organizer 2, pages 1–3

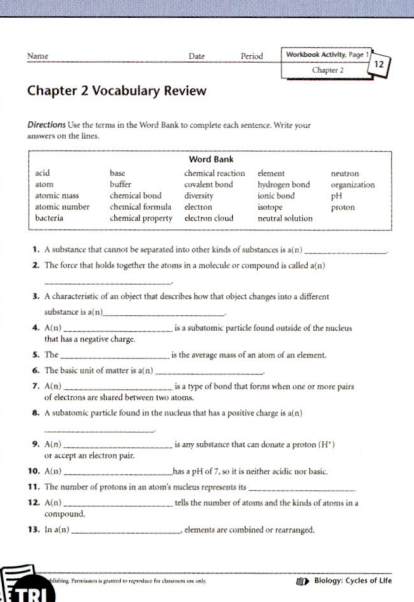

Workbook Activity 12, pages 1–3

Chapter 2 REVIEW

Word Bank
acid
atomic number
base
buffer
chemical bond
chemical reaction
covalent bond
crystalline
hydrophilic
hydrophobic
ionic bond
isotope
matter
neutron
pH
physical property
polar molecule
proton
radical
radioactive

Vocabulary Review

On a sheet of paper, write the word or words from the Word Bank that best complete each sentence.

1. Two atoms are held together by a(n) _____ when an electron transfers from one atom to the other.

2. A(n) _____ molecule can be dissolved in a water solution, but a(n) _____ molecule does not mix with water.

3. The ability of water to change from solid to liquid is a(n) _____ of water.

4. A(n) _____ is a tiny particle in the nucleus of an atom that has a positive electrical charge.

5. Atoms with a(n) _____ share electrons.

6. A(n) _____ of an atom has the same atomic number but a different atomic mass.

7. A solution with a _____ of 7.0 is considered to be neutral.

8. A(n) _____ is a group of atoms that behave like they are one ion.

9. The number of protons in the nucleus of the atom is called the _____.

10. A(n) _____ donates hydrogen ions to a solution, but a(n) _____ accepts hydrogen ions.

11. A(n) _____ has no charge and is found in the nucleus.

12. Anything that has mass and takes up space is _____.

13. A solution that can receive moderate amounts of acid or base without changing its pH is a(n) _____.

Review continued on next page

Basic Chemistry Chapter 2 65

Chapter 2 Review

Use the Chapter Review to prepare students for tests and to reteach content from the chapter.

Chapter 2 Mastery Test

The Teacher's Resource Library includes two forms of the Chapter 2 Mastery Test. Each test addresses the chapter Goals for Learning. An optional third page of additional critical-thinking items is included for each test. The difficulty level of the two forms is equivalent.

Review Answers

Vocabulary Review

1. ionic bond 2. hydrophilic, hydrophobic
3. physical property 4. proton 5. covalent bond 6. isotope 7. pH 8. radical 9. atomic number 10. acid, base 11. neutron
12. matter 13. buffer

Review Answers
14. chemical reaction 15. polar molecule
16. radioactive 17. chemical bond
18. crystalline

Teacher Alert

In the Chapter Review, the Vocabulary Review activity includes a sample of the chapter's vocabulary terms. The activity will help determine students' understanding of key vocabulary terms and concepts presented in the chapter. Other vocabulary terms used in the chapter are listed below.

atom	empirical
atomic mass	formula
bacteria	hydrogen bond
binary	ion
compound	ionic
chemical	compound
formula	mass
chemical	molecular
process	molecule
chemical	neutral
property	solution
chemistry	nucleus
compound	organization
diversity	product
electron	radioisotope
electron cloud	reactant
electron shell	solvent
element	subatomic
element symbol	particle

Concept Review
19. A 20. C 21. D

Chapter 2 REVIEW – continued

14. The rearranging of the chemical makeup of matter is called a(n) _____.
15. Water is a(n) _____ because its opposite ends have opposite electric charges.
16. As they change to another substance over time, _____ elements give off energy.
17. Two or more atoms linked by a(n) _____ form a molecule.
18. A(n) _____ substance has a regularly repeating arrangement of atoms.

Concept Review
On a sheet of paper, write the letter of the answer that completes each sentence correctly.

19. The central part of an atom is the _____.
    - **A** nucleus
    - **B** neutron
    - **C** proton
    - **D** molecule

20. Water is made up of two _____ atoms and one _____ atom.
    - **A** oxygen, hydrogen
    - **B** sodium, hydroxide
    - **C** hydrogen, oxygen
    - **D** carbon, oxygen

21. Which of the following is a radical?
    - **A** H
    - **B** O
    - **C** H_2O
    - **D** OH

66 Chapter 2 Basic Chemistry

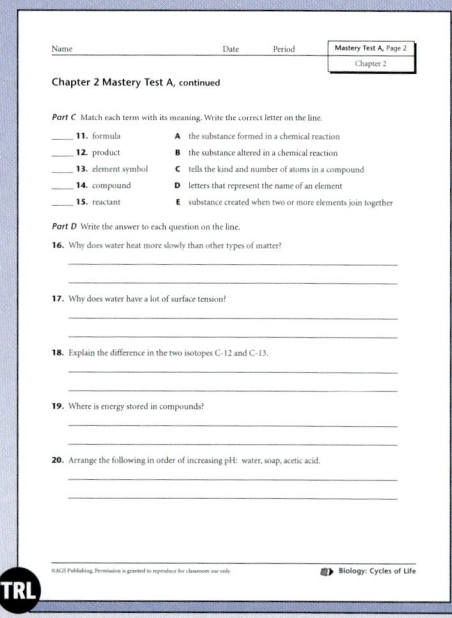

Chapter 2 Mastery Test A, pages 1–3

Critical Thinking

On a sheet of paper, write the answers to the following questions. Use complete sentences.

22. Explain the trend that atoms of certain elements give up or accept electrons based on their position in the Periodic Table.

23. What are the reactants and the product in the following reaction? $C + O_2 \longrightarrow CO_2$

24. Give an example that shows water is an excellent solvent.

25. Explain three ways the special properties of water make it an important biological solvent.

Research and Write

Research the most recent addition to the Periodic Table. Find the name of the element and write a description of it. Include its atomic number, its properties, and a brief description of how the element was created.

Test-Taking Tip To prepare for a test, study in short sessions rather than in one long session. During the week before a test, spend time each day reviewing your notes.

Critical Thinking

22. On the periodic table, atoms on the left side generally give up electrons to atoms on the right side, beginning with the row that has chlorine. **23.** Reactants are C and O (carbon and oxygen), and the product is CO_2 (carbon dioxide). **24.** Answers will vary, but should include any example of a substance dissolving in water. **25.** Hydrogen bonds allow water to resist temperature change, which keeps stability. Frozen water expands, allowing liquid water to remain below surface ice and support life. Water is a polar molecule, which allows it to dissolve most organic substances.

Research and Write

Many printed references will be outdated on the subject of this feature, so instruct students to work in pairs and conduct an Internet search to investigate the most recent addition to the periodic table. Students' findings will vary, as some newly discovered elements are pending widespread recognition in the scientific community. One of the most recent elements to receive a name and be added to the periodic table is Darmstadtium, discovered in 1994 and named after the city in Germany where it was found.

ALTERNATIVE ASSESSMENT

Alternative Assessment items correlate to the student Goals for Learning at the beginning of this chapter.

- Have students list five living things that are made of matter.
- Have students explain how elements can be recombined.
- Ask students to list the seven energy levels of an atom. (K, L, M, N, O, P, Q) Have them explain how the levels differ in the amount of electrons they can hold. (K:2, L:8, M:18, N:32, O:50, P:72, Q:98)
- Have students write a short description of water's unique properties.
- Have students explain why most chemical reactions are acid-base reactions.

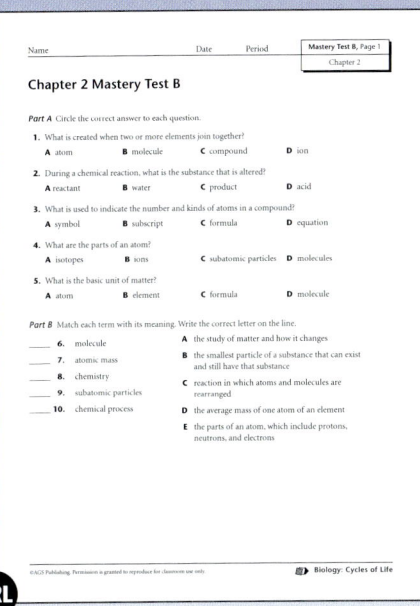

Chapter 2 Mastery Test B, pages 1–3

Chapter 3

Planning Guide
Chemistry at the Cellular Level

		Student Pages	Vocabulary	Lesson Review	Critical-Thinking Questions
Lesson 1	What Are Organic Molecules?	70–76	✔	✔	✔
Lesson 2	Carbohydrates	77–81	✔	✔	✔
Lesson 3	Lipids	82–87	✔	✔	✔
Lesson 4	Proteins	88–93	✔	✔	✔
Lesson 5	Nucleic Acids	94–97	✔	✔	✔

Chapter Activities

Teacher's Resource Library
Community Connection 3:
  The Diet Fads
Graphic Organizer 3:
  Organic Molecules

Teacher's Edition
Opener Activity

Assessment Options

Student Text
Chapter 3 Review

Teacher's Resource Library
Chapter 3 Mastery Tests A and B

Teacher's Edition
Chapter 3 Alternative Assessment

	Student Text Features									Teaching Strategies						Learning Styles					Teacher's Resource Library			
	Achievements in Science	Science at Work	Biology in Your Life	Investigation/Discovery	Biology in the World	Express Lab	Link to	Research and Write	Technology and Society	ELL/ESL Strategy	Background Information	Science Journal	Applications (Home, Career, Community, Global, Environment)	Online Connection	Teacher Alert	Auditory/Verbal	Body/Kinesthetic	Interpersonal/Group Learning	Logical/Mathematical	Visual/Spatial	Workbook Activities	Alternative Workbook Activities	Lab Manual	Self-Study Guide
				75		74				72	70	73	73		72	73					13	13	11–13	✔
		81					✔			79	77		80		79, 80						14	14	14	✔
			86					84	84	84	82		84, 85							83	15	15	15	✔
	89		91							93	88	91			90, 92		90		91		16	16		✔
					97			101		95	94		96	97				95			17–18	17–18		✔

Pronunciation Key

a	hat	e	let	ī	ice	ô	order	ù	put	sh	she
ā	age	ē	equal	o	hot	oi	oil	ü	rule	th	thin
ä	far	ėr	term	ō	open	ou	out	ch	child	ᴛʜ	then
â	care	i	it	ȯ	saw	u	cup	ng	long	zh	measure

ə { a in about / e in taken / i in pencil / o in lemon / u in circus }

Alternative Workbook Activities

The Teacher's Resource Library (TRL) contains a set of lower-level worksheets called Alternative Workbook Activities. These worksheets cover the same content as the regular Workbook Activities but are written at a second-grade reading level.

Skill Track Online

Use Skill Track Online for *Biology: Cycles of Life* to monitor student progress and meet the demands of adequate yearly progress (AYP). Make informed instructional decisions with individual student and class reports of online lesson and chapter assessments. With immediate and ongoing feedback, students will also see what they have learned and where they need more reinforcement and practice.

Chapter at a Glance

Chapter 3: Chemistry at the Cellular Level
pages 68–101

Lessons

1. What Are Organic Molecules?
   pages 70–76

   Investigation 3 pages 75–76

2. Carbohydrates
   pages 77–81

3. Lipids
   pages 82–87

   Discovery Investigation 3
   pages 86–87

4. Proteins
   pages 88–93

5. Nucleic Acids
   pages 94–97

   Biology in the World page 97

Chapter 3 Summary page 98

Chapter 3 Review pages 99–101

Audio CD

Skill Track Online for Biology: Cycles of Life

Teacher's Resource Library

   Workbook Activities 13–18

   Alternative Workbook Activities 13–18

   Lab Manual 11–15

   Community Connection 3

   Graphic Organizer 3

   Resource File 5–6

   Chapter 3 Self-Study Guide

   Chapter 3 Mastery Tests A and B

(Answer Keys for the Teacher's Resource Library begin on page 675 of the Teacher's Edition. The Materials List for the Lab Manual activities begins on page 720.)

Opener Activity

Have students read the Nutrition Facts on several different processed foods. Assess students' prior knowledge by having a discussion about the groups of organic molecules listed (carbohydrates, fats, and proteins). Ask students: Can you define any of these molecules? How are these molecules used by the body? *(Sample answer: They help body cells grow and function.)* Have students make a list of questions they have about these molecules. As they read the chapter, they can record the answers to their questions.

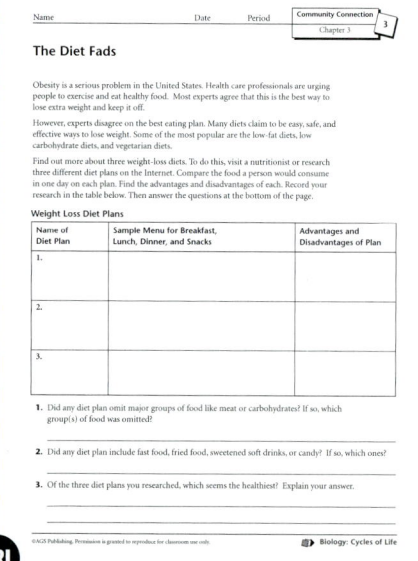

Community Connection 3

Chapter 3

Chemistry at the Cellular Level

What do the items in the photograph have in common? All come from living things and all contain organic molecules. When you eat food, your body uses organic molecules for energy and growth. In Chapter 3, you will find out what an organic molecule is. You will learn about the four major kinds of organic molecules that make up living things and what each one does.

Organize Your Thoughts

Organic molecules
- Carbohydrates
  - Energy
  - Structure
- Lipids
  - Long-term energy storage
  - Hormones
- Proteins
  - Structure
  - Storage
  - Transport
  - Enzymes
- Nucleic acids
  - Information storage

Goals for Learning

- To recognize that all living things share common biological molecules
- To compare carbohydrates, lipids, and proteins
- To identify foods for nutritional balance
- To describe the role of DNA and RNA in protein synthesis

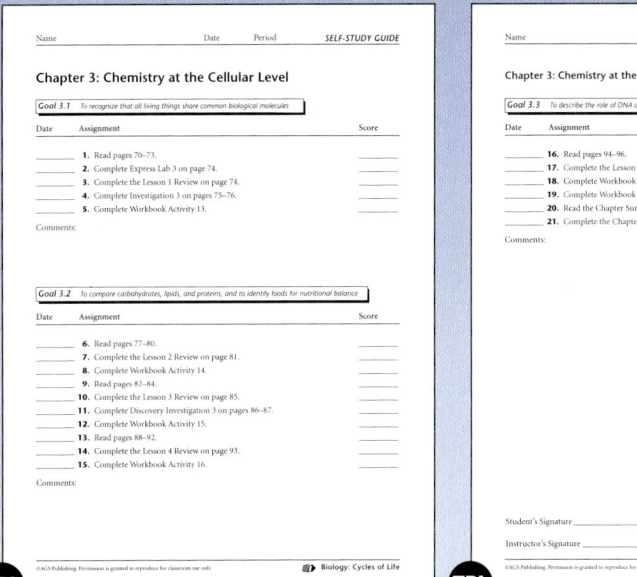
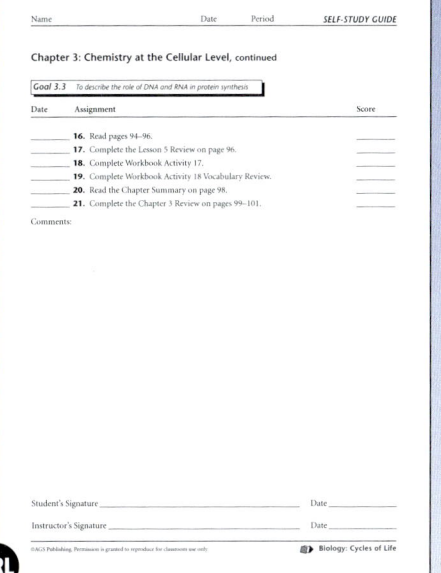

Chapter 3 Self-Study Guide

Introducing the Chapter

Ask students: What do you know about organic molecules? Encourage students to write what they know in the first column of a three-column chart. Ask them to write questions they have about the structure of matter in the second column of the chart. As students read the chapter, they can use the third column of the chart to write answers to their questions.

Have students copy the Organize Your Thoughts chart on this page and then expand it as they read the chapter. Students can then use it to review the chapter.

Notes and Math Tips

Ask volunteers to read the notes and math tips that appear in the margins throughout the chapter. Then discuss them with the class.

TEACHER'S RESOURCE

The AGS Publishing Teaching Strategies in Science Transparencies may be used with this chapter. The transparencies add an interactive dimension to expand and enhance the *Biology: Cycles of Life* program content.

CAREER INTEREST INVENTORY

The AGS Publishing Harrington-O'Shea Career Decision-Making System-Revised (CDM) may be used with this chapter. Students can use the CDM to explore their interests and identify careers. The CDM defines career areas that are indicated by students' responses on the inventory.

Chemistry at the Cellular Level 69

Lesson at a Glance

Chapter 3 Lesson 1

Overview In this lesson, students learn about the major groups of organic compounds essential for living things.

Objectives

- To explain that organic compounds contain carbon
- To understand that carbon atoms are versatile
- To identify the four classes of organic compounds essential for living things
- To tell that cells can break down and put together macromolecules

Student Pages 70–76

Teacher's Resource Library

Workbook Activity 13
Alternative Workbook Activity 13
Lab Manual 11–13
Resource File 5

Vocabulary

amino acid	lipid
carbohydrate	macromolecule
dehydration synthesis	monomer
	monosaccharide
fat	nucleic acid
fatty acid	nucleotide
functional group	organic compound
glycerol	polymer
hydrocarbon	polysaccharide
hydrolysis	

Have students work in small groups to make a word search using all of the vocabulary terms in this lesson. Have groups exchange and solve one another's word searches.

Background Information

Foods are made up of macromolecules. These macromolecules all contain chemical energy that can be converted to heat energy and/or kinetic energy in the body. The heat energy of food is measured in calories. A calorie is the amount of heat energy needed to raise the temperature of 1 kilogram of water 1°C.

Lesson 1 What Are Organic Molecules?

Objectives

After reading this lesson, you should be able to
- explain that organic compounds contain carbon
- understand that carbon atoms are versatile
- identify the four classes of organic compounds essential for living things
- tell that cells can break down and put together macromolecules

Organic compound
A compound that contains carbon (except carbon dioxide, carbon monoxide, and carbonates)

Organic Molecules

A cell is made mostly of water. The rest of the cell is mainly molecules that contain carbon. These carbon-based molecules are called **organic compounds**. They are made up of carbon atoms and other atoms bonded together. Look at the structural diagram of an organic molecule in Figure 3.1.1. One line between atoms represents a single bond. Notice that four carbon atoms are bonded in a straight line. Each carbon also bonds to two or three hydrogen atoms.

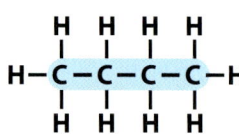 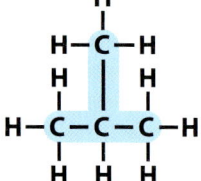

Figures 3.1.1 and 3.1.2 Here are two examples of carbon-based structural diagrams.

Look at Figure 3.1.2. Count the number of carbon atoms and hydrogen atoms in Figures 3.1.1 and 3.1.2. What did you find? Both molecules have the same number of hydrogen and carbon atoms. However, they are different compounds because of their bonding patterns. Figure 3.1.1 is a straight chain carbon compound. Figure 3.1.2 is a branched carbon compound.

Look at Figure 3.1.3. Two lines between atoms represent a double bond. Notice that some carbon atoms form double bonds with other carbon atoms. As a result, each carbon atom can bond with only one hydrogen atom. This structure is called a carbon ring.

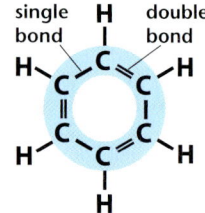

Figure 3.1.3 This is an example of a molecule with double carbon bonds.

70 Chapter 3 Chemistry at the Cellular Level

Functional group

A group of atoms within a molecule that causes the molecule to react in a specific way

A carbon atom can bond with up to four other atoms to fill its outer electron shell. Think about a carbon atom like an intersection of two roads. The carbon atom can form up to four bonds. A carbon atom can bond with another carbon atom. Or, it can bond with other atoms, such as hydrogen or oxygen. This means you can make an endless number of carbon compounds that differ in size and pattern. Unlike carbon, the hydrogen atom can bond with only one atom.

Each organic molecule has a characteristic and complex shape. Molecules recognize each other by shape. The groups of atoms bonded to carbon atoms usually take part in chemical reactions. These groups of atoms are called **functional groups.** A functional group is a group of atoms within a molecule that causes the molecule to react in a specific way. Many organic compounds contain functional groups.

Figure 3.1.4 shows one functional group, the hydroxyl group, or OH. It is found in sugars. The hydroxyl group is hydrophilic. It attracts water molecules. Figures 3.1.5 and 3.1.6 show a functional group called the carbonyl group, or CO. Carbonyl groups are also found in sugars.

Look at Figure 3.1.7. This is another functional group, the amino group, or NH_2. Amino groups are found in proteins. Recall from Chapter 2 that a protein is a compound that cells use to grow and work. Figure 3.1.8 shows a carboxyl group, or COOH. Carboxyl groups are found in proteins.

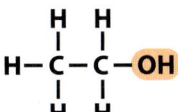

Figure 3.1.4 *Hydroxyl group*

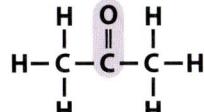

Figure 3.1.5 *Carbonyl group*

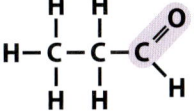

Figure 3.1.6 *Carbonyl group*

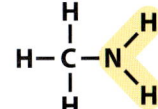

Figure 3.1.7 *Amino group*

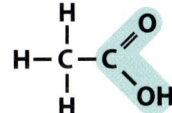

Figure 3.1.8 *Carboxyl group*

Warm-Up Activity

Food is the body's fuel. The organic molecules that make up food contain energy that is accessed when the food is broken down into its smaller components. Have students read and perform the Express Lab on page 74. Students will see that food contains three organic molecules essential to living things: carbohydrates, proteins, and fats.

Express Lab Answers

1. sugars, dietary fiber **2.** Answers will vary depending on the food but should be determined by dividing the number of calories from fat by the total number of calories.

Teaching the Lesson

Have students make flash cards for the four functional groups discussed in the lesson. On the front of the card, students should draw the functional group and put the name of the group on the back. The cards can be used to help students review for a quiz or test.

Have students make a chart to help them organize details about the four types of organic macromolecules important to living things: carbohydrates, lipids, proteins, and nucleic acids. The chart should include which monomers make up these macromolecules and which functional groups may be part of each.

To help students visualize dehydration synthesis, write on the board a simple equation showing this type of reaction. A good example is glucose and fructose bonding to form sucrose. Write the equation, using the structural formulas of each molecule. Have students examine the equation. Then circle the atoms that make up the water molecule formed at the end of the process.

3 Reinforce and Extend

ELL/ESL Strategy

Language Objective: *To summarize vocabulary terms in this lesson*

Have students learning English make a graphic organizer that summarizes the information presented about the four macromolecules on pages 72–73. Students may want to make a chart, a concept map, or a word web. After students have completed their graphic organizer, have them review the organizer orally, filling in any definitions of terms used in the organizer that they can.

Teacher Alert

Compounds that have a carboxyl group have acidic qualities and are called carboxylic acids or organic acids. When a carboxylic acid is in solution, the hydrogen ion of the carboxyl group dissociates from the oxygen atom. This meets the definition of an acid: a substance that gives off hydrogen ions in solution. One example of a carboxylic acid that students are familiar with is vinegar. Vinegar is acidic with a pH of about 3. Another carboxylic acid is formic acid. Formic acid is the substance that some ants inject into victims when the ants sting.

Lab Activities

Chapter 3 has Investigation and Discovery Investigation lab activities. Two additional lab activities for Chapter 3 appear in the Biology: Cycles of Life Lab Manual and on the Teacher's Resource Library CD-ROM.

Hydrocarbon
A molecule that contains carbon and hydrogen

Carbohydrate
A sugar or starch that living things use for energy

Lipid
A macromolecule that is not soluble in water

Nucleic acid
A large macromolecule that stores important information in a cell

Macromolecule
A molecule composed of a very large number of atoms

Monomer
A small molecular structure that can chemically bond to other monomers to form a polymer

Polymer
A very large molecule made from simple units

Amino acid
A molecule that makes up proteins

Monosaccharide
A carbohydrate made of one sugar

If one or more carbon atoms bond to only hydrogen atoms, that molecule is called a **hydrocarbon**. An example of a hydrocarbon is CH_4, or methane. Methane is made up of one carbon bonded to four hydrogens. Methane is abundant in natural gas. It is in the digestive systems of grazing animals like cows. Hydrocarbons contain only carbon and hydrogen. Other organic molecules contain nitrogen, sulfur, or oxygen as well as carbon and hydrogen.

Macromolecules

The four important types of organic molecules are proteins, **carbohydrates, lipids,** and **nucleic acids.** These four large molecules are called **macromolecules.** Macromolecules are made of hundreds or thousands of atoms. Macromolecules are strings of units. The individual units in macromolecules are called **monomers.** Think of a macromolecule like a string of beads. Each bead represents a monomer. The entire string of beads represents a **polymer.** A polymer is a very large molecule made from many small monomers.

Organic molecules are often large. When carbon atoms are joined in long chains or in rings, the molecule is less reactive. The longer the chain, the less reactive the molecule is. Most foods are macromolecules.

Food macromolecules are biological polymers. Biological polymers are chains of repeating units of smaller monomers linked together. The monomers in proteins are **amino acids.** A **monosaccharide** is a carbohydrate made of one sugar. Monosaccharides are the simplest group of carbohydrates. A **polysaccharide** is a long polymer chain made up of monosaccharides. **Nucleotides** are the monomers in nucleic acids.

Unlike nucleotides, lipids are not organized in repeating units of monomers. Lipids are made up of **glycerol, fatty acids,** and other components. Glycerol is a sweet, syrupy alcohol with three hydroxyl groups (OH). Many fatty acids are found in animal and vegetable **fats** and oils. Lipids store large amounts of energy.

Polysaccharide
A carbohydrate that can be broken down by hydrolysis into two or more monosaccharides

Nucleotide
The repeating monomer in nucleic acid; consists of a nitrogen base, a sugar, and a phosphate group

Glycerol
A sweet, syrupy alcohol with three hydroxyl groups (OH)

Fatty acid
A long hydrocarbon with a carboxyl group at the end

Fat
A chemical that stores large amounts of energy

Dehydration synthesis
The process of joining monomers by removing a molecule of water

Hydrolysis
A chemical process in which a molecule is separated into two parts by adding a molecule of water

When cells link monomers into a chain, the process is called **dehydration synthesis.** Dehydration means "removing water." Synthesis means "to put together." When a monomer is added to a polymer chain, a molecule of water forms. The water comes from the release of two hydrogen atoms and one oxygen atom from the monomers. Dehydration synthesis is shown in Figure 3.1.9.

Cells must also break down food macromolecules to access the monomers for assembly into new macromolecules. The opposite process occurs, which is called **hydrolysis.** Hydrolysis means "to break with water." As you can see in Figure 3.1.10, adding water during hydrolysis breaks down bonds between monomers.

Dehydration Synthesis

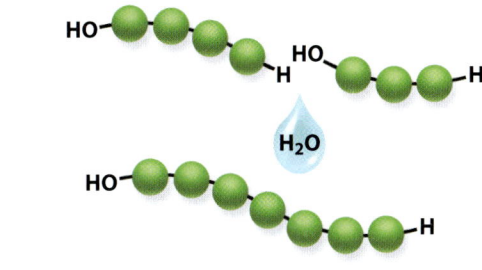

Hydrolysis

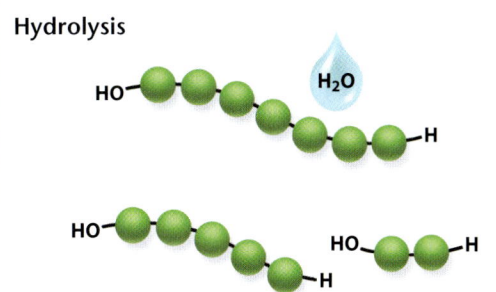

Figures 3.1.9 and 3.1.10 Figure 3.1.9 shows dehydration synthesis. Figure 3.1.10 shows hydrolysis.

SCIENCE JOURNAL

Food, which is composed of macromolecules, is the body's fuel. Have students write a paragraph about how they feel when they are low on fuel, or hungry. Encourage them to use adjectives and analogies to describe how they feel.

CAREER CONNECTION

Dieticians help people plan nutritious meals and learn more about eating a balanced diet. Dieticians study the organic molecules that are essential to living things. They use this knowledge to plan meals and diets that promote health. Have students find more information about dieticians, such as what educational background is needed and what organizations or institutions employ dieticians.

LEARNING STYLES

Auditory/Verbal
Have students explain the processes of dehydration synthesis and hydrolysis, using Figures 3.1.9 and 3.1.10 as a guide.

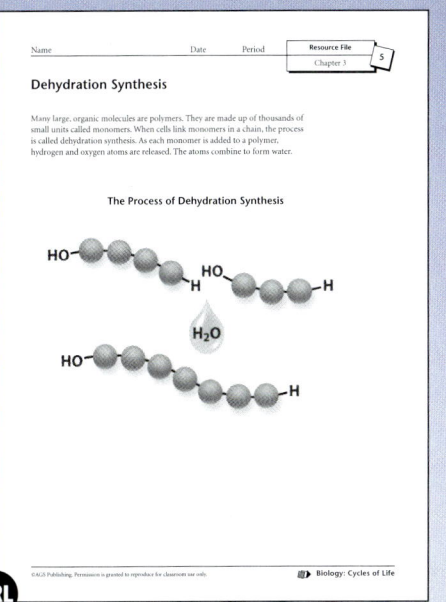

Resource File 5

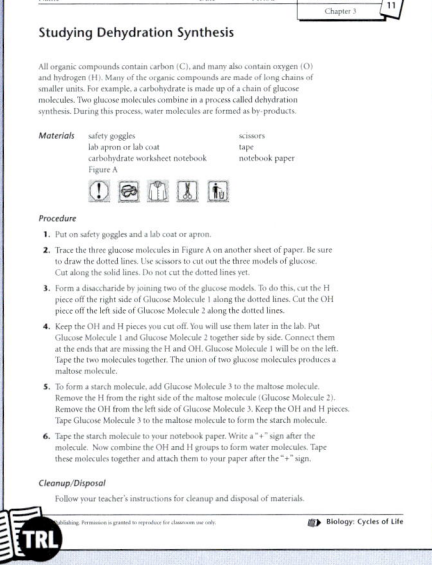

Lab Manual 11, pages 1–2

Lesson 1 Review Answers

1. organic **2.** protein **3.** carbon
4. Macromolecules such as carbohydrates are made of repeating units. Just as beads join together to form a necklace, amino acids join together to form proteins. Monosaccharides join together to form carbohydrates. **5.** Carbohydrates are made from repeating monomers called monosaccharides, which link together. Lipids are made of a glycerol molecule and fatty acids.

Portfolio Assessment

Sample items include:
- Express Lab answers
- Paragraph from Science Journal
- Lesson 1 Review answers

Lesson 1 REVIEW

On a sheet of paper, write the word that completes each sentence correctly.

1. Carbon-based molecules are known as _____ compounds.
2. A(n) _____ is made of many amino acids.
3. Groups of atoms called functional groups are attached to _____ atoms and take part in chemical reactions.

Critical Thinking

On a sheet of paper, write the answers to the following questions. Use complete sentences.

4. How do macromolecules form? Give some examples of macromolecules.
5. Compare and contrast carbohydrates and lipids.

Express Lab 3

Materials
- Food labels with Nutrition Facts

Procedure
1. Select one food label.
2. Read the label. Determine the amount of fat, carbohydrates, and protein in one serving of the food.
3. Compare your food label with a different food label chosen by a classmate. Which food is higher in fat, carbohydrates, and protein?

Analysis
1. What kinds of carbohydrates are listed on the label?
2. Calculate the percentage of calories from fat in one serving.

74 Chapter 3 Chemistry at the Cellular Level

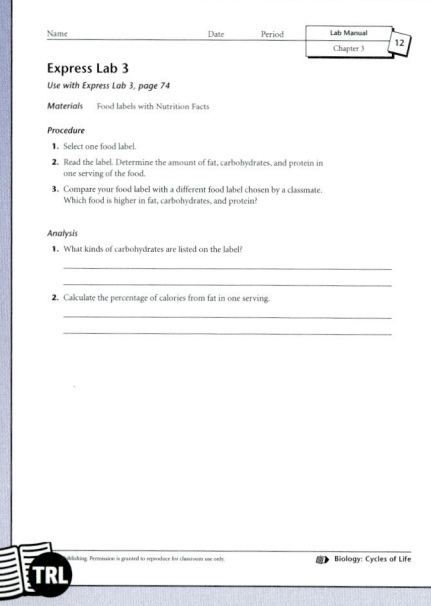

Workbook Activity 13   **Lab Manual 12**

74 Chapter 3

INVESTIGATION 3

Materials
- safety goggles
- lab coat or apron
- wax pencil
- test tubes
- test tube rack
- graduated cylinder
- distilled water
- egg albumin solution
- 5% milk solution
- 5% starch solution
- dropper bottle of biuret solution

Amino Acids and Proteins

Proteins are made of monomers called amino acids. How can you tell if a food contains proteins? In this investigation, you will test for proteins.

Procedure

1. To record your data, make a data table like the one shown here.

Solution	Color	Protein
1. distilled water		
2. egg albumin solution		
3. 5% milk solution		
4. 5% starch solution		

2. Put on safety goggles and a lab coat or apron. **Safety Alert: Do not touch or taste any chemicals.**

3. With a wax pencil, label four test tubes from 1 to 4. Add 3 mL of each solution to the correct tube:

   Test Tube 1 distilled water

   Test Tube 2 egg albumin solution

   Test Tube 3 5% milk solution

   Test Tube 4 5% starch solution

Investigation 3

Encourage students to read the investigation steps and formulate their own questions before beginning the investigation. Discuss with students the question in the first paragraph. Encourage students to share their thoughts.

Objectives
- To perform chemical tests
- To determine whether proteins are present in solutions of unknown composition
- To recognize the role of a control in a scientific experiment

Skills
Measuring, observing, using science lab equipment, collecting information, organizing information, classifying and categorizing, recording data, comparing and contrasting, making inferences, analyzing data, drawing conclusions

Background
All proteins are made of amino acids. The biuret test for proteins is based on a chemical reaction that occurs in an alkaline solution between certain amino groups present in a protein and copper sulfate. Under alkaline conditions, certain amino acid groups react to form with copper sulfate, turning purple in the presence of proteins or pink when combined with small fragments of a large protein that contains only a few amino acids.

Time Frame
One class period

Procedure
- To prepare biuret reagent from scratch, dissolve 8.0 g sodium hydroxide (NaOH) in 100 mL water in a flask. Add 1.0 g copper sulfate. Stopper the flask tightly and shake to mix. Dispense in dropper bottles.

- If you do not use biuret reagent, ask students to add 2 mL of 10% sodium hydroxide (NaOH) solution and five drops of 1% copper sulfate ($CuSO_4$) solution to each test tube.

- Be sure students use clean glassware to measure each test substance.

Safety Alert
- Be sure that students have read and understand all safety rules for working in the lab. Discuss the Safety Alerts with students.
- Make sure students wear safety goggles and a lab coat or apron.

- To prepare a 1% starch solution, add 1 g soluble starch to a small amount of cold water. Dilute to 100 mL with boiling water, and stir until dissolved. Cool before using. Do not store.

- To prepare an albumin solution, add 10 g powdered albumin to a small amount of water. Dilute to 100 mL with water, and stir until dissolved. Do not store.

- To prepare a gelatin solution, dissolve one package of plain Knox gelatin in 1,000 mL distilled water.

- Students should work together in pairs to complete the activity.

Cleanup/Disposal
When students have finished the lab, provide them with hot, soapy water, test-tube brushes, and test-tube racks to clean their test tubes. Instruct students in proper cleanup and disposal of any other materials.

Continued on page 76

Continued from page 75

Results

Solution	Color	Protein
1. distilled water	blue	no
2. egg albumin solution	violet	yes
3. 5% milk solution	pale purple or pink	yes
4. 5% starch solution	blue	no

Egg albumin is a protein. Milk contains several proteins including casein, the principal protein of cow's milk. Starch is a carbohydrate, not a protein, so it does not produce a color change.

Analysis Answers

1. Test Tubes 2 and 3 contain a protein.
2. When a protein is present, the liquid in the tube turns pink or purple.
3. Test Tube 1 is the control. Students should explain why they were or were not surprised by the results.

Conclusions Answers

1. All proteins are made of amino acids linked together. Substances that are not proteins do not produce a color change because they do not contain amino acids.
2. Test Tube 1 contained distilled water because it was the control. Distilled water will not react with the other solutions used in the experiment. A control is always included to ensure that results are due only to the factor being tested or examined in the experiment. In this experiment, the control tube is identical to the other tubes except for one factor: It does not contain a substance to be tested.
3. Answers will vary. For example, students may suggest comparing different methods of preparing food samples for testing, or examining the effects of temperature on the testing.

Explore Further Answers

Results will vary depending on the foods selected by students. Students will need to prepare dilute suspensions of foods they want to test. If students need help choosing another food, suggest a 1% solution of powdered gelatin. Gelatin is a soluble mixture of polypeptides, and it will produce a purple color.

4. Add a dropperful of biuret solution to each tube. Mix gently. Look at the color of each tube. A protein will cause a color change.
5. In your data table, write down your observations.

Cleanup/Disposal
Before leaving the lab, clean up your materials and wash your hands.

Analysis
1. Which tubes contain a protein?
2. What color change do you see if the tube contains a protein?
3. Which tube is a control? Did any of the results surprise you? Explain your answer.

Conclusions
1. What do all proteins have in common?
2. Why do you think Test Tube 1 contained distilled water?
3. Write a new question about testing for proteins that you could explore in another investigation.

Explore Further
Use the same procedure to test for proteins in other foods.

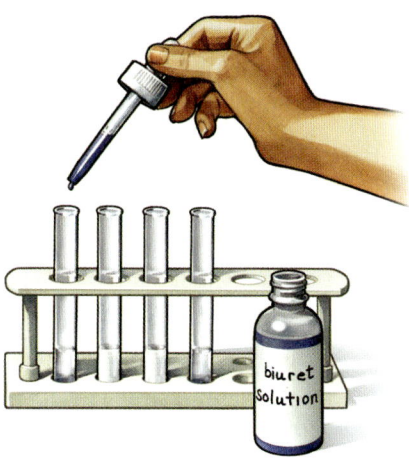

76 Chapter 3 Chemistry at the Cellular Level

Assessment

Check to see that students have correctly recorded results in their data table. You might include the following items from this investigation in student portfolios:

- Data table
- Answers to Analysis and Conclusions questions
- Student proposal for additional work in response to Explore Further

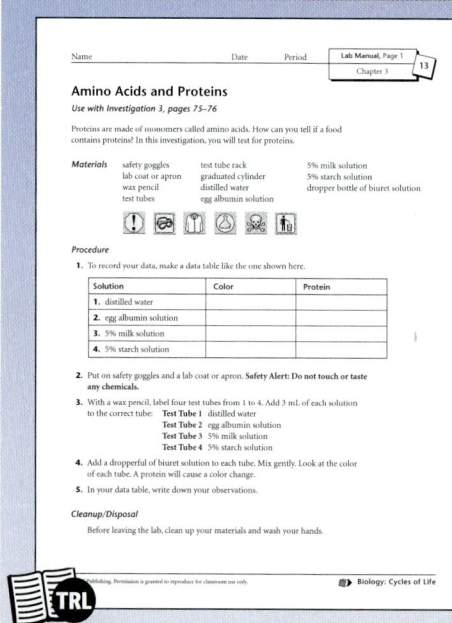

Lesson 2 Carbohydrates

Objectives

After reading this lesson, you should be able to

- explain that saccharides are carbohydrates
- understand that carbohydrates store energy used to carry out the many functions of cells

You may call them carbs. Carbs or carbohydrates are sugar molecules in potatoes, pasta, and soft drinks or sodas. These organic compounds contain only carbon, hydrogen, and oxygen. Most carbohydrates are grouped as monosaccharides, **disaccharides,** or polysaccharides. The word **saccharide** means sugar. *Mono* means "one," *di* means "two," and *poly* means "many." This naming refers to the number of sugars in the molecule. A disaccharide has two monosaccharides.

Disaccharide *A sugar formed from two monosaccharide molecules*

Saccharide *A simple sugar*

Fructose *A form of sugar found in fruit and honey*

Glucose *A monosaccharide used as a source of energy in animals and plants*

Monosaccharides

Monosaccharides are simple sugars. Monosaccharides are a source of energy for the cell. When monosaccharides are broken down in the cell, energy is released from the bonds and carbon dioxide (CO_2) is given off. Cells also use monosaccharides to make other kinds of organic molecules.

In carbohydrates, the ratio of C, H, and O atoms is 1:2:1. The formula for carbohydrates is $C_nH_{2n}O_n$. The number of carbon atoms equals the number of oxygen atoms. The number of hydrogen atoms equals twice the number of either the carbon atoms or the oxygen atoms.

The two most common monosaccharides are **fructose** and **glucose.** Fructose is found in fruit and honey. Glucose is a source of energy in animals and plants. Look at Figures 3.2.1 and 3.2.2. Notice that fructose and glucose each have six carbons. The chemical formula for both sugars is $C_6H_{12}O_6$. What difference do you see between the fructose and glucose figures?

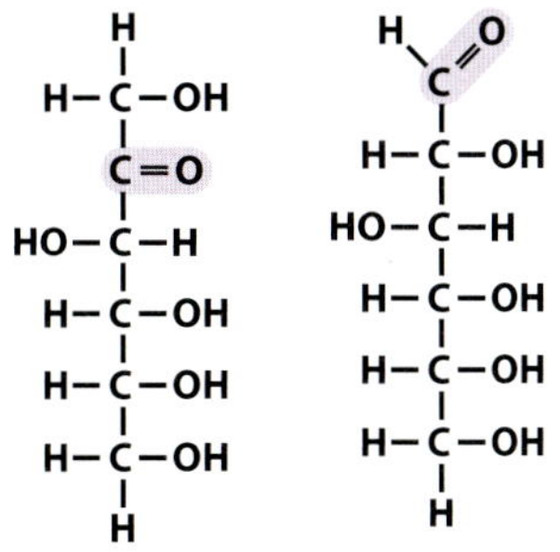

Figures 3.2.1 and 3.2.2 *Glucose and fructose are isomers.*

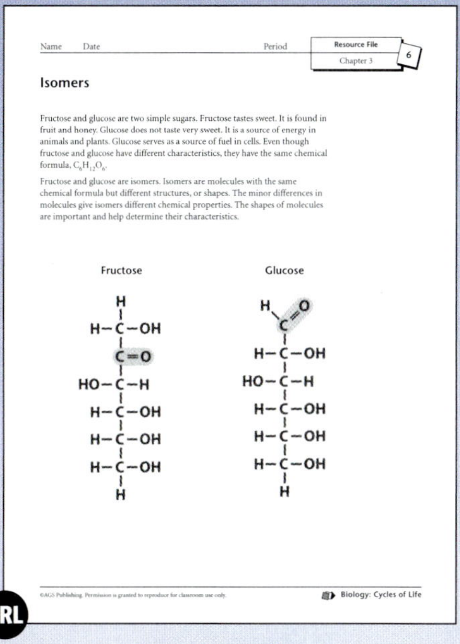

Name Date Period Resource File 6 Chapter 3

Isomers

Fructose and glucose are two simple sugars. Fructose tastes sweet. It is found in fruit and honey. Glucose does not taste very sweet. It is a source of energy in animals and plants. Glucose serves as a source of fuel in cells. Even though fructose and glucose have different characteristics, they have the same chemical formula, $C_6H_{12}O_6$.

Fructose and glucose are isomers. Isomers are molecules with the same chemical formula but different structures, or shapes. The minor differences in molecules give isomers different chemical properties. The shapes of molecules are important and help determine their characteristics.

Fructose Glucose

©AGS Publishing. Permission is granted to reproduce for classroom use only. Biology: Cycles of Life

TRL

Resource File 6

Lesson at a Glance

Chapter 3 Lesson 2

Overview In this lesson, students learn about the different groups of carbohydrates and common carbohydrates from each group.

Objectives

- To explain that saccharides are carbohydrates
- To understand that carbohydrates store energy used to carry out the many functions of cells

Student Pages 77–81

Teacher's Resource Library TRL

Workbook Activity 14

Alternative Workbook Activity 14

Lab Manual 14

Resource File 6

Vocabulary

cellulose	isomer
disaccharide	membrane
fructose	plastid
glucose	saccharide
glycogen	starch

Have students make flash cards to help learn the vocabulary terms in this lesson. Students should write the term on one side and the definition on the other. Have students work in groups to quiz each other on the terms by holding up the flash cards. If the word is displayed, students should give the definition. If the definition is displayed, students should supply the word.

Background Information

One type of carbohydrate, cellulose, is the most common organic compound on Earth. Plants produce about 100 billion tons of cellulose per year. Very few organisms have the ability to digest cellulose. Organisms that can digest cellulose include some types of bacteria and fungi. Cows have cellulose-digesting bacteria in their digestive system. These bacteria break down cellulose in the grass that cows eat. The bacteria then convert the glucose derived from the cellulose to other nutrients that the cow can use.

1 Warm-Up Activity

Bring in the Nutrition Facts and lists of ingredients for several different foods that are high in added sugar, such as fruit juice drinks, cereal, and peanut butter. Write on the board the ingredients of each item and have students try to identify which ingredients are sugars. Examples of sugars include high fructose corn syrup, corn syrup, fructose, sucrose, maltose, lactose, honey, molasses, and fruit juice concentrate. Tell students that if the terms appear first or second in the list of ingredients, or if several of the terms appear, the food is probably high in added sugars. Read the Nutrition Facts to find out how many grams of sugar are in one serving of each item and include that information on the board. Have students arrange the foods from highest to lowest amount of sugar.

2 Teaching the Lesson

Have students copy the following on a sheet of paper:

I. Monosaccharides—
   1.
   2.
II. Disaccharides—
   1.
   2.
   3.
III. Polysaccharides—
   1.
   2.
   3.

As students read the lesson, have them write the definition for each word along with examples of each.

Draw on the board the structural formulas for fructose and glucose. Have students identify the similarities and differences between them. *(They each have the same number of carbon, hydrogen, and oxygen atoms. The atoms are bonded to each other in a different configuration. They are not the same structurally.)*

Bring in a carbonated soft drink and have students read the label to find out how many grams of sugar are in one serving. Use a scale to measure the same amount of table sugar in one serving. Four grams of sugar is equal to one teaspoon of sugar. Table sugar and other sugars added to foods are refined sugars that are simple carbohydrates.

Isomer
One of two or more compounds with the same molecular formula but different structures

Starch
A polymer of glucose found in plants

Cellulose
A woody polymer of glucose

Glycogen
The main storage form of glucose found in animal cells

Link to ▶▶▶
Chemistry
Artificial sweeteners provide sweetness but have few or no calories and no nutritional value. Saccharin was the first commercially available artificial sweetener. American chemist Ira Remsen and German chemist Constantin Fahlberg discovered saccharin in 1879. Saccharin is 200 to 700 times sweeter than granulated sugar.

The difference is where the double-bonded oxygen is located in the molecule. Fructose and glucose are **isomers.** Isomers are molecules with the same molecular formula but different structures and shapes.

Remember that the shape of molecules is important. Minor differences in molecules give isomers different chemical properties. For example, fructose tastes sweeter than glucose.

Disaccharides

Disaccharides are two monosaccharides bonded together. Monosaccharides bond when the H from one sugar molecule combines with the OH of another sugar molecule during dehydration synthesis. Two examples of disaccharides are maltose and lactose. Maltose is a disaccharide formed by joining two glucose monomers. Lactose is found in milk. Some people are lactose intolerant, which means they cannot drink milk from cows. They may drink soy milk instead.

Sucrose, or table sugar, is another disaccharide. It is made up of one molecule of glucose and one molecule of fructose. It is obtained from sugarcane and sugar beet roots. In the early 1980s, manufacturers began to change the glucose in corn syrup into fructose. The new product was called high fructose corn syrup (HFCS). Today, HFCS has replaced much of the sucrose in prepared foods such as bread and cold cereals. HFCS has little nutrient value other than being a carbohydrate. Our diets need more complex polysaccharides.

Polysaccharides

Polysaccharides are repeated units of simple sugars. The most common polysaccharides are **starch, cellulose,** and **glycogen.** Starch, cellulose, and glycogen are polymers of glucose. The difference between them is in the way the monomers are linked. In living things, polysaccharides are used to store sugar and to build structural parts of cells. Glycogen is the main storage form of glucose in animal cells. Animals store glycogen in liver and muscle cells. Plants store starch in **plastids.** Cellulose is part of plant cell walls. It provides structure for the plant.

---

3 Reinforce and Extend

Link to
Chemistry. Have students read the Link to Chemistry feature. Another artificial sweetener, sucralose, was first approved by the Food and Drug Administration in 1998. Sucralose is the only no-calorie artificial sweetener that is actually made from sugar, specifically sucrose. Since sucralose cannot be digested, it does not add any calories to food. Sucralose is 600 times sweeter than sugar.

Plastid
A small, special part of a plant cell

Membrane
A wall made of different molecules that separate a cell from its surroundings

Link to
Health
Fructose is a sugar found in honey and fruits. It is also found in the high fructose corn syrup used in many juices, sodas, and snack foods. Many processed foods contain fructose because it is cheaper to use than sucrose, or table sugar. Fructose can cause digestive problems because it is not easily absorbed by the body. The body can more easily absorb sucrose, which contains glucose.

Carbohydrates and Health

You may have heard the term *carbo-loading*, or eating large amounts of starchy foods the day before a sports event. The body changes starch to glycogen, which is readily available as a source of energy. Starch is the form in which plants store glucose.

Cellulose is important to plant structure because it is a strong, rigid molecule. It is used for plant structures such as stems, leaves, and wood. This strength is why wood is used to build houses. Animals such as cows can change cellulose into a digestable form, but people cannot digest cellulose. For example, we cannot digest wood. If you eat cellulose, it is considered dietary fiber.

Although not a source of nutrients, fiber keeps the digestive system healthy. Vegetables, whole grains, beans, and fruits have fiber. Cellulose is the structural material of plants. Cotton is about 90 percent cellulose. When you use a cotton towel to dry dishes, the towel does not dissolve because it is mostly cellulose.

Figure 3.2.3 shows foods that are good sources of carbohydrates. Carbohydrates are a main source of energy for the body. They are important in cellular functions. For example, they are involved in cells recognizing each other and in the **membrane** structure of cells. A membrane is a wall made of different molecules that separate a cell from its surroundings.

Figure 3.2.3 *Foods high in carbohydrates include whole grains, beans, vegetables, and fruits.*

TEACHER ALERT

Carbohydrates can be classified as simple or complex. Simple carbohydrates include monosaccharides and disaccharides. Complex carbohydrates are polysaccharides. Simple carbohydrates occur naturally in fruits and milk, but processed and refined sugars are also added to foods. Refined sugars do not have any nutritional value, but still contain calories. It is recommended that a person get 40–60 percent of his or her daily calories from carbohydrates. Most of these calories should come from complex carbohydrates, which are found in whole grains and legumes such as beans and lentils.

Link to

Health. Ask a volunteer to read aloud the feature about fructose on this page. Fructose is also found naturally in onions, artichokes, pears, and wheat. Fructose is not digested as it passes through the small intestine. When fructose reaches the large intestine, bacteria that are naturally present there break it down. This results in the production of intestinal gas.

PRONUNCIATION GUIDE

Use the pronunciation shown here to help students pronounce difficult words in this lesson. Refer to the pronunciation key on the Chapter Planning Guide for the sounds of the symbols.

saccharin (sa´kə rən)

aspartame (as´pər tām)

ELL/ESL STRATEGY

Language Objective: *To classify different types of carbohydrates*

Have students draw examples of foods that contain the different types of carbohydrates presented in the lesson. Depending on their level of English proficiency, students could draw and label their own pictures or students could be given a list of the different forms of carbohydrate they should represent in their drawings. For example, students could draw foods that contain monosaccharides such as fruits and honey (fructose), foods that contain disaccharides such as table sugar (sucrose) and milk (lactose), and foods that contain polysaccharides such as lettuce (cellulose) and items made from whole grains (fiber).

In the Community

Students may have seen foods in grocery stores or on restaurant menus labeled *low-carb*, *carb-wise*, or *carb-fit*. These are terms created by the manufacturers of foods and are not regulated or defined by the Food and Drug Administration (FDA). In the past, the FDA has defined terms such as *low-fat* for food labels. For example, for a food to be considered low-fat, it must contain 3 grams of fat or less per serving. This has not yet been done for terms such as *low-carb*.

Have students make a list of foods they can find in grocery stores that have some type of low-carb label. For each food, have them read the Nutrition Facts and record how many carbohydrates are in one serving of the food. Have students answer the following questions: How do the products on the list compare with one another? Is there any consistency to the labeling?

Teacher Alert

Tell students that the Dietary Guidelines Committee reviews and updates the Food Pyramid every five years. The current version of the Pyramid is under revision and the new Pyramid will be released in late 2005. Proposed changes include updated information about food intake patterns, a new graphic presentation of the Pyramid, and new educational materials for the public. For more information on the proposed changes to the Food Guide Pyramid visit www.usda.gov/cnpp/pyramid.html. For more information on dietary guidelines and the current Food Guide Pyramid visit www.healthierus.gov/dietaryguidelines/.

Science Myth

Myth: To gain muscle mass, some athletes and bodybuilders take dietary supplements containing amino acids.

Fact: For most people, a well-balanced diet with enough protein provides the necessary amino acids needed for muscle growth. The main sources of amino acids are lean meats, beans, and dairy products. Extra proteins in the diet are lost in urine.

Carbohydrates also help the body use fats and remove foreign substances. Extra glucose is stored as glycogen or fat in the body.

The average American adult eats about 8 ounces of carbohydrates each day. Some common foods contain mostly carbohydrates. Examples are bread, rice, potatoes, pasta, fruits, vegetables, and baked goods. Many of these foods contain both starch and fiber. The body can digest starch, but it cannot digest fiber.

You may have heard about low carb diets. The nitrogen balance in the body can be harmed if a person does not get enough carbohydrates. The body needs carbohydrates for energy. Without carbohydrates, the body will break down certain tissues to use their proteins. For example, proteins from muscles could be used for energy. This use of protein for energy will harm the body's defense functions.

Healthy Eating

Every day, your body needs many different nutrients to keep healthy. A guide to good nutrition is the Food Guide Pyramid, shown in Figure 3.2.4. The Pyramid can help you choose what and how much to eat from each food group to get the nutrients you need. The U.S. government provides the Food Guide Pyramid and guidelines for a healthy diet and exercise.

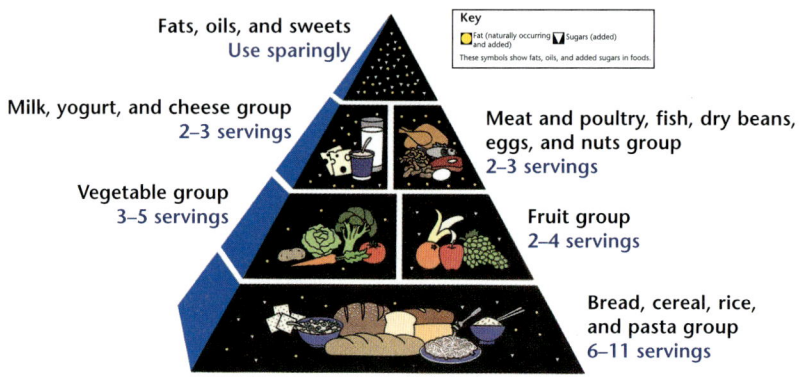

Figure 3.2.4 Food Guide Pyramid. Source: U.S. Department of Agriculture

---

Science Myth

Have students read the Science Myth feature. Advertisements for dietary supplements that promote muscle development appear in sports magazines and on television. Students may have read or seen news stories about athletes who use dietary supplements to help build muscle. Extra protein does not help muscle develop because it cannot be stored by the body as protein. Excess protein is either burned for energy or stored as fat.

Lesson 2   REVIEW

Word Bank
glyogen
energy
fructose

On a sheet of paper, write the word from the Word Bank that completes each sentence correctly.

1. Monosaccharides are a source of _____ for the cell.
2. The simple sugar _____ is found in fruits.
3. Animals store sugar in the form of _____ in the liver and muscle cells.

Critical Thinking

On a sheet of paper, write the answers to the following questions. Use complete sentences.

4. How can you recognize the chemical formula of a carbohydrate?
5. Compare and contrast monosaccharides and disaccharides.

Science at Work

Biochemist

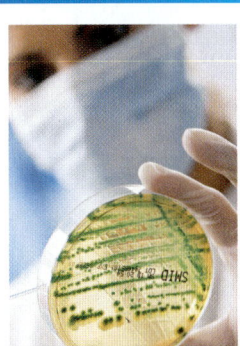

Biochemists study the complex chemical reactions in living things. A biochemist combines knowledge of chemistry and biology. They study life processes at a molecular or cellular level. Biochemists work with many kinds of organisms.

Some biochemists work in basic research. Biochemists who work in applied research develop new drugs and medical treatments. Many biochemists work for federal, state, or local governments. Others work for drug companies, universities, or in hospitals or research and teaching laboratories.

Biochemists work independently or as part of research teams. They need strong communication skills to present their research findings and get research funding. A Ph.D. is required to do independent research. Biochemists with a bachelor's or master's degree hold a wide variety of jobs.

Chemistry at the Cellular Level Chapter 3

Lesson 2 Review Answers

1. energy 2. fructose 3. glycogen 4. The chemical formula for a carbohydrate contains carbon, hydrogen, and oxygen and may be written as $C_nH_{2n}O_n$. The number of carbon atoms equals the number of oxygen atoms. The number of hydrogen atoms equals twice the number of either the carbon atoms or the oxygen atoms. 5. Monosaccharides are simple sugars. Disaccharides are two monosaccharides that are bonded together. Both are carbohydrates that contain carbon, hydrogen, and oxygen.

Portfolio Assessment

Sample items include:
- Flash cards from Vocabulary activity
- Outline from Teaching the Lesson
- Lesson 2 Review answers

Science at Work

Have a volunteer read aloud the feature about biochemists. Discuss the idea that biochemists are doing important work in the medical field. Biochemists are involved in the search for cures to diseases such as cancer and AIDS. Work done in the field of biochemistry has also led to the development of DNA analysis and the production of human insulin.

Lesson at a Glance

Chapter 3 Lesson 3

Overview In this lesson, students learn how lipids are used in the body and what the three main types of lipids are.

Objectives

- To explain that lipids are water-insoluble molecules used for food storage, membranes, and hormones
- To describe the three main types of lipids

Student Pages 82–87

Teacher's Resource Library

Workbook Activity 15
Alternative Workbook Activity 15
Lab Manual 15

Vocabulary

lipid bilayer	steroid
phospholipid	trans fat
polyunsaturated fatty acid	triglyceride
saturated fatty acid	unsaturated fatty acid

Have students write a sentence using each vocabulary term in context. Have students share their sentences.

Background Information

Fats are one type of lipid. Fats are used as energy in the body, to help make structures such as the cell membrane, to help protect vital organs, and as insulation. Eating a diet that contains no fats may result in a deficiency of certain essential fatty acids. It is recommended that no more than 30 percent of total daily calories in a person's diet come from fats. Only 10 percent of daily calories should come from saturated fats.

82 Chapter 3

Lesson 3 Lipids

Objectives

After reading this lesson, you should be able to

- explain that lipids are water-insoluble molecules used for food storage, membranes, and hormones
- describe the three main types of lipids

Phospholipid
A lipid with two fatty acid molecules joined by a molecule of glycerol

Steroid
A lipid containing four attached carbon rings

Triglyceride
A lipid made of three fatty acids and one molecule of glycerol

Saturated fatty acid
A fatty acid containing no double carbon bonds and the maximum number of hydrogen atoms

Lipids in the diet are an energy source for cells. Lipids are also important because they carry fat-soluble vitamins and essential fatty acids to cells. Cells need these to make various molecules. A fat-free diet results in a deficiency, or lack, of essential fatty acids in the body. Examples of food containing lipids are butter, lard, and cooking oils.

In living things, lipids are structural parts of cell membranes. They are sources of insulation and a means of energy storage. Lipids are made up of carbon, hydrogen, and oxygen atoms. Examples of lipids are fats, **phospholipids,** and **steroids.**

Fats and Fatty Acids

The three most common forms of lipids in the body are fats, phospholipids, and steroids. Fats are **triglycerides.** Most fats you eat are triglycerides. Your body stores fats as triglycerides. To form a triglyceride, one molecule of glycerol and three fatty acids join by dehydration synthesis. Fatty acids are long hydrocarbons that store large amounts of energy. Fats provide a source of stored energy for your body to use when it needs it. People need to have a stored source of energy or fuel reserve.

Three kinds of fatty acids are **saturated, unsaturated,** and **polyunsaturated.** A saturated fatty acid contains no double carbon bonds and the maximum number of hydrogen atoms. An unsaturated fatty acid contains double or triple bonds and has less than the maximum number of hydrogen atoms. A polyunsaturated fatty acid contains many double or triple bonds. Figure 3.3.1 shows examples of foods that are good sources of saturated and unsaturated fatty acids.

Animal fats such as lard and butter have a high proportion of saturated fatty acids. This arrangement allows them to stack on top of each other. This means they are usually solid at room temperature.

82 Chapter 3 Chemistry at the Cellular Level

Unsaturated fatty acid
A fatty acid containing double or triple bonds and less than the maximum number of hydrogen atoms

Polyunsaturated fatty acid
A fatty acid containing many double or triple bonds

Trans fat
An unsaturated fat that has been changed to a saturated fat

Eating too much animal fat over time may increase the chance of heart disease. Lipid deposits build up in the walls of blood vessels. This reduces blood flow and increases the risk of heart attack.

Some fish oils and vegetable oils, such as corn oil and olive oil, are high in unsaturated fatty acids. Because of the bent shape of their fatty acids, unsaturated oils stay liquid at room temperature. However, tropical plant oils such as cocoa butter are different. Cocoa butter, a tropical plant oil, is an ingredient in chocolate. Because it is a mixture of saturated and unsaturated fatty acids, cocoa butter is solid at room temperature, but melts in your mouth.

Trans fats are unsaturated fatty acids that have been changed to saturated fatty acids. Manufacturers make trans fats by adding hydrogen to vegetable oil. Trans fats increase the stability, or long life, of foods. Trans fats are found in vegetable shortenings, some margarines, crackers, cookies, and snack foods. A small amount of trans fat is found naturally, mainly in dairy products, some meat, and other animal-based foods.

Figure 3.3.1 *Sources of fats include butter, lard, and vegetable oil.*

Warm-Up Activity

Ask students to name foods that have a high fat content. *(Sample answers: butter, bacon, fried foods, cream)* Cut a paper grocery bag into small pieces. Choose several foods that have a high fat content and several foods that do not. Examples: a piece of butter, a peanut, a potato chip, a piece of an apple, a flake from a box of cereal, and a banana. Label each paper bag piece so that it corresponds to one of the food items chosen. Have volunteers place the food on the paper bag for 30 seconds. Time students during this step for accuracy. Have students predict which foods they think will leave grease stains on the paper. Record the predictions on the board. Let the paper pieces sit overnight. The next day, have students examine the stains left on the paper pieces. The foods that leave grease stains have a high fat content.

Teaching the Lesson

Remind students that, like carbohydrates, the chemical and molecular structures of fats are important to their properties. The differences between saturated fats and unsaturated fats occur because of the different chemical bonds each have.

Have students make a table to organize the material on fats in this lesson. Column titles could include *Chemical Makeup, How Used in the Body,* and *Examples.* Row titles should include the three types of fats discussed in the lesson: *Triglycerides, Phospholipids,* and *Steroids.*

Reinforce and Extend

LEARNING STYLES

Visual/Spatial

Have students make a poster that depicts different examples of foods that contain saturated fats and unsaturated fats. Students can cut out photographs from magazines, use labels from foods, or make their own drawings of the foods. Encourage students to be creative but accurate in their presentation of the material.

Research and Write

Have students read the feature about anabolic steroids. These are manufactured substances that are similar to the hormone testosterone. They are legal only when prescribed by a physician. Some people, such as athletes, may illegally take anabolic steroids to help build muscle and enhance performance. Remind students to find reputable sources on the Internet, such as medical journals, and to avoid commercial sites as they conduct their research.

ELL/ESL Strategy

Language Objective: *To describe various lipids*

Have students work together in groups of three to write a short presentation about lipids. Each student should talk about one of the types of fat. Presentations should include a definition of the type of fat being discussed, how it is used by the body, and examples of the foods in which it can be found. Students can read from notes or index cards during the presentation. Students may write an outline on the board if it will help them during their presentation. Encourage students to use visual aids such as magazine advertisements or food labels as they discuss sample foods.

Technology and Society

Have students read the Technology and Society feature. Foods that contain hydrogenated oil or partially hydrogenated oil contain high amounts of trans fat. The FDA requires food manufacturers to include the amounts of saturated fat and cholesterol on the labels of food products. Beginning in 2006, companies will also be required to include the amount of trans fat a product contains. Have students discuss why knowing the amounts of these fats is beneficial.

Lipid bilayer
Two layers of phospholipids

Research and Write

Use the Internet to prepare a group report on the use of anabolic steroids among athletes. Describe the health risks posed by their use.

Phospholipids

Phospholipids are like triglycerides except that a phosphate group replaces a fatty acid chain. The phosphate group interacts with water. Phospholipids contain two fatty acid tails and one negatively charged phosphate head. The tails are hydrophobic (water-hating), which means the fatty acids do not mix with water. The head is hydrophilic (water-loving). The two fatty acid chains position themselves away from water. The phosphate end positions itself toward water. Phospholipids line up with the heads together and the tails together.

Phospholipids can form a double layer called a **lipid bilayer,** or two layers of phospholipids. Cell membranes are made up of a lipid bilayer.

Steroids

Steroids are lipids containing four attached carbon rings. Cholesterol, vitamin D, and hormones are examples of steroids. Cholesterol is an important steroid. It is a common part of animal cell membranes. Various hormones in the body such as estrogen and testosterone are steroids created from cholesterol. However, a high level of cholesterol in the body over time may cause various diseases.

Technology and Society

Food companies use a process called hydrogenation to change liquid corn oil into corn oil margarine. Hydrogenation adds hydrogen to the double-bonded carbon atoms found in unsaturated fats. As a result, the unsaturated double bonds are replaced with single bonds. Hydrogenation increases the shelf life of fats. Foods made with hydrogenated fats can stay fresh a long time. However, hydrogenation also increases the saturation of fats, making hydrogenated foods less healthy.

---

84   Chapter 3   *Chemistry at the Cellular Level*

Global Connection

The amount and type of fats consumed in a person's diet may be influenced by culture. Have students research the diets of different cultures and find answers to the following questions: What differences in diet exist in other cultures compared to the diet of many Americans? What health issues occur as a result of diet in different cultures? Have students share the results of their research with the class.

Pronunciation Guide

Use the pronunciation shown here to help students pronounce a difficult word in this lesson. Refer to the pronunciation key on the Chapter Planning Guide for the sounds of the symbols.

hydrogenation (hī drä′jə nā′shən)

Lesson 3 REVIEW

On a sheet of paper, write the word or words that complete each sentence correctly.

1. In an unsaturated fatty acid, some carbon atoms are joined by _____ bonds.
2. A(n) _____ is a lipid that contains a phosphate group.
3. A(n) _____ fatty acid has no double bonds between carbon atoms.

On a sheet of paper, write the letter of the answer that completes each sentence correctly.

4. A triglyceride is made up of three fatty acids and one molecule of _____.
   - A water
   - B glycerol
   - C phospholipid
   - D glucose

5. Animal fats such as _____ have a high proportion of saturated fatty acids.
   - A butter
   - B some fish oils
   - C olive oil
   - D corn oil

6. Unsaturated fatty acids that have been changed to saturated fatty acids are called _____.
   - A oils
   - B trans fats
   - C steroids
   - D lipids

Critical Thinking

On a sheet of paper, write the answers to the following questions. Use complete sentences.

7. Why are lipids necessary for the body to function?
8. Compare and contrast animal fats and plant and fish oils.
9. Explain the relationship between a diet high in saturated fatty acids and heart disease.
10. What are steroids? Name some examples of steroids.

Lesson 3 Review Answers

1. double **2.** phospholipid **3.** saturated **4.** B **5.** A **6.** B **7.** Lipids are structural components of cell membranes, sources of insulation, and a means of energy storage. **8.** Animal fats such as lard and butter have a high proportion of saturated fatty acids. Because of their linear arrangement, animal fats are usually solid at room temperature. Plant oils and some fish oils are high in unsaturated fatty acids. They have bent shapes and are less likely to form solids, so they are usually liquid at room temperature. **9.** Saturated fatty acids have long, straight fatty acids chains, which form a stacked arrangement. As a result, they are usually solid at room temperature, which can allow lipid deposits to build up in the walls of blood vessels. This buildup reduces blood flow and increases the risk of heart attack. **10.** Steroids are a type of lipid characterized by four joined carbon rings. Examples of steroids are estrogen and testosterone.

Portfolio Assessment

Sample items include:
- Report from Research and Write
- Poster from Learning Styles Visual/Spatial
- Research from Global Connection
- Lesson 3 Review answers

At Home

Have students read the list of ingredients on processed foods such as margarine, crackers, cookies, and other snack foods to see if they contain hydrogenated oil or partially hydrogenated oil. Have students make a list of foods at home that contain these oils. Ask students what food items could be substituted that are better for their health.

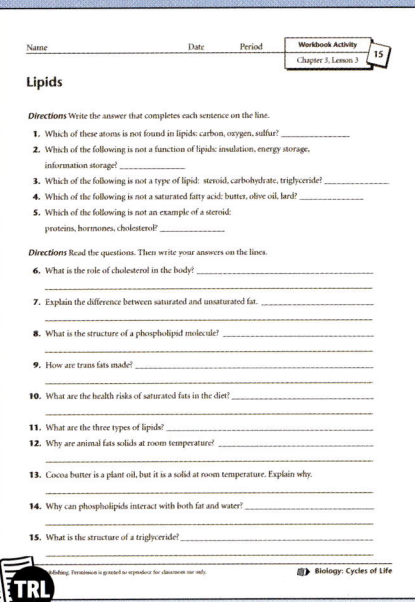

Workbook Activity 15

Discovery Investigation 3

This investigation is less structured than the first investigation in this chapter. It offers students more challenge and requires more teacher facilitation. Encourage students to read the investigation steps and formulate their own questions before beginning the investigation. Discuss with students the question in the first paragraph. Encourage students to share their thoughts.

Objectives

- To perform chemical tests to determine observable characteristics of a lipid
- To become familiar with using the scientific method
- To perform chemical tests to determine whether a substance of unknown identity is a lipid

Skills

Measuring, observing, using science lab equipment, recording and interpreting data, describing, comparing and contrasting, making inferences, designing an experiment, communicating, analyzing data, drawing conclusions

Background

Unlike carbohydrates, lipids are made of a glycerol molecule attached to three fatty acid chains. The tails of the fatty acid chains are hydrophobic (water-hating) or nonpolar, which results in fatty acids not mixing with water. Carbohydrates such as glucose are polar and mix with water.

Sudan III is a large organic molecule with an affinity for fats. Sudan III solution is nonpolar and will mix with other nonpolar substances, such as vegetable oil. Methylene blue solution mixes with water but does not mix with nonpolar substances such as vegetable oil.

Time Frame

One class period

Procedure

- Sudan III solution and methylene blue dye solution are available commercially.
- To create an unknown solution, prepare a dilute solution of imitation maple syrup. Imitation maple syrup contains glucose, which dissolves easily in water.

Hold the solution until after students have completed the first part of the experiment.

- Be sure students understand what a control is *(a group or an individual that serves as a standard of comparison; a control is identical to other groups or individuals, except for one factor)*. Ask students to identify which test tube is the control. *(test tube 1)*
- Have students work together in groups to complete the activity.
- Have students answer the Analysis questions after completing Step 5. You may want to discuss students' answers before students do Step 6.
- Students should document the procedure they suggest, including the list of materials needed, the preparation and safety alerts required, and any information necessary for someone else to repeat students' experiment. Have students record their results.

DISCOVERY INVESTIGATION 3

Materials
- safety goggles
- lab coat or apron
- wax pencil
- test tubes
- test tube rack
- water
- vegetable oil
- unknown liquid
- Sudan III dye solution
- methylene blue dye solution

Testing for Lipids

Lipids contain carbon, hydrogen, and oxygen atoms, but not in the same ratio as carbohydrates. If you were given an unknown substance, how could you tell if it is a lipid? You will find out in this lab.

Procedure

1. To record your data, make a data table like the one shown here.

Solution	Sudan III	Methylene Blue
1. water		
2. vegetable oil		
3. water + oil		

2. Put on safety goggles and a lab coat or apron. **Safety Alerts: Do not touch or taste any chemicals.**

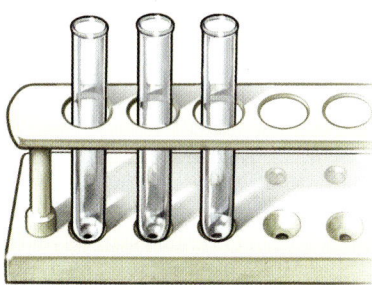

SAFETY ALERT

- Make sure that students have read and understand all safety rules for working in the lab. Discuss the Safety Alerts with students.
- Be sure students wear safety goggles and a lab coat or apron.
- Remind students to handle glass with care and dispose of broken glass properly.

3. With a wax pencil, label three test tubes from 1 to 3. Add the following solutions to the correct tube:

   Test Tube 1 2 mL water

   Test Tube 2 2 mL vegetable oil

   Test Tube 3 1 mL water + 1 mL vegetable oil

4. Add 3 drops of Sudan III to each test tube. Then add 3 drops of methylene blue to Test Tube 3. Shake the test tubes well. Allow them to settle.

5. In your data table, write down your observations.

6. In a small group, discuss how you could determine if an unknown liquid is a lipid. Write a hypothesis that could be tested with an experiment using the unknown liquid.

7. Write a procedure for your experiment. Include Safety Alerts.

8. Have your hypothesis, procedure, and Safety Alerts approved by your teacher. Then carry out your experiment. Record your results.

Cleanup/Disposal
Before leaving the lab, clean up your materials and wash your hands.

Analysis
1. What differences did you notice between Test Tube 1 and Test Tube 2?
2. Explain how Sudan III and methylene blue behave differently as dyes.

Conclusions
1. Was your hypothesis supported by the results of your investigation?
2. How do the structural differences between lipids and carbohydrates explain your results?

Explore Further
In your group, discuss other ways that you could test an unknown substance to determine if it is a lipid.

- Ask students to discuss any problems they had performing the experiment. Ask them which part of the procedure, if any, they would change if they were going to perform the experiment again.

Cleanup/Disposal
When students have finished the lab, provide them with hot, soapy water, test-tube brushes, and test-tube racks to clean their test tubes. Instruct students in proper cleanup and disposal of any other materials.

Results
Sample data table:

Solution	Sudan III	Methylene Blue
1. water	does not mix	mixes
2. vegetable oil	mixes	does not mix
3. water + oil	mixes with oil	mixes with water

Students will discover that Sudan III will mix with the vegetable oil, but will not mix with water. Methylene blue will not mix with the vegetable oil, but will mix with water. If dilute pancake syrup is used as an unknown, it will mix with the methylene blue, but not with the Sudan III. Therefore, the unknown is not a lipid.

Answers to Analysis, Conclusions, and Explore Further begin on page 670 of this Teacher's Edition.

Assessment
Check to see that students have recorded results in their data table. Review group hypotheses and experiment procedures. You might include the following items from this investigation in student portfolios:

- Hypothesis and experimental procedure
- Data table
- Answers to Analysis and Conclusions questions
- Student proposal for question to investigate in Explore Further

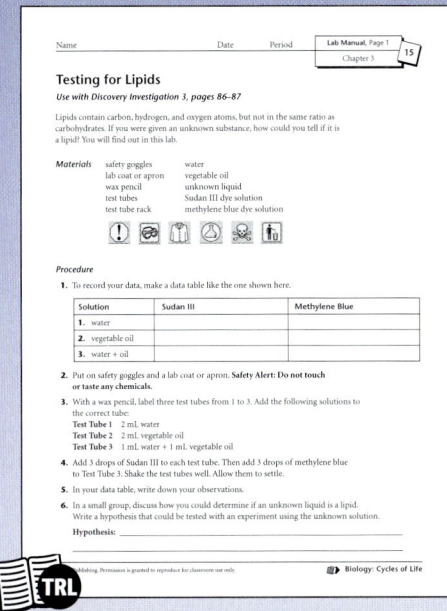

Lab Manual 15, pages 1–2

Lesson at a Glance

Chapter 3 Lesson 4

Overview In this lesson, students learn the structure of a protein and how proteins are used by the body.

Objectives

- To tell how proteins are used in many ways in the body
- To explain that amino acids are the monomers of proteins

Student Pages 88–93

Teacher's Resource Library

Workbook Activity 16
Alternative Workbook Activity 16

Vocabulary

codon	insoluble
complete protein	peptide
contractile	peptide bond
dipeptide	polypeptide
enzyme	sequence
gene	synthesize
hemoglobin	truncate

Have students work in small groups to create a crossword puzzle using all of the vocabulary terms from this lesson. Have groups exchange and solve one another's crossword puzzles.

Background Information

Proteins are complex molecules that have four levels of organization. The primary structure of a protein is the sequence of amino acids. The primary structure of a protein is determined by genes. The secondary structure of a protein is how the amino acids twist or fold within the polypeptide. For example, the amino acids may twist to form a helix shape or fold to make pleats. Hydrogen bonds between amino acids cause the secondary structure of a protein. The tertiary structure of a protein is the three-dimensional shape of the protein. Some proteins have more than one polypeptide chain. The arrangement of one polypeptide chain to another within a protein is its quaternary structure.

Lesson 4 Proteins

Objectives

After reading this lesson, you should be able to

- tell how proteins are used in many ways in the body
- explain that amino acids are the monomers of proteins

Proteins are the most complicated molecules in living things. Figure 3.4.1 shows different foods that are good sources of protein. Proteins are made of amino acids. Amino acids contain carbon, hydrogen, oxygen, and nitrogen atoms. Amino acids are often called the building blocks of life. A protein is many amino acids strung together in a certain order. It is then folded into a particular shape.

Twenty different amino acids are found in proteins. The human body contains hundreds of thousands of different types of proteins. Each protein is unique and essential for life. A single cell has about 100 million protein molecules.

Figure 3.4.1 *Foods high in protein include meat, poultry, eggs, and dairy products.*

Compare this with the 26 letters in the English alphabet. Thousands of words can be made from different arrangements of these letters. Think about how words are made from strings of letters in a particular order. *Bat* and *tab* have the same letters, but the different order of the letters creates different words. The order of amino acids spells out a particular protein.

Each of the 20 amino acids has a central carbon atom with four covalent bonds. These bonds link the carbon atom to an amino group (NH_2), a carboxyl group (COOH), a hydrogen atom (H), and an R group.

Chapter 3 Chemistry at the Cellular Level

Contractile
Able to become shorter or longer

Hemoglobin
An iron-containing protein in red blood cells that carries oxygen

Enzyme
A protein that brings about a chemical reaction in an organism

The R group can be a carbon side chain, a hydrogen atom, or a functional group. The R group gives a particular amino acid its special chemical properties.

What Proteins Do

Some proteins provide the support needed for hair, feathers, ligaments, and spider webs. Some proteins are used as storage in seeds and eggs. Some proteins are **contractile,** or able to become shorter or longer.

Contractile proteins allow muscles to shorten or lengthen. Some proteins are used for transport. **Hemoglobin** is an iron-containing protein in red blood cells. It carries oxygen. Other proteins are **enzymes.** An enzyme is a protein that brings about a chemical reaction in an organism.

About 25 percent of the protein in your body is collagen. Collagen is a major structural protein. It forms molecular cables, or fibrils, that strengthen the tendons. Collagen also supports the skin and internal organs. Bones and teeth are made by adding minerals to collagen.

Achievements in Science

Protein Structure

Most proteins are complex molecules containing from 100 to more than 10,000 amino acids. Because they are so large, proteins can be difficult to study. How do scientists discover the molecular structure of a protein?

They start by determining the sequence of amino acids in the protein. To do this, they use acids and enzymes to split the protein at certain amino acids. The English biochemist Frederick Sanger developed this technique. He was the first scientist to show that each protein has a specific amino acid sequence. In 1958, Sanger was awarded the Nobel Prize for Chemistry for his work to determine the amino acid sequence of insulin. Insulin, a small protein made by the body, breaks down carbohydrates and fats.

To find the shape of larger proteins, scientists crystallize the protein. Then they shoot X-rays at the crystal. The X-rays scatter when they strike the crystal and form an image. Patterns within the image reveal the protein's molecular structure and shape.

Chemistry at the Cellular Level   Chapter 3   89

1 Warm-Up Activity

Have students work in groups to compose a list of everything they know about proteins. When groups have completed their lists, have a volunteer from each group write the list on the board. Review the list together with students, looking for any repeated information. After students have finished reading the lesson, have them return to the lists and check the items for accuracy. Have them correct any inaccurate information on the original lists.

2 Teaching the Lesson

Explain to students that proteins are large molecules that can be broken down into smaller components, just like carbohydrates and lipids. The building blocks of carbohydrates are monosaccharides. The building blocks of lipids are fatty acids and glycerol. Similarly, the building blocks of proteins are amino acids.

Draw on the board a simple representation of an amino acid, showing the amine group (NH_2), the carboxyl group (COOH), a hydrogen (H), and an R (to represent the R group). Next to that, draw the simplest amino acid, glycine. Glycine has the same structure as the model already on the board except that the R group is replaced with a hydrogen atom (H).

3 Reinforce and Extend

Achievements in Science

Have a volunteer read the Achievements in Science feature aloud. Frederick Sanger is only one of four people to receive two Nobel Prizes. Besides the Nobel Prize he won in 1958, he was jointly awarded the Nobel Prize along with two other scientists in 1980. Sanger, along with Paul Berg and Walter Gilbert, was awarded the Nobel Prize for determining the sequence of nucleotides in nucleic acids. Have students research more information about Sanger's background. They can present the results of their research in an oral report to the class.

Pronunciation Guide

Use the pronunciation shown here to help students pronounce a difficult word in this lesson. Refer to the pronunciation key on the Chapter Planning Guide for the sounds of the symbols.

collagen (käˊlə jən)

LEARNING STYLES

Body/Kinesthetic

Help students understand how peptide bonds are formed by explaining that a peptide bond always forms between the carbon atom of the carboxyl group and the nitrogen atom of the amine group of an amino acid. The OH and H atoms from the end of each group bond together to form water. This is how a peptide bond is formed through dehydration synthesis.

Draw the structural formula for a glycine molecule on a sheet of paper, leaving the OH atoms of the carboxyl group blank. On another smaller sheet of paper, add the OH atoms. Tape the smaller sheet of paper in place over the blank spot on the glycine molecule. On a third sheet of paper, draw the structural formula for alanine, leaving the H atom blank at the end of the amine group. On a smaller sheet of paper, add the H atom. Tape the smaller sheet of paper in place over the blank spot on the amine group.

Have three students come to the front of the room. One student should hold the glycine molecule and another should hold the alanine molecule. Have students act out dehydration synthesis and the formation of a peptide bond by pulling off the taped pieces of paper (with the OH and H atoms on them) and handing them to the third student. The first two students should hold their pieces of paper together to show the bond that now exists between the C and the N atoms. The third student has a new water molecule that has been produced by the formation of the peptide bond.

Peptide
A compound made up of two or more amino acids; peptides combine to make proteins

Dipeptide
Two amino acids joined by a peptide bond

Peptide bond
A covalent bond between two amino acids

Polypeptide
Several amino acids joined to form a chain

Sequence
A continuous or connected series

Gene
The information about a trait that a parent passes to its offspring; a section of DNA

Codon
A specific sequence of three consecutive nucleotides that is part of a gene

Peptides

A **peptide** is a compound made up of two or more amino acids. Peptides combine to make proteins. When two amino acids bond, they form a **dipeptide** and a water molecule. The water molecule is removed by dehydration synthesis to form the **peptide bond.** A peptide bond is a covalent bond between two amino acids.

When several amino acids join into a string, the compound is called a **polypeptide.** When the polypeptide chain twists and folds, it forms a protein. In other words, a long chain of amino acids is called a protein. Proteins usually have 100 or more amino acids. The peptide bonds in a protein can be broken by adding water, or hydrolysis.

Making Proteins

To function, proteins must have the necessary amino acids in a specific **sequence** and be folded into a specific shape. A sequence is a continuous or connected series. Proteins loop, coil, and crinkle into complicated shapes. The shapes are like a messy group of wire coat hangers rather than a stack of neatly folded dish towels.

Your **genes** have the instructions to make proteins. A gene is a section of DNA that carries information that a parent passes to its offspring. Each gene is made up of **codons,** which are like the words of the instructions. A codon is a specific sequence of three nucleotides. Each nucleotide contains one of four bases, which are the "letters" of the genetic alphabet. You will find out more about nucleotides in Lesson 5.

Proteins and Health

Proteins are essential molecules used in all types of cellular activity and life. An example of a protein is an enzyme. Most enzymes are proteins. Enzymes are essential for any cell to function. Most proteins in the body are in continuous breakdown and formation. To maintain health, the body must have a supply of amino acids to replace the proteins that are broken down.

TEACHER ALERT

Kwashiorkor is a type of malnutrition that occurs when a person does not get enough proteins in his or her diet. This is not necessarily related to a lack of calories. A person suffering from kwashiorkor can be getting enough calories from food, however, the foods do not contain adequate amounts of protein to sustain the body.

The initial symptoms of kwashiorkor include fatigue, lethargy, and irritability. Later symptoms are more severe and include loss of muscle mass, stunted growth in children, and lessened immunity. Although eating a balanced diet can extinguish the condition, children suffering from kwashiorkor may have permanent mental and physical damage.

The occurrence of kwashiorkor is low in developed countries. It is more prevalent in developing countries and in countries that are struck by repeated natural disasters such as drought.

Synthesize
To make into a whole substance

Truncate
To shorten

Complete protein
A protein source that provides the body with the essential amino acids

The human body cannot **synthesize,** or make nine amino acids. These nine amino acids are called essential amino acids. The nine essential amino acids are: histidine, isoleucine, lysine, methionine, phenylalanine, threonine, tryptophan, and valine. They must be provided in the diet in adequate amounts because cells cannot make them. A cell will stop making a protein even if one essential amino acid is missing. The result is a **truncated,** or shortened, polypeptide.

A diet that does not include **complete proteins** will negatively affect health. A complete protein is a protein source that provides the body with all nine essential amino acids.

Biology in Your Life

Consumer Choices: Choosing a Vegetarian Diet

Proteins play many roles in the body. The body cannot make nine of the 20 essential amino acids. For cells to make proteins, your diet must include these nine essential amino acids. Complete proteins are those that have all essential amino acids. Eggs, milk, and most meat products are sources of complete proteins.

Most of us get the essential amino acids in our daily diets. For example, the protein in animal products has all the amino acids needed for health. What about a diet that does not include animal products? A vegetarian diet excludes all forms of animal flesh, such as meat, fowl, and fish. Some vegetarians eat eggs and dairy products. Vegetarians who do not eat any animal products are called vegans.

Plant products, such as lettuce, rice, and pasta, do not have all the essential amino acids. Even plant products high in protein, such as beans, are low in one or more of

the essential amino acids. For this reason, a healthy vegetarian diet requires planning. Vegetarians need to eat a wide variety of foods to get all essential amino acids every day. Vegetarians who eat some animal foods regularly, such as eggs or dairy products, probably get enough amino acids.

1. What is a complete protein?
2. Why does a healthy vegetarian diet require careful planning?
3. Describe one example of a healthy vegetarian diet.

Teacher Alert

If the shape of a protein is lost, a protein is said to be denatured. A denatured protein no longer functions properly. Denaturation can occur if a protein is exposed to extreme temperature or pH. A classic example of a denatured protein is the protein albumin in egg whites. When an egg is raw, the albumin is a thick, clear fluid. When the egg is heated, the albumin is denatured and changes to a solid white substance. Denaturation is permanent, as can be seen in the case of albumin. Once an egg is cooked, the protein does not return to its liquid state after the egg cools.

Teacher Alert

Enzymes play an important role in the chemistry and maintenance of the body. In some cases, if an enzyme is absent or cannot function properly, it can lead to a life-threatening situation. Galactosemia is a condition that results because the enzyme that breaks down the monosaccharide galactose is absent. Galactose, along with glucose, makes up lactose, the main sugar in milk. If an infant with galactosemia is given milk, derivatives of galactose collect in the blood and the infant will fail to thrive. Treatment for galactosemia is to replace regular milk with a formula that does not contain lactose. If left untreated, the condition can result in liver and kidney damage, the formation of cataracts, mental retardation, or death.

Insoluble
Not able to dissolve in water

Foods such as meat, eggs, and beans are made of giant protein molecules. Enzymes must digest, or break down, the protein molecules before they can be used to build and repair body tissues.

An enzyme in the juice of the stomach starts the digestion, or breakdown, of swallowed protein. The small intestine completes further digestion. Here, several enzymes from pancreatic juice and the lining of the intestine break down protein molecules into amino acids. These small molecules are absorbed from the small intestine into the blood and then are carried to all parts of the body to build cells.

If the temperature or the pH changes in a cell, proteins may come apart and lose their shape. Recall that pH is a number that tells whether a substance is an acid or a base. What happens when you cook an egg? Eggs are a good source of protein. Look at Figures 3.4.3 and 3.4.4. The photos show what happens to an egg as it heats up. The egg white turns from clear to white. The shiny, yellow yolk turns a firm, dark yellow. This happens because the proteins become **insoluble,** or not able to dissolve in water. The proteins form a solid. When this happens, proteins lose their shape and cannot function. A certain protein must have a particular shape to perform a particular job.

Figures 3.4.3 and 3.4.4 *Notice the changes in an egg's protein after heat has been applied.*

Lesson 4 REVIEW

On a sheet of paper, write the word or words that complete each sentence correctly.

1. When two amino acids join, they form a(n) _____.
2. Genes contain the instructions to make _____.
3. The words for the instructions in genes are called _____.

On a sheet of paper, write the letter of the answer that completes each sentence correctly.

4. Proteins contain _____ atoms, which are not found in carbohydrates.
   - A hydrogen
   - B carbon
   - C oxygen
   - D nitrogen
5. Contractile proteins are found in _____.
   - A seeds
   - B muscles
   - C feathers
   - D eggs
6. The shape of a protein resembles _____.
   - A beads on a string
   - B folded dishtowels
   - C a messy group of coat hangers
   - D a flat stack of three straight chains

Critical Thinking

On a sheet of paper, write the answers to the following questions. Use complete sentences.

7. Why is the R group in an amino acid important?
8. How are proteins used in the body?
9. What are essential amino acids? Why are they essential?
10. What do you think could happen if a protein in a cell twists into the wrong shape?

Chemistry at the Cellular Level Chapter 3

Lesson 4 Review Answers

1. dipeptide **2.** proteins **3.** codons **4.** D **5.** B **6.** C **7.** The R group gives a particular amino acid its special chemical properties. **8.** Proteins are used in the body as support, as contractile proteins to allow muscles to shorten, for transport, and as enzymes. **9.** Essential amino acids are the nine amino acids the body cannot synthesize. They must be provided in the diet. Without them, the body cannot make certain proteins. **10.** The protein would not have the right shape to do its job in the cell.

Portfolio Assessment

Sample items include:
- Revised lists from Warm-Up Activity
- Paragraph from Science Journal
- Poster from Learning Styles Logical/Mathematical
- Lesson 4 Review answers

ELL/ESL Strategy

Language Objective: *To explain the meaning of lesson vocabulary terms*

Have students work in small groups to make flash cards for the vocabulary terms in this lesson. The front of the card should have the vocabulary term and a pronunciation below it. The back of the card should have the definition. Have students quiz each other, using the cards. As each card is presented, the student being quizzed should pronounce the word and then give a definition.

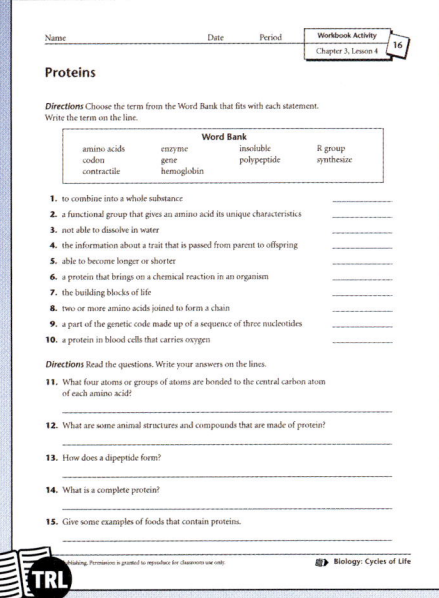

Workbook Activity 16

Lesson at a Glance

Chapter 3 Lesson 5

Overview In this lesson, students learn about the two types of nucleic acids.

Objectives

- To explain that nucleic acids are informational macromolecules
- To understand that the monomers of nucleic acids are nucleotides
- To tell that DNA and RNA contain the instructions for assembling proteins

Student Pages 94–97

Teacher's Resource Library

Workbook Activity 17–18

Alternative Workbook Activity 17–18

Vocabulary

deoxyribose	ribose
helix	RNA

Have students write a paragraph using all the vocabulary terms in this lesson.

Background Information

Nucleic acids get their name because they were first discovered within the nucleus of a cell. Nucleic acids are made up of carbon, hydrogen, oxygen, nitrogen, and phosphorus. DNA contains genes. Genes determine which traits a person inherits as well as protein synthesis within the cell. RNA is involved in protein synthesis.

 Warm-Up Activity

Show students three-dimensional models of DNA and RNA molecules. Ask students to point out the similarities and differences between the two molecules. Ask students what adjectives they would use to describe these molecules.

Lesson 5 Nucleic Acids

Objectives

After reading this lesson, you should be able to

- explain that nucleic acids are informational macromolecules
- understand that the monomers of nucleic acids are nucleotides
- tell that DNA and RNA contain the instructions for assembling proteins

RNA
A molecule that works together with DNA to make proteins

Helix
A twisted shape like a spiral staircase

Nucleic acids serve as information storage molecules. They provide the directions to make proteins. Two important nucleic acids are DNA (**d**eoxyribo**n**ucleic **a**cid) and **RNA** (**r**ibo**n**ucleic **a**cid). DNA contains genes, the hereditary blueprints for all life.

Genes are sections of DNA. Genes program the amino acid sequence of proteins. However, RNA must first translate this genetic code in DNA. RNA is essential for protein synthesis. You will learn about this process in Chapter 11.

Both DNA and RNA are polymers. They are both made up of thousands of linked monomers called nucleotides. Nucleotides join to form nucleic acids. Two nucleic acid strands join to form DNA. RNA is one nucleic acid strand.

As seen in Figure 3.5.1, each nucleotide is a complicated molecule with three parts: a sugar, a phosphate, and a base. The sugar and phosphate are the same in all nucleotides. Only the nitrogen base varies. In DNA, the four nitrogen bases are adenine (A), guanine (G), cytosine (C), and thymine (T). These four types of nucleotides can bond in any order. They can form many unique strands of DNA. Figure 3.5.2 on page 95 shows part of a DNA strand and the four types of nitrogen bases.

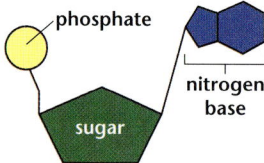

Figure 3.5.1 *A nucleotide is a complicated molecule with three parts.*

DNA is a ladder-like structure. It is made up of two nucleic acid strands twisted together. This structure is called a double **helix**. A helix is a twisted shape like a spiral staircase as you can see in Figure 3.5.3. Covalent bonds between the sugar of one nucleotide and the phosphate of the next nucleotide bond nucleotides together in a strand. This is called a sugar-phosphate backbone. The backbone forms the sides of the DNA ladder.

94 Chapter 3 Chemistry at the Cellular Level

Ribose
The five-carbon sugar in RNA

Deoxyribose
The five-carbon sugar in DNA

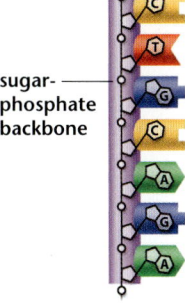

Figure 3.5.2 Four types of nucleotides make up DNA strands.

The bases in the two strands then bond to form the rungs of the ladder. These bonds are weak hydrogen bonds. When the DNA strands are zipped together into a double helix, it is very stable.

The four steps to make a DNA double helix are:

1. Two nucleic acid strands line up next to each other.
2. The sugar-phosphate backbone of the two strands form the sides of the ladder.
3. The bases of the two strands bond to one another with hydrogen bonds and form the rungs of the ladder.
4. The ladder twists into a spiral to form a double helix.

Only certain bases can bond with other bases. For example, adenine (A) pairs with thymine (T). Guanine (G) pairs with cytosine (C). If the sequence of one strand of the double helix is known, the other strand's sequence of bases can be determined.

RNA differs from DNA in four ways. RNA has an extra OH group, or hydroxyl group. RNA uses a base called uracil (U) instead of the base thymine (T). RNA is a single-stranded molecule and takes various unique shapes. It can even form base pairs with itself so that it can fold into many shapes. RNA uses the sugar **ribose**. DNA uses the sugar **deoxyribose**. Table 3.5.1 shows the differences between DNA and RNA.

Table 3.5.1 Characteristics of DNA and RNA		
Characteristic	DNA	RNA
Structure	Double-stranded	Single-stranded
Bases	Adenine, cytosine, guanine, thymine	Adenine, cytosine, guanine, uracil
Sugar	Deoxyribose	Ribose

Figure 3.5.3 The DNA double helix is made up of two nucleic acid strands twisted together.

2 Teaching the Lesson

Provide students with unlabeled diagrams of a nucleotide, a DNA molecule, and an RNA molecule. As students read the lesson and study Figures 3.5.1 and 3.5.2, have them fill in the labels on each diagram. For the nucleotide, they should label the three main parts: the sugar, the phosphate, and the base. For the DNA and RNA, they should label the sugar (deoxyribose or ribose), the phosphate, and the bases as they correctly correspond to each other.

3 Reinforce and Extend

LEARNING STYLES

Interpersonal/Group Learning

Have students work in small groups to make models of the DNA molecule. Provide students with scissors, glue, and different colored sheets of construction paper. Before students begin, decide which colors will represent each of the four different bases. Display the completed models around the classroom.

ELL/ESL STRATEGY

Language Objective: To compare and contrast DNA and RNA

Have students learning English study Table 3.5.1, which compares and contrasts the characteristics of DNA and RNA. After they have studied the table, have students explain how DNA and RNA are similar and how they are different. For example, they could write sentences such as "Both DNA and RNA contain four types of bases. Three of the bases are the same for each: adenine, cytosine, and guanine. The fourth base for each is different. DNA contains thymine, and RNA contains uracil."

Lesson 5 Review Answers

1. DNA, RNA **2.** helix **3.** nucleotide **4.** D
5. B **6.** D **7.** DNA carries a code that contains the instructions for making proteins. RNA translates this code to make proteins. **8.** The three parts of a nucleotide are a sugar, a phosphate, and a base. The sugar and phosphate are the same in all nucleotides. Only the base varies. **9.** DNA is like a four-letter alphabet because it has four types of nucleotides, each with a different nitrogen base. These four types of nucleotides can be arranged to code for different proteins. **10.** Only certain bases pair with other bases by hydrogen bonds. Such pairing provides stability to the rungs of the double-helix ladder.

Portfolio Assessment

Sample items include:
- Labeled diagrams from Teaching the Lesson
- DNA models from Learning Styles Interpersonal/Group Learning
- Lesson 5 Review answers

IN THE ENVIRONMENT

Exposure to certain environmental hazards can damage DNA molecules irreparably. For example, exposure to radiation, such as radon gas, can cause mutations in genetic material that can lead to cancer. Radon gas is released naturally into the air as uranium rock beneath Earth's surface decays to form radium, the source of radon. Cigarette smoke can also cause mutations to DNA that can lead to cancer. Some communities have instituted bans on smoking in public to reduce exposure to cigarette smoke. Discuss the laws or policies that exist in your local community in regard to smoking in public places.

Lesson 5 REVIEW

On a sheet of paper, write the word or words that complete each sentence correctly.

1. Two important nucleic acids are _____ and _____.
2. DNA forms a ladder-like structure called a double _____.
3. A(n) _____ has three parts: a sugar, a phosphate, and a base.

On a sheet of paper, write the letter of the answer that completes each sentence correctly.

4. In DNA, only the _____ varies from one nucleotide to another.
   - **A** sugar
   - **B** phosphate
   - **C** amino acid
   - **D** base

5. Nucleotides are the _____ of nucleic acids.
   - **A** proteins
   - **B** monomers
   - **C** polymers
   - **D** amino acids

6. The rungs of the DNA ladder are made from _____.
   - **A** sugars
   - **B** carbon and hydrogen
   - **C** phosphate
   - **D** bases

Critical Thinking

On a sheet of paper, write the answers to the following questions. Use complete sentences.

7. Compare and contrast the roles and structures of DNA and RNA.
8. What are the three parts of a nucleotide? Which part(s) vary? Which part(s) remain the same?
9. How are the bases in DNA like a four-letter alphabet?
10. Explain why it is important that only certain bases pair with other bases.

Workbook Activity 17

BIOLOGY IN THE WORLD

Vitamin A and Blindness

Vitamins are organic compounds that the body needs. Each vitamin plays a different role. For example, vitamin A is needed for healthy eyesight. Your body needs vitamin A to make a substance that absorbs light and lets you see. Vitamin A is a fat-soluble vitamin, which means that it is stored by the body.

Your body does not make most vitamins. Instead, they must come from foods you eat. But no one food has all of the vitamins you need. This is why it is important to eat a balanced daily diet that includes a wide variety of foods.

In some parts of the world, many kinds of foods are in short supply. As a result, daily diets may be missing certain vitamins. For example, lack of vitamin A is the most common cause of blindness among children in developing countries. In these areas, many adults and children have poor diets.

Infants are often born with little vitamin A stored in their bodies. After birth, their diets are low in vitamin A. Without enough vitamin A, many children do not develop normal eyesight.

The World Health Organization (WHO) and its partners have found a low-cost solution to vitamin A deficiency. They give young children a high-dose vitamin A capsule every six months. These organizations also train parents to serve the right kinds of foods. A balanced diet means that children will get enough vitamin A as they grow.

1. Why do children need vitamin A?
2. In developing countries, why is vitamin A given to children once every six months instead of daily?
3. For further study, find out what foods contain vitamin A.

BIOLOGY IN THE WORLD

Have volunteers take turns reading the Biology in the World feature.

After students have determined which foods contain vitamin A, have them keep track of how much of these foods they eat in a day. Ask students to determine if they are they getting enough vitamin A. Have students research other problems that can result from a vitamin A deficiency. *(increased risk of respiratory, urinary, and digestive system infections; night blindness; and poor development of bones and teeth)*

Biology in the World Answers

1. Children need vitamin A in order to develop normal eyesight. If an infant is born with little vitamin A stored in the body and his or her diet lacks vitamin A after birth, normal eyesight will not develop. **2.** This is a low-cost solution when children are not getting vitamin A every day through their diets. **3.** Foods that contain vitamin A include orange and green vegetables such as carrots, sweet potatoes, mangoes, cantaloupe, spinach, and kale; liver; eggs; milk; and fortified cereals.

ONLINE CONNECTION

A Web site that students may find useful for completing the Learning Styles Activity on page 91 is provided by the Food and Drug Administration at www.health.gov/dietaryguidelines/dga2000/document/frontcover.htm. Instruct students to click on *Build a Healthy Base* and then *Let the Pyramid guide your food choices.*

A Web site that students may find useful when researching information about vitamin A deficiency is provided by the Office of Dietary Supplements and the National Institutes of Health at www.ods.od.nih.gov/index.aspx. Tell students to click on *Health Information,* and then *Vitamin and Mineral Supplement Fact Sheets,* and then *Vitamin A.*

One Web site students may find interesting after completing Chapter 3 is the Food and Nutrition Information Center at www.nal.usda.gov/fnic/etext/000020.html, which has information on the nutritional value of foods, the sugar content of foods, and the amount of trans fats in foods.

Chapter 3 Summary

Have volunteers read aloud each summary item on page 98. Ask volunteers to explain the meaning of each item. Direct students' attention to the Vocabulary box on the bottom of page 98. Have them read and review each term and its definition.

Graphic Organizer

As students read Chapter 3, have them finish completing the concept map on Graphic Organizer 3: Organic Molecules. Encourage students to read each lesson of the chapter and then have them fill in the portion of the concept map that pertains to the lesson. When they have completed the concept map, ask them to answer the questions.

Chapter 3 SUMMARY

- Living things are made of organic compounds. Organic compounds contain carbon.

- There are four main types of organic compounds: carbohydrates, proteins, lipids, and nucleic acids. These four compounds are macromolecules, which are large molecules made of many atoms.

- Some macromolecules are made of repeating units called monomers.

- Carbohydrates are made of simple sugars called monosaccharides. Carbohydrates are made of carbon, hydrogen, and oxygen atoms in a 1:2:1 ratio. Carbohydrates are the body's main source of energy.

- Polysaccharides are made up of repeated units of monosaccharides. Starch, cellulose, and glycogen are examples of polysaccharides.

- Lipids provide long-term energy storage. Oils and fats are examples of lipids.

- A triglyceride is made of one molecule of glycerol and three fatty acids.

- Proteins are made of amino acids. Proteins play many roles in cells, including support, storage, and structure.

- Enzymes are proteins that bring about a chemical reaction in an organism.

- The monomers in nucleic acids are nucleotides.

- Nucleic acids are long strands of nucleotides. DNA is made up of two nucleic acids twisted into a double helix. Genes are sections of DNA. Genes contain the instructions to make proteins. A second nucleic acid called RNA translates the DNA instructions to form proteins.

Vocabulary

amino acid, 72	functional group, 71	monomer, 72	RNA, 94
carbohydrate, 72	gene, 90	monosaccharide, 72	saccharide, 77
cellulose, 78	glucose, 77	nucleic acid, 72	saturated fatty acid, 82
codon, 90	glycerol, 73	nucleotide, 73	sequence, 90
complete protein, 91	glycogen, 78	organic compound, 70	starch, 78
contractile, 89	helix, 94	peptide, 90	steroid, 82
dehydration synthesis, 73	hemoglobin, 89	peptide bond, 90	synthesize, 91
deoxyribose, 95	hydrocarbon, 72	phospholipid, 82	trans fat, 83
dipeptide, 90	hydrolysis, 73	plastid, 79	truncate, 91
disaccharide, 77	insoluble, 92	polymer, 72	triglyceride, 82
enzyme, 89	isomer, 78	polypeptide, 90	unsaturated fatty acid, 83
fat, 73	lipid, 72	polysaccharide, 73	
fatty acid, 73	lipid bilayer, 84	polyunsaturated fatty acid, 83	
fructose, 77	macromolecule, 72	ribose, 95	
	membrane, 79		

Chapter 3 Chemistry at the Cellular Level

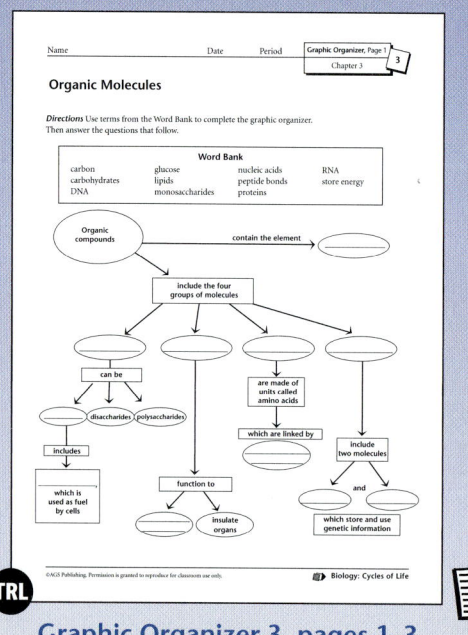

Graphic Organizer 3, pages 1–3

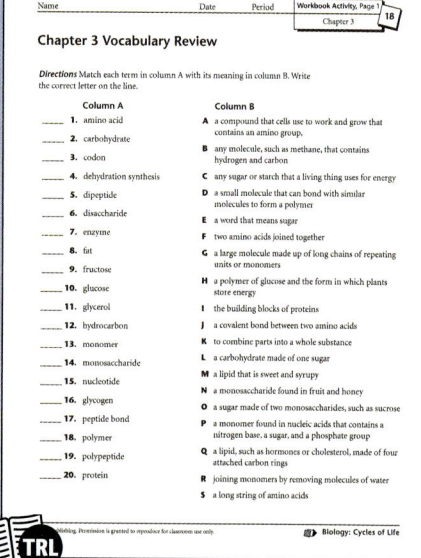

Workbook Activity 18, pages 1–3

Chapter 3 REVIEW

Word Bank
amino acid
carbohydrate
codon
disaccharide
enzyme
fructose
gene
glucose
hemoglobin
macromolecule
nucleic acid
organic compound
peptide bond
phospholipid
polymer
RNA
starch
triglyceride

Vocabulary Review
On a sheet of paper, write the word or words from the Word Bank that best complete each sentence.

1. A(n) _____ is two simple sugars bonded together.
2. Two amino acids can be joined by a(n) _____.
3. A(n) _____ is a large molecule made of many atoms.
4. Single-stranded _____ molecules translate the code for making proteins.
5. A(n) _____ is a section of DNA that contains hereditary information.
6. A compound that contains carbon is called a(n) _____.
7. A(n) _____ is made up of three fatty acids and a glycerol molecule.
8. A polymer of glucose that stores energy in plants is _____.
9. A(n) _____ is a building block found in proteins.
10. An iron-containing protein in red blood cells that carries oxygen is _____.
11. DNA is made of two _____ strands.
12. A(n) _____ is an organic compound containing carbon, hydrogen, and oxygen in a 1:2:1 ratio.
13. A(n) _____ is a specific sequence of three consecutive nucleotides.
14. A lipid can be a fat, _____, or steroid.
15. A protein that brings about a reaction in an organism is a(n) _____.

Review continued on next page

Chapter 3 Review
Use the Chapter Review to prepare students for tests and to reteach content from the chapter.

Chapter 3 Mastery Test
The Teacher's Resource Library includes two forms of the Chapter 3 Mastery Test. Each test addresses the chapter Goals for Learning. An optional third page of additional critical-thinking items is included for each test. The difficulty level of the two forms is equivalent.

Review Answers
Vocabulary Review
1. disaccharide 2. peptide bond
3. macromolecule 4. RNA 5. gene
6. organic compound 7. triglyceride
8. starch 9. amino acid 10. hemoglobin
11. nucleic acid 12. carbohydrate
13. codon 14. phospholipid 15. enzyme

Review Answers

16. polymer 17. fructose, glucose

TEACHER ALERT

In the Chapter Review, the Vocabulary Review activity includes a sample of the chapter's vocabulary terms. The activity will help determine students' understanding of key vocabulary terms and concepts presented in the chapter. Other vocabulary terms used in the chapter are listed below.

cellulose	membrane
complete protein	monomer
contractile	monosaccharide
dehydration synthesis	nucleotide
deoxyribose	peptide
dipeptide	plastid
fat	polypeptide
fatty acid	polysaccharide
functional group	polyunsaturated fatty acid
glycerol	ribose
glycogen	saccharide
helix	saturated fatty acid
hemoglobin	sequence
hydrocarbon	steroid
hydrolysis	synthesize
insoluble	trans fat
isomer	truncate
lipid	unsaturated fatty acid
lipid bilayer	

Concept Review

18. C 19. A 20. A 21. B 22. D

Chapter 3   REVIEW - continued

16. A(n) _____ is a very large molecule made from many simple units.

17. The two most common monosaccharides are _____ and _____.

Concept Review

On a sheet of paper, write the letter of the word or words that complete each sentence correctly.

18. _____ is a sugar found in fruit.
    - **A** Glucose
    - **B** Lactose
    - **C** Fructose
    - **D** Sucrose

19. Animals store glucose in the form of _____ in liver and muscle cells.
    - **A** glycogen
    - **B** body fat
    - **C** cellulose
    - **D** starch

20. During _____, bonds between monomers are broken by adding water.
    - **A** hydrolysis
    - **B** dehydration synthesis
    - **C** polymerization
    - **D** carbohydrate loading

21. A complete protein provides the body with the nine essential _____.
    - **A** proteins
    - **B** amino acids
    - **C** carbohydrates
    - **D** polymers

22. DNA and RNA are made of units called _____.
    - **A** glycerol
    - **B** amino acids
    - **C** fatty acids
    - **D** nucleotides

Chapter 3   Chemistry at the Cellular Level

Chapter 3 Mastery Test A, pages 1–3

Critical Thinking

On a sheet of paper, write the answers to the following questions. Use complete sentences.

23. Why are some lipids solid at room temperature?
24. Explain how peptide bonds form.
25. Which kinds of macromolecules store energy? Explain.

Research and Write

Write a report on the role of dietary animal fats in human heart disease. Describe how changes in diet can reduce the risk of heart disease.

Test-Taking Tip When answering multiple-choice questions, read the sentence completely using each choice. Then choose the one that makes the most sense when the entire sentence is read.

Critical Thinking

23. Some fatty acids are solid at room temperature because they have long, straight chains. This enables the molecules to stack tightly, which makes them solid at room temperature. 24. Peptide bonds form between two amino acids during dehydration synthesis. When the two amino acids join, a molecule of water is formed from the release to two hydrogen atoms and one oxygen atom. 25. Carbohydrates and lipids store energy in cells. When carbohydrates are broken down in the cell, energy is extracted from the bonds of monosaccharides. A lipid molecule contains long hydrocarbon chains, which contain a lot of energy.

Research and Write

Have students read the Research and Write feature on this page. Ask students to consider one food item that they know has a direct effect on the health of their heart. If students are having problems choosing a direction for their report, encourage them to reread the section on trans fats in Lesson 3. Also tell them that a helpful keyword to use when they begin their research is *cholesterol*.

ALTERNATIVE ASSESSMENT

Alternative Assessment items correlate to the student Goals for Learning at the beginning of this chapter.

- Ask students to define an organic compound and give several examples. Have students explain how organic compounds have different characteristics even though they all contain carbon.
- Have students write a paragraph that summarizes how DNA and RNA are involved in protein synthesis.
- Have students make a list of foods that each contain carbohydrates, fats, and proteins. Have students choose from the foods on their lists to make one day's worth of food that represents a diet with a balance of complex carbohydrates, proteins, and fats.

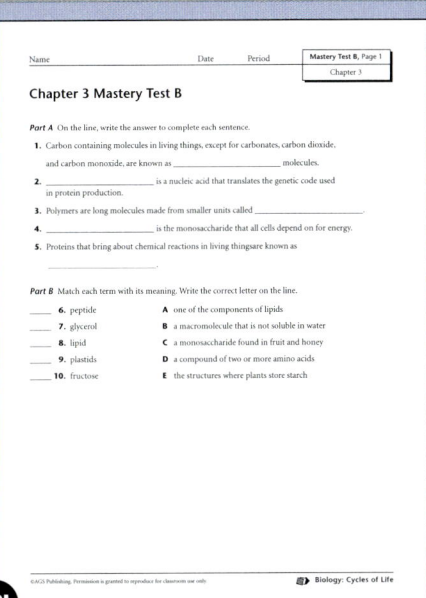
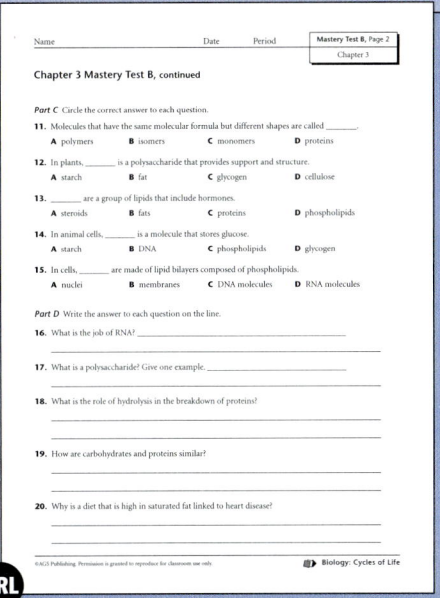

Chapter 3 Mastery Test B, pages 1–3

Chapter 4

Planning Guide
Cells: The Basic Units of Life

	Student Pages	Vocabulary	Lesson Review	Critical-Thinking Questions
Lesson 1 What Is a Cell?	104–110	✔	✔	✔
Lesson 2 Cellular Structure and Function	111–115	✔	✔	✔
Lesson 3 What Kind of Cell Is It?	116–122	✔	✔	✔
Lesson 4 After the Cell	123–127	✔	✔	✔

Chapter Activities

Teacher's Resource Library
Community Connection 4:
  Kidney Dialysis
Graphic Organizer 4:
  Cells: The Basic Units of Life

Teacher's Edition
Opener Activity

Assessment Options

Student Text
Chapter 4 Review

Teacher's Resource Library
Chapter 4 Mastery Tests A and B

Teacher's Edition
Chapter 4 Alternative Assessment

Achievements in Science	Science at Work	Biology in Your Life	Investigation/Discovery	Biology in the World	Express Lab	Link to	Research and Write	Technology and Society	ELL/ESL Strategy	Background Information	Science Journal	Applications (Home, Career, Community, Global, Environment)	Online Connection	Teacher Alert	Auditory/Verbal	Body/Kinesthetic	Interpersonal/Group Learning	Logical/Mathematical	Visual/Spatial	Workbook Activities	Alternative Workbook Activities	Lab Manual	Self-Study Guide
			109		107	✔			107	104		106, 107		107		105	108			19	19	16–18	✔
						✔		115	114	111	114	113, 114		114	112				113	20	20	19	✔
118			121			✔			119	116	117			118				117		21	21	20	✔
	124	125	127				131		125	123	127	125	127						124	22–23	22–23		✔

Pronunciation Key

a	hat	e	let	ī	ice	ô	order	ủ	put	sh she
ā	age	ē	equal	o	hot	oi	oil	ü	rule	th thin
ä	far	ėr	term	ō	open	ou	out	ch	child	ᴛʜ then
â	care	i	it	ȯ	saw	u	cup	ng	long	zh measure

ə { a in about, e in taken, i in pencil, o in lemon, u in circus }

Alternative Workbook Activities

The Teacher's Resource Library (TRL) contains a set of lower-level worksheets called Alternative Workbook Activities. These worksheets cover the same content as the regular Workbook Activities but are written at a second-grade reading level.

Skill Track Online

Use Skill Track Online for *Biology: Cycles of Life* to monitor student progress and meet the demands of adequate yearly progress (AYP). Make informed instructional decisions with individual student and class reports of online lesson and chapter assessments. With immediate and ongoing feedback, students will also see what they have learned and where they need more reinforcement and practice.

Chapter at a Glance

Chapter 4: Cells: The Basic Units of Life
pages 102–131

Lessons

1. **What Is a Cell?**
   pages 104–110

   Investigation 4 pages 109–110

2. **Cellular Structure and Function**
   pages 111–115

3. **What Kind of Cell Is It?**
   pages 116–122

   Discovery Investigation 4
   pages 121–122

4. **After the Cell**
   pages 123–127

   Biology in the World page 127

Chapter 4 Summary page 128

Chapter 4 Review pages 129–131

Audio CD

Skill Track Online for Biology: Cycles of Life

Teacher's Resource Library

- Workbook Activities 19–23
- Alternative Workbook Activities 19–23
- Lab Manual 16–20
- Community Connection 4
- Graphic Organizer 4
- Resource File 7–8
- Chapter 4 Self-Study Guide
- Chapter 4 Mastery Tests A and B

(Answer Keys for the Teacher's Resource Library begin on page 675 of the Teacher's Edition. The Materials List for the Lab Manual activities begins on page 720.)

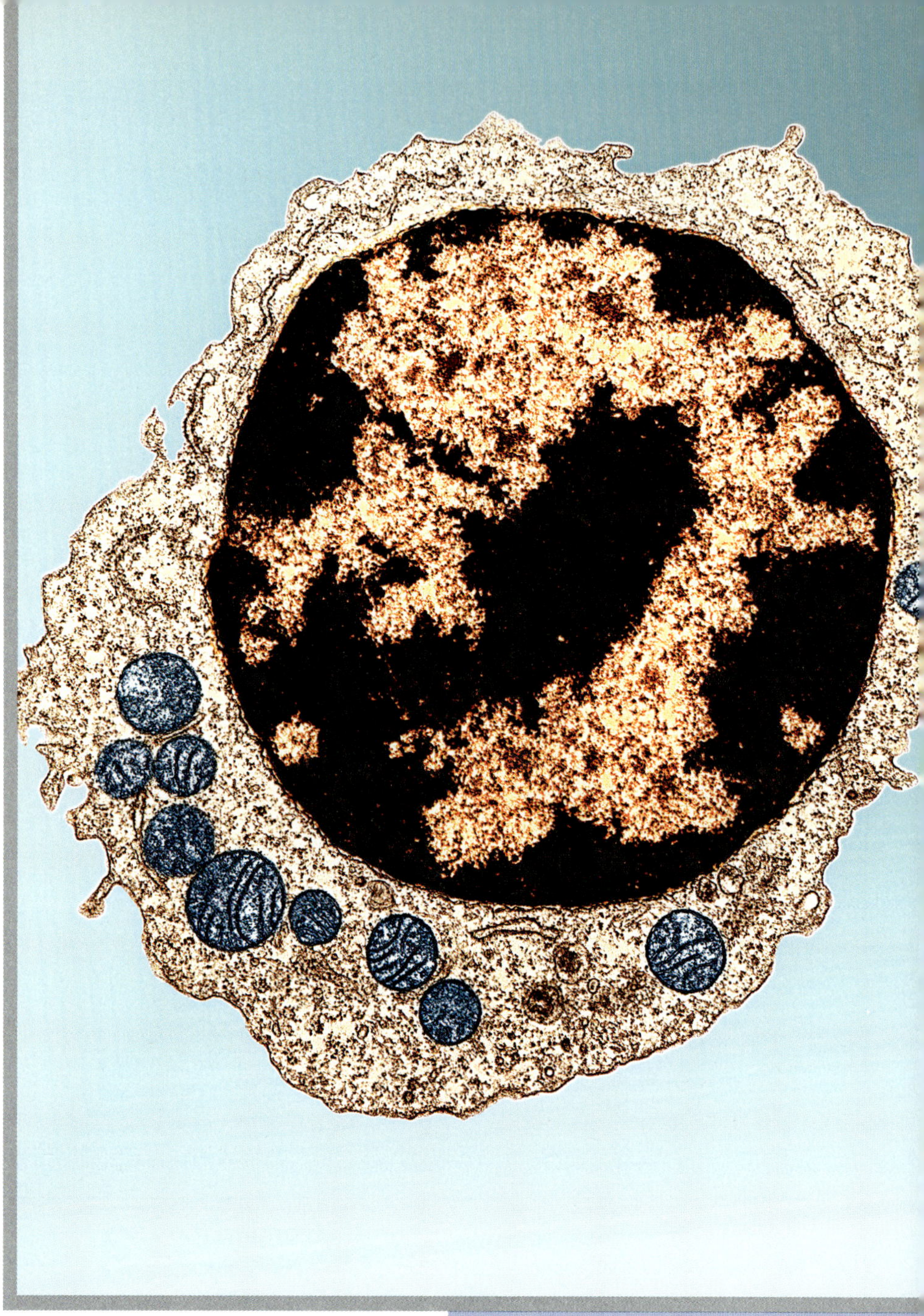

Opener Activity

Dilute with water a small amount of yogurt that contains live acidophilus cultures. Have students examine drops of the yogurt mixture under a high-powered microscope. Have them observe and draw the *Lactobacillus* bacteria they see. Explain that these simple organisms consist of a single living unit—a cell—while humans consist of many more complex cells.

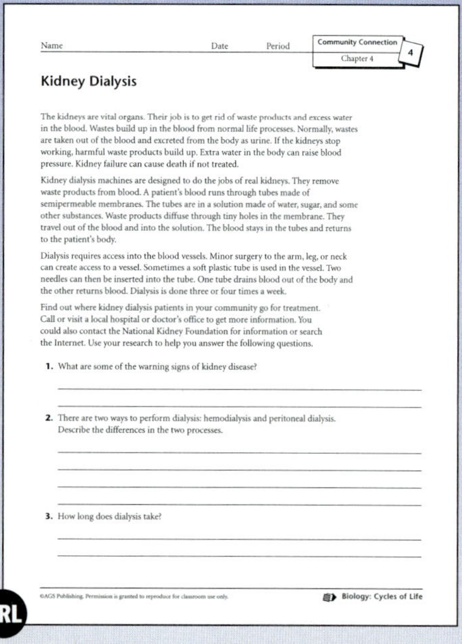

Community Connection 4

102 Chapter 4

Chapter 4
Cells: The Basic Units of Life

The object in the photograph is a white blood cell seen through a microscope. Notice that the inside of the cell is organized. This organization is important to large cells like this white blood cell. Some cells do not have the same amount of organization. Yet they do all of the things that make organisms alive. In Chapter 4, you will learn what cells are and what they do. You will also learn about the two basic types of cells that make up living things.

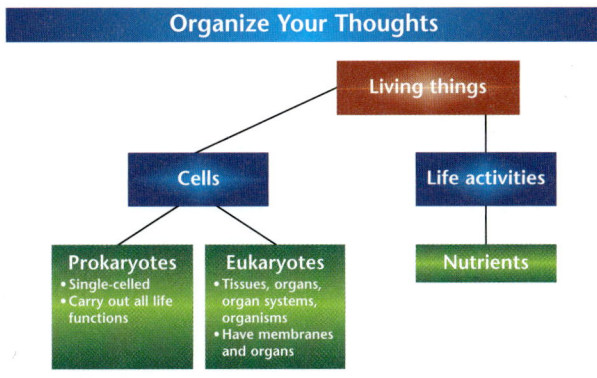

Organize Your Thoughts

- Living things
  - Cells
    - Prokaryotes
      - Single-celled
      - Carry out all life functions
    - Eukaryotes
      - Tissues, organs, organ systems, organisms
      - Have membranes and organs
  - Life activities
    - Nutrients

Goals for Learning

- To learn how cells serve as the basic unit of life
- To know that cells perform many common activities
- To explain how cells use diffusion and osmosis
- To understand that cells perform different functions
- To explain how cells are grouped by structure

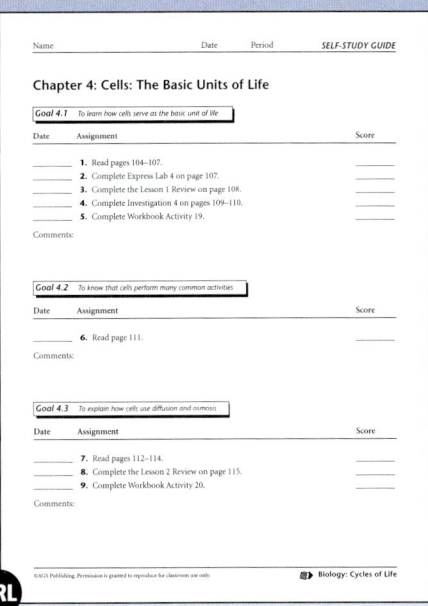

Chapter 4 Self-Study Guide

Introducing the Chapter

Have students estimate how many cells are in the human body. Explain that there are more than 100,000,000,000,000 (10^{14}) cells in the body and that these cells differ in the types of jobs they do. Have students read the Goals for Learning and note that in this chapter, they will learn about the organization of living systems and the function of the parts of these systems.

Ask students to examine the photograph of the white blood cell on page 102 and tell how it relates to their understanding of cells. Then read the introduction aloud. Discuss the Organize Your Thoughts chart.

Have students write questions about what they want to know about the structures and functions of cells. For example, students might ask "What kinds of molecules are found in cells?" or "What types of jobs do cells perform in the human body?" Students can use their questions to help set a purpose for reading.

Notes and Math Tips

Ask volunteers to read the notes and math tips that appear in the margins throughout the chapter. Then discuss them with the class.

Teacher's Resource

The AGS Publishing Teaching Strategies in Science Transparencies may be used with this chapter. The transparencies add an interactive dimension to expand and enhance the *Biology: Cycles of Life* program content.

Career Interest Inventory

The AGS Publishing Harrington-O'Shea Career Decision-Making System-Revised (CDM) may be used with this chapter. Students can use the CDM to explore their interests and identify careers. The CDM defines career areas that are indicated by students' responses on the inventory.

Lesson at a Glance

Chapter 4 Lesson 1

Overview In this lesson, students learn what cells are, how cells were discovered, and what molecules make up cell parts.

Objectives
- To identify what a cell is
- To list the types of molecules found in a cell
- To explain how cells were discovered
- To define *cell theory*

Student Pages 104–110

Teacher's Resource Library

Workbook Activity 19

Alternative Workbook Activity 19

Lab Manual 16–18

Vocabulary

ATP hormone
cell theory microscope

Have students make index cards with visual clues that help them remember the definition of each term. For example, to remember the term *ATP*, students might draw a cartoon of a cell visiting an "ATP ATM machine" to withdraw the cell's energy currency—adenosine triphosphate. Encourage visual learners to refer to these cards when they study.

Background Information

The structure and composition of the molecules that make up cells helps determine their function in the cell. For example, carbohydrates contain many high-energy bonds. Breaking and reforming these bonds allows the cell to release and store energy. The specific combination of amino acids in a protein determines the shape of the protein and therefore its function in the cell.

1 Warm-Up Activity

In preparation for the Express Lab on page 107, prepare a hay infusion at least one week before class. To prepare a hay infusion, add pieces of hay to a jar filled with pond water. Cover the jar loosely.

Lesson 1 What Is a Cell?

Objectives

After reading this lesson, you should be able to
- identify what a cell is
- list the types of molecules found in a cell
- explain how cells were discovered
- define the cell theory

In Chapter 3, you found out that many different types of molecules are in organisms. How do all of these different molecules come together to create a living thing? Organisms get different molecules from the foods they eat. By breaking down food, organisms can harvest all the extra molecules they need to function and live.

Carbohydrate, lipid, protein, and nucleic acid molecules organize themselves into different structures. For example, sometimes proteins and lipids work together to make certain structures. Other times, nucleic acids and proteins work together. The four different types of molecules can work together or separately. They create different structures that help organisms to live.

Organisms are a collection of different combinations of molecules. However, living things are more than a collection of different molecules. All these combinations of molecules come together to form the first level of organization, the cell. A cell is the smallest unit of life.

Major Functions of Cells

The cells in our body perform many important functions. By breaking down food we eat, energy is produced inside cells. Cells use the oxygen we take in. The water in sweat comes from cells. Cells reproduce themselves to make more cells. The instructions for life, found in DNA, are stored in cells.

Nucleic acids, carbohydrates, lipids, and proteins come together in many combinations to make a cell. Each kind of molecule has unique properties, like polarity. These different properties allow each kind of molecule to perform certain actions.

ATP
Adenosine triphosphate; a molecule in all living cells that acts as fuel

Hormone
A chemical signal used to control body function

Carbohydrates have several functions in a cell. Their main use is for energy. The cell can break the bonds of carbohydrate molecules. When it breaks these bonds, energy is released. This energy is used to make adenosine triphosphate, also called **ATP.** ATP is a cell's main fuel source.

Cells use carbohydrates for other jobs. Many cells communicate with each other using small sugar molecules. Cells use larger complex carbohydrates, such as starch and glycogen, to store energy. Complex carbohydrates also provide support because of their rigid structure.

Like carbohydrates, lipids store energy for cells. Lipids are a form of long term energy storage. Cells use lipids only when carbohydrates are not available. Lipids perform other functions. All cells are surrounded by a membrane. A membrane acts as a barrier for a cell. A membrane separates a cell from the rest of the world.

The main molecules found in membranes are lipids. Lipids are hydrophobic, or water hating. They act as a barrier because they do not mix with water or solutions made with water. Lipids are also the base molecules our body uses to make **hormones.** Hormones are special chemical signals the body uses to direct some of its activities.

Proteins have many different roles in the cell. Many proteins help keep the structure of a cell steady. Other proteins are found inside the membrane. Cells use these proteins to communicate with each other. These proteins also help control what comes in and out of a cell.

Science Myth

Myth: All living things are made of cells, not molecules.

Fact: Living things contain many different kinds of molecules. In living organisms, molecules come together to form the first level of organization, the cell.

Cells: The Basic Units of Life Chapter 4 **105**

After about a week, the jar will contain a large population of microorganisms. To keep the infusion going, add hay and pond water each week. After several weeks, samples may include ciliates, flagellates, and diatoms.

Have students read and perform the Express Lab. Explain that some organisms are made up of only one cell. Many such single-celled organisms can be found in one drop of water. If students have trouble identifying cells on the slides, provide them with a class set of images showing these cells.

Express Lab Answers

1. Answers will vary. Students may see algae, ciliates, flagellates, and diatoms. They may also see large bacteria if magnification is sufficient. **2.** Answers will vary.

 Teaching the Lesson

Have students look at Chapter 3 to see how the structures and compositions of carbohydrates, proteins, and nucleic acids differ. Remind students that all of these molecules contain carbon and hydrogen and are thus considered organic molecules. All three can exist as long chains of repeating units.

 Reinforce and Extend

LEARNING STYLES

Body/Kinesthetic
Tincture of iodine turns dark blue in the presence of the carbohydrate starch. Have students use a solution of tincture of iodine to compare the starch content of different foods, such as granulated sugar, cornstarch, bread, crackers, sliced apples, and sliced turkey. Extend the activity by having students compare the starch content of a fresh cracker and a piece of cracker that has been chewed and spit out. (*Saliva breaks the starch down into simpler carbohydrates, which do not turn iodine dark blue.*)

Science Myth

Have students read the Science Myth feature. Remind students that all matter is made up of atoms and molecules. Living things are made up of matter, and so they are made up of atoms and molecules. Relate the structures of life to the structure of a building. A building is made up of bricks containing bits of rock, which is made up of atoms. The essential building unit is the brick, but the brick is not the simplest unit of matter.

Career Connection

Have students research the career of a nutritionist. If possible, have them interview a nutritionist and report their findings to the class. Encourage students to ask questions about the person's education, the types of services he or she provides, and the applications of his or her field of study.

Link to

Chemistry. Have students read the Link to Chemistry feature. The electrostatic force is the attraction between oppositely charged particles and the repulsion between like charges. Ionic bonds form between oppositely charged ions. Explain that methylene blue and crystal violet, which are positively charged, form ionic bonds with negatively charged molecules in cell parts. Ask students: What kinds of cell parts are not stained by these dyes? *(Cell parts that contain only positively charged molecules are not stained.)*

In the Community

Plan a field trip to a hospital, medical clinic, or research facility that uses high-powered microscopes to analyze biological samples. Have students compare the magnification capabilities of the compound microscopes in the classroom with those at the professional facility.

Pronunciation Guide

Use the pronunciation shown here to help students pronounce a difficult word in this lesson. Refer to the pronunciation key on the Chapter Planning Guide for the sounds of the symbols.

von Leeuwenhoek (von lā´vun hůk)

Microscope
An instrument used to magnify things

Link to ➢➢➢
Chemistry

When seen under the light microscope, many cells appear transparent. Biologists often use chemical dyes to make cells easier to see. Many dyes, such as methylene blue and crystal violet, are positively charged molecules. They combine with negatively charged cell parts, such as nucleic acids. Some stains color only certain parts of the cell. Scientists use stains to identify cells and cell parts.

Many proteins are used as enzymes. Remember that enzymes bring about a chemical reaction in an organism. Enzymes have specific shapes that determine the kind of job they do. Proteins come in various shapes and sizes. Each protein is unique.

Nucleic acids are the main information molecules in cells. The instructions to make all the proteins we need are in cells found in DNA. The order of bases in a DNA molecule acts as a code to make proteins. RNA helps make the protein coded in DNA. All these different molecules work together to allow a cell to function and live.

Microscopes and Cells

All living things are made of a collection of cells. Cells are so small that we cannot see them with the naked eye. We see cells by using a special piece of equipment called a **microscope.** A microscope is an instrument used to magnify things. Some microscopes use natural light to help magnify an object. These are called light microscopes. Other microscopes use a beam of electrons to create a larger image of an object. These are called electron microscopes.

Microscopes were invented in the late 1500s in Europe. Their invention was important to learning about life. They allowed scientists to see life forms that they normally could not see.

Using the microscope, several scientists made great discoveries about cells. In 1665, Robert Hooke, an English scientist, began to look at thin slices of cork. Cork is a dead wood material. He found that the interior of cork is an ordered collection of little boxes. He looked at other types of plants and found the same pattern. Hooke called these little boxes *cells.* About ten years later, a Dutch scientist named Anton von Leeuwenhoek was the first person to view living cells under a microscope.

The work of Hooke and von Leeuwenhoek was made famous about 150 years later. The new ideas from their research took time to be accepted by other scientists. This is often true in science. In the 1800s, German scientists Matthias Schleiden and Theodor Schwann helped advance a new idea about the cell.

Cell theory
A theory that all living things are made of cells, that cells are the basic units of structure and function in living things, and that cells only come from already present cells

Schleiden showed that all plants are made of cells, and Schwann did the same for animals. Another German scientist in the 1800s, Rudolf Virchow, discovered that cells can only come from other cells.

The Cell Theory

All of these discoveries are grouped together to create the **cell theory**. The cell theory has three parts:
- All living things are made of cells. All cells have some structures in common, such as DNA.
- Cells are the basic units of structure and function in living things.
- Cells only come from already present cells.

Express Lab 4

Materials
- safety goggles
- lab coat or apron
- eyedropper
- pond water or hay infusion
- microscope slide
- coverslip
- microscope

Procedure
1. Put on safety goggles and a lab coat or apron.
2. Use the eyedropper to get a drop of pond water or hay infusion.
3. Place the drop on a microscope slide. Hold a coverslip at a 45° angle from the slide and at the edge of the drop of solution. Gently lower the coverslip over the drop. **Safety Alert: Handle glass microscope slides with care. Dispose of broken glass properly.**
4. Use a microscope to examine the slide under low power and then under high power. Describe the different kinds of cells you see.
5. When finished, wash your hands well.

Analysis
1. How many kinds of cells did you find?
2. Were any cells moving? If so, describe them.

TEACHER ALERT

Be sure that students understand that cells can come only from other cells and that they cannot be made artificially from cell parts. Brainstorm other things that cannot be constructed from parts but must come from similar things, such as living organisms. Just as the cells that compose a multicelled organism must come from other cells, entire organisms cannot be built by humans from spare organs and body parts. Entire organisms can be produced only by natural reproduction by mating or budding from like organisms.

ELL/ESL Strategy

Language Objective: *To summarize*

Have students form groups that include both students learning English and students with strong English skills. Have each group create a skit that summarizes the history of the discovery of cells from the invention of the microscope to the development of the cell theory. Students may research scientists such as Hooke, von Leeuwenhoek, Schleiden, and Schwann. Have students perform their skits.

GLOBAL CONNECTION

Plasmodium is a single-celled organism that causes malaria, a serious disease with cycles of high fever and chills. Have students research the reproduction and life cycle of *Plasmodium* and report their findings to the class. Be sure they include a description of the types of regions in which malaria is common and the ways of preventing the spread of the disease in those areas.

LAB ACTIVITIES

Chapter 4 has Investigation and Discovery Investigation lab activities. Two additional lab activities for Chapter 4 appear in the Biology: Cycles of Life Lab Manual and on the Teacher's Resource Library CD-ROM.

Lesson 1 Review Answers

1. ATP **2.** hormone **3.** microscope **4.** C
5. B **6.** D **7.** A cell is surrounded by a cell membrane. A cell performs all of the major functions necessary for living things, such as reproducing and breaking down food to release energy. DNA, which contains the instructions for life, is stored in cells. **8.** The order of bases in a DNA molecule functions as a code for making proteins. **9.** DNA contains the instructions for making proteins. RNA serves as a "code-breaker" and helps to make the protein coded for in DNA. **10.** The cell theory states that cells are an organism's basic unit of structure and function, that all living things are made of cells, and that cells only come from other cells that are already present.

Portfolio Assessment

Sample items include:
- Express Lab answers
- Report for Global Connection
- Lesson 1 Review answers

LEARNING STYLES

Interpersonal/Group Learning

Divide the class into four groups and have each group write at least two questions for each of the following categories: cell functions, molecules in cells, discovery of cells, and cell theory. Then have each group choose one member to be part of the judging panel. This panel will consist of a scorekeeper, a moderator, a question reader, and a fact checker. Have the groups turn in their questions to the question reader. After a question is read aloud, the moderator will choose the student who first raises his or her hand to answer the question. The fact checker will quickly check the lesson to see if the answer is correct. The scorekeeper will award a point to a team when a member provides a correct answer.

Lesson 1 REVIEW

Word Bank
ATP
microscope
hormone

On a sheet of paper, write the word from the Word Bank that completes each sentence correctly.

1. Another name for adenosine triphosphate is _____.
2. A(n) _____ is a chemical signal our body uses to direct some of its activities.
3. An instrument used to magnify an object is called a(n) _____.

On a sheet of paper, write the letter of the answer that completes each sentence correctly.

4. A cell's main fuel source is _____.
   - **A** DNA
   - **B** RNA
   - **C** ATP
   - **D** proteins

5. The cell membrane is mainly made of _____.
   - **A** nucleic acids
   - **B** lipids
   - **C** proteins
   - **D** carbohydrates

6. Enzymes have specific _____ that determine the kind of job they do.
   - **A** lipids
   - **B** carbohydrates
   - **C** starches
   - **D** shapes

Critical Thinking

On a sheet of paper, write the answer to the following questions. Use complete sentences.

7. What are the characteristics of a cell?
8. How do nucleic acids carry information?
9. Compare and contrast the roles of DNA and RNA.
10. What does the cell theory state?

108 Chapter 4 Cells: The Basic Units of Life

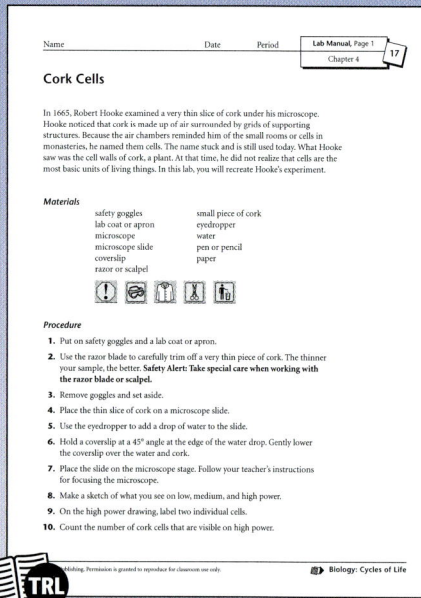

Workbook Activity 19

Lab Manual 17, pages 1–2

INVESTIGATION 4

Living Cells

Materials
- safety goggles
- lab coat or apron
- 100 mL beaker
- sucrose
- warm water (38°C to 43°C)
- glass rod
- 1 envelope active dry yeast
- eyedropper
- microscope slide
- dropper bottle of iodine solution
- coverslip
- microscope

The cell is the basic unit of life. Yeasts are single-celled organisms. In this lab, you will see how yeast cells perform the functions needed for life.

Procedure

1. Put on safety goggles and a lab coat or apron.
2. In a 100 mL beaker, add 4 g of sucrose to 60 mL of warm water. With a glass rod, stir in one envelope of active dry yeast. Let the mixture stand for 10 minutes.
3. Describe the appearance of the mixture in the beaker.

Cells: The Basic Units of Life Chapter 4 **109**

Investigation 4

Encourage students to read the investigation steps. Discuss questions they may have before beginning the investigation.

Objectives

- To prepare a wet-mount slide to view under the microscope
- To use a compound light microscope at low power and at high power
- To recognize life functions of living cells

Skills

Measuring, observing, describing, collecting information, using science lab equipment, making inferences, analyzing data, drawing conclusions

Background

All living cells must perform the major functions necessary for living things. Like all cells, yeast cells produce energy by breaking down food (in this case, sucrose). Yeast cells are surrounded by cell membranes containing lipids, which separate the cell from the surrounding environment.

Time Frame

One class period

Procedure

- If class time is limited, prepare a yeast-glucose solution 1–4 hours before class begins instead of having students make their own solutions. To do this, dissolve one packet of dried yeast in 200 mL of a 20% glucose solution. Keep the solution in a warm place (approximately 38°C to 43°C) until lab time. To prepare a 20% sucrose solution, dissolve 100 g sucrose (table sugar) in distilled water for a total volume of 500 mL.
- To use dried active yeast sold in jars, note that $2\frac{1}{4}$ teaspoons of dried yeast is equivalent to one packet of dried yeast.
- Optional: If time allows, ask students to also add 4 g sucrose to 60 mL warm water (38°C to 43°C) in a second beaker without yeast. This will serve as a control.
- Before beginning the activity, review with students the correct way to carry, use, and store the microscope.

SAFETY ALERT

- Be sure that students have read and understood all safety rules for working in the lab. Discuss the Safety Alerts with students.
- Be sure students wear safety goggles and a lab coat or apron.
- Remind students to handle glass microscope slides with care and to dispose of broken glass properly.
- Tell students that iodine is a poison and an eye irritant. It will stain skin and clothing.

- Have students work together in pairs to complete the activity.
- Have students describe the appearance of the mixture in the beaker.
- Ask students to offer an explanation for adding iodine in Step 5 to the microscope slide. *(to stain the yeast cells so they can be seen more easily)* Ask students to name a familiar food that smells like the yeast solution. *(bread)*
- Have students begin viewing slides by using the objective with the lowest power. Show students how to slowly lower the objective while viewing the microscope from the side, taking care

Continued on page 110

Cells: The Basic Units of Life **109**

Continued from page 109

to stop before the objective touches the slide. Then use the coarse-focus knob to focus up (and away) from the slide until the image comes into view. Use the fine-focus knob to sharpen the image. Have students who successfully focus a slide help those having trouble.

- Students should take turns viewing the slide under each level of magnification. Have one student watch while the other focuses the microscope to make sure the objective lens does not get forced into the slide accidentally.
- Have students record their observations of the yeast cells, including their shape.

Cleanup/Disposal

Instruct students in proper cleanup and disposal of materials.

Results

After 10 minutes, the beaker containing warm water, sugar, and yeast will begin to look bubbly and somewhat frothy. When viewed under the microscope, yeast cells will appear oval or round in shape. Students may see some yeast cells that are dividing by budding.

Analysis Answers

1. Sucrose is the energy source for the yeast cells.
2. A cell membrane surrounds each yeast cell.

Conclusions Answers

1. The cell membrane acts as a barrier for the cell, separating it from the surrounding environment.
2. Students may suggest comparing different carbohydrates (such as sucrose, lactose, and fructose) to learn which carbohydrate provides the most energy for yeast.

Explore Further Answers

Students could examine the effects of a variety of temperatures (cool, room temperature, warm, hot) on the ability of living yeast cells to grow. Yeast requires warm temperatures (38°C to 43°C) to grow. Temperatures that are too cool or too hot will prevent growth.

4. Use the eyedropper to place one drop of the mixture onto a clean glass microscope slide. **Safety Alert: Handle glass microscope slides with care. Dispose of broken glass properly.**

5. Add one drop of iodine solution to the mixture on the slide. **Safety Alert: Iodine stains skin and clothing. It is a poison and an eye irritant.**

6. Hold a coverslip at a 45° angle at the edge of the drop of iodine solution. Gently lower the coverslip over the drop. You have prepared a wet mount.

7. Place the wet mount on the microscope stage. Follow instructions from your teacher to focus and adjust the microscope.

8. Observe several yeast cells. Make note of their shape.

Cleanup/Disposal
Before leaving the lab, clean up your materials and wash your hands.

Analysis
1. What is the energy source for yeast cells?
2. What cell structure surrounds each yeast cell?

Conclusions
1. What is the role of the cell membrane?
2. Write a new question about energy and living cells that you could explore in another investigation.

Explore Further
Design a similar procedure to test the effects of temperature on living yeast cells.

Assessment

Monitor students as they use the microscopes to ensure that they follow correct procedures. Review student descriptions of yeast cells as viewed under the microscope. You might include the following items from this investigation in student portfolios:

- Description of the solution in the beaker
- Description of yeast cells under the microscope
- Answers to Analysis and Conclusions questions
- Student proposal for additional work in response to Explore Further

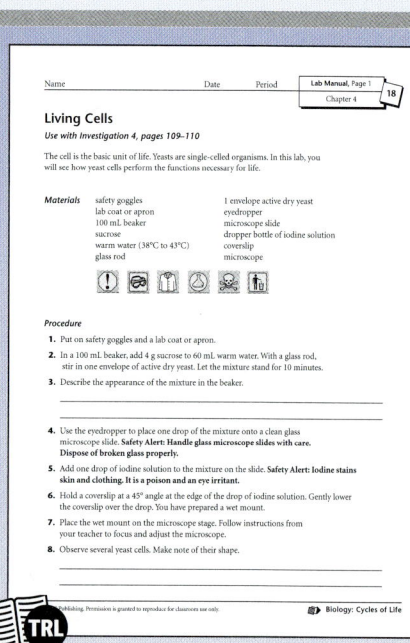

Lesson 2: Cellular Structure and Function

Objectives

After reading this lesson, you should be able to

- relate a cell's structure to function
- define homeostasis
- predict the direction of diffusion
- identify the three different kinds of osmotic environments

Homeostasis
The ability of organisms to maintain their internal conditions

A cell's structure determines its function, or the activities a cell can perform. A cell's structure is the collection of molecules that make up that cell. All cells have some structural features in common. All cells have DNA. The difference lies in the code of the DNA. All cellular membranes are made of lipids. But differences in proteins in the membrane create differences in cell function.

How do structure and function relate? The molecules in a cell do different activities. If a cell does not have a certain kind of molecule, it cannot perform a certain function. Some molecules are only present in a cell when it needs to do a certain function. The cell produces many of these molecules when needed, then breaks them down when they are not needed.

There are many different types of activities because there are many different kinds of cells. All cells use some basic functions to stay alive. Many of these activities maintain a biological balance with the cell's surrounding environment. This overall balance is known as **homeostasis**. Homeostasis is the ability of organisms to maintain their internal conditions. In homeostasis, the amounts of molecules inside and outside the cell are kept at certain levels to maintain a balance. Figure 4.2.1 shows the two ways that cells maintain homeostasis.

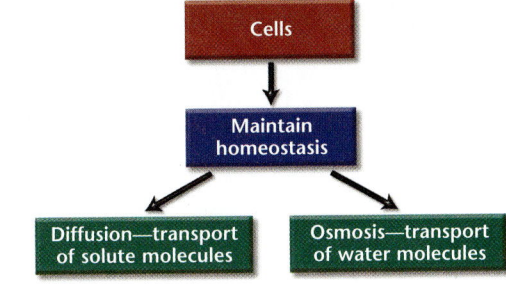

Figure 4.2.1 Cells maintain homeostasis in two ways.

in constant motion, the particles in a solution naturally spread out evenly over time. If you add more of a certain chemical to a solution, it will eventually spread out evenly over the entire solution. If two solutions are separated by a barrier that is permeable to a specific chemical, the molecules of that chemical will pass through the barrier and spread out evenly over the two solutions. In this way, the molecules move from an area of high concentration to an area of low concentration.

Lesson at a Glance

Chapter 4 Lesson 2

Overview In this lesson, students learn how cell structures and physical processes contribute to homeostasis.

Objectives

- To relate a cell's structure to its function
- To define *homeostasis*
- To predict the direction of diffusion
- To identify the three different kinds of osmotic environments

Student Pages 111–115

Teacher's Resource Library
Workbook Activity 20
Alternative Workbook Activity 20
Lab Manual 19
Resource File 7–8

Vocabulary

concentration	hypotonic
concentration gradient	isotonic
	osmosis
diffusion	selectively permeable membrane
equilibrium	
homeostasis	solute
hypertonic	transport

Have students look up the meanings of the prefixes *hypo-*, *hyper-*, and *iso-*. Have them use a dictionary to make a list of words that come from these prefixes, such as *hyperactive*, *hypoallergenic*, and *isoscelese*. Encourage students to use their lists to devise a mnemonic device to help them remember the difference between the terms *hypotonic*, *hypertonic*, and *isotonic*.

Background Information

Solutions are homogenous mixtures of two or more substances. In living systems, solutions are usually made up of different chemicals dissolved in water. One property that describes a solution is concentration. Concentration is the number of molecules of one type of compound or element in a given region or amount of solution. Because the particles that make up solutions are

Warm-Up Activity

Have a volunteer spray a small amount of air freshener in one corner of the classroom. Have students raise their hands when they can smell the scent. Students closest to the sprayer will smell the scent first, and those farthest away will smell it last. Explain that the particles of air freshener diffuse throughout the solution of air in the room in a way similar to a drop of dye dispersing passively throughout a liquid solution.

Teaching the Lesson

Compare diffusion of molecules to groups of students eating in a cafeteria during lunch. At the beginning of lunchtime, students file in through the doors. The concentration of students is greatest near the doors and in line to get food. As students leave the food line, they spread out somewhat evenly throughout the cafeteria. On a typical day, it is not likely that all students would eat in one corner, leaving most of the cafeteria empty. Molecules in solution spread out in a similar way.

Reinforce and Extend

Link to

Social Studies. Have students read the Link to Social Studies feature. Have them research recipes and methods for salting and curing foods. For example, jerky and salt-cured meats such as beef, bacon, ham, or salmon can keep unrefrigerated for many months. Encourage students to try out one of the recipes at home.

LEARNING STYLES

Auditory/Verbal
Have students work in small groups to prepare a poem, skit, song, rap, or cheer that includes the terms *diffusion, concentration gradient, osmosis, hypotonic, hypertonic, isotonic,* and *equilibrium.* Ask students to put on an informal talent show in which they perform their creative work for the class.

Transport
To move molecules from one side of a membrane to the other

Concentration
A measurement of the amount of dissolved substance in a fixed amount of solvent

Diffusion
The movement of molecules from an area of high concentration to an area of low concentration

Link to ≫≫≫
Social Studies

Because salt draws water out of cells, it is used to preserve some foods, such as bacon and fish. Salt has been widely used throughout history. People did not need fresh foods if they had salted, preserved foods to eat. Salt-preserved foods also allowed people to travel long distances by land or sea.

Sometimes a cell moves molecules in or out of itself to achieve balance. This activity is called **transport.** Transport means to move molecules from one side of a membrane to the other.

You already know that molecules are constantly in motion. In general, molecules tend to spread out, not group, as they move around. To concentrate molecules means to gather molecules together in one area.

An area having many of the same molecules has a high **concentration** of those molecules. An area of low concentration has only a few molecules. Molecules generally move to an area where they have the most space available. Molecules naturally move from areas of high concentration to areas of low concentration. The movement of molecules from an area of high concentration to an area of low concentration is called **diffusion.**

Figure 4.2.2 shows the process of diffusion. In the first beaker, a sugar cube is dissolving in water. Sugar molecules are moving by diffusion. In the second beaker, sugar molecules have equally distributed themselves in the water. Remember, water is a solvent, a substance that can dissolve one or more other substances.

Figure 4.2.2 *Diffusion is seen when a sugar cube dissolves in a beaker of water.*

Selectively permeable membrane
A membrane that allows some molecules to pass but blocks other molecules from coming through

Concentration gradient
A difference in the concentration of a substance across a distance

Osmosis
The movement of water through a cell membrane

Science Myth

Myth: For best performance, athletes should always have sports drinks during a workout.

Fact: During most exercise, plain water is the best choice to replace lost fluids. Sports drinks may help during long workouts.

Cells use diffusion to control the concentrations of their molecules. A cell's membrane is the main barrier that separates a cell from its environment. Some chemicals can easily cross cell membranes. Large molecules may need help from the cell to pass through its membrane. Polar molecules have difficulty passing through the hydrophobic inside of the cell's membrane.

A cell has a **selectively permeable membrane.** The membrane allows some molecules to pass, but blocks other molecules from coming through. A cell's membrane controls the concentrations of different molecules. A **concentration gradient** forms when different concentrations of a molecule are on either side of the membrane. A concentration gradient is the difference in the concentration of a substance across a distance. Cells use concentration gradients to direct some of their activities. Cells have other ways to control molecule concentrations.

Osmosis: A Special Type of Diffusion

Water is the main solvent for most chemicals in an organism's body. How much water is used to dissolve the chemicals affects the concentration of the chemicals. Cells control the concentration of other molecules by changing the concentration of water molecules. Cells do this by performing **osmosis.** Osmosis is the movement of water through a cell membrane.

Water easily crosses the membrane of a cell. Water also moves from areas of high to low concentration. By moving water molecules around, cells can raise or lower the concentrations of other molecules.

How can scientists tell which molecules move where? Recall that all molecules naturally move from areas of high to low concentration. Moving water molecules around can completely change a cell's inside and outside environment. Three different environments explain the movement of molecules. In these three different environments, the movement of water molecules, or osmosis, is the focus.

Cells: The Basic Units of Life Chapter 4 **113**

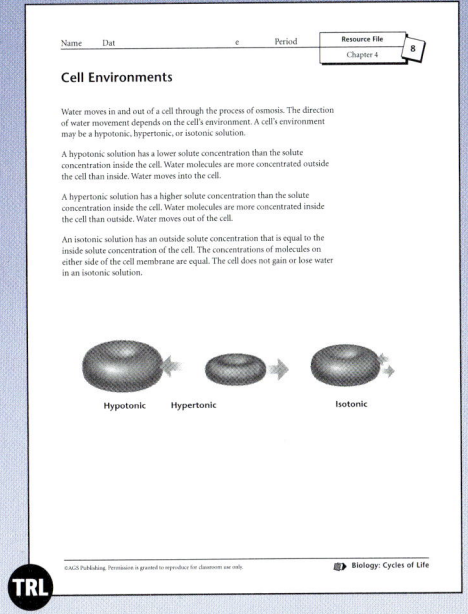

Resource File 8

LEARNING STYLES

Visual/Spatial

Students can compare a selectively permeable membrane to a sieve. A sieve will allow small particles of flour to pass through. However, larger particles, such as beads, will not pass through. The sieve is selectively permeable to flour. Explain that membranes are selectively permeable to molecules that vary not just by size, but also by polarity and shape.

Science Myth

Have a volunteer read aloud the first sentence of the Science Myth feature. Have students discuss why they think sports drinks help during a workout. Students may have heard that these drinks replenish fluids and electrolytes. They also contain carbohydrates, which are used by cells for energy. Have students read the rest of the feature and then discuss why they think that plain water might be best for replacing lost fluids during shorter workouts. Students may discuss the fact that consuming extra sugar is not always necessary during shorter workouts.

IN THE ENVIRONMENT

Water can be treated by using a process called reverse osmosis. In reverse osmosis, a solution that contains contaminants is separated from a clean solution by a membrane permeable only to water. If pressure is applied to the side containing the contaminated solution, water can diffuse across the membrane, increasing the volume of clean solution on the other side. Many desalination plants use reverse osmosis to generate fresh water. Ask students if they know of equipment used in homes that makes use of reverse osmosis. Reverse osmosis is used on a smaller scale in some home water-filtration systems. Encourage discussion of how this type of home water-filtration system works.

Cells: The Basic Units of Life **113**

AT HOME

Have students place slices of carrot or potato in freshwater and saltwater solutions or grapes in freshwater and sugar-water solutions. Have them compare the texture, shape, size, and masses of each sample before and after the solutions soak overnight. *(Samples placed in hypertonic solutions, such as a carrot placed in salt water, will shrink due to loss of water to the external solution. Samples placed in hypotonic solutions, such as a grape placed in fresh water, will expand in size due to osmosis.)* Have students relate their observations to the results of cooking practices such as pickling and salting.

SCIENCE JOURNAL

Have students write a description of what happens when cells are surrounded by hypertonic, hypotonic, and isotonic solutions.

TEACHER ALERT

Many students have trouble understanding that molecules and cellular structures lack will. They might find it easier to personify cells or particles in living systems. However, doing so can propagate misconceptions. Avoid using phrases such as "molecules want to move" or "molecules like to be." Instead, use wording such as "molecules tend to move" or "molecules are more likely to be" when describing the nature of chemicals in living systems.

Hypotonic
A solution whose solute concentration is lower than the solute concentration of another solution

Solute
A dissolved substance

Hypertonic
A solution whose solute concentration is higher than the solute concentration of another solution

Isotonic
A solution whose solute concentration is equal to the solute concentration of another solution

Equilibrium
A state where concentrations are equal in all parts of an area

Compared to human body fluids, seawater is a hypertonic solution. If a person drinks a lot of seawater, water leaves the body's cells to dilute the salt in the seawater. The body's cells shrink and die. This leads to dehydration and death.

Hypotonic is the first environment shown in Figure 4.2.3. A hypotonic solution has a solute concentration that is lower than the solute concentration of another solution. *Hypo* is a prefix that means "lower." The word *tonic* refers to the **solute** molecules, not water. A solute is a dissolved substance. If the environment outside a cell is hypotonic, it has fewer solute molecules than the environment inside the cell. In other words, water molecules are more concentrated on the outside of the cell than inside the cell. In this type of environment, water molecules will move into the cell. If too much water enters, the cell could burst.

Hypertonic is the second environment. Look at Figure 4.2.4. A hypertonic solution has a solute concentration that is higher than the solute concentration elsewhere. The prefix *hyper* means "higher." If the environment outside a cell is hypertonic, the water concentration is higher inside the cell than outside the cell. In this type of environment, water molecules will move out of the cell. If too much water leaves, the cell could shrink.

If the environment outside a cell is hypotonic, then the environment inside the cell is hypertonic. If the outside is hypertonic, then the environment inside the cell is hypotonic. Hypotonic and hypertonic describe solute concentration. They do not describe water concentration.

Isotonic is the third concentration environment shown in Figure 4.2.5. An isotonic solution has a concentration that is equal to the inside solute concentration of another solution. The concentrations of solute molecules on both sides of the membrane are equal. In this state, the whole environment is in **equilibrium.** Equilibrium is a state of equal concentrations in all parts of an area. Reaching equilibrium with different outside environments is one way cells maintain homeostasis.

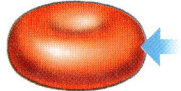

Figures 4.2.3, 4.2.4, and 4.2.5 *The same cell is shown in outside environments that are hypotonic, hypertonic, and isotonic. The arrows indicate movement.*

114   Chapter 4   Cells: The Basic Units of Life

ELL/ESL Strategy

Language Objective: *To explain difficult concepts*

Have students form pairs that include both a student learning English and a student with strong English skills. Have students take turns reading each paragraph on page 114 and explaining the content of the paragraph to their partner in their own words. Students may wish to use simple diagrams to illustrate their explanations. Encourage students to provide a helpful critique of their partner's explanation by pointing out any details that might have been left out. As a class, make a list of the important points discussed in the text. Have students save these notes to study for quizzes or tests.

Lesson 2 REVIEW

On a sheet of paper, write the word or words that complete each sentence correctly.

1. A cell maintains a biological balance known as _____.
2. When there are different concentrations of a molecule on either side of the cell membrane, a _____ results.
3. A cell reaches _____ when solute concentrations inside and outside the cell are equal.

Critical Thinking

On a sheet of paper, write the answers to the following questions. Use complete sentences.

4. How does a cell maintain homeostasis?
5. Why is a cell membrane selectively permeable?

Technology and Society

Physiological saline is a sterile solution of sodium chloride. It is isotonic to body fluids. Doctors use it to replace body fluids lost during bleeding, burns, or excessive sweating. Without enough fluid in the body, blood pressure drops. The sudden loss of blood pressure can damage the brain, heart, and kidneys. In medical emergencies, physiological saline saves many lives.

Cells: The Basic Units of Life Chapter 4   115

Lesson 2 Review Answers

1. homeostasis **2.** concentration gradient **3.** equilibrium **4.** A cell maintains homeostasis by transporting molecules in or out to achieve balance. **5.** A cell membrane is selectively permeable because it easily allows some molecules to pass, but not others.

Portfolio Assessment

Sample items include:
- Description from Science Journal
- Write-up of creative work from Learning Styles Auditory/Verbal
- Lesson 2 Review answers

Technology and Society

Explain that sodium chloride is a common compound used in cooking. Ask students: What is sodium chloride better known as? *(table salt)* Have a volunteer read aloud the Technology and Society feature. Explain that the saline solutions found at the drug store for contact lenses are chemically similar to human tears. Guide students to the conclusion that tears taste salty because they contain dissolved salts such as sodium chloride.

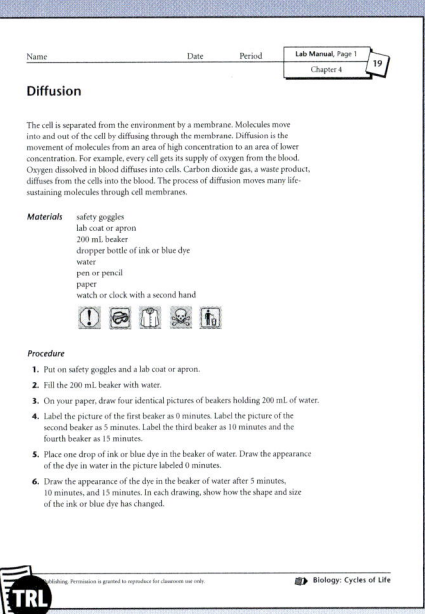

Lab Manual 19, pages 1–2

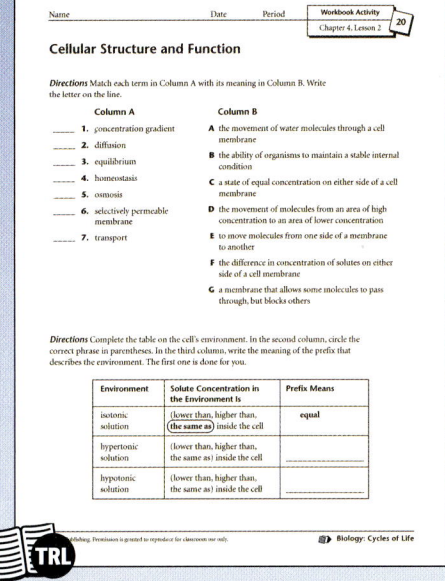

Workbook Activity 20

Lesson at a Glance

Chapter 4 Lesson 3

Overview In this lesson, students compare different types of cells, their general structure, and the types of organisms they make up.

Objectives

- To identify the two major categories of cells
- To compare the major structural differences between cells
- To describe the kinds of organisms that cells make

Student Pages 116–122

Teacher's Resource Library TRL

Workbook Activity 21

Alternative Workbook Activity 21

Lab Manual 20

Vocabulary

binary fission	organelle
eukaryote	prokaryote

The word *binary* comes from the Latin word *bini*, which means "two by two." The word *fission* comes from the Latin word *fissio*, which means "split." Have students predict the meaning of the term *binary fission* from this etymological information. *(Binary fission occurs when a cell reproduces by splitting into two cells.)*

Background Information

Some scientists theorize that eukaryotes developed when smaller bacteria began to live inside larger bacteria. This theory, called endosymbiosis, suggests that ATP-producing bacteria became mitochondria, the eukaryotic organelles responsible for energy production. Other bacteria that produce carbohydrates by using sunlight became chloroplasts, the eukaryotic organelles responsible for generation of glucose in plants.

Lesson 3 What Kind of Cell Is It?

Objectives

After reading this lesson, you should be able to
- identify the two major categories of cells
- compare the major structural differences between cells
- describe the kinds of organisms that cells make

As you have learned, an important cell function is to maintain homeostasis. Cells perform other functions. Cells can be grouped in many different ways, such as by structure. Since structure determines function, these structural groupings can also be the basis of grouping by function.

Prokaryotic Cells

Membranes are the first structures used to group cells together. Some cells have only one membrane. This membrane separates the cell from the outside world. All other cell parts and molecules, including the DNA, float freely inside the cell. This is a prokaryotic cell or **prokaryote.** A prokaryote has only one outside membrane. It has no nucleus or other internal structures.

Prokaryote
A cell with only one outside membrane and no nucleus or other internal structures

Prokaryotic cells are the simplest organisms. Organisms commonly called bacteria are prokaryotes. Remember that bacteria are the simplest single cells that carry out all basic life activities.

Some people think all bacteria are harmful. That is not true. Only some bacteria cause disease. People clean themselves and their surroundings to prevent harmful bacteria from spreading.

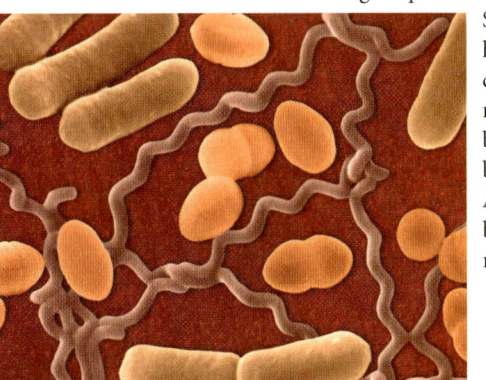

Some bacteria help us live. They help us break down food and use chemicals. Bacteria can also help make different kinds of food, like bread, cheese, and yogurt. Most bacteria are harmless to people. As seen in Figure 4.3.1, most bacteria come in three shapes: rods, spirals, and spheres.

Figure 4.3.1 Most bacteria are shaped like rods, spirals, or spheres.

116   Chapter 4   Cells: The Basic Units of Life

 ### Warm-Up Activity

Have students use calculators to demonstrate how a single bacterium can produce millions of bacteria. Ask them to determine the following: if each cell divides (producing two cells) once an hour, after how many hours would there be over 1,000,000 bacteria? *(20 hours)*

Binary fission
Reproduction in which a bacterial cell divides into two cells that look the same as the original cell

Eukaryote
A cell with several internal structures, including the nucleus, that are surrounded by membranes

Organelle
A tiny membrane-bound structure inside a cell

Since prokaryotes do not have many specific structures, they do not have many specific functions. Prokaryotes' main goal is to live. To reach this goal, they eat and remove waste from their inside. Both of these functions are controlled by the one membrane that surrounds the cell. To live, prokaryotes must find the right environment. This environment depends on the type of prokaryote. Prokaryotes live in every part of the world. Prokaryotes can be found in any type of environment, even inside other organisms.

Because their structure is so simple, prokaryotes can grow quickly. To reproduce, prokaryotes make copies of their DNA and then divide in two. This process is known as **binary fission**, which we will discuss in Chapter 9. Binary fission is the reproduction of bacteria. In binary fission, a bacterial cell divides into two cells that look the same as the original cell. Prokaryotes reproduce quickly because making cells is simple. One cell can divide enough times to make over a million cells in less than one day!

Eukaryotic Cells

Many prokaryotes live in the world. What about the rest of the organisms on the planet, including humans? These organisms are more complex than prokaryotes. Because of this, they have more complex cells. These complex cells have more structures compared to prokaryotes. If a cell is not prokaryotic, it is a **eukaryote**. A eukaryotic cell has several structures, including a nucleus. In a cell, the nucleus controls growth and reproduction. The nucleus and other cell structures are surrounded by membranes. Eukaryotes include many kinds of organisms, such as mushrooms, molds, plants, and animals.

A eukaryotic cell has more membranes than the one separating it from the outside. The other membranes are found inside the cell and create separate areas called **organelles**. An organelle is a tiny, membrane-bound structure inside a cell. Each organelle has a different function.

Link to

Health

An antibiotic is a drug that kills bacteria. Unlike animal cells, bacteria have a cell wall surrounding the cell membrane. Many antibiotics, such as penicillin, interfere with cell wall production. These antibiotics kill bacteria, but leave eukaryotes unharmed.

Cells: The Basic Units of Life Chapter 4 **117**

---

2 Teaching the Lesson

Point out to students that membranes are an important component of cellular structures. Many important chemical reactions and exchanges of materials take place on and through cell membranes. For this reason, the efficiency of cell processes is greatly improved when the surface area of membranes in cells is maximized in relation to the volume of the cell. This balance is why most cells are very tiny. The efficiency of many of life's processes is greatest when there is a high ratio of cell surface area to cell volume, a characteristic of small cells.

3 Reinforce and Extend

LEARNING STYLES

Logical/Mathematical
Have students determine how surface area of a cell is related to cell volume by using modeling clay. Have them make a lump of clay into a cube shape and use a ruler to measure and calculate the cube's volume and surface area. With a plastic knife, they can cut the cube in half. Have them compare the total volume and surface area of the two smaller shapes with that of the larger cube. Students can show that, as the clay is cut into smaller pieces, the ratio of surface area to volume increases.

Link to

AT HOME

Certain conditions encourage the reproduction of bacteria. Many safe practices in the kitchen come from the need to prevent bacteria reproduction. Cooking and maintaining foods at certain temperatures prevents bacteria from multiplying. Keeping food refrigerated slows bacterial growth, as well as the decay of food. Have students research food safety with respect to the spread and growth of bacteria and relate it to cooking practices in their home.

Health. Have students read the Link to Health feature. Bacteria build strong cell walls using an enzyme called transpeptidase. Penicillin prevents this enzyme from performing its function. When bacteria reproduce in the presence of penicillin, the cell walls built are too weak to contain the cell contents, causing the new cells to rupture and die. Have students predict what penicillin will do to the helpful bacterial that live in the intestine. Explain that antibiotics such as penicillin prevent the reproduction of other bacteria in the body, even the beneficial ones.

TEACHER ALERT

Some students think that because all prokaryotes are single cells, all single-celled organisms are prokaryotes. However, many eukaryotes are also single cells. The simplest way to differentiate between eukaryotes and prokaryotes is the presence or lack of a nucleus. In eukaryotes, the cell's DNA is enclosed in the nucleus. In prokaryotes, the cell's DNA floats freely in the cell's cytoplasm. Most prokaryotes are single-celled organisms that have rigid cell walls. Some eukaryotes, such as amoebas, are single-celled organisms, while others, such as humans, have many cells.

Achievements in Science

Ask volunteers to read aloud the Achievements in Science feature. Have students find out more about growing cancer cells in tissue cultures. For example, have them find out what a biopsy is and how it can be used to determine if a tumor is cancerous.

All eukaryotic cells have a nucleus. Remember that the nucleus is the information and control center of a cell. It contains most of a cell's DNA.

The nucleus is the main organelle used to identify eukaryotic cells. It is usually the largest organelle inside a cell. All eukaryotic cells have a nucleus surrounded by a membrane. Prokaryotic cells do not have a nucleus surrounded by a membrane.

Eukaryotic cells have other organelles. Each organelle has a specific function. Some organelles produce fuel for the cell. Others help a cell move around. Still other organelles help cells talk to one another. All of these different organelles and their functions are controlled by the activities of the nucleus.

Achievements in Science

Growing Cells in the Lab

Soon after cells were discovered, scientists wanted to learn how living cells function. But they faced a puzzling question: How can you study living cells? In 1907, American scientist Ross Granville Harrison answered this question. He became the first scientist to grow cells outside of an organism. Harrison invented lab techniques to grow frog nerve cells in dishes.

Growing animal or plant cells in an artificial environment is known as tissue culture. Scientists collect one or more cells, and then raise the cells in a special solution called a culture medium. The medium is at a temperature close to that of the organism's normal environment. The cells divide and make new cells. They create a continuous population, or cell line.

From studying tissue culture, scientists have learned that normal cells lose their ability to multiply after 50 to 100 cell divisions. However, cancer cells continue to divide. Many researchers today use the HeLa cell line. These are cancer cells from Henrietta Lacks, who died in 1951 from cancer. Her cells have been a great benefit to modern scientific research.

Since they are complex, eukaryotic cells have many different methods to control their activities. Even reproduction is more complex in eukaryotic cells and happens through a series of steps. We will discuss eukaryotic reproduction in Chapter 9.

Different eukaryotic cells have different amounts and kinds of organelles. The organelles in a eukaryotic cell determine the main function of the cell. A cell's main function affects the kinds of proteins produced by the cell. For example, plant cells have many organelles that store water because they need water constantly. Look at Figure 4.3.2. Muscle cells have many organelles that produce energy. They need energy to work. A cell's structure and its function are closely related to each other. We will discuss different organelles and their functions in Chapter 5.

Figure 4.3.2 *Muscle cells have many organelles that produce energy because these cells need energy to work.*

ELL/ESL Strategy

Language Objective: *To compare and contrast prokararyotic and eukaryotic cells*

Have students form groups that include both students learning English and students with strong English skills. Provide groups with a variety of materials such as pipe cleaners, yarn, felt, construction paper, poster board, colored markers, and glue. Have students design and create a visual display that compares prokaryotic and eukaryotic cells. Be sure that students clearly label their displays and provide either an oral or a written description on the differences and similarities of the two types of cells. Have students include a brief explanation of why they chose the materials they did to portray the two types of cells and their structures.

Lesson 3 Review Answers

1. organelles **2.** binary fission **3.** nucleus
4. A **5.** B **6.** D **7.** The organelles present in a cell are based on the major function of that cell. For example, plant cells have organelles that can store water, since they need water on a constant basis. **8.** Binary fission is the reproduction of bacteria. Bacteria are prokaryotes. Prokaryotes are the simplest organism, having only one cell. One cell can divide many times to make more than one million cells in less than a day. **9.** Both prokaryotes and eukaryotes must contain DNA because it contains the instructions needed to make proteins, which are essential for life. **10.** A prokaryotic cell lacks a nucleus. A eukaryotic cell contains a nucleus plus several other membrane-bound organelles.

Portfolio Assessment

Sample items include:
- Calculations from Warm-Up Activity
- Chart from Learning Styles Logical/Mathematical
- Reports from ELL/ESL Strategy
- Lesson 3 Review answers

Lesson 3   R E V I E W

On a sheet of paper, write the word or words that complete each sentence correctly.

1. Structures with different functions inside a eukaryotic cell are called _____.
2. Prokaryotes reproduce by a process called _____.
3. The largest organelle inside a cell is usually the _____.

On a sheet of paper, write the letter of the answer that completes each sentence correctly.

4. The simplest organisms are _____.
   - **A** bacteria
   - **B** plants
   - **C** molds
   - **D** animals

5. Prokaryotes contain all of the following except _____.
   - **A** DNA
   - **B** a nucleus
   - **C** molecules floating inside
   - **D** a cell membrane

6. Cells found in _____ have many organelles that produce energy.
   - **A** hair
   - **B** skin
   - **C** plants
   - **D** muscles

Critical Thinking

On a sheet of paper, write the answer to the following questions. Use complete sentences.

7. How are organelles related to a cell's function?
8. Why is binary fission a fast way for a cell to reproduce?
9. Explain why both prokaryotic cells and eukaryotic cells contain DNA.
10. How could you distinguish a prokaryotic cell from a eukaryotic cell?

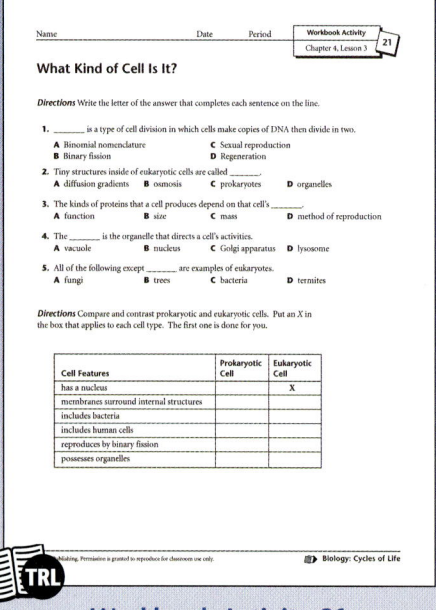

Workbook Activity 21

DISCOVERY INVESTIGATION 4

Materials
- safety goggles
- lab coat or apron
- microscope slide
- forceps
- *Elodea* leaf
- dropper bottle of distilled water
- coverslip
- microscope
- dropper bottle of 10% NaCl solution

Osmosis in Cells

Water enters and leaves cells by osmosis. In this investigation, you will predict the direction of water movement across a cell membrane. Under what conditions will water enter a cell? Under what conditions will water leave a cell?

Procedure

1. Put on safety goggles and a lab coat or apron.
2. Use forceps to get a small *Elodea* leaf. Use the dropper to put a drop of distilled water onto a clean glass microscope slide. Place the leaf over the drop of water. Carefully place a coverslip on the leaf. **Safety Alert: Handle glass microscope slides with care. Dispose of broken glass properly.**

Discovery Investigation 4

This investigation is less structured than the first investigation in this chapter. It offers students more challenge and requires more teacher facilitation. Encourage students to read the investigation steps and formulate their own questions before beginning the investigation. Discuss with students the two questions in the first paragraph on page 121. Encourage students to share their thoughts.

Objectives
- To prepare a wet-mount slide to view under the microscope
- To use a compound light microscope at low power and at high power
- To predict the direction of water movement into or out of a cell
- To design an experiment to test a hypothesis

Skills
Observing, describing, using science lab equipment, comparing and contrasting, making inferences, designing an experiment, predicting outcomes, recognizing cause and effect, analyzing data, drawing conclusions

Background
In living organisms, water serves as the main solvent for the chemicals needed to sustain life. Water moves from areas of high concentration (few solutes) to areas of low concentration (many solutes). Under normal conditions when sufficient water is present, *Elodea* cells appear bright green, and the cell cytoplasm completely fills the cells.

However, if *Elodea* cells are surrounded by a hypertonic solution, such as salt water, water will leave the cells and the cell contents will collapse inside the cell wall. To reverse the loss of water in the cells, students can place a tiny piece of paper towel at the edge of the cover slip, then place a drop of distilled water at the opposite edge of the cover slip. Students will see the cell contents regain their normal shape as water reenters the cells.

Time Frame
One class period

SAFETY ALERT
- Make sure that students have read and understood all safety rules. Discuss the Safety Alerts.
- Be sure students wear safety goggles and a lab coat or apron.
- Check that students understand the correct procedures for working with the microscope.
- Remind students to handle glass microscope slides with care and to dispose of broken glass properly.
- Discourage students from placing the plants near their mouth or skin. Be sure they wash their hands after the investigation.

Procedure
- *Elodea* is an inexpensive freshwater aquatic plant that is commonly sold in pet shops or aquarium stores. It must be kept submerged or very wet, or it will quickly die. Be sure that students keep the *Elodea* underwater before and after they select a leaf.
- If not available locally, *Elodea* is readily available from a supplier of science education materials. Some are listed on page 723.
- Have students work together in small groups to complete the activity.

Continued on page 122

Continued from page 121

- Review the use of the terms *solute* and *solvent*. Remind students that water moves from areas of high concentration (few solutes) to areas of low concentration (many solutes). Tell students that distilled water, unlike tap water, does not contain dissolved solutes.

- Help students remember that the terms *hypotonic* and *hypertonic* describe solute concentrations, not water.

- Have students document the procedure they suggest, including the list of materials needed, the preparation and safety alerts required, and any information necessary for someone else to repeat students' experiment. Have students record their results.

- Ask students to discuss any problems they had performing the experiment. Ask them which part of the procedure, if any, they would change if they were going to perform the experiment again.

Cleanup/Disposal

Instruct students in proper cleanup and disposal of materials.

Results

Because *Elodea* is a plant, its cells are surrounded by cell walls. Students will discover that *Elodea* cells in distilled water are bright green with the cell cytoplasm completely filling the cells and pushing up against the cell walls. If *Elodea* cells are mounted in a drop of 10% NaCl solution, water will exit the cells as it moves from its higher concentration inside the cell towards its lower concentration (the salt water outside the cell). As water rushes out of the cell, students will see the cytoplasm contract and pull away from the cell wall.

Answers to Analysis, Conclusions, and Explore Further begin on page 670 of this Teacher's Edition.

---

3. Place the wet mount on the microscope stage. Follow instructions from your teacher to focus and adjust the microscope.

4. Describe what you see. Do you think water is entering the *Elodea* cells or leaving the cells? Explain your answer.

5. In a small group, discuss how you could determine the conditions that cause water to enter and exit the cell. Write a hypothesis that you could test with an experiment.

6. Write a procedure for your experiment. Include Safety Alerts.

7. Have your hypothesis, procedure, and Safety Alerts approved by your teacher. Then carry out your experiment. Record your results.

Cleanup/Disposal
Before leaving the lab, clean up your materials and wash your hands.

Analysis
1. Is distilled water a hypotonic or hypertonic environment compound to *Elodea* cells?
2. In what direction do you think water would move if *Elodea* cells were surrounded by saltwater?

Conclusions
1. Was your hypothesis supported by the results of your investigation?
2. Plant fertilizers contain salts. Why is it important to use the correct amount of fertilizer?

Explore Further
In your group, discuss how you could find out if the events you have just seen are reversible.

Assessment

Check to see that students have correctly recorded their descriptions of the *Elodea* slide. Monitor students as they use the microscope to ensure they follow correct procedures. Review group hypotheses and experiment procedures. You might include the following items from this investigation in student portfolios:

- Hypothesis and experimental procedure
- Answers to Analysis and Conclusions questions
- Student proposal for question to investigate in Explore Further

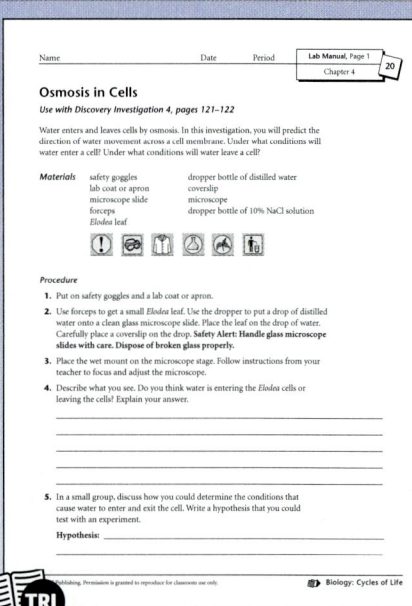

Lesson 4: After the Cell

Objectives

After reading this lesson, you should be able to
- name the four levels of organization in complex organisms
- identify examples of each level of organization

Tissue
A group of cells that are similar and work together

Epithelial cell
A skin cell

Nervous tissue
Nerves made from collections of nerve cells

In the last lesson, we looked at the two major classifications of cells: prokaryotes and eukaryotes. Remember that prokaryotes are single-cell organisms that can carry out all the functions necessary for life.

The cells that make up larger organisms have different functions based on their structures. The different kinds of cells are not found everywhere in an organism. All cells do not perform all activities. Different kinds of cells rely on each other to keep an organism alive. Cells in complex organisms are put together in an ordered way.

Cells can be grouped together into **tissues.** A tissue is a group of cells that are similar and work together. For example, skin is made up of **epithelial cells,** or skin cells. Epithelial cells work together as skin tissue to protect parts of your body. Nerve cells work together to form **nervous tissue.** Nervous tissue forms nerves that relay messages to and from the brain. Nerves run throughout your body. Muscle tissue is made of muscle cells that work together to make muscles move.

Figure 4.4.1 The human body is made up of cells, tissues, organs, and organ systems.

Cells: The Basic Units of Life   Chapter 4   123

Lesson at a Glance

Chapter 4 Lesson 4

Overview In this lesson, students learn about the levels of organization of living systems.

Objectives
- To name the different levels of organization in complex organisms
- To identify examples of each level of organization

Student Pages 123–127

Teacher's Resource Library (TRL)
Workbook Activity 22–23
Alternative Workbook Activity 22–23

Vocabulary

circulatory system   organ
epithelial cell   organ system
nervous tissue   tissue

Have students work in pairs to organize the vocabulary terms into four different levels in order from smallest division to largest division. *(epithelial cell, tissue and nervous tissue, organ, organ system, and circulatory system)*

Background Information

Though many parts of the human body must work together to carry out daily functions, some parts work together more closely than others. Groups of organs that work together are called organ systems. Just as eukaryotic cells are made up of organelles with specific functions that help the cell maintain homeostasis, organ systems are made up of organs with specific functions that help the human organism survive.

 Warm-Up Activity

Have students describe and order different levels of geographic organization such as planet, continent, country, state, county, zip code, neighborhood, street address, house, and room. Lead students to understand that, as with the organization of living systems, in general, there are greater numbers of the most specific levels of organization.

Cells: The Basic Units of Life   **123**

2 Teaching the Lesson

Epithelial cells are found in skin tissue, and they also make up the tissues that line internal organs. Epithelial cells that line the windpipe produce a sticky mucus that traps potentially dangerous particles that are inhaled. Blood vessels are also lined with a thin layer of epithelial cells that allow nutrients and oxygen to enter and exit the blood. A layer of similar epithelial cells is called epithelial tissue, which is one type of tissue found in the human body.

3 Reinforce and Extend

LEARNING STYLES

Visual/Spatial
Have students compose structures using stacking or interlocking building blocks. Then have them examine one another's structures. Ask them to write a paragraph that compares the strength, complexity, and flexibility of different structures composed by the different blocks. Tell them to consider if the materials, shapes, and design of the individual blocks affect the final structures. Discuss the importance of the component structures on the overall structure and function of the blocks and relate this to living systems.

Science at Work

As a class, read the Science at Work feature about the career of a developmental biologist. Have interested students find out more about the different stages of human development from a single cell that divides, differentiates, and develops into tissues, organs, and complex organ systems.

Organ
A group of different tissues that work together to perform specific functions

Organ system
A group of organs that work together to perform specific connected tasks

Circulatory system
A collection of organs, including the heart, which moves blood and gases throughout the body

Tissues can be grouped together into **organs.** The organ is the next level of organization in complex organisms. Organs are a group of different tissues that work together to perform specific functions. The heart is an example of an organ. Muscle tissue in the heart contracts. This movement causes the heart to beat and pump blood. The heart is separated from the rest of the body by a covering of epithelial cells. Nervous tissue relays messages from the brain to the heart.

Organs can be grouped together into **organ systems.** An organ system is a group of organs that work together to perform several connected tasks. The heart, an organ, pumps blood through the arteries. Blood is a tissue made of blood cells. Blood carries oxygen to all the parts of a body. The veins carry blood back to the lungs to get more oxygen for the body. All of these organs and tissues are grouped together in the **circulatory system.** The circulatory system is an organ system that includes the heart, arteries, and veins. It moves blood and gases throughout the body.

Science at Work

Developmental Biologist

During development, a single eukaryotic cell gives rise to dividing cells. These cells become different from one another. This process is called *differentiation*. Developmental biologists find out how cells divide, differentiate, and form tissues and organs. They study how genes control development. Developmental biologists learn about structural changes that take place as an organism develops. They also discover how the environment, drugs, or chemicals affect development.

Developmental biologists often specialize. Many study errors in development that cause diseases or disorders. They seek to understand how development occurs so that diseases or birth defects can be prevented or treated.

Most jobs in developmental biology require a master's degree. A Ph.D. degree is needed to do independent research. Developmental biologists must be patient, curious, and detailed-oriented.

Organ systems are the final level of organization in an organism. Humans, like other animals and plants, have these four levels of organization: cells, tissues, organs, and organ systems. These levels differ for different organisms. We will discuss organ systems found in the human body in Chapters 11 and 12.

Biology in Your Life

Technology:
Artificial Blood

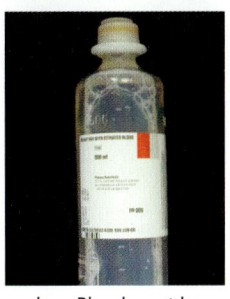

Many accident victims often need blood cells to replace those they have lost. Blood cells carry oxygen throughout the body. Quick replacement of lost blood is needed to survive. A blood transfusion can mean the difference between life and death. However, people must receive blood that matches their blood type. Supplies of donated blood sometimes run low. Blood must be refrigerated, and it does not stay fresh for long.

Researchers are now developing and testing artificial blood substitutes. These products carry oxygen to body tissues. Artificial blood products do not last a long time in the body. They help a patient survive until the person receives real blood.

Unlike real blood, artificial blood can be given to a person of any blood type. It can be stored at room temperature. Scientists think artificial blood products will soon save lives during medical emergencies.

1. What is the function of blood cells?
2. How does artificial blood differ from real blood?
3. Do you know what blood type you are? If not, how can you find out? Why might it be important to know your blood type?

CAREER CONNECTION

Invite a phlebotomist or nurse to visit the classroom and discuss the need for blood donors and the practice of safely donating blood and providing blood transfusions. If possible, have the person provide a demonstration or an explanation for determining blood type. Have students prepare questions about the training, challenges, and rewards of having a career as a phlebotomist or nurse.

ELL/ESL STRATEGY

Language Objective:
To use visuals

Have students form pairs that include both a student learning English and a student with strong English skills. Provide students with a list of the vocabulary terms in the lesson. Have students take turns describing a vocabulary term in their own words and using the term in a sentence.

Biology in Your Life

Have students read the Biology in Your Life feature about artificial blood and answer the questions at the bottom of the page. Have interested students research blood typing, blood transfusions, the history of blood banks, or dialysis to find out more about blood.

Biology in Your Life Answers

1. Blood cells carry oxygen throughout the body. **2.** Unlike real blood, artificial blood can be given to a person of any blood type. It can also be stored at room temperature. **3.** Answers may vary. Accept all reasonable responses. It is important to know your blood type in case you need a transfusion.

Lesson 4 Review Answers

1. organ system 2. cells 3. organ 4. A
5. B 6. B 7. In prokaryotes, each cell must perform all of the tasks necessary for life. In eukaryotes, different kinds of cells perform different activities. 8. An organ is a group of issues working together to perform a specific function. Organs and tissues work together within an organ system. 9. Some tissues, such as blood, are found in more than one organ system. 10. Organ systems in the body must all work together. For example, the respiratory system provides the oxygen needed by the circulatory system.

Portfolio Assessment

Sample items include:
- Paragraph from Learning Styles Visual/Spatial
- Questions prepared for the visiting phlebotomist or nurse in the Career Connection
- Lesson 4 Review answers

Lesson 4 REVIEW

Word Bank
cells
organ system
organ

On a sheet of paper, write the word or words from the Word Bank that complete each sentence correctly.

1. A(n) _____ is made up of different organs that work together to perform a specific connected tasks.
2. A tissue is a group of _____ with similar structures that work together to do a common function.
3. The heart is an example of a(n) _____.

On a sheet of paper, write the letter that answers each sentence correctly.

4. The role of epithelial cells is to _____.
   A protect parts of the body
   B break down food
   C carry oxygen
   D transmit information
5. Blood is an example of a(n) _____.
   A cell   B tissue   C organ   D organ system
6. Messages are carried to and from the brain by _____ cells.
   A muscle   B nerve   C skin   D blood

Critical Thinking

On a sheet of paper, write the answer to each of the following questions. Use complete sentences.

7. Compare the ways in which prokaryotes and eukaryotes perform the tasks necessary for life.
8. Describe the relationship among tissues, organs, and organ systems.
9. Are some tissues found in more than one organ system? Explain your answer.
10. How are organ systems in the body related to one another? Provide an example.

126 Chapter 4 Cells: The Basic Units of Life

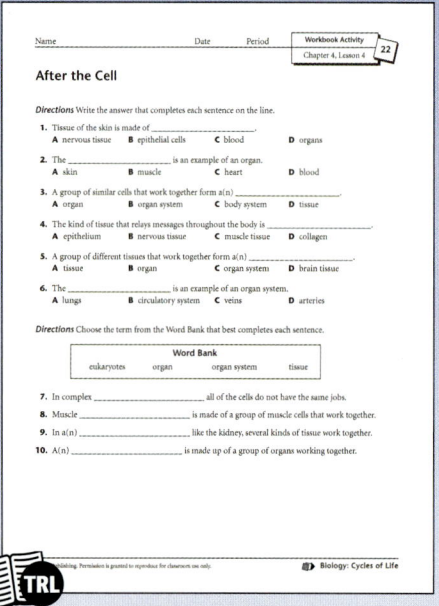

Workbook Activity 22

BIOLOGY IN THE WORLD

Stem Cells

Many diseases and injuries, such as Parkinson's disease, spinal cord injuries, and damaged heart muscle tissue, involve damage to the body's cells. Currently, many of these diseases and injuries have no cures. New technology in the area of stem cell research may offer solutions.

Stem cells are special cells that can serve as a repair system for the body. They have three properties that allow them to perform this function: 1) They can divide and renew themselves for long periods of time; 2) They do not have a specific task or function; 3) They can become specialized cells, such as muscle cells or nerve cells.

All animals, including humans, start life as one cell. This single cell divides and becomes multiple cells. In three to five days, a small number of stem cells have formed. These cells become hundreds of different kinds of cells that will make up the adult organism. Later in life, stem cells are still present in our bodies. Adult stem cells can replace damaged or worn out cells. Scientists are trying to use adult stem cells as a treatment for diseases that destroy cells.

Doctors treat people with blood diseases such as leukemia by transplanting blood-forming stem cells from bone marrow. Stem cells might be used as replacement cells to treat other conditions.

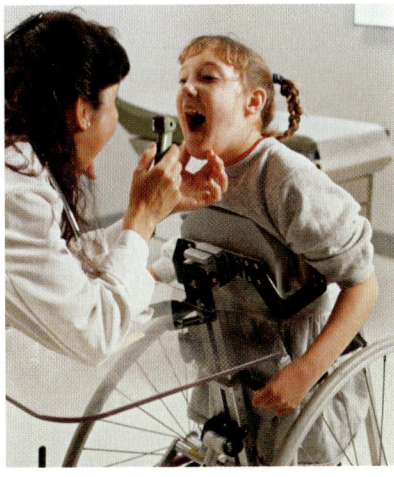

This includes diabetes, spinal cord injury, and Alzheimer's disease. Scientists have been able to cause stem cells to become nerve cells similar to those destroyed by Parkinson's disease. Someday, these nerve cells might replace damaged nerve cells, helping those who have Parkinson's disease.

1. What three properties of stem cells make them special?

2. What kinds of diseases can doctors treat with stem cells? What diseases do they hope to treat in the future?

3. What steps might a doctor take to use stem cells to treat someone who has damaged heart muscle tissue?

ONLINE CONNECTION

 Students can visit www.cellsalive.com to see images of cells that were captured for educational and medical research.

To find news articles on research and discoveries concerning structures and functions in the human body, have students click on *Human Body* at www.sciencenewsforkids.org.

BIOLOGY IN THE WORLD

Have students read the Biology in the World feature about stem cells and answer the questions at the bottom of the page. Then have students research and discuss the debate over stem-cell research in the United States. Have students answer the following questions: What social issues are brought up by the use of stem cells in disease-prevention research? What alternatives are suggested for using stem cells? Are these alternatives effective? Have students engage in a mock debate, using the information that they have gathered.

Biology in the World Answers

1. They can divide and renew themselves for long periods of time. They do not have a specific task or function. They can become specialized cells. 2. Doctors can treat blood diseases such as leukemia. They hope to treat Parkinson's disease, diabetes, spinal cord injuries, and Alzheimer's disease. 3. Sample answer: First, the stem cells would be grown in culture. Then the cells would be injected into the heart muscle. The cells would multiply and become heart muscle cells, replenishing the damaged area.

SCIENCE JOURNAL

 Have students write a letter to the editor describing their opinion and arguments for or against the use of stem cells in research. Remind them to include a description of what stem cells are and what their functions in natural systems are.

PRONUNCIATION GUIDE

Use the pronunciation shown here to help students pronounce difficult words in this lesson. Refer to the pronunciation key on the Chapter Planning Guide for the sounds of the symbols.

leukemia (lü kē′mē ə)

diabetes (dī′ə bē′tēz)

Alzheimer's (älts′hī′mərz)

Chapter 4 Summary

Have volunteers read aloud each summary item on page 128. Ask volunteers to explain the meaning of each item. Direct students' attention to the Vocabulary box on the bottom of page 128. Have them read and review each term and its definition.

Graphic Organizer

As students read Chapter 4, have them finish completing the concept map on Graphic Organizer 4: Cells: The Basic Units of Life. Encourage students to read each lesson of the chapter and then have them fill in the portion of the concept map that pertains to the lesson. When they have completed the concept map, ask them to answer the questions.

Chapter 4 SUMMARY

- Cells are the smallest units of life. The cell performs many functions necessary for life.
- Carbohydrates, lipids, proteins, and nucleic acids are macromolecules serve different roles in cells.
- Cells can be viewed through a microscope.
- The three-part cell theory sums up the role of cells. First, the cell is an organism's basic unit of structure and function. Second, all living things are made of cells. Third, cells come from other cells that are already present.
- A cell's structure determines its function. Living things maintain a biological balance with their environment. This balance is known as homeostasis.
- A cell maintains homeostasis by transporting molecules in or out through the cell's membrane.
- In the process of diffusion, solute molecules enter or exit a cell as they move from areas of high concentration to areas of low concentration.
- In the process of osmosis, water molecules enter or exit a cell depending on the concentrations of solutes inside and outside of the cell.
- A cell's selectively permeable membrane controls the molecules that enter and exit the cell. Water molecules easily cross the cell membrane.
- There are two kinds of cells, prokaryotes and eukaryotes. Prokaryotes are single-celled organisms that lack a nucleus. Eukaryotes are more complex cells. They contain a nucleus and other membrane-bound organelles.
- Complex organisms are made up of many kinds of cells. Each kind of cell has a different function. Cells with the same function work together to form a tissue.
- A tissue is a group of similar cells with a common function. An organ is a group of different tissues working together to perform specific functions. An organ system is a group of organs working together to perform related tasks.

Vocabulary

ATP, 105
binary fission, 117
cell theory, 107
circulatory system, 124
concentration, 112
concentration gradient, 113
diffusion, 112
epithelial cell, 123
equilibrium, 114
eukaryote, 117
homeostasis, 111
hormone, 105
hypertonic, 114
hypotonic, 114
isotonic, 114
microscope, 106
nervous tissue, 123
organ, 124
organ system, 124
organelle, 117
osmosis, 113
prokaryote, 116
selectively permeable membrane, 113
solute, 114
tissue, 123
transport, 112

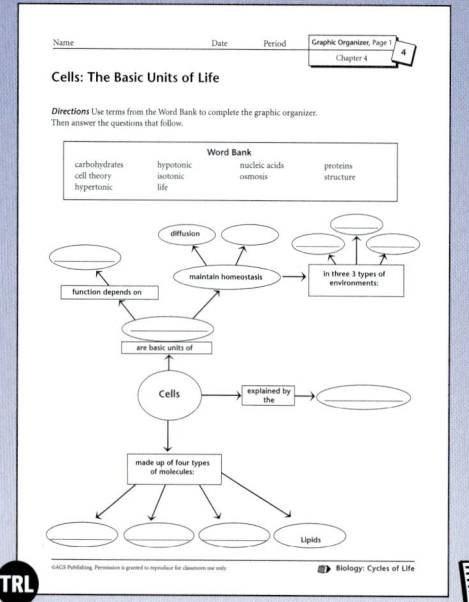

Graphic Organizer 4, pages 1–3   Workbook Activity 23, pages 1–2

Chapter 4 REVIEW

Word Bank
ATP
diffusion
equilibrium
eukaryote
homeostasis
hormone
hypertonic
hypotonic
isotonic
microscope
organ
organ system
organelle
osmosis
prokaryote
tissue

Vocabulary Review

On a sheet of paper, write the word or words from the Word Bank that complete each sentence.

1. In a(n) _____ environment, the solute concentration is equal both inside and outside of the cell.
2. A group of similar cells with similar functions is a(n) _____.
3. The movement of molecules from areas of high concentration to low concentration is called _____.
4. A(n) _____ is a cell with internal structures surrounded by membranes.
5. In a(n) _____ environment, the solute concentration is higher than elsewhere.
6. A biological balance that all organisms work to maintain is known as _____.
7. A scientist would use a(n) _____ to view cells.
8. In a(n) _____ environment, the solute concentration is lower than elsewhere.
9. A(n) _____ is a group of different tissues working together to perform specific functions.
10. The diffusion of water molecules is called _____.
11. A cell with only one outer membrane and no specific internal structures is a(n) _____.
12. A(n) _____ is a special chemical signal the body uses to direct some of its activities.
13. A state where concentrations are equal in all parts of an area is _____.
14. A group of organs that work together to perform several connected tasks is called a(n) _____.

Review continued on next page

Cells: The Basic Units of Life Chapter 4   129

Chapter 4 Review

Use the Chapter Review to prepare students for tests and to reteach content from the chapter.

Chapter 4 Mastery Test

The Teacher's Resource Library includes two forms of the Chapter 4 Mastery Test. Each test addresses the chapter Goals for Learning. An optional third page of additional critical-thinking items is included for each test. The difficulty level of the two forms is equivalent.

Review Answers

Vocabulary Review

1. isotonic 2. tissue 3. diffusion
4. eukaryote 5. hypertonic 6. homeostasis
7. microscope 8. hypotonic 9. organ
10. osmosis 11. prokaryote 12. hormone
13. equilibrium 14. organ system

Review Answers

15. ATP 16. organelle

TEACHER ALERT

In the Chapter Review, the Vocabulary Review activity includes a sample of the chapter's vocabulary terms. The activity will help determine students' understanding of key vocabulary terms and concepts presented in the chapter. Other vocabulary terms used in the chapter are listed below.

binary fission
cell theory
circulatory system
concentration
concentration gradient
epithelial cell
equilibrium
nervous tissue
selectively permeable membrane
solute
transport

Concept Review

17. D 18. B 19. C 20. C 21. A

Critical Thinking

22. In an isotonic solution, the concentrations of solute on the inside and outside of the cell are equal. The environment is said to be in equilibrium, which will enable the cells to maintain homeostasis and remain alive. 23. A salty environment is a hypertonic environment. Water molecules leave the food cells by osmosis. 24. Plant cells, animal cells, and bacteria are surrounded by an outer membrane and contain DNA. Plant cells and animal cells have a nucleus, which bacteria lack. Plant cells and animal cells divide by mitosis. Bacteria divide by binary fission. 25. Prokaryotes are able to reproduce quickly because their structure is very simple. They make copies of their DNA, then divide by binary fission.

Chapter 4 REVIEW – continued

15. The cell's main fuel source is _____.
16. A small, membrane-bound structure in a eukaryotic cell is called a(n) _____.

Concept Review

On a sheet of paper, write the answer that completes each sentence correctly.

17. Cells use diffusion and osmosis to _____.
    A make ATP C move
    B capture prey D maintain a stable environment

18. In cells, the main function of carbohydrates is to _____.
    A act as the major molecule found in membranes
    B provide energy
    C store information
    D help to make chemical reactions possible

19. Prokaryotic cells _____.
    A lack a cell membrane
    B form organs
    C reproduce by binary fission
    D have a nucleus

20. The heart, blood, arteries, and veins work together as a(n) _____.
    A tissue C organ system
    B organ D organism

21. Examples of prokaryotes are _____.
    A bacteria C mushrooms
    B plants D animals

Chapter 4 Cells: The Basic Units of Life

Chapter 4 Mastery Test A, pages 1–3

Critical Thinking

On a sheet of paper, write the answer to each of the following questions. Use complete sentences.

22. A research scientist who is collecting cells places them in an isotonic solution. Explain why the scientist does this.
23. Salt preserves certain foods by removing moisture. Why can salt be used to remove water from foods?
24. How are plant cells, animal cells, and bacteria similar? How are they different?
25. Why are prokaryotes able to reproduce quickly?

Research and Write

With a partner, interview a medical professional and prepare a report on the medical condition known as shock. Describe the causes and treatment of shock.

Test-Taking Tip Take time to organize your thoughts before answering a question that requires a written answer. Jot down notes before answering the question if necessary.

Research and Write

Before students interview the medical professional, suggest that they first research the causes and treatment of shock in order to form a list of useful questions they might ask during the interview. Suggest that students share their research with the class in the form of a written report, in an oral presentation, or as part of an informative poster.

Research and Write Answer

Shock describes the failure of the circulatory system to circulate blood. Shock most commonly occurs as a result of a massive loss of blood (for example, from extensive bleeding due to an accident or severe burns). Intravenous replacement of fluids is usually the first course of action during treatment.

ALTERNATIVE ASSESSMENT

Alternative Assessment items correlate to the student Goals for Learning at the beginning of this chapter.

- Have pairs of students explain to each other how cells serve as the basic unit of life in both prokaryotic organisms and eukaryotic organisms.
- Have students make a list of a typical cell's common activities.
- Have students draw diagrams that illustrate a cell placed in solutions that are hypertonic, hypotonic, and isotonic.
- Display labeled images of a blood cell, a nerve cell, and a muscle cell. Have students explain what these cells have in common and how they differ in the kind of functions they perform for the human body.
- Provide students with some analogies for living systems, such as a solar system, a city, a neighborhood, or a population. Have students relate the organization of the analogous system to the organization of living systems into cells, tissues, organs, and organ systems.

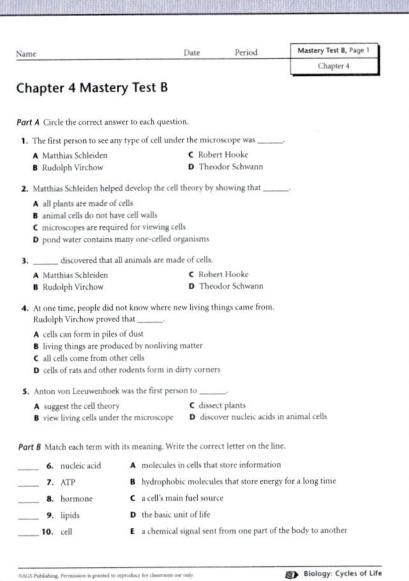

Chapter 4 Mastery Test B, pages 1–3

Chapter 5

Planning Guide
A Journey into the Eukaryotic Cell

	Student Pages	Vocabulary	Lesson Review	Critical-Thinking Questions
Lesson 1 What Are Cell Membranes?	134–137	✔	✔	✔
Lesson 2 What Do Membranes Do?	138–141	✔	✔	✔
Lesson 3 Information Organelles	142–145	✔	✔	✔
Lesson 4 Energy Organelles	146–149	✔	✔	✔
Lesson 5 The Endomembrane System	150–153	✔	✔	✔
Lesson 6 The Cytoskeleton	154–158	✔	✔	✔
Lesson 7 Plant Cells	159–163	✔	✔	✔

Chapter Activities

Teacher's Resource Library
Community Connection 5:
 Cell Organization
Graphic Organizer 5:
 Traits of Plant and Animal Cells

Teacher's Edition
Opener Activity

Assessment Options

Student Text
Chapter 5 Review

Teacher's Resource Library
Chapter 5 Mastery Tests A and B

Teacher's Edition
Chapter 5 Alternative Assessment

132A

	Student Text Features									Teaching Strategies						Learning Styles					Teacher's Resource Library			
	Achievements in Science	Science at Work	Biology in Your Life	Investigation/Discovery	Biology in the World	Express Lab	Link to	Research and Write	Technology and Society	ELL/ESL Strategy	Background Information	Science Journal	Applications (Home, Career, Community, Global, Environment)	Online Connection	Teacher Alert	Auditory/Verbal	Body/Kinesthetic	Interpersonal/Group Learning	Logical/Mathematical	Visual/Spatial	Workbook Activities	Alternative Workbook Activities	Lab Manual	Self-Study Guide
						135				136	134				135, 136	137					24	24	21	✔
			140							139	138	140	140						141		25	25		✔
							✔	143	143	145	142	144	144								26	26		✔
	148						✔			147	146							149			27	27		✔
		150					✔		151	152	150		152		152						28	28	22	✔
					157					156	154		155							155	29	29	23–24	✔
				161	163				167	159	159		163	163				160			30–31	30–31	25	✔

Pronunciation Key

a	hat	e	let	ī	ice	ô	order	ů	put	sh	she	ə { a in about
ā	age	ē	equal	o	hot	oi	oil	ü	rule	th	thin	e in taken
ä	far	ėr	term	ō	open	ou	out	ch	child	ŦH	then	i in pencil
â	care	i	it	ȯ	saw	u	cup	ng	long	zh	measure	o in lemon
												u in circus

Alternative Workbook Activities

The Teacher's Resource Library (TRL) contains a set of lower-level worksheets called Alternative Workbook Activities. These worksheets cover the same content as the regular Workbook Activities but are written at a second-grade reading level.

Skill Track Online

Use Skill Track Online for *Biology: Cycles of Life* to monitor student progress and meet the demands of adequate yearly progress (AYP). Make informed instructional decisions with individual student and class reports of online lesson and chapter assessments. With immediate and ongoing feedback, students will also see what they have learned and where they need more reinforcement and practice.

Chapter at a Glance

Chapter 5:
A Journey into the Eukaryotic Cell
pages 132–167

Lessons

1. What Are Cell Membranes?
   pages 134–137

2. What Do Membranes Do?
   pages 138–141

3. Information Organelles
   pages 142–145

4. Energy Organelles
   pages 146–149

5. The Endomembrane System
   pages 150–153

6. The Cytoskeleton
   pages 154–158

   Investigation 5
   pages 157–158

7. Plant Cells
   pages 159–163

   Discovery Investigation 5
   pages 161–162

   Biology in the World page 163

Chapter 5 Summary page 164

Chapter 5 Review pages 165–167

Audio CD 🎧

Skill Track Online
for Biology: Cycles of Life

Teacher's Resource Library (TRL)

Workbook Activities 24–31

Alternative Workbook Activities 24–31

Lab Manual 21–25

Community Connection 5

Graphic Organizer 5

Resource File 9–10

Chapter 5 Self-Study Guide

Chapter 5 Mastery Tests A and B

(Answer Keys for the Teacher's Resource Library begin on page 675 of the Teacher's Edition. The Materials List for the Lab Manual activities begins on page 720.)

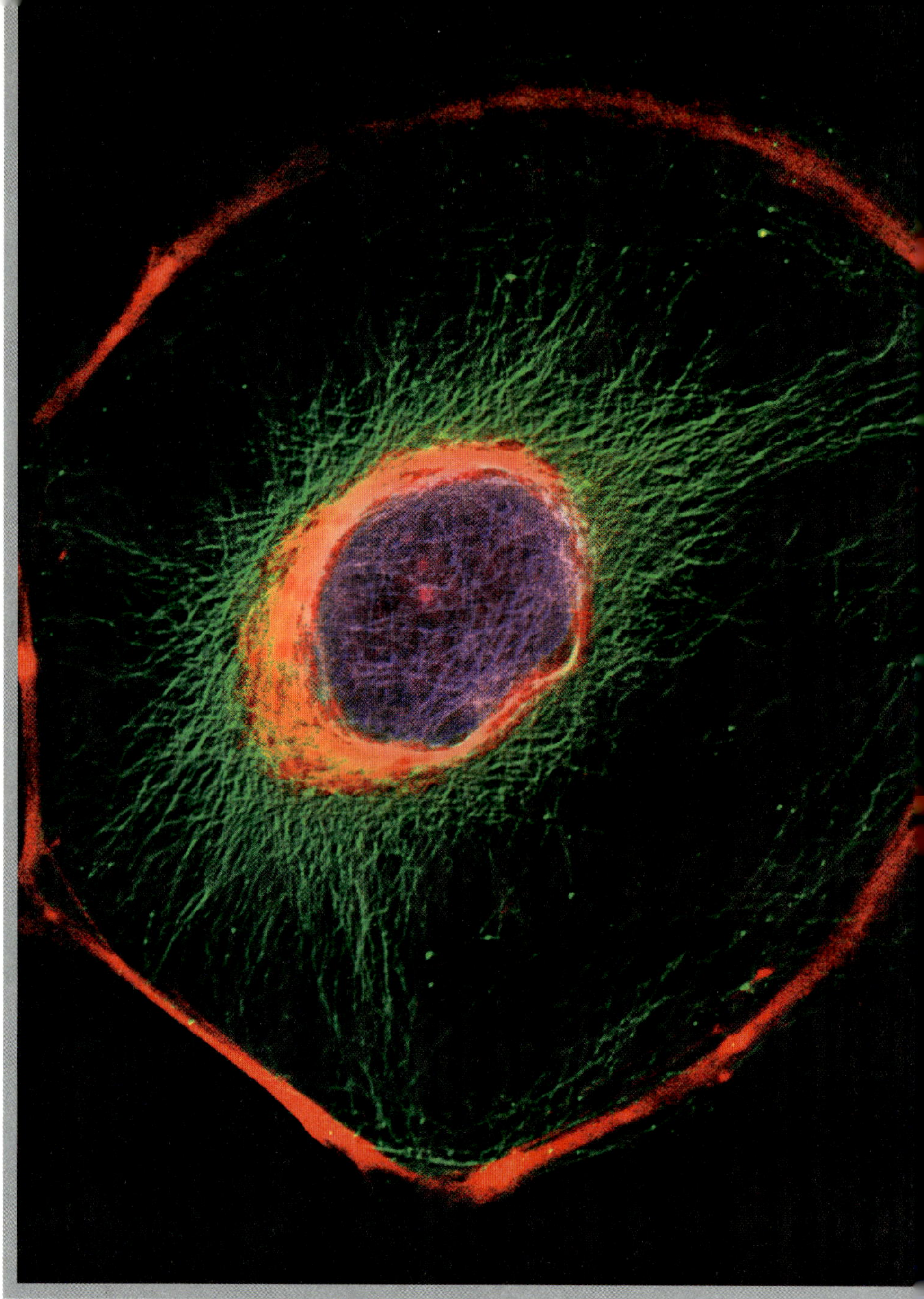

Opener Activity

Display drawings, photographs, posters, or prepared slides of eukaryotic cells. Have students describe what they see. As students read the chapter, let them refer back to these items to reinforce what they are reading.

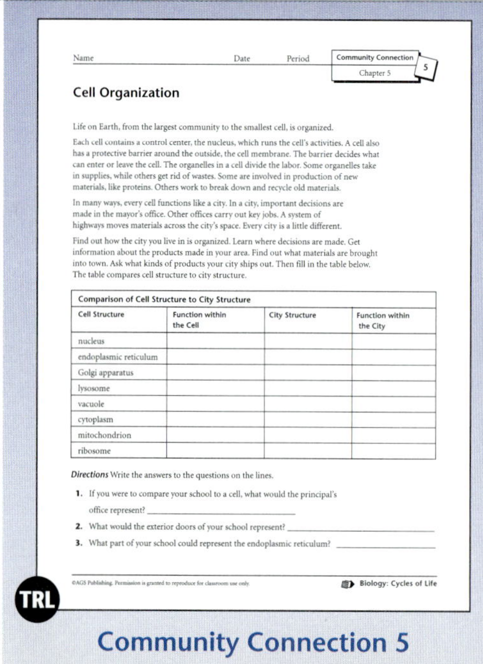

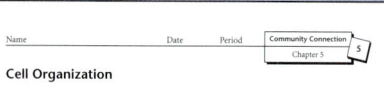

Community Connection 5

Chapter 5
A Journey into the Eukaryotic Cell

The object in the photograph may look like something you would see in outer space. However, this is a cell from a mouse. Notice all the structures that make up the cell. Animal cells contain the same types of structures. Plant cells have structures that are different from animal cells. In Chapter 5, you will learn about the many structures in cells. You will also find out how materials move within, through, and around cells.

Organize Your Thoughts

Eukaryotic cells have membranes.
- Plasma membrane outside cell
  - Controls transport
  - Supports signal pathways
  - Provides support and protection
- Membranes create
  - Information organelles
  - Factory organelles
  - Energy organelles
  - Support organelles

Goals for Learning

- ◆ To identify the structure and activities of cell membranes
- ◆ To describe information organelles
- ◆ To describe energy organelles
- ◆ To understand the endomembrane system
- ◆ To describe the cytoskeleton
- ◆ To identify plant cell structures and functions

Introducing the Chapter

Have students write the headings *What I Know, What I Want to Know,* and *What I Learned* across the top of a sheet of paper. Then have them write statements under the first two headings about the following subtopics: cell membranes, information organelles, energy organelles, the endomembrane system, cytoskeleton, and plant cells. As students read the lessons, they can add statements under the third heading.

As a class, read aloud the Goals for Learning. Encourage students to add more statements to the chart they just made. Answer any questions that students may have about the Goals for Learning.

Notes and Math Tips

Ask volunteers to read the notes and math tips that appear in the margins throughout the chapter. Then discuss them with the class.

TEACHER'S RESOURCE

The AGS Publishing Teaching Strategies in Science Transparencies may be used with this chapter. The transparencies add an interactive dimension to expand and enhance the *Biology: Cycles of Life* program content.

CAREER INTEREST INVENTORY

The AGS Publishing Harrington-O'Shea Career Decision-Making System-Revised (CDM) may be used with this chapter. Students can use the CDM to explore their interests and identify careers. The CDM defines career areas that are indicated by students' responses on the inventory.

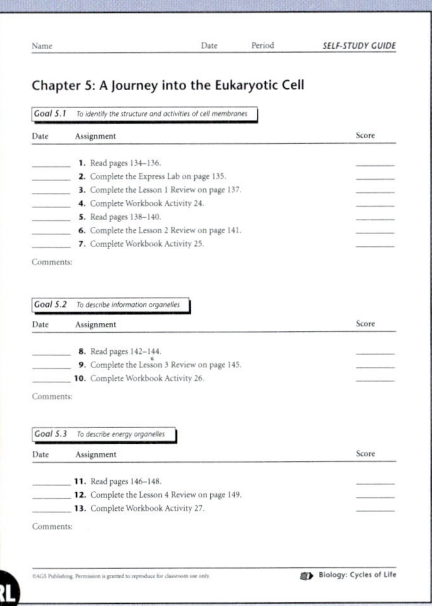

Chapter 5 Self-Study Guide

Lesson at a Glance

Chapter 5 Lesson 1

Overview In this lesson, students learn the internal structure of plant and animal cells.

Objectives
- To explain the bilayer structure of cellular membranes
- To identify the function of other molecules found in a cellular membrane
- To describe a cell's inside environment

Student Pages 134–137

Teacher's Resource Library

Workbook Activity 24
Alternative Workbook Activity 24
Lab Manual 21
Resource File 9

Vocabulary
bilayer
cytoplasm
cytosol
extracellular matrix
fluid mosaic model
plasma membrane
transport protein

Have students use a dictionary to find the meanings of the vocabulary terms and the prefixes *bi-*, *trans-*, and *extra-*. Then ask students to write a paragraph that uses each of the terms.

Background Information
The cell membrane controls what enters and leaves the cell and provides protection and support for the cell. The cell membrane is composed of two lipid layers, hence the term *lipid bilayer* or *bilayer*. In addition to lipids, many cell membranes contain proteins embedded in the membrane. Often carbohydrates are attached to the proteins. These proteins and carbohydrates help control what enters and leaves the cell.

Lesson 1: What Are Cell Membranes?

Objectives
After reading this lesson, you should be able to
- explain the bilayer structure of cellular membranes
- identify the function of other molecules found in a cellular membrane
- describe a cell's inside environment

Bilayer
Two layers

As you learned in Chapter 4, eukaryotic cells are more complex than prokaryotic cells. For example, eukaryotic cells contain organelles. Organelles are surrounded by membranes that perform special functions. Both cell and organelle membranes are important in determining what a cell does. Membranes control the activities of a cell. Understanding the structure of membranes will help you understand how membranes control cell activities.

Cell Membrane Structure

Cell membranes are made of phospholipids. Remember that a phospholipid is a lipid molecule with a head and a tail. The head is a phosphate group (PO_4) joined to a glycerol molecule. The phosphate group has a negative charge. The head of the molecule is polar and hydrophilic (water-loving). The tail of a phospholipid is made of two fatty acid chains attached to the same glycerol molecule. The fatty acids have no charge. They are nonpolar and hydrophobic (water-hating).

Look at Figure 5.1.1. When phospholipids pack together, the polar heads interact with each other. The nonpolar tails also interact with each other. The phospholipids form a **bilayer,** or two layers. In the bilayer, the hydrophilic heads move to the outside of the layer. The hydrophobic tails move to the inside. This phospholipid bilayer is called a membrane.

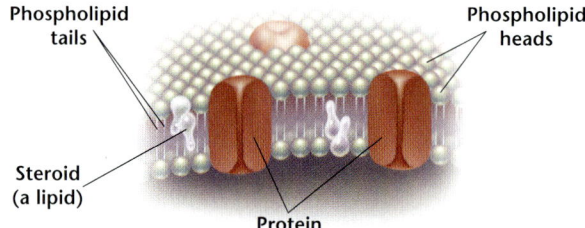

Figure 5.1.1 *Cell membranes are made of two layers of phospholipids.*

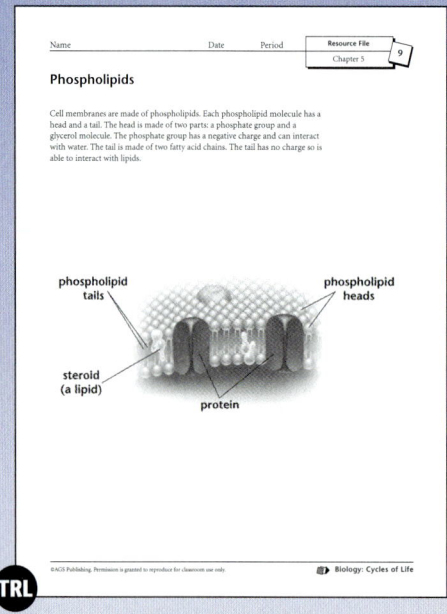

Resource File 9

Cell Membrane Function

The hydrophilic outside of a membrane allows cells and organelles to interact with their fluid environments. The inside of a membrane is a divider for the cell. The chemical nature of the membrane limits the size and type of molecules that can cross it. Because of this characteristic, the membrane is selectively permeable. Remember that a selectively permeable membrane allows some molecules to pass. It blocks other molecules from coming through. The membrane that surrounds a cell and separates it from the environment is called the **plasma membrane.**

Plasma membrane
The membrane that surrounds a cell and separates it from the environment

Express Lab 5

Materials
- safety goggles
- lab coat or apron
- medium-sized beaker
- warm tap water
- vegetable oil

Procedure
1. Put on safety goggles and a lab coat or apron.
2. Fill the beaker about one-quarter full of water. **Safety Alert: Be careful when working with glassware.**
3. Add vegetable oil until the beaker is about half full of liquid.
4. Observe the liquids in the beaker. Gently tilt the beaker back and forth. Observe how the liquids respond to the motion.

Analysis
1. Which liquid is like the head of a phospholipid? Which liquid is like the tail?
2. How did the liquids respond when you tilted the beaker sideways? How is this similar to a plasma membrane?

1 Warm-Up Activity

Have students perform the Express Lab. Ask students: What is an everyday example of an oil-and-water mixture? *(vinegar and oil salad dressing; vinegar contains mostly water)* Ask students to describe how the water and oil mix. *(They do not mix; they form separate layers.)*

Express Lab Answers

1. The water is similar to the polar head, and the vegetable oil is similar to the nonpolar tail. 2. The layers stay separated no matter what motion occurs. This accurately represents the fluid mosaic model of the plasma membrane, which allows motion and shifting while still maintaining the layers.

2 Teaching the Lesson

As students read the lesson, have them write down the main ideas from each paragraph. Encourage them to ask questions about any concept they do not understand. Then have students add any additional information that helps them understand the concept.

Go through the lesson as a class. Have volunteers explain the concepts in each paragraph. Clear up any misconceptions that students may have.

3 Reinforce and Extend

TEACHER ALERT

To help students understand the concept of selectively permeable, tell them that the cell membrane is similar to a window screen. It is selectively permeable because it will allow air through, but it does not allow most insects through.

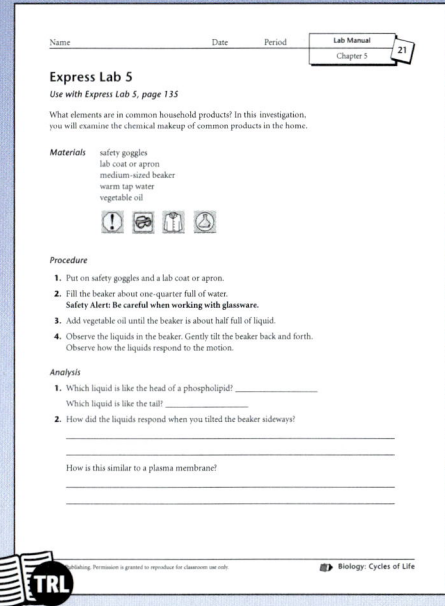

ELL/ESL Strategy

Language Objective:
To compare a mosaic to a cell membrane

Have students research what a mosaic is. Then have them write a paragraph comparing a cell membrane to a mosaic. Encourage students to share their comparisons with the class and to use photographs and drawings with their presentation.

Teacher Alert

Lipids are large molecules composed of glycerol and three fatty acids. If one of the fatty acids is replaced by a phosphate group, there will be a phospholipid. A phospholipid consists of a glycerol attached to two fatty acids and a phosphate group. The cellular membrane is composed of two layers of these phospholipids.

Lab Activities

Chapter 5 has Investigation and Discovery Investigation lab activities. Two additional lab activities for Chapter 5 appear in the Biology: Cycles of Life Lab Manual and on the Teacher's Resource Library CD-ROM.

Fluid mosaic model
A plasma membrane model where proteins float freely through the phospholipid bilayer

Transport protein
A protein in the plasma membrane that helps move molecules across the membrane

Extracellular matrix
A sticky coating outside the plasma membrane of animal cells that joins cells together

Cytoplasm
The area inside a cell; contains organelles and cytosol

Cytosol
The fluid base of the cytoplasm; contains molecules used and made by the cell

Although the plasma membrane is selectively permeable, many different molecules can enter and leave the cell. These molecules are often helped by proteins in the plasma membrane. Some membrane proteins are on one side of the membrane. Others stretch across the entire width of the membrane. Some membrane proteins stay in one place. Others float around and through the membrane. The plasma membrane shifts constantly. Phospholipids and proteins move around together. This model of the plasma membrane is called the **fluid mosaic model.** Proteins in the plasma membrane that help molecules to cross are called **transport proteins.** We will discuss the function of transport proteins in Lesson 2.

Extra Cellular Matrix

Animal cells have another layer on the outside of the plasma membrane. This layer is called the **extracellular matrix.** It is a sticky coating made and given off by animal cells. The extracellular matrix keeps cells joined together. It allows them to pass molecules between them. Fibers in this layer connect cells to each other. Those fibers are also connected to the interior of the cell. These connections help similar cells in similar tissues act together.

Inside the Plasma Membrane

Eukaryotic cells contain organelles bound by membranes. These membranes have the same structure as the plasma membrane. They function in the same way because they control the activities of the individual organelles. Organelles process information and energy for the cell. They also provide support and movement.

Inside the cell, organelles float in an area called the **cytoplasm.** Cytoplasm is made of organelles and a fluid called **cytosol.** Cytosol is a water-based mixture of molecules the cell needs. Molecules made by the cell and molecules taken in by the cell move throughout the cytoplasm. Organelles in the cell use or change these molecules.

Lesson 1 REVIEW

On a sheet of paper, write the letter of the answer to complete each sentence correctly.

1. The fluid mosaic model describes _____.
   A the extracellular matrix
   B the movement of proteins in and out of the cell
   C the plasma membrane
   D the organization of organelles in the cytoplasm

2. The characteristics that best describe the tail of a phospholipid molecule are _____.
   A neutral charge, nonpolar, and hydrophobic
   B neutral charge, polar, and hydrophobic
   C negative charge, polar, and hydrophilic
   D negative charge, nonpolar, and hydrophobic

3. The organelles and fluid in a cell together make up the _____.
   A cytosol   B plasma   C cytoplasm   D matrix

On a sheet of paper, write the word or words to complete each statement correctly.

4. Unlike prokaryotic cells, eukaryotic cells contain _____.
5. The plasma membrane is _____ permeable.
6. The extracellular matrix is on the outside of the _____.

Critical Thinking

On a sheet of paper, write the answers to the following questions. Use complete sentences.

7. Describe the functions of the plasma membrane.
8. What might happen if a cell's plasma membrane is not partially hydrophobic?
9. Why do cells need a hydrophilic part to the plasma membrane?
10. What is the function of cytosol in a cell?

A Journey into the Eukaryotic Cell Chapter 5

Lesson 1 Review Answers

1. C 2. A 3. C 4. organelles 5. selectively 6. plasma membrane 7. The plasma membrane covers the outside of eukaryotic cells and their organelles. Plasma membranes determine which proteins and molecules go in and out of cells and organelles. 8. Water could rush into the cell, causing it to burst. 9. The hydrophilic outside of the plasma membrane allows the cell to come into contact with watery solutions that contain nutrients and other materials that the cell needs. 10. Cytosol is the medium that suspends the organelles and carries the molecules needed by the cell and its organelles.

Portfolio Assessment

Sample items include:
- Express Lab answers
- Paragraphs comparing cell membranes to mosaics
- Lesson 1 Review answers

LEARNING STYLES

Auditory/Verbal
Auditory learners may benefit from listening to an audio CD of this lesson. Many of the concepts are complex. If an audio CD is not available, assign pairs of students to work together. Each student can read a paragraph to the other. Allow students to discuss the content.

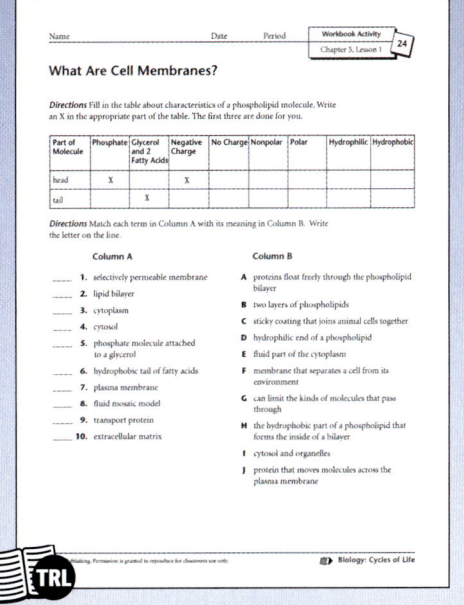

Workbook Activity 24

Lesson at a Glance

Chapter 5 Lesson 2

Overview In this lesson, students learn about how molecules are moved across the plasma membrane.

Objectives

- To compare active and passive transport
- To compare exocytosis and endocytosis
- To list ways animal cells are joined

Student Pages 138–141

Teacher's Resource Library

Workbook Activity 25
Alternative Workbook Activity 25

Vocabulary

active transport	facilitated diffusion
endocytosis	gap junction
exocytosis	passive transport

Create a word search puzzle with the vocabulary terms from this lesson. Have students work together to solve the puzzle.

Background Information

Cells must move substances in and out of the cell to maintain homeostasis. Four ways in which cells move molecules across the plasma membrane are active transport, passive transport, endocytosis, and exocytosis. Passive transport is the only one that does not require the cell to expend energy. Endocytosis and exocytosis are used when large particles must be moved across the plasma membrane. Endocytosis is the movement of substances inside the cell. Exocytosis is the movement of substances outside the cell. Both endocytosis and exocytosis involve surrounding the particle with a plasma membrane. Then the plasma membrane disconnects itself from the primary plasma membrane. It encapsulates the particle in the separated plasma membrane.

138 Chapter 5

Lesson 2 What Do Membranes Do?

Objectives

After reading this lesson, you should be able to
- compare active and passive transport
- compare exocytosis and endocytosis
- list ways animal cells are joined

Passive transport
The movement of molecules across a membrane when the movement requires no energy

Facilitated diffusion
Passive transport that involves membrane proteins

Active transport
The movement of molecules across a membrane when the movement requires energy

The plasma membrane's main function is to control how molecules enter and leave the cell. Some molecules are small enough or have a certain chemical nature so they can cross the plasma membrane. They cross by diffusion. Remember that diffusion is the movement of molecules from an area of high concentration to an area of low concentration.

Diffusion, also called **passive transport,** does not need energy. A cell does not use ATP for diffusion and osmosis (the diffusion of water). Molecules that diffuse across a membrane follow their concentration gradient. They move from a high concentration to a low concentration.

Some molecules have shapes that do not allow them to naturally diffuse. However, they do not require ATP to be transported. These molecules experience **facilitated diffusion.** This type of passive transport uses membrane proteins to help molecules across. The proteins act in one of two ways. One way is when proteins open up a channel in the membrane, like a hole. The channel allows molecules to travel across. The second way is when proteins bind to a specific molecule on one side. Then the membrane opens on the other side to release the specific molecule.

Cells need molecules that cannot passively cross the membrane. To get these molecules, cells perform **active transport.** Active transport is when a cell uses energy to bring a molecule across its membrane. Cells use ATP, the energy molecule, as the fuel for active transport. Transport proteins inside the plasma membrane are involved in active transport.

These proteins use ATP to attach molecules to themselves and then change shape. The proteins push the molecules through the membrane. Transport proteins need energy because the molecules are moving against their concentration gradient. They are going from a low concentration to a high concentration.

138 Chapter 5 A Journey into the Eukaryotic Cell

Endocytosis
A process in which a cell membrane surrounds and encloses a substance to bring the substance into the cell

Exocytosis
A process in which a substance is released from a cell through a pouch that transports the substance to the cell surface

Sometimes a cell needs to move substances that are too large for transport proteins to handle. The plasma membrane must change its structure to move these substances. The cell uses two processes to do this. One process is to digest needed substances. The other process is to get rid of unwanted substances.

Endocytosis is the process a cell uses to bring large substances inside the cell. Figure 5.2.1 shows this process. The plasma membrane folds inward to surround the substances. The plasma membrane then pinches off the newly formed package. The cell moves the package to where it is needed inside.

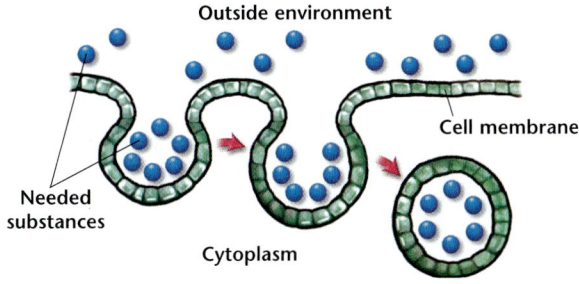

Figure 5.2.1 *Cells use endocytosis to bring in large substances.*

The reverse of this process is **exocytosis**. Figure 5.2.2 shows the process of exocytosis. A cell removes unwanted substances by packing them into a membrane. The cell moves this package to the plasma membrane. The two membranes fuse together. Then the cell pushes the waste outside of the cell.

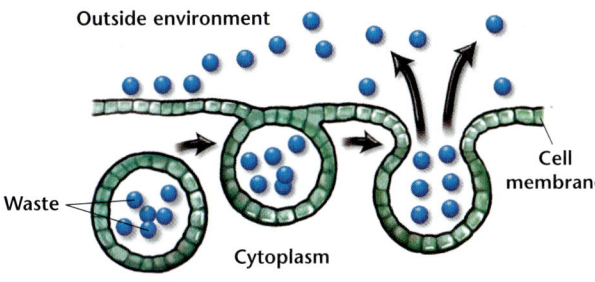

Figure 5.2.2 *Cells use exocytosis to get rid of waste.*

1 Warm-Up Activity

Have students discuss why they think it is important for cell membranes to control what enters and leaves the cell. *(The cell membranes must control what enters and leaves the cell to keep the cell healthy.)* Ask students: What types of things enter and leave the cell? *(Food or energy sources and waste products will enter and leave the cell.)*

2 Teaching the Lesson

Ask volunteers to read aloud each paragraph in the lesson. Discuss the main ideas in each paragraph. Clarify any misconceptions that students may have about the content. Have students write down the main ideas from each paragraph.

Fill a plastic bag with partially set gelatin. Explain to students that the plastic bag acts like a cell membrane. The plastic bag controls what enters and leaves the bag just as the cell membrane controls what enters and leaves the cell. Explain to students that the cell membrane can open and close, allowing particles to enter and leave the cell.

3 Reinforce and Extend

ELL/ESL STRATEGY

Language Objective: *To explain each vocabulary word, using images*

Have students create an illustrated glossary. Students should first write a vocabulary word and its definition on a sheet of paper. (Students may write the definition in English and in their native language.) Then instruct students to draw an illustration that helps to explain the meaning of the word. Have them create a page for each vocabulary term in the lesson.

Biology in Your Life

Bring several antibacterial products to class for students to view. Bring only over-the-counter products, not prescription drugs. Encourage students to read the labels to see if the product contains triclosan. Ask volunteers to read aloud the feature on antibacterial products. Then ask students: Why is it important that we use antibacterial products sparingly? *(Some bacteria are becoming resistant to antibacterial products.)*

Biology in Your Life Answers

1. Antibiotic drugs work to kill bacterial cells directly or to stop them from reproducing. **2.** Triclosan blocks the active site and prevents the cell from manufacturing fats. **3.** Some ways to keep antibiotics working are to take them only when necessary and to not use antibacterial soap when regular soap will do.

SCIENCE JOURNAL

Ask students to write a paragraph that describes a situation in which they may want to use an antibacterial product in their home.

IN THE COMMUNITY

Food preparation is one area in which it is important to keep unwanted bacteria growth under control. Invite the supervisor of the school cafeteria or a local health inspector to make a presentation to the class. Ask the visitor to share what precautions are taken in cafeterias and restaurants to ensure the food is safe to eat. Ask the visitor to give tips about how students can prepare foods that are free of contamination.

Gap junction
Connections between cells made for support and communication

The plasma membrane also helps cells communicate with each other. Carbohydrates on the outside of the plasma membrane act as signals. Cells use these signals to recognize each other. Cells with the same markers stick together and eventually work together as a tissue. When this happens, the plasma membranes form **gap junctions.** Gap junctions are connections between cells made for support and communication. Cells send messages back and forth through gap junctions.

Biology in Your Life

Consumer Choices: Antibacterial Products

You probably have several cleaning products or medicines in your home that are antibacterial or antibiotic. The prefix *anti-* means "against" or "preventing." These products work by destroying cells. Doctors may prescribe antibiotic drugs for bacterial infections. Antibiotics are important weapons against deadly bacterial diseases such as tuberculosis, a lung disease. Antibiotics work in two ways. They cause problems with the cell walls of bacteria, which kills the bacteria. They can also stop bacteria from reproducing.

Most antibacterial soaps and cleaning products contain a chemical called triclosan. Triclosan works by finding active sites on an important enzyme in bacterial and fungal cells. A fungus is an organism that usually has many cells and decomposes material for its food. When triclosan blocks this active site, the cell cannot make some fats it needs to survive.

Many health professionals think antibiotics should be used as little as possible. The more we use them, the less likely they are to work. That is because some bacteria no longer react to the antibiotics.

Instead, they reproduce quickly and create new strains of bacteria that do not react to the antibiotics. Antibiotics do not work on viruses, which cause many common illnesses. Many health professionals also think antibacterial soaps are not necessary. They say washing with regular soap and warm water removes bacteria. Not all bacteria harm humans. Antibiotics and antibacterial products destroy both good and bad bacteria.

1. In what ways do antibiotic drugs work to stop bacteria?
2. How does triclosan in antibacterial cleaning products destroy bacterial cells?
3. What can you do to keep antibiotics working?

Chapter 5 A Journey into the Eukaryotic Cell

PRONUNCIATION GUIDE

Use the pronunciation shown here to help students pronounce difficult words in this lesson. Refer to the pronunciation key on the Chapter Planning Guide for the sounds of the symbols.

antibacterial (an′ti bak tir′ē əl)

triclosan (trī klō′san′)

Lesson 2 REVIEW

Word Bank
active transport
facilitated diffusion
passive transport

On a sheet of paper, write the words from the Word Bank that complete each statement correctly.

1. The type of cellular transport that uses proteins for movement, but not ATP, is called _____.
2. The type of cellular transport that does not use proteins or ATP is called _____.
3. The type of cellular transport that uses ATP and transport proteins is called _____.

On a sheet of paper, write the word or words to complete each statement correctly.

4. The process of removing waste from a cell by fusing the membranes is called _____.
5. Cells communicate with other cells through _____.
6. The process called _____ is used to bring substances into a cell.

Critical Thinking

On a sheet of paper, write the answers to the following questions. Use complete sentences.

7. Describe how facilitated diffusion works.
8. When does a cell need to use energy to transport a molecule across the plasma membrane?
9. Explain how the plasma membrane helps cells communicate with each other.
10. How would the transport abilities of your body's cells be affected if you did not eat properly?

Lesson 2 Review Answers

1. facilitated diffusion 2. passive transport 3. active transport 4. exocytosis 5. gap junctions 6. endocytosis 7. Facilitated diffusion works by either opening up a hole in the membrane, allowing the molecule to pass, or by attaching to a molecule and creating an opening on the other side. 8. Proteins must use energy when a molecule is passing from an area of low concentration to an area of high concentration. 9. The plasma membrane helps cells communicate with each other by using carbohydrates outside of the plasma membrane. The carbohydrates act as signals for cells to recognize each other. Cells with the same markers stick together and form gap junctions, which are connections between cells for support and communication. Cells send messages back and forth through gap junctions. 10. The cells in your body might lack the proper proteins to transport molecules. If you are not eating enough nourishing food, your body may lack the energy, or ATP, to perform active transport.

Portfolio Assessment

Sample items include:
- List of main ideas from each paragraph
- Illustrated glossary from ELL/ESL Strategy
- Graphic organizer from Learning Styles Logical/Mathematical
- Lesson 2 Review answers

LEARNING STYLES

Logical/Mathematical

Have students create their own graphic organizer of the material in this lesson. The graphic organizer should contain all of the lesson objectives. Students should share their graphic organizers with the class.

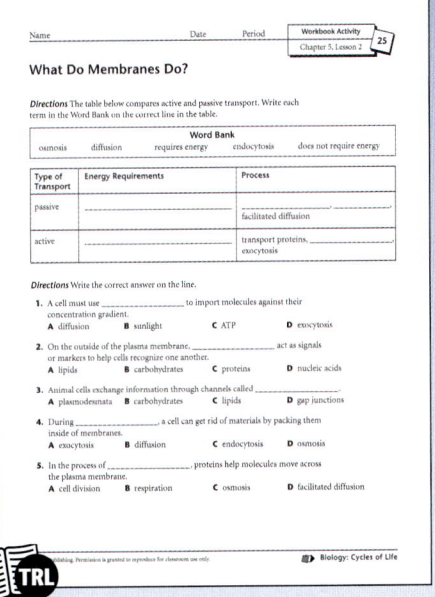

Workbook Activity 25

Lesson at a Glance

Chapter 5 Lesson 3

Overview In this lesson, students learn about information organelles such as the nucleus, the nucleolus, and ribosomes.

Objectives
- To identify the nucleus of a cell
- To describe structures found in the nucleus
- To explain the structure and function of ribosomes
- To discuss how the nucleus directs cell activities

Student Pages 142–145

Teacher's Resource Library TRL
Workbook Activity 26
Alternative Workbook Activity 26

Vocabulary

chromosome   nucleolus
genome   pore
nuclear envelope   ribosome

Discuss the meaning of each vocabulary term with students. Have students write sentences using each term.

Background Information

The nucleus contains the coded instructions for making proteins and other important particles. Proteins are assembled at the ribosomes of a cell. The nucleolus is where the assembly of ribosomes begins.

Warm-Up Activity

Ask students: Who controls all of the scheduling of activities, classes, and programs in the school? *(the central office, principal's office, or main office)* Tell students that the nucleus of a cell is similar to this office. The nucleus is the control center of the cell. The nucleus contains the DNA, which holds the instructions for making an organism.

Lesson 3 Information Organelles

Objectives

After reading this lesson, you should be able to
- identify the nucleus of a cell
- describe structures found in the nucleus
- explain the structure and function of ribosomes
- discuss how the nucleus directs cell activities

The rest of this chapter will look at the structure and function of various organelles in eukaryotic cells. One group of organelles controls information in the cell.

The Nucleus

The major organelle that controls information in the cell is the nucleus. It is the largest organelle in a eukaryotic cell. If you look at a cell under a microscope, the nucleus is a large, dark circle. It is surrounded by a membrane called the **nuclear envelope**. This membrane is a bilayer with holes, called **pores**, in it. Pores in the nuclear envelope help the nucleus send and receive messages inside the cell.

Inside the nucleus is a ball of fibers called the **nucleolus**. The nucleolus makes an information organelle called the **ribosome**. Figure 5.3.1 shows a eukaryotic cell and its nucleus.

Nuclear envelope
The membrane surrounding the nucleus of a cell

Pore
A hole in the nuclear envelope used to send and receive messages

Nucleolus
A ball of fibers in the nucleus that makes ribosomes

Ribosome
An information organelle that uses the instructions in DNA to make a protein

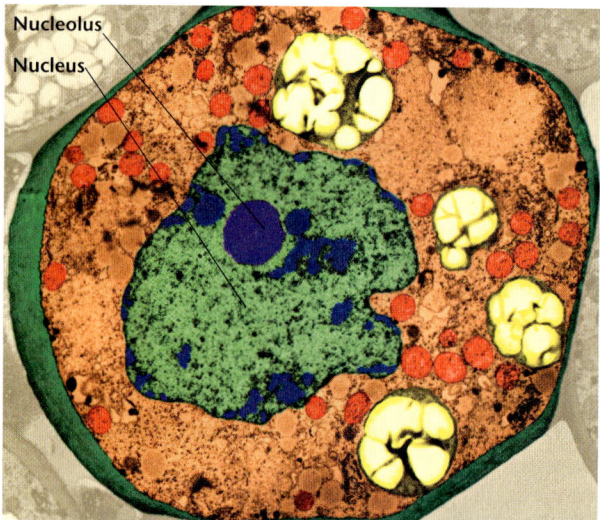

Figure 5.3.1 *The nucleus is the largest organelle in a eukaryotic cell.*

142 Chapter 5 *A Journey into the Eukaryotic Cell*

Genome
The entire DNA found in a cell

Chromosome
A structure in the nucleus made of individual DNA molecules folded and coiled together with proteins

If the DNA found in one human cell was laid out in one long molecule, it would be about three feet long.

Research and Write

Use the Internet to research DNA mutations. Create a chart listing the activities or materials that cause mutations and the health problems that occur as a result.

The nucleus of a cell acts like the control center. That is because an organism's entire DNA is inside the nucleus. DNA is a double strand of nucleic acid that contains all the directions to make an organism. The entire DNA for an organism is called its **genome.**

How does DNA fit inside a cell's nucleus? First, an organism's DNA in the nucleus is in separate molecules called **chromosomes.** Chromosomes are structures made of DNA and proteins. The proteins bind the DNA molecule and help it fold and coil to become smaller.

This folding is the second reason why DNA fits into a small space. Each chromosome is one molecule of DNA. Many different sets of instructions can be in that DNA molecule. Each chromosome contains different sections called genes. A gene is a specific sequence in DNA that carries instructions to make a specific protein. The proteins made from genes make an organism unique. One way to understand an organism's DNA is to think of it as a set of books. Each chromosome is a book. Each gene is a specific sentence in a book.

Ribosomes

Other information organelles in eukaryotic cells are ribosomes. Ribosomes make proteins from the directions found in DNA. Ribosomes are made from a combination of RNA and other proteins. Remember that RNA is a single strand of nucleic acid made with a different sugar molecule than DNA.

Technology and Society

Scientists use a variety of microscopes to look at cells. Electron microscopes allow scientists to observe cells and their organelles. Electron microscopes work by shooting beams of electrons onto a sample to create an image. Using electrons instead of light allows scientists to see microscopic images in finer detail than ever before. This has allowed scientists to make great progress in their research, especially in the field of medicine.

A Journey into the Eukaryotic Cell Chapter 5

Teaching the Lesson

Divide the class into small groups. Have each student in the group pick a section from the lesson. Tell students to first read aloud their chosen section and then explain it to the other members of their group.

Have each student make a large illustration of a cell. Tell students to label all of the components that are mentioned in this lesson. Below the illustration or on another sheet of paper, students should describe what each component does. Check students' illustrations and descriptions to make sure they have included all of the information from this lesson.

Reinforce and Extend

Research and Write

Have students read the directions for their project in the Research and Write feature. Tell them that the Internet contains a variety of sources for information and therefore they need to be sure the Web sites they use are reliable. Suggest that students use the National Institutes of Health Web site at www.nih.gov.

Technology and Society

Have a volunteer read aloud the Technology and Society feature. Have students do research and create a time line showing when various types of microscopes were invented. Tell students to provide a brief description of each type of microscope. Allow students to present their time lines to the class.

Link to

Math. Have students read the Link to Math feature. The surface area to volume ratio of a cell is a limiting factor in the size of the cell. As the size of a cell increases, the volume increases at a much larger rate than the surface area of the cell. In this case, the plasma membrane would not have enough surface area through which oxygen, nutrients, and wastes must pass. As a result, the cell would either starve from lack of nutrients or die because of toxic buildup of wastes.

Science Journal

Have students write a paragraph explaining the link between improving microscope technology and our understanding of how a cell works.

Global Connection

Biologists from many universities and organizations are working together to map the genomes of many species. Biologists are seeking a better understanding of the evolution of organisms and the cause for diseases that genetically pass from generation to generation. Information is shared by biologists around the world.

Have small groups work together to locate where this research is taking place. Have them mark the locations of the countries on a globe or world map.

Math Tip

The human genome is made up of a total of 46 chromosomes. You inherited 23 chromosomes from your mother and 23 chromosomes from your father.

Link to ▸▸▸
Math

Cells are limited in size. As a cell's outside area increases, the volume inside increases at a much larger rate. Doubling or tripling the size of a cell requires vast amounts of cellular material. Creating too much volume would make it hard for a cell to work. So most cells are very small.

Ribosomes are found throughout the cell. Ribosomes float freely in the cell or attach to other organelles. They help interpret the instructions found in the genes of a cell. Ribosomes use the sequences of DNA and RNA as a guide. Ribosomes then put together individual amino acids to make a protein. Since a cell is always making many different proteins, large numbers of ribosomes are inside a cell. The small red dots in Figure 5.3.2 are ribosomes.

Because they control the creation of proteins, the nucleus and ribosomes help control cell activities. Most cellular activities require some kind of protein, mainly enzymes. The instructions for these proteins are in genes. The nucleus controls which proteins are made by controlling which genes get used. The cell uses different genes at different times. Ribosomes make proteins. Ribosomes also control which proteins are made first and how quickly they are made.

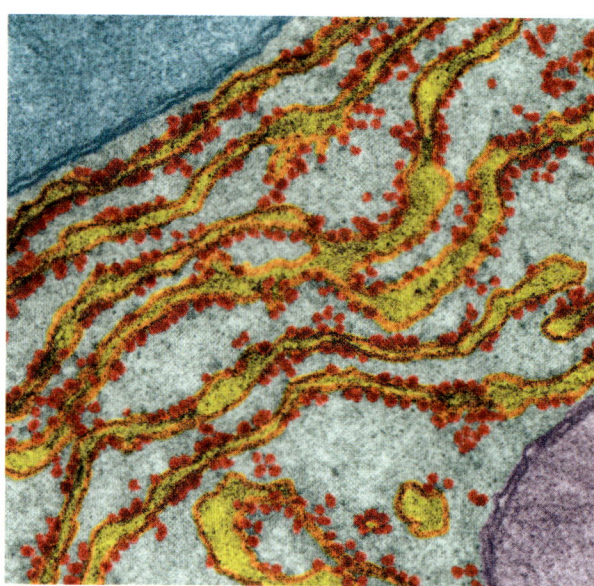

Figure 5.3.2 *The red dots in this cell are ribosomes. Some float freely. Some ribosomes attach to other organelles in the cell.*

144 Chapter 5 A Journey into the Eukaryotic Cell

Lesson 3   REVIEW

Word Bank
nucleus
nucleolus
pores

On a sheet of paper, write the word from the Word Bank that completes each statement correctly.

1. Ribosomes are created in the _____.
2. Messages are transported in and out of the nucleus through _____.
3. The largest organelle in a eukaryotic cell is the _____.

On a sheet of paper, write the letter of the answer to complete each sentence correctly.

4. Sections of DNA that code for a particular protein are called _____.
   - **A** chromosomes **B** genes **C** genomes **D** RNA
5. Ribosomes are made up of _____.
   - **A** DNA
   - **B** RNA
   - **C** DNA and proteins
   - **D** RNA and proteins
6. A genome includes all the DNA in _____.
   - **A** a gene
   - **B** a chromosome
   - **C** an organism
   - **D** the biosphere

Critical Thinking

On a sheet of paper, write the answers to the following questions. Use complete sentences.

7. How can a three-foot long section of DNA fit in the nucleus of one cell?
8. How could a scientist looking at two different cells under a microscope tell which cell makes more proteins?
9. Explain why almost any cell function can be traced back to activity in the nucleus.
10. Why can scientists use a person's DNA to determine if they are likely to develop a disease?

A Journey into the Eukaryotic Cell   Chapter 5

Lesson at a Glance

Chapter 5 Lesson 4

Overview In this lesson, students learn about energy organelles such as chloroplasts and mitochondria.

Objectives

- To identify chloroplasts and mitochondria
- To describe unique molecules found in chloroplasts
- To discuss how a cell processes energy
- To explain the importance of surface area in energy organelles

Student Pages 146–149

Teacher's Resource Library

Workbook Activity 27
Alternative Workbook Activity 27

Vocabulary

cellular respiration	matrix
chlorophyll	mitochondrion
chloroplast	photosynthesis
cristae	stroma
grana	thylakoid

Have students look up each vocabulary term in the Glossary. Answer any questions that students may have about the definition of each term. Have students write each vocabulary term in a sentence.

Background Information

The sun provides energy for most living things on Earth. Green plants that contain chlorophyll are able to capture the energy from the sun and convert it to simple sugars. Green plants form the basis of a food chain or food web for most organisms. There are only a few known organisms that do not use photosynthesis as their ultimate source of energy. Some of these organisms live in extreme environments such as near deep-sea vents.

Lesson 4: Energy Organelles

Objectives

After reading this lesson, you should be able to

- identify chloroplasts and mitochondria
- describe unique molecules found in chloroplasts
- discuss how a cell processes energy
- explain the importance of surface area in energy organelles

Cells have many different jobs. All cells take in nutrients, remove waste, reproduce, and most importantly, make proteins. To do these activities, cells use a molecule called ATP as a source for energy. ATP stores energy in its chemical bonds. Energy stored in ATP ultimately comes from the sun. Two organelles, **chloroplasts** and **mitochondria,** harvest and transform the sun's energy for cell use.

Chloroplasts

Chloroplasts are energy organelles found only in plant cells. They harvest energy in sunlight and convert it into other forms. Chloroplasts use a molecule called **chlorophyll** to trap energy. Chlorophyll absorbs energy from sunlight, and then passes that energy to other molecules in the chloroplasts.

These molecules transform the energy through a process called **photosynthesis.** Photosynthesis is a set of many chemical reactions that produce glucose. Energy from the sun is stored in the chemical bonds of glucose. Glucose produced by a plant can be used as a source of energy by other organisms or by the plant itself. We'll discuss the process of photosynthesis in Chapter 8.

Chloroplasts in plant cells have unique structures to harvest light energy. Bean-shaped chloroplasts have two membranes surrounding them. Inside the inner membrane is a space filled with a thick fluid called **stroma.** The sugar-making part of photosynthesis takes place in the stroma.

Chloroplast
An energy organelle in plants that harvests energy from the sun

Mitochondrion
An energy organelle that converts energy from bonds in glucose into ATP (plural is mitochondria)

Chlorophyll
A molecule in chloroplasts that traps energy from sunlight

Photosynthesis
A process that chloroplasts use to convert energy from the sun into chemical energy stored in glucose

Link to >>>

Environmental Science

Plants take in carbon dioxide, use it in photosynthesis, and then release oxygen. People and animals breathe in the oxygen that plants give off. Scientists think that cutting down trees in tropical rainforests contributes to the increase of carbon dioxide in the air. Fewer plants are available to absorb carbon dioxide.

146 Chapter 5 A Journey into the Eukaryotic Cell

Link to

Environmental Science. Have a volunteer read aloud the environmental science feature. Ask students: Why do scientists think there is a link between the cutting down of trees and increased amounts of carbon dioxide in the atmosphere? *(Cutting down trees decreases the number of trees available to absorb carbon dioxide and to release oxygen.)* What can be done to correct this problem? *(Stop cutting down trees in the tropical rain forests and replant trees to replace those that have been cut down.)*

Stroma
A thick fluid inside chloroplasts

Thylakoid
A membrane sac that contains chlorophyll

Grana
Stacks of thylakoids inside chloroplasts

Cellular respiration
The process in which cells break down food to release energy

Matrix
A thick fluid inside mitochondria

Chlorophyll produces a green color. That is why most leaves are green or have green parts.

In the stroma are membrane sacs, or pouches, called **thylakoids.** Thylakoids contain chlorophyll. Thylakoid sacs are piled together into stacks called **grana.**

Thylakoids are connected to each other inside the chloroplast. Chlorophyll molecules are bound in the membranes of the thylakoids. Chlorophyll traps the sun's energy, transfers the energy into different forms, and stores it in glucose. Figure 5.4.1 shows a chloroplast and its structures.

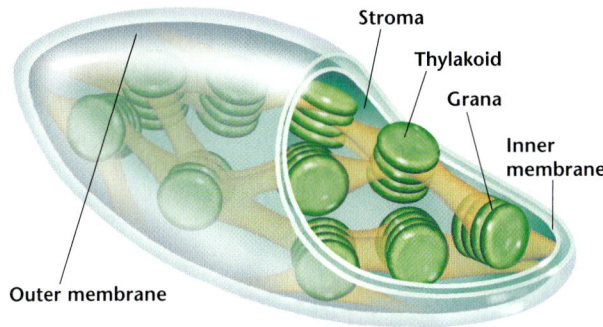

Figure 5.4.1 Only plant cells have chloroplasts.

Mitochondria

Mitochondria are energy organelles found in both plant and animal cells. Mitochondria get energy out of glucose so cells can use it. To do this, mitochondria use **cellular respiration.** Cellular respiration uses oxygen to break down glucose molecules. This process involves many chemical reactions similar to photosynthesis. As glucose is broken down, the released energy is stored in the bonds of ATP. We'll discuss cellular respiration in Chapter 7.

Mitochondria are bean-shaped organelles with two membranes. Because mitochondria produce fuel for the cell, they are often called the powerhouse of the cell. **Matrix** is a thick fluid inside the mitochondria.

Warm-Up Activity

Obtain prepared slides of plant cells for students to view. If slides and a microscope are not available, use photographs, posters, or drawings. Have students study the images to identify the chloroplasts and mitochondria in the cells.

Teaching the Lesson

Have volunteers read aloud each paragraph in the lesson. Point out the structures discussed in the paragraph.

Have students write a paragraph about each vocabulary term, describing what the term means and what role it plays in the process of converting sunlight into usable energy.

Reinforce and Extend

ELL/ESL Strategy

Language Objective: *To explain how energy is obtained and converted to ATP in the cell*

Divide students into small groups. Ask each group to create a presentation for the class on how cells convert sunlight to ATP. Suggest that students make posters, do computer presentations, or use other visual aids. Encourage students to use the lesson vocabulary terms in their presentations.

> **Cristae**
> The folded layers of the inner membrane inside mitochondria

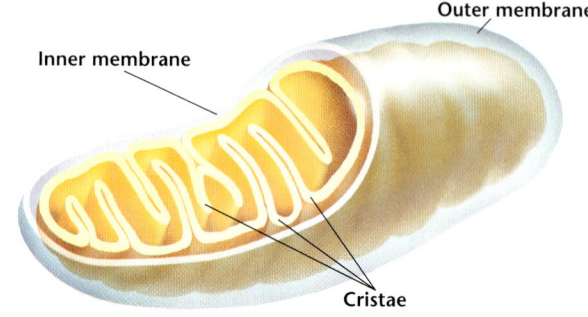

Figure 5.4.2 *Mitochondria break down glucose to release energy.*

The inner membrane inside the mitochondria folds. This creates many layers. These layers are called **cristae.** The inner membrane contains proteins and other molecules used during cellular respiration. The ATP made from this process diffuses out of mitochondria to the rest of the cell. Figure 5.4.2 shows a mitochondrion and its structures.

Both chloroplasts and mitochondria have a lot of membranes inside of them. The membranes are where the main activities of chloroplasts and mitochondria take place. More membranes means more surface area for a cell. More surface area means more space for photosynthesis and cellular respiration. This helps the cell produce more energy.

> **Link to**
> **Chemistry**
> Photosynthesis is an endothermic reaction, meaning energy is absorbed. Respiration is an exothermic reaction, meaning energy is given off.

Achievements in Science

An understanding of plant disease is important to food growers. Since ancient times, people have lost valuable crops to insects or disease-causing organisms. The first effective use of chemicals for disease control occurred in the late 1800s. Grapes for winemaking were under constant attack from a disease called downy mildew. Alexis Millardet, a French botany professor, noticed that grape plants sprayed with a mixture of limestone and copper sulfate discouraged people from stealing the grapes. The spray also killed the fungus that caused downy mildew.

Millardet's discovery led to the widespread use of a spray called Bordeaux mixture. The spray controls fungi and bacteria that harm plants. Bordeaux mixture is still used today, as are other chemicals, to control plant diseases.

148   Chapter 5   *A Journey into the Eukaryotic Cell*

Lesson 4   REVIEW

Word Bank
grana
sunlight
cristae

On a sheet of paper, write the word from the Word Bank to complete each statement correctly.

1. The stacks of thylakoids in chloroplasts are called _____.
2. The folded membrane layers in mitochondria are called _____.
3. Photosynthesis captures energy from _____ for use by organisms.

On a sheet of paper, write the letter of the answer to complete each sentence correctly.

4. To break down glucose for cellular respiration, _____ is needed.

   A sunlight   B water   C ATP   D oxygen

5. Mitochondria produce energy in the form of _____.

   A glucose   B ATP   C matrix   D heat

6. Energy is captured for photosynthesis by _____ molecules.

   A ATP   B chlorophyll   C glucose   D cristae

Critical Thinking

On a sheet of paper, write the answers to the following questions. Use complete sentences.

7. Why do mitochondria have folded inner membranes?
8. Why would you expect to find more mitochondria in muscle cells than in fat cells?
9. What part of a plant do you think contains cells with the most chloroplasts? Explain your answer.
10. Humans and animals do not have chloroplasts in their cells and cannot photosynthesize. Why are they still dependent on the sun for energy?

A Journey into the Eukaryotic Cell   Chapter 5   149

Lesson 4 Review Answers

1. grana **2.** cristae **3.** sunlight **4.** D **5.** B **6.** B **7.** The folded membrane allows more surface area to fit into the organelles. Having more surface area allows more reactions to take place. **8.** Muscle cells need more energy to work, since they are responsible for moving the body and performing physical labor. **9.** Most plants have more chloroplasts in their leaves. This is the part of the plant that receives the most sunlight. Because plants have chloroplasts in the leaves, they can catch more sunlight for photosynthesis. **10.** Humans and animals still get their energy from plants that have used photosynthesis to make glucose. Almost all life gets energy ultimately from the sun.

Portfolio Assessment

Sample items include:
- Paragraphs from Teaching the Lesson
- Short report from Achievements in Science
- ELL/ESL Strategy visual aids
- Lesson 4 Review answers

LEARNING STYLES

Interpersonal/Group Learning
Divide students into small groups. Have each group create a board game that uses the lesson material. Have groups exchange and play each other's games.

Workbook Activity 27

A Journey into the Eukaryotic Cell   149

Lesson at a Glance

Chapter 5 Lesson 5

Overview In this lesson, students learn about the endomembrane system.

Objectives

- To identify the organelles of the endomembrane system
- To discuss the function of endomembrane organelles
- To describe the overall function of the endomembrane system

Student Pages 150–153

Teacher's Resource Library

Workbook Activity 28
Alternative Workbook Activity 28
Lab Manual 22

Vocabulary

endomembrane system	lysosome
endoplasmic reticulum	secrete
Golgi apparatus	vacuole

Have students make flash cards to study the vocabulary terms. Instruct students to write a term on one side of a card and its definition on the reverse side. Encourage students to include a sentence that correctly uses the term below its definition.

Background Information

The endoplasmic reticulum (ER) is the site where lipids and proteins are made. Ribosomes are attached to the surface of the ER where they carry out the synthesis of proteins. The ribosomes cause the ER to look rough, so it is called the rough ER. Areas of the ER that do not contain ribosomes appear smooth, so they are called smooth ER. Smooth ER is responsible for many biochemical activities including making lipids and carbohydrates and breaking down toxic substances.

The lysosomes serve the function of cleanup crew for the cell. Lysosomes contain digestive enzymes that digest worn-out organelles, food particles, viruses, and bacteria.

150 Chapter 5

Lesson 5 The Endomembrane System

Objectives

After reading this lesson, you should be able to
- identify the organelles of the endomembrane system
- discuss the function of endomembrane organelles
- describe the overall function of the endomembrane system

As you have learned, a main cell activity is to make proteins and other molecules. What does a cell do with these molecules? Eukaryotic cells have a large network of organelles called the **endomembrane system**. The prefix *endo-* means "inside." Endomembrane means "inside the membrane." The organelles in the endomembrane system are mostly made of membranes. Together, these organelles help cells make, adjust, package, ship, and receive many different molecules.

Endoplasmic Reticulum

A member of the endomembrane system is an organelle called the **endoplasmic reticulum**, or ER. The ER is a group of membranes throughout the cell that make different molecules. Two kinds of ER, rough and smooth, work together in the cell.

Endomembrane system
A group of organelles that help a cell make and use different molecules

Endoplasmic reticulum (ER)
An organelle that makes different molecules

▼◄▲▼◄▲▼◄▲▼◄▲▼◄▲▼◄▲▼◄▲▼◄▲▼◄▲▼◄▲▼

Science at Work

Plant Pathologist

Did you know that plants get sick? Plants get diseases caused by bacteria, viruses, and fungi. They also face problems from insects and other organisms.

Plant pathologists examine plants to diagnose their problems and to develop and give treatments. The government uses plant pathologists to keep diseases and pests from spreading. A person with a degree in plant pathology can work for universities, farmers, greenhouses, environmental agencies, or in research.

Plant pathologists need a bachelor's degree from a university. Most government agencies that employ plant pathologists require a master's degree. Working in research or as a professor requires a Ph.D.

150 Chapter 5 A Journey into the Eukaryotic Cell

Science at Work

Have a volunteer read aloud the feature about plant pathologists. Ask students: Why is it important for plant pathologists to examine fruits and vegetables that are imported from other countries? *(The imported fruits and vegetables may carry diseases that can be spread to crops in the United States.)*

Secrete
To make and then give off

Golgi apparatus
An organelle made of stacked membrane sacs that makes final changes to and packages molecules made in the cell

Vacuole
A membrane sac that transports and stores molecules

Rough ER has ribosomes attached to it. It looks rough under the microscope. Ribosomes make many different proteins that a cell uses or **secretes**. Secrete means "to make and give off." After the ribosomes make proteins, the ER packages and sends them to the next organelle.

Smooth ER acts the same as rough ER, except that it produces other molecules. Smooth ER has enzymes bound inside its membrane, so it looks smooth under a microscope. Those enzymes help the smooth ER make lipids and carbohydrates. Smooth ER also helps cells handle poisonous substances.

Golgi Apparatus

After different molecules are made, the ER sends them to the **Golgi apparatus** for necessary changes. This organelle is a stack of flat membrane sacs. Under a microscope, it looks like a stack of pancakes. Once molecules are ready, the Golgi apparatus packages them. Then it sends the packages elsewhere in the cell or to the outside of the cell.

Vacuoles

Both the ER and Golgi apparatus use organelles called **vacuoles** to send their molecules around. Vacuoles are membrane sacs formed from the membranes of other organelles. They can form from the ER, Gogli apparatus, or plasma membrane. They fuse with other membranes to become part of them. Cells take in materials by forming a vacuole from the plasma membrane.

Technology and Society

High-Tech Medications

Some new cancer treatments use liposomes, which are hollow bodies made of phospholipids. Liposomes are filled with a cancer drug. The liposomes deliver the drug to cancer cells. The cancer cells absorb the liposomes. The liposomes then break down their phospholipid walls. This releases the drug which poisons the cancer cells.

---

1 Warm-Up Activity

Have a volunteer write a simple flowchart on the board, showing the function of a factory. *(raw materials>product made >product packaged>product shipped)* Explain to students that the endomembrane system is a type of "factory" for the cell.

2 Teaching the Lesson

Have students make an outline of the lesson. Remind them to include enough information so the outline can be used to study for tests and quizzes.

Tell students that the endoplasmic reticulum makes different types of molecules for the cell. The rough ER makes proteins for the cell. The smooth ER produces lipids and carbohydrates. The Golgi apparatus packages the molecules in vacuoles so they can be transported to other parts of the cell. The lysosomes clean up the cell.

As a class, create a graphic organizer for this lesson. Have students brainstorm the type of graphic organizer they want to use. Ask volunteers for suggestions and write them on the board. After the graphic organizer is complete, have students copy it for reference.

3 Reinforce and Extend

Technology and Society

Have students read the Technology and Society feature. Ask students: Why is it beneficial to have cancer drugs delivered directly to the cancer cells? *(A higher concentration of the drug can target only the cancer cells, not the healthy cells.)* Have students research and find other hi-tech medications. Students can report their findings to the class.

Teacher Alert

Cells that produce proteins for export to other parts of the body, such as white blood cells, are dense in rough ER. Cells that metabolize lipids and carbohydrates, such as skeletal and cardiac muscle cells, are dense in smooth ER. Cells that detoxify the body, such as liver cells, also are dense in smooth ER.

ELL/ESL Strategy

Language Objective: To understand the meanings of the vocabulary terms

Divide students into small groups. Have each group use the vocabulary terms to create a set of flash cards. The vocabulary terms should be on one set of cards and the definitions on a different set. Have students shuffle both sets separately. Tell them to then match the definitions and terms correctly for all of the cards.

Link to

Health. Have a volunteer read aloud the Link to Health feature about natural dyes. Most of the food colorings used today are synthetic. In 1900 there were about 80 synthetic color additives available for use in foods. The Food and Drug Act of 1906 tightly regulated color additives that could be added to foods. The act permitted only seven synthetic color additives for foods. These controls helped ensure that the food supply was safe for consumption. Today there are still only seven certified colors approved for use in foods.

At Home

Have students read the labels on five processed food products and find the type of food coloring used. Have them report their findings to the class.

Lysosome
A membrane sac with special enzymes used to break down large molecules

This ability allows vacuoles to perform several functions. Vacuoles ship molecules within a cell or to the outside of the cell. Vacuoles also store material for later use.

Lysosomes

Another member of the endomembrane system is an organelle called a **lysosome.** Lysosomes are sacs like vacuoles, but they contain special enzymes. The enzymes help the cell digest, or break down, large molecules so it can use them. These enzymes digest many kinds of molecules. They must be contained in lysosomes so they do not destroy the rest of the cell.

A Factory and Delivery Service

The endomembrane system supports the main activities of a cell by making, packaging, sending, receiving, and digesting different molecules. The endomembrane system acts like a cell's factory and delivery service.

> **Link to ▶▶▶**
>
> **Health**
>
> Chlorophyll is the only natural dye approved by the U.S. Food and Drug Administration (FDA) for use in products. The FDA is a government agency that protects the public's health. The FDA approves the use of chlorophyll in very small amounts. Currently, chlorophyll is used as a coloring in some cosmetics and drugs. Chlorophyll has not been approved as a coloring for food products.

Lesson 5 REVIEW

Word Bank
endoplasmic reticulum
Golgi apparatus
vacuole

On a sheet of paper, match each description with a term in the Word Bank.

1. a packaging and distribution center
2. a storage unit
3. a factory

On a sheet of paper, write the word to complete each statement correctly.

4. Rough endoplasmic reticulum looks rough under the microscope because it has _____ on its surface.
5. Lysosomes contain _____ that help to digest molecules.
6. Endoplasmic reticulum, the Golgi apparatus, vacuoles, and lysosomes in a eukaryotic cell are made up mostly of _____

Critical Thinking

On a sheet of paper, write the answers to the following questions. Use complete sentences.

7. Describe the two types of endoplasmic reticulum and the materials each makes.
8. Explain what vacuoles do.
9. What does the Golgi apparatus do?
10. How are the organelles of the endomembrane system alike? How are they different?

A Journey into the Eukaryotic Cell Chapter 5 153

Lesson 5 Review Answers

1. Golgi apparatus 2. vacuole 3. endoplasmic reticulum 4. ribosomes 5. enzymes 6. membranes 7. Rough ER is covered with ribosomes and makes proteins. Smooth ER has no ribosomes and makes lipids and carbohydrates. 8. Vacuoles are used to transport material from the ER and Golgi apparatus. Vacuoles also safely store the enzymes used to break down material in lysosomes. In addition, vacuoles are an important part of transporting material in and out of the cell. 9. The Golgi apparatus packages molecules and sends them elsewhere in the cell or to the outside of the cell. 10. All of the endomembrane system organelles are mostly made of membranes. Each of the organelles has a different function: to make, adjust, package, ship, or receive molecules.

Portfolio Assessment

Sample items include:
- Outlines of the lesson
- Research on hi-tech medicines from Technology and Society
- Findings from At Home
- Lesson 5 Review answers

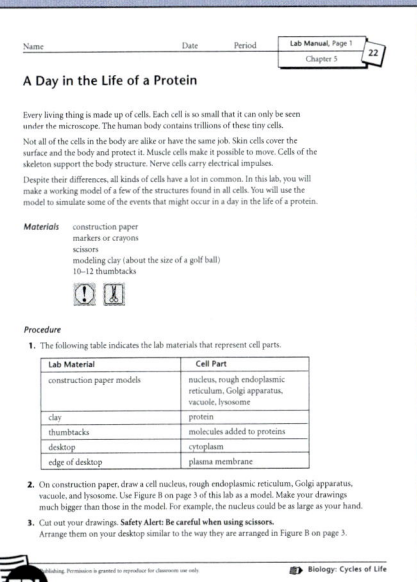

Lab Manual 22, pages 1–3

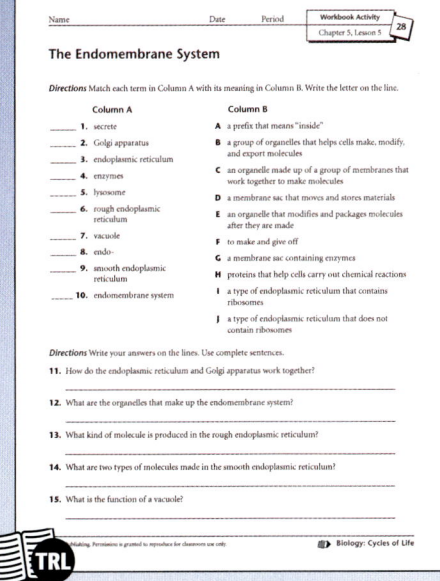

Workbook Activity 28

Lesson at a Glance

Chapter 5 Lesson 6

Overview In this lesson, students learn about the cytoskeleton.

Objectives

- To describe the primary functions of the cytoskeleton
- To identify three types of fibers in the cytoskeleton
- To explain the unique structure of cilia and flagella

Student Pages 154–158

Teacher's Resource Library

Workbook Activity 29

Alternative Workbook Activity 29

Lab Manual 23–24

Vocabulary

actin	intermediate filament
cilia	microfilament
cytoskeleton	microtubule
flagella	tubulin

Discuss the meaning of each vocabulary term. Have students write sentences using each term correctly.

Background Information

The cytoskeleton gives cells support, anchors organelles, and allows cells to move. The cytoskeleton is composed of a network of protein filaments. There are three types of protein fibers that compose the cytoskeleton: microfilaments, intermediate filaments, and microtubules. These fibers vary in shape and function.

 Warm-Up Activity

Display a photograph, a transparency, or an illustration of a human skeleton. Ask students: What is the function of a skeleton? *(It supports the body and allows the body to move.)* Tell students that the cytoskeleton does the same thing for the cell.

Lesson 6 The Cytoskeleton

Objectives

After reading this lesson, you should be able to

- describe the primary functions of the cytoskeleton
- identify three types of fibers in the cytoskeleton
- explain the unique structure of cilia and flagella

A group of organelles that helps cells perform many activities is the **cytoskeleton.** *Cyto* means "cell," so *cytoskeleton* means "cell skeleton." That is exactly what it is.

Cytoskeleton Structure and Function

The cytoskeleton is made of many fibers that stretch across the inside of the cell. These fibers give the cell support and help it keep its shape. Some organelles in the cell, like the nucleus, use these fibers to anchor themselves in a certain position in the cytoplasm. Other organelles move around in the cytoplasm, such as lysosomes and vacuoles. They use the cytoskeleton fibers like a train uses tracks. By using these fibers, organelles stay connected to one another. This allows the cell to function as one unit.

The fibers of the cytoskeleton help the cell in movement. If a cell needs to move around, which many do, it needs muscle. That muscle is the cytoskeleton. Cytoskeleton fibers are like the muscles in the human body that stretch and shrink to help the body move. When a cell moves around, the cytoskeleton fibers add more fiber molecule to the moving end. At the same time, the other end of the fibers remove fiber molecules. This causes the end of the fibers to shorten.

Three Types of Cytoskeleton Fibers

The three types of cytoskeleton fibers are made from different types of protein. **Microfilaments** are fibers made of a ball-shaped protein called **actin.** Actin molecules are connected together in long strings. These strings of protein are twisted together to make long fiber molecules. Microfilaments are mainly responsible for moving the whole cell around.

The second type of cytoskeleton fibers are the **intermediate filaments.** These fibers are made from long, string-like proteins. The proteins coil together like rope to form rods that add strength to the shape of the cell. Organelles anchor themselves to these rods.

Cytoskeleton
A group of fibers running throughout the inside of a cell that supports the cell and helps the cell move

Microfilament
A long cytoskeleton fiber used to move the cell

Actin
A ball-shaped protein used to make microfilaments

Intermediate filament
A rod-like cytoskeleton fiber used to strengthen the cell's shape; organelles anchor themselves to these rods

154 *Chapter 5 A Journey into the Eukaryotic Cell*

Microtubule
A tube-like cytoskeleton fiber used by organelles to move around

Tubulin
A ball-shaped protein used to make the hollow tube structure of microtubules

Cilia
Small, hair-like structures made of microtubules; found on the outside of some cells to aid in movement

Flagella
Long, tail-like structures made of microtubules; found on the outside of some cells to aid in movement

The third type of cytoskeleton fibers are **microtubules.** Microtubules are made from units of a ball-shaped protein called **tubulin.** Tubulin molecules come together to form a hollow tube that supports the cell's shape. Organelles use microtubules to move around.

Microtubules also work outside the cell. These fibers anchor to and extend out of the plasma membrane. They form two types of structures, **cilia** and **flagella.** Cilia are small, hair-like structures on the outside of some cells. Flagella are long, tail-like structures. Only one flagellum or two flagella are found on certain kinds of cells. Both cilia and flagella help an unattached cell move around. These structures also help move substances across an attached cell. Figure 5.6.1 shows some of the organelles in a eukaryotic cell.

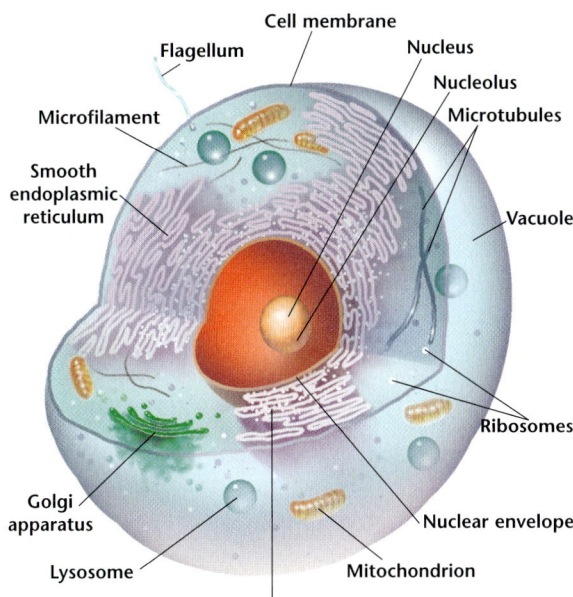

Figure 5.6.1 *Eukaryotic cells contain many organelles with specialized functions.*

 Teaching the Lesson

Have students write *cytoskeleton, microfilaments, intermediate filaments,* and *microtubules* on a sheet of paper. Ask them to write details about each of these as they read the lesson, including the relationship with one another and their function in the cell.

 Reinforce and Extend

IN THE ENVIRONMENT

 One interesting eukaryote lives in the gut of termites. This creature uses flagella for locomotion. Termites cannot digest wood, but this eukaryote produces an enzyme that digests wood. Have students find out more about this beneficial relationship. Ask each student to present one interesting fact.

LEARNING STYLES

 **Visual/Spatial**
Have students draw a eukaryotic cell, using colored pencils to clearly define each structure. Remind them to label all the parts.

Lesson 6 Review Answers

1. microfilaments **2.** microtubules
3. intermediate filaments **4.** actin **5.** balls
6. cell skeleton **7.** Microtubules can take the form of cilia, which are small, hairlike structures, or flagella, which are long tails. **8.** Fibers will lengthen and add more material to the end of the cell in the direction of movement. On the other end, fibers are removed, causing the cytoskeleton to shorten. **9.** Both cilia and flagella are made up of nine pairs of microtubules surrounding a pair of microtubules in the center. **10.** The cytoskeleton helps to maintain the shape of the cell. It helps to anchor or provide movement for organelles in the cell. It helps the cell move through its outside environment.

Portfolio Assessment

Sample items include:
- Sentences using the vocabulary terms
- Drawings from Learning Styles Visual/Spatial
- Lesson 6 Review answers

ELL/ESL Strategy

Language Objective: *To explain the lesson concepts*

Assign each English language learner a partner. Have the partner explain the lesson concepts paragraph by paragraph. Then have students change roles. Encourage students to ask questions if they do not understand a concept.

156 Chapter 5

Lesson 6 REVIEW

Word Bank
intermediate filaments
microfilaments
microtubules

On a sheet of paper, write the word or words from the Word Bank that match each description.

1. the part of the cytoskeleton mainly responsible for moving the cell around
2. the part of the cytoskeleton that helps organelles move inside the cell
3. the part of the cytoskeleton that adds strength to the shape of the cell

On a sheet of paper, write the word or words to complete each statement correctly.

4. Microfilaments are made up of a protein called _____.
5. Microtubules and microfilaments are made from proteins that are shaped like _____.
6. The word *cytoskeleton* means _____.

Critical Thinking

On a sheet of paper, write the answers to the following questions. Use complete sentences.

7. Describe the two types of microtubule structures that work outside of a cell.
8. Explain how cytoskeleton fiber activity can cause a cell to move.
9. Describe the structure of fibers that make up cilia and flagella.
10. List three ways that the cytoskeleton helps a cell work.

156 Chapter 5 *A Journey into the Eukaryotic Cell*

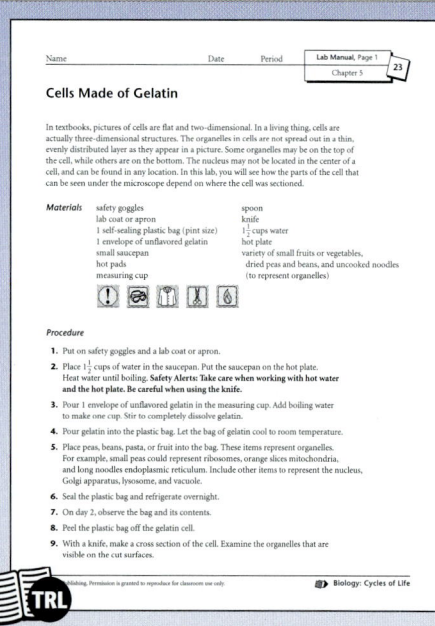

Workbook Activity 29   **Lab Manual 23, pages 1–2**

INVESTIGATION 5

Materials
- safety goggles
- lab coat or apron
- tweezers
- onion
- glass slide
- dropper bottle of iodine solution
- coverslip
- microscope
- prepared slide of human cheek cells

Comparing Plant and Animal Cells

All organisms are made up of cells. All cells have some things in common. However, some key differences exist between the cells that make up plants and the cells that make up animals. In this lab, you will examine plant cells and animal cells, noting their similarities and differences. You will learn more about plant cells in Lesson 7.

Procedure

1. Put on safety goggles and a lab coat or apron.
2. Using tweezers, peel a small, thin piece of tissue from an inside section of the onion.

A Journey into the Eukaryotic Cell Chapter 5 **157**

SAFETY ALERT

- Make sure that students have read and understood all safety rules for working in the lab. Discuss the Safety Alerts with students.
- Be sure students wear safety goggles and a lab coat or apron.
- Remind students to handle glass microscope slides with care and to dispose of broken glass properly.
- Have students exercise caution using the iodine solution. Emphasize that only a drop of stain is needed.

Investigation 5

Encourage students to read the investigation steps. Discuss questions they may have before beginning the investigation.

Objectives

- To prepare and observe animal and plant cells
- To draw and identify the various components of the cells
- To compare and contrast the different characteristics of the two types of cells
- To infer information about the organisms the cells came from

Skills

Observing, using science lab equipment, drawing, identifying samples, comparing and contrasting, making inferences, communicating, analyzing data, drawing conclusions

Background

Students will get experience preparing basic slides and using microscopes. After learning about plant and animal cells in Lessons 1–6, this lab gives students a hands-on experience observing samples. It also prepares students for Lesson 7.

Time Frame

One class period

Procedure

- Have students work together in groups to complete the activity.
- Peel off the onion skin before setting the onions out to ensure that students use live tissue for their slide mounts. You can also substitute prepared slides or prepare and show the slides as a demonstration to the class.
- Check to see that students understand the correct procedures for handling and using a microscope.
- Examine students' drawings to be sure they have included everything they have observed. Have students label all the structures they can identify. Also, have them record the name of the sample they are observing and the magnification they are using along with their drawings.

Continued on page 158

A Journey into the Eukaryotic Cell **157**

Continued from page 157

Cleanup/Disposal
Instruct students in proper cleanup and disposal of materials.

Results
Students should prepare two drawings: one of onion cells they observed and the other of human cheek cells they observed. Students should label the structures in their drawings and note the magnification they used.

Analysis Answers
1. Answers will vary. Students should be able to identify the nucleus and cytoplasm in both cells. In the onion cell, students should be able to identify the cell wall and probably the central vacuole.
2. Students should note the shape and structure of the plant cell because of the presence of a cell wall. Some students may identify the central vacuole, which helps give the plant cell its rigidity.

Conclusions Answers
1. Students probably will not find the smaller organelles, such as mitochondria, nucleolus, and the parts of the endomembrane system. These organelles are generally too small to be found, even under high resolution. Students will not find chloroplasts in the onion cell because the onion bulb is not photosynthetic.
2. The onion plant requires a cell wall to remain rigid and function under different environmental conditions. Animal cells in the cheek do not need this structure and instead are much more fluid.

Explore Further Answers
There will be some slight variation in the shape of the onion cells and the position of organelles within the cells, but generally, the cells will be similar.

---

3. Place the piece of onion tissue on a glass slide. Be sure the piece of onion is small enough to fit on the slide. **Safety Alert: Handle glass microscope slides with care. Dispose of broken glass properly.**
4. Add one drop of iodine solution to the onion piece on the slide. **Safety Alert: Iodine stains skin and clothing. It is a poison and an eye irritant.**
5. Hold a coverslip at a 45° angle at the edge of the drop of iodine solution. Gently lower the coverslip.
6. Look at the onion cells under the microscope. Observe the cells at various magnifications until you get a clear, sharp image.
7. Make a drawing of what you see under the microscope. Label your drawing.
8. Next, look at the prepared slide of human cheek cells under the microscope. Make a drawing of what you see. Label your drawing.

Cleanup/Disposal
Before leaving the lab, clean up your materials and wash your hands.

Analysis
1. Which cell parts could you identify in the onion and cheek cells?
2. What differences did you observe between the two types of cells?

Conclusions
1. What organelles were you not able to find as you observed the cells? Why do you think you could not find them?
2. How do the differences in the two types of cells reflect the differences in the organisms the cells belong to?

Explore Further
Observe cells from other sections of the onion. How do they compare with the first cells you observed?

158   Chapter 5   *A Journey into the Eukaryotic Cell*

Assessment
Check students' drawings to be sure they have labeled the structures correctly. You might include the following items from this investigation in student portfolios:
- Drawings
- Answers to Analysis and Conclusions questions
- Answers to Explore Further

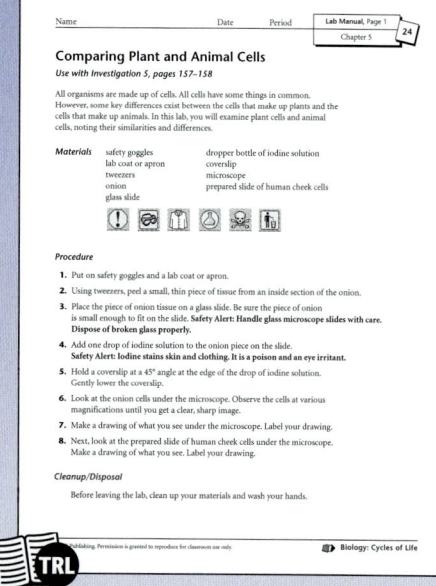

Lesson 7: Plant Cells

Objectives

After reading this lesson, you should be able to
- identify special structures found in plant cells
- describe the main functions of special plant structures

Cell wall
The rigid layer of cellulose outside the plasma membrane of plant cells

Plasmodesmata
Openings in the cell wall used for communication and transport of molecules

Central vacuole
Large membrane sac in the center of a plant cell used for water storage

Plant cells are eukaryotic cells. They have organelle structures. We have already discussed one organelle unique to plant cells—a chloroplast. Most plant cells have several chloroplasts, especially if they are in the leaves of the plant. Cells in a plant's roots may not have any chloroplasts because they are not exposed to sunlight. Plant cells have other unique structures.

Plant cells are surrounded by a plasma membrane and a **cell wall**. The cell wall is made of a complex carbohydrate called cellulose. Remember that cellulose is a rigid molecule. It makes the cell wall a firm structure. The cell wall rarely changes shape.

Plasmodesmata are openings in the cell wall. Plant cells use these openings to communicate with each other. Plant cells use their cell walls to connect with other plant cells and to transport molecules. Connected plant cells form plant tissue.

When plants are watered, the water collects each cell in a **central vacuole**. Plant cells have one large central vacuole that takes up a lot of space. Plant cells store water and poisons in the central vacuole, which is usually in the center of the cell. If a plant wilts, it is because of a lack of water in the cells. The cell inside the cell wall will shrivel and die, but the wall will stay firm.

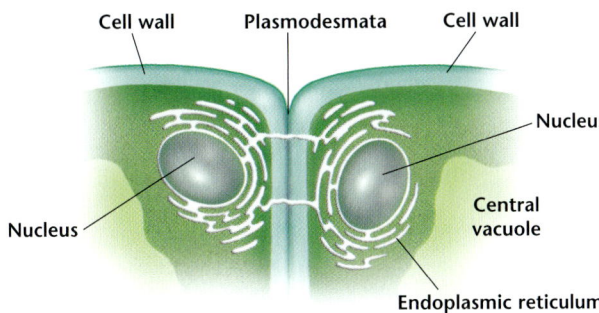

Figure 5.7.1 Plants cells have some structures that animal cells do not have.

A Journey into the Eukaryotic Cell   Chapter 5

Lesson at a Glance

Chapter 5 Lesson 7

Overview In this lesson, students learn about plant cells.

Objectives
- To identify special structures found in plant cells
- To describe the main functions of special plant structures

Student Pages 159–163

Teacher's Resource Library
- Workbook Activity 30–31
- Alternative Workbook Activity 30–31
- Lab Manual 25
- Resource File 10

Vocabulary

cell wall   plasmodesmata
central vacuole

Tell students to use context clues to understand the terms in this lesson. Then have them write a paragraph, correctly using the terms.

Background Information

Plant and animal cells have many similarities, but they also have some differences. Plant cells, in general, are larger than animal cells. Plant cells have cell walls and chloroplasts. Plant cells usually have one large vacuole. Animal cells have centrioles, and plant cells do not. Animal cells often have many small vacuoles.

1 Warm-Up Activity

Display an illustration of a plant cell that has the parts of the cell labeled. See if students can identify the structures that are unique to plant cells.

2 Teaching the Lesson

Have volunteers read the lesson to the class. Have another volunteer point out the structure being discussed on the illustration used in the Warm-Up Activity.

3 Reinforce and Extend

ELL/ESL Strategy

 **Language Objective:** *To compare plant and animal cells*

Have students create a Venn diagram of plant and animal cells. One circle should contain only the organelles that plant cells contain. The other circle should contain the organelles that only animal cells contain. Students should place organelle structures that both cells contain in the area where the circles overlap.

A Journey into the Eukaryotic Cell **159**

Lesson 7 Review Answers

1. eukaryotic 2. cellulose 3. Chloroplasts
4. B 5. A 6. D 7. Central vacuoles contain mostly water, along with some toxins that have been stored. 8. Plant cells remain rigid because their walls are made of cellulose, which is stiff. 9. Plant leaves contain lots of chloroplasts. Plant roots generally contain few or no chloroplasts. Plant stems can vary in the amount of chloroplasts they contain. 10. Plant cells contain one large vacuole that is located near the center and takes up a lot of space. Animal cells contain many smaller vacuoles located throughout the cell.

Portfolio Assessment

Sample items include:
- Paragraphs using vocabulary terms
- Lesson 7 Review answers

Science Myth

Have a volunteer read the Science Myth to the class. While displaying an image of a plant cell, explain that it has both a cell wall and a cell membrane.

LEARNING STYLES

Body/Kinesthetic

Have students make a three-dimensional model of a plant cell and an animal cell. Have students label each part of the cells. Students can use inexpensive materials in their models, such as plastic bags, pipe cleaners, and pasta.

Lesson 7 REVIEW

Science Myth

Myth: Plant cells have cell walls instead of cell membranes.

Fact: A membrane surrounds every plant and animal cell. Plant cells also have a cell wall that lies outside the cell membrane.

On a sheet of paper, write the word or words to complete each statement correctly.

1. Plants have _____ cells, meaning they contain membranes and organelles.
2. The cell wall of a plant cell is made from _____.
3. _____ are organelles found in plant cells, but not in animal cells.

On a sheet of paper, write the letter of the answer to complete each sentence correctly.

4. A plant cell contains a(n) _____ that stores water and poisons.
   - **A** cell wall
   - **B** central vacuole
   - **C** cell membrane
   - **D** nucleus
5. The purpose of plasmodesmata is to _____.
   - **A** communicate with other cells
   - **B** protect and shape the cell
   - **C** conduct photosynthesis
   - **D** store water
6. Plant cell walls connect with other plant cell walls to create plant _____.
   - **A** organelles **B** megacells **C** vacuoles **D** tissue

Critical Thinking

On a sheet of paper, write the answers to the following questions. Use complete sentences.

7. What would you expect to find in a central vacuole?
8. A plant that is not watered will wilt, but the tissues and cells will stay rigid. Explain what causes plant tissue to keep its shape.
9. Describe a plant part that has lots of chloroplasts and a part that has few chloroplasts.
10. How do plant cell vacuoles and animal cell vacuoles differ?

160 Chapter 5 A Journey into the Eukaryotic Cell

Workbook Activity 30

DISCOVERY INVESTIGATION 5

Comparing Plant Cells

Materials
- *Elodea* plant
- safety goggles
- lab coat or apron
- tweezers
- eyedropper
- distilled water
- glass slide
- coverslip
- microscope
- prepared slide of onion root tip (longitudinal section)
- prepared slide of corn stem (cross section)

The cells in different parts of a plant are different, depending on the jobs of those particular cells. In this lab, you will examine cells from different parts of a plant. You will discover how cells differ according to their functions.

Procedure

1. Put on safety goggles and a lab coat or apron.
2. In a small group, observe an *Elodea* plant. Discuss the structure of its leaves, stems, and roots. Make a table that lists the characteristics of each plant part.
3. Predict what differences you will find in the cells of the three plant parts.
4. Make a wet mount of one *Elodea* leaf using a drop of water.

A Journey into the Eukaryotic Cell Chapter 5 **161**

SAFETY ALERT

- Make sure that students have read and understood all safety rules for working in the lab. Discuss the Safety Alerts with students.
- Be sure students wear safety goggles and a lab coat or apron.
- Check that students understand the correct procedures for working with a microscope.
- Remind students to handle glass microscope slides with care and to dispose of broken glass properly.

Discovery Investigation 5

This investigation is less structured than the first investigation in this chapter. It offers students more challenge and requires more teacher facilitation. Encourage students to read the investigation steps. Discuss questions they may have before beginning the investigation.

Objectives

- To infer information about different cell structures and functions
- To prepare a slide of leaf cells for observation
- To organize information on a table for comparison
- To hypothesize about different plant structures and cells

Skills

Observing, communicating, drawing, identifying samples, describing, collecting and recording information, using science lab equipment, making inferences, analyzing data, drawing conclusions

Background

Plant cells have several characteristics that make them different from animal cells. Plant cells have a thick cell wall, a central vacuole, and chloroplasts. Different plant structures, such as roots, stems, and leaves, have different functions, and the cells that make up these structures differ to reflect these functions.

Time Frame

One class period

Procedure

- Have students work together in pairs or groups to complete the activity.
- Make sure students are familiar with the parts of a plant cell. Encourage them to discuss what the different structures of a plant do. Guide the discussion as needed.
- Have students create a table to list the characteristics of each plant structure. They might write their predictions and compare them later.

Continued on page 162

Continued from page 161

- Guide or demonstrate the procedure for making a wet mount. Make sure that students understand to use only a small amount of plant tissue, usually just one leaf, and one or two drops of distilled water under the coverslip.
- Have students make detailed drawings with notes and labels of what they see.
- If time permits, have students prepare slides of stems and roots. Live slides of leaves are desired so that students can see the live chloroplasts floating in the cytoplasm.

Cleanup/Disposal

Instruct students in proper cleanup and disposal of materials.

Results

Answers will vary. Generally, students should observe that cells in the leaves contain a large number of chloroplasts in order to maximize the amount of photosynthesis done by the plant. Since leaves are exposed to the sun, they contain the majority of the plant's chloroplasts. Stems may contain chloroplasts, depending on how much exposure to the sun they get. Stem cross sections will show many cells with very thick walls and no internal organelles that provide support and transport water and nutrients. Roots will show no chloroplasts, but a variety of cells in various stages of elongation with thinner cell walls due to the function of roots (especially at the tip) to grow downward and find water.

Answers to Analysis, Conclusions, and Explore Further begin on page 670 of this Teacher's Edition.

Assessment

Check to see that students listed characteristics in their tables and that they labeled the cells in their drawings correctly. You might include the following items from this investigation in student portfolios:

- Data table and prediction
- Drawings
- Answers to Analysis and Conclusions questions
- Research and predictions for Explore Further

5. Examine the wet mount under a microscope. Observe the cells at various magnifications until you get a clear, sharp image. Discuss what you see. Record your observations. Make a drawing of the cells you observe. Label the cell parts in your drawing. **Safety Alert: Handle glass microscope slides with care. Dispose of broken glass properly.**

6. Observe the cells in the prepared slide of a corn stem. Discuss and record your observations. Make and label a drawing of the cells.

7. Observe the cells in the prepared slide of an onion root tip. Discuss and record your observations. Make and label a drawing of the cells.

Cleanup/Disposal

Before leaving the lab, clean up your materials and wash your hands.

Analysis

1. What plant organelles did you see?
2. What differences did you notice in the cells and arrangements of cells in the three plant parts?

Conclusions

1. How accurate were your predictions compared with what you observed?
2. As a group, select another type of plant. Predict what you might find in different parts of the plant you have selected.

Explore Further

Research one of the following plant structures: potato, thorn, celery stalk, lettuce, or onion bulb. Is the structure a root, stem, or leaf? What makes this structure different from a typical root, stem, or leaf? What would you expect to find if you examined its cells?

162 Chapter 5 *A Journey into the Eukaryotic Cell*

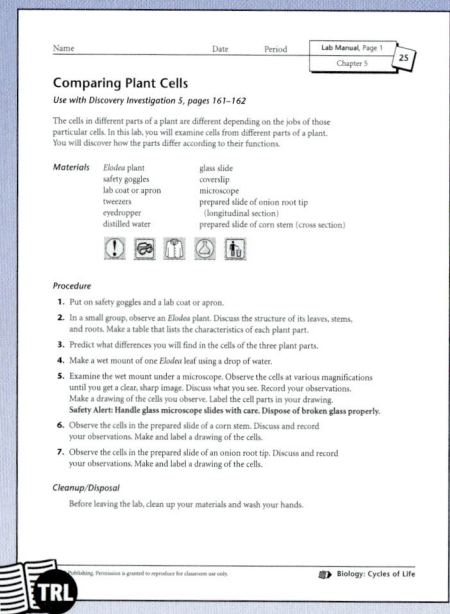

Lab Manual 25, pages 1–2

BIOLOGY IN THE WORLD

Mitochondrial DNA—A New Tool of Discovery

Forensic investigators use DNA to find criminals. Genealogists use DNA to find ancestors. Genealogists trace or study the history of a person or family. DNA is a great tool, but there are some problems with using it. An individual's DNA is made of a mix of his or her parents' DNA. This means that an almost endless stream of combinations can exist, depending on which chromosomes were passed on. Also, over time DNA can break down when exposed to light or heat.

The discovery that mitochondria have their own DNA is a breakthrough for scientists. Mitochondria make copies of themselves by dividing. This means that the small amount of DNA present in the mitochondria does not change. Also, mitochondrial DNA is only inherited from the mother. The DNA in the mitochondria of your cells is basically the same DNA that existed in your mother's mitochondria and in her mother's mitochondria, all the way back as far as samples can be found. Genealogists use mitochondrial DNA to trace ancestry through many generations of mothers and to make family trees.

Mitochondrial DNA is not as fragile as the DNA that makes up the genome in the nucleus. A genome is the entire DNA of an organism. Some cells have one large mitochondria. Most have thousands. Every cell has mitochondrial DNA.

A small sample of body tissue or blood usually contains enough mitochondrial DNA to test.

Using mitochondrial DNA, investigators have tracked down the parents of political prisoners. Mitochondrial DNA has helped prove the relationship between a parent and his or her children. Recently, scientists used samples from 200,000-year-old bones from Africa to track down what they think is the most direct ancestral mother of modern humans.

1. What property of mitochondrial DNA makes it helpful to criminal investigators?
2. In what kind of situation would mitochondrial DNA not be useful when tracing a family tree?
3. Mitochondrial disorders cause some diseases. What evidence would lead you to think that a disease was inherited through mitochondrial DNA?

Chapter 5 Summary

Have volunteers read aloud each summary item on page 164. Ask volunteers to explain the meaning of each item. Direct students' attention to the Vocabulary box on the bottom of page 164. Have them read and review each term and its definition.

Graphic Organizer TRL

As students read Chapter 5, have them finish completing the chart on Graphic Organizer 5: Traits of Plant and Animal Cells. Encourage students to read each lesson of the chapter and then have them fill in the portion of the chart that pertains to the lesson. When they have completed the chart, ask them to answer the questions.

Chapter 5 SUMMARY

- Eukaryotic cells contain organelles with membranes. Cellular membranes are made up of a bilayer of phospholipids.

- The plasma membrane surrounds the cell and controls molecules that pass through.

- Passive transport is when molecules pass through the plasma membrane without needing energy. Facilitated transport is a type of passive transport that uses membrane proteins to help molecules cross the plasma membrane. A molecule requiring energy to cross the plasma membrane undergoes active transport.

- Cells use their membranes to communicate with other cells and their environment.

- The largest organelle in a eukaryotic cell is the nucleus. It contains the nucleolus and the cell's DNA.

- Proteins are produced by the cell using ribosomes and RNA.

- Plant cells contain organelles called chloroplasts that change sunlight into glucose through photosynthesis.

- Both plant and animal cells transform energy from sugars for their use through respiration. This takes place in organelles called mitochondria.

- Eukaryotic cells contain an endomembrane system that packages and transports molecules. This system includes the endoplasmic reticulum, Golgi apparatus, vacuoles, and lysosomes.

- Cells have a network of fibers that make up a cytoskeleton. The cytoskeleton provides support and movement, and anchors organelles.

- Plant cells have a rigid cell wall and one large, central vacuole.

Vocabulary

actin, 154	cytosol, 136	Golgi apparatus, 151	plasma membrane, 135
active transport, 138	endocytosis, 139	grana, 147	plasmodesmata, 159
bilayer, 134	endomembrane system, 150	intermediate filament, 154	pore, 142
cell wall, 159	endoplasmic reticulum, 150	lysosome, 152	ribosome, 142
cellular respiration, 147	exocytosis, 139	matrix, 147	secrete, 151
central vacuole, 159	extracellular matrix, 136	microfilament, 154	stroma, 147
chloroplast, 146	facilitated diffusion, 138	microtubule, 155	thylakoid, 147
chlorophyll, 146	flagella, 155	mitochondrion, 146	transport protein, 136
chromosome, 143	fluid mosaic model, 136	nuclear envelope, 142	tubulin, 155
cilia, 155	gap junction, 140	nucleolus, 142	vacuole, 151
cristae, 148	genome, 143	passive transport, 138	
cytoplasm, 136		photosynthesis, 146	
cytoskeleton, 154			

164 Chapter 5 A Journey into the Eukaryotic Cell

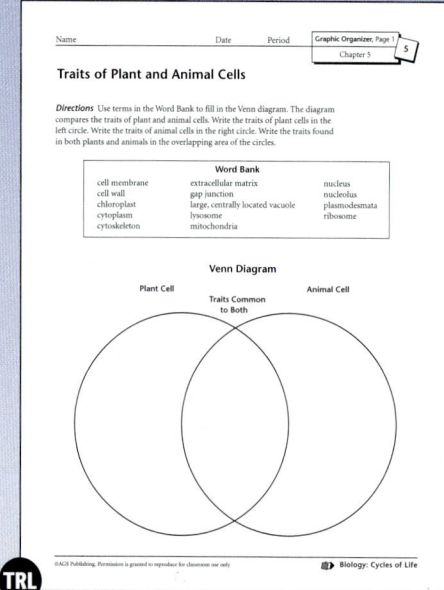

Graphic Organizer 5, pages 1–3

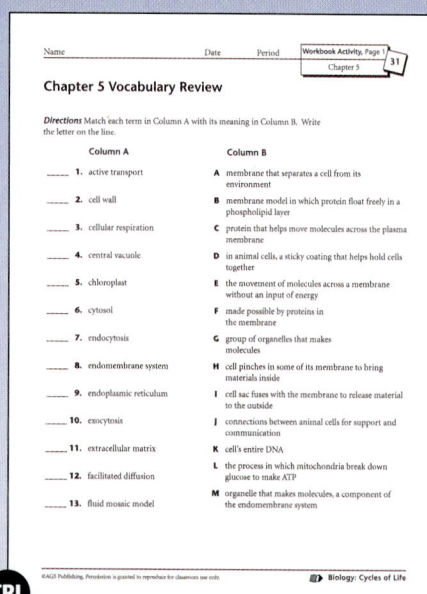

Workbook Activity 31, pages 1–3

Chapter 5 REVIEW

Word Bank
active transport
cellular respiration
chloroplast
cilia
cytoplasm
cytoskeleton
endomembrane system
flagella
genome
mitochondrion
nucleolus
passive transport
photosynthesis
plasma membrane
plasmodesmata
ribosome
vacuole

Vocabulary Review

On a sheet of paper, write the word or words from the Word Bank that complete each sentence correctly.

1. A membrane sac that transports and stores molecules is _____.

2. A molecule that moves through a membrane using _____ requires no energy.

3. Made of RNA and proteins, a(n) _____ puts together amino acids to make proteins.

4. The process of _____ transforms energy from sugars to ATP.

5. All the DNA in the cell is contained in the _____.

6. Energy in the form of ATP is required to move molecules through a membrane by _____.

7. Small, hairlike structures made of microtubles are _____.

8. A(n) _____ is an organelle found only in plant cells.

9. Plant cells communicate through _____.

10. An organelle called a(n) _____ transforms energy through respiration.

11. A selectively permeable _____ surrounds the outside of cells and regulates which molecules enter and exit the cell.

12. Ribosomes are made in the _____.

13. Plants use chlorophyll in the process of _____, which traps the sun's energy.

14. The area inside a cell that contains organelles is _____.

15. The endoplasmic reticulum, Golgi apparatus, vacuoles, and lysosomes all make up a cell's _____.

Review continued on next page

Review Answers

16. cytoskeleton 17. flagella

TEACHER ALERT

In the Chapter Review, the Vocabulary Review activity includes a sample of the chapter's vocabulary terms. The activity will help determine students' understanding of key vocabulary terms and concepts presented in the chapter. Other vocabulary terms used in the chapter are listed below.

actin	gap junction
bilayer	Golgi apparatus
cell wall	grana
central vacuole	intermediate filament
chlorophyll	lysosome
chromosome	matrix
cristae	microfilament
cytosol	microtubule
endocytosis	nuclear envelope
endoplasmic reticulum	pore
exocytosis	secrete
extracellular matrix	stroma
facilitated diffusion	thylakoid
fluid mosaic model	transport protein
	tubulin

Concept Review

18. C 19. C 20. B 21. A

Critical Thinking

22. You could examine the cells of the organism for clues. If the cells contain chloroplasts, it is more likely a plant. A better test would be to find out what makes up the cell walls. If the cell walls contain cellulose, then it is almost certainly a plant. 23. The ER and Golgi apparatus must be able to package molecules in membranes for transport. Lysosomes must have a membrane surrounding them to prevent their enzymes from destroying parts of the cell.

Chapter 5 REVIEW - continued

16. The _____ is made up of fibers that support and give the cell its shape.
17. Two structures made of microtubules that aid in movement are cilia and _____.

Concept Review

On a sheet of paper, write the letter of the answer that completes each sentence correctly.

18. Both plant and animal cells have _____.
    A mitochondria and chloroplasts
    B chloroplasts and a nucleus
    C a nucleolus and mitochondria
    D a nucleus and a cell wall

19. Molecules move between the nucleus and the rest of the cell through _____.
    A membranes   C pores
    B plasmodesmata   D vacuoles

20. Facilitated diffusion is a form of _____.
    A active transport
    B passive transport
    C pores
    D neither active nor passive transport

21. Actin makes up cytoskeleton fibers called _____.
    A microfilaments   C intermediate filaments
    B pores   D microtubules

166 Chapter 5 A Journey into the Eukaryotic Cell

Critical Thinking

On a sheet of paper, write the answers to the following questions. Use complete sentences.

22. You have discovered an organism that could be a plant or a mushroom. How would you decide what it is?
23. Each organelle of the endomembrane system is surrounded by a membrane. Why is this important?
24. Describe the structures that make up a chloroplast. Also describe which steps of photosynthesis take place at each structure.
25. Why can many physical differences in people be traced to differences in their DNA?

Research and Write

How did some cells develop membrane-bound organelles? Use the Internet and print resources to research the work of American scientist Lynn Margulis. Her work led to what is known as the endosymbiotic theory. This theory is one of the most famous and groundbreaking ideas in biology. Write a short paragraph or make a poster that describes her theory.

Test-Taking Tip If a word on a test is new to you, take the word apart. Compare the parts to other words you know.

---

24. Chloroplasts contain membrane sacs called thylakoids that are stacked together as grana. Chlorophyll molecules are bound onto the membrane, and light energy is collected here. Inside the membrane is a fluid called stroma where glucose is produced. 25. Having different sequences of DNA means that cells in a person's body will make different proteins. Therefore, each person will react differently to things in the environment. Many of these differences are easily seen, such as eye color or height.

Research and Write

Divide the class into small groups. Have each group present an oral presentation to the class. Encourage students to use a variety of sources of information, such as reference books, journals, textbooks, encyclopedias, and the Internet. Have students use visual aids, such as posters, during their oral presentation.

ALTERNATIVE ASSESSMENT

Alternative Assessment items correlate to the student Goals for Learning at the beginning of this chapter.

- Have students draw a diagram identifying the structure and activities of cell membranes.
- Have students write a description about information organelles.
- Have students orally describe energy organelles.
- Have students explain the endomembrane system to a partner.
- Have students orally describe the cytoskeleton.
- Have student pairs identify and draw sketches of plant structures. They should label and describe the function of each structure.

Chapter 5 Mastery Test B, pages 1–3

Chapter 6

Planning Guide
ATP and Energy Cycles

	Student Text Lesson			
	Student Pages	Vocabulary	Lesson Review	Critical Thinking Questions
Lesson 1 What Is Energy?	170–173	✔	✔	✔
Lesson 2 Making ATP	174–179	✔	✔	✔
Lesson 3 Enzymes and Energy Flow	180–183	✔	✔	✔
Lesson 4 More About Enzymes	184–189	✔	✔	✔

Chapter Activities

Teacher's Resource Library
Community Connection 6:
 Enzyme Cleaners
Graphic Organizer 6:
 Cells Use Energy

Teacher's Edition
Opener Activity

Assessment Options

Student Text
Chapter 6 Review

Teacher's Resource Library
Chapter 6 Mastery Tests A and B

Teacher's Edition
Chapter 6 Alternative Assessment

168A

Student Text Features									Teaching Strategies						Learning Styles					Teacher's Resource Library			
Achievements in Science	Science at Work	Biology in Your Life	Investigation/Discovery	Biology in the World	Express Lab	Link to	Research and Write	Technology and Society	ELL/ESL Strategy	Background Information	Science Journal	Applications (Home, Career, Community, Global, Environment)	Online Connection	Teacher Alert	Auditory/Verbal	Body/Kinesthetic	Interpersonal/Group Learning	Logical/Mathematical	Visual/Spatial	Workbook Activities	Alternative Workbook Activities	Lab Manual	Self-Study Guide
					172	✔			171	170		172							173	32	32	26	✔
	176		178			✔			175	174	176			175	175		176			33	33	27–28	✔
		181				✔		182	181	180		182				182				34	34		✔
186			187	189		✔	193		185	184	186	189	189					186		35–36	35–36	29–30	✔

Pronunciation Key

a	hat	e	let	ī	ice	ô	order	u̇	put	sh	she
ā	age	ē	equal	o	hot	oi	oil	ü	rule	th	thin
ä	far	ėr	term	ō	open	ou	out	ch	child	ᴛʜ	then
â	care	i	it	ȯ	saw	u	cup	ng	long	zh	measure

ə { a in about, e in taken, i in pencil, o in lemon, u in circus }

Alternative Workbook Activities

The Teacher's Resource Library (TRL) contains a set of lower-level worksheets called Alternative Workbook Activities. These worksheets cover the same content as the regular Workbook Activities but are written at a second-grade reading level.

Skill Track Online

Use Skill Track Online for *Biology: Cycles of Life* to monitor student progress and meet the demands of adequate yearly progress (AYP). Make informed instructional decisions with individual student and class reports of online lesson and chapter assessments. With immediate and ongoing feedback, students will also see what they have learned and where they need more reinforcement and practice.

Chapter at a Glance

Chapter 6: ATP and Energy Cycles
pages 168–193

Lessons

1. **What Is Energy?**
   pages 170–173

2. **Making ATP**
   pages 174–179

   Investigation 6 pages 178–179

3. **Enzymes and Energy Flow**
   pages 180–183

4. **More About Enzymes**
   pages 184–189

   Discovery Investigation 6
   pages 187–188

   Biology in the World page 189

Chapter 6 Summary page 190

Chapter 6 Review pages 191–193

Audio CD 🎧

Skill Track Online
for Biology: Cycles of Life

Teacher's Resource Library TRL

- Workbook Activities 32–36
- Alternative Workbook Activities 32–36
- Lab Manual 26–30
- Community Connection 6
- Graphic Organizer 6
- Resource File 11–12
- Chapter 6 Self-Study Guide
- Chapter 6 Mastery Tests A and B

(Answer Keys for the Teacher's Resource Library begin on page 675 of the Teacher's Edition. The Materials List for the Lab Manual activities begins on page 720.)

Opener Activity

Instruct students to bring in magazines and newspapers from home. Ask them to cut out a picture of an energy source, such as food, and an activity that requires energy, such as running. Have students glue or tape the pictures on a sheet of paper. Then ask them to choose a vocabulary term and use it in a sentence that relates to the pictures.

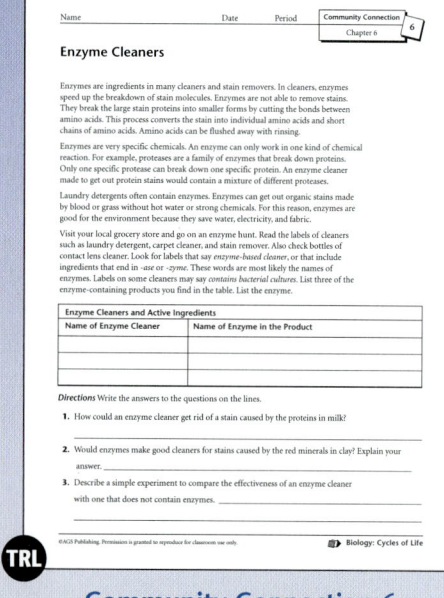

Community Connection 6

Chapter 6: ATP and Energy Cycles

You can see fireflies easily on a summer night. The photograph shows why. Fireflies give off light. The light is the result of a chemical process that requires energy. That energy comes from an organic molecule called ATP. An ATP molecule transfers energy to an enzyme. The enzyme starts a chemical reaction that gives off light. In Chapter 6, you will learn about the flow of energy in living things. You will also learn how ATP and enzymes are important to the transfer of energy in cells.

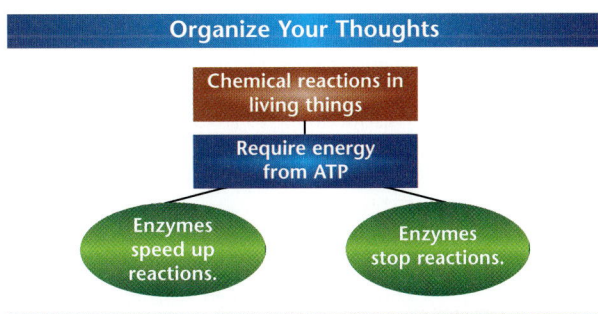

Organize Your Thoughts

Chemical reactions in living things → Require energy from ATP → Enzymes speed up reactions. / Enzymes stop reactions.

Goals for Learning

- To explain how chemical reactions in cells use or release energy
- To describe how ATP transfers energy within cells
- To identify the roles of enzymes in cells
- To explain how enzymes assist reactions to overcome energy barriers
- To describe how enzymes bind with specific molecules

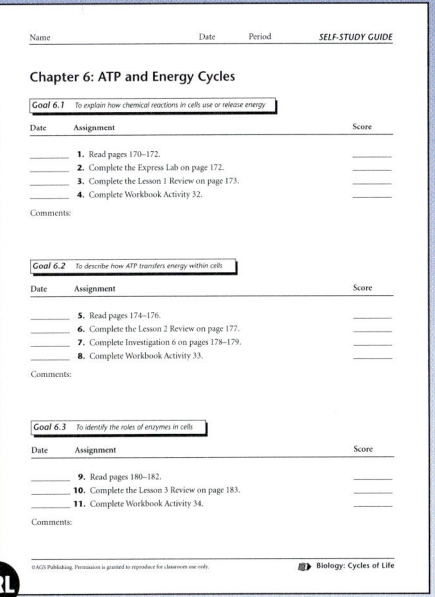

Chapter 6 Self-Study Guide

Introducing the Chapter

Ask students to look at page 168 and write down one or two questions they have about the firefly in the photograph. Then have a volunteer read the opening paragraph aloud. Ask students: What makes a firefly glow?

Lead a discussion in which students name cycles that occur in nature and what characteristics those cycles share. For example, in the water cycle, water is not created or destroyed, but rather changes form as it moves above, below, and on the earth. Connect this discussion to the lesson content by explaining that energy is similarly converted and transferred in cells of living things.

Have students copy each goal from Goals for Learning onto a separate index card. As they read the lessons, have students add information to their cards.

Notes and Math Tips

Ask volunteers to read the notes and math tips that appear in the margins throughout the chapter. Then discuss them with the class.

TEACHER'S RESOURCE

The AGS Publishing Teaching Strategies in Science Transparencies may be used with this chapter. The transparencies add an interactive dimension to expand and enhance the *Biology: Cycles of Life* program content.

CAREER INTEREST INVENTORY

The AGS Publishing Harrington-O'Shea Career Decision-Making System-Revised (CDM) may be used with this chapter. Students can use the CDM to explore their interests and identify careers. The CDM defines career areas that are indicated by students' responses on the inventory.

Lesson at a Glance

Chapter 6 Lesson 1

Overview In this lesson, students learn what ATP is and how energy in food changes forms to be used by cells.

Objectives

- To explain how food molecules provide a source of energy to living things
- To describe how ATP acts as energy currency at the cellular level
- To recognize that ATP hydrolysis releases energy
- To recognize that ATP synthesis requires energy

Student Pages 170–173

Teacher's Resource Library

Workbook Activity 32
Alternative Workbook Activity 32
Lab Manual 26

Vocabulary

adenine	metabolism
calorie	potential energy
kinetic energy	

Have students compose sentences using each of the vocabulary terms. Ask them to try using as many related words as possible in one sentence.

Background Information

There are fundamental laws of science that are important to this lesson. The laws of conservation of matter and energy state that both matter and energy are neither created nor destroyed, but rather change forms. For example, sunlight is transferred into stored chemical energy during photosynthesis. Animals then eat plants, and the stored chemical energy is broken down during cellular respiration to power processes in cells. The energy thereby changes from potential energy to kinetic energy. Scientists acknowledge the sun as the foremost source of energy.

Lesson 1 What Is Energy?

Objectives

After reading this lesson, you should be able to
- explain how food molecules provide a source of energy to living things
- describe how ATP acts as energy currency at the cellular level
- recognize that ATP hydrolysis releases energy
- recognize that ATP synthesis requires energy

Adenine
A nitrogen-containing compound found in ATP, DNA, and RNA

Metabolism
The collection of the chemical reactions that occur in the cell

Potential energy
Stored energy

Kinetic energy
Energy of motion

The human body does not waste energy, which means it is efficient. Energy is transferred in living things through the breakdown of nutrients. The body takes in food and uses it as a source of energy. If the body cannot use the energy right away, it stores the energy for later use.

Imagine you are watching a race. Where does a person get the energy to run? You may think it comes from simple sugars like glucose. However, the energy comes from the breakdown of glucose in the body. When glucose breaks down, the energy is used to form other molecules. One molecule is adenosine triphosphate, or ATP. ATP provides immediate energy.

ATP is called the energy currency of life. Like currency (money units), the cell can covert, or change, ATP from one form to another. Recall that ATP is a high-energy molecule that stores energy needed by cells. In animals, ATP is assembled in the mitochondria. ATP is made up of ribose, three phosphate groups, and **adenine.** Ribose is a five-carbon sugar. A phosphate group is a group of molecules made up of phosphorus and oxygen. Adenine is a nitrogen-containing compound. Adenine is also found in DNA and RNA.

Potential and Kinetic Energy

Living things need energy to stay alive. Living things use energy for growth, repair, reproduction, and **metabolism.** Metabolism is the collection of chemical reactions that occur in a cell. The following ideas help explain how living things access energy.

Think about lifting a pencil above your head. You provided the energy to lift the pencil. The pencil now has **potential energy,** or stored energy. Potential energy is energy that results from position. If you let go of the pencil, it drops. When the pencil drops, its potential energy transforms into **kinetic energy,** or energy of motion.

170 Chapter 6 ATP and Energy Cycles

---

1 Warm-Up Activity

Have students conduct several trials of the Express Lab on page 172. Instruct them to eliminate the extreme values (the highest and lowest measurements) and average the remaining values. Explain that the accuracy of their results improves as each additional trial is averaged with the rest.

Express Lab Answers

1. The ball dropped from the shelf or the high place had the most potential energy. **2.** The ball on the ground had the least potential energy. **3.** Energy was transferred by pushing the balls off objects and allowing gravity to take over.

4. The bounce height corresponds to the amount of kinetic energy, which is directly proportional to the amount of potential energy due to the balls' position above the ground. The greater the potential energy, the greater is the kinetic energy.

Calorie
A unit used to measure the amount of energy food contains

Link to >>>
Earth Science

Cyanobacteria were the first organisms that were able to photosynthesize and release oxygen. These organisms evolved about 2.5 billion years ago. At that time, they began releasing oxygen into the atmosphere as a product of photosynthesis. This oxygen-rich atmosphere paved the way for modern life.

Remember that energy cannot be created or destroyed. Energy can only be converted from one form to another. Cells take in chemical potential energy and convert it to kinetic energy to use in cellular activities. This cycle is repeated throughout the life of a cell.

Food and Potential Energy

Food has chemical potential energy, especially carbohydrates and fats, which are energy rich. The body processes the potential energy of food to release chemical energy. This process requires oxygen. Inside body cells, food is oxidized. Oxidation releases heat as energy. The energy is used to make ATP.

About 60 percent of the energy from the breakdown of food is converted to body heat. A person needs to keep a temperature of 98.6°F, even in a cold environment. The remaining 40 percent of the energy from food is converted to do work in the cells.

Study the food label in Figure 6.1.1. How many **calories** are in one serving? The calorie is a unit used to measure the amount of energy in food. The calorie count represents the energy content. Calories are energy units.

Figure 6.1.1 *Many packaged foods provide consumers with nutrition facts.*

---

2 Teaching the Lesson

Ask students to make a flowchart connecting metabolism, oxidation, and cellular respiration. Instruct them to leave space so they can add notes about each process. Metabolism is the most general term. It refers to all chemical processes in cells and should be listed first.

Students can also make charts to organize examples and characteristics of potential and kinetic energy.

Offer students some examples and definitions of calories. Tell them that a plain bagel has 195 calories and a large apple has 115. The text defines a calorie as a measure of energy. More specifically, a calorie is the amount of energy required to raise the temperature of one gram of water one degree Celsius.

3 Reinforce and Extend

Link to

Earth Science. Have students read the Link to Earth Science feature. Tell students that Earth is estimated to have been formed 4.5 billion years ago. In terms of Earth's age, 2.5 billion years is a significant span of time. To expand on this topic of geologic time, display a copy of the geologic time scale, which appears in Appendix D.

ELL/ESL Strategy

Language Objective: *To compare related words*

Write *oxygen*, *oxidized*, and *oxidation* on the board. Explain that when something is *oxidized*, oxygen has been added to it. Similarly, *oxidation* is the combination of a substance with oxygen. Show how these words contain the prefix *oxy-* (or *ox-*), which means "containing oxygen."

Pronunciation Guide

Use the pronunciation shown here to help students pronounce a difficult word in this lesson. Refer to the pronunciation key on the Chapter Planning Guide for the sounds of the symbols.

cyanobacteria (sī´ə nō bak tir´ē a)

At Home

Have students keep a daily journal of the foods they eat. Ask them to estimate their caloric intake by consulting food labels and searching for food calorie charts on the Internet. Students can also investigate how many calories they burn while doing everyday activities.

Global Connection

Divide students into groups and have them use the Internet to contact students in other countries. Ask them to compare and contrast food labels on processed foods. Have students write answers to the following questions: Are diets based on 2,000 calories as in the label in Figure 6.1.1 on page 171? Do food labels in other countries use the same units of measurement (grams, milligrams, calories)?

Lab Activities

Chapter 6 has Investigation and Discovery Investigation lab activities. Two additional lab activities for Chapter 6 appear in the Biology: Cycles of Life Lab Manual and on the Teacher's Resource Library CD-ROM.

Different types of foods provide different amounts of calories. Each gram of fat contains 9 calories. Each gram of protein or carbohydrate contains 4 calories. This is why one serving of high-fat food contains more energy and calories than one serving of a protein-rich or carbohydrate-rich food.

The potential energy of food does not provide energy directly to cells. Instead, these food molecules are broken down during cellular respiration. Energy is released to make ATP molecules. ATP provides energy for cells to meet their energy needs. In other words, ATP captures, transfers, and stores energy. ATP acts like a type of energy currency.

The process of releasing the chemical energy of food is called cellular respiration. We will discuss this process in detail in Chapter 7. Cellular respiration harvests energy for the cell in the form of ATP. You already know that this process occurs in the mitochondria.

Express Lab 6

Materials
- 3 tennis balls
- meterstick

Procedure
1. Set one tennis ball on the ground. Set a second tennis ball on a desk or a table. Set a third tennis ball on a shelf or a place that is higher than the desk or table.
2. Push the tennis ball off the desk or table. With a meterstick, measure how high the tennis ball bounces. Record this measurement.
3. Push the tennis ball off the shelf or from the high place. With a meterstick, measure how high the tennis ball bounces. Record this measurement.

Analysis
1. Which tennis ball had the most potential energy?
2. Which tennis ball had the least potential energy?
3. How did you transfer the potential energy of the tennis balls to kinetic energy?
4. What do the bounce height measurements tell you about the kinetic and potential energy of the three tennis balls?

172 Chapter 6 ATP and Energy Cycles

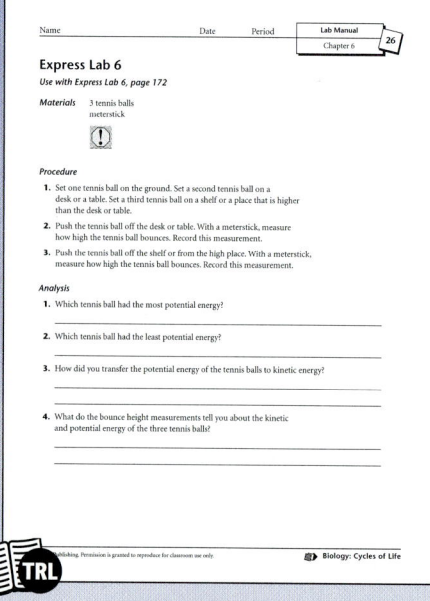

Lesson 1 REVIEW

On a sheet of paper, write the letter of the answer to complete each sentence correctly.

1. Adenosine triphosphate, or ATP, is used by the body as _____.
   - A material to make membranes
   - B a reactant to make sugars
   - C a means of removing waste
   - D a source of energy

2. The energy of motion is called _____.
   - A weight
   - B mass
   - C potential energy
   - D kinetic energy

3. Calories are units that measure _____.
   - A weight   B mass   C energy   D sugars

On a sheet of paper, write the word or words to complete each sentence correctly.

4. Food has chemical _____ energy.
5. Cellular respiration occurs in the _____ of a cell.
6. _____ is made up of ribose, three phosphate groups, and adenine.

Critical Thinking

On a sheet of paper, write the answers to the following questions. Use complete sentences.

7. Describe two ways the body uses energy from food. What proportion is used for each purpose?
8. Where does the energy supplied by ATP come from?
9. How would your eating habits change if you could use only glucose to supply energy to your body? Explain why this would not work well.
10. Explain how ATP operates as a type of energy currency.

ATP and Energy Cycles Chapter 6 173

Lesson 1 Review Answers

1. D 2. D 3. C 4. potential 5. mitochondria 6. ATP 7. Approximately 60 percent of the energy is converted to body heat. The remaining energy is used to do work in the cells. 8. Energy supplied by ATP is released by breaking chemical bonds that hold together phosphate molecules. 9. You would have to eat very small amounts of food continuously because, without ATP, glucose would release all of its energy at one time as it was digested by your body. This would be impossible, because your body requires different amounts of energy at various times. Also, your body would have to deal with excess energy, or food, by creating heat. 10. ADP adds a phosphate molecule by using energy from the breakdown of sugars and fats. This energy is stored in the phosphate bonds and changes the ADP to ATP. When energy is needed, the bonds break. This releases the phosphate molecule and the energy from the bond. Cells use this energy, and the ATP molecule becomes ADP again.

Portfolio Assessment

Sample items include:
- Express Lab answers
- Answers from Global Connection
- Lesson 1 Review answers

LEARNING STYLES

Visual/Spatial

Students may gain a greater understanding of what ATP is if they see a model of the compound. Ask students to use the Internet or reference books to find the chemical formula for ATP. Then help them construct models, using atomic modeling sets or plastic-foam balls with elements labeled. Students could also look for diagrams of an ATP compound on the Internet.

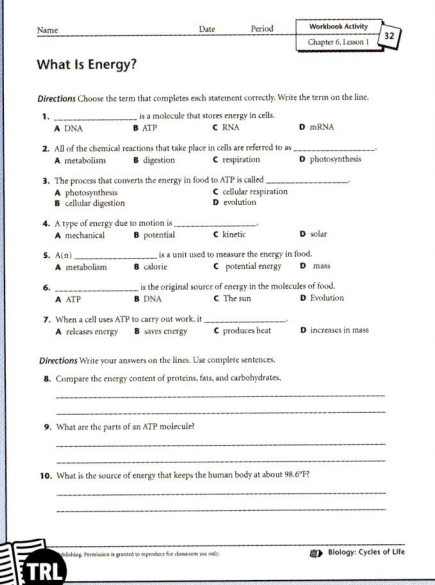

Workbook Activity 32

ATP and Energy Cycles 173

Lesson at a Glance

Chapter 6 Lesson 2

Overview In this lesson, students learn how ATP is made in plants and animals.

Objectives

- To explain how ATP is made from ADP
- To describe how ATP powers chemical reactions
- To compare how plants and animals make ATP

Student Pages 174–179

Teacher's Resource Library TRL

Workbook Activity 33
Alternative Workbook Activity 33
Lab Manual 27–28
Resource File 11

Vocabulary

ADP   phosphorylation

Have students use a dictionary to find the word history for each vocabulary term. Tell them to find the components that make up each of the terms.

Background Information

A phosphate is a polyatomic ion or a radical, typically composed of one phosphorus atom and four oxygen atoms. A radical is a group of two or more atoms that act like one atom and is unaltered in a chemical reaction. Phosphate groups that are negatively charged carry a -3 charge, as expressed in the formula PO_4^{3-}, which means that it has gained three electrons. A free phosphate ion in solution is called inorganic phosphate. This is what is exchanged during phosphorylation to change ADP into ATP. In Figure 6.2.1, the inorganic phosphate group is denoted as P_i.

The Krebs cycle is named for Sir Hans Kreb, a German biochemist who worked in the 1930s to explain how glucose is transformed into ATP.

Lesson 2 Making ATP

Objectives

After reading this lesson, you should be able to

- explain how ATP is made from ADP
- describe how ATP powers chemical reactions
- compare how plants and animals make ATP

ADP
Adenosine diphosphate; a molecule converted to ATP by the addition of a phosphate

Phosphorylation
The addition of a phosphate group to a molecule

Food that you eat is broken down by digestion into macromolecules. Macromolecules travel in the blood to all body cells. Cells take in macromolecules as needed. Inside the cell, energy stored in the bonds of the macromolecules is made available to the cell.

Making ATP and ADP

Recall that mitochondria are sites in cells where energy from food macromolecules is released. This energy is released when bonds in the macromolecules are broken. The energy is used to join a phosphate group to **ADP**, or adenosine diphosphate, to make ATP. Adding a phosphate group to a molecule is called **phosphorylation**.

Because the phosphate groups are negatively charged, they repel each other. It takes a large amount of energy to join them. This means ATP is an energy-rich molecule. The bonds between the phosphate groups in ATP have large amounts of chemical potential energy.

After ATP forms, it moves out of the mitochondria by diffusion to another site in the cell. It is stored until the cell needs energy to cause a chemical reaction to take place. Then ATP is hydrolyzed to provide energy for the reaction. The energy used to make ATP is released when ATP is hydrolyzed, or reacts to water. Hydrolysis removes a phosphate group from ATP. After hydrolysis, an ATP molecule becomes an ADP molecule. ADP is then available to become recharged.

Link to >>>

Health

ATP provides energy for your body by adding and losing phosphate groups. Phosphate groups are made from phosphorus, a nutrient required for all living things. In addition to being part of your energy cycle, phosphorous is found in your bones and in the walls of your body cells. Foods rich in phosphorus include milk, meat, fish, and eggs.

174 Chapter 6 ATP and Energy Cycles

Link to

Health. After students have read the feature about phosphorus, ask them to investigate what other high-energy foods contain phosphorus. List students' findings on the board and discuss the connection between phosphorus and proteins. Then ask students to observe their personal intake of phosphorus by keeping a journal of the foods they eat for a week.

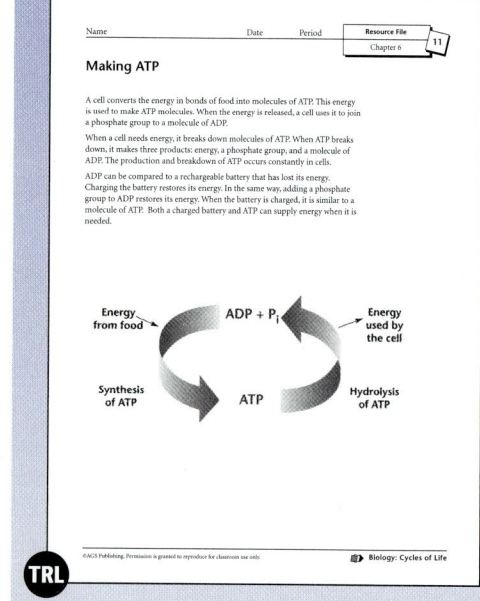

Resource File 11

Figure 6.2.1 sums up this cyclic process. A phosphate group is represented by P_i in the figure.

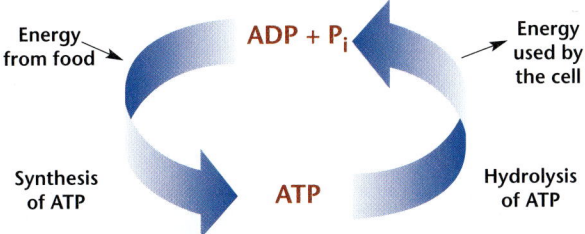

Figure 6.2.1 *In a cyclic process, cells release energy stored in food. This energy is then available for cellular activities.*

Making ATP in Plants and Animals

Plants use the energy in sunlight, carbon dioxide, and water to assemble energy-rich sugars to store as food. Plants use the stored food as a source of energy or to build materials for cells. Plants making food is an example of the transfer of matter and energy between an organism and its environment.

Animals that eat plants use the stored food as a source of energy for cellular processes. Animals that eat plants also use the stored food as a source of raw materials to build and repair cells. This is an example of the transfer of matter and energy between two organisms. Usually organisms can respond quickly to new demands.

Energy from food molecules is used to return ADP to the high-energy state of ATP. In Chapter 7, you will learn more about this process, called the Krebs cycle or the ATP/ADP cycle.

TEACHER ALERT

Students might have trouble remembering the difference between ATP and ADP. Tell them that the "T" in ATP signifies triphosphate, and *tri-* means "three" (as in three phosphates). Similarly, the "D" in ADP signifies diphosphate, and *di-* means "two" (as in two phosphates).

LEARNING STYLES

Auditory/Verbal

Have students read the section "Making ATP and ADP" aloud. Instruct them to make a sequential list of the cycle steps. Next have students read their lists aloud and record them on tape. Then invite them to play their tapes as they perform physical work, such as raising their hands or standing up. Doing so will help students make a connection between physical work and the chemical reactions taking place inside their bodies that power such movement.

Warm-Up Activity

Have students read the section "Making ATP and ADP." Then pass out magnets to students. Ask them to try pushing two negative poles together so they touch. Students will feel some resistance. Ask students: What does the magnet activity model? *(It models the large amount of energy needed to join two negatively charged phosphate groups.)* What sentences in the text support your answer? *(The first two sentences of the second paragraph of the section supports the answer.)*

 Teaching the Lesson

As they read, instruct students to keep a running list of every instance of energy transfer. For example, students should include the breakdown of sugars and fats releasing energy to assemble ATP, which then reacts with water and releases energy to drive cell processes.

Encourage students to look at word parts, context clues, or a dictionary to find out the meanings of some difficult words, such as *macromolecules* (p. 174), *diffusion* (p. 174), and *hemoglobin* (p. 176).

Reinforce and Extend

ELL/ESL STRATEGY

Language Objective: *To classify different parts of speech*

Make sure students know that *hydrolyze* and *hydrolysis* are different parts of speech. Tell students that *-ize* usually denotes a verb, while *-sis* or *-ion* denotes a noun. Ask students to find another example of two similar words that are different parts of speech. The term *synthesis* is used in Figure 6.2.1 on page 175. Ask students: What part of speech is *synthesis*? *(noun)* What is a verb form of the word? *(synthesize)*

Science at Work

Have students read the feature and then work together to make a list of questions they would ask a pharmacy technician. Help students brainstorm appropriate questions, such as the following: What are the most common prescriptions you fill? What illnesses do those medicines treat? How important is chemistry in what you do? What are common problems or obstacles that you deal with? How is what you do different from what a pharmacist does?

Select volunteers to go to local pharmacies and seek answers to the questions. You may want to call each pharmacy before you send students.

LEARNING STYLES

Logical/Mathematical

Ask students to reflect on what they have learned. Have them skim the lesson and write down any questions they still have about the content. Then help students answer their questions by looking at the text more closely. You might suggest outside sources for students to consult.

SCIENCE JOURNAL

Ask students to write a paragraph describing the ATP cycle, including how ATP is made, altered, and reassembled in living things. Make sure they use the following terms: *food, energy, phosphate groups, ADP, mitochondria, hydrolysis, phosphorylation,* and *cellular processes*. If students need help, suggest they refer to Figure 6.2.1 and describe the cycle that is pictured there.

Some macromolecules, such as DNA, are stable and rarely break down. Others break down quickly. For example, the hemoglobin in red blood cells lasts about 100 days. Some enzymes only last a few hours.

Without ATP, life as we understand it could not exist. ATP is the main source of energy for thousands of reactions that occur in all forms of life.

Science at Work

Pharmacy Technician

Pharmacists supply patients with the medicines they need to fight illness. More and more prescriptions today are being written for a growing and aging population. Pharmacists rely on skilled pharmacy technicians to help them handle the work.

Pharmacy technicians receive prescriptions from doctors and hospitals. They verify insurance information and help the pharmacist with everyday duties. Technicians even help prepare prescriptions under the guidance of a pharmacist.

Pharmacy technicians must have a high school degree. They must also complete a training program or have a two-year degree from a technical school.

Lesson 2 REVIEW

Word Bank
phosphorylation
energy
ATP

On a sheet of paper, write the word from the Word Bank that completes each sentence correctly.

1. Converting ADP to _____ is a key reaction for all life processes.
2. The addition of a phosphate group to a molecule is _____.
3. Most chemical reactions in cells require _____ to occur.

On a sheet of paper, write the letter of the answer that completes each sentence correctly.

4. The bonds between the phosphate groups in ATP have large amounts of chemical _____ energy.
   - **A** kinetic   **B** potential   **C** rich   **D** low

5. The main source of energy for reactions that occur in all living organisms is _____.
   - **A** diffusion   **C** ADP
   - **B** phosphate   **D** ATP

6. ATP captures _____ when it forms.
   - **A** energy   **B** nitrogen   **C** sugars   **D** fats

Critical Thinking

On a sheet of paper, write the answers to the following questions. Use complete sentences.

7. Describe how converting ADP to ATP is a key reaction in organisms.
8. Explain the process of phosphorylation.
9. Why do you think some macromolecules last longer than others in living organisms?
10. Why is the breakdown and replacement of enzymes in living organisms important?

ATP and Energy Cycles Chapter 6 177

Lesson 2 Review Answers

1. ATP **2.** phosphorylation **3.** energy **4.** B **5.** D **6.** A **7.** Converting ADP to ATP is a key reaction that supplies energy for life processes. In the ATP/ADP cycle, the breakdown of sugar and fats releases energy to assemble ATP. ATP loses one phosphate group when it reacts with water. It then releases energy to drive cell processes. **8.** Phosphorylation is the addition of a phosphate group to a protein or small molecule. This process requires energy. **9.** Some macromolecules are stable and rarely break down, so they last a long time. **10.** Enzymes are necessary for thousands of chemical reactions in living organisms.

Portfolio Assessment

Sample items include:
- Lists of instances of energy transfer
- Descriptions written for Science Journal
- Lesson 2 Review answers

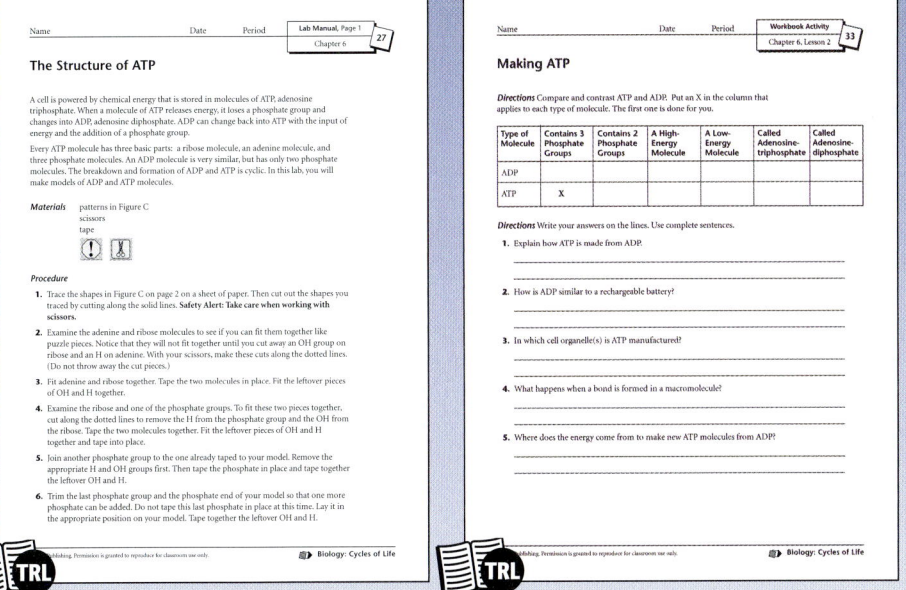

Lab Manual 27, pages 1–2   Workbook Activity 33

Investigation 6

Encourage students to read the investigation steps. Discuss questions they may have before beginning the investigation.

Objectives

- To perform an experiment using a common enzyme
- To observe how digestive enzymes work
- To test for sugars and starches present in reactants and products

Skills

Observing, using science lab equipment, measuring, organizing, collecting and recording information, analyzing data, drawing conclusions

Background

When starches such as potatoes are eaten, the body needs to digest them. Students will observe how amylase breaks up starch into simple sugars. The iodine test will reveal which samples contain starches. The Benedict's reagent will reveal which samples contain simple sugars.

You may want to write a simple reaction equation on the board, such as the following:

starch + amylase → maltose + maltose

Or you could draw a simple picture to show students what is happening in the reaction.

Time Frame

One class period

Procedure

- Have students work together in pairs or small groups to complete the activity.
- You may order the starch and maltose solutions prepared or prepare them yourself. The starch solution can be prepared by boiling chopped-up potatoes in water and using the starch extracted from the boiling.

INVESTIGATION 6

Materials
- safety goggles
- lab coat or apron
- wax pencil
- 6 test tubes
- test tube rack
- maltose solution
- starch solution
- 1% amylase solution
- 250 mL beaker
- warm water
- eyedropper
- iodine solution
- Benedict's reagent

Enzymes in Saliva

Your body uses enzymes to help digest food. When you eat, enzymes in your saliva help break down the sugars in food for your cells to use. In this lab, you will observe how the enzyme amylase found in saliva breaks down starches. You will test reactions with Benedict's reagent and iodine solution. Benedict's reagent changes color from blue to yellow if a sugar, such as maltose, is present. Iodine turns blue or black in the presence of starch.

Procedure

1. To record your data, make a data table like the one shown here.

Test Tube	Contents	Iodine Test	Benedict's Test
1	maltose (sugar)		
2	starch + amylase		
3	starch + maltose (sugar)		

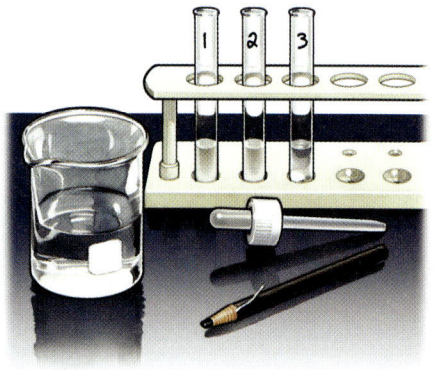

178   Chapter 6   ATP and Energy Cycles

Safety Alert

- Make sure that students have read and understood all safety rules for working in the lab. Discuss the Safety Alerts with students.
- Be sure students wear safety goggles and a lab coat or apron.
- Remind students to handle the solutions with care to avoid spills.
- Tell students not to drink or eat anything during the experiment.
- Be sure the warm-water bath is not hot or boiling. It is meant to simulate the warm environment of the human body.

2. Put on safety goggles and a lab coat or apron.
3. With a wax pencil, label three test tubes 1, 2, and 3. Label a second set of three test tubes in the same way and set these aside.
4. Add 2 mL of maltose solution to Test Tube 1.
5. Add 2 mL of starch solution to Test Tubes 2 and 3.
6. Add 4 mL of water to Test Tubes 1 and 3.
7. Add 4 mL of amylase solution to Test Tube 2.
8. To make a warm water bath, fill a 250 mL beaker with 150 mL of warm water.
9. Place all three test tubes in the warm water bath for 15 minutes. Be sure the test tubes stand upright. Do not allow water to enter the test tubes.
10. Remove the test tubes from the water bath. Pour half of the contents of each test tube into the empty test tubes with the same label.
11. For each pair, use the pencil to label one Test Tube I for iodine test and the other B for Benedict's test.
12. Place two drops of iodine solution in Test Tube 1-I. Gently swirl the test tube. Record your observations in the data table. Place two drops of Benedict's reagent in Test Tube 1-B. Gently swirl the tube. Record your observations.
13. Repeat Step 12 for Test Tubes 2-I and 2-B, and 3-I, and 3B.

Cleanup/Disposal
Before leaving the lab, follow your teacher's instructions to clean up and dispose of your materials.

Analysis
1. What happened to the starch when amylase was added to it?
2. Which solutions tested positive for sugar? Which solutions tested positive for starch?

Conclusions
1. Why did you use maltose in one of your test tubes?
2. How does amylase work in your body? Where in your body do these processes take place?
3. Why is it important for you to chew your food well when you eat?

Explore Further
Try the test again using a starchy food such as corn, rice, or potatoes. Be sure you chop up the food before putting it in the test tube. The chopping represents the action of chewing before digestion.

Cleanup/Disposal
Instruct students in proper cleanup and disposal of materials.

Analysis Answers
1. Amylase broke down the starch into simple sugars.
2. Test Tube 1 (maltose solution) and Test Tube 2 (starch solution with amylase) give a positive test for sugars with the Benedict's reagent. Test Tube 2 may give a positive test for starch with the iodine if the amylase has not broken down the entire sample. Test Tube 3 (starch control) tests negative for sugars and positive for starch.

Conclusions Answers
1. The maltose was a control to compare a known positive result with the experimental test tube (amylase + starch).
2. Amylase works to break down the starchy foods you eat. This process takes place in your mouth as you chew.
3. Chewing your food well gives amylase a chance to digest the food properly before it goes to your stomach.

Explore Further Answers
Encourage students to use small amounts of food and chop them into small pieces for easier digestion. You may need to add more enzyme to break down the food particles. Be sure to point out that the physical breakdown of food—chewing—influences the rate of digestion by enzymes by increasing the surface area of the food.

Assessment
Check to be sure that students have correctly recorded results in their data table. You might include the following items from this investigation in student portfolios:
- Data table
- Answers to Analysis and Conclusions questions
- Student proposal for additional work in response to Explore Further

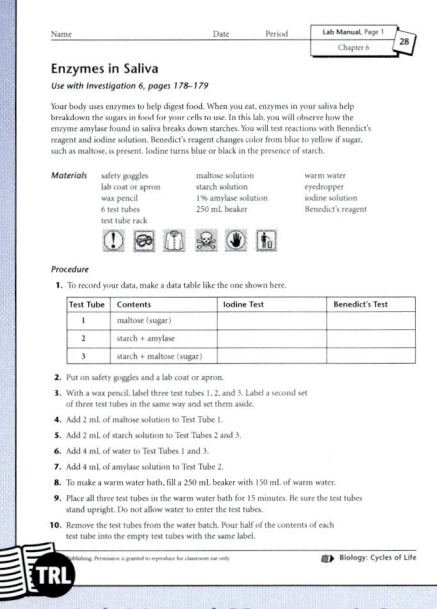

Lab Manual 28, pages 1–2

Lesson at a Glance

Chapter 6 Lesson 3

Overview In this lesson, students learn what enzymes are and how they regulate energy flow in living things.

Objectives

- To explain that enzymes act as catalysts for chemical reactions
- To describe how enzymes speed up chemical reactions
- To recognize that living organisms make most enzymes

Student Pages 180–183

Teacher's Resource Library

Workbook Activity 34

Alternative Workbook Activity 34

Vocabulary

catalyst   pepsin
diabetes   saliva
obesity

Have students make crossword puzzles using the vocabulary terms in this lesson. Instruct them to use the definitions as the clues. After they have made their puzzles, have students exchange papers and complete their partner's puzzle.

Background Information

Amino acids are often called the building blocks of life. More than 500 amino acids can be found in nature, but only a core group of 20 amino acids are said to be proteinogenic, or protein building. Proteins, such as enzymes, are made up of these amino acids.

Almost every living thing uses a standard genetic code to make proteins. These 20 amino acids are part of that code. The code is represented by a very long molecule called DNA, or deoxyribonucleic acid.

Lesson 3 Enzymes and Energy Flow

Objectives

After reading this lesson, you should be able to

◆ explain that enzymes act as catalysts for chemical reactions
◆ describe how enzymes speed up chemical reactions
◆ recognize that living organisms make most enzymes

Catalyst
A chemical that helps in a chemical reaction, but is not consumed or changed in the reaction

Enzymes are proteins in living things. They are made of amino acids. Specific enzymes help in the chemical reactions in living organisms. Enzymes help organisms control the chemical environment at the cellular level. Enzymes can speed up chemical reactions. They can also stop chemical reactions from occurring. Enzymes act as **catalysts.** A catalyst is a chemical that helps a chemical reaction, but is not consumed or changed in the reaction.

Living things get energy for cellular processes by breaking down energy-rich food molecules. Getting nutrients and energy from food involves many chemical reactions. These reactions need catalysts. Catalysts lower the energy level required for chemical reactions to occur.

The Role of Enzymes

Most biological catalysts, or enzymes, are specific to certain chemical reactions. Cells create an enzyme with one purpose—to act as a catalyst for one specific biochemical reaction.

Enzymes are part of every chemical reaction in living organisms. They assist digestion, growth, and building of cells. They help break down substances such as vitamins and nutrients. Enzymes also support all reactions involving energy transfer.

Enzymes control the rate and site of chemical reactions. For example, enzymes speed the creation of RNA and DNA. Enzymes also specify the sites for building RNA. Once RNA is formed, enzymes help make proteins that the cell needs.

The breakdown of chemical bonds releases energy. Enzymes control the release of energy in chemical reactions so that the proper amount of energy is released.

Chapter 6 ATP and Energy Cycles

Obesity
A condition of being greatly overweight

Diabetes
A genetic disease in which a person has too much sugar in his or her blood

The Importance of Enzymes

Enzymes play a very important role in health. An imbalance or lack of certain enzymes can cause many health problems in people. For example, protease is an enzyme that digests proteins. A lack of protease can result in low blood sugar, kidney problems, and bone problems. Another enzyme, amylase, digests carbohydrates. A lack of amylase can result in skin rashes and liver disease.

Lipase is an enzyme that digests fats. If there is not enough lipase in the body, health problems can result. This includes **obesity, diabetes,** and heart and blood vessel disease.

Biology in Your Life

Consumer Choices: Enzyme Products

The human body uses enzymes constantly to do a wide variety of jobs. Some people do not have the enzymes needed to digest certain foods. Taking enzyme products before or while they eat allows them to enjoy these foods.

The most common enzyme-related food problem is lactose intolerance. Lactose is a sugar in dairy products such as milk, cheese, and yogurt. Most people have an enzyme called lactase that allows them to break down and digest lactose.

People who do not have lactase cannot digest lactose. They have stomach problems if they eat dairy foods. Lactose intolerance is common in older people or people of African, Asian, and Mediterranean backgrounds. If you have lactose intolerance, you can use a tablet or liquid product that contains lactase. It will break down the lactose as you eat dairy products.

Other food enzyme products are available to address problems with eating beans and other vegetables. These enzymes help digest the complex sugars in vegetables. The enzymes work the same way lactase does. You add it to your food as you eat, and it helps digest the food in your stomach.

1. Why do some people have trouble eating dairy products?
2. How do enzyme products help people with food intolerances?
3. Do you or someone you know have trouble eating certain foods? If yes, what can the person do to help digestion?

ATP and Energy Cycles   Chapter 6   181

Warm-Up Activity

Conduct the following demonstration of an enzyme at work. Gather two transparent plastic cups, some milk, some meat tenderizer, and a teaspoon. Label one cup "control" and the other "enzyme." Put 4 teaspoons of milk in each cup. Then add 2 teaspoons of meat tenderizer to the "enzyme" cup. Stir and have students make observations. After 35 minutes, have them make observations again. The meat tenderizer is an enzyme that breaks down the proteins in milk. Students should observe that a white solid mass similar to yogurt has formed.

Teaching the Lesson

Instruct students to make a three-column KWL chart to catalog what they already know about enzymes and what they want to know about enzymes. After completing the lesson, have students add to the third column what they learned about enzymes.

Have students take notes as they read by listing characteristics and examples of enzymes.

Reinforce and Extend

Biology in Your Life

Have students read the feature about enzyme products. Then ask students to conduct a survey among family members and friends to find out how common enzyme-related food problems are. Students should specifically ask what enzyme deficiency or ailment a person has.

Biology in Your Life Answers

1. Some people's bodies do not produce the enzyme lactase naturally. Lactase breaks down the sugars in dairy products. **2.** Enzyme products add a particular enzyme to food as the person eats. The enzyme is then present in the stomach to digest the food. **3.** Answers will vary. Students should indicate that consuming enzyme products before or while eating will help people digest foods they are intolerant of.

ELL/ESL Strategy

Language Objective: *To compare and contrast enzyme imbalances and deficiencies*

Group English language learners with partners proficient in English. Have pairs read through this page and create a visual that shows several of the health problems on pages 181–182. Tell students that they need to present the information so that the cause of each health problem is clear.

ATP and Energy Cycles   181

IN THE COMMUNITY

Have students investigate whether enzymes are being used in local landfills, wastewater treatment plants, or bioreactors. Students should start by visiting their community's Web site or going to their city hall or municipal offices. For more detailed information, students could conduct an interview with a municipal official. Help them generate a list of appropriate questions.

LEARNING STYLES

Body/Kinesthetic

Make labels of enzymes and substances that enzymes react with by writing the following terms on separate index cards: *saliva, pepsin, starches,* and *proteins.* Give a card to each student, and then line up the enzymes (*saliva* and *pepsin*) on one side of the room, and the substances that enzymes react with (*starches* and *proteins*) on the opposite side. Instruct students to find their match. (*"Saliva"* should match with *"starches,"* and *"pepsin"* should match with *"proteins."*) Have students research other enzymes and the substances that they react with.

Science Myth

Before students read the myth, ask them: Do you think enzymes are living organisms like cells? Then ask a volunteer to read the feature aloud. Ask students: Can heat kill enzymes? (*No, enzymes are proteins, not living things.*) Can heat affect enzymes? (*Yes, it can change an enzyme's shape and ability to function.*)

Technology and Society

After students have read the feature, ask them to research specific cases in which the use of enzymes has helped cleanup operations. The Environmental Protection Agency's Web site at www.epa.gov is a good starting place. Have students report their findings to the class.

182 Chapter 6

Saliva
A liquid produced by glands in the mouth that helps in chewing and starts digestion

Pepsin
An enzyme produced in the stomach for digestion

Science Myth

Myth: Heat kills enzymes.

Fact: Enzymes are proteins, not living things, so they cannot be killed. High temperatures can change the shape of enzymes so that they cannot function. Most enzymes regain their original shape when the temperature returns to normal.

Obesity is a condition of being greatly overweight. Diabetes is an inherited disease in which people have too much sugar in their blood. This results in a high blood glucose level.

People with diabetes may have to take insulin regularly to help in the metabolism of carbohydrates. As seen in Figure 6.3.1, insulin is given by injections, or shots. Insulin is a chemical signal. It causes specific enzymes to work in response to blood glucose levels.

Human **saliva** and the digestive tract have high concentrations of enzymes. Saliva contains an enzyme that converts starches into sugars. Enzymes assist in digestion. The stomach combines the enzyme **pepsin** with acid to speed up the digestion of proteins. Enzymes are carried to the intestines to help the digestion of fats.

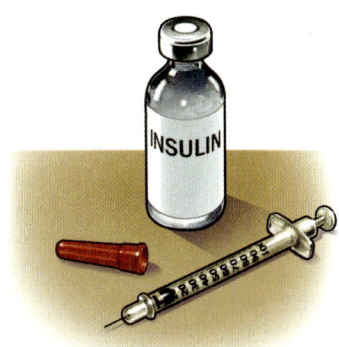

Figure 6.3.1 *People with diabetes may need to take insulin.*

Technology and Society

Engineers use the power of enzymes to clean up polluted soils and streams. They create huge containers of enzymes called bioreactors. These bioreactors are specially mixed to clean up the chemicals in a polluted area. The chemicals are then added to the bioreactor and digested by the enzymes. This process models the way enzymes in your body digest food.

182   Chapter 6   ATP and Energy Cycles

CAREER CONNECTION

A geneticist is a biologist who studies genetics. Genetics can be summarized as the branch of biology that deals with heredity. This involves the study of cells and DNA. Clinical geneticists diagnose, study, and treat genetic disease. The development and growth of genetically modified organisms has also increased the demand for experts in genetics. Direct students to the following Web site to ask questions of a geneticist: www.thetech.org/askScientist/askquestion.php.

Students can also visit the Princeton Review's Web site and access its career center for more information on geneticists: www.princetonreview.com/cte/profiles/dayInLife.asp?careerID=202.

Lesson 3 REVIEW

Link to
Home and Career

Researchers are developing coffee plants that produce decaffeinated beans genetically. Normal coffee plants use an enzyme to make the caffeine in their beans. By changing the DNA of the coffee plant, researchers hope to turn off the gene that produces the enzyme. This will produce caffeine-free beans.

On a sheet of paper, write the letter of the answer that completes each sentence correctly.

1. Enzymes allow chemical reactions to occur _____.
   - **A** faster
   - **B** stronger
   - **C** more often
   - **D** slower

2. Enzymes work by _____.
   - **A** lowering the energy needed to break bonds
   - **B** adding heat to a reactant molecule
   - **C** making the reactants water-soluble
   - **D** increasing the speed of electrons

3. Enzymes are _____.
   - **A** acids
   - **B** sugars
   - **C** fats
   - **D** proteins

On a sheet of paper, write the word or words that complete each sentence correctly.

4. Enzymes are also called _____ because they support a reaction, but do not change during the reaction.

5. Enzyme action controls the _____ and _____ of a reaction.

6. In humans, _____ and the _____ have high concentrations of enzymes to help the breakdown of food.

Critical Thinking

On a sheet of paper, write the answers to the following questions. Use complete sentences.

7. How do enzymes control chemical reactions?

8. List and describe three health problems caused by an imbalance or lack of certain enzymes.

9. Describe how enzymes assist in the digestion process.

10. Why are enzymes important in living organisms?

ATP and Energy Cycles   Chapter 6   183

Lesson at a Glance

Chapter 6 Lesson 4

Overview In this lesson, students learn more about enzymes.

Objectives

- To describe how pH affects enzyme activity
- To define *activation energy* and explain its importance
- To recognize that an enzyme only works in a specific chemical reaction
- To recognize that enzymes change shape during chemical reactions, but are not changed chemically

Student Pages 184–189

Teacher's Resource Library

Workbook Activity 35–36

Alternative Workbook Activity 35–36

Lab Manual 29–30

Resource File 12

Vocabulary

activation energy   substrate
active site

Write each vocabulary term and definition in random order on the board. Have students match each term with the appropriate definition.

Background Information

Most people credit English chemist Joseph Priestley with starting the study of photosynthesis. In the late 1700s, he did an experiment in which a burning candle "injured" the air in a jar, causing the candle to extinguish itself before the wax and wick were consumed. Other scientists, such as Jean Senebier and Theodore de Saussure, expanded on Priestley's work. Senebier proved that carbon dioxide was the "injured" air and was absorbed by plants, and Saussure demonstrated that an increase in plant mass was not due only to the absorbed carbon dioxide, but also to water. The reactants in photosynthesis are carbon dioxide and water; the products are glucose and oxygen.

184 Chapter 6

Lesson 4 — More About Enzymes

Objectives

After reading this lesson, you should be able to

- describe how pH affects enzyme activity
- define activation energy and explain its importance
- recognize that an enzyme only works in a specific chemical reaction
- recognize that enzymes change shape during chemical reactions, but are not changed chemically

Activation energy
The amount of energy needed to start a chemical reaction

Plants transfer the energy from sunlight into food that has chemical energy. Plants use sunlight, carbon dioxide, and water to make energy-rich sugars. Enzymes are involved in the chemical reactions that make these sugars. This process is called photosynthesis, and it is the basis of all life. Only plants perform photosynthesis.

Enzymes are at work wherever there is life. Yeast cells use enzymes when they raise bread dough. Bacteria use enzymes to break down cellulose fiber in the stomachs of cows and termites. Plants, animals, and bacteria use enzymes to control chemical reactions in their cells. Reproduction, growth, metabolism, and synthesis involve enzymes that regulate reactions in all living things.

Some enzymes stop reactions. This keeps the cell from using valuable resources. An example is penicillin, a substance that gets rid of harmful bacteria. Penicillin works by stopping an enzyme that bacteria use to make their cell walls.

Activation Energy

Most chemical reactions in cells need enzymes. A chemical reaction has inputs called reactants and outputs called products. Remember that a reactant is altered in a chemical reaction. To begin the reaction, the chemical bonds of the reactants must be broken. This requires energy, usually heat energy. This energy is called **activation energy**. It is the energy needed to activate the chemical reaction.

Under normal temperatures in organisms, only a few reactants have enough energy to exceed this activation energy. Adding heat would give reactants more energy. This is not an option in living things. Instead, enzymes lower the activation energy of reactions. In other words, enzymes allow reactions to occur at cooler temperatures. Figure 6.4.1 illustrates how enzymes lower the amount of activation energy needed to break the chemical bonds of reactants.

184 Chapter 6 ATP and Energy Cycles

Pronunciation Guide

Use the pronunciation shown here to help students pronounce a difficult word in this lesson. Refer to the pronunciation key on the Chapter Planning Guide for the sounds of the symbols.

penicillin (pe nə si′lən)

Substrate and Active Site

There are many different kinds of enzymes. Each enzyme works on only a certain chemical reaction. The enzyme recognizes the shape of its reactant molecule. The reactant molecule is called a **substrate**. A substrate is the molecule on which an enzyme reacts.

The enzyme has a special shape called the **active site**. The shape of its active site fits the substrate more snugly. When they come together, the active site changes shape. Think about how your hand changes shape when you shake someone's hand so you have a better fit.

Substrate
A reactant molecule; the molecule on which an enzyme reacts

Active site
The area on an enzyme where the substrate fits in shape and chemistry

Link to >>> Health

Most drugs used to treat the HIV virus that causes AIDS stop enzymes from working. These drugs stop the enzymes the virus needs to survive and reproduce. Often the drugs that work against HIV also damage mitochondria. The side effects of HIV drugs are often weakness and failure of body tissues that need lots of energy.

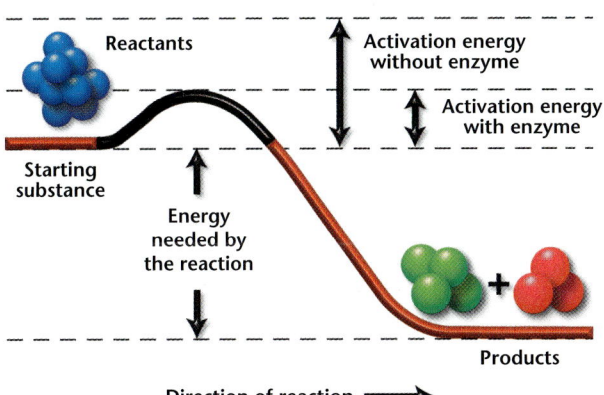

Figure 6.4.1 Enzymes lower activation energy to allow chemical reactions in the cell to take place.

---

1 Warm-Up Activity

Divide the class into groups. Gather some pieces of a jigsaw puzzle that fit together. Organize the fitting pieces into assembled pairs (one pair for each group), and then split them up, distributing one of the fitting pieces to each group of students. Tell students the piece they have represents a chemical compound to be used in a chemical reaction. Then pass out other pieces of the puzzle, the piece that fits the "compound," along with some that do not. Ask students to try to match the "compound" with the piece that fits. Ask students: What does the piece that fits the "compound" represent? *(an enzyme)* Why are pieces of a jigsaw puzzle appropriate as a model? *(because cells create an enzyme with one purpose—to act as a catalyst for one specific biochemical reaction—just as each puzzle piece has one specific piece that fits it)*

Note: Make sure that each "compound" distributed fits only one "enzyme."

2 Teaching the Lesson

Remind students that energy is stored in chemical bonds. Make sure students understand that activation energy is the energy needed to break those bonds so the elements in reactants can be rearranged in reactions that form products. A quick review of chemistry vocabulary (Chapter 2) may be helpful.

3 Reinforce and Extend

Link to

Health. AIDS is an acronym for Acquired Immunodeficiency Syndrome. HIV is the virus that causes AIDS. Cells of HIV attack and kill cells of the body's immune system that normally fight off microbes and infection. When the immune system is thus weakened, it becomes less effective at fighting opportunistic diseases such as pneumonia. HIV is transmitted primarily through unprotected sexual intercourse and sharing of infected syringes. Avoiding such activities is the best way to avoid infection. There is no cure for AIDS, but there are drugs that slow its progress. Some of these drugs bind to and disable proteins, such as reverse transcriptase and protease, which HIV uses to copy and replicate itself.

Resource File 12

ELL/ESL Strategy

Language Objective: *To explain a photosynthesis diagram*

Have students learning English explain the effect an enzyme has on the activation energy needed by a starting substance in a reaction with the aid of Figure 6.4.1. Have partners study the diagram and explain it to each other in their own words. Invite pairs to reproduce the diagram on the board and to explain to the class the concept of activation energy provided by enzymes.

Lesson 4 Review Answers

1. reactants, products 2. substrate 3. activation energy 4. Each enzyme works on only a certain chemical reaction. The enzyme recognizes the shape of the reactant molecule, or substrate. The active site of the enzyme fits the substrate. After they fit together, the active site changes shape. This changes the chemical reaction. 5. Penicillin stops a reaction between a bacteria and the enzyme it uses to make its cell walls.

Portfolio Assessment

Sample items include:
- Science Journal summaries
- Lesson 4 Review answers

Achievements in Science

Have students read the feature about diabetes. Ask students to ask any relatives with diabetes what the testing kits are like. Then have students search the Internet to find information about recent advances in home monitoring for people with diabetes.

LEARNING STYLES

Interpersonal/Group Learning

Organize students into groups of three or four and have them compile a master list of characteristics and examples of enzymes. Some students will include information that other students have neglected. Then have a representative from each group read their list to the class. Hearing the characteristics repeated will help students remember them.

SCIENCE JOURNAL

Ask students to write a summary of why they think enzymes are important to life.

Lesson 4 REVIEW

Word Bank
activation energy
products
reactants
substrate

On a sheet of paper, write the word or words from the Word Bank to complete each sentence correctly.

1. A chemical reaction has inputs called _____ and outputs called _____.
2. The active site of an enzyme fits the _____.
3. The amount of energy needed to start a chemical reaction is called the _____.

Critical Thinking

On a sheet of paper, write the answers to the following questions. Use complete sentences.

4. How does an enzyme work in a chemical reaction?
5. Give an example of an enzyme that stops a reaction.

Achievements in Science

Over 18 million people, or 6.3 percent of the population, have diabetes. Diabetes happens when the body cannot produce or properly use insulin. The body secretes insulin. This hormone changes sugar, starches, and other food into energy for daily life. Without enough insulin, the body cannot keep the right amount of sugar in the blood.

People with diabetes must inject insulin and monitor their blood-sugar levels constantly. Man-made insulin first became available in the 1920s. People had to make regular trips to the doctor to have their sugar levels checked and get treatment.

A breakthrough came in the 1940s. Then, Helen Free and her husband, Alfred, invented a test to check blood-sugar levels at home. Anyone could easily use this "dip-and-read" test at anytime. Today, many people with diabetes use in-home tests.

186 Chapter 6 ATP and Energy Cycles

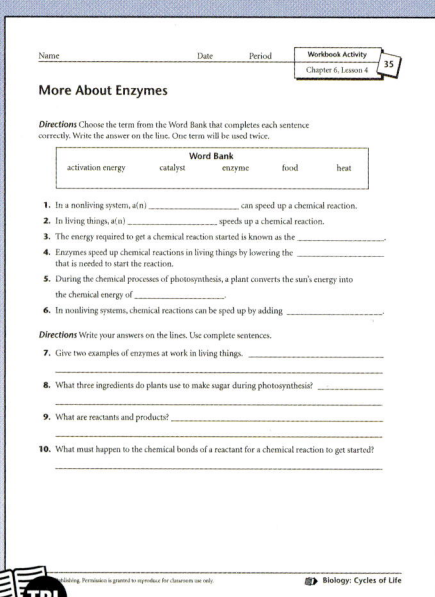

Workbook Activity 35

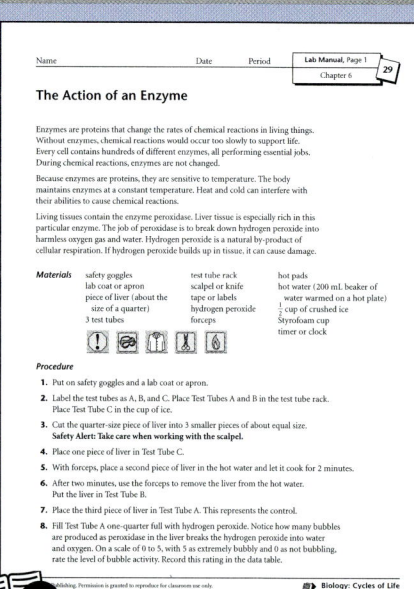

Lab Manual 29, pages 1–3

DISCOVERY INVESTIGATION 6

How Does pH Affect Stomach Enzymes?

Materials
- safety goggles
- lab coat or apron
- 6 test tubes
- test tube rack
- 2% pepsin solution
- cool tap water
- diluted sodium hydroxide
- diluted hydrochloric acid
- wax pencil
- pieces of boiled egg whites
- eyedropper
- large beaker
- warm water

Pepsin is an enzyme that digests proteins. The stomach releases pepsin to break down proteins into peptides and amino acids for digestion. The stomach's environment is full of dilute hydrochloric acid, or HCl. HCl is a strong, irritating acid. Pepsin works well in an acidic environment. In this lab, you will create a procedure to test the activity of pepsin over time at different pH levels. You will use pieces of boiled egg as the protein substrate. You will test samples at different times to see how quickly the egg is digested at different pH levels.

Procedure

1. Put on safety goggles and a lab coat or apron.
2. Fill five test tubes half full of the 2% pepsin solution. Be sure each test tube contains the same amount of solution. Create a control by filling a sixth test tube half full of cool tap water. Using the wax pencil, label the control C.

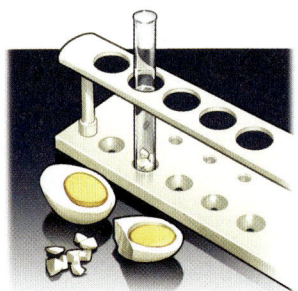

ATP and Energy Cycles Chapter 6 **187**

SAFETY ALERT

- Make sure that students have read and understood all safety rules for working in the lab. Discuss the Safety Alerts with students.
- Be sure students wear safety goggles and a lab coat or apron.
- Remind students to use caution when handling the diluted hydrochloric acid and sodium hydroxide.

Discovery Investigation 6

This investigation is less structured than the first investigation in this chapter. It offers students more challenge and requires more teacher facilitation. Encourage students to read the investigation steps. Discuss with students the question in the title of this investigation.

Objectives
- To design and conduct an experiment
- To observe the activity of an enzyme at different pH levels
- To organize information in a table for comparison

Skills
Measuring, observing, designing an experiment, using science lab equipment, collecting and recording information, making inferences, organizing, communicating, analyzing data, drawing conclusions

Background
Pepsin is an enzyme in the stomach that digests proteins. Pepsin works best at a pH range of 1 to 3. To maintain this pH, the stomach secretes hydrochloric acid. In this lab, students will organize test tubes filled with pepsin enzyme solution at different pH levels and observe how quickly egg whites are digested.

Time Frame
One class period

Procedure
- Have students work together in groups to complete the activity.
- Prepare the pieces of hard-boiled egg whites ahead of time. Boil the eggs and separate the yolks from the whites. Chop the egg whites into small pieces about the size of a pencil eraser. Small pieces will give the best results. Be sure all pieces are the same size so students can easily compare how much the egg whites have been "digested" from one test tube to another.

Continued on page 188

Continued from page 187

- Review students' data tables and the pH levels they have chosen before the investigation begins.
- Optional: Use a pH meter or testing strips to test the pH levels of the various test tubes. Be sure students use a suitable hydrochloric acid solution and that they add the acid to the solution carefully. You can substitute vinegar for hydrochloric acid.
- Be sure students make at least one test tube with a basic solution. Encourage students to test a variety of pH levels. An ideal setup would include the control and four solutions of varying acidity.
- You can easily convert this lab into an investigation of how surface area affects protein digestion. Instead of changing the pH level, have students use different-sized pieces of egg white and observe how the different sizes affect the rate of digestion. Ask them to infer how chewing is important for digestion. If you have extra time, you can add this investigation to the pH investigation.

Sample Data Table

Test Tube pH	% Egg Is Broken Down
1. control	
2.	
3.	
4.	
5.	

Cleanup/Disposal

Instruct students in proper cleanup and disposal of materials.

Results

Answers will vary. Students will discover that pepsin works best at a pH of 1 to 3. Their results should reflect that an acidic environment is necessary for pepsin to work well. At higher pH levels, the pepsin enzyme is completely ineffective.

If surface area is investigated, students should find that the greater the surface area (the smaller the pieces), the quicker digestion occurs.

Answers to Analysis, Conclusions, and Explore Further begin on page 670 of this Teacher's Edition.

---

3. Determine the pH levels you want to use in your experiment.
4. You should test a minimum of three pH levels (acidic, neutral, and basic), but you can test up to five. With a wax pencil, number the test tubes. On a sheet of paper, write each pH level and assign it a test tube number. This is your data table. Have your teacher approve your pH levels and data table.
5. Using the eyedropper, add sodium hydroxide to the basic test tube(s) and hydrochloric acid to the acidic test tube(s). Add different amounts according to the variety of pH levels you want. For the neutral pH and control test tubes, do not add either. **Safety Alert: Be careful with diluted hydrochloric acid. Although diluted, it can damage skin, eyes, and clothing. If it spills, rinse the area immediately.**
6. Add a piece of boiled egg white to every test tube. Be sure the pieces are all the same size.
7. Fill the beaker half full with warm water. The water level should be below the top of the test tubes. Place the test tubes in this warm water bath. Be sure the test tubes stand upright with their openings clear of the surface. Water should not enter the test tubes.
8. Observe how the pepsin breaks down the egg whites at each pH level. Record your observations in your data table. At regular time intervals, estimate how much of the egg white is broken down in each test tube. Use your control for comparison.

Cleanup/Disposal

Ask your teacher for guidance in disposing of the solutions. Before leaving the lab, wash your hands.

Analysis

1. How did pH affect the rate at which the egg white was digested?
2. At what pH level did the pepsin work best?

Conclusions

1. What kind of environment does your stomach need to maintain to digest proteins well?
2. Why did you place the test tubes in a warm water bath?

Explore Further

Why do people take antacids? What effect do you think antacids have on your stomach and digestion?

Assessment

Check students' data tables to be sure they have recorded data correctly. You might include the following items from this investigation in student portfolios:
- Data table
- Answers to Analysis and Conclusions questions
- Answers to Explore Further questions

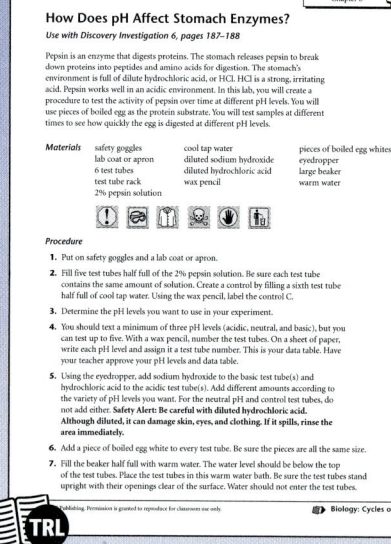

Lab Manual 30, pages 1–2

BIOLOGY IN THE WORLD

Catalytic Converters

Enzymes and catalysts play important roles in our bodies. These chemicals are also used for other purposes. For example, engineers use catalysts to clean the pollution that comes from vehicles.

The exhaust fumes from cars contain several types of pollution. Among them is carbon monoxide, which is poisonous to animals and humans. Exhaust fumes also include nitrogen oxides, which cause acid rain. Hydrocarbons in exhaust fumes help form smog.

By the 1970s, pollution from cars had become a big problem in the United States. By then, more and more people were driving in cities. The result was a severe drop in the quality of air. Many big cities developed smog problems.

To reduce smog, Congress passed several laws that required cars to have catalytic converters. Today, all cars have catalytic converters that reduce air pollution by as much as 90 percent.

Catalytic converters work by using metals as catalysts to change air pollutants into safer substances. As the exhaust fumes move through the catalytic converter, the metal catalysts cause reactions. The reactions change the pollutants into nitrogen, oxygen, carbon dioxide, and water. Although air pollution is still a

problem in most urban areas, the use of catalytic converters has helped make the air cleaner for everyone.

1. Why were catalytic converters invented?
2. What is an advantage of using catalysts as filters?
3. Besides using catalytic converters, what do you think improves the quality of air?

Chapter 6 Summary

Have volunteers read aloud each summary item on page 190. Ask volunteers to explain the meaning of each item. Direct students' attention to the Vocabulary box on the bottom of page 190. Have them read and review each term and its definition.

Graphic Organizer

As students read Chapter 6, have them finish completing the chart on Graphic Organizer 6: Cells Use Energy. Encourage students to read each lesson of the chapter and then have them fill in the portion of the chart that pertains to the lesson. When they have completed the chart, ask them to answer the questions.

Chapter 6 SUMMARY

- Cells use ATP to provide energy as needed. ATP is made up of a five-carbon sugar, three phosphate groups, and a nitrogen-containing compound.

- Food macromolecules have potential chemical energy in their bonds. Energy from food is released in the mitochondria when these bonds are broken.

- The released energy is used to add a phosphate group to ADP, creating ATP. The bonds that hold the phosphate groups are high in energy.

- When a phosphate group breaks off ATP, it releases energy that the cell uses. The result is an ADP molecule.

- ADP and ATP cycle back and forth, storing and releasing energy as the organism needs it.

- Plants and animals use food as a source of energy for cellular processes.

- Plants and animals use food as a source of raw materials to build and repair cells.

- The energy in plant sugars comes from light energy. Light energy is converted to chemical energy by photosynthesis.

- Matter and energy are transferred between an organism and its environment, and from one organism to another.

- Enzymes are proteins that cause or prevent chemical reactions in living things.

- Enzymes work by lowering the activation energy needed for a reaction to occur.

- Each enzyme works on a specific reactant molecule. The enzyme recognizes the molecule by matching its active site to the molecule.

- Enzymes work to maintain homeostasis, or a stable environment, in living things.

Vocabulary

activation energy, 184	diabetes, 181	potential energy, 174
active site, 185	kinetic energy, 170	saliva, 182
adenine, 170	metabolism, 170	substrate, 185
ADP, 174	obesity, 181	
calorie, 171	pepsin, 182	
catalyst, 180	phosphorylation, 174	

190 Chapter 6 ATP and Energy Cycles

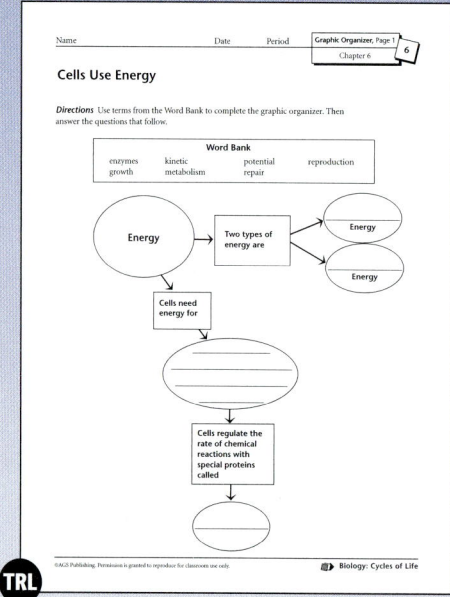

Graphic Organizer 6, pages 1–3

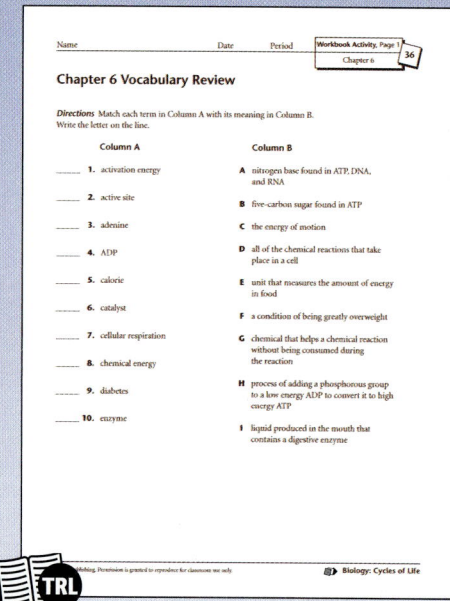

Workbook Activity 36, pages 1–2

Chapter 6 REVIEW

Word Bank
activation energy
active site
ADP
calorie
catalyst
diabetes
kinetic energy
metabolism
obesity
pepsin
phosphorylation
potential energy
saliva
substrate

Vocabulary Review

On a sheet of paper, write the word or words from the Word Bank that best complete each sentence.

1. The stomach releases the enzyme _____ to aid digestion.
2. A unit used to measure the amount of energy that food contains is a(n) _____.
3. The area on an enzyme where the substrate fits in shape and chemistry is the _____.
4. Together, all the chemical reactions in a cell make up the _____.
5. Food contains _____ that must be released to be used.
6. The process of _____ adds a phosphate group to ADP, creating ATP.
7. A molecule made up of ribose, adenine, and two phosphate groups is known as _____.
8. A chemical that speeds up a reaction, but is not involved in the reaction is a(n) _____.
9. A person who has _____ has trouble regulating the amount of sugar in the bloodstream.
10. As food is chewed, enzymes in the _____ help break down starches for easier digestion.
11. A condition of being greatly overweight is called _____.
12. The energy of motion is also called _____.
13. The amount of energy needed to start a chemical reaction is known as _____.
14. A reactant molecule is a(n) _____.

Review continued on next page

Chapter 6 Review
Use the Chapter Review to prepare students for tests and to reteach content from the chapter.

Chapter 6 Mastery Test
The Teacher's Resource Library includes two forms of the Chapter 6 Mastery Test. Each test addresses the chapter Goals for Learning. An optional third page of additional critical-thinking items is included for each test. The difficulty level of the two forms is equivalent.

Review Answers
Vocabulary Review
1. pepsin 2. calorie 3. ribose
4. metabolism 5. potential energy
6. phosphorylation 7. ADP 8. catalyst
9. diabetes 10. saliva 11. obesity
12. kinetic energy 13. activation energy
14. cellular respiration

TEACHER ALERT

In the chapter review, the Vocabulary Review Activity includes a sample of the chapter's vocabulary terms. The activity will help determine students' understanding of key vocabulary terms and concepts presented in the chapter. Other vocabulary terms used in the chapter are listed below.

active site   adenine

Concept Review

15. A 16. C 17. C 18. B 19. C 20. C

Critical Thinking

21. If you eat foods with lots of calories, you may gain weight. If you burn more calories than you eat through physical activity, you may lose weight. **22.** ATP is the main source of energy for thousands of reactions that occur in all forms of life. **23.** Enzymes lower the activation energy of reactions, so less heat energy is needed. **24.** Enzymes in saliva cause food to be digested. Enzymes in penicillin block cell wall construction in specific bacteria. **25.** Enzymes act as catalysts for chemical reactions in cells. Enzymes help build cells and support energy transfer reactions.

Chapter 6 REVIEW - continued

Concept Review

On a sheet of paper, write the letter of the answer to complete each sentence correctly.

15. ATP reacts with _____ to release energy.

    A water **B** phospholipids **C** ADP **D** DNA

16. The bonds in ATP are full of energy because _____.

    A water molecules are being split

    B oxygen is burning food molecules

    C the phosphate groups repel each other

    D the sun's energy is being absorbed

17. When a cell needs energy, ATP is hydrolyzed to produce _____.

    A glucose **B** oxygen **C** ADP **D** ATP

18. ATP is a(n) _____ molecule.

    A energy-poor

    B energy-rich

    C catalyst

    D substrate

19. Enzymes act like _____ in their role of speeding up reactions.

    A water **B** pH **C** heat **D** acid

20. The _____ is the molecule on which an enzyme reacts.

    A catalyst   **C** substrate

    B cell wall   **D** active site

Chapter 6 Mastery Test A, pages 1–3

Critical Thinking

On a sheet of paper, write the answers to the following questions. Use complete answers.

21. In what two ways does the calorie content of your food affect your weight?
22. Life would not exist without ATP. Explain why this statement is true.
23. Explain how enzymes allow chemical reactions to occur at cooler temperatures.
24. Give an example of an enzyme that causes a reaction. Give an example of an enzyme that prevents a reaction.
25. Explain the role of enzymes in cells.

Research and Write

You know that enzymes are important to the workings of a healthy cell. Research some health problems and diseases caused by a lack of enzymes or by enzymes that do not work properly. Choose one condition or disease. Make a poster that explains how enzymes are connected to the problem.

Test-Taking Tip When answering a multiple-choice question, first identify the choices you know are not true.

Research and Write

Have partners search library catalogs for medical journals or search government Web sites on the Internet. The National Institutes of Health (NIH) is a good site to explore at www.nih.gov. If students type *enzyme deficiencies* into the search field of the NIH site, a host of links will be listed. Approve students' ideas before they make their poster so two groups do not present research on the same condition or disease.

ALTERNATIVE ASSESSMENT

Alternative Assessment items correlate to the student Goals for Learning at the beginning of this chapter.

- Have students describe with a partner why chemical reactions in cells use or release energy.
- Have students draw a diagram of the ATP cycle in cells and narrate the flow of energy in the cycle.
- Have students first write a definition of *enzyme* and then a description of the role of enzymes in cells.
- Have students discuss in groups how enzymes assist reactions to overcome energy barriers.
- Have students draw a picture of enzymes binding with specific molecules. Ask them to label the active site and explain why the shape of both enzyme and molecule is important.

Chapter 7

Planning Guide
Cellular Respiration in Energy Cycles

	Student Pages	Vocabulary	Lesson Review	Critical-Thinking Questions
Lesson 1 What Is Cellular Respiration?	196–199	✔	✔	✔
Lesson 2 The Stages of Cellular Respiration	200–207	✔	✔	✔
Lesson 3 Fermentation	208–213	✔	✔	✔
Lesson 4 Controlling Cellular Respiration	214–217	✔	✔	✔

Student Text Lesson

Chapter Activities

Teacher's Resource Library
Community Connection 7:
 Dairy Products and Fermentation
Graphic Organizer 7:
 Cellular Respiration

Teacher's Edition
Opener Activity

Assessment Options

Student Text
Chapter 7 Review

Teacher's Resource Library
Chapter 7 Mastery Tests A and B

Teacher's Edition
Chapter 7 Alternative Assessment

Student Text Features								Teaching Strategies					Learning Styles					Teacher's Resource Library			
Achievements in Science	Science at Work	Biology in Your Life	Investigation/Discovery	Biology in the World	Express Lab	Link to	Research and Write	Technology and Society	ELL/ESL Strategy	Background Information	Science Journal	Applications (Home, Career, Community, Global, Environment)	Online Connection	Teacher Alert	Auditory/Verbal	Body/Kinesthetic	Interpersonal/Group Learning	Logical/Mathematical	Visual/Spatial	Workbook Activities	Alternative Workbook Activities	Lab Manual	Self-Study Guide
					198	✔			198	196	199								198	37	37	31	✔
205			206			✔			203	200		204		202	203	202				38	38	32	✔
	210		212			✔		208	211	208	209	210		209			210			39	39	33–34	✔
		215		217		✔	221		217	214		215, 217	217	215				216		40–41	40–41	35	✔

Pronunciation Key

a	hat	e	let	ī	ice	ô	order	ù	put	sh	she	ə { a in about
ā	age	ē	equal	o	hot	oi	oil	ü	rule	th	thin	e in taken
ä	far	ėr	term	ō	open	ou	out	ch	child	ŦH	then	i in pencil
â	care	i	it	ò	saw	u	cup	ng	long	zh	measure	o in lemon, u in circus

Alternative Workbook Activities

The Teacher's Resource Library (TRL) contains a set of lower-level worksheets called Alternative Workbook Activities. These worksheets cover the same content as the regular Workbook Activities but are written at a second-grade reading level.

Skill Track Online

Use Skill Track Online for *Biology: Cycles of Life* to monitor student progress and meet the demands of adequate yearly progress (AYP). Make informed instructional decisions with individual student and class reports of online lesson and chapter assessments. With immediate and ongoing feedback, students will also see what they have learned and where they need more reinforcement and practice.

Chapter at a Glance

Chapter 7: Cellular Respiration in Energy Cycles
pages 194–221

Lessons

1. **What Is Cellular Respiration?**
   pages 196–199

2. **The Stages of Cellular Respiration**
   pages 200–207

   Investigation 7 pages 206–207

3. **Fermentation**
   pages 208–213

   Discovery Investigation 7
   pages 212–213

4. **Controlling Cellular Respiration**
   pages 214–217

   Biology in the World page 217

Chapter 7 Summary page 218

Chapter 7 Review pages 219–221

Audio CD

Skill Track Online
for Biology: Cycles of Life

Teacher's Resource Library (TRL)

- Workbook Activities 37–41
- Alternative Workbook Activities 37–41
- Lab Manual 31–35
- Community Connection 7
- Graphic Organizer 7
- Resource File 13–14
- Chapter 7 Self-Study Guide
- Chapter 7 Mastery Tests A and B

(Answer Keys for the Teacher's Resource Library begin on page 675 of the Teacher's Edition. The Materials List for the Lab Manual activities begins on page 720.)

Opener Activity

Explain to students the analogy between the fuel that an automobile needs to run properly and the fuel that the human body needs to function properly. Have students draw a cartoon that depicts the analogy, including the idea that when an automobile or a human is out of fuel, neither has the energy to do work.

Community Connection 7

Chapter 7

Cellular Respiration in Energy Cycles

Like all living organisms, horses get energy from food. How does the energy get to the muscles of the running horses? Cells transfer the energy in food to ATP. The molecules of ATP provide energy when needed. Cells carefully control this process. In Chapter 7, you will learn the process of cellular respiration. You will find out how the right amount of energy is made available to cells to do their work.

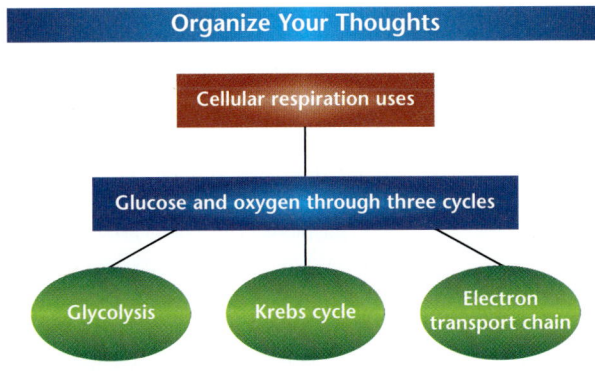

Organize Your Thoughts

Cellular respiration uses → Glucose and oxygen through three cycles → Glycolysis, Krebs cycle, Electron transport chain

Goals for Learning

- To understand that cells perform chemical reactions to gain energy
- To identify the three stages of cellular respiration
- To trace the steps in cellular respiration
- To describe various methods to create ATP
- To explain how cells control energy reactions

Introducing the Chapter

Have students list things they do every day that require energy. Remind students that even such activities as breathing, digesting food, and sleeping require the body to use energy. This energy comes from the food they eat. Have students describe how they feel when they have missed a meal and are very hungry. When students respond that they feel weak or tired, explain that this is because their cells are running out of energy.

Have students examine the photograph of the horses running on page 194. Ask students: What do horses eat to get energy? *(grass, hay, straw)* Have students read the Goals for Learning and note that the first part of the chapter will focus on how the body accesses the energy in food.

Notes and Math Tips

Ask volunteers to read the notes and math tips that appear in the margins throughout the chapter. Then discuss them with the class.

TEACHER'S RESOURCE

The AGS Publishing Teaching Strategies in Science Transparencies may be used with this chapter. The transparencies add an interactive dimension to expand and enhance the *Biology: Cycles of Life* program content.

CAREER INTEREST INVENTORY

The AGS Publishing Harrington-O'Shea Career Decision-Making System-Revised (CDM) may be used with this chapter. Students can use the CDM to explore their interests and identify careers. The CDM defines career areas that are indicated by students' responses on the inventory.

Chapter 7 Self-Study Guide

Lesson at a Glance

Chapter 7 Lesson 1

Overview In this lesson, students learn about cellular respiration and the major chemical reactions it involves.

Objectives

- To define *cellular respiration*
- To connect cellular respiration to human breathing
- To discuss the purpose of redox reactions

Student Pages 196–199

Teacher's Resource Library TRL

Workbook Activity 37
Alternative Workbook Activity 37
Lab Manual 31
Resource File 13

Vocabulary

electron carrier	redox reaction
NADH	reduction
oxidation	respiration

Write on the board the equation for cellular respiration. Have students describe the reaction, using the vocabulary terms from this lesson. *(Sample answer: The entire equation represents cellular respiration, the process by which cells release energy from food. The oxidation part of the reaction occurs when glucose loses electrons and hydrogen. The reduction part of the reaction occurs when oxygen gains electrons and hydrogen.)*

Background Information

Respiration means "breathing." Scientific terms distinguish stages as the blood carries oxygen from the lungs to cells and returns carbon dioxide from cells to the lungs. External respiration is the exchange of oxygen and carbon dioxide between the lungs and the blood. Internal respiration is the exchange of oxygen and carbon dioxide between the blood and cells. Cellular respiration is the metabolic reaction that takes place within cells and produces ATP.

Lesson 1 — What Is Cellular Respiration?

Objectives

After reading this lesson, you should be able to
- define cellular respiration
- connect cellular respiration to human breathing
- discuss the purpose of redox reactions

All cells need energy to do their work. Enzymes use energy in the form of ATP to help reactions happen. Energy is used to move materials in and out of cells. A cell gets this energy from the food an organism eats. How does a cell change the energy from food into the form of ATP? Recall that the reactions a cell uses to create and use ATP are called cellular respiration.

Cellular Respiration

You may have heard the word **respiration.** Respiration is about breathing. When you breathe air in and out, you respire. You breathe in oxygen and breathe out carbon dioxide. Cellular respiration is the process a cell uses to transform chemical potential to energy. The cell uses this energy for metabolism and growth. Study the equation for cellular respiration.

$$C_6H_{12}O_6 + 6O_2 \longrightarrow 6CO_2 + 6H_2O + ATP$$

glucose + oxygen yields carbon dioxide + water + ATP

Respiration
The process by which living things release energy from food

This equation shows that cellular respiration uses O_2 (oxygen) and produces CO_2 (carbon dioxide). This is similar to human respiration. The oxygen in the air you breathe in is used in cellular respiration. The oxygen enters the lungs and is absorbed into the blood. The blood carries the oxygen to all the cells in your body. Cells use this oxygen for cellular respiration.

In addition to oxygen, cellular respiration uses glucose. Recall that glucose has the chemical formula $C_6H_{12}O_6$. Organisms use glucose as their main energy source. You get glucose from the food you eat.

Cellular respiration produces carbon dioxide. This gas is absorbed back into the blood. The blood carries the carbon dioxide back to the lungs. You breathe carbon dioxide out as a gas.

To sum up, you inhale oxygen into your lungs from the air. Your blood carries the oxygen from your lungs to the cells for use in cellular respiration. Your blood carries carbon dioxide produced from cellular respiration back to the lungs, where it is exhaled.

How a Cell Gets Energy from Glucose

How does a cell get energy from glucose? Remember that glucose is a sugar molecule. Glucose has energy stored in its bonds. When these bonds break, they release energy. The energy released is in the form of electrons. The electrons are transferred from glucose to other molecules involved in cellular respiration. The chemical reactions that transfer these electrons are called **redox reactions.**

The word *redox* is formed from two words, **reduction** and **oxidation.** Reduction refers to chemical reactions in which a molecule gains electrons. Oxidation refers to chemical reactions in which a molecule loses electrons. The two words are joined because one molecule gains electrons from another molecule losing them.

Figure 7.1.1 shows that glucose undergoes oxidation and loses electrons during cellular respiration. Through many reactions, the electrons are transferred to the oxygen molecules. As oxygen is reduced, it bonds with hydrogen ions in the cell. The result is water, or H_2O. Water is another product of cellular respiration.

Redox reaction
A chemical reaction in which electrons are transferred between atoms

Reduction
A chemical reaction that results in a gain of electrons

Oxidation
A chemical reaction that results in a loss of electrons

Link to >>> Chemistry

The formation of rust is a redox reaction. Rust is iron oxide. It forms when iron or steel is exposed to air and moisture. Oxygen, water, and iron are needed for rust to occur. When rust forms, the iron loses electrons. The oxygen gains electrons. Iron rusts faster at higher ion concentrations, such as when salts are spread on roads.

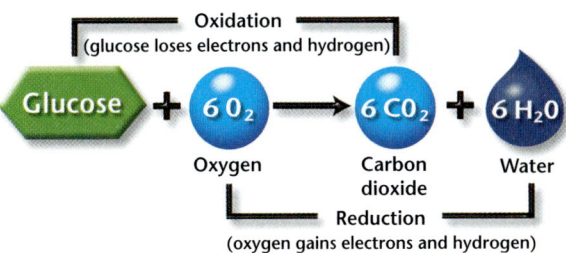

Figure 7.1.1 Oxidation and reduction are chemical reactions in cells.

1 Warm-Up Activity

Before doing the Express Lab, have students recall the major organic molecules that living things need: carbohydrates, proteins, fats, and nucleic acids. The first three are compounds found in the Nutrition Facts on labels of processed foods. Remind students that carbohydrates can be simple or complex. Simple carbohydrates include sugars such as glucose and lactose. Complex carbohydrates include starch and fiber.

Express Lab Answers

1. Answers will vary depending on the labels selected. For example, granola and granola bars often contain several forms of sugar. **2.** Answers will vary depending on the labels selected. Sweetened breakfast cereals, cookies, and cakes are high in sugar.

2 Teaching the Lesson

Remind students that breathing and eating are two processes necessary for survival. To help students organize the information on cellular respiration, have them make a flowchart that includes the major steps, reactants, and products of cellular respiration in the body. Have students identify which reactant comes from air *(oxygen)* and which comes from food *(glucose)*.

Students may be confused by the idea that a molecule *gains* electrons during a *reduction* reaction. Explain that although this seems contradictory, electrons have a negative charge. (Each electron has a charge of −1.) If a molecule gains electrons, the overall charge of the molecule is reduced. For example, if a molecule of iron with a charge of +3 gains one electron, the overall charge of the iron molecule changes to +2. Have students make a number line to help them calculate with negative numbers.

3 Reinforce and Extend

Link to Chemistry

Chemistry. Have a volunteer read the Link to Chemistry feature aloud. Have students think of examples of rust they have seen. For example, rust forms on the steel hulls of ships in salt water. In cold climates where salt is spread on roads in winter, the salt may accelerate the rusting process on the undersides of cars.

ELL/ESL Strategy

Language Objective: *To learn vocabulary in a content area*

To help students learning English become familiar with the vocabulary terms in this lesson, have students make flash cards. They may also make flash cards for other terms in the lesson that give them difficulty. The front of the flash card should have the term along with the pronunciation beneath it. The back should contain a definition along with any helpful examples or chemical reactions drawn out. Use the flash cards to show students how the term *redox* is made from the first parts of the terms *reduction* and *oxidation*. Students can use the flash cards to review for quizzes and tests.

Science Myth

Have a volunteer read the Science Myth feature aloud. Explain that even though plants make their own food through the process of photosynthesis, they still need to change the energy from glucose into a form that plant cells can use. Because plants undergo aerobic respiration, they need oxygen as well as carbon dioxide.

Learning Styles

Visual/Spatial
To help students understand the idea that respiration occurs in the lungs and cellular respiration occurs in cells, have students make a poster that shows the different steps of respiration and cellular respiration that occur in the body. For example, students could draw a human body and make callouts of the lungs and the cells. They could explain what happens in the lungs during respiration and what happens in the cells during cellular respiration. Students can use arrows to show how these two processes are related.

Electron carrier
A molecule that carries electrons from one set of reactions to another

NADH
Nicotinamide adenine dinucleotide; the main electron carrier involved in cellular respiration

Science Myth

Myth: Plants perform photosynthesis instead of cellular respiration.

Fact: All living things carry out respiration. Using energy from sunlight, plants capture carbon dioxide and make sugars during photosynthesis. During respiration, plants release the energy stored in these sugars.

When hydrogen combines with oxygen to make water, the reaction is explosive. Combining hydrogen gas and oxygen gas releases a lot of energy quickly. A cell does not force these two gases together. Instead, it uses many chemical reactions to slowly release this energy in a step-by-step process. As this energy is released, the cell uses it to create ATP.

The slow release of energy happens by transferring electrons through several different molecules. **Electron carriers** are special molecules that help the cell with redox reactions. Specifically, cellular respiration uses an electron carrier called NAD^+.

When electrons are transferred to this molecule, NAD^+ reacts with hydrogen in the cell to form **NADH.** The many reactions involved in cellular respiration produce NADH. The amount of NADH produced helps determine how much overall ATP is produced.

Cellular respiration involves many different chemical reactions. These reactions are grouped into three stages. In Lesson 2, we will discuss the activities and results of each stage.

Express Lab 7

Materials
- ingredients list from a food label
- dictionary or encyclopedia

Procedure
1. Select a food label.
2. Read the ingredients list on your label. Which items are sugars? Look up unfamiliar ingredients in a dictionary or encyclopedia.
3. Compare your ingredients list with those of your classmates.

Analysis
1. Which food label has the largest number of different sugars?
2. Which food labels list a carbohydrate as the first, second, or third ingredient?

Lesson 1 REVIEW

Word Bank
respiration
oxidation
reduction

On a sheet of paper, write the word from the Word Bank that completes each statement correctly.

1. During cellular respiration, glucose undergoes _____ and loses electrons.

2. During cellular respiration, oxygen undergoes _____ and gains electrons.

3. During _____, a cell takes in oxygen and releases carbon dioxide.

On a sheet of paper, write the letter of the answer that completes each sentence correctly.

4. NADH is a special molecule called a(n) _____ carrier.
   A electron   C carbon dioxide
   B glucose   D oxygen

5. Cellular respiration does not produce _____.
   A CO_2 B H_2O C glucose   D ATP

6. To perform reduction, a cell uses both _____ and oxygen.
   A water   C ATP
   B carbon dioxide   D glucose

Critical Thinking

On a sheet of paper, write the answers to the following questions. Use complete sentences.

7. Compare and contrast human respiration and cellular respiration.

8. Without oxygen, cellular respiration will stop. Explain why.

9. Describe the two events that occur during a redox reaction.

10. Why do cells need electron carrier molecules during cellular respiration?

Cellular Respiration in Energy Cycles Chapter 7   199

Lesson 1 Review Answers

1. oxidation 2. reduction 3. respiration 4. A 5. A 6. D 7. Human respiration is the process of breathing or taking in oxygen. Cellular respiration is the metabolic pathway used to harvest energy, in the form of ATP, for the cell. 8. Cellular respiration will stop without oxygen because oxygen and glucose are the necessary reactants to start the chemical formula for respiration. 9. During a redox reaction, one molecule gains electrons and another molecule loses electrons. 10. Electron carrier molecules are needed during cellular respiration because they enable energy to be released slowly in a step-by-step process.

Portfolio Assessment

Sample items include:
- Express Lab answers
- Poster from Learning Styles Visual/Spatial
- Lesson 1 Review answers

SCIENCE JOURNAL

Have students write a short paragraph about breathing based on personal experience and relate it to the lesson in some way. For example, they might describe breathing extra hard when running. They might conclude that is because their cells need more oxygen to produce the extra energy needed for running.

LAB ACTIVITIES

Chapter 7 has Investigation and Discovery Investigation lab activities. Two additional lab activities for Chapter 7 appear in the Biology: Cycles of Life Lab Manual and on the Teacher's Resource Library CD-ROM.

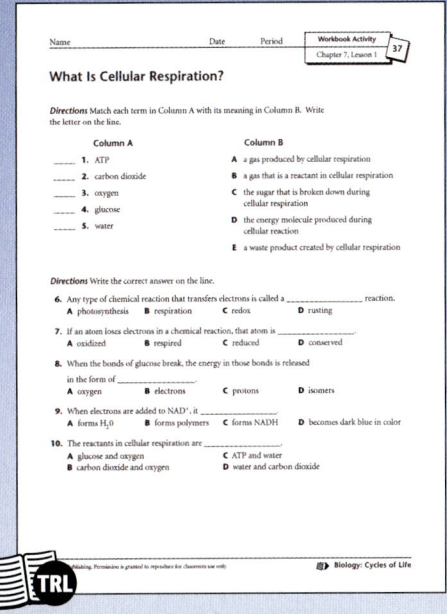

Workbook Activity 37

Cellular Respiration in Energy Cycles 199

Lesson at a Glance

Chapter 7 Lesson 2

Overview In this lesson, students learn details of the three stages of cellular respiration.

Objectives

- To describe the overall activity of each stage
- To compare locations of each stage of cellular respiration
- To discuss the molecules created and used by each stage

Student Pages 200–205

Teacher's Resource Library

Workbook Activity 38

Alternative Workbook Activity 38

Lab Manual 32

Resource File 14

Vocabulary

acetic acid
acetyl CoA
ATP synthase
coenzyme A
electron transport chain
FADH$_2$
glycolysis
Krebs cycle
pyruvic acid

Have students make a three-column chart to organize the vocabulary terms. The headings of the columns should be *Glycolysis, Krebs Cycle,* and *Electron Transport Chain*. Under each heading, have students list the terms associated with the stage of cellular respiration and explain how it is related to the stage.

Background Information

The body metabolizes fats and proteins for energy. These compounds cycle through the same stages of cellular respiration as carbohydrates do, but first they must be broken down and converted to glucose or other substances. Fats are broken down into glycerol and fatty acids. Further processes convert glycerol into pyruvic acid and fatty acids into acetyl CoA, which can enter the Krebs cycle. Proteins are broken down into amino acids, which are then converted to substances such as acetyl CoA.

Lesson 2: The Stages of Cellular Respiration

Objectives

After reading this lesson, you should be able to

- describe the overall activity of each stage
- compare locations of each stage of cellular respiration
- discuss the molecules created and used by each stage

Glycolysis
The first stage of cellular respiration in which glucose is first split

Pyruvic acid
A major product of glycolysis

In this lesson, we will discuss the three stages of cellular respiration.

Stage 1: Glycolysis

Glycolysis is the first stage of cellular respiration. It begins the breakdown of glucose. Recall that glucose comes from food an organism eats. Other carbohydrates in food are converted to glucose for glycolysis.

Glycolysis begins by using two ATP molecules. Although cellular respiration makes ATP, some reactions in cellular respiration use ATP. The amount used is small compared to the total amount of ATP made from these reactions.

Figure 7.2.1 shows the process of glycolysis. To begin glycolysis, the cell divides one glucose molecule in half using the two ATP molecules. Each half goes through several reactions. Bonds in the molecules break and release energy in the form of electrons. As a result, NAD$^+$ is reduced to make two NADH molecules. (The third stage of cellular respiration uses these NADH molecules.) Four ATP molecules are created during glycolysis. These ATP molecules can be used as cellular fuel. In addition, two molecules of **pyruvic acid** are created.

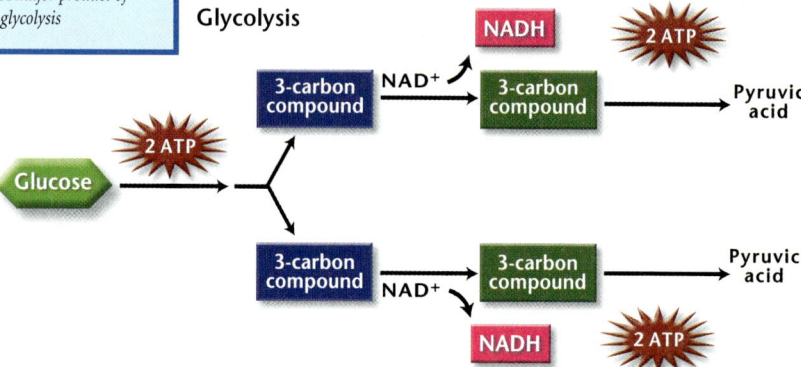

Figure 7.2.1 Glycolysis is the first stage of cellular respiration. It begins with the splitting of glucose.

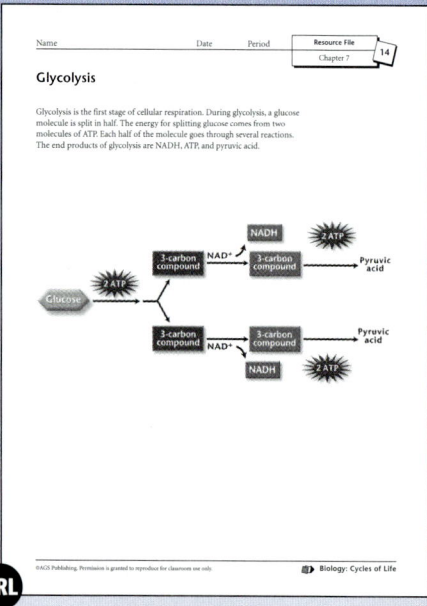

Resource File 14

Acetic acid
A sharp-smelling, colorless acid formed from the breakdown of pyruvic acid

Coenzyme A
An organic molecule that helps move the products of glycolysis into mitochondria

Acetyl CoA
A compound made from the bonding of coenzyme A and acetic acid

Krebs cycle
The second stage of cellular respiration

$FADH_2$
An electron carrier produced by the Krebs cycle

To sum up, glycolysis produces four ATP molecules, two NADH molecules, and two pyruvic acid molecules. These eight products come from one glucose molecule and two ATP molecules. As a result, the overall gain in glycolysis is two ATP molecules.

Recall that mitochondria are the sites of cellular respiration. However, glycolysis does not take place inside of mitochondria. Glycolysis happens in the cytoplasm of the cell. The second and third stages of cellular respiration happen inside of mitochondria.

Before the pyruvic acid molecules can move inside the mitochondria, they need more conversion. The cell breaks off one molecule of carbon dioxide from each pyruvic acid molecule. This creates **acetic acid.** To move into the mitochondria, acetic acid needs help from another molecule called **coenzyme A.** Coenzyme A and acetic acid bond to form one **acetyl CoA** molecule and one NADH molecule. Acetyl CoA crosses the membrane of the mitochondria. It releases acetic acid into the mitochondrial matrix. From one original glucose molecule, two acetic acid molecules enter the second stage of cellular respiration. This stage is called the **Krebs cycle.**

Stage 2: The Krebs Cycle

The Krebs cycle occurs inside of mitochondria in the thick fluid called the matrix. This set of reactions is called a cycle. This is because the beginning and the end of the reactions are the same. Two acetic acid molecules from glycolysis enter the matrix. Each acetic acid molecule bonds to the starting molecule in the cycle. From there, a series of reactions breaks and forms new bonds in the molecules.

As the Krebs cycle continues, two molecules of CO_2 (carbon dioxide) form. They are given off as waste. Most of the CO_2 from cellular respiration is produced here. As the Krebs cycle continues, an ATP molecule is created. The cycle also creates three NADH molecules and one **$FADH_2$** molecule. $FADH_2$ is another electron carrier used in the same way as NADH.

 Warm-Up Activity

Have students write out step-by-step directions that explain how to tie a shoelace. Have a volunteer read his or her directions to the class. See if students can tie their shoes according to the instructions or if a step was left out. Explain to students that the step-by-step processes used to carry out many activities in daily life are comparable to the step-by-step process of cellular respiration. One step must be completed before the next step can occur.

2 Teaching the Lesson

To help students better understand each stage of cellular respiration, have them make three large circles with the three headings *Glycolysis, Krebs Cycle,* and *Electron Transport Cycle* on a sheet of paper. The *Glycolysis* circle should be in one corner of the page, the *Krebs Cycle* circle should be in the middle of the page, and the *Electron Transport Cycle* circle should be in the opposite corner of the page. For each cycle, have students identify the molecules that begin the process and the end products of each stage. Students can use arrows from one circle to another to show how each of the end products is subsequently processed by the body. Some arrows may go to the edge of the page instead of to another circle.

For example, glycolysis begins with glucose. Of its end products, the ATP is used for energy, the NADH enters the electron transport chain, and the pyruvic acid molecules are further converted before entering into the Krebs cycle. The Krebs cycle gives off ATP as energy, CO_2 as waste (exhaled), and NADH and $FADH_2$ molecules, which enter the electron transport chain. The end products of the electron transport chain are water and ATP molecules. Encourage students to compare the complex patterns made by their arrows. The class may want to make one big collective chart on the board.

3 Reinforce and Extend

LEARNING STYLES

Body/Kinesthetic

Have students "act out" the stages of cellular respiration by labeling cards that have the molecules produced by the substeps of each of the three stages of cellular respiration. Label cards as follows, without indicating the group number: *(group 1)* glycolysis, 1 glucose molecule, 2 pyruvic acid molecules, 2 NADH molecules, 2 ATP molecules, 2 acetyl CoA molecules; *(group 2)* 2 CO_2 molecules, 2 NADH molecules, Krebs cycle, 2 ATP molecules, 4 CO_2 molecules, 6 NADH molecules, 2 $FADH_2$ molecules; *(group 3)* electron transport chain, 34 ATP molecules. Distribute cards to students and have them organize themselves into groups that represent each of the three stages of cellular respiration with the reactants and products in the appropriate groups. Have each student explain how what is written on his or her card fits into the process of cellular respiration.

TEACHER ALERT

Remind students that a key result of these processes is ATP production for energy. Help students track how many ATP molecules are produced at each stage from one molecule of glucose. Glycolysis yields 4 ATP molecules and uses 2, so the net gain is 2. The Krebs cycle yields 2 ATP molecules. In the electron transport chain, 10 NADH and 2 $FADH_2$ molecules are converted to up to 34 ATP molecules (10 × 3 + 2 × 2). Thus, up to 38 molecules of ATP are produced from one molecule of glucose.

Electron transport chain
The third stage of cellular respiration

ATP, NADH, and $FADH_2$ are the main products of the Krebs cycle, shown in Figure 7.2.2. These products are reactants in the **electron transport chain,** the third stage of cellular respiration. In total, six ATP, eight NADH, and two $FADH_2$ molecules are made from one glucose molecule. This amount includes the two NADH molecules from glycolysis.

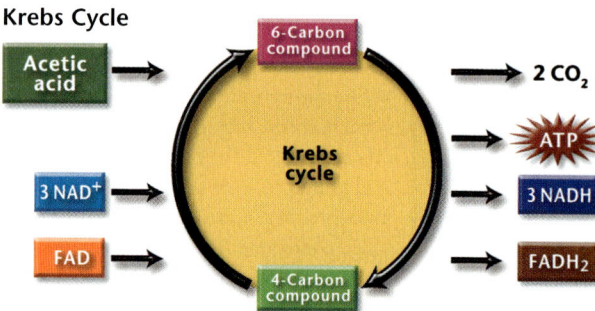

Figure 7.2.2 *The Krebs cycle is the second stage of cellular respiration. Its main products are ATP, NADH, and $FADH_2$.*

Stage 3: The Electron Transport Chain

The third stage of cellular respiration is the electron transport chain. This stage has two parts: an electron transport chain and ATP production. Recall that mitochondria have an inner membrane and an outer membrane with a space between them. The electron transport chain is found in a group of structures inside the mitochondria's inner membrane. In this space are special chains of proteins and electron carriers.

To begin, NADH transfers electrons to the first electron carrier in the chain. From there, the high-energy electrons are passed down the chain of electron carriers. $FADH_2$ also interacts with the electron transport chain. This happens at a point farther down the chain.

Each time the electrons are passed down the chain, a little energy is released. Proteins in the chain use energy to pump hydrogen ions (H^+) across the inner membrane of the mitochondria. Hydrogen ions are naturally present throughout the cell. The pumping action of the chain produces a H^+ concentration gradient between the two membranes.

ATP synthase
An enzyme at the end of the electron transport chain that helps drive the bonding of a phosphate to ADP to create ATP

As electrons pass down the chain, they lose energy to allow water to form. Electrons from the original glucose molecule lose much of their starting energy. This decrease allows the electrons to react with O_2 and H^+ to form water.

We discussed in Lesson 1 that the formation of water can be an explosive reaction. Why don't cells explode when they form water? The electron transport chain slowly decreases the energy to reduce oxygen. Oxygen also helps pull the electrons down the chain. The cell uses the water formed at the end of the chain in other ways.

With the help of **ATP synthase,** the electron transport chain produces ATP. ATP synthase is an enzyme found in the inner mitochondrial membrane. ATP synthase uses the H^+ concentration gradient to produce ATP.

Remember that the concentration gradient is created by the proteins in the electron transport chain. As H^+ ions collect between the membranes, they move toward areas of lower H^+ ion concentrations. ATP synthase uses energy from this movement to bind a phosphate group to an ADP molecule. The result is a new ATP molecule that the cell can use for energy in metabolic processes. Figure 7.2.3 sums up the electron transport chain.

Electron Transport Chain

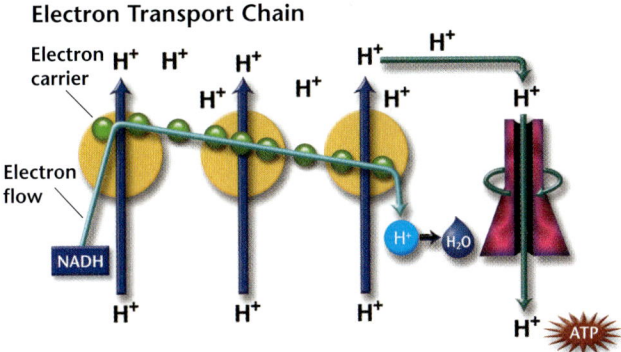

Figure 7.2.3 *The electron transport chain is the third stage of cellular respiration.*

LEARNING STYLES

Auditory/Verbal
Have students explain the processes of glycolysis, the Krebs cycle, and the electron transport chain, using Figures 7.2.1, 7.2.2, and 7.2.3 as guides.

ELL/ESL STRATEGY

Language Objective:
To communicate in oral and written words and diagrams

Have students who are learning English make their own diagrams that outline the steps involved in each of the three stages of cellular respiration. Encourage them to include labels and vocabulary terms where appropriate. Also, encourage them to add other basic vocabulary terms from earlier chapters and lessons, such as *cell* or *molecule*, as appropriate to their level of English language skills. Nontechnical terms such as *convert* may be appropriate as well for some students. More advanced English language learners may be invited to explain their diagrams orally to a small group.

Link to

Earth Science. Have students read the Link to Earth Science feature. Almost 90 percent of limestone is formed through the biochemical process of marine organisms removing calcium from seawater to make shells and other hard parts. One type of limestone, called coquina, is a rock made up of whole and broken shells that are cemented together. Another type of limestone is chalk, which is made up of the hard parts of microscopic marine organisms found in plankton.

In the Environment

Humans and many other species get oxygen for cellular respiration by inhaling air. Having clean, unpolluted air to breathe is an important health concern. Breathing polluted air can cause irritation and illness within the respiratory system. Have students research the types of pollutants that are being released into the air. For each pollutant, have them also find out what can be done or is being done to reduce the amount being released. Have students present the results of their research to the class in the form of an oral report.

Link to

Earth Science

Over time, some of Earth's carbon is incorporated into minerals such as calcite. Calcite is formed from the shells of marine mollusks and other organisms. These mineral-containing carbon substances are called carbonates. One carbonate mineral, limestone, is used to make cement. Limestone begins to form when marine organisms such as clams and oysters remove minerals from seawater.

The electron transport chain uses all of the NADH and $FADH_2$ made from glycolysis and the Krebs cycle. This means that many H^+ ions are pumped into the space between the mitochondrial membranes. In turn, ATP synthase uses the movement of these H^+ ions to form ATP.

The electron transport chain alone produces about 34 ATP molecules for one glucose molecule. Cellular respiration produces a maximum of 38 ATP molecules for every glucose molecule. This seems like a lot of energy for the cell, but the cell needs all of it. The high output of ATP from cellular respiration is necessary for cells to live. Some cells use up to 10 million ATP molecules per second.

Figure 7.2.4 shows that cellular respiration is a cyclic process. Cellular respiration includes many individual cycles. One cycle is the Krebs cycle. Another cycle is the movement of H^+ ions back and forth across the mitochondrial membrane. This movement drives ATP synthase to produce ATP. The enzymes in these reactions also cycle. Life's most basic processes happen in a cycle.

Cellular Respiration

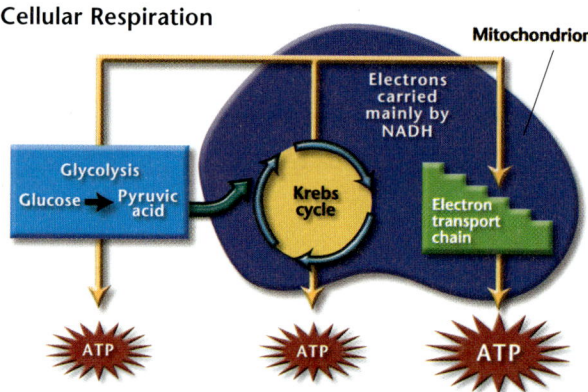

Figure 7.2.4 *Cellular respiration is a cyclic process.*

Lesson 2 REVIEW

Word Bank
energy
Krebs cycle
glucose

On a sheet of paper, write the word or words from the Word Bank that complete each statement correctly.

1. The splitting of _____ begins the process called glycolysis.
2. As electrons are passed down a chain of electron carriers, _____ is released.
3. Three molecules of NADH and one molecule of $FADH_2$ are products of the _____.

Critical Thinking

On a sheet of paper, write the answers to the following questions. Use complete sentences.

4. Which stage of cellular respiration produces the most ATP? Explain your answer.
5. Why is the Krebs cycle considered a cycle?

Achievements in Science

Discovering Biochemical Pathways

Cellular respiration is a set of reactions that occur in sequence. Each reaction is called a biochemical pathway. The product of one pathway becomes the starting material for the next pathway.

Starting in the late 1920s, German scientists Gustav Embden and Otto Meyerhof learned the steps of glycolysis. Glycolysis is the first stage of cellular respiration. These steps are known as the Embden-Meyerhof pathway. In 1937, British biochemist Sir Hans Krebs discovered a series of reactions that became known as the Krebs cycle. The Krebs cycle produces electron carriers, which carry energy to the electron transport chain. Krebs was awarded the 1953 Nobel Prize for Physiology or Medicine.

Then in the late 1930s, biochemist Gerty Cori and her husband Carl F. Cori learned how the body converts glucose to glycogen for short-term energy storage. In 1947, the Coris won the Nobel Prize for Physiology or Medicine. Gerty Cori was the first American woman to receive a Nobel Prize in the sciences.

Investigation 7

Encourage students to read the investigation steps. Discuss questions they may have before beginning the investigation.

Objectives

- To list the reactants and products of cellular respiration
- To recognize the role of respiration in living cells
- To predict the products of respiration

Skills

Measuring, observing, describing, comparing and contrasting, making inferences, recognizing cause and effect, analyzing data, drawing conclusions

Background

During cellular respiration, cells release carbon dioxide. The amount of carbon dioxide released is a measure of the rate of respiration. During exercise, cells require more oxygen and thus release more carbon dioxide as respiration occurs at a faster rate.

Time Frame

One class period

Procedure

- Have students work together in groups to complete the activity.
- Review the concept of pH with students. Remind them that the concentration of H+ ions represents the acidity of a solution, which is measured as a pH value. A compound that donates H+ ions to a solution is an acid.
- You can buy a 0.1% bromothymol blue indicator from a supplier of science education materials. Some are listed on page 699.
- Tell students that indicators are dyes that turn different colors in solutions of different pH. Bromothymol blue is an indicator. It is yellow in solutions with a pH between 3 and 8. It turns blue at pH 10 or higher.
- You can substitute a small flask for the beaker.

Cleanup/Disposal

Instruct students in proper cleanup and disposal of materials.

INVESTIGATION 7

Materials
- safety goggles
- lab coat or apron
- small beaker
- ruler
- bromothymol blue
- plastic wrap
- soda straw

Products of Cellular Respiration

During cellular respiration, cells use glucose and oxygen to make energy in the form of ATP. Cells also release carbon dioxide (CO_2) and water. When carbon dioxide dissolves in water, it forms carbonic acid (H_2CO_3). In this lab, you will see evidence of cellular respiration.

Procedure

1. Put on safety goggles and a lab coat or apron.
2. Using a ruler to measure, pour 1 inch of bromothymol blue into a small beaker. On a sheet of paper, describe the color of the liquid in the beaker. **Safety Alert: Be careful when working with glassware and the solution.**
3. Cover the beaker with plastic wrap. With the soda straw, poke a small hole through the plastic. Fit the soda straw through the hole.
4. Gently blow through the straw into the beaker. **Safety Alert: Be careful not to splash or inhale the solution.**
5. On a sheet of paper, write a description of your results.

Safety Alert

- Make sure that students have read and understood all safety rules for working in the lab. Discuss the Safety Alerts with students.
- Be sure students wear safety goggles and a lab coat or apron.
- Remind students to handle glassware carefully.
- Tell students to blow through the straw slowly, taking care not to splash or inhale the bromothymol blue solution.

Cleanup/Disposal
Before leaving the lab, clean up your materials and wash your hands.

Analysis
1. When you blow through the soda straw, what happens to the color of the liquid?
2. Why does the air you exhale cause this result?
3. What is the source of the carbon atoms in the CO_2 that is released during cellular respiration?

Conclusions
1. What product of cellular respiration causes the result you observed?
2. How do you think exercise affects cellular respiration? Explain your answer.

Explore Further
Use the procedure above to test the effects of exercise on cellular respiration.

Cellular Respiration in Energy Cycles Chapter 7

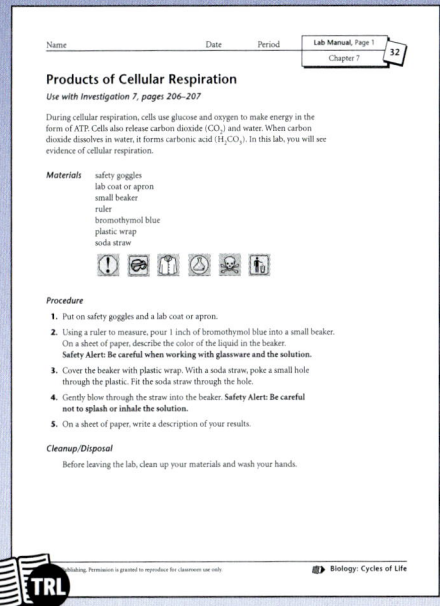

Lab Manual 32, pages 1–2

Results
Students will observe that the bromothymol blue solution turns green, then yellow as they continue to blow through the straw. The faster the color change in the bromothymol blue, the higher the level of CO_2.

Analysis Answers
1. It becomes green, then yellow.
2. The exhaled air contains carbon dioxide, which dissolves in the bromothymol blue solution to form carbonic acid. The carbonic acid changes the bromothymol blue to a yellow color.
3. Glucose is the source of the carbon atoms in the CO_2 released during cellular respiration.

Conclusions Answers
1. Carbon dioxide causes the bromothymol blue solution to turn yellow.
2. Exercise increases the rate of cellular respiration. As exercise occurs, cells need more oxygen and break down more glucose, so more carbon dioxide is released.

Explore Further Answers
Encourage students to propose different methods to test the effects of exercise on cellular respiration. For example, students may want to examine the effect of exercise, such as bench-stepping or running in place, just prior to blowing into the bromothymol blue. Be sure that proposed methods will be respectful of those students who are less physically fit and students with physical disabilities.

Assessment
Observe students to be sure they are measuring correctly. Check to see that students have written detailed descriptions of their results. You might include the following items from this investigation in student portfolios:

- Descriptions of experiment results
- Answers to Analysis and Conclusions questions
- Student proposal for additional work in response to Explore Further

Cellular Respiration in Energy Cycles 207

Lesson at a Glance

Chapter 7 Lesson 3

Overview In this lesson, students learn the process of fermentation.

Objectives

- To compare aerobic species to anaerobic species
- To relate fermentation to cellular respiration
- To describe different products of fermentation

Student Pages 208–213

Teacher's Resource Library

Workbook Activity 39
Alternative Workbook Activity 39
Lab Manual 33–34

Vocabulary

aerobic	fermentation
anaerobic	lactic acid
ethyl alcohol	

Have students write a sentence using each vocabulary term in context. Ask volunteers to share their sentences with the class.

Background Information

Organisms that require oxygen for cellular respiration are called obligate aerobes. Some types of bacteria use oxygen if it is available but can survive by fermentation when necessary. They are called facultative anaerobes. *E. coli* is an example of a facultative anaerobe. An obligate anaerobe is an organism that cannot use oxygen for cellular respiration. Many obligate anaerobes cannot survive when exposed to oxygen. Examples of obligate anaerobes include *Clostridium botulinum*, which causes botulism, and *Clostridium tetani*, which causes tetanus.

Lesson 3 Fermentation

Objectives

After reading this lesson, you should be able to
- compare aerobic species to anaerobic species
- relate fermentation to cellular respiration
- describe different products of fermentation

Aerobic
Requiring oxygen

Anaerobic
Not requiring oxygen

Fermentation
An anaerobic process for making ATP

Humans use oxygen to help drive cellular respiration. Because of this, humans are an **aerobic** species. An aerobic species breathes and requires oxygen to live.

Anaerobic Species

Not all species are aerobic. Many bacterial species are **anaerobic.** They cannot use oxygen to drive cellular respiration or other metabolic reactions. In these species, oxygen is a poison. If exposed to oxygen, they are severely damaged or destroyed.

Anaerobic species only exist in places not exposed to the atmosphere or another source of oxygen. Anaerobic species live in closed-in environments with limited resources. They require energy to live. They use **fermentation** to create ATP. Fermentation is an anaerobic process for making ATP.

The reactions for fermentation are the same reactions that occur during glycolysis in cellular respiration. Remember that oxygen is not used in cellular respiration until the electron transport chain. Anaerobic species are prokaryotic and do not have mitochondria.

This is not a problem for anaerobic species. Glycolysis occurs in the cytoplasm, which prokaryotes have. Prokaryotes harvest a small amount of ATP from these reactions. Anaerobic species break down sugars in the same manner. However, the products of these fermentation reactions are different from pyruvic acid.

Technology and Society

Industrial fermentation is the use of fermentation to produce valuable products. Pharmaceutical companies use fermentation carried out by microorganisms to make antibiotics, hormones, and specialized proteins. These proteins include the protein insulin and a variety of antibodies. In many cases, the microorganisms have been genetically changed to produce a specific substance.

208 Chapter 7 Cellular Respiration in Energy Cycles

Technology and Society

One product of industrial fermentation is monoclonal antibodies, which are identical molecules produced from the clone of a cell. Monoclonal antibodies can be produced in large quantities. They are used in medical laboratories to test for the presence of bacteria such as streptococcus in cultures from the human body. Monoclonal antibodies are used to help reduce the body's rejection of transplanted organs. Research on cancer treatment is also being done using monoclonal antibodies.

PRONUNCIATION GUIDE

Use the pronunciation shown here to help students pronounce a difficult word in this lesson. Refer to the pronunciation key on the Chapter Planning Guide for the sounds of the symbols.

pharmaceutical (fär′mə sü′ti kəl)

Lactic acid
An organic waste produced by anaerobic fermentation

Ethyl alcohol
A colorless liquid waste produced by anaerobic fermentation

Link to >>>

Social Studies

For centuries, people have used fermentation to bake. By 2600 B.C., the Egyptians were using the fermentation process to make bread. To do this, they maintained an ongoing culture of fermentation microorganisms.

Two Types of Fermentation

The two main types of fermentation are based on the products they form. The first type is **lactic acid** fermentation. This process is shown in Figure 7.3.1. Recall that fermentation is an anaerobic process to make ATP. Lactic acid is an organic waste produced by anaerobic fermentation. Instead of forming pyruvic acid, these reactions use NADH from glycolysis to form lactic acid.

People use anaerobic species to produce certain kinds of food, like cheese and yogurt. Their slightly sour flavor is a result of lactic acid.

People are exposed to lactic acid in another way. Human muscle cells use a lot of ATP and oxygen to function. During major physical activity like exercising, muscle cells need more oxygen. If muscle cells do not get enough oxygen, they use lactic acid fermentation to produce ATP. As muscle cells use these anaerobic reactions, lactic acid builds up in the cells as waste. This buildup causes sore muscles.

Some anaerobic species use another type of fermentation called **ethyl alcohol** fermentation. Ethyl alcohol is a colorless liquid waste product produced by anaerobic fermentation. It is also the main chemical in alcoholic beverages. Ethyl alcohol fermentation breaks down glucose into two products, carbon dioxide and ethyl alcohol.

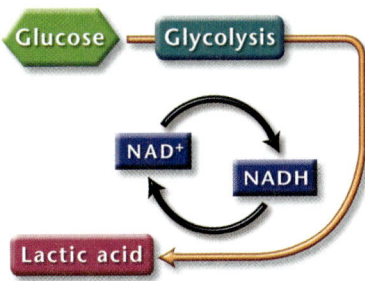

Figure 7.3.1 *During lactic acid fermentation, NADH from glycolysis forms lactic acid.*

Cellular Respiration in Energy Cycles Chapter 7 **209**

Science Journal

 Have students write a short paragraph explaining how the use of fermentation to make foods affects their lives. Paragraphs should answer these questions: Which of the foods made using fermentation have they eaten? Do they enjoy the taste of these foods? Which foods would they like to try (excluding alcoholic beverages)?

1 Warm-Up Activity

Prepare two pieces of bread dough before class; refrigerate overnight if needed. Include yeast in one piece and leave yeast out of the other piece. At the beginning of class, place each piece in a loosely covered bowl. Place both bowls in a warm, sunny location. After 30 minutes, have students compare the pieces of dough. Ask students: Which piece has yeast in it? *(The one with the yeast should rise as a result of the carbon dioxide given off as the yeast ferments the sugar in the bread dough. The piece without the yeast will not rise.)*

2 Teaching the Lesson

Have students make a chart to compare and contrast lactic acid fermentation and ethyl alcohol fermentation. Column headings could be *Lactic Acid Fermentation* and *Ethyl Alcohol Fermentation*. Row headings could include *Reactants, End Products,* and *Uses by Humans.*

3 Reinforce and Extend

TEACHER ALERT

 Another important difference between fermentation and cellular respiration is the number of ATP molecules produced by each process. Cellular respiration yields up to 38 ATP molecules per molecule of glucose. Most of the ATP is produced in the electron transport chain, which is not a part of anaerobic respiration. Fermentation yields only two molecules of ATP per molecule of glucose.

Link to

Social Studies. Have a volunteer read the Link to Social Studies feature aloud. Certain breads, such as sourdough and rye, get their unique tangy tastes because of the yeast used to make the dough rise. Some people use yeast for sourdough that has been passed down in families from one generation to the next.

Cellular Respiration in Energy Cycles **209**

Learning Styles

Interpersonal/Group Learning

Have students work in groups to research more examples of foods that are made using fermentation. Have each group make a poster that depicts examples of the different foods. Students can cut out photographs from magazines, use labels from foods, print photographs from the Internet, or make their own drawings of the foods. Examples of foods that are made using fermentation include bread, cheese, buttermilk, sour cream, yogurt, fermented milk, beer, wine, sake, sauerkraut, pickles, olives, cured ham, and soy sauce.

Global Connection

Certain species of anaerobic bacteria live in extreme environments such as hot springs, hydrothermal vents, or freezing soil in Antarctica. Bacteria that live in extreme environments are called extremophiles. Have students research more information about the places in the world where certain anaerobic extremophiles can be found. Students can write a report to share with the class about the conditions of the environment and how the bacteria survive.

Science at Work

Have students read the Science at Work feature. Invite a certified athletic trainer (ATC) to speak to the class. Have students write down questions that they have about being an ATC beforehand. Make sure the discussion includes the effect of lactic acid buildup in muscles and how to avoid or treat it.

Figure 7.3.2 The spaces in this bread represent carbon dioxide bubbles that escaped during baking.

People rely on ethyl alcohol fermentation when they use yeast to make bread. Yeasts are aerobic bacteria that perform ethyl alcohol fermentation and glycolysis. When yeasts are put into dough, they separate from oxygen. Yeasts break down the sugars in the dough mixture to get fuel. As they ferment the sugars, they produce carbon dioxide. Bubbles of CO_2 gas are trapped in the dough and cause it to rise. Bakers allow this process to happen so the dough will rise and the taste is right.

Look at Figure 7.3.2. The white, soft part of bread has many tiny air bubbles trapped inside the crust. The spaces are where CO_2 bubbles were trapped during baking.

Science at Work

Certified Athletic Trainer

A certified athletic trainer (ATC) prevents, assesses, and manages injuries resulting from physical activity. An ATC works under the direction of a physician. ATCs cooperate with health care professionals, administrators, and parents. When a sports injury occurs, an ATC can provide emergency care. ATCs work with patients and other health care team members to develop plans for treatment and rehabilitation.

Certified athletic trainers work in schools, colleges, sports medicine clinics, professional sports programs, hospitals, and the military. Most jobs in athletic training require a bachelor's degree from a college with an accredited athletic training curriculum. After completing a bachelor's degree, people can take a national certification exam to become certified.

Lesson 3 REVIEW

Word Bank
aerobic
ethyl alcohol
lactic acid

On a sheet of paper, write the word or words from the Word Bank that complete each statement correctly.

1. Because humans use oxygen, they are a(n) _____ species.
2. Cheese and yogurt are formed by _____ fermentation.
3. The bubbles produced by _____ fermentation cause yeast bread to rise.

On a sheet of paper, write the letter of the answer that completes each sentence correctly.

4. Anaerobic species include certain _____.
   - **A** bacteria **B** plants **C** protists **D** animals
5. Ethyl alcohol fermentation produces all of the following except _____.
   - **A** carbon dioxide **C** ethyl alcohol
   - **B** ATP **D** oxygen
6. Lactic acid fermentation occurs in muscle cells when _____ is in low supply.
   - **A** water **C** oxygen
   - **B** carbon dioxide **D** ethyl alcohol

Critical Thinking

On a sheet of paper, write the answers to the following questions. Use complete sentences.

7. Describe a situation that could cause lactic acid to build up in human muscle cells.
8. How is fermentation similar to cellular respiration? How is it different?
9. How might an organism benefit by carrying out fermentation instead of cellular respiration?
10. Compare and contrast lactic acid fermentation with ethyl alcohol fermentation.

Cellular Respiration in Energy Cycles Chapter 7 211

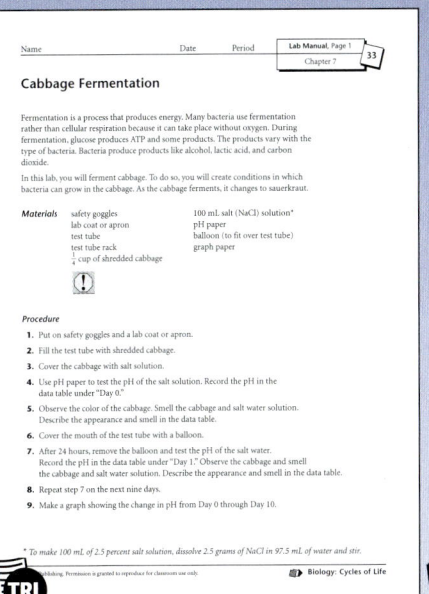

Lab Manual 33, pages 1–2

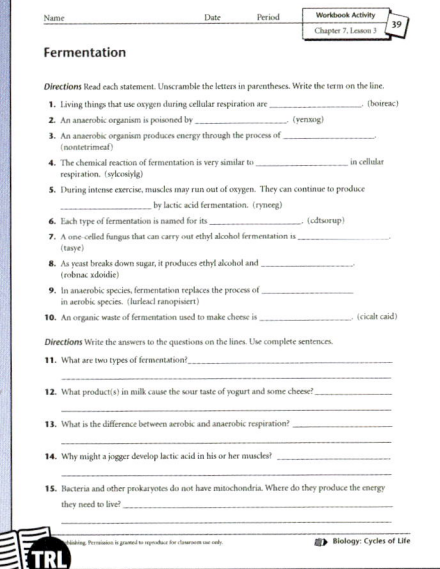

Workbook Activity 39

Lesson 3 Review Answers

1. aerobic 2. lactic acid 3. ethyl alcohol
4. A 5. D 6. C 7. Lactic acid can build up in human muscle cells during periods of sustained exercise. 8. Both fermentation and cellular respiration require glucose and produce ATP. However, fermentation does not require O_2. It also produces less ATP than cellular respiration does.
9. An organism might benefit by carrying out fermentation instead of cellular respiration because it would enable the organism to live in an environment without oxygen. 10. Lactic acid fermentation produces lactic acid. Humans use lactic acid to produce cheese and yogurt. Lactic acid can also occur in muscle cells when oxygen is in short supply. Ethyl alcohol fermentation produces ethyl alcohol and carbon dioxide. Humans use it in baking and brewing. Both lactic acid fermentation and ethyl alcohol fermentation occur in the absence of oxygen. Both produce a small amount of ATP.

Portfolio Assessment

Sample items include:
- Compare-and-contrast chart from Teaching the Lesson
- Paragraph from Science Journal
- Poster from Learning Styles Interpersonal/Group Learning
- Lesson 3 Review answers

ELL/ESL Strategy

Language Objective: *To practice outlining skills*

Have students learning English make an outline of the lesson. Headings within the outline could include *Anaerobic Species, Fermentation, Lactic Acid Fermentation,* and *Ethyl Alcohol Fermentation.* Encourage students to make the outlines as thorough as they can.

Cellular Respiration in Energy Cycles 211

Discovery Investigation 7

This investigation is less structured than the first investigation in this chapter. It offers students more challenge and requires more teacher facilitation. Discuss with students the questions in the first paragraph on page 212. Encourage students to read the investigation steps and formulate their own questions before beginning the investigation.

Objectives

- To determine the products of fermentation
- To predict the effects of temperature on the rate of fermentation
- To develop a testable hypothesis
- To design an experiment to test a hypothesis

Skills

Observing, measuring, designing an experiment, using science lab equipment, describing, comparing and contrasting, measuring, making inferences, predicting outcomes, recognizing cause and effect, analyzing data, drawing conclusions

Background

Yeast cells perform ethyl alcohol fermentation. This form of fermentation breaks down glucose to produce carbon dioxide, ethyl alcohol, and a small amount of ATP. In baking, the carbon dioxide gas produces holes that cause the bread dough to rise. The ethyl alcohol evaporates during baking.

Time Frame

One class period

Procedure

- Have students work together in groups to complete the activity.
- Before class, prepare a 20% sucrose solution by dissolving 100 g of sucrose (table sugar) in distilled water for a total volume of 500 mL.
- To begin the lab, prepare a yeast-sucrose solution by adding one packet of dried yeast per every 200 mL of a 20% sucrose solution. Give each team enough yeast-sucrose solution to fill a large test tube approximately $\frac{1}{2}$ to $\frac{2}{3}$ full.
- If you use dried active yeast in jars, note that $2\frac{1}{4}$ teaspoons of dried yeast equals one packet of dried yeast.
- As a substitute for the large beaker, use a large jar such as a mason jar, mayonnaise jar, or spaghetti sauce jar.
- Don't allow students to insert the gas delivery tubes into the one-hole rubber stoppers. Assemble them before students arrive for lab.
- To make a glass delivery tube, insert 5 cm of glass tubing into a one-hole rubber stopper. As you insert the tubing, be careful not to break it. To help with insertion, lubricate the glass with a little oil or water. Place a 50-cm piece of rubber tubing over the upper end of the glass tubing.

DISCOVERY INVESTIGATION 7

Materials
- safety goggles
- lab coat or apron
- large beaker
- warm water (38° to 43°C)
- large test tube
- solution of yeast and sucrose
- one-hole rubber stopper with gas delivery tube
- small beaker
- tap water
- limewater

Making ATP Without Oxygen

When oxygen is not present, some species use fermentation to make ATP. What are the products of fermentation? Does temperature affect the rate of fermentation? You will find out the answers to these questions in this lab.

Procedure

1. Put on safety goggles and a lab coat or apron.
2. Fill a large beaker half full with warm water.
3. Fill a large test tube nearly full with the solution of yeast and sucrose. Cap the test tube with the one-hole rubber stopper with the gas delivery tube.
4. **Safety Alert: Be careful when working with glassware.** Place the test tube in the beaker of warm water. Keep the test tube upright. Do not stir or mix the yeast and sucrose solution in the test tube.

212 Chapter 7 Cellular Respiration in Energy Cycles

SAFETY ALERT

- Make sure that students have read and understood all safety rules for working in the lab. Discuss the Safety Alerts with students.
- Be sure students wear safety goggles and a lab coat or apron.
- Don't allow students to use very hot water.
- Remind students not to stir the yeast solution with the glass test tube.

5. Fill a small beaker nearly full with tap water. Put the end of the gas delivery tube in the small beaker of tap water. Watch for gas bubbles at the end of the tube. Count the number of gas bubbles released per minute.

6. In a small group, discuss what gas is given off in this setup. Write a hypothesis about how you could identify this gas. The hypothesis should be one that you could test using limewater.

7. Write a procedure and Safety Alerts for your experiment.

8. Have your hypothesis, Safety Alerts, and procedure approved by your teacher. Then carry out your experiment.

Cleanup/Disposal
Before leaving the lab, clean up your materials and wash your hands.

Analysis
1. How do yeast cells make ATP?
2. Is fermentation occurring during your experiment? Describe the evidence that supports your answer.

Conclusions
1. Was your hypothesis supported by the results of your experiment?
2. Does temperature affect the rate of fermentation? Suggest an experiment that you could perform to find out.

Explore Further
In your group, discuss how you could measure the effect of temperature on bread making.

Assessment
Check student procedures and observe students as they perform their experiments. Review student predictions and hypotheses for Explore Further. You might include the following items from this investigation in student portfolios:

- Hypothesis and experimental procedure
- Answers to Analysis and Conclusions questions
- Student proposal for question to investigate in Explore Further

- You can buy a 0.1% bromothymol blue indicator from a supplier of science education materials. Some are listed on page 723.
- Tell students that indicators are dyes that turn different colors in solutions of different pHs. Bromothymol blue is an indicator. It is yellow in solutions with a pH between 3 and 8. It turns blue at pH 10 or higher.
- Have students document the procedure they suggest, including the list of materials needed, the preparation and safety alerts required, and any information necessary for someone else to repeat their experiment. Have students record their results.
- Ask students to discuss any problems they had in performing the experiment. Ask them which part of the procedure, if any, they would change if they were going to perform the experiment again.

Cleanup/Disposal
Instruct students in proper cleanup and disposal of materials.

Results
Students should observe that the bromothymol blue solution in the small beaker turns green, then yellow in the presence of bubbles from the solution of yeast and sucrose. Fermentation produces carbon dioxide, which dissolves in the bromothymol blue solution to form carbonic acid. The carbonic acid changes the bromothymol blue to a yellow color. The faster the color change in the bromothymol blue, the greater is the rate of fermentation.

Yeast cells need warm temperatures (38° to 43°C) to thrive. Students will find that the largest number of bubbles will be produced at this temperature. Warmer or colder temperatures will greatly slow the rate of fermentation.

Answers to Analysis, Conclusions, and Explore Further begin on page 670 of this Teacher's Edition.

Lab Manual 34, pages 1–2

Lesson at a Glance

Chapter 7 Lesson 4

Overview In this lesson, students learn how cellular respiration is controlled in the body.

Objectives

- To relate energy needs to controlling respiration
- To discuss other molecules that cellular respiration can use

Student Pages 214–217

Teacher's Resource Library (TRL)

Workbook Activity 40–41

Alternative Workbook Activity 40–41

Lab Manual 35

Vocabulary

feedback inhibition

Have students look up the word *inhibit* in a dictionary. Ask students: How does the definition of *inhibit* relate to the concept of feedback inhibition? *(To inhibit is to hold something in check or restrain it. Feedback inhibition restrains processes from going too fast or too slow.)* Ask students: Where have you heard the word *feedback*? How does that relate to feedback inhibition? *(Answers will vary. Sample answer: Feedback is getting information or response in reaction to what one has done. When a process goes outside normal bounds, a feedback reaction restores it.)*

Background Information

There are two types of feedback loops in the body: negative feedback systems and positive feedback systems. Most metabolic activities are controlled by negative feedback loops, in which a controlled condition is kept from moving outside a normal range. An example is glucose levels in the blood. In a positive feedback system, rather than returning to normal, the change is intensified. An example is labor contractions. Once the cycle starts, the contractions grow stronger until the birth of the baby.

Lesson 4 Controlling Cellular Respiration

Objectives

After reading this lesson, you should be able to

◆ relate energy needs to controlling respiration

◆ discuss other molecules that cellular respiration can use

Feedback inhibition

A process used by cells to control metabolic pathways

Cellular respiration and fermentation are the main pathways all life uses to create energy. These regulated and controlled reactions are part of an organism's metabolism. If an organism is resting, its cells do not produce much ATP. Cellular respiration slows down. When an organism is active, respiration reactions work harder to supply energy. Like other metabolic pathways, cellular respiration is strictly controlled. Over time, organisms have developed these controls to save energy.

Many cells use the enzymes involved in these reactions to control the same reactions. The product of a reaction in a pathway can interact with molecules from another reaction in that pathway. For example, the product from one reaction may stop the enzyme of another reaction. When that product becomes concentrated, it causes the enzyme from the other reaction to stop working. The pathway begins to work again when the concentration of the product drops. In this way, a cell can stop a pathway from producing too many molecules. This process of control is called **feedback inhibition.** Feedback inhibition uses energy cycles to control metabolism.

What happens to cellular respiration if glucose is not available? Because cellular respiration is a metabolic process, it interacts with other metabolic reactions. When glucose is not available, cells create glucose from other molecules.

For example, cells use polysaccharides, like starch, by pulling off one glucose monomer at a time. Cells use lipids by breaking them down into parts. By rearranging these parts, cells create molecules needed in different stages of cellular respiration. Feeding these molecules into those stages moves the process along. Because lipids have long fatty acid chains, they store more energy than carbohydrates.

Cells also use proteins for energy. Cells separate proteins into their different amino acids. In this way, cells transform the amino acids into molecules needed in different stages.

214 Chapter 7 Cellular Respiration in Energy Cycles

 Warm-Up Activity

Have students count and record the number of breaths they take in 30 seconds while sitting quietly. Next, have students jog in place for one minute (if able) and then immediately start counting how many breaths they take in 30 seconds. Ask students: What is the relationship among your rate of breath, the rate of cellular respiration, and your body's need for energy? *(Running takes more energy than sitting, so the cells need more ATP, so more oxygen is needed for the electron transport chain stage of cellular respiration, so one breathes faster to take in more oxygen.)*

 Teaching the Lesson

Help students understand how a feedback inhibition loop works by drawing a simple example on the board. When blood glucose levels are too low, the body releases the hormone glucagon, which stimulates liver cells to release glucose into the blood. Blood glucose levels rise as a result. If blood glucose levels are too high, the body releases insulin that stimulates cells to absorb glucose. Blood glucose levels fall as a result. The cycle begins again when blood glucose levels drop too low.

214 Chapter 7

The goal of cellular respiration is to obtain energy for the cells of an organism. An organism must eat to provide the molecular fuel for cellular respiration. An organism breaks down food into smaller molecules. The cells of the organism use these molecules for many purposes, including making ATP. When an organism has enough ATP to function, the cells use ATP in other ways.

An organism often stores unused fuel molecules as fat. The fat is stored until the organism uses it. An organism uses fat when its cells cannot find other fuel molecules. For example, people who want to lose weight try to use stored fat molecules. To use this fat, they must limit the number of calories they eat and increase the amount of energy their cells need. By doing both, cells begin to harvest needed energy from stored fat molecules.

Biology in Your Life

Technology: Carbon Monoxide Detectors

Carbon monoxide poisoning is the main cause of accidental poisoning deaths in the United States. Carbon monoxide is a colorless and odorless gas. When inhaled, carbon monoxide binds to hemoglobin. Hemoglobin is a protein found in red blood cells that carries oxygen throughout the body. Carbon monoxide displaces oxygen. Respiration then slows or stops. Carbon monoxide at low levels causes headaches, nausea, vomiting, and weakness. At higher levels, carbon monoxide can be deadly.

Carbon monoxide is produced when fuel such as wood, gasoline, or oil is burned incompletely. Flame-fueled devices such as gas stoves, water heaters, and grills are sources of carbon monoxide. When these devices are vented properly, carbon monoxide escapes harmlessly to the outside air.

Carbon monoxide detectors in homes save lives. They sound an alarm when there is too much carbon monoxide. When an alarm sounds, people should leave the house quickly and telephone for help.

1. Why is carbon monoxide deadly?
2. How does a carbon monoxide detector work?
3. What flame-fueled devices do you have in your home?

3 Reinforce and Extend

TEACHER ALERT

Excess carbohydrates, proteins, and fats are all processed and stored in the body as fat. Any excess fuel for the body is converted to triglycerides, phospholipids, or cholesterol and stored to be used as energy when needed. Triglycerides are the main form of storage in the body.

Biology in Your Life

Have volunteers read the Biology in Your Life feature aloud. Each year, approximately 500 people in the United States die as a result of accidental carbon monoxide poisoning. Another 5,000 are treated at hospitals for exposure to carbon monoxide. At low levels, exposure to carbon monoxide can cause shortness of breath, nausea, and headaches. Exposure to moderate levels can cause dizziness, severe headaches, mental confusion, and loss of consciousness.

Biology in Your Life Answers

1. Carbon monoxide is deadly because it binds to hemoglobin, a protein found in red blood cells. Hemoglobin carries oxygen throughout the body. Carbon monoxide binds to hemoglobin more tightly than oxygen. This prevents hemoglobin from carrying oxygen around the body. Carbon monoxide is also a dangerous gas because it cannot be seen or smelled. **2.** Carbon monoxide detectors work by triggering an alarm based on an accumulation of carbon monoxide over time. **3.** Flame-fueled devices at students' homes may include gas stove tops, ranges, water heaters, grills, clothes dryers, and automobiles.

AT HOME

With a parent or guardian, have students check and record what flamed-fueled devices, if any, are used in their homes and if they are properly vented. Ask students: Does your home have a carbon monoxide detector? Does everyone in your family know what to do if the detector alarm goes off? *(open windows, ventilate home with fresh air, have a professional check heating system or appliances; if feeling dizzy or drowsy, leave the home and call 911 for possible carbon monoxide poisoning)*

IN THE COMMUNITY

Have students think of ways they can raise awareness in their community about the risk of accidental carbon monoxide poisoning. Have them research steps people can take to help reduce the risk of carbon monoxide poisoning. (See Online Connection on page 217.) Encourage them to make posters, flyers, or pamphlets with this information to post or distribute in their community.

Lesson 4 Review Answers

1. controlled 2. stop 3. resting 4. A 5. B 6. D 7. Cells use feedback inhibition to control metabolic pathways by shutting down pathways when sufficient amounts of the pathway's product are present. When the product amount decreases, cells will turn on the pathway again. 8. Cellular respiration and fermentation are two examples of metabolic pathways used by living organisms. 9. When a food contains polysaccharides, cells remove one glucose monomer at a time. When a food contains lipids, cells break the lipid molecules into different parts to form other molecules, which can then enter the stages of cellular respiration. When a food contains proteins, cells break down the proteins into amino acids, which can become transformed into molecules used in different stages of cellular respiration. 10. When a teaspoon of sugar is lit with a match, its energy is immediately released as light and heat. The breakdown of sugar in the body, however, is a slow process during which energy is gradually released in a series of controlled steps during cellular respiration.

Portfolio Assessment

Sample items include:
- Poster/pamphlet from In the Community
- Feedback loop from Learning Styles Logical/Mathematical
- Lesson 4 Review answers

Link to

Home and Career. Ask students: What would happen in the metal strip if the thermostat were to break in half? *(The thermostat would no longer function properly. The "receptor" that changes in response to temperature changes would not send signals to control the heat.)*

LEARNING STYLES

Logical/Mathematical

Have students make a diagram that shows the cyclical nature of the feedback inhibition that maintains the temperature of a room that has a thermostat.

216 Chapter 7

Lesson 4   R E V I E W

Link to »»

Home and Career

How are a cell and a thermostat alike? Both use feedback inhibition. A cell uses feedback inhibition to control metabolism. A thermostat also uses this process to control a room's temperature.

A thermostat uses a metal strip that coils and uncoils in response to changes in temperature. The metal strip causes the heat to turn on when the temperature drops below a certain level. It causes the heat to turn off when the temperature reaches a desired level.

On a sheet of paper, write the word that completes each statement correctly.

1. In cells, metabolic pathways are _____ to avoid wasting energy.
2. A metabolic pathway will _____ if it is producing more molecules than necessary.
3. When an organism is _____, cellular respiration slows.

On a sheet of paper, write the letter of the answer that completes each sentence correctly.

4. Organisms will store unused fuel molecules as _____.
   A fat   **B** glucose   **C** water   **D** ATP
5. Cells can break down polysaccharides, like starch, by removing one _____ monomer at a time.
   A lipid   **C** fatty acid chain
   B glucose   **D** amino acid
6. Limiting calories and increasing exercise will cause cells to harvest energy from _____ molecules.
   A polysaccharide   **C** carbohydrate
   B protein   **D** fat

Critical Thinking

On a sheet of paper, write the answers to the following questions. Use complete sentences.

7. How do cells use feedback inhibition to control metabolic pathways?
8. Describe two examples of metabolic pathways used by living organisms.
9. How does cellular respiration harvest energy from food molecules other than glucose?
10. A teaspoon of sugar burns up quickly when lit with a match. Compare the burning of sugar to the breakdown of sugar in the body.

216   Chapter 7   Cellular Respiration in Energy Cycles

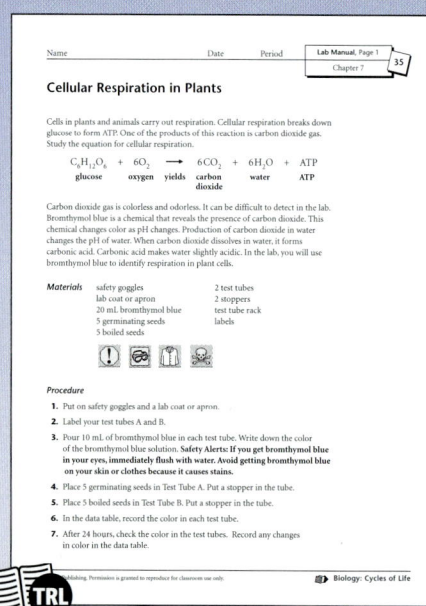

Workbook Activity 40   **Lab Manual 35, pages 1–2**

BIOLOGY IN THE WORLD

Boosting Cellular Respiration

Think about the last time you exercised hard. Were you out of breath? Were your muscles sore and tired? Providing energy is the job of cellular respiration. This process requires oxygen. When you breathe, oxygen enters your lungs. Oxygen is carried throughout your body by a vast number of red blood cells. Red blood cells travel through your body tissues and deliver oxygen to every cell.

Sometimes red blood cells cannot transport enough oxygen to meet tissue demands. Then the kidneys release a hormone called erythropoietin. Erythropoietin, also called EPO, tells the body to make new red blood cells. Most new red blood cells replace those that are old and worn out.

Blood loss, regular aerobic exercise, or moving to a high elevation also triggers the release of EPO. This causes the body to produce more red blood cells. The extra red blood cells result in more cellular respiration and better delivery of oxygen to body tissues.

Athletes sometimes train at high elevations. This causes their bodies to release EPO and make more red blood cells. Extra red blood cells deliver more oxygen to working muscles. As a result, high elevation training improves speed and endurance.

Sometimes cancer or kidney failure can cause a shortage of red blood cells in people. Doctors may prescribe EPO to increase red blood supply. This helps relieve fatigue. Some athletes take EPO illegally to gain a competitive advantage. However, the dangers of EPO misuse are high. Too many red blood cells cause blood to become thick. This increases the risk of blood clots or stroke.

1. Why do athletes sometimes train at high elevations?
2. Why do you think taking EPO helps people with kidney failure feel less tired?
3. Why is it dangerous for athletes to take EPO?
4. Why does regular aerobic exercise or moving to a higher elevation trigger the release of EPO?

ONLINE CONNECTION

 While working on the In the Community activity in Lesson 4, students may find it useful to consult the EPA Web site at www.epa.gov/iaq/pubs/coftsht.html. It has information about how to reduce the risk of carbon monoxide poisoning.

After completing Chapter 7, students may want to use the Medline Plus Web site at www.nlm.nih.gov/medlineplus/foodnutritionandmetabolism.html. It has links to information on food, nutrition, and metabolism.

ELL/ESL STRATEGY

 **Language Objective:** *To summarize information*

Have English language learners read the last two paragraphs on this page. Then have them write a short summary of the information presented in the paragraphs.

BIOLOGY IN THE WORLD

Have volunteers read the Biology in the World feature aloud. The release of erythropoietin is controlled by feedback inhibition within the body. When the kidneys detect low levels of oxygen in the blood, increased amounts of erythropoietin are released into the blood. This stimulates the production of more red blood cells. As the number of red blood cells increases and blood oxygen levels increase, the kidneys reduce the amount of erythropoietin released.

Biology in the World Answers

1. Athletes sometimes train at higher elevations because their bodies will release EPO and make more red blood cells, improving speed and endurance. **2.** EPO tells the body to make more red blood cells, which transport oxygen throughout the body, increasing cellular respiration and producing more energy in persons with kidney failure. **3.** It is dangerous for athletes to take EPO because too many red blood cells cause blood to become unnaturally thick, increasing the risk of blood clots or stroke. **4.** Regular aerobic exercise causes tissues to demand more oxygen than red blood cells can transport, which triggers the release of EPO. Moving to a higher elevation also causes tissues to demand more oxygen than red blood cells can transport because the air contains less oxygen at higher elevations.

CAREER CONNECTION

 Medical Laboratory Technician (MLT) is a career that involves analyzing blood samples. This may include determining the number of red and white blood cells present, the amount of triglycerides in the blood, and the levels of certain hormones in the blood. MLTs are required to complete a Medical Laboratory Technician program at an accredited community college. They must also take a national certification exam. Recommended high school courses include biology, chemistry, and math.

Chapter 7 Summary

Have volunteers read aloud each summary item on page 218. Ask volunteers to explain the meaning of each item. Direct students' attention to the Vocabulary box on the bottom of page 218. Have them read and review each term and its definition.

Graphic Organizer

As students read Chapter 7, have them finish completing the chart on Graphic Organizer 7: Cellular Respiration. Encourage students to read each lesson of the chapter and then have them fill in the portion of the chart that pertains to the lesson. When they have completed the chart, ask them to answer the questions.

Chapter 7 SUMMARY

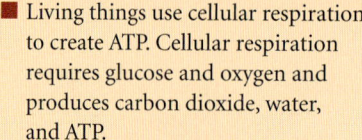

- Living things use cellular respiration to create ATP. Cellular respiration requires glucose and oxygen and produces carbon dioxide, water, and ATP.

- Energy is released from glucose as electrons. Electrons are gained in reduction and lost in oxidation. Glucose is oxidized during cellular respiration.

- Cellular respiration occurs in three stages: glycolysis, the Krebs cycle, and the electron transport chain.

- Glycolysis occurs in a cell's cytoplasm. In glycolysis, glucose splits to produce two molecules of pyruvic acid. Pyruvic acid becomes acetyl CoA, which releases acetic acid for the next stage of cellular respiration.

- In the mitochondria, the Krebs cycle produces the electron carriers NADH and $FADH_2$. These electron carriers are used in the last stage of cellular respiration.

- In the mitochondria, the electron transport chain passes electrons down a series of electron carriers. The released energy is used to make ATP. The electron transport chain makes most of the ATP produced during cellular respiration.

- Fermentation occurs in a cell's cytoplasm. This process does not require oxygen.

- Prokaryotes produce ATP by using lactic acid fermentation, which produces ATP and lactic acid. Lactic acid fermentation can occur in muscle cells. Ethyl alcohol fermentation produces ATP and ethyl alcohol.

- Cells use feedback inhibition to control metabolic pathways. Feedback inhibition stops a pathway when its product is not needed. It starts a pathway when its product is needed.

Vocabulary

acetic acid, 201	electron transport chain, 202	lactic acid, 209
acetyl CoA, 201	ethyl alcohol, 209	NADH, 198
aerobic, 208	$FADH_2$, 201	oxidation, 197
anaerobic, 208	feedback inhibition, 214	pyruvic acid, 200
ATP synthase, 203	fermentation, 208	redox reaction, 197
coenzyme A, 201	glycolysis, 200	reduction, 197
electron carrier, 198	Krebs cycle, 201	respiration, 196

218 Chapter 7 Cellular Respiration in Energy Cycles

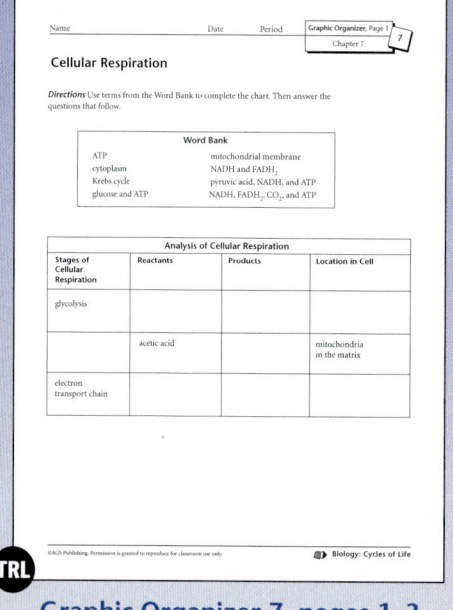

Graphic Organizer 7, pages 1–3

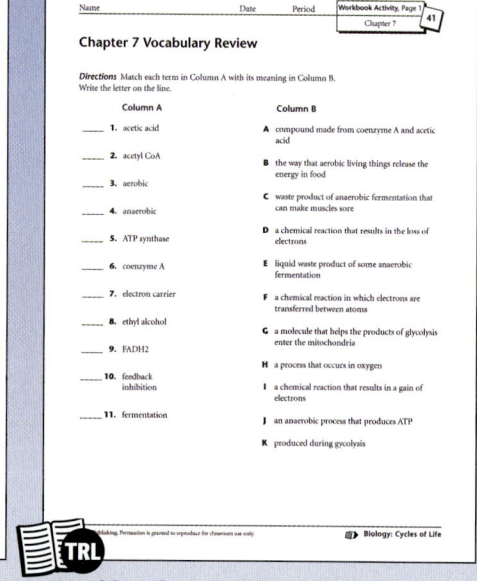

Workbook Activity 41, pages 1–2

Chapter 7 REVIEW

Word Bank
aerobic
anaerobic
ATP synthase
electron carrier
electron transport chain
ethyl alcohol
feedback inhibition
fermentation
glycolysis
Krebs cycle
lactic acid
NADH
oxidation
pyruvic acid
redox reaction
reduction
respiration

Vocabulary Review

On a sheet of paper, write the word or words from the Word Bank that complete each sentence correctly.

1. The process of breathing or taking in oxygen is called _____.

2. During the electron transport chain, an enzyme called _____ uses the H^+ concentration gradient to produce ATP.

3. A(n) _____ process is a process that requires oxygen.

4. Glucose is split in half during _____.

5. A(n) _____ is a chemical reaction involving the transfer of electrons.

6. Cells use a process of control known as _____ to regulate metabolic pathways.

7. Any molecule that transports electrons from one set of reactions to another is called a(n) _____.

8. In a(n) _____ reaction, a molecule loses electrons.

9. When oxygen is not present, living things use a series of reactions called _____ to make ATP.

10. The main electron carrier involved in cellular respiration is NAD^+, which becomes _____ after reacting with hydrogen.

11. Glycolysis produces two molecules of _____.

12. Alcoholic beverages and bread are made using an anaerobic process called _____ fermentation.

13. The second stage of cellular respiration is a series of reactions called the _____, which takes place inside mitochondria.

14. During the last stage of cellular respiration, a group of electron carriers called the _____ gradually releases energy from shared electrons.

Review continued on next page

Review Answers

15. anaerobic **16.** lactic acid **17.** reduction

TEACHER ALERT

In the Chapter Review, the Vocabulary Review activity includes a sample of the chapter's vocabulary terms. The activity will help determine students' understanding of key vocabulary terms and concepts presented in the chapter. Other vocabulary terms used in the chapter are listed below.

acetic acid   coenzyme A
acetyl CoA $FADH_2$

Concept Review

18. B **19.** A **20.** B **21.** D

Critical Thinking

22. Fermentation in anaerobic bacteria does not require oxygen and produces only a small amount of ATP. Cellular respiration in humans requires oxygen and produces a comparatively large amount of ATP. **23.** The final stage of cellular respiration, the electron transport chain, requires oxygen. Oxygen is necessary because it serves as the final electron acceptor.

Chapter 7 REVIEW - continued

Vocabulary Review

15. A(n) _____ process does not use oxygen.

16. An anaerobic process used to make cheese and yogurt is called _____ fermentation.

17. In a(n) _____ reaction, a molecule gains electrons.

Concept Review

On a sheet of paper, write the letter of the answer that completes each sentence correctly.

18. Cells use _____ to create ATP.

    A DNA   **C** photosynthesis

    B cellular respiration   **D** CO_2

19. After exercise, a buildup of _____ in your muscles can cause soreness.

    A lactic acid   **C** ethyl alcohol

    B carbon dioxide   **D** oxygen

20. Inside the cell, the reactions of the electron transport chain occur in the _____.

    A nucleus   **C** cytoplasm

    B mitochondria   **D** chloroplasts

21. Organisms use _____ as their main carbohydrate energy source.

    A ATP   **B** starch   **C** fats   **D** glucose

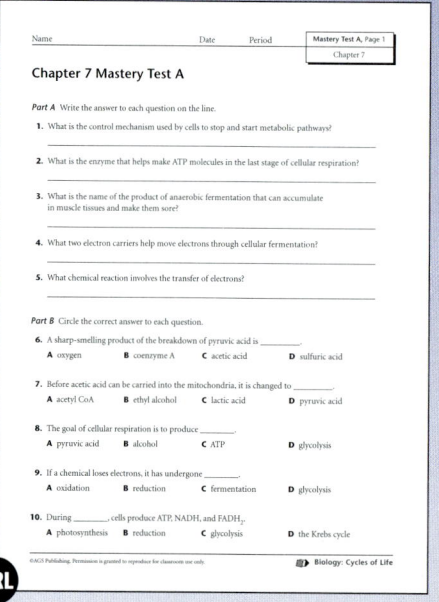
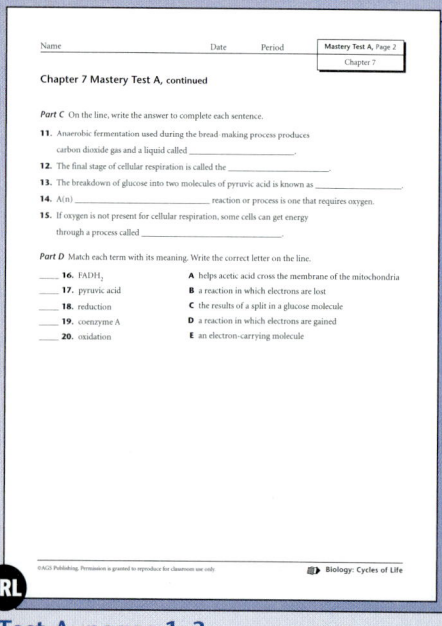

Chapter 7 Mastery Test A, pages 1–3

Critical Thinking

On a sheet of paper, write the answer to each of the questions. Use complete sentences.

22. Compare and contrast fermentation in anaerobic bacteria with cellular respiration in humans.

23. What stage of cellular respiration requires oxygen? Explain the role of oxygen in this stage.

24. Why do cells with a great need for energy, such as heart muscle cells, have more mitochondria than other cells?

25. Anaerobic cells cannot perform cellular respiration. Why?

Research and Write

Write a report on some common anaerobic bacteria. Describe how they can affect the body. Use both print and electronic resources. You might also gather information from a medical professional.

Test-Taking Tip When studying for a test, review any previous tests or quizzes that cover the same information. Be sure you have the correct answers for items you missed.

---

24. The Krebs cycle and the electron transport chain both occur in the mitochondria. Cells with a great need for energy need a large supply of ATP. This means they have more mitochondria than other cells have. **25.** Anaerobic cells cannot perform cellular respiration because they do not have mitochondria. Mitochondria are active in the Krebs cycle and the electron transport chain. Anaerobic cells also cannot be in an environment that contains oxygen.

Research and Write

A good source for students to use for this activity is a microbiology book, which will provide them with examples of anaerobic bacteria and the effects they have on the body. Examples of common anaerobic bacteria include *Clostridium botulinium*, *Clostridium tetani*, *Clostridium perfringens*, *E. coli*, and *Salmonella spp.*

ALTERNATIVE ASSESSMENT

Alternative Assessment items correlate to the student Goals for Learning at the beginning of this chapter.

- Have students write out the equation for cellular respiration. Ask them to identify where each of the reactants comes from and how the products are formed.
- Have students list the three stages of cellular respiration and write a one-sentence summary of what happens in each stage.
- Give students a partially filled-in diagram that shows the steps involved in cellular respiration. Ask them to fill in the missing steps.
- Ask students to define *fermentation*. Then have them compare and contrast lactic acid fermentation and ethyl alcohol fermentation.
- Ask students to define *feedback inhibition*. Then have them explain how it is related to cellular respiration.

Chapter 7 Mastery Test B, pages 1–3

Chapter 8

Planning Guide
Photosynthesis in Energy Cycles

	Student Text Lesson			
	Student Pages	Vocabulary	Lesson Review	Critical-Thinking Questions
Lesson 1 What Is Photosynthesis?	224–229	✔	✔	✔
Lesson 2 The Light Reaction	230–237	✔	✔	✔
Lesson 3 The Dark Reaction: The Calvin-Benson Cycle	238–241	✔	✔	✔

Chapter Activities

Teacher's Resource Library
Community Connection 8:
  Xeriscaping
Graphic Organizer 8:
  Respiration and Photosynthesis

Teacher's Edition
Opener Activity

Assessment Options

Student Text
Chapter 8 Review

Teacher's Resource Library
Chapter 8 Mastery Tests A and B

Teacher's Edition
Chapter 8 Alternative Assessment

Achievements in Science	Science at Work	Biology in Your Life	Investigation/Discovery	Biology in the World	Express Lab	Link to	Research and Write	Technology and Society	ELL/ESL Strategy	Background Information	Science Journal	Applications (Home, Career, Community, Global, Environment)	Online Connection	Teacher Alert	Auditory/Verbal	Body/Kinesthetic	Interpersonal/Group Learning	Logical/Mathematical	Visual/Spatial	Workbook Activities	Alternative Workbook Activities	Lab Manual	Self-Study Guide
		227	228		226	✔			225	224		226					226	226		42	42	36–37	✔
			236			✔		231	232	230		233, 234, 235		232, 233		231			232	43	43	38	✔
239	240			241			245		240	238	239, 241	239	241		239					44–45	44–45	39–40	✔

Pronunciation Key

a	hat	e	let	ī	ice	ô	order	ù	put	sh she
ā	age	ē	equal	o	hot	oi	oil	ü	rule	th thin
ä	far	ėr	term	ō	open	ou	out	ch	child	ŦH then
â	care	i	it	ȯ	saw	u	cup	ng	long	zh measure

ə { a in about, e in taken, i in pencil, o in lemon, u in circus }

Alternative Workbook Activities

The Teacher's Resource Library (TRL) contains a set of lower-level worksheets called Alternative Workbook Activities. These worksheets cover the same content as the regular Workbook Activities but are written at a second-grade reading level.

Skill Track Online

Use Skill Track Online for *Biology: Cycles of Life* to monitor student progress and meet the demands of adequate yearly progress (AYP). Make informed instructional decisions with individual student and class reports of online lesson and chapter assessments. With immediate and ongoing feedback, students will also see what they have learned and where they need more reinforcement and practice.

Chapter at a Glance

Chapter 8: Photosynthesis in Energy Cycles
pages 222–245

Lessons

1. What Is Photosynthesis?
   pages 224–229

   Investigation 8 pages 228–229

2. The Light Reaction
   pages 230–237

   Discovery Investigation 8
   pages 236–237

3. The Dark Reaction: The Calvin-Benson Cycle
   pages 238–241

   Biology in the World page 241

Chapter 8 Summary page 242

Chapter 8 Review pages 243–245

Audio CD 🎧

Skill Track Online 🖱
for Biology: Cycles of Life

Teacher's Resource Library (TRL)

Workbook Activities 42–45

Alternative Workbook Activities 42–45

Lab Manual 36–40

Community Connection 8

Graphic Organizer 8

Resource File 15–16

Chapter 8 Self-Study Guide

Chapter 8 Mastery Tests A and B

(Answer Keys for the Teacher's Resource Library begin on page 675 of the Teacher's Edition. The Materials List for the Lab Manual activities begins on page 720.)

Opener Activity

The nongreen pigments in leaves are always present, even when the leaves are green. Illustrate this fact by using a drawing program on a computer to show a small number of red, orange, and yellow dots and a significantly larger number of green dots randomly arranged on a page. Explain that each dot represents a pigment. Point out that the overall effect of the dots is green in color. However, when the green dots are removed, representing the breakdown of chlorophyll, the page looks orange. This demonstration also works with overlay transparencies on an overhead projector.

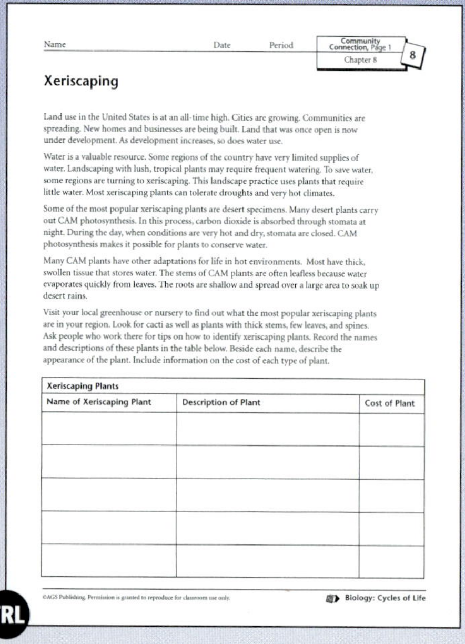

Community Connection 8, pages 1–2

Chapter 8

Photosynthesis in Energy Cycles

The giant kelp in the photograph is part of a forest. Like the forests on land, ocean forests play an important role in the cycling of energy. Sunlight shining through the water is taken in and used to make energy-rich molecules. This process is called photosynthesis. The energy-rich molecules made by kelp are food for animals. Now, take a deep breath. The oxygen you just took in may have come from kelp. Kelp uses the same process as land plants to make oxygen. In Chapter 8, you will learn about photosynthesis and how important this process is to life on Earth.

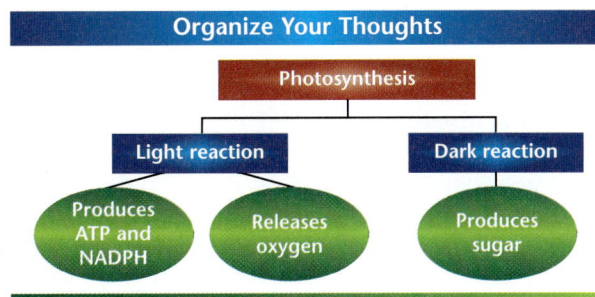

Goals for Learning

- ◆ To understand that photosynthesis is an energy conversion process to produce energy-rich molecules and oxygen
- ◆ To explain how plants and some microorganisms transform solar energy into chemical energy
- ◆ To describe the light reaction of photosynthesis
- ◆ To describe the dark reaction of photosynthesis

Introducing the Chapter

Ask students: How do you get the energy you need to perform your daily activities? *(by eating food)* Explain that plants cannot consume food as we do, but like animals, plants need energy to carry out their functions. The energy comes from sunlight. Plants use sunlight to make their own food in the form of sugars. Have students read the Goals for Learning and note that in this chapter, they will learn how plants and many microorganisms use photosynthesis to get energy from sunlight.

Have students examine the photograph of kelp on page 222. Ask students: How do you think the photograph relates to photosynthesis? Then read the chapter introduction aloud. Discuss the Organize Your Thoughts chart and the ways that plants get the energy they need for survival.

Notes and Math Tips

Ask volunteers to read the notes and math tips that appear in the margins throughout the chapter. Then discuss them with the class.

TEACHER'S RESOURCE

The AGS Publishing Teaching Strategies in Science Transparencies may be used with this chapter. The transparencies add an interactive dimension to expand and enhance the *Biology: Cycles of Life* program content.

CAREER INTEREST INVENTORY

The AGS Publishing Harrington-O'Shea Career Decision-Making System-Revised (CDM) may be used with this chapter. Students can use the CDM to explore their interests and identify careers. The CDM defines career areas that are indicated by students' responses on the inventory.

Chapter 8 Self-Study Guide

Lesson at a Glance

Chapter 8 Lesson 1

Overview In this lesson, students learn about how plants use photosynthesis to make sugar.

Objectives

- To explain how plants change the earth's atmosphere by removing carbon dioxide
- To identify the relationship between photosynthesis and respiration
- To explain what chloroplasts do in plant cells
- To describe how chlorophyll captures light energy

Student Pages 224–229

Teacher's Resource Library (TRL)

Workbook Activity 42
Alternative Workbook Activity 42
Lab Manual 36–37
Resource File 15–16

Vocabulary

autotroph	stoma
mesophyll	vascular bundle

Have students look up the meanings of *auto-* ("self") and *troph-* ("feeding"). Tell them that *heterotroph* refers to organisms that must feed on other organisms to meet their energy needs. Ask students: What do you think *autotroph* means?

Background Information

The equation for photosynthesis is a summary of many smaller chemical reactions that take place during the two stages of photosynthesis: the light and dark reactions. The simplified equation in the text is often simplified even further by canceling out six molecules of water on each side:

photosynthesis: $6 CO_2 + 6 H_2O + light \rightarrow C_6H_{12}O_6 + 6 O_2$

The general equation for cellular respiration, discussed in Chapter 7 on pages 196–197, is the opposite of the general equation for photosynthesis:

cellular respiration: $C_6H_{12}O_6 + 6 O_2 \rightarrow 6 CO_2 + H_2O + ATP$

The products for one equation are the reactants of the other equation. The form of energy is different in each reaction. Photosynthesis takes in light energy. Cellular respiration releases energy in the form of chemical bonds in ATP.

The two processes interact in a cyclical way as animals eat plants for sugars, the animals exhale carbon dioxide, and plants use the carbon dioxide to produce more sugars. The cycle that results is often called the carbon-oxygen cycle.

Lesson 1: What Is Photosynthesis?

Objectives

After reading this lesson, you should be able to

- explain how plants change the earth's atmosphere by removing carbon dioxide
- identify the relationship between photosynthesis and respiration
- explain what chloroplasts do in plant cells
- describe how chlorophyll captures light energy

Autotroph
A self-nourishing organism that makes its own food

Sunlight is the source of energy for living things. Living things need energy to grow and to carry out life processes. Recall that living things usually get energy from molecules of glucose. Where does the chemical energy stored in the bonds of glucose come from? The energy comes from photosynthesis. Photosynthesis changes the energy of sunlight into the chemical energy stored in glucose bonds. Photosynthesis is the connection between the sun and the energy needs of living systems.

Photosynthesis

Photosynthesis occurs in plants. Plants are **autotrophs**. An autotroph makes its own food. Plants use energy from sunlight in photosynthesis. They use this energy to combine CO_2 (carbon dioxide) and H_2O (water) to make glucose. Study the chemical equation for photosynthesis.

$6CO_2 + 12H_2O + light \longrightarrow C_6H_{12}O_6 + 6O_2 + 6H_2O$
carbon dioxide — water — energy — yields — glucose — oxygen — water

Within this equation are two important ideas in biology. First, living things need energy to maintain life. The energy usually comes from glucose. During photosynthesis, CO_2 and water molecules are rearranged to become energy-rich sugar molecules.

Second, many living things eat plants, or they eat animals that have eaten plants. Both plants and animals break down glucose in their cells. They use the chemical energy stored in the bonds of glucose. This energy is transferred to the bonds of ATP. The energy in ATP is then readily available as cells need it. Recall that the process of breaking down glucose to form ATP is called cellular respiration.

To sum up, plants use photosynthesis to make glucose. Plants and animals use cellular respiration to harvest the energy in the bonds of glucose.

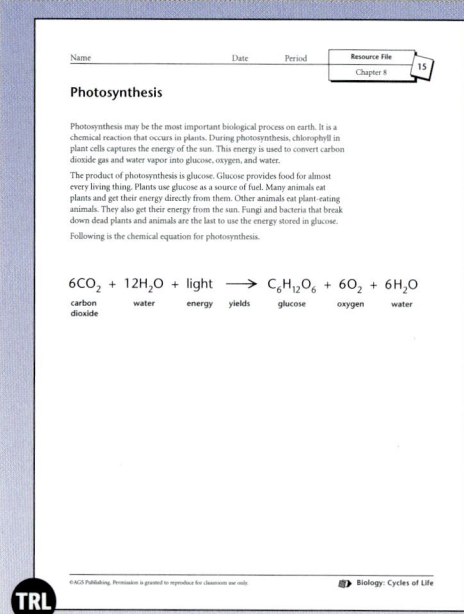

Resource File 15

Stoma
An opening on the underside of a leaf for gas exchange (plural is stomata)

Vascular bundle
A vein in a leaf that transports water and food

Mesophyll
The green tissue inside a leaf

Science Myth

Myth: Plants obtain the raw materials for photosynthesis just from the soil.

Fact: Plants obtain the materials for photosynthesis from the soil and the air.

Green Leaves

Photosynthesis takes place mostly in the leaves of plants or in certain algae and bacteria. If you study a leaf under a microscope, you can see various structures. These structures are important in photosynthesis.

Figure 8.1.1 shows the structures in a leaf. The top layer of the leaf is a transparent waxy layer. It takes in sunlight. This layer also prevents the loss of water from evaporation. A **stoma** is a tiny pore, or hole, that allows gas to move in and out of the leaf. Many stomata are on the underside of a leaf. Stomata take in carbon dioxide and release oxygen.

The veins in a leaf are called **vascular bundles.** They carry water from the roots to the leaf. Vascular bundles also carry food out of the leaf to other parts of the plant.

Mesophyll cells make up the green tissue inside a leaf. They contain organelles called chloroplasts that are the sites of photosynthesis. Chloroplasts contain a green pigment called chlorophyll. A pigment is a chemical that absorbs only certain wavelengths of visible light. You will learn more about wavelengths of light in Lesson 2.

Recall that each chloroplast has an outer and inner membrane. The inner membrane contains stroma, a thick fluid. Suspended in the stroma are thylakoids. Recall from Chapter 5 that thylakoids are sacs arranged in stacks called grana.

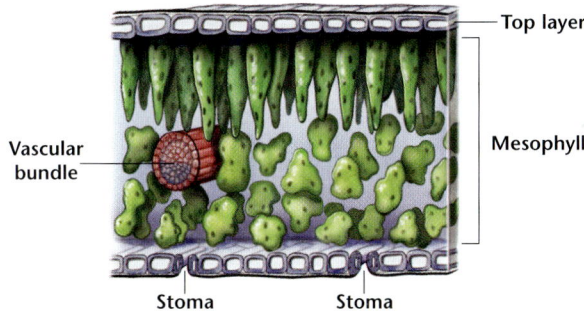

Figure 8.1.1 *The structures in leaves are important in photosynthesis.*

ELL/ESL Strategy

Language Objective:
To use visuals

Help students interpret the chemical equation given in the text by diagramming it on the board. Write the balanced general equation for photosynthesis. Draw a line underneath the equation. Have volunteers write out the formulas for each of the molecules represented underneath that part of the equation. Lead students to notice that the number of atoms of any one element is the same on both sides of the equation.

Science Myth

Have students read the Science Myth feature. Have students examine the equation for photosynthesis on page 224. Ask students: What inputs does photosynthesis require? *(carbon dioxide, water, and light)* What forms do these inputs have? *(Carbon dioxide is a gas, water is a liquid, and light is a form of energy.)* Lead students to conclude that plants obtain water primarily from the soil through their roots and carbon dioxide primarily from the air through the stomata in their leaves.

1 Warm-Up Activity

Explain that the process of a seed sprouting is called germination. Most seeds will sprout only when the conditions are best for producing a plant that is likely to survive. For example, dry or freezing conditions are not ideal for most plants, so many seeds will not germinate under these conditions.

Have students read and perform the Express Lab on page 226. Students can work in groups to complete the lab. Point out that the only difference between the two sets of seeds is the presence or absence of light. Remind students that seeds usually sprout underground.

Express Lab Answers

1. After 7 days, the bean seedlings raised in the light are green. The bean seedlings raised in the dark are pale white with elongated stems. After 14 days, the stems may be slightly longer than before but will eventually stop growing. **2.** The elongated stems of the seedlings raised in darkness help the growing seedling reach the light sooner.

2 Teaching the Lesson

Demonstrate that leaves contain multiple colors of pigment by performing chromatography. Place a green leaf over a long, narrow strip of chromatography paper. Use a quarter to scratch the top of the leaf so that it leaves a mark of pigment onto the paper below. The mark should be at least 1 cm from one end of the paper. Make a solvent mixture of 9 teaspoons lighter fluid (petroleum ether) and 1 teaspoon acetone. Stand the paper up in a beaker with the marked end of the paper at the bottom. Use a pencil to prevent the paper from touching the sides of the beaker. Add enough solvent mixture so that the liquid level is just below the mark on the paper. Cover the beaker loosely with aluminum foil and place it under a fume hood or outside. The different pigments will travel up the chromatography paper at different speeds, separating to show their different colors.

3 Reinforce and Extend

LEARNING STYLES

Logical/Mathematical

Tell students that coefficients are the numbers found before the chemical formulas in a chemical equation. Explain that coefficients tell the ratios of the reactants (chemicals to the left of the arrow) and products (chemicals to the right of the arrow) in a chemical reaction. Students can predict the number of molecules of a certain substance that would be produced by a given quantity of reactants. For example, the equation for photosynthesis given on page 224 shows that, for every six molecules of carbon dioxide that react, one molecule of glucose is produced. Ask students: How many molecules of carbon dioxide would be needed to produce 12 molecules of glucose by photosynthesis? *(72)*

Link to

Earth Science. Have students read the Link to Earth Science feature. Remind them that the equation for photosynthesis on page 224 is a general equation involving only three elements (carbon, oxygen, and hydrogen). The equation is actually a summary of many chemical equations that represent smaller steps in the process. These smaller steps involve many different molecules that contain additional elements, such as nitrogen and phosphorus.

IN THE COMMUNITY

Plan a field trip to a park, forest, botanical garden, or nature preserve that allows collection of samples. Have students use field guides to identify native plants. Encourage them to collect, examine, and categorize various leaves from different types of plants. If possible, invite a local expert to discuss the water and light needs for propagation of different species of trees, shrubs, and plants.

Link to ►►► Earth Science

Plants take in water and minerals from soil. They need minerals in tiny quantities. Each mineral is essential for healthy plant growth. Minerals assist chemical reactions during cellular respiration and photosynthesis.

Chlorophyll molecules and other pigments are in the membranes of the thylakoids. When sunlight strikes the pigments, they absorb the light.

Have you wondered why some green leaves change color in the fall? A leaf is green because of chlorophyll. During the plant's growing season, these green pigments are plentiful. They mask pigments of other colors such as red and yellow. In the fall, the chloroplasts die. Then red and yellow pigments become the main color of the leaves.

Some bacteria carry on photosynthesis although they do not have chloroplasts. Instead, they have photosynthetic membranes within their cells. These membranes allow them to produce sugar.

Express Lab 8

Materials
- lab coat or apron
- 8 paper towels
- tap water
- 10 bean seeds
- 2 containers, such as plastic cups or self-sealing plastic bags

Procedure
1. Put on a lab coat or apron.
2. Moisten the paper towels with tap water.
3. Put 5 bean seeds between the layers of 4 paper towels. Repeat with the other 5 bean seeds and paper towels.
4. Put each set of paper towels and seeds upright in a container.
5. Put one container in a sunny place, such as a windowsill. Put the other container in a dark, lightproof place, such as a closet.
6. After 7 days, examine the seeds. Examine the seeds after 14 days.

Analysis
1. After 7 days, how do the two sets differ? How do they differ after 14 days?
2. Describe the growth form of the seedlings raised in darkness. How is this helpful to the seedlings?

LEARNING STYLES

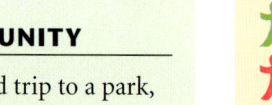

Interpersonal/Group Learning

Divide the class into small groups. Have them design a presentation for teaching this lesson to a group of younger students. Have each student choose one of these concepts: (1) plants make their own food; (2) leaves contain stomata, vascular bundles, and mesophyll cells. Each student should provide a brief oral report, a visual prop, and two quiz questions with answers. Have students give their presentations to a group of younger students.

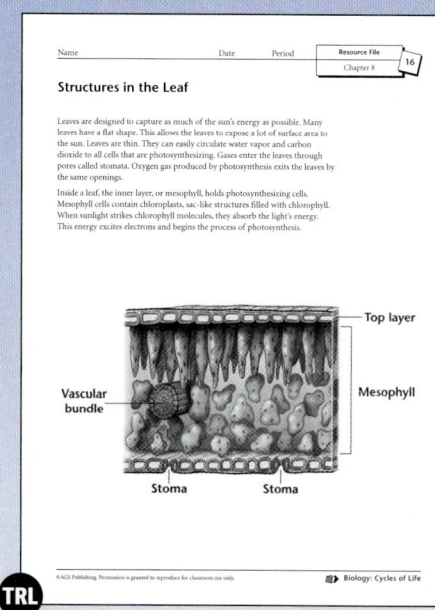

Resource File 16

Lesson 1 REVIEW

Word Bank
chloroplasts
glucose
autotroph

On a sheet of paper, write the word from the Word Bank that completes each statement correctly.

1. An organism that make its own food is a(n) _____.
2. In photosynthesis, plants change CO_2 and water into _____.
3. Plant cells contain small structures called _____, which are sites of photosynthesis.

Critical Thinking

Write the answer to each of the following questions.

4. Compare cellular respiration and photosynthesis.
5. Photosynthesis does not occur in plant roots. Explain why.

Biology in Your Life

Technology: Fluorescent Lightbulbs for Plant Growth

Have you seen plant growth lamps at a plant nursery or garden center? If you look closely, you will see these lamps use light bulbs with a red or blue tinge. These lightbulbs are designed to produce light that is most beneficial to plants.

Visible light and other forms of electromagnetic radiation are made of different wavelengths of light. Scientists know which wavelengths plants use. Chlorophyll *a* is the most important photosynthetic pigment. It absorbs blue light (short wavelength) and red light (long wavelength).

Ordinary incandescent lightbulbs provide red light, but little blue light. Ordinary fluorescent lightbulbs provide green, yellow, and blue light.

They do not produce much red light. Plant growth lamps contain fluorescent lightbulbs especially made for plant growth. These lightbulbs provide the blue and red light needed for photosynthesis.

1. How do fluorescent bulbs for plant growth differ from ordinary fluorescent bulbs?
2. Fluorescent lightbulbs for plant growth do not contain green light. Explain why.
3. Why would plant growth lamps produce healthier indoor plants than ordinary lightbulbs?

Photosynthesis in Energy Cycles Chapter 8 227

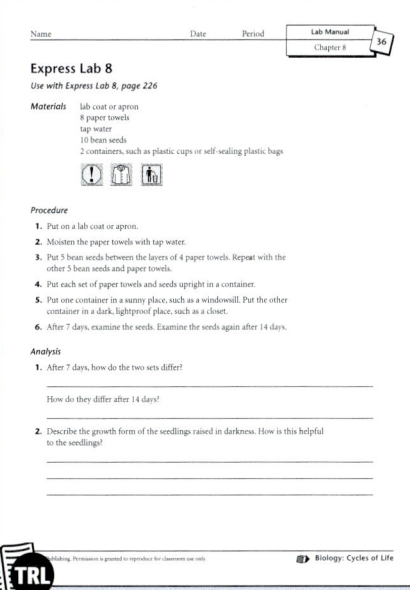

Lab Manual 36   Workbook Activity 42

Lesson 1 Review Answers

1. autotroph 2. glucose 3. chloroplasts
4. Cellular respiration breaks down glucose to obtain energy for the cell in the form of ATP. Photosynthesis uses energy from sunlight to combine carbon dioxide and water to make glucose.
5. Photosynthesis does not occur in plant roots because they are underground where no light is available.

Portfolio Assessment

Sample items include:
- Analysis answers from Express Lab 8
- Leaf collection from In the Community
- Lesson 1 Review answers

Biology in Your Life

Have students read the Biology in Your Life feature and answer the questions. Have students design an experiment that determines the best kind of light for promoting plant growth. For example, an experiment might involve growing plants using different types of household or commercial light bulbs, direct and indirect sunlight, and different color filters that change the color of light that reaches the plants.

Biology in Your Life Answers

1. Fluorescent bulbs made for plant growth provide blue and red light. Ordinary fluorescent bulbs provide green, yellow, and blue light. 2. Green light is reflected by plants. Because plants reflect green light, it is not useful for photosynthesis. 3. Plants need blue and red light for photosynthesis. Ordinary lightbulbs don't have red light and have little blue light.

LAB ACTIVITIES

Chapter 8 has Investigation and Discovery Investigation lab activities. Two additional lab activities for Chapter 8 appear in the Biology: Cycles of Life Lab Manual and on the Teacher's Resource Library CD-ROM.

Photosynthesis in Energy Cycles 227

Investigation 8

Encourage students to read the investigation steps. Discuss questions they may have before beginning the investigation.

Objectives

- To list the reactants and products of photosynthesis
- To recognize the role of photosynthesis in plant cells
- To predict the products of photosynthesis

Skills

Measuring, using science lab equipment, observing, collecting and recording information, comparing and contrasting, making inferences, recognizing cause and effect, analyzing data, drawing conclusions

Background

Plants use sunlight, carbon dioxide, and water to make sugars. When photosynthesis occurs, oxygen is released. In aquatic plants, carbon dioxide is obtained from CO_2 dissolved in the water. The release of O_2 can be seen as bubbles leaving the aquatic plant.

Time Frame

One class period

Procedure

- Have students work together in groups to complete the activity.
- For best oxygen production, use fresh *Elodea*. *Elodea* is an inexpensive freshwater aquatic plant commonly sold in pet shops or aquarium stores.
- *Elodea* must be kept submerged or very wet, or it will die quickly. Remind students to keep the *Elodea* underwater or covered with wet paper towels before they place it in the test tubes.
- If not available locally, *Elodea* is readily available from a supplier of science education materials. Some are listed on page 723.
- After the sprigs are selected and ends are cut at a 45° angle, remove some *Elodea* leaves near the cut end.
- Be sure each *Elodea* sprig is completely submerged in each test tube.
- You can use a beaker in place of a test-tube rack to hold the test tubes.
- Ask students: What do you think happens to distilled water when it is boiled and then cooled? *(The carbon dioxide dissolved in the water is driven off.)*

INVESTIGATION 8

Materials
- safety goggles
- lab coat or apron
- scissors
- 2 *Elodea* sprigs
- heavy-duty thread
- 2 glass rods
- 2 large test tubes
- wax pencil
- 0.25% sodium bicarbonate ($NaHCO_3$) solution
- cooled, boiled distilled water
- test tube rack
- lamp

Oxygen Production During Photosynthesis

During photosynthesis, plants use energy from sunlight to combine carbon dioxide (CO_2) and water to make glucose. Plants release oxygen (O_2) and water. In this investigation, you will see the roles of carbon dioxide and oxygen during photosynthesis.

Procedure

1. Put on safety goggles and a lab coat or apron.
2. Using scissors, remove two healthy sprigs of *Elodea*. Then recut the end of each sprig at a 45° angle. **Safety Alert: Be careful when using scissors.**
3. Use two pieces of thread to tie each sprig to a glass rod.

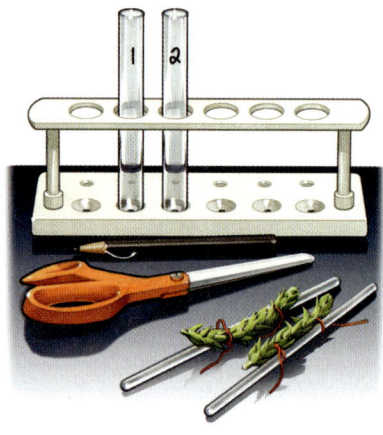

Safety Alert

- Make sure that students have read and understood all safety rules for working in the lab. Discuss the Safety Alerts with students.
- Be sure students wear safety goggles and a lab coat or apron.
- Remind students to handle scissors and glass rods carefully.
- Tell students to avoid touching the parts of the lamp that may be hot.

4. With the sprig's cut side up, place each rod into a test tube.

5. With a wax pencil, label the test tubes 1 and 2. Fill Test Tube 1 with 0.25% sodium bicarbonate solution. Be sure the *Elodea* sprig is covered with the solution. Fill Test Tube 2 with boiled and cooled distilled water. Be sure the *Elodea* sprig is covered with the distilled water.

6. Place the test tubes into a test tube rack. Place the rack so that both tubes are 1 meter from the lamp. Turn the lamp on.

7. Wait 5 minutes. Then watch both *Elodea* sprigs for bubbles that form at the cut end. Record your observations. Then turn the lamp off.

Cleanup/Disposal
Before leaving the lab, clean up your materials and wash your hands.

Analysis
1. In which test tube did bubbles appear?
2. What do the bubbles contain?

Conclusions
1. What was the role of the sodium bicarbonate solution?
2. Why did bubbles not appear in one of the test tubes?

Explore Further
Use a similar procedure to test the effect of light on photosynthesis.

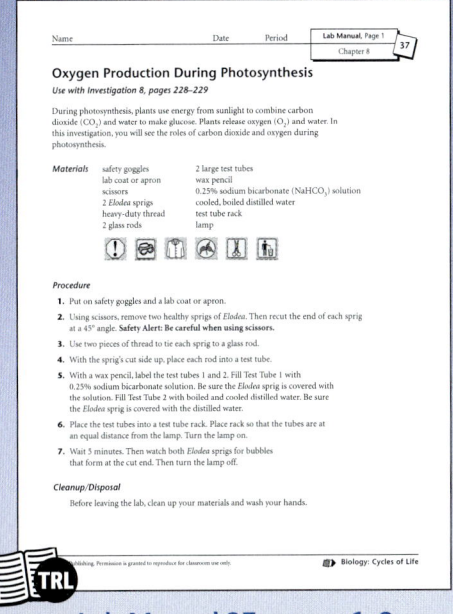

Lab Manual 37, pages 1–2

Cleanup/Disposal
Instruct students in proper cleanup and disposal of materials.

Results
When photosynthesis occurs, the release of oxygen is seen in the form of large, distinct bubbles at the cut surface of the *Elodea* stem. Photosynthesis takes place in the tube containing sodium bicarbonate ($NaHCO_3$) solution because it serves as a carbon dioxide source. Photosynthesis will not occur in the cooled, boiled distilled water because boiling drives away any CO_2 dissolved in the water.

Analysis Answers
1. Bubbles appeared in Test Tube 1, containing sodium bicarbonate ($NaHCO_3$) solution, at the cut surface of the *Elodea* stem.
2. The bubbles contain oxygen.

Conclusions Answers
1. Sodium bicarbonate serves as a source of the carbon dioxide needed for photosynthesis.
2. Bubbles do not appear at the cut surface of the *Elodea* stem in Test Tube 2 containing cooled, boiled distilled water. This is because boiling has driven away the CO_2 dissolved in the water, so photosynthesis cannot take place.

Explore Further Answers
Encourage students to propose different methods to test the effects of light on photosynthesis.

Assessment
Check to see that students recorded their observations in the data table. You might include the following items from this investigation in student portfolios:
- Answers to Analysis and Conclusions questions
- Student proposal in response to Explore Further

Lesson at a Glance

Chapter 8 Lesson 2

Overview In this lesson, students learn how plant cells convert energy from the sun to chemical energy

Objectives

- To recognize that sunlight is made up of different wavelengths
- To explain that pigments in green leaves absorb light
- To describe how light energy is used to produce ATP and NADPH
- To recognize that photosynthesis is responsible for the oxygen in the air

Student Pages 230–237

Teacher's Resource Library TRL

Workbook Activity 43
Alternative Workbook Activity 43
Lab Manual 38

Vocabulary

absorb	G3P
Calvin-Benson cycle	photon
carotenoid	photosystem
electromagnetic radiation	reaction center
electromagnetic spectrum	wavelength

Have students study the vocabulary terms associated with light: *absorb, electromagnetic radiation, electromagnetic spectrum, photon,* and *wavelength.* After they have defined the terms, ask students: How can you define these terms more simply in your own words?

Background Information

Visible light makes up a very small portion of the electromagnetic light spectrum. High-energy light of very short wavelengths beyond the visible spectrum includes ultraviolet (UV) light, X-rays, and gamma rays. Low-energy light of very long wavelengths beyond the visible spectrum includes infrared light, microwaves, and radio waves.

Lesson 2 The Light Reaction

Objectives

After reading this lesson, you should be able to

- recognize that sunlight is made up of different wavelengths
- explain that pigments in green leaves absorb light
- describe how light energy is used to produce ATP and NADPH
- recognize that photosynthesis is responsible for the oxygen in the air

The energy produced by the sun travels through space as waves called **electromagnetic radiation.** Electromagnetic radiation is made up of electric and magnetic waves. This radiation reaches the earth in the form of light.

The smallest unit of light is the **photon.** It is too small to be seen. A photon has a fixed amount of energy. Photons of light are **absorbed,** or retained, by pigments in leaves. In this absorption process, photons act like particles of light. However, when photons of light travel from the sun to leaves, they act like waves.

Electromagnetic radiation from the sun is made up of different **wavelengths** of energy. A wavelength is the distance between repeating units of a wave pattern. Light of shorter wavelengths has more energy than light of longer wavelengths. Study the **electromagnetic spectrum** in Figure 8.2.1. This is the spectrum, or range, of wavelengths of electromagnetic radiation. Visible light—the light that humans can see—is in the middle of the spectrum.

Electromagnetic radiation
Radiation that is made up of electric and magnetic waves

Photon
The smallest unit of light

Absorb
To retain

Wavelength
The distance between repeating units of a wave pattern

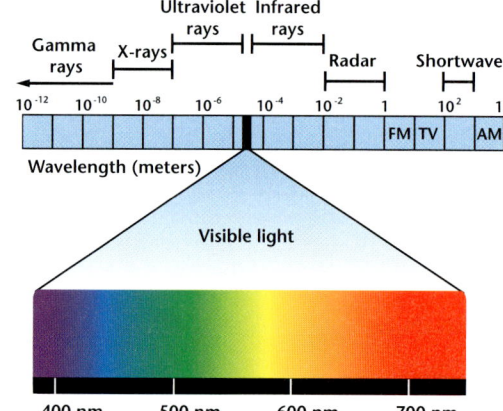

Figure 8.2.1 *Humans can only see a small portion of the electromagnetic spectrum.*

230 Chapter 8 Photosynthesis in Energy Cycles

Warm-Up Activity

Have students use a halogen flashlight and a prism to refract a narrow beam of white light into a spectrum of different wavelengths. Allow students to adjust the width of the flashlight beam and the positions of the flashlight, prism, and a sheet of white paper to obtain the most distinct visible spectrum. Have students draw the final arrangement and the spectrum that results.

Electromagnetic spectrum
The range of wavelengths of electromagnetic radiation

Humans can see light that is between 400 nm and 700 nm. Nm is the abbreviation for nanometer. A nanometer is one billionth of a meter. Wavelengths of light are measured in nanometers.

Most life depends on the energy of the visible part of the spectrum. Photons of visible light contain just enough energy to excite electrons without hurting the cell. Photons of ultraviolet light contain too much radiation for most biological systems. Photons of infrared light do not contain enough energy to maintain biological systems.

When passed through a prism, we see the different wavelengths of visible light as different colors. Have you seen a rainbow after it rains? The rainbow appears because drops of water act like small prisms.

The Energy of Visible Light and Photosynthesis

Chlorophyll does not absorb all the wavelengths of visible light equally. Chlorophyll *a* is the most important light-absorbing pigment in plants. Chlorophyll *a* does not absorb light in the green part of the spectrum. The absorption of light by chlorophyll *a* is highest at two wavelengths. These wavelengths are 430 nm (blue light) and 662 nm (red light). The rate of photosynthesis at different wavelengths of visible light also shows two peaks. These peaks are close to the absorption peaks of chlorophyll *a*.

> **Link to Physics**
>
> A prism separates visible light into different wavelengths. The wavelengths are visible as different colors. A man-made prism is a piece of glass or other transparent material cut at precise angles. Objects in nature, such as drops of water, can also serve as prisms. A rainbow forms when tiny water droplets separate light into its many colors.

> **Technology and Society**
>
> Commercial greenhouses sometimes use carbon dioxide generators to add carbon dioxide to the air. Carbon dioxide generators are machines that burn natural gas or propane and then release carbon dioxide. This extra carbon dioxide increases the rate of photosynthesis. It helps plant growth. Lower carbon dioxide levels decrease plant growth. This can cause flowers and fruit to drop off the plant.

2 Teaching the Lesson

To help students understand the relationship between wavelength and energy, compare light waves to water waves. Have students imagine that they are sitting on a raft in a swimming pool. If a friend makes a series of 6-inch waves with a long wavelength (crests spread far apart), the raft will move up and down with the wave slowly. If the friend makes a series of 6-inch waves with a short wavelength (crests close together), the raft will move up and down with the wave rapidly. Moving the raft up and down more often in the same span of time requires more energy.

3 Reinforce and Extend

Link to

Physics. Have students read the Link to Physics feature. Explain that a prism forms a spectrum because it refracts, or bends, light. Light travels at different speeds in different materials. When it passes from air into glass or water, it slows down. If it strikes the glass or water at an angle, changing speed bends its path. (You can illustrate this by rolling a toy car at an angle from a smooth to a rough surface. The car will swerve.) The different wavelengths of light are slowed down at different rates through the glass in a prism or raindrop. Thus, the different wavelengths of light bend at different angles, causing them to spread out and form a spectrum, or rainbow.

Technology and Society

Explain that one way to speed up a chemical reaction is to increase the quantity of reactants (or ingredients) available. Ask students: How could you use this information to increase the rate of photosynthesis? *(Increase the amount of water and carbon dioxide that are available, or increase the exposure to light.)* Then have students read the Technology and Society feature, which tells how commercial greenhouses maximize the rate of photosynthesis and plant growth.

LEARNING STYLES

Body/Kinesthetic
To help students understand the relationship between wavelength and energy, compare light waves to jumping rope. Explain that swinging a jump rope represents the crests (high points) and troughs (low points) of a wave. A single wavelength is represented by the amount of "wave" between adjacent times that the rope hits the floor. Swinging a rope slowly represents a longer wavelength, because the number of times that the rope hits the floor (trough) is small in a certain period of time. For example, to represent a longer wavelength, have students jump rope at a rate of one swing per second for 20 seconds. Then to represent a shorter wavelength, have students jump rope at a rate of two swings per second for 20 seconds. They will note that the "wave" with the shorter wavelength (higher frequency) took significantly more energy to produce.

TEACHER ALERT

Students may confuse the abbreviations NADPH, ATP, and G3P with chemical formulas such as CO_2, H_2O, and O_2. Explain that these abbreviations do not indicate the numbers and types of atoms of each element in the compound as chemical formulas do. Instead, they represent shortened versions (abbreviations) of a longer word. For example, ATP stands for adenosine triphosphate.

ELL/ESL STRATEGY

Language Objective:
To classify using visuals

Provide students with construction paper, glue, and yarn. Have them make three different models of waves: one with a short wavelength on blue or violet paper, one with a long wavelength on red paper, and one with an intermediate wavelength on yellow paper. The waves should all have similar heights (amplitudes). Have a volunteer sketch on the board a diagram of the electromagnetic light spectrum, indicating the different colors of visible light and relative wavelength and energy. Have additional volunteers indicate where each of their three models could be placed on the diagram. Have students label their models to indicate the color of light each represents and the relative wavelength and energy. For example, they might write "red, longer wavelength, less energy."

Carotenoid
Any yellow, orange, or red pigment found widely in plants and animals

Besides chlorophyll *a*, plants depend on other pigments. The other pigments, called accessory pigments, absorb light of different wavelengths. One accessory pigment is chlorophyll *b*. It is similar to chlorophyll *a* in structure. Chlorophyll *b* absorbs the orange and blue ranges of the visible spectrum. Plants usually contain about half as much chlorophyll *b* as they do chlorophyll *a*.

Other accessory pigments are **carotenoids.** A carotenoid is a yellow-orange pigment that absorbs blue-green light. Carotenoids pass energy to chlorophyll *a*. Carotenoids also protect the plant by getting rid of extra light energy that could harm chlorophyll. Figure 8.2.2 compares the light absorption of chlorophyll and carotenoids.

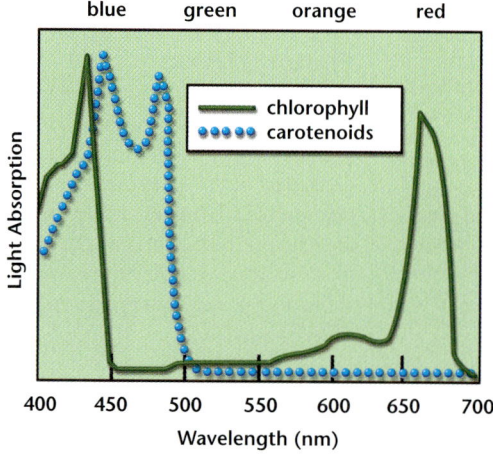

Figure 8.2.2 Chlorophyll and carotenoids absorb visible light differently.

The Two Processes of Photosynthesis

Photosynthesis is made up of two processes. Each process is a series of steps. One process is the light reaction. In the light reaction, plant cells convert energy from the sun to chemical energy. This reaction produces ATP and NADPH. NADPH is an electron carrier. The electrons from water are used to form NADPH.

LEARNING STYLES

Visual/Spatial

Show students pictures of a carrot, a cooked shrimp, a salmon steak, and a cooked lobster. Ask students: Which food do you think gets its characteristic color from carotenoids? *(carrots)* Tell students that the color of all of these foods is due in large part to carotenoids. Explain that animals cannot produce their own carotenoids, but get these pigments from the plants that they eat.

Calvin-Benson cycle
A process in photosynthesis that produces sugar

G3P
A sugar molecule

Reaction center
A special molecule of chlorophyll *a* in which electron transfer occurs

The other process is the dark reaction, or the **Calvin-Benson cycle.** During the Calvin-Benson cycle, cells produce sugar from carbon dioxide. ATP produced during the light reaction is the energy source for making **G3P,** a sugar. Some of this G3P is converted to glucose.

Study Figure 8.2.3. Find the relationship between the light reaction and the dark reaction. Notice that both reactions take place inside the chloroplast. To start the light reaction, light strikes the chloroplast. ATP and NADPH are produced. Oxygen is released into the air. In the dark reaction, or Calvin-Benson cycle, the cell produces sugar.

Link to
Language Arts
The word *photosynthesis* combines two words. First is the word *photo*, which comes from the Greek word for "light." Second is the word *synthesis*, which comes from the Latin word meaning "to put together." The word *photosynthesis* also describes its two-part nature. During the light reaction, light is captured. During the dark reaction, carbon dioxide is used to make sugar.

Figure 8.2.3 *In the chloroplast, photosynthesis is made up of a light reaction and a dark reaction. The light reaction produces ATP and NADPH, and the dark reaction produces glucose.*

The Light Reaction

Electrons become excited when photons of light strike pigments. Electrons in the pigments move to a higher energy level. Think of this process as electrons being boosted uphill. The cell transfers the excited electrons to a **reaction center.** A reaction center is a special molecule of chlorophyll *a* in which electron transfer occurs. At the reaction center, the electrons enter an electron transport chain. This chain forms NADPH and ATP. The energy of the excited electrons is captured in these ATP molecules. The ATP and NADPH are used later in the dark reaction to make sugar.

TEACHER ALERT

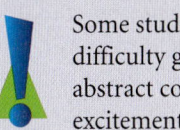 Some students may have difficulty grasping the abstract concept of excitement of electrons. Electrons in the excited state are similar in potential energy to a cart at the top of a hill. Moving the cart to the top of the hill is like light striking the pigments and exciting the electrons. When a person lets go of the cart, its potential energy converts to kinetic energy as it speeds down the hill. The potential energy of electrons in the excited state is converted to chemical energy in the bonds that form when NADPH and ATP molecules are produced.

IN THE ENVIRONMENT

 Solar energy is light energy from the sun. Just as plants use the energy of sunlight to excite electrons and break bonds in molecules, people can use solar energy to do work. Solar energy is clean and does not introduce pollutants into the environment. Simple solar collectors use the sun's radiation to heat water or food. Solar cells are more complicated. Like photosynthetic pigments in plants, they rely on excited electrons to carry out a task. Solar cells are devices that convert sunlight to electrical energy. Solar cells contain semiconducting materials (such as doped silicon) that cause electrons to flow when the material is illuminated. The flow of electrons through wires is electricity.

Link to

Language Arts. Have students read the Link to Language Arts feature. Ask students: What are some other words that are related to the words *photo* and *synthesis*? (*Photograph, photon, photosphere,* and *photosensitive all include the root word* photo. *Synthesis, synthesize, and synthesizer are related to the word* synthesis.) Have students look up the words they suggest in a dictionary.

Link to

Social Studies. Have students read the Link to Social Studies feature. Ask students: Why do you suppose you can eat some plants (such as rice, wheat, and corn) to obtain energy, but other nonpoisonous plants (such as many grasses and shrubs) are not edible? Explain that not all carbohydrates can be processed by humans as food. The plant carbohydrates that humans can digest include starch, glucose, fructose, and sucrose. Cows rely on bacteria in their digestive tracts to digest cellulose, a carbohydrate found in grasses and hay. Enzymes from the bacteria break down cellulose into nutrients that cows can digest.

AT HOME

Many of the carbohydrates that people consume come from starches in foods such as rice, corn, potatoes, and wheat products. Have students examine an extremely thin slice of uncooked potato under a microscope. Starch granules are large, pale bodies in which potato cells store starch. Stain a slice of potato with a dilute solution of tincture of iodine and have students examine it under a microscope. Iodine turns starch dark blue, so the starch granules become stained.

PRONUNCIATION GUIDE

Use the pronunciation shown here to help students pronounce a difficult word in this lesson. Refer to the pronunciation key on the Chapter Planning Guide for the sounds of the symbols.

photophosphorylation
(fō´tō fos´fôr ə lā´shən)

Photosystem
An assembly of proteins and pigments through which electrons are transferred to reaction centers

Link to ▶▶▶
Social Studies

Agriculture began when humans realized that plants are food or could be used to make food. Some early crop plants were cereals, including rice, wheat, barley, and maize (corn). Cereals store carbohydrates in energy-rich, dry seeds called grains. Grains are easy to harvest. They store well and do not spoil easily.

At the same time, the chloroplast splits water molecules into hydrogen and oxygen. It takes a large amount of energy to do this. The energy to split water molecules comes from sunlight. The hydrogen is carried along with the electrons in the electron transport chain.

The Electron Transport Chain

Pigments are arranged on the surface of the chloroplast in groups called **photosystems.** A photosystem is an assembly of proteins and pigments through which electrons are transferred to reaction centers. Photophosphorylation occurs in a photosystem. Recall that phosphorylation is the addition of a phosphate group to a molecule.

In the light reaction, photophosphorylation is a process that generates ATP. In this process, energy-rich electrons from a reaction center lose their energy. The energy loss happens as the electrons move along a chain of molecules called the electron transport chain. The cell uses the energy lost by the electrons to make ATP.

There are two types of reaction centers, Photosystem I and Photosystem II. In Photosystem I, chlorophyll P700 absorbs red light and produces ATP. Then the electrons return to the reaction center. In Photosystem II, chlorophyll P680 also absorbs red light. The electrons in the chlorophyll become excited and move to Photosystem I. Photosystem II replaces these electrons with the electrons gained from splitting water. During this water-splitting process, oxygen is released. The release of oxygen from photosynthesis maintains Earth's supply of oxygen.

To sum up, the light reaction converts solar energy to the chemical energy of ATP and NADPH. Oxygen is released. No sugar is produced. In Lesson 3, you will learn more about the dark reaction.

Lesson 2 REVIEW

Word Bank
absorb
visible light
more

On a sheet of paper, write the word or words from the Word Bank that complete each sentence correctly.

1. Pigments in green leaves _____ light.
2. Light of shorter wavelengths has _____ energy than light of longer wavelengths.
3. Plants use energy in the _____ part of the spectrum.

On a sheet of paper, write the letter of the answer that completes each sentence correctly.

4. Chlorophyll *a* does not absorb light in the _____ part of the spectrum.
   - A blue
   - B green
   - C red
   - D orange

5. A _____ is a yellow-orange pigment that absorbs blue-green light.
   - A carotenoid
   - B chlorophyll
   - C spectrum
   - D prism

6. Particles of light are called _____.
   - A waves
   - B photons
   - C rays
   - D electromagnetic radiation

Critical Thinking

On a sheet of paper, write the answers to the following questions. Use complete sentences.

7. What are accessory pigments? Explain what they do.
8. During which process of photosynthesis is light absorbed? During which process is sugar produced?
9. What are reaction centers? Explain what they do.
10. When is oxygen released during photosynthesis?

Lesson 2 Review Answers

1. absorb 2. more 3. visible 4. B 5. A 6. B 7. Accessory pigments such as carotenoids absorb light of different wavelengths and pass energy along to chlorophyll, the main photosynthetic pigment. 8. Light is absorbed during the light reactions. Sugar is produced during the dark reactions (Calvin-Benson cycle). 9. Reaction centers are special molecules of chlorophyll *a* where electron transfer happens. 10. Oxygen is released when water is split during the light reaction.

Portfolio Assessment

Sample items include:
- Drawings from Warm-Up Activity
- Wave models from ELL/ESL Strategy
- Lesson 2 Review answers

GLOBAL CONNECTION

In most physical processes and chemical reactions, energy is lost to the surroundings. This is true for every step of photosynthesis. Thus, much of the original light energy absorbed by a plant's pigments is lost without being stored in the bonds of glucose molecules that are the final product of photosynthesis. Even more energy is lost when the plant uses the glucose molecules in cellular respiration. The same thing happens when animals eat plants to obtain energy. Energy is lost at every step. The end result is that the higher up in the food chain an organism is, the more plants and animals must die to feed that organism, and thus the more energy is lost along the way. It takes a great deal of energy from sunlight to support one animal that eats other animals that eat plants. For this reason, carnivores and omnivores have more impact on Earth's energy resources than do herbivores.

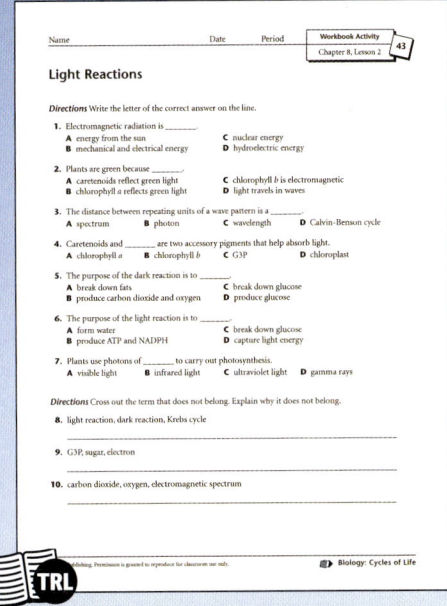

Workbook Activity 43

Discovery Investigation 8

This investigation is less structured than the first investigation in this chapter. It offers students more challenges and requires more teacher facilitation. Discuss with students the question in the first paragraph on page 236. Encourage students to read the investigation steps and formulate their own questions before beginning the investigation.

Objectives

- To recognize the role of light in photosynthesis
- To predict the relationship between the amount of light and the rate of photosynthesis
- To develop a testable hypothesis
- To design an experiment to test a hypothesis

Skills

Measuring, using science lab equipment, observing, collecting and recording information, describing, designing an experiment, comparing and contrasting, making inferences, predicting outcomes, recognizing cause and effect, analyzing data, drawing conclusions

Background

Plants need light to perform photosynthesis. When photosynthesis occurs, oxygen is released. In aquatic plants, the release of O_2 can be seen as bubbles leaving the plant.

Time Frame

One class period

Procedure

- Have students work together in groups to complete the activity.
- For best oxygen production, use fresh *Elodea*. *Elodea* is an inexpensive freshwater aquatic plant commonly sold in pet shops or aquarium stores. If not available locally, *Elodea* is readily available from a supplier of science education materials. Some are listed on page 699.
- *Elodea* must be kept submerged or very wet, or it will die quickly. Remind students to keep the *Elodea* underwater or covered with wet paper towels before they place it in the test tubes.
- After the sprigs are selected and ends are cut at a 45° angle, have students remove some of the *Elodea* leaves near the cut end.
- The addition of sodium bicarbonate ($NaHCO_3$, or baking soda) assists photosynthesis because the $NaHCO_3$ serves as a carbon dioxide source.
- Be sure that each *Elodea* sprig is completely submerged in each test tube. To allow time for photosynthesis to begin before the first time trial, let the flask stand in front of the lamp for 5 minutes before beginning to count bubbles.

DISCOVERY INVESTIGATION 8

Materials
- safety goggles
- lab coat or apron
- large flask
- cool tap water
- scissors
- *Elodea* sprig
- heavy-duty thread
- glass rod
- large test tube
- 0.25% sodium bicarbonate ($NaHCO_3$) solution
- meterstick
- lamp
- stopwatch

Light and Photosynthesis

Plants need light to perform photosynthesis. Does the amount of light affect the rate of photosynthesis? You will find out in this lab.

Procedure

1. Put on safety goggles and a lab coat or apron.
2. Fill the flask with cool tap water.
3. Use scissors to cut a healthy sprig of *Elodea*. **Safety Alert: Be careful when using scissors.** Be sure the sprig will fit inside the large test tube. Recut the end of the sprig at a 45° angle. With a piece of thread, tie the sprig securely to the glass rod.
4. With the cut end up, place the glass rod into the test tube. Fill the test tube with 0.25% sodium bicarbonate solution. Be sure the *Elodea* sprig is covered with the solution.

236 Chapter 8 Photosynthesis in Energy Cycles

SAFETY ALERT

- Make sure that students have read and understood all safety rules for working in the lab. Discuss the Safety Alerts with students.
- Be sure students wear safety goggles and a lab coat or apron.
- Remind students to handle scissors and glass rods carefully.
- Tell students to avoid touching parts of the lamp that may be hot.

5. Place the test tube into the flask. Place the flask 1 meter from the lamp. Turn on the lamp.

6. Wait 5 minutes. Then watch the *Elodea* sprig for bubbles that form at the cut end. Once bubbles start to appear, count the number of bubbles that form each minute. Do this for 5 minutes, recording your observations in a data table.

7. Write a hypothesis about the relationship between the amount of light and the rate of photosynthesis.

8. Write a procedure for an experiment to test your hypothesis. Include Safety Alerts. Hint: Consider using different distances between the lamp and the *Elodea* sprig.

9. Have your hypothesis, Safety Alerts, and procedure approved by your teacher. Then carry out your experiment.

Cleanup/Disposal
Before leaving the lab, clean up your materials and wash your hands.

Analysis
1. What is the purpose of the water in the flask?
2. At which distance from the light source was the rate of photosynthesis greatest?

Conclusions
1. Was your hypothesis supported by the results of your experiment?
2. Do you think temperature affects the rate of photosynthesis? Suggest an experiment that you could perform to find out.

Explore Further
How could you find out the effects of different colors of light on photosynthesis?

Photosynthesis in Energy Cycles Chapter 8 **237**

- **Important:** After each 5-minute time period in front of the lamp, students must remove the test tube from the flask and replace the tap water in the flask with fresh, cool tap water. Changing the water in the flask prevents heat accumulation from influencing the rate of photosynthesis.
- Have students document the procedure they suggest, including the list of materials needed, the preparation and safety alerts required, and any information necessary for someone else to repeat their experiment. Have students record their results.
- Ask students to discuss any problems they had in performing the experiment. Ask them which part of the procedure, if any, they would change if they were going to perform the experiment again.
- Optional for Explore Further: Students can make a simple cellophane light filter by cutting a square of cellophane and framing it in lightweight cardboard to add support. Cellophane is available in different colors at craft stores. It is sold in rolls and can easily be cut to the desired size.

Cleanup/Disposal
Instruct students in proper cleanup and disposal of materials.

Results
When photosynthesis occurs, the release of oxygen can be seen in the form of large, distinct bubbles at the cut surface of the *Elodea* stem. The number of bubbles per minute serves as an indicator of the rate of photosynthesis. As the distance to the lamp decreases, the rate of photosynthesis generally increases. An example of a possible data table is shown here:

Distance from Light Source (cm)	Time Interval 1 2 3 4 5 (min)	Avg. Number of Bubbles/min
100		
80		
40		
20		
10		
5		

Answers to Analysis, Conclusions, and Explore Further begin on page 670 of this Teacher's Edition.

Assessment
Check to see that students have filled in the data table. You might include the following items from this investigation in student portfolios:

- Hypothesis and experimental procedure
- Data table
- Answers to Analysis and Conclusions questions
- Student proposal for procedure to investigate the question in Explore Further

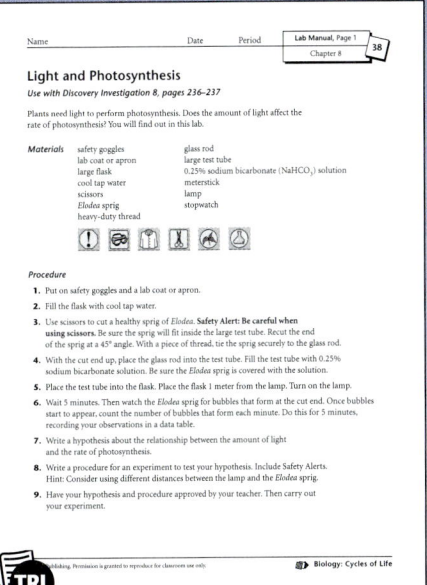

Lab Manual 38, pages 1–2

Photosynthesis in Energy Cycles **237**

Lesson at a Glance

Chapter 8 Lesson 3

Overview In this lesson, students learn how plant cells produce sugar from carbon dioxide in the Calvin-Benson cycle, or the dark reaction.

Objectives

- To recognize that the dark reaction uses the ATP and NADPH produced in the light reaction
- To explain that ATP and NADPH are used to produce energy-rich carbohydrate molecules
- To describe the Calvin-Benson cycle
- To describe plants that have adapted to their environment

Student Pages 238–241

Teacher's Resource Library

Workbook Activity 44–45

Alternative Workbook Activity 44–45

Lab Manual 39–40

Vocabulary

C_4 plant	PGA
CAM plant	RuBP

Some students may have difficulty distinguishing among the vocabulary terms that include abbreviations of unfamiliar words, such as *PGA* and *RuBP*. Encourage students to come up with simple mnemonic devices to help them tell the terms apart. For example, the term *PGA* has three letters and describes a molecule with three carbons.

Background Information

Transpiration is the loss of water vapor from plant leaves. Water evaporates from the leaf surface through tiny pores called stomata. Stomata regulate the amount of water released into the air and the amount of carbon dioxide that enters a plant. Thus, when stomata are open, carbon dioxide can enter the plant and water can exit.

Lesson 3 The Dark Reaction: The Calvin-Benson Cycle

Objectives

After reading this lesson, you should be able to

- recognize that the dark reaction uses the ATP and NADPH produced in the light reaction
- explain that ATP and NADPH are used to produce energy-rich carbohydrate molecules
- describe the Calvin-Benson cycle
- describe plants that have adapted to their environment

RuBP
Ribulose bisphosphate; a five-carbon carbohydrate that combines with CO_2 in the first step of the Calvin-Benson cycle

PGA
Phosphoglycerate; a three-carbon molecule formed in the first step of the Calvin-Benson cycle

Think of the Calvin-Benson cycle as a sugar factory. The factory is inside the stroma of the chloroplast. Like a factory, the Calvin-Benson cycle changes its input, mainly carbon dioxide, into a final product. The final product is a small sugar molecule called G3P. The cell uses this sugar molecule to make glucose and other compounds.

One input into the Calvin-Benson cycle is carbon dioxide from the air. A second input is energy from ATP that is made in the light reaction. A third input is high-energy electrons from NADPH, also produced in the light reaction. From these inputs, the Calvin-Benson cycle produces G3P. G3P is an energy-rich sugar molecule.

Figure 8.3.1 shows the four main steps in the Calvin-Benson cycle. In Step 1, CO_2 molecules and the sugar **RuBP** (**ribu**lose **b**is**p**hosphate) combine to make **PGA** (**p**hospho**g**lycer**a**te). An enzyme assists this chemical reaction. In Step 2, energy from ATP and electrons from NADPH combine to form G3P. In Step 3, G3P produces glucose and other compounds needed for metabolism and growth. In Step 4, energy from ATP is added to the remaining G3P molecules to make RuBP. The Calvin-Benson cycle is now complete and begins again.

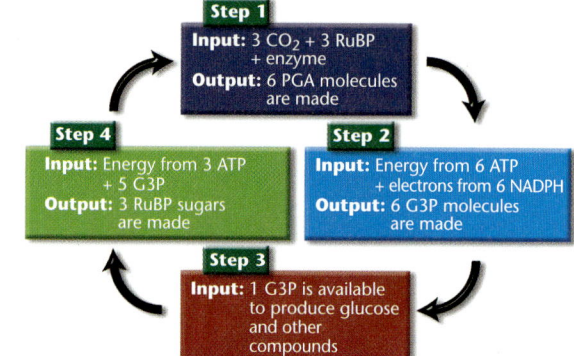

Figure 8.3.1 *The Calvin-Benson cycle is like a four-step sugar factory.*

Warm-Up Activity

Allow students to determine the rate of transpiration in a sprig of coleus or some other houseplant. Have students fill two test tubes with the same amount of water. Place a cutting of a houseplant in one test tube. Have students mark the water levels on the outside of both test tubes. After 24 hours, have students mark the new water levels on the outside of the test tubes. The difference in the water levels represents the amount of water lost to transpiration rather than to evaporation from the surface of the water.

Teaching the Lesson

Lead students to notice that C_4 plants and CAM plants are adapted to hot, dry climates in different ways. They differ in the function of special structures that regulate dark reactions. C_4 plants have adapted to dry, hot weather by closing their stomata during dry conditions. They use an enzyme to incorporate carbon dioxide into organic acids in certain cells and then carry out the Calvin-Benson cycle in separate cells even when the stomata are closed.

C_4 plant
A plant that photosynthesizes in hot, dry weather

CAM plant
A plant that takes in CO_2 only during the night

Science Myth

Myth: The dark reaction takes place only in the dark.

Fact: The dark reaction can occur in the dark or in the light. It will occur if ATP and NADPH are supplied from the light reactions. In most plants, the Calvin-Benson cycle occurs during the daylight hours.

C_4 Plants and CAM Plants

When the weather is hot and dry, water evaporates from plants quickly. To save water, the stomata close and no more CO_2 enters the plant. Photosynthesis stops. Some plants conserve, or save, water differently. **C_4 plants** such as corn and crabgrass, have a special enzyme in their leaves. This enzyme grabs CO_2 and turns it into a four-carbon compound. This means C_4 plants can photosynthesize in hot, dry weather.

Another group of plants that photosynthesize in hot, dry conditions are **CAM plants** like cacti and pineapple. CAM plants close their stomata during the hot day. They open their stomata at night to store CO_2 for use during the day.

These plants have adjusted their cycles in response to their environment. The life-giving reactions of photosynthesis can continue in the day or night. Photosynthesis feeds into a larger energy cycle with cellular respiration. Oxygen and glucose made from photosynthesis are used in cellular respiration. In turn, the water and carbon dioxide given off during cellular respiration are used in photosynthesis. This allows the energy cycle in living things to continue.

Achievements in Science

Discovering Photosynthesis

In 1771, English chemist Joseph Priestley was the first scientist to study photosynthesis. Priestley burned a candle in a sealed, glass jar until the candle went out. He opened the jar, put in a small plant, and sealed the jar again. After several days, he lit a candle in the jar. The candle burned. Priestley thought the plant had released a substance that supported burning.

That substance was oxygen. In 1779, Dutch physician Jan Ingenhousz showed that a plant produces oxygen only when exposed to light. Experiments in the early 1800s by Nicholas de Saussure from France showed that plants absorb carbon dioxide from the air. By the mid-1800s, scientists had learned that plants store light energy from the sun as chemical energy.

CAM plants have adapted to dry, hot weather by closing their stomata during the day to slow transpiration and conserve water. They incorporate carbon dioxide into organic acids at night, when the stomata are open, and carry out the Calvin-Benson cycle during the day.

3 Reinforce and Extend

Science Myth

Have students read the Science Myth feature. Help students distinguish between the light reaction, which can occur only when there is sunlight available, and the dark reaction, which can occur at any time. In fact, in many plants, the dark reaction occurs during the day when the light reaction is providing energy needed for the Calvin-Benson cycle. Be sure that students do not confuse the distinction between the light and dark reactions with the distinctions between steps of the Calvin-Benson cycle, which may occur both during the day and night.

Achievements in Science

Have students read the Achievements in Science feature and research more about the lives, experiments, and discoveries of the three scientists named. Encourage students to present their findings in a written report or in an illustrated poster that indicates which aspect of photosynthesis was discovered by each scientist.

Science Journal

Have students write a fictional story from the point of view of a carbon atom in a carbon dioxide molecule that becomes involved in photosynthesis. Have them include creative descriptions of what happens at each stage of photosynthesis.

Learning Styles

Auditory/Verbal

Have students work in small groups to write lyrics about the Calvin-Benson cycle, using the tune of a familiar song. Be sure students include descriptions of the four main steps of the Calvin-Benson cycle. Students may wish to use tunes from current popular music or from an old folk song such as *She'll Be Coming Around the Mountain*.

Career Connection

Invite a botanist or horticulturalist to visit the classroom and discuss how different plants require different kinds of care. If possible, have the visitor provide examples of C_3 plants, C_4 plants, and CAM plants. Have students prepare questions about the training, challenges, and rewards of a career as a botanist or horticulturalist.

Lesson 3 Review Answers

1. sugar **2.** can **3.** open **4.** When you eat a meal, you obtain carbon from the foods you eat. During the Calvin-Benson cycle, plants obtain carbon from the carbon dioxide in the air. **5.** C_4 plants and CAM plants have methods of photosynthesis that are very efficient for hot, dry climates. C_4 plants have a special enzyme that turns CO_2 into a four-carbon compound. CAM plants close their stomata during the day when it is hot. They capture CO_2 at night for use later during the daytime.

Portfolio Assessment

Sample items include:
- Reports on agricultural plant scientists from Science at Work
- Reports or posters from Achievements in Science
- Questions prepared for the visiting botanist or horticulturalist in the Career Connection
- Lesson 3 Review answers

ELL/ESL Strategy

Language Objective: *To use visuals*

Pair a student who is learning English with a student who has strong English skills. Have each pair write on note cards the following terms: *ATP, carbon dioxide, G3P, electron, enzyme, glucose, hydrogen, NADPH, oxygen, PGA, pigment, reaction center, RuBP, sunlight,* and *water*. Have students take turns reviewing the light and dark reactions of photosynthesis, using the cards as props in a visual demonstration. Encourage them to follow the text as they summarize the steps in photosynthesis.

Science at Work

As a class, read the Science at Work feature about the career of an agricultural plant scientist. Have students find out more about problems that agricultural plant scientists solve, such as managing the use of fertilizers, organic farming, pesticides, and crop rotation. Encourage students to present their findings in a report.

240   Chapter 8

Lesson 3 REVIEW

On a sheet of paper, write the word in parentheses that best completes each sentence.

1. The Calvin-Benson cycle makes an energy-rich _____ (electron carrier, sugar, wavelength) known as G3P.
2. The reactions of the Calvin-Benson cycle _____ (always, can, cannot) occur during the daylight hours.
3. In most plants, stomata on a leaf must be _____ (open, closed, made) during the Calvin-Benson cycle.

Critical Thinking

On a sheet of paper, write the answers to the following questions. Use complete sentences.

4. How does a person eating a meal resemble the Calvin-Benson cycle in plants?
5. How do C_4 plants and CAM plants differ from other plants?

Science at Work

Agricultural Plant Scientist

Agricultural plant scientists solve problems in agriculture. They help improve the breeding and management of food crops. They improve seed quality and nutrition levels in crops. Agricultural plant scientists help farmers become more productive. They help conserve, or save, natural resources and maintain the environment.

Agricultural plant scientists in research usually work in offices and labs. Some spend a lot of time outdoors performing research on farms and at agricultural research stations.

Many work for state governments. Others work for companies that produce foods or agricultural chemicals, supplies, or machines. A bachelor's degree is needed to assist in basic research. A master's or doctoral degree is required to perform or direct research.

240   Chapter 8   Photosynthesis in Energy Cycles

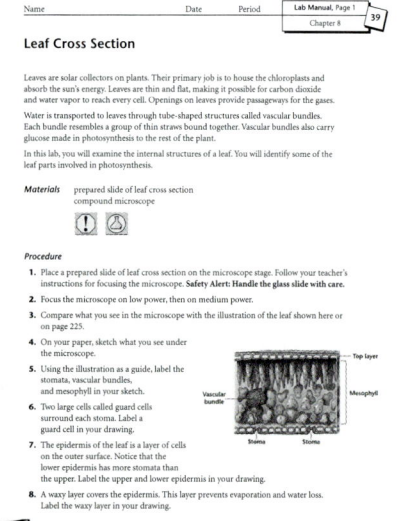

Workbook Activity 44   **Lab Manual 39, pages 1–2**

BIOLOGY IN THE WORLD

Worldwide Photosynthesis

Where do you think most of the world's photosynthesis takes place? You may think it occurs in tropical rain forests. Or maybe you think it occurs in the vast evergreen forests in northern regions. These would be good guesses, but they are not correct. Most photosynthesis occurs in the oceans.

The upper layers of the oceans are home to microscopic organisms called plankton. Some plankton, such as bacteria and algae, carry out photosynthesis. These plankton are called phytoplankton. Although tiny, phytoplankton are very important. Phytoplankton performs more than 40 percent of the photosynthesis that takes place on the earth. They provide food, directly or indirectly, for all other marine animals.

Like plants on land, phytoplankton use carbon dioxide and release oxygen. Carbon dioxide and oxygen are reused in global cycles. Each cycle involves many living things, including humans. For example, the burning of coal, oil, and gasoline releases carbon dioxide. About one-half of this human-produced carbon dioxide goes into the atmosphere.

Scientists do not know how much of the remaining carbon dioxide is taken up by phytoplankton. They are not sure how much carbon dioxide is dissolved in ocean water. They also do not know how much of the earth's oxygen is produced by phytoplankton. Scientists who study the oceans have found that global changes in temperature influence phytoplankton growth. Many scientists think the world is becoming warmer. This could increase the numbers of phytoplankton.

1. Where does most of the earth's photosynthesis take place?
2. Why do phytoplankton live in the upper layers of the ocean?
3. How do phytoplankton affect the amount of oxygen on the earth?

BIOLOGY IN THE WORLD

Have students read the Biology in the World feature about worldwide photosynthesis and answer the questions at the bottom of the page. Have students research and discuss the idea of photosynthesis on a global scale. Suggest that students find answers to the following questions: What effects does the burning of fossil fuels and deforestation have on the amount of carbon dioxide in the atmosphere? How does this excess carbon dioxide affect the environment? How do the ozone layer and the production of chemicals such as chlorofluorcarbons play a role in the debate over global warming? What alternatives to current energy production practices might solve environmental problems commonly associated with the buildup of greenhouse gases? Are these alternatives effective? Have students engage in a mock debate using the information that they have gathered.

Biology in the World Answers

1. Most of Earth's photosynthesis takes place in the oceans. 2. Phytoplankton live in the upper layers of the ocean waters because these areas receive sunlight. 3. Phytoplankton add to the amount of oxygen on Earth.

SCIENCE JOURNAL

Have students write an essay or a letter to the editor describing their opinions and predictions about the effects of fossil fuel use in the global cycle described in Biology in the World. Remind students to include in their essay or letter a description of how photosynthesis is involved on a global scale.

PRONUNCIATION GUIDE

Use the pronunciation shown here to help students pronounce a difficult word in this lesson. Refer to the pronunciation key on the Chapter Planning Guide for the sounds of the symbols.

phytoplankton (fī tō plank′ tən)

ONLINE CONNECTION

Have students visit this site for more in-depth descriptions of the stages of photosynthesis: www.emc.maricopa.edu/faculty/farabee/BIOBK/BioBookPS.html.

Students can read this article to find out more about why leaves change color in the fall: www.forestry.about.com/od/fallcolor/a/why_leaf_color.htm?terms=photosynthesis.

Students can learn more about fertilizers at this Web site: www.howstuffworks.com/question181.htm.

Lab Manual 40, pages 1–2

Chapter 8 Summary

Have volunteers read aloud each summary item on page 242. Ask volunteers to explain the meaning of each item. Direct students' attention to the Vocabulary box on the bottom of page 242. Have them read and review each term and its definition.

Graphic Organizer

As students read Chapter 8, have them finish completing the chart on Graphic Organizer 8: Respiration and Photosynthesis. Encourage students to read each lesson of the chapter and then have them fill in the portion of the chart that pertains to the lesson. When they have completed the chart, ask them to answer the questions.

Chapter 8 SUMMARY

- During photosynthesis, plants use carbon dioxide (CO_2) to make sugar. During this process, plants release oxygen (O_2) into the atmosphere.

- Plants use energy from sunlight to combine carbon dioxide (CO_2) and water (H_2O), making glucose.

- The cells of plants and animals break down glucose to release energy during cellular respiration.

- The oxygen released during photosynthesis is used by plants and animals during cellular respiration.

- Visible light is the light we see. Visible light is part of the electromagnetic spectrum.

- Photosynthesis takes place in green leaves. Pigments in chloroplasts absorb certain wavelengths of visible light. Chlorophyll *a* is the main light-absorbing pigment in plants.

- Photosynthesis consists of two processes, the light reaction and the dark reaction. The dark reaction is also known as the Calvin-Benson cycle.

- During the light reaction, light energy is converted to chemical energy in the form of ATP and NADPH. Water is split and oxygen is released.

- The ATP and NADPH from the light reaction are needed by the dark reaction.

- During the dark reaction, the energy from ATP and NADPH is used. The carbon in CO_2 is used to make an energy-rich sugar called G3P. G3P is used by the cell to make glucose and other compounds for metabolism and growth.

Vocabulary

absorb, 230	electromagnetic radiation, 230	photosystem, 234
autotroph, 224	electromagnetic spectrum, 231	reaction center, 233
C_4 plant, 239	G3P, 233	RuBP, 238
Calvin-Benson cycle, 233	mesophyll, 225	stoma, 225
CAM plant, 239	PGA, 238	vascular bundle, 225
carotenoid, 232	photon, 230	wavelength, 230

242 Chapter 8 *Photosynthesis in Energy Cycles*

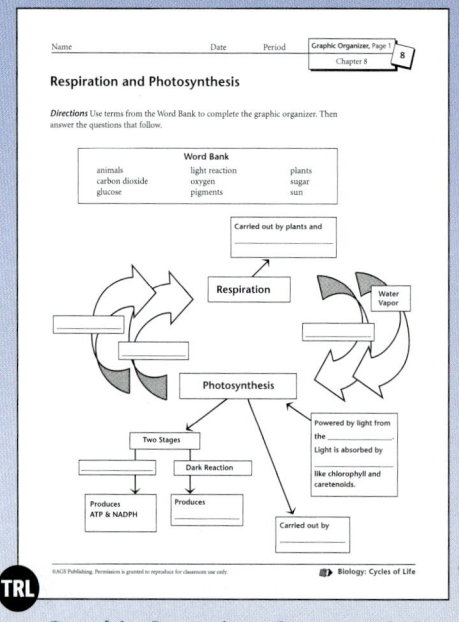

Graphic Organizer 8, pages 1–3

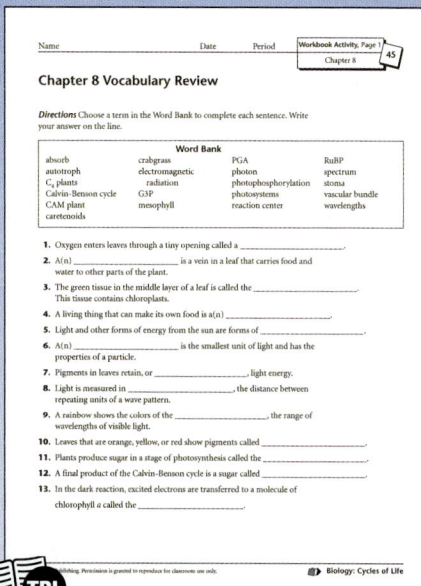

Workbook Activity 45, pages 1–2

Chapter 8 REVIEW

Word Bank
autotroph
C_4 plant
Calvin-Benson cycle
CAM plant
carotenoid
electromagnetic radiation
electromagnetic spectrum
G3P
mesophyll
PGA
photon
photosystem
reaction center
RuBP
stoma
vascular bundle
wavelength

Vocabulary Review

On a sheet of paper, write the word or words from the Word Bank that complete each sentence correctly.

1. A small pore called _____ allows air to enter and exit the leaf.
2. The five-carbon carbohydrate that combines with CO_2 in the first step of the Calvin-Benson cycle is called _____.
3. An organism that makes its own food is a(n) _____.
4. The green tissue inside a leaf is called the _____.
5. An assembly of proteins and pigments known as a(n) _____ is found in chloroplasts.
6. A(n) _____ is a particle of light.
7. A(n) _____ is a special molecule of chlorophyll *a* in which electron transfer occurs.
8. A yellow-orange pigment called a(n) _____ passes energy to chlorophyll *a*.
9. The distance between repeating units of a wave pattern is called a(n) _____.
10. A three-carbon molecule formed in the first step of the Calvin-Benson cycle is _____.
11. The dark reaction is also known as the _____.
12. An energy-rich sugar molecule called _____ is produced during the dark reaction.
13. A(n) _____ closes its stomata during the day and opens them at night.

Review continued on next page

Chapter 8 Review

Use the Chapter Review to prepare students for tests and to reteach content from the chapter.

Chapter 8 Mastery Test

The Teacher's Resource Library includes two forms of the Chapter 8 Mastery Test. Each test addresses the chapter Goals for Learning. An optional third page of additional critical-thinking items is included for each test. The difficulty level of the two forms is equivalent.

Review Answers

Vocabulary Review

1. stoma 2. RuBP 3. autotroph
4. mesophyll 5. photosystem 6. photon
7. reaction center 8. carotenoid
9. wavelength 10. NADPH 11. Calvin-Benson cycle 12. G3P

Review Answers

13. CAM plant 14. electromagnetic radiation 15. electromagnetic spectrum 16. absorption 17. vascular bundle 18. C_4 plant

Teacher Alert

In the Chapter Review, the Vocabulary Review activity includes a sample of the chapter's vocabulary terms. The activity will help determine students' understanding of key vocabulary terms and concepts presented in the chapter. Other vocabulary terms used in the chapter are listed below.

absorb

Concept Review

19. C 20. A 21. B

Chapter 8 REVIEW - continued

14. Radiation that is made up of electric and magnetic waves is called _____.
15. The _____ is the range of wavelengths of electromagnetic radiation.
16. The process of retaining energy when light strikes chlorophyll is called _____.
17. Inside a leaf, a vein or _____ transports food and water.
18. Unlike other plants, a(n) _____ captures CO_2 and turns it into a four-carbon compound.

Concept Review

On a sheet of paper, write the letter of the answer that completes each sentence correctly.

19. The product of photophosphorylation is _____.
    A oxygen   B carbon dioxide   C ATP   D sugars
20. Oxygen is released when _____.
    A water is split   C carbon dioxide enters the leaf
    B G3P is made   D light is absorbed
21. The light reaction produces _____.
    A sugars   C carbon dioxide
    B ATP and NADPH   D chlorophyll

244 Chapter 8 Photosynthesis in Energy Cycles

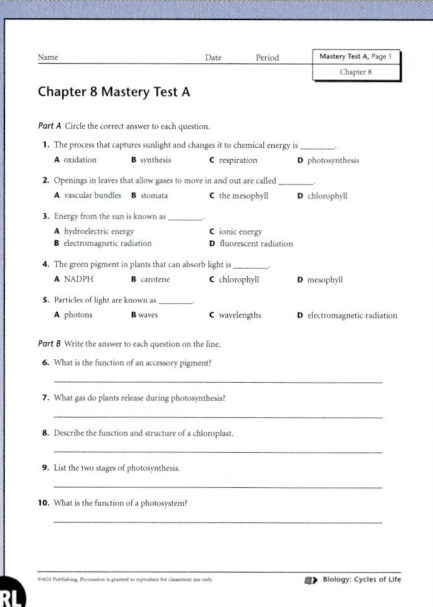

Chapter 8 Mastery Test A, pages 1–3

Critical Thinking

On a sheet of paper, write the answers to the following questions. Use complete sentences.

22. Describe the relationship between the processes of cellular respiration and photosynthesis.
23. Why are C_4 plants and CAM plants found in hot, dry climates?
24. Why do plants appear green?
25. Why do you think plants that grow in dense, tropical rain forests often have large, flat leaves?

Research and Write

Write a report on the role of beta-carotene in the human diet. Explain why it is important to eat foods containing beta-carotene.

Test-Taking Tip Before you start a test, look it over so you can plan how to use your time.

Critical Thinking

22. Cellular respiration requires oxygen and glucose, both of which are produced by photosynthesis. **23.** C_4 plants and CAM plants have very efficient methods to obtain carbon dioxide. C_4 plants have a special enzyme that turns CO_2 into a four-carbon compound. CAM plants close their stomata during the day when it is hot. They capture CO_2 at night for use later during the daytime. **24.** Plants appear green because chlorophyll does not absorb light in the green portion of the visible spectrum. **25.** Light is in short supply in dense tropical rain forests. Plants with large, flat leaves are able to absorb more light for photosynthesis.

Research and Write

Direct students to the Internet or the library to find out more about the importance of beta-carotene in the human diet. Students may wish to do this research individually, in pairs, or in small groups.

ALTERNATIVE ASSESSMENT

Alternative Assessment items correlate to the student Goals for Learning at the beginning of this chapter.

- Display images of a plant and a plant cell and an animal and an animal cell. Have students use the examples to write a paragraph that explains how each organism gets its energy and whether its cells carry out photosynthesis, cellular respiration, or both.
- Have students make a drawing of the electromagnetic light spectrum and label the relative energy and wavelengths of visible light. Then have students indicate on the spectrum which portion of the visible part of solar energy is absorbed by plant pigments.
- Divide the class into groups of four students. Have each group member stand in a circle representing the Calvin-Benson cycle. Have each student in turn say what happens in his or her stage of the cycle and what is being passed on to the next stage.

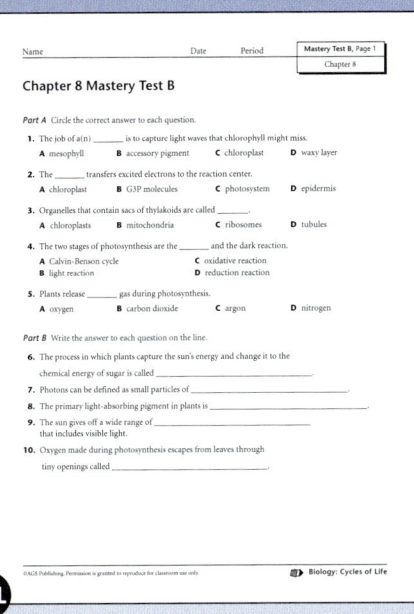
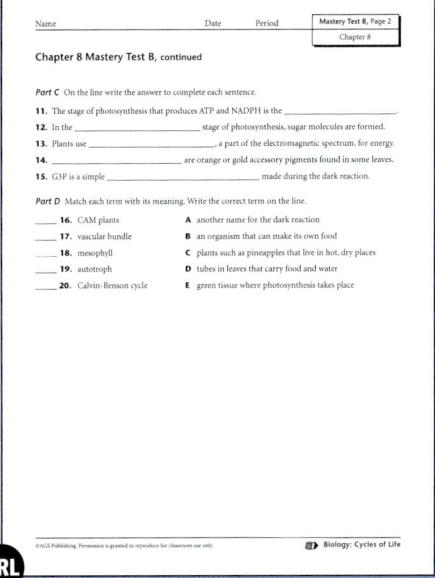

Chapter 8 Mastery Test B, pages 1–3

Chapter 9

Planning Guide
The Life Cycles of Cells and Reproduction

	Student Pages	Vocabulary	Lesson Review	Critical-Thinking Questions
Lesson 1 The Cell Cycle and Mitosis	248–251	✔	✔	✔
Lesson 2 What Is Cancer?	252–255	✔	✔	✔
Lesson 3 Meiosis: The Life Cycle of Sex Cells	256–259	✔	✔	✔
Lesson 4 The Human Reproductive System	260–264	✔	✔	✔
Lesson 5 Human Development	265–271	✔	✔	✔

Chapter Activities

Teacher's Resource Library
Community Connection 9:
 Family Planning
Graphic Organizer 9:
 Mitosis and Meiosis

Teacher's Edition
Opener Activity

Assessment Options

Student Text
Chapter 9 Review

Teacher's Resource Library
Chapter 9 Mastery Tests A and B

Teacher's Edition
Chapter 9 Alternative Assessment

Student Text Features								Teaching Strategies						Learning Styles					Teacher's Resource Library			
Achievements in Science	Science at Work	Biology in Your Life	Investigation/Discovery	Biology in the World	Express Lab	Link to	Research and Write	Technology and Society	ELL/ESL Strategy	Background Information	Science Journal	Applications (Home, Career, Community, Global, Environment)	Online Connection	Teacher Alert	Auditory/Verbal	Body/Kinesthetic	Interpersonal/Group Learning	Logical/Mathematical	Visual/Spatial	Workbook Activities	Alternative Workbook Activities	Lab Manual	Self-Study Guide
					250	✔			250	248				250	249				249	46	46	41–42	✔
			254			✔		253	252		253									47	47	43	✔
						✔			258	256				257				258	258	48	48	44	✔
	261					✔			262	260	263			261, 263		262				49	49		✔
268		267	269	271			275		267	265	266	266, 267	271	267				271		50–51	50–51	45	✔

Pronunciation Key

a	hat	e	let	ī	ice	ô	order	u̇	put	sh	she
ā	age	ē	equal	o	hot	oi	oil	ü	rule	th	thin
ä	far	ėr	term	ō	open	ou	out	ch	child	ᴛʜ	then
â	care	i	it	ȯ	saw	u	cup	ng	long	zh	measure

ə { a in about, e in taken, i in pencil, o in lemon, u in circus }

Alternative Workbook Activities

The Teacher's Resource Library (TRL) contains a set of lower-level worksheets called Alternative Workbook Activities. These worksheets cover the same content as the regular Workbook Activities but are written at a second-grade reading level.

Skill Track Online

Use Skill Track Online for *Biology: Cycles of Life* to monitor student progress and meet the demands of adequate yearly progress (AYP). Make informed instructional decisions with individual student and class reports of online lesson and chapter assessments. With immediate and ongoing feedback, students will also see what they have learned and where they need more reinforcement and practice.

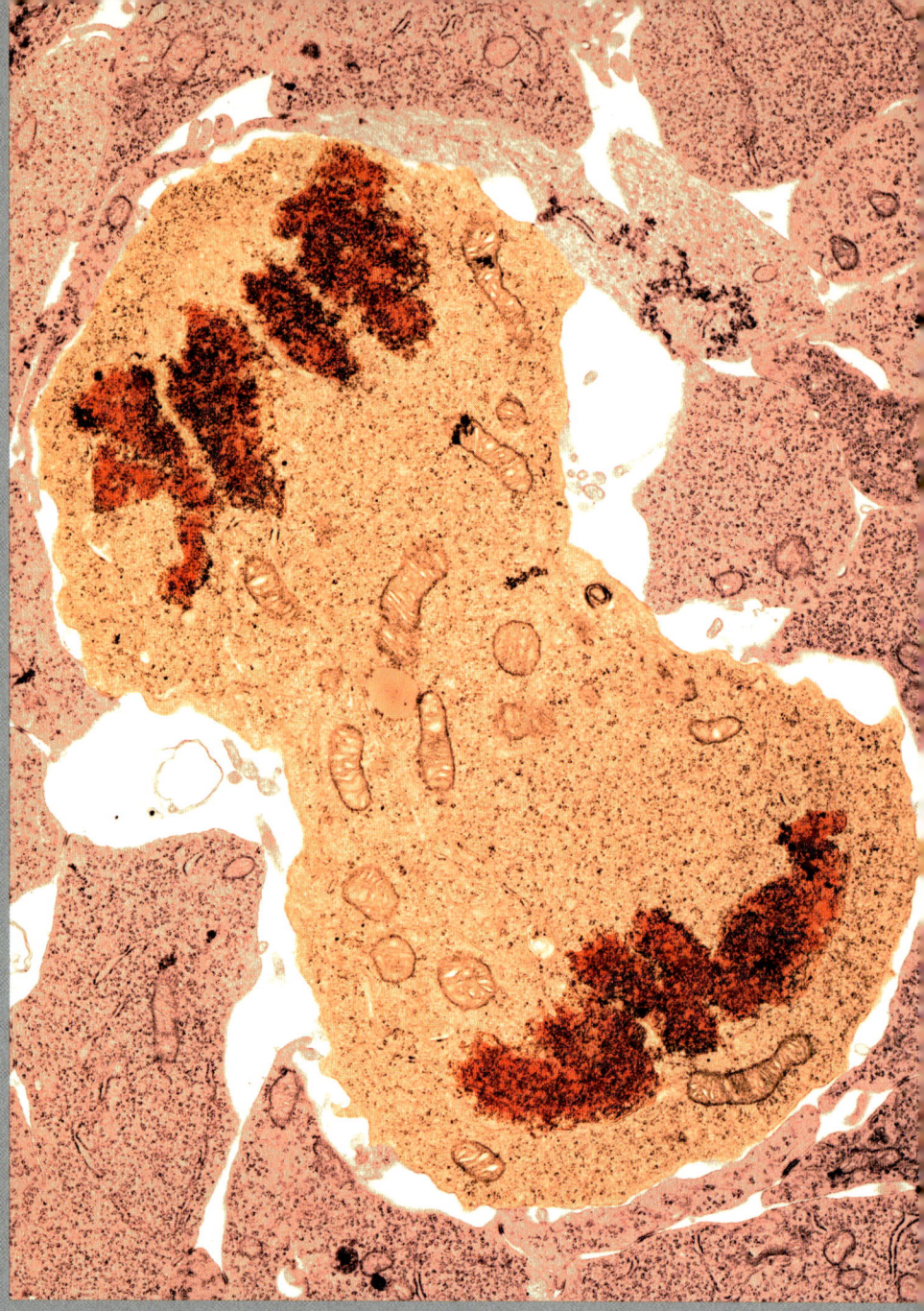

Chapter at a Glance

Chapter 9: The Life Cycles of Cells and Reproduction
pages 246–275

Lessons

1. The Cell Cycle and Mitosis
   pages 248–251
2. What Is Cancer?
   pages 252–255

   Investigation 9 pages 254–255
3. Meiosis: The Life Cycle of Sex Cells pages 256–259
4. The Human Reproductive System pages 260–264
5. Human Development
   pages 265–271

   Discovery Investigation 9
   pages 269–270

   Biology in the World page 271

Chapter 9 Summary page 272

Chapter 9 Review pages 273–275

Audio CD 🎧

Skill Track Online for Biology: Cycles of Life

Teacher's Resource Library (TRL)

   Workbook Activities 46–51

   Alternative Workbook Activities 46–51

   Lab Manual 41–45

   Community Connection 9

   Graphic Organizer 9

   Resource File 17–21

   Chapter 9 Self-Study Guide

   Chapter 9 Mastery Tests A and B

(Answer Keys for the Teacher's Resource Library begin on page 675 of the Teacher's Edition. The Materials List for the Lab Manual activities begins on page 720.)

Opener Activity

Make a seven-column chart on the board, using the following headings: *Mitosis, Meiosis, Fertilization, Development During Pregnancy, Development During Infancy, Development During Childhood,* and *Development During the Teen Years.* Test students' prior knowledge by asking them to share what they know about any of these column headings. Fill in the table with the facts students contribute.

Community Connection 9

246 Chapter 9

Chapter 9

The Life Cycles of Cells and Reproduction

The photograph shows one cell about to become two cells. The cell is undergoing cell division, a form of reproduction. Notice the other cells surrounding the dividing cell. The dividing cell is part of a much larger organism. As you know, cells are the basic units of life. They can do all the things that make something alive, including reproduction. In Chapter 9, you will find out how cells reproduce. You will also learn how cellular reproduction makes it possible for living things to inherit traits.

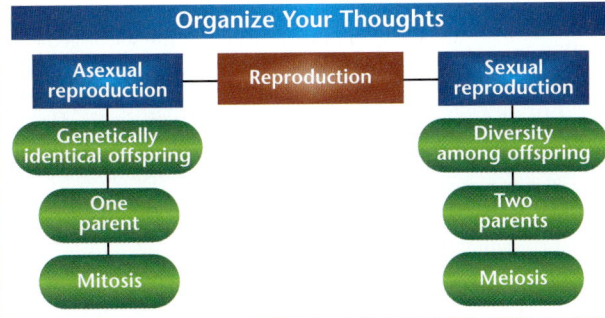

Goals for Learning

- ◆ To explain the phases of a cell's life cycle
- ◆ To describe the process of mitosis
- ◆ To explain how cancer is the breakdown of mitosis
- ◆ To describe the process of meiosis
- ◆ To describe the formation and function of gametes
- ◆ To explain the process of human reproduction

247

Introducing the Chapter

Have students recall the differences between asexual reproduction and sexual reproduction. Both are important to the growth and development of a multicellular organism. Cells divide asexually in order for an organism to grow and to replace or repair damaged cells. Sexual reproduction continues the species by producing offspring that have genetic material from both parents.

Have students study the photograph of the cell dividing. Have them list reasons why cells need to reproduce.

After students read the Goals for Learning, explain that although each of these processes takes place at the cellular level, each also affects the body as a whole. As students read the chapter, have them ask and answer the question "How does this affect the body as a whole?" for each of the processes listed in the Goals for Learning.

Notes and Math Tips

Ask volunteers to read the notes and math tips that appear in the margins throughout the chapter. Then discuss them with the class.

TEACHER'S RESOURCE

The AGS Publishing Teaching Strategies in Science Transparencies may be used with this chapter. The transparencies add an interactive dimension to expand and enhance the *Biology: Cycles of Life* program content.

CAREER INTEREST INVENTORY

The AGS Publishing Harrington-O'Shea Career Decision-Making System-Revised (CDM) may be used with this chapter. Students can use the CDM to explore their interests and identify careers. The CDM defines career areas that are indicated by students' responses on the inventory.

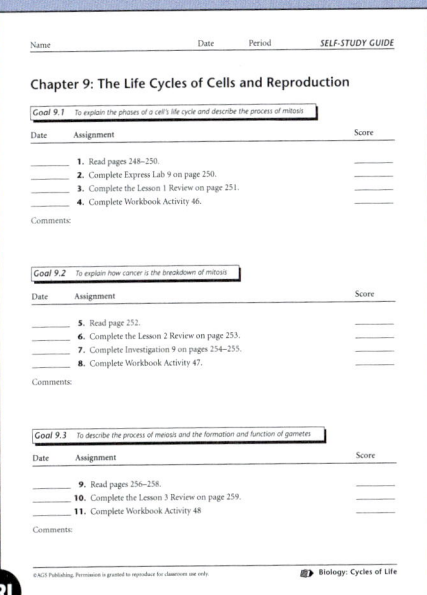

Chapter 9 Self-Study Guide

Lesson at a Glance

Chapter 9 Lesson 1

Overview In this lesson, students learn about the cell cycle and the stages of mitosis.

Objectives

- To identify the phases of the cell cycle
- To discuss the activities of each phase of mitosis
- To compare the genetic makeup of cells before and after mitosis
- To compare reproduction in eukaryotic and prokaryotic cells

Student Pages 248–251

Teacher's Resource Library

Workbook Activity 46
Alternative Workbook Activity 46
Lab Manual 41–42
Resource File 17

Vocabulary

cell cycle	metaphase plate
centromere	mitosis
cleavage furrow	sister chromatid
cytokinesis	spindle
interphase	

Read the definition for each vocabulary term to the class. After each term, have students supply an expanded definition of the term. For example, an expanded definition for the term *mitosis* could include naming the four stages of mitosis and a brief description of what occurs during each stage.

Background Information

The length of the cell cycle varies depending on the type of cell. Typically, interphase is the longest phase, accounting for up to 90 percent of the cell cycle. The mitotic division of a cell occurs quickly in comparison to the time the cell spends in interphase. A typical mammal cell completes its cell cycle in about 24 hours. The G_1 stage may last 8–10 hours. The S phase lasts about 6–8 hours. The G_2 phase lasts about 4–6 hours. Mitosis occurs in less than 1 hour.

Lesson 1 — The Cell Cycle and Mitosis

Objectives

After reading this lesson, you should be able to
- identify the phases of the cell cycle
- discuss the activities of each phase of mitosis
- compare the genetic makeup of cells before and after mitosis
- compare reproduction in eukaryotic and prokaryotic cells

Cells are the basic unit of life. As a cell lives, it goes through common stages of activity. These stages combine into the **cell cycle**, or life cycle, of a cell. The cell cycle begins when a new cell is created. It ends when it divides to make new cells. When a cell divides, it performs reproduction. Reproduction is the process of living things making more living things. Both the nucleus and cytoplasm divide in eukaryotic cell division.

Interphase

When a eukaryotic cell is created, it begins its life in **interphase**. Interphase is the longest phase of the life cycle of a cell. Interphase is divided into three stages based on how the cell grows. The first stage is called G_1. G stands for "growth." During the G_1 stage, a cell performs its typical activities, such as cellular respiration. The cell also grows to a mature size.

The second stage of interphase is the S stage. S stands for *synthesis*. A cell in S stage makes a copy of its entire DNA. The copies of each chromosome stay together as **sister chromatids**. Sister chromatids are joined tightly at the **centromere**.

The third stage of interphase is the G_2 stage. In this stage, a cell makes copies of its organelles and doubles in size. These activities prepare the cell for the next part of the cell cycle stage, **mitosis**, or the M phase. The M stands for *mitosis*, which is the process of cellular reproduction. During mitosis, a cell undergoes division to make two identical daughter cells.

Mitosis

Mitosis is the process of creating two identical nuclei. Mitosis has four phases. Figure 9.1.1 shows the four phases of mitosis. Prophase is the first phase. In prophase, a cell's nuclear envelope breaks down. The cell forms a network of fibers called the **spindle**. Spindle fibers move chromosomes around during reproduction. Some spindle fibers attach to each set of sister chromatids near their centromere.

> **Cell cycle**
> *The life cycle of a cell from its beginning until it divides*
>
> **Interphase**
> *The phase of a cell cycle in which a cell grows to mature size and carries out typical activities*

248 Chapter 9 The Life Cycles of Cells and Reproduction

Interphase may last for hours, days, or years, depending on the type of cell. A human liver cell, for example, takes over a year to complete its cell cycle.

1 Warm-Up Activity

Have students recall the role of a chromatin in the cell. Chromatin contains DNA and proteins that control the activation of genes. When a cell replicates its DNA before mitosis occurs, the chromatin condenses to form pairs of sister chromatids. Have students perform the Express Lab on page 250.

Express Lab Answers

1. The sister chromatid was created by making an exact copy of the chromosome, using the same colored beads in the same sequence. **2.** The beads represent the genes on the chromosome. The twist tie represents a centromere. **3.** The sister chromatid is created in the S phase of mitosis.

Sister chromatid
One of a pair of identical chromosomes created before a cell divides

Centromere
The area where two sister chromatids are tightly joined together

Mitosis
The process of dividing a cell's nucleus to make two identical nuclei

Spindle
A network of fibers that move chromosomes during mitosis

Metaphase plate
The middle of a cell where chromosomes line up in metaphase

Metaphase is the second phase of mitosis. In metaphase, the spindle fibers line up the sister chromatids in the center of the cell. This area is called the **metaphase plate.**

The third phase in mitosis is anaphase. In anaphase, the sister chromatids separate at their centromeres. They become individual chromosomes. The spindle fibers move the separated chromosomes to opposite sides of the cell.

Telophase is the fourth phase. In telophase, two nuclear envelopes form around each set of chromosomes. The spindle fibers break down. **Cytokinesis** also occurs along with telophase. Cytokinesis is the process of dividing the cytoplasm of a cell into two daughter cells. As the two nuclei form, a ring of fibers forms around the outside of the cell. The fibers begin pinching in the cell membrane to form a **cleavage furrow.** The fibers shorten until they pinch the cell in two.

Mitosis results in two identical daughter cells from one parent cell. DNA in the daughter cells is an exact copy of the parent DNA.

Mitosis

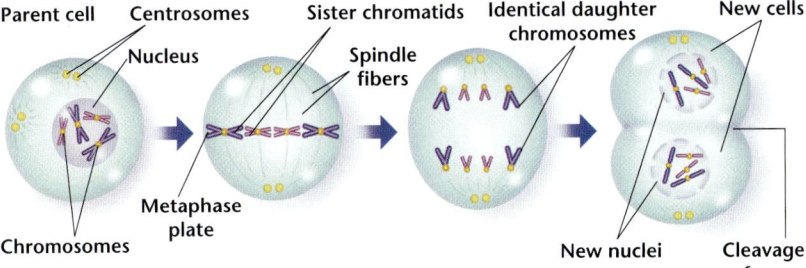

Prophase: The chromosomes in DNA have been copied. Chromosomes are paired.

Metaphase: The nucleus disappears. Paired chromosomes line up in the center of the cell.

Anaphase: Pairs of chromosomes separate. They move to opposite sides of the cell.

Telophase: Two nuclei form. The cell divides into two identical daughter cells.

Figure 9.1.1 Mitosis occurs in four phases.

2 Teaching the Lesson

Have students make an outline of the material presented in the lesson. On a sheet of paper have them copy the following:

I. Interphase
   A.
      1.
   B.
      1.
   C.
      1.

II. Mitosis
   A.
      1.
   B.
      1.
   C.
      1.
   D.
      1.

For each of the stages of interphase and mitosis, have students fill in one related detail.

Using light microscopes, set up sample slides that show the different stages of the cell cycle of an animal cell. Have another microscope in which students can examine slides of mitosis and find different stages on their own.

3 Reinforce and Extend

LEARNING STYLES

Visual/Spatial
Provide students with various materials such as yarn, pipe cleaners, thread, buttons, beads, glue, scissors, colored markers, and poster board. Using the materials, have students make a poster that shows the stages of mitosis. Students can use the thread to represent spindle fibers, the buttons to represent centromeres, and the yarn or pipe cleaners to make chromosomes. Display the completed posters around the classroom.

LEARNING STYLES

Auditory/Verbal
Have students explain the stages of mitosis, using Figure 9.1.1 as a guide.

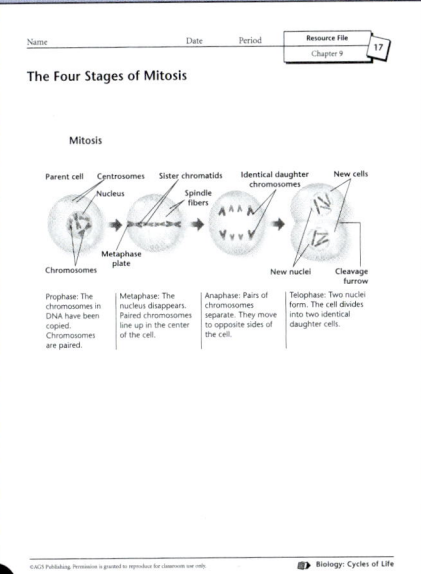

Resource File 17

TEACHER ALERT

Another aspect of the cell cycle is the death of a cell. Apoptosis is the genetically programmed death of a cell. Apoptosis results when genes begin to produce enzymes that damage a cell's nucleus and cytoskeleton. Cellular DNA is damaged, and the cell begins to shrink. The dying cell is eventually ingested by phagocytes. Phagocytes are cells that eat infected cells and pathogens.

ELL/ESL STRATEGY

Language Objective: *To summarize lesson content*

Have students learning English work with a partner to answer the Lesson 1 Review questions. Have partners take turns reading the questions aloud.

Link to

Chemistry. Have students read the Link to Chemistry feature. Explain the idea that control of the cell cycle stages is often compared to the control of a washing machine cycle. Each control system proceeds according to an internal clock. Both control systems can be influenced by external cues as well as internal cues. Cyclin is an example of an internal cue in the control system of a cell cycle.

PRONUNCIATION GUIDE

Use the pronunciation shown here to help students pronounce a difficult word in this lesson. Refer to the pronunciation key on the Chapter Planning Guide for the sounds of the symbols.

kinase (kī′nās)

Cytokinesis
The process of dividing the cytoplasm of a cell in two

Cleavage furrow
A structure that is formed when fibers pinch in the membrane of a dividing cell

Link to ▶▶▶
Chemistry

The cell cycle depends on enzymes called kinases. Kinases start and stop mitosis in cells by attaching to a cyclin. Cyclin is a protein that regulates the cell cycle. When many kinase enzymes are in a cell, the cell usually divides. When the amount of kinase is low, the cell does not go through mitosis.

Some cells, such as muscle and nerve cells, do not go through the entire cell cycle. These cells are in G_0 stage, a nondividing stage. However, most cells reproduce through mitosis. This process is important for organisms. Through reproduction, organisms replace used or damaged cells. For example, skin cells heal a cut by reproducing more cells. Because cells reproduce, organisms can grow from small children to larger adults. Mitosis is a constant cycle that allows life to continue.

Prokaryotes and Binary Fission

Only eukaryotic cells go through mitosis, which is the division of the nucleus. Prokaryotic cells do not have a nucleus. They reproduce by binary fission. In binary fission, a prokaryotic cell copies its DNA and doubles in size. The two copies separate and the plasma membrane pinches. Then the membrane separates. Two identical prokaryotic cells result.

Express Lab 9

Materials
- 20 different colored beads
- 2 pieces of string or twine
- twist tie

Procedure
1. String together 10 beads of various colors on a piece of string or twine. To keep the beads in place, knot the ends. This is a model of a chromosome.
2. Exchange your chromosome model with another classmate. Use 10 more beads and string to create a sister chromatid for the chromosome you received.
3. Tie the sister chromatids together near the center with a twist tie.

Analysis
1. How did you create the sister chromatid?
2. What do the different colored beads represent? What does the twist tie represent?
3. In which stage of interphase are sister chromatids created?

250 Chapter 9 The Life Cycles of Cells and Reproduction

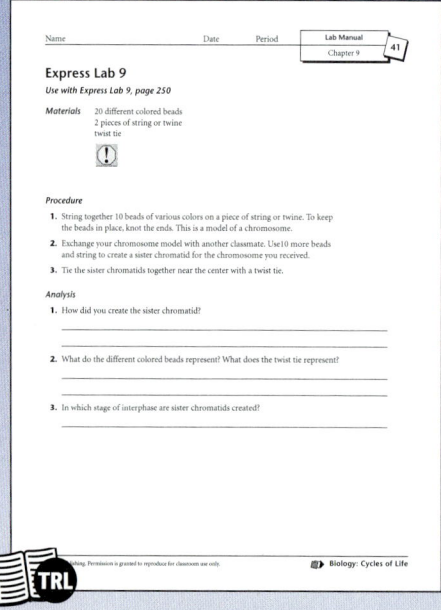

Lab Manual 41

Lesson 1 REVIEW

On a sheet of paper, write the letter of the answer that completes each sentence correctly.

1. A cell reproduces by dividing to create _____.
   - **A** two daughter cells
   - **C** two parent cells
   - **B** four daughter cells
   - **D** four parent cells

2. The size of the cell doubles in the _____.
   - **A** G_1 stage
   - **B** G_2 stage
   - **C** S stage
   - **D** M phase

3. The process of creating two identical cells is _____.
   - **A** centromere
   - **C** metaphase
   - **B** interphase
   - **D** mitosis

On a sheet of paper, write the word or words that complete each statement correctly.

4. A chromosome attached by a centromere to another identical chromosome is known as a(n) _____.

5. During _____, the cell creates a network of spindle fibers.

6. Cells that do not reproduce stay in _____ phase.

Critical Thinking

On a sheet of paper, write the answers to the following questions. Use complete sentences.

7. Why do eukaryotic cells reproduce?

8. Bacterial cells are prokaryotic cells. They divide and split much like human cells do. Why is this not mitosis?

9. What happens during cytokinesis?

10. Give an example of a type of cell that reproduces often and a type of cell that rarely reproduces.

The Life Cycles of Cells and Reproduction Chapter 9   251

Lesson 1 Review Answers

1. A **2.** B **3.** D **4.** sister **5.** prophase **6.** G_0 **7.** Eukaryotic cells reproduce to replace used or damaged cells and to grow. **8.** Bacterial cells do not have a nucleus. A nucleus is required for mitosis. **9.** Cytokinesis occurs along with telophase. Cytokinesis is the process of dividing the cytoplasm of a cell into two. As the two new nuclei form, a ring of fiber forms around the outside of the cell. This fiber begins pinching in the cell membrane to form a cleavage furrow. The fiber shortens until it pinches the cell in two. **10.** Skin cells must reproduce often to heal cuts or other damage. Muscle and nerve cells may never reproduce.

Portfolio Assessment

Sample items include:
- Express Lab answers
- Poster from Learning Styles Visual/Spatial
- Lesson 1 Review answers

LAB ACTIVITIES

Chapter 9 has Investigation and Discovery Investigation lab activities. Two additional lab activities for Chapter 9 appear in the Biology: Cycles of Life Lab Manual and on the Teacher's Resource Library CD-ROM.

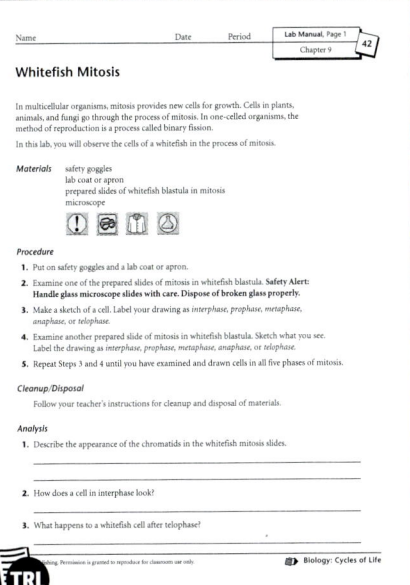

Lab Manual 42, pages 1–2

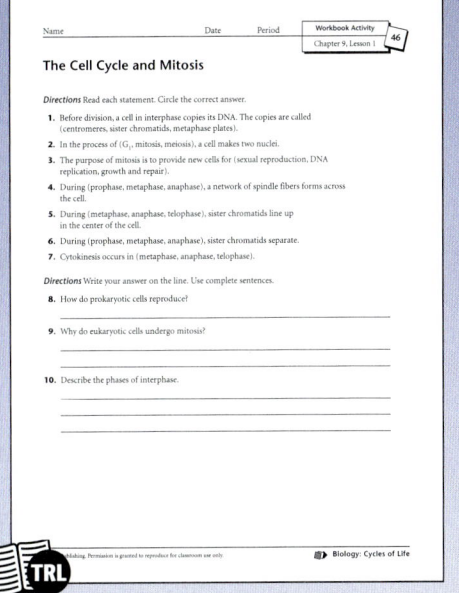

Workbook Activity 46

Lesson at a Glance

Chapter 9 Lesson 2

Overview In this lesson, students learn what happens when a cell divides uncontrollably.

Objectives

- To define *cancer*
- To define *benign tumors* and *malignant tumors*
- To discuss how cancer spreads
- To identify certain methods used to treat cancer

Student Pages 252–255

Teacher's Resource Library

Workbook Activity 47
Alternative Workbook Activity 47
Lab Manual 43

Vocabulary

benign tumor   metastasis
cancer   tumor
malignant tumor

Have students write a paragraph that uses all of the vocabulary terms in this lesson.

Background Information

The branch of medicine that involves the study of tumors is called oncology. Cancer names are based on the type of tissue in which the cancer develops. For example, melanoma begins in melanocytes, the cells in the skin that produce the pigment melanin. Lymphoma begins in lymphatic tissues, such as the lymph nodes.

 Warm-Up Activity

Provide students with photographs that show the ABCDs of monitoring spots on the skin. People should check for **A**symmetry (one half of a spot does not match the other); irregular **B**orders (the border is ragged or blurred); changes in **C**olor, especially when the pigmentation is not the same throughout the spot; and changes in the **D**iameter of a spot. Dermatologists recommend that people regularly check moles and other skin spots, looking for changes.

Lesson 2 What Is Cancer?

Objectives

After reading this lesson, you should be able to
- define cancer
- define benign tumors and malignant tumors
- discuss how cancer spreads
- identify certain methods used to treat cancer

Cancer is a physical condition in which a cell grows without control and divides too much. Human bodies have signal molecules that control cell division. One cause of cancer is when these control systems break. They produce more signal molecules than needed. This causes a cell to divide too much. A cancer cell divides through mitosis. It creates a ball of cells called a **tumor**.

A **benign tumor** grows in only one area of the body. Tumors can spread to other body areas. Cells from the original tumor break away and enter the blood. Tumor cells travel through the body and attach to other areas. Once attached, the cells grow and divide into a new tumor. **Metastasis** is the process of cancerous cells spreading to other body areas. A tumor that has spread is a **malignant tumor.**

Doctors use different methods to rid the body of tumors. If a tumor is found early, doctors can often remove it with surgery. Doctors may treat malignant tumors with radiation therapy. This process uses beams of radiation aimed at the tumor. Radiation kills cells in the tumor by breaking them apart. Doctors may also use chemotherapy to treat cancer. Chemotherapy uses drugs that poison the tumor cells. Because radiation and chemotherapy can hurt normal cells, doctors try to find and remove tumors before they spread.

Cancer
A condition in which a cell grows without control and divides too much

Tumor
A ball of cells made from the extra divisions of a cancer cell

Benign tumor
A tumor that is only in the area where it began

Metastasis
The process of cancer cells spreading from one body area to another

Malignant tumor
A tumor that has spread from its original site to other body areas

Link to ▶▶▶
Health

Every year, more than one million new cases of skin cancer are diagnosed in the United States. Skin cancer causes 9,800 deaths every year. Most skin cancer is caused by too much exposure to the sun. To reduce your risk of skin cancer, use sunscreens, sunglasses, and hats that protect against ultraviolet (UV) rays.

---

2 Teaching the Lesson

Have students practice their note-taking skills as they read this lesson. Instruct them to summarize the material presented in the lesson as they read.

Link to

Health. Have a volunteer read the Link to Health feature. Explain to students that there are three types of skin cancer. The most common type, basal cell carcinoma, results from the abnormal growth of cells in the lowest layer of the epidermis. Squamous cell carcinoma occurs when cells in the middle layer of the epidermis undergo abnormal growth. Melanoma, the most deadly form of skin cancer, occurs when the cells that make the pigment melanin are affected. Ask students: What precautions can you take to reduce the risk of developing skin cancer later in life?

Lesson 2 REVIEW

On a sheet of paper, write the word that completes each statement correctly.

1. A(n) _____ is a tumor that has spread through metastasis.
2. A condition in which a cell grows without control and divides too much is _____.
3. A ball of cells made from the extra divisions of a cancer cell is a(n) _____.

Critical Thinking

On a sheet of paper, write the answers to the following questions. Use complete sentences.

4. How do the extra cells created by cancer harm the body?
5. How could cancer spread from the lungs to the liver?

Technology and Society

The DNA microarray, or gene chip, is a cancer-fighting tool. To create microarrays, scientists put hundreds of samples of DNA on a slide. They apply a fluorescent dye to find gene segments that have made proteins recently. Next, they compare gene segments from cancer patients with the gene segments of healthy people. The DNA microarray helps scientists identify the gene segments that are causing the cancer.

The Life Cycles of Cells and Reproduction Chapter 9 253

Workbook Activity 47

Global Connection

Explain to students that cancer clusters sometimes occur in areas around the world. A cancer cluster occurs when a statistically significant number of people in a given area, during a given time period, have the same or related types of cancers. Have students research an area of the world in which a cancer cluster has occurred. Have students answer these questions: What type of cancer did people develop? Was a cause determined? Then have students share their results with the class.

---

3 Reinforce and Extend

At Home

A person may have an increased risk of developing certain diseases, including certain types of cancer, if other family members have had the disease. Doctors are encouraging patients to know their family health history in order to increase awareness about early warning signs and early detection of some cancers. Have students interview family members to find out more about their family health history.

Lesson 2 Review Answers

1. malignant tumor 2. cancer 3. tumor 4. Extra cells take nutrients and resources from the other cells that need them. This causes an imbalance that makes the body sick. 5. Cancer cells from a tumor in the lungs can enter the blood stream and travel to the liver. If the cells attach to the liver, they can begin to grow and create a new tumor there.

Portfolio Assessment

Sample items include:
- Notes from Teaching the Lesson
- Lesson 2 Review answers

Technology and Society

Have students read the Technology and Society feature. Scientists have been able to isolate genes that are associated with certain types of cancers, including breast cancer and kidney cancer. These genes are abnormal or have been altered through mutation. Genes such as p53, BRCA1 (**BR**east **CA**ncer gene 1), and BRCA2 have all been found to be altered in patients with breast cancer.

The Life Cycles of Cells and Reproduction 253

Investigation 9

Encourage students to read the investigation steps. Discuss questions they may have before beginning the investigation.

Objectives

- To observe cells in various stages of the cell cycle
- To draw and label specific parts of the cell in various stages
- To infer knowledge of the cell cycle through observation

Skills

Observing, using science lab equipment, drawing, inferring, analyzing data, drawing conclusions

Background

Onion roots offer a good way to observe cells in various stages of the cell cycle. Because the tips of the roots are constantly growing, cells in various stages should be easily identifiable. Students should be able to identify cells in the different stages of the cycle and make drawings of the important characteristics that define each stage.

Time Frame

One class period

Procedure

- Have students work together in small groups to complete the activity.
- Prepared slides of onion roots in mitosis can be obtained from a supplier of education materials. Some are listed on page 723.

INVESTIGATION 9

Materials
- safety goggles
- lab coat or apron
- prepared slide of onion root
- microscope

Observing Cell Cycle Phases

Cells grow during interphase. They also make copies of their DNA and organelles during this phase. Cells reproduce to make new cells during mitosis and cytokinesis. As cells enter mitosis, they separate the DNA copies. During cytokinesis, the cells grow larger and divide in two. Making new cells allows an organism to grow larger or replace damaged cells. In this investigation, you will examine the cells of an onion root. You will observe cells in different phases of the cell cycles.

Procedure

1. Put on safety goggles and a lab coat or apron.
2. Examine the prepared slide of an onion root. **Safety Alert: Handle glass microscope slides with care. Dispose of broken glass properly.**
3. Find a cell in interphase. On a sheet of paper, draw what you observe. Label the parts of the cell that you recognize.
4. Find examples of cells in mitosis. Draw examples of a cell in prophase, metaphase, anaphase, telophase, and cytokinesis. Label the cell parts you recognize.

SAFETY ALERT

- Be sure that students have read and understood all safety rules for working in the lab. Discuss the Safety Alerts with students.
- Make sure that students understand the correct procedures for handling and using the microscope.
- Remind students to handle glass microscope slides with care and to dispose of broken glass properly.

Cleanup/Disposal
When you are finished, return the prepared slide to your teacher.

Analysis
1. What cell parts were you able to identify easily?
2. What cell parts were difficult or impossible to identify?

Conclusions
1. How did you recognize a cell in interphase?
2. What were the main characteristics of the cells in mitosis?
3. How did you identify a cell undergoing cytokinesis?

Explore Further
In which phase were most of the cells you observed? What can you infer about the life of a cell from this observation?

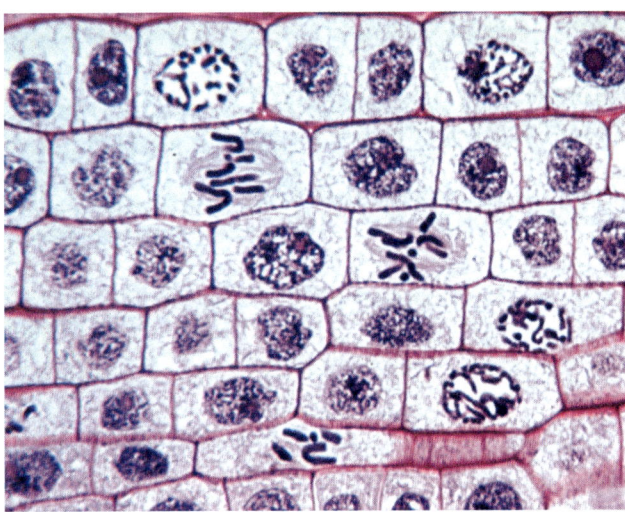

Cleanup/Disposal
Instruct students in proper cleanup and disposal of materials.

Analysis Answers
1. Students should be able to identify the nucleus (when present) and chromosomes during mitosis. They should notice that the nucleus has broken down during mitosis.
2. Students will likely not be able to identify spindle fibers. In addition, they may not be able to identify DNA during interphase or cytokinesis.

Conclusions Answers
1. Students should recognize that the nucleus is intact in interphase.
2. Students should identify and recognize the state and position of chromosomes in the cell during the different phases and the activity that is occurring.
3. Students may be able to witness the cell wall being built to separate two new cells as part of cytokinesis.

Explore Further Answers
Students can count and identify that most cells are in interphase. They should infer that a cell spends most of its life cycle in interphase. They may also notice more cells in mitosis around the tip of the root than in the middle because of the active growth of the root.

Assessment
You might include the following items from this investigation in student portfolios:
- Student drawings of different stages of mitosis
- Answers to Analysis and Conclusions questions
- Answers to Explore Further questions

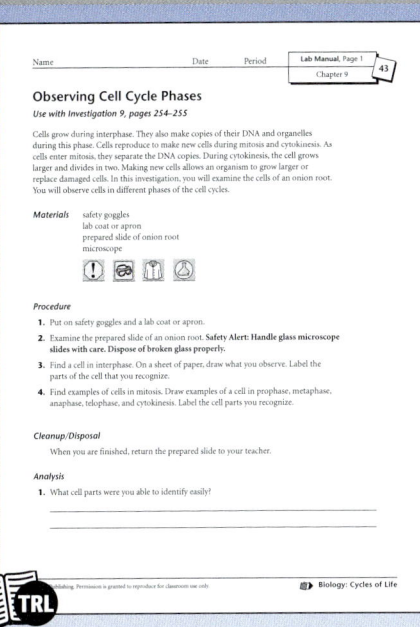

Lab Manual 43, pages 1–2

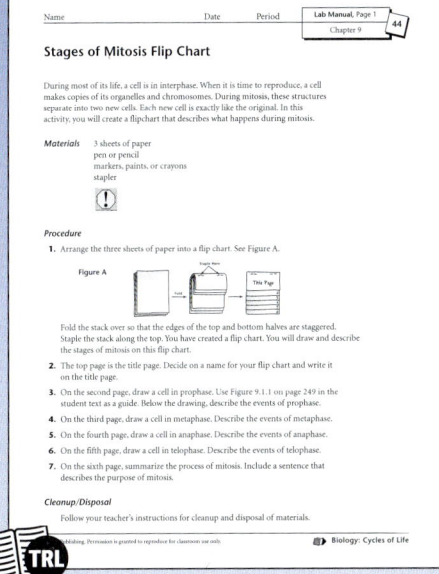

Lab Manual 44, pages 1–2

Lesson at a Glance

Chapter 9 Lesson 3

Overview In this lesson, students learn the steps involved in meiosis.

Objectives

- To identify male and female gametes
- To compare chromosome numbers between somatic cells and gametes
- To describe the stages of meiosis
- To compare meiosis and mitosis

Student Pages 256–259

Teacher's Resource Library

   Workbook Activity 48

   Alternative Workbook Activity 48

   Lab Manual 44

   Resource File 18

Vocabulary

crossing over	meiosis
diploid	somatic cell
egg	sperm
fertilization	tetrad
gamete	zygote
haploid	
homologous chromosome	

Read the vocabulary terms to the class. For each term, have a volunteer supply the definition.

Background Information

Of the 23 pairs of homologous chromosomes in human cells, 22 pairs are called autosomes. The remaining pair of chromosomes are the sex chromosomes, which determine a person's gender. In females, the homologous pair of sex chromosomes contains two X chromosomes. In males, the homologous pair contains an X chromosome and a Y chromosome.

Lesson 3: Meiosis: The Life Cycle of Sex Cells

Objectives

After reading this lesson, you should be able to

- identify male and female gametes
- compare chromosome numbers between somatic cells and gametes
- describe the stages of meiosis
- compare meiosis and mitosis

Gamete
A sex cell; sperm or an egg

Egg
The female gamete

Sperm
The male gamete

Somatic cell
A cell that is not a sex cell

Diploid
Having two copies of each kind of chromosome

Homologous chromosome
One of a matching pair of chromosomes that comes from each parent

Gametes, or sex cells, do not perform mitosis. Gametes are cells involved in sexual reproduction. The female gamete is called an **egg.** The male gamete is called **sperm.** Most cells in an organism are **somatic cells,** not sex cells. A human somatic cell has 46 chromosomes in its nucleus. Because there are 23 human chromosomes, each somatic cell is a **diploid** cell. A diploid cell has two copies of each chromosome, called **homologous chromosomes.** One copy of each chromosome comes from the father. The other copy comes from the mother.

Gametes and Meiosis

Gametes are **haploid** cells. They have one set of chromosomes. Both sperm and eggs cells have 23 chromosomes inside their nuclei. Humans create more humans by joining one egg cell with one sperm cell. **Fertilization** is the process of combining an egg cell and a sperm cell. After fertilization, a new diploid cell is formed, called a **zygote.** A zygote goes through many rounds of mitosis, eventually creating a new organism.

Gametes have a special type of reproduction called **meiosis.** Meiosis is similar to mitosis. However, there are some key differences in the formation of haploid cells. In contrast to mitosis, meiosis involves two divisions, meiosis I and meiosis II. In meiosis I, homologous chromosomes are separated from each other. In meiosis II, sister chromosomes are separated. The resulting cells are haploid.

Meiosis I

Figure 9.3.1 shows the four stages of meiosis I. Meiosis I begins with prophase I. In this phase, the sister chromatids for each chromosome shrink. Spindle fibers appear and attach to the centromeres. A special feature of prophase I is synapsis. In synapsis, homologous chromosomes pair together and form a **tetrad.** One copy of each chromosome pairs up with the other copy. Each copy has the same DNA in the same location.

256   Chapter 9   The Life Cycles of Cells and Reproduction

Haploid
Having one copy of each kind of chromosome

Fertilization
The joining of male and female gametes to create a new organism

Zygote
A fertilized cell

Meiosis
A process that results in sex cells

Tetrad
A pair of homologous chromosomes joined together

Crossing over
The process of homologous chromosomes in a tetrad trading pieces of similar DNA

While the chromosomes are paired, they trade DNA pieces with each other. This trade is called **crossing over.** Crossing over makes every organism unique. This process creates different chromosomes that are passed on to offspring.

In metaphase I, the tetrads line up randomly. They line up in the middle of the cell along the metaphase plate. In anaphase I, homologous chromosomes separate. They move toward opposite ends of the cell. Each end now has a haploid daughter nucleus. The nucleus has only one set of chromosomes. Each chromosome is made up of two sister chromatids. In telophase I and cytokinesis, the nuclei and cytoplasm divide in half. Two haploid daughter cells form. Each haploid cell contains two copies of the same set of chromosomes.

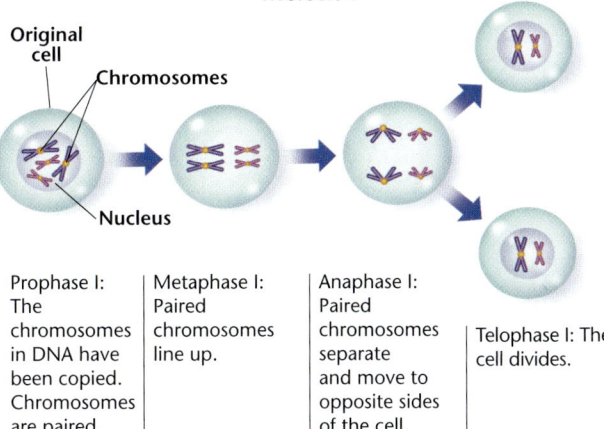

Figure 9.3.1 *Meiosis I occurs in four phases.*

Meiosis II

Meiosis II is similar to meiosis I. However, DNA is not copied in meiosis II. Meiosis II starts with prophase II. In this stage, the nuclei and the sister chromatids stay tightly packed. Spindle fibers attach to each pair of sister chromatids. The spindle fibers move the sister chromatids to the center of the cells.

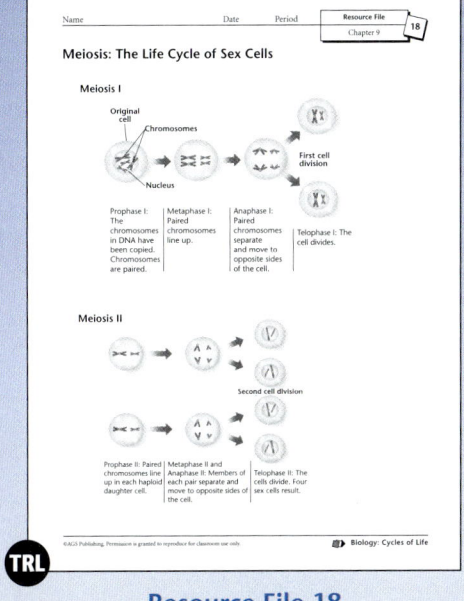

Resource File 18

1 Warm-Up Activity

Present students with two labeled diagrams: one that shows the stages of mitosis and one that shows the stages of both meiosis I and meiosis II. Have students spend a few minutes studying the diagrams. Ask students to explain the similarities and differences between the stages of mitosis and meiosis. (*The stages of mitosis and meiosis have the same names and essentially the same actions take place in each stage. The difference between mitosis and meiosis is that nuclear division occurs twice during meiosis. The end product of mitosis is two cells identical to the parent cell. The end product of meiosis is four cells, each with half the amount of chromosomes as the parent cell.*)

2 Teaching the Lesson

Have students make a chart to help organize information about the stages of meiosis I and meiosis II. Students should include a brief description of what occurs during each stage. Using human cells as an example, students should include details about the number of chromosomes present during the different stages and the number of cells produced at the end of meiosis I and meiosis II.

3 Reinforce and Extend

TEACHER ALERT

Disorders can occur as a result of a person missing chromosomes or having too many chromosomes. Down syndrome occurs when the homologous chromosome 21 does not properly separate during meiosis I. As a result, a person is born with an extra chromosome 21. This causes mental retardation and affects physical development. Organs such as the heart may not develop normally. Klinefelter's syndrome occurs when males are born with an extra X chromosome. This results in sterility and can affect mental functioning.

LEARNING STYLES

Logical/Mathematical

Scientists use the letter n to represent the number of haploid chromosomes an organism has. The denotation $2n$ represents the number of chromosomes in a diploid cell. Have students determine the haploid or diploid number of chromosomes for the following organisms, given the information below:

Chimpanzee: $2n = 48$, $n = ?$
Horse: $n = 32$, $2n = ?$
Frog: $2n = 26$, $n = ?$
Fruit fly: $n = 4$, $2n = ?$
(24, 64, 13, 8)

ELL/ESL Strategy

Language Objective: *To compare meiosis and mitosis*

Have students write a paragraph describing the similarities and differences between meiosis and mitosis.

Science Myth

Have students read the Science Myth feature. During interphase, cells replicate DNA and cell organelles to get ready for cell division. Make the analogy to preparing to bake a cake. All of the ingredients needed to make the cake must be gathered ahead of time. The cell is actively preparing for cell division during interphase.

Science Myth

Myth: When not dividing in mitosis, cells rest during interphase.

Fact: Cells are more active during interphase than during mitosis. Interphase is the phase when growth takes place.

In metaphase II, the sister chromatids reach the metaphase plate. In anaphase II, the sister chromatids separate at their centromeres. The separated chromatids become individual chromosomes. They move to opposite ends of the cells. In telophase II, four nuclei are created. Cytokinesis divides the two cells into four haploid daughter cells. Each gamete cell has 23 chromosomes. When the gametes fertilize, the resulting zygote has a diploid set of 46 chromosomes. Figure 9.3.2 shows the process of meiosis II.

Meiosis II

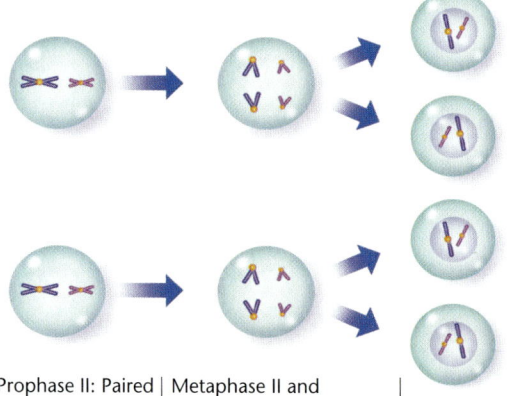

Prophase II: Paired chromosomes line up in each haploid daughter cell.

Metaphase II and Anaphase II: Members of each pair separate and move to opposite sides of the cell.

Telophase II: The cells divide. Four sex cells result.

Figure 9.3.2 *Meiosis II creates four new gamete cells.*

Like mitosis, meiosis is a cycle of division and reproduction that supports life. Mitosis and meiosis are alike, but different. In mitosis, one cell undergoes one division, creating two somatic cells. In meiosis, one cell undergoes two divisions to create four gamete cells. Because most cells in an organism are somatic, mitosis occurs more often than meiosis.

LEARNING STYLES

Visual/Spatial

Cover the diagram labels on TRL Resource File 18 (Figures 9.3.1 and 9.3.2). Make copies of Resource File 18 for students to use. Ask students to fill in labels, using as many vocabulary terms as possible. Students should also label each stage of meiosis I and meiosis II.

Lesson 3 REVIEW

Link to
Social Studies

A group of New York doctors and businessmen formed the American Cancer Society, or the ACS, in 1913. The society's goals were to educate the public about cancer and to raise money for cancer research. Today, the ACS has over 2 million volunteers who work around the world.

On a sheet of paper, write the word or words that complete each statement correctly.

1. Human cells that are not gametes are called _____ cells.
2. Sex cells have a total of _____ chromosomes, and all other cells have a total of _____ chromosomes.
3. Gametes are created during a dividing process called _____.

On a sheet of paper, write the letter of the word or words that complete each sentence correctly.

4. Tetrads form during _____.
   - **A** prophase I
   - **B** metaphase I
   - **C** prophase II
   - **D** metaphase II

5. The main difference between meiosis I and meiosis II is that _____ in meiosis II.
   - **A** the nuclei do not divide
   - **B** cytokinesis is not involved
   - **C** no spindle fibers form
   - **D** no new DNA is created

6. After completing meiosis II, human sex cells have a total of _____ chromosomes.
   - **A** 2
   - **B** 4
   - **C** 23
   - **D** 46

Critical Thinking

On a sheet of paper, write the answers to the following questions. Use complete sentences.

7. How do chromosomes during meiosis I change to cause unique offspring?
8. Why are cells that have completed meiosis I not diploid?
9. Describe an egg cell, a sperm cell, and a somatic cell in these terms: diploid, haploid, male, female.
10. What problems would humans have if they reproduced without using meiosis?

The Life Cycles of Cells and Reproduction Chapter 9 259

Lesson 3 Review Answers

1. somatic **2.** 23, 46 **3.** meiosis **4.** A **5.** D **6.** C **7.** During meiosis I in prophase, homologous chromosomes line up and trade pieces of DNA in a process called crossing over. **8.** Although the cells have two of each type of chromosome, they are sister chromatids, not different chromosomes that have joined through fertilization. **9.** A female egg cell is a haploid cell. A male sperm cell is also a haploid cell. A somatic cell is diploid and can be male or female. **10.** There would be much less diversity. Without allowing chromosomes to combine in different pairs, the offspring would all be very similar to the parent.

Portfolio Assessment

Sample items include:
- Paragraph from ELL/ESL Strategy
- Diagrams from Learning Styles Visual/Spatial
- Lesson 3 Review answers

Link to

Social Studies. Have a volunteer read aloud the Link to Social Studies feature. Students can visit the American Cancer Society (ACS) Web site at www.cancer.org and enter their zip code to find out more about local events sponsored by the ACS. These include Relays for Life, speeches and lectures, and information about the Great American Smokeout.

Workbook Activity 48

The Life Cycles of Cells and Reproduction 259

Lesson at a Glance

Chapter 9 Lesson 4

Overview In this lesson, students learn about the human male and female reproductive systems.

Objectives

- To describe spermatogenesis and oogenesis
- To identify structures in the male and female reproductive systems
- To discuss how sperm and eggs travel through the reproductive system

Student Pages 260–264

Teacher's Resource Library

Workbook Activity 49

Alternative Workbook Activity 49

Resource File 19–21

Vocabulary

ejaculation	penis
embryo	scrotum
estrogen	semen
fallopian tube	seminiferous tubule
follicle	spermatogenesis
gonad	spermatogonia
menopause	testis
menstruation	testosterone
oocyte	urethra
oogenesis	uterus
ovary	vas deferens
ovulation	

Have students work in small groups to make a word search puzzle for all of the vocabulary terms in this lesson. Have groups exchange and solve each other's puzzles.

Background Information

The ovaries and testes are part of the reproductive system, but they also function as endocrine glands. The ovaries produce the hormones estrogen, progesterone, inhibin, and relaxin. Other reproductive hormones released by the pituitary gland are follicle-stimulating hormone (FSH) and luteinizing hormone (LH). Together these hormones control the menstrual cycle, maintain pregnancy, prepare the body for labor and delivery of a baby, and stimulate the mammary glands to lactate. The testes produce the hormones testosterone and inhibin. FSH and LH are also released by the pituitary gland in males. All of these hormones play a role in the production of sperm as well as the development of secondary sex characteristics in males.

Lesson 4 The Human Reproductive System

Objectives

After reading this lesson, you should be able to

- describe spermatogenesis and oogenesis
- identify structures in the male and female reproductive systems
- discuss how sperm and eggs travel through the reproductive system

Humans reproduce sexually. Their gametes are part of an organ system called the reproductive system. The reproductive system is made of various organs and differs for males and females. The process of creating gametes in males and females also differs.

The Male Reproductive System

Male gametes, or sperm, are made through meiosis. This process, called **spermatogenesis,** takes place in the **testes.** The testes in a sexually active male make more than 200 million sperm cells every day. The testes, also called **gonads,** are the organs that produce gametes in males. The testes also produce the male sex hormone **testosterone.** Testosterone causes male characteristics, such as facial hair and a low voice. Testes are kept in the **scrotum,** a sac outside of the male body. Because the scrotum is outside the body, it is about 2°C cooler than the rest of the body. Sperm cells are sensitive to heat. The lower temperature of the scrotum helps sperm to live. Figure 9.4.1 shows the main reproductive organs of the human male.

Spermatogenesis
The process of making a sperm cell

Testis
The male sex organ that produces sperm cells (plural is testes)

Gonad
An organ that makes gametes

Testosterone
A male sex hormone

Scrotum
A sac that holds the testes

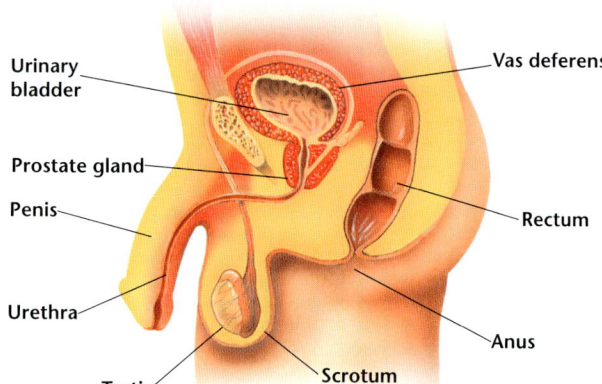

Figure 9.4.1 The male reproductive system is made of many organs.

260 Chapter 9 The Life Cycles of Cells and Reproduction

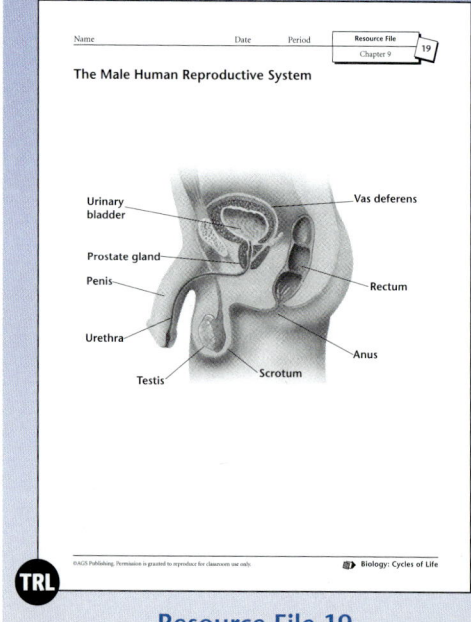

Resource File 19

Spermatogonia
Early gamete cells that have not grown into sperm

Seminiferous tubule
The tissue in the testes where spermatogenesis happens

Vas deferens
The tubes that connect the testes to the urethra

Urethra
The tube that carries urine and semen out of the body

Semen
A mixture of fluid and sperm cells

Penis
The male organ that delivers sperm to the female body

Ejaculation
The release of semen from the penis

Once a human male is sexually mature, spermatogenesis begins and continues for the male's life. Inside the testes, the original diploid cells that begin meiosis are called **spermatogonia.** They are found in tissue called **seminiferous tubules,** which make up the testes. Once they begin meiosis, they create four haploid sperm cells that are stored until needed.

Sperm cells are released during male sexual activity. When released, sperm cells travel through muscular tubes called the **vas deferens.** These tubes come from each of the testes and carry sperm cells to the **urethra.** The urethra is a tube that carries both **semen** and urine. Semen is a thick, milky fluid that feeds and carries sperm cells outside of the body. When sperm cells reach the urethra, they mix with other chemicals to make semen. Semen is made of mucus, sugars, and enzymes that help the sperm survive outside of the body.

Semen travels down the urethra into the **penis.** The penis is a tube of special tissue that surrounds the urethra. Semen is released through a small opening in the penis tip connected to the urethra. The process of releasing sperm is called **ejaculation.**

Science at Work

Laboratory Technician

Laboratory technicians analyze scientific samples. They may observe cells and run experiments. Laboratory technicians work closely with scientists or doctors. Technicians develop good procedures and follow them carefully. They often read test results and analyze data. A technician uses a variety of laboratory equipment, including microscopes and culture equipment. Laboratory technicians work with a variety of samples. These samples include plants, animals, chemicals, soils, and blood. Technicians must have a bachelor's degree or a two-year associate's degree in a scientific field.

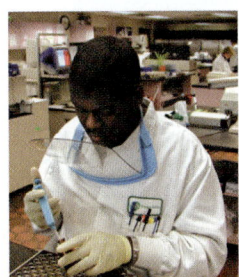

---

1. Warm-Up Activity

Set up several microscopes with slides of mature human sperm cells and cross sections of human ovaries with an ovum present. Have students describe the differences between a sperm cell and an egg cell.

2. Teaching the Lesson

Cover the diagram labels on TRL Resource Files 19–21 (Figures 9.4.1, 9.4.2, and 9.4.3). Make copies of TRL Resource Files 19–21 for students to use. As students read the lesson, have them label the structures of the male and female reproductive systems.

Have students make a flowchart to sequence the steps of the female menstrual cycle.

3. Reinforce and Extend

TEACHER ALERT

Students may need clarification that the male urethra cannot carry semen and urine at the same time. A reflex controls the sphincter muscle at the base of the urinary bladder. At the time of ejaculation, the reflex closes the sphincter. Urine cannot enter the urethra, and semen cannot enter the urinary bladder.

Science at Work

Have a volunteer read the Science at Work feature aloud. Ask students: Why is it important that a lab technician follow experimental procedures carefully? *(to be sure that results are accurate and to make sure that samples are not tainted)* Why is it important to follow laboratory rules when working in the lab? *(for safety and to help keep lab equipment in good condition)*

ELL/ESL Strategy

Language Objective: *To describe the human reproductive system*

Have students write a list of questions they have about the male and/or female reproductive system. They can record the answers as they read the chapter or use other resources to find the answers.

Learning Styles

Body/Kinesthetic
Provide students with models of the male and female reproductive systems. Allow students to use the models to study and learn the structures and functions of each reproductive system.

Oogenesis
The process of creating an egg cell

Ovary
The female organ that makes egg cells

Oocyte
An early egg cell that has not finished meiosis

Estrogen
A female sex hormone

Follicle
A ball of cells with a growing oocyte found inside

Ovulation
The process of releasing an egg from an ovary

Fallopian tube
A tube through which eggs pass from an ovary to the uterus

Uterus
An organ in most female mammals that holds and protects an embryo

Females are born with about 400,000 oocytes that are produced and stored in the ovaries.

The Female Reproductive System

Figure 9.4.2 shows the main reproductive organs of the human female. A female's gametes, or eggs, are produced through a process called **oogenesis**. This process happens in the **ovaries**. When a female is born, her two ovaries contain all the cells that will become eggs. These cells, called **oocytes**, are in prophase I of meiosis. When a female becomes sexually mature, the oocytes go through the remaining stages of meiosis. The oocytes grow into egg cells during a monthly cycle.

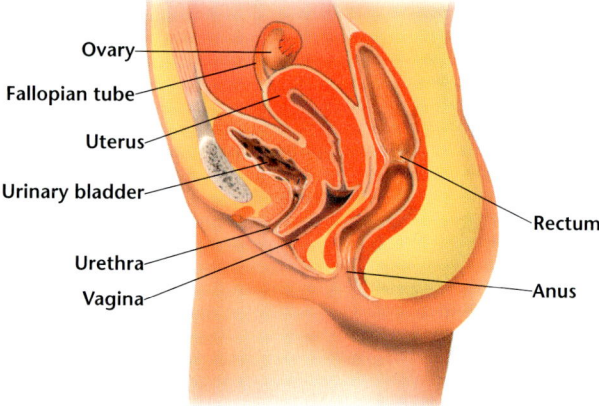

Figure 9.4.2 *The female reproductive system is made of many organs.*

Hormones control this monthly cycle. A main female sex hormone is **estrogen**. At the beginning of the monthly cycle, the ovaries and other organs in the body produce estrogen. As estrogen levels increase during the cycle, one oocyte grows into an egg in one ovary.

This growth begins in a ball of cells called a **follicle**. Each follicle contains the oocyte and other cells that feed and nurture the oocyte. As the follicle grows, the oocyte continues with meiosis. However, meiosis in females produces one egg cell, not four. The other cells from meiosis break down.

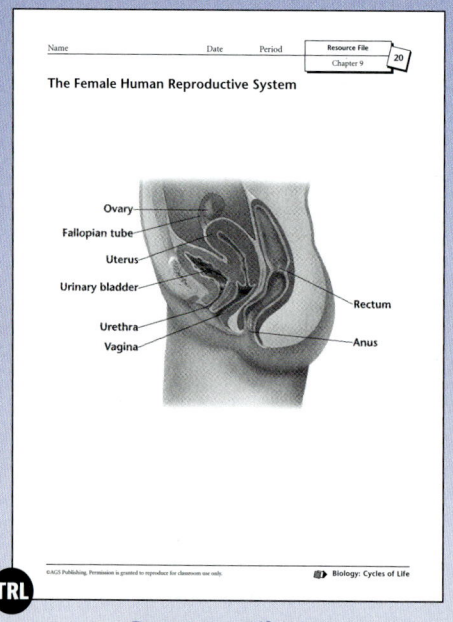

Resource File 20

Embryo
An early stage in the development of an organism

Menstruation
The process during which an unfertilized egg, blood, and pieces of the lining of the uterus exit the female body

Menopause
The period when menstruation naturally stops; usually occurs between the ages of 45 and 55

After about 14 days, the follicle releases the egg cell into the **fallopian tube.** This process is called **ovulation.** A fallopian tube is near each ovary. Both tubes connect to the **uterus.**

The inside lining of the uterus grows with blood-rich tissue during the monthly cycle of a female. The lining can hold and nourish a fertilized egg. If an egg is fertilized, it quickly divides and attaches to the lining of the uterus. Here, it develops into an **embryo.**

You can follow the path of an oocyte in Figure 9.4.3. If an egg is not fertilized during a cycle, the egg, blood, and pieces of the lining break off. These materials leave the body through the vagina. This process is called **menstruation.** It signals the end of a female's monthly cycle, about 28 days long. After menstruation, the cycle begins again.

Menstruation continues for many years. Eventually, the ovaries stop releasing eggs. This usually happens between the ages of 45 and 55. This event is called **menopause.** After menopause, a woman stops ovulating.

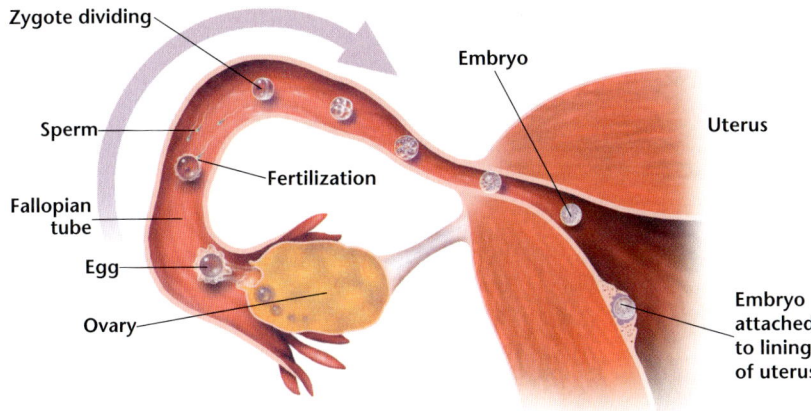

Figure 9.4.3 *A zygote divides in a fallopian tube, becomes an embryo, and attaches to the uterus.*

Teacher Alert

Explain to students that not every female's menstrual cycle will be exactly 28 days. Although 28 days is considered the average length of a menstrual cycle, a cycle can range from 23 days to 35 days and still be considered normal. When females first begin menstruating, the length of time between each period can be irregular for several years. Even if cycles become regular, changes in diet, exercise, or stress can cause a cycle to be longer or shorter than normal.

Science Journal

Have students write a list of questions they have about reproductive health that they could ask on their next visit to a health-care professional.

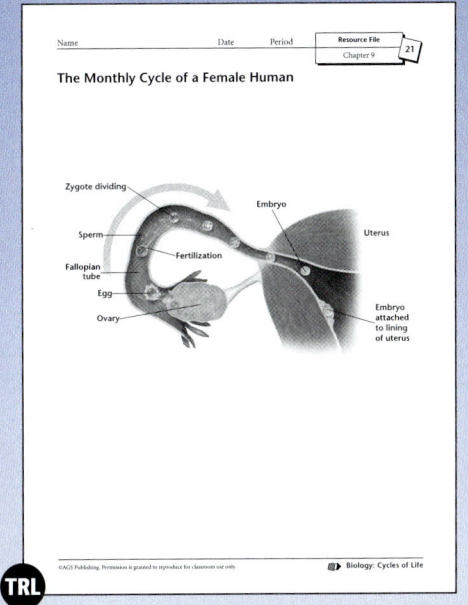

Resource File 21

Lesson 4 Review Answers

1. testes **2.** estrogen **3.** spermatogenesis, oogenesis **4.** D **5.** D **6.** A **7.** Sperm are being constantly created in the testes. Eggs are created when the female is born and then stay in prophase I until released. **8.** The testes produce and store sperm. The scrotum holds testes and regulates temperature. The penis releases sperm for fertilization. **9.** Oocytes are contained in the ovaries when a female is born. Spermatogonia are contained in the testes, beginning at sexual maturity. **10.** A fertilized egg becomes a zygote. As the zygote grows through mitosis, it becomes an embryo. The embryo continues to grow, and cells differentiate to create a fetus. The fetus leaves the mother's body to become a baby. An unfertilized egg is released from the body every month through menstruation.

Portfolio Assessment

Sample items include:
- Flowchart from Teaching the Lesson
- Lesson 4 Review answers

Link to

Physics. Have students read the Link to Physics feature. Sperm cells are mobile because they have a flagellum, a whiplike tail that propels them. Egg cells are moved through the fallopian tubes by cilia, which are short, hairlike structures that line the inside of the tubes and push egg cells to the uterus.

264 Chapter 9

Lesson 4 REVIEW

Link to >>>

Physics

Although sperm and egg cells are both haploid gametes, they differ in size and weight. The sperm cell is the smallest cell in the human body. The egg cell is the largest. About 175,000 sperm cells equal the weight of one egg cell.

On a sheet of paper, write the word or words that complete each statement correctly.

1. The male hormone is produced in the _____.
2. A hormone called _____ controls the activities of the female reproductive system.
3. The process of creating a sperm cell is _____, and the process of creating an egg cell is _____.

On a sheet of paper, write the letter of the word or words that complete each sentence correctly.

4. Male facial hair is caused by the production of _____.
   - **A** sperm cells
   - **B** semen
   - **C** estrogen
   - **D** testosterone
5. Sperm cells are created in the _____.
   - **A** vas deferens
   - **B** seminiferous tubules
   - **C** scrotum
   - **D** testes
6. An unfertilized egg is _____.
   - **A** released from the body through menstruation
   - **B** recycled and returned to the ovaries
   - **C** destroyed and reabsorbed
   - **D** kept in the uterus

Critical Thinking

On a sheet of paper, write the answers to the following questions. Use complete sentences.

7. Contrast the time periods in which eggs and sperm are created.
8. What are three organs of the male reproductive system? What are their functions?
9. Contrast the meiosis of the female oocyte and the meiosis of spermatogonia.
10. What are the pathways a fertilized egg and an unfertilized egg can take?

264 Chapter 9 The Life Cycles of Cells and Reproduction

Workbook Activity 49

Lesson 5 Human Development

Objectives

After reading this lesson, you should be able to
- describe human fertilization and development
- explain childbirth
- compare infancy and the teen years

Vagina
The tube-like canal in the female body through which sperm enter the body

Cervix
An opening that connects a female's uterus and vagina

Pregnancy
The development of a fertilized egg into a baby inside a female's body

Gestation time
The period of development of a mammal, from fertilization until birth

Placenta
A tissue that provides the embryo with food and oxygen from its mother's body

For fertilization to happen, sperm must be delivered to the egg. To deliver sperm, an erect penis enters the **vagina**. After ejaculation, sperm enter the vagina and travel through the **cervix**. The cervix is the other opening of the uterus. It connects the uterus and vagina. Sperm travel through the uterus and into the fallopian tubes. One sperm fertilizes one egg.

What Happens During Pregnancy?

The fertilized egg is a diploid cell. It attaches to the blood-rich lining of the uterus. The fertilized egg continues mitosis and becomes a zygote. After a few days, the zygote is called an **embryo**. It is now a hollow ball of cells. When a fertilized egg attaches to the uterus, the female becomes **pregnant**. Pregnancy is the development of a fertilized egg into a baby inside a female's body. This period of growth in the uterus is called **gestation time**. Human gestation lasts about nine months.

As the embryo grows through mitosis, the lining of the uterus becomes the **placenta**. The placenta is blood-rich tissue that nourishes a growing embryo during pregnancy. The **umbilical cord** connects the placenta to the embryo. The umbilical cord contains blood vessels that provide the embryo with food and oxygen.

A three-week-year-old embryo has three cell layers that will develop into different body parts. Around four weeks, its heart beats and blood vessels have formed. The embryo has a head and buds for arms and legs. The embryo is smaller than a fingernail. In another week, hands and fingers appear. Eyes look like black spots. By week nine, the embryo is called a **fetus**. It has all the major structures found in babies.

By the end of three months, the fetus can suck its thumb. It can turn its head and move its arms and legs. During the next three months of pregnancy, the fetus increases in length and can be active.

The Life Cycles of Cells and Reproduction Chapter 9 265

Lesson at a Glance

Chapter 9 Lesson 5

Overview In this lesson, students learn about human development from fertilization to the teen years.

Objectives
- To describe human fertilization and development
- To explain childbirth
- To compare infancy and the teen years

Student Pages 265–271

Teacher's Resource Library

Workbook Activity 50–51

Alternative Workbook Activity 50–51

Lab Manual 45

Vocabulary

adolescence	placenta
cervix	pregnancy
fetus	umbilical cord
gestation time	vagina

Have students use each vocabulary term in a sentence. Have students share their sentences with the class.

Background Information

Although 300–500 million sperm may be released during ejaculation, less than 1 percent actually reach the egg in the female reproductive tract. Only one sperm cell fuses with the egg during fertilization. Immediately following fertilization, the cell membrane undergoes changes that block any other sperm from fusing with the egg. This prevents polyspermy, which is fertilization by more than one sperm cell. If polyspermy does occur, it causes abnormal development and the embryo dies.

Warm-Up Activity

Provide students with photographs of a developing fetus. Explain that pregnancy is divided into three stages, or trimesters. The photographs should include the fetus during each trimester. Have students discuss the differences in the appearance of the fetus during each trimester.

Teaching the Lesson

Have students make a timeline to help organize the information in the lesson. The timeline should begin with fertilization and include stages of pregnancy, how an infant develops after birth, and what happens during adolescence. Encourage students to leave room on their timeline to fill in details about events that occur during development.

Reinforce and Extend

CAREER CONNECTION

Certified nurse-midwives (CNMs) are registered nurses who are also trained as midwives. CNMs provide care to pregnant women, such as medical examinations and delivery of babies. Requirements for becoming a CNM include being a registered nurse, having a four-year college degree, and completing a one-year training program in midwifery.

Umbilical cord
The cord that connects an embryo to the placenta

Fetus
An embryo after eight weeks of development in the uterus

Adolescence
The teenage years of a human

At birth, the average human baby is 40 to 50 cm long and weighs 2.7 to 4.5 kilogram (7–12 pounds). It is about the size of a small watermelon.

Over the last three months, the fetus becomes larger. Muscles and bones become stronger. The fetus has less room to move in the mother's uterus and is usually less active.

Childbirth

When the fetus reaches full size, the fetus and placenta leave the uterus through the vagina. Figure 9.5.1 gives an example of how a baby is positioned in the mother's body. Muscles in the uterus and vagina squeeze together, or contract, and push the fetus and placenta through. The umbilical cord is clamped and cut. Now the baby can survive outside of the mother's body. After this, the cycle of human reproduction can begin again.

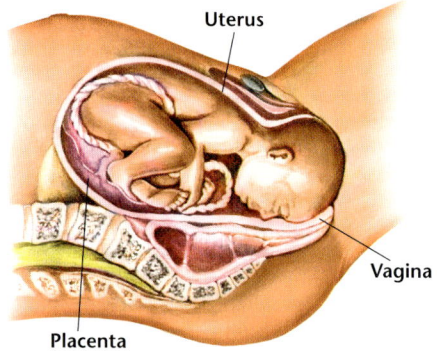

Figure 9.5.1 *A baby leaves the uterus through the vagina.*

Infancy

A human baby, or infant, is born helpless. People must provide constant care for a baby. After a year or so, a baby walks, communicates, and eats solid food. People care for children as they go through the teen years, called **adolescence.**

Rapid growth and physical changes occur during adolescence. The male's voice becomes lower. Hair grows on the face, under the arms, and around the sex organs. For females, hair also grows under the arms and around the sex organs. The breasts enlarge and menstruation begins. Teens learn about becoming an adult. They take on more responsibility. They learn more about themselves and their place in the world.

266   Chapter 9   The Life Cycles of Cells and Reproduction

IN THE COMMUNITY

Explain to students that exercise at all ages is an important part of maintaining a healthy lifestyle and a healthy weight. Regular exercise helps reduce the risk of developing heart disease, diabetes, and certain cancers. Exercise can help manage stress and can be a way to socialize. Have students find out what resources exist in their community for exercise, such as a community center or a local park with walking trails.

SCIENCE JOURNAL

Explain to students that learning how to do things that are complex and involve many steps is part of human development. Have students remember when they were learning how to do something that seemed difficult. Have students write a paragraph describing what they learned, how they learned, and how they felt while learning and afterward.

Biology in Your Life

The Environment: What Causes Cancer?

Cancer is caused when a cell does not cycle properly and reproduces repeatedly. What causes the cell cycle to go wrong? Scientists know that the cause is often genetic. Some people are more likely than others to get cancer, depending on the genes they inherited.

Some cancers are linked to things encountered in daily life. Things that can cause cancer are called *carcinogens*. Common carcinogens are radiation, tobacco smoke, and asbestos.

Radiation in large doses can damage a person's DNA. If the damage is severe enough, cancer can result. Radiation includes long exposure to the sun. Tobacco smoke contains dozens of carcinogens. Over time, exposure to tobacco smoke can cause lung cancer. This is true even if a person does not smoke.

Asbestos once was a common building material because it does not burn. However, asbestos breaks down into very small fibers that can be inhaled and cause lung cancer. Many countries ban the use of asbestos.

Carcinogens do not cause cancer in all people. Whether someone gets cancer due to a carcinogen depends on three factors: 1) how much of the carcinogen they are exposed to; 2) how long they are exposed to it; 3) and their genetic makeup.

1. Why should you avoid or limit your exposure to carcinogens?
2. How can some people be exposed to carcinogens and stay healthy, while others who are exposed get cancer?
3. What lifestyle changes can you make to lower your chances of getting cancer from a known carcinogen?

ELL/ESL Strategy

Language Objective: *To explain personal changes*

Have students explain how they have changed since they were children. Encourage them to explain how they have changed physically and to include things that they have learned.

Teacher Alert

Students may question why radiation is used in the treatment of cancer if it is a known carcinogen. When used to treat cancer, the radiation is concentrated and aimed directly on the cancer cells. The radiation destroys the cells by damaging their DNA. The cells can no longer grow and divide, thus reducing the size of a tumor. The goal of radiation therapy is to destroy as many cancer cells as possible while harming as few healthy cells as possible.

Biology in Your Life

Have students read the Biology in Your Life feature. Explain that there are some risk factors associated with cancer that an individual can control and others that cannot be controlled. Risk factors a person can avoid include reducing exposure to known carcinogens and making lifestyle changes, such as changes in diet and amount of exercise. Genetic predisposition, race, age, and gender are risk factors that cannot be controlled.

Biology in Your Life Answers

1. Carcinogens are materials that can cause cancer. **2.** Some people are more likely to get cancer depending on the genes they inherited. **3.** Lifestyle changes include not smoking, avoiding breathing in someone else's tobacco smoke, avoiding prolonged exposure to strong sunlight by using sunscreen, wearing a hat, and wearing sunglasses.

IN THE ENVIRONMENT

Exposure to certain chemicals such as asbestos, PCBs, radon, benzene, or vinyl chloride is associated with an increased risk in developing cancer. Have students research a known environmental carcinogen. Ask them to find out if there are any laws to reduce the use or release of the substance into the environment.

Lesson 5 Review Answers

1. fetus **2.** nine **3.** placenta, embryo
4. Rapid growth and physical changes occur during adolescence. The male's voice becomes lower. Hair grows on the face, under the arms, and in the area around the sex organs. For females, hair also grows under the arms and around the sex organs. The breasts enlarge, and menstruation begins. Teens learn about becoming an adult. They take on more responsibility. **5.** An egg becomes fertilized by a sperm. The fertilized egg attaches to the uterus, undergoes mitosis, and becomes an embryo. The placenta attaches the embryo to the mother's uterus. By three weeks, three cell layers have formed. The embryo has a head and buds for arms and legs. By four weeks, the embryo has hands and fingers. The eyes look like black spots. By week nine, at the end of the first trimester, the embryo is called a fetus and has all the major structures found in babies.

Portfolio Assessment

Sample items include:
- Paragraph from Science Journal
- Research from In the Environment
- Lesson 5 Review answers

Achievements in Science

Have students read the Achievements in Science feature. Explain that as scientists learn more about cancer, its causes, successful treatments, and possible prevention, the rates of cancer development are beginning to decrease for certain cancers. The death rates from certain cancers are also beginning to decrease. Ask students: Why is it important that the public be well informed about cancer? *(Being well informed can help people make lifestyle changes that reduce risk factors. Being able to recognize the early signs and symptoms of cancer is an important part of early detection. The earlier that cancer is detected, in many cases, the higher is the chance of survival.)*

Lesson 5 REVIEW

Word Bank
nine
placenta
fetus
embryo

On a sheet of paper, write the the word or words from the Word Bank that complete each sentence correctly.

1. At week nine, an embryo is called a(n) _____.
2. The human gestation period lasts about _____ months.
3. The umbilical cord connects the _____ to the _____.

Critical Thinking

On a sheet of paper, write the answers to the following questions. Use complete sentences.

4. What kinds of physical changes take place during adolescence?
5. Pregnancies are often referred to as trimesters. A trimester is about three months long. What developments occur in a fetus during the first trimester?

Achievements in Science

Cancer in people has been noted throughout recorded history. The word *cancer* was first used by Hippocrates, an ancient Greek doctor. Since then, several doctors have made important discoveries about human cancer. During the 1700s, the Scottish doctor John Hunter began removing malignant tumors from people. Hunter helped develop this surgery. Soon, other doctors began removing tumors for people.

In 1761, John Hill, a British doctor, recognized that tobacco use could cause cancer. An American scientist, Francis Peyton Rous, discovered a virus that caused cancer.

The work of Hill, Rous, and others led to the discovery of other substances that could cause cancer, such as radiation and certain chemicals.

In the late 1800s, Thomas Beatson, a Scottish surgeon, found a link between hormones produced by the ovaries and breast cancer. Beaston's work led the way for hormone treatment of cancer. Scientists discovered radiation in the late 1800s and early 1900s. This discovery led to the use of X-rays to find cancer tumors. Later, scientists discovered how to use radiation therapy to destroy tumors. Today, scientists and doctors worldwide continue to identify sources of cancer and develop new cancer treatments.

268 Chapter 9 The Life Cycles of Cells and Reproduction

Workbook Activity 50

DISCOVERY INVESTIGATION 9

Materials
- lab coat or apron
- modeling clay in different colors

Modeling the Movement of Chromosomes

DNA is organized into sections called chromosomes. Each chromosome contains many genes. Human chromosomes come in pairs, with one chromosome coming from each parent. The genes on a chromosome are mixed and distributed during meiosis. In meiosis I, chromosomes trade genetic information by crossing over. In meiosis II, the chromosome pairs are separated and redistributed in gametes.

In this investigation, you will create models of chromosomes with different-colored clay. You will use your models to show how meiosis I and meiosis II cause genes to mix, creating different chromosomes.

Meiosis I:	Meiosis I:	Meiosis I:	Meiosis II:
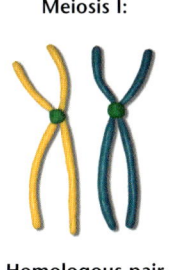			
Homologous pair lines up	Crossover	Result	Result

Discovery Investigation 9

This investigation is less structured than the first investigation in this chapter. It offers students more challenge and requires more teacher facilitation. Encourage students to read the Discovery Investigation steps. Discuss questions they may have before beginning the investigation.

Objectives
- To create accurate models of chromosome pairs
- To accurately model the activity of chromosomes during meiosis
- To observe and understand the differences in chromosome activity during meiosis I and meiosis II

Skills
Observing, designing, communicating

Background
Genetic recombination occurs in different ways in meiosis I and meiosis II. In meiosis I, chromosomes exchange some genetic material in crossing over. In meiosis II, chromosomes are pulled apart, which separates chromatids into gamete cells for reproduction.

Time Frame
One class period

Procedure
- Have students work in groups. Encourage students to be creative.
- Review how DNA is organized into chromosomes and DNA.
- Students should be aware that sections of each chromosome make up genes that code for specific proteins and/or traits. Students should account for different chromosomes or chromatids by using different colors so that they will be easily visible when sections are switched during crossing over or when they are recombined in meiosis II.
- For easy comparison, groups should start with the same types of models for number, size, and color.

Continued on page 270

Continued from page 269

Cleanup/Disposal

Instruct students in proper cleanup and disposal of materials.

Results

Students should illustrate that portions of chromosomes (genes) will move from one sister chromatid to another during meiosis I. The sister chromatids will separate and form a variety of combinations within gametes in meiosis II.

For a more effective illustration, have students model meiosis II, using the end products of another group that modeled meiosis I.

Answers to Analysis, Conclusions, and Explore Further begin on page 670 of this Teacher's Edition.

Assessment

You might include the following items from this Investigation:
- Student models
- Answers to Analysis and Conclusions questions
- Answers Student research and predictions for Explore Further

Procedure

1. Form small groups. Select either meiosis I or meiosis II to model.
2. Put on a lab coat or apron.
3. Use the modeling clay to design and create chromosome models. Determine the size and color of your models. Keep your models simple.
4. On paper, diagram the process your group wants to model (meiosis I or meiosis II). Label the activities that occur during each phase of the process.
5. Now use your chromosome models to show each phase of the process. Show how the chromosomes move or change. Use different clay colors to make this clear.
6. Compare the models your group created with the models of other groups. Compare how each group showed that the genes on their chromosomes have moved.

Cleanup/Disposal

When you are finished, return any unused modeling clay to the proper place. Wash your hands in warm, soapy water.

Analysis

1. Compare your models with models of the same process created by another group. How do the two sets differ?
2. Compare your models with models of a different process created by another group. How different are the two sets?

Conclusions

1. In meiosis I, how does the size of the chromosome and the site of crossing over affect the number and type of genes that are transferred? Are some genes more likely to be transferred in crossing over than others?
2. Suppose one of the groups modeling meiosis II used chromosomes that had crossed over in meiosis I as their starting materials. How would this affect offspring?

Explore Further

Compare the models of gamete cells from the end of meiosis II with another group's gamete cells. How much does this affect offspring?

270 Chapter 9 The Life Cycles of Cells and Reproduction

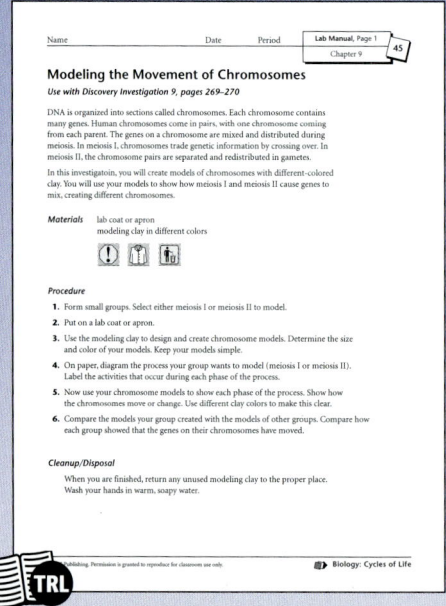

Lab Manual 45, pages 1–2

BIOLOGY IN THE WORLD

Life Without DNA

All living organisms on Earth have one thing in common—they all use DNA to replicate, or make copies of themselves. A cell's DNA is like a library of all of its parts and activities. DNA controls the production of proteins that make up the cell. It also acts as a blueprint to transmit information from one generation of cells to the next.

Scientists have long wondered how the first DNA molecules were created and whether DNA is necessary for life to exist. They also wonder if other life forms in the universe exist without DNA. Many scientists think RNA may have once done all the work that DNA does now.

Scientists think RNA acts like a messenger for DNA. Scientists have run experiments that show that RNA can behave like DNA as an information carrier. RNA may also act as a protein in carrying out cellular functions.

Recently, scientists have tried to create a type of primitive life-form from RNA. In one experiment, scientists mixed materials that make up RNA with water and a certain type of clay. The materials assembled themselves into a cell-like structure as seen in the photograph. This structure may have been the ancestor to cells as we know them today.

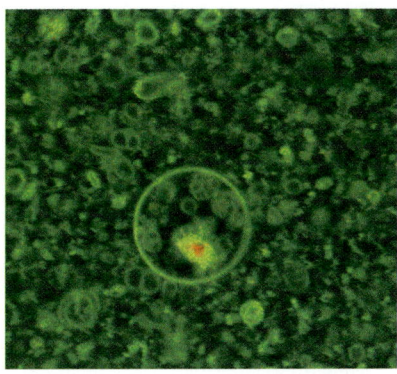

Experiments recreating primitive life without DNA are interesting to both biologists and astronomers looking for life in the universe. Currently, space probes are searching for life based on the life structures we know on Earth. By finding new ways that life can exist, we may be better equipped to search for different types of life elsewhere.

1. What was the importance of the experiment that showed RNA could carry information and do cellular functions?
2. Why do scientists think the first cells may have used RNA instead of DNA?
3. How could information from these RNA experiments be useful in space missions?

The Life Cycles of Cells and Reproduction Chapter 9

ONLINE CONNECTION

A Web site students may find interesting after completing Chapter 9 is the Centers for Disease Control and Prevention Web site at www.atsdr.cdc.gov/COM/cancer-fs.html, which has information about cancer and risk factors. Another Web site is from the National Cancer Institute at http://cis.nci.nih.gov, which has a collection of cancer fact sheets.

BIOLOGY IN THE WORLD

Have volunteers read aloud the Biology in the World feature. There are several theories about the origin of the organic molecules within cells, including DNA, RNA, and proteins. Some scientists hypothesize that RNA was the first organic molecule that led to the formation and functioning of early cells. These scientists believe that over time DNA replaced RNA as the molecule that held genetic material because it is a more stable molecule for storage than RNA. The structure of DNA is a double helix, whereas RNA exists only as a single strand of genetic material.

Biology in the World Answers

1. It showed that RNA could function like DNA does in a cell. **2.** Experiments showed that RNA would partially assemble itself in a cell-like structure when added to clay and water. **3.** A space probe could use information about different life-forms to widen its search for extraterrestrial life.

LEARNING STYLES

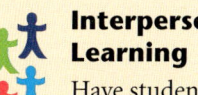

Interpersonal/ Group Learning

Have students work in small groups to research the most current information and theories of the possibility of life on other planets or moons in our solar system. One of the essential requirements for life as we know it is water. Ask students: Which planets and moons do scientists think might have water? What type of life on other planets are scientists looking for? Have students present the results of their research in the form of a newspaper article, including art.

Chapter 9 Summary

Have volunteers read aloud each summary item on page 272. Ask volunteers to explain the meaning of each item. Direct students' attention to the Vocabulary box on the bottom of the page 272. Have them read and review each term and its definition.

Graphic Organizer

As students read Chapter 9, have them finish completing the chart on Graphic Organizer 9: Mitosis and Meiosis. Encourage students to read each lesson of the chapter and then have them fill in the portion of the chart that pertains to the lesson. When they have completed the chart, ask them to answer the questions.

Chapter 9 SUMMARY

- Cells go through cycles. A cell cycle begins when a new cell is created. It ends when the cell divides to make new cells.

- A cell spends most of its life in interphase carrying out its typical cell activities.

- During mitosis, a cell divides to create two daughter cells. Daughter cells from mitosis are identical copies of the parent cell, with the same DNA.

- Cancer is a condition in which cell cycles are uncontrolled.

- Human sex cells, or gametes, undergo meiosis to make new sex cells. Gametes from meiosis are haploid cells and have one set of chromosomes. Cells with two sets of chromosomes are called diploid cells.

- Meiosis I results in two cells with two copies of the same chromosomes. Meiosis II results in four haploid daughter cells, each with one copy of each type of chromosome.

- The male reproductive system produces and delivers sperm to the female uterus to fertilize an egg for reproduction. The female reproductive system produces a haploid egg cell in the ovaries. An unfertilized egg cell is released through menstruation.

- Reproduction takes place when a haploid sperm fertilizes a haploid egg cell. This results in a diploid zygote that grows through mitosis.

- A fertilized egg develops into a zygote, undergoes mitosis, and becomes an embryo. An embryo grows into a fetus, then into a baby.

Vocabulary

adolescence, 266	fertilization, 257	metastasis, 252	spermatogenesis, 260
benign tumor, 252	fetus, 266	mitosis, 249	spermatogonia, 261
cancer, 252	follicle, 262	oocyte, 262	spindle, 249
cell cycle, 248	gamete, 256	oogenesis, 262	testis, 260
centromere, 249	gestation time, 265	ovary, 262	testosterone, 260
cervix, 265	gonad, 260	ovulation, 262	tetrad, 257
cleavage furrow, 250	haploid, 257	penis, 261	tumor, 252
crossing over, 257	homologous chromosome, 256	placenta, 265	umbilical cord, 266
cytokinesis, 250	interphase, 248	pregnancy, 265	urethra, 261
diploid, 256	malignant tumor, 252	scrotum, 260	uterus, 262
egg, 256	meiosis, 257	semen, 261	vagina, 265
ejaculation, 261	menopause, 263	seminiferous tubule, 261	vas deferens, 261
embryo, 263	menstruation, 263	sister chromatid, 249	zygote, 257
estrogen, 262	metaphase plate, 249	somatic cell, 256	
fallopian tube, 262		sperm, 256	

272 Chapter 9 The Life Cycles of Cells and Reproduction

Graphic Organizer 9, pages 1–3

Workbook Activity 51, pages 1–4

Chapter 9 REVIEW

Word Bank
benign tumor
cytokinesis
egg
gonad
haploid
interphase
meiosis
menstruation
mitosis
ovulation
placenta
pregnancy
somatic cell
sperm
zygote

Vocabulary Review

On a sheet of paper, write the word or words from the Word Bank that best complete each sentence.

1. A cell that has undergone _____ results in four cells.
2. A cell that has undergone _____ results in two cells.
3. The process of dividing everything in a cell except the nucleus is called _____.
4. The process of _____ marks the end of the female monthly reproductive cycle.
5. A(n) _____ is a collection of rapidly dividing cells that has not spread from its beginning area.
6. The phase of the cell cycle in which a cell grows and carries out its normal activities is called _____.
7. A(n) _____ cell contains only one copy of each chromosome.
8. The female gamete cell is called a(n) _____.
9. The process of releasing an egg from an ovary is called _____.
10. An organ responsible for making gametes is called a(n) _____.
11. A fertilized cell is called a(n) _____.
12. In the human body, a cell that is not a gamete is called a(n) _____.
13. The _____ nourishes a developing embryo during pregnancy.
14. The haploid gamete produced by males is called _____.
15. The development of a fertilized egg into a baby inside a female's body is called _____.

Review continued on next page

The Life Cycles of Cells and Reproduction Chapter 9 273

Chapter 9 Review

Use the Chapter Review to prepare students for tests and to reteach content from the chapter.

Chapter 9 Mastery Test

The Teacher's Resource Library includes two forms of the Chapter 9 Mastery Test. Each test addresses the chapter Goals for Learning. An optional third page of additional critical-thinking items is included for each test. The difficulty level of the two forms is equivalent.

Review Answers

Vocabulary Review

1. meiosis 2. mitosis 3. cytokinesis
4. menstruation 5. benign tumor
6. interphase 7. haploid 8. egg 9. ovulation
10. gonad 11. zygote 12. somatic cell
13. placenta 14. sperm 15. pregnancy

TEACHER ALERT

In the Chapter Review, the Vocabulary Review activity includes a sample of the chapter's vocabulary terms. The activity will help determine students' understanding of key vocabulary terms and concepts presented in the chapter. Other vocabulary terms used in the chapter are listed below.

adolescence	metastasis
cancer	oocyte
cell cycle	oogenesis
centromere	ovary
cervix	penis
cleavage furrow	scrotum
crossing over	semen
diploid	seminiferous tubule
ejaculation	
embryo	sister chromatid
estrogen	spermatogenesis
fallopian tube	spermatogonia
fertilization	spindle
fetus	testis
follicle	testosterone
gamete	tetrad
gestation time	tumor
homologous chromosome	umbilical cord
	urethra
malignant tumor	uterus
	vagina
menopause	vas deferens
metaphase plate	

The Life Cycles of Cells and Reproduction 273

Concept Review

16. B **17.** D **18.** C **19.** C **20.** B

Critical Thinking

21. A cancerous cell has a problem with its control system. Because of this problem, it continually divides and creates a mass of cells. **22.** If a tumor is found early, it can be surgically removed. This can eliminate all the cancer. If the tumor is not found early, cancer may spread to other body tissues. In that case, tumor removal is not enough. Drugs and/or radiation would be necessary.

Chapter 9 REVIEW - continued

Concept Review

On a sheet of paper, write the letter of the answer that completes each sentence correctly.

16. In mitosis, chromatids line up in the middle of the cell during _____.

  A anaphase **B** metaphase **C** prophase **D** telophase

17. In mitosis, separate nuclear envelopes form around the two sets of chromosomes during _____.

  A anaphase **B** metaphase **C** prophase **D** telophase

18. During meiosis, spindle fibers appear during _____.

  A anaphase **B** metaphase **C** prophase **D** telophase

19. During _____ of meiosis, sister chromatids are separated and pulled to opposite ends of the cell.

  A anaphase I   **C** anaphase II
  B metaphase I   **D** metaphase II

20. Chromosomes are duplicated to create sister chromatids during _____.

  A meiosis I and meiosis II
  B meiosis I and mitosis
  C meiosis II and mitosis
  D mitosis only

274 Chapter 9 The Life Cycles of Cells and Reproduction

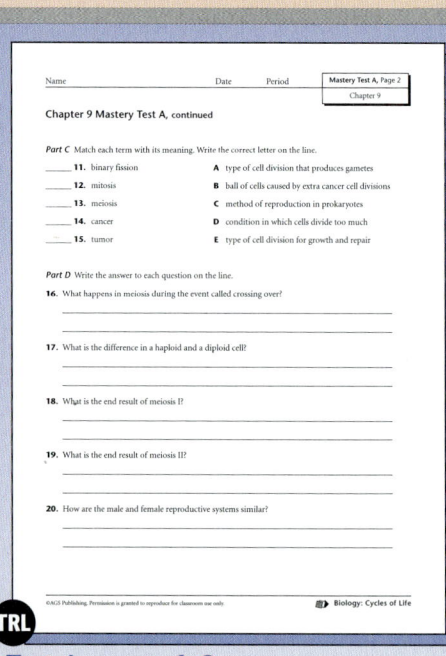

Chapter 9 Mastery Test A, pages 1–3

Critical Thinking

On a sheet of paper, write the answers to the following questions. Use complete sentences.

21. What is the difference between a cancer cell and a normal cell that is dividing?

22. Some people have cancer tumors removed, and their cancer never returns. Other people with cancer must be treated with drugs and radiation. Explain why.

23. How do cells combine and reproduce to create different combinations of DNA in babies?

24. What is a disadvantage to an organism that reproduces by binary fission? What is an advantage?

25. Describe the production of male and female gametes. Explain how the two work to help humans reproduce. Include the terms *mitosis* and *meiosis* in your description.

Research and Write

Spindle fibers attach to sister chromatids at the centromere. Research to find where the other end of the spindle fibers attach. Compare and contrast how spindle fibers attach in plant and animal cells.

 **Test-Taking Tip** If you cannot think of the right words to answer a question, try recalling pictures. Make a drawing to help you think.

The Life Cycles of Cells and Reproduction Chapter 9 **275**

---

23. During meiosis, cells divide and split their DNA in half to create different combinations in gametes. The gametes of the mother and father combine to create a cell with a full set of DNA. This cell has a mixture of half of each parent's DNA and will divide in mitosis as a new baby. 24. A disadvantage of producing by binary fission is that new organisms are created with few differences between them. This is because the DNA is the same. An advantage of binary fission is that reproduction can take place without needing two organisms. 25. Gametes do not perform mitosis. They reproduce by a similar type of reproduction called meiosis. In meiosis, one cell undergoes two divisions to create four gamete cells. The male and female gamete cells combine (fertilization) and form a zygote cell. The zygote goes through many rounds of mitosis to become a new organism.

Research and Write

Have students work individually to prepare a written report that provides enough information so that someone who has not read this chapter would still understand the details about spindle fibers.

ALTERNATIVE ASSESSMENT

Alternative Assessment items correlate to the student Goals for Learning at the beginning of this chapter.

- Have students draw and label the cells in different stages of mitosis.
- Have students explain how a tumor forms and the difference between a benign tumor and a malignant tumor.
- Have students draw and label cells in the different stages of meiosis I and meiosis II.
- Have students work with a partner to make a graphic organizer, such as a flowchart, that shows the steps involved in fertilization.

Chapter 10

Planning Guide
Inheritance Patterns in Life Cycles

		Student Pages	Vocabulary	Lesson Review	Critical-Thinking Questions
Lesson 1	What Did Mendel Discover?	278–283	✔	✔	✔
Lesson 2	Different Ways Alleles Cooperate	284–291	✔	✔	✔
Lesson 3	The Importance of Sex Chromosomes	292–299	✔	✔	✔

Chapter Activities

Teacher's Resource Library
Community Connection 10:
  Genetic Counseling
Graphic Organizer 10:
  Mendel's Work

Teacher's Edition
Opener Activity

Assessment Options

Student Text
Chapter 10 Review

Teacher's Resource Library
Chapter 10 Mastery Tests A and B
Chapters 1–10 Midterm Mastery Test

Teacher's Edition
Chapter 10 Alternative Assessment

Student Text Features									Teaching Strategies						Learning Styles					Teacher's Resource Library			
Achievements in Science	Science at Work	Biology in Your Life	Investigation/Discovery	Biology in the World	Express Lab	Link to	Research and Write	Technology and Society	ELL/ESL Strategy	Background Information	Science Journal	Applications (Home, Career, Community, Global, Environment)	Online Connection	Teacher Alert	Auditory/Verbal	Body/Kinesthetic	Interpersonal/Group Learning	Logical/Mathematical	Visual/Spatial	Workbook Activities	Alternative Workbook Activities	Lab Manual	Self-Study Guide
					283	✔			282	278	280	281		283	280			282	279	52	52	46	✔
			288	290		✔	289	287	286	284	288	286, 287, 289	287			286				53	53	47	✔
296	294		297	299		✔	303		295	292		294	299				293			54–55	54–55	48–50	✔

Pronunciation Key

a	hat	e	let	ī	ice	ô	order	ú	put	sh	she	
ā	age	ē	equal	o	hot	oi	oil	ü	rule	th	thin	
ä	far	ėr	term	ō	open	ou	out	ch	child	ŦH	then	
â	care	i	it	ȯ	saw	u	cup	ng	long	zh	measure	

ə { a in about; e in taken; i in pencil; o in lemon; u in circus }

Alternative Workbook Activities

The Teacher's Resource Library (TRL) contains a set of lower-level worksheets called Alternative Workbook Activities. These worksheets cover the same content as the regular Workbook Activities but are written at a second-grade reading level.

Skill Track Online

Use Skill Track Online for *Biology: Cycles of Life* to monitor student progress and meet the demands of adequate yearly progress (AYP). Make informed instructional decisions with individual student and class reports of online lesson and chapter assessments. With immediate and ongoing feedback, students will also see what they have learned and where they need more reinforcement and practice.

Chapter at a Glance

Chapter 10: Inheritance Patterns in Life Cycles
pages 276–303

Lessons
1. **What Did Mendel Discover?** pages 278–283
2. **Different Ways Alleles Cooperate** pages 284–291

   Investigation 10 pages 290–291
3. **The Importance of Sex Chromosomes** pages 292–299

   Discovery Investigation 10 pages 297–298

Biology in the World page 299

Chapter 10 Summary page 300

Chapter 10 Review pages 301–303

Audio CD

Skill Track Online for Biology: Cycles of Life

Teacher's Resource Library

- Workbook Activities 52–55
- Alternative Workbook Activities 52–55
- Lab Manual 46–50
- Community Connection 10
- Graphic Organizer 10
- Resource File 22–24
- Chapter 10 Self-Study Guide
- Chapter 10 Mastery Tests A and B
- Chapters 1–10 Midterm Mastery Test

(Answer Keys for the Teacher's Resource Library begin on page 675 of the Teacher's Edition. The Materials List for the Lab Manual activities begins on page 720.)

Opener Activity

Display photographs of organisms and their offspring. Vary the photographs by showing different kinds of organisms such as horses, cats, flowers, and fish. Point out to students that all offspring inherit traits from their parents.

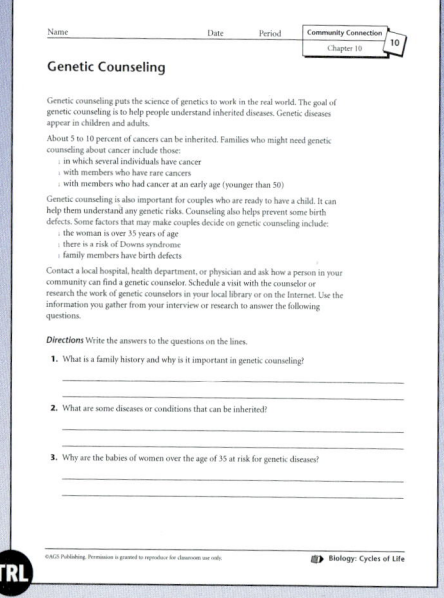

Community Connection 10

Chapter 10
Inheritance Patterns in Life Cycles

Look at the photograph of a chromosome. Near the bottom, find the threads that separate from the dark orange mass. These threads are sections of a DNA molecule coiled inside the chromosome. As you know, DNA is genetic material that contains instructions for life. Before DNA could be seen with a microscope, researchers had observed what DNA does. In Chapter 10, you will learn about early research on heredity—the passing of traits from parents to offspring. You will also learn about the structures that store and transmit traits and what can happen if the structures are damaged.

Organize Your Thoughts

- Genetics
  - Experiments
    - Mendel
    - Morgan
  - Heredity
    - Alleles
    - Sex chromosomes
    - Environment
    - Genetic disorders

Goals for Learning

♦ To explain how genes pass traits from parents to offspring
♦ To describe the role of chromosomes in heredity
♦ To identify patterns of heredity in humans

Introducing the Chapter

Have students look at the photograph on page 276. Ask students: What do scientists mean when they say that DNA contains instructions for life?

Discuss the Organize Your Thoughts chart. Then ask students: How is genetics related to heredity?

Read aloud the Goals for Learning. Help students write questions about what they want to find out about heredity. For example, students might write "Why does a dog have short hair while its mother has long hair?" Students can use their questions to help set a purpose for reading.

Notes and Math Tips

Ask volunteers to read the notes and math tips that appear in the margins throughout the chapter. Then discuss them with the class.

TEACHER'S RESOURCE

The AGS Publishing Teaching Strategies in Science Transparencies may be used with this chapter. The transparencies add an interactive dimension to expand and enhance the *Biology: Cycles of Life* program content.

CAREER INTEREST INVENTORY

The AGS Publishing Harrington-O'Shea Career Decision-Making System-Revised (CDM) may be used with this chapter. Students can use the CDM to explore their interests and identify careers. The CDM defines career areas that are indicated by students' responses on the inventory.

Chapter 10 Self-Study Guide

Lesson at a Glance

Chapter 10 Lesson 1

Overview In this lesson, students learn about genetics and heredity.

Objectives
- To relate heredity to human characteristics
- To describe Mendel's work with pea plants
- To identify the law of segregation
- To identify the law of independent assortment
- To draw a Punnett square

Student Pages 278–283

Teacher's Resource Library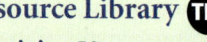

Workbook Activity 52

Alternative Workbook Activity 52

Lab Manual 46

Resource File 22–23

Vocabulary

allele	law of independent
cross-fertilization	assortment
dihybrid cross	law of segregation
dominant gene	monohybrid cross
F_1 generation	P generation
F_2 generation	pollen
heredity	Punnett square
heterozygous	recessive gene
homozygous	trait
hybrid	

Have students create crossword puzzles using the vocabulary terms. Then have students exchange puzzles and solve them.

Background Information

For thousands of years, humans have improved their food crops and livestock through genetics, even though the word *genetics* wasn't used until the twentieth century. This allowed more people to be fed with less land and fewer animals. Humans have been concerned about their own genetics, too, but it has taken thousands of years to develop the knowledge and technology to understand the complexities of human genetics.

Lesson 1 What Did Mendel Discover?

Objectives

After reading this lesson, you should be able to
- relate heredity to human characteristics
- describe Mendel's work with pea plants
- identify the law of segregation
- identify the law of independent assortment
- draw a Punnett square

Trait
A characteristic of an organism

Heredity
The passing of traits from parents to offspring

Cross-fertilization
A process in which pollen from one plant fertilizes the eggs in a flower of a different plant

Pollen
Tiny grains containing sperm; the male plant gamete

Many families have characteristics common among all the members. Some offspring have the same eye or hair color as a parent. Others have the same nose shape as a grandparent. All organisms, including humans, pass **traits** to their offspring during reproduction. A trait is a characteristic of an organism. A trait can be a physical characteristic like eye color, height, or face shape. Traits are inherited through gametes. **Heredity** is the study of how traits are passed from parents to offspring.

Mendel's Studies

The science of heredity began in the mid-1800s. An Austrian scientist named Gregor Mendel noticed common traits in pea plants. Each trait had two forms. For example, pea plants were tall or short. Flowers were purple or white. Mendel decided to study seven traits. He studied plant height, flower position, flower color, seed color, seed shape, pod color, and pod shape. Mendel studied almost 20,000 pea plants.

To begin, Mendel grew many generations of plants until he had true-breeding for each trait. True-breeding plants have offspring that always show the same form of the trait. For example, true-breeding tall plants always produce tall plants.

Mendel now began to cross-fertilize. **Cross-fertilization** is a process in which **pollen** from one plant fertilizes the eggs in a flower of a different plant. Pollen is the male plant gamete. Mendel used pollen from a tall plant to fertilize an egg of a short plant. He made similar crosses between plants with opposite forms of traits.

The F_1 Generation

Mendel called the first round of plants the parental generation, or the **P generation**. The P generation is the first two individuals that mate in a genetic cross. Mendel called the offspring the F_1 **generation.**

278 Chapter 10 Inheritance Patterns in Life Cycles

---

1 Warm-Up Activity

Have students perform the Express Lab on page 283. Ask students if they understand what the term *probability* means. *(the likelihood that an event will occur)* Ask students: How is the coin toss similar to inheriting a trait from a parent? *(The likelihood of an offspring inheriting a trait from a parent is often a question of probability.)*

Probabilities can be expressed in words, as fractions, as percentages, or as decimals. The use of two coin tosses serves as a model of a monohybrid cross. Ask students to make a simple four-box Punnett square to summarize this lab.

P generation
Parental generation; the first two individuals that mate in a genetic cross

F₁ generation
The offspring that result when two different kinds of pure plants are cross-pollinated

Hybrid
The offspring of two different true-breeding plants

Monohybrid cross
A cross between two plants that differ in only one trait

F₂ generation
The offspring that result when two hybrid plants are crossed

Allele
One form of a gene

Dominant gene
A gene that shows up in an organism

Recessive gene
A gene that is hidden by a dominant gene

The F_1 generation plants were **hybrids.** Hybrids are the offspring of two different true-breeding plants. The parent plants differed only in one trait. Another name for this type of cross is a **monohybrid cross.** Mendel carried out monohybrid crosses to study each of the seven traits. The offspring from monohybrid crosses always gave similar results. For every trait, he saw only one form of that trait in the F_1 generation. The other form seemed to disappear. Mendel wondered if the form truly had disappeared, or if something else was happening.

The F_2 Generation

Mendel then used F_1 plants to fertilize each other, creating an F_2 **generation.** Mendel found two results. First, some offspring in the F_2 generation showed the same trait forms as the F_1 generation. Second, the trait forms that had disappeared in the first cross now appeared. These traits had only been hidden in the F_1 generation.

For example, Mendel's pea plants had a gene for tall plants and a gene for short plants. When he crossed a true-breeding tall plant and a true-breeding short plant, all F_1 generation plants were tall. When he crossed F_1 generation plants, some F_2 generation plants were tall. Some were short. The short gene had been hidden by the tall gene in the F_1 generation. This means a gene can take two or more forms. **Alleles** are different forms of the same gene.

Recall from Chapter 9 that an organism receives an allele from each parent. When the parent gametes fertilize, two alleles are inside the new cells. These alleles can be the same or different. If the alleles are the same, both genes show the same form of a trait. If they are different, one is a **dominant gene** and shows its form of the trait. The other allele is a **recessive gene.** It is hidden by the dominant gene and does not show its form of the trait.

> **Link to** >>>
> **Language Arts**
> The term F_1 generation means "first filial generation." Filial means "of or relating to a son or daughter."

Express Lab Answers
1. Alleles are different versions of the same gene. For example, the gene for height in pea plants had two alleles: tall and short. Each coin toss also has two possibilities: heads or tails. **2.** In the Punnett square, write the probability of each possible outcome along the top and side: $\frac{1}{2}$ heads, $\frac{1}{2}$ tails. The square will show a typical genotypic ratio of $\frac{1}{4}$ heads-heads, $\frac{2}{4}$ heads and tails, $\frac{1}{4}$ tails-tails.

 Teaching the Lesson

As students read the lesson, have them write down the main ideas from each paragraph. Encourage them to ask questions about any concept they do not understand. Have them write down any additional information that helps them understand the concept.

Go through the lesson as a class. Have volunteers explain the concepts in each paragraph. Clear up any misconceptions students may have.

3 Reinforce and Extend

Pronunciation Guide

Use the pronunciation shown here to help students pronounce a difficult word in this lesson. Refer to the pronunciation key on the Chapter Planning Guide for the sounds of the symbols.

Mendel (men´dl)

Learning Styles

 **Visual/Spatial**
Have students help prepare a visual display showing animals with inherited traits. Students can search magazines and other sources for pictures. Ask them to clip the pictures and label the inherited traits. Display the pictures in the classroom.

> **Link to**
> **Language Arts.** Have a volunteer read aloud the Link to Language Arts feature. Ask students to write a paragraph explaining why the genetic term F_1 is an appropriate name. *(The F_1 generation is the first son or daughter of the parental generation.)*

SCIENCE JOURNAL

 Invite students to write a paragraph describing traits they have inherited from their parents. Students should include characteristics such as hair color, eye color, height, and face shape.

LAB ACTIVITIES

Chapter 10 has Investigation and Discovery Investigation lab activities. Two additional lab activities for Chapter 10 appear in the Biology: Cycles of Life Lab Manual and on the Teacher's Resource Library CD-ROM.

LEARNING STYLES

Auditory/Verbal

 Have students work with partners with one student reading page 280 to the other student. Encourage each student to quiz the other about the material being read. Then have them switch roles and read page 281. Again, students should quiz each other about the material on the page.

Law of segregation
A law that states that pairs of homologous chromosomes separate in meiosis and each gamete receives one gene of a pair

Homozygous
Having chromosomes that contain an identical pair of genes for a particular trait

Heterozygous
Having chromosomes that contain a pair of genes that do not code for the same trait form

Dihybrid cross
A cross between two plants that differ in two traits

Law of Segregation

From his results, Mendel came up with the **law of segregation**. This law states that pairs of homologous chromosomes pull apart in meiosis. Each gamete receives one gene of a pair. Genes that come together with the same alleles are **homozygous**. Genes that come together with different alleles are **heterozygous**. The dominant allele is displayed in a heterozygous pair.

Law of Independent Assortment

Mendel wondered if certain trait forms and their alleles were inherited together. For example, would round seeds always be yellow? Would wrinkled seeds always be green? To find out, Mendel made **dihybrid crosses.** He used a P generation that differed in only two traits. Each parent displayed two dominant trait forms or two recessive trait forms. He crossed these plants with each other. His F_1 generation always displayed both dominant trait forms. Next, he let the F_1 plants fertilize each other. If certain alleles always inherit together, he would see only those allele pairings in the F_2 generation.

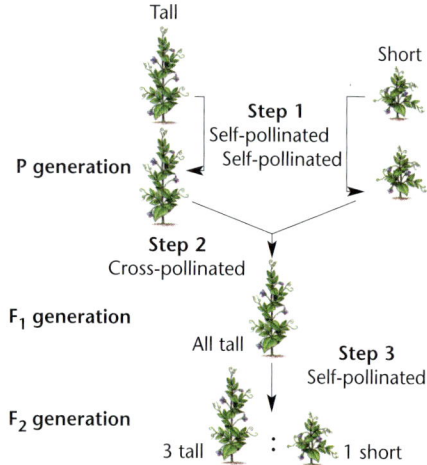

Figure 10.1.1 Mendel's studies involved three generations. The results were always the same.

280   Chapter 10   Inheritance Patterns in Life Cycles

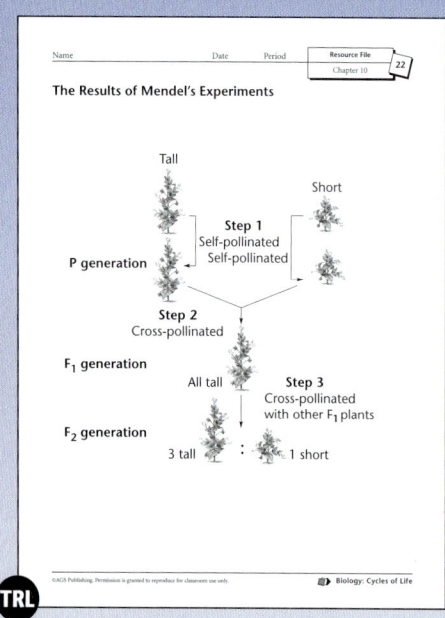

Resource File 22

Law of independent assortment
A law that states that each pair of chromosomes separates independently of other pairs of chromosomes in meiosis

Punnett square
A model used to represent crosses between organisms

For any two traits, Mendel's results always showed the ratio of 9:3:3:1. For example, for seed color and shape, the F_2 generation had nine yellow round seeds and three green round seeds. It also had three yellow wrinkled seeds and one green wrinkled seed. He saw the same ratio for all pairings of his seven traits.

From these results, Mendel came up with the **law of independent assortment.** This law states that each pair of chromosomes separates on its own in meiosis. Four pairings of alleles are possible. Figure 10.1.1 sums up the results of Mendel's experiments.

Punnett Squares

A model called a **Punnett square** can help explain the results of Mendel's crosses. The Punnett square in Figure 10.1.2 shows Mendel's cross of true-breeding tall plants with true-breeding short plants.

TT stands for a pure tall parent plant, and *tt* stands for a pure short parent plant. The capital *T* stands for the dominant gene for plant height (tallness). The lowercase *t* stands for the recessive gene for plant height (shortness). As Figure 10.1.2 shows, all F_1 pea plants were tall. But they also carried the recessive gene for shortness.

Science Myth

Myth: More dominant alleles exist than recessive alleles.

Fact: The frequency of a specific allele is not due to its dominance. Frequency is the number of times an allele appears. The frequency of an allele is due to whether the allele helps an organism survive.

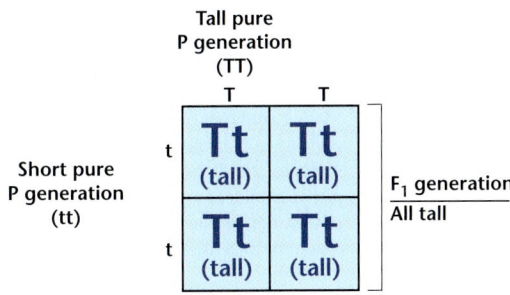

Figure 10.1.2 *This Punnett square shows Mendel's F_1 generation.*

Science Myth

Have a volunteer read aloud the Science Myth. Ask students: Why are alleles that help a species survive found frequently in a population? *(Organisms that do not contain alleles that contribute to survival do not survive and reproduce in large numbers. Traits that do not contribute to the survival of the species are found in increasingly smaller numbers as time passes.)*

GLOBAL CONNECTION

Tell students that genealogy is the study of family histories and that many families trace their ancestors back for centuries. Have students research the genealogy of a royal family. Many of these genealogies are a study of how families are related and how families intermarried. Ask students: Why were these genealogies important? *(They determined who would be the next king or queen, as well as who might receive favors from the current royal family.)*

Link to

Chemistry. Have students read the Link to Chemistry feature. Explain that approximately 1 in 60 people is a carrier of the gene that causes PKU. Two people who are carriers of the gene but who do not exhibit the condition have a 25 percent chance of having a child who has PKU, a 50 percent chance of having a child who carries the gene but is unaffected, and a 25 percent chance of having a normal child.

LEARNING STYLES

Logical/Mathematical

Use a Punnett square to show students how the above statistics for PKU can be calculated. Each carrier parent will have one normal gene and one that causes PKU. Let N stand for the normal gene and P stand for the gene that carries the disorder. The results of the Punnett square are NN, NP, NP, and PP. The children with NP genes are the carriers. The children with NN genes are normal. The children with PP genes have PKU.

ELL/ESL STRATEGY

Language Objective: *To summarize the main ideas in the lesson*

Help students create a graphic organizer using information in this lesson. Have students fold a sheet of notebook paper in half lengthwise and put the headings *Mendel's Studies* for one column and *Punnett Squares* for the other. Students should write facts in each column as they read the lesson. Encourage them to use their graphic organizers to study for quizzes and tests.

Math Tip

In Mendel's F_2 generation, he always got three tall plants and one short plant.

Mendel grew another generation of pea plants, the F_2 generation, by crossing the F_1 generation. Mendel saw that some short pea plants showed up in the F_2 generation. The Punnett square in Figure 10.1.3 shows Mendel's results. Three dominant allele plants showed up for every one recessive allele plant. In other words, for every three tall plants, there was one short plant. Mendel wrote this ratio as 3:1. Figure 10.1.3 sums up the results of Mendel's experiments.

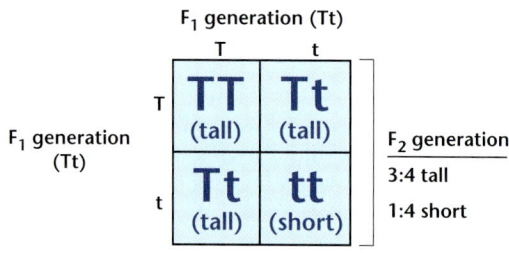

Figure 10.1.3 *This Punnett square shows Mendel's F_2 generation.*

In Mendel's dihybrid crosses, the F_2 generation results were always the same. He always got the ratio 9:3:3:1. For example, he made dihybrid crosses for seed color and shape. He always got nine yellow round seeds, three yellow wrinkled seeds, three green round seeds, and one green-wrinkled seed.

Link to ≫≫≫

Chemistry

Many genetic disorders are caused by a mistake in a chemical pathway. For example, a missing enzyme causes a rare genetic disorder called phenylketonuria (PKU). The enzyme breaks down phenylalanine, an amino acid. Without the enzyme, brain damage occurs. Babies with PKU can be identified at birth and placed on a low-phenylalanine diet. Foods high in phenylalanine include milk and eggs.

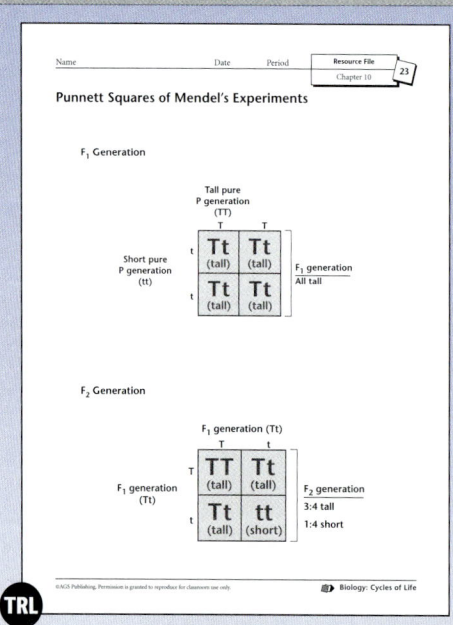

Lesson 1 REVIEW

Word Bank
- monohybrid crosses
- F_2
- homozygous
- F_1

On a sheet of paper, write the word or words from the Word Bank that complete each sentence correctly.

1. Recessive genes can be hidden in the _____ generation, but can reappear in the _____ generation.
2. If genes come together with the same alleles, they are _____.
3. To study a single trait, Mendel carried out _____.

Critical Thinking

On a sheet of paper, write the answers to the following questions. Use complete sentences.

4. What are true-breeding plants?
5. In each generation, Mendel counted the number of pea plants having each trait form. Why was this important?

Math Tip
To find the probability in Step 4 of Express Lab 10, multiply 0.5 by 0.5.

Express Lab 10

Materials
- safety goggles
- 2 coins

Procedure
1. Put on safety goggles.
2. Probability is the likelihood that a specific event will occur. Toss a coin into the air. What is the probability that the coin will land head up? Tail up?
3. Toss the second coin. Does the way that the first coin landed affect how the second coin landed?
4. What is the probability that both coins will land head up? To find out, multiply the separate probabilities of each event.

Analysis
1. How is each coin toss similar to an allele?
2. How can you use a Punnett square to show your results?

Lesson at a Glance

Chapter 10 Lesson 2

Overview In this lesson, students learn how alleles are expressed in living things.

Objectives

- To compare dominant and recessive alleles
- To describe how alleles work together
- To relate the influence of the environment on traits
- To explain linked genes

Student Pages 284–291

Teacher's Resource Library

Workbook Activity 53

Alternative Workbook Activity 53

Lab Manual 47

Vocabulary

codominance	phenotype
genetics	pleiotropy
genotype	polygenic
incomplete	trait
dominance	sickle-cell
linkage map	disease
linked gene	simple dominance
multiple allele	testcross

Have students look up each vocabulary term in a dictionary. Then have them write sentences using the terms.

Background Information

Alleles are two or more genes that result in a particular trait or phenotype. Alleles may exist in pairs, or there may be a number of alleles responsible for a particular trait. Traits controlled by two or more genes are said to be polygenic traits. For example, there are probably three different genes that control human skin color. Polygenetic traits result in a wide range of possible phenotypes as demonstrated by the wide range of human skin colors.

Lesson 2: Different Ways Alleles Cooperate

Objectives

After reading this lesson, you should be able to

- compare dominant and recessive alleles
- describe how alleles work together
- relate the influence of the environment on traits
- explain linked genes

Pairs of alleles come together during fertilization of a female gamete by a male gamete. As the zygote develops, the pairs of alleles are copied many times. Pairs of alleles exist in all cells except haploid gametes. Pairs of alleles work together in different ways. Some pairs behave differently from other pairs.

Simple Dominance

Let's look at how different alleles are created. Over time, DNA changes. Recall that genes make up chromosomes, which are sections of DNA. When the gene for a certain trait changes, it may produce a change in the form of that trait. The new form may help the organism survive better. If the organism reproduces, it will pass the new gene and allele to its offspring. Even if the allele does not help survival, it will still pass on the new trait form to its offspring.

Genetics is the study of DNA changes and how genes are passed through generations. Genetics is the study of heredity.

The most common relationship among alleles is **simple dominance.** In simple dominance, one allele is dominant to a recessive allele. When two dominant alleles come together in a homozygous pair, the dominant trait shows. When two recessive alleles come together in a homozygous pair, the recessive form of the trait shows. What happens when a dominant allele and a recessive allele come together in a heterozygous pair? The dominant form of the trait shows. Many human genes have simple dominance.

Genotypes and Phenotypes

An organism's combination of genes for a trait is called its **genotype.** The genotype of Mendel's F_1 pea plants was *Tt*. These plants were tall. What an organism looks like as a result of its genes is its **phenotype.** An organism has both a genotype and a phenotype for all traits.

Genetics
The study of heredity

Simple dominance
One allele is dominant to a recessive allele

Genotype
An organism's combination of genes for a trait

Phenotype
An organism's appearance as a result of its combination of genes

284 Chapter 10 Inheritance Patterns in Life Cycles

Testcross
A test that determines an unknown genotype of an organism by crossing it with a homozygous recessive organism

Multiple allele
One of more than two forms of a gene

Determining Unknown Genotypes

How can scientists tell if an organism with a dominant form of a trait has homozygous or heterozygous allele pairs? They perform a **testcross**. In a testcross, an individual of unknown genotype, but dominant phenotype, is bred with a homozygous recessive individual. The appearance of the offspring from the testcross will indicate the genotype of the unknown parent. A testcross relies on simple dominance.

Other Allele Relationships

Less common relationships also exist among alleles. Some genes have **multiple alleles.** A multiple allele is a genetic trait with more than two alleles. An example of a multiple allele is human blood type. As seen in Figure 10.2.1, people have A, B, AB, or O blood type.

These blood types are created by three different alleles: A, B, and O. The A and B alleles are dominant. The O allele is recessive. A person with blood type A has two A alleles or an A allele and an O allele. A person with blood type B has two B alleles or a B allele and an O allele. A person with blood type O has two O alleles.

Link to >>>
Environmental Science

Changes in global temperature can change the way a trait appears. For example, in some rabbits a black coat is controlled by an enzyme. This enzyme is active only at low temperatures. In temperate climates, most rabbits are mostly white. Only the cooler regions of the body—the tips of the feet, tail, ears, and nose—are black.

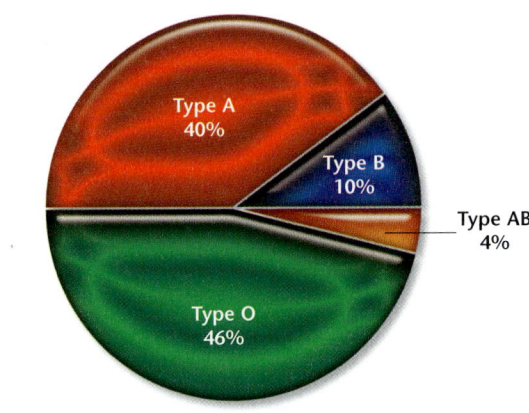

Figure 10.2.1 There are four blood types in the United States.

---

1. Warm-Up Activity

Divide students into small groups. Assign half the groups the topic *food crops* and half the groups the topic *livestock*. Ask students to brainstorm the following question: Why is it important to control the traits or characteristics of the plants or animals? Have students prepare a list of traits they would want to control. *(Possible answers: Dairy farmers would want cows that produce the most milk. Beef producers would want cows that produce quality meat. Corn growers would want to plant corn that produces the best ears of corn.)*

2. Teaching the Lesson

This lesson contains many unfamiliar scientific terms. Students will benefit by going through this lesson in small groups. Have students take turns reading paragraphs from the lesson. After each paragraph is read, tell students to discuss the meaning of any vocabulary terms. Help students clarify any unknown terms. Write the difficult terms on the board along with a definition provided by students.

3. Reinforce and Extend

Link to

Environmental Science. Have a volunteer read aloud the Link to Environmental Science feature. Explain to students that this demonstrates the effect the environment has on a trait. Point out that not all traits are sensitive to temperature and that rabbits are a special case.

LEARNING STYLES

Body/Kinesthetic
Have students write *A*, *B*, and *O* on two sets of note cards. This will represent the three blood type alleles. Have students arrange the cards to show the different blood types possible. Then have them write the arrangements on a sheet of paper and note which blood type is dominant and which is recessive.

IN THE COMMUNITY

Ask students to contact a local support group for sickle-cell anemia or to e-mail a state group. Have them ask who is at risk, how to prevent permanent damage from the disease, and how newborns are screened and treated for the disease.

ELL/ESL STRATEGY

Language Objective: *To summarize the concept of incomplete dominance*
Have students write a paragraph explaining incomplete dominance.

Codominance
Two different alleles come together and produce both trait forms

Incomplete dominance
Two different alleles come together and produce a trait form that is neither dominant nor recessive

Pleiotropy
One gene that affects many traits

Sickle-cell disease
A genetic disease in which a person's red blood cells have a sickle shape

People with blood type AB have both an A and B allele. Both alleles display their trait form. The two alleles have **codominance.** Codominance is when two different alleles come together and both show their trait form.

Another relationship between alleles is **incomplete dominance.** In heterozygous pairs, the dominant allele usually hides the recessive allele. In incomplete dominance, the dominant and recessive alleles work together. These create a trait form that is between the dominant and recessive trait forms. For example, red is a dominant color in snapdragon flowers. White is a recessive color. The heterozygous pair produces pink flowers. Pink is between the dominant red and recessive white.

In **pleiotropy,** one gene affects many traits. An example of pleiotropy is a genetic disease called **sickle-cell disease.** A different allele for a protein in red blood cells causes sickle-cell disease. Look at Figure 10.2.2. The gene that affects the protein also affects cell shape. This causes red blood cells to become sickle shaped. Sickle-shaped red blood cells have difficulty passing through small blood vessels. Less blood reaches the body. Tissue that does not receive normal blood flow becomes damaged.

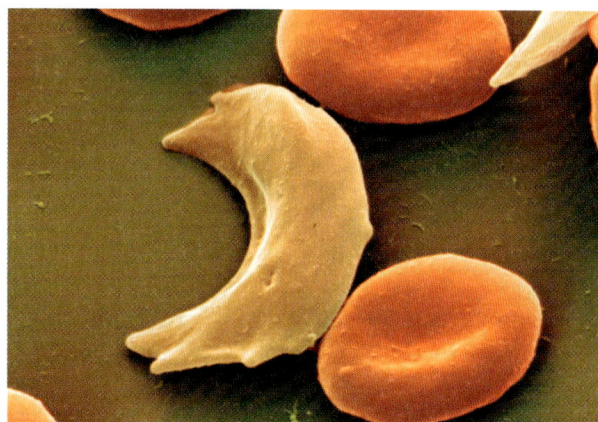

Figure 10.2.2 Compare the shape of normal red blood cells and sickle-shaped red blood cells.

Polygenic trait
A trait controlled by two or more genes

Linked gene
A gene close to another gene on a chromosome, causing their alleles to be inherited together

Linkage map
A map that shows distances between linked genes on a chromosome

A trait controlled by two or more genes is called a **polygenic trait**. Examples of human polygenic traits are eye color, skin color, and height. Many genes are involved in polygenic traits.

Linked Genes
When genes are on separate chromosomes, they sort independently during meiosis. **Linked genes** located on the same chromosomes tend to be inherited together. They tend to stay together during meiosis. Sometimes, the alleles of linked genes are separated. Scientists count the number of separations in a group of organisms. Then they create a **linkage map** of the separations. A linkage map tells the distance between different genes on the same chromosome.

The Role of Genetics and Environment
When scientists study traits of organisms, they look at genes and the environment. All organisms live in a unique environment. Environmental factors often play an important role in developing genes or alleles. For example, several genes affect the color of human skin. However, skin color can change based on how much sunlight it absorbs. Traits of all organisms are affected by the organisms' environment. Traits are also affected by organisms' inherited genes.

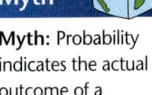

Science Myth

Myth: Probability indicates the actual outcome of a genetic cross.

Fact: Probability is the likelihood that a specific event will happen. Probabilities are used only to predict the possible outcome of a genetic cross.

Technology and Society
The blood of people with hemophilia lacks a substance that allows it to clot. In the most common form of hemophilia, the missing clotting factor is called factor VIII, or antihemophilic globulin (AHG). To treat hemophilia, physicians give people clotting factors. The clotting factors come from donated human blood. To prevent blood-borne diseases, clotting factors are heated.

IN THE ENVIRONMENT

Ask students: Why would a white rabbit have a higher chance of survival in an area that received a lot of snow than a brown rabbit would? *(The white rabbit could blend in better with its surroundings than a brown rabbit could.)* Would you expect to find more alleles for white rabbits or brown rabbits in a snowy area? Why? *(white; because more white rabbits lived to reproduce)*

Science Myth
Have a volunteer read aloud the Science Myth feature. Tell students that probability is a scientific guess as to what the outcome will be. Probability is a method that scientists use to make predictions. Scientists use mathematics as a basis for this prediction.

Technology and Society
Have a volunteer read aloud the Technology and Society feature. Ask students: Why are clotting factors important in blood? *(Clotting factors cause blood to clot when a person is injured. Without clotting factors, a person will bleed for a longer period of time than a person with clotting factors.)*

TEACHER ALERT

Currently there is no cure for hemophilia, only treatment for the disorder. If treated, a person with hemophilia is expected to live about 10 years less than a person without hemophilia. Without treatment, many hemophiliacs do not reach adulthood.

Biology in Your Life

Have volunteers read aloud the Biology in Your Life feature. Ask students: What are two types of evidence that doctors look for in genetic testing? *(large evidence—a missing or added piece of chromosome or an entire chromosome; smaller evidence—extra or missing chemical base in a gene)* Why would couples want to know if they are carriers of a genetic disorder before they had children? *(to determine whether or not they were at risk of passing the disorder on to their children)*

Biology in Your Life Answers

1. Genetic testing is the examination of a person's DNA to search for a disease or a disorder. **2.** If cystic fibrosis or Tay-Sachs runs in their family or in their spouse's family, a couple may want to know if they are both carriers before deciding to have children. **3.** If they have this gene and are at risk, they can seek early and frequent screenings for this cancer.

Science Journal

Have students write a paragraph explaining whether or not they would want to be tested to find out if they were a carrier of a cancer-risk gene.

Biology in Your Life

Technology: Genetic Testing

Genetic testing is the process of examining a person's DNA to search for a disease or a disorder. Some genetic tests looks for large evidence. This includes a missing or extra chromosome or piece of a chromosome. Other tests look for smaller evidence. This includes an extra or missing base in a gene.

Many genetic tests look for inherited disorders that appear in families. Testing can reveal if a person is a carrier for genetic diseases such as cystic fibrosis or Tay-Sachs. A carrier is an organism that carries an allele, but does not show the effects of the allele. Cystic fibrosis is an inherited disease that affects sodium in the body. It causes respiratory and digestive problems. Tay-Sachs disease is fatal. Harmful amounts of a fatty substance collect in the brain's nerve cells.

Both parents must be carriers to have a child with cystic fibrosis or Tay-Sachs. People with a family history of these and other genetic disorders can be tested before deciding to have children.

Scientists have developed genetic tests for several types of cancer that show up in families. Most forms of breast and colon cancer are not inherited. However, a small number of people carry an allele that greatly increases their risk. For these persons, a genetic test shows if they need regular screenings for cancer.

1. What is genetic testing?

2. When might people want to know if they are carriers for cystic fibrosis or Tay-Sachs?

3. Why is it helpful for people to know if they have an allele for an inherited type of cancer?

Lesson 2 REVIEW

Word Bank
- codominance
- dominant
- phenotype
- recessive

Research and Write

Use the Internet and print resources to write a report on Manx cats. Manx cats do not have a tail. Explain how not having a tail in these cats is controlled by a deadly allele.

On a sheet of paper, write the word from the Word Bank that completes each statement correctly.

1. In simple dominance, one allele is _____ to its _____ allele.
2. What an organism looks like as a result of its genes is its _____.
3. Two alleles have _____ when both produce their trait.

On a sheet of paper, write the letter of the answer that completes each sentence correctly.

4. In AB blood, the A and the B alleles have _____.
   - A simple dominance
   - B pleiotrophy
   - C codominance
   - D incomplete dominance

5. To perform a testcross, scientists cross an organism with an unknown genotype with a _____ organism.
   - A homozygous recessive
   - B heterozygous
   - C homozygous dominant
   - D true-breeding

6. A ratio of 3 tall plants to 1 short plant suggests that _____.
   - A height is controlled by pleiotropic alleles
   - B tall is dominant and short is recessive
   - C short is dominant and tall is recessive
   - D the alleles for height are codominant

Critical Thinking

On a sheet of paper, write the answers to the following questions. Use complete sentences.

7. Why are linked genes often inherited together?
8. How is a linkage map created?
9. Explain the inheritance of blood type in humans.
10. Describe an example of a polygenic trait in humans.

Inheritance Patterns in Life Cycles Chapter 10 289

Lesson 2 Review Answers

1. dominant, recessive 2. phenotype 3. codominance 4. C 5. A 6. B 7. Linked genes are often inherited together because they are located close to one another on the same chromosome. 8. To create a linkage map, scientists first count the number of separations in a group of organisms. Then they create a linkage map of the separations. 9. The inheritance of blood type in humans is controlled by multiple alleles: A, B, and O. Every person has two of these three alleles. Alleles A and B are codominant. Allele O is recessive. 10. Height, eye color, and skin color are examples of human polygenic traits. Polygenic traits are controlled by several genes at the same time.

Portfolio Assessment

Sample items include:
- List of traits from Warm-Up Activity
- Paragraph from Science Journal
- Lesson 2 Review answers

Career Connection

Have students research the work and educational requirements of a genetic counselor. Have students explain why genetic counseling can be a rewarding career.

Research and Write

Students may wish to do their research on Manx cats in pairs or in small groups. Suggest that students share their research with the class

Research and Write Answers

In Manx cats, the presence or absence of a tail is controlled by two codominant alleles. A normal allele produces a normal spine. An abnormal allele produces an abnormal, short spine. Cats with two normal alleles have tails. Heterozygous cats are tail-less (Manx) cats. Cats with two abnormal alleles do not develop a spine and die early in development. The abnormal allele is a lethal allele in homozygous cats.

Workbook Activity 53

Inheritance Patterns in Life Cycles 289

Investigation 10

Encourage students to read the investigation steps. Discuss questions they may have before beginning the investigation.

Objectives

- To apply knowledge of inheritance to construct and interpret Punnett squares
- To predict the results of genetic crosses of pea plants, using Punnett squares

Skills

Communicating, collecting information, following written directions, applying information, drawing conclusions, making inferences, understanding concepts, analyzing data, drawing conclusions

Background

A Punnett square is a tool to help students see all possible allele combinations that can result from a genetic cross. Each box inside the Punnett square shows an equally probable combination of alleles.

When used for a monohybrid cross, a Punnett square follows the inheritance of one trait. A monohybrid Punnett square contains four boxes. Each allele possessed by one parent is shown along the top, with one allele per column. Each allele possessed by the other parent is shown along the side, with one allele per row.

When used for a dihybrid cross, a Punnett square follows the inheritance of two traits. A dihybrid Punnett square contains 16 boxes. Each possible pair of alleles for the two traits is shown along the top and side of the Punnett square.

The Punnett square is named after its inventor, English geneticist Reginald Crundall Punnett (1875–1967). Punnett studied many fundamental aspects of Mendelian genetics, including linkage and sex determination. He used poultry and sweet peas as his research organisms.

Time Frame

One class period

Procedure

- Have students work together in pairs or groups to complete the activity.
- Remind students that each pea plant has two alleles for flower color. One allele comes from one parent. The other allele comes from the other parent.
- Explain that a letter of the alphabet is used to symbolize a gene. The letter is often the first letter of the name of the dominant form of the trait. For example, *P* is for purple. A capital letter represents a dominant allele, and a lowercase letter represents a recessive allele.
- Students sometimes confuse the terms *gene* and *allele*. To give them a concrete analogy, tell them that a gene is like a house, and an allele is like a person who lives in that house. Mendel's gene for flower color in garden peas consists of two alleles, just as a house can have two inhabitants.

INVESTIGATION 10

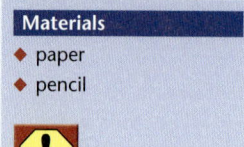

Materials
- paper
- pencil

Using Punnett Squares

A Punnett square is a tool used to predict the possible offspring of a cross. In a Punnett square, a capital letter stands for a dominant allele. A lowercase letter stands for a recessive allele. Each parent carries two alleles. If the parent is true breeding, the alleles are the same. In this investigation, you will use Punnett squares to predict the offspring of genetic crosses.

Procedure

1. In pea plants, a flower color of purple is dominant over the color white. Use capital *P* to stand for the allele for purple. Use a lowercase *p* to stand for the allele for white. In his experiments, Mendel crossed a true-breeding purple-flowering plant with a true-breeding white-flowering plant. On a sheet of paper, write the symbols for these two parental (P-generation) plants.

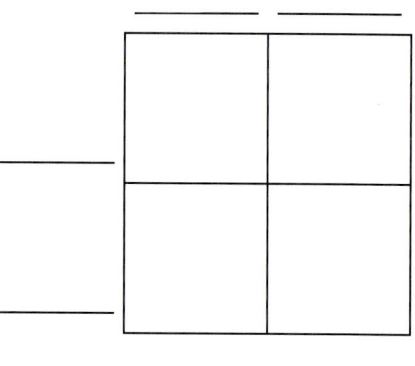

290   Chapter 10   Inheritance Patterns in Life Cycles

2. Draw a Punnett square like the one shown on page 290. Separate and write each of the alleles from one parent in the indicated spaces along the top. Separate and write each allele from the other parent along the side. Fill in the four boxes in the Punnett square. Each box shows the F_1 combination of the allele from one parent (along the top) with the allele from the other parent (along the side).

3. Draw a new Punnett square. Cross two F_1 plants with each other. The new Punnett square will show the resulting F_2 individuals.

Analysis

1. What allele combinations and flower colors are possible among the F_1 plants?
2. What allele combinations are possible among the F_2 plants? What flower colors are possible? Write the ratios of combinations and flower colors in this generation.

Conclusions

1. Why did Mendel use true-breeding plants for each parental cross?
2. Write a new question about genetic crosses that you could explore in another investigation.

Explore Further

Use the procedure above to show the offspring of a dihybrid cross.

Assessment

You might include the following items from this investigation in student portfolios:

- Answers to Analysis and Conclusions questions
- Student proposal for additional work for Explore Further

Results

Help students see that each box represents an intersection of a vertical line (the gametes of the parent shown at the left) and a horizontal line (the gametes of the parent shown at the top). As students fill in their Punnett squares, remind them that each box in a monohybrid Punnett square can contain only two alleles. Each box in a dihybrid Punnett square can contain only four alleles.

Analysis Answers

1. All F_1 individuals resulting from this cross are purple-flowering pea plant flowers. All F_1 individuals have the allele combination Pp.
2. The allele combinations PP, Pp, and pp appear in the F_2 pea plants. These allele combinations are found in a ratio of 1 PP: 2 Pp: 1pp in the F_2 pea plants. The F_2 pea plants have purple or white flowers. These colors appear in a 3 purple: 1 white ratio.

Conclusions Answers

1. For each trait that he studied, Mendel used true-breeding pea plants for each parental cross. He knew these plants would always produce only pea plants with the same form of that trait.
2. Answers will vary depending on students' questions. For example, students may want to prepare Punnett squares showing the inheritance of Mendel's factors for height in pea plants.

Explore Further Answers

Encourage students to draw a Punnett square to show the offspring of a dihybrid cross. Students could follow the inheritance of flower color and height, two traits described in Lesson 1. For example, students could prepare a 16-box dihybrid Punnett square to show a cross between two heterozygous, purple-flowering, tall plants.

Lab Manual 47, pages 1–2

Lesson at a Glance

Chapter 10 Lesson 3

Overview In this lesson, students learn about the importance of sex chromosomes.

Objectives

- To describe how an organism's sex is determined
- To compare different types of sex chromosomes
- To explain how sex-linked traits are inherited

Student Pages 292–299

Teacher's Resource Library TRL

Workbook Activity 54
Alternative Workbook Activity 54
Lab Manual 48–50
Resource File 24

Vocabulary

autosome	sex chromosome
carrier	sex-linked inheritance
hemophilia	sex-linked trait

Read each vocabulary term and have students provide the definition. Then have volunteers use the terms in complete sentences.

Background Information

Another condition that is passed to children on the X chromosome is Duchenne's muscular dystrophy. Usually only males get this disease. Males with this disorder experience progressive muscle weakness and often die by the age of 25.

 Warm-Up Activity

Draw on the board the Punnett square from Figure 10.3.1. Explain how the chance of producing a male or a female is 50 percent.

Lesson 3 The Importance of Sex Chromosomes

Objectives

After reading this lesson, you should be able to
- describe how an organism's sex is determined
- compare different types of sex chromosomes
- explain how sex-linked traits are inherited

Sex chromosome
A chromosome that determines the sex of an organism

Autosome
A chromosome other than a sex chromosome

An important trait in an organism is its sex, whether it is male or female. Chromosomes other than **sex chromosomes** are called **autosomes**. Sex chromosomes determine the sex of an organism. Recall that all organisms have two sex chromosomes in each cell, except for gamete cells. Only one sex chromosome is present in gamete cells. The types of sex chromosomes that pair up determine the sex of an organism.

Determining the Sex of an Organism

Humans have two types of sex chromosomes, X and Y. A human zygote with two X chromosomes (XX) is female. A human zygote with an X and a Y chromosome (XY) is male. During meiosis, the sex chromosomes separate. The sex chromosomes that pair in fertilization depend on the sex chromosomes in the gametes.

The sex of an organism depends on the Y chromosome. If a Y chromosome is present, the zygote becomes male. It produces certain chemicals found in males. If a Y chromosome is not present, the zygote becomes female. It produces certain chemicals found in females. The Punnett square in Figure 10.3.1 shows a 50 percent chance of producing either a female or male offspring.

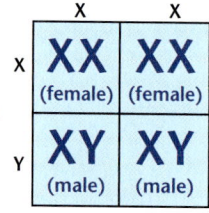

Figure 10.3.1 Human sex chromosomes determine the sex of an offspring. The chance of producing either a female (XX) or male (XY) is 50 percent.

292 Chapter 10 Inheritance Patterns in Life Cycles

Sex-linked trait
A trait determined by an organism's sex chromosomes

Hemophilia
A genetic disease in which a person's blood fails to clot

Link to >>>
Social Studies

Hemophilia has played a role in Europe's history. England's Queen Victoria was a carrier of hemophilia. Through her offspring, hemophilia appeared in other royal families of Europe in Russia, Spain, and Prussia. A descendant is a person born of a certain family. For example, Queen Victoria's granddaughter Alexandra married Nicholas II of Russia. Their only son, Alexis, had hemophilia.

Some human females and males have an extra X chromosome. Some human males have an extra Y chromosome. The extra chromosome comes from an error during meiosis in one of their parent cells.

Sex chromosomes of many organisms follow this XY pattern. Other patterns also determine sex. In many insect species, only the X sex chromosome exists. Males have one X chromosome. Females have two X chromosomes. Other species have the ZW sex chromosome system. In this system, male organisms have two Z sex chromosomes (ZZ). Females have Z and W chromosomes (ZW).

Genetic Disorders

Sex chromosomes carry many genes in their DNA. Not all of these genes are involved in deciding sex. An organism's sex chromosomes determine **sex-linked traits**. This is true in people, especially for the X chromosome. The X chromosome contains genes important for other functions. Genes on the X chromosome may control genetic diseases such as **hemophilia**. People with hemophilia have blood that does not clot. Because the gene involved in hemophilia is sex-linked, it is inherited differently in males and females.

Every person gets an X chromosome from her or his mother. The mother only has an X sex chromosome in her gametes. The father's gametes can have an X or a Y chromosome. The sex of an offspring depends on which chromosome is present in the sperm that fertilizes the egg. The inheritance of sex-linked traits is also controlled by the pairing of sex chromosomes.

Let's look at hemophilia. Its allele is on the X chromosome. The allele for hemophilia is recessive. A mother with hemophilia carries two alleles for hemophilia. Any X chromosome she passes on will have the hemophiliac allele. This means a son will receive the hemophiliac allele and have hemophilia. Any daughters may or may not have hemophilia. This depends on if the father's X chromosome has the hemophilia allele.

2 Teaching the Lesson

Have students make an outline of the lesson. Students should include the main ideas from each paragraph, as well as detail statements. Encourage students to ask questions about any section they do not understand. Have students refer to their outlines as they study for tests and quizzes.

3 Reinforce and Extend

Link to

Social Studies. Have a volunteer read aloud the Link to Social Studies feature. Tell students that in addition to the male heir, there were four daughters. Lead a discussion about the chances of one of Alexis's four older sisters also having hemophilia.

LEARNING STYLES

Interpersonal/Group Learning

The Russian royal family was not the only royal family affected by hemophilia. Divide the class into small groups. Have the groups research Queen Victoria's legacy of hemophilia. Have students make a poster showing Queen Victoria's family tree. Students should note members of the family who were affected and how they were affected. Have students present their posters and information to the class.

Carrier
An organism that carries an allele but does not show the effects of the allele

Daughters with normal blood can have two normal alleles or one normal and one hemophiliac allele. A **carrier** is an organism that carries an allele but does not show the effects of the allele. For any disorder, a human carrier has one dominant normal allele and one recessive allele. Carriers pass these alleles to offspring. For hemophilia, if a father has a normal allele, the daughter will be a carrier. If a father has the hemophiliac allele, the daughter will have hemophilia.

Sex-Linked Inheritance

In the early 1900s, an American scientist named Thomas Morgan studied chromosomes and genes. He used fruit flies because their cells have four pairs of chromosomes. The chromosomes are large and easy to see under a microscope. He also used fruit flies because they reproduce quickly. It is easy to tell the male fruit fly from the female.

▼◄▲▼◄▲▼◄▲▼◄▲▼◄▲▼◄▲▼◄▲▼◄▲▼◄▲▼◄▲▼

Science at Work

Genetic Counselor

Genetic counselors help people understand the chances of inheriting a genetic disease. Many people who see genetic counselors have a family history of an inherited disease or disorder. A genetic counselor can help them understand medical information about inherited diseases.

Genetic counselors are members of a team of health professionals. They work with physicians, nurses, dieticians, social workers, and lab technicians. Most genetic counselors work in university medical centers or private hospitals.

Genetic counselors enjoy helping people and working as part of a team. They need experience in biology, nursing, genetics, public health, or psychology. Any jobs require graduate degrees in medical genetics and counseling.

Sex-linked inheritance
The passing on of traits with genes located on the X chromosome

Fruit flies usually have red eyes. Morgan noticed that one male fruit fly had white eyes. To produce an F_1 generation, he mated the white-eyed male with a red-eyed female. All offspring had red eyes. Morgan concluded that the allele for red eyes was dominant in fruit flies.

Morgan mated the flies from the F_1 generation to produce an F_2 generation. Some offspring had red eyes and some had white eyes. All white-eyed flies were males. None of the females had white eyes. Morgan concluded that eye color in fruit flies is a sex-linked trait.

Morgan showed that the father plays an important role in determining the sex-linked traits of offspring. The father shares the one copy of his X chromosome. A disorder allele on his X chromosome is passed to all of his daughters. The father is the only source of Y chromosomes for his sons. **Sex-linked inheritance** has special patterns. The genes on one chromosome may or may not be found on the other chromosome. Sex-linked inheritance is the passing on of traits with genes located on the X chromosome.

The Punnett squares in Figure 10.3.2 show Morgan's results. Notice that only the X chromosome carries a gene for eye color. The genotypes $X_R X_R$ and $X_R X_r$ represent a red-eyed female fly. The genotype $X_R Y$ represents a red-eyed male. White-eyed males have the genotype $X_r Y$.

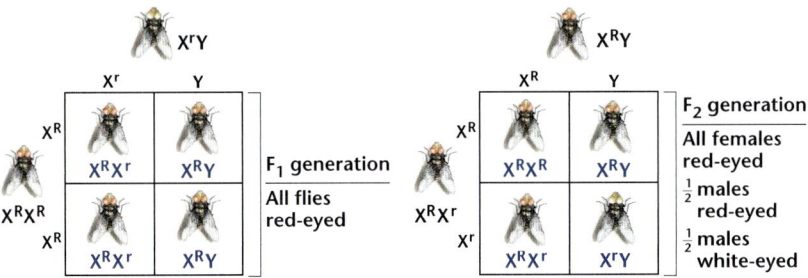

Figure 10.3.2 These Punnett squares show the results of Morgan's experiment with fruit flies.

ELL/ESL STRATEGY

Language Objective: *To explain sex-linked inheritance*

Have partners read the section Sex-Linked Inheritance. Then have one partner explain the section to the other partner. Encourage the listening student to ask questions about anything he or she does not understand. Then have students exchange roles and repeat the process.

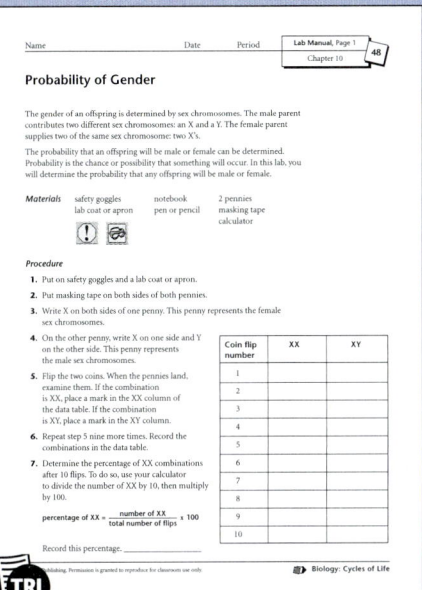

Lab Manual 48, pages 1–2

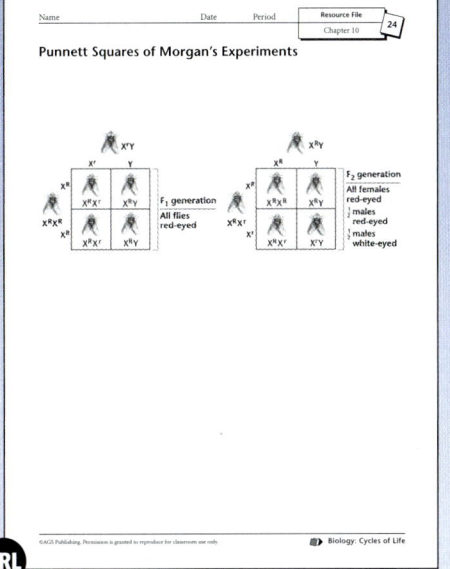

Resource File 24

Lesson 3 Review Answers

1. autosome 2. Y 3. sperm 4. A man cannot be a carrier for hemophilia because he has only one X chromosome and the allele for hemophilia is recessive. 5. Sex-linked disorders usually occur in men because they have only one X chromosome. If a man inherits a sex-linked disorder, he will express the allele even if it is recessive, because he does not have a second X chromosome.

Portfolio Assessment

Sample items include:
- Outline from Teaching the Lesson
- Lesson 3 Review answers

Achievements in Science

Have a volunteer read aloud the feature about discovering genes for genetic diseases. Ask students: Why is it necessary to collect genetic data from so many people in a geographic area? *(to find a specific gene and trace its occurrence through a population)* Why is it important to find the gene that causes a disease or disorder? *(so that a cure or treatment can be found)*

PRONUNCIATION GUIDE

Use the pronunciation shown here to help students pronounce a difficult word in this lesson. Refer to the pronunciation key on the Chapter Planning Guide for the sounds of the symbols.

Kári Stefánsson (kä´ rē stef ən´ sən)

Lesson 3   R E V I E W

Word Bank
autosome
sperm
Y

On a sheet of paper, write the word or letter from the Word Bank that completes each sentence correctly.

1. A(n) _____ is a chromosome other than a sex chromosome.
2. A sex-linked gene is found on the _____ chromosome.
3. The sex of an offspring depends on the _____.

Critical Thinking

On a sheet of paper, write the answers to the following questions. Use complete sentences.

4. A man cannot be a carrier for hemophilia. Why.
5. Why do sex-linked disorders usually occur in men?

Achievements in Science

Discovering Genes for Genetic Diseases

Hard work and new ideas help researchers find disease-causing genes. For example, in 1979, Dr. Nancy Wexler studied families in Venezuela where Huntington's disease was common. This genetic disease destroys the nervous system. She collected family information and blood samples from thousands of people. She then traced the inheritance of Huntington's disease.

Based on Wexler's data, scientists found the Huntington's gene in 1993. An error in the gene causes it to make a defective protein. This protein builds up in the brain, resulting in death.

Finding a gene is often the first step toward finding a cure. Genomics is the development of new treatments based on an organism's genes.

In 1996, Dr. Kári Stefánsson began a genomics project. He collected modern disease information and genetic data. He also studied historical records from over a thousand years ago. Stefánsson identified parts of genes shared by related people and some disease-causing genes. Based on his data, scientists can now find treatments and cures for some diseases.

296 Chapter 10 Inheritance Patterns in Life Cycles

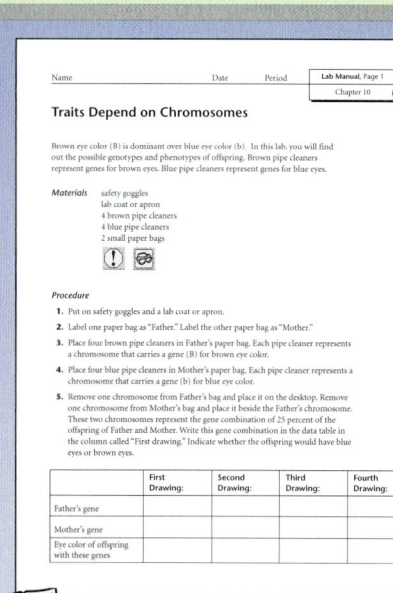

Workbook Activity 54   **Lab Manual 49, pages 1–2**

DISCOVERY INVESTIGATION 10

Materials
- paper
- pencil

Interpreting Pedigrees

A pedigree is a chart that traces a family's genetic history for a certain trait. In this lab, you will learn how to interpret a pedigree.

Procedure

1. On a sheet of paper, copy the pedigree shown below. Circles represent females. Squares represent males. A horizontal line between a male and a female represents marriage. A vertical line that comes down from a married couple leads to their children. A Roman numeral indicates each generation.

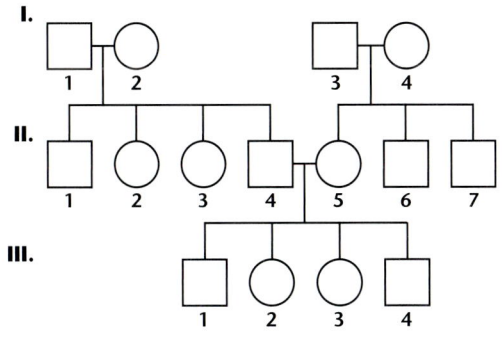

Inheritance Patterns in Life Cycles   Chapter 10   297

Discovery Investigation 10

This investigation is less structured than the first investigation in this chapter. It offers students more challenge and requires more teacher facilitation. Encourage students to read the Discovery Investigation steps. Discuss questions they may have before beginning the investigation.

Objectives
- To recognize the role of pedigrees in understanding patterns of inheritance
- To predict the likelihood of an individual inheriting a genetic disease

Skills
Communicating, collecting information, following written directions, applying information, making inferences, understanding concepts, predicting outcomes, recognizing cause and effect, analyzing data, drawing conclusions

Background
Like a family tree, a pedigree shows family members across generations. Pedigree analysis can reveal if a disease or trait is dominant, recessive, codominant, or sex-linked. To build a pedigree, as much information as possible is collected about a family's history for a particular trait. The information is put into a pedigree. Then the results can be analyzed.

Time Frame
One class period

Procedure
- Have students work together in groups to complete the activity.
- Have students document the procedure they suggest, including any information necessary for someone else to repeat their experiment.
- Help students become familiar with the term *mode of inheritance*. This term describes how a trait is inherited. In this chapter, students have learned that a trait can be dominant, recessive, codominant, or sex-linked.

Continued on page 298

Continued from page 297

- To help students understand the use of Roman numerals for each generation, tell them to think of Generation I as grandparents, Generation II as parents, and Generation III as children.
- Pedigrees are often constructed with incomplete information. Students will discover that they sometimes cannot be sure of an individual's phenotype or a genotype based on the information at hand. They may need to determine what other information must be obtained before an individual's phenotype or a genotype can be known for certain.

Results

Students will discover that attached earlobes is an recessive trait. Two parents with free earlobes (Ff) can produce a child with attached earlobes. This means attached earlobes are homozygous recessive (ff). ABO blood type is controlled by multiple alleles. It is an example of codominance. A type AB parent has an A allele and a B allele. A type O person always has two O alleles, because O is recessive. A type A person can have two A alleles or one A allele and one O allele. A type B person can have two B alleles or one B allele and one O allele.

Answers to Analysis, Conclusions, and Explore Further begin on page 670 of this Teacher's Edition.

Assessment

You might include the following items from this investigation in student portfolios:

- Student hypothesis and completed pedigree
- Answers to Analysis and Conclusions questions
- Student proposal for question to investigate in Explore Further

2. Read the following information. It applies to the pedigree on page 297.

- Attached earlobes are attached to the side of the head. Free earlobes are not attached to the side of the head. Persons I-3 and I-4 have free earlobes. So does their son, II-7. Their daughter, II-5, and son, II-6, have attached earlobes. Their daughter's husband, II-4, also has attached earlobes.
- Person I-1 has type A blood. His wife, I-2, has type B blood. They have four children: son II-1 (type O), daughter II-2 (type AB), daughter II-3 (type A), and son II-4 (type B).

3. Write a procedure describing how you could determine the possible phenotypes and genotypes of the Generation III individuals.

4. Have your procedure approved by your teacher. Write the possible phenotypes and genotypes for Generation III.

Analysis
1. Write the phenotypes and genotypes of the persons described in Step 2.
2. Which two persons are adopted?

Conclusions
1. Is either the earlobe trait or blood type trait a sex-linked trait? Explain your answer.
2. What are the possible phenotypes and genotypes for Generation III?

Explore Further
How can a pedigree reveal a child's risk of inheriting a genetic disease?

298 Chapter 10 Inheritance Patterns in Life Cycles

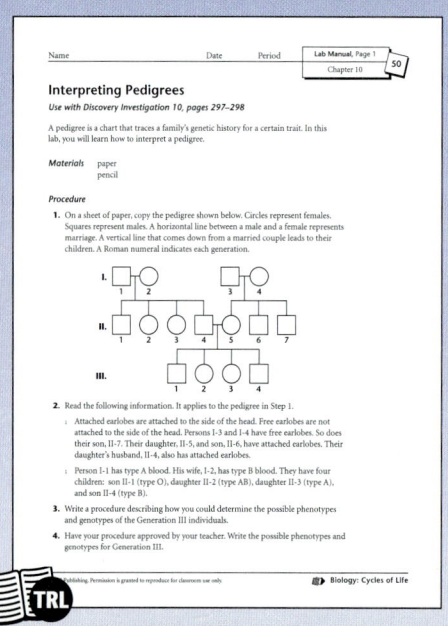

Lab Manual 50, pages 1–2

BIOLOGY IN THE WORLD

Karyotyping

A karyotype is a picture of the chromosomes from an individual cell. In the 1920s, scientists prepared a karyotype to show the four chromosomes of the fruit fly. In the mid-1950s, scientists determined that humans have 46 chromosomes.

To prepare a karyotype, a tissue sample (usually blood) is obtained from the organism. Then researchers add a substance to the blood sample to start cell division. This is done because chromosomes are only visible when a cell is undergoing mitosis or meiosis.

Researchers then add a chemical to stop the dividing cells at metaphase. Then they treat the cells with a solution that causes them to swell. The cells are placed on microscope slides.

Next, researchers stain the cells with dyes to create banding patterns in each chromosome. Because the banding patterns are unique, researchers can recognize each chromosome.

Finally, researchers photograph the chromosomes. They cut out the photos and arrange them in pairs according to size.

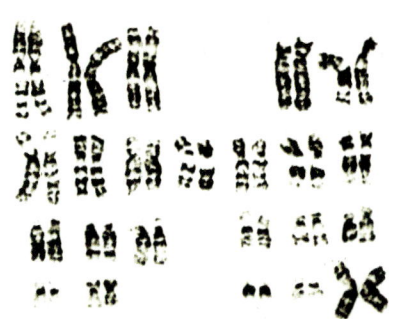

Researchers can identify genetic disorders with karyotypes. Humans usually have 22 pairs of autosomes and one pair of sex chromosomes. A karyotype can show an abnormal chromosome number. Researchers also spot missing or extra material within a chromosome.

1. What are the steps to prepare a karyotype?
2. Why are dividing cells used for karyotyping?
3. Why do researchers use karyotypes?

Chapter 10 Summary

Have volunteers read aloud each summary item on page 300. Ask volunteers to explain the meaning of each item. Direct students' attention to the Vocabulary box on the bottom of page 300. Have them read and review each term and its definition.

Graphic Organizer

As students read Chapter 10, have them finish completing the chart on Graphic Organizer 10: Mendel's Work. Encourage students to read each lesson of the chapter and then have them fill in the portion of the chart that pertains to the lesson. When they have completed the chart, ask them to answer the questions.

Chapter 10 SUMMARY

- Scientist Gregor Mendel studied the inheritance of genetic traits by working with garden peas. Mendel summed up his work in two laws.

- The law of segregation states that an organism has two genes for each trait, one from each parent. The two genes separate during meiosis and come back together in fertilization.

- The law of independent assortment states that alleles separate independently of each other in meiosis.

- A genotype is an organism's combination of genes for a given trait. A phenotype is the appearance that results from the genotype.

- Multiple alleles occur when more than two alleles govern a genetic trait.

- In simple dominance, one allele is dominant to a recessive allele.

- In codominance, both alleles display their form of the trait. In incomplete dominance, both alleles work together to create a new form of the trait.

- Two or more pairs of genes at the same time determine a polygenic trait.

- Sex chromosomes determine the sex of an organism. All other chromosomes are autosomes.

- A human male has an X and a Y sex chromosome. A human female has two X chromosomes.

- A carrier is an organism that carries an allele but does not show the effects of the allele.

- Genes found on the X chromosome are called sex-linked genes.

- Human females can carry a sex-linked trait. Males who inherit a sex-linked allele will show it. Females must have two copies of a sex-linked allele to show it.

Vocabulary

allele, 279
autosome, 292
carrier, 294
codominance, 286
cross-fertilization, 278
dihybrid cross, 280
dominant gene, 279
F_1 generation, 279
F_2 generation, 279
genetics, 284
genotype, 284
hemophilia, 293
heredity, 278
heterozygous, 280
homozygous, 280
hybrid, 279
incomplete dominance, 286
law of independent assortment, 281
law of segregation, 280
linkage map, 287
linked gene, 287
monohybrid cross, 279
multiple allele, 285
P generation, 279
phenotype, 284
pleiotropy, 286
pollen, 278
polygenic trait, 287
Punnett square, 281
recessive gene, 279
sex chromosome, 292
sex-linked inheritance, 295
sex-linked trait, 293
sickle-cell disease, 286
simple dominance, 284
testcross, 285
trait, 278

300 Chapter 10 Inheritance Patterns in Life Cycles

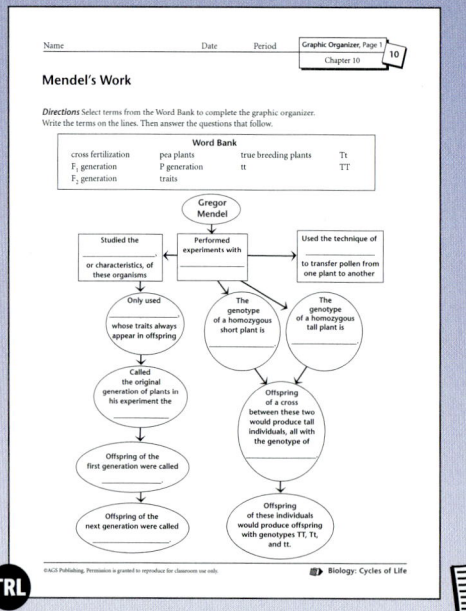

Graphic Organizer 10, pages 1–3

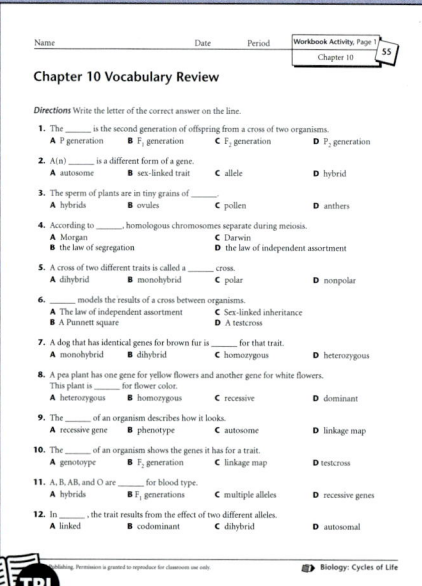

Workbook Activity 55, pages 1–3

300 Chapter 10

Chapter 10 REVIEW

Word Bank
allele
carrier
codominance
dihybrid cross
F_1 generation
F_2 generation
genotype
heredity
heterozygous
homozygous
hybrid
incomplete dominance
law of independent assortment
law of segregation
monohybrid cross
multiple allele
P generation
phenotype
Punnett square
recessive gene
sex chromosome
sex-linked trait

Vocabulary Review

On a sheet of paper, write the word or words from the Word Bank that complete each sentence correctly.

1. The study of how traits are passed through generations is called _____.
2. A(n) _____ involves parents that differ in only one trait. A(n) _____ follows the inheritance of two traits.
3. The original pair of individuals involved in a cross is called the _____.
4. Each different form of the same gene is called a(n) _____.
5. The _____ are the offspring of the original organisms involved in a cross. When this second generation of individuals produces offspring, the new generation is the _____.
6. A(n) _____ will be hidden unless the individual is homozygous.
7. The _____ states that an organism has two alleles for each trait, one from each parent, which come together during fertilization.
8. A(n) _____ is the product of gametes from two different sources.
9. A(n) _____ is the physical form of a trait produced in an organism. A(n) _____ is an organism's combination of genes for a certain trait.
10. According to the _____, alleles separate independently of each other during meiosis.

Review continued on next page

Inheritance Patterns in Life Cycles Chapter 10 301

Review Answers

11. homozygous, heterozygous
12. multiple allele **13.** codominant
14. Punnett square **15.** incomplete dominance **16.** sex-linked trait **17.** sex chromosome **18.** carrier

TEACHER ALERT

In the Chapter Review, the Vocabulary Review activity includes a sample of the chapter's vocabulary terms. The activity will help determine students' understanding of key vocabulary terms and concepts presented in the chapter. Other vocabulary terms used in the chapter are listed below.

autosome	polygenic trait
cross-fertilization	sex-linked inheritance
dominant gene	sickle-cell disease
genetics	simple dominance
hemophilia	testcross
linkage map	trait
linked gene	
pleiotropy	
pollen	

Concept Review

19. C **20.** B **21.** B

Critical Thinking

22. Some traits seemed to disappear in subsequent generations because they were controlled by recessive alleles, which are not expressed in the presence of a dominant allele. **23.** A testcross is a mating between a homozygous recessive individual and an individual with an unknown genotype. Since the homozygous recessive individual has a known genotype, the results of the testcross will reveal whether the unknown individual is homozygous dominant (all offspring will have the dominant trait) or heterozygous (offspring will have either the dominant or recessive trait).

302 Chapter 10

Chapter 10 REVIEW - continued

11. If both alleles of a gene are the same, the gene is _____. If both alleles of a gene are different, the organism is _____.

12. A trait controlled by a(n) _____ has more than two alleles for that gene.

13. When two different alleles come together and both produce their form of the trait, that pair of alleles is in _____.

14. A(n) _____ is a tool used to predict the possible results of a genetic cross.

15. When a trait is controlled by _____, the resulting form is between the dominant and recessive form.

16. A trait determined by the X or Y chromosome is a(n) _____.

17. A(n) _____ determines whether an individual is male or female.

18. For a recessive genetic disorder, a(n) _____ has one dominant normal allele and one recessive allele.

Concept Review

On a sheet of paper, write the letter of the answer that completes each sentence correctly.

19. Recessive traits often reappear in _____.
 A the parental generation **C** the F_2 generation
 B the F_1 generation **D** heterozygous individuals

20. A(n) _____ shows the distances between genes located on the same chromosome.
 A pedigree **C** dihybrid cross
 B linkage map **D** Punnett square

302 Chapter 10 Inheritance Patterns in Life Cycles

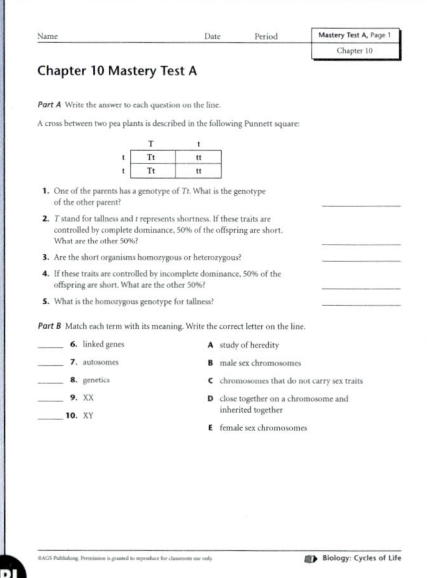
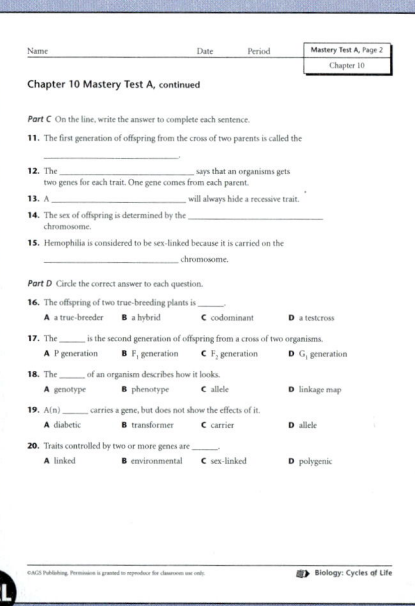

Chapter 10 Mastery Test A, pages 1–3

21. A carrier can transmit a genetic disorder when they pass on _____.

   A one dominant normal allele
   B one recessive abnormal allele
   C one dominant abnormal allele
   D one recessive normal allele

Critical Thinking

On a sheet of paper, write the answers to the following questions. Use complete sentences.

22. In Mendel's studies, why did one form of a trait seem to disappear?
23. How can a testcross determine the unknown genotype of an organism?
24. How can you tell if the inheritance of a trait is sex-linked?
25. A scientist crossed a red-eyed female fruit fly with a white-eyed male fruit fly. All F_1 offspring had red eyes. Then the scientist bred the F_1 flies to create an F_2 generation. All F_2 females were red-eyed. One-half of the F_2 males were red-eyed. One-half were white-eyed. Why were none of the F_2 females white-eyed?

Research and Write

With a partner, prepare a report on Tay-Sachs disease. In addition to using the Internet and the library, interview a doctor or other healthcare professional. Describe the cause of the disease. Explain why it is more common in certain populations.

Test-Taking Tip: Answer all questions you are sure of first. Then go back and answer the others.

---

24. If a trait is sex-linked, expression of the trait depends on the sex of the individual. The pattern of inheritance differs for males and females. If a trait is autosomal, equal numbers of males and females will express the trait.

25. The gene for eye color is sex-linked. The allele for white eyes is recessive. None of the F_2 females were white-eyed because they received the X chromosome with the allele for red eyes from their male F_1 parent.

Research and Write

Have a volunteer read aloud the Research and Write feature. Encourage students to give an oral presentation on Tay-Sachs disease.

Research and Write Answers

Tay-Sachs disease is caused by a defective allele that fails to produce an enzyme needed to break down a lipid found in brain cells. The lipid collects in the brain, causing death in early childhood. Jews of Central European ancestry who mate are at a higher risk of producing a baby with Tay-Sachs disease. Approximately 4 percent of these individuals are carriers.

ALTERNATIVE ASSESSMENT

Alternative Assessment items correlate to the student Goals for Learning at the beginning of this chapter.

- Ask students to write a short paragraph explaining how genes pass traits from parents to offspring.
- Have students describe the role of chromosomes in heredity.
- Have students construct a Punnett Square to identify a pattern of heredity in humans.

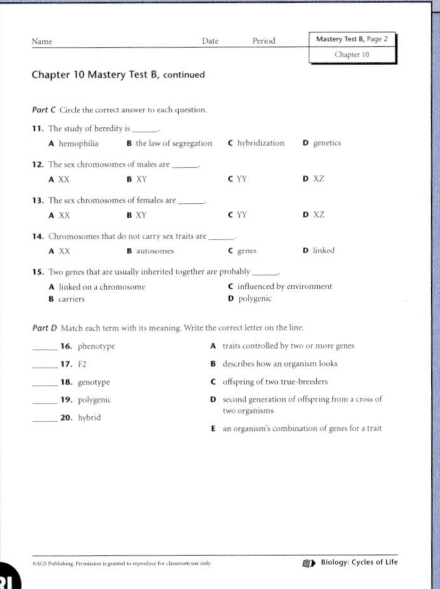

Chapter 10 Mastery Test B, pages 1–3

Chapter 11

Planning Guide
Genetic Information Cycles

	Student Pages	Vocabulary	Lesson Review	Critical-Thinking Questions
Lesson 1 How Are Molecules of Life Involved in Heredity?	306–309	✔	✔	✔
Lesson 2 DNA Replication	310–315	✔	✔	✔
Lesson 3 The Path of Genetic Information	316–320	✔	✔	✔
Lesson 4 What Are Viruses?	321–324	✔	✔	✔
Lesson 5 Using the Path of Genetic Information	325–331	✔	✔	✔
Lesson 6 Natural Defenses Against Disease	332–337	✔	✔	✔

Chapter Activities

Teacher's Resource Library
Community Connection 11:
  Childhood Vaccinations
Graphic Organizer 11:
  DNA Structure

Teacher's Edition
Opener Activity

Assessment Options

Student Text
Chapter 11 Review

Teacher's Resource Library
Chapter 11 Mastery Tests A and B

Teacher's Edition
Chapter 11 Alternative Assessment

Student Text Features									Teaching Strategies						Learning Styles					Teacher's Resource Library			
Achievements in Science	Science at Work	Biology in Your Life	Investigation/Discovery	Biology in the World	Express Lab	Link to	Research and Write	Technology and Society	ELL/ESL Strategy	Background Information	Science Journal	Applications (Home, Career, Community, Global, Environment)	Online Connection	Teacher Alert	Auditory/Verbal	Body/Kinesthetic	Interpersonal/Group Learning	Logical/Mathematical	Visual/Spatial	Workbook Activities	Alternative Workbook Activities	Lab Manual	Self-Study Guide
					307		307		308	306		307						308		56	56	51	✔
			314						312	310				313	312					57	57	52	✔
	318					✔			319	316	317			318						58	58	53	✔
						✔			322	321	323	322					323			59	59		✔
			330			✔		328	327	325	328	327, 328		328					326	60	60	54–55	✔
334		336	337				341		333	332		335	337				334			61–62	61–62		✔

Pronunciation Key

a hat	e let	ī ice	ô order	ù put	sh she	ə { a in about
ā age	ē equal	o hot	oi oil	ü rule	th thin	e in taken
ä far	ėr term	ō open	ou out	ch child	ᴛʜ then	i in pencil
â care	i it	ȯ saw	u cup	ng long	zh measure	o in lemon
						u in circus

Alternative Workbook Activities

The Teacher's Resource Library (TRL) contains a set of lower-level worksheets called Alternative Workbook Activities. These worksheets cover the same content as the regular Workbook Activities but are written at a second-grade reading level.

Skill Track Online

Use Skill Track Online for *Biology: Cycles of Life* to monitor student progress and meet the demands of adequate yearly progress (AYP). Make informed instructional decisions with individual student and class reports of online lesson and chapter assessments. With immediate and ongoing feedback, students will also see what they have learned and where they need more reinforcement and practice.

Chapter at a Glance

Chapter 11: Genetic Information Cycles
pages 304–341

Lessons

1. **How Are Molecules of Life Involved in Heredity?** pages 306–309

2. **DNA Replication** pages 310–315

   Investigation 11 pages 314–315

3. **The Path of Genetic Information** pages 316–320

4. **What Are Viruses?** pages 321–324

5. **Using the Path of Genetic Information** pages 325–331

   Discovery Investigation 11 pages 330–331

6. **Natural Defenses Against Disease** pages 332–337

   Biology in the World page 337

Chapter 11 Summary page 338

Chapter 11 Review pages 339–341

Audio CD

Skill Track Online for Biology: Cycles of Life

Teacher's Resource Library TRL

   Workbook Activities 56–62

   Alternative Workbook Activities 56–62

   Lab Manual 51–55

   Community Connection 11

   Graphic Organizer 11

   Resource File 25–26

   Chapter 11 Self-Study Guide

   Chapter 11 Mastery Tests A and B

(Answer Keys for the Teacher's Resource Library begin on page 675 of the Teacher's Edition. The Materials List for the Lab Manual activities begins on page 720.)

Opener Activity

Show students pictures of a spiral staircase and a spring. Explain that each shows a helix, or coil. The spiral staircase is an example of a double helix, because it contains two coils. Explain that an important biological molecule, DNA, is shaped like a double helix. Have students make models of a double helix, using pipe cleaners. First, have them arrange, bend, and twist pipe cleaners so that they make a flat ladder shape. Then have them twist the ladder so that it is like a spiral staircase. The result is a double helix similar to the shape of DNA.

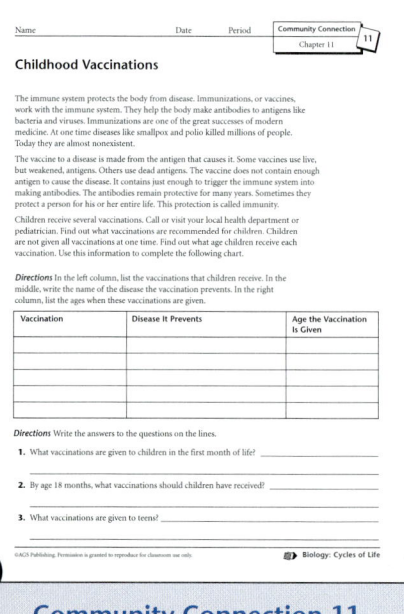

Community Connection 11

Chapter 11
Genetic Information Cycles

Genes that produce traits are part of DNA. Scientists can determine much of the information that DNA stores. Lab images of DNA show patterns of dark and light bands like the ones in the photograph. By interpreting these patterns, scientists have made maps of the genes in chromosomes for many living things. In Chapter 11, you will learn about DNA and how it transmits genetic information. You will find out how scientists use knowledge of DNA to understand and treat certain diseases.

Organize Your Thoughts

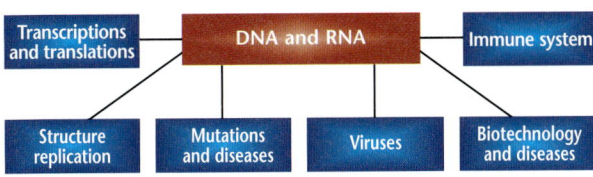

Goals for Learning

♦ To describe the structure and function of DNA
♦ To identify that viruses are special pieces of DNA
♦ To explain some changes in DNA that can lead to health problems
♦ To explain that organisms have systems to fight diseases

Introducing the Chapter

Have students discuss what they already know about heredity, genetics, and DNA. Ask students: What function do you think DNA performs in cells? Explain that the DNA in each of their cells stores information for coding more than 20,000 proteins. Have students read the Goals for Learning and note that in this chapter, they will learn about the nucleic acids such as DNA and RNA in relation to inheritable traits, viruses, fighting disease, and biotechnology.

Have students read the Goals for Learning again. Have them write questions about what they want to find out about genetic information cycles. For example, students might ask "What roles do DNA and RNA play in the body?" or "How is the body affected by disease, and how does it respond to disease?" Students can use their questions to help set a purpose for reading.

Notes and Math Tips

Ask volunteers to read the notes and math tips that appear in the margins throughout the chapter. Then discuss them with the class.

TEACHER'S RESOURCE

The AGS Publishing Teaching Strategies in Science Transparencies may be used with this chapter. The transparencies add an interactive dimension to expand and enhance the *Biology: Cycles of Life* program content.

CAREER INTEREST INVENTORY

The AGS Publishing Harrington-O'Shea Career Decision-Making System-Revised (CDM) may be used with this chapter. Students can use the CDM to explore their interests and identify careers. The CDM defines career areas that are indicated by students' responses on the inventory.

Lesson at a Glance

Chapter 11 Lesson 1

Overview In this lesson, students learn about the structure and base pairing of nucleic acids such as DNA and RNA.

Objectives

- To describe the structure of nucleotides
- To explain the structure of a DNA molecule
- To explain complementary base pairing

Student Pages 306–309

Teacher's Resource Library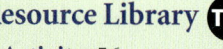

Workbook Activity 56

Alternative Workbook Activity 56

Lab Manual 51

Resource File 25

Vocabulary

complementary base pairing	nitrogenous base
cytosine (C)	sugar-phosphate backbone
guanine (G)	thymine (T)
	uracil (U)

Have students make a graphic organizer using all of the vocabulary terms and the following connecting phrases: parts of nucleotides include, held together by, between, which is double ringed, which is single ringed, found only in RNA, found only in DNA. (for example: parts of nucleotides include → sugar-phosphate backbone, nitrogenous base → held together by → complimentary base pairing → between → guanine [→ which is double ringed], cytosine [→ which is single ringed])

Background Information

Energy is required to break the hydrogen bonds between the nitrogenous bases that hold the two strands of DNA together. When you heat samples of DNA, the added energy causes the hydrogen bonds to break and the strands to come apart. The exposed nitrogenous bases can then pair with the complementary nitrogenous bases of free nucleotides, which can bond together to form a second strand when

306 Chapter 11

Lesson 1 How Are Molecules of Life Involved in Heredity?

Objectives

After reading this lesson, you should be able to

- describe the structure of nucleotides
- explain the structure of a DNA molecule
- explain complimentary base pairing

Sugar-phosphate backbone
The negatively charged backbone of a nucleic acid strand

Nitrogenous base
A nitrogen-containing molecule attached to a nucleotide

Guanine (G)
A double-ringed nitrogenous base found in DNA and RNA

As you know, traits are inherited from parents through the activities of chromosomes in cells. A trait is a characteristic of an organism. DNA stores information about an organism's traits. Recall that chromosomes are sections of DNA. Chromosomes contain genes for traits. An allele is one of several forms that a particular gene can take. Alleles differ slightly in their molecular structure. These slight differences determine the traits that an organism inherits. DNA stores the genetic information of an organism.

The Parts of DNA

To understand how DNA instructs life, let's look at the parts of DNA. Remember that DNA is a nucleic acid. It is made up of many smaller molecules called nucleotides. Nucleotides have three parts. One part is a sugar molecule. DNA has the sugar deoxyribose. RNA, the other nucleic acid, has the sugar ribose. Both sugar molecules have five carbon atoms along with oxygen and hydrogen atoms.

Nucleotides also have a phosphate group. This group is important for creating nucleic acid strands. The phosphate group of one nucleotide forms a covalent bond with the sugar of another nucleotide. The repeating pattern of bonded nucleotides forms a long strand called a **sugar-phosphate backbone.** The phosphate groups are negatively charged. This causes the nucleic acid strand to have a negative charge.

Nucleotides also have a **nitrogenous base.** The nitrogenous base is a molecule made of carbon, nitrogen, hydrogen, and oxygen. It is attached to the sugar of the nucleotide. Study the base structures in Figure 11.1.1. The double-ringed bases are adenine (A) and **guanine (G).** The single-ringed bases are **thymine (T), cytosine (C),** and **uracil (U).** DNA nucleotides have a phosphate group, deoxyribose, and A, G, C, or T. RNA nucleotides have a phosphate group, ribose, and A, G, C, or U.

306 Chapter 11 Genetic Information Cycles

---

the sample is cooled again. The result is two identical molecules of DNA. The process can be repeated many times, producing many copies of DNA. This technique is called polymerase chain reaction, or PCR. PCR is used to make great quantities of DNA from a very small sample so that the DNA can be analyzed.

Figure 11.1.1 *There are five nitrogenous bases found in DNA and RNA.*

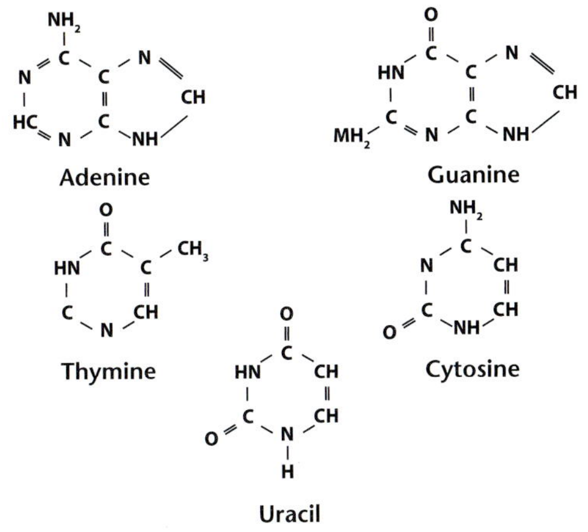

Thymine (T)

A single-ringed nitrogenous base found in DNA

Cytosine (C)

A single-ringed nitrogenous base found in DNA and RNA

Uracil (U)

A single-ringed nitrogenous base found only in RNA

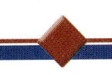

James Watson and Francis Crick used tin and wire to make DNA models. Their research earned them the Nobel Prize.

The Discovery of DNA's Structure

For many years, scientists wanted to know the structure of DNA. In 1949, Austrian scientist Erwin Chargraff researched the DNA of many organisms. He found the amount of adenine always equaled the amount of thymine. He also found that the amount of guanine always equaled the amount of cytosine.

In the early 1950s, British scientists Rosalind Franklin and Maurice Wilkins took X-ray photographs of DNA. Their photographs did not show details of the structure. However, they did show that the shape of DNA was a helix.

Meanwhile, British scientists James Watson and Francis Crick were also trying to determine the structure of DNA. They built many models. None worked. Then they saw one of Franklin's X-ray photographs. Using this photograph, Watson and Crick created a new model of DNA. Their model was two strands of nucleotides that wound around each other. The strands formed a double helix. A double helix is a twisted shape like a spiral staircase. Watson and Crick put the sugar-phosphate backbone on the outside of the double helix. They put the nitrogenous bases on the inside.

Research and Write

Prepare a report on the research of Rosalind Franklin. Describe how her X-ray studies of DNA helped Watson and Crick discover its structure.

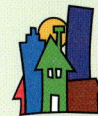

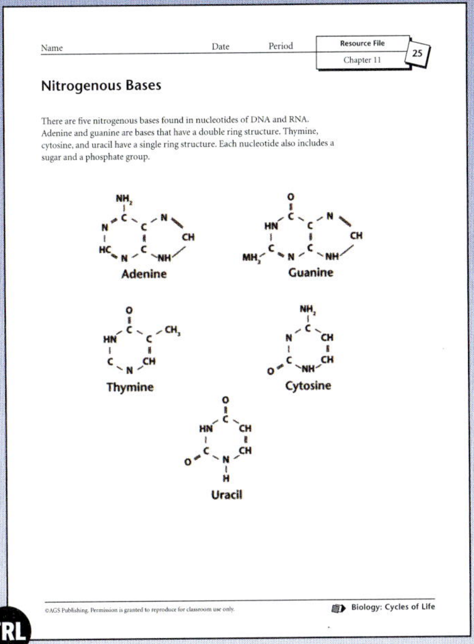

1 Warm-Up Activity

Have students read and perform the Express Lab on page 308. Have students compare the percentages of each type of base within one organism. Explain that if certain bases pair only with each other, then there should be similar percentages of each base in a pair.

Express Lab Answers

1. Cytosine and thymine are single-ringed bases. Adenine and guanine are double-ringed bases. **2.** The proportions vary slightly among different living things, but A and T, and also G and C, are always present in the same relative amounts. This suggests that DNA has the same fundamental structure in all living things.

2 Teaching the Lesson

Help students compose a mnemonic device to remember which nitrogenous bases pair. For example, "**C**ows like **G**rass" might help them remember that **C**ytosine pairs with **G**uanine. "**A**lligators have **T**eeth and **U**se them" might help students remember that **A**denine pairs with **T**hymine and **U**racil.

3 Reinforce and Extend

Research and Write

Have students use the library or Internet to find out more about the life and work of Rosalind Franklin. Have them make a timeline of the discoveries associated with her and her contemporaries' work. Students might find it interesting to know that she died before Watson and Crick were awarded the Nobel prize, which is awarded only to living recipients. Students may wish to do this research individually, in pairs, or in small groups. Suggest that students share their research with the class as a written report, in a presentation using visual or audio aids, or as part of an informative poster.

At Home

Have students research how to isolate DNA by using materials in their kitchen. Simple procedures include common materials such as salt, water, liquid detergent, meat tenderizer, and rubbing alcohol to isolate DNA from onions, liver, or spinach. Remind students to use the same safety precautions at home that they would use in the classroom laboratory.

Name Date Period — Resource File 25, Chapter 11

Nitrogenous Bases

There are five nitrogenous bases found in nucleotides of DNA and RNA. Adenine and guanine are bases that have a double ring structure. Thymine, cytosine, and uracil have a single ring structure. Each nucleotide also includes a sugar and a phosphate group.

Adenine

Guanine

Thymine

Cytosine

Uracil

©AGS Publishing. Permission is granted to reproduce for classroom use only. Biology: Cycles of Life

TRL

Resource File 25

ELL/ESL STRATEGY

Language Objective: To summarize

Have students form groups that include both students learning English and students with strong English skills. Have each group create an oral presentation that summarizes the work of one of the scientists or scientific teams mentioned in the lesson. Students may wish to expand upon the information given in the lesson by going to the library or using the Internet to find out more about the scientists Erwin Chargaff, James Watson and Francis Crick, and Maurice Wilkins and Rosalind Franklin. Have students include visual aids when they give their presentations to the class.

LEARNING STYLES

Logical/Mathematical

Have students imagine that they are researching a fictitious alien species whose DNA has six kinds of nitrogenous bases. Write on the board the following percentages for each base: silline 13.1%, wackine 22.8%, fooline 12.9%, goofine 23.1%, ludicrine 13.9%, ridiculine 14.2%. Have students use Chargaff's rule as a model to determine which nitrogenous bases pair. *(Silline pairs with fooline, wackine pairs with goofine, and ludicrine pairs with ridiculine.)*

Complementary base pairing
The pairing of the nitrogenous bases adenine to thymine and cytosine to guanine in DNA strands

Watson and Crick thought the nitrogenous bases on one strand formed hydrogen bonds with nitrogenous bases on the other strand. The hydrogen bonds kept the two strands of nucleotides the same distance apart. Watson and Crick wondered how the bases were paired between the two strands. They knew the pairings were due to the size of the bases and the forming of hydrogen bonds.

Watson and Crick turned to Chargaff's discovery. They found that the nitrogenous bases follow a pattern called **complementary base pairing.** Each base always pairs with its complement base. Adenine in one strand always pairs with thymine in the other strand. Guanine always pairs with cytosine. The pairing of a single-ringed base with a double-ringed base maintains the same distance between strands. The sequence of nucleotides along the length of each DNA strand can vary. Watson and Crick published their model in 1953. It was a milestone in biology.

Express Lab 11

Materials
- paper
- pen

Procedure
Erwin Chargaff analyzed the amounts of nitrogenous bases in the DNA of various organisms. Some of his results are shown in the table below.

Analysis
1. Which nitrogenous bases are single-ringed bases? Which are double-ringed bases?
2. How do Chargaff's results vary? What do his results suggest about DNA?

Organism	Adenine	Guanine	Cytosine	Thymine
Human	30.4%	19.6%	19.9%	30.1%
Ox	29.0%	21.2%	21.2%	28.7%
Sea urchin	32.8%	17.7%	17.3%	32.1%

308 Chapter 11 Genetic Information Cycles

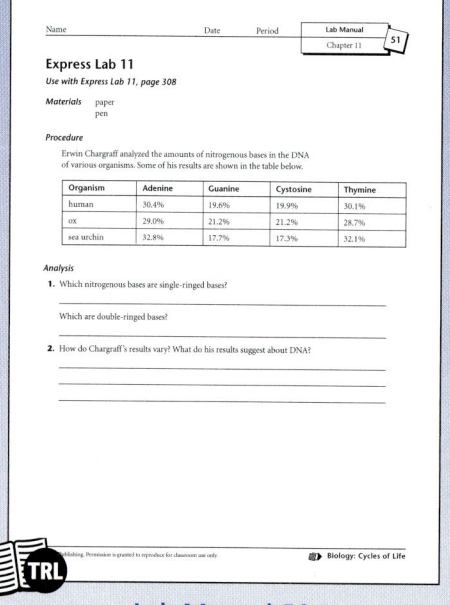

Lesson 1 REVIEW

On a sheet of paper, write the word or words in parentheses that complete each statement correctly.

1. DNA contains the sugar _____ (deoxyribose, ribose, guanine), and RNA contains the sugar _____ (guanine, deoxyribose, ribose).
2. Complementary pairing of _____ (phosphate groups, nitrogenous bases, sugars) ensures that the strands of DNA maintain an even distance.
3. In DNA, adenine pairs with _____ (thymine, ribose, cytosine) guanine pairs with _____ (thymine, guanine, cytosine).

On a sheet of paper, write the letter of the answer that completes each sentence correctly.

4. In RNA, the base _____ replaces thymine.
   A uracil B guanine C adenine D cytosine
5. A molecule of DNA contains two _____.
   A phosphate groups C sugar molecules
   B nitrogenous bases D nucleotide chains
6. A nucleotide contains each of the following except a(n) _____.
   A nitrogenous base C amino acid
   B sugar molecule D phosphate group

Critical Thinking

On a sheet of paper, write the answers to the following questions. Use complete sentences.

7. What is the role of nucleotides in DNA structure?
8. Explain how DNA resembles a twisted ladder.
9. What is complementary base pairing?
10. How did the work of other scientists help Watson and Crick determine the structure of DNA?

Lesson 1 Review Answers

1. deoxyribose, ribose **2.** nitrogenous bases **3.** thymine, cytosine **4.** A **5.** D **6.** C **7.** Nucleotides are the building blocks of DNA structure. **8.** DNA resembles a twisted ladder because it consists of two nucleotide chains, each with a sugar-phosphate backbone. Pairs of nitrogenous bases make the rungs of the ladder. **9.** Complementary base pairing is the matchup between adenine and thymine and between cytosine and guanine. **10.** After viewing the research of other scientists, Watson and Crick were able to determine what was missing from their models. From the photographs of DNA taken by Rosalind Franklin and Maurice Wilkens, they learned that the shape of DNA was a helix. From Erwin Chargaff's research, they learned how the bases were paired.

Portfolio Assessment

Sample items include:
- Graphic organizer from Vocabulary
- Report on Rosalind Franklin from Research and Write
- Write-up from At Home
- Lesson 1 Review answers

LAB ACTIVITIES

Chapter 11 has Investigation and Discovery Investigation lab activities. Two additional lab activities for Chapter 11 appear in the Biology: Cycles of Life Lab Manual and on the Teacher's Resource Library CD-ROM.

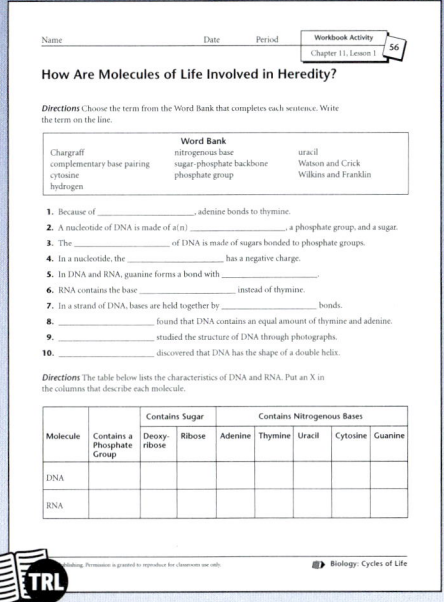

Workbook Activity 56

Lesson at a Glance

Chapter 11 Lesson 2

Overview In this lesson, students learn about how DNA is replicated in prokaryotes and eukaryotes.

Objectives
- To explain semi-conservative replication
- To compare prokaryotic and eukaryotic replication
- To describe enzymes involved in DNA replication

Student Pages 310–315

Teacher's Resource Library TRL

Workbook Activity 57
Alternative Workbook Activity 57
Lab Manual 52
Resource File 26

Vocabulary

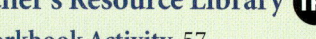

bacteriophage
DNA ligase
DNA polymerase
lagging strand
leading strand
marker
origin of replication
replication
replication bubble
replication fork
semi-conservative replication
template
virus

Direct students to the diagram of DNA replication on page 312. Point out on the diagram the origin of replication, replication bubble, replication fork, lagging strand, and leading strand. Have students make drawings that compare the common words within each vocabulary term. For example, students might draw a picture that compares the tines of a fork or a fork in the road to the two strands in the replication fork.

Background Information

Before Meselson and Stahl's experiments, scientists proposed that DNA could replicate in one of three ways: conservative replication, semi-conservative replication, or dispersive replication. In conservative replication, the new DNA molecule would be made up of entirely new nucleotides in both strands, while the original molecule would contain only original nucleotides. In semi-conservative replication, each of the resulting DNA molecules is made up of a strand of new nucleotides and a strand of the original nucleotides. In dispersive replication, both DNA molecules would be made up of strands that contained both new nucleotides and some of the original nucleotides.

Meselson and Stahl replicated DNA in the presence of new nucleotides that contained a heavy isotope of nitrogen. When they analyzed the DNA resulting from the first replication, they found molecules of only one weight. The molecules each contained a strand of heavy DNA and a strand of light DNA, a result of semi-conservative replication. They knew conservative replication had not occurred, because it would have resulted in a mix of heavier new molecules and lighter original molecules. They knew the DNA was not replicated through dispersive replication, because after a second replication, some of the strands were made entirely from heavy nucleotides.

310 Chapter 11

Lesson 2 DNA Replication

Objectives

After reading this lesson, you should be able to
- explain semi-conservative replication
- compare prokaryotic and eukaryotic replication
- describe enzymes involved in DNA replication

Replication
The process DNA uses to copy itself

Bacteriophage
A virus that infects bacteria

Virus
A type of germ that is not living

Marker
A material, such as an atom, used to mark an item

Semi-conservative replication
A model of DNA replication in which an old strand of DNA is used to make a new strand of DNA

The process of copying DNA in a cell is called **replication**. Scientists discovered this process in the 1950s.

The Experiments of Hershey and Chase

How did scientists learn that DNA transferred information from parents to offspring? Until the 1950s, some scientists thought proteins were the genetic material. Other scientists thought that DNA was the genetic material.

To find out, American scientists Alfred Hershey and Martha Chase ran experiments in 1952. They used **bacteriophages** containing both DNA and protein. Bacteriophages are **viruses** that infect bacteria. You will learn more about viruses in Lesson 4.

Hershey and Chase put special atoms called **markers** into the DNA and protein of the viruses. The markers identified the DNA and the protein. Viruses with the marked atoms infected bacteria. The bacteria reproduced. The offspring bacteria had DNA and proteins. However, only the DNA contained markers. The experiments of Hershey and Chase showed that DNA passed from parent to offspring.

DNA as a Template

Scientists wondered how instructions in DNA were passed from parents to offspring. Watson and Crick thought that complementary base pairing was important. Recall that complementary base pairing in DNA is the matching of single-ringed bases with double-ringed bases.

American scientists Matthew Meselson and Franklin Stahl proved this theory during 1957 and 1958. They also showed that DNA is copied through **semi-conservative replication**. In this process, the original molecule serves as a **template** for making new DNA molecules. A template is a pattern used for copying.

310 Chapter 11 Genetic Information Cycles

Template
A pattern used for copying

Origin of replication
A site where DNA replication begins

Replication bubble
An area in which DNA replication is occurring with both strands unwound and being used as templates

Replication fork
The end of a replication bubble in which DNA polymerase is actively adding nucleotide bases to a new strand

DNA polymerase
An enzyme that adds new nucleotide bases to a new strand during DNA replication

While reproducing, the double helix unwinds. The strands separate. Each old strand becomes a template for a new strand. Remember that in DNA, adenine pairs with thymine, and guanine pairs with cytosine. As new nucleotides form and bond, they make a new strand to complement the old strand.

DNA replication creates two DNA molecules from the unwound original molecule. Each new DNA molecule contains one old strand and one new strand. This makes the two DNA molecules semi-conservative. Using this method, the instructions in DNA can be copied many times.

How DNA Replicates

DNA replication begins in areas of DNA molecules called **origins of replication.** These areas have nucleotide bases arranged in certain orders called sequences. Sequences of bases are the signals for all processes involving DNA. Each molecule of DNA has several origins of replication.

Recall from Chapter 9 that chromosomes reproduce in S phase. Each chromosome is made of one piece of DNA and proteins. In S phase, the DNA molecule unwinds at each sequence. As the strands unwind, they create **replication bubbles.** Several bubbles are on every DNA molecule during replication. The bubbles grow on each side as new strands are made inside. The growing bubbles combine into larger bubbles. All the bubbles grow together and create two new molecules of DNA.

In the replication bubbles, enzymes help in DNA replication. To begin, enzymes unwind DNA at the origin of replication. This creates a small replication bubble. There is a **replication fork** on each side of the bubble. At the replication fork, new nucleotide bases attach, creating the new strand. **DNA polymerase,** an enzyme, helps bond the new nucleotides. These nucleotides are complementary to the nucleotides on the template strand.

Genetic Information Cycles Chapter 11 311

Warm-Up Activity

Show students two long strips of Velcro® that are stuck together. Explain that together they represent a single molecule of DNA. Pull the strips apart at one end and demonstrate how two new DNA molecules can be produced by adding additional strips of Velcro to the unwound portions of the strip. Continue pulling apart the original strands and adding the new strands until you have two complete DNA molecules. Explain that the two new molecules of DNA each contain a strand from the original molecule. Demonstrate the replication bubble by showing an origin of replication that is in the center of the strips, rather than at one of the ends.

Teaching the Lesson

Have students use modeling clay to demonstrate semi-conservative replication. They should arrange the clay on two strips of paper that can be easily pulled apart to separate the model DNA strands. Have them use green clay to make two long ropes that represent the sugar-phosphate backbone of a single DNA molecule with two strands. Then have them make small balls of clay to represent the nitrogenous bases: red (cytosine), blue (thymine), yellow (adenine), and white (guanine). Students can use their knowledge from Lesson 1 to show how the bases pair. Have them model the process of replication by building a second strand onto each of the original strands. Explain that semi-conservative means that half (*semi-*) of the DNA is saved (conserved) to be used in the new molecule. Have students draw what they have modeled with the clay.

Reinforce and Extend

PRONUNCIATION GUIDE

Use the pronunciation shown here to help students pronounce a difficult word in this lesson. Refer to the pronunciation key on the Chapter Planning Guide for the sounds of the symbols.

polymerase (pə lim′ə rās)

Genetic Information Cycles 311

ELL/ESL Strategy

Language Objective: To explain how to use a model

Have students form pairs composed of a student learning English and a student with strong English skills. Provide students with construction paper, scissors, and tape. Have students devise a model of DNA replication, using the materials. Have one student use the model to explain what happens at the leading strand, and have the other student explain what happens at the lagging strand. Remind students to illustrate the roles of DNA polymerase and DNA ligase in their explanations. They may choose not to represent the nitrogenous bases in great detail. Instead have them focus on the differences in the ways that the strands are built.

Learning Styles

Auditory/Verbal

Have students write jokes that include terms from the lesson. *(For example: Why did the geneticist call the waiter to the table? He needed a new replication fork.)* Encourage students to share their jokes with the class and follow up each joke with an explanation of the actual definition of the term or concept in the joke.

Leading strand
The side of the replication fork where the newly made DNA is in one piece

Lagging strand
The side of the replication fork where the newly made DNA is in several small pieces

DNA ligase
An enzyme that bonds all pieces of newly made DNA to make one strand

DNA polymerase uses both old strands as templates. It bonds the phosphate group of a new nucleotide to the sugar of the last nucleotide in a growing strand. DNA polymerase adds bases in only one direction. At each replication fork, one new strand is made as one piece. This side of the fork is called the **leading strand.** The other side of the fork, called the **lagging strand,** is made from many small pieces of DNA.

As DNA polymerase adds bases, the new strand at each fork becomes longer. The replication bubbles grow and combine. **DNA ligase,** an enzyme, connects the pieces of the new DNA strand. DNA ligase makes sugar-phosphate bonds between nucleotides. When all the small pieces of DNA have been bonded together, two new DNA double helixes are created. These two new strands have the same sequence of nucleotides. Figure 11.2.1 shows DNA replication.

DNA replication occurs constantly in organisms. DNA is replicated every time a cell divides. Replication produces exact copies that are passed to new cells through mitosis or meiosis. The cycle of division, growth, and reproduction keeps life going. It allows genetic information to be passed on.

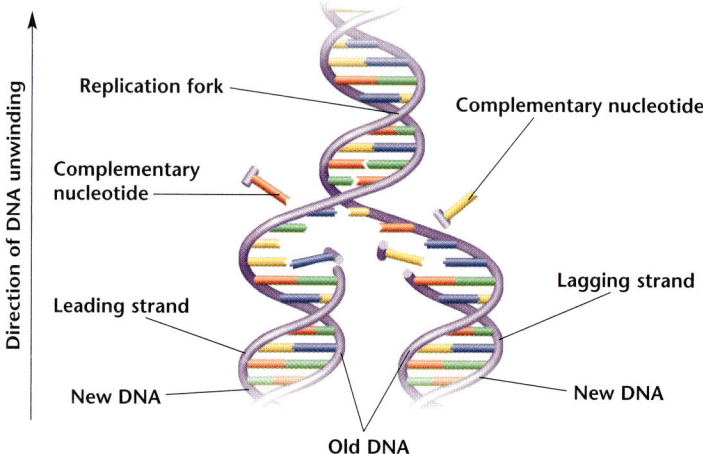

Figure 11.2.1 DNA replication occurs constantly in organisms.

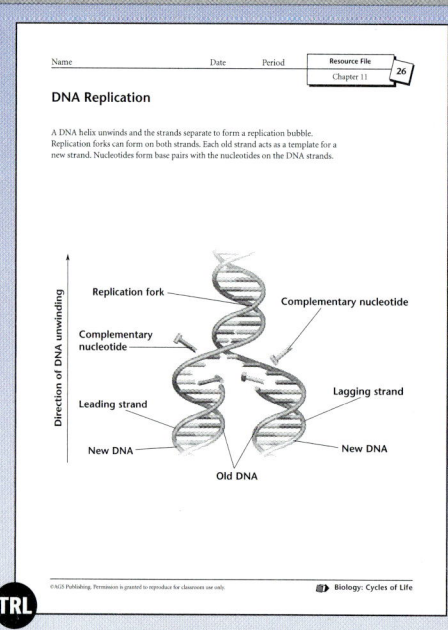

Resource File 26

Lesson 2 REVIEW

Word Bank
DNA
DNA polymerase
viruses

On a sheet of a paper, write the word or words from the Word Bank that complete each sentence correctly.

1. During replication, an enzyme called _____ adds new nucleotide bases to the new DNA strand.
2. Experiments performed by Hershey and Chase showed that _____ is passed from parent to offspring.
3. Bacteriophages are _____ that infect bacteria.

On a sheet of paper, write the letter of the answer that completes each sentence correctly.

4. During replication, DNA _____.
   - **A** is used to make RNA
   - **C** directs protein synthesis
   - **B** remains intact
   - **D** is copied

5. When DNA is replicated, the original molecule serves as a(n) _____.
   - **A** template
   - **B** replication fork
   - **C** enzyme
   - **D** marker

6. Before DNA replication can begin, the DNA must _____.
   - **A** undergo translation
   - **C** join with a ribosome
   - **B** unwind
   - **D** leave the nucleus

Critical Thinking

On a sheet of paper, write the answers to the following questions. Use complete sentences.

7. What is semi-conservative replication?
8. When does DNA replication occur?
9. What happens at a replication fork?
10. Compare and contrast the roles of DNA polymerase and DNA ligase.

Genetic Information Cycles Chapter 11 313

Lesson 2 Review Answers

1. DNA polymerase **2.** DNA **3.** viruses **4.** D **5.** A **6.** B **7.** Semi-conservative replication is DNA replication in which one old chain of DNA is used as a model for a new chain. Thus, half of a new molecule of DNA is new and half is old. **8.** DNA replication occurs whenever mitosis or meiosis takes place. **9.** In DNA replication, a replication fork is the site of attachment for new bases. **10.** DNA polymerase helps bond new nucleotides to the growing strand. DNA ligase makes the sugar-phosphate bonds along the sides of the new DNA strand.

Portfolio Assessment

Sample items include:
- Drawings from Teaching the Lesson
- Models from ELL/ESL Strategy
- Jokes from Learning Styles Auditory/Verbal
- Lesson 2 Review answers

TEACHER ALERT

Some students will want to know why the building of DNA strands is different at the leading and lagging strand. Explain that the sugar-phosphate backbone of DNA is directional. Each nucleotide can be added in only one direction on a strand, because the enzymes can make the bond only between an open sugar on the existing strand and a phosphate group on the free nucleotide. A molecule of DNA polymerase, the enzyme that controls the addition of nucleotides, attaches to each strand at the replication fork. As the fork moves down the molecule, the DNA polymerase on the leading strand continues adding in a single direction with the fork. The DNA polymerase on the lagging strand adds in the direction opposite the fork. As the fork moves down the molecule, the DNA polymerase on the lagging strand must stop after a short while and reattach closer to the fork. The addition of nucleotides in short pieces on the lagging strand is called discontinuous synthesis.

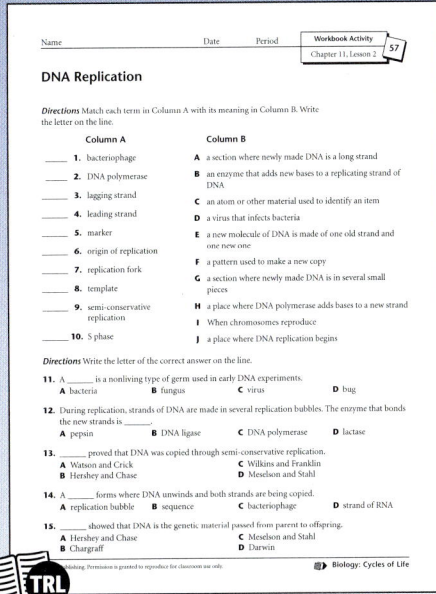

Workbook Activity 57

Genetic Information Cycles 313

Investigation 11

Encourage students to read the investigation steps. Discuss questions they may have before beginning the investigation.

Objectives

- To list the three components of a nucleotide
- To group nitrogenous bases in pairs according to the rules of complementary base pairing
- To construct a model of the DNA double helix

Skills

Using models, comparing and contrasting, interpreting visuals, recognizing patterns, analyzing data, drawing conclusions

Background

Simple DNA models provide concrete examples that will help students later visualize abstract processes such as DNA replication, transcription, and translation. Using models, students will learn that each DNA nucleotide is made of a sugar called deoxyribose, a phosphate group, and one of four different nitrogenous bases.

Time Frame

One class period

Procedure

- Have students work in groups.
- Provide each group with a large sheet of construction paper to serve as a background for their DNA model.
- Use the analogy of a ladder to remind students that the DNA helix is a consistent width along its entire length.
- Students will need six different colors for the different parts of each DNA model. Suggested colors are listed below. To de-emphasize the sugar-phosphate backbone, you may wish to use white, gray, or black for the sugars and the phosphates. To help students learn the rules of nucleotide pairing, use warm colors for A and T and cool colors for C and G.

  Sugar (deoxyribose) = color #1
  Phosphate group = color #2
  Thymine = color #3 (red)
  Cytosine = color #4 (blue)

INVESTIGATION 11

Materials
- safety goggles
- lab coat or apron
- paper models for sugar, phosphate group, cytosine (C), thymine (T), adenine (A), guanine (G)
- large sheet of paper
- tape
- wooden craft sticks
- ruler

Modeling DNA

DNA is made of two strands of nucleotides arranged in the form of a double helix. Each nucleotide is made of a sugar called deoxyribose, a phosphate group, and one of four nitrogenous bases.

Procedure

1. Put on safety goggles and a lab coat or apron.
2. Place a large sheet of paper on your desk. The paper represents the width of a DNA molecule.
3. Select a model of deoxyribose and a model of a phosphate group. Position them along one side of the paper. Show how they form the sugar-phosphate backbone of one strand of the double helix. Tape them to the paper.

314   Chapter 11   Genetic Information Cycles

Adenine = color #5 (yellow)
Guanine = color #6 (green)

- You may wish to use die-cut paper cutouts in the following shapes: circle (phosphate group), pentagon (deoxyribose), and hexagon (thymine, cytosine). Use a hexagon taped to a pentagon of the same color to represent a double-ring base (adenine or guanine).
- Both of the double-ring bases (adenine and guanine) must be the same size as each other.
- The two single-ring bases (thymine and cytosine) must be the same size as each other.
- You may substitute plastic coffee stir sticks for wooden craft sticks.

Safety Alert

- Instruct students to dispose of broken craft sticks with sharp edges.

4. Select two nitrogenous bases for your first base pair. Follow the rules of complementary base pairing. Tape one base to the sugar of one strand. Tape the second base to the other sugar.

5. Position wooden craft sticks to represent hydrogen bonds between the bases. **Safety Alert: Broken craft sticks may have sharp edges. Do not use them.**

6. Select another sugar model and phosphate group model. Position them along the other side of the paper. They represent the second side of the sugar-phosphate backbone of the second strand. Be sure the sugars are directly across from each other. Then tape down the models to the paper.

7. Repeat Steps 2 through 6, adding two more nitrogenous bases to your DNA molecule.

8. Use a ruler to measure the widths of the two sets of base pairs in your model. Record your data.

Cleanup/Disposal
When you are finished, put away the tape and ruler.

Analysis
1. Are the two sets of base pairs in your model equal in width? Explain your answer.
2. Which nitrogenous bases can be correctly paired?

Conclusions
1. A DNA double helix is the same width throughout. What does this suggest about base pairing?
2. Write a new question about DNA structure that you could explore in another investigation.

Explore Further
Combine your finished model with other students' models to create a longer double helix.

Cleanup/Disposal
Instruct students in cleanup and disposal of materials.

Results
Help students see that a double-ring base must always be paired with a single-ring base. Adenine and thymine are always paired together. Guanine and cytosine are always paired together. If students mistakenly pair two double-ring bases or two single-ring bases, their DNA ladder will be too wide or too narrow.

Analysis Answers
1. Both sets of base pairs are approximately equal in width. This is because a double-ring base can pair only with a single-ring base.
2. Adenine and thymine are always paired together. Guanine and cytosine are always paired together.

Conclusions Answers
1. Complementary base pairing ensures that a DNA double helix is the same width throughout, since a double-ring base always pairs with a single-ring base.
2. Answers will vary. Students may wish to explore the relationship between DNA structure and proteins, which would set the stage for Lesson 3.

Explore Further Answers
Encourage students to join their base pairs with those of another group to lengthen the DNA molecule. Make sure that both groups follow the rules of complementary base pairing.

Assessment
You might include the following items from this investigation in student portfolios:
- Answers to Analysis and Conclusions questions
- Student models of a longer double helix

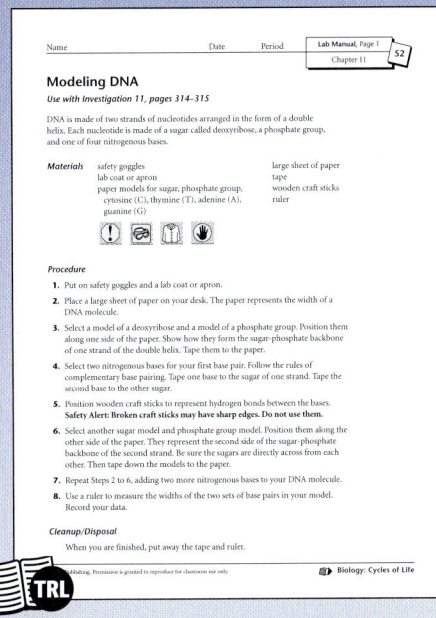

Lab Manual 52, pages 1–2

Lesson at a Glance

Chapter 11 Lesson 3

Overview In this lesson, students learn about the roles of different types of RNA in the production of proteins, using DNA as a template and the mutations that can result when DNA is translated improperly.

Objectives

- To describe transcription and RNA splicing
- To compare the three types of RNA
- To describe translation
- To list examples of mutations

Student Pages 316–320

Teacher's Resource Library

Workbook Activity 58

Alternative Workbook Activity 58

Lab Manual 53

Vocabulary

anticodon	ribosomal RNA
deletion	(rRNA)
exon	RNA polymerase
genetic code	RNA splicing
insertion	substitution
intron	terminator
messenger RNA	transcription
(mRNA)	transfer RNA
mutagen	(tRNA)
mutation	translation
promoter	

Have students use a dictionary to look up the meanings of common words within the vocabulary terms, such as *deletion, insertion, messenger, promoter, substitution, terminator, transcription,* and *translation*. Then have them relate the meaning of the word in a day-to-day context with the biological meaning associated with DNA and protein synthesis. For example, a transcription is a written copy of an audio recording. In biology, transcription is the process of making an RNA copy of the information encoded in DNA. Both meanings have to do with making a copy of something.

Lesson 3   The Path of Genetic Information

Objectives

After reading this lesson, you should be able to

- describe transcription and RNA splicing
- compare the three types of RNA
- describe translation
- list examples of mutations

Transcription
The creation of an RNA molecule using the bases in a DNA molecule as a template

Translation
The creation of a protein using the bases in an RNA molecule as a template

RNA polymerase
An enzyme that adds RNA nucleotides to a new RNA molecule

Messenger RNA (mRNA)
An RNA molecule that carries instructions for the order of amino acids in a protein

Instructions in DNA are found in the order of its nitrogenous bases. Genes are certain sequences of DNA found on the chromosomes. Bases in these sequences are a code. A cell reads the code and gives directions to make proteins. These proteins become enzymes or other structures that allow life to continue.

To read the code in DNA, a cell uses RNA, enzymes, and other molecules. Two processes happen when a cell reads the instructions in DNA: **transcription** and **translation.** Through these processes, genetic information flows from DNA to RNA to protein.

Transcription and RNA Splicing

The first step in making a protein is the reading of DNA. This step is called transcription. It happens inside the nucleus of a cell. Transcription produces complementary RNA to DNA sequences. When a cell needs to make a protein, it uses **RNA polymerase,** an enzyme. RNA polymerase helps make a molecule of **messenger RNA,** also called mRNA.

Messenger RNA helps interpret, or read, the DNA code. To make messenger RNA, RNA polymerase attaches to specific sequences called **promoters.** Promoters are located at the beginning of genes. RNA polymerase attaches to the promoter sequence on one DNA strand. The promoter sequence determines which strand goes through transcription.

After RNA polymerase attaches to the promoter sequence, it unwinds the DNA. Then it begins creating an RNA strand. RNA polymerase moves down the DNA. It brings in RNA nucleotides complementary to the DNA nucleotides. Finally, RNA polymerase comes to a **terminator** in DNA. Terminator sequences stop RNA polymerase and transcription. The new strand of mRNA is released. The new mRNA is an RNA copy of the DNA gene.

316   *Chapter 11 Genetic Information Cycles*

Background Information

Because introns are removed after transcription, the mRNA copy of a gene can be significantly shorter than the segment of DNA that contains the gene. Though only the exons code for proteins, scientists hypothesize that introns do serve a purpose. They may allow multiple proteins to be made from the same gene by the removal of some introns at certain times and other introns at other times. They may also serve an evolutionary purpose by promoting protein diversity.

316   Chapter 11

Promoter
The sequence of DNA at the beginning of genes

Terminator
The sequence of DNA that signals the end of transcription

RNA splicing
The removal of introns from an mRNA strand

Intron
A part of mRNA that does not have protein-making instructions

Exon
A part of mRNA that has protein-making instructions

Ribosomal RNA (rRNA)
An RNA molecule found in ribosomes that positions mRNA during translation

Transfer RNA (tRNA)
An RNA molecule that brings in amino acids during translation

Genetic code
A specific code used to translate base sequences in RNA into amino acid sequences in proteins

During transcription, RNA polymerase adds RNA nucleotides. Ribose is the sugar of RNA nucleotides. If a cytosine base is in the DNA nucleotide, RNA polymerase adds a nucleotide containing guanine to the new RNA. RNA polymerase adds a uracil nucleotide for every adenine nucleotide in DNA.

Cap and tail structures are then added to the ends of the new mRNA strand. It also undergoes **RNA splicing.** During this process, enzymes cut out certain parts of the mRNA strand. These parts, called **introns,** do not produce proteins. The strand parts that produce proteins are called **exons.** After these changes, mRNA leaves the nucleus.

Ribosomal RNA (rRNA) and **transfer RNA (tRNA)** are made in the nucleus by transcription of certain genes. These two RNAs are important in translation. Translation is the next step in making a protein.

Translation

Translation happens in a cell's cytoplasm. Translation produces proteins based on the sequence of nucleotide bases in mRNA. An organism's **genetic code** is found in codons. Codons are sets of three bases in mRNA. Codons can be any combination of the four RNA bases. Each combination codes for a specific amino acid. Recall that amino acids are the building blocks of proteins. The AUG codon is the start signal for translation. UAA, UAG, and UGA are the three stop codons. They signal the end of translation.

Translation uses ribosomes in the cytoplasm. Ribosomes are made of rRNA and protein. At the start of translation, the rRNA in ribosomes line up with the mRNA. The ribosome moves down the mRNA until it reaches the start codon. Then tRNAs enter the ribosome with amino acids attached.

Genetic Information Cycles Chapter 11

Warm-Up Activity

Show students a diagram of a typical animal cell. Explain that the cell's DNA never leaves the nucleus during normal cellular activity. The protein-producing ribosomes always stay outside of the nucleus. However, the ribosomes require the information in DNA to construct proteins. Have students hypothesize ways that the small bits of information needed to make the different proteins could be conveyed to ribosomes. Explain that cells use small copies of DNA (called mRNA) to transfer the information for different genes to the ribosome.

Teaching the Lesson

Have students use modeling clay to demonstrate transcription similar to the way they modeled replication in Lesson 2, using the same color coding for the bases. Have them use orange clay to represent the sugar-phosphate backbone of RNA and purple clay to represent uracil. Have them model the process of transcription by using as a template a model DNA strand that has the following sequence of bases: red-yellow-blue-blue-white-red-yellow. *(The RNA strand should have the following colors representing the bases: white-purple-yellow-yellow-red-white-purple.)* Have students make drawings of what they modeled with the clay.

Reinforce and Extend

SCIENCE JOURNAL

Have students write a fictional story from the point of view of a ribosome, messenger RNA, transfer RNA, an amino acid, a protein, or another cellular component. In their story, they should describe how proteins are made by ribosomes, using nucleic acid templates. They should include a complete description of protein synthesis.

TEACHER ALERT

Many students may not realize that some mutations in DNA cause few or no changes in the resulting proteins. This is because multiple codons code for the same amino acid. If a single-base substitution changes a codon that codes for the same amino acid as that of the original codon, the mutation has no effect on the protein that is produced. A particularly devastating mutation called a frameshift mutation arises when a deletion or an insertion causes the ribosome to read the codons one or two bases off. Demonstrate this effect to the class by using the following sentences as models:

message from original "DNA strand": THE MAN SAT ONA MAT.

single substitution with insignificant result: THE MAN SIT ONA MAT.

single deletion with frameshift mutation: THE MNS ATO NAM AT.

Link to

Environmental Science. Have students read the Link to Environmental Science. Some scientists propose that mutation due to UV radiation may increase as the molecules of ozone in the UV-deflecting ozone layer are depleted. Despite differences in opinion on the seriousness of changes to the amount of UV radiation reaching the surface of the earth, most scientists agree that there is a direct relationship between a person's degree of exposure to sunlight and the likelihood that the person may develop mutations that lead to skin cancer. To protect against damaging effects of UV radiation, it is important to use sunscreens rated SPF (Sun Protection Factor) 15 or higher, wear clothing that covers the skin, and minimize exposure to the sun.

Anticodon
A complementary three-base sequence to the codon found in tRNA

Link to

Environmental Science

The sun's ultraviolet (UV) radiation can cause the joining of thymine bases in DNA. If the joined thymine bases are not fixed by repair enzymes, they interfere with DNA replication. They may cause skin cancer. The earth is protected from UV radiation by a layer of ozone molecules. The use of chemicals called CFCs has caused ozone levels to decrease.

Each tRNA has a base sequence called an **anticodon.** Anticodons are complementary to the codons in mRNA. For example, if an mRNA codon is GAU, the tRNA anticodon is CUA.

For each mRNA codon, the tRNA with the complementary anticodon binds to it. This tRNA brings an amino acid, which becomes attached to a growing protein chain. The ribosome moves down the mRNA. The ribosome trades used tRNAs for new tRNAs. The chain of amino acids grows. Finally, the ribosome reaches a stop codon. Translation stops. The amino acid chain releases and folds into a protein. The mRNA leaves the ribosome.

Science at Work

Pharmaceutical Researcher

Pharmaceutical researchers work in teams to discover and develop new drugs. A pharmaceutical researcher may be trained as a chemist, a biologist, a virologist, or a physician. A virologist studies viruses. Scientists working to discover new drugs can identify and test molecules that could be used as a drug. After a new drug is developed, it must be tested to ensure that it is safe and effective. Pharmaceutical researchers study how the drug is absorbed and used by the body.

The growing field of genomics has increased the pace of new drug development. Genomics is uncovering new information about genes and the proteins they make. In turn, scientists are learning more about the roles of these proteins. Many pharmaceutical researchers are studying the interaction of a person's genetic makeup and his or her response to a drug.

Pharmaceutical researchers must be willing to learn new things. They must also work as team members.

Science at Work

Have students read the Science at Work feature about the career of a pharmaceutical researcher. Have students find out more about some of the problems that pharmaceutical researchers solve, such as developing ways to cure or prevent the spread of diseases or to lessen the harmful side effects of medications. Encourage students to present their findings in an oral or a written report.

Mutation
A change in the sequence of DNA

Mutagen
A physical or chemical material that cause changes in DNA

Substitution
A mutation in which one nucleotide base is replaced with another

Deletion
A mutation in which one or more nucleotide bases are removed from a DNA sequence

Insertion
A mutation in which one or more nucleotide bases are added to a DNA sequence

Myth: A mutation occurs because of an environmental need.

Fact: Mutations occur at random. By chance, a mutation may increase an organism's odds of survival.

Transcription and translation happen constantly inside of cells. Cells must make proteins they need, such as enzymes. An mRNA created in transcription is translated many times before it is lost. Then the genetic information cycle starts over again by creating another mRNA.

Mutations

How do genes change to make alleles? Alleles are created by **mutations.** Mutations are changes in a DNA sequence. Mutations happen for several reasons. Sometimes, DNA mutates randomly and naturally.

Mutations are also caused when mistakes happen during DNA replication and transcription. DNA polymerase usually corrects these mistakes. Another cause of mutations is **mutagens.** Mutagens are physical or chemical materials that cause changes in DNA. Mutagens include ultraviolet radiation from the sun, tar and nicotine in cigarette smoke, and X-rays.

Some mutations are harmless. Others can be harmful. Mutations can change the structure of an amino acid that becomes part of a protein. This change can cause the protein to not function.

One type of mutation is a **substitution.** Substitution occurs when one nucleotide base is replaced with another. This can change a codon structure in mRNA. As a result, a different amino acid might be built into a protein.

Deletions happen when nucleotides are removed from DNA. **Insertions** happen when extra nucleotides are added to a DNA sequence. These types of mutations can greatly change the amino acid structure of a protein.

Any of these mutations create new alleles—new forms of a gene. New alleles can cause a new phenotype to be displayed in organisms.

ELL/ESL Strategy

Language Objective: *To use analogies*

Write the following sentence on the board: start-FAT-DOG-SAT-ONA-MAT-stop. Explain that it is similar to a sequence of mRNA because it has three-letter "codons" that each code for a certain word. Have each group draw cartoons that represent how the sentence changes under three different circumstances: a substitution, a deletion, and an insertion. For example, a cartoon of a dog sitting on a cat represents a substitution of C for the M in the last codon, a cartoon of a dog sitting on a woman represents a deletion of T from the last codon, and a cartoon of a dog sitting on a map represents an insertion of P after A in the last codon.

Science Myth

Have students read the Science Myth feature. Remind them that mutations can be beneficial to, harmful to, or have no effect on an organism. Beneficial mutations can include mutations that lead to the production of a protein that helps an organism survive in its environment. Explain that though an environment naturally selects organisms with a beneficial mutation over those with a harmful mutation, the mutation itself is a random event. The trait that results from the mutation may determine whether or not the organism survives.

Lesson 3 Review Answers

1. transcription, translation 2. mutations, mutagen 3. nucleus, cytoplasm 4. B 5. A 6. C 7. Introns are sequences of mRNA that do not contain instructions for making proteins. Exons are sequences of mRNA that contain instructions for making proteins. 8. Promoters indicate the beginnings of genes, enabling RNA polymerase to begin transcription. Terminators signal the end of transcription and tell RNA polymerase where to detach. 9. Each tRNA delivers the correct amino acid according to the mRNA code. 10. The rRNA in ribosomes helps align the tRNA and the mRNA.

Portfolio Assessment

Sample items include:
- Drawings from Teaching the Lesson
- Reports from Science at Work
- Cartoons from ELL/ESL Strategy
- Lesson 3 Review answers

Link to

Chemistry. Have students read the Link to Chemistry feature. Explain that DNA molecules are not as tidy as they appear in the models in this lesson. Deletions, substitutions, and insertions can result when a very small change occurs in the structure of a single nitrogenous base. Have students compare the structures of cytosine and uracil on page 307. Ask students: What is the main difference between these two bases? *(Uracil has a double-bonded oxygen, while cytosine has a NH$_2$ group.)* The mutagen nitrous acid changes cytosine to uracil. This seemingly small change affects the numbers of hydrogen bonds the nitrogenous base can form and thus the base pairing it undergoes.

Lesson 3 REVIEW

Word Bank
cytoplasm
mutagen
mutations
nucleus
transcription
translation

On a sheet of paper, write the word from the Word Bank that completes each sentence correctly.

1. RNA molecules are made during _____. Proteins are made during _____.
2. Changes in the sequence of DNA are called _____. Such a change might be caused by a _____.
3. Transcription takes place in the _____. Translation occurs in the _____.

Link to >>>
Chemistry

Chemical mutagens cause mutations. Some chemical mutagens are like normal nitrogenous bases. However, they pair incorrectly during replication. An example is 2-amino purine. This compound is similar to adenine. Other mutagens cause chemical changes in bases. This changes their pairing abilities. Nitrous acid changes cytosine to uracil, which then forms hydrogen bonds with adenine instead of guanine.

On a sheet of paper, write the letter of the answer that completes each statement correctly.

4. Molecules of mRNA and tRNA line up with the cell's _____ to begin translation.
   A DNA   B ribosomes   C nucleus   D cell membrane
5. Introns are removed from mRNA because they _____.
   A lack protein-making instructions
   B slow down transcription
   C are missing uracil
   D contain mutations
6. When _____ occurs, a nucleotide is removed from DNA.
   A a substitution   C a deletion
   B an insertion   D transcription

Critical Thinking

On a sheet of paper, write the answers to the following questions. Use complete sentences.

7. Compare and contrast introns and exons.
8. Why are promoters and terminators needed?
9. Describe the roles of tRNA.
10. Describe the role of rRNA.

Chapter 11 Genetic Information Cycles

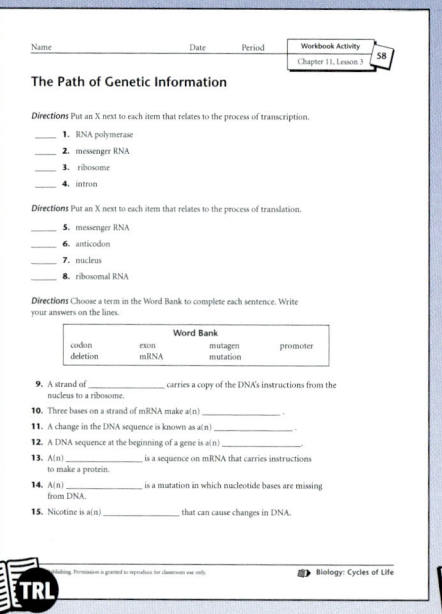

Workbook Activity 58

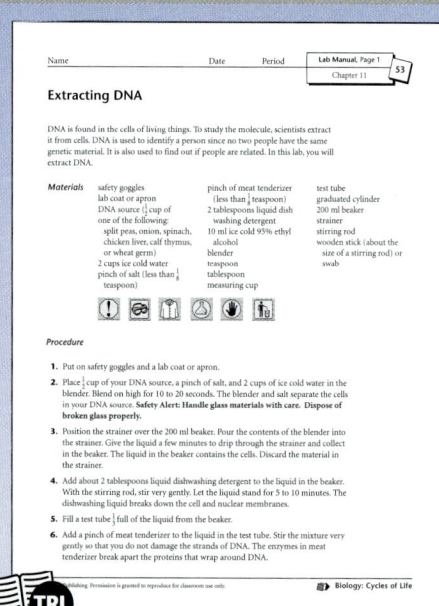

Lab Manual 53, pages 1–2

Lesson 4: What Are Viruses?

Objectives

After reading this lesson, you should be able to
- describe the structures of viruses
- compare the life cycles of viruses
- discuss how vaccines work

Parasite
An organism that absorbs food from a living organism and harms it

Capsid
The protein shell of a virus

Evolve
To change biologically

The path of genetic information from DNA to RNA to protein supports life. Living things use genetic information to grow, function, and reproduce. Viruses use this path only to survive. Viruses are not living and do not produce their own energy. They do not have organelles. They cannot reproduce by themselves.

Viruses are pieces of DNA or RNA wrapped in a protein shell. Viruses are cellular **parasites.** Parasites need other living things to grow and reproduce. Viruses use cells to make molecules and reproduce.

The Structure of Viruses

Viruses have two main structures. One structure is the **capsid.** It is the outside protein shell of the virus. It is made of protein and has different shapes. Some viruses have molecules on the outside of this shell to help them attach to cells.

The second structure in a virus is its genetic material. This can be DNA or RNA. The genetic material of a virus contains genes to make more viruses. Viral genetic material is smaller than cellular genetic material. Just one mutation in viral DNA can have a great effect on that virus. Viruses can quickly change, or evolve. Figure 11.4.1 shows an influenza, or flu, virus.

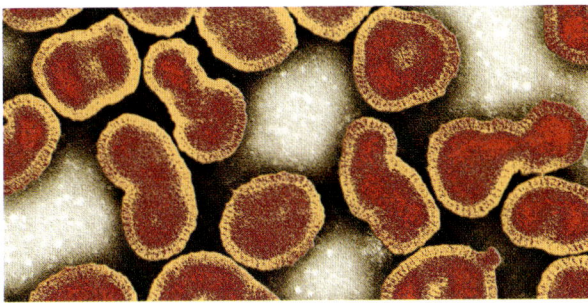

Figure 11.4.1 This is an influenza, or flu, virus. It can be passed from person to person.

Lesson at a Glance

Chapter 11 Lesson 4

Overview In this lesson, students learn about viruses and vaccines.

Objectives
- To describe the structures of viruses
- To compare the life cycles of viruses
- To discuss how vaccines work

Student Pages 321–324

Teacher's Resource Library TRL
Workbook Activity 59
Alternative Workbook Activity 59

Vocabulary

capsid	lysogenic cycle
evolve	lytic cycle
host cell	parasite
immune system	vaccine
infect	

Explain that the terms *lysogenic cycle* and *lytic cycle* come from the Greek word *luein*, which means "to loosen." The term *lysogenic cycle* also contains the root *gen-*, which means "to give birth." Lead students to conclude that the lytic cycle involves producing viruses that break open ("loosen") the cell membrane, while the lysogenic cycle produces cells with DNA that have the ability in the future to produce ("give birth to") the viruses that destroy the cell.

Background Information

Computer viruses are given that name because their method of transmission is comparable to biological viruses. Like biological viruses, computer viruses do not contain the working mechanisms of their hosts (computers). Instead, they are simply programs that cause the computer to run operations not intended by the user. Just as a biological virus contains no organelles that produce proteins, a computer virus does not contain hardware or a user interface that allows the user to control the program.

Warm-Up Activity

Draw a 1-cm line on the board. Next to it, draw a 1-m line. Explain that the lines represent the approximate lengths of a typical virus and a typical bacterium. On this scale, 1 centimeter represents 100 nanometers. Ask students: Why are viruses not typically larger than bacteria or eukaryotic cells? *(In order to enter the cell, the virus must be smaller than its host.)*

 ## Teaching the Lesson

On the board, make a chart with two boxes, labeling them *Lytic Cycle* and *Lysogenic Cycle*. Have students copy the chart and write in each box a brief description of the life cycle, the way the viruses are replicated, the effect on the host organism, and the relative difficulty of curing the viral disease.

 ## Reinforce and Extend

IN THE COMMUNITY

 If possible, have a representative of a hospital, hospice, or medical clinic that provides services for people with HIV and AIDS speak about the life cycle of HIV. Have students prepare questions ahead of time to ask about disease prevention, treatment, and research for cures or vaccines.

ELL/ESL STRATEGY

 **Language Objective:** *To use analogies*

Have students devise an analogy for a virus, using common objects in the real world. For example, students could compare a virus to a stray piece of paper that falls into a pile of papers that someone is about to photocopy. Have them present their analogy to the class in an oral report or a poster. Be sure they include in their analogy references to the virus, the host cell, and the type of reproductive pathway.

Infect
To cause disease or an unhealthy condition by introducing germs and viruses

Host cell
A cell infected and used by a virus

Lytic cycle
A cycle in which a virus uses a host cell to make more virus particles until the host cell is destroyed

Many viruses cause colds in people. These different viruses are almost the same except for small mutations. Doctors cannot cure colds because there are so many variations.

How Viruses Infect

Scientists group viruses by what organism they **infect,** or use for their needs. Some viruses only infect plants that have RNA. Many animal viruses infect only certain species. They do not harm other animal species. However, viruses can mutate to infect new species.

When a virus infects an organism, it attaches to the membrane of a cell, called the **host cell.** The virus opens a hole in the membrane. It pushes its genetic material inside. Once inside, two pathways are possible for the genetic material.

The first pathway is the **lytic cycle.** In this cycle, the virus uses the host to make more viruses. The host cell makes copies of the DNA or RNA and new capsid proteins. This process continues until the cell is full of viruses. Then the cell bursts open and dies. New viruses are released.

> **Science Myth**
>
> **Myth:** Antibiotics treat a cold.
>
> **Fact:** Viruses cause colds. Antibiotics are effective only against bacteria. Doctors sometimes prescribe antibiotics for people with colds to treat other bacterial infections, such as strep throat. These infections sometimes occur because a cold weakens the immune system.

Science Myth

Have students read the Science Myth feature. Antibiotics are generally nonspecific and act on all types of bacteria, even those that benefit the body. If the person has no bacterial infections, the antibiotic may deplete the beneficial bacteria in the body.

Lysogenic cycle
A cycle in which a virus hides its genetic information in the host cell until it switches to the lytic cycle

Vaccine
A material that causes the body to make antibodies against a specific virus

Immune system
The body's most important defense against diseases

The second pathway is the **lysogenic cycle.** In this cycle, viral DNA hides itself in the host's DNA. Viral DNA can hide for years. If the cell undergoes stress, the viral DNA comes out and switches to the lytic cycle. Because viruses can hide, it is hard to cure a viral infection.

Vaccines

As seen in Figure 11.4.2, there are many **vaccines** available to fight viral diseases in people. By getting a vaccine, an individual introduces a virus to his or her **immune system.** The immune system is a natural defense system against disease. The immune system remembers what a virus looks like. The immune system identifies and destroys cells infected by that virus. You will learn more about the immune system in Lesson 6.

The measles vaccine and other vaccines are made from very weakened viruses. Vaccines for influenza, also called flu, and other vaccines are made from dead, whole viruses. Other vaccines are made with parts or products of a virus.

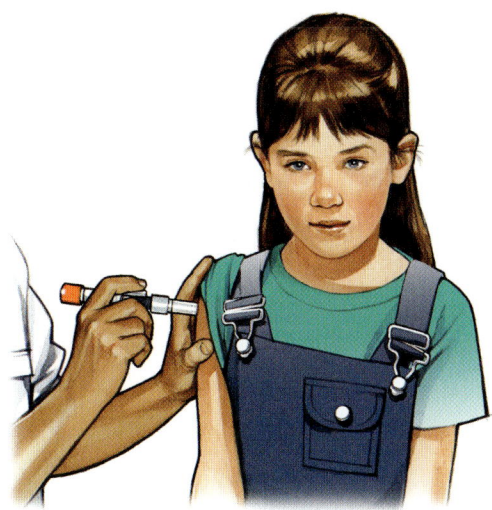

Figure 11.4.2 *This young girl is receiving a vaccine.*

LEARNING STYLES

Body/Kinesthetic

Have students model how a cell uses genetic information from DNA to produce proteins by comparing it to a "song factory." Have partners use several pieces of paper that represent DNA. On each piece of paper, write a set of instructions such as the following: 1st student writes: "Mary had a little lamb." 2nd student writes: "Its fleece was white as snow." or 1st student writes: "Oh say can you see." 2nd student writes: "By the dawn's early light." Have students write the lyrics to songs on index cards according to the instructions on the "DNA." The index cards with song lyrics represent the proteins that the cell produces. Then give each pair of students a piece of paper with the following instructions: 1st student writes: "1st student writes: 1st student writes." 2nd student writes: "2nd student writes: 2nd student writes." Explain that the cell is now producing instructions to produce more instructions. Discuss with students how this process is similar to the way a virus uses a cell's machinery to produce more viruses.

SCIENCE JOURNAL

Have students write a short play about a viral attack on an organism or a cell. In their play, they may wish to personify the key structures that make up the host cells and viruses. Students should include creative descriptions of what happens during the lytic and lysogenic cycles.

Lesson 4 Review Answers

1. parasites **2.** host cell **3.** genetic material **4.** A **5.** D **6.** B **7.** Viruses are considered nonliving because they do not have a nucleus or other organelles, and they cannot reproduce without invading a living cell. **8.** A vaccine protects against a specific virus because it contains weakened viruses of that same type. These viruses stimulate the immune system to produce antibodies against that virus. These antibodies will protect the vaccinated person from becoming infected by that virus. **9.** In the lytic cycle, the host cell makes more viruses, then bursts. In the lysogenic cycle, the viral DNA enters the host cell's DNA, where it may remain hidden for years. It may later switch to the lytic cycle at any time. **10.** Viruses can quickly evolve because their genetic material is small and simple. A single mutation can thus have a great effect.

Portfolio Assessment

Sample items include:
- Completed charts from Teaching the Lesson
- Analogies from the ELL/ESL Strategy
- Questions prepared for the visitor for In the Community
- Script of play from Science Journal
- Lesson 4 Review answers

Link to

Language Arts. Have students read the Link to Language Arts feature. Encourage students to find out more about the history of viruses such as smallpox (also called variola) and cowpox (also called vaccinia). Though cowpox is related to the deadly smallpox, cowpox is not dangerous to humans and causes only minor skin irritations. Jenner experimented with both vaccination and "variolation," which he found to be a significantly more dangerous method of preventing the spread of smallpox. The smallpox virus is now thought to be eradicated due to vaccination using Jenner's concept.

324   Chapter 11

Lesson 4   REVIEW

Word Bank
- genetic material
- host cell
- parasites

On a sheet of paper, write the word or words from the Word Bank that complete each sentence correctly.

1. Viruses are cellular _____, using other cells to make molecules and reproduce.
2. Viruses can be grouped according to the kind of _____ they infect.
3. When a virus invades a host cell, it pushes its _____ inside the cell.

On a sheet of paper, write the letter of the answer that completes each sentence correctly.

4. A virus contains a(n) _____.
   - **A** type of nucleic acid
   - **B** organelle
   - **C** nucleus
   - **D** ribosome

5. Viruses have two main structures, a(n) _____ and genetic material.
   - **A** organelle
   - **B** vaccine
   - **C** host cell
   - **D** capsid

6. Some vaccines are made from _____.
   - **A** capsids
   - **B** severely weakened viruses
   - **C** RNA
   - **D** antibiotics

Critical Thinking

On a sheet of paper, write the answers to the following questions. Use complete sentences.

7. Why are viruses nonliving?
8. Why does a vaccine work only against a specific virus?
9. Compare and contrast the lytic cycle and the lysogenic cycle.
10. Why can viruses evolve quickly?

Link to Language Arts

The word *vaccine* comes from the Latin word *vacca*, which means "cow." In 1796, British physician Edward Jenner gave the world's first vaccination. He used the harmless cowpox virus to protect people against smallpox. Cowpox virus is related to the smallpox virus. Smallpox is a deadly disease.

324   Chapter 11   Genetic Information Cycles

Workbook Activity 59

Chapter 11, Lesson 4

What Are Viruses?

Directions Write a sentence using the following words.
1. parasite, virus, DNA
2. host cell, lytic cycle, infect
3. host cell, lysogenic cycle, lytic cycle

Directions Each statement is a clue. Unscramble the letters in parentheses that follow each statement. Write the term on the line.

4. Nonliving parasites called _____ are made of DNA or RNA wrapped in protein. (susirev)
5. In the _____, a virus hides in the DNA of a host cell. (escgiynol leycc)
6. A virus is covered with a(n) _____, or a protein shell. (isadcp)
7. Viruses _____ when their DNA changes. (levevo)
8. A(n) _____ can help protect against viruses by causing the production of antibodies. (cenaivc)
9. The _____ defends the body against disease. (emnmui myests)
10. A virus infects a(n) _____ and uses its DNA. (otsh lelc)
11. During the _____, a virus uses a cell to make new virus particles. (tcyil ceycl)
12. A(n) _____ absorbs food from an organism and harms it. (tasiepar)
13. A virus can _____ a cell and cause disease. (fcntei)
14. Stress can cause a virus to switch from the lysogenic cycle to the _____. (yiclt yelc)
15. The _____ for influenza is made from dead viruses. (caenciv)

Lesson 5: Using the Path of Genetic Information

Objectives

After reading this lesson, you should be able to
- define biotechnology and how it works
- describe new products made through biotechnology
- identify medical conditions caused by changes in genetic information
- relate the activities of chromosomes to disease
- identify the genetic parts of cancer

Scientists use genetic information to help make life better. **Biotechnology** uses living organisms and their genetics to make medicines and better food crops. Biotechnology changes an organism's genetic makeup to make new molecules, such as proteins. These molecules are used to help that organism, or other organisms.

How Biotechnology Changes Genetic Makeup

How does biotechnology change genetic makeup? Scientists have figured out the DNA sequence of various simple organisms. Scientists compare these genes and their proteins to human genes and proteins. They have found many similarities, even with bacterial genes and proteins. Bacteria are valuable organisms in biotechnology.

Bacteria are simple organisms with only one chromosome. They have small rings of DNA called **plasmids**. Plasmids have few genes on them. Plasmids can be passed from one bacterium to another. **Biotechnologists** use plasmids to make new gene products.

Because bacterial DNA is simple, it can take on new genetic information easily. Biotechnologists take interesting genes and put them into bacterial DNA. First, they use enzymes called **restriction endonucleases** to cut out the gene. These enzymes recognize certain nucleotide base sequences. They break DNA molecules at that sequence.

Biotechnologists then insert the gene into another piece of DNA, usually a plasmid. To do this, they cut the plasmid with restriction endonucleases. They mix in the desired gene. Then they use DNA ligase to bond the genetic material together. The new gene becomes part of a plasmid. Then biotechnologists put the new plasmids into bacteria. The process of adding foreign DNA to a bacterial cell is called **transformation**.

Biotechnology
The use of organisms and their genetics in industry to make products

Plasmid
A small, circular piece of DNA, usually found in bacteria

Biotechnologist
A scientist who studies biotechnology

Lesson at a Glance

Chapter 11 Lesson 5

Overview In this lesson, students learn how changes in DNA can lead to diseases and how biotechnology products are developed.

Objectives
- To define *biotechnology* and how it works
- To describe new products made through biotechnology
- To identify medical conditions caused by changes in genetic information
- To relate the activities of chromosomes to disease
- To identify the genetic parts of cancer

Student Pages 325–331

Teacher's Resource Library
Workbook Activity 60
Alternative Workbook Activity 60
Lab Manual 54–55

Vocabulary
biotechnologist	nondisjunction
biotechnology	plasmid
Down syndrome	restriction endonuclease
genetically modified food	transformation
growth factor	

Break down the meanings of the more complicated vocabulary terms to help students remember them. For example, *junction* means "joining" or "coming together" and *disjunction* means "disjoining" or "separating." When a nondisjunction occurs, the chromosomes do not separate. As another example, explain that the suffix *-ase* indicates that the enzyme makes or breaks bonds in a chemical. The prefix *endo-* means "inside." An endonuclease breaks the bonds that hold two strands of nucleic acids together, the bonds between the nitrogenous bases. Restriction refers to the fact that these enzymes work only on strands of nucleic acids with very specific sequences.

Background Information

Splicing plasmids or short sequences of DNA into other molecules of DNA is called recombinant DNA technology. Recombinant DNA technology is used in a wide range of applications, including the development of genetically modified organisms with desired traits or capable of producing desired protein products. It is also used in gene therapy, in which cells with ineffective genes receive recombinant DNA containing effective genes.

Warm-Up Activity

Bring in a grafted cactus plant in which the top part of the plant is one color or shape and the bottom part of the plant is another. Explain that grafting is cutting two plants and placing the top part of one on the bottom part of the other. The resulting grafted plant has the beauty or productivity of one part and the hearty root system of the other part. Ask students: Which of the two plants used to make part of the grafted cactus most likely has a heartier root system? *(Most likely the bottom part is used for its hearty root system.)* Explain that biotechnologists use a similar idea with genes. They "graft" (splice) genes into the DNA of an organism to benefit from the proteins or characteristics of one organism and the productivity or heartiness of another. Have students discuss why biotechnologists might splice a gene for a human protein into bacteria DNA. *(The scientists want to produce lots of the protein, but cannot get it from humans for ethical reasons.)*

 Teaching the Lesson

Explain that restriction endonucleases are specific to certain base sequences. Some may be more specific than others, cutting DNA after longer sequences than others. Ask students: What effects might a restriction endonuclease with a very short (and not very specific) target sequence have on a long DNA molecule? *(The DNA molecule might be cut in several places rather than just at one very specific site.)*

Reinforce and Extend

Learning Styles

 **Visual/Spatial**

Have students cut off a strip of notebook paper and write the following letters to represent a sequence of bases in DNA: ACCGATTGAACCGTTAT. Have them write the complementary DNA base sequence underneath the given sequence, according to the pairing rules given in Lesson 1. *(The complementary sequence is TGGCTAACTTGGCAATA.)*

Explain that this strip of paper represents a DNA molecule. Have students cut the DNA molecule into two pieces to the right of the following sequence on the lower line: TTGG. The pieces that result represent molecules of DNA that have been cut by a restriction endonuclease. The following sets of letters represent the results:

ACCGATTGAACC GTTAT
TGGCTAACTTGG CAATA

Restriction endonuclease
An enzyme that cuts DNA molecules at specific sequences

Transformation
The process of adding foreign DNA to a bacterial cell

The bacteria treat the new plasmids like their own genes and make proteins from them. Biotechnologists also use the DNA of cows, pigs, and other organisms to take on new genes and make new proteins.

Improvements Through Biotechnology

Biotechnologists improve many medicines and foods. For example, biotechnologists have developed a new way to make insulin. People with diabetes do not produce enough of the protein insulin. They need insulin shots regularly. Biotechnologists have removed and copied the human insulin gene and put it into bacteria. The transformed bacteria make insulin. Most insulin used to treat diabetes is made this way.

Biotechnology has improved other medicines, such as antibiotics. Antibiotics are medicines that help people fight infection caused by bacteria.

Biotechnology has improved farming and growing crops such as cotton. Plants can take on new genetic information easily. Farmers often spray chemicals on plants to stop insects from destroying them. Some plants make these chemicals naturally. Biotechnologists put the genes of plants that make these chemicals into plants without them. Biotechnology helps more crops survive. Figure 11.5.1 shows a cotton plant that has been improved through biotechnology.

Figure 11.5.1 *Biotechnology has improved many crops, including cotton.*

Genetically modified food
A food product with genes that have been changed

Down syndrome
A medical condition caused by cells having an extra chromosome 21

Nondisjunction
Chromosomes that do not separate during anaphase, resulting in extra chromosomes in some cells

Growth factor
A protein that helps control the growth and division of cells

Scientists also have improved the flavor and freshness of fruits and vegetables through biotechnology. Food changed through biotechnology must be labeled **genetically modified food.**

Understanding the Genetics of Diseases

Knowledge of genetic information has helped scientists understand the genetics of diseases and other medical conditions. Some conditions are caused by the number of chromosomes in cells. One such condition is **Down syndrome.** People with Down syndrome have cells with three copies of chromosome 21.

Nondisjunction causes Down syndrome. Nondisjunction occurs when chromosomes do not separate during meiosis. This causes some gametes to have extra chromosomes that are passed on to offspring. Extra chromosomes give humans cells too much information. This causes conditions like Down syndrome.

Small mutations in DNA sequences for particular proteins cause many diseases. Some mutations change the amino acid order by changing or removing an amino acid. Proteins with these mutations do not function normally.

Sickle-cell disease arises from an amino acid change in the protein hemoglobin. People with sickle-cell disease have jagged and curved red blood cells. Normal red blood cells are smooth and round. Hemoglobin in red blood cells carries oxygen to other cells.

Link to ▶▶▶
Social Studies
DNA plays an important role in forensic science. Forensic science is used in the justice system, often to solve crimes. DNA analysis can help identify potential suspects whose DNA may match evidence left at a crime scene.

IN THE ENVIRONMENT

Many people are concerned that genetically modified organisms are dangerous for ecosystems. When farmers or ranchers raise plants or animals that have genes that make them better able to survive in an ecosystem than competitor species can, they may dominate over competitors and cause the native species to die out. This could also become a problem if the genetically modified organisms are able to breed with native species and produce offspring that carry the genetically modified trait. If native traits are not naturally selected over genetically modified traits, biodiversity can decrease. Have students research health concerns about crops that have been genetically modified.

ELL/ESL STRATEGY

Language Objective:
To compare and contrast

Have students form pairs composed of a student learning English and a student with strong English skills. Provide each pair with karyotypes of a female with Down syndrome and a female that does not have Down syndrome. Have students determine how the two karyotypes differ. *(The karyotype representing the individual with Down syndrome will have an extra chromosome 21.)* Have students review with each other the process of meiosis. Have them write descriptions of how a person with Down syndrome came to have an extra chromosome in his or her genome.

Link to

Social Studies. Have students read the Link to Social Studies feature. Biotechnologists can determine the "DNA fingerprint" of an individual by using a very small sample of DNA. A DNA fingerprint is the pattern or sequence of bases in a person's genome. Like an actual fingerprint, a DNA fingerprint can be used to link physical evidence to an individual's identity. All actual fingerprints are unique. Even identical twins have different fingerprints. A person's DNA sequence, however, is not entirely unique because identical twins have the same DNA fingerprints.

GLOBAL CONNECTION

The development of some genetically modified foods has generated global controversy. Some people believe that genetically modified foods damage native ecosystems and traditional farming practices. Others believe that genetically modified foods can save many communities from lack of land, water, and other resources that contribute to the nutritional needs of local populations. Have students research the use of genetically modified foods in government relief programs and international politics. Have them present a persuasive speech for or against the use of genetically modified foods to solve world hunger.

SCIENCE JOURNAL

Have students write an essay or a letter to the editor describing their opinions about the availability of genetic information and privacy issues. They may choose to address the advantages and disadvantages of being able to identify people and the genetic disorders they may have, based on their unique DNA sequences.

Technology and Society

Have students read the Technology and Society feature. Biotechnology has allowed scientists to determine the sequence of a person's entire genome. This includes as many as 3 billion nitrogenous base pairs. As computer technology improves, this large quantity of information can become stored on smaller and smaller storage devices.

People with sickle-cell disease have hemoglobin that makes crystals. The crystals cause the sickle shape. One mutated nucleotide base in a gene causes the different hemoglobin.

Problems with DNA can cause cancer. Cancer starts when cells do not stop growing and dividing. This extra growth leads to tumors. Mutations in certain genes cause tumors. These genes produce **growth factor** proteins. Growth factors control when and how fast cells grow and divide. Changes in the genes for these proteins can cause them to not work or to work too much.

Much research focuses on the changes in cells that lead to cancer. Research has helped doctors determine if someone is at risk to develop cancer. People can take genetic tests to find out if they have mutations associated with most cancer.

Doctors can test people to see if they have genetic diseases. These tests look for odd DNA sequences or proteins that are not functioning. Science, including biotechnology, makes treating and curing some diseases possible.

Technology and Society

Many scientists think that a person's entire genome can soon be placed on a digital chip. A genome is all the genetic material in all of the chromosomes of an organism. Doctors could then use this DNA information to diagnose and treat diseases. Over time, scientists will develop more diagnostic tests that can be run on genome chips.

TEACHER ALERT

Be sure that students understand that cancer can result from multiple factors, both environmental and genetic. While mutagens such as UV radiation and certain chemicals can cause changes in DNA molecules, individuals can inherit mutated genes that make them more likely to develop cancer when exposed to mutagens. If cell growth is controlled by multiple factors, it may take mutations in multiple genes to set off uncontrolled cell growth (cancer). Some of these mutations may be inherited, while others may develop in an individual over his or her lifetime.

Lesson 5 REVIEW

Word Bank
plasmids
restriction endonuclease
transformation

On a sheet of paper, write the word or words from the Word Bank that complete each sentence correctly.

1. Small rings of bacterial DNA are _____.
2. Enzymes called _____ cut DNA molecules at specific sequences.
3. The addition of foreign DNA to a cell is known as _____.

On a sheet of paper, write the letter of the answer that completes each sentence correctly.

4. _____ are useful organisms in biotechnology.
   - A Bacteria
   - B Proteins
   - C Growth factors
   - D Antibiotics

5. Down syndrome results from _____.
   - A a deletion
   - B nondisjunction
   - C a substitution
   - D antibiotics

6. A disease called _____ is the result of uncontrolled cell growth.
   - A sickle-cell disease
   - B Down syndrome
   - C diabetes
   - D cancer

Critical Thinking

On a sheet of paper, write the answers to the following questions. Use complete sentences.

7. What is biotechnology?
8. Describe one way that biotechnology might benefit you or a member of your family.
9. How do biotechnologists produce insulin?
10. What advantages do bacteria offer biotechnologists?

Genetic Information Cycles Chapter 11 329

Lesson 5 Review Answers

1. plasmids 2. restriction endonucleases 3. transformation 4. A 5. B 6. D
7. Biotechnology is the use of organisms and their genetics in industry to make medicines and improved food crops.
8. Biotechnology can make insulin less expensive and easier to obtain. It can improve other medicines such as antibiotics or growth hormones. It can provide larger supplies of improved crops. 9. The gene for human insulin production has been placed into bacteria, which then produce insulin. 10. Bacteria have simple genetics that are easy to control. Because they also have small rings of DNA called plasmids, it is easy to add genes to a plasmid, then add the new plasmids to bacteria.

Portfolio Assessment

Sample items include:
- DNA models from Learning Styles Visual/Spatial
- Written descriptions from the ELL/ESL Strategy
- Essays or letters to the editors from Science Journal
- Lesson 5 Review answers

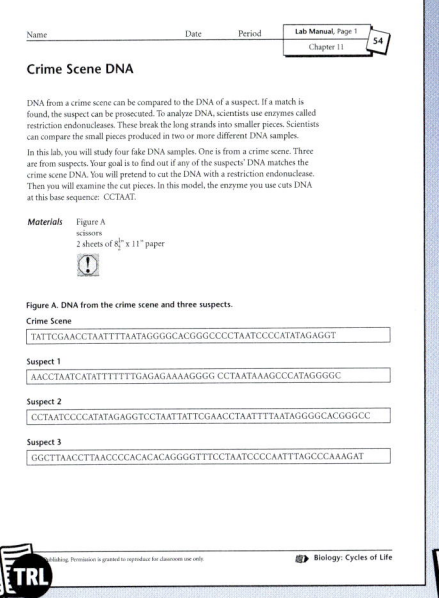

Lab Manual 54, pages 1–3   Workbook Activity 60

Genetic Information Cycles 329

Discovery Investigation 11

This investigation is less structured than the first investigation in this chapter. It offers students more challenge and requires more teacher facilitation. Encourage students to read the Discovery Investigation steps. Discuss questions they may have before beginning the investigation.

Objectives

- To compare and contrast the structures of DNA and RNA
- To distinguish between transcription and translation
- To recognize the role of mRNA in translation
- To determine how a mutation can affect a protein

Skills

Applying information, comparing and contrasting, identifying similarities and differences, making inferences, understanding concepts, predicting outcomes, recognizing cause and effect, recognizing patterns, drawing conclusions

Background

Hemoglobin carries oxygen throughout the body. A normal hemoglobin molecule consists of four polypeptide chains: two identical alpha chains and two identical beta chains. Each polypeptide consists of about 150 amino acids. In people with sickle-cell disease, a mutation causes an incorrect amino acid (valine instead of glutamic acid) at amino acid #6 in the beta polypeptide chains.

Time Frame

One class period

Procedure

- Have students work in small groups to complete the activity.
- Help students unfamiliar with the term *faulty*. Ask other students to suggest words or phrases (such as *out of order, defective, broken down, not working, damaged,* or *flawed*) that are synonyms.

DISCOVERY INVESTIGATION 11

Materials
- paper
- pencil

A Faulty Protein

The nucleic acid DNA contains the directions for making proteins. A mutation is a change in the sequence of DNA nucleotides. In this investigation, you will learn how a mutation can affect a blood protein called hemoglobin, causing sickle-cell disease.

Procedure

1. Write the following DNA nucleotide sequence on a sheet of paper:
   T G A G G A C T C C T C.

2. Write the complementary mRNA sequence.

3. Table 11.1 on page 331 shows the possible codons in mRNA. Each codon, or set of three nucleotide bases, codes for one amino acid. Use this table to translate the mRNA sequence in Step 2. Write the amino acid sequence that the mRNA sequence will produce.

Chapter 11 Genetic Information Cycles

4. Write the following DNA nucleotide sequence:
   T G A G G A C A C C T C.
   Does this DNA sequence match the one in Step 3?

Analysis

1. In Step 2, what is the complementary mRNA sequence? How many codons does it contain?

2. In Step 3, what is the amino acid that the mRNA sequence will produce?

3. In Step 4, what is the complementary mRNA sequence for the DNA sequence? What is the amino acid sequence that this mRNA sequence produces?

Conclusions

1. What process is occurring in Step 2?

2. What process is occurring in Step 3?

3. Identify the DNA mutation shown in Step 4. What type of mutation is this?

Explore Further

When might a genetic mutation fail to affect a protein? Change the DNA sequence in Step 1 to show how a gene can undergo a mutation and still produce a normal protein.

Table 11.1 Codons in mRNA

First Base	Second Base				Third Base
	U	C	A	G	
U	UUU, UUC Phenylalanine; UUA, UUG Leucine	UCU, UCC, UCA, UCG Serine	UAU, UAC Tyrosine; UAA, UAG Stop	UGU, UGC Cysteine; UGA Stop; UGG Tryptophan	U C A G
C	CUU, CUC, CUA, CUG Leucine	CCU, CCC, CCA, CCG Proline	CAU, CAC Histidine; CAA, CAG Glutamine	CGU, CGC, CGA, CGG Arginine	U C A G
A	AUU, AUC, AUA Isolecine; AUG Start	ACU, ACC, ACA, ACG Threonine	AAU, AAC Asparagine; AAA, AAG Lysine	AGU, AGC Serine; AGA, AGG Arginine	U C A G
G	GUU, GUC, GUA, GUG Valine	GCU, GCC, GCA, GCG Alanine	GAU, GAC Aspartic acid; GAA, GAG Glutamic acid	GGU, GGC, GGA, GGG Cysteine	U C A G

- When students are asked to write the corresponding mRNA sequence in Step 2, remind them that uracil (U) replaces thymine (T) in RNA and pairs with adenine (A).
- Tell students to use the genetic code chart to determine the amino acid coded for by each mRNA codon.

Results

The DNA nucleotide sequence shown in Step 1 codes for amino acids 4–7 in the beta polypeptide chains of human hemoglobin. In Step 4, students will discover a trio of DNA nucleotides that contain a mutation: "CTC" (normal hemoglobin) now reads "CAC" (sickle-cell hemoglobin). This single-nucleotide mutation will change the normal mRNA codon from "GAG" to "GUG." As a result, valine will replace glutamic acid, resulting in sickle-cell disease.

Answers to Analysis, Conclusions, and Explore Further begin on page 670 of this Teacher's Edition.

Assessment

You might include the following items from this investigation in student portfolios:

- Student hypothesis and proposed procedure
- Answers to Analysis and Conclusions questions
- Student proposal to investigate in Explore Further

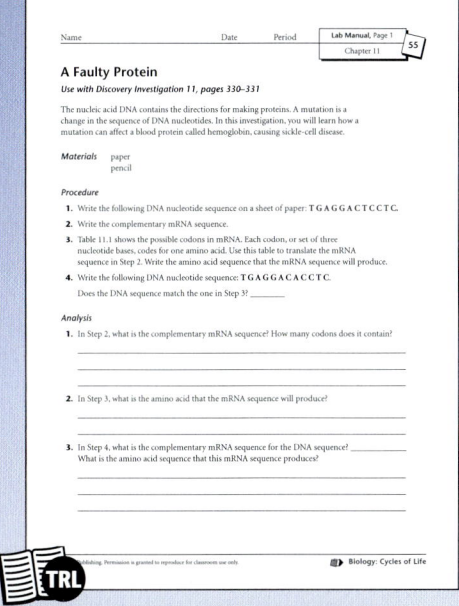

Lab Manual 55, pages 1–2

Lesson at a Glance

Chapter 11 Lesson 6

Overview In this lesson, students learn about the structures, roles, and responses of the immune system.

Objectives

- To identify the three parts of nonspecific defense against disease
- To describe the inflammatory response
- To discuss how the body has specific defenses against disease
- To compare the functions of B cells and T cells

Student Pages 332–337

Teacher's Resource Library

Workbook Activity 61–62

Alternative Workbook Activity 61–62

Vocabulary

antigen	lymph system
B lymphocyte	lymphocyte
complement protein	macrophage
cytotoxic T cell	memory cell
helper T cell	nonspecific defense
immunity	pathogen
infectious disease	phagocyte
inflammatory response	specific defense
	T lymphocyte
	white blood cell

Have students work in pairs to organize the lesson vocabulary terms into three groups: structures produced by the human body (*B lymphocyte, complement protein, cytotoxic T cell, helper T cell, lymph system, lymphocyte, memory cell, phagocyte, T lymphocyte, white blood cell*), agents that invade the human body (*antigen, infectious disease, pathogen*), and types of responses (*immunity, inflammatory response, nonspecific defense, specific defense*).

Lesson 6: Natural Defenses Against Disease

Objectives

After reading this lesson, you should be able to

- identify the three methods of nonspecific defense
- describe the inflammatory response
- discuss how the body has specific defenses against disease
- compare the functions of B cells and T cells

The human immune system is made up of a system of organs and cells that fight disease. It also protects against some cancer cells. If enough germs get into the body, they can start causing an infection. An **infectious disease** occurs when viral or bacterial germs invade body cells, causing sickness. The invading organisms are called **pathogens.**

The Lymph System

The immune, nervous, endocrine, and **lymph systems** work together to regulate internal body functions and behavior. The lymph system is a network of small vessels and organs. The organs include the spleen, thymus, and lymph nodes. Lymph nodes contain billions of **white blood cells.** White blood cells multiply rapidly to fight germs. During illness, lymph nodes fill with millions of extra white blood cells and dead germs. When you are healthy, lymph nodes are about the size of a pea or grape. When you are ill, lymph nodes can swell to the size of a golf ball.

The lymph system carries hormones and other chemicals throughout the body. White blood cells use the lymph system to travel. The immune and lymph systems defend against disease in two ways, **nonspecific defense** and **specific defense.**

Nonspecific Defense

The first part of nonspecific defense is the skin. Skin keeps out most invaders. It covers most of the body. Body areas without skin that are exposed to the outside environment have a mucus cover. Mucus is a thick fluid given off by cells. Mucus protects the surface of body areas. Mucus traps pathogens. Chemicals in mucus make it hard for pathogens to survive.

If the skin and mucus barriers are broken, pathogens can infect a person. Then the second part of nonspecific defense begins to work. **Complement proteins** fight pathogens. They open holes in the membranes of invading pathogens. They also signal the **phagocytes.**

Infectious disease
An illness that can pass from person to person

Pathogen
A germ

Lymph system
A human organ system that transports hormones and human immune cells throughout the body

White blood cell
A cell of the immune system

332 Chapter 11 Genetic Information Cycles

Background Information

Antibodies are specific to certain proteins (called antigens) on pathogens. Antibodies prevent sickness in two ways: through clumping of pathogens so that they are easily destroyed by white blood cells and through triggering an immune response that makes it difficult for the disease to propagate in the future. Someone can develop immunity after getting a disease the first time or in response to vaccination. Vaccines are harmless versions of a pathogen that introduces an antigen to the body and triggers a specific immune response without causing sickness.

Nonspecific defense
The use of a skin barrier, complement proteins, and the inflammatory response to defend against pathogens

Specific defense
The use of lymphocytes to recognize antigens and attack infected cells based on antigens

Complement protein
A protein that breaks the membranes of pathogens

Phagocyte
A cell that eats infected cells and pathogens

Inflammatory response
An increase in blood flow to infected body tissue

Lymphocyte
A white blood cell that has receptor proteins that recognize antigens

B lymphocyte
A white blood cell that produces antibodies

T lymphocyte
A specific defense cell that signals and destroys infected cells

Phagocytes are a type of white blood cell. Phagocytes eat infected and foreign cells. They move around the body in the blood. Phagocytes find pathogens or infected cells and surround them. Then they bring the invaders inside their membrane. Enzymes in phagocytes break down the infected cells or pathogens.

The third method of nonspecific defense is the **inflammatory response.** Cells near an infection site send out chemical signals. The signals increase blood flow to the area. Complement proteins arrive. They signal phagocytes. When phagocytes arrive, they eat infected cells and pathogens. After the invaders are gone, the damaged tissue heals.

The body sometimes uses fever in the inflammatory response. Fever results from an increase in body temperature. This stops bacteria from growing and helps phagocytes work faster.

Specific Defense

Specific defenses use the **lymphocytes.** Lymphocytes are a type of white blood cell. There are two types, **B lymphocytes** and **T lymphocytes.** Each lymphocyte has thousands of receptor proteins in its membranes. Receptor proteins recognize **antigens.** Antigens are molecules or pieces of molecules not usually found in the body. Antigens are often molecules in bacterial membranes or viral capsids.

B lymphocytes mainly defend against bacteria and viruses found in body fluids outside of cells. B lymphocytes produce antibodies in response to antigens found in body fluids. An antigen receptor on a B lymphocyte binds to the matching antigen receptor on a pathogen. The B lymphocyte then grows and produces an identical B lymphocyte through mitosis. These soon form millions of identical B lymphocytes.

Each B lymphocyte produces and secretes antibodies specific to the antigen on the pathogen. The binding of antibodies stops the pathogen from reproducing. It also causes pathogens to stick together. Phagocytes then destroy the clumps of pathogens.

 Warm-Up Activity

Bring in a lock that requires a key, its key, and several similar keys that will not open the lock. Ask a volunteer: How could you determine which key opens the lock? *(Try each key in the lock until one opens it.)* Point out that the shape of the key is specific to the lock. To make a second key that will open the lock, someone must cut a key with the exact shape. Explain that the body's immune system has an analogous system of proteins that are shaped so that they fit very specific foreign invaders (antigens). Have students write a paragraph explaining the analogy.

 Teaching the Lesson

Help students make a graphic organizer that illustrates the specific and nonspecific defenses. To help students sequence the events that take place during each process, go over the lesson as a class while students make their graphic organizers. Be sure they include all the cells and proteins associated with each process.

 Reinforce and Extend

ELL/ESL Strategy

 **Language Objective:** *To explain difficult concepts*

Have students in pairs take turns reading each paragraph about specific defense and explaining the content to their partner. Students may wish to use simple diagrams to illustrate their explanations. Encourage students to provide a helpful critique of their partner's explanation by pointing out any details they might have left out. As a class, make a list of the important points discussed in the lesson. Have students save these notes for studying for tests and quizzes.

LEARNING STYLES

Interpersonal/Group Learning

Have groups of students perform skits in which they model nonspecific and specific defenses. Cell roles that students might play in the skits include pathogens, phagocytes, T lymphocytes, B lymphocytes, helper T cells, cytotoxic T cells, and memory cells. Have students work together to think of ways to model the different proteins involved, such as complement proteins, antibodies, and receptor proteins.

Achievements in Science

Have students read the Achievements in Science feature about the history of HIV. Explain that HIV infects certain cells in the immune system and not others. People infected with HIV can have the disease but show no signs of it until they begin to lose important immune cells called helper T cells, which eventually can cause the infected people to develop the devastating effects of full-blown AIDS. Have students find out more about the different stages of HIV infection and the role of mutation in the spread of the disease.

Antigen
A foreign molecule that activates the immune system

Cytotoxic T cell
A lymphocyte that scans for antigens and then destroys infected cells

T lymphocytes work differently than B lymphocytes. They directly attack host cells that contain bacteria or viruses. Host cells are infected body cells. Every T lymphocyte has receptors for a specific antigen. A pathogen that has infected a body cell displays its antigens on the surface of the body cell. The antigens bind to the receptors on the matching T lymphocyte.

The T lymphocyte then grows and produces an identical T lymphocyte through mitosis. These soon form millions of identical T lymphocytes. The identical T lymphocytes develop into **cytotoxic T cells.**

The cytotoxic T cell binds to an infected cell's membrane. They secrete a protein which pokes holes in the membrane. The infected cell spills fluid, breaks open, and dies. Phagocytes then restore the dead host cell.

Achievements in Science

Finding HIV

In 1981, doctors in California and New York were puzzled. They were seeing several young men with an unusual kind of pneumonia. Pneumonia is a lung disease. Other men had a rare form of cancer.

Within months, scientists learned that a new disease was in the United States. This disease weakened the immune system, resulting in death. The disease was named acquired immune deficiency syndrome, or AIDS. Researchers worldwide looked for the cause of AIDS.

In 1983, Dr. Luc Montagnier in Paris reported that he had found a new virus, LAV, associated with AIDS. Several months later, Dr. Robert Gallo announced that a virus caused AIDS. He named the virus HTLV-III. In 1986, the AIDS virus was renamed human immunodeficiency virus, or HIV.

The identification of AIDS and its cause was an important first step in the fight against AIDS. Scientists have developed drugs that slow the progress of the disease. However, there is no cure. From 1981 through 2003, 20 million people worldwide have died from AIDS.

Helper T cell
A lymphocyte that scans for antigens

Macrophage
A large white blood cell that eats pathogens and cellular waste

Memory cell
A lymphocyte that is activated if an antigen causes another infection

Immunity
The ability of the body to fight off a specific pathogen

Both B lymphocytes and cytotoxic T cells get help from a type of lymphocyte called a **helper T cell.** Like all lymphocytes, every helper T cell has receptors that recognize a specific antigen on macrophages. **Macrophages** are white blood cells that eat pathogens. Helper T cells secrete chemicals that attract both cytotoxic T cells and B lymphocytes.

Immunity

Most of the cells involved in overcoming an infection die. However, some B lymphocytes and T lymphocytes live in the body. The become **memory cells.** A memory cell is a lymphocyte that is activated if an antigen causes another infection.

Thanks to memory cells, the immune system remembers some antigens. These antigens will activate lymphocytes that have receptor proteins specific to the antigens. If a pathogen tries to invade a second time, memory cells recognize it right away. They divide quickly and make active lymphocytes to fight the pathogen. They then get rid of the pathogen before it can cause a disease.

People develop **immunity** from diseases. Immunity happens when antigens cannot cause sickness because lymphocytes remember the antigen and destroy it. For example, people are sick with chickenpox only once. After the first infection, the immune system identifies and destroys newly infected cells.

Career Connection

Have students research the career of a nurse or physician. If possible, have them interview a nurse or physician about pathogens, natural immunity, vaccinations, and antibiotics. Encourage students to ask questions about the person's education, the types of services he or she provides, and the applications of his or her field of study. Encourage students to report their findings to the class.

Lesson 6 Review Answers

1. nonspecific **2.** antigens **3.** lymph **4.** The inflammatory response increases blood flow to the affected area. Complement proteins arrive and signal phagocytes. Phagocytes devour the infected cells. Sometimes the inflammatory response includes fever, which can stop bacteria from growing and help phagocytes to work faster. **5.** Humans develop immunity after exposure to a certain disease, either through a natural encounter with the disease or through vaccination. Memory cells help the immune system remember some antigens.

Portfolio Assessment

Sample items include:
- Paragraph from Warm-Up Activity
- Graphic organizers from Teaching the Lesson
- Diagrams and lists from the ELL/ESL Strategy
- Questions prepared for the visiting nurse or doctor from the Career Connection
- Lesson 6 Review answers

Biology in Your Life

Have students read the Biology in Your Life feature about vaccine delivery. Have students research the different types of vaccines available and the benefits and drawbacks of each type.

Biology in Your Life Answers

1. Viruses are very small, making it possible for them to enter the body through the mucous membranes of the nose and throat. **2.** Most vaccines are large molecules that would be broken down and destroyed in the stomach before they could be absorbed into the bloodstream. **3.** Needle-free vaccination is painless and quick. It also protects health-care workers from dangerous diseases that can be transmitted by accidental needle sticks.

Lesson 6   REVIEW

Word Bank
antigens
lymph
nonspecific

On a sheet of paper, write the word from the Word Bank to complete each sentence correctly.

1. When the body is attacked by a foreign substance, the _____ defenses are the first to react.
2. Foreign molecules called _____ activate the immune system.
3. A network of small vessels and organs known as the _____ system carries chemicals throughout the body.

Critical Thinking

On a sheet of paper, write the answers to the following questions. Use complete sentences.

4. How does the inflammatory response fight infection?
5. How do people develop immunity from a certain pathogen?

Biology in Your Life

Technology: Vaccine Delivery

In the past, most vaccines were given as a shot. There are needle-free options for some vaccines. A nasal vaccine that protects against influenza, or flu, contains inactive flu viruses. The vaccine is sprayed up the nostrils and enters the blood.

People can get a vaccine by a needle-free injector. The injector uses a jet of helium gas to deliver the vaccine to the blood. Other devices use a spring to shoot drugs into the muscle or just below the skin. People can swallow some vaccines. A fatty acid surrounds tiny, vaccine-filled particles. The fatty acid protects the vaccine from being broken down and digested in the stomach. When the drug reaches the lower intestine, it is absorbed and enters the blood.

Injection-free methods are painless. They protect health care workers from accidental needle pricks. These methods are also fast. This is important when large numbers of people must be vaccinated quickly. This can happen during flu season, for example.

1. Why can a viral vaccine be delivered in a nasal spray?
2. Most vaccines cannot be swallowed. Explain why.
3. What are advantages of needle-free vaccination for you?

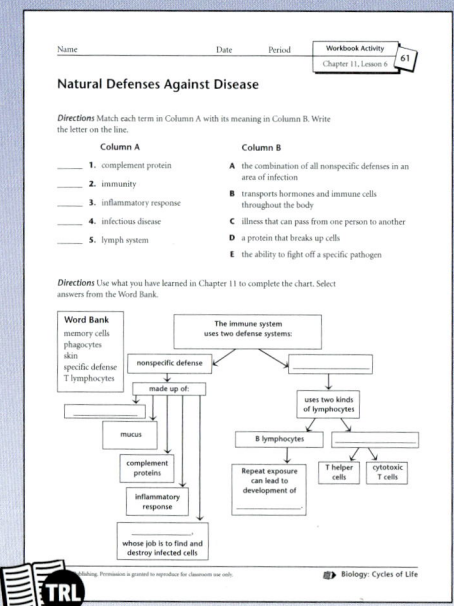

Workbook Activity 61

BIOLOGY IN THE WORLD

The Human Genome Project

Launched in 1990, the Human Genome Project was a 13-year research effort to analyze human DNA. The U.S. Department of Energy and the National Institutes of Health funded the project. One goal of the Human Genome Project was to identify all genes in human DNA. Another goal was to determine the base pair sequences that make up each gene.

Researchers also studied the genes of several other organisms. These included certain species of bacteria and yeast, the fruit fly, and laboratory mice. Researchers can use genes from these simpler organisms to study similar genes found in humans.

Scientists completed the sequencing of the human genome in April 2003. The information gained from the Human Genome Project helped create a new field of study called genomics. Genomics is the study of genes and their functions.

During the Human Genome Project, scientists identified about 1.4 million locations in human DNA in which single-nucleotide DNA differences, or SNPs, occur. These differences make each person unique. SNPs will make it possible to find the DNA sequences for heart disease, diabetes, arthritis, Alzheimer's disease, and certain forms of cancer.

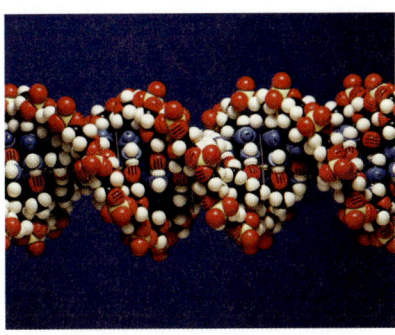

Scientists are using genomic information from the Human Genome Project to find new ways to diagnose and treat genetic disorders and diseases. Detailed genetic maps will make it possible to develop treatments that target the cause of the disease instead of the symptoms. Scientists will be able to design new drugs to match a person's genetic makeup. These custom drugs will be based on a person's genetic profile.

1. Why did scientists want to discover the DNA sequences of other organisms?
2. What is genomics?
3. How can the Human Genome Project lead to the development of new drugs?

Chapter 11 Summary

Have volunteers read aloud each Summary item on page 338. Ask volunteers to explain the meaning of each item. Direct students' attention to the Vocabulary box on the bottom of page 338. Have them read and review each term and its definition.

Graphic Organizer

As students read Chapter 11, have them finish completing the concept map on Graphic Organizer 11: DNA Structure. Encourage students to read each lesson of the chapter and then have them fill in the portion of the chart that pertains to the lesson. When they have completed the chart, ask them to answer the questions.

Chapter 11 SUMMARY

- The double helix structure of DNA allows it to carry coded instructions to make proteins.

- Each nucleotide in DNA contains the sugar deoxyribose, a phosphate group, and one of four nitrogenous bases. Each base follows a pattern called complementary base pairing: adenine pairs with thymine, and guanine pairs with cytosine. RNA is a single strand of nucleotides. RNA nucleotides contain uracil instead of thymine and ribose instead of deoxyribose.

- Two new copies of DNA form during DNA replication. During replication, the double helix unwinds. Each strand serves as a template for a new strand.

- Transcription is the creation of an RNA molecule. During translation, a protein is created based on the sequence of bases in mRNA.

- A virus is a nonliving particle. A virus invades a host cell to reproduce.

- Biotechnology is the use of organisms and their genetics to make medicines and improve food crops.

- The immune system defends the body against infections. Nonspecific defenses, such as the inflammatory response, are the body's first line of defense. Specific defenses, such as antibodies, attack infected cells based on the presence of certain antigens.

- Immunity results when the immune system recognizes previous antigens.

Vocabulary

anticodon, 318
antigen, 334
B lymphocyte, 333
bacteriophage, 310
biotechnologist, 325
biotechnology, 325
capsid, 321
complement protein, 333
complementary base pairing, 308
cytosine, 307
cytotoxic T cell, 334
deletion, 319
DNA ligase, 312
DNA polymerase, 311
Down syndrome, 327
evolve, 321
exon, 317
genetic code, 317

genetically modified food, 327
growth factor, 327
guanine, 306
helper T cell, 335
host cell, 322
immune system, 323
immunity, 335
infect, 322
infectious disease, 332
inflammatory response, 333
insertion, 319
intron, 317
lagging strand, 312
leading strand, 312
lymph system, 332
lysogenic cycle, 323
lymphocyte, 333
lytic cycle, 322
macrophage, 335

marker, 310
memory cell, 335
messenger RNA, 316
mutagen, 319
mutation, 319
nitrogenous base, 306
nondisjunction, 327
nonspecific defense, 333
origin of replication, 311
parasite, 321
pathogen, 332
phagocyte, 333
plasmid, 325
promoter, 317
replication, 310
replication bubble, 311
replication fork, 311
restriction endonuclease, 326
ribosomal RNA, 317
RNA polymerase, 316

RNA splicing, 317
semi-conservative replication, 310
specific defense, 333
substitution, 319
sugar-phosphate backbone, 306
T lymphocyte, 333
template, 311
terminator, 317
thymine, 307
transcription, 316
transfer RNA, 317
transformation, 326
translation, 316
uracil, 307
vaccine, 323
virus, 310
white blood cell, 332

338   Chapter 11   Genetic Information Cycles

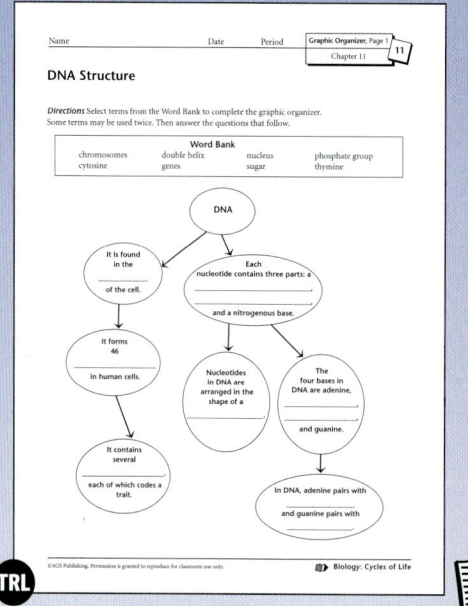

Graphic Organizer 11, pages 1–3

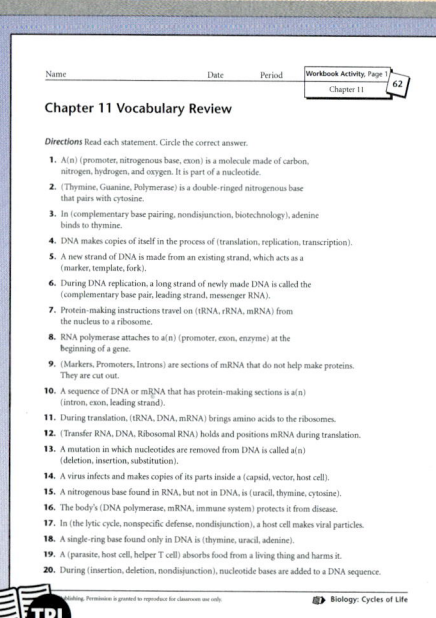

Workbook Activity 62, pages 1–5

Chapter 11 REVIEW

Word Bank
- anticodon
- antigen
- biotechnology
- DNA polymerase
- host cell
- immunity
- lymphocyte
- messenger RNA
- mutation
- nitrogenous base
- nonspecific defense
- phagocyte
- plasmid
- replication fork
- restriction endonuclease
- ribosomal RNA
- semi-conservative replication
- specific defense
- transcription
- transfer RNA
- transformation
- translation
- vaccine
- virus

Vocabulary Review

On a sheet of paper, write the word or words from the Word Bank that best complete each sentence.

1. The building block that makes up a nucleic acid is a(n) _____.

2. During _____, a protein is created from the coded sequences of bases in the RNA molecule.

3. Nucleotide bases are attached to a new strand of DNA at the _____.

4. An enzyme called _____ bonds new nucleotides to the nucleotides on the template strand.

5. When _____ occurs, an RNA molecule is created based on the sequence of bases in a DNA molecule.

6. A molecule called _____ interprets the DNA codes and carries the coded instructions for the order of amino acids in a protein. Another molecule called _____ delivers the correct amino acids. During translation, _____ helps position the amino acids.

7. Three complementary base units known as a(n) _____ ensure that the correct amino acid is delivered.

8. A(n) _____ is made up of nonliving pieces of DNA or RNA wrapped in a protein shell.

9. A white blood cell that has receptor proteins that recognize antigens is a(n) _____.

10. DNA is copied during _____.

Review continued on next page

Genetic Information Cycles Chapter 11 **339**

Review Answers

11. immunity, vaccine **12.** nitrogenous base **13.** biotechnology, plasmid **14.** mutation **15.** antigen **16.** host cell **17.** restriction endonuclease, transformation **18.** nonspecific defense, specific defense

TEACHER ALERT

In the Chapter Review, the Vocabulary Review activity includes a sample of the chapter's vocabulary terms. The activity will help determine students' understanding of key vocabulary terms and concepts presented in the chapter. Other vocabulary terms used in the chapter are listed below.

adenine	leading strand
B lymphocyte	lymph system
bacteriophage	lysogenic cycle
biotechnologist	lytic cycle
capsid	macrophage
complement protein	marker
complementary base pairing	memory cell
	mutagen
	nondisjunction
cytosine	origin of replication
cytotoxic T cell	
deletion	parasite
DNA ligase	pathogen
Down's syndrome	phagocyte
	promoter
evolve	replication
exon	replication bubble
genetic code	
genetically modified food	RNA polymerase
	RNA splicing
growth factor	sequence
guanine	substitution
immune system	sugar-phosphate backbone
infect	
infectious disease	T lymphocyte
inflammatory response	template
	terminator
insertion	thymine
intron	uracil
lagging strand	white blood cell

Concept Review
19. C **20.** A **21.** D

340 Chapter 11

Chapter 11 REVIEW - continued

11. The ability of the immune system to recognize and remember an antigen is known as _____. A(n) _____ contains a weakened virus that prepare the body to fight and destroy cells infected by that particular virus.

12. In DNA, a(n) _____ can be cytosine, thymine, adenine, or guanine.

13. The use of organisms and their genetics to make medicines and improve food crops is called _____. A(n) _____ is a small circular piece of DNA.

14. A(n) _____ is a change in the sequence of DNA.

15. A foreign molecule that activates the immune system is called a(n) _____.

16. A virus infects an organism by entering a(n) _____.

17. Scientists use an enzyme called _____ to cut a DNA molecule and remove a specific sequence. During a process known as _____, foreign DNA is added to a bacterial cell.

18. When any foreign substance appears, the immune system will first use its _____ to attack. Later, the immune system will use its _____ to attack infected cells based on the presence of antigen molecules.

Concept Review

On a sheet of paper, write the letter of the answer that completes each sentence correctly.

19. A vaccine helps the body _____.

A make new DNA **C** fight viruses
B repair mutations **D** make proteins

340 Chapter 11 Genetic Information Cycles

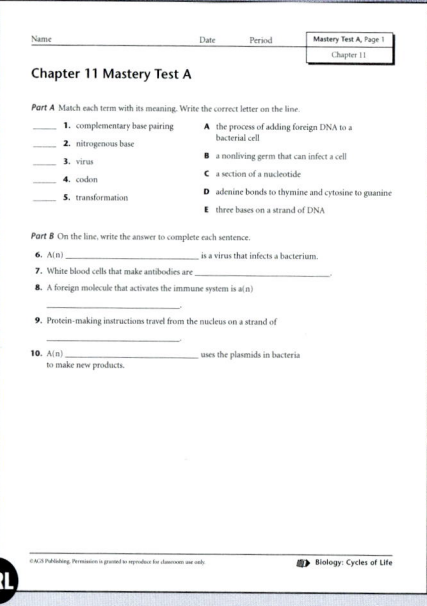

Chapter 11 Mastery Test A, pages 1–3

20. A molecule called _____ carries the genetic code from the nucleus into the cell cytoplasm.

   A mRNA   C rRNA
   B tRNA   D DNA polymerase

21. A specific defense is a(n) _____.

   A inflammation   C skin barrier
   B fever   D lymphocyte

Critical Thinking

On a sheet of paper, write the answers to the following questions. Use complete sentences.

22. Compare and contrast transcription and translation.
23. What would happen to the human body if helper T cells disappeared?
24. Why is DNA replication called semi-conservative?
25. Compare and contrast antigens and antibodies.

Research and Write

Write a report on the development of the vaccine for polio.

Test-Taking Tip To answer a multiple-choice question, read every choice before you answer the question. Cross out the choices that you know are wrong. Choose the best answer from the remaining choices.

Critical Thinking

22. Transcription produces molecules of RNA that are complementary to the sequence of bases in a DNA molecule. Translation produces a protein from the coded sequence of bases in an RNA molecule. **23.** If helper T cells disappeared, the body could not identify a specific infection or subsequently send signals to activate cytotoxic T cells. **24.** DNA replication is called semi-conservative because half of a new strand is old and half is new. **25.** Antigens are molecules or pieces of molecules not typically found in the body. Because they are recognized as foreign, they alert the immune system to the presence of invaders. Antibodies are proteins produced by the immune system that bind to antigens, signaling phagocytes to destroy the invading cells or viruses.

Research and Write

Have students use the library or the Internet to find out more about polio and the development of a vaccine for the disease. *(There are two widely used polio vaccines, the injectible killed-virus vaccine developed by Jonas Salk and the oral attenuated live-virus vaccine developed by Albert Sabin.)* Students may wish to do this research individually, in pairs, or in small groups. Suggest that students share their research with the class.

ALTERNATIVE ASSESSMENT

Alternative Assessment items correlate to the student Goals for Learning at the beginning of this chapter.

- Have pairs of students explain to each other the similarities and differences among replication, transcription, and translation. Have them compare and contrast the molecules and structures involved and the substances produced by each process.
- Have students make models of a virus and a host cell and use their models to explain the lytic and lysogenic cycles.
- Have students draw diagrams that illustrate what happens during the specific and nonspecific defenses.

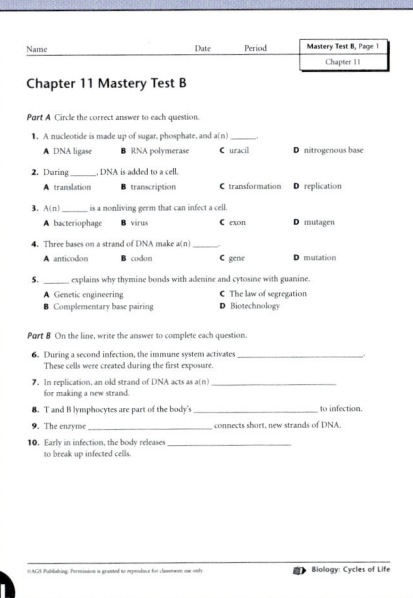

Chapter 11 Mastery Test B, pages 1–3

Chapter 12 Planning Guide
Human Body Systems

	Student Pages	Vocabulary	Lesson Review	Critical-Thinking Questions
Lesson 1 The Digestive System	344–347	✔	✔	✔
Lesson 2 The Respiratory System	348–351	✔	✔	✔
Lesson 3 The Circulatory System	352–358	✔	✔	✔
Lesson 4 The Excretory System	359–361	✔	✔	✔
Lesson 5 The Nervous System	362–366	✔	✔	✔
Lesson 6 The Sensory System	367–371	✔	✔	✔
Lesson 7 The Endocrine System	372–374		✔	✔
Lesson 8 The Skeletal and Muscular Systems	375–381	✔	✔	✔

(Student Text Lesson)

Chapter Activities

Teacher's Resource Library

Community Connection 12: The Effects of Smoking on the Human Body

Graphic Organizer 12: Comparing Body Systems

Teacher's Edition

Opener Activity

Assessment Options

Student Text

Chapter 12 Review

Teacher's Resource Library

Chapter 12 Mastery Tests A and B

Teacher's Edition

Chapter 12 Alternative Assessment

	Student Text Features								Teaching Strategies						Learning Styles					Teacher's Resource Library			
Achievements in Science	Science at Work	Biology in Your Life	Investigation/Discovery	Biology in the World	Express Lab	Link to	Research and Write	Technology and Society	ELL/ESL Strategy	Background Information	Science Journal	Applications (Home, Career, Community, Global, Environment)	Online Connection	Teacher Alert	Auditory/Verbal	Body/Kinesthetic	Interpersonal/Group Learning	Logical/Mathematical	Visual/Spatial	Workbook Activities	Alternative Workbook Activities	Lab Manual	Self-Study Guide
					346	✔			346	344		346		344				346	347	63	63	56	✔
									351	348		350		350		349		350		64	64	57–58	✔
			356	357		✔			353	352	355	355			354, 355			354		65	65		✔
									360	359		361						360		66	66		✔
365						✔			364	362		364				365		365		67	67		✔
								370	369	367	370	369		368	369, 370	369			368, 370	68	68		✔
	373								373	372								374	374	69	69		✔
			379	381		✔	385		375	375		377	377	381						70–71	70–71	59–60	✔

Pronunciation Key

a	hat	e	let	ī	ice	ô	order	ủ	put	sh	she
ā	age	ē	equal	o	hot	oi	oil	ü	rule	th	thin
ä	far	ėr	term	ō	open	ou	out	ch	child	ᴛʜ	then
â	care	i	it	ȯ	saw	u	cup	ng	long	zh	measure

ə { a in about, e in taken, i in pencil, o in lemon, u in circus }

Alternative Workbook Activities

The Teacher's Resource Library (TRL) contains a set of lower-level worksheets called Alternative Workbook Activities. These worksheets cover the same content as the regular Workbook Activities but are written at a second-grade reading level.

Skill Track Online

Use Skill Track Online for *Biology: Cycles of Life* to monitor student progress and meet the demands of adequate yearly progress (AYP). Make informed instructional decisions with individual student and class reports of online lesson and chapter assessments. With immediate and ongoing feedback, students will also see what they have learned and where they need more reinforcement and practice.

Chapter at a Glance

Chapter 12: Human Body Systems
pages 342–385

Lessons

1. The Digestive System
   pages 344–347

2. The Respiratory System
   pages 348–351

3. The Circulatory System
   pages 352–358

   Investigation 12 pages 357–358

4. The Excretory System
   pages 359–361

5. The Nervous System
   pages 362–366

6. The Sensory System
   pages 367–371

7. The Endocrine System
   pages 372–374

8. The Skeletal and Muscular Systems
   pages 375–381

   Discovery Investigation 12
   pages 379–380

   Biology in the World page 381

Chapter 12 Summary page 382

Chapter 12 Review pages 383–385

Audio CD 🎧

Skill Track Online 🖱
for Biology: Cycles of Life

Teacher's Resource Library (TRL)

   Workbook Activities 63–71
   Alternative Workbook Activities 63–71
   Lab Manual 56–60
   Community Connection 12
   Graphic Organizer 12
   Resource File 27–30
   Chapter 12 Self-Study Guide
   Chapter 12 Mastery Tests A and B

(Answer Keys for the Teacher's Resource Library begin on page 675 of the Teacher's Edition. The Materials List for the Lab Manual activities begins on page 720.)

Opener Activity

Before starting the chapter, have students write the names of any human body systems they know of. If students need help, refer them to Organize Your Thoughts on page 343. Then have students bring in photographs and pictures from home that show people engaged in activities that make use of these body systems. For example, a person playing a sport demonstrates the function of the skeletal and muscular systems. A person eating illustrates the digestive system.

Community Connection 12

Chapter 12: Human Body Systems

Think about what the swimmer in the photograph must do to create motion through water. Every body system is involved in producing and controlling motion. Muscles, bones, skin, lungs, heart, ears, eyes, brain, and stomach are all in action at the same time. Imagine building a machine that could move like a swimmer! In Chapter 12, you will learn about the systems of the human body. You will find out how the systems interact and how their activities are coordinated.

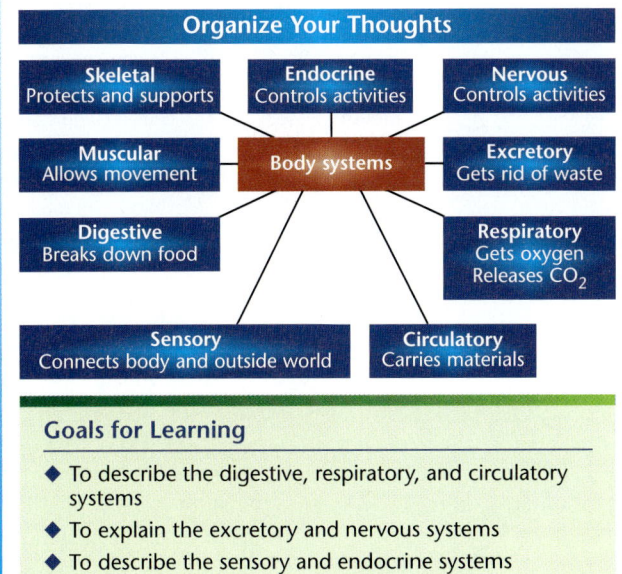

Organize Your Thoughts

- Skeletal — Protects and supports
- Endocrine — Controls activities
- Nervous — Controls activities
- Muscular — Allows movement
- Body systems
- Excretory — Gets rid of waste
- Digestive — Breaks down food
- Respiratory — Gets oxygen Releases CO_2
- Sensory — Connects body and outside world
- Circulatory — Carries materials

Goals for Learning

- ◆ To describe the digestive, respiratory, and circulatory systems
- ◆ To explain the excretory and nervous systems
- ◆ To describe the sensory and endocrine systems
- ◆ To explain the skeletal and muscular systems

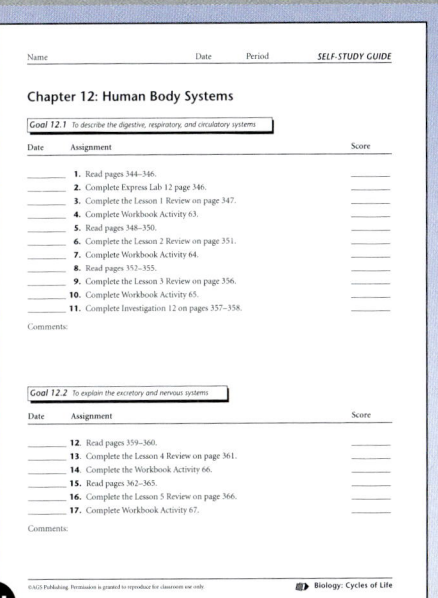

Chapter 12 Self-Study Guide

Introducing the Chapter

Have students look at the photograph on page 342 and write down one or two questions they have about it.

Ask students: How would you define a "system" in your own words? Then have them improve their definition by consulting a dictionary. (*A system is a group of interrelated, interacting, independent elements that form a complex whole.*)

Have students look at the body systems and their corresponding functions in Organize Your Thoughts. Ask students: Do any names of systems look familiar? Have students jot down any general or specific information they know about the systems. Then ask students: Do any two systems in the diagram have similar functions? (*Nervous and endocrine systems both control activities.*) As they read, instruct students to look for what makes these systems different from one another.

Notes and Math Tips

Ask volunteers to read the notes and math tips that appear in the margins throughout the chapter. Then discuss them with the class.

TEACHER'S RESOURCE

The AGS Publishing Teaching Strategies in Science Transparencies may be used with this chapter. The transparencies add an interactive dimension to expand and enhance the *Biology: Cycles of Life* program content.

CAREER INTEREST INVENTORY

The AGS Publishing Harrington-O'Shea Career Decision-Making System-Revised (CDM) may be used with this chapter. Students can use the CDM to explore their interests and identify careers. The CDM defines career areas that are indicated by students' responses on the inventory.

Lesson at a Glance

Chapter 12 Lesson 1

Overview In this lesson, students learn about the structure and function of the digestive system.

Objectives

- To trace the path of food through the digestive system
- To explain how and where digestive chemicals act on food
- To describe what happens to undigested food

Student Pages 344–347

Teacher's Resource Library

Workbook Activity 63
Alternative Workbook Activity 63
Lab Manual 56
Resource File 27

Vocabulary

bile	peristalsis
chyme	pharynx
feces	rectum
gallbladder	reflex
ingestion	villi

Encourage students to think of mnemonic devices to help them remember new vocabulary. For example, in**g**estion is the first stage of di**g**estion. **F**eces means **f**ood that has not been digested.

Background Information

An enzyme is a chemical catalyst that speeds up chemical reactions in all living organisms. Enzymes are unchanged in chemical reactions. Amino acids are biochemical building blocks of proteins.

Pronunciation Guide

Use the pronunciation shown here to help students pronounce difficult words in this lesson. Refer to the pronunciation key on the Chapter Planning Guide for the sounds of the symbols.

salivary amylase (sa´lə ver ē a´mə lās´)
esophagus (i sä´fə gəs)

344 Chapter 12

Lesson 1 The Digestive System

Objectives

After reading this lesson, you should be able to

- trace the path of food through the digestive system
- explain how and where digestive chemicals act on food
- describe what happens to undigested food

Ingestion
The intake of food; the first stage of digestion

Reflex
An automatic response

People need nutrients, minerals, and vitamins from food to live. The human body uses these materials as a source of energy and to build and maintain new cells. The body breaks down food in the digestive system. The main part of the digestive system is the digestive tract. The digestive tract is a long tube that is open at each end of the body. The digestive tract begins at the mouth, where food and liquids enter the body. The tract ends at the anus, where wastes leave the body. The journey of food through the digestive system takes about 24 to 33 hours. As you read about digestion, refer to Figure 12.1.1, which shows the digestive tract.

The Four Stages of Digestion

The first stage of digestion is **ingestion.** Food is taken into the mouth. The teeth chew food into a soft pulp. While food is in the mouth, a **reflex** triggers the release of saliva. A reflex is an automatic response. As you know, saliva is a liquid produced by glands in the mouth. Saliva helps in chewing and starts digestion. Food mixes with saliva and becomes moist and slippery. Saliva also kills bacteria in food. An enzyme in saliva called salivary amylase begins to break down starch and glycogen.

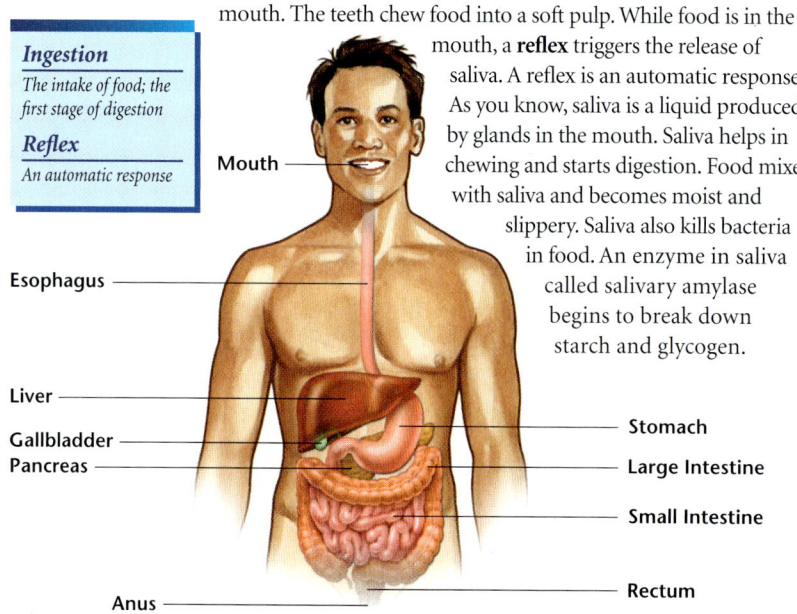

Figure 12.1.1 The human digestive tract can measure up to 30 feet.

344 Chapter 12 Human Body Systems

Teacher Alert

Point out to students that saliva kills some bacteria, not all bacteria. Salmonella and other bacteria that are not killed by saliva can cause food poisoning and other illnesses.

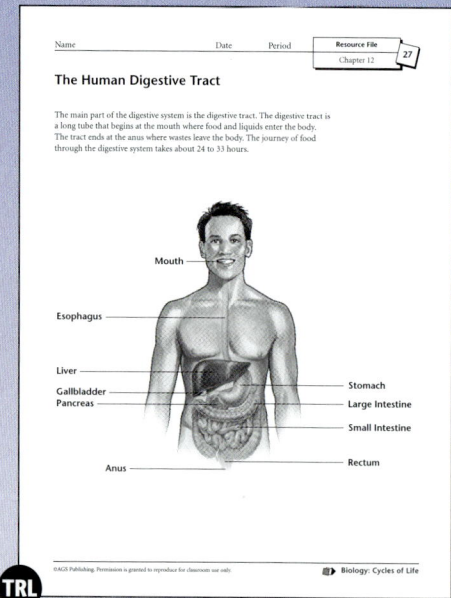

Resource File 27

Pharynx
The passageway between the mouth and the esophagus for air and food

Peristalsis
The movement of digestive organs that pushes food through the digestive tract

Gallbladder
The digestive organ that stores bile

Chyme
The liquid food in the digestive tract that is partially digested

Villi
The tiny, fingerlike structures in the small intestine through which food molecules enter the blood

Bile
A substance made in the liver that breaks down fats

Bacteria can cause an ulcer, or a break, in the stomach lining. Ulcers can be treated with antibiotics.

With the help of the tongue, the food passes to the **pharynx.** The food enters the esophagus. The esophagus connects the mouth and the stomach. The food moves through the esophagus by **peristalsis,** or waves of muscle contraction.

Once food enters the stomach, the second stage of digestion begins. The swallowed food mixes with digestive juices from the liver, **gallbladder,** pancreas, and glands in the intestinal wall. The digestive juices contain enzymes that further digest food. Thick muscles in the walls of the stomach contract. They mash food into a soup called **chyme.**

Stomach acid is very strong. It can dissolve an iron nail. However, the stomach is protected by a lining of mucus. Stomach lining is replaced every three days.

The third stage of digestion is absorption. Chyme enters the small intestine. The small intestine is the longest part of the digestive tract. If unrolled, it would be nearly 20 feet long. The small intestine has fingerlike projections on its surface called **villi.** Villi increase the rate of absorption of food and minerals into the blood.

In the small intestine, enzymes continue to chemically break down food. During this process, the gallbladder releases **bile.** The liver makes bile, a substance that breaks down fats. As chyme arrives in the small intestine, bile flows from the liver to the gallbladder and into the intestine.

Nutrients from food are now small molecules. They can pass through the lining of the small intestine and into the blood. Nutrients are carried to the liver and other body parts to be processed, stored, and distributed. The liver works like a food-processing factory. The liver stores some nutrients. It also changes nutrients to different forms, then releases them into the blood. The nutrients travel to each body cell. Cells absorb the small molecules, such as amino acids and simple sugars. The cells then reassemble these molecules for growth and repair or for ATP production.

Human Body Systems Chapter 12

 Warm-Up Activity

Have students read and perform the Express Lab on page 346. Make sure the food labels provided are from foods that contain fiber. Fiber is indigestible plant matter that stimulates peristalsis. Cellulose is a complex carbohydrate made of glucose units. It is the main part of cell walls in plant cells and is composed of 6 carbon atoms, 10 hydrogen atoms, and 5 oxygen atoms.

Express Lab Answers

1. Cellulose is a type of dietary fiber. Cellulose and all other types of fiber are not digested by the digestive system; they pass right through. **2.** It is recommended that adults have about 24 grams of dietary fiber each day. **3.** Fiber helps keep the digestive system working properly and eliminates waste.

Teaching the Lesson

Obtain a model with removable organs or a large diagram of the human body. Point out the location of the liver, gallbladder, pancreas, and intestines.

Encourage students to use clues in the lesson to take notes. For example, when skimming, students should look for words that signal new thoughts. *First, second, third,* and *fourth* are used in this lesson to describe each of the four stages of digestion.

Give students Resource File 27, which has a diagram of Figure 12.1.1. Have them write *1, 2, 3,* and *4* on the part of the digestive tract where the first, second, third, and fourth stages of digestion occur. Then have students label each number with its corresponding process (ingestion, dissolving and digestion, absorption, elimination) and any other vocabulary terms that are relevant to that stage of digestion.

3 Reinforce and Extend

AT HOME

Have students perform this simple experiment at home to observe salivary amylase at work. Instruct students to put one small piece of bread in water and another in their mouth (without chewing it). After some time has passed, they should observe that the bread in their mouth has not only become soggy from the saliva but also changed texture, as starch has begun to break down chemically. Have students compare and contrast this texture with the texture of the bread in water.

Link to

Environmental Science. After students have read the environmental science feature about *E. coli*, encourage them to research recent outbreaks of the bacteria. Research might include the types of food in which bacteria have been found, symptoms of bacterial infection, and ways to avoid bacterial infection.

ELL/ESL Strategy

Language Objective: *To understand idioms*

English language learners may have trouble with idioms. Tell students that an idiom is an expression in a particular language that cannot be understood from the individual meanings of the words in the idiom. For example, *break down* does not involve movement in a downward direction. *Break down* means "decompose." Similarly, *takes up* on this page does not mean "rises" or "moves upward," but rather "absorbs." Challenge students to find other idioms in the lesson. Help students think of synonyms to clarify the meaning of each idiom.

Feces
The solid waste material remaining in the large intestine after digestion

Rectum
The lower part of the large intestine where feces are stored

Link to >>>
Environmental Science

Escherichia coli is a bacterium commonly found in the digestive tract of humans. Although humans interact with *E. coli* often, nearly all strains are harmless. Sometimes, a bacteria strain harmful to humans can develop. It might be passed along in food. That is why it is important to follow clean practices in food packaging and food preparation.

The fourth stage of digestion is elimination. Undigested food moves to the large intestine and water is recovered. Useful substances are absorbed through the walls of the large intestine and released into the blood. Undigested material passes out of the digestive tract as **feces** through the **rectum** and anus.

Humans absorb 80 to 90 percent of the organic matter in food. Humans cannot digest the cellulose from plant cell walls. Vegetables and fruits are not absorbed as completely as meat, fats, and simple carbohydrates.

Glucose and Glycogen

During digestion, liver cells and muscle cells store glucose as glycogen. Liver cells take up glucose from blood. They store excess glucose as glycogen and change it back to glucose when needed. Glycogen is made of many glucose units. Glucose is the main fuel molecule for the body's cells.

Hormones regulate metabolism. For example, the glycogen storage areas may be full. If people eat more calories than needed, the extra calories are stored as fat in adipose, or fat, cells. If people eat fewer calories than needed, the stored fuel is removed from the storage areas. It is then used as fuel for the body's cells.

Express Lab 12

Materials
- Food products with nutrition labels

Procedure
1. Study the food labels of two different types of food.
2. Look at the ingredients list on each label. Note the amount of fiber in each type of food.

Analysis
1. What is the connection between cellulose and fiber?
2. How much fiber is recommended each day as part of a healthy diet?
3. Why is fiber important to a healthy diet?

346 Chapter 12 Human Body Systems

LEARNING STYLES

Logical/Mathematical

Direct students to the last two sentences on page 345. Have them reflect on what they learned about ATP in Chapter 6. Have them copy passages about energy and ATP synthesis into their notes for this lesson. Students should refer to parts of the chapter that are about the ATP cycle and describe how energy is transferred from food to chemical bonds in ATP. Students can also refer to graphics and diagrams.

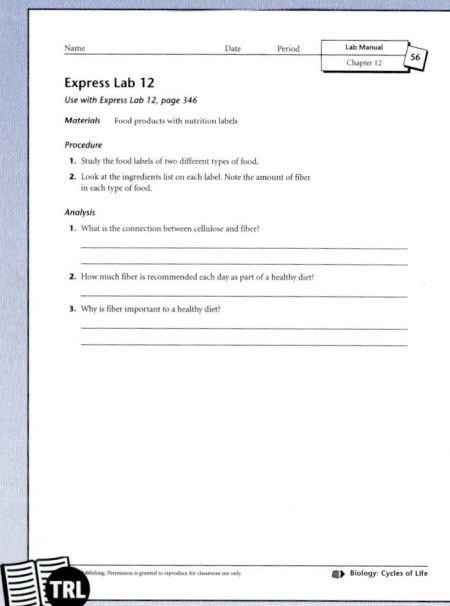

Lesson 1   R E V I E W

Word Bank
- anus
- chyme
- mouth
- villi

On a sheet of a paper, write the word from the Word Bank that completes each sentence correctly.

1. The surface of the small intestine has fingerlike projections called _____ that increase the rate of absorption.

2. Food that has been mashed into a soup in the stomach is _____.

3. The digestive tract begins at the _____ and ends at the _____.

On a sheet of paper, write the letter of the answer that completes each sentence correctly.

4. Your body's metabolism is regulated by _____.
   - **A** hormones   **B** glucose   **C** enzymes   **D** adipose cells

5. The body stores extra glucose as _____.
   - **A** sucrose   **B** ATP   **C** bile   **D** glycogen

6. Bile aids digestion by _____.
   - **A** neutralizing stomach acid
   - **B** breaking down fats
   - **C** converting glucose to glycogen
   - **D** storing vitamins and minerals

Critical Thinking

On a sheet of paper, write the answers to the following questions. Use complete sentences.

7. Why is it helpful for the small intestine to have villi?

8. How do nutrients reach all the cells in the body?

9. List the three roles that saliva plays in digestion.

10. Why does the strong acid in the stomach not dissolve the organs in the digestive system, including the stomach?

Human Body Systems Chapter 12 347

Lesson 1 Review Answers

1. villi **2.** chyme **3.** mouth, anus **4.** A **5.** D **6.** B **7.** Villi increase the rate of absorption. **8.** Blood carries nutrients from one part of the body to another. **9.** Saliva mixes with food to make it moist and slippery. Saliva helps kill bacteria that are in the food. An enzyme in saliva begins to break down starch and glycogen. **10.** A layer of mucus lines the stomach and is constantly being replaced.

Portfolio Assessment

Sample items include:
- Answers to Express Lab questions
- Annotated diagram of digestive tract from Teaching the Lesson
- Research report from Link to Environmental Science
- Flowchart from Learning Styles Visual/Spatial
- Lesson 1 Review answers

LEARNING STYLES

Visual/Spatial
Have students look back over the lesson and draw a flowchart or similar graphic organizer for the material. Alternatively, have students draw a picture of the digestive tract, with labels of the four stages and related vocabulary.

LAB ACTIVITIES

Chapter 12 has Investigation and Discovery Investigation lab activities. Two additional lab activities for Chapter 12 appear in the Biology: Cycles of Life Lab Manual and on the Teacher's Resource Library CD-ROM.

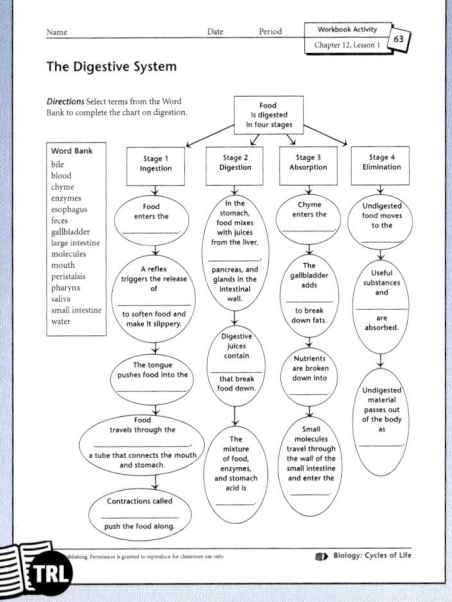

Workbook Activity 63

Human Body Systems 347

Lesson at a Glance

Chapter 12 Lesson 2

Overview In this lesson, students learn about the structure and function of the respiratory system.

Objectives

- To identify the function and parts of the respiratory system
- To describe the process of gas exchange in the lungs
- To describe the process of breathing
- To list some respiratory diseases

Student Pages 348–351

Teacher's Resource Library

Workbook Activity 64

Alternative Workbook Activity 64

Vocabulary

alveolus	epithelium
asthma	glottis
bronchiole	larynx
bronchitis	sleep apnea
bronchus	trachea
capillary	

Have students write a sentence using each vocabulary term in context. Ask volunteers to share their sentences with the class.

Background Information

Diffuse is the verb form of *diffusion*. *Diffusion* has several different dictionary definitions. In this lesson, diffusion refers to the process by which dissolved substances move from an area of higher concentration to an area of lower concentration.

Lesson 2 The Respiratory System

Objectives

After reading this lesson, you should be able to
- identify the function and parts of the respiratory system
- describe the process of gas exchange in the lungs
- describe the process of breathing
- list some respiratory diseases

Epithelium
A thin layer of cells forming a tissue that covers body surfaces and lines some organs

Capillary
A blood vessel through which oxygen and food molecules pass to body cells

Glottis
The opening to the windpipe

Larynx
The voice box

Body cells use oxygen to release energy from food. This process is cellular respiration. During this process, carbon dioxide is produced as waste. The body takes in oxygen and releases carbon dioxide into the environment. The exchange of oxygen and carbon dioxide occurs in the lungs. That is why the lungs are the most important organs in the respiratory system.

Oxygen from inhaled air diffuses across the **epithelium** in the lungs into the blood. The epithelium is a thin layer of cells forming a tissue that covers body surfaces and lines some organs. The blood circulates to the body's tissues through **capillaries.** Capillaries are blood vessels that have a wall that is one cell thick. Oxygen and food molecules pass through the capillaries to body cells. Carbon dioxide, a waste product of the body, diffuses from the blood into the lungs to be exhaled.

Respiration

Respiration begins when air is inhaled. Air enters the nose through the nostrils. Small nasal hairs filter the air. The nostrils warm and humidify the air. Then the air flows to the pharynx. The digestive tract and respiratory tract cross at the pharynx.

When the **glottis** is open, air passes through. The glottis is the opening to the windpipe. When food is swallowed, the **larynx** moves up and tips the epiglottis over the glottis. The epiglottis is a thin, soft material. It prevents swallowing and inhaling at the same time.

From the larynx, air passes to the **trachea.** The trachea divides into two branches called bronchi. Each **bronchus** leads to one lung. The lungs have a spongy texture and are lined with cilia and mucus. Cilia are hair-like structures. Mucus traps dust, pollen, and other particles. The cilia move the mucus up where it is swallowed. This process cleans the respiratory system.

348 Chapter 12 Human Body Systems

 Warm-Up Activity

To help students grasp the concept of diffusion, remind them how air particles move from areas of higher concentration to areas of lower concentration. To model this, have students blow up a balloon and then let it deflate. Air rushes out. Similarly, dissolved substances in blood pass from areas of higher concentration to areas of lower concentration. The air rushing out of the balloon is analogous to dissolved particles such as oxygen passing from alveoli to capillaries, where the concentration is lower.

Trachea
The tube that carries air to the bronchi

Bronchus
A tube that connects the trachea to a lung (plural is bronchi)

Bronchiole
A tube that branches off the bronchus

Alveolus
A tiny air sac at the end of each bronchiole that holds air (plural is alveoli)

In the United States, nearly 87 percent of lung cancer cases are connected to smoking.

From the bronchi, the lungs branch into **bronchioles.** At the tip of each bronchiole is a cluster of air sacs called alveoli. An **alveolus** is a tiny air sac. There are millions of alveoli. Gas exchange happens at the alveoli. Oxygen enters the alveoli and dissolves in the moist mucus. It diffuses across the epithelium into a network of capillaries. Capillaries are wrapped around the alveoli. Capillary walls are very thin and close to each other. Oxygen easily seeps through them and into the blood. At the same time, carbon dioxide in the blood seeps into the alveoli. Carbon dioxide is removed from the body when exhaled.

Breathing

Figure 12.2.1 shows the respiratory system. Breathing alternates between inhaling and exhaling. During inhalation, the muscles around the lungs and the diaphragm contract. The diaphragm is a strong, thin muscle below the lungs. The rib cage expands and lung volume increases. Air rushes into the lungs. During exhalation, the diaphragm and other muscles around the lungs relax. Lung volume decreases. Air is pushed up the breathing tubes and out the mouth and nostrils.

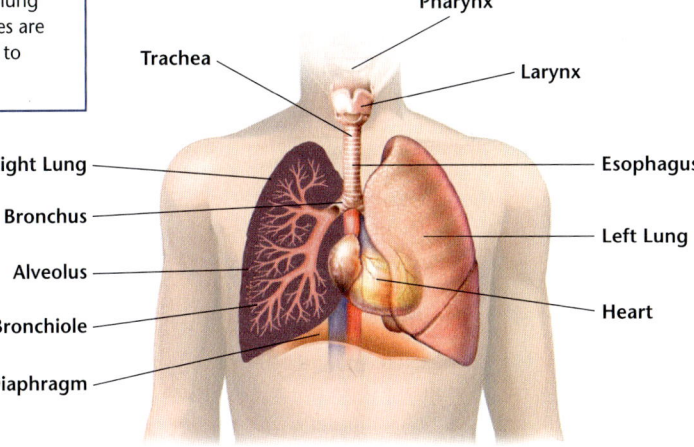

Figure 12.2.1 *The respiratory system takes in oxygen and gets rid of carbon dioxide.*

2 Teaching the Lesson

Ask students: Where have you encountered the term *respiration* in earlier chapters? *(cellular respiration in Chapter 7, photosynthesis in Chapter 8)* In photosynthesis, respiration refers to the exchange of carbon dioxide and oxygen between a plant and the atmosphere. Have students compare and contrast this type of respiration with the respiration that occurs during breathing.

Tell students that in addition to cancer, emphysema, and heart disease, smoking has other dangerous effects on health. Encourage students to research what smoking does to the respiratory system. Smoking damages the cilia, first slowing their movement and then paralyzing them altogether. As a result, mucus must be moved up through the lungs and bronchi in a different way, by coughing. This results in what is called a smoker's cough.

Ask students: Why do people breathe faster when they are exercising? *(There is an increase in cellular respiration to produce the energy to perform the exercise, so people need to take in more oxygen and exhale more carbon dioxide.)*

3 Reinforce and Extend

LEARNING STYLES

Body/Kinesthetic
Have students close their eyes and feel the parts of their body that move as they inhale and exhale. They will feel the rib cage expanding. Make sure they do not confuse the rib cage with the diaphragm or stomach. Students will not be able to feel their diaphragm contracting and relaxing.

Singers train themselves to use their diaphragm and respiratory system to produce more and better sound. If possible, get a music or voice teacher to visit your class and demonstrate how inhalation can be maximized and how exhalation is used to sustain sound.

PRONUNCIATION GUIDE

Use the pronunciation shown here to help students pronounce a difficult word in this lesson. Refer to the pronunciation key on the Chapter Planning Guide for the sounds of the symbols.

cystic fibrosis (sis′tik fī brō′səs)

IN THE COMMUNITY

Invite an otolaryngologist to visit your class and make a presentation on common respiratory illnesses such as asthma, allergies, bronchitis, and pneumonia. Make sure the doctor discusses prevention and treatments for respiratory illnesses.

IN THE ENVIRONMENT

Have students research ways that environmental decisions by governments affect public health. For example, exposure to increased levels of ozone, an air pollutant, can worsen symptoms for those who suffer from allergies or asthma. At least one study provided strong evidence that exposure to increased levels of ozone in the air may actually cause asthma in children.

LEARNING STYLES

Logical/Mathematical

Ask students: If a person breathes 12 times a minute, how many seconds does the person take to complete one full breath? *(one breath every five seconds)*

Sleep apnea
A condition in which short periods of not breathing occur during sleep

Asthma
A condition that narrows or blocks the airways and makes breathing difficult

Bronchitis
An inflammation of the bronchial tubes

At rest, you usually breathe about 12 times a minute.

The contracting and relaxing of muscles control the rate of expansion (increase) and constriction (decrease) of the lungs. That means you can control your breathing by holding your breath. You can breathe deeper or faster. Breathing is usually automatic. You breathe without thinking about it.

Sometimes this automatic system does not work correctly. People with **sleep apnea** stop breathing up to 300 times a night. When breathing stops, oxygen levels decrease. Then carbon dioxide levels increase in the blood. The decreased oxygen and increased carbon dioxide usually signal the brain to breathe. The person wakes up so breathing can restart.

Changes in altitude can change breathing. As altitude increases, atmospheric pressure decreases. Decreased pressure reduces the amount of oxygen that enters the blood. To get more oxygen, mountain climbers breathe more quickly as they climb. They also lose carbon dioxide faster.

Respiratory System Diseases

Some people have respiratory system diseases. **Asthma** is a condition that narrows or blocks the airways. This causes shortness of breath and makes breathing difficult. The airways narrow when they overreact to certain substances, such as dust, smoke, or cold air.

Bronchitis is another respiratory system disease that reduces airflow. Over time, exposure to lung irritants causes bronchitis. Irritants include cigarette smoke and air pollutants. Cystic fibrosis is a genetic disease. It causes mucus to build up in the lungs and clog the airways.

The circulatory system, which you will learn about in Lesson 3, works together with the respiratory system. The respiratory system supplies oxygen to the body and gets rid of carbon dioxide. This process supports the work of cells. The circulatory system transports these gases from the lungs to the cells and back to the lungs. This process is a continual cycle.

TEACHER ALERT

To avoid confusion, make sure students recognize the singular and plural form of terms such as *alveoli* and *bronchi*. The lesson makes the distinction in the last paragraph on page 348. The word *bronchi* is plural because it refers to two branches, while the word *each* suggests that *bronchus* is singular. Students can remember the distinction (*-i* means "more than one," *-us* means "one") by recalling that the convention is opposite the use of the pronouns *I* (singular) and *us* (plural).

Lesson 2 REVIEW

Word Bank
carbon dioxide
cystic fibrosis
oxygen
sleep apnea

On a sheet of a paper, write the word or words from the Word Bank that complete each sentence correctly.

1. An inherited respiratory disease is ____.
2. A condition that causes a person to stop breathing at night is ____.
3. Gas exchange involves taking in ____ and getting rid of ____.

On a sheet of paper, write the letter of the answer that completes each sentence correctly.

4. The ____ traps dust and other particles in the lungs.
   A alveoli   B cilia   C glottis   D mucus

5. Respiration begins when ____.
   A the lungs stretch   C air is inhaled
   B the diaphragm contracts   D the mouth opens

6. An increase in altitude changes breathing by ____.
   A slowing carbon dioxide loss from blood
   B reducing the amount of oxygen entering the blood
   C increasing dehydration in blood
   D decreasing muscle activity in the diaphragm

Critical Thinking

On a sheet of paper, write the answers to the following questions. Use complete sentences.

7. Why can't a person breathe when swallowing food?
8. How does oxygen taken in by the lungs reach the body's cells?
9. Why are the lungs the most important organs in the respiratory system?
10. Describe three respiratory diseases.

Human Body Systems Chapter 12 351

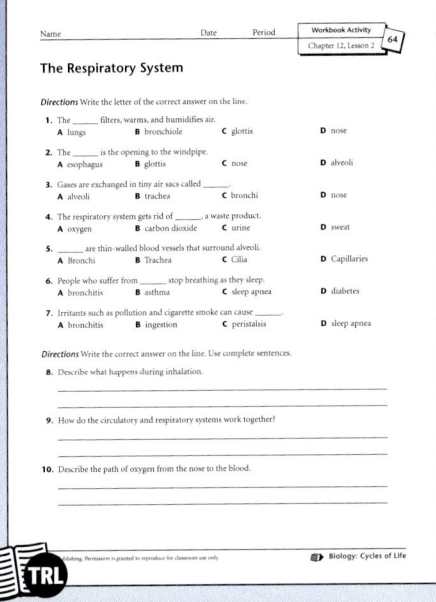

Workbook Activity 64

Lesson at a Glance

Chapter 12 Lesson 3

Overview In this lesson, students learn about the structure and function of the circulatory system.

Objectives

- To identify the major parts of the circulatory system and their functions
- To compare and contrast arteries and veins
- To trace the flow of blood through the heart
- To describe the parts of blood and explain their functions

Student Pages 352–358

Teacher's Resource Library TRL

- Workbook Activity 65
- Alternative Workbook Activity 65
- Lab Manual 57–58
- Resource File 28

Vocabulary

aorta	hypertension
artery	inferior vena cava
atherosclerosis	interstitial fluid
atrium	plasma
cardiac	platelet
cardiovascular disease	superior vena cava
	thrombus
connective tissue	ventricle
fibrinogen	

Write the vocabulary terms in one column on the board. Write the definitions in random order in a second column. Have students match each term with the correct definition by drawing lines from the terms to their definitions.

Background Information

A hormone is a substance that affects and regulates physiological activity such as growth or metabolism. An antibody is a protein substance in blood or tissue that destroys or weakens a harmful bacterium or toxin. Hormones are important to growth and development. Antibodies are important to the immune system.

Lesson 3 The Circulatory System

Objectives

After reading this lesson, you should be able to
- identify the major parts of the circulatory system and their functions
- compare and contrast arteries and veins
- trace the flow of blood through the heart
- describe the parts of blood and explain their functions

Cardiac
Relating to the heart

The circulatory system transports gases, nutrients, hormones, and antibodies within the body. Blood delivers oxygen and nutrients to the body's cells. Blood also carries away waste materials.

The Heart

Figure 12.3.1 shows the heart. The heart is the main organ of the circulatory system. It pumps blood through the body. The heart is about the size of a fist. It is located between the lungs in the chest cavity. The heart is made mostly of thick muscular tissue called **cardiac** muscle. The heart contracts and relaxes in a regular manner know as the heartbeat. The heart works automatically. A person does not have to think about it to make the heart beat.

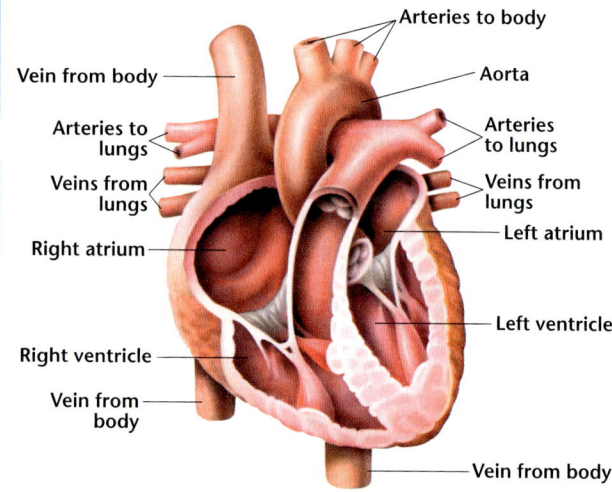

Figure 12.3.1 The heart is the main organ of the circulatory system.

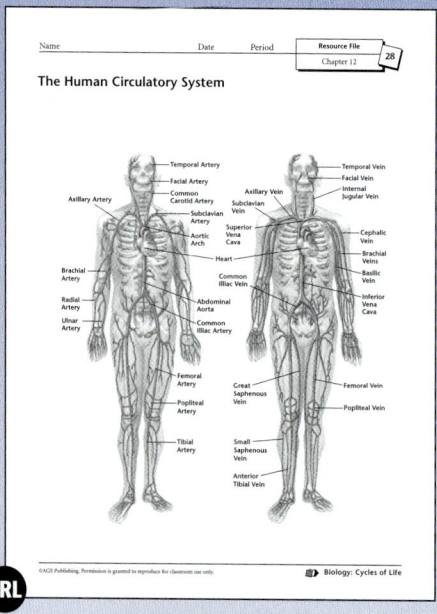

Resource File 28

Atrium
A heart chamber that receives blood returning to the heart (plural is atria)

Ventricle
A heart chamber that pumps blood out of the heart

Artery
A blood vessel that carries blood away from the heart (plural is arteries)

Aorta
A large vessel through which the left ventricle sends blood to the body

Interstitial fluid
A fluid that fills the space around cells and exchanges nutrients and wastes with blood

Superior vena cava
A large vein that carries blood from the head, neck, and arms to the heart

Inferior vena cava
A large vein that carries blood from the trunk and legs to the heart

The heart has two sides, left and right. Each side has an upper chamber called the **atrium** and a lower chamber called the **ventricle.** The atrium is the smaller chamber and has thin walls. It receives blood from the body. From the atrium, blood flows into the larger ventricle. The ventricle has thick, strong walls that contract to pump blood.

How Blood Circulates

Blood travels in one direction to form a circle pattern. Arteries are blood vessels that carry blood away from the heart. An **artery** carries blood full of oxygen. The **aorta** is the largest artery. Arteries become smaller as they move away from the heart.

From the aorta, blood flows through arteries to the heart muscle. Other branches lead to capillaries in the head, arms, stomach, and legs. From capillaries, the blood travels to body cells. **Interstitial fluid** fills the space around body cells. It exchanges nutrients and wastes with the blood. Blood gives up oxygen and picks up carbon dioxide produced by cellular respiration.

Blood that contains waste products flows back to the heart through veins. Oxygen-poor blood from the head, arms, and neck goes to a large vein called the **superior vena cava.** Another large vein called the **inferior vena cava** carries blood from the trunk and legs. These large veins take blood into the right atrium of the heart. The oxygen-poor blood flows into the right ventricle.

Only one artery carries blood high in carbon dioxide. This artery carries oxygen-poor blood from the right ventricle to the lungs. As blood flows through capillaries into the lungs, it loads oxygen and unloads carbon dioxide. Oxygen-rich blood returns from the lungs to the left heart atrium and to the left ventricle. The left ventricle pumps the oxygen-rich blood into the aorta, and the cycle repeats.

Human Body Systems Chapter 12 353

Warm-Up Activity

Students can feel their circulatory system at work by feeling their heartbeat and their pulse. Instruct students to take their pulse by counting the number of beats in a minute. You may need to demonstrate how to do this. One way to find your pulse is to place two fingers in the groove on your wrist under your thumb. (Make sure your palms are facing up.) Slide your fingers in the groove until you feel the pulsing of the radial artery. (The radial artery transports blood to the hand.) You can also find your pulse along the carotid artery that supplies blood to the neck and head. Run two fingers along your windpipe about two inches below your chin.

Teaching the Lesson

Have students write down what they think the prefix *inter-* means, based on the definition of *interstitial fluid* in the lesson. (*Inter-* means "between, among, in the midst of.")

Ask students: What analogies can you think of for the circulatory system? *(One good analogy is transportation systems. Major roads and interstate highways represent major arteries. Driveways represent capillaries, while houses, factories, and schools represent individual cells.)*

Reinforce and Extend

ELL/ESL Strategy

Language Objective:
To understand use of hyphens

Some students who are learning English may not recognize the function of the hyphen in terms such as *oxygen-rich* and *oxygen-poor*. Tell students that a hyphen is used to connect a noun, *oxygen*, with an adjective, *rich*. The hyphen makes both words function together as a single compound unit, an adjective that modifies the noun *blood*. Have students make other compounds with *rich* and *poor* and use them in sentences. (Example: The rainforest is a plant-rich habitat.)

Human Body Systems 353

LEARNING STYLES

Logical/Mathematical

According to the Centers for Disease Control, in 2001, the average life expectancy in the United States was 77.2 years. Ask students: How could you use the information in the lesson to calculate the number of times a heart beats in a lifetime if the average life expectancy is 77.2 years? To simplify the calculation, tell students to ignore leap years and assume a lifetime average of 70 beats per minute. *(Students should calculate the number of minutes in a day; multiply that by 365 to get minutes in a year; multiply the result by 77.2 to determine minutes in a lifetime; and finally multiply the resulting figure by 70, the number of beats per minute.)*

Link to

Chemistry. Chemistry is important to blood. Recall that healthy blood has a pH between 7.35 and 7.45. Have students refer back to the "Blood and pH" Biology in the World feature in Chapter 2 on page 63 for more information on the chemistry of blood. Tell students that the average life span of a red blood cell is 100–120 days.

LEARNING STYLES

Auditory/Verbal

Have students look up *fiber* in a dictionary. *(They will find several definitions, of which the first will most likely define fiber as a threadlike structure.)* Next, have students look up the prefix *fibr-*. *(It means "fiber" or "fibrous tissue.")* Direct students' attention to the definition of *fibrinogen* in the lesson. Point out that the definition mentions the word *threads*. Have students use a dictionary to list and define other words with the prefix *fibr-*.

Connective tissue
The supporting framework of the body and its organs

Plasma
The liquid part of blood

Platelet
A tiny piece of cell that helps form clots

Link to ▸▸▸

Chemistry

Red blood cells are one of the few human cells that do not contain DNA. As they mature, red blood cells lose their cell nucleus. DNA is stored in the nucleus. Mature red blood cells also contain no mitochondria.

Heart valves prevent blood from flowing backwards. A defect in a valve is called a heart murmur. It sounds like hissing as blood squirts backward through a valve. The elastic walls of arteries expand when they receive blood from the ventricles. When you take your pulse, you can detect this movement. A pulse represents the rhythmic stretching of the arteries. Blood pressure is the contractions of the ventricles, which cause stretching.

The heart beats about 70 times a minute in adults who are sitting or standing quietly. That is over 100,000 beats per day pumping more than 7,000 liters of blood. Some body hormones increase heart rate. An increase in body temperature also increases heart rate. A fever causes body temperature and pulse rate to increase. Exercise increases heart rate, which delivers more oxygen to the muscles to do the extra work.

Capillaries in the brain, heart, kidneys, and liver are always filled with blood. The amount of blood varies in other body sites. After eating, blood is moved to the digestive tract. You may feel cold after eating because of this. During exercise, blood is moved away from the digestive tract and sent to the skin and muscles.

Blood Cells

Blood is **connective tissue.** Connective tissue is the supporting framework of the body and its organs. Blood contains cells held in **plasma.** Plasma is the liquid part of blood. The three types of blood cells are red blood cells, white blood cells, and **platelets.**

Red blood cells, also called erythrocytes, transport oxygen. Hemoglobin is a protein in red blood cells that contains iron. Hemoglobin transports oxygen.

White blood cells are larger than red blood cells. There is about one white blood cell for every 700 red blood cells. White blood cells fight infection in the body. White blood cells usually stay outside the circulatory system in the interstitial fluid.

Fibrinogen
A protein in the platelets that forms into threads, creating a clot

Thrombus
A clot of blood formed within a blood vessel

Cardiovascular disease
A disease of the heart and blood vessels

Atherosclerosis
A disease that harms the arteries by narrowing them

Hypertension
High blood pressure

Science Myth

Myth: The blood in arteries is red. The blood in veins is blue.

Fact: All blood is red. Blood vessels near the skin look blue because you look at blood through skin. Illustrations often have red for arteries and blue for veins. This is to show that arteries carry more oxygen than veins.

Platelets are pieces of cells used in blood clots. A protein in the platelets, called **fibrinogen,** forms into threads, creating a clot. An inherited defect in clotting is hemophilia. A person who has hemophilia can have trouble stopping the flow of blood, even from a minor cut. The blood does not clot well.

In some people, platelets form a clot, or a **thrombus,** when there is no injury. A thrombus blocks the flow of blood. A thrombus can form in people who have heart disease.

Heart Diseases

Diseases of the heart and blood vessels are called **cardiovascular diseases.** Cardiovascular diseases cause more than half of all deaths each year in the United States. Heart attacks and strokes result from a thrombus that clogs an artery. A blocked artery causes cardiac muscle tissue to die. Blocked arteries in the brain can cause a stroke.

Many people who have had a heart attack have **atherosclerosis.** This disease causes a buildup of fatty substances. Over time, this buildup causes blood vessels to harden and narrow. The risk of a heart attack or stroke increases. Another condition called **hypertension,** or high blood pressure, increases the chance of stroke or heart attack. Hypertension happens when the force of blood against the artery walls is too strong.

Keeping Fit

Being overweight increases a person's chances of cardiovascular diseases. Most people become overweight because they eat too many calories and do not exercise enough. Exercise has many more benefits than helping maintain a healthy body weight. Regular exercise makes the heart stronger and more efficient. It helps strengthen muscles, bones, and joints. It also helps reduce the risk of diabetes, colon cancer, and cardiovascular and other diseases.

Everyone needs exercise to stay healthy. Most people should be physically active daily for at least 30 minutes. Keeping fit can include playing sports, walking, biking, or swimming.

Human Body Systems   Chapter 12   **355**

Learning Styles

Auditory/Verbal
Tell students that another name for low blood pressure is hypotension. *Hypo-* means "less than normal." *Hyper-* means "excessive" or "beyond." These prefixes are opposites, so it follows that hypertension and hypotension are opposite classifications. Have students work in pairs to identify and define other pairs of words starting with prefixes that have opposite meanings, using a dictionary if needed. (Example: *subsaturated, supersaturated*)

At Home

Tell students that blood pressure is measured in two ways: a systolic reading that measures the greatest pressure when the heart is constricted, and a diastolic reading that measures the greatest pressure when the heart is relaxed. Generally, a normal range for an adolescent under 18 is around 90 mmHg systolic and under 60 mmHg diastolic (where mmHg is a distance in millimeters, the pressure exerted by the heart would force a column of mercury to rise, much like a thermometer).

Have students try to obtain their most recent blood pressure readings from their doctor, with parental help. Ask students: Does your blood pressure fall within the normal range?

Science Journal

Have students write a first-person paragraph describing how their digestive, respiratory, and circulatory systems cooperate to carry out bodily functions, and how this relates to their lives. *(Example: My digestive system breaks down food into macromolecules that then pass into my blood, and are distributed to other parts of my body through the circulatory system. That's how molecules from my breakfast cereal got to the cells that gave my muscles the energy to walk to school this morning.)*

Science Myth

Ask a volunteer to read the Science Myth feature aloud. Tell students that blood is red because red blood cells make up 40–45 percent of blood. (By contrast, platelets and white blood cells make up only about 1 percent of blood.) Red blood cells are red because of the iron in hemoglobin. Iron combines well with oxygen. The more oxygen blood has, the redder it is. So while it is true that blood containing more oxygen is redder, venous blood containing less oxygen is simply less red than arterial blood.

Lesson 3 Review Answers

1. atrium **2.** plasma **3.** arteries **4.** When an artery is blocked, cardiac muscle tissue dies, and a heart attack can result. **5.** Red blood cells contain hemoglobin, which transports the oxygen in the blood.

Portfolio Assessment

Sample items include:
- Lesson 3 Review answers

Biology in Your Life

Read aloud the Biology in Your Life feature about blood pressure. Then have students recall the last time they had a physical. Ask students: Can you remember having your blood pressure taken? How did the doctor or nurse measure your blood pressure? *(Probably it was measured with a sphygmomanometer, using a blood pressure cuff.)* Have students describe the device used. Then tell students how it works. Typically, a cuff is wrapped around the arm. Air is pumped into the cuff to cut off the flow of blood for a couple of seconds. Then a valve is released so pressure eases gradually, and a stethoscope is used to determine at what pressure the blood flows into the limb again.

Biology in Your Life Answers

1. High blood pressure often does not show any symptoms. **2.** High blood pressure can cause heart attack or stroke. **3.** Treatments for mild high blood pressure include losing weight and exercising. Also, risk factors such as smoking, drinking, and stress should be reduced or eliminated. If blood pressure is high enough, medication may be necessary.

Lesson 3 REVIEW

Word Bank
arteries
atrium
plasma

On a sheet of a paper, write the word from the Word Bank that completes each sentence correctly.

1. The _____ is the smaller chamber of the heart.
2. The liquid part of blood is _____.
3. Atherosclerosis is caused by fatty substances that are deposited on the inner walls of _____.

Critical Thinking

On a sheet of paper, answer the following questions. Use complete sentences.

4. How does cardiovascular disease cause a heart attack?
5. What part of red blood cells helps to transport oxygen?

Biology in Your Life

Consumer Choices: What Does Blood Pressure Mean?

The American Heart Association estimates that about 25 percent of adults have high blood pressure. High blood pressure is also called hypertension. Many people do not know when they have hypertension. It often does not cause obvious problems.

Blood pressure tells how hard the heart works to pump blood throughout the body. Sometimes arteries get clogged or become narrow. Blood moves slower through the body and the heart must work harder. This builds pressure. The person may be at risk for heart attack or stroke.

Smoking, too much alcohol, and high stress can cause hypertension. To control hypertension, doctors tell people to exercise regularly and lose weight, and eat more fruits, vegetables, and whole grains.

People may have to take medications to reduce hypertension.

1. Why can someone who feels healthy have high blood pressure?
2. What are dangers of high blood pressure?
3. Do you know someone who has high blood pressure? What do they do to treat it?

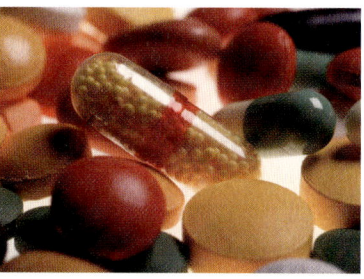

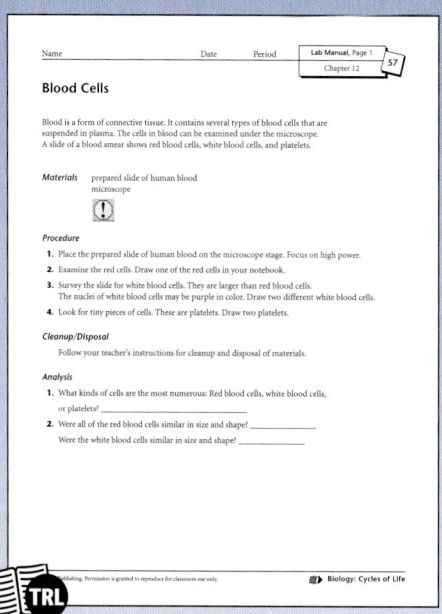

Lab Manual 57, pages 1–2

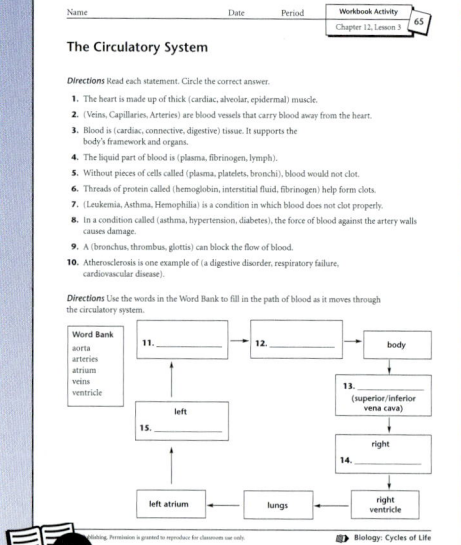

Workbook Activity 65

INVESTIGATION 12

Materials
- graph paper
- clock with a second hand

How Exercise Affects Heart Rate

Heart rate is usually measured by taking a person's pulse. Each time your heart beats, it sends blood rushing through your arteries. The arteries stretch a little as blood rushes through them. You can feel this stretching as a small bump or beat at a pressure point. The easiest pressure points to use are on your neck or on the inside of your wrist. By counting the beats, you will find your heart rate, or pulse rate. In this lab, you will find out how your heart rate changes with exercise.

Procedure

1. To record your observations, draw a table like the one shown below on a sheet of graph paper.

2. To find your resting heart rate, take your pulse. To do this, sit quietly in a chair for two minutes. Then place your first two fingers on your inner wrist near the base of your thumb. Press lightly to feel your pulse. If you do not feel a pulse, move your fingers around a little until you do.

Activity	Heart Rate
Sitting quietly	
After running for 1 minute	
After resting for 2 minutes	
After resting for 4 minutes	
After resting for 6 minutes	
After resting for 8 minutes	
After resting for 10 minutes	

Human Body Systems Chapter 12 357

SAFETY ALERT

- Be sure students do not perform an exercise that could cause injury. Check with the school nurse to find out if any students require special consideration or alternative exercises.

Investigation 12

Encourage students to read the investigation steps. Discuss questions they may have before beginning the investigation.

Objectives
- To learn to take and record heart rates
- To collect data and display it on a graph
- To connect the changes in heart rates to level of physical activity

Skills
Observing, collecting data, finding averages, displaying data, inferring

Background
Students do not always make the connection between body systems and the environment. Although they know that physical exertion causes them to breathe harder and to sweat, they often do not realize that these things happen as a response to the environment to maintain homeostasis.

In this investigation, students learn to take and record their pulse rate during different levels of activity. As the body exercises more intensely, it requires more oxygen for respiration to supply the needed energy. As a result, breathing increases to take in more oxygen, and the heart rate increases to deliver the oxygen to the cells.

Time Frame
One class period

Procedure
- Be sure students have enough room to perform their exercise. The investigation calls for students to run in place, but they can perform another exercise, such as doing steps. Students should perform a safe exercise that will raise their heart rates, but not cause overexertion or injury. Be sure to include students with physical disabilities in this investigation, as almost any type of physical activity will give results.

Continued on page 358

Human Body Systems 357

Continued from page 357

Analysis Answers

1. As the level of exercise increases, the heart rate increases.
2. After the exercise has stopped and the person begins to rest, his or her heart rate begins to drop to the resting rate.

Conclusions Answers

1. The heart responds to the need for more oxygen by the cells in the body. As exercise increases, energy is used and oxygen is required.
2. Heart rate responds to the intensity of the exercise. As you increase intensity, the heart rate also increases. As you rest, your heart rate drops back down.

Explore Further Answers

Have students show the link between heart rate, respiration rate, and activity.

Assessment

Check students' data tables and the graph they created. Check students' answers to the Analysis and Conclusions questions. You might include the following items from this investigation in student portfolios:

- Answers to Analysis and Conclusions questions

3. Watching the second hand on a clock, count the beats you feel for exactly one minute. Record this number in your table.
4. Run in place for one minute. **Safety Alert: Tell your teacher if you should not do this physical activity.**
5. Immediately measure your heart rate for one minute. Record this information.
6. Sit quietly for one minute. Then measure your heart rate for one minute. Repeat until you have recorded five measurements after your run.
7. On graph paper, make a graph from your data to show how your heart rate changed before, during, and after exercise.

Analysis

1. How did exercise affect your heart rate?
2. What happened to your heart rate when you stopped exercising and rested?

Conclusions

1. What needs do you think your heart responded to when your heart rate changed?
2. What do you think heart rate tells you about the level of exercise you are performing?

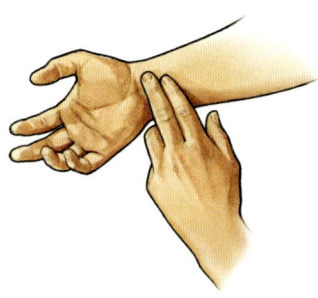

Explore Further

Measure your heart rate for one minute while you run in place. At the same time, have a partner measure your respiration rate (the number of breaths you take in a minute). How are respiration rate and heart rate related?

Lab Manual 58, pages 1–2

Lesson 4: The Excretory System

Objectives

After reading this lesson, you should be able to
- explain how the excretory system regulates water balance in the body
- explain how the excretory system removes waste from the body
- describe how hormones control water absorption in the body

Ureter
A tube that carries urine from the kidney to the urinary bladder

Urine
Liquid waste formed in the kidneys

The excretory system regulates water balance in the body and removes waste. Wastes from interstitial fluid are carried by blood capillaries. The capillaries deposit the waste at a collection point for removal from the body. The excretory system also regulates the chemical makeup of body fluids. It keeps the proper amounts of water, salts, and nutrients in the body fluids. The excretory system includes the kidneys, **ureters,** bladder, urethra, liver, lungs, and skin.

Your cells make nitrogen wastes, which are poisonous. The excretory system gets rid of these wastes. The body has two bean-shaped kidneys. The kidneys are the main organs of the excretory system. Each kidney is about 10 centimeters long. Blood flows to and from the kidneys through the renal artery and renal vein. The kidneys take the nitrogen wastes from the blood and form **urine.** Urine leaves each kidney through the ureter. The ureter is a duct, or body tube. A ureter from each kidney drains into the bladder. From the bladder, urine leaves the body through the urethra. Follow the path of urine through the excretory system in Figure 12.4.1.

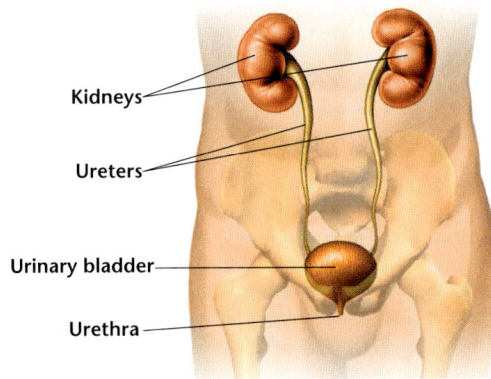

Figure 12.4.1 The body produces about 1.5 liters (6 cups) of urine in one 24-hour period.

Lesson at a Glance

Chapter 12 Lesson 4

Overview In this lesson, students learn about the structure and function of the excretory system.

Objectives
- To explain how the excretory system regulates water balance in the body
- To explain how the excretory system removes waste from the body
- To describe how hormones control water absorption in the body

Student Pages 359–361

Teacher's Resource Library TRL
Workbook Activity 66
Alternative Workbook Activity 66

Vocabulary

antidiuretic hormone (ADH)	glomerulus
dermis	nephron
epidermis	perspiration
fatty layer	ureter
	urine

Have students make crossword puzzles using the vocabulary terms in this lesson. Instruct them to use the definitions as the clues. After they have made their puzzles, have students exchange papers and fill in the solution to their partner's puzzle.

Background Information

The human body is made mostly of water. Drinking too much or too little water can disrupt the other function of the excretory system, which is to regulate the removal of wastes, particularly salts.

1. Warm-Up Activity

Have students design their own model of a nephron by constructing a filtering device. Provide these materials: coffee filters, a rubber band, a toilet paper roll, and a liquid containing large particles such as coffee grounds.

2 Teaching the Lesson

Ask students: If an antidiuretic hormone controls the reabsorption of water back into the body, what do you think a diuretic does? *(A diuretic increases the amount of urine that is expelled from the body and can lead to dehydration.)* Tell students that caffeine and alcohol are diuretics.

Have students recall that there are 1,000 milliliters in a liter. A milliliter is a relatively small unit. Ask students: How would you calculate the number of liters filtered by nephrons in one day? *(Multiply 125 milliliters by 60 [minutes/hour], then multiply that product by 24 [hours/day] to determine number of milliliters; then divide that number by 1,000 to determine the number of liters.)*

To help students remember vocabulary, draw their attention to word parts. Remind students that *epi-* means "above" or "over." Ask students: Why is the top layer of skin called the epidermis? *(because it is the layer that lies over the dermis)* Point out that some terms have the prefix *ur-* (ureter, urine). *Ur-* means "urine" and comes from the Greek word *ouron*. *Ex-* is a prefix that means "outside, out of, away from."

Review the concept of evaporation. Ask students: Why do you think perspiration leaves the skin feeling cool? *(because energy is lost when water changes from a liquid to a gas)*

3 Reinforce and Extend

LEARNING STYLES

Visual/Spatial

Draw a 10-cm vertical line on the board so students can observe the actual length of a kidney. Have students close their books and draw a picture of the excretory system as you read the second paragraph on page 359.

Nephron
A small tube that is the excretory unit of the kidney

Glomerulus
A group of capillaries that make up a tiny tube in nephrons

Antidiuretic hormone (ADH)
A hormone that controls the absorption of water back into the body

Epidermis
The thin outer layer of skin

Dermis
The thick layer of cells below the epidermis

Fatty layer
The layer of skin that protects organs and keeps in heat

Perspiration
A liquid waste made of heat, water, and salt released through skin

Nephrons filter about 125 milliliters of body fluid per minute. They filter all body fluid about 16 times every day.

Inside the kidney are millions of **nephrons.** A nephron is a tiny tube made up of the **glomerulus,** a group of capillaries. Blood flows into the kidney from the renal artery. The renal artery branches into capillaries in the glomerulus. Pressure from the arteries causes water and solutes from blood to filter into the nephrons. Fluid flows through the nephrons into a collecting duct. Capillaries surrounding the nephrons receive fluids and solutes. Nephrons filter water and solutes from blood. They replace water and molecules in the blood. They secrete waste products from surrounding capillaries into the ureters.

Antidiuretic hormone, or **ADH,** controls the absorption of water back into the body. A low fluid level in the blood causes the release of more ADH into the blood. ADH causes the kidneys to increase water absorption and produce less urine. This puts more water into the blood. When there is too much fluid, ADH in the blood is reduced. The kidneys absorb less water and produce more urine. Infection, poisons such as mercury, and genetic diseases can harm kidney function.

Many wastes leave the body through the skin. Figure 12.4.2 shows the three layers of skin. The **epidermis** is the top layer. It protects the deep layers of the skin. Under the epidermis is the **dermis.** This thick layer of skin contains blood vessels, nerves, and glands. The next layer is the **fatty layer.** It protects the body's organs and keeps in heat.

The body carries water and salt to sweat glands. These wastes form **perspiration.** Thousands of sweat glands in the skin release perspiration through pores on the skin's surface. Perspiration cools the body when water evaporates from the skin.

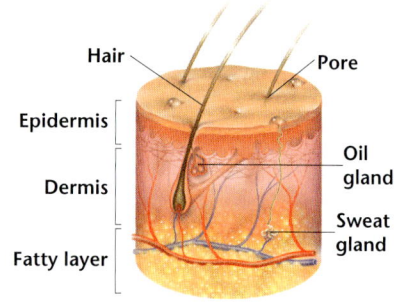

Figure 12.4.2 *Skin is made up of the epidermis, dermis, and fatty layer.*

360 Chapter 12 Human Body Systems

ELL/ESL STRATEGY

Language Objective: *To build vocabulary*

Make sure students do not confuse *secrete* with *secret*. *Secrete* is a verb that means "to generate and separate a substance (secretion) from a cell or tissue." Have them use a dictionary to see what else they can learn about *secrete*, *secret*, and related words.

Lesson 4 REVIEW

Word Bank
ADH
dermis
mercury

On a sheet of a paper, write the word from the Word Bank that completes each sentence correctly.

1. Kidneys can be damaged by poisons such as _____.
2. Absorption of water back into the body is controlled by _____.
3. The three layers of skin are the epidermis, the _____, and the fatty layers.

On a sheet of paper, write the letter of the answer that completes each sentence correctly.

4. The _____ is not a part of the excretory system.
   A kidney   B liver   C stomach   D skin

5. A nephron is made up of a group of _____ that together make up the glomerulus.
   A arteries   B capillaries   C veins   D ureters

6. Urine leaves each kidney through a _____.
   A ureter   C renal vein
   B renal artery D bladder

Critical Thinking

On a sheet of paper, write the answers to the following questions. Use complete sentences.

7. What kinds of wastes are released through the skin?
8. Describe the path that wastes take as they are processed by the kidneys.
9. How does ADH control activity in the excretory system?
10. What three functions does a nephron perform?

Lesson 4 Review Answers

1. mercury 2. ADH 3. dermis 4. C 5. B 6. A 7. Water and salt are released as perspiration through the sweat glands. 8. Blood travels to and from the kidneys through the renal artery and renal vein. Urine leaves the kidney through the ureter and enters the bladder. Urine then leaves the bladder and exits the body through the urethra. 9. ADH is a hormone that controls the reabsorption of water. When there is not enough fluid available, ADH increases and causes more water to enter the bloodstream. When there is too much water, ADH is reduced and water is eliminated from the system. 10. A nephron filters water and solutes from the blood, reabsorbs water and molecules into the blood, and secretes waste products from capillaries into the ureters.

Portfolio Assessment

Sample items include:
- Drawings of the excretory system from Learning Styles Visual/Spatial
- Reports on mercury from In the Environment
- Lesson 4 Review answers

PRONUNCIATION GUIDE

Use the pronunciation shown here to help students pronounce a difficult word in this lesson. Refer to the pronunciation key on the Chapter Planning Guide for the sounds of the symbols.

dialysis (dī a´ lə səs)

IN THE ENVIRONMENT

Have groups of students conduct Internet research about the rising levels of mercury in the United States. Questions students might consider include: Why is it a hazard? *(Students should note the effects of mercury on developing fetuses in pregnant women.)* Why is it increasing? What is being done to curb mercury pollution? Have groups present their findings to the class in a brief oral summary.

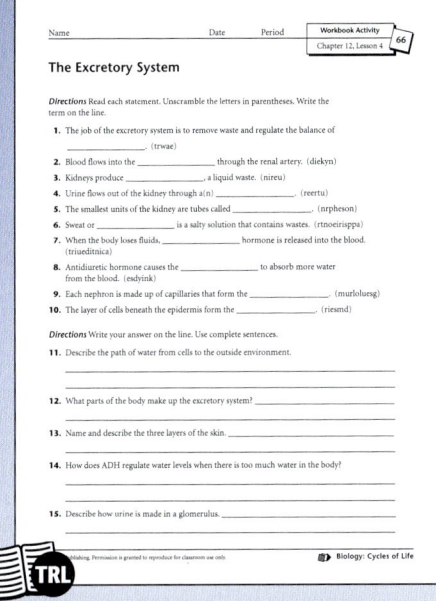

Workbook Activity 66

Lesson at a Glance

Chapter 12 Lesson 5

Overview In this lesson, students learn about the structure and functions of the nervous system.

Objectives

- To describe the structures and functions of the nervous system
- To identify the function of the spinal cord
- To describe how the nervous system operates
- To explain the purpose of reflex actions

Student Pages 362–366

Teacher's Resource Library

Workbook Activity 67
Alternative Workbook Activity 67
Resource File 29

Vocabulary

axon	limbic system
brain stem	neuron
cerebellum	neurotransmitter
cerebral cortex	pituitary gland
dendrite	synapse
diencephalon	thalamus
hypothalamus	

Have students make a three-column chart for the vocabulary in this lesson. Instruct students to write down each word in the first column. In the second, they should write the definition that is supplied in the lesson. (You may choose to have them define each term in their own words rather than copying definitions out of the book.) Then have students look up each term in a dictionary and write in the third column any additional information they find.

Lesson 5 The Nervous System

Objectives

After reading this lesson, you should be able to
- describe the structures and functions of the nervous system
- identify the function of the spinal cord
- describe how the nervous system operates
- explain the purpose of reflex actions

Brain stem
The part of the brain that controls automatic activities and connects the brain and the spinal cord

Cerebellum
The part of the brain that controls balance

Limbic system
The part of the brain that registers feelings

Diencephalon
The front of the brain

For all your body systems to work, they need to be coordinated. Body parts have to know what to do and when to do it. Your nervous system coordinates all your body parts. It is the body's communication network. It is also the most complex body system.

The nervous system is made up of two systems. The central nervous system is made up of the brain and spinal cord. The central nervous system controls the activities of the body, including the sense organs. The peripheral nervous system is made up of nerves outside the central nervous system. The peripheral nervous system carries messages between the central nervous system and other body parts.

The Brain

The brain is at the center of the nervous system. It is divided into five areas: the **brain stem, cerebellum, limbic system, diencephalon,** and **cerebral cortex.** The brain stem connects the brain and the spinal cord. It controls automatic activities including heart rate, digestion, respiration, and circulation. It coordinates muscles that move without you thinking about them, such as stomach muscles.

Above the brain stem is the cerebellum. This area of the brain controls balance. It also helps muscles work together so that you walk and write smoothly. The limbic system registers your feelings, especially fear, anger, and pleasure.

The front of the brain is called the diencephalon. It includes the **thalamus** and **hypothalamus.** The thalamus directs incoming sensory messages so that you see, hear, and smell. The hypothalamus regulates hormones, the pituitary gland, body temperature, and other activities. The **pituitary gland** produces secretions that regulate basic body functions. You will learn more about the thalamus, hypothalamus, and pituitary gland in Lesson 7.

362 Chapter 12 Human Body Systems

Background Information

The study of the brain is an ever-changing discipline. Scientists are constantly learning more about how our brains and nervous systems work. The left part of the brain controls the right side of the body, and vice versa. A stroke in an artery on the right side of the brain may cause nerve and tissue damage and possible paralysis on the left side of the body.

Much of what has been learned about the human brain has been made possible through the use of magnetic resonance imaging (MRI) technology. In addition to studying the brain, MRIs are used to diagnose and observe the progress of many diseases.

Cerebral cortex
The part of the brain in which most of the high-level functions take place

Thalamus
The part of the brain that directs sensory messages

Hypothalamus
The part of the brain that regulates hormones, the pituitary gland, body temperature, and other activities

Pituitary gland
A gland in the brain that produces secretions that regulate basic body functions

The cerebral cortex makes up most of the brain. Most high-level functions take place in the cerebral cortex. The cerebral cortex is made up of two halves. Each half is divided into four lobes: frontal, parietal, temporal, and occipital. Each lobe is responsible for different body functions. Some lobes are involved in vision, hearing, touch, movement, and smell. Others are involved in thinking, reasoning, and memory.

Areas in the frontal lobes are used for short-term memory. Short-term memory stores a small amount of information for a short time, about 35 to 40 seconds. If the information is needed for a longer period of time, long-term memory is activated. Long-term memory stores information in the brain for a long time. If the information is needed, it is brought into working memory. Figure 12.5.1 shows the human brain.

The Spinal Cord

The spinal cord is a thick bunch of nerves that start at the brain stem and go down the back. The spinal cord runs through the backbone. The backbone protects the spinal cord. The brain sends and receives information through the spinal cord. Thirty-one pairs of spinal nerves branch off from the spinal cord.

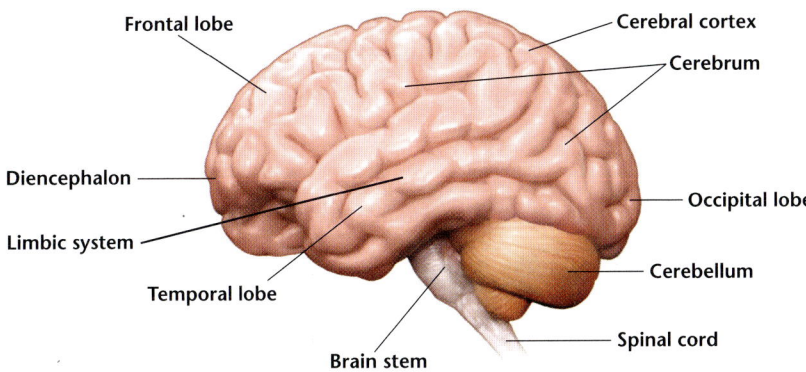

Figure 12.5.1 *The human brain is at the center of the nervous system.*

1 Warm-Up Activity

If possible, borrow several baseball gloves and a baseball from the physical education department of your school, or invite students to bring baseball gloves and balls from home. Have students line up in groups of three or four and toss the ball among them. Ask students: How do you think this activity models the nervous system?

Read aloud the last paragraph on page 363. Ask students: Now how do you think the ball activity modeled the nervous system? *(Students should realize that the student represents a neuron, the ball represents a neurotransmitter, the glove [or the hands] of the person receiving the ball represents the dendrite, and the space between them represents the synapse.)*

2 Teaching the Lesson

Read aloud the definitions on page 363, which lists the functions of the hypothalamus. Ask students: What is the normal human body temperature? *(98.6° Fahrenheit)* What do people do with a thermometer when they feel ill? *(take their temperature)* Ask students to recall the last time they had a fever. Explain that a fever reflects the body reacting appropriately. During a fever, the heart beats faster, which circulates white blood cells at a faster rate. The production rate of antibodies and other infection-fighting cells increases as well.

Have students make a chart to organize the characteristics of the three types of neurons (sensory neurons, motor neurons, and association neurons). Brainstorm examples and scenarios of events that trigger impulses in each of the three types.

3 Reinforce and Extend

ELL/ESL Strategy

Language Objective: *To recognize acronyms*

Point out the acronym ALS on page 365. Tell English language learners that an acronym is a word or an abbreviation formed from the first letters of the words in a name. The letters in an acronym are often capitalized, and the letters usually form a word (such as NATO or scuba). Encourage students to think of other acronyms they have heard. *(Examples: CD, DVD, AIDS, ATM)* Ask students: Why do you think people use acronyms? *(Acronyms take less time to write or say than unabbreviated versions.)*

Career Connection

A neurologist is a doctor specializing in neurology, the study of the nervous system and disorders that affect it. Neurologists monitor and treat patients who suffer from motor-neuron diseases such as multiple sclerosis (MS), Parkinson's disease, and Alzheimer's disease. It is a challenging profession, but extremely important. Neurologists rely on cutting-edge technology. In 2004, California passed a proposition to provide funding for stem cell research, which could have enormous benefits in the field of neurology. Have students who are interested in learning more about neurology research current topics in the field and prepare a written report.

Dendrite
A thin branch of the cell body that receives information from other cells

Axon
A long extension of the nerve cell that carries information to other cells

Neuron
A nerve cell

Synapse
A tiny gap between neurons

Neurotransmitter
A substance that transmits nerve impulses across a synapse

Neurons

Information moves through your body by traveling along many nerve cells. Nerve cells are called **neurons.** Neurons send signals in the form of electrical signals throughout the body. These messages are called impulses. An impulse quickly carries information from one neuron to the next. Neurons do not touch each other. Impulses must cross a small gap, or **synapse,** between neurons.

An impulse travels from one end of a neuron to the other end. When the impulse reaches the end of a neuron, a chemical called a **neurotransmitter** is released. The neurotransmitter moves into the synapse and touches the next neuron. This starts another impulse.

Each neuron has a cell body. Thin, spider-like **dendrites** branch out from the cell body. Dendrites receive information from other cells. Each neuron also has an **axon,** a long, wire-like nerve fiber that extends from the cell body. The axon carries information to other cells. The axon's ends are branched and have button-shaped axon bulbs.

With the help of neurotransmitters, nerve impulses travel along the axon. Then they jump across synapses to other nerve cells. Find the parts of the two neurons in Figure 12.5.2.

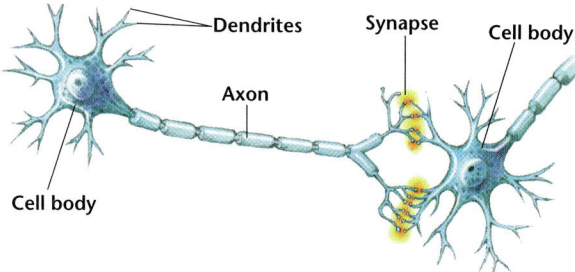

Figure 12.5.2 *Neurons transmit information throughout the body.*

364   Chapter 12   Human Body Systems

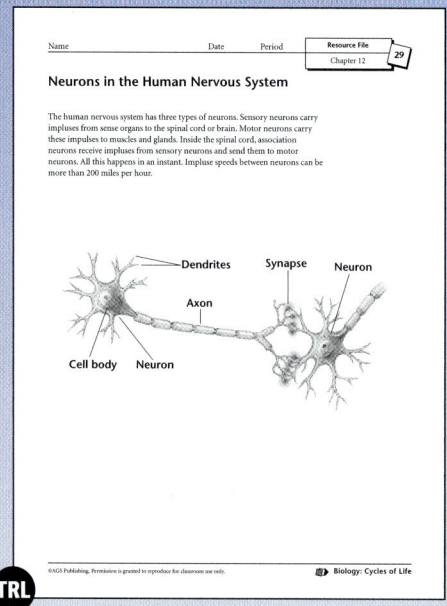

Resource File 29

364   Chapter 12

Link to ▶▶▶
Social Studies

Amyotrophic lateral sclerosis (ALS) is a rare disease that destroys nerve cells in the spinal cord. A person with ALS slowly loses motor abilities and becomes paralyzed. People with ALS lose the ability to move, but still think clearly. Lou Gehrig, a Yankee baseball player, had ALS. ALS is also known as Lou Gehrig's disease.

The nervous system has three types of neurons. Sensory neurons carry impulses from sense organs to the spinal cord or brain. Motor neurons carry these impulses to muscles and glands. Inside the spinal cord, association neurons receive impulses from sensory neurons and send them to motor neurons. All of this happens in an instant. Impulse speeds between neurons can be more than 200 miles per hour.

Reflex Actions

Sneezing, coughing, and blinking are reflex actions. They happen automatically. Many reflex actions protect the body from injury.

Achievements in Science

People once thought that the food they ate changed into blood. Blood was then burned up as energy. In 1628, William Harvey, a British doctor, published a description of the circulatory system. Other doctors criticized Harvey's work. Over time, however, they accepted the idea that blood circulates constantly in the body.

In 1818, James Blundell, another British doctor, performed the world's first successful blood transfusion. A blood transfusion is the transferring of blood from a donor to another person. A donor is someone who donates, or gives, blood. Since then, doctors have saved millions of lives by blood transfusions. In 1901, Austrian scientist Karl Landsteiner discovered that proteins in blood cells create different blood types. Doctors soon realized they needed to match blood types in transfusions. Today, all blood is typed and matched between donors and the people who receive donated blood.

In 1967, Christiaan Barnard, a South African doctor, transplanted the world's first human heart. He took the heart of a woman who had just died and placed it into the body of a 55-year old man. The man lived 18 days. This historic event led to successful transplants of hearts and other organs.

Link to

Social Studies. The influence of sports on history and social action is well-documented in the case of Lou Gehrig, a famous baseball player of the 1930s. Among his achievements is his record for career grand slams. He also held the record for consecutive games played until Cal Ripken broke the record in 1995. Despite his endurance in the game, however, Gehrig succumbed to ALS less than two years after leaving baseball. Recently, the drug Rilutek has showed some signs of slowing the progression of ALS.

LEARNING STYLES

Body/Kinesthetic

Have students recall the last time they went to a doctor. Ask students: Can you think of any reflex actions the doctor tested? *(The doctor may have used a light rubber hammer to tap a certain spot on the knee.)* Ask students: Can you think of any other reflex actions? *(When you hit your funny bone, there is a reflex action.)*

LEARNING STYLES

Visual/Spatial

Find a detailed diagram of the brain to photocopy and distribute to students. Cover any labels with paper so students can label the different areas of the brain themselves. Then have them write the characteristics and functions of each area in the margins around the diagram. Have students draw lines connecting their written notes to the related areas of the brain.

Achievements in Science

Divide the class into groups of four and have each student read a portion of the Achievements in Science feature aloud. (Tell students to split the second paragraph so one student reads about James Blundell and the other reads about Karl Landsteiner.) Then ask students to find out more information concerning the life and work of the doctor they read about. You might also prompt them to research other advancements in the practice of organ transplants. Encourage students to explore how a person's nervous system can send signals to and from transplanted organs.

Lesson 5 Review Answers

1. synapses **2.** electrical impulses **3.** central nervous system **4.** C **5.** A **6.** D **7.** A nerve cell is made up of a main cell body with thin dendrites attached and one long, wire-like nerve fiber. **8.** Short term memory is information that is stored for only about 35–40 seconds. Short-term memory information is stored in the frontal lobes. When information is needed for a longer period of time, long-term memory is activated. **9.** The brain stem controls many of the main living activities such as digestion, respiration, and circulation. **10.** The nerve impulse travels from the nerve cell along its axon. When it reaches the end of the axon, a neurotransmitter is released, and this moves into the synapse and touches the next nerve cell.

Portfolio Assessment

Sample items include:
- Chart of neurons from Teaching the Lesson
- Research report about neurology from Career Connection
- Annotated diagram from Learning Styles Visual/Spatial
- Lesson 5 Review answers

Lesson 5 REVIEW

Word Bank
central nervous system
electrical impulses
synapses

On a sheet of a paper, write the word or words from the Word Bank that complete each sentence correctly.

1. Gaps between neurons are _____.
2. Nerves cells transmit information as _____.
3. The _____ is made up of the brain and the spinal cord.

On a sheet of paper, write the letter of the answer that completes each sentence correctly.

4. The control center of the body is the _____.
   - **A** heart
   - **B** spinal cord
   - **C** brain
   - **D** hypothalamus

5. The part of the brain that is responsible for balance is the _____.
   - **A** cerebellum
   - **B** limbic system
   - **C** brain stem
   - **D** cerebral cortex

6. The limbic system of the brain is responsible for _____.
   - **A** movement
   - **B** body temperature
   - **C** memory
   - **D** feelings

Critical Thinking

On a sheet of paper, write the answers to the following questions. Use complete sentences.

7. Describe the parts that make up a nerve cell.
8. How does the brain handle information for short-term and long-term memory?
9. What are the functions of the brain stem?
10. Describe how a nerve impulse travels through a nerve cell to another nerve cell.

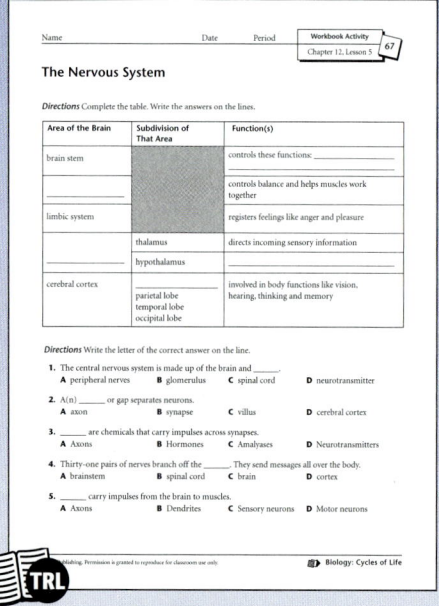

Workbook Activity 67

Lesson 6: The Sensory System

Objectives

After reading this lesson, you should be able to

- describe how sensations that begin as forms of energy are detected by sensory receptor cells
- explain how the brain distinguishes any type of stimulus
- name the five sensory receptors
- trace the interactions among the senses, nerves, and brain that allow humans to cope with their environment

Effector cell
A muscle or gland cell that carries out the body's responses to stimuli

Sensory receptor
A specialized neuron that detects sensory stimuli, then converts them to nerve impulses that go to the brain

The sense organs connect the body with the outside world. The five main sense organs are the eyes, ears, skin, nose, and tongue. Receptor cells in these organs receive information about the outside world. Receptor cells send impulses to your brain through sensory neurons. Your brain processes these impulses. Then you see, hear, feel, smell, and taste.

How the Sensory System Works

The nervous system transmits and understands sensory information. Once sensory information gets to the brain, it is sent to an integration center. When the information is received, signals from the integration center communicate to **effector cells.** Effector cells are muscle or gland cells that carry out the body's responses to stimuli. Recall that nerves carry information along nerve pathways by transmitting electrical impulses.

Sensations begin as different forms of energy, such as mechanical energy, light, heat, and chemical energy. The five types of **sensory receptors** are mechanoreceptors, pain receptors, photoreceptors, thermoreceptors, and chemoreceptors. Each receptor is a specialized neuron that can detect a tiny stimulus. A photoreceptor can detect a single photon of light. A chemoreceptor can detect a single molecule that creates an odor or a taste.

Mechanoreceptors respond to stimuli such as pressure, touch, stretch, motion, and sound. These are forms of mechanical energy. Receptors that detect touch are close to the surface of the skin. Receptors responding to pressure and vibration are in deep skin layers. Other receptors, such as hair cells in the ear, detect motion through movement.

Pain receptors are in the epidermis. Recall that the epidermis is the outer layer of the skin. Pain receptors respond to high temperature, heavy pressure, or specific chemicals. These stimuli result in a reaction. For example, if you touch a hot stove (stimulus), you will remove your hand quickly (reaction).

Lesson at a Glance

Chapter 12 Lesson 6

Overview In this lesson, students learn about the structure and function of the sensory system.

Objectives

- To describe how sensations that begin as forms of energy are detected by sensory receptor cells
- To explain how the brain distinguishes any type of stimulus
- To name the five sensory receptors
- To trace the interactions among the senses, nerves, and brain that allow humans to cope with their environment

Student Pages 367–371

Teacher's Resource Library
Workbook Activity 68
Alternative Workbook Activity 68

Vocabulary

auditory nerve	iris
cochlea	optic nerve
cornea	pupil
eardrum	retina
effector cell	sensory receptor

Write each vocabulary term in one column on a sheet of paper. Write the definitions in random order in a second column. Photocopy and distribute the papers, and instruct students to connect each term with the correct definition by drawing a line.

Background Information

Electromagnetic receptors detect forms of radiation energy such as sunlight. The electromagnetic spectrum is a range of radiation wavelengths. Radio waves have the longest wavelengths in the spectrum, and gamma rays have the shortest. Between them, ranging from longer to shorter wavelengths, are microwaves, infrared light, visible light, ultraviolet waves, and X-rays. As wavelength increases, frequency decreases. Gamma rays have short wavelengths; their high frequencies make them a dangerous form of high-energy radiation.

Visible light is only a portion of the electromagnetic spectrum. Photoreceptors respond to visible light. There are two kinds of photoreceptors in the eye: rods, which are used when there is less illumination, and cones, which are used when there is more illumination. Rods are especially attuned to motion; cones, to color.

1 Warm-Up Activity

Have students read the first paragraph on page 367 and then ask them to reflect on their morning. Lead a discussion in which students talk about the first stimulus to each of their five main sense organs. For example, the first thing they heard may have been an alarm clock. The first thing they smelled may have been breakfast. The first thing they tasted may have been orange juice.

2 Teaching the Lesson

Point out to students the prefixes in four of the five types of sensory receptors on page 367. Then tell students to look up each prefix in a dictionary and use it to write their own definition of each type of sensory receptor. *(For example, thermo- means "heat," so a thermoreceptor is a sensory receptor that responds to temperature.)*

Ask students: What enables us to see colors? *(Visible light is a range of different wavelengths that the brain interprets as colors. The surfaces of different materials reflect the light of certain wavelengths, and that reflected light enters the eye. Photoreceptors then convey signals to the brain, which interprets them as different colors.)*

Use a diagram of the brain to review with students the location of the temporal lobes and parietal lobes.

3 Reinforce and Extend

TEACHER ALERT

Some students might think electricity and magnetism are forms of radiation. Point out that visible light is a form of radiation, but electricity and magnetism are not. Magnetism is a force exerted by electric currents on other electric currents. Electricity is a phenomenon that depends on electrons and protons and the fact that particles with like charges repel, while particles with opposite charges attract.

Cornea
A clear layer of the eye that light passes through

Pupil
The black circle in the center of the iris

Iris
The part of the eye that controls the amount of light that enters

Photoreceptors detect energy as different wavelengths of radiation, such as visible light. Thermoreceptors respond to heat or cold. They help regulate body temperature. Chemoreceptors respond to specific molecules. Taste buds on the tongue detect sour and sweet, for example.

When a sensory receptor cell detects stimuli, it sends a signal to the brain. Information about sounds or visual objects is sent to the temporal lobes of the brain. Information about motion and location is sent to the parietal lobes of the brain. Once the brain is aware of sensations, it interprets them. Then we see, hear, feel, smell, and taste.

The Sense of Sight

The human eye is an organ that detects colors and forms images of objects. Figure 12.6.1 shows the parts of the eye. Light rays enter the eye through the **cornea**. The cornea is a clear layer of tissue that light passes through. The cornea bends rays of light toward the **pupil**. The pupil is the dark, round opening in the center of the **iris**. The pupil opens and closes to control the amount of light that enters.

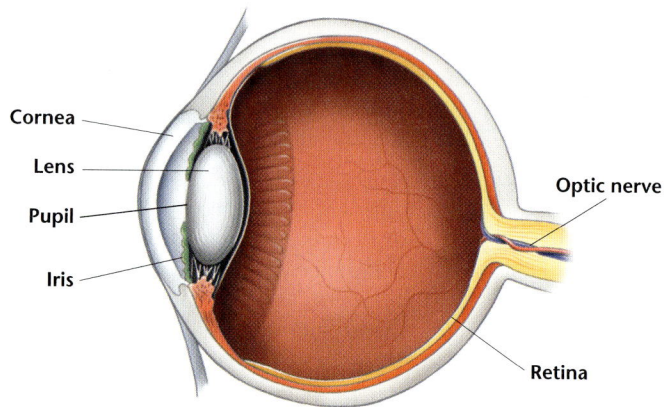

Figure 12.6.1 *The human eye is a complex organ.*

LEARNING STYLES

Visual/Spatial
Have students create a Venn diagram that compares and contrasts effector cells and receptor cells.

Retina
The back part of the eye where light rays are focused

Optic nerve
A bundle of nerves that carry impulses from the eye to the brain

Eardrum
A thin tissue in the middle ear that vibrates when sound waves strike it

Cochlea
The organ in the ear that sends impulses to the auditory nerve

Auditory nerve
A bundle of nerves that carry impulses from the ear to the brain

Behind the pupil is the lens. The lens focuses light rays onto the **retina**. The retina lies at the back of the eye. The retina has a membrane that contains photoreceptors. Photoreceptors change light rays into electrical impulses. The impulses are sent through the **optic nerve** to the brain. The brain translates the impulses into the images you see.

The Sense of Hearing

Your ears transform sound waves into electrical impulses. Review Figure 12.6.2 as you read how the ears work. When something makes a sound, it sends sound waves, or vibrations, into the air. The outer ear collects sound waves. The waves enter the ear opening and go down the ear canal. The vibrations strike the tympanic membrane, or **eardrum.** The eardrum is a thin tissue that vibrates, or shakes, when sound waves strike it.

The vibrations pass through three small bones in the middle ear. The bones are called the malleus, incus, and stapes. The sound waves enter the inner ear. They cause fluid in the **cochlea** to vibrate. The cochlea is a hollow, coiled tube that contains fluid and thousands of mechanoreceptors. Mechanoreceptors vibrate when sound waves strike them. These cells send impulses to the **auditory nerve,** which goes to the brain. The brain interprets the impulses as sounds you hear.

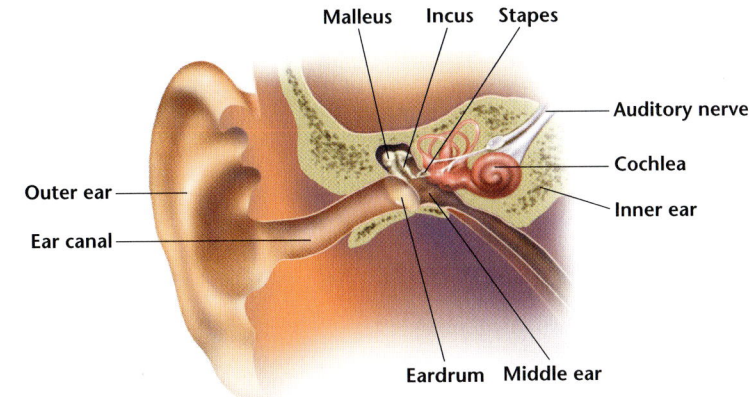

Figure 12.6.2 *The ears are sensory organs.*

LEARNING STYLES

Auditory/Verbal
Have students write paragraphs describing what happens as sound waves go through the ear. Then have students take turns recording their scripts on an audio recorder. Make sure they understand that what they are hearing are sound waves. Students can use the tapes to study.

LEARNING STYLES

Body/Kinesthetic
Encourage students to close their eyes, pinch their nose, or wear headphones or earplugs to impair one of their five senses. Tell them to notice their surroundings by using their other senses.

IN THE ENVIRONMENT

Noise pollution is environmental sound that is annoying, alarming, or physically harmful. Sound is usually measured in decibels. Hearing damage occurs when high-decibel sounds damage hair cells (called stereocilia) in the cochlea and inner ear. Have students search the Internet for a chart listing the decibel measure of common sources of noise pollution. Then ask students what sources of noise pollution are common in daily life.

ELL/ESL STRATEGY

Language Objective:
To classify

Provide students who are learning English with a list of sensory adjectives such as *loud, sweet,* and *bright.* Have them classify the adjectives under the five senses. Then have them write additional adjectives under each sense.

The Sense of Touch

The skin receives messages about heat, cold, pressure, and pain. Sensory receptors in the skin send nerve impulses to the brain. The brain interprets the impulses to tell if something is cold, hot, smooth, or rough. The fingertips and lips have the most receptors and are very sensitive to touch.

The Senses of Taste and Smell

Taste buds are receptor cells on the tongue that can sense taste. The four kinds of tastes are sweet, sour, bitter, and salty. When food touches the tongue, taste buds send impulses to the brain. The brain interprets these impulses as tastes.

Much of the sense of taste depends on the sense of smell. Receptors in the nose sense smells. The brain needs these impulses from the nose and impulses from the tongue to interpret taste.

Technology and Society

Some people who wear corrective lenses—eyeglasses or contact lenses—decide to have laser surgery. Laser surgery, also called LASIK, uses computers to map the cornea of the eye. The cornea is cut and reshaped using a laser, knife, or heat device. The corrected cornea transmits a sharper image to the brain. LASIK surgery corrects vision problems.

LEARNING STYLES

Auditory/Verbal
Have students write a list of their favorite foods. Then have them classify each food as sweet, sour, bitter, or salty. Have students compare and contrast their responses with one another in groups.

LEARNING STYLES

Visual/Spatial
Have students make diagrams of sensory organs based on information in the lesson, write the function of each part of the organ in the margin, and then draw a line connecting the description to the part of the diagram it describes.

SCIENCE JOURNAL

Have students write a paragraph assessing their sensory systems. The paragraph should answer the following questions: How is your eyesight? Sense of hearing? Sense of touch? Do you wear glasses or a hearing aid? Do you think some senses are stronger than others?

Technology and Society

LASIK surgery is not without risk. As the technology improves, so does the success rate of LASIK surgery, but that does not eliminate the possibility that something will go wrong. After students have read the feature, have them research the topic of LASIK surgery. Research should include associated risks and side effects.

Lesson 6 REVIEW

Word Bank
cochlea
cold
heat
sensory receptor

On a sheet of paper, write the word or words from the Word Bank that complete each sentence correctly.

1. Thermoreceptors respond to _____ or _____.
2. The _____ is an organ in the ear that transforms vibrations into nerve impulses for the brain to interpret.
3. A specialized neuron that detects sensory stimuli is a(n) _____.

On a sheet of paper, write the letter of the word or words that complete each sentence correctly.

4. _____ receptors are located in the epidermis of the skin.
   A Pain   B Touch   C Vibration   D Motion
5. _____ cannot be detected by a mechanoreceptor.
   A Pressure   B Touch   C Sound   D Light
6. The _____ controls the amount of light that enters the eye.
   A pupil   B iris   C retina   D cornea

Critical Thinking

On a sheet of paper, write the answers to the following questions. Use complete sentences.

7. What are different types of sensory receptors? What do they do?
8. How do effector cells work in the body?
9. Explain how the parts of the eye transmit stimuli to the brain.
10. People sometimes ask, "If a tree falls in the forest and no one is around, does it make a sound?" What is the scientific answer to this question?

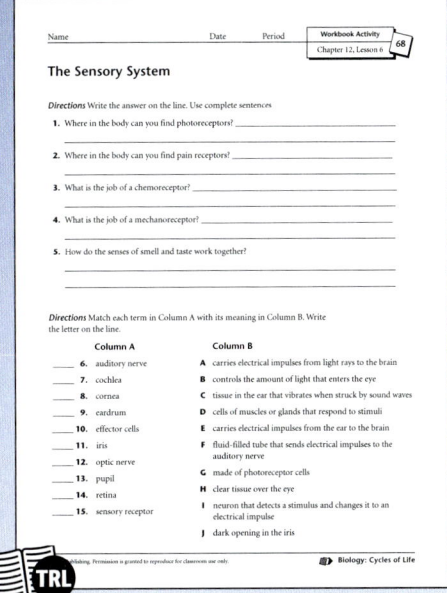

Workbook Activity 68

Lesson 6 Review Answers

1. heat, cold **2.** cochlea **3.** sensory receptor **4.** A **5.** D **6.** A **7.** The five types of sensory receptors are mechanoreceptors, pain receptors, thermoreceptors, chemoreceptors, and photoreceptors. Mechanoreceptors respond to forms of mechanical energy, such as pressure, touch, and sound. Pain receptors respond to stimuli with a reaction, such as pulling hand away from a sharp object. Thermoreceptors help regulate body temperature. Chemoreceptors can detect specific molecules that create odor and taste. Photoreceptors respond to light. **8.** Effector cells receive signals from the brain through integration centers. The effector cells are the muscle or gland cells that then carry out the actions commanded by the brain. **9.** Light enters the eye through the cornea, which bends it through the pupil. The pupil opens and closes to control how much light enters. The lens behind the pupil focuses the light onto the retina, which contains the photoreceptor cells that change the light into electrical impulses for the brain to interpret. **10.** Sensory information such as sound is a result of a stimulus being interpreted by the brain. Since there is no one near the tree, no ear to collect the stimulus, and no brain to interpret the stimulus, then it does not really make a sound.

Portfolio Assessment

Sample items include:
- Venn diagram from Learning Styles Visual/Spatial
- Recorded paragraphs from Learning Styles Auditory/Verbal
- Paragraph for Science Journal
- Lesson 6 Review answers

Lesson at a Glance

Chapter 12 Lesson 7

Overview In this lesson, students learn about the structure and function of the endocrine system.

Objectives
- To explain what hormones do
- To explain how a feedback loop works
- To describe the stress response

Student Pages 372–374

Teacher's Resource Library (TRL)
- Workbook Activity 69
- Alternative Workbook Activity 69

Background Information

The endocrine system is a communication system that uses hormones to carry signals among glands and cells to control the body's internal functions. Hormones are chemical messengers that flow through the bloodstream to attach to target cells. Target cells then interpret the hormone's instructions. Most hormones are steroids. Students may be familiar with anabolic steroids in the context of performance-enhancing drugs. However, steroids do occur naturally in the body and are essential for growth and development. Have students recall estrogen and testosterone. Estrogen is a hormone produced in the ovaries and testes. It is more abundant in women than in men. By contrast, testosterone is the male sex hormone. Estrogen and testosterone are especially active during puberty, the stage of adolescence when people become physiologically capable of sexual reproduction.

Lesson 7 The Endocrine System

Objectives
After reading this lesson, you should be able to
- explain what hormones do
- explain how a feedback loop works
- describe the stress response

The endocrine system produces hormones, which regulate body functions. Table 12.7.1 lists glands in the body that produce hormones. Figure 12.7.1 shows that glands are found throughout the body. There are more than 30 different hormones. Hormones affect everything from kidney functions to growth and development. They work by attaching to certain cells, then changing the function of the cells.

The endocrine system can take minutes, hours, or days to act. It takes time for hormones to be produced and carried in the blood to target organs.

Table 12.7.1 Eight Glands and What They Do

Gland Name	What It Does
Adrenal glands	Increase metabolic activity and raise the level of glucose in the blood
Gonads	Produce sperm in males and estrogen in females
Hypothalamus	Regulates the pituitary gland
Pancreas	Regulates the level of glucose in the blood
Pineal gland	Secretes melatonin to regulate sleep
Pituitary gland	Maintains water and salt balance
Thymus gland	Helps certain white cells develop and plays a part in the body's defenses
Thyroid gland	Regulates calcium in the blood

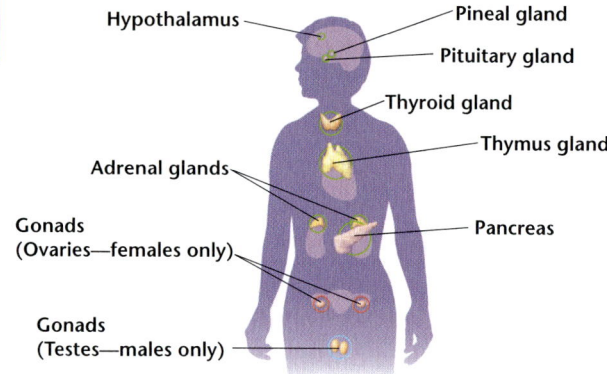

Figure 12.7.1 The glands secrete more than 30 different hormones in the body.

---

1. Warm-Up Activity

Have students form groups of four to model the feedback loop. The four students in each group will represent the gland that secretes the hormone, the hormone itself, the cell that receives the hormone, and the chemical signal sent from the cell back to the gland. Have the hormone carry a note describing a simple test message that the cell will perform. Have the cell give the chemical signal a note telling the gland to either keep sending hormones or to stop sending them.

Each gland must secrete the correct amount of hormones for the body to work properly. After hormones reach the cells, the cells send a chemical signal back to the gland. This signal tells the gland to continue or to stop secreting the hormones. This process is called a feedback loop.

The body reacts when it is stressed. People under stress sweat more, their heart beats faster, and they breathe faster. This is the stress response. When a person feels scared or excited, the adrenal glands secrete a hormone called adrenaline. Adrenaline causes stress changes in the body.

The stress response can be negative if it goes on for a long time. A person can become depressed. The stress response can also be positive. If you are running a race, your heart rate increases and more oxygen is sent to your muscles. Adrenaline increases the amount of glucose in your muscles. After the race, your body returns to normal.

Science at Work

Forensic Technician

Forensic technicians investigate crimes. They collect and analyze physical evidence. They perform tests on weapons or substances such as fiber, hair, tissue, or body fluid. Forensic technicians use technology, including DNA analysis, to investigate crimes.

Forensic technicians prepare reports on their findings. They provide information to investigators.

When criminal cases go to trial, forensic technicians often provide testimony (information). Their testimony can include laboratory findings about the substances and materials found at a crime scene.

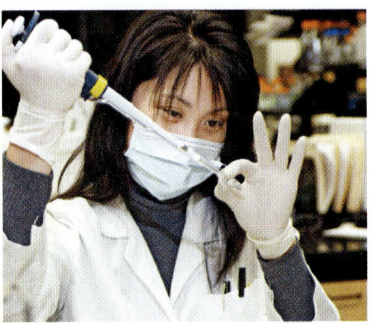

Forensic technicians must have a high school degree and an associate's degree or two years of specialized training. Many obtain a four-year college degree and become forensic investigators.

2 Teaching the Lesson

Ask students: Can you think of any analogies for the process of the endocrine system feedback loop? *(Example: A thermostat works much the same way. When the temperature falls below a certain temperature, the thermostat signals the furnace to produce more heat. Once the temperature has been raised, the thermostat signals the furnace to stop.)*

Ask students: Can you remember an event that caused you to feel extreme fear or excitement? Tell them the "rush" they probably felt was adrenaline, released from the adrenal glands to fuel a fight or flight response.

Ask students if they have ever heard someone tell a story about a physical reaction, such as a burst of energy, in an emergency situation. Have them share their stories with the class or write an imaginary news article of the event.

3 Reinforce and Extend

ELL/ESL STRATEGY

Language Objective: *To build conversational skills*

Invite students who share a native language other than English to discuss lesson content in that language. Students who are learning English may be able to learn from one another if they are given freedom to communicate freely, without having to concentrate on English translation and grammar. Have students discuss the feedback loop. Then have them write in English a description of the feedback loop.

Science at Work

The investigative arm of the law depends on forensic evidence collected from crime scenes. DNA evidence is a relatively new tool of forensic investigators and technicians. It has profound ramifications in the prosecution of legal cases about alleged crimes. For example, Illinois placed a moratorium on the death penalty after a several convicted prisoners were proven innocent through an analysis of DNA evidence. Have students conduct research and report to the class about ways that forensic evidence has affected specific criminal cases.

Lesson 7 Review Answers

1. hormones **2.** gonads **3.** glucose **4.** C
5. B **6.** A **7.** After hormones reach the cells, the cells send chemical signals back to the gland, telling the gland to either keep releasing hormones or to stop. **8.** The hypothalamus is a gland that regulates the pituitary gland. The pancreas is another gland, and it regulates the level of glucose in the blood. The pineal gland regulates sleep. The thymus gland helps with the body's defenses. The thyroid gland regulates calcium in the blood.
9. Stress from the environment signals the adrenal glands to release adrenaline.
10. The stress response is how the body reacts when it is stressed.

Portfolio Assessment

Sample items include:
- Flowcharts from Learning Styles Visual/Spatial
- Lesson 7 Review answers

LEARNING STYLES

Visual/Spatial
Show students an example of a flowchart. Then have them draw a flowchart of the feedback loop with labels. After they complete their flowcharts, have students trade them with partners and describe the process shown in their partner's flowcharts.

LEARNING STYLES

Interpersonal/Group
Tell students that hormones work much like catalysts in that they target certain cells and stimulate a specific reaction. Divide the class into groups of three or four and have students discuss how the endocrine system works. Then encourage the groups to think of analogies for the endocrine system. *(Example: television or radio signals that are broadcast everywhere, but only picked up by certain frequencies)*

Lesson 7 REVIEW

Word Bank
glucose
gonads
hormones

On a sheet of a paper, write the word from the Word Bank that completes each sentence correctly.

1. The endocrine system produces _____ that regulate body functions.
2. Sperm and estrogen are produced in the _____.
3. The pancreas regulates the level of _____ in the blood.

Match the following descriptions with the correct gland. Write the letter of your answer on a sheet of paper.

4. increases metabolic activity and raises the level of glucose in the blood
5. maintains water and salt balance
6. regulates calcium in the blood

A thyroid gland   **C** adrenal gland
B pituitary gland   **D** thymus gland

Critical Thinking

On a sheet of paper, write the answers to the following questions. Use complete sentences.

7. Explain how the feedback loop works between cells and glands to regulate the release of hormones.
8. What are five glands and their functions?
9. How do the adrenal glands respond to stress?
10. What is the stress response?

Workbook Activity 69

Lesson 8: The Skeletal and Muscular System

Objectives

After reading this lesson, you should be able to
- identify the functions of bone
- explain how bones and muscles work together to produce movement
- describe the different kinds of muscle

Skeletal system
The network of bones in the body

Red marrow
The spongy material in bones that makes blood cells

Osteoporosis
A disease in which bones become lighter and break easily

The Skeletal System

The 206 bones of the human body make up the **skeletal system.** The skeleton has five major jobs. First, it protects vital organs such as the brain, heart, and lungs. For example, the rib cage protects the lungs and heart. Vertebrae protect the spinal cord. The pelvis protects reproductive organs. The skull protects the brain. Second, bones give the body shape. Bones form a framework that supports the softer tissues of the body.

Third, the skeletal system allows movement. Because muscles are attached to bones, when muscles move, bones move. The body has big bones, small bones, flat bones, wide bones, and bones with unusual shapes. The variety of bones helps a person move in different ways. Fourth, blood cells are formed in bones. Bones contain spongy material called **red marrow.** Red marrow has special cells that make blood cells. Fifth, bones store minerals such as calcium, phosphorous, and magnesium.

Bones

Bones are alive and change constantly. They have nerves and blood vessels. Bones are built up and broken down throughout life. This is a normal process. For example, enzymes break down bone tissue when the body needs calcium. Calcium is released into the blood. If calcium is not replaced in bone tissue, a person can develop **osteoporosis.** Osteoporosis is a disease in which bones become lighter and break easily. Exercising on a regular basis and taking in more calcium can help prevent osteoporosis.

A typical bone has an outer layer of hard bone. This layer is strong, dense, and tough. Beneath the hard bone is a layer of spongy bone. It looks like a honeycomb. It is light and slightly flexible. In the middle of some bones is red marrow. The red marrow makes blood cells.

Human Body Systems Chapter 12 375

Lesson at a Glance

Chapter 12 Lesson 8

Overview In this lesson, students learn about the structure and function of the skeletal and muscular systems.

Objectives

- To identify the functions of bone
- To explain how bones and muscles work together to produce movement
- To describe the different kinds of muscle

Student Pages 375–381

Teacher's Resource Library

Workbook Activity 70–71

Alternative Workbook Activity 70–71

Lab Manual 59–60

Resource File 30

Vocabulary

involuntary muscle skeletal system
ligament   tendon
osteoporosis   voluntary muscle
red marrow

Have students write each vocabulary term on an index card. On the opposite side, have them write any definitions, examples, and characteristics described in the lesson. Then have students use each term in a sentence without looking at their cards.

Background Information

There are over 600 muscles in the human body. Skeletal muscle makes up the most body mass of the three muscle types (cardiac, smooth, and skeletal) and accounts for 23 percent of a woman's body weight and 40 percent of a man's. The smallest muscle in the body is called the stapedius. It is connected to the stirrup and mediates movement of vibrations from the eardrum to the inner ear. One of the largest muscle is the latissimus dorsi, which is in the back.

ELL/ESL Strategy

Language Objective: *To understand idioms*

Point out the phrases *built up* and *broken down* on this page. Explain that in this context, *up* and *down* do not refer to a direction. Invite students to rewrite sentences in their own words. For example, after reading "Bones are built up and broken down throughout life," they might rewrite the sentence as "Bones gain mass and lose mass throughout life."

Resource File 30

Human Body Systems 375

Warm-Up Activity

Obtain a large poster or diagram of the skeletal and muscular systems. Display it in the classroom.

Take a survey of the class. Ask students: Have you or someone you know ever broken a bone or torn a muscle? Have students point out the injury on the poster or diagram of the skeletal system or muscular system.

Teaching the Lesson

Have students make a two-column chart of the five functions of the skeletal system listed on page 375. As they read, have them fill in information for each function.

Ask students: What bones are exposed after you eat a chicken wing? Have them draw a picture and label the cartilage and ligaments. If some students do not eat chicken, pair them with students who do. If possible, bring in a chicken wing for students to observe.

The lesson states that an infant has about 350 bones. Refer students back to the beginning of the lesson, which states that there are 206 bones in the human body. Have students investigate which bones fuse together as infants develop.

Have students compare and contrast ligaments and tendons. Have them make a drawing of each.

Ask students: What common muscles can you name? For each muscle named, ask students: Is that muscle voluntary or involuntary?

Ask students: Where have you seen or heard the word *antagonistic* before? *(An antagonist in a story is the character who opposes or works against the protagonist. People who oppose or work against something are said to be antagonistic toward it.)*

Ligament
A strong tissue that connects bone to bone

Most bones start out as cartilage. Cartilage is a thick, smooth, tough tissue. It is softer than bone. Parts of your body are cartilage. Feel the end of your nose and outer ear. These body parts are made of cartilage. Before birth, the entire skeleton is cartilage. It is gradually replaced by bone. Infants have about 350 bones. As people grow, some bones fuse together.

Cartilage covers the end of each bone. Where two bones meet, cartilage at the bone ends is covered by a thin film of slippery fluid. This keeps bones from scratching and bumping against each other when they move. Strips of strong tissue called **ligaments** connect bones to each other. Ligaments stretch to allow the bones to move.

Joints

Bones meet at joints. Three types of joints allow for flexibility in movement. One type of skeletal joint is the ball-and-socket joint. This joint allows the arms and legs to rotate. Figure 12.8.1 shows another type of joint, the hinge joint. The knee is a hinge joint. Hinge joints allow movement only in one direction. A third type of joint is the pivot joint. This joint allows limited rotation. The forearm at the elbow is a pivot joint.

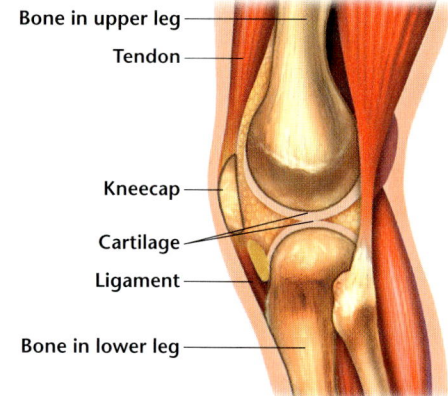

Figure 12.8.1 *The knee is a hinge joint.*

376 Chapter 12 Human Body Systems

Tendon
A tough tissue that attaches muscles to bones

Voluntary muscle
A muscle that a person can control

Involuntary muscle
A muscle that a person cannot control

The Muscular System

The muscular system consists of more than 640 muscles in the human body. Almost half the body's weight is muscle. The skeletal and muscular systems work together to produce movement. Tough strips of tissue called **tendons** attach muscles to bones.

Muscle tissue is made up of long cells. Muscles can contract, or shorten, when they receive a signal from the brain. Muscles pull on tendons when they contract. Tendons pull on the bones and cause limbs to move. Muscles are attached in antagonistic pairs. This means the muscles in a pair work against each other. One muscle pulls the body part one way. The other muscle pulls it back. As one muscle pulls, the other muscle relaxes and stretches.

There are three types of muscle tissue: skeletal, smooth, and cardiac. Most muscle is skeletal muscle. Skeletal muscles are attached to bones. Skeletal muscles cause voluntary movement. This means you can choose when to use them. **Voluntary muscles** are in your face, arms, and legs.

Smooth muscle is found in the lining of the digestive tract, arteries, and other organs. Smooth muscles are **involuntary muscles.** This means that you cannot choose when to use them. These muscles use peristalsis, or wavelike motions, to do their job. For example, food moves through the digestive tract by peristalsis. The heart is made of cardiac muscle. Cardiac muscle is involuntary.

Link to ➤➤➤
Home and Career
Some people choose to donate their organs when they die. They are often given a special symbol on their driver's license to tell others of their wish. Currently, not enough organs are donated to fill the need for saving lives. If you want to become an organ donor, tell your family and friends so that they are aware of your wish.

---

3 Reinforce and Extend

SCIENCE JOURNAL

Have students write a paragraph describing how the muscular and skeletal systems work together to produce movement. Then have them write a second paragraph assessing how smoothly their muscular and skeletal systems cooperate to make movement. If they need help getting started, ask the following questions: Are you prone to muscle injuries, or brittle or broken bones? Do you have any problems performing physical activities? Have you ever had physical therapy?

GLOBAL CONNECTION

Invite students to research the origin of our species and the evolution of humans from primate to *Homo sapiens*. Students should focus their research on changes to bone and body structure (the skull in particular) that anthropologists have discovered. Have students find out in what part of the world these discoveries took place and where modern humans originated.

Link to

Home and Career. After students have read the Home and Career feature about organ donation, ask them to survey family members to learn if they (1) have listed themselves as potential organ donors; (2) know anyone who has already donated living tissue, such as a kidney; or (3) know anyone who has received a donated organ.

Lesson 8 Review Answers

1. involuntary 2. red marrow 3. tendons
4. D 5. C 6. A 7. Their bodies do not get enough calcium and break down bone tissue to get more. As a result, their bones become lighter and weaker. 8. Skeletal muscle is found all over the body, attached to the skeleton. Cardiac muscle makes up the heart. Smooth muscle is spiral muscle that lines internal organs. 9. Most of the time, breathing is an involuntary muscle action. Your lungs breathe normally without being told to, just like your heart beats. However, breathing can also become voluntary, as you have the ability to change your breathing or even hold your breath. 10. The ball and socket joint allows rotation of arms and legs. A hinge joint allows movement in one direction only. A pivot joint allows rotation of the forearm at the elbow.

Portfolio Assessment

Sample items include:
- Drawings of ligaments and tendons from Teaching the Lesson
- Paragraphs for Science Journal
- Lesson 8 Review answers

378   Chapter 12

Lesson 8 REVIEW

Word Bank
involuntary
red marrow
tendons

On a sheet of a paper, write the word or words from the Word Bank that complete each sentence correctly.

1. Muscle actions that activate the heart and lungs are _____.
2. New blood cells are created in the _____.
3. The skeletal system is connected to muscle tissue by _____.

On a sheet of paper, write the letter of the answer that completes each sentence correctly.

4. Muscles move the body by _____.
   A twisting   B lengthening   C pushing   D pulling

5. The area of the skeletal system that protects the heart is the _____.
   A skull   C rib cage
   B backbone   D limb and pelvis

6. The skeletal system does not _____.
   A stimulate growth of the body
   B protect the vital organs
   C give shape to the body
   D allow movement

Critical Thinking

On a sheet of paper, write the answers to the following questions. Use complete sentences.

7. Why do some people develop osteoporosis?
8. What are the three types of muscle tissue? Where is each type found?
9. Is breathing a voluntary muscle action or an involuntary muscle action? Explain your answer.
10. Describe the three types of skeletal joints that allow movement.

378   Chapter 12 Human Body Systems

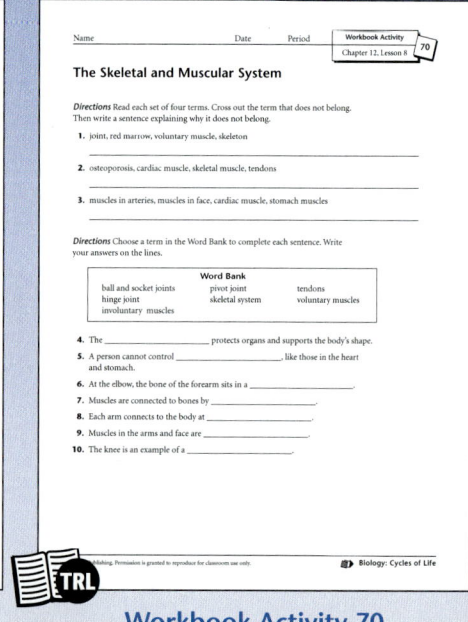

Lab Manual 59, pages 1–3   Workbook Activity 70

DISCOVERY INVESTIGATION 12

Materials
- safety goggles
- lab coat or apron
- assorted materials to model joints such as screws, washers, hinges, ball-like lollipops, bottle caps, craft sticks, pipe cleaners, modeling clay, push pins, glue

Constructing Models of Human Joints

The human skeletal system uses three types of joints that allow movement. The ball-and-socket joint allows rotation. The hinge joint moves back and forth in one direction. The pivot joint allows limited rotation. By working together, these joints allow the human skeleton to move in many different ways.

In this investigation, you will be given a variety of materials to make your own models of these joints.

Procedure

1. In a small group, write a procedure with Safety Alerts to make one type of joint. You may use any of the materials listed. Write the procedure as if you were giving directions to another person.

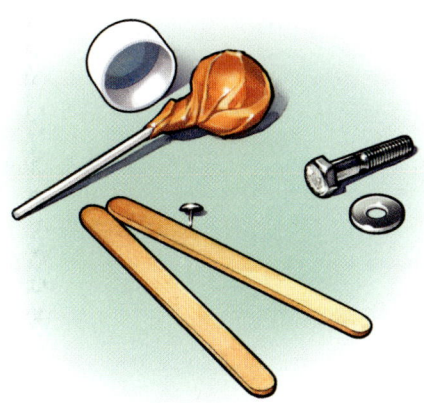

SAFETY ALERT
- Make sure that students have read and understood all safety rules for working in the lab. Discuss the Safety Alerts with students.
- Students should wear safety goggles and lab coats or aprons during this exercise. Select items from a local hardware store that can be used safely by students.
- Monitor the materials used by students to be sure they are working responsibly.

Discovery Investigation 12

This investigation is less structured than the first investigation in this chapter. It offers students more challenge and requires more teacher facilitation. Encourage students to read the Discovery Investigation steps. Discuss questions they may have before beginning the investigation.

Objectives
- To investigate and understand how different types of human joints work
- To use simple hardware materials to make models of human joints
- To infer the workings and limitations of different joints

Skills
Constructing models, inferring, communicating, comparing and contrasting

Background
Chapter 12 discusses the three different types of human joints and how they work in various areas of the body. This investigation challenges students to use their creativity to construct models of those three joints. In the process, they gain a deeper understanding of how these joints work in different areas of the body. You should be able to find a variety of hinges and joints in your local hardware store. Try to find an assortment of different materials that students might use.

Time Frame
One class period

Procedure
- Have students work in groups.
- Students should create a procedure, or a set of directions and diagrams, that shows how to construct the joint they have made.

Cleanup/Disposal
Instruct students in proper cleanup and disposal of materials.

Continued on page 380

Continued from page 379

Results

Students will use their imaginations to create examples of different joints. Be sure their models follow the basic principles of each joint type and also the limitations of each joint type. Any differences between the workings of a model and the joint it is modeled after should be noted and explained by students.

Answers to Analysis, Conclusions, and Explore Further begin on page 670 of this Teacher's Edition.

Assessment

You might include the following items from this investigation in student portfolios:

- Answers to Analysis and Conclusions questions

2. Put on safety goggles and a lab coat or apron.

3. Follow your procedure to construct the model. **Safety Alert: Be careful when working with materials that have sharp edges.**

Cleanup/Disposal

When you are finished, clean up your area and put extra materials away.

Analysis

1. What factors did you consider when making your joint?
2. Where is the actual joint located in the human body?
3. What are the limitations of your joint model?

Conclusions

1. Describe how your joint model is different from the body joint it represents.
2. What limitations did you have with the materials?
3. What are the advantages of body joints compared to mechanical joints?

Explore Further

Add a motor or pulley system to make your model move. Try to mimic the movements of the body joint. Be creative in your materials and methods.

380 Chapter 12 Human Body Systems

Lab Manual 60, pages 1–2

BIOLOGY IN THE WORLD

Blood Donations

You probably have seen blood drives. You or family members may have donated blood. People often need blood when a natural disaster or medical emergency happens in a community. The need for blood during emergencies is constant and urgent. A supply of blood for emergencies must always be available.

The donor's blood type must match the blood type of the person receiving the blood. Blood type is determined by the types of proteins on the surface of red blood cells. Donated blood that does not match can clot, causing death for the person who receives it. A person with type AB blood can only donate blood to other AB blood types. However, people with type AB blood can receive blood from all other blood types.

For this reason, people with AB blood are called universal receivers. People with type O blood can donate to all blood types, but they can receive only type O blood. People with type O blood are called universal donors.

Health professionals must test donated blood for disease agents, such as the viruses that cause AIDS and hepatitis. Hepatitis is a liver disease. New screening procedures include testing for the nucleic acids that make up harmful viruses.

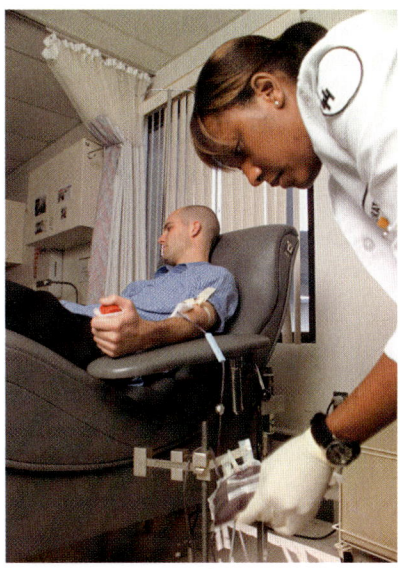

These new tests are more accurate than older tests. Older tests looked for antibodies. These new tests are also faster than the old tests. This allows donated blood to be used more quickly.

1. What steps are taken to be sure a community's blood supply is safe?
2. Every medical facility keeps a supply of type O blood. Why?
3. What must health professionals do to blood that has been donated?

Chapter 12 Summary

Have volunteers read aloud each summary item on page 382. Ask volunteers to explain the meaning of each item. Direct students' attention to the Vocabulary box on the bottom of page 382. Have them read and review each term and its definition.

Graphic Organizer

As students read Chapter 12, have them finish completing the chart on Graphic Organizer 12: Comparing Body Systems. Encourage students to read each lesson of the chapter and then have them fill in the portion of the chart that pertains to the lesson. When they have completed the chart, ask them to answer the questions.

Chapter 12 SUMMARY

- During digestion, food changes into a form that can enter cells. The large intestine eliminates undigested food.

- The respiratory system brings oxygen into the lungs and releases carbon dioxide from the lungs.

- The circulatory system moves materials to and from cells. The heart is the main organ in this system. Blood contains different cell types that bind with oxygen, prevent bleeding, and fight infection.

- The excretory system removes waste and regulates water balance in the body. The kidneys filter the blood to get rid of toxic wastes. The wastes leave the body as urine.

- The nervous system controls and coordinates body activities. Impulses carry information from nerve cell to nerve cell. The brain is the control center.

- The five main sense organs are the eyes, ears, skin, nose, and tongue. Sensory receptors in sense organs gather information and send nerve impulses to the brain.

- The endocrine system produces hormones that regulate many body functions.

- The skeletal and muscular systems work together to produce movement. Blood cells are made inside some bones. Bones store minerals, protect organs, and give the body shape.

Vocabulary

alveolus, 349	cerebral cortex, 363	inferior vena cava, 353	rectum, 346
antidiuretic hormone (ADH), 360	chyme, 345	ingestion, 344	red marrow, 375
aorta, 353	cochlea, 369	interstitial fluid, 353	reflex, 344
artery, 353	connective tissue, 354	involuntary muscle, 377	retina, 369
asthma, 350	cornea, 368	iris, 368	sensory receptor, 367
atherosclerosis, 355	dendrite, 364	larynx, 348	skeletal system, 375
atrium, 353	dermis, 360	ligament, 376	sleep apnea, 350
auditory nerve, 369	diencephalon, 362	limbic system, 362	superior vena cava, 353
axon, 364	eardrum, 369	nephron, 360	synapse, 364
bile, 345	effector cell, 367	neuron, 364	tendon, 377
brain stem, 362	epidermis, 360	neurotransmitter, 364	thalamus, 363
bronchiole, 349	epithelium, 348	optic nerve, 369	thrombus, 355
bronchitis, 350	fatty layer, 360	osteoporosis, 375	trachea, 349
bronchus, 349	feces, 346	peristalsis, 345	ureter, 359
capillary, 348	fibrinogen, 355	perspiration, 360	urine, 359
cardiac, 352	gallbladder, 345	pharynx, 345	villi, 345
cardiovascular disease, 355	glomerulus, 360	pituitary gland, 363	ventricle, 353
cerebellum, 362	glottis, 348	plasma, 354	voluntary muscle, 377
	hypertension, 355	platelet, 354	
	hypothalamus, 363	pupil, 368	

382 Chapter 12 Human Body Systems

Graphic Organizer 12, pages 1–3

Workbook Activity 71, pages 1–5

Chapter 12 REVIEW

Word Bank
artery
capillary
chyme
effector cell
epithelium
fibrinogen
glottis
ligament
nephron
neuron
peristalsis
plasma
red marrow
sensory receptor
synapse
tendon
trachea

Vocabulary Review

On a sheet of paper, write the word or words from the Word Bank that best complete each sentence.

1. A(n) _____ is a cell that specializes in conducting electrical impulses throughout the body.
2. A(n) _____ detects stimuli and converts them to nerve impulses that are sent to the brain.
3. Food is pushed along the digestive tract through the action of _____.
4. The _____ must be closed when swallowing food in order to protect the windpipe.
5. Information from an integration center goes to a(n) _____, which carries out the body's response.
6. Blood cells are made in _____.
7. A(n) _____ connects bones to each other.
8. Oxygen that is breathed in diffuses across the _____ into the blood.
9. A bone is connected to a muscle with a(n) _____.
10. Nerve impulses pass between two nerve cells through a(n) _____.
11. Food that is being digested takes the form of _____ when it enters the small intestine.
12. A small tube that is the excretory unit of the kidney is a(n) _____.
13. The liquid part of blood is _____.
14. Blood reaches an individual cell through a(n) _____.

Review continued on next page

Human Body Systems   Chapter 12   **383**

Chapter 12 Review

Use the Chapter Review to prepare students for tests and to reteach content from the chapter.

Chapter 12 Mastery Test

The Teacher's Resource Library includes two forms of the Chapter 12 Mastery Test. Each test addresses the chapter Goals for Learning. An optional third page of additional critical-thinking items is included for each test. The difficulty level of the two forms is equivalent.

Review Answers

Vocabulary Review

1. neuron 2. sensory receptor 3. peristalsis
4. glottis 5. effector cell 6. red marrow
7. ligament 8. epithelium 9. tendon
10. synapse 11. chyme 12. nephron
13. plasma 14. capillary 15. trachea
16. fibrinogen 17. vein

Teacher Alert

In the Chapter Review, the Vocabulary Review activity includes a sample of the chapter's vocabulary terms. The activity will help determine students' understanding of key vocabulary terms and concepts presented in the chapter. Other vocabulary terms used in the chapter are listed below.

adrenaline	ingestion
alveolus	inferior vena cava
antidiuretic hormone	involuntary muscle
asthma	iris
auditory nerve	larynx
axon	limbic system
bile	neurotransmitter
brain stem	optic nerve
bronchiole	osteoporosis
bronchitis	perspiration
bronchus	pharynx
cerebellum	pituitary gland
cerebral cortex	pupil
cochlea	rectum
connective tissue	reflex
cornea	retina
dendrite	skeletal system
dermis	sleep apnea
diencephalon	superior vena cava
eardrum	thalamus
epidermis	ureter
fatty layer	urine
feces	ventricle
gallbladder	villi
glomerulus	voluntary muscle
hypertension	
hypothalamus	

Concept Review
18. C **19.** A **20.** B **21.** D

Critical Thinking
22. Muscles can only move by pulling. In order to move in both directions, two muscles must work in different directions.

Chapter 12 REVIEW – continued

15. Air travels through the _____ to reach the bronchi.

16. The protein in blood that forms clots is _____.

17. Blood traveling in a(n) _____ is moving away from the heart.

Concept Review
On a sheet of paper, write the letter of the answer that completes each sentence correctly.

18. Blood in an artery is usually _____.
- **A** rich in oxygen and moves toward the heart
- **B** poor in oxygen and moves toward the heart
- **C** rich in oxygen and moves away from the heart
- **D** poor in oxygen and moves away from the heart

19. High-level functions such as learning, thinking, and memory functions are carried out by the _____.
- **A** cerebral cortex
- **C** limbic system
- **B** cerebellum
- **D** spinal cord

20. The liver works to help the body by _____.
- **A** producing stomach acid
- **B** processing food to get nutrients
- **C** releasing bile into the stomach
- **D** extracting water from waste

21. Platelets can form a clot, or a _____.
- **A** red blood cell
- **C** plasma
- **B** white blood cell
- **D** thrombus

Chapter 12 Human Body Systems

Chapter 12 Mastery Test A, pages 1–3

Critical Thinking

On a sheet of paper, write the answers to the following questions. Use complete sentences.

22. Why must muscles work in pairs to allow a complete range of movement?
23. Describe the two main systems that make up the nervous system.
24. Describe the process of respiration.
25. How can the stress response be negative or positive?

Research and Write

Investigate government regulations for the handling and preparation of food products. What new technologies are being introduced in the meat industry to prevent food from becoming infected by pathogens? Describe some arguments that support these methods. Describe some of the criticism of the methods.

Test-Taking Tip Read test questions carefully. Identify questions that require more than one answer.

---

23. The nervous system is made up of the central nervous system, which includes the brain and spinal cord, and the peripheral nervous system, which includes all the nerves outside of the central nervous system. **24.** Respiration begins when air is inhaled. Air passes through the nose, pharynx, trachea, and bronchi, which lead into the lungs. The lungs branch into bronchioles, which have alveoli at their tips. Oxygen then passes from the alveoli to capillaries and into the blood. At the same time, carbon dioxide in the blood passes into the alveoli. Then air is exhaled and carbon dioxide is removed. **25.** The stress response can be positive while playing a sport. The response will cause more oxygen to be sent to muscles. If a stress response, such as increased heart rate, continues for a long time then negative effects can begin.

Research and Write

Divide students into groups of three or four. They can search library catalogs for medical journals or search government Web sites on the Internet. The Food and Drug Administration Web site (www.fda.gov) is a good starting point.

ALTERNATIVE ASSESSMENT

Alternative Assessment items correlate to the student Goals for Learning at the beginning of this chapter.

- Write on the board *protects and supports, allows movement, breaks down food, controls activities, carries materials, gets rid of waste, connects body with outside world,* and *gets oxygen, releases CO_2.* Have students write the name of the system next to each function. *(skeletal, muscular, digestive, endocrine and nervous, circulatory, excretory, sensory, respiratory)*
- Divide the class into eight groups and assign each group one of the body systems described in this chapter. Have each group create a poster with vocabulary, functions, and illustrations of systems and processes.

Chapter 13

Planning Guide
Evolution and Natural Selection

	Student Pages	Vocabulary	Lesson Review	Critical-Thinking Questions
Lesson 1 What Is Biological Evolution?	388–391	✔	✔	✔
Lesson 2 Evidence of Evolution	392–396	✔	✔	✔
Lesson 3 Rates of Evolutionary Change	397–403	✔	✔	✔
Lesson 4 Processes in Evolution	404–409	✔	✔	✔
Lesson 5 Natural Selection	410–415	✔	✔	✔
Lesson 6 Microevolution and Macroevolution	416–421	✔	✔	✔

(Column group header: **Student Text Lesson**)

Chapter Activities

Teacher's Resource Library
Community Connection 13:
  Local Threatened and Endangered Organisms
Graphic Organizer 13:
  Evolution and Natural Selection

Teacher's Edition
Opener Activity

Assessment Options

Student Text
Chapter 13 Review

Teacher's Resource Library
Chapter 13 Mastery Tests A and B

Teacher's Edition
Chapter 13 Alternative Assessment

Achievements in Science	Science at Work	Biology in Your Life	Investigation/Discovery	Biology in the World	Express Lab	Link to	Research and Write	Technology and Society	ELL/ESL Strategy	Background Information	Science Journal	Applications (Home, Career, Community, Global, Environment)	Online Connection	Teacher Alert	Auditory/Verbal	Body/Kinesthetic	Interpersonal/Group Learning	Logical/Mathematical	Visual/Spatial	Workbook Activities	Alternative Workbook Activities	Lab Manual	Self-Study Guide
						✓			389	388	391	390		389			390			72	72		✓
			393			✓			395	392		395		394	393					73	73	61–62	✓
			402			✓			398	397		399, 400		399			399			74	74	63–64	✓
409	408							404	408	404	407			407				406		75	75		✓
		412	414						411	410		411							412	76	76	65	✓
					421	✓		425	418	416	419		421	417						77–78	77–78		✓

Pronunciation Key

a	hat	e	let	ī	ice	ô	order	ù	put
ā	age	ē	equal	o	hot	oi	oil	ü	rule
ä	far	ėr	term	ō	open	ou	out	ch	child
â	care	i	it	ȯ	saw	u	cup	ng	long

sh	she		a in about
th	thin		e in taken
ᴛʜ	then	ə	i in pencil
zh	measure		o in lemon
			u in circus

Alternative Workbook Activities

The Teacher's Resource Library (TRL) contains a set of lower-level worksheets called Alternative Workbook Activities. These worksheets cover the same content as the regular Workbook Activities but are written at a second-grade reading level.

Skill Track Online

Use Skill Track Online for *Biology: Cycles of Life* to monitor student progress and meet the demands of adequate yearly progress (AYP). Make informed instructional decisions with individual student and class reports of online lesson and chapter assessments. With immediate and ongoing feedback, students will also see what they have learned and where they need more reinforcement and practice.

Chapter at a Glance

Chapter 13: Evolution and Natural Selection
pages 386–425

Lessons

1. **What Is Biological Evolution?** pages 388–391
2. **Evidence of Evolution** pages 392–396
3. **Rates of Evolutionary Change** pages 397–403

   Investigation 13 pages 402–403
4. **Processes in Evolution** pages 404–409
5. **Natural Selection** pages 410–415

   Discovery Investigation 13 pages 414–415
6. **Microevolution and Macroevolution** pages 416–421

   Biology in the World page 421

Chapter 13 Summary page 422

Chapter 13 Review pages 423–425

Audio CD

Skill Track Online for Biology: Cycles of Life

Teacher's Resource Library

- Workbook Activities 72–78
- Alternative Workbook Activities 72–78
- Lab Manual 61–65
- Community Connection 13
- Graphic Organizer 13
- Resource File 31–32
- Chapter 13 Self-Study Guide
- Chapter 13 Mastery Tests A and B

(Answer Keys for the Teacher's Resource Library begin on page 675 of the Teacher's Edition. The Materials List for the Lab Manual activities begins on page 720.)

Opener Activity

Display photographs of the finches that Darwin found on the Galapagos Islands. Have students observe the beaks of the different species. Point out to students that the different beak shapes help the finches find food.

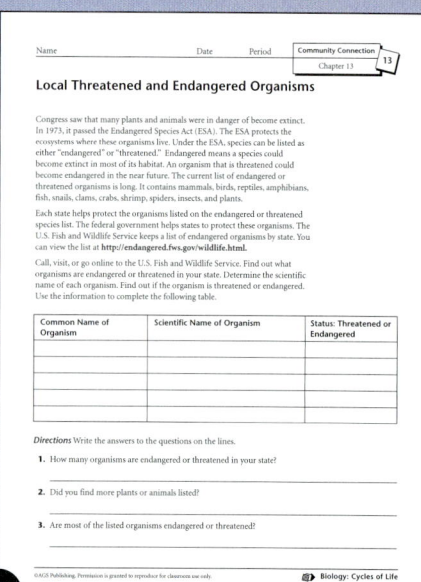

Community Connection 13

386 Chapter 13

Chapter 13

Evolution and Natural Selection

Can you see the leopard in the tree in the photograph? The leopard's spots help it blend with the spotted pattern in the tree bark. This keeps the leopard hidden. The spots make the leopard a better hunter. Traits like the leopard's spots are called adaptations. Adaptation improves the chance that an organism survives and reproduces in an environment. In Chapter 13, you will learn about biological evolution. You will find out how species adapt through natural selection.

Organize Your Thoughts

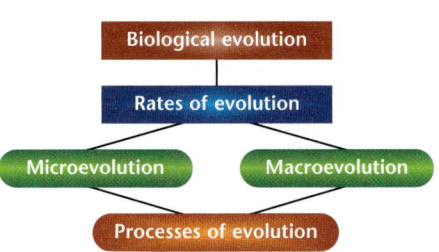

Goals for Learning

- ◆ To describe the theory of evolution and the evidence that supports evolution
- ◆ To describe the rates of evolutionary change
- ◆ To explain how changes occur in the gene pool
- ◆ To define natural selection, microevolution, and macroevolution

387

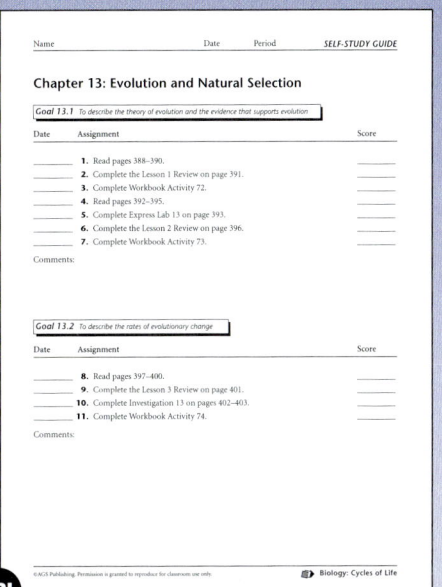

Chapter 13 Self-Study Guide

Introducing the Chapter

Ask students: Have you ever noticed that different animals have different characteristics that aid them in survival?

Look at the photograph on page 386. What characteristics do leopards have that help them survive? *(The markings on leopards' fur help them blend into their environment. They are able to run at tremendous speeds that allow them to catch prey.)*

Have students read the Goals for Learning. Help students write questions about what they want to find out about evolution and natural selection. For example, students might ask "Why is the study of evolution important?" or "Why is the study of evolution important to me?" Students can use their questions to help set a purpose for reading.

Notes and Math Tips

Ask volunteers to read the notes and math tips that appear in the margins throughout the chapter. Then discuss them with the class.

TEACHER'S RESOURCE

The AGS Publishing Teaching Strategies in Science Transparencies may be used with this chapter. The transparencies add an interactive dimension to expand and enhance the *Biology: Cycles of Life* program content.

CAREER INTEREST INVENTORY

The AGS Publishing Harrington-O'Shea Career Decision-Making System-Revised (CDM) may be used with this chapter. Students can use the CDM to explore their interests and identify careers. The CDM defines career areas that are indicated by students' responses on the inventory.

Evolution and Natural Selection   387

Lesson at a Glance

Chapter 13 Lesson 1

Overview In this lesson, students learn about biological evolution.

Objectives
- To define *evolution*.
- To state the two theories that came from Darwin's work
- To explain why Mendel's work supported evolution
- To describe the modern synthesis theory

Student Pages 388–391

Teacher's Resource Library

Workbook Activity 72

Alternative Workbook Activity 72

Vocabulary

acquired trait
adapt
biological evolution
common descent
descent with modification
fossil
gene pool
modern synthesis
natural selection
population

Have students read the terms and definitions. Then have students write complete sentences, correctly using each term.

Background Information

Charles Darwin was a British scientist who lived from 1809 to 1882. After graduating from Cambridge, he served aboard the HMS *Beagle* as an unpaid naturalist. On this scientific expedition around the world, Darwin observed many plants, animals, fossils, and geological formations. The observations on this trip provided Darwin with the inspiration to write his book *On the Origin of Species by Means of Natural Selection*. This book created a great deal of controversy because it opposed the accepted views of the time and it opposed theological viewpoints.

Lesson 1 — What Is Biological Evolution?

Objectives

After reading this lesson, you should be able to
- define evolution
- state the two theories that came from Darwin's work
- explain why Mendel's work supported evolution
- describe the theory of modern synthesis

Fossil
The remains or impressions of an organism that lived in the past

Population
A group of organisms of the same species that live in the same area

Biological evolution
The change in the gene pool of a population over time

Gene pool
The genes found within a population

Millions of different types of organisms live on the earth today. They differ in structures, behaviors, and genes. Living things are also alike in many ways. They reproduce, use energy, and exchange substances with the environment. Living things share the same pattern of genetic code. How do scientists explain the differences and similarities in living things?

To answer this question, scientists look at the history of living things. They do this by looking at **fossils** in rocks. Fossils are the remains or impressions of organisms that lived in the past. Fossils show that ancient organisms are like modern organisms, but are also different. Scientists look at other types of evidence that support a theory called evolution. Evolution is the changes in a **population** over time. You will study these types of evidence in Lesson 2. Scientists use the theory of evolution to explain the similarity and differences in living things.

Biological evolution is the change in the gene pool of populations of organisms over time. **Gene pool** is the genes found within a population. Biological evolution explains how living things that appear to be different are related. This theory also explains how differences develop among living things.

Lamarck's Ideas About Evolution

In the early 1800s, French scientist Jean Baptiste de Lamarck published ideas about evolution. He thought a relationship between fossils and modern living things was due to the idea that life evolves. He thought organisms change as they adjust to changes in the environment. The changes are passed to offspring.

For example, Lamarck thought ancient giraffes ate the lower leaves on trees. To eat the higher leaves, they stretched their necks. Lamarck thought stretching caused offspring to be born with longer necks. He thought a giraffe's long neck was an **acquired trait**. An acquired trait would come from an organism's behavior and is passed to offspring. Scientists rejected Lamarck's ideas. However, scientists accepted the idea that adaptation resulted from interactions between living things and their environments.

388 Chapter 13 *Evolution and Natural Selection*

Acquired trait
A trait that comes from an organism's behavior

Descent with modification
The theory that more recent species of organisms are changed descendants of earlier species

Natural selection
The process by which organisms best suited to the environment survive, reproduce, and pass their genes to the next generation

Common descent
A theory that present organisms descend from past organisms

Darwin's Theories of Decent with Modification and Natural Selection

From 1831 to 1836, British scientist Charles Darwin sailed around the world. On his travels, Darwin studied living things. He observed that organisms were alike in many ways, but were also different.

Darwin suggested organisms living today descended, or evolved, from organisms that lived millions of years ago. These early descendants spread to different areas. Then they changed to fit different ways of life. Darwin called this idea **descent with modification.** This theory states that more recent species of organisms are changed descendants of earlier species.

On his travels, Darwin observed that species created large numbers of offspring. However, not all survived. He also observed great variation among members in a population. He suggested individuals with survival traits best suited to their environment are more likely than others to reproduce. Darwin called this idea **natural selection.**

In 1859, Darwin published his ideas in a book, *On the Origin of Species.* Natural selection is the process by which organisms best suited to the environment survive, reproduce, and pass their genes to the next generation.

Darwin explained evolution with two ideas. His first idea was **common descent.** He stated that present organisms are related to past organisms. Darwin thought all species had come from one or a few original life-forms. For example, he thought all birds and mammals came from an animal that lived in the distant past. Darwin's theory explains why organisms have offspring that are similar. Common descent basically says that evolution occurs in nature.

Darwin's second idea was natural selection. Darwin thought that natural selection explained how evolution occurs. In this theory, new variations within populations happen constantly. Some variations give individuals an advantage in survival. These individuals produce more offspring than individuals without the variations.

Evolution and Natural Selection Chapter 13

Warm-Up Activity

Show students a picture of a white rabbit and a brown rabbit. Ask students: Which rabbit is more likely to survive in a snowy environment and which is more likely to survive on a prairie? Why? *(The white rabbit is more likely to survive in a snowy environment because it will blend into the environment better. It will be less visible to predators. Likewise, the brown rabbit is more likely to survive on a prairie for the same reasons.)*

Explain that this is the type of reasoning Darwin used to explain natural selection. The white rabbits found in snowy environments are more likely to survive and reproduce more white rabbits. Brown rabbits found in snowy environments will probably be eaten by predators and will not reproduce. The number of white rabbits will increase, and the number of brown rabbits will decrease.

Teaching the Lesson

As students read the lesson, have them write down the main ideas from each paragraph. Have students include supporting details so that they have enough information to understand the concept or theory. Encourage them to ask questions about any concept or theory they do not understand.

Reinforce and Extend

TEACHER ALERT

Some students may find this material offensive. Be sensitive to the opinions of these students to prevent any unnecessary misunderstandings.

ELL/ESL STRATEGY

Language Objective: *To summarize the main ideas in the lesson*

Have students create their own graphic organizer for this lesson. They can use their graphic organizers to study for quizzes and tests.

LEARNING STYLES

Interpersonal/Group Learning
Have students work with partners to make a table comparing and contrasting Lamarck's ideas, Darwin's theories, and the theory of modern synthesis.

GLOBAL CONNECTION

Have students research the fossilized human remains that scientists have found in northern Africa. Have students present their research findings to the class. Students should use a world map to identify where the fossilized remains were found.

Link to

Social Studies. Have students read the Link to Social Studies feature. Ask them to find northern Africa on a world map. Have students brainstorm ways that humans could have migrated from northern Africa to populate the world as it is today. *(Accept all reasonable responses and explanations.)*

Adapt
To change genetically over generations to become more suited to the environment

Modern synthesis
A theory that states evolution involves changes in a population's gene pool over time

Link to ▸▸▸
Social Studies

By examining the DNA of many people, scientists have found that we are all very closely related. The genetic diversity between any two humans is very small. Scientists have evidence that all humans descended from a very small population in northern Africa. These people lived between 70,000 and 140,000 years ago.

Individuals in a population with traits best suited to the environment increase in numbers. They are more likely to survive. They are also more likely to pass their genes to their offspring. The entire population **adapts** to its environment as more offspring with the favored traits are created. Over many generations, the entire population and the whole species evolve with the adaptations.

Sometimes, natural selection can cause a new species to arise from an old species. The new species cannot reproduce with the old species. The two species often become separated by natural barriers, such as rivers and mountains. This reproductive separation causes the two species to evolve differently.

The Transfer of Genetic Material
Remember from Chapter 10 Gregor Mendel's experiments with pea plants. In 1866, Mendel determined how traits combined to produce patterns of inheritance. Based on Mendel's data, scientists later determined how genetic material was passed to offspring. In all organisms, genes carry the information about traits from parents to offspring.

Modern Synthesis
Darwin and Mendel laid the groundwork for the modern study of life. Darwin explained that all living things are connected. He proposed the theory of natural selection to explain how organisms changed. Mendel developed the theory of genetics. Recall from Chapter 10 that genetics is the basis for biological inheritance.

Today, scientists support a theory of evolution called **modern synthesis.** The theory of modern synthesis explains that populations evolve. Individuals do not evolve. Modern synthesis combines the ideas of Darwin, Mendel, and other scientists. Modern synthesis states that evolution involves changes in a population's gene pool over time. Genes determine the traits of all living things.

Lesson 1 REVIEW

Word Bank
acquired trait
common descent
gene pool

On a sheet of paper, write the word or words from the Word Bank that complete each sentence correctly.

1. Darwin's idea of _____ states that today's organisms are related to past organisms.
2. The theory of modern synthesis states that evolution involves changes in a population's _____.
3. Lamarck's ideas about evolution stated that a giraffe's long neck was a(n) _____.

On a sheet of paper, write the letter of the answer that completes each sentence correctly.

4. Mendel developed the theory of _____.
   A natural selection   C evolution
   B modern synthesis   D genetics

5. Darwin thought _____ was needed for a species to change.
   A extinction   C genetic mutation
   B natural selection   D an acquired trait

6. A current theory of evolution is _____.
   A species isolation   C behavior change
   B barrier   D modern synthesis

Critical Thinking

On a sheet of paper, write the answers to the following questions. Use complete sentences.

7. Describe the process Darwin thought caused a species to evolve into another species.
8. Describe the modern synthesis theory of evolution.
9. What are fossils? What do they show scientists?
10. What were Lamarck's ideas about evolution?

Evolution and Natural Selection Chapter 13

Lesson 1 Review Answers

1. common descent **2.** gene pool **3.** acquired trait **4.** D **5.** B **6.** D **7.** Darwin thought that new species were created when members of the same species were separated by a barrier. Each population, prevented from reproducing with each other, would evolve separately. **8.** According to the modern synthesis theory, evolution involves changes in a population's gene pool over time. Individuals do not evolve. **9.** Fossils are the remains or impressions of organisms that lived in the past. The similarities and differences between these ancient organisms and modern organisms provide scientists with evidence of evolution **10.** Lamarck thought organisms change as they adjust to changes in the environment. He thought an acquired trait could be passed to offspring.

Portfolio Assessment

Sample items include:
- Main ideas of lesson from Teaching the Lesson
- Student's graphic organizer from ELL/ESL Strategy
- Lesson 1 Review answers

SCIENCE JOURNAL

Have students write a paragraph describing what they think about Lamarck's ideas, Darwin's theories, and the theory of modern synthesis.

LAB ACTIVITIES

Chapter 13 has Investigation and Discovery Investigation lab activities. Two additional lab activities for Chapter 13 appear in the Biology: Cycles of Life Lab Manual and on the Teacher's Resource Library CD-ROM.

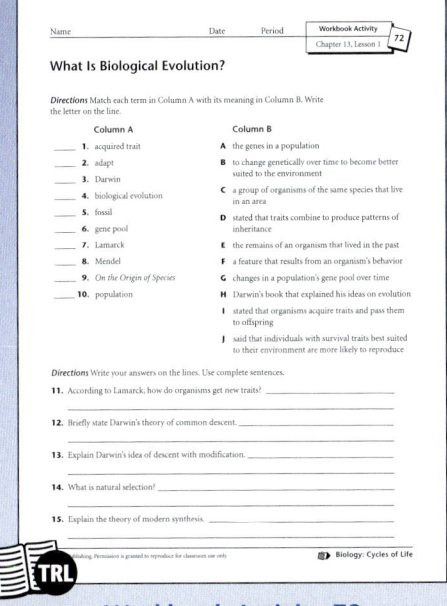

Workbook Activity 72

Lesson at a Glance

Chapter 13 Lesson 2

Overview In this lesson, students learn about the evidence found to support the theory of modern synthesis.

Objectives

- To describe why fossils support the theory of evolution
- To explain why biogeography supports the theory of evolution
- To explain why anatomy provides evidence of evolution
- To describe why molecular biology provides evidence of evolution

Student Pages 392–396

Teacher's Resource Library

Workbook Activity 73
Alternative Workbook Activity 73
Lab Manual 61–62
Resource File 31

Vocabulary

anatomy
biogeography
comparative anatomy
fossil record
homologous structures
molecular biology
sedimentary rock

Have students use a dictionary to find the meaning of prefixes and root words in the vocabulary terms.

Background Information

Scientists have found that geographic barriers have caused members of the same species to evolve to such an extent that they must be classified as subspecies. Geographic barriers include seaways, rivers, mountain ranges, and deserts. Islands separated from the mainland provide excellent examples of this biodiversity. The finches on the Galapagos Islands and the birds called honeycreepers on the Hawaiian Islands are two examples of species that evolved to fill different niches.

392 Chapter 13

Lesson 2 Evidence of Evolution

Objectives

After reading this lesson, you should be able to

- describe why fossils support the theory of evolution
- explain why biogeography supports the theory of evolution
- explain why anatomy provides evidence of evolution
- describe why molecular biology provides evidence of evolution

Sedimentary rock
The rock formed from pieces of other rock and organic matter that have been pressed and cemented together

Fossil record
The history of life on the earth, based on fossils that have been discovered

Scientists use different types of evidence to support the theory of modern synthesis. Scientists have found fossils of organisms similar to modern organisms. They have found patterns in the way living things are distributed on the earth. Organisms that look different may have similar body structures. Scientists have also found that the DNA of each species is different, but alike. Let's look at each type of evidence of evolution.

Fossil Record

Fossils are evidence that species lived long ago. The earth today is very different than it was billions of years ago. The continents were once in different locations. The climate was different. Scientists have found that **sedimentary rock** contains a **fossil record**, or diary, of the earth's history. Sedimentary rock is rock formed from pieces of other rock and organic matter that have been pressed and cemented together. Sedimentary rock often has layers.

By examining the fossils in each rock layer, scientists can estimate when certain organisms lived. Fossils in the lower layers represented species that lived before species in the upper layers. The fossil record also shows how organisms have changed over time. By comparing fossils to modern organisms, scientists have found many similarities.

Biogeography

Scientists have found patterns in the way living things are distributed, or spread out, on the earth. The study of the geographical distribution of fossils and living organisms is called **biogeography.** For example, kangaroos are only found in Australia. Scientists think kangaroos evolved in isolation from regions where other animals diversified.

392 Chapter 13 Evolution and Natural Selection

Biogeography
The study of the geographical distribution of fossils and living organisms

Charles Darwin observed that the animals on the Galapagos Islands were similar to animals in South America. The Galapagos Islands are a group of islands 600 miles west of Ecuador in South America.

Darwin thought that Galapagos species evolved from animals that came from South America. He thought the differences between parents and offspring happened through natural selection. By using biogeography, scientists today have evidence that supports Darwin's observations.

Express Lab 13

Materials
- marker
- 3 flat sponges

Procedure
1. Form small groups.
2. Using a marker, make a shape like an ×, □, or ○ on the long side of each sponge. Make each mark different. The marks represent fossils. The sponges represent layers of rock.
3. Put the sponges on top of each other so that the fossils face you. Observe the order of fossils from top to bottom.
4. Hold the layers of sponges tightly on both ends. Moving your hands toward each other, push inward against the sponges. Observe what happens to the order of fossils from top to bottom.

Analysis
1. Which fossil is the oldest in Step 3?
2. How did the order of fossils change in Step 4?
3. What does a scientist need to know about a rock to tell if one fossil is older than another fossil?

Evolution and Natural Selection Chapter 13 **393**

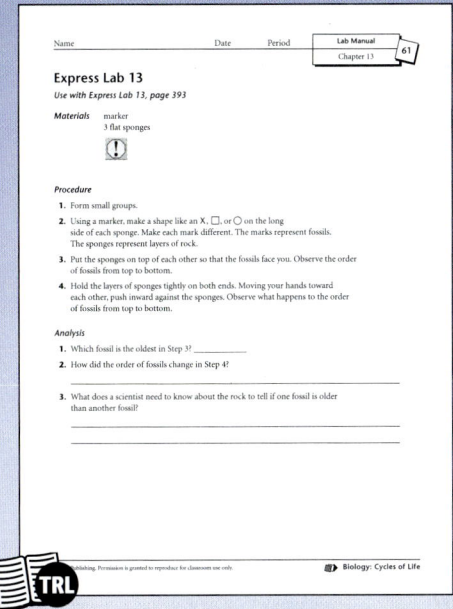

Lab Manual 61

1 Warm-Up Activity

Have students perform the Express Lab on page 393. Ask students: Why is it important to determine the order in which the fossils formed? *(The order of fossil formation provides historical information about the area.)* How is the sponge similar to soil and rock? *(The sponge represents the layers of separation between the fossils. In real life, soil and rock separate the fossils.)*

Express Lab Answers

1. The oldest fossil is in the bottom rock layer (sponge). **2.** As the sponges folded, the order of fossils changed. A fossil that was on top may have ended up in the middle or on the bottom. **3.** The scientist needs to know whether the rock has been folded greatly or overturned.

2 Teaching the Lesson

Have a volunteer read the section about biogeography. Have students brainstorm reasons why the animals on the Galapagos Islands and the animals in South America can be similar even though they are separated by the ocean. *(Sample answers: The animals were brought to the islands by travelers on ships. The islands and the continent of South America were once connected but have since drifted apart.)* Ask students: Can you think of other examples of animals in different parts of the world that are similar but are classified as different species? *(Sample answers: polar bears and grizzly bears; African elephants and Asian elephants)*

Have students outline this lesson, using the main ideas and details from each section. Encourage students to use their outlines as study guides.

3 Reinforce and Extend

LEARNING STYLES

Auditory/Verbal

Assign each small group one of these sections: Fossil Record, Biogeography, Comparative Anatomy, or Molecular Biology. Have students explain the concepts in the section to the group. Have each group explain their section to the class.

Evolution and Natural Selection **393**

Teacher Alert

Remind students that it is possible that all of the continents once formed one large supercontinent—Pangaea. The continents of South America, Africa, and Australia separated from Pangaea to form a smaller landmass called Gondwanaland. A group of flightless birds provides evidence of the existence of Gondwanaland: the cassowary and emu in Australia, the rhea in South America, and the ostrich in Africa. Fossil evidence and DNA analysis show that these birds are related. Have students research and compare pictures of these flightless birds.

Anatomy
The structure of an organism

Comparative anatomy
The study of anatomy of different species

Homologous structure
The body parts that are similar in related animals

Comparative Anatomy

To look for clues suggesting evolution, scientists compare the **anatomy** of species. Anatomy is the structure of an organism. **Comparative anatomy** is the study of anatomy of animals of different species. Sometimes species look different, but their structures are similar.

Look at the front limbs of the four animals in Figure 13.2.1. Notice how similar the bones are. The limbs are **homologous structures.** Body parts that are similar in different animals are homologous structures. However, the function of the limbs differs for each animal. Some scientists think homologous structures appeared in an ancestor common to all organisms.

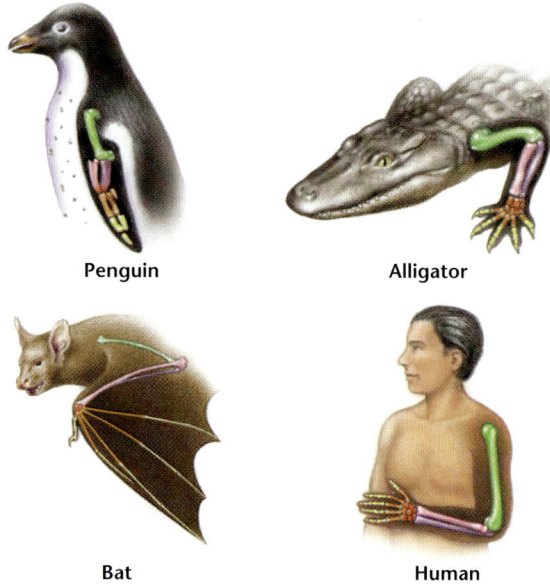

Figure 13.2.1 *The front limbs of these different animals are similar.*

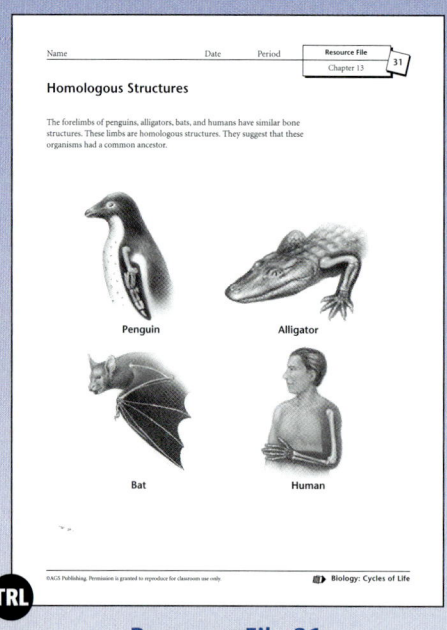

Resource File 31

Molecular Biology

Molecular biology
The study of the biochemical and molecular processes within cells

Scientists use **molecular biology** to examine the basis of life. Molecular biology is the study of the biochemical and molecular processes within cells. Scientists use molecular studies as evidence of evolution. For example, scientists use DNA analysis to show that life has evolved. They have found that similar forms of organisms have more recent common ancestors than less similar forms. They have also found that the early stages of embryos of different animals are very similar.

The evidence for these patterns is in the DNA sequences of organisms. Remember that a cell makes a new copy of its DNA before dividing to produce two daughter cells. Cells may make mistakes when copying its DNA nucleotides. A few nucleotides may change each time a cell divides.

Over time, two organisms with a common ancestor will have differences in their DNA sequences. The more cell divisions that occur, the more differences in DNA sequences will result. By comparing these differences, scientists can understand how species are related.

Scientists have methods to find the sequence of DNA nucleotides in chromosomes. In 2003, the Human Genome Project identified the entire sequence of human DNA. Recall from Chapter 5 that a genome is the entire DNA found in a cell. Scientists also have found the sequences of other species' genomes. By comparing these sequences and other evidence, scientists are putting together the history of life on the earth.

Link to >>>
Chemistry

Scientists once thought prokaryotes did not have organelles. Recently, they discovered a primitive organelle that exists in some bacteria. These tiny organelles are like pouches. These pouches contain enzymes. The pouches are also found in some eukaryotes. Scientists think this may be an important evolutionary link between bacteria and eukaryotic cells.

ELL/ESL Strategy

Language Objective: *To explain the meaning of molecular biology*

Have students write and act out a short skit that explains the meaning of molecular biology and describes what a molecular biologist does.

Career Connection

Have students research molecular biology as a career. Ask students to identify high school courses that should be taken as preparation for a career in molecular biology. In addition, have them find colleges and universities in their area that offer degrees in molecular biology as well as facilities that offer employment to molecular biologists after graduation.

Link to

Chemistry. Have students read the Link to Chemistry feature. Ask students: How does this provide a possible evolutionary link between prokaryote and eukaryote cells? *(It is possible that eukaryotes evolved directly from prokaryotes. These pouches found in prokaryotes could have evolved into the organelles found in eukaryotes.)*

Lesson 2 Review Answers

1. sedimentary rock **2.** nucleotides
3. molecular biology **4.** B **5.** B **6.** C
7. By comparing the DNA sequences with the common ancestor, a scientist can see how closely the sequences match. Generally, an organism that matches an ancestor is more closely related to it.
8. Scientists can get information about when an organism lived by examining the fossil record. Scientists can also compare the fossils to modern organisms to see how an organism changed over time.
9. The Galapagos animals looked like South American animals. **10.** The Human Genome Project has mapped the entire sequence of genes in humans. By sequencing other species, DNA can be compared and evolutionary relationships can be better determined.

Portfolio Assessment

Sample items include:
- Section outlines from Teaching the Lesson
- Skit from ELL/ESL Strategy
- Lesson 2 Review answers

Lesson 2   R E V I E W

Word Bank
molecular biology
nucleotides
sedimentary rock

On a sheet of paper, write the word or words from the Word Bank that complete each sentence correctly.

1. Pieces of rock and organic material pressed together form _____.
2. DNA sequences between two related organisms will often have a few different _____ due to copying errors.
3. The study of biochemical and molecular processes within cells is _____.

On a sheet of paper, write the letter of the answer that completes each sentence correctly.

4. The layers of sedimentary rock form a _____.
   A biogeography   C continent
   B fossil record   D climate

5. The body structures of some species support Darwin's theories because they _____.
   A have similar functions   C are the same
   B have similar limbs   D are very different

6. The study of biogeography includes information about the location of _____.
   A rocks   C fossils and living organisms
   B homologous structures   D the fossil record

Critical Thinking

On a sheet of paper, write the answers to the following questions. Use complete sentences.

7. How could a scientist use DNA sequences of two organisms to find which is more closely related to a common ancestor?
8. What can scientists find by examining the fossil record?
9. Why did Darwin think animals on the Galapagos Islands evolved from animals in South America?
10. How has the Human Genome Project contributed to knowledge about evolution?

396   Chapter 13   Evolution and Natural Selection

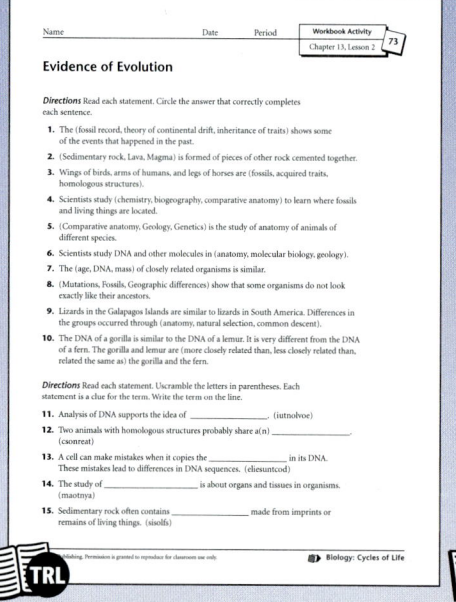

Workbook Activity 73

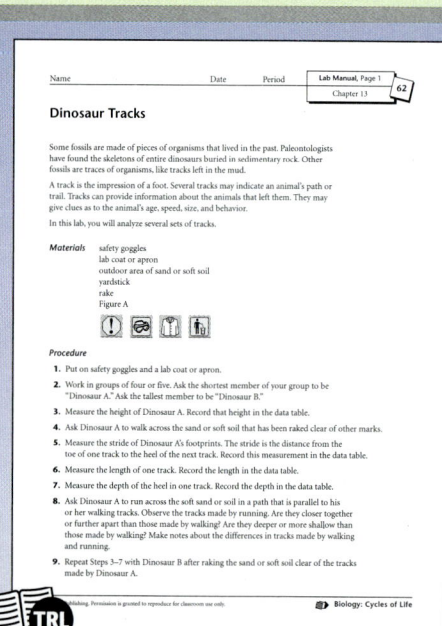

Lab Manual 62, pages 1–2

Lesson 3   Rates of Evolutionary Change

Objectives

After reading this lesson, you should be able to
- define geologic time
- explain how a rock's age determines a fossil's age
- describe how the geologic time scale relates to evolutionary change
- explain how continental drift and plate tectonics relate to evolutionary change

Geologic time
All the time that has passed since the earth formed

Paleontologist
A scientist who studies fossils

Many modern organisms are very different in structure and behavior from organisms that lived in the past. For example, modern horses are much larger than early horses. Early horses had four toes on each foot. As the horse evolved, its four toes became a single hoof.

The diversity of organisms today and in the past is the result of evolution. Evolution has occurred on the earth over many millions of years. Scientists look for evidence of evolutionary change in the earth's history.

Geological Time

Most events in the earth are compared to **geologic time**. Geologic time is all the time that has passed since the earth formed. Scientists estimate that the earth is about 4.6 billion years old. They base this estimate on meteorites and moon rocks. Meteorites are pieces of rock that hit the surface of a planet or moon after traveling through space. Both meteorites and moon rocks formed about the same time as the earth.

Fossils are an important record of the earth's history. Recall from Lesson 1 that fossils are the remains or impressions of organisms preserved in rocks. Fossils are evidence that certain kinds of life existed.

Paleontologists are scientists who look for and study fossils. Their findings have formed a fossil record. The fossil record tells about the organisms that once lived on the earth. The fossil record also shows how organisms have changed over time.

A fossil can be a preserved organism or an impression of an organism. Fossils of an organism's activities are called trace fossils, such as foot prints.

Evolution and Natural Selection   Chapter 13   397

Lesson at a Glance

Chapter 13 Lesson 3

Overview In this lesson, students learn about the rates of evolutionary change.

Objectives

- To define *geologic time*
- To explain how a rock's age determines a fossil's age
- To describe how the geologic time scale relates to evolutionary change
- To explain how continental drift and plate tectonics relate to evolutionary change

Student Pages 397–403

Teacher's Resource Library (TRL)
- Workbook Activity 74
- Alternative Workbook Activity 74
- Lab Manual 63–64
- Resource File 32

Vocabulary

amphibian	magma
continental drift	paleontologist
crust	plate
geologic time	plate tectonics
geologic time scale	radioactive element
	reptile
invertebrate	vertebrate

Have students create a crossword puzzle using the vocabulary terms. Then have students exchange puzzles and solve each other's puzzles.

Background Information

Carbon-14 dating is widely used to determine the age of fossils or other once-living organisms. All living organisms contain amounts of the radioactive isotope carbon-14. When a living organism dies, the amount of carbon-14 in it begins to decline at a known rate. Scientists can test the specimen to determine the amount of carbon-14 remaining and determine the age of the specimen. Carbon-14 dating can date specimens up to 50,000 years old.

A new method of carbon-14 dating called accelerator mass spectrometer counts the actual number of carbon-14 atoms remaining in an object instead of the rate of decay. This method can date objects up to 90,000 years old.

Evolution and Natural Selection   397

Warm-Up Activity

Show students pictures of the evolution of the horse. Have students note the differences in the horses through time. Show students pictures of mammoths and elephants. Discuss the similarities and differences of these two animals.

 Teaching the Lesson

Have students make a timeline to help organize the information in the lesson. The timeline should include the following developments: Earth, bacteria, multicelled animals, invertebrates, vertebrates, and single landmass breakup. Encourage students to leave room on their timeline to fill in details about each development.

 Reinforce and Extend

ELL/ESL STRATEGY

 **Language Objective:** *To explain the geologic time scale*

Have students make their own geologic time scale, using art materials such as markers, colored pencils, and poster board. Have students present their geologic time scale to the class.

Radioactive element
An element that decays to form another element

Geologic time scale
A table that divides the earth's history into time periods

Invertebrate
An animal that does not have a backbone

Vertebrate
An animal that has a backbone

Amphibian
A vertebrate that lives at first in water and then on land

Reptile
An egg-laying vertebrate that breathes with lungs

The oldest known rocks on the earth are in Greenland. They are about 3.8 billion years old.

Paleontologists can determine the relative ages of fossils by comparing their locations in rock. Relative age shows whether a fossil is older or younger than another fossil. Fossils in lower layers of rock are older than fossils in upper layers of rock. The lower rock layers were formed first. More recent rock layers contain fossils that look more like existing species.

Paleontologists can also estimate the actual ages of fossils. Actual age tells the number of years ago a fossil formed. Scientists use **radioactive elements** to date fossils. A radioactive element decays to form another element. This decay happens at a constant rate. To determine the age of fossils found in a rock, paleontologists compare the amounts of different elements in the rock.

Geologic Time Scale

Using fossils, paleontologists have put together the **geologic time scale.** This table is shown in Appendix D. The geologic time scale is a table that divides the earth's history into different time periods. The table shows the kinds of organisms that first appeared during each time period.

Scientists have found small fossils that show evidence of bacteria living 3.5 to 3.8 billion years ago. They have found evidence that animals of two or more cells lived 670 million years ago. However, the organisms that lived between these two dates did not have hard body parts. They seldom became fossils.

In the Cambrian period about 570 million years ago, there was a dramatic change on the earth. At the beginning of this period, animals with hard shells and other body coverings appeared. Fossils from the Cambrian period show that a variety of **invertebrates** lived in the seas. An invertebrate is an animal that does not have a backbone.

The earliest **vertebrate** fossils are from about 500 million years ago. A vertebrate is an animal with a backbone. Early **amphibians** and **reptiles** appeared next. An amphibian is a vertebrate that lives at first in water and then on land. A reptile is an egg-laying vertebrate that breathes with lungs.

Dinosaurs appeared about 225 million years ago. They disappeared suddenly about 160 million years later. Birds and mammals appeared in the fossil record about 200 million years ago.

Geologic Time

One of the greatest scientific theories is that geologic time represents billions of years. Using radioactive dating methods, scientists measure the age of radioactive elements and fossils. Scientists used this new knowledge along with an understanding of **plate tectonics.** Plate tectonics is a theory that states the earth's crust is made of large sections of crust that move. Scientists knew evolutionary change that resulted in new species occurred very slowly. The rate of evolutionary change happens over millions of years.

The study of plate tectonics discusses the theory of **continental drift.** This theory states that the major landmasses of the earth move. In 1912, German scientist Alfred Wegener published the theory of continental drift. He thought the earth's continents were once a single, large landmass. Wegner thought this landmass began to break up about 200 million years ago. The continents slowly moved to their present positions. Figure 13.3.1 shows their movement. For a detailed map of the continents today, see Appendix E.

> **Plate tectonics**
> A theory that the earth's surface is made of large sections of crust that move
>
> **Continental drift**
> A theory that the major landmasses of the earth move

225 million years ago   180 million years ago   Present day

Figure 13.3.1 *The theory of continental drift states that the major landmasses move over time.*

Link to

Earth Science. Have students read the Link to Earth Science feature. Explain that this fossil was found in the northern region of Venezuela. Unlike today's guinea pig, this one was too large to be a burrowing mammal. Scientists think this rodent sat up on its hind legs to scout for danger and then ran if it was threatened.

At Home

Have students use the Internet to research the weight of small cars. Ask them to find a car that is the approximate weight of the fossilized guinea pig found in 2003. Tell them to visualize an actual guinea pig that large.

Pronunciation Guide

Use the pronunciation shown here to help students pronounce a difficult word in this lesson. Refer to the pronunciation key on the Chapter Planning Guide for the sounds of the symbols.

guinea (gi′ nē)

Magma
Hot, liquid rock inside the earth

Plate
A large section of the earth's crust that moves

Crust
The outer layer of the earth

As evidence, Wegener found fossils on one continent that were similar to those on other continents. He thought mountain ranges and rock layers continued from one continent to another. In the 1950s, scientists used new instruments to determine if Wegener's theory was supported. They did this by mapping the ocean floor.

Scientists found long mountain ranges called mid-ocean ridges along the ocean floor. Mid-ocean ridges wind along the entire earth. Scientists found that **magma** once pushed apart the **plates** on which continents were located. Magma is hot, liquid rock inside the earth. Magma pushes up when volcanos erupt. A plate is a large section of the earth's **crust,** or outer layer, that moves. By the late 1960s, scientists accepted the theory of continental drift.

The theory of continental drift led to another important theory in science—plate tectonics. This theory states that the earth's crust is made of large sections, or plates. Most plates include ocean crust and continental crust. Over a long time, plates move. The positions of the continents change. Thus, as the continents moved apart, each became a separate evolutionary area. The living things of the different biogeographic regions diversified. The living things of different biogeographic regions adapted and evolved.

Link to ➤➤➤

Earth Science

In 2003, paleontologists uncovered the complete skeleton of an ancestor to the modern guinea pig. Guinea pigs are rodents which are small gnawing mammals. The skeleton belonged to the largest rodent ever discovered. Unlike modern rodents, this ancestor was the size of a horse. It measured over 9 feet long and weighed more than 1,500 pounds.

Lesson 3 REVIEW

Word Bank
continental drift
geologic time scale
paleontologist

On a sheet of paper, write the word or words from the Word Bank that complete each sentence correctly.

1. A scientist who studies fossils is a _____.
2. The _____ is a measurement of the earth's history, divided into time periods.
3. Today's continents may have existed as one large landmass that separated due to _____.

On a sheet of paper, write the letter of the answer that completes each sentence correctly.

4. Fossils before the Cambrian period are rare because _____.
   A little life existed then
   B little sediment existed to form fossils
   C organisms lacked hard parts
   D organisms lived mainly in the ocean

5. Plate tectonics states that the earth's crust is made of _____.
   A plates   C meteorites
   B magma   D moon rocks

6. A fossil found under a layer of rock is usually _____.
   A younger than the rock
   B older than the rock
   C evolved from the rock
   D made from a different type of rock

Critical Thinking

On a sheet of paper, write the answers to the following questions. Use complete sentences.

7. Why do scientists think the earth is 4.6 billion years old?
8. What is the theory of continental drift?
9. What is the theory of plate tectonics?
10. How do scientists find the actual age of a fossil?

Evolution and Natural Selection Chapter 13 401

Lesson 3 Review Answers

1. paleontologist **2.** geologic time scale **3.** continental drift **4.** C **5.** A **6.** B **7.** Radioactive dating dates moon rocks and meteorites to 4.6 billion years ago, and Earth formed at about the same time. **8.** Continental drift states that over time, the earth's major landmasses move. **9.** This theory states that the earth's crust is made of several large sections, called plates, that move. **10.** Scientists compare the amounts of different elements in the rock that contained the fossil.

Portfolio Assessment

Sample items include:
- Timeline from Teaching the Lesson
- Geologic time scale from ELL/ESL Strategy
- Lesson 3 Review answers

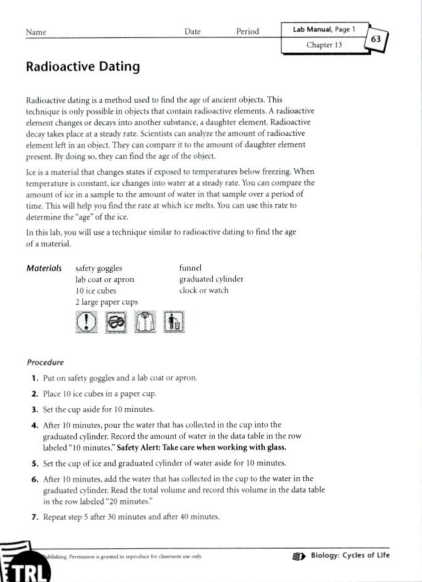

Lab Manual 63, pages 1–2

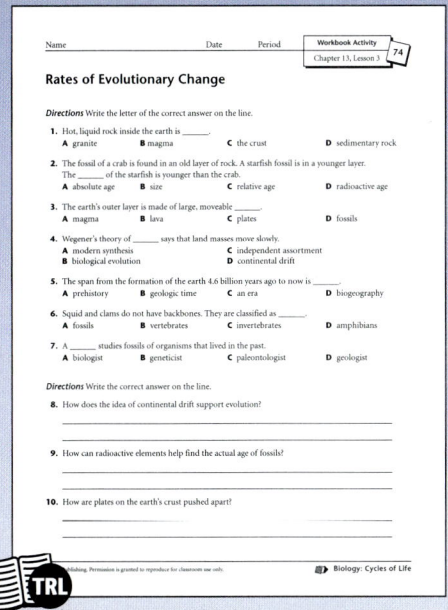

Workbook Activity 74

Investigation 13

Encourage students to read the investigation steps. Discuss questions they may have before beginning the investigation.

Objectives

- To create and run a basic simulation of natural selection
- To collect data and display it in a chart
- To infer the mechanics of natural selection through observation

Skills

Observing, running a simulation, collecting and analyzing data, inferring, drawing conclusions

Background

Using colored plastic chips and a simple example of natural selection in a simulation helps students comprehend what actually happens before, during, and after natural selection. By keeping a census of individuals expressing a certain gene, students can see how some mutations enhance survival and are passed on through reproduction.

Time Frame

One class period

Procedure

- Have student pairs work together to complete the activity.
- Provide students with a supply of colored plastic chips and six-sided number cubes. The colors of the chips and the details of the example can be changed to illustrate any reasonable genetic mutation.

INVESTIGATION 13

Materials
- about 50 blue plastic chips
- about 50 white plastic chips
- blue pencil
- red pencil

Natural Selection in Action

Mutations are random changes in DNA. Mutations create differences in organisms. When the environment changes, some organisms can survive and reproduce due to characteristics from mutations. Natural selection may remove organisms without these characteristics. Then their genes are less likely to be passed on. In this investigation, you will demonstrate how a mutation affects the survival rate and reproduction of organisms in a certain environment.

Procedure

1. Make a data table like the one shown on page 403.
2. Scatter 12 white plastic chips and 12 blue plastic chips on your desktop. The white chips represent organisms that can survive in temperatures above 0°C. This is the normal temperature range for the species. The blue chips represent organisms of the same species with a mutation. The mutation allows them to survive in temperatures below 0°C and in the normal temperature range. These organisms are cold-tolerant. The desktop represents the environment for all the organisms. Record the number of blue chips, white chips, and total chips.

402   Chapter 13   *Evolution and Natural Selection*

3. In the first event of this investigation, the temperature is above 0°C. To have the organisms reproduce, add a white chip or a blue chip for each pair of chips of the same color. For example, in the first round of reproduction, you start with 12 white chips (6 pairs). Add 6 more white chips to the environment. You also have 12 blue chips (6 pairs). Add 6 more blue chips to the environment. Record the number of white chips, blue chips, and the total chips after this event.

4. Follow the directions and events described by your teacher. After each event, allow your organisms to reproduce as in Step 2.

5. Make a graph to compare the population growth of the white and blue organisms. Label the y-axis "Number of Organisms." Label the x-axis "Time" and mark off increments of 10,000 years. Use a blue pencil to track the population of the blue chips. Use a red pencil to track the population of the white chips.

Cleanup/Disposal
When you are finished, return the materials to your teacher.

Analysis
1. How was the number of normal-range organisms (white chips) affected by cold weather?
2. How was reproduction by both normal-range and cold-tolerant organisms affected by a colder climate?

Conclusions
1. If the climate stays cold, what predictions can you make about the blue and white populations?
2. What would happen if the climate became warmer?
3. What information is missing from this investigation?

Explore Further
Try the simulation again introducing the missing element referred to in Question 3.

	Start	1st Event	2nd Event	3rd Event	4th Event	5th Event
Blue						
White						
Total						

Cleanup/Disposal
Instruct students in proper cleanup and disposal of materials.

Analysis Answers
1. The population of normal-range organisms dropped due to the cold environment.
2. The cold-tolerant organisms reproduced at an increasingly greater rate as normal-range organisms were selected out.

Conclusions Answers
1. The population will slowly be replaced by cold-tolerant organisms.
2. The change would stabilize. Normal-range organisms would no longer be selected out of the population and would begin to reproduce at the same rate as the cold-tolerant organisms. However, if the warm weather was detrimental to the cold-tolerant organisms, the trend could reverse entirely.
3. Sample answers: 1. Reproduction could combine the genes from cold-tolerant organisms with normal-range organisms. 2. Natural death should occur within the cold-tolerant organisms, although this death would be applied to both organisms at the same rate in addition to the deaths caused by selection.

Explore Further Answers
Encourage students to add a natural death percentage into the exercise or to somehow determine a method for recombining the genes.

Assessment
Check to see that students have created their data tables and charts correctly. You might include the following items from this investigation in student portfolios:
- Data table and chart
- Answers to Analysis and Conclusions questions
- Results of Explore Further

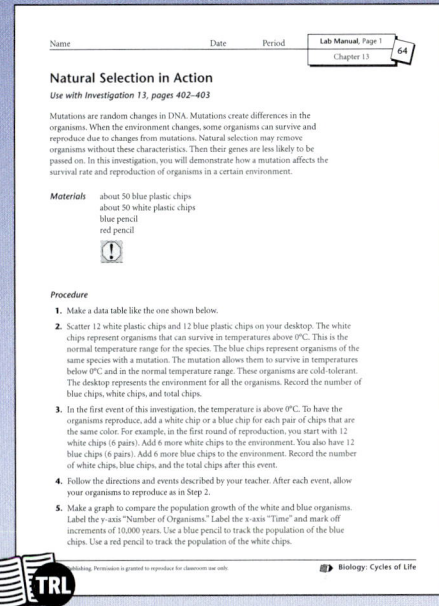

Lab Manual 64, pages 1–2

Lesson at a Glance

Chapter 13 Lesson 4

Overview In this lesson, students learn about the processes that affect evolution.

Objectives

- To describe processes that add new alleles to the gene pool
- To describe processes that remove alleles from the gene pool

Student Pages 404–409

Teacher's Resource Library

Workbook Activity 75

Alternative Workbook Activity 75

Vocabulary

endangered	habitat
extinction	Hardy-Weinberg
gene flow	equilibrium
genetic drift	recombination

Have students in small groups discuss the meaning of each term. Have groups look up the definition of each term in the Glossary. Then have students write sentences using each term.

Background Information

Humans have 23 chromosomes, with a diploid number of 46 chromosomes. Health problems or disabilities can occur when the chromosomes fail to recombine correctly. Down syndrome, Turner's syndrome, and some types of leukemia are examples of some conditions that may occur.

Technology and Society

Have students read the Technology and Society feature. Then ask students to research the current status of DNA-repair lotion. Have students report their findings to the class.

Lesson 4: Processes in Evolution

Objectives

After reading this lesson, you should be able to
- describe processes that add new alleles to the gene pool
- describe processes that remove alleles from the gene pool

The diversity of organisms today and in the past is the result of evolution. There are processes that allow evolution to continue. There are also processes that slow evolution. Remember that individual organisms do not evolve. Although they change as they grow and develop, these changes are not evolution. Evolution is the change that occurs in the gene pool of a population over time. A population is made up of individuals of the same species that live in the same place. Members of the same species mate and reproduce. How do changes in the gene pool of a population occur? They can occur through mutation, recombination, gene flow, genetic drift, and natural selection.

Mutation

Recall that random change in the nucleotide sequence of DNA is a mutation. Mutations are the source of new genetic variations. Radiation or chemicals in the environment can change genes. Germ-cell mutations can occur in an organism's gametes, or germ cells. Genes can change if they are copied incorrectly during DNA replication. For example, one nucleotide in a DNA strand could replace another nucleotide. This could change the protein made by RNA. If the protein function changes, this could harm the organism.

A mutation could help an organism. A mutation sometimes results in a trait that improves an organism's chances for survival. An organism that survives is more likely to reproduce. The favorable mutation is passed to offspring. As the mutation is passed on to future generations, it becomes more common within the population.

Technology and Society

One of the most common causes of skin cancer is exposure to the sun's ultraviolet (UV) rays. These rays damage the DNA in skin cells. This can create a mutation that causes skin cancer. Recently, scientists developed a skin lotion with DNA-repair enzymes that enter the cells. Scientists hope enzyme lotions can also be developed to treat other skin diseases.

Recombination
The creation of new combinations of alleles in offspring

Science Myth

Myth: A gene and an allele are the same thing.

Fact: A gene is a segment of DNA that codes for a particular product, such as a protein. Mutations of the same gene create different alleles, or forms of the trait. For example, one allele for eye color may code for green eyes. Another allele may code for brown eyes.

Mutations are important because every individual has thousands of genes. Many populations have thousands or millions of individuals. Over time, mutations become the source for variation in genes.

The variation is then subject to natural selection. For example, some insects are resistant to chemicals used to destroy them. Insects that are resistant to the chemicals survive and reproduce. The gene for resistance is passed to the offspring. This means the offspring are also resistant to these chemicals.

Recombination

Every chromosome in sperm or egg cells is a mixture of genes from the parents. This is due to a process called **recombination.** Recombination is the creation of new combinations of alleles in offspring. Remember that an allele is a different form of the same gene.

Think of recombination as reshuffling. Recombination is a process of evolution. It adds new alleles and combinations to the gene pool.

Here is how recombination happens. Genes are at specific locations along the chromosomes. Most sexually reproducing organisms have two of each chromosome type in every cell. One chromosome is inherited from the mother. The other chromosome is inherited from the father. Recall that when an organism produces gametes (sex cells), the gametes have only one of each chromosome.

During meiosis, each chromosome of a pair breaks in several places. The chromosome pieces are rejoined to form two new chromosomes. Later, these chromosomes are split into two cells that divide and become gametes. Both chromosomes are a mix of alleles from the mother and the father because of recombination.

Recombination creates new combinations of alleles. Alleles that arise at different times and different places can be brought together. Recombination can occur between genes and within genes.

1. Warm-Up Activity

Show students pictures of the finches that Darwin found on the Galapagos Islands. Have students closely observe the beaks of the finches. The variations in the beaks are due to mutations in the genes. Some mutations improved the chances of survival for the finches in their habitat.

2. Teaching the Lesson

Have students create a chart for this lesson. Tell them to use the following as column headings: *Mutation, Recombination, Gene Flow, Genetic Drift, Hardy-Weinberg Equilibrium,* and *Natural Selection.* As students read the lesson, have them write facts about each topic under the correct heading.

3. Reinforce and Extend

Science Myth

Have students read the Science Myth feature. Remind students that a gene controls the production of proteins and the cell cycle. An allele is an alternative form of a gene for each variation of a trait in an organism.

Gene flow	The movement of genes into or out of a population
Genetic drift	The random changes in the gene pool of a small population
Endangered	A condition in which there are almost no organisms of a certain species
Extinction	The death of all members of a species
Habitat	The place where an organism lives

Gene Flow

A population may gain or lose alleles when it combines with another population. New individuals can enter a population by moving from another population. If they mate, they can bring new alleles to the local gene pool. This is called **gene flow.**

Suppose that pollen from a population of white flowers is blown to a population of red flowers. Recall that pollen is the tiny grains of a seed plant that contain sperm cells. If the pollen fertilizes the red flowers, new alleles are introduced. Over time, genetic differences between the two populations will be reduced.

Genetic Drift

One generation in a population represents the gene pool of the previous generation. The size of the population could greatly decrease if disaster strikes. Natural disasters include floods, droughts, fires, and earthquakes. Natural disasters often happen by chance.

A population that survives a disaster may not represent the parent population's gene pool. Some alleles may be removed. These changes result in loss of gene variety. The population cannot adapt well to a quickly changing environment. This leads to **genetic drift.** Genetic drift is the random changes in the gene pool of a small population.

Figure 13.4.1 Cheetahs are an endangered species.

All populations have genetic drift. Genetic drift can greatly change small populations. The loss of gene variation could reduce the ability of a population to adapt to environmental change. It can lead to an **endangered** species or the **extinction** of a species. An endangered species, such as the cheetah in Figure 13.4.1, has almost no organisms left. Extinction is the death of all members of a species.

Today, there are only three small populations of cheetahs in the wild. The loss of gene variation and loss of their **habitat** raise concerns about the future of cheetahs. Habitat is the place where an organism lives.

LEARNING STYLES

Logical/Mathematical

Plants and animals that are endangered or extinct are listed by the U.S. Fish and Wildlife Service. The statistics on these organisms are available at the U.S. Fish and Wildlife Service Web site. Have students find this data and use the data to create their own graphs. Tell them to use the symbols from this site to create a bar graph showing endangered animals in the United States.

Hardy-Weinberg Equilibrium

Hardy-Weinberg equilibrium
A principle that states the frequencies of alleles in a population do not change unless evolutionary factors act on the population

Scientists must study and analyze population's gene pools to understand how they change. To do this, scientists must first assume that a population is in **Hardy-Weinberg equilibrium.** What is this principle? Hardy-Weinberg equilibrium means that frequencies of alleles in a population do not change unless evolutionary factors act on the population. In other words, a population stays in Hardy-Weinberg equilibrium unless outside factors change its gene pool. Gene flow and genetic drift are factors that can take a population out of Hardy-Weinberg equilibrium, for example.

Godfrey Harold Hardy and Wilhelm Weinberg are the two scientists who came up with this principle. For their idea to work, they had to make assumptions about a population. The main assumption is that a population does not change. This means its gene pool does not change. For this to happen, the population size must be large. The population also cannot experience natural selection, mutation, or other changes. However, in the natural world, populations usually change. The Hardy-Weinberg equilibrium is useful because it provides a starting point to understand when a gene pool is changing.

Scientists use the Hardy-Weinberg principle to predict genotype frequencies. The Hardy-Weinberg principle is written as an equation: $p^2 + 2pq + q^2 = 1$. This equation describes each of the possible allele combinations in a population. The p and q represent the frequency of the dominant (p) and the recessive (q) alleles in a population. Since all the alleles for a certain point will be dominant or recessive, then $p + q = 1$ (or 100%).

This means that all homozygous dominant individuals would have two dominant alleles ($p \times p = p^2$). Recall that homozygous means having an identical pair of genes. Homozygous recessive individuals would have two recessive alleles ($q \times q = q^2$). Heterozygous individuals would have one of each allele. Those pairs can be made in two different ways. This depends on which parent donates an allele ($2 \times p \times q = 2pq$).

TEACHER ALERT

The Hardy-Weinberg principle was derived in 1908 by Wilhelm Weinberg, a German physician, and Godfrey Harold Hardy, a British mathematician. Medical geneticists sometimes use this principle to determine if mutations are occurring in a population due to processes such as radiation from industry, medical procedures, or nuclear fallout.

SCIENCE JOURNAL

Write a paragraph describing why it would be useful to know if industrial processes, medical procedures, or nuclear fallout were introducing mutated genes in a population.

ELL/ESL Strategy

Language Objective: *To compare and contrast adding and removing alleles to the gene pool*

Have one student in a pair describe a process that adds new alleles to the gene pool. Encourage the listening student to ask any questions that he or she does not understand. Then have the other student describe a process that removes alleles from the gene pool. Have students compare and contrast these processes.

Science at Work

Have a volunteer read aloud the Science at Work feature about paleontology technicians. Ask students: Where are possible locations in which a paleontology technician might work? *(Sample answers: out in the field where a dig is taking place, in museums, at universities)*

Encourage students to go online and find technical schools, colleges, or universities that offer training for paleontology technicians.

Natural Selection

Natural selection can increase or decrease the number of times an allele appears in a population. Natural selection that weeds out harmful alleles is called negative selection. Natural selection that increases the number of helpful alleles is called positive selection. You will learn more about natural selection in Lesson 5.

Summing Up

As you know, evolution is a change in the gene pool of a population over time. Evolution can occur due to various processes. Processes that add new alleles to the gene pool are mutation, recombination, gene flow, and natural selection.

Processes that remove alleles are genetic drift and natural selection. Genetic drift removes alleles randomly from the gene pool. Natural selection removes the frequency of harmful alleles from the gene pool. The genetic variation in a population results from the balance between these processes.

Science at Work

Paleontology Technician

A paleontologist studies fossils to learn about ancient life. Paleontology technicians assist paleontologists by collecting and preparing fossil specimens. They may work with a paleontologist to collect and record data and to catalog samples. In addition, paleontology technicians may create fossil displays for teaching.

To become a paleontology technician, a high school degree and some technical training is required. Most technicians have a degree in college or go to a technical school. Some may be able to work with a paleontologist in an entry-level job. As they take on more responsibilities, they can earn the title of paleontology technician.

Lesson 4 REVIEW

On a sheet of paper, write the word that completes each sentence correctly.

1. Recombination shuffles genes by recombining _____.
2. Genetic drift can lead to the formation of a(n) _____ species.
3. Individuals do not evolve, but _____ evolve.

Critical Thinking

On a sheet of paper, write the answers to the following questions. Use complete sentences.

4. Explain how gene flow and genetic drift affect a population.
5. Can individuals experience evolution? Explain.

Achievements in Science

Scientists continue to learn about the genes that make living things function. One research area is the human Y chromosome in males. The Y chromosome is more likely than other chromosomes to contain mistakes and lose pieces. These mistakes are passed on to male children. There is no second Y chromosome in males to correct mistakes.

The Y chromosome is inherited only by males. By analyzing the Y chromosome, scientists can track male ancestors. In 2003, scientists mapped the Y chromosome.

They found that most genes on the Y chromosome are involved in producing sperm. They also found that genes on the Y chromosome affect body size. This finding supports a theory that the changing of the Y chromosome over time helps males. These changes make males bigger and stronger.

Currently, scientists are collecting blood samples from males worldwide. They will use the Y chromosome sequencing to track where the first people lived. They will also try to determine how people have moved throughout the world.

Evolution and Natural Selection Chapter 13 409

Lesson 4 Review Answers

1. alleles 2. endangered 3. populations
4. Gene flow can add new alleles, bringing genetic variation to a population. Genetic drift can cause loss of gene variety in a population through the removal of some alleles. 5. An individual organism keeps the same genes throughout life. This means an individual cannot evolve. Only by mutating, reproducing, and selecting can evolution occur in a population.

Portfolio Assessment

Sample items include:
- Chart from Teaching the Lesson
- Graph from Learning Styles Logical/Mathematical
- Lesson 4 Review answers

Achievements in Science

Have students read the Achievements in Science feature. Then ask them to research and find more information about tracking male ancestors by using the Y chromosomes. Have students report their findings to the class. Encourage students to bring visual aids, such as photographs, drawings, or maps, to show during their presentation.

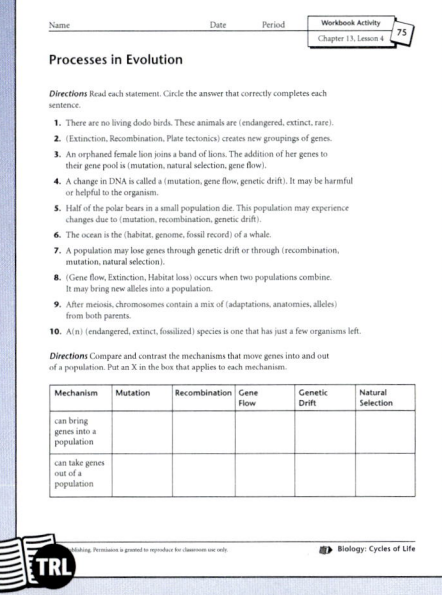

Workbook Activity 75

Evolution and Natural Selection 409

Lesson at a Glance

Chapter 13 Lesson 5

Overview In this lesson, students learn about natural selection.

Objectives
- To define *artificial selection*
- To explain the purpose of natural selection

Student Pages 410–415

Teacher's Resource Library

Workbook Activity 76
Alternative Workbook Activity 76
Lab Manual 65

Vocabulary

artificial selection   malaria

Read each word to the class and have a volunteer supply the definition.

Background Information

Artificial selection is a common practice in farm animals. Farmers and ranchers breed cattle to perform specific functions. For example, ranchers breed some cattle to be good milk producers. Dairy farmers want cattle that produce the most milk. Cattle ranchers that produce beef want cattle that produce enough milk for their young but not overproduce. They want the cattle's energy resources to go to producing muscle instead of milk. By selectively breeding cattle, farmers and ranchers can produce cattle that best serve their needs.

Lesson 5: Natural Selection

Objectives

After reading this lesson, you should be able to
- define artificial selection
- explain the purpose of natural selection

Artificial selection
A process of changing a species by people who select the breeding of certain traits

British scientist Charles Darwin published *On the Origins of Species by Means of Natural Selection* in 1859. The book presented his ideas about evolution and natural selection. Darwin became famous for his ideas. You will learn more about natural selection in this lesson.

Artificial Selection

Darwin knew that people who bred animals and plants used variations among the offspring of the parents. For example, breeders mated pigeons. The offspring had different colors, beaks, necks, feet, and tails. The breeders then selected specific traits in the offspring. They bred those offspring.

Darwin called this process **artificial selection.** Through artificial selection, pigeon breeders created many different-looking pigeons. Figure 13.5.1 shows an example of a pigeon created by artificial selection. All pigeons belong to the same species. However, they have differences in their genetic makeup.

Figure 13.5.1 *Pigeon breeders can create many different-looking pigeons through artificial selection. Here is an example of a pigeon created by artificial selection.*

410   Chapter 13   Evolution and Natural Selection

Malaria
A disease that causes chills and fever

The sickle-cell allele occurs most often in areas of Africa where malaria is common.

Darwin knew that animals living in the wild struggled for survival. Some birds, for example, were good at finding scarce food in a severe winter. They also avoided being eaten by larger animals. These birds had a better chance of surviving and reproducing offspring.

Darwin called this process natural selection. He chose this term to show that artificial selection was different than natural selection. In natural selection, events in the natural environment determine which animals survive. The animals that survive can then mate to produce offspring.

Natural Selection

Natural selection keeps life going over time. Environments always change. New generations must adapt to survive and reproduce. If they did not adapt, individuals would die as their environment changed.

Natural selection does not always stop a new allele from increasing. If a new allele helps the organism survive, natural selection will favor it.

An example of natural selection is the allele of sickle cell. Variation in a single gene determines whether red blood cells are shaped normally or sickled. The sickle shape prevents cells from carrying normal levels of oxygen.

About one in every 500 African Americans has sickle-cell disease. This disease results from being homozygous (having an identical pair of genes) for the recessive sickle-cell allele. One in every 11 African Americans is heterozygous and a carrier. This means they do not get the disease. But they may pass the recessive gene to their children.

Heterozygous individuals are more resistant to **malaria** than individuals who are homozygous. Malaria is a disease in the tropics caused by a parasite. This parasite is a major cause of death in certain areas of Africa. Heterozygous individuals pass on both sickle-cell alleles and normal alleles to offspring. Thus, both alleles remain in the gene pool.

1 Warm-Up Activity

Show students pictures of different types of horses. Have students discuss why artificial selection has been used to produce these animals. For example, draft horses have been bred to pull heavy loads. Miniature horses have been bred to make small pets.

2 Teaching the Lesson

Have students make a graphic organizer comparing and contrasting artificial and natural selection. After students have completed their graphic organizer, discuss the similarities and differences.

3 Reinforce and Extend

ELL/ESL Strategy

Language Objective: *To describe natural selection*

Have students in small groups take turns describing how natural selection happens. Every member of the group should take a turn. Encourage each group to think of more examples of natural selection.

In the Environment

Contact a local zoo and ask if there is a staff member available who could give your class a tour of the zoo and discuss natural and artificial selection. Many zoos have education departments that work with schools.

LEARNING STYLES

Visual/Spatial

Have students collect pictures of dogs that were bred by artificial selection for a purpose. Students should create a poster showing the groups of dogs. Groups might include herding dogs, hounds, nonsporting and sporting dogs, terriers, toy breeds, and working dogs.

Biology in Your Life

Have a volunteer read the Biology in Your Life feature about X-rays. Ask if anyone in the class has had an X-ray and would like to share their experience with the class. Have someone describe the apronlike shield the dentist uses to protect the patient's body. Ask students: What did the person taking the X-ray do and why? *(The X-ray technician left the room or stayed behind a shield so that he or she would not be exposed to the X-rays. People who give X-rays have to protect their body from overexposure.)*

Biology in Your Life Answers

1. X-rays can cause damage to the DNA in cells. **2.** Cells can either repair the damaged DNA or destroy themselves. **3.** X-rays should only be given when necessary and at the lowest radiation level that is effective. Protective lead equipment should be used to protect other body parts.

Biology in Your Life

**Technology:
Safe X-rays?**

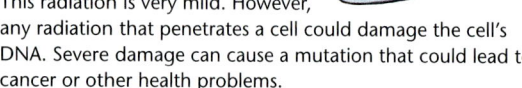

Have you had X-rays taken at a doctor's or dentist's office? You were probably given protective clothing to wear. Doctors and dentists commonly use X-rays to learn about people's health and dental problems.

X-rays use a type of radiation that penetrates skin and muscle tissue. This radiation is very mild. However, any radiation that penetrates a cell could damage the cell's DNA. Severe damage can cause a mutation that could lead to cancer or other health problems.

Cells with damaged DNA due to X-rays work quickly to repair the damage. Cells with mild damage from X-rays often will self-destruct. Then they do not pass on DNA damage.

To reduce possible DNA damage, health professionals use precautions when giving X-rays. They use X-rays only when necessary. They use the lowest dosage of radiation needed. Health professionals cover areas not being viewed by X-rays with protective lead aprons. People who operate X-ray machines use lead shields as protection.

1. What possible damage to cells can result from X-rays?
2. How do cells respond to DNA damage?
3. If you get an X-ray, what safety precautions should be used?

Chapter 13   Evolution and Natural Selection

Lesson 5 REVIEW

Word Bank
artificial selection
environment
reproduce

On a sheet of paper, write the word or words from the Word Bank that complete each sentence correctly.

1. Natural selection gives an advantage to some organisms that make them more likely to survive and _____.
2. Without being able to adapt, species would die as their _____ changed.
3. Changes in a species caused by people who breed the species for certain traits is _____.

On a sheet of paper, write the letter of the word or words that complete each sentence correctly.

4. _____ alleles for sickle-cell disease remain in the gene pool.
   A Two   B One   C Four   D Zero

5. Sickle-shaped red blood cells help prevent _____.
   A oxygen   B malaria   C alleles   D mosquitoes

6. _____ individuals pass on both sickle-cell and normal alleles to offspring.
   A Old   C Heterozygous
   B Homozygous   D Recessive

Critical Thinking

On a sheet of paper, write the answers to the following questions. Use complete sentences.

7. Compare and contrast natural selection and artificial selection.
8. A person breeds dogs for a specific color. How does this affect the genetic makeup of the population of the dogs?
9. Why is the sickle-cell allele in the human population?
10. How does natural selection help ensure that a population survives over time?

Evolution and Natural Selection Chapter 13   413

Lesson 5 Review Answers

1. reproduce **2.** environment **3.** artificial selection **4.** A **5.** B **6.** C **7.** Artificial selection involves actively breeding organisms for desired traits. Natural selection shapes the gene pool of a population due to natural events that influenced survival. **8.** By selecting specific individuals for breeding, the person is increasing the frequency of the desired alleles and causing the population to have a similar genetic makeup. **9.** Because sickle cells offer some protection against malaria, they are also selected for it when the disease is present. **10.** Through evolution and natural selection, a population as a whole is able to diversify and survive environmental changes that eliminate parts of the population.

Portfolio Assessment

Sample items include:
- Graphic organizer from Teaching the Lesson
- Poster of dogs from Learning Styles Visual/Spatial
- Lesson 5 Review answers

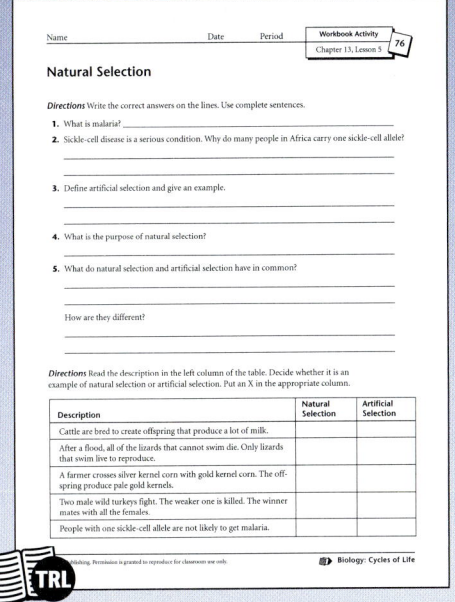

Workbook Activity 76

Discovery Investigation 13

This investigation is less structured than the first investigation in this chapter. It offers students more challenge and requires more teacher facilitation. Encourage students to read the Discovery Investigation steps. Discuss questions they may have before beginning the investigation.

Objectives

- To track and understand how alleles move through reproduction in a population
- To infer the alleles of specific blood types
- To predict the blood types and alleles that individuals inherit
- To use randomization to assign alleles
- To infer that some alleles are dominant and some are recessive

Skills

Observing, diagramming, inferring, predicting, communicating, analyzing data, drawing conclusions

Background

Students have learned that alleles are passed on and mixed through recombination in a population. The alleles that determine blood types is one example. Students should be able to track alleles as they move through a population, charting whether the alleles increase or disappear.

Time Frame

One class period

Procedure

- Have students work in small groups to complete the activity.
- Have students copy on a sheet of paper the chart from the textbook. You may also want to have them create physical models of the alleles or create a computer program that illustrates the alleles and blood types. Encourage students to use different-colored pens or markers to distinguish the alleles.

DISCOVERY INVESTIGATION 13

Materials
- Blood Type Allele Chart
- coin

Tracking Blood Type Alleles

A person's blood type is determined by the inheritance of one of three alleles—A, B, or O—from each parent. The alleles together determine the blood type of that person. The allele combinations that create blood types are shown in the following table:

Blood Type	Allele Pairings	
A	AO	AA
B	BO	BB
O		OO
AB		AB

In this investigation, you will track alleles and blood types in a family. You will also examine how alleles are passed from parents to offspring.

Procedure

1. On a sheet of paper, copy the Blood Type Allele Chart on page 415. The chart represents three generations of a family. For each person, the top two squares show the person's blood type alleles. The bottom square shows the blood type that resulted from the combination of the two alleles.

2. Fill in the allele blanks for Child W and Child K. Determine each child's blood type.

3. Determine the blood types of Spouse W and Spouse K.

4. Choose which alleles will be passed from the second generation to the third generation. You may want to flip a coin to determine the allele a grandchild will receive.

5. Determine the blood types for all grandchildren.

Analysis

1. What blood types are possible for the grandchildren from Child W and Spouse W? Explain your answer.

2. What blood types are possible for the grandchildren from Child K and Spouse K? Explain your answer.

3. What allele was removed from the Child K–Spouse K branch to result in Grandchildren L and M?

Conclusions

1. What effect does the O allele have on determining blood type?

2. In this investigation, is it appropriate to use a coin flip to determine the alleles that are inherited? Explain your answer.

3. How could the offspring of Grandchild L or Grandchild M reclaim the lost allele?

Explore Further

A blood type also has a Rh factor. Parents pass on a positive Rh allele or a negative Rh allele. Go through the chart again and assign Rh alleles to all blood types.

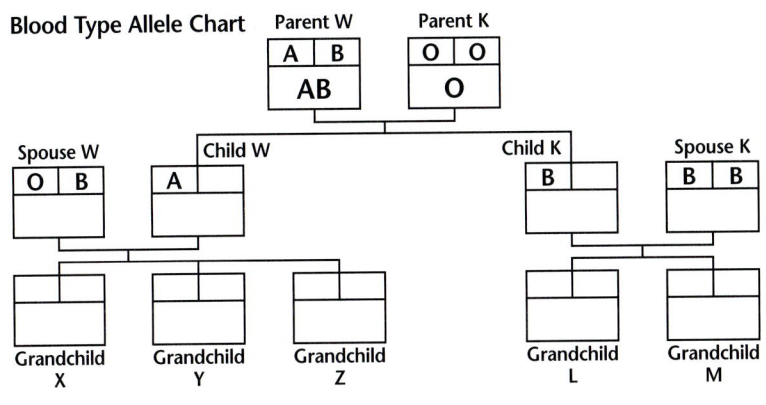

Cleanup/Disposal

Instruct students in proper cleaning and disposal of materials.

Results

Spouse W will be blood type B. Child W will have alleles A and O and be blood type A. Child K will have alleles B and O and be blood type B. Spouse K will be blood type B. Grandchildren X, Y, and Z can have any variety of alleles and blood types. Grandchildren L and M can have either alleles B and B or alleles B and O, and will both be blood type B.

Answers to Analysis, Conclusions, and Explore Further begin on page 670 of this Teacher's Edition.

Assessment

You might include the following items from this investigation in student portfolios:

- Allele chart
- Answers to Analysis and Conclusions questions
- Answers to Explore Further

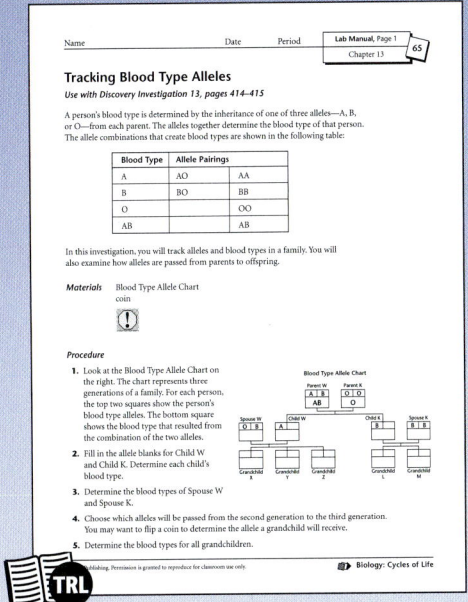

Lab Manual 65, pages 1–2

Lesson at a Glance

Chapter 13 Lesson 6

Overview In this lesson, students learn about microevolution and macroevolution.

Objectives
- To define *microevolution*
- To define *macroevolution*
- To give an example of microevolution
- To describe Darwin's four main ideas about natural selection
- To compare phenotype changes and evolution
- To define *evolutionary biology*

Student Pages 416–421

Teacher's Resource Library

Workbook Activity 77–78

Alternative Workbook Activity 77–78

Vocabulary

differential reproduction	frequency
evolutionary biology	macroevolution
	microevolution
	overproduction

Have students look in a dictionary to find the meaning of the prefixes and root words for the vocabulary terms.

Background Information

The eel catfish living in the rain forests of central Africa provides an example of microevolution. This eel burrows into the mud to find worms for food. The eel catfish does not have pectoral or pelvic fins—an adaptation for burrowing. However, one biologist was surprised to find that a reproductive pair of laboratory specimens produced larvae with fully developed pectoral fins. Biologists examined various specimens and found that about two-thirds of the eel catfish also had pectoral fins and that a few had both pectoral and pelvic fins. The bodies of the specimens with both types of fins were shaped more like fish than eels. Biologists hypothesized that fin loss and body elongation are adaptations of the eel catfish for burrowing.

Lesson 6 — Microevolution and Macroevolution

Objectives

After reading this lesson, you should be able to
- define microevolution
- define macroevolution
- give an example of microevolution
- describe Charles Darwin's four main ideas about natural selection
- compare phenotype changes and evolution
- define evolutionary biology

Microevolution
The minor changes in a population's allele-frequencies from generation to generation

Macroevolution
The large-scale changes in a population over long periods of time

Frequency
The rate of occurrence

Scientists refer to evolution as **microevolution** and **macroevolution.** Microevolution are the minor changes in a population's allele-frequencies from generation to generation. These changes may be due to these processes: mutation, gene flow, genetic drift, and natural selection.

Macroevolution refers to large-scale changes over long periods of time. Macroevolution produces evolutionary trends. Macroevolution also includes mass extinctions that have occurred during the history of life. These extinctions involved losses of large numbers of species. Macroevolution may result in the evolution of new species.

Scientists sometimes have difficulty telling the difference between microevolution and macroevolution. Over time, tiny mutations like those in microevolution can build up in populations. Eventually, a new species can result. This is macroevolution.

Scientists have shown the process of microevolution in the laboratory. To explain the process of macroevolution, scientists use the fossil record.

An Example of Microevolution

Scientists have studied many examples of microevolution. One example happened in England in the 1800s. During this time, scientists kept track of moths named *Biston betularia*. The moths were either light or dark in color.

Before 1848, dark moths made up less than two percent of the population. However, the **frequency**, or numbers, of the dark moth began to increase. By 1898, 95 percent of the moths in English cities were dark. Scientists noted that there were fewer dark moths in rural areas.

Over 50 years, the moth population had changed from mostly light-colored moths to mostly dark-colored moths. Figure 13.6.1 shows the two moths. Scientists wondered why this change happened. The color of the *Biston betularia* moth is mainly determined by one gene. The change in the number of the dark moths meant a change in the gene pool. Dark moths meant a change in the allele-frequencies of the moth gene pool. A change in the gene pool of this population is evolution.

The increase in the numbers of the dark moth was due to natural selection. The Industrial Revolution took place in the late 1800s. During the Industrial Revolution, people used power-driven machines in factories to make goods. People built factories in the cities.

As the machines ran, they gave off a black powder called soot. The soot covered the nearby birch trees. The trees became dark. Moths landed on these trees. When birds looked for moths to eat, they saw only the light-colored moths.

The dark moths stayed alive because the birds could not see them. The dark moths reproduced. The greater number of offspring from the dark moths caused their increase. These members in the population of moths were naturally selected to live and reproduce.

Figure 13.6.1 *Scientists in the 1800s kept track of the light-colored and dark-colored moths named* Biston betularia.

Warm-Up Activity

Find pictures of some type of plant or animal that has an assortment of markings. Describe the organism's habitat to the class. Then have students brainstorm reasons why certain markings would be beneficial over other markings for the survival of the organism. Or find pictures of plants or organisms that are camouflaged by their color and markings. Have students brainstorm why the markings are beneficial for the organism's survival.

Teaching the Lesson

Have students make an outline of the lesson. Students should include the main ideas from each paragraph as well as detail statements. Encourage students to ask questions about any section they do not understand. Have students refer to their outlines as they study for tests and quizzes.

Reinforce and Extend

TEACHER ALERT

After England enacted Clean Air legislation in 1956, the occurrence of dark moths began to decline. Beginning in 1959, the population of *Biston betularia* was sampled outside of Liverpool, England, each year. The numbers of dark moths dropped from a high of 94% in 1960 to 19% in 1994. Similar statistics have occurred in other locations throughout England. The drop in the number of dark moths correlates to the drop in air pollution, particularly in the drop of sulfur dioxide that darkened the bark of the trees.

Link to

Health. Ask students to read the Link to Health feature about performance-enhancing drugs. Performance-enhancing drug use or steroid use by athletes is an ongoing issue in all sports and in the Olympics. Have students search for news articles about athletes who have been caught using these drugs. Have students share their information with the class.

ELL/ESL STRATEGY

Language Objective: *To compare and contrast microevolution and macroevolution*

Have pairs of students compare and contrast microevolution and macroevolution. Have students share their ideas with the class. Correct any misconceptions that students may have.

Overproduction
When organisms produce more offspring than can survive

Differential reproduction
When individuals leave more offspring than other individuals

Link to ▶▶▶
Health

Many professional sports teams use drug tests. They use the tests to be sure that athletes do not cheat by using performance-enhancing drugs. Performance-enhancing drugs are often swallowed or injected by needles. Today, some athletes may be putting performance-enhancing genes directly into their muscles. Scientists are working on tests to detect the genetic changes caused by this action.

Darwin's Four Main Ideas of Natural Selection

Darwin's ideas can be applied to both microevolution and macroevolution. The following four ideas sum up his theory of natural selection:

- Organisms tend to produce more offspring than can survive. This is called **overproduction**. For example, frogs lay thousands of eggs. Only a few live to be adult frogs.

- Individuals in a population vary in many traits. Frogs in a population may differ slightly in color, length, or speed. Alleles for specific traits are inherited.

- Individuals with alleles best suited to the environment are more likely to survive.

- Individuals with alleles best suited to the environment usually leave more offspring. The offspring survive and reproduce. This leads to **differential reproduction** within a species. Differential reproduction is when individuals leave more offspring than other individuals. Over time, the gene pool in the population changes.

Phenotypes and Evolution

An organism's phenotype is determined by its genes and its environment. Remember that a phenotype is an organism's appearance. For example, people are larger now than in the recent past. This is a result of better diet and new medicines. It is not a result of gene changes.

Phenotypic changes are not necessarily due to evolution. There is no change in the genes. In other words, a phenotypic change is not passed on to an organism's offspring. Most changes due to environment are slight, such as size differences. However, large-scale phenotypic changes are due to genetic changes. Thus, they are considered evolution.

> **Evolutionary biology**
> The study of genetic changes within and among populations of organisms

Scientific Study of Evolution

Scientists seek to understand nature—how natural facts and events relate to other natural facts and events. Scientists look for causes and effects. They have developed explanations for the diversity of living things due to natural selection. Scientists continue to develop better explanations for the causes of natural facts and events.

Scientists use theories to group together scientific information. Scientists can never be sure an explanation or theory is complete and final. For that reason, scientists continue to investigate theories. Scientists change theories if new scientific information is accepted after repeated experiments or observations.

The theory of evolution talks about experiments and observations that show life has changed over time. This theory explains why there are different kinds of life on the earth. Changes in living things, as shown in the fossil record and in the DNA of organisms, support the theory of evolution. Based on many tests and careful analysis, scientists are confident about the theory of evolution.

In this chapter, you have learned that **evolutionary biology** provides new insights into the world. Evolutionary biology is the study of genetic changes within and among populations of organisms. This includes genetic changes that are occurring or have occurred.

Evolutionary biology links basic scientific research to knowledge needed to meet important needs of society. This includes preservation, or the saving of the earth's environment. You will learn more about preservation in Chapter 19.

SCIENCE JOURNAL

 Have students write a paragraph about why studying evolutionary biology is important.

Lesson 6 Review Answers

1. macroevolution 2. microevolution
3. evolutionary biology 4. D 5. A 6. C
7. The theory of microevolution has been tested extensively and has held up over time. 8. Soot from the factories colored the tree barks black. The black moths, which had been only about 2 percent of the population, blended in with the trees and were less likely to be eaten by birds than were the light-colored moths. In time, the population of the dark-colored moths grew. 9. Scientists must rely on fossils as evidence for macroevolution. 10. 1. Organisms tend to produce more offspring than can survive. 2. Individuals in a population vary in traits that can be inherited. 3. Individuals with traits best suited to their environment are more likely to survive. 4. Individuals with traits best suited to the environment produce more offspring than those not as well suited. Over time the population changes.

Portfolio Assessment

Sample items include:
- Outline from Teaching the Lesson
- Paragraph for Science Journal
- Lesson 6 Review answers

Lesson 6   R E V I E W

Word Bank
evolutionary biology
macroevolution
microevolution

On a sheet of paper, write the word or words from the Word Bank that complete each sentence correctly.

1. Large changes in gene frequency over a long period of time is _____.
2. Evolution that involves small gene changes over a few generations is _____.
3. The study of genetic changes within and among populations of organisms is _____.

On a sheet of paper, write the letter of the answer that completes each sentence correctly.

4. An organism's phenotype is determined by its _____.
   - **A** mutation
   - **B** macroevolution
   - **C** microevolution
   - **D** genes and environment

5. The formation of a new species can result from _____.
   - **A** macroevolution
   - **B** microevolution
   - **C** phenotypes
   - **D** macroevolution or microevolution

6. The increase in the numbers of black moths in England in the 1800s was due to _____.
   - **A** genetic drift
   - **B** gene flow
   - **C** natural selection
   - **D** recombination

Critical Thinking

On a sheet of paper, write the answers to the following questions. Use complete sentences.

7. Why do scientists support the theory of microevolution?
8. Describe how microevolution caused a change in the populations of light- and dark-colored moths in England during the 1800s.
9. What evidence exists for macroevolution?
10. What are Darwin's four main ideas that sum up his theory of natural selection?

420   Chapter 13   Evolution and Natural Selection

Workbook Activity 77

BIOLOGY IN THE WORLD

Problems with Animal Breeding

All dogs carry defective, or not perfect, genes. Defective genes are usually recessive. A recessive gene is hidden by a dominant gene.

Since genes come in pairs, normal genes hide most defective genes. Dogs usually have four to seven defective genes in their DNA. In contrast, humans usually have 10 to 12 defective genes.

Most people who breed animals have a purpose. For example, people breed race horses for their speed. Breeding closely related animals allows breeders to get traits they want.

When dogs are bred, there is some inbreeding. Inbreeding is the breeding of closely related individuals to get desired characteristics and to remove unwanted characteristics. With inbreeding, two closely related animals share genes for certain traits. When these two animals are bred, the desired form of a trait, such as a specific fur color, appears.

While good traits are achieved through inbreeding, some bad traits are also found in the offspring. If inbreeding continues, the bad traits build up. This leads to genetic problems.

Some human populations have been inbred. Sometimes this happens because of isolation. Isolation can occur because of barriers like mountains. Mutations are concentrated in inbred populations. For example, hemophilia often appears in some royal families when relatives marry and have children.

1. Why are most defective genes not a problem for an organism?
2. Why do people inbreed some domestic animals?
3. Some states have laws that do not allow marriage between closely related people such as first cousins. Why are these laws in place?

Chapter 13 SUMMARY

- Life on the earth is diverse. Organisms change constantly. New species form. Some species become extinct.

- Charles Darwin stated organisms evolve into different species over time. He also stated the theory of natural selection, in which organisms with some traits survive better than others. They breed more offspring, and the traits become more common.

- Gregor Mendel's experiments showed that traits in organisms are passed on through genetic material. Mendel's discoveries and Darwin's theories explained how a population's gene pool changes over time.

- New species arise from parent species when similar organisms become reproductively isolated from each other.

- Fossils give clues about older life-forms, including body structures and how long ago they lived. Scientists find evidence for evolution in fossils, distribution of organisms, anatomy, and molecular biology. Scientists can date fossils relatively by their position in the earth. They can date fossils more exactly with radioactive dating.

- The position of the continents has changed due to continental drift.

- Mutations occur randomly. This causes diversity within populations. Diversity can help organisms survive and reproduce.

- Mechanisms of microevolution are genetic drift, gene flow, mutations and natural selection.

Vocabulary

acquired trait, 389
adapt, 390
adaption, 389
amphibian, 398
anatomy, 394
artificial selection, 410
biogeography, 393
biological evolution, 388
common descent, 389
comparative anatomy, 394
continental drift, 399
crust, 400

descent with modification, 389
differential reproduction, 418
endangered, 406
evolutionary biology, 419
extinction, 406
fossil, 388
fossil record, 392
frequency, 416
gene flow, 406
gene pool, 388

genetic drift, 406
geologic time, 397
geologic time scale, 398
habitat, 406
Hardy-Weinberg equilibrium, 407
homologous structure, 393
invertebrate, 398
macroevolution, 416
magma, 400
malaria, 411
microevolution, 416

modern synthesis, 390
molecular biology, 395
natural selection, 389
overproduction, 418
paleontologist, 397
plate, 400
plate tectonics, 399
population, 388
radioactive element, 398
recombination, 405
reptile, 398
sedimentary rock, 392
vertebrate, 398

422 Chapter 13 Evolution and Natural Selection

Chapter 13 REVIEW

Word Bank
acquired trait
anatomy
artificial selection
biogeography
biological evolution
extinction
fossil
gene flow
gene pool
genetic drift
macroevolution
microevolution
molecular biology
overproduction
plate tectonics
radioactive element
recombination

Vocabulary Review
On a sheet of paper, write the word or words from the Word Bank that complete each sentence

1. A(n) _____ provides direct evidence of a species that once lived.
2. The _____ are all the genes present in a species or population.
3. A species that has difficulty surviving may face _____ and disappear.
4. Small-scale changes in gene frequencies in a population that occur over a few generations is _____.
5. Large evolutionary changes in a population over a long period of time is _____.
6. A(n) _____ decays, or breaks apart, to form another element.
7. A theory from the 1800s said that a(n) _____ comes from an organism's behavior.
8. New combinations of alleles in offspring are created through _____.
9. The theory of _____ says that the earth's surface is made of large sections of crust that move over time.
10. The random changes in the gene pool of a small population is _____.
11. A process that adds alleles to or removes alleles from a population is _____.
12. The study of the geographical distribution of fossils and living organisms is _____.
13. A change in the gene pool of a population over time is _____.

Review continued on next page

Chapter 13 Review
Use the Chapter Review to prepare students for tests and to reteach content from the chapter.

Chapter 13 Mastery Test
The Teacher's Resource Library includes two forms of the Chapter 13 Mastery Test. Each test addresses the chapter Goals for Learning. An optional third page of additional critical-thinking items is included for each test. The difficulty level of the two forms is equivalent.

Review Answers
Vocabulary Review
1. fossil 2. gene pool 3. extinction
4. microevolution 5. macroevolution
6. radioactive element 7. acquired trait
8. recombination 9. plate tectonics
10. genetic drift 11. gene flow
12. biogeography 13. biological evolution

Review Answers

14. overproduction **15.** artificial selection
16. anatomy **17.** molecular biology

TEACHER ALERT

 In the Chapter Review, the Vocabulary Review activity includes a sample of the chapter's vocabulary terms. The activity will help determine students' understanding of key vocabulary terms and concepts presented in the chapter. Other vocabulary terms used in the chapter are listed below.

adapt	geologic time scale
amphibian	habitat
biological evolution	Hardy-Weinberg equilibrium
common descent	homologous structure
comparative anatomy	invertebrate
continental drift	magma
crust	malaria
descent with modification	modern synthesis
differential reproduction	natural selection
endangered	paleontologist
evolutionary biology	plate
fossil record	population
frequency	reptile
geologic time	sedimentary rock
	vertebrate

Concept Review

18. D **19.** A **20.** D **21.** C

Critical Thinking

22. Modern synthesis combines the ideas of Darwin, Mendel, and other scientists. This theory states that evolution involves changes in a population's gene pool over time. **23.** Mutations occur when a cell divides and creates a copy of its DNA. If a mutation causes a different protein to be made, then it will cause a change in the organism. If the mutation does not cause a different protein to be made, it will make no difference.

Chapter 13 REVIEW - continued

14. Organisms tend to practice _____ by producing more offspring than can survive.

15. People change a species through _____, which is the breeding of organisms for specific traits.

16. The structure of an organism is _____.

17. The study of DNA and its expression in cells is an area of _____.

Concept Review

On a sheet of paper, write the letter of the answer that completes each sentence correctly.

18. Darwin's theory of common descent stated that all organisms _____.

　A evolve at a constant rate
　B evolve due to acquired traits
　C evolve until they are selected
　D evolved from past organisms

19. The deeper a fossil is found in sedimentary rock, the _____.

　A older the fossil is
　B more likely the fossil has evolved
　C less complete the fossil is
　D more worn the fossil is

20. The earliest organisms to appear on the earth were _____.

　A algae　B fishes　C plants　D bacteria

21. When two populations combine, the result is often _____.

　A recombination　C gene flow
　B genetic drift　D mutation

Chapter 13 Mastery Test A, pages 1–3

Critical Thinking

On a sheet of paper, write the answers to the following questions. Use complete sentences.

22. What is the theory of modern synthesis?
23. How do mutations create genetic diversity? Why do some mutations not cause any change?
24. How does the allele that causes sickle-cell disease both help and harm people?
25. Do mutations that survive through natural selection always improve a species? Explain your answer.

Research and Write

Work with a partner to research two hoaxes about evolution and fossils. People have found fake fossils and presented them as real. Some fake fossils have fooled scientists. Write a description of the hoaxes. Include how scientists proved that the fossils were not real.

Test-Taking Tip Before writing out an answer on a test, read the question twice to be sure you understand what it is asking.

24. When someone has two sickle-cell alleles, they develop sickle-cell disease and have trouble getting oxygen. However, someone who has one sickle-cell allele and one normal allele does not get the disease, and is also protected from getting malaria. 25. Mutations that survive natural selection help an organism survive specific environmental conditions that other mutations might not. It does not always make an organism stronger or better. Sometimes a mutation will select for a trait that does not help the organism in any way other than to survive a random condition, much like the moths in England.

Research and Write

Encourage students to use a variety of sources such as newspapers, reference books, journals, textbooks, encyclopedias, and the Internet to find information about fossil hoaxes. Remind students to check their sources to make sure they are reliable. Have students present their research findings to the class as an oral report, using a visual aid that they have created.

ALTERNATIVE ASSESSMENT

Alternative Assessment items correlate to the student Goals for Learning at the beginning of this chapter.

- Have students describe the theory of evolution to a partner.
- Have students make a list of evidence that supports evolution.
- Have students write a paragraph describing the rates of evolutionary change.
- Have students work with a partner to create a chart listing and defining the processes that change gene pools.
- Have students write a definition in their own words for each of the following terms: *natural selection*, *microevolution*, and *macroevolution*.

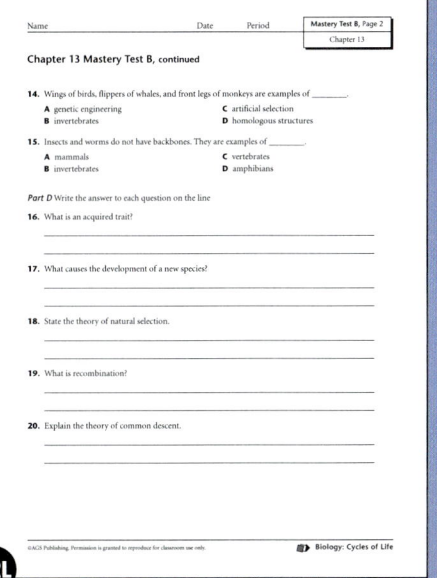

Chapter 13 Mastery Test B, pages 1–3

Chapter 14

Planning Guide
Speciation and Punctuated Equilibrium

	Student Pages	Vocabulary	Lesson Review	Critical-Thinking Questions
Lesson 1 What Is Speciation?	428–433	✔	✔	✔
Lesson 2 Classifying Species	434–439	✔	✔	✔
Lesson 3 Conditions for Speciation to Occur	440–446	✔	✔	✔
Lesson 4 Conditions That Affect Species Survival	447–451	✔	✔	✔

Chapter Activities

Teacher's Resource Library
Community Connection 14:
 Prevent the Spread of Antibiotic-
 Resistant Bacteria
Graphic Organizer 14:
 Speciation and Punctuated Equilibrium

Teacher's Edition
Opener Activity

Assessment Options

Student Text
Chapter 14 Review

Teacher's Resource Library
Chapter 14 Mastery Tests A and B

Teacher's Edition
Chapter 14 Alternative Assessment

Student Text Features									Teaching Strategies						Learning Styles					Teacher's Resource Library			
Achievements in Science	Science at Work	Biology in Your Life	Investigation/Discovery	Biology in the World	Express Lab	Link to	Research and Write	Technology and Society	ELL/ESL Strategy	Background Information	Science Journal	Applications (Home, Career, Community, Global, Environment)	Online Connection	Teacher Alert	Auditory/Verbal	Body/Kinesthetic	Interpersonal/Group Learning	Logical/Mathematical	Visual/Spatial	Workbook Activities	Alternative Workbook Activities	Lab Manual	Self-Study Guide
		432		433					430	428	431	429		430, 431		432	432			79	79	66	✓
436			438			✓		437	437	434		436			435					80	80	67–68	✓
	442		445			✓			442	440	442		441						443	81	81	69	✓
					451	✓	455		448	447		449, 451	451	448			450	449		82–83	82–83	70	✓

Pronunciation Key

a	hat	e	let	ī	ice	ô	order	ú	put	sh	she
ā	age	ē	equal	o	hot	oi	oil	ü	rule	th	thin
ä	far	ėr	term	ō	open	ou	out	ch	child	ᵺ	then
â	care	i	it	ò	saw	u	cup	ng	long	zh	measure

ə { a in about, e in taken, i in pencil, o in lemon, u in circus }

Alternative Workbook Activities

The Teacher's Resource Library (TRL) contains a set of lower-level worksheets called Alternative Workbook Activities. These worksheets cover the same content as the regular Workbook Activities but are written at a second-grade reading level.

Skill Track Online

Use Skill Track Online for *Biology: Cycles of Life* to monitor student progress and meet the demands of adequate yearly progress (AYP). Make informed instructional decisions with individual student and class reports of online lesson and chapter assessments. With immediate and ongoing feedback, students will also see what they have learned and where they need more reinforcement and practice.

Chapter at a Glance

Chapter 14: Speciation and Punctuated Equilibrium
pages 426–455

Lessons

1. **What Is Speciation?**
   pages 428–433

2. **Classifying Species**
   pages 434–439

   Investigation 14 pages 438–439

3. **Conditions for Speciation to Occur** pages 440–446

   Discovery Investigation 14
   pages 445–446

4. **Conditions That Affect Species Survival** pages 447–451

   Biology in the World page 451

Chapter 14 Summary page 452

Chapter 14 Review pages 453–455

Audio CD

Skill Track Online
for Biology: Cycles of Life

Teacher's Resource Library TRL

Workbook Activities 79–83

Alternative Workbook Activities 79–83

Lab Manual 66–70

Community Connection 14

Graphic Organizer 14

Resource File 33–34

Chapter 14 Self-Study Guide

Chapter 14 Mastery Tests A and B

(Answer Keys for the Teacher's Resource Library begin on page 675 of the Teacher's Edition. The Materials List for the Lab Manual activities begins on page 720.)

Opener Activity

Have students write down questions they have about species and speciation. *(Sample questions: What is a species? How do scientists determine whether two similar organisms are the same species? How does a new species evolve? What happens when a new species is discovered?)* As they read the chapter, students should record the answers to their questions when they find them in the text.

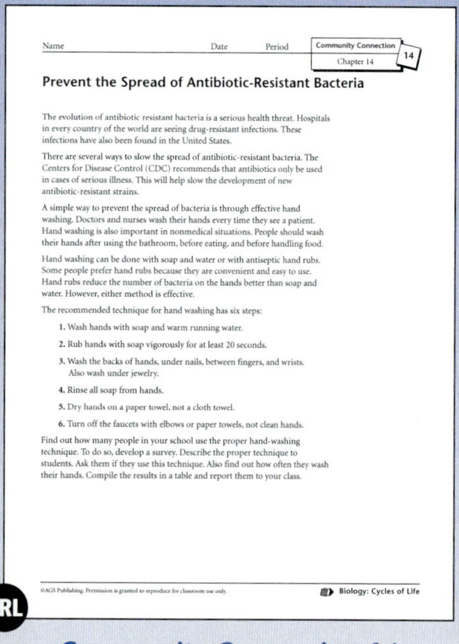

Community Connection 14

Chapter 14
Speciation and Punctuated Equilibrium

The bird in the photograph is a medium ground finch. Charles Darwin observed this species in the Galapagos Islands. Just as Darwin thought, the key to this bird's success is the size of its beak. The kinds and sizes of seeds that these finches eat change every year, depending on the rainfall in their area. Variation in the trait of beak size helps the species adapt to changes. In Chapter 14, you will learn about the formation of species, or speciation. You will also learn about the rates at which speciation occurs.

Organize Your Thoughts

Species
- Stability
- Change in environment
  - Species extinction
  - Speciation

Goals for Learning

- To define speciation and explain how it occurs
- To identify the classification systems of living things
- To identify conditions for speciation to occur
- To describe conditions that affect the survival of species

Introducing the Chapter

Have students study the photograph of the medium ground finch on page 426. Have them consider the following scenario. Suppose you are a scientist looking at this bird for the first time. How would you determine what species the bird is? Is it a new species? What characteristics would you use to compare this bird to other birds that are somewhat similar? (Encourage students to consider ideas beyond just gross anatomy and morphology.) What type of information would definitively determine if this bird is a new species? *(Sample answers: DNA analysis, number of chromosomes, specific biochemistry, inability to successfully reproduce with other species that are similar to it)*

Have students read the Goals for Learning. Explain that in this chapter students will learn how a species is defined and the different ways a new species may come into existence.

Notes and Math Tips

Ask volunteers to read the notes and math tips that appear in the margins throughout the chapter. Then discuss them with the class.

TEACHER'S RESOURCE

The AGS Publishing Teaching Strategies in Science Transparencies may be used with this chapter. The transparencies add an interactive dimension to expand and enhance the *Biology: Cycles of Life* program content.

CAREER INTEREST INVENTORY

The AGS Publishing Harrington-O'Shea Career Decision-Making System-Revised (CDM) may be used with this chapter. Students can use the CDM to explore their interests and identify careers. The CDM defines career areas that are indicated by students' responses on the inventory.

Lesson at a Glance

Chapter 14 Lesson 1

Overview In this lesson, students learn about how new species come into existence.

Objectives

- To describe methods scientists use to classify living things
- To describe Charles Darwin's speciation ideas
- To list causes of speciation
- To explain the biological species concept
- To explain the ecological species concept
- To describe three types of speciation

Student Pages 428–433

Teacher's Resource Library TRL
- Workbook Activity 79
- Alternative Workbook Activity 79
- Lab Manual 66

Vocabulary

allopatric speciation
asexual reproduction
biochemistry
biological species concept
classify
ecological species concept
fertile
interbreed
mammary gland
morphology
niche
reproductively isolated
subpopulation
subspecies
sympatric speciation

Have students write a short paragraph that includes five vocabulary terms used correctly in context. Encourage students to choose vocabulary terms that are related to one another in order to make a well-constructed paragraph.

Lesson 1 What Is Speciation?

Objectives

After reading this lesson, you should be able to
- describe methods scientists use to classify living things
- describe Charles Darwin's speciation ideas
- list causes of speciation
- explain the biological species concept
- explain the ecological species concept
- describe three types of speciation

Classify
To group

Mammary gland
A milk-producing structure on a mammal

Morphology
The study of differences in body forms of organisms

In Chapter 13, you learned that living things are similar, but different. To study living things, scientists classify organisms into groups based on their similarities and differences. **Classify** means "to group." For example, scientists classify humans into the group *Homo sapiens*. Humans belong to a larger group called mammals. Mammals are animals that have **mammary glands.** Mammary glands are milk-producing structures on a mammal. Humans also belong to a larger group called animals.

You have also learned that scientists make decisions about how to compare and contrast living things. They may use **morphology** to classify living things. Morphology is the study of the differences in the body form of organisms. For example, the body form of a bird differs from the body form of a cat. Scientists classify birds and cats into different morphology groups. Scientists also classify living things based on differences in **biochemistry,** body function, or behavior.

Species: Most Specific Level of Classification

Scientists group members of a population into a classification level called species. As you know, a species is a group of living things that can breed with each other. They produce offspring that are like themselves and are **fertile.** Scientists classify animals and plants by a classification system. Species is the most specific level of the classification system. You will learn more about this classification system in Lesson 2.

Darwin's Theories on Speciation

Scientists want to find what causes differences in living things to happen. To find the answers, scientists investigate how a species changes over time. Scientists also study how one species evolves into two or more different species.

Charles Darwin, a British scientist, traveled around the world from 1831 to 1836. He wanted to learn how and why living things change over time. To find out, Darwin studied many organisms, including the finches on the Galapagos Islands.

428 Chapter 14 Speciation and Punctuated Equilibrium

Background Information

Charles Darwin traveled aboard the HMS *Beagle* as the ship's naturalist from 1831 to 1836. The ship's main goal was to map the South American coastline, of which little was known. Darwin recorded information about the organisms he saw in different areas of South America. Darwin reviewed his data and the samples he collected after he returned to Britain. He worked and wrote about his theories for almost 15 years before publishing *On the Origin of Species by Means of Natural Selection* in 1859. In his book, Darwin presented his theory that natural selection was the mechanism of evolution.

428 Chapter 14

Biochemistry
Chemistry that deals with the chemical compounds and processes in organisms

Fertile
Capable of producing offspring

Reproductively isolated
A division between populations that once mated, but can no longer mate and produce fertile offspring

Interbreed
To breed together

The Galapagos Islands are on the equator in the Pacific Ocean. They are 600 miles (960 kilometers) west of Ecuador, South America.

Darwin observed that the Galapagos finches looked alike. However, some groups of finches did not reproduce with each other. He noticed that the different species had specific differences. Some had beaks for eating seeds. Others ate insects. Some finches had beaks like a woodpecker. They used their beaks to drill holes in tree bark. Then they held a cactus spine in their beaks to dig out insects. Some finches lived on the ground. Others lived in trees.

Darwin found 13 species of finches on the Galapagos Islands. He wondered if these species had a common ancestor. The ancestor would be the original species. Finding the ancestor of the finches would help Darwin figure out how speciation happened. Today, scientists think the original species of finches came from Central or South America. The 13 species of Galapagos finches developed from the original species. This speciation took several million years.

Causes of Speciation

As you know, speciation is the creation of new species. There are different explanations as to how speciation occurs. Geographical barriers can separate the members of a population. Recall that a population is a group of organisms of the same species that live in the same area.

Over time, if separated populations come into contact and members interbreed, speciation does not occur. However, if members from the separated populations do not reproduce with each other, speciation occurs. Populations that do not reproduce with each other are **reproductively isolated.**

Any factor that prevents two species from reproducing living, fertile offspring contributes to reproductive isolation. Over time, the gene pools in each of the separated populations change. The populations can no longer **interbreed** even if they come in contact with each other. That is because they are reproductively isolated. Recall from Chapter 13 that a gene pool is the genes found within a population.

---

1 Warm-Up Activity

Have students read and perform the Express Lab on page 433. Give students at least ten everyday objects on a tray. Students may decide to classify the objects according to size, shape, color, what they are made of, or what they are used for.

Express Lab Answers

1. Answers will vary. **2.** Answers will vary, but should include a reasonable explanation of how the objects are related. **3.** Answers will vary.

2 Teaching the Lesson

Have students make a Venn diagram to organize the similarities and differences between the biological species concept and the ecological species concept.

Have students make a list of the different ways species can become reproductively isolated.

3 Reinforce and Extend

GLOBAL CONNECTION

Have students find the Galapagos Islands on a world map. The Galapagos Islands were made famous because of Darwin's research on the finches living there. Have students find out more information about the Galapagos Islands by answering the following questions: What other organisms live there? Why are these islands a good place to study how speciation occurs? Why is it important that these islands be preserved and protected? Have students share their research with the class.

Students may wish to visit the Library of Congress Web site at www.loc.gov/rr/international/hispanic/galapagos.html, which has links to resources about the Galapagos Islands and current environmental issues concerning the islands.

PRONUNCIATION GUIDE

Use the pronunciation shown here to help students pronounce a difficult word in this lesson. Refer to the pronunciation key on the Chapter Planning Guide for the sounds of the symbols.

Galapagos (gə lä′ pə gəs)

ELL/ESL Strategy

Language Objective: *To pronounce and use vocabulary terms*

Pair students who are learning English with students proficient in English. Have students use the Glossary to look up the pronunciation of any vocabulary terms they do not know how to pronounce. Have students practice pronunciation by using each term in a sentence.

Teacher Alert

Be sure that students understand the full definition of the biological species concept. The individuals of a species not only interbreed, but also produce viable, fertile offspring. Students may be confused by news stories of hybrids produced by the interbreeding between lions and tigers, sheep and goats, or zebras and Shetland ponies. Although these animals may interbreed and produce healthy offspring, the offspring are sterile, that is, they cannot reproduce successfully. Therefore, the definition of the biological species concept is not met. The two parent organisms remain two different species.

Biological species concept
A principle that defines a species as populations that can interbreed and produce offspring

Insects are the most diverse organisms on the earth.

Defining Species: Biological Species Concept

Scientists classify sexually reproducing species using the **biological species concept.** This principle defines species as groups of interbreeding populations reproductively isolated from other groups. Species cannot interbreed with members of another species. Reproductive barriers between species isolate their gene pools.

Genetic exchange is possible among members of a species. However, genetic exchange is not possible among members of different species. Look at the horse and donkey in Figure 14.1.1. Horses and donkeys are closely related. If these two species interbreed, the offspring are mules. A mule is not fertile. For this reason, scientists classify horses and donkeys as two species.

Fireflies may look similar, but different species of fireflies do not mate. Many factors prevent mating. For example, the two species may live in different habitats of an area. They do not come in contact with each other. This reproductive isolation occurred with Darwin's finches. Some finches lived in trees. Some lived on the ground.

Different species of fireflies may breed at different times of day or in different seasons. Male fireflies use specific signals to attract females. A firefly from one species would not use or recognize the signals of another species.

Figure 14.1.1 *How are a donkey and a horse alike? How are they different?*

430 Chapter 14 Speciation and Punctuated Equilibrium

Asexual reproduction
Reproduction that involves one parent and no egg or sperm

Ecological species concept
A principle that defines species as populations that can interbreed and produce offspring based on their niche

Niche
The way of life of a species

Subspecies
A division of a species

Allopatric speciation
When similar organisms do not interbreed due to physical barriers

Sympatric speciation
When similar organisms live nearby, but do not interbreed due to differences in behavior

Defining Species: Ecological Species Concept

Scientists cannot use the biological species concept for species that reproduce asexually. **Asexual reproduction** involves one organism and no egg or sperm. Scientists define asexually reproducing species by the **ecological species concept.** This principle states that species are defined based on their **niche.** A niche describes the way of life of a species, or how a species adapts to a role in its environment.

A niche refers to more than an organism's physical surroundings. It includes the organism's living and nonliving interactions with its environment. Sometimes scientists define species by both the biological species concept and the ecological species concept.

Two Classification Questions

To classify living things, scientists usually ask two questions. First, does a species differ from other species? Second, will a species remain different in the future? Scientists answer the first question by looking at structure, reproduction, and niches.

To answer the second question, scientists decide if a **subspecies** will become isolated. A subspecies is a division of a species. If a subspecies becomes isolated, natural selection or genetic drift will produce different gene pools. Remember from Chapter 13 that genetic drift is the random change in the gene pool of a small population.

Mechanisms of Speciation

Before a new species arises, the gene pool of a population is cut off from other populations of the parent species. The population with the isolated gene pool now evolves on its own. This reproductive isolation can follow two different development paths in forming a new species. One path is **allopatric speciation.** The other path is **sympatric speciation.**

Allopatric speciation means that similar organisms do not interbreed due to a physical barrier. A physical barrier could be mountains, forests, deserts, rivers, or oceans. A physical barrier isolates populations. This occurred with the finches on the Galapagos Islands.

SCIENCE JOURNAL

Have students choose an organism and write a description of the organism. Encourage students to give a specific and detailed description of the organism as if they were collecting data to classify the organism based on its physical features.

TEACHER ALERT

Students may have difficulty understanding how sympatric speciation can occur. Plant species provide some of the best examples of sympatric speciation. If, during cell division and reproduction, a mutation occurs, the mutated offspring can be reproductively isolated from the rest of the population. For example, one mutation that occurs in many plant species results in an extra set of chromosomes. This means that the mutant organism cannot interbreed successfully with the other organisms in the population.

Biology in Your Life

Have students read the Biology in Your Life feature. Remind students that there are nearly 400 breeds of the domestic dog. Although each breed has a different appearance, all breeds are the same species, *Canis familiaris*. The DNA of dogs is almost identical to the DNA of wolves. How many students have dogs as pets? How is their pet different from a wolf in both appearance and behavior?

Biology in Your Life Answers

1. Scientists think less aggressive wolves either learned to get food from begging or from humans' garbage. **2.** Traits that developed included floppy ears, curly tails, smaller teeth, shorter legs **3.** The genes for some traits may be located close to desirable traits in the genome.

LEARNING STYLES

Body/Kinesthetic

Provide students with marbles, construction paper, cardboard pieces, scissors, glue, and colored markers. Have students model allopatric speciation, using the materials. For example, the marbles represent a population of organisms. Students could make a mountain range out of the other materials and place it so that some of the marbles are separated from the rest of the group. Have students explain what type of organism the marbles represent and how they have chosen to model allopatric speciation. Have them predict what may happen to each of the two groups after they are separated.

Subpopulation
A division of a population

Sympatric speciation occurs when a **subpopulation** becomes reproductively isolated while living among the parent population. The lack of interbreeding occurs because of differences in behavior. Sympatric speciation is not a common method among animal species. However, sympatric speciation accounts for about 25 percent of plant species. This mechanism accounts for many plant species grown for food.

Biology in Your Life

The Evolution of Dogs: The Environment

Dogs have evolved for the last 10,000 to 14,000 years for one main purpose—to coexist with humans. Dogs originally evolved from wolves. They have changed greatly and are now very different animals. Scientists have studied dogs to learn how having them as pets could cause so many changes. The answer probably depends on how dogs first became tame and began to coexist with humans. Scientists have several theories about how this happened, but do not know for sure. Perhaps less aggressive wolves found that they could get food from humans by begging. Perhaps tamer wolves were not frightened by humans and began to live near their garbage.

The evolution of wolves into dogs marked several distinct changes. Many of these changes cannot be explained. For example, many breeds of dogs and other pets developed short legs. Their tails became curled. Their ears became floppy. Other traits are more logical. For example, dogs have much smaller teeth than wolves. This makes sense because pets do not need their teeth for hunting and tearing meat from bones like wolves do.

Scientists also are studying how foxes change when they are selected over several generations to become pets. Many of the same traits, such as short legs and floppy ears, begin to show up as well. These traits are not essential in pet animals. They may develop because they are located close to desirable traits in the genome.

1. What theories try to explain how wolves started to become pets?

2. What kinds of traits developed in dogs as a result of becoming pets?

3. Why do scientists think other traits also developed?

LEARNING STYLES

Interpersonal/Group Learning

Have students work in small groups to describe a "new" species by answering the following questions: What characteristics will it have? What will it look like? How will it be different from other species that are closely related to it? What characteristics will make it unique? What habitat will it live in? How was it discovered? Encourage students to be creative but realistic in their efforts to describe their species.

Lesson 1 REVIEW

Word Bank
fertile
morphology
speciation

On a sheet of paper, write the correct word from the Word Bank that completes each question correctly.

1. To group organisms, scientists use _____, or the differences in body form.
2. Organisms that are the same species can breed and produce living, _____ offspring.
3. The creation of a new species is _____.

Critical Thinking

On a sheet of paper, write the answers to the following questions. Use complete sentences.

4. How does Darwin's study of the Galapagos finches relate to the concept of niche?
5. What can cause speciation to occur?

Express Lab 14

Materials
◆ buttons or other objects

Procedure
1. Examine the buttons or other objects. Each object represents a different organism.
2. Working with a partner, develop a way to group these organisms into different "species."
3. When you are finished, be prepared to explain your method to your classmates.

Analysis
1. What are the unique characteristics of each species?
2. Which species are most closely related? How can you tell?
3. List more characteristics to classify these organisms if they were actual living things.

Speciation and Punctuated Equilibrium Chapter 14

Lesson 1 Review Answers

1. morphology 2. fertile 3. speciation 4. Darwin's study showed that each of the 13 finch species had adapted to different ecological niches. The species had different habitats, diets, and methods of finding food. 5. Geographical barriers can cause reproductive isolation, which leads to speciation.

Portfolio Assessment

Sample items include:
- Express Lab answers
- Description from Science Journal
- Lesson 1 Review answers

LAB ACTIVITIES

Chapter 14 has Investigation and Discovery Investigation lab activities. Two additional lab activities for Chapter 14 appear in the Biology: Cycles of Life Lab Manual and on the Teacher's Resource Library CD-ROM.

Lab Manual 66

Workbook Activity 79

Lesson at a Glance

Chapter 14 Lesson 2

Overview In this lesson, students learn about the different systems used by scientists to classify organisms.

Objectives

- To describe the three types of classification systems
- To explain the two-word name of species
- To define the three-domain system

Student Pages 434–439

Teacher's Resource Library

Workbook Activity 80
Alternative Workbook Activity 80
Lab Manual 67–68
Resource File 33

Vocabulary

Archaea	kingdom
division	phylum
Eukarya	three-domain
genus	system

Have students make and fill in a three-column chart to organize information about the vocabulary terms. Column headings should be *Vocabulary Term*, *Definition*, and *Example*. Encourage students to use information from other chapters, if needed, to find examples for the vocabulary term.

Background Information

Assigning organisms a two-part scientific name, genus and species, allows scientists to communicate in a universal language. Using the common name for an organism is less precise. Common names for the same organism can differ from one area of the world to the next. Also, the same common name may refer to more than one species. Using scientific names for organisms eliminates confusion.

Lesson 2 Classifying Species

Objectives

After reading this lesson, you should be able to
- describe the three types of classification systems
- explain the two-word name of species
- define the three-domain system

Genus
A group of similar species

Kingdom
A group of similar phyla or divisions

Phylum
A subdivision of the animal kingdom (plural is phyla)

Division
A subdivision of the plant kingdom

Scientists use a system to group and classify extinct and living species of organisms.

Linnaeus Classification System

In 1753, Carolus Linnaeus, a Swedish scientist, developed a new system to classify plants and animals. Scientists use his system today to classify new organisms. Linnaeus grouped species by physical characteristics.

Under the Linneaus system, each species has a two-word name. The first word is the **genus**. For example, maple trees belong to the genus Acer. The scientific names of all maple trees begin with the word *Acer*. The second word is the species. The scientific name of the sugar maple tree is *Acer saccharum*. The scientific name of the red maple is *Acer rubrum*.

In the Linneaus system, each organism belongs to seven levels. Look at Figure 14.2.1. From the most general to the most specific, the seven layers are: **kingdom, phylum or division,** class, order, family, genus, and species.

Scientists have used the Linneaus system for over two centuries. You will learn more about this classification system in Chapter 15.

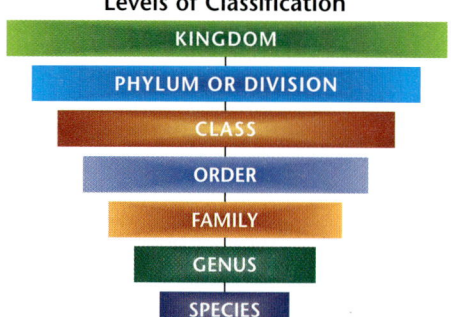

Figure 14.2.1 Each organism belongs to seven levels in the Linneaus system.

434 Chapter 14 Speciation and Punctuated Equilibrium

---

1 Warm-Up Activity

Show students side-by-side photographs of the arctic fox (*Alopex lagopus*) with its winter coat and its summer coat. Also, show students side-by-side photographs of the eastern meadowlark (*Sturnella magna*) and the western meadowlark (*Sturnella neglecta*). For each pair of photographs, ask students: Are these two organisms the same species or different species? Why or why not? (*The summer and winter arctic fox are the same species; they have the same scientific name, are the animal at different times of year, and can reproduce fertile offspring. The eastern and western meadowlarks are different species, as shown by the second word of their scientific name; they occupy different niches and cannot reproduce fertile offspring.*) Tell students the correct answers; then hold a short discussion about the characteristics that scientists use to identify a species. Relying on visual examination alone is not enough to determine if organisms are the same species. Looking closely at morphology and biochemistry are important components of determining the species of an organism.

Link to ››› Language

Most species have Latin or Greek names. The scientific name for humans, *Homo sapiens,* comes from two Latin words. *Homo* means "man" and *sapiens* means "wise." Some species are named after the people who discovered or named them. For example, Johann Wilhelm Weinmann discovered and named *Weinmannia silvicola,* a tree native to New Zealand.

Study Figures 14.2.2 and 14.2.3. The figures show two species, the fruit fly and the sweetbay magnolia. How are these species alike? How do they differ?

Grouping Species by Ancestors

In the 1960s, scientists also began to group species by ancestors. Scientists continue to use characteristics that are alike in species to group them. Some characteristics include DNA, biochemistry, and morphology.

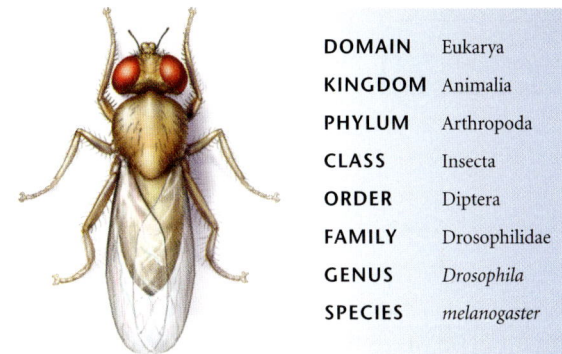

DOMAIN	Eukarya
KINGDOM	Animalia
PHYLUM	Arthropoda
CLASS	Insecta
ORDER	Diptera
FAMILY	Drosophilidae
GENUS	*Drosophila*
SPECIES	*melanogaster*

Figure 14.2.2 *Fruit fly,* Drosophila melanogaster

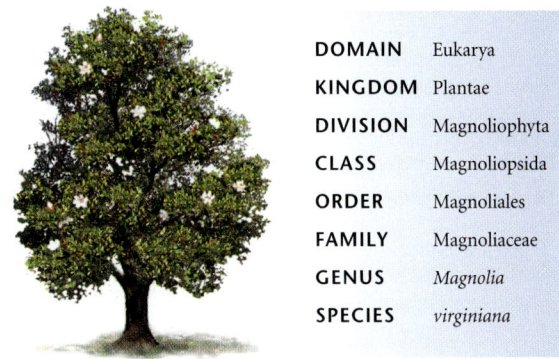

DOMAIN	Eukarya
KINGDOM	Plantae
DIVISION	Magnoliophyta
CLASS	Magnoliopsida
ORDER	Magnoliales
FAMILY	Magnoliaceae
GENUS	*Magnolia*
SPECIES	*virginiana*

Figure 14.2.3 *Sweetbay magnolia,* Magnolia virginiana

Speciation and Punctuated Equilibrium Chapter 14   435

2 Teaching the Lesson

Have students examine the representation of Linnaeus's classification system shown in Figure 14.2.1. Point out that the levels of classification are like an upside-down pyramid. The broadest group, kingdom, is on the top. The groups subsequently narrow to the most restrictive group, species.

Have students design and complete a chart in which they compare and contrast the three different systems of classification.

3 Reinforce and Extend

Link to

Language Arts. Have students read the Link to Language Arts feature. Many of the names in the classification system are derived from Latin and Greek roots related to characteristics of organisms in that group. For example, the order name Carnivora (the order of mammals that includes dogs, cats, and bears) comes from the Latin roots *carn,* which means "flesh," and *vorus,* which means "to devour."

LEARNING STYLES

Auditory/Verbal

Have students use a dictionary to find out how the genus and/or species names of the following organisms are related to their characteristics.

Canis lupus (gray wolf)
Canis rufus (red wolf)
Vulpes velox (swift fox)
Alopex lagopus (Arctic fox)

(*Lupus* means "wolf." *Rufus* means "red." *Vulpes* means "fox" and *velox* means "quick." *Alopex* means "fox.") Note that animals in more than one genus share the common name "fox." They are in the same family, Canidae, together with dogs and wolves.

PRONUNCIATION GUIDE

Use the pronunciation shown here to help students pronounce a difficult word in this lesson. Refer to the pronunciation key on the Chapter Planning Guide for the sounds of the symbols.

Linnaeus (lə nē′ əs)

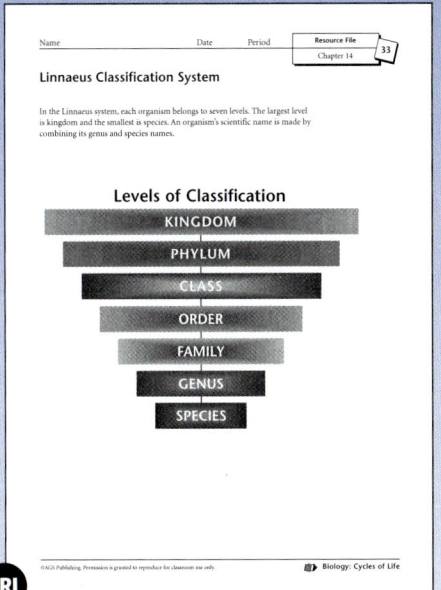

Resource File 33

AT HOME

Have students think of ways that other things are organized or classified. Library books are categorized by topic and are organized using the Dewey Decimal or the Library of Congress systems. Grocery stores classify and organize food items into certain groups in aisles. Have students find examples of how objects have been classified and organized in their homes. For example, they may have organized a CD or DVD collection. The food in cabinets or the refrigerator may be organized in a certain way. Have students write a short paragraph describing an organization scheme that exists in their home.

Achievements in Science

Have students read the Achievements in Science feature. Have them focus on the last sentence of the feature. Remind students that despite the best efforts of scientists, some questions about human ancestry still remain unanswered. Also, there is considerable debate among scientists about how to link the different fossils together to form a tree explaining human ancestry. Ask students: Why is it so difficult for scientists to definitively determine human ancestry? *(Sample answers: It is difficult to discover and uncover fossils. The fossil record remains incomplete. Different scientists make different interpretations of the existing data.)*

Three-domain system
A system that classifies all living things into three broad groups

Archaea
The domain of prokaryotic organisms that are not bacteria

Eukarya
The domain of eukaryotic organisms

Three-Domain System

Recently, scientists began using a **three-domain system.** In this system, scientists classify living things into three broad groups: Bacteria, **Archaea,** or **Eukarya.** The fruit fly, sweetbay magnolia, and human belong to the Eukarya domain. You will learn more about the three-domain system in Chapter 15.

Differences Used to Classify Species

Scientists look for differences in living things to classify an organism as a member of a population. The difference must be clear and constant. Scientists often ignore small differences when classifying species.

Sometimes scientists cannot isolate one main difference when assigning an organism to a species. For example, they look at several factors to assign a tree to the correct species. They may compare the color of flowers, buds, and bark. They also compare the number of flowers, and the shape of the leaves and fruit.

Achievements in Science

Discovering Human Ancestors

Humans are the only living species that belong to the genus *Homo.* Modern humans and our ancestors are hominids. Hominids walk upright on two legs and have thumbs for gripping. Early hominid fossils generally belong to the genus *Australopithecus.* This genus is an ancestor to the *Homo* species.

Raymond Dart, an Australian scientist, found the first hominid fossil in 1924. He found a skull that was larger than an ape's skull. The skull was about 2 million years old and resembled both humans and apes. Dart named this organism *Australopithecus africanus.*

In 1974, American paleontologists working in Ethiopia found a nearly complete skeleton of *Australopithecus afarensis.* They named the 3-million-year-old skeleton Lucy. In 1994, another group of American paleontologists found a 4.4-million-year-old skeleton. Scientists classified this skeleton as a new genus, *Ardipithecus ramidus.*

Between 1997 and 1999, Yohannes Haile-Selassie found fossil fragments of a subspecies of *Ardipithecus ramidus* in his native Ethiopia. He called the new fossils *Ardipithecus ramidus kadabba.* These fragments are about 5.2 million years old. Scientists continue to search for evidence of the earliest hominids and fill in the gaps of human ancestry.

Lesson 2 REVIEW

Word Bank
- genus
- morphology
- species
- three-domain system

On a sheet of paper, write the word or words from the Word Bank that complete each question correctly.

1. Scientists use the _____ to classify living things into three broad groups.

2. The first word of a scientific name is the _____ of the organism. The second word is the _____.

3. Scientists use DNA, biochemistry, and _____ to name and classify living things.

Critical Thinking

On a sheet of paper, write the answers to the following questions. Use complete sentences.

4. List the seven levels of Linneaus classification from most general to most specific.

5. Why do scientists consider many factors when assigning an organism to a species?

Technology and Society

Recently, scientists have begun looking for new organisms in the world's oceans. To do this, they sample seawater and analyze DNA. Currant data shows that there is more life and diversity in the sea than scientists had thought. The first sample of seawater contained 1.2 million unrecorded genes and 1,800 new microorganisms.

Speciation and Punctuated Equilibrium Chapter 14   437

Investigation 14

Encourage students to read the investigation steps. Discuss questions they may have before beginning the investigation.

Objectives

- To examine the effects of antibiotics on bacterial growth and population
- To observe the effects of natural selection on a population of organisms
- To infer the long-range effects on the genetic diversity of the selected bacteria

Skills

Observing, inferring, collecting and analyzing data, drawing conclusions

Background

Students have learned that natural selection can change the gene pool of a population. This investigation allows them to observe selection firsthand and infer the long-term effects that occur as a result.

Time Frame

One class period to set up, then observations over the next several class periods

Procedure

- Have students work with partners or in small groups to complete the activity.
- Demonstrate how to effectively streak the petri dishes.
- In Step 7, be sure the dishes are sealed, then invert them, and place them in a temperature- and light-controlled environment. If you do not have an environment-controlled chamber, place the dishes in a desk drawer or a closet.

Cleanup/Disposal

Instruct students in proper cleanup and disposal of materials.

INVESTIGATION 14

Materials
- safety goggles
- lab coat or apron
- gloves
- wax pencil
- 2 nutrient agar petri dishes
- Bunsen burner
- inoculation loop
- bacteria culture
- forceps
- antibiotic disk

Natural Selection in Bacteria

People use antibiotics to destroy bacteria that can cause disease. Medicines, soaps, and other cleaners may contain antibiotics. Antibiotics kill bacteria or change their ability to reproduce or function. Through natural selection, some bacteria adapt and become resistant to antibiotics. This makes it more difficult to kill harmful bacteria with antibiotics. In this investigation, you will observe the effects of natural selection in bacteria.

Procedure

1. Put on safety goggles, a lab coat or apron, and gloves.
2. Using a wax pencil, label the bottom of one petri dish A. Label the bottom of the other petri dish B. Write your name and the date on the bottom of each petri dish.
3. Follow your teacher's instructions to light the Bunsen burner.

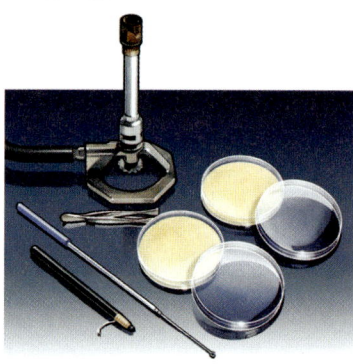

438   Chapter 14   Speciation and Punctuated Equilibrium

Safety Alert

- Be sure that students have read and understood all safety rules for working in the lab. Discuss the Safety Alerts with students.
- Be sure students take care in handling the bacteria cultures. Have students wash their hands after handling the cultures and dishes.
- Students should be careful when using Bunsen burners. Have them wear protective clothing and secure hair and loose objects.

4. To sterilize the inoculation loop, pass it through the flame. **Safety Alert: Be careful when working with an open flame.**

5. Collect a small amount of bacteria culture by putting the inoculation loop on the surface of the bacteria culture. With the inoculation loop, make a zigzag streak from top to bottom on the nutrient agar in petri dish A and petri dish B. Do not break the surface of the nutrient agar.

6. Using the forceps, pick up an antibiotic disk. Put the disk on petri dish A.

7. Cover both petri dishes. Put both petri dishes in a light- and temperature-controlled area as directed by your teacher.

8. Over the next three days, check your petri dishes every 24 hours. Record your observations.

Cleanup/Disposal
When you are finished, clean your lab area. Dispose of used petri dishes according to your teacher's directions. Wash your hands well with soap and warm water.

Analysis
1. Compare the growth of the bacteria on petri dish A and petri dish B.
2. Describe the differences in the bacterial growth between your petri dish B and the petri dish B of other classmates. What factors cause these differences in growth?

Conclusions
1. What effect did the antibiotic disk have on the bacteria population on petri dish A?
2. What is occurring on petri dish A? What changes are occurring in the bacterial population as a result?
3. What problems can result by using antibiotics too often?

Explore Further
Take a sample of bacteria growing close to the antibiotic disk from petri dish A. Streak this sample onto a clean petri dish. Add an antibiotic disk. Cover the petri dish. Put this dish in a light- and temperature- controlled area as directed by your teacher. Check your dish every 24 hours over the next three days. Record your observations. Compare the growth of the bacteria on this dish with the growth on your petri dish A from the investigation. What could cause the differences in bacteria growth?

Analysis Answers
1. The antibiotic disks should suppress the growth of bacteria.
2. Some bacteria will be more successful growing in the presence of the disks than other populations. This is likely because of genetic differences in the populations, as well as some environmental differences between the dishes and techniques of different students. Some bacteria have genetic resistance that makes the antibiotic less effective.

Conclusions Answers
1. The antibiotic suppressed the growth of the bacteria on petri dish B to different degrees.
2. The bacteria that do not have resistance to the antibiotic are being killed or not reproducing. The bacteria with resistance are surviving and reproducing. The resistant bacteria are increasing as a percentage of the bacterial population.
3. If antibiotics are used frequently, the general population of bacteria that cause illness in humans becomes more resistant to antibiotics. If this trend continues, it becomes increasingly likely that people will become sick due to bacteria that cannot be treated with antibiotics.

Explore Further Answers
Students may notice that their second bacteria culture is more resistant to the antibiotics. They have selected for a population that is more resistant than the first. Look at students' notes to be sure they are making observations about the growth on their petri dishes.

Assessment
You might include the following items from this investigation in student portfolios:
- Data table with student observations
- Answers to Analysis and Conclusions questions
- Student observations and answer to Explore Further question

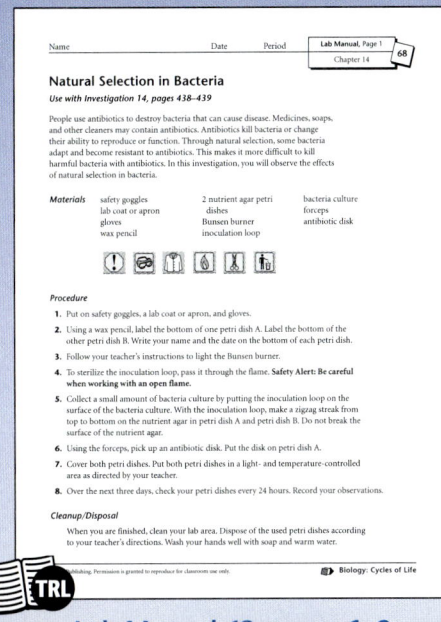

Lab Manual 68, pages 1–2

Lesson at a Glance

Chapter 14 Lesson 3

Overview In this lesson, students learn theories about different mechanisms through which speciation can occur.

Objectives

- To explain how speciation happens
- To describe early theories of the rate of speciation
- To describe the punctuated equilibrium theory
- To describe the coordinated stasis theory

Student Pages 440–446

Teacher's Resource Library

Workbook Activity 81

Alternative Workbook Activity 81

Lab Manual 69

Resource File 34

Vocabulary

coordinated stasis
punctuated equilibrium
stasis

Randomly read the definitions of the vocabulary terms to students. After each definition, have students write the corresponding term on a sheet of paper.

Background Information

The geographical isolation of individuals in a population can lead to reproductive isolation and speciation. Lava flows from volcanic eruptions, mountain formation, glacial movement, and changes in the surface level of water masses can create geographical barriers between populations. Factors such as genetic drift, natural selection, and mutations continue to act on the gene pools of the separated groups. At some point, the gene pool of each isolated group is altered enough so that the groups can no longer successfully interbreed and produce fertile offspring.

Lesson 3 — Conditions for Speciation to Occur

Objectives

After reading this lesson, you should be able to

- explain how speciation happens
- describe early theories of the rate of speciation
- describe the punctuated equilibrium theory
- describe the coordinated stasis theory

Link to >>> Social Studies

In 1859, Charles Darwin published a book about his theories of evolution. *On the Origin of Species by Means of Natural Selection* is one of the world's most important science books.

Speciation occurs when a single species becomes two or more species. Speciation usually takes much longer than a person's lifetime to happen. To study speciation, scientists look at changes in the geography of the area where populations live. Scientists then look at how the characteristics of living things differ between geographic areas. For example, related species could live in nearby areas, but are separated by a barrier.

How Speciation Occurs

Scientists think speciation begins when members of a species become separated by geography. The species becomes two populations that live in different environments. Members of each species do not move between the populations. The two populations do not interbreed. They do not exchange genes. Over time, they evolve with differences in the gene pool.

The two populations become very different. If they come together, they cannot interbreed. The two populations are reproductively isolated. Scientists classify members of the two populations as separate species.

The Rate of Speciation

Scientists think speciation happens by different methods. Recall from Chapter 13 that speciation may be the result of many smaller changes occurring. These changes occur over a vast period of time.

In the 1800s, Charles Darwin explained that the origin of species is through adaptation by natural selection. Isolated populations evolve differences gradually as they adapt to the environment. Paleontologists find evidence of gradual changes in the fossil record.

440 Chapter 14 *Speciation and Punctuated Equilibrium*

Link to

Social Studies. Have students read the Link to Social Studies feature. After spending almost 15 years working on the manuscript of *On the Origin of Species by Means of Natural Selection*, Darwin was finally forced to finish and publish it in 1859. Another scientist, Alfred Wallace, had developed a theory of natural selection as the mechanism of evolution that was very similar to Darwin's theory. Wallace sent the summary of his theory to Darwin to read and pass on for publication. When Darwin read the essay by Wallace, he was prompted to finish his own publication.

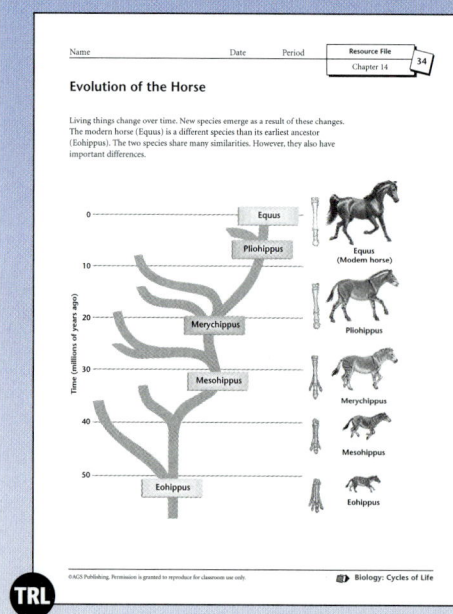

Resource File 34

Stasis
Showing little change over time

Punctuated equilibrium
A theory that states species stay the same for a long time, then new species evolve suddenly due to global changes and mass extinctions

In the 1930s, two American scientists, Theodosius Dobzhansky and Ernst Mayr, published a new theory about speciation. They thought members of a species separated by geography, such as a barrier, become separate species. Dobzhansky and Mayr thought that geographic isolation happens before speciation. Their theory is called allopatric speciation, which was discussed in Lesson 1.

Both theories link environmental change with evolution. Darwin's theory of natural selection is linked with environmental change. The Dobzhansky-Mayr theory states that speciation happens in populations isolated by geography. The change in geography results from environmental change. This means changes in the environment are related to speciation.

Punctuated Equilibrium

Some scientists support the sudden appearance of new species. These scientists think speciation occurs in thousands of years rather than in millions of years. They think that species are in **stasis** most of the time. Stasis means showing very little change over time.

Some species can survive without change for millions of years. Then, a huge change happens in the environment. For example, a meteor crashes into the earth. Or the sea level rises because polar ice caps melt. This pattern of speciation is called **punctuated equilibrium.**

The punctuated equilibrium theory states that species stay the same for long periods of time. Then, the species changes quickly because of changes in the environment. Changes in the environment change the living conditions of species.

Scientists have found examples of punctuated equilibrium over the past 1.65 million years. For example, the earth has had four main periods of global warming. During periods of global warming, glacial ice moved into North America, Europe, and Asia. As a result, ecosystems moved south. Recall from Chapter 1 that an ecosystem is the living and nonliving things found in an area.

Warm-Up Activity

Show students side-by-side photographs of two squirrels: *Ammospermophilus harrisi* and *Ammospermophilus leucurus*. Ask students: Do you think the squirrels are the same species? Why or why not? *(Answers will vary.)* Explain to students that these squirrels are a classic example of allopatric speciation. The two squirrels live on opposite sides of the Grand Canyon. The geographical isolation, or the few miles that separate the original populations, led to reproductive isolation. *A. leucurus* is smaller, has a shorter tail, and has different coloration compared to *A. harrisi*. The squirrels are two different species.

Teaching the Lesson

Point out to students that new scientific theories are often presented while more research on a topic is in process. This idea is reflected in the text in this lesson. Although new theories have been developed about how speciation occurs, this does not mean that all previous theories have been discarded.

Reinforce and Extend

TEACHER ALERT

Whether evolution occurs gradually (as Darwin proposed) or in spurts (following the theory of punctuated equilibrium) is still a much debated topic in the scientific community. Different groups of organisms seem to have different rates of evolution. The fossil record provides clear evidence for both theories. Some groups, such as African mammals, have evolved gradually. Other groups, such as the marine invertebrate bryozoa, have evolved according to the punctuated equilibrium theory.

ELL/ESL Strategy

Language Objective: *To learn how to take notes*

Have students take notes on the lesson as they read. They may choose to make a detailed outline of the material, or they may organize the material in a different way. Remind students that whatever way they choose, they should have clear, organized, accurate notes on the information presented in the lesson.

Science Journal

Have students compare and contrast the two theories: (1) that speciation results from gradual changes in species and (2) that speciation occurs in punctuated equilibrium. Students may choose to write a paragraph or present the information in the form of a graphic organizer.

Science at Work

Have students take turns reading the Science at Work feature aloud. If possible, bring in a carefully illustrated scientific book such as *Gray's Anatomy*, which includes very detailed, accurate illustrations of the systems of the human body. Have students look through their text to find figures that have been illustrated and examine the level of detail involved.

Coordinated stasis
A pattern where most species appear at about the same time

Plant and animal species survived if they could live in the changed areas. These species stayed the same. Other species became extinct. They could not live in the changed areas. Or they did not move away from the original area to a new area where they could survive.

Coordinated Stasis

Paleontologists study life in the past by studying fossils. As you know, fossils are the remains or impressions of organisms that lived in the past. The findings of paleontologists have formed a fossil record that shows how organisms have changed over time.

Paleontologists think evolution happens in a common process. The ancestors of species that live in an area evolved in the same way. Many species show similar patterns of evolution. After extinction, new species often appear at about the same time. Scientists call this pattern **coordinated stasis.**

▼◄▲◄▼◄▲◄▼◄▲◄▼◄▲◄▼◄▲◄▼◄▲◄▼◄▲◄▼◄▲◄▼

Science at Work

Scientific Illustrator

A scientific illustrator creates art for scientific purposes. A scientific illustrator may create drawings, paintings, or models. The art must be accurate.

Scientific illustrators work in all areas of science. They often work with scientists. For example, a scientific illustrator might work with a paleontologist. The scientific illustrator would make a painting of a newly discovered dinosaur. A scientific illustrator's artwork may appear in museums, brochures, magazines, textbooks, and other books.

Most scientific illustrators have a high school degree and some science education from a university or technical school. Many have completed a degree from an art school. Many scientific illustrators have computer training to create images, models, and animation.

An example of coordinated stasis is a global cooling that began about 2.8 million years ago. Cooler and drier conditions in Africa resulted. The African ecosystems changed suddenly.

As seen in Figure 14.3.1, dry grasslands replaced wet forests. Some species survived. Other species moved. Some species became extinct because they could not adapt to the new environment. At the same time, animal species moved to the African grasslands. Speciation also occurred during this time.

To sum up, classifying the many living things on the earth is a continuing process. Scientists debate about how organisms evolve. They look for evidence as to whether living things gradually change over time, as Darwin thought. Or they look for evidence as to whether punctuated equilibrium leads to the diversity in species.

Figure 14.3.1 *The African grasslands replaced wet forests due to global warming about 2.8 million years ago.*

Learning Styles

Visual/Spatial

Have students choose an organism to illustrate, preferably something they can observe in three dimensions such as a pet dog, cat, hamster, or fish; a squirrel or pigeon in a local park; or a person. Instruct them to draw the organism as accurately as possible, with features to scale and in the correct proportions. Students can display their work around the classroom.

Lesson 3 Review Answers

1. stasis 2. coordinated stasis 3. punctuated equilibrium 4. C 5. D 6. C 7. Dobzhansky and Mayr thought that when species became geographically separated, they evolved into different species. 8. Closely related species living near each other were most likely the same species before speciation occurred. 9. Scientists study speciation by examining changes in the geography of the area in which organisms live or by comparing how the characteristics of organisms differ between two locations. 10. The two populations are isolated and do not interbreed. After time, the populations have evolved differently. At some point, the evolutionary differences become big enough that the populations cannot breed even if they come back into contact with each other. At this point, they have become different species.

Portfolio Assessment

Sample items include:
- Paragraph from Science Journal
- Drawing from Learning Styles Visual/Spatial
- Lesson 3 Review answers

Lesson 3 REVIEW

Word Bank
coordinated stasis
punctuated equilibrium
stasis

On a sheet of paper, write the word or words from the Word Bank that complete each question correctly.

1. A species that shows little change over time is in _____.
2. A pattern where most new species appear at about the same time is _____.
3. A theory says species stay the same for a long time, then change quickly because of environmental changes. This theory is _____.

On a sheet of paper, write the letter of the answer that completes each sentence correctly.

4. Today, most species are in _____.
   A change   C stasis
   B coordinated statis   D isolation

5. When glacial ice moved into North America, some organisms survived without changing by _____.
   A breeding with new species
   B reproducing in larger numbers
   C using fewer resources
   D moving to new areas

6. A pattern where most species appear at about the same time is _____.
   A speciation   C coordinated stasis
   B punctuated equilibrium   D stasis

Critical Thinking

On a sheet of paper, write the answers to the following questions. Use complete sentences.

7. Describe the Dobzhansky-Mayr theory.
8. Explain why closely related species are often located near each other.
9. How do scientists study speciation?
10. What often happens when a species becomes geographically divided into two populations?

444 Chapter 14 Speciation and Punctuated Equilibrium

Workbook Activity 81

DISCOVERY INVESTIGATION 14

Materials
- safety goggles
- lab coat or apron
- moss plant
- fern plant
- coniferous tree branch
- flowering tree branch

Plant Evolution

The DNA of life forms changes over generations. Many changes are slight and make little difference in the lives of the organisms. Environmental changes can cause organisms to change. Environmental changes allow some organisms with slight differences to grow and reproduce better than other organisms. Over time, these differences may cause new species to develop. In this investigation, you will examine several types of plants. You will determine how changes caused new species of plant life to develop.

Procedure

1. Put on safety goggles and a lab coat or apron.
2. Examine the plants your teacher provided. Read the notes and descriptions that go with each plant.

Procedure
- Have students work in groups to complete the activity.
- Prepare a brief information card that describes each plant, its life cycle, environment, and reproductive cycle for students to use. Include the following information:

Moss
Description: Moss plants are nonvascular plants. Mosses are very small and do not have true roots, stems, or leaves.
Environment: A moss plant must live in a moist environment. The plant has no vascular tissue or roots to transport water, minerals, or sugars.
Reproductive cycle: When conditions are right, the moss plant's reproductive structure releases spores, which grow into a new plant if the temperature and moisture level are right.

Fern
Description: A fern is a seedless vascular plant. Ferns have roots, stems, and leaves.
Environment: Ferns have roots and vascular tissue that enable them to grow upright and transport water, minerals, and sugar throughout the plant.

Continued on page 446

Discovery Investigation 14

This investigation is less structured than the first investigation in this chapter. It offers students more challenge and requires more teacher facilitation. Encourage students to read the Discovery Investigation steps. Discuss questions they may have before beginning the investigation.

Objectives
- To observe a series of plants that have evolved and diversified
- To use observations to infer information about diversification and evolution

Skills
Observing, inferring, thinking critically, communicating, analyzing data, drawing conclusions

Background
Students have learned that organisms often diversify and experience speciation when the environment changes or creates new niches to be exploited. This investigation gives them hands-on experience observing some basic evolutionary diversification. Students will discuss what they observe and draw conclusions from those observations. Students should determine that moss is the most primitive plant, because it has no vascular tissue or seeds. Moss must be in contact with water at all times to survive and reproduce. Ferns evolved next, with vascular tissue that allows them to grow upright from the ground. Conifers evolved after ferns and developed seeds that could stay viable until conditions were right to germinate. Flowering plants developed most recently. Flowering plants have vascular tissue and seeds. They also use flowers, which often involve insects and other animals to pollinate and carry seeds to different locations.

Time Frame
One class period

Continued from page 445

Reproductive cycle: Ferns reproduce using spores. The spores must land where the right temperature and moisture levels can allow new plant life.

Conifer

Description: Conifers are gymnosperms. These plants produce seeds but no flowers.

Environment: The conifer can exist in many different environments. Conifers can send down deep roots to get water and transport water, minerals, and sugars through vascular tissue.

Reproductive cycle: The conifer plant produces uncovered, or naked, seeds that can withstand dry conditions and extreme temperatures. The seed stays ready until conditions are right before sprouting to produce a new plant.

Flowering Plant

Description: A flowering plant is an angiosperm. Angiosperms produce seeds and flowers. Flowering plants produce seeds in fruits.

Environment: Flowering plants can exist in many different environments. Flowering plants have roots and vascular tissue.

Reproductive cycle: A flowering plant produces flowers. The flowers are pollinated and produce seeds enclosed in a fruit. These fruits are often eaten or distributed by animals. The seed can withstand unfriendly environments until temperatures and moisture is right to produce a new plant.

Results

Students should gain the above information through their observations, reading, and class discussion. They should be able to answer the *Analysis* questions.

Answers to Analysis, Conclusions, and Explore Further begin on page 670 of this Teacher's Edition.

Assessment

You might include the following items from this investigation in student portfolios:

- Answers to Analysis and Conclusions questions
- Answer to Explore Further question

3. In small groups, observe and discuss each plant. Record your observations. Your teacher will help guide your discussion and answer questions.

4. Use the notes provided by your teacher and your own observations to answer the Analysis questions.

Cleanup/Disposal

When you are finished, clean your lab area.

Analysis

1. What differences did you see between the moss and the other plants? Would each difference be an advantage or disadvantage? Explain your answer.

2. How are the moss and the fern different from the other two plants?

3. The coniferous plant and the flowering plant are adapted to what kind of niche?

4. What advantage does the flowering plant have compared to the other three plants? Why do you think this is an advantage?

Conclusions

Using your observations and the information provided, determine the order in which the four plants evolved. List the four plants, in order, from the earliest to the most recent.

Explore Further

Research the physical and biological characteristics of blue-green algae. Do you think blue-green algae evolved sooner, the same time, or later compared to the four plants in this investigation? Explain your answer.

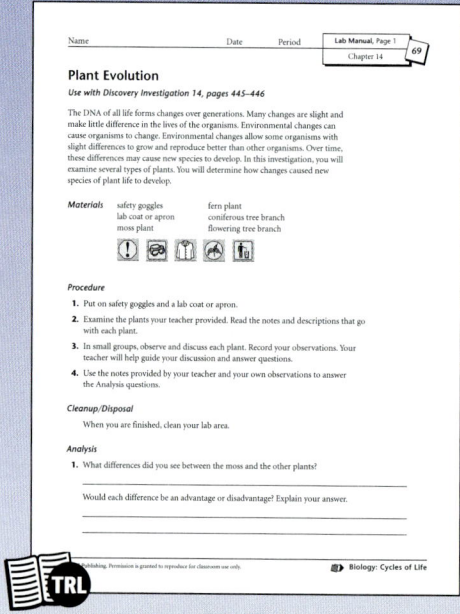

Lab Manual 69, pages 1–2

Lesson 4: Conditions That Affect Species Survival

Objectives

After reading this lesson, you should be able to
- explain the effect of mass extinction on surviving species
- describe the process of speciation in new areas
- define instantaneous speciation
- explain the genetic health of a species
- describe the current loss of species in the world

Mass extinction
The dying out of large numbers of species in a short period of time

Community
A group of different populations that live in the same area

Many factors affect the survival of species. You will learn about some of these factors in this lesson.

Mass Extinction

Scientists have found periods of **mass extinction** from the fossil record. Mass extinction is the dying out of large numbers of species in a short period of time. A species becomes extinct when its habitat is destroyed. Recall from Chapter 13 that a habitat is the place where an organism lives.

A species can become extinct if its environment changes. For example, if the ocean changed a few degrees in temperature, many organisms would die. Some species may become extinct. Other species would not become extinct. Over time, they would adapt to their new environment.

One mass extinction happened 250 million years ago. Another mass extinction happened 65 million years ago. Some scientists think a large comet or asteroid hit the earth both times. As a result, the earth's crust moved and volcanoes erupted. Hot, liquid rock inside the earth pushed up through volcanoes. Sunlight may have been blocked for many years. Plants and animals died from lack of food.

Other scientists think a gradual process of volcanic eruptions and continental drift caused the two mass extinctions. As you have learned, continental drift describes how the major landmasses of the earth move. Species that survive mass extinction fill new roles in the changed environment.

Diversity in New Areas

Species in a new area go through a cycle in populating and creating diversity. For example, after an island forms, many species move to the island. The species interact with one another. They form a **community**. A community is a group of different populations that live in the same area.

Lesson at a Glance

Chapter 14 Lesson 4

Overview In this lesson, students learn about different conditions that affect species survival.

Objectives
- To explain the effect of mass extinction on surviving species
- To describe the process of speciation in new areas
- To define *instantaneous speciation*
- To explain the genetic health of a species
- To describe the current loss of species in the world

Student Pages 447–451

Teacher's Resource Library

Workbook Activity 82–83

Alternative Workbook Activity 82–83

Lab Manual 70

Vocabulary

co-adaptation   mass extinction
community
instantaneous
  speciation

Before beginning the lesson, write the vocabulary terms on the board. Have students use the Glossary to find the definition of each term. Have students write the definition of each term before reading the lesson.

Background Information

Past extinctions are thought to have been caused by catastrophic events such as ice ages or meteors slamming into the earth's surface. Today, extinction rates are high, and biodiversity across the world is threatened. Human actions have led to habitat loss though destruction, pollution, and disruption of habitats. Some species are endangered because of overhunting or overharvesting for food and other commercial value. Other activities such as introducing new species into an established ecosystem can also bring a species to the brink of extinction.

Warm-Up Activity

Read aloud the definition of the term *community* (a group of different populations that live in the same area). Have students think about the community in which they live. Have students make a list of the different populations of organisms (including animals and plants) that are part of their community. Ask students: What might happen if any of those populations disappeared from the community? *(Answers will vary.)*

 Teaching the Lesson

Have students make an outline of the material presented in the lesson. The headings should match the main headings in the text with room for important points to be made.

I. Mass Extinction
   1.
   2.

II. Diversity in New Areas
   1.
   2.
   3.

III. Genetic Health of Species
   1.
   2.

IV. Today's Loss of Species
   1.
   2.

 Reinforce and Extend

ELL/ESL STRATEGY

 **Language Objective:** *To explore word meanings*

Have students look up the words *extinct, community, endangered,* and *instantaneous* in a dictionary. These words can all be used in everyday conversation. Have students write sentences that use the words in an everyday context.

Co-adaptation
One species becoming dependent on another species

Instantaneous speciation
A new species formed in one to several generations

Many scientists think a meteor hit the earth and caused the extinction of dinosaurs. Scientists have found a large meteor crater measuring about 112 miles (180 kilometers) in diameter on the ocean floor. This giant crater is on the Yucatan Peninsula of Mexico and in the Gulf of Mexico. The crater is the same age as the extinction of the dinosaurs.

Rapid evolution then occurs. The new populations adapt to the island's environment. Speciation occurs if members of the population are geographically isolated and do not come together to interbreed.

Scientists have found examples of speciation on the islands of Hawaii. They have found a small number of original species on the islands. These species evolved into many species over hundreds or thousands of years. That is a short time compared to evolution in other areas of the world.

Some of these new island species interacted regularly. As they continued to evolve, they underwent **co-adaptation.** Co-adaptation happens when species interact so much that they change in response to each other. Over time, these species become dependent on each other for survival.

The land along the equator has more species than areas north or south of the equator. There are more species in a large landmass than a small island. For example, South America has more species than small islands in the Pacific Ocean. The more stable an area, the more species there are in the area. This happens because the species have more time to adapt. This process results in more diversity.

A new species can be formed in a few generations. For example, plants in one generation can create offspring that cannot breed with the parent plants in only one generation. This is an example of **instantaneous speciation.**

Sympatric speciation sometimes produces new species in a short time. For example, some fruit flies breed on one kind of a plant. Others breed on a different kind of plant. Still others breed at different seasons. These differences happen because existing genes mutate or recombine in a short time. It is possible for a new species to form within a few years. Most species do not form that quickly.

TEACHER ALERT

 Students may be familiar with the term *extinction* in reference to a single species dying out. Point out that mass extinctions occur when many different species die out at about the same time. At the end of the Permian period, about 250 million years ago, a mass extinction occurred in which as many as 96 percent of all species may have died out.

Science Myth

Myth: Humans lived at the same time as dinosaurs.

Fact: Some movies and television programs show humans living at the same time as dinosaurs. However, humans did not appear on the earth until many millions of years after dinosaurs became extinct.

Genetic Health of Species

Scientists have observed that the size of a population influences the genetic health of a species. When a population falls below 100 individuals, harmful genes in the population occur in greater frequencies. This can result in death. In large populations, harmful genes occur less frequently.

Biologists think a population with 50 members is too small for genetic health. They are concerned when the population size becomes too small to remain healthy. Populations of 500 or more members usually stay healthy. In Chapter 13, for example, you learned that scientists are concerned about the small cheetah population.

Today's Loss of Species

Today, scientists around the world are concerned that some species are disappearing quickly. Species are disappearing at almost a thousand times faster than they are forming. This extinction is mainly because people are changing the environment.

In one person's lifetime, it is possible to lose half the species of the world. That would mean a huge change in a short period of time. It took thousands or millions of years for most species to develop. Scientists want to protect living things from extinction.

Link to >>>
Earth Science

Scientists have found a layer of metal called iridium in ancient rock layers. Iridium formed about the time dinosaurs disappeared. Iridium is rare on the earth, but it is very common in meteors.

Link to
Earth Science. Have students read the Link to Earth Science feature. Explain to students that the cause of the dinosaurs' mass extinction is a highly debated topic among scientists. One theory is that dinosaurs became extinct when a large meteor struck Earth about 65 million years ago, at the end of the Cretaceous period. The impact of the meteor could have caused global forest fires. The particles thrown into the atmosphere from the impact could have blocked out the Sun for months. During this time, dinosaurs became extinct and mammals began to dominate. One piece of evidence that seems to support this theory came to light in the 1980s when it was discovered that the layer of rock marking the end of the Cretaceous period contained high amounts of iridium. Iridium is rare on Earth, but very abundant in meteors. Although many scientists believe that a meteor did strike Earth, whether or not this caused dinosaur extinction is still being debated.

Science Myth

The mammals that lived at the same time as dinosaurs were tiny—about the size of mice. Dinosaurs became extinct about 65 million years ago. At this time, larger and more varied species of mammals began to evolve.

IN THE COMMUNITY

Have students investigate if there are any threatened or endangered species in their local area. If there are none, have students check the entire state. Ask students: What events led to the organism being threatened? What actions are being taken to help prevent the extinction of the species? Have students present their research to the class.

LEARNING STYLES

Logical/Mathematical
Some scientists have estimated that the world will lose as much as 20 percent of its biodiversity through extinctions in the next 30 years. Have students calculate the projected loss of the groups of organisms listed below, using the 20 percent estimate:

Currently 250,000 species of plants
Currently 20,000 species of butterflies
Currently 9,000 species of birds

(50,000 species of plants projected to be lost; 4,000 species of butterflies projected to be lost; 1,800 species of birds projected to be lost)

Lesson 4 Review Answers

1. community 2. instantaneous speciation
3. mass extinction 4. D 5. C 6. A 7. A comet or an asteroid may have struck Earth, blocking sunlight that caused the food chain to collapse. Volcanic eruptions and continental drift also may have created the extinctions. 8. A new species formed in one or two generations is an example of instantaneous speciation.
9. A larger area with a larger population is more diverse. When this happens, harmful genes occur with less frequency and the population stays healthy. 10. Scientists are seeing species become extinct about a thousand times faster than they appear.

Portfolio Assessment

Sample items include:
- Outline from Teaching the Lesson
- Research from In the Community
- Lesson 4 Review answers

LEARNING STYLES

Interpersonal/Group Learning

Present students with the following scenario and then have them debate the situation.

A proposal has been made in a rural area to build a shopping mall. The mall means more jobs will be available both during construction and after completion. The mall owner has agreed to donate a percentage of the profits from the first year of sales to the local school district. However, the remaining area of forest will have to be cleared in order to build the mall. The forest is an area where a species of hawk makes its nests and raises its young. If the forest is cleared, scientists predict that hawks of this species may become extinct. The hawk is also a predator of field mice and snakes.

Have students begin with these pros and cons and continue to make more complete lists. Have students choose a moderator for the debate.

Lesson 4   R E V I E W

Word Bank
community
instantaneous speciation
mass extinction

On a sheet of paper, write the word or words from the Word Bank that complete each question correctly.

1. A group of different populations that live in the same area is a(n) _____.
2. A new species that forms in only one generation is an example of _____.
3. The fossil record shows that periods of _____ are followed by diversity in organisms.

On a sheet of paper, write the letter of the answer that completes each sentence correctly.

4. The more stable an area, the more _____ are in the area.
   A instantaneous speciations   C mass extinctions
   B endangered species   D species

5. When organisms populate a new area and are isolated geographically from other populations of the same species, _____.
   A the population decreases   C speciation occurs
   B mass extinctions occur   D evolution slows down

6. A species becoming dependent on another species is _____.
   A co-adaptation   C population
   B instantaneous speciation   D community

Critical Thinking
On a sheet of paper, write the answers to the following questions. Use complete sentences.

7. Describe two theories for the mass extinctions that occurred 250 million and 65 million years ago.
8. What is instantaneous speciation?
9. Why is a large population generally healthier than a small population?
10. What current trends are scientists observing about speciation and extinction?

450   Chapter 14   Speciation and Punctuated Equilibrium

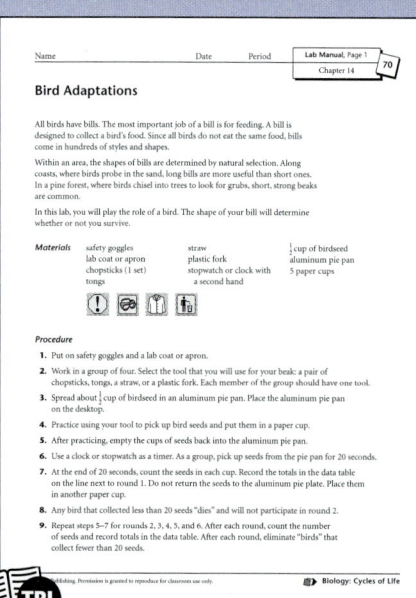

Workbook Activity 82   **Lab Manual 70, pages 1–2**

BIOLOGY IN THE WORLD

Discoveries of New Species

Scientists have identified over 2.5 million species alive on the earth today. Many more species remain to be discovered. Scientists are constantly searching for new species of plants and animals. Many places, such as rainforests, are dense with organisms and have not been fully explored by scientists.

Scientists estimate that they have identified only a small percentage of the bacteria on the earth. Bacteria and other microorganisms are too small to be observed in the environment. They must be observed under a microscope to be identified.

Not all newly discovered species are tiny. In 2001, scientists discovered a new species of evergreen tree in Vietnam. The tree, found clinging to the side of a rock, was named the Golden Vietnamese Cypress.

In 2003, British scientists discovered a new plant species. They named the species *Senecio eboracensis*. The plant resulted from the mating of two different weed plants. It evolved into a separate species. This happened because of a change in the plant's flowering time. It flowered at a different time than the parent plants and could no longer reproduce with them.

The discovery of new plant species provides information about the environment and ecosystem they belong to. Plants are also a common source of medicine. Finding new plants may lead to the creation of important new medical treatments.

1. Why are many species undiscovered?
2. What caused the plant discovered in Britain to be considered a separate species?
3. What benefits can result from the discovery of new plant species?

Speciation and Punctuated Equilibrium Chapter 14

ONLINE CONNECTION

 Students can find information about the threatened and endangered species of plants and animals in the United States at this Web site of the U. S. Fish & Wildlife Service at http://endangered.fws.gov/wildlife.html.

BIOLOGY IN THE WORLD

Have volunteers read aloud the Biology in the World feature. Discuss the importance of discovering new species of microorganisms, plants, and animals.

Biology in the World Answers

1. They live in areas, such as rain forests, that have not been fully explored. **2.** It evolved separately until it was unable to reproduce with the parent plants. **3.** New species provide information about the ecosystem they belong to, and they may be used to make new medicines.

IN THE ENVIRONMENT

 Have students research new species that have recently been discovered. Have students answer questions such as the following: What characteristics does it have? Where can it be found? What type of habitat does it live in? Other students might examine the "big picture" of species discovery by researching questions such as the following: What percentage of species is estimated to still be undiscovered? How does habitat destruction threaten the discovery of new species? Have students present a report on their research to the class.

GLOBAL CONNECTION

 The area of Vietnam where the golden Vietnamese cypress tree was discovered is biologically diverse. The team of scientists that discovered the tree has found many other new species of plants in the area. Other new plants include species of orchids, shrubs, and herbs. The team has scientists from the United States, Vietnam, Russia, and the United Kingdom. Dr. Nguyen Tien Hiep is the coordinator of the Vietnam Botanical Project. One of his areas of expertise is conifers.

Chapter 14 Summary

Have volunteers read aloud each summary item on page 452. Ask volunteers to explain the meaning of each item. Direct students' attention to the Vocabulary box on the bottom of page 452. Have them read and review each term and its definition.

Graphic Organizer

As students read chapter 14, have them finish completing the chart on Graphic Organizer 14: Speciation and Punctuated Equilibrium. Encourage students to read each lesson of the chapter and then have them fill in the portion of the chart that pertains to the lesson. When they have completed the chart, ask them to answer the questions.

Chapter 14 SUMMARY

- Scientists classify all organisms into groups. Scientists use morphology, biochemistry, body functions, and behavior to classify organisms.

- A species is the first level of classification. Members of the same species are very similar to each other. They can breed with one another to produce fertile offspring.

- Scientists classify sexually reproducing species by the biological species concept. They classify asexually reproducing species by the ecological species concept.

- Living things change over time. New species sometimes emerge as a result of these changes. Mechanisms of speciation include allopatric speciation and sympatric speciation.

- Scientists give every species a two-part scientific name. The scientific name is made up of the genus and the species.

- Scientists use the Linneaus system to classify animals and plants. Each organism belongs to seven levels. These levels, from general to specific, are: kingdom, phylum, class, order, family, genus, and species.

- Speciation, or the creation of new species, happens when a single species becomes two or more species. Speciation usually occurs because two populations of the same species separate. They evolve and cannot breed with each other.

- Speciation often follows periods of mass extinction. Populations that survive take over new resources.

- Currently, scientists believe that species are disappearing much faster than new species are emerging.

Vocabulary

allopatric speciation, 431
Archaea, 436
asexual reproduction, 431
biochemistry, 429
biological species concept, 430
classify, 428
co-adaptation, 448
community, 447
coordinated stasis, 442
division, 434
ecological species concept, 431
Eukarya, 436
fertile, 429
genus, 434
instantaneous speciation, 429
interbreed, 430
kingdom, 434
mammary gland, 428
mass extinction, 447
morphology, 428
niche, 431
phylum, 434
punctuated equilibrium, 441
reproductively isolated, 429
stasis, 441
subpopulation, 432
subspecies, 431
sympatric speciation, 431
three-domain system, 436

452 Chapter 14 Speciation and Punctuated Equilibrium

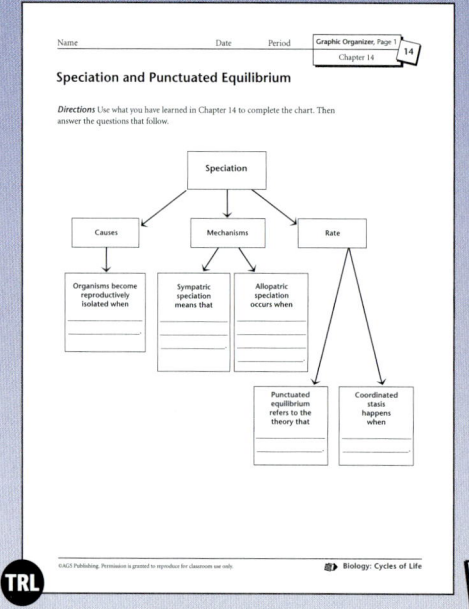

Graphic Organizer 14, pages 1–3

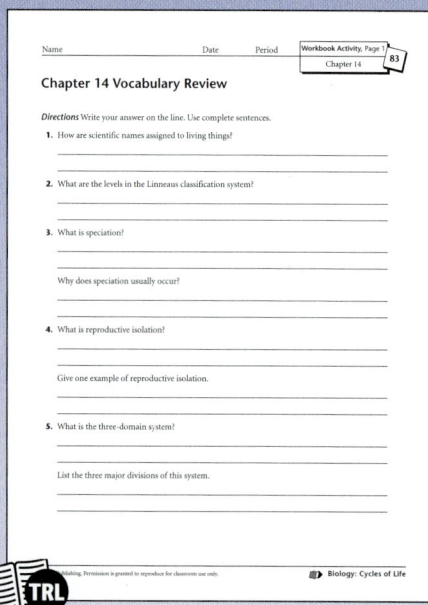

Workbook Activity 83, pages 1–3

Chapter 14 REVIEW

Word Bank
- allopatric speciation
- Archaea
- asexual reproduction
- co-adaptation
- coordinated stasis
- Eukarya
- genus
- kingdom
- mass extinction
- morphology
- niche
- punctuated equilibrium
- reproductively isolated
- stasis
- subspecies
- sympatric speciation
- three-domain system

Vocabulary Review

On a sheet of paper, write the word or words from the Word Bank that best complete each sentence.

1. Reproduction that involves one parent and no egg or sperm is _____.
2. A system that classifies all living things into three broad groups is the _____.
3. A theory that states species stay the same for a long time, then new species suddenly evolve due to global changes and mass extinctions is _____.
4. The study of differences in body forms of organisms is _____.
5. A population in _____ is not changing.
6. Two populations that were separated by a barrier become different species through _____.
7. A subpopulation becomes a different species by being reproductively isolated even when living with the parent population through _____.
8. A(n) _____ describes the way of life a species, or how a species adapts to its role in its environment.
9. The domain of prokaryotic organisms that are not bacteria is _____.
10. The domain of eukaryotic organisms is _____.
11. A group of similar phyla is a(n) _____.
12. A group of similar species is a(n) _____.
13. A(n) _____ occurs when large numbers of species disappear suddenly.

Review continued on next page

Speciation and Punctuated Equilibrium Chapter 14 453

Review Answers
14. subspecies 15. coordinated stasis
16. reproductively isolated
17. co-adaptation

Teacher Alert

In the Chapter Review, the Vocabulary Review activity includes a sample of the chapter's vocabulary terms. The activity will help determine students' understanding of key vocabulary terms and concepts presented in the chapter. Other vocabulary terms used in the chapter are listed below.

biochemistry	fertile
biological species concept	instantaneous speciation
classify	interbreed
community	mammary gland
division	phylum
ecological species concept	subpopulation

Concept Review
18. C 19. D 20. B 21. C 22. B

Chapter 14 REVIEW - continued

14. A division of a species is called a(n) _____.

15. A pattern where most species appear at about the same pattern is _____.

16. Two populations of birds that no longer reproduce with each other are _____.

17. Species that are dependent on each other have developed _____.

Concept Review
On a sheet of paper, write the letter of the answer that best completes each sentence.

18. In the species name *Homo sapiens*, the word *Homo* is the name of the _____.

  A kingdom **B** family **C** genus **D** species

19. If parents belong to the same _____, they can produce fertile offspring.

  A kingdom **B** speciation **C** niche **D** species

20. Sympatric speciation means that subpopulations _____.

  A are reproductively isolated while living among the parent population

  B are geographically separated form the parent population

  C can breed with each other to produce fertile offspring

  D are created due to a period of mass extinctions

21. A species that survives mass extinction _____.

  A eventually becomes extinct

  B becomes weak

  C diversifies to fill niches

  D undergoes a period of stasis

454   Chapter 14   *Speciation and Punctuated Equilibrium*

22. Scientists classify sexually reproducing species by the _____.

   A ecological species concept
   B biological species concept
   C punctuated equilibrium theory
   D coordinated stasis pattern

Critical Thinking

On a sheet of paper, write the answers to the following questions. Use complete sentences.

23. Place these seven classification levels of Linnaeus in order from the most specific to the most general: class, family, genus, kingdom, order, phylum, species.

24. A biologist is studying a new tree whose leaves are the same shape as another familiar tree. Should the biologist classify the new tree as the same species as the familiar tree? Explain your answer.

25. How do mass extinctions cause diversity in other species?

Research and Write

Use the Internet and print resources to select a country in which species are becoming extinct. Identify and investigate some endangered species. What are people doing to preserve plant and animal diversity in that country? Share your research with the class.

 **Test-Taking Tip** When studying for a test, learn the most important points. Practice writing this material or explaining it to someone else.

Speciation and Punctuated Equilibrium Chapter 14 455

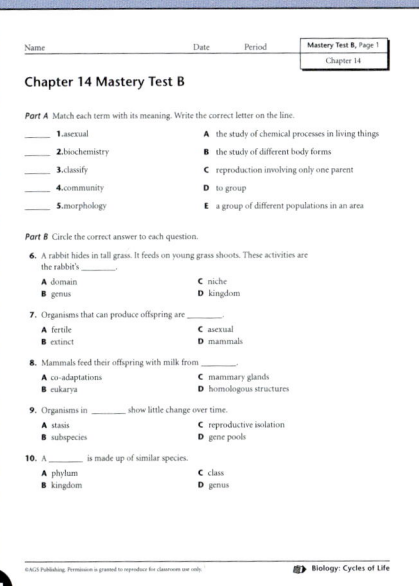

Chapter 14 Mastery Test B, pages 1–3

Critical Thinking

23. The seven levels from the most specific to the most general are kingdom, phylum, class, order, family, genus, and species. 24. The biologist should not classify the tree as the same species based on leaf shape alone. Scientists consider a number of factors when assigning an organism to a species. Leaf shape alone is not enough. They consider other characteristics such as flower color, bark, and buds. 25. A mass extinction like the dinosaurs causes more resources and geographic area to be available to the surviving species. These species then spread out and become isolated from each other, creating diversification and causing speciation that results in large numbers of new species.

Research and Write

A Web site students may find helpful for this assignment is http://species.enviroweb.org/oes.html, which has links to lists of endangered species by country. They can also visit the National Geographic Society's Web site at www.nationalgeographic.com/wildworld, which highlights 200 of the world's most endangered areas and ecosystems.

ALTERNATIVE ASSESSMENT

Alternative Assessment items correlate to the student Goals for Learning at the beginning of this chapter.

- Have students define the biological species concept and the ecological species concept. Have them explain why scientists need two different methods to define a species.
- Have students identify the three different classification systems used by scientists and give details of how the systems differ.
- Have students compare and contrast the different theories of how speciation occurs: through gradual evolutionary changes, through punctuated equilibrium, or through coordinated stasis.
- Have students list different environmental conditions or events that impact the survival of a species and explain their impact.

Speciation and Punctuated Equilibrium 455

Chapter 15

Planning Guide
Phylogenies and Classifying Diversity

	Student Pages	Vocabulary	Lesson Review	Critical-Thinking Questions
Lesson 1 How Do Scientists Classify Living Things?	458–463	✔	✔	✔
Lesson 2 The Kingdom Protista	464–467	✔	✔	✔
Lesson 3 The Kingdom Fungi	468–471	✔	✔	✔
Lesson 4 The Kingdom Plantae	472–478	✔	✔	✔
Lesson 5 The Kingdom Animalia	479–481	✔	✔	✔
Lesson 6 Invertebrates	482–488	✔	✔	✔
Lesson 7 Vertebrates	489–496	✔	✔	✔
Lesson 8 Humans	497–499	✔	✔	✔

Chapter Activities

Teacher's Resource Library
Community Connection 15:
  Grocery Store Plants and Animals
Graphic Organizer 15:
  Phylogenies and Classifying Diversity

Teacher's Edition
Opener Activity

Assessment Options

Student Text
Chapter 15 Review

Teacher's Resource Library
Chapter 15 Mastery Tests A and B

Teacher's Edition
Chapter 15 Alternative Assessment

Student Text Features									Teaching Strategies						Learning Styles					Teacher's Resource Library			
Achievements in Science	Science at Work	Biology in Your Life	Investigation/Discovery	Biology in the World	Express Lab	Link to	Research and Write	Technology and Society	ELL/ESL Strategy	Background Information	Science Journal	Applications (Home, Career, Community, Global, Environment)	Online Connection	Teacher Alert	Auditory/Verbal	Body/Kinesthetic	Interpersonal/Group Learning	Logical/Mathematical	Visual/Spatial	Workbook Activities	Alternative Workbook Activities	Lab Manual	Self-Study Guide
			462		460	✔			460	458				459					459	84	84	71–72	✔
466						✔			465	464				466		466				85	85		✔
			470			✔			469	468		469–471								86	86	73	✔
	474					✔			473	472			475	474, 477	476	475	477			87	87		✔
									480	479	480									88	88	74	✔
								484	485	482				486		483		487	487	89	89		✔
				495		✔			492	489	493	491							493	90	90	75	✔
			499			✔	503		498	497				499						91–92	91–92		✔

Pronunciation Key

a	hat	e	let	ī	ice	ô	order	ủ	put	sh	she
ā	age	ē	equal	o	hot	oi	oil	ü	rule	th	thin
ä	far	ėr	term	ō	open	ou	out	ch	child	ŦH	then
â	care	i	it	ȯ	saw	u	cup	ng	long	zh	measure

ə { a in about / e in taken / i in pencil / o in lemon / u in circus }

Alternative Workbook Activities

The Teacher's Resource Library (TRL) contains a set of lower-level worksheets called Alternative Workbook Activities. These worksheets cover the same content as the regular Workbook Activities but are written at a second-grade reading level.

Skill Track Online

Use Skill Track Online for *Biology: Cycles of Life* to monitor student progress and meet the demands of adequate yearly progress (AYP). Make informed instructional decisions with individual student and class reports of online lesson and chapter assessments. With immediate and ongoing feedback, students will also see what they have learned and where they need more reinforcement and practice.

Chapter at a Glance

Chapter 15: Phylogenies and Classifying Diversity
pages 456–503

Lessons

1. **How Do Scientists Classify Living Things?** pages 458–463

    Investigation 15 pages 462–463

2. **The Kingdom Protista** pages 464–467

3. **The Kingdom Fungi** pages 468–471

4. **The Kingdom Plantae** pages 472–478

5. **The Kingdom Animalia** pages 479–481

6. **Invertebrates** pages 482–488

7. **Vertebrates** pages 489–496

    Discovery Investigation 15 pages 495–496

8. **Humans** pages 497–499

    Biology in the World page 499

Chapter 15 Summary page 500

Chapter 15 Review pages 501–503

Audio CD

Skill Track Online for Biology: Cycles of Life

Teacher's Resource Library TRL

- Workbook Activities 84–92
- Alternative Workbook Activities 84–92
- Lab Manual 71–75
- Community Connection 15
- Graphic Organizer 15
- Resource File 35–36
- Chapter 15 Self-Study Guide
- Chapter 15 Mastery Tests A and B

(Answer Keys for the Teacher's Resource Library begin on page 675 of the Teacher's Edition. The Materials List for the Lab Manual activities begins on page 720.)

Opener Activity

Tell students that this chapter is about how living organisms are classified into levels of organization. Lead a class discussion of other classification systems and make a list on the board of student responses. For example, students may have heard of the Dewey decimal classification system used in libraries.

Community Connection 15

Chapter 15
Phylogenies and Classifying Diversity

A patch of mushrooms grows on the tree trunk in this photograph. The mushrooms began with the growth of a single spore. Then they appeared when conditions were right for reproduction. Scientists think life on the earth began with one living cell. Life then spread throughout the earth's surface. The millions of different species we see today gradually replaced earlier, simpler life-forms. In Chapter 15, you will learn about the evolutionary history, or phylogeny, of the major groups of living things. You will also learn how biologists classify living things.

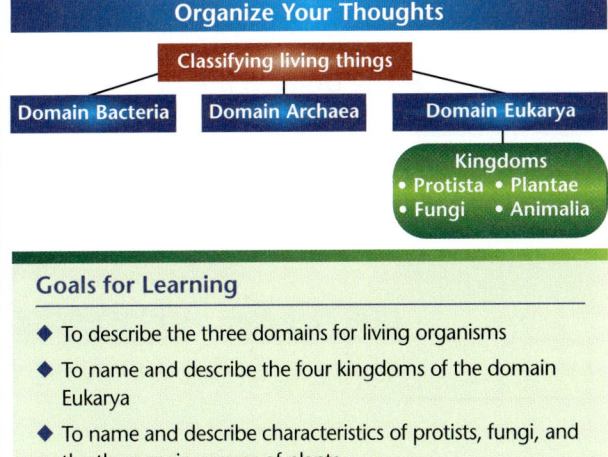

Goals for Learning

- To describe the three domains for living organisms
- To name and describe the four kingdoms of the domain Eukarya
- To name and describe characteristics of protists, fungi, and the three main groups of plants
- To list the eight common features of animals and to describe the characteristics of invertebrates and vertebrates

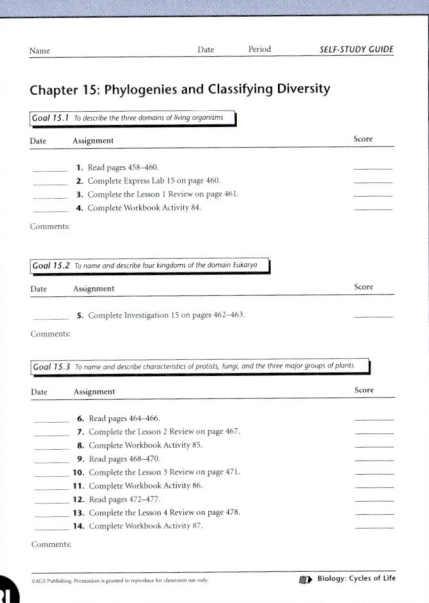

Chapter 15 Self-Study Guide

Introducing the Chapter

Remind students that they can refer back to page x for a step-by-step guide to beginning a new chapter.

Ask students: How many different plants can you name? What are some characteristics they share? What are some characteristics that make them different from one another? Explain to students that scientists have classified living things into a system that shows both biological diversity and organization.

Have students make a chart listing each of the Goals for Learning as a column heading. Encourage them to fill in each column with appropriate information as they read the chapter.

Notes and Math Tips

Ask volunteers to read the notes and math tips that appear in the margins throughout the chapter. Then discuss them with the class.

TEACHER'S RESOURCE

The AGS Publishing Teaching Strategies in Science Transparencies may be used with this chapter. The transparencies add an interactive dimension to expand and enhance the *Biology: Cycles of Life* program content.

CAREER INTEREST INVENTORY

The AGS Publishing Harrington-O'Shea Career Decision-Making System-Revised (CDM) may be used with this chapter. Students can use the CDM to explore their interests and identify careers. The CDM defines career areas that are indicated by students' responses on the inventory.

Phylogenies and Classifying Diversity

Lesson at a Glance

Chapter 15 Lesson 1

Overview In this lesson, students learn about taxonomy as they are introduced to the domains Bacteria, Archaea, and Eukarya.

Objectives
- To name the three domains for classifying living things
- To describe the kinds of organisms that belong to each domain

Student Pages 458–463

Teacher's Resource Library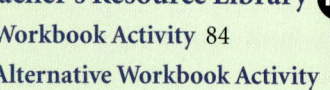
- Workbook Activity 84
- Alternative Workbook Activity 84
- Lab Manual 71–72

Vocabulary
taxonomist
taxonomy

Ask students to look up the vocabulary terms in a dictionary. Instruct them to note what part of speech each term is. Then have them use the two terms in one sentence.

Background Information

The convention of classifying living things by assigning them two-part Latin names is called binomial nomenclature. According to this system, an organism is assigned a genus name and an epithet, or descriptor. A genus is a larger group of living organisms made up of similar species. A species is the most specific level of organization for the classification system. Together, the two constitute an organism's scientific name, or species name. It is written in italics, with the genus name capitalized. For instance, the scientific name for humans is *Homo sapiens*. However, as technology improves and DNA analysis becomes more common, organisms once grouped together because of shared features are reshuffled within the evolving taxonomic hierarchy.

Lesson 1  How Do Scientists Classify Living Things?

Objectives

After reading this lesson, you should be able to
- name the three domains for classifying living things
- describe the kinds of organisms that belong to each domain

Taxonomy
The science of classifying organisms based on the features they share

Taxonomist
A scientist who classifies and assigns scientific names to organisms

Humans have about 100,000 million bacteria living in every square centimeter of their skin.

In Chapter 13, you learned that scientists use different systems to group and classify organisms. **Taxonomy** is the science of classifying organisms based on features they share.

Taxonomists classify and assign scientific names to organisms. They assign a two-part Latin name to each species. They classify species according to several classification systems. You will study the three-domain system in this chapter.

The Three-Domain Classification System

Taxonomists use three domains to represent the highest level of classification. Figure 15.1.1 shows the three domains: bacteria, archaea, and eukarya. As you learned in Chapter 14, taxonomists classify living things into other levels. After grouping organisms into a domain, they classify organisms into kingdom, then phylum (for animals) or division (for plants and fungi). The next levels are class, order, family, genus, and species. In this chapter, you will learn about the features of each domain and kingdom. You will also learn about the evolutionary history and features of some animal phyla and plant divisions.

The Domain Bacteria

Recall from Chapter 1 that bacteria are the simplest single cells that carry out all basic life activities. There are thousands of species of bacteria. Bacterial cells live as individuals or in clusters. Some bacteria move. Others never move.

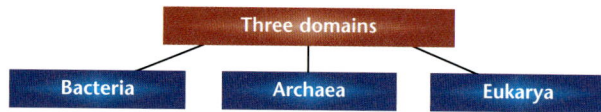

Figure 15.1.1 *Scientists classify living things into three domains.*

458 Chapter 15 Phylogenies and Classifying Diversity

Bacteria are prokaryotes. Bacterial cells do not have a nucleus or other organelles. Bacteria have cell walls like plants. However, their cell walls lack a protein found in plant cell walls. Bacteria live on or in nearly every material and environment on the earth. They live in soil, water, and air.

Some bacteria perform photosynthesis. They make food from sunlight and get rid of oxygen. Other bacteria absorb food from the material they live on or in. Some bacteria can cause disease in animals.

Other bacteria are helpful. For example, millions of *E. coli* bacteria live in the stomach. They help the body digest food. They also produce some vitamins the body needs.

The Domain Archaea

Archaea are prokaryotes that look like bacteria. Although archaea have genes like eukaryotes, their genes are only found in the domain Archaea. Many archaea live in extreme conditions. For example, some live in polar ice or very salty conditions such as the Dead Sea in Jordan. Archaea have molecules and enzymes that protect them from extreme temperatures and harsh conditions. Many archaea also live in ordinary temperatures and conditions. Archaea have a pigment in their cells that reacts with light to make ATP.

The Domain Eukarya

All eukaryotes belong to the domain Eukarya. Some eukaryotes are single-celled organisms. Others have many cells that do different tasks. Taxonomists classify eukaryotes as animals, plants, fungi, or protists. Recall that protists are one-celled organisms and have plantlike or animal-like properties.

Eukaryotic cells are usually larger than prokaryotic cells. Every eukaryotic cell has organelles that include a nucleus, DNA, chromosomes, and ribosomes. Most eukaryotes also have Golgi apparatus and mitochondria. Plants and algae have chloroplasts that carry out photosynthesis.

The Dead Sea is located at the lowest point on the earth's surface, 390 meters (about 1,300 feet) below sea level.

 Warm-Up Activity

Have students read and perform the Express Lab on page 460. As students create classification systems in the Express Lab, it may be helpful to provide examples of features that can be used as criteria. For instance, the type of pet (fish, dog, cat), the color, the size, the breed, and the length of hair are all features that can be used to group pets into a classification system.

Express Lab Answers

1. Students may consider such things as color, size, number of legs, amount of hair, what the pet eats, etc. **2.** Both the students' and scientists' classification systems are based on physical observations about the organisms. The students' classification system is limited to very basic observations, while a biological classification system uses more in-depth information such as chemical composition, DNA analysis, and evolutionary relationships.

 Teaching the Lesson

Have students create an outline for this lesson's content. Encourage them to use heads and topic sentences for main ideas. They might also create a three-column chart with the headings "Domain Bacteria," "Domain Archaea," and "Domain Eukarya." They can then put information in the appropriate column.

 **Reinforce and Extend**

TEACHER ALERT

 Students may be surprised to learn that *E. coli* is helpful in digestion. They may be more familiar with a strain of the bacteria called *E. coli* 0157:H7, which receives more media attention because it causes severe illness.

LEARNING STYLES

Visual/Spatial
Have students arrange the levels of taxonomic organization in a vertical flowchart, ranging from the most general down to the most specific level. *(domain, kingdom [phylum or division], class, order, family, genus, species)* They can also add descriptions of each level to their flowcharts.

ELL/ESL Strategy

Language Objective: *To explain the structure of a classification system*

Divide the class into small groups. Assign each group one of the three domains. Remind students how words such as *highest* and *next* indicate a sequence or hierarchy. Encourage students to substitute their own words and prepare a presentation explaining the structure of their assigned domain. Tell students to provide analogies in their presentations.

Link to

Health. Have students read the Link to Health feature. Explain that chemistry is important to taxonomy because DNA and RNA are chemical compounds containing genetic information. Genetic information, in turn, is fundamental to classifying organisms. However, viruses, despite having genetic information, are not classified as living things. Viruses invade the cells of living organisms and use host cells' organelles to reproduce.

Pronunciation Guide

Use the pronunciation shown here to help students pronounce a difficult word in this lesson. Refer to the pronunciation key on the Chapter Planning Guide for the sounds of the symbols.

retrovirus (re′trō vī′rəs)

Link to ≫≫≫
Health

Viruses are not living, but they have their own genetic material. Viruses contain DNA or RNA. A subset of RNA viruses are retroviruses. The HIV virus that causes AIDS is a retrovirus.

Many eukaryotes have flagella for movement or cilia to sense the environment. Reproduction occurs by mitosis. In most eukaryotic animals and plants, sexual reproduction occurs by meiosis. You will learn more about the domain Eukarya later in this chapter.

Nonliving Viruses

Recall that viruses are not living things. Taxonomists do not classify them in a domain. As you know, a virus is made up of genetic material inside a capsid, a protein coat. Viruses are everywhere. They infect all types of living things. However, viruses are specific to certain living things. For example, plant viruses infect certain plants cells and not animal cells. Scientists classify viruses by the kind of organism they infect, their shape, and the molecules they use.

Express Lab 15

Materials
◆ pictures of pets

Procedure
1. Bring to class a photograph, drawing, or magazine picture of a pet.
2. Using all of the pictures brought by your classmates, create your own classification system for the pets. Organize them in a way that makes sense. Create three or more different levels of organization.
3. Create an organizational chart for your classification system.

Analysis
1. On what features did you base your classification system?
2. How is your classification system similar to the three-domain system? How is it different?

460 Chapter 15 Phylogenies and Classifying Diversity

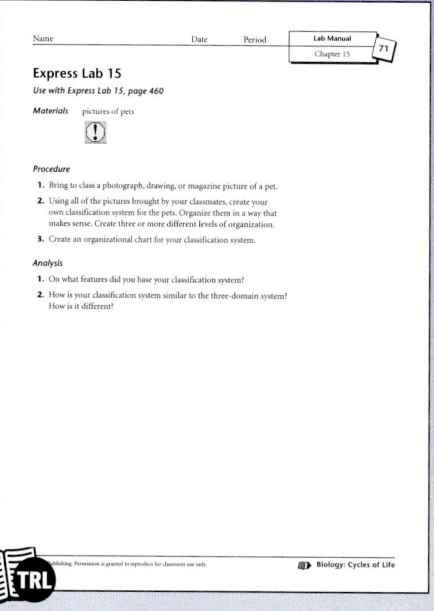

Lesson 1 REVIEW

Word Bank
archaea
domain
living
taxonomist

On a sheet of paper, write the word from the Word Bank that completes each sentence correctly.

1. Viruses are not _____ things and are not classified in a _____.
2. A _____ classifies and assigns scientific names to organisms.
3. Many _____ live in extreme conditions.

On a sheet of paper, write the letter of the answer that completes each sentence correctly.

4. _____ are members of the domain Eukarya.
   A Fungi   **B** Bacteria   **C** Virus   **D** Archaea

5. In most eukaryotic cells, sexual reproduction is by _____.
   A ribosomes   **B** mitosis   **C** meiosis   **D** pigments

6. The science of classifying organisms based on shared features is _____.
   A ecology   **C** biogeography
   B paleontology **D** taxonomy

Critical Thinking

On a sheet of paper, answer the following questions. Use complete sentences.

7. Compare the organisms that make up the domain Bacteria and the domain Archaea.
8. How can bacteria be helpful? How can they be harmful?
9. You are given a sample of single-celled organisms. You must classify the sample as bacteria or eukarya. By using a microscope, what clues could you look for?
10. People cannot be infected by a virus carried by a plant. Explain why.

Phylogenies and Classifying Diversity Chapter 15 461

Lesson 1 Review Answers

1. living, domain **2.** taxonomist **3.** archaea **4.** A **5.** C **6.** D **7.** Both are mostly single-celled. Both are prokaryotes. The genes of archaeans are different from bacteria, and archaeans can live in environments that most other organisms cannot tolerate. **8.** Some bacteria produce needed vitamins for the human body. Other bacteria can be harmful by causing disease. **9.** You would look for a cell nucleus or other cell organelles. If the cell has any of these organelles, you know it belongs to Domain Eukarya. **10.** Viruses are specific for different types of organisms. Plant viruses cannot infect animals, and animal viruses cannot infect plants.

Portfolio Assessment

Sample items include:
- Flowchart from Learning Styles Visual/Spatial
- Presentation from ELL/ESL Strategy
- Lesson 1 Review answers

LAB ACTIVITIES

Chapter 15 has Investigation and Discovery Investigation lab activities. Two additional lab activities for Chapter 15 appear in the Biology: Cycles of Life Lab Manual and on the Teacher's Resource Library CD-ROM.

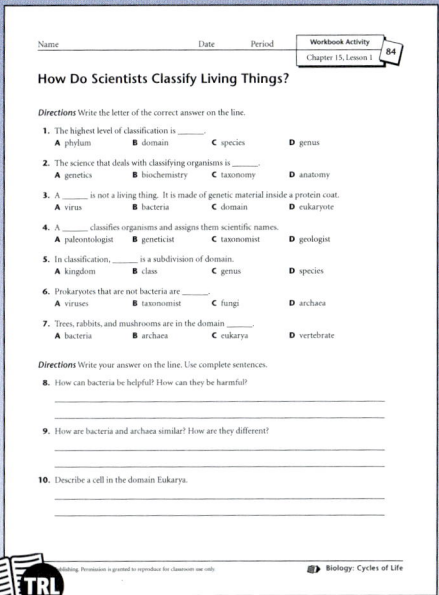

Workbook Activity 84

Phylogenies and Classifying Diversity 461

Investigation 15

Encourage students to read the Investigation steps. Discuss questions they may have before beginning the investigation.

Objectives

- To classify organisms based on their similarities and differences
- To make a classification chart based on observations

Skills

Observing, inferring, organizing information, comparing, contrasting

Background

Providing students with a variety of examples of organisms with classification information allows them to observe how classification works. With assistance from classification labels that are provided with the samples, students can make their own classification charts, using the same logic that scientists use.

Time Frame

One class period

Procedure

- Have students work together in small groups to complete the activity.
- Use photographs or live specimens for the organisms. Use photographs for organisms such as archaeans and animals that cannot be used as live specimens.
- Put a classification card that shows how the organism is classified from domain to species next to each specimen. Include as large an assortment of organisms as can be managed effectively in class. Be sure to include specimens from each domain and each kingdom. Try to include at least two samples that are classified the same all the way down to the genus so that students can observe that some organisms are very closely related. Your list of pictures or specimens might include two different plants, an insect, a picture of any animal, a mushroom (from grocery store), a bacteria slide set up under a microscope, (or a picture of bacteria) algae, and a picture of archaea.

INVESTIGATION 15

Materials
- pictures of different organisms

Classifying Organisms

Scientists classify all organisms by domain, kingdom, phylum or division, class, order, family, genus, and species. In this investigation, you will see that the more related organisms are, the higher the classification level they share.

Procedure

1. Note the differences and similarities between the organisms in the pictures.

2. On a sheet of paper, make a classification chart. To start, list the three domains. Choose one organism from the pictures to represent each domain. List each organism next to its domain on your chart. Write a brief description of each organism and why it is classified in its domain.

3. Choose one organism from the pictures to represent each kingdom. List these on your classification chart. Write a brief description of each organism and why it is classified in its kingdom.

4. List the remaining organisms from the pictures on your chart.

SAFETY ALERT

- Take care with any live specimens that could be dangerous.
- Be sure bacteria are sealed in petri dishes and are not opened.
- Be sure students do not handle any specimens.
- Be aware of student allergies to guide your choice of which plant and animal specimens to include. Although you should strive to use as many live specimens as possible, substitute photographs for any organisms that could be troublesome or impractical to have live in class.

Cleanup/Disposal
When you are finished, be sure your lab area is clean.

Analysis
1. What differences did you see in the sizes of the organisms in the three domains?
2. Where are the organisms in each domain usually found?

Conclusions
1. What features do scientists use to classify organisms into domains?
2. What differences did you notice between organisms in different kingdoms?

Explore Further
Say that you have discovered a new species. Make some notes about this new organism. Include its size, where it lives, and how and what it eats. Trade your information with a classmate. Decide how you would classify each other's organisms.

Cleanup/Disposal
Instruct students in proper cleaning and disposal of materials.

Analysis Answers
1. Students should notice that organisms in domains Archaea and Bacteria are small and single-celled, while organisms in domain Eukarya are mostly larger and multicelled.
2. Bacteria are found almost everywhere, although they are too small to be seen without a microscope. Eukaryans inhabit a variety of environments. Archaeans are found in extreme conditions, such as very hot, very cold, or extremely salty environments.

Conclusions Answers
1. Scientists use information about the cells that make up an organism to classify the organisms into the domains.
2. Answers will vary. Students should make general observations about some kingdoms, such as that the organisms in kingdom Plantae are green and photosynthetic.

Explore Further Answers
Students can create and interpret the key characteristics that allow classification with their organisms.

Assessment
You might include the following items from this investigation in student portfolios:
- Classification table
- Answers to Analysis and Conclusions questions
- Answers to Explore Further

Lesson at a Glance

Chapter 15 Lesson 2

Overview In this lesson, students learn about the kingdom Protista.

Objectives

- To name the four kingdoms in the domain Eukarya
- To describe the kingdom Protista
- To describe features of three types of protists
- To name three classification levels in the kingdom Protista
- To describe features of algae
- To describe features of slime molds

Student Pages 464–467

Teacher's Resource Library TRL

Workbook Activity 85
Alternative Workbook Activity 85
Resource File 35

Vocabulary

algae	protozoan
amoeba	pseudopod
dysentery	slime mold
euglena	spore

Make a word search puzzle on the board. Then ask students to raise their hands as they locate vocabulary terms in the puzzle. Invite students to come to the board and circle the terms they can identify.

Background Information

The kingdom Protista is, in some respects, a sort of miscellaneous category of taxonomic organization. It now includes protozoa, some types of plankton, algae, and some other random organisms that cannot be classified as a plant, an animal, a fungus, or a bacterium. Some scientists think the kingdom Protista should be divided into separate kingdoms.

Lesson 2 The Kingdom Protista

Objectives

After reading this lesson, you should be able to

- ◆ name the four kingdoms in the domain Eukarya
- ◆ describe the kingdom Protista
- ◆ describe features of three types of protists
- ◆ name three classification levels in the kingdom Protista
- ◆ describe features of algae
- ◆ describe features of slime molds

Protozoan
A protist that ingests food and usually lives in water (plural is protozoa)

Algae
A protist that makes its own food and usually lives in water

Euglena
A protist that make its own food

The domain Eukarya has four kingdoms: Protista, Fungi, Plantae, and Animalia. This lesson will discuss the kingdom Protista. The kingdom Protista is made up of many eukaryotic organisms such as protozoa, **algae, euglenas,** and **slime molds.** Most protists are one-celled organisms. A few have many cells. Some protists make their own food. Others absorb food from outside sources. All protists carry out basic life activities.

Protozoa

A **protozoan** is an animal-like protist that moves. Protozoa have stomach-like parts for digesting food. Some protozoa have properties of animals and plants. They behave like animals by getting food and moving. They eat bacteria, other protozoa, and fungi. In turn, they give off nitrogen, an element needed by plants. Some protozoa make their own food in sunlight. There are about 65,000 species of protozoa. They live in many different environments.

Most protozoa are harmless. A few can cause disease. For example, a type of **amoeba** can live in the human intestines. It feeds on red blood cells and causes **dysentery,** a disease of the intestines.

There are three groups of protozoa. The largest group is the ciliates. These one-celled organisms have cilia, or hairlike structures that help them move around. An example of a ciliate is the paramecium. Look at Figure 15.2.1 on page 465. The paramecium is covered by cilia. The cilia move the paramecium through water and sweep food into its mouthlike opening.

The second group of protozoa is the amoebas. Find the amoeba in Figure 15.2.1. Amoebas move by **pseudopods.** A pseudopod sticks out like a foot and pulls an amoeba along. Amoebas also use their pseudopod to surround food and bring it inside.

464 Chapter 15 Phylogenies and Classifying Diversity

Amoeba
A protozoan that moves by pushing out parts of its cell

Dysentery
A disease of the intestines

Pseudopod
A part of some one-celled organisms that sticks out like a foot and moves the cell along

The third group is the flagellates. They are the smallest protozoa. They have one or more flagella. Recall that flagella are long, whiplike tails that help move protozoa and other organisms through water.

The euglena in Figure 15.2.1 is a flagellate. One flagellum is shown. Euglenas behave like both plants and animals. Like plants, they make their own food in sunlight. Like animals, they absorb food from the environment. They absorb food when sunlight is not present.

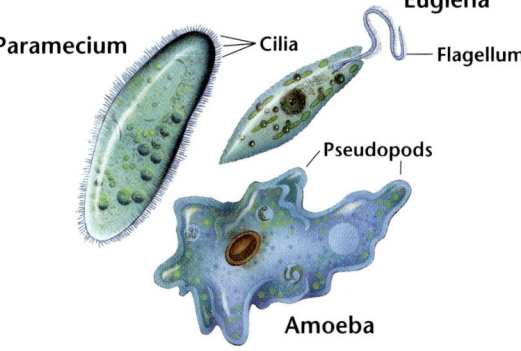

Figure 15.2.1 *Protozoa probably evolved about 1.5 billion years ago.*

Link to
Language Arts
The word *protozoa* means "first animals." Protozoans are probably the ancestors of modern animals.

Algae range in size from microscopic organisms to large seaweed. Some seaweed can grow as long as a football field.

Other Protists

Brown algae belong to the division Phaeophyta. They are the largest and most complex algae. They are often called seaweed. There are also red algae and green algae species. Algae are plant-like protists. They grow in moist areas, on trees, and on rocks. Most algae live in fresh water and saltwater. You may have seen algae that grow as a green scum on a pond or lake. The green scum is thousands of tiny algae.

Some algae get their nutrients from living things. For example, *Pfiesteria* produces harmful substances that stun passing fish and cause bleeding sores. *Pfiesteria* feed on the fish blood and fluids. Most algae make their own food. They use energy from sunlight and release oxygen. Algae produce a large amount of the oxygen that other organisms use. However, algae are not plants because they do not have roots, stems, or leaves.

Phylogenies and Classifying Diversity Chapter 15 **465**

 Warm-Up Activity

Have volunteers bring in samples of water from a local pond or stream. Instruct groups of students to mount a drop of water on a slide and then analyze it under a microscope. Ask them to use Figure 15.2.1 to try and identify any protists in the water sample. Alternatively, you could obtain a prepared microscope slide set for students to use with a microscope.

 Teaching the Lesson

Have students create an outline to organize the taxonomic hierarchy discussed in this lesson. Remind them to include the main ideas from each paragraph, as well as detail statements.

 Reinforce and Extend

ELL/ESL Strategy

 **Language Objective:** *To describe the features of a protozoa*

Have students work in small groups to make a poster showing one type of protozoa. Have them draw and label each part of the protozoan. Tell students to include as many properties as they can find listed in the text. Then have each group present their poster to the class. Encourage the group to divide up the description of the poster so that all members of the group can speak.

Link to

Language Arts. Ask students to read the Link to Language Arts feature in groups. Then instruct each group to conduct research into the etymology of "protozoa." If students need help, tell them that modern Latin is used heavily in scientific terminology. *(The word* protozoa *has a modern Latin etymology. The German zoologist Georg A. Goldfuss first used it in 1818.)*

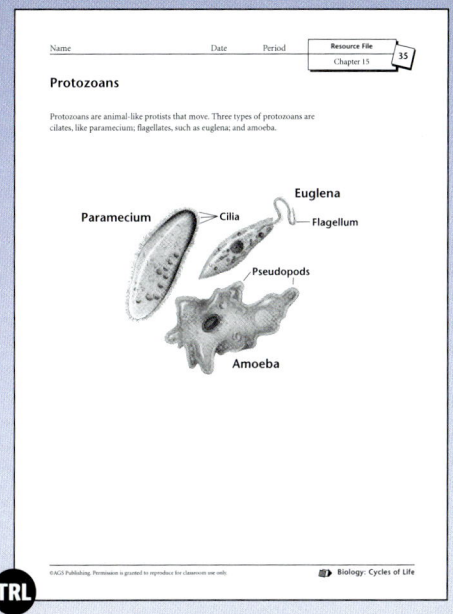

Resource File 35

TEACHER ALERT

Students may think amoebae, flagellates, and slime molds should be classified as animals since they can move. Emphasize that these protists have animal-like qualities, but remain classified in the kingdom Protista because of the other qualities they possess.

LEARNING STYLES

Body/Kinesthetic

Have students make models of each type of protist described in Lesson 2. They can make models out of clay or cut out shapes from index cards. Have them add distinguishing features such as cilia, flagella, and pseudopods. Make sure the ciliate models are the largest and the flagellate models are the smallest. If possible, obtain samples of algae and/or slime molds for students to handle and observe.

Achievements in Science

Ask volunteers to read aloud the Achievements in Science feature. Then organize students into groups and have each group prepare a K-W-L chart. After reading the selection, they can fill out the first two columns. Then encourage students to research the topics in the *Want to Know* column. Tell them to write their findings in the *What I Learned* column.

Slime mold
A protist that lives as an individual cell, then joins other slime mold cells to form a community that produces spores

Spore
A reproductive cell of some organisms

Diatoms are another example of useful protists. A diatom has a hard shell made out of silica. Silica is used to make glass. Shell remains of diatoms are used to make paint for roads and grit for toothpaste.

The Phylum Amoebozoa

The phylum Amoebozoa is made up of **slime molds.** This phylum is in the kingdom Protista. Slime molds are like fungi and animals. They have amoebalike cells that digest fungi and bacteria. They usually grow on damp soil, rotting logs, or other decomposing matter in moist areas. Many slime molds are yellow or red. Some are white.

If food or water is scarce, slime molds gather together and form one structure. The new community becomes a slimy covering and moves toward food or water. Once they move to their new location, they begin to reproduce. Some slime mold cells become **spores.** A spore is a reproductive cell. When food and water are present, a spore becomes a new slime mold cell.

Achievements in Science

The History of Classification Systems

An ancient Greek, Aristotle, developed the first classification system. His system had four categories: plants, animals with blood, animals without blood, and other things. Scientists used Aristotle's classification system for centuries.

In 1753, Carolus Linnaeus developed the classification system that scientists use today. Linnaeus took Aristotle's system and expanded it. He made it more complex. Linnaeus introduced hierarchy, in which organisms in larger categories are divided into smaller and more precise groups.

Linnaeus grouped organisms into the animal kingdom or the plant kingdom. Then he used differences in how the organisms looked or functioned to further classify them. His hierarchy levels are kingdom, phylum, class, order, family, genus, and species.

Through the years, scientists have expanded Linnaeus's classification system. They have analyzed the chemical structures of organisms and their DNA. As a result, they adjusted how some organisms are classified. They expanded the kingdom level to include more organisms. They also added the domain level above the kingdom level. The domain level represents genetic differences between organisms.

Chapter 15 Phylogenies and Classifying Diversity

Lesson 2   REVIEW

Word Bank
cilia
pseudopod
sunlight

On a sheet of paper, write the word from the Word Bank that completes each sentence correctly.

1. Protozoa use _____ to move and capture food.
2. Amoebas use a _____, or false foot, to move and to surround food.
3. Most algae get their energy from _____.

On a sheet of paper, match each term with one of the descriptions listed below.

A algae   **B** protozoa   **C** slime molds

4. protista that act like animals
5. protista that behave like plants
6. protista that act like fungi

Critical Thinking

On a sheet of paper, answer the following questions. Use complete sentences.

7. In what ways do humans use diatoms?
8. In what ways are protozoa dangerous to humans?
9. Describe the positive and negative impact that algae have on humans.
10. Describe the life cycle of a slime mold.

Phylogenies and Classifying Diversity   Chapter 15   467

Lesson 2 Review Answers

1. cilia **2.** pseudopod **3.** sunlight **4.** B **5.** A **6.** C **7.** Diatom shells are used to make paint and toothpaste. **8.** Protozoa are mainly harmless to humans. However, some amoebas can cause disease. One type of amoeba can live in the human intestine and cause dysentery. **9.** Algae help humans by producing oxygen for the atmosphere. When too much algae grows, unsightly green scum can form a layer on top of a pond or lake. **10.** Slime molds work as individual cells in a single structure when conditions are not favorable. When conditions favor the slime mold, some cells form reproductive structures, such as spores. These spores then become whole new slime mold cells.

Portfolio Assessment

Sample items include:
- Outline from Teaching the Lesson
- Posters from ELL/ESL Strategy
- Lesson 2 Review answers

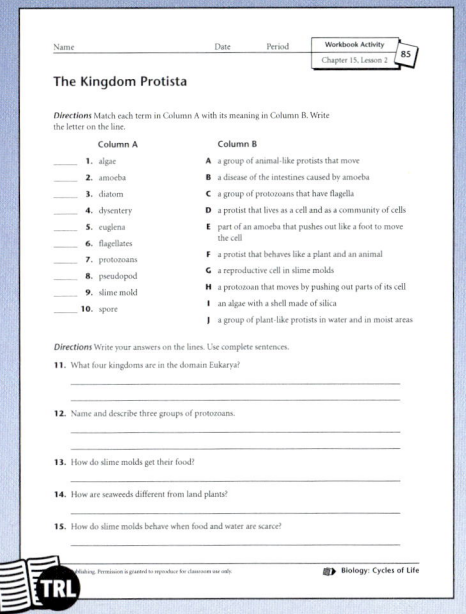

Workbook Activity 85

Phylogenies and Classifying Diversity   467

Lesson at a Glance

Chapter 15 Lesson 3

Overview In this lesson, students learn about the kingdom Fungi.

Objectives
- To describe the kingdom Fungi
- To describe features of fungi
- To describe lichens

Student Pages 468–471

Teacher's Resource Library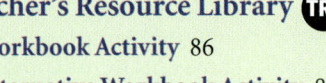
Workbook Activity 86
Alternative Workbook Activity 86
Lab Manual 73

Vocabulary

cyanobacterium   mold
hyphae   mycelium
lichen

Before starting the lesson, and before students have looked at the text, write each vocabulary term on the board. Then read the definition of each term in random order and ask students to provide the appropriate term. Encourage pairs of students to repeat this activity at the conclusion of the lesson.

Background Information

Mycology is the specialized field of fungi study and taxonomy. The kingdom Fungi is broken down into four divisions. Most mushrooms belong to the division Basidiomycota, while most yeasts and *Penicillium*, the fungus used to make penicillin, belong to the division Ascomycota. Approximately 60 percent of identified fungi belong to the division Ascomycota. Bread mold belongs to the division Zygomycota. Members of the division Chytridiomycota are the most primitive fungi. Many are aquatic and have flagella, and some have been linked to declining frog populations.

Lesson 3 The Kingdom Fungi

Objectives

After reading this lesson, you should be able to
- describe the kingdom Fungi
- describe features of fungi
- describe lichens

Mold
A fungus that grows quickly on a surface

Hyphae
Threadlike fibers containing membranes and cytoplasm

Mycelium
The underground feeding network of a fungus

The fungus *Armillaria ostoyae* is the size of 1,600 football fields. It weighs hundreds of tons and may be the world's largest organism. *Armillaria ostoyae* is between 2,400 and 8,500 years old.

Have you seen mushrooms in the grocery store or **mold** on bread? Both are members of the fungi kingdom. You will learn about the kingdom Fungi in this lesson.

Some fungi are single-celled, such as yeast. Most fungi are bunches of many cells, such as mushrooms or mold. Fungi are eukaryotic organisms. Their DNA is in the cell nucleus. Some fungi look like plants. However, fungi cannot carry on photosynthesis. Fungi are more closely related to animals than to plants. Scientists have identified about 100,000 fungi species.

Fungi decompose, or break down, dead organisms for food. They absorb sugars through their cell walls. To take in more complex food, fungi give off enzymes. The enzymes break down complex food into simpler forms. The fungi then absorb the food. After fungi digest the food, they give off carbon and nitrogen. Other organisms use these chemicals.

Fungi usually grow in slightly acidic environments. They do not need much moisture. Fungi live in soil, in houses, on plants and animals, and in fresh water and seawater. Some fungi spread by forming reproductive spores, or sex cells. A fungus can produce trillions of spores. Wind, water, birds, and animals carry away the spores. If conditions in the new areas are right, the spores will grow into new fungi.

Most fungi are made of **hyphae.** Hyphae are threadlike fibers that contain membranes and cytoplasm. Hyphae form a mat called a **mycelium.** This is the underground feeding network of fungi. Although fungi cannot move, hyphae grow and spread quickly. Some hyphae can grow up to a kilometer (0.62 miles) in one day. The mushroom you see growing on the ground is the reproductive structure of the fungus. Most of the fungal body lies underground as mycelium.

468 Chapter 15 Phylogenies and Classifying Diversity

---

1 Warm-Up Activity

Obtain some samples of fungi and lichen for students to see and handle. (Mushrooms and yeast are easy to obtain.) Prepare slides of the samples so students can see the structure of the fungi through a microscope. Have students write down their observations.

468 Chapter 15

Lichen
An organism that is made up of a fungus, a green alga, and a cynobacterium

Cyanobacterium
A blue-green algae

Link to >>>
Social Studies

The potato famine caused by the fungus *Phytophthora infestans* resulted in a large wave of immigration from Ireland to the United States. These immigrants included the great-grandparents of President John F. Kennedy.

Helpful and Harmful Fungi

Some fungi are useful, such as the fungus in penicillin. Penicillin is an antibiotic used to destroy bacteria that cause disease. People add fungi to milk to make cheese. People use yeast, a fungus, to make bread rise.

Some fungi cause diseases in plants, animals, and people. The fungus *Phytophthora infestans* caused the Great Potato Famine in Ireland in the mid-1800s. Millions of people died when this fungus ruined their potato crops. Fungi ruin about a quarter to half of harvested fruits and vegetables each year. Fungi can harm wood in houses, clothing, and some plastics, such as shower curtains.

Lichens

A **lichen** is made up of a fungus, a green algae, and **cyanobacterium.** Taxonomists classify lichens as a species. The algae provide food. The bacteria provide nitrogen. The fungi provide a physical environment for growth. Lichens are usually found on rocks and trees. Some lichens are thousands of years old. There are two lichens in Figure 15.3.1.

Figure 15.3.1 *Lichens are usually found on rocks and trees.*

In the Environment

In terms of ecological significance, fungi occupy two main niches: decomposer and parasite. A niche is the role an organism plays within an ecosystem. As decomposers, fungi are essential to the carbon and nitrogen cycles. Some fungi are symbiotically beneficial to other organisms. Lichen, for example, are made in large part of fungi that keep the lichen from drying out. Lichens are commonly found in extreme environments such as in high latitudes and on mountains.

Have students research the role of lichen in an extreme environment. Ask volunteers to share their discoveries.

2 Teaching the Lesson

If students have difficulty remembering all of the information presented in this lesson, prompt them to focus on main ideas and supporting details. They can look at headings, topic sentences, and vocabulary terms for guidance, and make flowcharts or outlines to organize the information.

Students have probably heard of some of the more annoying examples of fungi that are infections common to people. Ringworm is actually a fungus, as is athlete's foot.

After students view yeast cells through a microscope in the Warm-Up Activity, tell them that yeast is a unicellular type of fungus that has many uses. Not only are some yeasts used in bread and other foods, but also "baker's yeast" *(Saccharomyces cerevisiae)* is very popular with biologists in the laboratory. This is because it is easy to culture and manipulate, grows rapidly, is largely nonpathogenic, and is similar in structure to plant and animal cells. Thus, it is a model organism for studying genetics and the cell cycle in eukaryotic cells. In fact, bakers yeast was the first eukaryote whose genome was completely sequenced.

3 Reinforce and Extend

Link to

Social Studies. The Irish Potato Famine is a good example of the importance fungi hold in human society. After students have read the Link to Social Studies feature, have them conduct further research about the famine. It was especially devastating because the fungus that caused it spreads very quickly.

ELL/ESL Strategy

Language Objective:
To describe a member of the kingdom Fungi

Pair students learning English with students proficient in English. Have each student pick a fungus to describe to his or her partner. Tell them to provide enough information so that their partner can name the fungus that is being described.

Biology in Your Life

Have volunteers read aloud the Biology in Your Life feature. Students may have heard substances described as biodegradable or nonbiodegradable. Biodegradation is the process of converting matter back into carbon dioxide and water through microbial action. Some paper products are biodegradable, while most plastics are not. However, some materials will take longer than a few weeks to decompose, as stated in the feature. While most foods will compost after a few weeks, paper products can take two to five months. Orange peels can take up to six months. Organize students into groups and prompt them to conduct research to come up with a list of things that compost quickly versus things that take some time to decompose.

Biology in Your Life Answers

1. Composting is the act of breaking down trash or dead organic material and converting it into a useable substance, such as fertilizer or mulch.
2. Microorganisms, such as fungi and bacteria, are used for composting.
3. You can begin by piling newspapers and kitchen scraps together. Then you need to add water to a compost pile in order to cause it to decompose. As microorganisms break down the material, the temperature in the pile increases and the decomposition speeds up.

Career Connection

 A mycologist is a scientist who studies various fungi—their properties, uses, and taxonomy. Their work is important, not only for classifying fungi, but also for taking advantage of the benefits fungi have to offer. Fungi are used in medicines (such as penicillin) and foods. Mycologists are also important for their ability to distinguish edible mushrooms from toxic mushrooms.

Have students create a list of questions that they would ask a mycologist in an interview.

Biology in Your Life

The Environment: Nature's Recycling System

What would happen if everything that died did not decompose, or break down? The surface of the earth would soon be covered in dead plants, animals, and microorganisms. Decomposition is part of the cycle of life. Fungi and bacteria constantly decompose organic matter. The leftovers are used by living organisms for growth, repair, and reproduction.

People use microorganisms to break down organic material in a process called composting. People compost because this process gets rid of waste. Composting provides fertilizer, or nutrients, for crops and gardens. Composting also reduces the amount of material in landfills.

Many things can be composted, such as leaves, wood, and grass clippings. Newspapers, coffee grounds, and food waste also can be composted. Composting is easy. To begin composting, pick a place and pile material there. Add a little water regularly. To speed up composting, turn the compost pile regularly. This allows air to enter the pile and allows gases to escape.

Microorganisms present on the composted materials begin to decompose. This raises the temperature in the pile. As the temperature increases, material decomposes more quickly. After a few weeks, you have compost—a fine-textured, fertile material. You can spread compost on top of soil, or dig it into soil.

1. What is composting?
2. What kinds of organisms are used for composting?
3. How can you begin composting? What happens during the process of composting?

Lesson 3 REVIEW

Word Bank
acidic
hyphae
mycelium

On a sheet of paper, write the word from the Word Bank that completes each sentence correctly.

1. The bodies of fungi are made of single strands of _____.
2. Fungi grow best in slightly _____ environments.
3. The body of a fungus that looks solid is a mat of fibers, or the _____.

On a sheet of paper, write the letter of the answer that completes each sentence correctly.

4. Molds and mushrooms are both _____.
   A lichens   B fungi   C bacteria   D algae

5. Lichens are a combination of fungi, algae, and _____.
   A bacteria   B cyanobacteria   C moss   D spores

6. Scientists have identified about _____ species of fungi.
   A 1,000   B 10,000   C 100,000   D 1,000,000

Critical Thinking
On a sheet of paper, answer the following questions. Use complete sentences.

7. How do fungi digest food?
8. Where can fungi live?
9. What are lichens? How do the three parts of lichens interact?
10. How can fungi help people? How can they harm people?

Phylogenies and Classifying Diversity Chapter 15 471

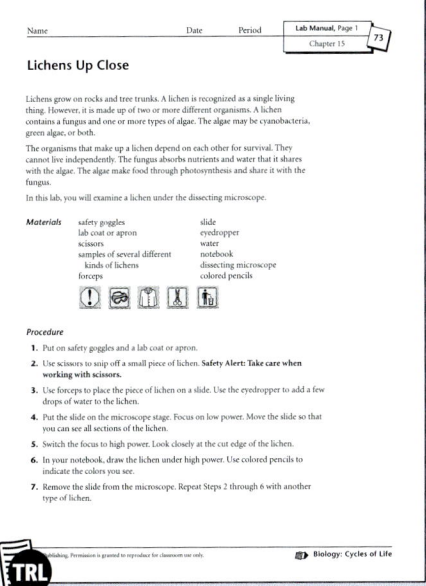

Lab Manual 73, pages 1–2   Workbook Activity 86

Lesson 3 Review Answers

1. hyphae **2.** acidic **3.** mycelium **4.** B **5.** B **6.** C **7.** Fungi digest food from outside their bodies. They release digestive enzymes that break down the food into nutrients that are absorbed through their cell walls. **8.** Fungi can live in soil, in houses, on plants and animals, and in fresh water and seawater **9.** Lichens are a species made up of fungi, algae, and cyanobacteria. The fungi provide a place for growth, the algae provide food, and the bacteria provide nitrogen. **10.** Fungi are useful by creating antibiotics and food products. Fungi also help break down dead plants and animals. Fungi harm humans by causing disease in plants, animals, and people.

Portfolio Assessment

Sample items include:
- Observation from Warm-Up Activity
- Interview questions from Career Connection
- Lesson 3 Review answers

AT HOME

Tell students to look for samples of fungi in their homes and yards. Have them write a description of each fungus found. Students might check old bread and fruit in their kitchens. Remind them that fungi are decomposers, and ask them to infer what outdoor environments decomposers might inhabit. Recesses in tree trunks and the underside of logs are good places for students to look. Advise them not to disturb any fungi that they find, and to leave everything as they found it.

Phylogenies and Classifying Diversity 471

Lesson at a Glance

Chapter 15 Lesson 4

Overview In this lesson, students learn about the kingdom Plantae.

Objectives

- To explain how plants are classified
- To define *vascular plants* and *nonvascular plants*
- To describe the features of mosses, ferns, gymnosperms, and angiosperms

Student Pages 472–478

Teacher's Resource Library
Workbook Activity 87
Alternative Workbook Activity 87

Vocabulary

alternation of generations	nonvascular plant
angiosperm	phloem
conifer	pistil
fern	pollination
fossil fuel	rhizoid
frond	seed
gametophyte	sori
germinate	sporophyte
gymnosperm	stamen
moss	stigma
mycorrhiza	vascular plant
nectar	vascular tissue
	xylem

Many of the above terms are plant parts and types of plants. Ask students to draw sketches as you read passages in the text that describe each term. Pronounce and spell each word slowly so students can write down the word, and emphasize words and phrases that are context clues. Then, as students read the lesson, instruct them to create a word web or description wheel by drawing lines and adding details.

Lesson 4 The Kingdom Plantae

Objectives

After reading this lesson, you should be able to
- explain how plants are classified
- define vascular plants and nonvascular plants
- describe the features of mosses, ferns, gymnosperms, and angiosperms

Seed
A plant part that contains a beginning plant and stored food

Fern
A seedless vascular plant

Moss
A nonvascular plant that has simple parts

Gymnosperm
A nonflowering seed plant

Angiosperm
A flowering seed plant

Vascular plant
A plant that has tubelike cells

Plants are eukaryotes that perform photosynthesis. Most plants live on land. Scientists have named more than 260,000 kinds of plants. Possibly tens of thousands of plants have not been found and named.

The kingdom Plantae is in the domain Eukarya. Scientists classify plants by body parts, such as **seeds**, roots, tubes, stems, and leaves. The three main groups of plants are **ferns, mosses,** and seed plants. Seed plants are divided into **gymnosperms** and **angiosperms.** You will learn more about each group in this lesson.

Vascular and Nonvascular Plants

Seed plants and ferns are **vascular plants.** Vascular plants have tubelike cells. These cells form tissue called **vascular tissue.** The tissue forms tubes that transport food and water throughout the plant. Vascular plants have leaves, stems, and roots.

Vascular plants are made of two types of tissue. One type is **xylem,** which is made of dead cells. Xylem transports water and minerals from the roots to the leaves. As you know, photosynthesis occurs in leaves. The second type of vascular tissue is **phloem.** Phloem is made up of living cells. Phloem takes sugars in the leaves to the roots. Photosynthesis does not occur in the roots.

Roots anchor plants in soil and rock. Roots absorb water and minerals, which are carried upward to the stems and then to the leaves. Some fungi live close to the roots of plants. The fungus absorbs minerals from the soil and shares them with the plant. In turn, the plant provides the fungus with some of the food it makes. The plant and fungus both benefit. This is called **mycorrhiza**.

Vascular tissue is important to plants. It allows food and water to be transported throughout the plant. A plant can grow tall because its leaves and stems do not need to be near the soil. A plant also grows tall because vascular tissue is thick. It provides support for the plant.

472 Chapter 15 Phylogenies and Classifying Diversity

Background Information

You may want to remind students that photosynthesis occurs primarily in leaves. Plant cells have organelles called chloroplasts that contain a pigment called chlorophyll. This pigment captures sunlight, which is the energy supply for photosynthesis. During the reaction, carbon dioxide enters the leaf through stomata, which are tiny openings, or pores, in the leaf. Carbon dioxide reacts with water and sunlight to produce glucose (which is stored chemical energy) and oxygen (which is released into the atmosphere through the stomata). Water vapor is also produced, and released through the stomata in a process called transpiration. Botanists theorize that transpiration is a good explanation for how water is transported from a plant's roots to its leaves.

Vascular tissue
A group of plant cells that form tubes through which food and water move

Xylem
The vascular tissue in plants that carries water and minerals from roots to stems and leaves

Phloem
The vascular tissue in plants that carries food from leaves to other parts of the plant

Mycorrhiza
A close relationship in which a fungus and the roots of a plant live together and help each other

Nonvascular plant
A plant that does not have tubelike cells

Rhizoid
A rootlike thread of a moss plant

Alternation of generations
A life cycle of mosses, algae, and some protists that alternates between a haploid phase and a diploid phase

Nonvascular plants are short and small because they do not have tubelike cells. They do not have tubes to transport water or provide support. They also do not have leaves, stems, or roots. Nonvascular plants usually grow in damp, shady areas on the ground and on the sides of trees and rocks.

The Phylum Bryophyta

Mosses belong to the phylum Bryophyta, a level in the kingdom Plantae. Scientists think mosses were the first plants to appear on the earth. A moss is a nonvascular plant that has simple leaflike and stemlike parts. Mosses grow in beds or clumps. They are low-growing plants.

Mosses need constant contact with moisture. They live in moist, shady areas. They get water through rootlike threads called **rhizoids.** Mosses have a waxy outer coat that prevents them from drying out.

Plants like mosses, algae, and some protists have a life cycle called **alternation of generations.** This means the life cycle takes turns, or alternates, between a haploid phase and a diploid phase. Recall that a haploid cell has one copy of each kind of chromosome. A diploid cell has two copies of each kind of chromosome.

The diploid phase in plants produces spores. A plant in this phase is called a **sporophyte.** Spores are produced by meiosis. This means a spore is a haploid reproductive cell. A spore can develop into an adult without fusing with another cell.

Science Myth

Myth: A plant makes tissue from the water and minerals it gets from soil.

Fact: Plant tissue is made from carbon. A plant gets carbon by taking in carbon dioxide from the air.

1 Warm-Up Activity

To give students an idea of what a plant's inner structure looks like, mount a small piece of a leaf on a slide and invite students to take a look at plant cells through a microscope. Repeat with a nonvascular sample, such as moss. You could also show them cross-section pictures or artists' renderings of plant tissues and structures such as phloem, xylem, and root systems.

2 Teaching the Lesson

There are many categories and types of plants discussed in Lesson 4. When teaching the alternation of generations and other difficult topics containing a lot of vocabulary, instruct students to rewrite content as individually numbered steps. After making their lists, have students read each step individually and visualize what happens.

Students might be easily confused by the high-level vocabulary presented in this lesson, especially if it is described with terms they may have forgotten. You may want to review the following terms: mitosis, meiosis, chromosome, haploid cell, diploid cell.

3 Reinforce and Extend

ELL/ESL Strategy

Language Objective: *To compare and contrast xylem and phloem*

Have students create illustrations of the processes that xylem and phloem perform. Students should first write the vocabulary term and its definition on a sheet of paper. (Students may write the definition in English as well as their primary language.) Then instruct students to draw an illustration that helps to compare and contrast these cells. Make sure students do not confuse phloem with phylum.

Science Myth

Tell students to read the Science Myth feature. Then write the chemical equation for photosynthesis on the board:

$12H_2O + 6CO_2 + sunlight = C_6H_{12}O_6$ (glucose) $+ 6O_2 + 6H_2O$

Point out that oxygen and water vapor are products released as gases. Explain that carbon is one of the more abundant elements on the earth. It can be found in all organic life and is the foundation for organic chemistry.

Teacher Alert

Just as fungi and bacteria decompose matter and release gases in a process fundamental to the life cycle of organisms, so too do plants convert these gases into matter during photosynthesis. Plants and fungi are at opposite ends of this cycle. Fungi biodegrade matter into carbon dioxide gas, water, and other products, and plants use that carbon dioxide and water to produce food and oxygen. In this respect, biodegradation and photosynthesis are opposite processes.

Science at Work

After students have read the Science at Work feature about museum guides, lead a discussion and brainstorm a list of general questions students would ask a museum guide. Encourage them to think of arboretums, nature museums, and conservatories in your area. Locate the contact information for staff at these institutions. Then have students draft and submit letters of inquiry, asking the questions the class brainstormed. Students can also include content-specific questions about plants.

Sporophyte
In alternation of generations, the diploid individual or generation that produces haploid spores

Gametophyte
In alternation of generations, the phase in which gametes are formed; a haploid individual that produces gametes

A spore then gives rise to a **gametophyte**. A gametophye produces gametes, or sex cells, by mitosis. The gametes fuse and give rise to the diploid phase. The sporophyte and gametophyte generations alternate in a plant's life cycle.

In mosses, millions of tiny spores form inside spore capsules on the end of a sporophyte stalk. Ripe spore cases break open. They shoot many spores into the air. Wind, rain, and animals carry the spores to new areas. There the spores grow by mitosis. They form gametophytes, or mature sex cells. The male gametophytes release sperm that swim through water to eggs in a female gametophyte. The diploid zygote develops as a sporophyte. The life cycle of the moss goes on.

Science at Work

Museum Guide

Museum guides teach students and visitors about the exhibits in a museum. The work of a museum guide varies, depending on the type of museum. For example, a guide in a natural history museum may describe fossils in exhibits. A guide in a science exploratory museum may perform experiments and demonstrations.

Guides must enjoy teaching and working with people. They must be able to answer questions for students and visitors.

To be a guide, a person must have a high school degree and complete training in the museum. Guides must stay current on changes in museum displays and in the research relating to the museum. Many guides get a higher degree. Then they may move to museum positions such as education director, display developer, or museum curator.

Frond
A large, feathery leaf of a fern

Sori
The clusters of reproductive cells on the underside of a frond

Fossil fuel
The fuel formed millions of years ago from the remains of plants and animals

Conifer
A cone-bearing gymnosperm

Link to >>>
Environmental Science
Some plants can tolerate air pollution better than other plants. Plants such as the Gingko tree are regularly planted in big cities. Gingko trees are not harmed by smog that damages many other plants.

The Phylum Polypodiophyta

Ferns belong to the phylum Polypodiophyta, a level in the kingdom Plantae. Ferns developed after mosses appeared. Scientists have found over 12,000 species of ferns. Many ferns live in tropical forests and temperate forests. Ferns are vascular plants. Fern leaves, or **fronds,** are usually large and flat.

On the underside of fronds are **sori.** Sori are small, round clusters that contain spores. Each cluster releases many haploid spores. These spores grow into tiny gametophytes on or just below the soil surface. On the underside of the gametophyte are sperm and egg-producing structures. Like mosses, fern sperm have flagella. The sperm swim through water to fertilize eggs. The zygote grows into the new sporophyte.

Over thousands of years, pressure and heat have changed the buried remains of ancient ferns and other plants and animals into coal. Coal, oil, and natural gas are **fossil fuels.** Fossil fuels provide energy for people. The amount of fossil fuels on the earth is limited. Scientists are looking into alternative sources of energy. You can learn more about different kinds of energy in Appendix F.

The Phylum Coniferophyta

After ferns appeared, gymnosperms such as **conifers** developed next. Conifers belong to the phylum Coniferophyta, a classification level in the kingdom Plantae. Gymnosperms are the first seed plants. Seed plants use seeds to reproduce. A seed is a plant part that contains a beginning plant and stored food.

The beginning plant is called an embryo. A seed has a coat that protects the embryo and holds in moisture. When conditions are right, the embryo grows into a full-sized plant.

Gymnosperms are nonflowering plants. The largest group of gymnosperms is conifers, or cone-bearing plants. Common conifers are pine trees, junipers, firs, cedars, redwoods, and spruces. Scientists have found about 700 species of conifers. Conifers can grow very large and tall, such as the giant redwoods in California. Gymnosperms are the main source of lumber and paper.

Link to
Environmental Science. Have a volunteer read aloud the feature about the Ginko tree. Tell students that *Ginkgo biloba* may be the oldest species of trees on Earth. It can live to be more than 1,000 years old and is native to China. Ginko trees are resistant to pollution, viruses, fungi, and pests, and have medicinal qualities beneficial to people.

LEARNING STYLES

Body/Kinesthetic
If possible, find a sample of a fern frond with sori for students to handle. Allow students to feel the texture of the sori. Explain that sori contain spores for the fern's reproduction.

IN THE ENVIRONMENT

Scientists are researching the uses of biomass as an alternative source of energy. Biomass is all around us. Biomass energy is harvested from organic matter such as leaves, sawdust, crops, animal waste, and many other materials. This organic matter can be burned directly for heat, although this practice produces soot and carbon dioxide. Another promising application is the refining of biomass for use in ethanol fuels. Ask students: What is the benefit to this research? *(This could prove to be a cleaner alternative to the limited supply of gasoline and other fossil fuels.)*

GLOBAL CONNECTION

While the redwoods of California's coastal range lay claim to the tallest trees in the world, the giant sequoias in the nearby Sierra Nevada mountain range are more massive because of their incredible width. The General Sherman tree in Sequoia National Forest is the classic specimen of the giant sequoia *(Sequoiadendron giganteum)*. Its mass is close to ten times that of a blue whale. For years, the General Sherman has been regarded as the largest living organism on Earth, although *Armillaria Ostoyae* may now rival it in size. (See page 468.) Have students research to find out where the world's largest organism lives. *(in Oregon)*

Learning Styles

Auditory/Verbal

If students have difficulty following the description of gymnosperms and reproduction of conifers, instruct them to close their eyes and visualize the process as a partner reads the passage to them.

Link to

Language Arts. Greek and Latin word parts have been used for scientific naming conventions since ancient times. Have students read the Link to Language Arts feature. See if they can guess what *gymno-* means. The prefix *gymno-* also has Greek roots; *gymnos* means "naked." Ask students: Why was the word part *gymnos* appropriate for naming the gymnosperm? *(because gymnosperm seeds are uncovered, under the scales of cones)*

Stamen
The male organ of reproduction in a flower, which includes the anther and filament

Link to ▸▸▸
Language Arts
The word *angiosperm* is made from the Greek words *angeion*, "capsule," and *sperma*, "seed."

Most conifers have green leaves all year. They are called evergreens. The leaves are shaped like needles. They do not lose water as easily as the bigger leaves of other trees. Because of their needles, conifers can survive well during dry periods.

Gymnosperm seeds are uncovered. They are under the scales of the cones. The reproductive organs of gymnosperms are in cones. Some cones are female. Some cones are male. Male cones are smaller than female cones. During reproduction, male cones release millions of pollen grains into the air. Some pollen grains reach female cones. The pollen grain grows a tube that reaches eggs in the ovary. When the pollen and egg meet, fertilization takes place.

The Phylum Anthophyta

After conifers appeared, angiosperms, or flowering plants, developed. Flowering plants belong to the phylum Anthophyta, a classification level in the kingdom Plantae. Most plants are angiosperms. Scientists have found about 250,000 species. Seed plants have the most advanced vascular tissue of all plants.

Study Figure 15.4.2. The flower is the part of an angiosperm that contains eggs and sperm. In a flower, the **stamens** are the male reproductive organs. The stamen includes the anther and filament. They produce pollen. Pollen contains sperm.

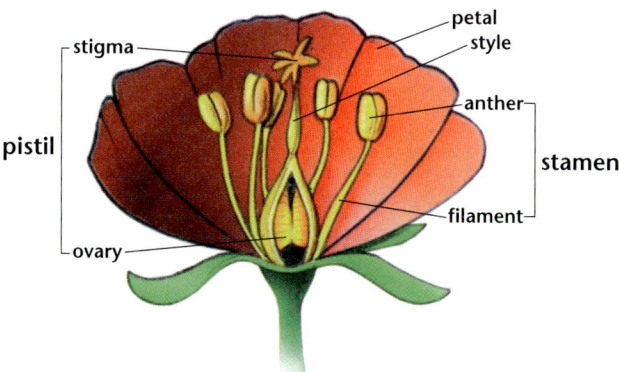

Figure 15.4.2 *A flower contains male and female reproductive organs.*

Pistil
The female organ of reproduction in a flower

Stigma
The upper part of the pistil on the tip of the style

Nectar
A sweet liquid that many flowers produce

Pollination
The process by which pollen is transferred from the stamen to the pistil

Germinate
To start to grow into a new plant

The **pistil** in a flower is the female reproductive organ. The upper part of the pistil is the **stigma**, which is sticky to catch pollen. The stigma is on the tip of the style. The lower part of the pistil is the ovary, which contains eggs.

Flowers attract insects and birds. They land on flowers to drink **nectar**, which is a sweet liquid many flowers produce. While insects and birds drink, pollen sticks to their bodies. They carry the pollen to the pistil of the same flower or other flowers. Wind, rain, and animals also spread pollen. **Pollination** occurs when pollen is transferred from the stamen to the pistil.

After pollination, the pollen grain grows a tube. The pollen tube grows down through the pistil to the eggs in the ovary. When the pollen inside the tube meets an egg, fertilization takes place. The ovary grows to become a fruit. Inside the fruit are seeds. The fruit protects the seeds. When the fruit is mature, it drops from the plant or is carried by another organism to a different area. For example, birds may eat the fruit. They will carry and drop the seeds in new areas. The seeds will **germinate** if conditions are right. The seeds then grow into new plants.

Angiosperms are valuable plants. They are a source of food for many living things. People use angiosperms for medicine and for fibers to make clothing. Some flowering plants are used to make perfume. Figure 15.4.3 sums up the three main groups of plants: mosses, seedless plants, and seed plants. Appendix G provides more information about the plant kingdom.

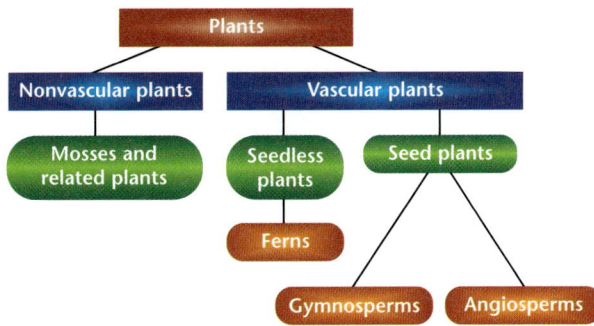

Figure 15.4.3 *Plants are classified according to their structures.*

TEACHER ALERT

To give students an idea of the evolution of plants on Earth, tell them that mosses originated about 500 million years ago (mya). While that may seem like a long time, it is relatively recent in terms of Earth's history, since it is estimated that Earth formed 4.5 billion years ago. Vascular plants such as ferns appeared sometime between 443 and 416 mya (during the Silurian period), and gymnosperms, the first seed-bearing plants, appeared between 360 and 300 mya (between the Devonian and Carboniferous periods). By that time there were forests of vascular plants. During the Triassic Period (about 250 mya), gymnosperms dominated the landscape. Angiosperms, flower-bearing plants, emerged between the Jurassic and Cretaceous Periods between 160 and 65 mya, when dinosaurs became extinct.

LEARNING STYLES

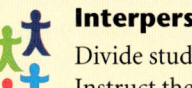

Interpersonal/Group
Divide students into groups. Instruct them to make a timeline using each of the major types of plants discussed in this lesson. Advise them to use poster board so they have lots of room to add notes from the text and from other groups' presentations. Then have each group present their poster to the class.

Lesson 4 Review Answers

1. rhizoids **2.** conifers **3.** sporophyte **4.** C
5. C **6.** D **7.** The male part of the flower is the stamen. The stamen is made of the anther and filaments. The female part is the pistil, which contains the stigma and the ovary. **8.** Plants often have fungi on their roots. The fungi absorb minerals for the plant to use. In return, the plant supplies the fungi with nutrients. **9.** Phloem is living vascular tissue that transports sugars from the leaves to the rest of the plant. Xylem is dead vascular tissue that transports water and minerals from the roots to the rest of the plant. **10.** Ferns that lived thousands of years ago died and became buried along with other plants and animal remains. Over time, pressure and heat changed this buried material to coal, which is used to create energy for humans today.

Portfolio Assessment

Sample items include:
- List of questions for museum guide
- Time line of plants
- Lesson 4 Review answers

Lesson 4 REVIEW

Word Bank
- conifers
- rhizoids
- sporophyte

On a sheet of paper, write the word from the Word Bank that completes each sentence correctly.

1. Mosses get water through rootlike threads called _____.
2. Most _____ have green leaves all year.
3. The seed of an angiosperm germinates to produce a _____.

On a sheet of paper, write the letter of the answer that completes each sentence correctly.

4. A plant is a _____.
   A one-celled eukaryote
   B one-celled prokaryote
   C multicellular eukaryote
   D multicellular prokaryote

5. Pollen is a _____.
   A female gametophyte   C male gametophyte
   B female sporophyte   D male sporophyte

6. Small, round clusters that contain spores on fronds are _____.
   A cones   B flowers   C seeds   D sori

Critical Thinking

On a sheet of paper, answer the following questions. Use complete sentences.

7. Describe the male and female parts that make up a flower.
8. How do plants and fungi work together to get nutrients?
9. Describe the two types of vascular tissue in plants.
10. How are ancient ferns and other plants connected to the way humans get energy today?

478 Chapter 15 Phylogenies and Classifying Diversity

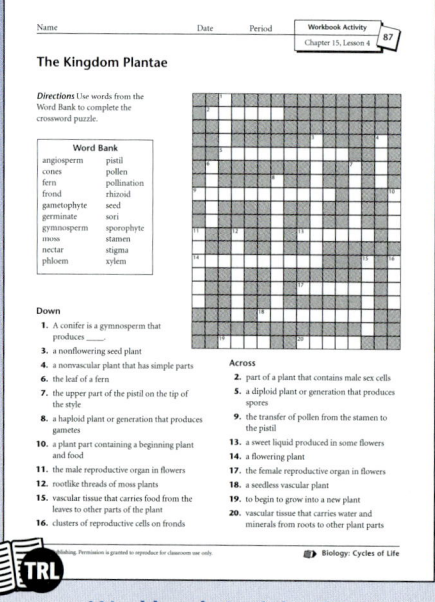

Workbook Activity 87

Lesson 5 The Kingdom Animalia

Objectives

After reading this lesson, you should be able to
◆ describe eight common features of organisms in the kingdom Animalia
◆ define vertebrates and invertebrates

Heterotroph
An organism that cannot make its own food

Multicellular
Made up of many cells

Blastula
A hollow ball of cells formed by cell divisions of a zygote

Animals are eukaryotes. The kingdom Animalia is in the domain Eukarya. Scientists have classified more than 1.5 million animals. Over half of these species are insects. New species are discovered every year. Scientists think there may be millions more species to find and classify.

Eight Common Features of Animals

Most animals share eight common features. One feature is that animals are **heterotrophs.** They cannot make their own food. They must eat food to supply energy and material for cell growth and repair. Animals eat live or dead organisms. Digestion occurs inside the animal's body.

Most animals have coordinated movement. They can also move quickly. Animals move by means of muscle cells. A nervous system controls their muscular and skeletal systems.

Another feature is that all animals are **multicellular.** They have many cells. This is true for tiny animals that can be seen only under a microscope and for huge animals such as whales and elephants.

Most animals are diploid. This means that most animals have two copies of each chromosome. One copy is inherited from the father. The other copy is inherited from the mother. Only their sex cells (sperm and egg) are haploid. They have one copy of each kind of sex chromosome.

Most animals reproduce sexually. They produce gametes, or eggs and sperm. Egg cells are much larger than sperm. Animal sperm cells have a flagella, which move the sperm cells.

When an egg is fertilized, it becomes a zygote, or a fertilized egg cell. The zygote divides again and again to form a hollow ball of cells called a **blastula.** All zygotes of animals develop a blastula. The formation of a blastula is another feature of animals. Cells within the blastula form three layers. These layers will become different parts of the body.

Lesson at a Glance

Chapter 15 Lesson 5

Overview In this lesson, students learn about the kingdom Animalia.

Objectives
- To describe eight common features of organisms in the kingdom Animalia
- To define *vertebrates* and *invertebrates*

Student Pages 479–481

Teacher's Resource Library
Workbook Activity 88
Alternative Workbook Activity 88

Vocabulary

blastula   multicellular
heterotroph

Tell students to use a dictionary to look up any word parts that stand out in the vocabulary terms. For instance, *troph-* is from the Greek word *trophe*, meaning "food, nourishment," and *multi-* is from the Latin word *multus*, which means "much, many." Ask students to describe why these and other word parts are appropriate for the vocabulary terms in which they are used.

Background Information

All the species of plants, animals, and microorganisms that have ever lived on Earth evolved from common ancestors. Early organisms inhabited a very different Earth environment. They would have been anaerobic (able to survive without the presence of atmospheric oxygen), hyperthermophilic (able to live in high-temperature environments), and autotrophic (able to produce its own food). The argument of a common origin for all life is affirmed by the facts that DNA and RNA are the basis for all living things, that all living things are made up of only 20 essential amino acids, and that ATP is the universal energy currency in all living cells.

Warm-Up Activity

Lead a class discussion in which students brainstorm the characteristics and features of animals. Ask students: What makes an animal an animal? Make a list on the board of student responses. Then read the passage describing the eight common features of animals. As a class, revise the list on the board so it matches the text by omitting incorrect student responses while modifying the more relevant ones.

 Teaching the Lesson

Students might remember each of the common features of animals more easily if they make a numbered list.

 **Reinforce and Extend**

SCIENCE JOURNAL

Have a volunteer read the fourth feature shared by all animals. Then ask students if they have seen the topic and terminology before. Ask them to reflect on the previous lesson's discussion of alternation of generations. Next, instruct students to write a paragraph in which they answer the following two questions: Which topic made more sense to you? Does reading one help you to understand the other?

ELL/ESL STRATEGY

 **Language Objective:** *To describe and summarize the common features of animals* Divide the class into small discussion groups. Have students discuss the eight common features of animals.

Only animal cells do not have rigid cell walls. This gives animal cells the ability to move. Remember from Chapter 11 that macrophages are white blood cells that move to different body parts. There, they surround and digest pathogens. If macrophages had rigid cell walls, they could not do this.

The cells of most animals are organized into tissues. Remember that a tissue is a group of cells that work together to perform a task. For example, muscle cells contract for movement. Here is a list of the eight features of animals:

- Heterotroph
- Coordinated movement and can move quickly
- Multicellular
- Diploid
- Reproduce sexually
- Develop a blastula
- No rigid cell walls
- Have tissues

Invertebrates and Vertebrates

Animals are either invertebrates or vertebrates. As you know, an invertebrate is an animal without a backbone. A vertebrate is an animal with a backbone. You will study invertebrates in Lesson 6, and vertebrates in Lessons 7 and 8.

Lesson 5 REVIEW

Word Bank
heterotrophs
invertebrate
nervous system
vertebrate

On a sheet of paper, write the word or words from the Word Bank that complete each sentence correctly.

1. Animals are _____ because they cannot make their own food.
2. Most animals have coordinated movement because their muscular and skeletal systems are controlled by a(n) _____.
3. A(n) _____ is an animal without a backbone, and a(n) _____ is an animal with a backbone.

On a sheet of paper, write the letter of the answer that completes each sentence correctly.

4. An animal zygote divides to form _____.
   A sperm   B an egg   C flagella   D a blastula

5. The cells of most animals are organized into _____.
   A tissues   B blastulas   C diploids   D haploids

6. All animals are _____, meaning they have many cells.
   A made up of rigid cell walls
   B haploid
   C multicellular
   D invertebrates

Critical Thinking

On a sheet of paper, answer the following questions. Use complete sentences.

7. In animals, what happens when an egg is fertilized?
8. How does having a nervous system help animals?
9. How are all animals alike as heterotrophs?
10. What are the eight features that most animals share?

Lesson 5 Review Answers

1. heterotrophs 2. nervous system 3. invertebrate, vertebrate 4. D 5. A 6. C 7. An egg is fertilized and becomes a zygote. The zygote divides several times to form a hollow ball of cells called a blastula. Cell layers in the blastula will become different parts of the body. 8. Animals are able to move their muscles using a nervous system. This enables them to chase and catch food. 9. All animals need food to survive. Heterotrophs are not capable of making their own food. 10. Most animals are heterotrophs, have coordinated movement, are multicellular, have two copies of each chromosome, reproduce sexually, develop a blastula during reproduction, have cells without rigid walls, and have tissues.

Portfolio Assessment

Sample items include:
- Paragraph in Science Journal
- Lesson 5 Review answers

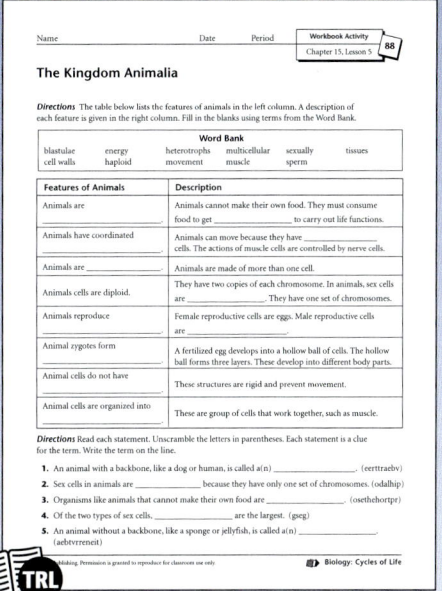

Workbook Activity 88

Lesson at a Glance

Chapter 15 Lesson 6

Overview In this lesson, students learn about invertebrates.

Objectives

- To describe the features of sponges and cnidarians
- To describe the features of flatworms, roundworms, and segmented worms
- To describe the features of mollusks, arthropods, and echinoderms

Student Pages 482–488

Teacher's Resource Library

Workbook Activity 89

Alternative Workbook Activity 89

Lab Manual 74

Resource File 36

Vocabulary

arachnid	metamorphosis
arthropod	mollusk
bilateral symmetry	molting
cnidarian	phylogeny
complete metamorphosis	radial symmetry
	radula
crustacean	roundworm
endoskeleton	segmented worm
exoskeleton	tentacle
flatworm	tube feet
incomplete metamorphosis	

Encourage students to explore and describe connections among related vocabulary terms. Help students write sentences that describe relationships, such as "Molting is the shedding of the exoskeleton" and "Crustaceans and arachnids are types of arthropods."

Lesson 6 Invertebrates

Objectives

After reading this lesson, you should be able to

◆ describe the features of sponges and cnidarians

◆ describe the features of flatworms, roundworms, and segmented worms

◆ describe the features of mollusks, arthropods, and echinoderms

Phylogeny
The origin and evolution of a species

Cnidarian
A group of invertebrates including jellyfish, corals, and hydras

Radial symmetry
An arrangement of body parts that resembles the spokes on a wheel

Tentacle
An armlike body part of cnidarians that is used to capture food

Invertebrates make up about 97 percent of all animal species. Recall from Chapter 13 that an invertebrate is an animal without a backbone. Invertebrates belong to more than 30 phyla. You will learn about eight phyla in this lesson.

Phylogeny is the origin and evolution of a species. Scientists use comparative anatomy and molecular biology to investigate animal phylogeny. In this lesson, you will learn about eight of the many phyla that belong to the kingdom Animalia and their evolutionary history.

The Phylum Porifera

The phylum Porifera is sponges. Sponges are the simplest animals. Their bodies are made up of two layers of cells. They do not have tissues or organs, and they do not move. They live in water and strain food from the water. Each cell of a sponge can sense and react to the environment. Scientists have found about 9,000 species of sponges.

The Phylum Cnidarian

Cnidarians appeared after sponges. Cnidarians include jellyfish, corals, and hydras. There are about 10,000 species of cnidarians. All live in water. All have **radial symmetry.** Radial symmetry is an arrangement of body parts that resembles the arrangement of spokes on a wheel. Cnidarians also have armlike **tentacles** with stinging cells. The tentacles capture food and push it into a baglike body cavity for digestion.

The Phylum Platyhelminthes

Flatworms developed after cnidarians. Flatworms are flat and thin. Their bodies have a left half and a right half. The halves are the same. This body type is called **bilateral symmetry.** Flatworms include planarians, flukes, and tapeworms. There are about 20,000 species of flatworms and most are parasites.

482 Chapter 15 Phylogenies and Classifying Diversity

Background Information

The Geologic Time Scale and fossil records are important to phylogeny. Fossil records and carbon deposit analysis (studying ratios of carbon isotopes produced by biological processes) suggest it was 3.5 billion years ago that life on Earth began with simple single-celled prokaryotes such as cyanobacteria (blue-green algae). Eukaryotes developed around 1.5 billion years ago. The fossil record from the Ediacaran period suggests that multicellular animals became common around 600 million years ago. Invertebrates came to dominate the evolving biosphere of Earth following the Cambrian explosion 545 million years ago.

Flatworm
A simple worm that is flat and thin

Bilateral symmetry
A body made of left and right halves that are the same

Roundworm
A worm with a smooth, round body and pointed ends

Segmented worm
A worm whose body is divided into sections

Mollusk
An invertebrate that has three body parts

The Phylum Nematoda

Roundworms, such as pinworms and hookworms, belong to the phylum Nematoda. They developed after cnidarians. There are about 90,000 species of nematodes, and there are probably more. Like flatworms, roundworms have bilateral symmetry. Roundworms live in wet soil or water. They eat dead leaves and other material. Some eat insects that destroy plant roots. Other roundworms destroy the roots of plants. Some roundworms live in humans and can cause them to become sick.

Roundworms have a complete digestive tract. This is a digestive tube with two openings. Animals with a complete digestive tract process food as it moves through different organs.

The Phylum Annelid

The annelids, or **segmented worms,** developed after roundworms. The round body of segmented worms is divided into many sections, or segments. Segmented worms live in moist soil, saltwater, and freshwater. There are more than 15,000 species of annelids.

Earthworms and leeches are two species of annelids. Earthworms tunnel through the soil to eat small food particles. Their tunnels loosen the soil and allow air to enter. This helps plants grow. Some leeches eat small invertebrates. Others attach to the skin of a vertebrate and feed on its blood. While feeding, the leech secretes a chemical so that the blood does not clot. Scientists are investigating this chemical as a medicine.

The Phylum Mollusca

Snails, slugs, oysters, clams, and octopuses belong to the phylum Mollusca. There are about 150,000 species of **mollusks.** Most live in saltwater and freshwater. They can swim quickly to find food. Some mollusks live on land. Mollusks have bilateral symmetry.

Every mollusk has a head, body, and muscular foot. The foot moves the animal around. Mollusks have soft bodies that contain organs. A hard outside shell protects most mollusks. The animal can fit inside this shell for protection.

Phylogenies and Classifying Diversity Chapter 15 **483**

Warm-Up Activity

Bring in lab specimens or pictures of organisms belonging to each of the eight phyla featured in this lesson. Allow students to view samples of smaller organisms, such as sponges and flatworms, through a microscope.

Teaching the Lesson

Encourage students to look for clues as they read. The word *after* is used in four of the sections about different phyla to set up the order or sequence with which these phylas' organisms evolved. Also encourage students to notice relationships. For example, *saltwater* and *freshwater* on page 483 are opposites.

Students will probably have trouble remembering each phylum by name and distinguishing one from the other. Break each phylum into syllables and pronounce it for students. Have students repeat the pronunciation of each word after you.

You might also instruct students to write the scientific name of each phylum on one side of an index card (Porifera, Platyhelminthes, Nematoda) and the common name, or examples, on the other side (sponges, flatworms, roundworms). Students can use the cards to quiz themselves.

Reinforce and Extend

LEARNING STYLES

Auditory/Verbal
Ask students: Have you ever collected or eaten a type of mollusk, such as a clam or an oyster? If students answer yes, ask them to describe the mollusk's features to the class.

Phylogenies and Classifying Diversity **483**

Technology and Society

As a class, read aloud the Technology and Society feature. Tell students that DNA technology and comparative analysis of genes prompted scientists to classify Archaea and Bacteria in separate domains. Archaea actually have base sequences of nucleic acids that are more similar to those in eukaryotes than those in bacteria.

A nautilus mollusk belongs to the genus *Nautilus*, which is the sole survivor of a subclass of mollusks that thrived 200 million years ago. The nautilus has gills, a spiral-shaped shell, and tentacles around the mouth for feeding. It swims backwards, propelling itself by squirting water through a funnel in the opposite direction.

Radula
A tonguelike organ covered with teeth that is used for feeding

Arthropod
A member of the largest group of invertebrates; this group includes insects

Crustacean
A class of arthropods that includes crabs, lobsters, crayfish, and pill bugs

Arachnid
A class of arthropods that includes spiders, scorpions, mites, and ticks

Exoskeleton
An external skeleton

Molting
The process by which an arthropod sheds its exoskeleton

Snails have a coiled shell. Slugs have a small internal shell. Snails and slugs make up the largest group of mollusks. Oysters, mussels, and scallops are protected by two shells hinged together. The hinged shells open and close. These animals live in mud or sand and use their foot for digging. Squid have a small internal shell, and octopuses have no shell. The brain of an octopus is large. Octopuses have good sense organs.

Mollusks feed by using a **radula.** A radula is a tonguelike organ covered with teeth that is used for feeding. A garden snail uses its radula to cut out pieces of leaves to eat. A squid's radula can rip apart food.

The Phylum Arthropoda

Arthropods belong to the phylum Arthropoda. There are about a million species of arthropods. They are the largest group of invertebrates. They make up more than three-fourths of all animal species. The five main groups of arthropods are **crustaceans,** millipedes, centipedes, **arachnids,** and insects.

Arthropods have segmented bodies with jointed legs. Most arthropods have antennae that allow them to feel, taste, and smell. Their body is covered with an **exoskeleton,** or an external skeleton. The exoskeleton can be thick or it can be very thin in places such as joints. As they grow, arthropods shed their exoskeleton and secrete a larger one. This process is called **molting.**

Technology and Society

DNA technology helps scientists classify organisms accurately. For example, nautilus mollusks were once classified into five species. Using DNA analysis, scientists found only two species of nautilus mollusks. Scientists are examining fossils for DNA evidence of ancient viruses that may have caused extinctions.

Metamorphosis
A major change in form that occurs as some animals develop into adults

Complete metamorphosis
The changes in form during development in which earlier stages do not look like the adult

Crabs, lobsters, crayfish, and shrimp are crustaceans. There are about 40,000 species of crustaceans. Most live in freshwater and saltwater. One group, called pill bugs, lives under moist leaves. Many crustaceans have five pairs of legs. Some legs have claws to help the animal handle food. The two legs closest to the head usually have powerful claws for protection.

Millipedes and centipedes have many body segments. They live on land and eat decaying plant matter. There are about 10,000 species of millipedes and 2,500 species of centipedes. Millipedes have two pairs of short legs on each body segment. Centipedes have poison claws that they use in defense and to paralyze insects and other animals. They have a pair of long legs on each body segment and can run quickly.

Arachnids are spiders, scorpions, mites, and ticks. There are about 70,000 species of arachnids. Most live on land. They have four pairs of legs and a pair of feeding limbs. Spiders produce threads of silk to spin webs and build nests. Spiders eat insects caught in their webs and nests. Some spiders catch small fish or frogs. Spiders inject their prey with poison to capture it. Scorpions use a stinger to inject poison into their prey. Mites and ticks live on mammals, including humans. Mites feed on hair and dead skin. Ticks feed by piercing the skin and eating blood.

There are about one million species of insects. They live almost everywhere, except in the deep ocean. Mosquitoes, flies, ants, and beetles are insects. Insects have three body parts: a head, thorax, and abdomen. The head has antennae and a pair of eyes. Mouth parts are varied for biting, chewing, and piercing skin.

Insects have three pairs of legs and one or two pairs of wings. Because insects can fly, they can escape predators. They can find food and move to new habitats. Insects are the only invertebrates that can fly.

Many insects go through **metamorphosis**. Metamorphosis is a major change in form that occurs as some animals develop into adults. **Complete metamorphosis** is the changes in the animal's form during development in which earlier stages do not look like the adult.

ELL/ESL Strategy

Language Objective:
To explain the meaning of the word arthropod

Tell students that a biologist named Karl Theodor Ernst von Siebold introduced the term *arthropod* in 1945. He combined the Greek word *arthron*, which means "joint," with *podos*, which means "foot." *Arthropoda* means "those with jointed feet." Organize students into small discussion groups. Have students try to further explain the meaning of the word *arthropod*.

Teacher Alert

Malaria is a disease that is transmitted by insects. Female mosquitoes carrying protozoan parasites spread it. Chagas disease, also spread by an insect, occurs primarily in Central and South America and Mexico. An arthropod called the "assassin bug" latches onto people in their sleep to suck their blood. The bug often leaves feces behind, and when people scratch the bitten area, usually around the nose and eyes, protozoa in the feces enter the bloodstream. The protozoa quickly spread, infesting organs in the body. In children, death from Chagas disease may come quickly. In adults, the disease may linger for many years with no visible symptoms. Eventually, the infested organs may burst, causing death.

Incomplete metamorphosis
The changes in form during development in which earlier stages look like the adult

Endoskeleton
An internal skeleton

Tube foot
A small structure used by echinoderms for attachment and movement

Look at Figure 15.6.1. The complete metamorphosis of a butterfly has four stages. The first three stages do not look like the adult butterfly. Some young insects, like grasshoppers, resemble adults. This is called **incomplete metamorphosis.** Crickets and cockroaches also develop by incomplete metamorphosis.

Many insects are pests. Fleas, ticks, and mosquitoes carry microorganisms that cause diseases. Grasshoppers and caterpillars destroy crops. They also serve as food for other organisms. Other insects are helpful. They make useful products such as honey, wax, and silk. Many insects pollinate flowers, which produce fruits.

The Phylum Echinodermata

Echinoderms belong to the phylum Echinodermata. Sea urchins, sand dollars, sea cucumbers, and sea stars belong to this group. All 7,000 species live in marine environments. Most do not move. Some move slowly. Echinoderms do not have body segments. They have radial symmetry. For example, starfish have parts that come out from the center like spokes.

Echinoderms have an **endoskeleton,** or an interior skeleton. They have a network of canals filled with water. These canals circulate water. The canals branch into **tube feet.** The tube feet attach firmly to surfaces and also move echinoderms.

Complete Metamorphosis

Stage 1 A butterfly egg hatches into a caterpillar.

Stage 2 A caterpillar feeds on leaves, molting several times as it grows.

Stage 3 When a caterpillar reaches its full size, it molts into a form called a pupa.

Stage 4 After a few weeks, the pupa molts into an adult butterfly.

Figure 15.6.1 *A butterfly metamorphosis has four stages.*

486 Chapter 15 Phylogenies and Classifying Diversity

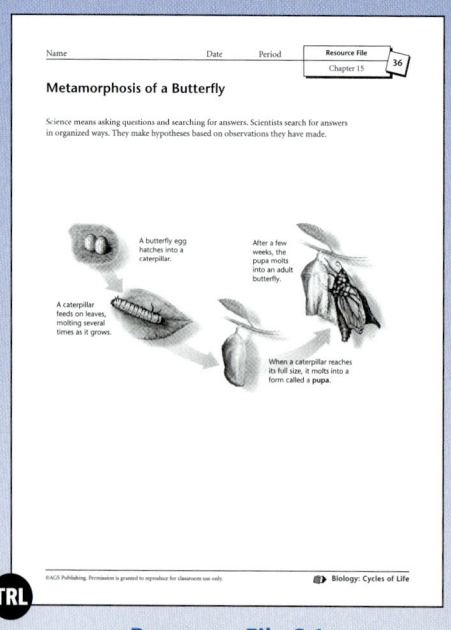

Resource File 36

Table 15.6.1 sums up the eight phyla covered in this lesson.

Table 15.6.1 Eight Invertebrate Phyla		
Phylum	Description	Examples
Porifera	Body wall of two cell layers; pores and canals; no tissues or organs; live in water; strain food from water	sponge
Cnidarian	Baglike body of two cell layers; one opening leading into a hollow body; tissues; radial symmetry; live in water	jellyfish, coral, hydra
Platyhelminthes	Flat, thin body; three cell layers; organs; digestive system with one opening; nervous system; bilateral symmetry; most are parasites	tapeworm, planarian, fluke
Nematoda	Round, slender body; digestive system with two openings; nervous system; bilateral symmetry	hookworm, pinworm
Annelid	Round, segmented body; digestive system, nervous system, circulatory system; bilateral symmetry; most are not parasites	earthworm, leech
Mollusca	Soft body covered by a fleshy mantle; move with muscular foot; some have shells; all have organ systems; bilateral symmetry; feed by using a radula	snail, slug, clam, oyster, scallop, squid, octopus
Arthropoda	Segmented body; jointed legs; most have antennae; all have organ systems; external skeleton	
	• Crustacean—two body parts; usually five pairs of legs two pairs of antennae; breathe with gills	crayfish, lobster, crab, shrimp, sow bug
	• Many body segments; from 15 to over 100; one or two pairs of legs in each segment	millipede centipede
	• Arachnid—two body segments; four pairs of legs; no antennae	spider, scorpion, tick mite
	• Insect—three body segments; three pairs of legs; one pair of antennae; most have two pairs of wings	fly, beetle, grasshopper, earwig, silverfish, water strider, butterfly, bee, ant
Echinodermata	Covered with spines; body has five parts; radial symmetry; live in ocean	sea star, sea urchin, sand dollar

LEARNING STYLES

Visual/Spatial

Have students make a two-column chart relating to Table 15.6.1. In the first column, they should list the names of each phyla. In the second column, students can sketch an animal that is an example of each phylum. Have students research an animal if they need more information to do a drawing.

LEARNING STYLES

Logical/Mathematical

Ask students to compare ratios of numbers of species in certain phyla. For instance, if there are 150,000 species of mollusks, and 15,000 species of annelids, then there are 10 species of mollusks for every species of annelid.

Lesson 6 Review Answers

1. radula **2.** sponges **3.** radial symmetry
4. B **5.** B **6.** C **7.** Both the exoskeleton and the endoskeleton provide protection and support. The exoskeleton covers the outside of a body. The endoskeleton is an interior skeleton. **8.** Arachnids have two body segments, four pairs of legs, and a pair of feeding limbs. Most live on land. Insects have three body segments and three pairs of legs. They are the only invertebrates that can fly. **9.** The mollusk uses a muscular foot to move. Most of the mollusk's organs are contained in a visceral mass. A fold of tissue called the mantle secretes a shell for protection. **10.** Worms till the soil as they tunnel through. Their tunnels allow air to enter the soil.

Portfolio Assessment

Sample items include:
- Ratios of numbers of species from Learning Styles Logical/Mathematical
- Lesson 6 Review answers

Lesson 6 REVIEW

Word Bank
radial symmetry
radula
sponges

On a sheet of paper, write the word or words from the Word Bank that complete each sentence correctly.

1. Mollusks feed by using a _____.
2. The simplest animals are _____.
3. Sea urchins, sand dollars, and sea cucumbers have _____.

On a sheet of paper, write the letter of the answer that completes each sentence correctly.

4. Three-fourths of all animal species are _____.
   A crustaceans   C annelids
   B arthropods   D poriferas

5. Flatworms have a body type called _____.
   A radial symmetry   C radula
   B bilateral symmetry D exoskeleton

6. Insects have _____ pairs of legs.
   A five   C three
   B four   D two

Critical Thinking

On a sheet of paper, answer the following questions. Use complete sentences.

7. Compare and contrast an endoskeleton and an exoskeleton.
8. Compare and contrast arachnids and insects.
9. Name and describe the three body parts of a mollusk.
10. Gardeners say that a garden filled with earthworms is good. Explain why.

488 Chapter 15 Phylogenies and Classifying Diversity

Lesson 7: Vertebrates

Objectives

After reading this lesson, you should be able to
- describe the main features of vertebrates
- describe the main features of the phylum Chordates
- list the evolutionary history of the phylum Chordates
- describe the features of eight vertebrate classes

Chordate
An animal that, in its embryo stage, has a dorsal nerve cord, a notochord, pharyngeal slits, and a tail that goes past the anus

Cartilage
A soft material found in vertebrate skeletons

Vertebra
One of the bones or blocks of cartilage that make up a backbone; (plural is vertebrae)

Dorsal
The back part of an animal

Scientists have classified about 50,000 species of vertebrates in the kingdom Animalia. The phylum Chordata is part of the kingdom Animalia. **Chordates** are vertebrates, or animals with backbones.

Features of Vertebrates

Vertebrates have three unique features. First, they have a skeleton inside their body. The skeleton is made of bone and **cartilage.** Cartilage is a soft material. Some invertebrates have an internal skeleton, but it is not made of bone. Second, vertebrates have a backbone. A **vertebra** is a bone or a block of cartilage that makes up a backbone. A backbone is made of many small vertebrae. Third, vertebrates have a skull. The skull surrounds and protects the brain.

Vertebrates live in most land habitats. Fish, which are vertebrates, live in freshwater and seawater.

The Phylum Chordata

Chordates share four common features when they are an embryo. First, they develop a **dorsal** nerve cord. The hollow nerve cord includes the brain and spinal cord. Second, a stiff **notochord,** or rod, develops along the dorsal side of the embryo.

Third, chordate embryos develop **pharyngeal slits,** or openings in the wall of the pharynx. The pharynx is the tube that connects the mouth to the digestive tract and windpipe. Fourth, chordate embryos have a tail that goes beyond the anus.

All chordates, including humans, have these features in their embryonic stage of development. These four features may be present for only a short time in some embryos.

Lesson at a Glance

Chapter 15 Lesson 7

Overview In this lesson, students learn about vertebrates.

Objectives
- To describe the main features of all vertebrates
- To describe the main features of the phylum Chordates
- To list the evolutionary history of the phylum Chordates
- To describe the features of eight vertebrate classes

Student Pages 489–496

Teacher's Resource Library
Workbook Activity 90
Alternative Workbook Activity 90
Lab Manual 75

Vocabulary

amniotic egg	larva
cartilage	marsupial
cephalaspidomorphi	myxini
chondrichthyes	notochord
chordate	operculus
cold-blooded	osteichthyes
dorsal	pharyngeal slit
ectotherm	swim bladder
endotherm	vertebra
gill	warm-blooded

Organize the class into pairs and have them use the Glossary to look up the vocabulary terms. Tell them to discuss each term.

Background Information

Mutations are the driving force behind evolution and can be credited with the diversity of life on Earth. Remind students that DNA is a nucleic acid that carries genetic information. DNA is encoded with four bases; these are the "building blocks" that form strands of double-stranded DNA: adenine (A), which pairs only with guanine (G), and thymine (T) which pairs with cytosine (C). Before cells divide, strands of DNA are copied during the process called replication (synthesis). Usually, the duplicated strand is identical to the original, but sometimes a base is left out (deletion) or inserted (insertion) or substituted, and a mutation occurs. Chemicals and radiation can cause mutations. Less favorable mutations can be removed from the gene pool through natural selection, while more favorable mutations help species adapt to stressful environmental conditions.

Warm-Up Activity

Ask students to skim the chapter and write the name of each class on a separate index card. Have them include examples of each type of vertebrate, such as "fish" or "bird." Then instruct students to list any characteristics that come to mind. Ask students: What characteristics make this class of vertebrates distinct? After reading the chapter, have students return to their index cards and compare them to Figure 15.7.1 on page 493.

Teaching the Lesson

Ask students to keep a log of what kinds of birds they see around their homes, around school, and in their community. If they do not know the common name of a bird, have them write down obvious features or characteristics and consult a field guide.

Ask students if they have ever seen an opossum. Then ask if they have specifically seen a mother opossum with young babies. Explain that the opossum is the only marsupial in North America.

Notochord
A rod found in the back of a chordate embryo

Pharyngeal slit
An opening in the wall of the pharynx of a chordate embryo

Myxini
A class of fish with a cartilage skeleton and no jaws or scales; hagfish

Cephalaspidomorphi
A class of fish with a cartilage skeleton and no jaws or scales; lampreys

Chondrichthyes
A class of fish with a flexible skeleton made of cartilage

Gill
A structure used by some animals to breathe in water

Osteichthyes
A class of bony fish with jaws and scales

Phylogeny

Vertebrates developed about 550 million years ago. The oldest vertebrate fossils are those of fish with no jaws. About 440 million years ago, ancestors of the first fish with jaws and a soft skeleton appeared. Bony fish evolved next.

About 370 million years ago, most amphibians resembled modern species. They became the first vertebrates to live on land. Reptiles arose from amphibians about 300 million years ago. Scientists think birds and mammals evolved from reptiles. Birds appeared about 220 millions years ago. Mammals are older, appearing 300 million years ago.

Eight Classes of Vertebrates

Scientists divide vertebrates into eight classes. Four classes are made up of different types of fish. These include fish without jaws, fish with jaws and soft skeletons, and bony fish. The other four classes are amphibians, reptiles, birds, and mammals.

Class Myxini and Class Cephalaspidomorphi

There are four classes of fish. One is the class **Myxini,** or hagfish. Another is the class **Cephalaspidomorphi,** which are lampreys. The fish have a skeleton made of soft cartilage. Both classes of fish have no jaws or scales.

Class Chondrichthyes and Class Osteichthyes

Class **Chondrichthyes** includes sharks, rays, and skates. Chondrichthyes have a flexible skeleton made of cartilage and paired fins. For example, sharks have a row of sensory organs along each side of the body. They sense changes in water pressure. This means they can detect vibrations caused by nearby fish. Chondrichthyes are fast swimmers. They have good sight and powerful jaws with rows of sharp teeth. Chondrichthyes swim to force water over their **gills** so they can breathe in oxygen.

The class **Osteichthyes** consist of bony fish. This includes tuna, trout, bass, salmon, goldfish, and many others. These fish have a jaw, scales, and a skeleton made of bone and paired fins. There are about 30,000 species of osteichthyes. They live in saltwater or freshwater. They have a keen sense of smell and eyesight.

Operculus
A protective flap over gills that allows a fish to breathe without swimming

Swim bladder
A gas-filled organ that allows a bony fish to move up and down in water

Larva
The immature form of an animal that looks different from the adult form

Amniotic egg
The egg of a vertebrate that lives on land

Cold-blooded
Having a body temperature that changes with the temperature of the surroundings

Ectotherm
An animal whose main source of body heat is its environment

Link to ▶▶▶

Language Arts

The word *amphibian* comes from two Greek words meaning "double life."

Bony fish have an **operculus.** This is a protective flap over their gills so they can breathe without swimming. Bony fish are covered with scales that protect the fish. Many bony fish also have a **swim bladder.** By changing the amount of gas in this organ, a bony fish can move up and down in water.

Class Amphibia

Amphibians belong to the class Amphibia. There are about 4,000 species of amphibians. Amphibians have four legs and a skeleton of bone. They produce jellylike eggs that develop in water. A frog is an amphibian. Frogs lay eggs in water, but live on land. A frog egg develops into a tadpole that lives in water. The tadpole is the **larva** stage. The tadpole has gills and a long tail. During metamorphosis, a tadpole grows legs and lungs and loses its gills and tail. It develops into an adult frog.

The skin of amphibians is thin. To keep from drying out, most amphibians live near water or in damp environments like swamps and rain forests. Their eggs do not have shells and would dry out if not in water. Amphibians breathe with lungs or through their skin as adults

Class Reptilia

Reptiles belong to the class Reptilia. There are about 6,500 species of reptiles, including snakes, lizards, turtles, alligators, and crocodiles. All reptiles have scales that waterproof their skin. Reptiles breathe in oxygen through their lungs. They have a skeleton of bone and claws. They also produce **amniotic eggs.** An amniotic egg has four membranes and is covered by a shell. The shell protects the egg on land. Some reptiles live on land. Some live in water.

Fish, amphibians, and reptiles are **cold-blooded** animals. They are **ectotherms.** Their body temperature changes with the temperature of their surroundings.

Dinosaurs were reptiles that appeared about 235 million years ago. They ranged in size from a four-story house to a modern cat. They became extinct about 65 million years ago.

---

 3 Reinforce and Extend

IN THE COMMUNITY

 Amphibians as a class of animals are particularly threatened by loss of habitat and pollution to water. Ask students if there are any large-scale construction projects going on in their community. Then organize students into groups and have them research the impact of development and pollution on local wetlands. Encourage them to contact local wildlife refuges or forest preserve agencies. You might also ask groups of students to seek out public records, such as land-impact studies and pollution studies, from their town hall or library. Have each group prepare a summary of their findings to present to the class.

Link to

Language Arts. Have students read the Link to Language Arts feature. Point out that the two Greek words are *amphi-*, which means "of both kinds," and *bios*, meaning "life." Ask students: Why would scientists choose these Greek words to describe amphibians? *(because they have two distinct stages of life)*

ELL/ESL Strategy

Language Objective: *To classify the class Reptilia*

Have students list as many members of the class Reptilia as they can recall without looking back at the text. Then tell them to turn to page 491 and check their list against the text under "Class Reptilia." Encourage students to understand any mistakes they made and to correct their lists.

Warm-blooded
Having a body temperature that stays the same

Endotherm
An animal that creates its own body heat through metabolism

The blue whale is the largest animal that has ever existed. Today, it is an endangered species.

Class Aves

Birds belong to the class Aves. There are about 8,600 species of birds. Like reptiles, birds produce amniotic eggs. They have scales on their legs. Unlike reptiles, birds have a bone structure for flying. Most birds fly. The bones of birds are hollow, strong, and light. Some birds, like eagles, have wings adapted to soar on air currents. Other birds like hummingbirds flap their wings constantly to stay in the air. Some birds, such as ostriches, do not fly.

Birds have feathers. Their feathers are made of protein. Feathers on their bodies help to regulate their body heat. Birds have no teeth. They use a gizzard to grind food. Female birds have only one ovary and lay eggs covered by a hard shell. All birds breathe with lungs and have a horny beak. Birds and mammals are **warm-blooded** because their body temperature stays the same. Warm-blooded animals are **endotherms.** They create body heat through metabolism.

Class Mammalia

Mammals belong to the class Mammalia. There are about 4,500 species of mammals. Most mammals live on land. There are about 1,000 species of mammals that have wings and fly, like bats. Other mammals live in water. These include blue whales, dolphins, and porpoises.

One feature of mammals is hair that covers most of their body. Hair helps keep a constant body temperature. A second feature mammals have is mammary glands on the chest or abdomen. Mammary glands produce milk for young offspring. A third feature mammals have is lungs.

Two mammals are egg-laying, the duck-billed platypus and the spiny anteater. After their eggs hatch, the young lick milk secreted onto the mother's fur.

Marsupial
A mammal with a pouch

About 300 species of mammals, such as kangaroos and koalas, are **marsupials.** Marsupials are animals with pouches. Marsupials give birth to tiny embryos that mature inside a pouch on the mother's abdomen. Milk is secreted inside the pouch for the embryos. More than 4,000 species of mammals have young that develop inside the mother. These include mice, tigers, elephants, dogs, cats, and humans.

Table 15.7.1 sums up the phylum Chordata.

\multicolumn{3}{c}{Table 15.7.1 Vertebrates}
Group	Description	Examples
Chordata Phylum	Internal skeleton of bone or cartilage; skull; sexual reproduction; bilateral symmetry Embryo—dorsal nerve cord, notochord, pharyngeal slits, tail	
Class Myxini Class Cephala-spidomorphi	Skeleton of cartilage; no scales or jaw; breathe with gills; live in water; cold-blooded	hagfish lamprey
Class Chondrichthyes	Skeleton of cartilage; toothlike scales; jaw; paired fins; breathe with gills; live in water; cold-blooded	shark, ray, skate
Class Osteichthyes	Skeleton of bone; bony scales; jaw; paired fins; breathe with gills; live in water; most have swim bladder; cold-blooded	trout, salmon, swordfish, goldfish
Class Amphibia	Skeleton of bone; moist, smooth skin; breathe with lungs or through skin as adults; young live in water, adults live on land; four legs; eggs lack shells; cold-blooded	newt, frog, toad
Class Reptilia	Skeleton of bone; dry, scaly skin; claws; breathe with lungs all stages; four legs except snakes; eggs have shell; cold-blooded	turtle, snake, alligator, lizard
Class Aves	Skeleton of bone; feathers; wings; beaks; claws; breathe with lungs all stages; eggs have shell; warm-blooded	hawk, goose, quail, robin, penguin
Class Mammalia	Skeleton of bone; hair; mammary glands; breathe with lungs all stages; young develop within mother; warm-blooded	bat, kangaroo, mouse, dog, whale, seal, human

SCIENCE JOURNAL

Ask students to write a paragraph in which they evaluate the taxonomic organization of this lesson's content. Ask students: Were you confused by the statement that this phylum contains two groups of invertebrates? Did the organization of vertebrate animals into classes make sense as you read about it?

LEARNING STYLES

Visual/Spatial

See if you can obtain old X-rays from a doctor's office, hospital, veterinary clinic, or zoo. Mention that you want the X-rays to show to students. Find an X-ray that illustrates the three unique features of vertebrates: skeletal system of bone (and, depending on the X-ray, cartilage), a skull, and a backbone with vertebra. Point out the features to students.

Lesson 7 Review Answers

1. endotherms, ectotherms 2. shells 3. amniotic eggs 4. B 5. A 6. B 7. There are two classes of fish that do not have jaws or scales. These are the class Myxini and the class Cephalaspidomorphi. A third class, Chondrichthyes, includes sharks. Fish in this class have strong jaws and swim fast. A fourth class is Osteichthyes. This class consists of bony fish. They have jaws, scales, and a skeleton made of bone. Many bony fish can move up and down in water. 8. The presence of lungs, body hair, and mammary glands are three distinguishing characteristics of mammals. 9. A shark must swim in order to take in oxygen, while a tuna can breathe without swimming. Sharks must also swim in order to move up and down, while a tuna uses a swim bladder to float up and down without swimming. The skeleton of a shark is flexible cartilage, and the skeleton of a tuna is hard and bony. 10. One key difference is the exteriors of each. Amphibians have smooth skin; reptiles have dry, scaly skin; birds have feathers; and mammals have hair. Another key difference is how each produce their young. An amphibian produces jellylike eggs. Reptiles and birds produce amniotic eggs. Most mammals have young that develop inside the mother.

Portfolio Assessment

Sample items include:
- List from ELL/ESL Strategy
- Paragraph from Science Journal
- Lesson 7 Review answers

Lesson 7   REVIEW

Word Bank
amniotic eggs
ectotherms
endotherms
shells

On a sheet of paper, write the word or words from the Word Bank that complete each sentence correctly.

1. Warm-blood animals are _____, and cold-blooded animals are _____.
2. Amphibians usually stay in the water because their eggs do not have _____ and would dry out on land.
3. Like reptiles, birds produce _____.

On a sheet of paper, write the letter of the answer that completes each sentence correctly.

4. The bones of _____ are light and hollow.
   A amphibians   **C** mammals
   B birds   **D** reptiles

5. Reptiles get oxygen through their _____.
   A lungs   **C** skin
   B gills   **D** swim bladder

6. By changing the amount of gas in its _____, a bony fish can move up and down in water.
   A notochord   **C** operculus
   B swim bladder   **D** lungs

Critical Thinking

On a sheet of paper, answer the following questions. Use complete sentences.

7. Describe the four classes of fish.
8. What are three features of mammals?
9. Describe some key differences between a shark and a tuna.
10. Describe some key differences between amphibians, reptiles, birds, and mammals.

Workbook Activity 90

DISCOVERY INVESTIGATION 15

Materials
- dichotomous key
- specimens or photos of several insects

Using a Dichotomous Key

To identify the species of an organism, scientists often use a dichotomous key. A dichotomous key allows the user to trace a path about the features of an organism. The user makes choices along the path based on observations about the organism. The dichotomous key splits into branches according to these choices until the user reaches the name of the organism. In this investigation, you will use a dichotomous key to identify the genus and species of several insects.

Procedure

1. Get a dichtomous key from your teacher.
2. Choose a specimen. Observe the specimen. **Safety Alert: Do not touch or harm the specimen.**
3. Look at the first branch of the dichtomous key. Determine which path to follow based on the features of your specimen.
4. Continue making observations and following the dichotomous key until you reach the name of the insect.
5. Use the dichotomous key to identify other specimens.

Phylogenies and Classifying Diversity   Chapter 15   495

SAFETY ALERT
- Be sure students have read and understood all safety rules for working in the lab.
- Be sure students do not handle specimens. They should be able to observe them.

Discovery Investigation 15

This investigation is less structured than the first investigation in this chapter. It offers students more challenges and requires more teacher facilitation. Encourage students to read the Discovery Investigation steps. Discuss questions they may have before beginning the investigation.

Objectives
- To understand how organisms are classified into dichotomous keys for identification
- To use a dichotomous key to identify an unknown organism
- To observe the different characteristics of various organisms

Skills
Observing, inferring, using information, identifying, thinking critically

Background
Students have learned about how organisms are classified. This investigation allows them to examine several unknown organisms and use a dichotomous key to identify them. Using a dichotomous key helps students understand the observations and logic that go into classifying organisms. The information on the dichotomous key shows the similarities and differences between organisms.

Time Frame
One class period

Procedure
- Have students work together in groups to complete the activity.
- Tailor the skill level to students in your class through the selection of the key and organisms.
- Use an existing dichotomous key or a simpler one that you create. If you make your own key, select organisms that are either closely related or very different, depending on the skill level of your students. Use scientific names or common names in your key.

Continued on page 496

Phylogenies and Classifying Diversity   495

Continued from page 495

- Take care in selecting the specimens that students will identify. Your county extension agent can help you find insect samples common in your area. Or use one of several computer programs that guide students through identification by using a dichotomous key if preparation of a hands-on investigation is too time-consuming.

Cleanup/Disposal

Instruct students in proper cleanup and disposal of materials.

Results

Students should successfully identify several organisms by using the dichotomous key. Be sure students understand how to follow the key as it branches. Students may need help interpreting descriptions on the key or identifying what they are observing on the specimen.

Answers to Analysis, Conclusions, and Explore Further begin on page 670 of this Teacher's Edition.

Assessment

You might include the following items from this investigation in student portfolios:

- Identification of specimens
- Answers to Analysis and Conclusions questions
- The dichotomous key in Explore Further

Cleanup/Disposal
When you are finished, be sure your lab area is clean.

Analysis
1. What kinds of observations did you need to make to identify your specimens?
2. What type of information is used in a dichotomous key?
3. What type of information is not used in a dichotomous key?

Conclusions
1. To be effective, should a dichotomous key include descriptions of all organisms that could be identified? Explain your answer.
2. In Investigation 15, you used descriptions and names to classify organisms. How is using a dichotomous key more helpful than relying on descriptions and names?

Explore Further
Using objects in everyday life, create your own dichotomous key. For example, create a dichotomous key that identifies different cars. Test your dichotomous key by having someone identify one object.

496 Chapter 15 Phylogenies and Classifying Diversity

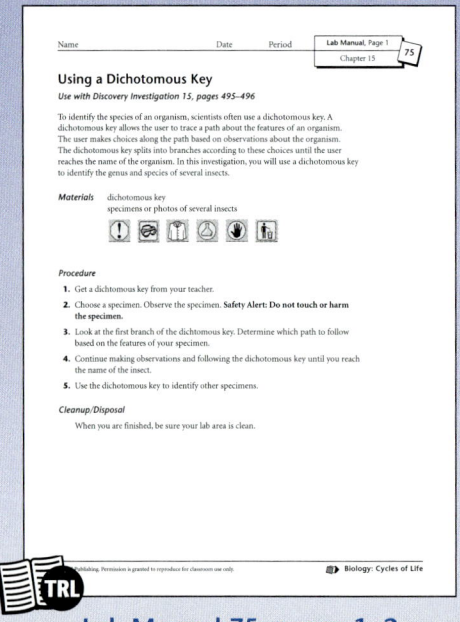

Lab Manual 75, pages 1–2

Lesson 8 Humans

Objectives

After reading this lesson, you should be able to
- define homo sapiens
- list features of humans

Culture
The languages, religions, customs, arts, and dress of a people

Bipedal locomotion
The ability to walk upright on two feet

Life span
The number of years an individual lives

Link to >>>
Language Arts

Homo sapiens comes from Latin and means "wise man."

Humans are classified as kingdom Animalia, phylum Chordata, subphylum Vertebrate, and class Mammalia. The species of humans is called *homo sapiens*. Humans are unique compared to other species. Humans develop language, have intelligence, and have **culture.** Culture is the languages, religions, customs, arts, and dress of a people. Humans use technology. They are naturally curious. They ask questions and find answers.

Humans have **bipedal locomotion.** They walk upright on two feet. Their hands have four fingers and one thumb. Human hands have opposable thumbs. Genetics, environmental conditions, and cultural factors like diet influence the body size of humans. Humans have the highest brain-to-body mass ratio of all large animals. Dolphins are second. Sharks have the highest brain-to-body mass ratio among fish. Octopuses have the highest ratio among invertebrates.

Homo sapiens are widespread on the earth. They are one of the most numerous mammals. Humans have a growing population. There are about 6.5 billion people on the earth today. Asia is the continent with the greatest population of humans. The rest live mainly in the Americas, Africa, and Europe.

Humans have much experience in changing their habitats. Humans change the environment by farming, building cities, developing transportation, and manufacturing products. This allows them to live in many areas of the world.

In wealthy nations, the human **life span** is about 80 years. Life span is the number of years an individual lives. The longest recorded life span for a human is 120 years. As new technology and new medicines are discovered, scientists think the average human life span will increase.

Phylogenies and Classifying Diversity Chapter 15   497

Lesson at a Glance

Chapter 15 Lesson 8

Overview In this lesson, students learn about humans.

Objectives
- To define *homo sapiens*
- To list features of humans

Student Pages 497–499

Teacher's Resource Library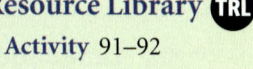
Workbook Activity 91–92
Alternative Workbook Activity 91–92

Vocabulary
bipedal locomotion   culture   life span

Have students look up each vocabulary term, first in a dictionary and then in an encyclopedia. Ask students to write an expanded definition for each term.

Background Information

Anthropology is the scientific study of the origins and physical, social, and cultural development of the human race. The genus *Homo* (*homo* means "man" in Latin) first emerged in Africa between 2 and 2.5 million years ago. The phylogeny of humans is a controversial subject, but anthropologists have been able to settle on at least three species of *Homo*: *H. habilis*, *H. erectus*, and *H. sapiens*. The criteria used to distinguish among them include changes in brain size and advancements in the use of tools made of stone and bone.

1 Warm-Up Activity

Ask students to look up the word *artifact* in a dictionary. Then ask them to brainstorm a list of modern devices that may one day be considered artifacts of our time. Write student responses on the board.

Link to

Language Arts. After reading the Link to Language Arts feature, have students look up the meaning of *erectus*. Ask students: What can you infer from its meaning? (*Erectus* is Latin for "upright." Students can infer that *Homo erectus* walked upright and was bipedal.)

Lesson 8 REVIEW

2 Teaching the Lesson

Have students create a mnemonic device for the succession of levels of taxonomic organization for humans. For example:
King (kingdom)   for (family)
Philip (phylum)   gold and (genus)
came (class)   silver (species)
over (order)

3 Reinforce and Extend

ELL/ESL Strategy

Language Objective: *To learn new content-specific vocabulary*

Ask students if they notice any word parts that are familiar to them in this lesson's vocabulary. Students should remember that *bi-* means two, and that *pede* means feet. Knowing this, ask them to write their own definition of *bipedal locomotion*.

Lesson 8 Review Answers

1. species 2. bipedal locomotion 3. brain 4. D 5. B 6. D 7. The size of a human body is influenced by genetics, environment, and cultural factors. 8. New technology and medicines continue to increase the life span. 9. Humans change their environments through agriculture, construction, transportation, and manufacturing. 10. Humans have the ability to think about concepts and ideas. Humans are naturally curious and can question and use logic.

Portfolio Assessment

Sample items include:
- Mnemonic from Teaching the Lesson
- Lesson 8 Review answers

498   Chapter 15

Word Bank
bipedal locomotion
brain
species

On a sheet of paper, write the word or words from the Word Bank that complete each sentence correctly.

1. There is only one _____ of humans.
2. Humans use _____, meaning they walk upright on two feet.
3. Humans have the highest ratio of _____ to body mass of any animal.

On a sheet of paper, write the letter of the answer that completes each sentence correctly.

4. The scientific name for humans is _____.
   A *Homo erectus*
   B *Homo habilis*
   C *Homo neanderthalensis*
   D *Homo sapiens*

5. Most humans live in _____.
   A the Americas   C Africa
   B Asia   D Europe

6. Unlike other mammals, human hands have _____.
   A five fingers   C fingernails
   B skin   D opposable thumbs

Critical Thinking

On a sheet of paper, answer the following questions. Use complete sentences.

7. What factors influence the body size of a human?
8. Why do scientists think the human life span will increase?
9. How do humans change their environments?
10. What are some features specific to humans?

498   Chapter 15   Phylogenies and Classifying Diversity

Workbook Activity 91

BIOLOGY IN THE WORLD

The Link Between Dinosaurs and Birds

Until the 1980s, most scientists thought that dinosaurs were heavy, slow creatures that looked like large lizards. Scientists get information about dinosaurs and other extinct animals mostly from fossils.

Recently, scientists have found many more dinosaur fossils. These fossils suggest that dinosaurs may be closely related to birds.

Recent fossils found in China show that dinosaurs had birdlike features. A dinosaur fossil of an early tyrannosaur shows clear imprints of feathers. Another smaller dinosaur was fossilized in a sleeping position. This position looks similar to the way modern birds curl up when they rest. These and other fossils show that many dinosaurs were small and quick. Some dinosaurs, for example, were the size of a chicken and could move fast.

The discovery of a dinosaur with feathers provided clues about the purpose of early feathers. Large dinosaurs like the tyrannosaur did not fly. Scientists think that feathers kept dinosaurs warm. After millions of years of evolution, birds began to use feathers on their wings for flight.

1. How do scientists learn about dinosaurs?
2. What evidence links dinosaurs to birds?
3. What purpose did feathers probably serve for dinosaurs?

Chapter 15 Summary

Have volunteers read aloud each summary item on page 500. Ask volunteers to explain the meaning of each item. Direct students' attention to the Vocabulary box on the bottom of page 500. Have them read each term and its definition.

Graphic Organizer

As students read Chapter 15, have them finish completing the chart on Graphic Organizer 15: Phylogenies and Classifying Diversity. Encourage students to read each lesson of the chapter and then have them fill in the portion of the chart that pertains to the lesson. When they have completed the chart, ask them to answer the questions.

Chapter 15 SUMMARY

- Scientists classify living organisms by their features and evolutionary history. The highest level of classification is the domain. Organisms are classified into the domains Archaea, Bacteria, or Eukarya.

- The kingdom Protista includes protozoa, algae, euglena, and slime molds. Members of the kingdom Fungi are eukaryotes with bodies made of strands of hyphae.

- Plants are classified into phyla by their evolutionary advancements. Phylum Bryophyta is mosses, and the phylum Polypodiophyta is ferns.

- The phylum Coniferophyta is conifers, and the phylum Anthophyta is flowering plants.

- Kingdom Animalia includes organisms that are multicellular eukaryotes. Animals are classified as invertebrates or vertebrates. Invertebrates include sponges, cnidarians, flatworms, mollusks, annelids, arthropods, and echinoderms. Vertebrates include fishes, amphibians, reptiles, birds, and mammals.

- There is only one species of humans, called *homo sapiens*.

Vocabulary

algae, 464	cyanobacterium, 469	marsupial, 493	radial symmetry, 482
alternation of generations, 473	dorsal, 489	metamorphosis, 485	radula, 484
amniotic egg, 491	dysentery, 465	mold, 468	rhizoid, 473
amoeba, 465	ectotherm, 491	mollusk, 483	roundworm, 483
angiosperm, 472	endoskeleton, 486	molting, 484	seed, 472
arachnid, 484	endotherm, 492	moss, 472	segmented worm, 483
arthropod, 484	euglena, 464	multicellular, 479	slime mold, 466
bilateral symmetry, 483	exoskeleton, 484	mycelium, 468	sori, 475
bipedal locomotion, 497	fern, 472	mycorrhiza, 473	spore, 466
blastula, 479	flatworm, 483	myxini, 490	sporophyte, 474
cartilage, 489	fossil fuel, 475	nectar, 477	stamen, 476
cephalaspidomorphi, 490	frond, 475	notochord, 490	stigma, 477
chondrichthyes, 490	gametophyte, 474	nonvascular plant, 473	swim bladder, 491
chordate, 489	germinate, 477	operculum, 491	taxonomist, 458
cnidarian, 482	gill, 490	osteichthyes, 490	taxonomy, 458
cold-blooded, 491	gymnosperm, 472	pharyngeal slit, 490	tentacle, 482
complete metamorphosis, 485	heterotroph, 479	phloem, 473	tube feet, 486
conifer, 475	hyphae, 468	phylogeny, 482	vascular plant, 472
crustacean, 484	incomplete metamorphosis, 486	pistil, 477	vascular tissue, 473
culture, 497	larva, 491	pollination, 477	vertebra, 489
	lichen, 469	protozoan, 464	warm-blooded, 492
	life span, 497	pseudopod, 465	xylem, 473

500 Chapter 15 *Phylogenies and Classifying Diversity*

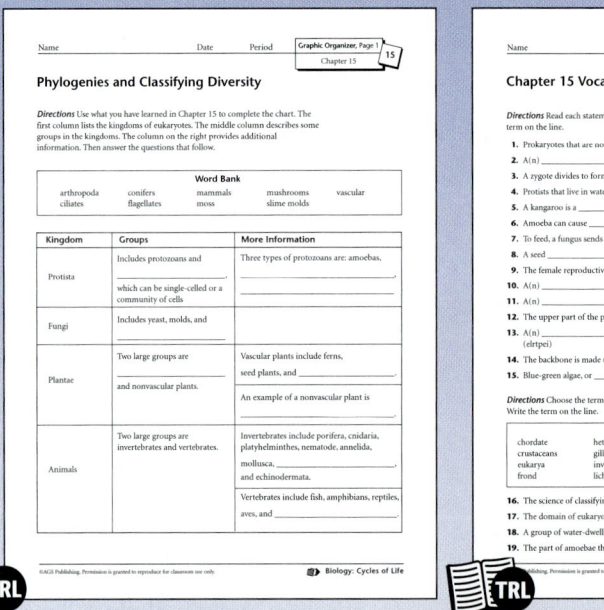

Graphic Organizer 15, pages 1–3   Workbook Activity 92, pages 1–4

Chapter 15 REVIEW

Word Bank
algae
alternation of generations
angiosperm
bilateral symmetry
gametophyte
gymnosperm
heterotroph
hyphae
larva
metamorphosis
mold
molting
phylogeny
pseudopod
slime mold
sporophyte
xylem

Vocabulary Review

On a sheet of paper, write the word or words from the Word Bank that complete each sentence correctly.

1. A(n) _____ consumes organic material for nutrition.
2. The _____ of a species includes information about its origin and evolution.
3. A body made of left and right halves that are the same is known as _____.
4. A protist that is yellow, red, or white and is like fungi and animals is a(n) _____.
5. An amoeba uses a(n) _____ to surround food and to move.
6. Mosses, algae, and some protists have a life cycle known as _____.
7. A protist that makes its own food and usually lives in water is _____.
8. During _____, arthropods shed their exoskeleton and secrete a larger one.
9. A fungus that grows quickly on a surface is a(n) _____.
10. A plant that is diploid is the _____.
11. A plant that is haploid is the _____.
12. Some organisms undergo _____, which involves several stages, as they develop into an adult.
13. A nonflowering seed plant is a(n) _____.
14. The bodies of fungi are made of strands of _____.
15. One stage of metamorphosis between embryo and adult for some organisms is the _____ stage.
16. A flowering plant is a(n) _____.

Review continued on next page

Chapter 15 Review
Use the Chapter Review to prepare students for tests and to reteach content from the chapter.

Chapter 15 Mastery Test
The Teacher's Resource Library includes two forms of the Chapter 15 Mastery Test. Each test addresses the chapter Goals for Learning. An optional third page of additional critical-thinking items is included for each test. The difficulty level of the two forms is equivalent.

Review Answers
Vocabulary Review

1. heterotroph 2. phylogeny 3. bilateral symmetry 4. slime mold 5. pseudopod 6. alteration of generations 7. algae 8. molting 9. mold 10. sporophyte 11. gametophyte 12. metamorphosis 13. gymnosperm 14. hyphae 15. larva 16. angiosperm 17. xylem

TEACHER ALERT

In the Chapter Review, the Vocabulary Review activity includes a sample of the chapter's vocabulary terms. The activity will help determine students' understanding of key vocabulary terms and concepts presented in the chapter. Other vocabulary terms used in the chapter are listed below.

amniotic egg
amoeba
arachnid
arthropod
bipedal locomotion
blastula
cartilage
cephalaspido-morphi
chondrichthyes
chordate
cnidarian
cold-blooded
complete metamorphosis
conifer
crustacean
culture
cyanobacterium
dorsal
dysentery
ectotherm
endoskeleton
endotherm
euglena
exoskeleton
fern
flatworm
fossil fuel
frond
germinate
gill
incomplete metamorphosis
lichen
life span
marsupial
mollusk
moss
multicellular
mycelium
myxini
nectar
nonvascular plant
notochord
operculus
osteichthyes
pharyngeal slit
phloem
pistil
pollination
protozoan
radial symmetry
radula
rhizoid
roundworm
seed
segmented worm
sori
spore
stamen
stigma
swim bladder
taxonomist
taxonomy
tentacle
tube feet
vascular plant
vascular tissue
vertebra
warm-blooded

Chapter 15 REVIEW - continued

17. The _____ is the vascular tissue in plants that carries water and minerals from the roots to the stems and leaves.

Concept Review

On a sheet of paper, write the letter of the answer that completes each sentence correctly.

18. The order of classification from highest to lowest level is _____.

  A domain, kingdom, phylum, class, order, family, genus, species

  B domain, species, kingdom, phylum, class, order, family, genus

  C species, domain, kingdom, phylum, class, order, family, genus

  D species, kingdom, phylum, class, order, family, genus, species, domain

19. The domain Eukarya has four kingdoms: Protista, Fungi, Plantae, and _____.

  A Protozoa   C Cnidarian
  B Animalia   D Phaeophyta

20. Bony fish have a(n) _____, or a protective flap over their gills.

  A radula   C swim bladder
  B notochord   D operculus

21. The phylum of plants that have vascular tissue but no seeds is _____.

  A Anthophyta   C Bryophyta
  B Coniferophyta   D Polypodiophyta

Chapter 15   Phylogenies and Classifying Diversity

Chapter 15 Mastery Test A, pages 1–3

Critical Thinking

On a sheet of paper, answer the following questions. Use complete sentences.

22. In what ways are birds, amphibians, and reptiles alike? In what ways are they different?

23. How are the four classes of fish alike? How are they different?

24. List the kingdom, phylum, and class of the species *Homo sapiens*.

25. Name the three groups of protozoans. Describe the structures each group uses for movement and catching food.

Research and Write

Do research to find information on key fossils of primitive humans. Explain the importance of each fossil find. Use this information and photos or art to create a poster. Include a map that shows where each fossil was found.

Test-Taking Tip To choose the answer that correctly completes a sentence, read the sentence using each answer choice. Then choose the answer that makes the most sense when the entire sentence is read.

Concept Review
18. A 19. B 20. D 21. D

Critical Thinking

22. Birds, amphibians, and reptiles all have bony skeletons and breathe with lungs at some stage. Birds have feathers and some can fly; amphibians have smooth skin and live in water when young; reptiles have dry, scaly skin that is waterproof. 23. All four classes of fish live in the water and are cold-blooded. The classes Myxini and Cephalaspidomorphi have skeletons made of soft cartilage and have no jaws or scales. The other two classes, Chondrichthyes and Osteichthyes, do have jaws and scales. The class Chondrichtyes contains fish that need to swim in order to breathe. The class Osteichthyes contains fish that can breathe without swimming. 24. The kingdom is Animalia, the phylum is Chordata, and the class is Mammalia. 25. Ciliates use hairlike projections called cilia to move and catch food. Amoebas use pseudopod projection to catch and engulf food. Flagellates use whiplike flagella to move through water.

Research and Write

Divide students into small groups to conduct research. They can search library databases and encyclopedias for "fossils" and "dinosaurs," or search the Internet for "important fossils" and "primitive humans."

ALTERNATIVE ASSESSMENT

Alternative Assessment items correlate to the student Goals for Learning at the beginning of this chapter.

- Facilitate a class discussion in which students compare and contrast the three-domain classification system with the six-kingdom classification system.
- Ask students to look over the chapter and create a diagram resembling a family tree. They can start with the kingdoms and then add the organisms that belong to each underneath.
- Have students create a miniaturized version of the Geologic Time Scale for eight phyla of the kingdom Animalia.

Chapter 16

Planning Guide
Behavioral Biology

	Student Pages	Student Text Lesson		
		Vocabulary	Lesson Review	Critical-Thinking Questions
Lesson 1 What Is Behavioral Biology?	506–512	✔	✔	✔
Lesson 2 Types of Behavior	513–519	✔	✔	✔
Lesson 3 Forms of Communication	520–529	✔	✔	✔

Chapter Activities

Teacher's Resource Library
Community Connection 16:
 Animal Behavior
Graphic Organizer 16:
 Behavioral Biology

Teacher's Edition
Opener Activity

Assessment Options

Student Text
Chapter 16 Review

Teacher's Resource Library
Chapter 16 Mastery Tests A and B

Teacher's Edition
Chapter 16 Alternative Assessment

	Student Text Features									Teaching Strategies						Learning Styles					Teacher's Resource Library			
	Achievements in Science	Science at Work	Biology in Your Life	Investigation/Discovery	Biology in the World	Express Lab	Link to	Research and Write	Technology and Society	ELL/ESL Strategy	Background Information	Science Journal	Applications (Home, Career, Community, Global, Environment)	Online Connection	Teacher Alert	Auditory/Verbal	Body/Kinesthetic	Interpersonal/Group Learning	Logical/Mathematical	Visual/Spatial	Workbook Activities	Alternative Workbook Activities	Lab Manual	Self-Study Guide
				511		509	✔			508	506		507, 509		509	509	510				93	93	76–77	✔
	518						✔			514	513	514	516		515			515		515	94	94	78	✔
		524	525	527	529		✔	533	522	521	520	524	524, 526	529	522			523		524	95–96	95–96	79–80	✔

Pronunciation Key

a	hat	e	let	ī	ice	ô	order	ù	put	sh she
ā	age	ē	equal	o	hot	oi	oil	ü	rule	th thin
ä	far	ėr	term	ō	open	ou	out	ch	child	ᴛʜ then
â	care	i	it	ȯ	saw	u	cup	ng	long	zh measure

ə { a in about, e in taken, i in pencil, o in lemon, u in circus }

Alternative Workbook Activities

The Teacher's Resource Library (TRL) contains a set of lower-level worksheets called Alternative Workbook Activities. These worksheets cover the same content as the regular Workbook Activities but are written at a second-grade reading level.

Skill Track Online

Use Skill Track Online for *Biology: Cycles of Life* to monitor student progress and meet the demands of adequate yearly progress (AYP). Make informed instructional decisions with individual student and class reports of online lesson and chapter assessments. With immediate and ongoing feedback, students will also see what they have learned and where they need more reinforcement and practice.

Chapter at a Glance

Chapter 16: Behavioral Biology
pages 504–533

Lessons

1. **What Is Behavioral Biology?**
   pages 506–512

   Investigation 16 pages 511–512

2. **Types of Behavior**
   pages 513–519

3. **Forms of Communication**
   pages 520–529

   Discovery Investigation 16
   pages 527–528

   Biology in the World page 529

Chapter 16 Summary page 530

Chapter 16 Review
pages 531–533

Audio CD

Skill Track Online
for Biology: Cycles of Life

Teacher's Resource Library TRL

   Workbook Activities 93–96

   Alternative Workbook Activities
   93–96

   Lab Manual 76–80

   Community Connection 16

   Graphic Organizer 16

   Resource File 37–38

   Chapter 16 Self-Study Guide

   Chapter 16 Mastery Tests A and B

(Answer Keys for the Teacher's Resource Library begin on page 675 of the Teacher's Edition. The Materials List for the Lab Manual activities begins on page 720.)

Opener Activity

Display photographs of animals engaged in different types of behavior. Examples might include a peacock displaying its tail feathers, a dog begging for food, or an animal running from a predator. Have students discuss what the animals are doing and why.

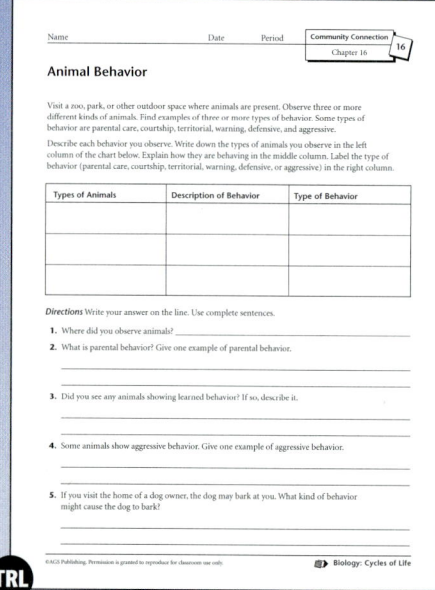

Community Connection 16

504 *Chapter 16*

Chapter 16: Behavioral Biology

Behavior is a response, or reaction, as a result of a stimulus. The bear's genes and changes in sunlight tell the bear that winter is coming. It's time for the bear to put on fat. The salmon know it's time to reproduce. Their genes tell them to return to their birthplace. They will lay eggs there. Some behaviors are innate, such as the salmon returning to their birthplace. Other behaviors are learned, such as the bear catching salmon. In Chapter 16, you will learn about animal behavior and its role in animal survival. You will also learn some processes that control animal behavior.

Goals for Learning

- ◆ To recognize that behaviors are responses to stimuli
- ◆ To identify behaviors as innate or learned
- ◆ To identify ways that animals communicate
- ◆ To recognize that behaviors help organisms survive

Introducing the Chapter

Have students label on a sheet of paper these three columns: "What I Know," "What I Want to Learn," and "What I Learned." Have them complete the first two columns about these topics: innate behavior, learned behavior, and animal communication. As they read the lessons, have them complete the third column.

Have students read the Goals for Learning. Students may want to add more topics to their paper after they have read the goals. Answer any questions that students may have.

Notes and Math Tips

Ask volunteers to read the notes and math tips that appear in the margins throughout the chapter. Then discuss them with the class.

TEACHER'S RESOURCE

The AGS Publishing Teaching Strategies in Science Transparencies may be used with this chapter. The transparencies add an interactive dimension to expand and enhance the *Biology: Cycles of Life* program content.

CAREER INTEREST INVENTORY

The AGS Publishing Harrington-O'Shea Career Decision-Making System-Revised (CDM) may be used with this chapter. Students can use the CDM to explore their interests and identify careers. The CDM defines career areas that are indicated by students' responses on the inventory.

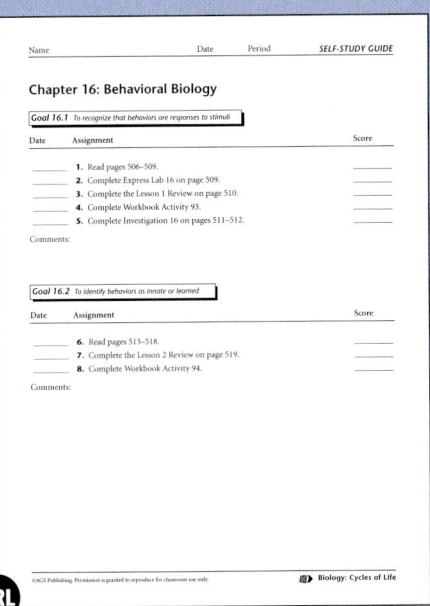

Chapter 16 Self-Study Guide

Lesson at a Glance

Chapter 16 Lesson 1

Overview In this lesson, students learn about the study of animal behavior.

Objectives
- To define and give examples of internal and external stimuli
- To define and give examples of innate and learned behavior

Student Pages 506–512

Teacher's Resource Library
Workbook Activity 93
Alternative Workbook Activity 93
Lab Manual 76–77

Vocabulary

behavior	fixed action
behavioral biology	pattern behavior
ethologist	innate behavior
external stimulus	internal stimulus
	learned behavior

Have students use a dictionary to look up the components of the vocabulary terms, such as *behavior, stimulus, internal, external,* and *innate.* Have students work in pairs to write a definition for each vocabulary term of two or more words, without using those words in the definition. *(Sample answers: behavioral biology: the study of the way living things act; internal stimulus: something that occurs inside an organism to which the organism reacts)* Then have students write complete sentences using the vocabulary terms.

Background Information

Ethologists study the behavior of animals. For example, ethologists may study how predators catch their young. They do not necessarily confine their research to one species but may study the techniques of many predators. Ethologists also may try to determine if a particular behavior is learned or innate. If the behavior is learned, they may study how the young are taught a particular behavior. If it is innate, they may try to determine the mechanism by which a particular behavior is passed on.

Lesson 1: What Is Behavioral Biology?

Objectives
After reading this lesson, you should be able to
- define and give examples of internal and external stimuli
- define and give examples of innate and learned behavior

You have probably watched animals over a period of time. You may have observed how a goldfish swims toward food. You may have watched how two dogs play. You may have observed how birds fly in flocks. These are examples of animal **behavior.** Behavior is the way an organism acts.

Behavioral biology is the study of the behavior of living things. A scientist who studies the behavior of animals is an **ethologist.** Ethologists observe animal behavior and then try to find out why the animals behaved in certain ways. Ethologists usually study animal behavior in their natural environments, such as flocks of birds flying. They also study behavior through experiments.

Behavior is usually observable. Scientists observe animals to see how they get food, reproduce, and avoid danger. Animals that are flexible in their behavior can adjust when their environment changes. These animals will change their behavior to fit the new environment.

Ethologists identify factors that shape behavior. They want to understand what stimuli cause animals to show a certain behavior. They also want to understand how behavior works and how animals learn a behavior.

Internal and External Stimuli

When organisms act, they are reacting to a stimulus. Recall from Chapter 1 that a stimulus is anything to which an organism reacts. For example, you eat because you feel hungry. Hunger is an **internal stimulus.** The behavior of eating is your reaction to this internal stimulus. A bird's song is an **external stimulus.** Birds use songs to attract mates. An external stimulus is one that occurs in an animal's environment.

Behavior
The way an organism acts

Behavioral biology
The study of the behavior of living things

Ethologist
A scientist who studies the behavior of animals

Internal stimulus
A stimulus that occurs inside of an organism

External stimulus
A stimulus that occurs outside of an organism

Sometimes animals may show the same behavior in all environments. Animals may also show certain behaviors only in certain environments. An animal's responses to external stimuli can result from interactions with members of its own species or other species. An animal also responds to nonliving elements in its environment.

Innate Behavior

Some responses are **innate behavior.** This behavior is inherited and does not have to be learned. Innate behavior is present at birth. For example, a spider's ability to spin a web does not require learning. When young spiders hatch, the mother dies. The young spiders make webs without seeing their mother make one.

Inheritance shapes behavior. Most animal behavior stays the same over time. This type of innate behavior is called **fixed action pattern behavior.** The behavior always occurs the same way. One species of spiders always spins webs by following the same steps in the same order. The behavior of web spinning is the same. Another species of spiders spins different webs. This species may use different steps in a different order.

Learned Behavior

Animals behave by observing and learning. This is called **learned behavior.** Animals invent and learn new behaviors. For example, scientists observed Japanese snow monkeys. These monkeys live near the ocean that surrounds Japan. The scientists threw pieces of potatoes near the monkeys. The monkeys wanted to eat the potatoes, but the pieces were covered with sand. The monkeys tried to brush off the sand, but the sand would not come off.

Then a female monkey dipped a piece of potato in the ocean. The water washed the sand away. She ate the potato. Some of the monkeys watched and learned this behavior. Other monkeys saw the behavior, but did not imitate it.

Innate behavior
A behavior that is present at birth

Fixed action pattern behavior
A behavior that always occurs the same way

Learned Behavior
A behavior that results from experience

 Warm-Up Activity

Ask students: What is an example of an innate behavior? *(Sample answers: spider spinning a web, baby crying)* Ask students: What is an example of a learned behavior? *(Sample answers: talking, a dog following commands)* Have students perform the Express Lab on page 509 and answer the questions.

Express Lab Answers

1. The second time should be shorter than the first time. The student learned from the first attempt and was able to do the maze faster. **2.** Answers may vary. The second student's time may be faster than the first student's first time but slower than that student's second attempt. The second student learned from watching the first student complete the maze, but may not be as proficient as someone who has already completed the maze. **3.** This is learned. The students are responding to stimuli (the maze) and learning how to solve it faster.

 Teaching the Lesson

Have students write down each subtopic (such as behavioral biology, internal and external stimuli, and innate behavior), leaving space between entries. As students read the lesson, have them write down facts about each subtopic.

Encourage students to ask questions about any concept they do not understand. Have them write down any additional information that helps them understand the concept.

Go through the lesson as a class. Have volunteers explain the concepts in each paragraph. Clear up any misconceptions students may have.

 Reinforce and Extend

AT HOME

 Have students keep a journal of family members reacting to stimuli for one evening. Journal entries might include items such as answering a phone or doorbell or coming to dinner when called. Have students share their entries with the class the next day.

Link to

Chemistry. Have students read the Link to Chemistry feature. The plant hormone, auxin, stimulates some plant cells to elongate and inhibits the elongation of other plant cells. For example, when a houseplant is placed near a window, the plant tends to bend toward the light. It is believed that auxin is destroyed where the light strikes the stem. The side of the stem away from the sun has more auxin present. The cells on this side of the stem elongate. This results in the plant bending toward the light.

When a plant is placed on its side, the plant responds to gravity. Gravity forces the auxin to the bottom side of the stem. The auxin forces the plant cells on this side of the stem to elongate, resulting in the plant growing upward. Auxin in the roots has the opposite effect on the plant cells. Auxin inhibits the elongation of the plant cells resulting in the roots turning downward.

ELL/ESL Strategy

Language Objective: *To explain concepts*

Divide the class into pairs. Have each pair of students compare and contrast internal and external stimuli. Then have students compare and contrast innate and learned behaviors. Have students share their ideas with the class.

Lab Activities

Chapter 16 has Investigation and Discovery Investigation lab activities. Two additional lab activities for Chapter 16 appear in the Biology: Cycles of Life Lab Manual and on the Teacher's Resource Library CD-ROM.

Link to >>>
Chemistry

Plants respond to stimuli. Tropisms are growth responses. They cause plants to grow toward or away from a stimulus. Tropisms are usually regulated by plant hormones, or chemicals, such as auxins. Phototropism is the growth of a plant toward or away from a light. Gravitropism is a plant's growth due to gravity.

The scientists tried another experiment. They threw grains of wheat near the monkeys. The monkeys could not get the sand off the small grains. A monkey put a handful of grain into the water. The sand sank. The grains of wheat floated on top of the water. The monkey skimmed off the wheat grains and ate them. Other monkeys watched and learned this new behavior. The new behavior was shared by imitation.

These experiments show that both genes and the environment affect behavior. Eating is an innate behavior. The snow monkeys modified their behavior by using a new method to clean their food. Figure 16.1.1 shows a group of Japanese snow monkeys.

Behavior Evolves Through Natural Selection

Scientists study behavior as evolutionary principles. They determine if a behavior is innate or learned. They also track changes in behavior over long periods of time. Patterns of behavior have evolved to ensure the reproductive success of a species. These changes in behavior evolved through natural selection.

Figure 16.1.1 *Some animals, such as Japanese snow monkeys, are flexible and can adapt to environmental changes.*

Scientists also investigate why certain behaviors are more favored by natural selection. They might ask, for example, why the mating behavior of many bird species occurs in the spring. This behavior may be due to available food in the spring for offspring.

Express Lab 16

Materials
- 3 copies of a maze puzzle
- stopwatch or clock with a second hand

Procedure
1. Work with a partner. Get a copy of a maze puzzle from your teacher.
2. Decide who will keep time and who will solve the maze puzzle. Time the person solving the puzzle. Stop timing the person when the puzzle is solved. Record this time.
3. Get another copy of the same maze puzzle. Have the same person solve the puzzle and the same person keep time. Record the time.
4. Get a third copy of the maze puzzle. Switch jobs with your partner.

Analysis
1. How did the time differ between the first attempt and the second attempt to solve the maze puzzle? What caused this difference?
2. How did the time in Step 4 compare to the first two times? What factors were different for the partner who solved the maze puzzle in Step 4?
3. Is the ability to solve the maze puzzle innate or learned?

IN THE COMMUNITY

Identify someone in the community who uses trained dogs or trains working dogs. Invite him or her to bring a trained dog and speak to the class, demonstrating how the dog responds to certain stimuli. Possible sources in the community are police departments and their drug-sniffing dogs, ranchers and their dogs that herd cattle, or dogs that help people with disabilities.

TEACHER ALERT

Students may benefit from a quick review of the principles of natural selection. Ask volunteers to explain the concept to the class. Answer any questions that students may have or clear up any misconceptions that arise.

LEARNING STYLES

Auditory/Verbal
Have volunteers read each section of the lesson to the class. Choose a different student for each section so that more students can participate in reading aloud. Have the other students follow along in their books. After a section has been read, have another student summarize the information that has just been read. More than one student may need to summarize the material so that no concepts are missed.

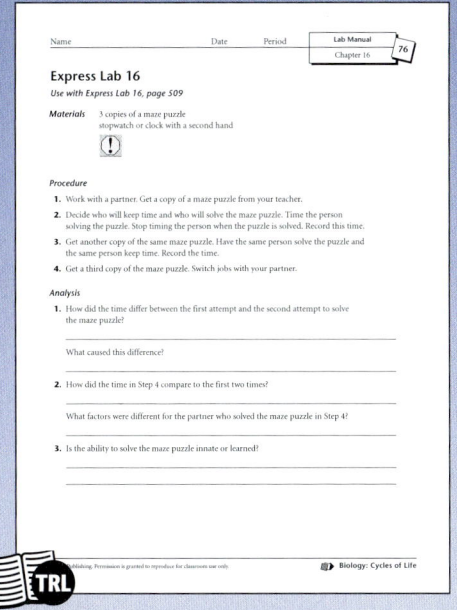

Lab Manual 76

Lesson 1 Review Answers

1. ethologist **2.** learned behavior **3.** innate behavior **4.** A **5.** B **6.** C **7.** Behaviors evolve to ensure the success of a species. Scientists believe that most behaviors evolved through natural selection, and those organisms that created a successful behavior pass it on to their offspring. **8.** An internal stimulus is one that comes from inside an animal, such as a hunger pain. An external stimulus comes from the environment, such as a cold breeze. Both cause a response. **9.** Spiders are born with the knowledge and ability to spin webs. Different species of spiders spin webs differently, but a young spider is able to spin its species' type of web without being taught. **10.** When monkeys were given wheat grains covered with sand, they tried different methods to clean it. When one monkey found a way to clean the food successfully, the other monkeys watched and copied the technique.

Portfolio Assessment

Sample items include:
- List of facts about each topic from Teaching the Lesson
- Journal of family members responding to various stimuli from At Home
- Lesson 16 Review answers

LEARNING STYLES

Body/Kinesthetic
Have a volunteer clap a short rhythm with his or her hands. Have the class try to clap the same rhythm with their hands. After students have successfully clapped the rhythm, have another volunteer clap a longer or more difficult rhythm. Ask students to repeat the rhythm. Tell students they are experiencing a learned behavior.

Lesson 1 REVIEW

Word Bank
ethologist
innate behavior
learned behavior

On a sheet of paper, write the word or words from the Word Bank that complete each sentence correctly.

1. A(n) _____ is a scientist who studies the behavior of animals.
2. A behavior that results from experience is _____.
3. A(n) _____ is a behavior that an animal is born with.

On a sheet of paper, write the letter of the answer that completes each sentence correctly.

4. A stimulus that occurs inside of an organism is a(n) _____.
   - **A** internal stimulus
   - **B** external stimulus
   - **C** innate behavior
   - **D** learned behavior

5. A stimulus that occurs outside of an organism is a(n) _____.
   - **A** internal stimulus
   - **B** external stimulus
   - **C** innate behavior
   - **D** learned behavior

6. The study of the behavior of living things is _____.
   - **A** fixed action pattern behavior
   - **B** stimuli
   - **C** behavioral biology
   - **D** learned behavior

Critical Thinking

On a sheet of paper, write the answers to the following questions. Use complete sentences.

7. How are behaviors linked with evolution and natural selection?
8. Compare an external stimulus and an internal stimulus.
9. Where does a spider's ability to spin a web come from?
10. Describe how snow monkeys learned new behaviors.

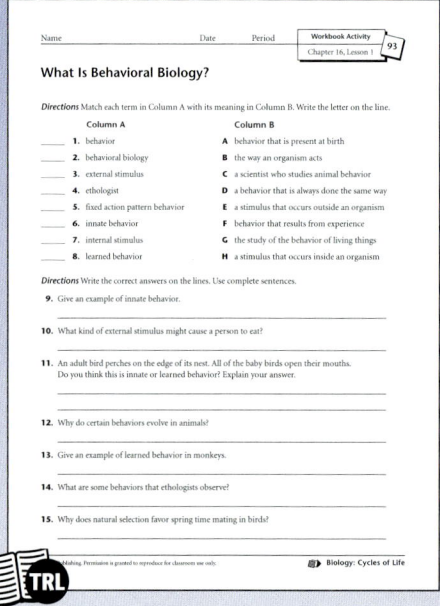

Workbook Activity 93

INVESTIGATION 16

Investigating Animal Behavior

Materials
- safety goggles
- lab coat or apron
- shoebox and lid
- scissors
- 6 paper towels
- tap water
- 10 sow bugs
- small lamp

Animals often react when their environment changes. They adapt to the change or move to a more suitable environment. Sow bugs often live under rocks in gardens and yards. They eat decayed organic material. In this investigation, you will observe what type of environment sow bugs prefer.

Procedure

1. Put on goggles and a lab coat or apron.
2. Make half of your shoebox dark. Make the other half open to light. To do this, use scissors to remove half of the shoebox lid. **Safety Alert: Be careful when using scissors to cut the shoebox lid.**

Behavioral Biology   Chapter 16

SAFETY ALERT

- Make sure that students are careful not to harm the sow bugs.
- Students should wash their hands after handling the sow bugs.
- Sow bugs should be kept in a dark, moist environment until they are ready to be used. After the investigation, the sow bugs can safely be returned to the outdoors.

Investigation 16

Encourage students to read the Investigation steps. Discuss questions they may have before beginning the investigation.

Objectives

- To observe animal behavior
- To collect data and reach a conclusion about sow bug behavior

Skills

Observing, experimenting, inferring, collecting and analyzing data, drawing conclusions

Background

Sow bugs are generally found in dark, damp places. Sow bugs avoid light and will usually move away from light into dark areas if available. This behavior protects the sow bug from predators and keeps it from drying out.

You can order sow bugs from a supplier of science educational materials. Some are listed on page 723. Or you can find sow bugs outdoors. If you wish to collect the sow bugs yourself, they can usually be found in a moderate climate by looking under rocks in a garden or yard setting.

Time Frame

One class period

Procedure

- You can use any type of container as the testing environment, as long as you are able to make half of the container fairly dark. Make sure that the container is large enough to hold all of the sow bugs comfortably, but small enough that the bugs can move around and find the dark environment easily.
- If your classroom is well-lit, the lamp may not be necessary, as the natural or classroom light will be enough of a stimulus.
- After placing the bugs into the box and putting on the lid, the sow bugs should begin to move almost immediately into the darker area.

Continued on page 512

Behavioral Biology

Continued from page 511

- Make sure that students place moist paper towels on the bottom of both sides of the box, as the sow bugs prefer dampness. The paper towels should be moist, but not completely wet.

Cleanup/Disposal
Instruct students in cleanup and disposal of materials.

Analysis Answers
1. Students should observe that most or all of the sow bugs move into the dark environment.
2. The stimulus in this investigation is the light. Sow bugs react to light by moving away from it.

Conclusions Answers
1. Sow bugs prefer a dark environment.
2. The behavior of the sow bugs is innate. Sow bugs naturally move into darker environments.
3. Sow bugs have evolved to prefer darker environments for many reasons. Some of the most likely reasons are to avoid predators and to avoid drying out.

Explore Further Answers
Students can create an additional investigation that shows that the sow bugs will seek out a moist environment.

Assessment
You might include the following items from this investigation in student portfolios:
- Answers to Analysis and Conclusions questions
- Procedure and hypothesis from Explore Further

512 Chapter 16

3. Dampen the paper towels with tap water. Put a layer of damp paper towels in the entire bottom of the box.

4. Put the sow bugs in the middle of the box. **Safety Alert: Handle the sow bugs gently. Do not harm them.** Put the lid on the box. Half of the box should be dark and half should be exposed to the light. To make the exposed half lighter, shine a small lamp onto it. Be sure the lamp only lights up half of the box. Keep the other half dark.

5. Wait five minutes. Count how many sow bugs are in the light half and how many are in the dark half of your box. Record the numbers.

Cleanup/Disposal
After handling the sow bugs, wash your hands. Follow your teacher's instructions for collecting the sow bugs and disposal of material. When you are finished, be sure your lab area is clean.

Analysis
1. In Step 5, how many sow bugs were in the light half of the box? How many were in the dark half?
2. What was the stimulus in this investigation? Describe the behavior the sow bugs displayed in response to this stimulus.

Conclusions
1. What type of environment do sow bugs prefer?
2. Do you think the behavior of the sow bugs in this investigation is innate or learned?
3. Why might sow bugs display this type of behavior?

Explore Further
Sow bugs are usually found in dark, damp environments. Design another investigation to determine whether sow bugs prefer a damp environment or a dry environment. Write a hypothesis. Have your procedure and Safety Alerts approved by your teacher. Conduct your investigation. Do your results support or refute your hypothesis?

512 Chapter 16 Behavioral Biology

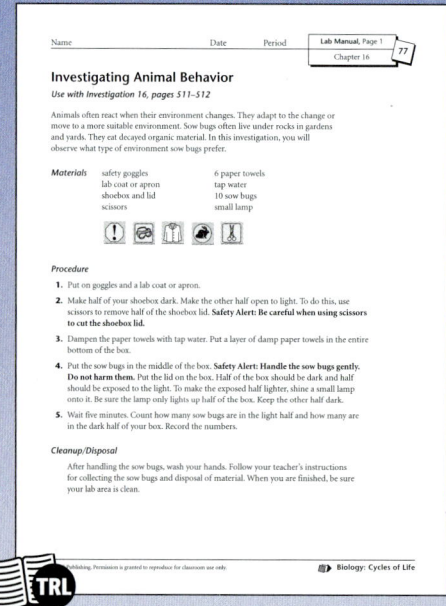

Lab Manual 77, pages 1–2

Lesson 2 Types of Behavior

Objectives

After reading this lesson, you should be able to

◆ describe parental care, courtship, defensive, and territorial behaviors
◆ give examples of spatial learning, imprinting, and observational learning
◆ give examples of inheritance and learned behavior together
◆ explain how behaviors help animals survive

Scientists investigate stimuli that trigger behaviors. To do this, scientists usually set up lab conditions to observe a behavior. For example, if a bird mates at a certain season, scientists might create lab conditions to **simulate** the season. Then, when placed in these conditions, the bird might show mating behavior, such as singing.

Scientists ask many questions to better understand animal behavior and why it happens. They may ask: How does a behavior affect an animal's chances of survival and reproduction? What are the stimuli that bring on a response? Has the response been changed by recent learning? Does a behavior change as an animal ages? What early experiences are necessary for a certain learned behavior? How does a behavior in one species compare with similar behavior in related species?

Categories of Innate Animal Behavior

Ethologists study many types of animal behavior. They want to find out how much of a behavior is due to inheritance or to learning. Ethologists group innate behaviors into various broad categories.

Simulate
To make the same conditions as the natural or original conditions

Parental care behavior
The caring for offspring by a parent

Courtship behavior
A behavior that helps attract a mate

One category is **parental care behavior.** This type of behavior ensures that offspring survive. For example, newly hatched birds open their mouths to get food from their parents. The young birds do this although their eyes are not yet open. This is an example of innate behavior. To live, the young birds must eat as soon as they are born. They have no time to learn how to eat.

Another category of innate animal behavior is **courtship behavior.** This behavior is used to attract a mate. Courtship behavior also helps animals recognize their own species. Courtship behavior differs for different animals. A male peacock displays his colorful tail to attract a female peacock. Other birds attract a mate with a certain song. Crickets have special mating sounds.

Behavioral Biology   Chapter 16   513

Lesson at a Glance

Chapter 16 Lesson 2

Overview In this lesson, students learn about categories of animal behavior.

Objectives

■ To describe parental care, courtship, defensive, and territorial behaviors
■ To give examples of spatial learning, imprinting, and observational learning
■ To give examples of inheritance and learned behavior together
■ To explain how behaviors help animals survive

Student Pages 513–519

Teacher's Resource Library
Workbook Activity 94
Alternative Workbook Activity 94
Lab Manual 78
Resource File 37

Vocabulary

aggressive behavior
courtship behavior
defensive behavior
imprinting
instinct
landmark
mimicry
observational learning
parental care behavior
predator
prey
releaser
simulate
spatial learning
territorial behavior
warning coloration

Have students create a crossword puzzle with the vocabulary words. They may base the clues on definitions or examples. Then have students exchange puzzles and solve each other's puzzles.

Background Information

Scientists have studied animal behavior for centuries. The discipline of ethology arose because of the work of European scientists. Konrad Lorenz of Austria, Niko Tinbergen of the United Kingdom, and Karl von Frisch of West Germany shared the Nobel Prize in 1973 for their discoveries in animal behavior.

Behavioral Biology   513

Warm-Up Activity

Show students a picture of a mother animal caring for her young. For example, show a picture of a bird feeding her chicks in a nest or a mother cat nursing her kittens. Explain to students that the picture shows an example of parental care behavior. Show a picture of a peacock spreading out its tail feathers. Explain to students that this is an example of courtship behavior. The male is trying to mate with a peahen. Show a picture of a predator chasing its prey. Explain to students that the prey is trying to avoid the predator. This is an example of defensive behavior.

 Teaching the Lesson

As students read the lesson, have them write down the main ideas from each paragraph. Have students include supporting details so that they have enough information to understand the concept. Encourage them to ask questions about any concept they do not understand.

 Reinforce and Extend

SCIENCE JOURNAL

 Have students write a paragraph about a scenario in which they have witnessed parental care behavior, courtship behavior, or defensive behavior on the part of animals in nature.

ELL/ESL STRATEGY

 **Language Objective:** *To make oral presentations*

Have a student learning English give a brief presentation to the class explaining one of the categories of innate animal behavior. This should be a simple description without visual aids. Have different students explain different categories of innate animal behavior.

Defensive behavior
A behavior to avoid or protect against predators

Predator
An organism that eats another organism

Prey
An organism that is eaten by another organism

Warning coloration
The bright colors or patterns on animals that scare off predators

Instinct
A pattern of innate behavior

Mimicry
A method of defense in which a species looks like another poisonous or dangerous species

Aggressive behavior
A behavior that warns predators not to approach

The light flashes that fireflies make in the summer are a form of courtship communication. The male makes a pattern of flashes. The female flashes back her response.

Defensive behavior is another category of innate animal behavior. In defensive behavior, animals avoid or protect themselves against **predators**. A predator eats another organism called its **prey**. Avoiding predators is very important to stay alive. Some animals improve their skills at avoiding predators. This is an example of animals adapting an innate behavior.

Some animals show certain defensive behaviors so that predators do not eat them. One example is **warning coloration**. Some species of wasps that can sting their predators are brightly colored. This warning coloration is a stimulus. It modifies, or changes, the behavior of predators. Based on experience or **instinct,** predators will not attack wasps with warning colorations. An instinct is an innate behavior.

Animals also use **mimicry** in defensive behavior. For example, hoverflies are colored like wasps but do not sting. Because some predators do not eat wasps, they also do not eat hoverflies. These predators think hoverflies are stinging wasps.

Some behavioral changes are defensive. For example, wolves may show **aggressive behavior** by growling and showing their teeth. They also flatten their ears. Aggressive behavior warns predators not to approach. These behaviors tell the predator that the hunted animal will fight. Rattlesnakes shake the rattle on their tail to warn predators that their bite is poisonous. Aggressive behavior is innate.

Animals sometimes combine aggressive behavior and warning coloration. For example, an amphibian may have a brightly colored belly. Recall from Chapter 15 that an amphibian is a vertebrate that lives in water and then on land. The rest of the amphibian's body is colored to blend with its surroundings. If threatened, the amphibian shows its belly. The colored belly tells a predator that the amphibian is poisonous.

514   Chapter 16   Behavioral Biology

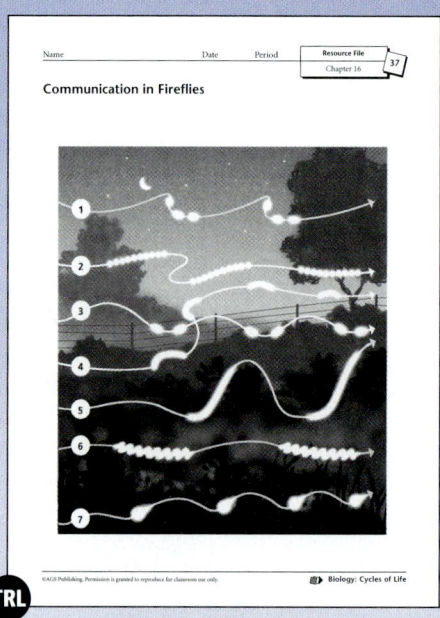

Resource File 37

Territorial behavior
A behavior that claims and defends an area

Releaser
A stimulus that brings out a certain behavior in another animal

Spatial learning
Learning by recognizing features

Imprinting
Learning in which an animal bonds with the first object it sees

Observational learning
Learning by watching or listening to another animal

Landmark
An object used to mark a location or position

Territorial behavior is another category of animal behavior. A territory is an area defined by an animal. The animal usually defends its territory from other animals of the same species. Territorial behavior helps animals survive. Animals can court, mate, produce offspring, and raise their young in their territories. Territorial behavior is an innate behavior.

Austrian ethologist Konrad Lorenz and Dutch ethologist Niko Tinbergen studied stimuli that cause territorial behavior. These stimuli are called **releasers.** Lorenz and Tinbergen studied territorial behavior in adult male robins.

During mating season, adult male robins often claim their territories with song. If this does not stop other male birds, the territorial birds display aggressive behavior. They attack other male robins that come into their territory. However, adult male robins do not show aggressive behavior toward young males. That is because the young males do not have red feathers yet. The red breast feathers on other adult males are the releasers for territorial behavior.

Innate and Learned Behavior Combine

Many patterns of behavior are a combination of innate and learned behavior. An animal's behavior may depend on both genetic inheritance and the environment. Three examples of animal behavior that have both genetic and learned parts are **spatial learning, imprinting,** and **observational learning.**

Spatial learning. To investigate spatial learning, Tinbergen looked at the behavior of a species of wasp. He wondered how an animal learns to recognize features in its area. He wanted to find out if a wasp can learn to find its nest by using **landmarks.** A landmark is an object used to mark a location or position.

Tinbergen observed that a female wasp digs an underground nest for each larva. The female wasp returns to her nest to care for each larva. Tinbergen wondered how each wasp found her nest. Did she use landmarks?

TEACHER ALERT

Explain to students that innate behaviors are due to natural selection. Animals that have these innate behaviors are better able to survive and reproduce than other members of the species that do not have these behaviors.

LEARNING STYLES

Visual/Spatial
Divide the class into small groups. Have each group select one of the categories of innate behavior in this lesson. Have students find photographs and make a collage of animals exhibiting their chosen innate behavior. Display students' collages in the classroom for other students to see and study.

LEARNING STYLES

Interpersonal/Group
Have the students who created a collage (above) make a presentation to the class about their collage. Each student in the group should speak. Have students explain how each photograph represents their chosen category of innate behavior.

PRONUNCIATION GUIDE

Use the pronunciation shown here to help students pronounce difficult words in this lesson. Refer to the pronunciation key on the Chapter Planning Guide for the sounds of the symbols.

Konrad Lorenz (kôn′rad lō′rents)

Niko Tinbergen (nē′kō tin′bər gən)

Link to

Social Studies. Have students read the Link to Social Studies feature. Ask students: Why do scientists think a protective wall was a sign of anger between two groups? *(because the wall appears to have been for protection, to keep other people out)* Ask students: Why do scientists think wars did not occur until people started living in groups? *(because people previously had few accumulated resources to motivate an attack)*

IN THE ENVIRONMENT

Have students observe animal behaviors outdoors. Have students find an animal and write a journal entry about what the animal is doing. Students should describe the animal's activity and explain how this exhibits innate or learned animal behavior. Allow students to share their observations with the class.

Link to ▶▶▶
Social Studies

Scientists think the first signs of aggressive behavior between groups of people, appeared over 3,000 years ago in a village in Mexico. There is evidence that a protective wall was built around the village. Scientists think that war did not occur until groups of people began to live together and gathered large amounts of resources.

To test this hypothesis, Tinbergen placed pinecones in a circle around the nest of a female wasp. The wasp continued to go to her nest. Then Tinbergen moved the pinecones away from the nest and put them in a circle. As you can see in the top half of Figure 16.2.1, the female wasp went to the center of the pinecone circle.

Next, Tinbergen put the pinecones into a triangle around the nest. Then he arranged rocks in a circle near the nest. Look at the bottom half of Figure 16.2.1. The female wasp flew to the rocks in a circle. Based on his experiments, Tinbergen showed that a landmark signals a wasp to its nest. The wasp used spatial learning.

Figure 16.2.1 A digger wasp finds her nest by noting how landmarks are arranged.

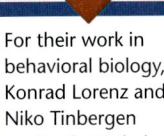

For their work in behavioral biology, Konrad Lorenz and Niko Tinbergen received a Nobel Prize in 1973.

Imprinting. Konrad Lorenz found that young birds bond with the first object they see. This behavior is called imprinting. Lorenz observed that young geese and chickens follow their mothers soon after they are hatched. He discovered this response could be transferred to another stimulus.

In one experiment, Lorenz removed goose eggs from their nest. He hatched the eggs in a lab. The baby geese saw Lorenz first. They imprinted on him. They thought Lorenz was their mother and followed him everywhere. The young geese did not recognize their real mother or other adults.

Lorenz repeated the experiment. This time he used boots and baby ducks. The young ducks imprinted on the boots.

Lorenz found that once imprinting is set, it cannot be changed. Imprinting helps animals survive. A result of imprinting is a strong bond that forms between a newborn and a parent. Young animals stay close to their mother. The mother feeds and protects her young. Lorenz also found that learning determines the result of this inherited behavior.

Observational learning. Birdsongs are both innate and learned. A bird raised alone will sing. Singing is innate behavior for birds. However, young birds must hear an adult male sing the species song. The song gets imprinted on the young birds. This type of behavior is called observational learning. Animals learn by watching or listening to another animal. As the young birds mature, they practice the species song. Their song eventually matches their memory of the imprinted song.

Science Myth

Myth: Some birds, such as parrots, can use human language.

Fact: Some birds can be taught to mimic human sounds. These birds say certain words or phrases. However, they are only reproducing what they hear. They do not understand the words. They are not communicating.

Achievements in Science

Read the Achievements in Science feature to the class. Have students research and find more information about animal behavior studies. Have students report their findings to the class. Encourage students to bring visual aids to show during their presentation.

Young birds raised in isolation that do not hear the species song cannot sing it. This means there is a period of time for young birds to learn the species song. As the birds mature, they perfect the song. This is another important period of time for learning the species song. If a bird becomes deaf after singing the song as a mature adult, it will continue to sing the song correctly.

Achievements in Science

Animal Behavior Research

Many scientists have contributed to the field of animal behavior. In the early 1900s, Russian scientist Ivan Pavlov investigated how dogs could be conditioned to show behavior. Conditioning is learning in which an animal connects one stimulus with another stimulus. Pavlov observed that dogs make saliva when they smell food. He rang a bell whenever he served food to the dogs. Soon the dogs associated the sound of the bell with food. The dogs made saliva whenever they heard the bell, whether food was present or not. The dogs' response was conditioned.

Austrian scientist Karl von Frisch studied the behavior of honeybees. He discovered that bees sense and react to different wavelengths of ultraviolet light. His most famous discovery was that honeybees communicate with each other through dance patterns.

These and many other scientists used patience, observation, and scientific methods to study animal behavior. Their work has provided insight into the animals with whom we share the earth.

518 *Chapter 16 Behavioral Biology*

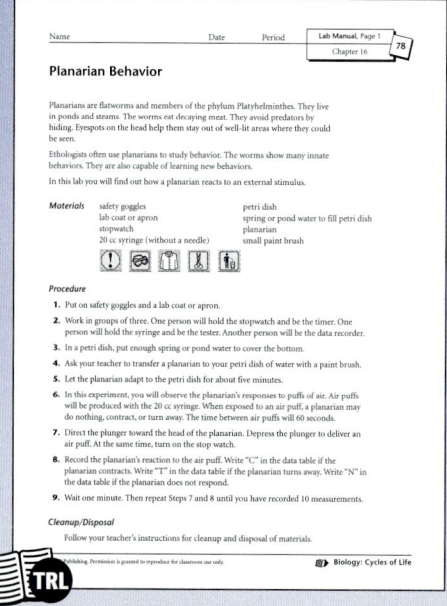

Lab Manual 78, pages 1–2

Lesson 2 REVIEW

Word Bank
defensive behavior
imprinting
observational learning

On a sheet of paper, write the word or words from the Word Bank that complete each sentence correctly.

1. Animals avoid or protect themselves against predators in _____.
2. Young birds form an attachment, called _____, to the first thing they see after they hatch.
3. Learning by watching or listening to another animal is _____.

On a sheet of paper, write the letter of the answer that completes each sentence correctly.

4. Rattlesnakes shake the rattle on their tail to _____.
   A attract a mate C warn predators
   B help find food D direct other rattlesnakes

5. Learning by recognizing features is _____.
   A aggressive behavior C spatial learning
   B parental care behavior D imprinting

6. Some amphibians display a brightly colored stomach to show that they are _____.
   A male B female C young D poisonous

Critical Thinking

On a sheet of paper, write the answers to the following questions. Use complete sentences.

7. Why is parental care behavior important? Give an example.
8. Describe Niko Tinbergen's experiments to determine how a female wasp finds its nest.
9. How do most birds learn to sing the species song?
10. How do animals use warning coloration and mimicry to protect themselves?

Lesson 2 Review Answers

1. defensive behavior **2.** imprinting **3.** observational learning **4.** C **5.** C **6.** D **7.** Parental care behavior increases an animal's chances of survival. An innate response, such as feeding offspring, is a parental behavior that ensures survival of offspring. **8.** Tinbergen moved landmarks from around the nest to another location. The wasps followed the landmarks, trying to find the nest. He also duplicated patters with different materials and learned that the wasps use shape-recognition to find the nests as well. **9.** Most birds must be taught to sing by an adult. They practice this song until they learn to sing it perfectly. **10.** Many animals will use coloring or other characteristics to warn potential predators that they are poisonous or dangerous to eat. Some harmless animals will replicate the appearance of a dangerous animal to fool predators.

Portfolio Assessment

Sample items include:
- Vocabulary crossword puzzle
- Collage showing innate animal behavior from Learning Styles Visual/Spatial
- Observations of animals exhibiting innate or learned behavior in the environment from In the Environment
- Lesson 2 Review answers

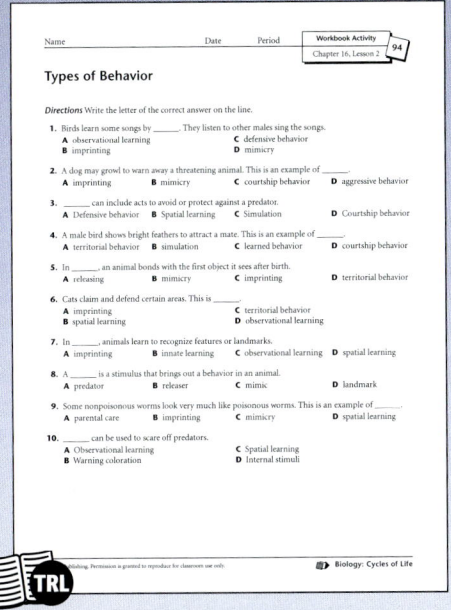

Workbook Activity 94

Lesson at a Glance

Chapter 16 Lesson 3

Overview In this lesson, students learn about animal communication.

Objectives

- To define *communication*
- To identify and give examples of social behaviors
- To give examples of animal communications
- To describe how communications can work together
- To explain how communication helps animals survive
- To give an example of an advanced communication system

Student Pages 520–529

Teacher's Resource Library

Workbook Activity 95–96

Alternative Workbook Activity 95

Lab Manual 79–80

Resource File 38

Vocabulary

agonistic interaction	metacommunication
cognition	pheromone
communication	scent
competitor	signal
cooperation	social behavior
dominant	sociobiologist
matched submission	

Have students look in a dictionary to find the meaning of the vocabulary words. Have students write the meaning of the words on a sheet of paper. Then have students write a complete sentence using each vocabulary word.

Background Information

Social behaviors must be distinguished from crowding behaviors. Social behaviors are cooperative efforts of a group working together to ensure the group's survival. While crowding conditions bring many animals together, these animals are competing for survival. The behaviors exhibited differ from those of species that work together for group survival.

Lesson 3 — Forms of Communication

Objectives

After reading this lesson, you should be able to
- define communication
- identify and give examples of social behaviors
- give examples of animal communications
- describe how communications can work together
- explain how communication helps animals survive
- give an example of an advanced communication system

When a bird sings, it is communicating. When a frog croaks, it is communicating. When a baby bear calls for its mother, it is communicating. In this lesson, you will learn different ways animals communicate.

What Is Communication?

Communication is sending information. People use language, speech, writing, art, and music to communicate. But there are other ways to communicate. Animals use actions, such as showing their teeth or wagging their tails. They also use smells and sounds. Communication has a purpose. Birds sing to find a mate or protect their territory. Dogs bark to warn that a stranger is approaching.

Social Behavior

Sociobiologists study how animals communicate and interact with each other. **Social behavior** is the interaction between two or more animals, usually of the same species. Some types of social behavior are aggressive behavior, courtship behavior, and **cooperation.** Social behavior influences the survival and reproduction of animals. Social behaviors are important adaptations in many species.

There are many types of aggressive behavior. In **agonistic interaction,** individuals have contests. Many species display aggressive behavior when they compete for food, find mates, and protect their territory. Birds, for example, sing songs during these contests. These songs warn other birds away.

Recall from Lesson 2 that animals establish a territory to protect their food supply and offspring. Some animals show aggressive behavior if their territory is threatened. They may also tell other members of their species about approaching predators. These are examples of aggressive behaviors.

Communication
Sending information

Sociobiologist
A scientist who studies how animals communicate and interact with each other

Social behavior
The interaction between two or more animals

Cooperation
A type of social behavior in which two or more individuals work or act together

Agonistic interaction
A type of social behavior in which individuals have contests and show aggressive behavior

Matched submission
A type of social behavior in which a threatened animal yields to a dominant animal

Dominant
Having the most influence or control

Signal
A behavior that causes a change in the behavior of another animal

Scent
Having a smell or odor

Competitor
An animal that tries to get the same resources as another animal

Another aggressive behavior is **matched submission**. A threatened animal shows submission to a **dominant** animal. For example, a small dog has a bone. A large dog wants the bone. The large dog snarls at the small dog. The large dog is showing aggressive behavior toward the small dog.

The small dog rolls over and shows its belly to the large dog. This behavior shows that the large dog is dominant. The large dog stops its aggressive behavior and takes the bone. Some species show behavior to indicate that the submissive animal is accepted.

You learned about courtship behavior in Lesson 2. Courtship behavior is a social behavior. Selection of a mate is important to ensure survival of the species. A **signal** is a behavior that causes a change in the behavior of another animal. Animals make signals to attract or keep the attention of a possible mate. Courtship signals are often a display of body parts, a call, or the release of a **scent**.

These signals are unique to a species. They make sure individuals mate with a member of their own species. Animals that form a lasting bond with one mate often show the same signals to each other. An example is a victory display shown between two penguins at their nest site.

Cooperation is when individual animals work together for the common good. For example, ants work together in an anthill to feed and raise offspring.

Communication Signals

Social behavior depends on methods of communication. Communication has three parts: sending a signal, receiving a signal, and responding to a signal. There are many kinds of signals and messages. A signal may be calls or sounds, facial expressions or body positions, scents, or specific movements. For example, when a bird sings, its message may tell **competitors** to stay away. Or the song may be a call for a mate. Other birds hear this stimulus and respond to it.

Warm-Up Activity

Find recordings of animals communicating with sounds. Play the recordings for the class. See if students can identify the animals that are making the sounds. Tell students that humans, as well as other animals, have ways of communicating with one another.

Teaching the Lesson

Have students create a detailed outline of the lesson as they read. Make sure students write down enough information so that the outline can be used to study for tests and quizzes.

Reinforce and Extend

ELL/ESL Strategy

Language Objective: *To write and act in a skit*

Have groups of students write and act out a short skit that explains the meaning of the term *communication*. Skits should include several examples of different types of communication.

Link to

Language Arts. Have a volunteer read aloud the Link to Language Arts feature. Encourage students to find out more information about humpback whales. If possible, find a recording of the sounds of the humpback whale to play for students.

Technology and Society

Have a volunteer read the Technology and Society feature to the class. Ask students: Do you know of any other devices that people with disabilities use to communicate? *(Sample answer: computers with voice synthesizers used by people who have had strokes)*

TEACHER ALERT

There are many different technologies available for people with various disabilities. For example, voice recognition systems enable a person to dial a telephone or write on a computer by speaking, without using hands or arms. Other devices are available to help people without full use of arms or hands. One such device tracks the movements of a tiny disposable dot placed on the forehead or eyeglasses. Head movements serve the same function as hand movements with a handheld computer mouse.

Metacommunication
A signal that changes the meaning of the next set of signals

Link to >>>
Language Arts

Humans are the only animals that use language. Many other animals have developed forms of communications similar to language. Humpback whales communicate with complex songs. Their songs have repeated elements that make up themes and phrases. This is like spoken or written language.

Some animal signals are related to food. Food calls tell a mate, offspring, or members of a group about a food source. Honeybees perform a dance that tells other honeybees where to find food. The dance patterns show other bees the direction and distance of flowers from the hive. Honeybees communicate by the pattern of their flight and how they move their bodies. This group of behaviors is called cooperation.

Some animals give alarm calls to signal that a predator is nearby. Alarm calls tell members of their species to run for cover. Sometimes members of other species will also hide. Instead of hiding, some animals may stop moving or gather into a group to reduce the risk of attack.

Metacommunications are signals that change the meaning of the next set of signals. For example, a dog shows a play face to another dog. This tells the other dog that the next aggressive signal is a play fight. It is not aggressive behavior.

Some predators deceive, or fool, prey by communication. For example, the angler fish has a small growth that hangs in front of its jaws. The growth looks like a lure, or food. When a small fish bites the fake lure, it is close to the mouth of the angler fish. The angler fish quickly captures the small fish.

Technology and Society

Scientists are developing new technology that allows people with disabilities to communicate effectively. People who are paralyzed may not be able to speak. They may not be able to use their hands to write or gesture. Scientists are developing a computer chip to be put into the brain. The computer chip would allow a person to control a computer cursor and keyboard using only their thoughts.

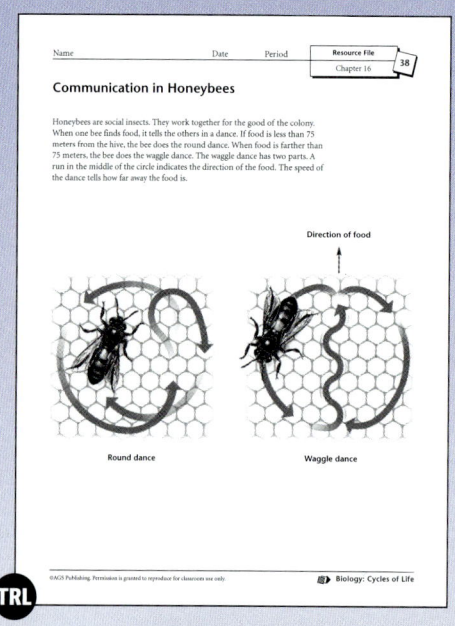

Resource File 38

Link to
Cultures

Humans, chimpanzees, and orangutans display cultural behavior. Cultural behavior is a behavior that is invented within a group and passed to the next generation. Cultural behavior in chimpanzees and orangutans includes activities such as using a tool to find food. These behaviors are found in some cultures, but not in others.

Signals Working Together

Animal communication often involves displaying a part of the body or a specific movement. Often these two communications occur together. The animal's movement shows off the body part.

Look at the bill of the adult herring gull in Figure 16.3.1. A parent herring gull shows its bill to its chicks in the nest. The bill of a herring gull is yellow with a red spot near the tip of the beak. When the parent returns to the nest with food, the parent stands over the chicks. The parent taps its bill on the ground in front of the chicks. This stimulus causes the hungry chicks to make begging responses. In turn, this action stimulates the parent to put the food in front of the chicks. The chicks eat the food. Once the chicks are fed, the parent leaves to find more food.

This communication cycle involves a body part, which is the red-spotted bill of the parent. It also includes a movement, which is the tapping on the ground. This helps the chicks see the red spot on the parent's bill. The red color causes a begging response from the herring gull chicks.

Animals have body parts to aid in communication. One example is the tail of the peacock. Sociobiologists think its tail is used in courtship behavior. Courtship behavior can lead to the growth of a feature that helps in selecting a mate.

Figure 16.3.1 *The red spot on the bill of the adult herring gull causes the chicks to beg.*

Link to

Cultures. Have a volunteer read aloud the Link to Cultures feature. Ask students: Why is a particular cultural behavior found in one group of chimpanzees or orangutans but not necessarily in another group of the same species? *(Because cultural behaviors are learned behaviors, group members learn a skill only if they have the opportunity to observe an animal that already has the skill.)*

Encourage students to research and find more information about cultural behavior in chimpanzees and orangutans. Have students share the information they find with the class.

LEARNING STYLES

Body/Kinesthetic

Divide the class into small groups. Have students make up a nonverbal communication system. Tell students they can use hand movements or body movements, but they cannot speak or write words. Allow students to communicate within the group, using their nonverbal communication system.

Science at Work

Have a volunteer read aloud the Science at Work feature about social workers. Ask students: How might social workers help other people function in their environment? Ask students: Why do you suppose this occupation is featured in this lesson? (*Social workers deal with interpersonal behavior, including communication.*)

SCIENCE JOURNAL

Have students write a paragraph about a time they have watched an animal use pheromones to mark its territory.

LEARNING STYLES

Logical/Mathematical
Divide the class into small groups. Have each group make up a communication system that uses a collection of symbols. Let students practice communicating within the group, using their new system. Then have each group write on the board a sentence using their new system and the key for their new system. Have students use the key to determine what the sentence says.

GLOBAL CONNECTION

People in several ancient civilizations had a written form of communication that used pictures to represent objects or ideas. This form of writing is called hieroglyphics. Ancient hieroglyphs have been found in Egypt, China, and Mesopotamia. Have students search the Internet, encyclopedias, or books for samples of these writings and share them with the class.

Pheromone
A chemical signal produced by an animal

Cognition
Knowledge

Scent Signals

Some animals communicate by odor. These chemical scent signals are called **pheromones.** Scent glands in the body make pheromones. Chemical signals are common among mammals and insects. Cats and dogs mark their territory with urine. Some hamsters have scent glands on their sides. To mark their territory, they leave their scent by rubbing their cheeks against objects.

Bees carry a pouch that contains material from their hive. When the bees return to their hive, they release the material. The odor of the material tells other bees that they are members of the hive. They can then enter the hive.

Advanced Signals

Alarm calls and courtship signals are innate responses to stimuli. Do animals understand the meaning of the signals they give and receive? This is a key question in the study of animal **cognition,** or knowledge.

Some signaling systems show an advanced understanding of communication. An example is the alarm calls by vervet monkeys. Vervet monkeys make different alarm calls in response to different predators.

Science at Work

Social Worker

Social workers help people function within their environment, maintain relationships, and solve personal problems. Social workers work one-on-one with a person or a group of people. A social worker may help two or more people communicate with each other so they can work together.

Both private organizations and government agencies employ social workers. Health care organizations and social service industries employ social workers. Most social workers specialize in providing a specific type of help.

To become a social worker, a bachelor's degree in social work, psychology, sociology, or a related field is required. Some positions in the health industry require a master's degree. Social workers must be licensed or certified by their state.

Their alarm calls are different for a leopard, snake, or eagle. The alarm calls allow other vervet monkeys to respond to the predator. Vervet monkeys develop the ability to make alarm calls over time.

Summing Up

Behavioral biology is the study of how animals react to stimuli and respond to predators and competitors. Behavioral biologists study mating behavior in animals. They study how animals interact with their own species to increase their chances of survival.

Biology in Your Life

Technology: Instant Wireless Communication

Over the years, people have created new ways to communicate with each other. The invention of the telegraph and the telephone in the 1800s allowed people to communicate over long distances. Today, cell phones and the Internet allow people to communicate quickly from nearly anywhere.

A new form of communication technology is radio frequency identification (RFID) chips. These tiny computer chips hold a lot of information. A radio receiver reads the information instantly.

Some companies use RFID chips in their products. The chips are very inexpensive. They are tiny and can be put on or into every product. When a product is shipped or sold, a radio reader identifies it and tracks it instantly. A computer then shows how many items have been sold or shipped at any time.

In the future, a tiny RFID chip with medical information could be put under a person's skin. Using the RFID chip, a doctor could

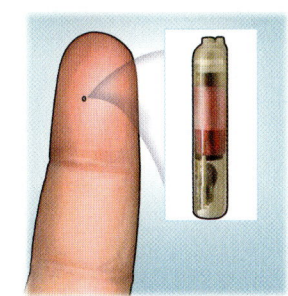

identify the person and get medical history instantly. RFID chips could be used to buy items in stores. You would take the items you want to buy and go to the front of the store. As you walked through the doorway, computers would read the identification of the items you bought. Computers would also read your credit card information from an RFID chip that you carry. This could mean no more lines at the cash register!

1. What does RFID stand for?
2. How are RFID chips used today?
3. In the future, how could RFID chips help you communicate instantly?

Biology in Your Life

Have a volunteer read aloud the feature about instant wireless communication. Ask students: What advantage would RFID chips have? *(Sample answers: inventory is easier and more reliable, information can be updated instantly, information can be accessed easily)* What disadvantages could these chips have? *(Answers will vary and may include privacy concerns.)*

Biology in Your Life Answers

1. RFID stands for radio frequency identification. 2. RFID chips are currently used to track products that are sold or shipped. 3. An RFID chip could be used to communicate instantly complex medical information for a person who is sick or injured to a doctor or an emergency room.

Lesson 3 Review Answers

1. agnostic interaction
2. metacommunication 3. signal 4. B
5. C 6. A 7. The three parts of communication are transmitting a signal, receiving a signal, and responding to a signal. 8. Animals use alarm signals to communicate when a threat is present in the form of a predator. The alarm tells other animals to run away, hide, or gather in numbers to face the threat. 9. Answers may vary. One example is the use of pheromones by honeybees. Bees carry some material from their hive. When they return to the hive, they release the material. The other bees can smell the material and allow the returning bee to enter the hive. 10. Scientists think that peacocks use the tail in sexual selection. Having a large, colorful tail exaggerates some of the characteristics that make a good mate.

Portfolio Assessment

Sample items include:
- Detailed outline from Teaching the Lesson
- Students' skit about communication from ELL/ESL Strategy
- Lesson 3 Review answers

CAREER CONNECTION

Have students research sociobiology as a career. Have them identify high school courses that should be taken as preparation for a career in sociobiology. In addition, have students identify colleges and universities in their area that offer degrees in sociobiology, as well as facilities that offer employment to sociobiologists after graduation.

Lesson 3 REVIEW

Word Bank
metacommunication
agonistic interaction
signal

On a sheet of paper, write the word or words from the Word Bank that complete each sentence

1. Individuals have contests and show aggressive behavior in _____.
2. A signal that changes the meaning of the next set of signals is _____.
3. A _____ is a behavior that causes a change in the behavior of another animal.

On a sheet of paper, write the letter of the answers that complete each sentence correctly.

4. A _____ is a chemical that has an odor.
   A metacommunication   C scent
   B pheromone   D cognition
5. Honeybees signal the location of food to other honeybees by _____.
   A releasing a scent   C dancing in patterns
   B changing color   D making sounds
6. Pheromones are _____.
   A chemical signals   C patterns of behavior
   B changes in appearance D mating behaviors

Critical Thinking

On a sheet of paper, write the answers to the following questions. Use complete sentences.

7. What are the three main parts of communication?
8. Give an example of how animals use alarm signals to communicate.
9. Give an example of how animals use pheromones to communicate.
10. Why do scientists think peacocks display colorful tails?

526 Chapter 16 Behavioral Biology

DISCOVERY INVESTIGATION 16

Materials
- index cards

Exploring Human Communication

People rely on spoken or written language to pass on information. They also use nonverbal methods to communicate. Some people may not realize that they use nonverbal communication. In this investigation, you will explore some ways humans communicate without using written or spoken language.

Procedure

1. In your group, discuss nonverbal ways animals and humans communicate. Examples are gestures, sounds, and body position. Record each example on an index card. Label the backs of the index cards Method.

2. Divide your group into two subgroups. One subgroup is the performers. The other subgroup is the audience.

3. In each subgroup, think of scenarios involving animal behavior. Examples are aggression and cooperation. Record each example on a card. Label the backs of the cards Scenario.

Behavioral Biology Chapter 16

- Students may benefit from using a video camera to capture some of the scenarios and play them back, looking for some of the more subtle gestures and body language that are displayed.

Continued on page 528

Discovery Investigation 16

This investigation is less structured than the first investigation in this chapter. It offers students more challenge and requires more teacher facilitation. Encourage students to read the Discovery Investigation steps. Discuss questions they may have before beginning the investigation.

Objectives
- To work as a group to explore different methods of nonverbal communication
- To interpret various social scenarios and communication methods
- To organize notes and information into a data table or chart

Skills
Observing, inferring, using information, identifying, thinking critically, analyzing data, drawing conclusions

Background
This chapter has given students information on the different ways that animals communicate. Students may believe that although animals display these behaviors and communication methods, people rely on speaking and writing. Through a series of exercises, students are encouraged to think of different scenarios and communication methods that humans use besides speaking and writing. By interpreting the scenarios in small groups, students will notice some actions, gestures, expressions, and tones people use to convey information.

Time Frame
One class period

Procedure
- Encourage students to think both analytically and creatively about how they communicate with one another.
- Students should not only use scenarios that wild animals might, but also everyday situations that humans encounter.
- Encourage students to use props when necessary.

Behavioral Biology

Continued from page 527

Results

Students should successfully identify many of the scenarios depicted. After observing and acting out many scenarios without using spoken language, they should become more aware of the many types of body language, sound tones, facial expressions, and other ways that people and animals both use as part of communication. Their data table or chart should include their observations.

Answers to Analysis, Conclusions, and Explore Further begin on page 670 of this Teacher's Edition.

Assessment

You might include the following items from this investigation in student portfolios:

- Data table or chart
- Answers to Analysis and Conclusions questions
- Data from Explore Further

4. Have the performers select one of their scenario cards. Do not show the card to the audience.

5. Have the audience select an index card from the method pile. Put this card face up on the table so everyone can see it.

6. Have the performers act out the scenario using the communication method on the card. Have the audience interpret the scenario and discuss what clues made the communication successful.

7. Alternate between the performers and audiences to interpret scenarios. Continue until all the scenario cards are used. Replace the method card after each scenario so it can be reused.

Cleanup/Disposal

When you are finished, be sure your lab area is clean.

Analysis

1. What clues led your subgroup to interpret the scenarios?
2. How do emotions play a part in communication?

Conclusions

1. What communication characteristics are associated with aggressive behavior, defensive behavior, and cooperative behavior?
2. Although people use spoken language to communicate ideas, words are only part of the communication. How do sounds and gestures communicate ideas? Give examples.

Explore Further

Gestures, tones, and expressions may send a different message from the words humans use. Design another investigation in which some students make truthful statements and others make untruthful statements. Try to decide who is untruthful.

528 *Chapter 16 Behavioral Biology*

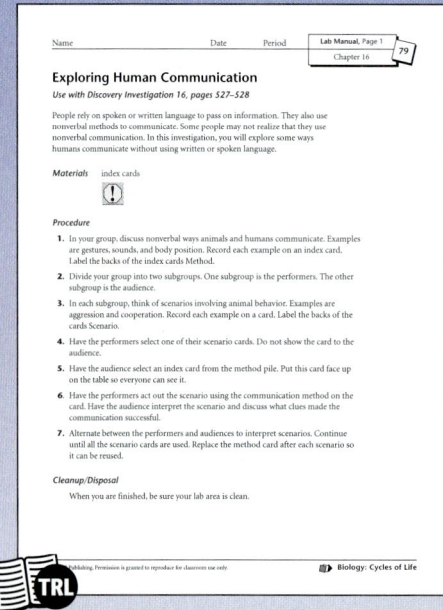

Lab Manual 79, pages 1–2

BIOLOGY IN THE WORLD

Behavior Studies of Twins

Animal behavior is determined by a mix of genetics and the environment. By studying twins, scientists can discover which behavior may be caused by the environment and which may be caused by genes.

Twins can be either fraternal or identical. Fraternal twins come from the union of two different eggs and two different sperm cells. Identical twins come from the same egg and sperm. The fertilized single egg splits. This creates two babies with the same DNA.

Since identical twins have the same DNA, most differences should be caused by their environment. Identical twins often share many behaviors. Some identical twins have been separated at birth and raised separately. Years later, as adults, they are still very similar.

Studying fraternal twins also provides information about how the environment shapes behavior and other traits. Scientists compare differences between fraternal and identical twins. For example, scientists have found that identical twins are much more likely to share smoking or nonsmoking behaviors than fraternal twins. This leads researchers to believe that there is a genetic tendency to be a smoker.

The same study showed that a twin who smoked died earlier than a twin who did not smoke. It did not matter whether the twin was identical or fraternal. In this case, the environment caused health problems, regardless of genetics.

1. What is the difference between identical and fraternal twins?
2. Why are scientists interested in studying differences in identical twins?
3. What information about smoking was discovered by studying twins?

BIOLOGY IN THE WORLD

Have volunteers read aloud the feature on behavior studies of twins. Ask students: Why is animal behavior a mixture of genetics and environment? *(Innate animal behavior is genetic, and learned behavior is acquired by observing and learning in the animal's environment.)* Ask students: Would siblings who are not twins be useful in this study? *(only in studying learned behaviors because siblings who are not twins do not have exactly the same genes)*

Biology in the World Answers

1. Identical twins have the same DNA. Fraternal twins do not have the same DNA. **2.** Since identical twins have the same DNA, differences in them must be mostly due to environmental differences. **3.** The study showed that genetics must be partially responsible for causing smoking behavior. Early death caused by smoking affected people regardless of their genetic makeup.

ONLINE CONNECTION

 For more information about humpback whales and their songs (and a link to hear their sounds), have students go to this Web site sponsored by The Whalesong Project: www.whalesong.net.

If students want to learn more about hieroglyphs, have them go to this Web site sponsored by the Public Broadcasting System: www.pbs.org/wgbh/nova/pyramid/hieroglyph.

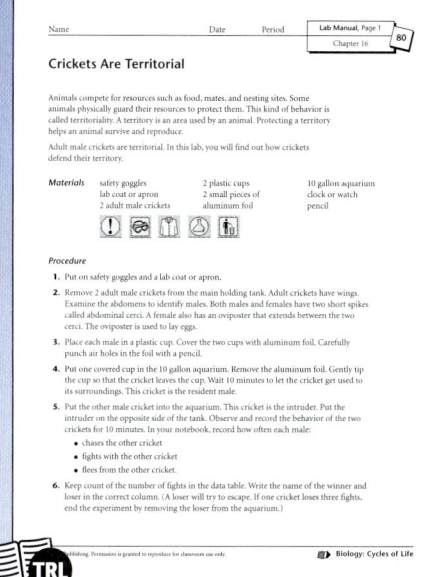

Lab Manual 80, pages 1–2

Chapter 16 Summary

Have volunteers read aloud each summary item on page 530. Ask volunteers to explain the meaning of each item. Direct students' attention to the Vocabulary box on the bottom of page 530. Have them read and review each term and its definition.

Graphic Organizer

As students read Chapter 16, have them finish completing the chart on Graphic Organizer 16: Behavioral Biology. Encourage students to read each lesson of the chapter and then have them fill in the portion of the chart that pertains to the lesson. When they have completed the chart, ask them to answer the questions.

Chapter 16 SUMMARY

- Behavioral biology is the study of the behavior of living things. Ethologists are scientists who study behavioral biology.

- Behaviors can be inherited or learned. Some behaviors evolve within species and are favored by natural selection.

- An innate behavior is a behavior an animal is born with. Mating and feeding behaviors are often innate.

- Physical characteristics, such as bright coloring, can be combined with behavior to ward off predators.

- Imprinting is behavior learned by a young animal.

- Some behaviors, such as birds learning songs, are a combination of imprinting and learning.

- Animals interact with one another in social behavior. Examples of social behavior are aggression, courtship, and cooperation.

- Courtship behavior between animals ensures partners are the same species.

- Animals use aggressive behavior to protect against predators or to defend territory.

- Animals may communicate as a means of cooperating within their community. Communication is used to warn of danger, signal the location of food, or identify members of a community.

Vocabulary

aggressive behavior, 514
agonistic interaction, 521
behavior, 506
behavioral biology, 506
cognition, 524
communication, 520
competitor, 521
cooperation, 521
courtship behavior, 513
defensive behavior, 514
dominant, 521
ethologist, 506
external stimulus, 506
fixed action pattern behavior, 507
imprinting, 515
innate behavior, 507
instinct, 514
internal stimulus, 506
landmark, 515
learned behavior, 507
matched submission, 521
metacommunication, 522
mimicry, 514
observational learning, 515
parental care behavior, 513
pheromone, 524
predator, 514
prey, 514
releaser, 515
scent, 521
signal, 521
simulate, 513
social behavior, 520
sociobiologist, 520
spatial learning, 515
territorial behavior, 515
warning coloration, 514

530 Chapter 16 Behavioral Biology

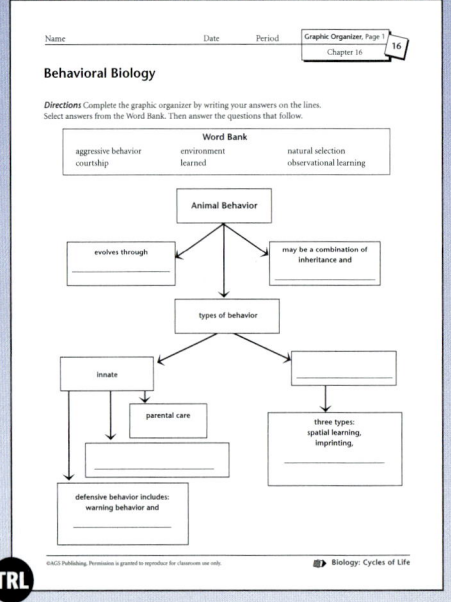

Graphic Organizer 16, pages 1–3

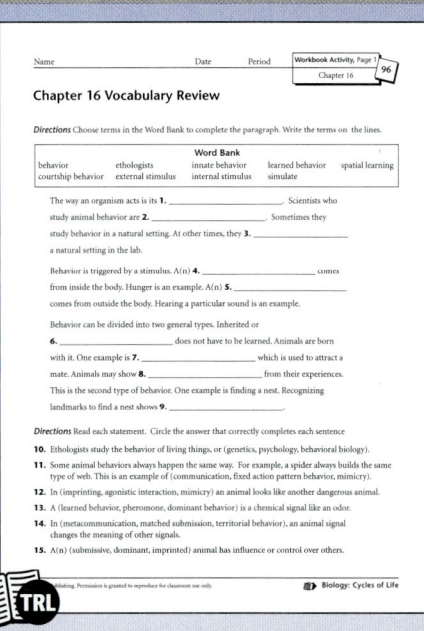

Workbook Activity 96, pages 1–2

Chapter 16 REVIEW

Word Bank
aggressive behavior
agonistic interaction
behavior
cognition
competitor
cooperation
dominant
ethologist
innate behavior
learned behavior
matched submission
predator
releaser
scent
signal
sociobiologist
warning coloration

Vocabulary Review
On a sheet of paper, write the word or words from the Word Bank that best complete each sentence.

1. An animal that is _____ shows influence or control over other animals.
2. Knowledge or recognition of another organism or surroundings is _____.
3. A scientist who studies the behaviors of animals is a(n) _____.
4. Growling and showing teeth are examples of _____.
5. A(n) _____ is present at birth.
6. A(n) _____ is behavior that results from experience.
7. Some animals use pheromones to communicate using _____.
8. A(n) _____ hunts and eats another animal.
9. The way an organism acts is _____.
10. The bright colors or patterns on animals that scare off predators is _____.
11. A(n) _____ tries to obtain the same resources as another animal.
12. A scientist who studies the factors that determine the social behavior of animals is a(n) _____.
13. A behavior that causes a change in the behavior of another animal is a(n) _____.
14. A type of social behavior in which individuals have contests and show aggressive behavior is _____.
15. The result of animals that display _____ is that one animal gets all the resources.

Review continued on next page

Behavioral Biology Chapter 16 531

Chapter 16 Review
Use the Chapter Review to prepare students for tests and to reteach content from the chapter.

Chapter 16 Mastery Test
The Teacher's Resource Library includes two forms of the Chapter 16 Mastery Test. Each test addresses the chapter Goals for Learning. An optional third page of additional critical-thinking items is included for each test. The difficulty level of the two forms is equivalent.

Review Answers
Vocabulary Review

1. dominant 2. cognition 3. ethologist
4. aggressive behavior 5. innate behavior
6. learned behavior 7. scent 8. predator
9. behavior 10. warning coloration
11. competitor 12. sociobiologist
13. signal 14. agnostic interaction
15. matched submission

Review Answers

16. releaser 17. cooperation

Teacher Alert

In the Chapter Review, the Vocabulary Review activity includes a sample of the chapter's vocabulary terms. The activity will help determine students' understanding of key vocabulary terms and concepts presented in the chapter. Other vocabulary terms used in the chapter are listed below.

behavioral biology
communication
courtship behavior
defensive behavior
external stimulus
fixed action pattern behavior
imprinting
instinct
internal stimulus
landmark
metacommunication
mimicry
observational learning
parental care behavior
pheromone
prey
simulate
social behavior
spatial learning
territorial behavior

Concept Review

18. B 19. C 20. A 21. D 22. C

Chapter 16 REVIEW - continued

16. A _____ is a stimulus that brings out a certain behavior in another animal

17. A type of social behavior in which animals work or act with another or others for a common purpose is _____.

Concept Review

On a sheet of paper, write the letter of the answer that best completes each sentence.

18. Imprinting takes place _____.
    A before an animal is born
    B when the animal is very young
    C when the animal matures
    D throughout an animal's life

19. An animal uses a courtship ritual to _____.
    A notify a mate or group of a food source
    B warn of danger
    C attract a suitable mate
    D protect its territory

20. A(n) _____ results from experience.
    A learned behavior
    B innate behavior
    C territorial behavior
    D courtship behavior

21. Learning in which an animal bonds with the first object it sees is _____.
    A spatial learning   C mimicry
    B defensive behavior D imprinting

532 Chapter 16 Behavioral Biology

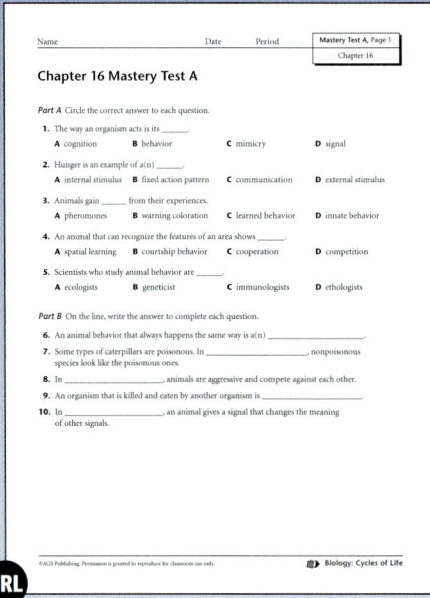

Chapter 16 Mastery Test A, pages 1–3

22. A fixed action pattern behavior is an action that _____.
    A sometimes changes   C always occurs the same way
    B always changes   D is a pheromone

Critical Thinking

On a sheet of paper, write the answer to the following questions. Use complete sentences.

23. Define fixed action pattern behavior. Give an example.
24. How does warning coloration help an animal survive predators?
25. Describe how inheritance and learning are both necessary for a bird to sing correctly.

Research and Write

Find an example of courtship behavior used by an animal species. Make a small presentation of the ritual. Use photos, audio sounds, or video. Explain how the ritual is accepted or turned down by the possible mate.

Test-Taking Tip If a question asks you to describe or explain something, try to answer the question as completely as possible. Use complete sentences.

Critical Thinking

23. Fixed action pattern behavior is a behavior known since birth that an animal does in the same way every time. A spider will take the exact same steps in the exact same order each time it spins a web. **24.** An animal may be brightly colored to warn a predator that it is poisonous. An animal may also be colored to resemble a more dangerous animal. **25.** A bird must be imprinted by hearing the song correctly when born. The bird will then practice to learn to sing the song it has been imprinted with. The ability to sing is a skill that the bird inherits.

Research and Write

Have students read and conduct the Research and Write feature. The best source for finding the necessary information is the Internet. Show students how to use a search engine and keywords to find helpful Web sites. You may want to have students work with partners or in small groups to complete this activity.

ALTERNATIVE ASSESSMENT

Alternative Assessment items correlate to the student Goals for Learning at the beginning of this chapter.

- Have students orally describe four or five behaviors that are responses to stimuli.
- Have students orally describe two or three behaviors that are innate and two or three that are learned.
- Have students write a paragraph describing at least three ways that animals communicate.
- Have students orally describe four or five behaviors that help organisms survive.

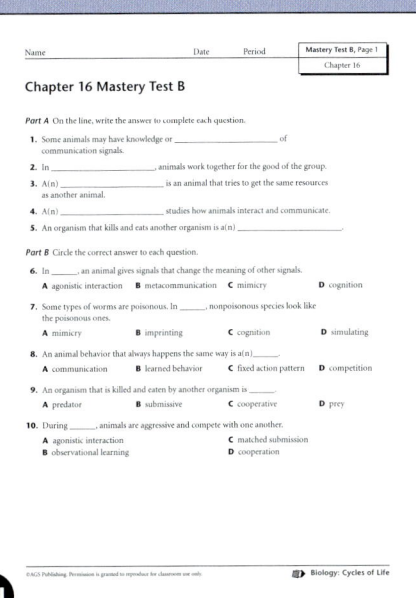
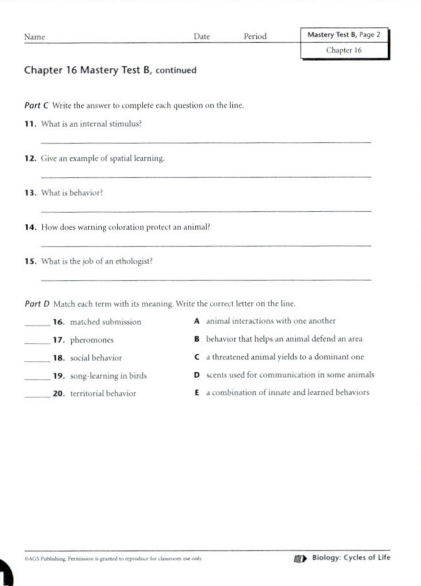

Chapter 16 Mastery Test B, pages 1–3

Chapter 17

Planning Guide
Populations and Communities

	Student Pages	Student Text Lesson		
		Vocabulary	Lesson Review	Critical-Thinking Questions
Lesson 1 Understanding Populations and Communities	536–540	✔	✔	✔
Lesson 2 Populations and Their Activities	541–547	✔	✔	✔
Lesson 3 Relationships in Communities	548–554	✔	✔	✔
Lesson 4 How Do Communities Start and Survive?	555–559	✔	✔	✔

Chapter Activities

Teacher's Resource Library
Community Connection 17:
 Grocery Store Plants and Animals
Graphic Organizer 17:
 Populations and Communities

Teacher's Edition
Opener Activity

Assessment Options

Student Text
Chapter 17 Review

Teacher's Resource Library
Chapter 17 Mastery Tests A and B

Teacher's Edition
Chapter 17 Alternative Assessment

534A

Student Text Features									Teaching Strategies						Learning Styles					Teacher's Resource Library			
Achievements in Science	Science at Work	Biology in Your Life	Investigation/Discovery	Biology in the World	Express Lab	Link to	Research and Write	Technology and Society	ELL/ESL Strategy	Background Information	Science Journal	Applications (Home, Career, Community, Global, Environment)	Online Connection	Teacher Alert	Auditory/Verbal	Body/Kinesthetic	Interpersonal/Group Learning	Logical/Mathematical	Visual/Spatial	Workbook Activities	Alternative Workbook Activities	Lab Manual	Self-Study Guide
						✓		538	538	536		537, 538			539			539		97	97	81	✓
542			546		544				544	541	544	543		542, 543						98	98	82	✓
	551		553			✓			550	548				551		550	551			99	99	83	✓
		557		559		✓	558, 563		557	555	559	556, 559	559						557	100–101	100–101	84–85	✓

Pronunciation Key

a	hat	e	let	ī	ice	ô	order	ù	put	sh	she	ə { a in about
ā	age	ē	equal	o	hot	oi	oil	ü	rule	th	thin	e in taken
ä	far	ėr	term	ō	open	ou	out	ch	child	ŦH	then	i in pencil
â	care	i	it	ò	saw	u	cup	ng	long	zh	measure	o in lemon, u in circus

Alternative Workbook Activities

The Teacher's Resource Library (TRL) contains a set of lower-level worksheets called Alternative Workbook Activities. These worksheets cover the same content as the regular Workbook Activities but are written at a second-grade reading level.

Skill Track Online

Use Skill Track Online for *Biology: Cycles of Life* to monitor student progress and meet the demands of adequate yearly progress (AYP). Make informed instructional decisions with individual student and class reports of online lesson and chapter assessments. With immediate and ongoing feedback, students will also see what they have learned and where they need more reinforcement and practice.

Chapter at a Glance

Chapter 17: Populations and Communities
pages 534–563

Lessons

1. **Understanding Populations and Communities** pages 536–540
2. **Populations and Their Activities** pages 541–547

   Investigation 17 pages 546–547
3. **Relationships in Communities** pages 548–554

   Discovery Investigation 17 pages 553–554
4. **How Do Communities Start and Survive?** pages 555–559

   Biology in the World page 559

Chapter 17 Summary page 560

Chapter 17 Review pages 561–563

Audio CD

Skill Track Online for Biology: Cycles of Life

Teacher's Resource Library

   Workbook Activities 97–101

   Alternative Workbook Activities 97–101

   Lab Manual 81–85

   Community Connection 17

   Graphic Organizer 17

   Resource File 39–40

   Chapter 17 Self-Study Guide

   Chapter 17 Mastery Tests A and B

(Answer Keys for the Teacher's Resource Library begin on page 675 of the Teacher's Edition. The Materials List for the Lab Manual activities begins on page 720.)

Opener Activity

Have students construct a bar graph showing the following data for the rate of growth for the world's population.

Year	Human Population (in Billions)
1800	0.98
1930	2.07
1960	3.02
1980	4.44
1990	5.27
2000	6.06

Discuss how the number of people in the world might affect the populations of other organisms. Explain that in this chapter, students will learn about populations and how they change and interact in communities.

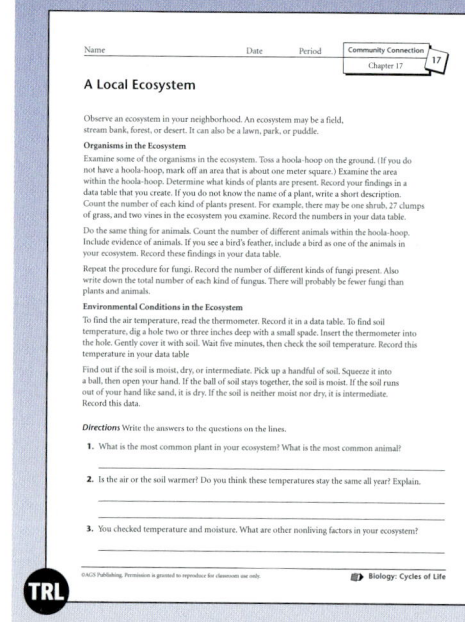

Community Connection 17

Chapter 17: Populations and Communities

The school of fish in the photograph is part of a coral-reef ecosystem. The organisms depend on each other for survival. Algae that live in the coral grow using energy from the sun. The algae become food for crustaceans, which are eaten by fish. Decomposers break down crustaceans and dead fish. This releases nutrients into the water. Crustaceans and fish hide in the coral to escape being eaten. In Chapter 17, you will learn about the living parts of an ecosystem—populations and communities. You will find out how the living things are woven together by the transfer of energy and materials.

Goals for Learning

- ◆ To explain the structure of populations and communities
- ◆ To describe factors affecting population growth
- ◆ To identify properties of communities
- ◆ To describe community interactions
- ◆ To explain how communities change

Introducing the Chapter

Have students discuss what they already know about the terms *population* and *community*. Have them tell what they think these terms have to do with organisms other than humans. Explain that in biology, a community consists of all the living things in an area, and a population consists of all the individuals of one species in an area. Have students read the Goals for Learning and note that in this chapter, they will learn about the different levels of organization in life, the meanings of the terms *population* and *community*, how populations are measured, and different properties of communities.

Have students examine the photograph of a school of fish and the surrounding marine plants on page 534. Ask students: How does the photograph relate to your understanding of populations and communities? (*Several populations of different types of fish and plants are parts of one community because they live in the same area.*)

Notes and Math Tips

Ask volunteers to read the notes and math tips that appear in the margins throughout the chapter. Then discuss them with the class.

TEACHER'S RESOURCE

The AGS Publishing Teaching Strategies in Science Transparencies may be used with this chapter. The transparencies add an interactive dimension to expand and enhance the *Biology: Cycles of Life* program content.

CAREER INTEREST INVENTORY

The AGS Publishing Harrington-O'Shea Career Decision-Making System-Revised (CDM) may be used with this chapter. Students can use the CDM to explore their interests and identify careers. The CDM defines career areas that are indicated by students' responses on the inventory.

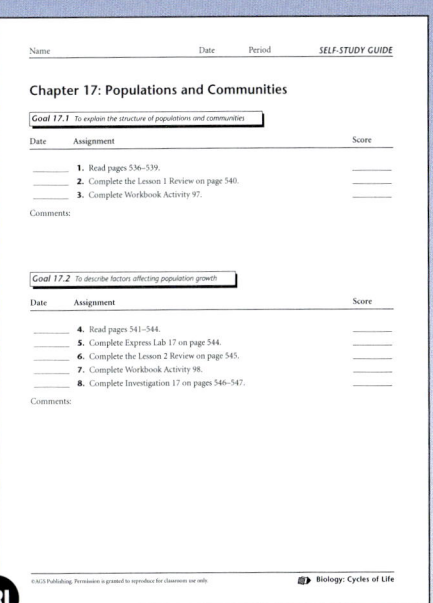

Chapter 17 Self-Study Guide

Lesson at a Glance

Chapter 17 Lesson 1

Overview In this lesson, students learn about the different levels of organization of the environment, including populations and communities.

Objectives

- To identify the levels of organization in life
- To define *population* and *community*
- To describe how populations are measured
- To identify properties of communities

Student Pages 536–540

Teacher's Resource Library TRL

Workbook Activity 97
Alternative Workbook Activity 97
Lab Manual 81
Resource File 39

Vocabulary

biome	population density
biosphere	sample
interact	stability

Have students use a dictionary to look up the meaning of the root *bio-*, which means "life." Have students list common words that contain the root, such as *biography, biology, bionic,* and *antibiotic.* Ask them to predict how the root relates to each word. Then have them use their new understanding of the root *bio-* to come up with their own definitions for the vocabulary terms *biosphere* and *biome.*

Background Information

In addition to the organization of the environment, biologists use other classification systems, such as the taxonomy of living things and the levels of body organization. Just as a kingdom is the highest level of organization for living things and species is the lowest, the biosphere is the highest level of organization for the environment and the individual organism is the lowest.

Lesson 1: Understanding Populations and Communities

Objectives

After reading this lesson, you should be able to

- identify the levels of organization in life
- define population and community
- describe how populations are measured
- identify properties of communities

Interact
To act upon or influence something

Biosphere
The total area of the earth that contains and supports life

You have now learned about the different levels and types of organization in life, from organism to molecule, and from kingdom to species. Every level acts upon, or **interacts** with, other levels. The many types of life also interact with nonliving things in their environments.

Recall from Chapter 1 that ecology is the study of how organisms interact with each other. Ecology is also the study of organisms interacting with the living and nonliving things in their environment.

Levels of Organization

Ecologists organize the environment into five levels: **biosphere,** ecosystem, community, population, and organism. The higher the level, the more interactions there are. Each level has unique properties because of the interactions of its parts. Organisms interact at different levels.

Study Figure 17.1.1. Notice that the highest level of organization is the biosphere.

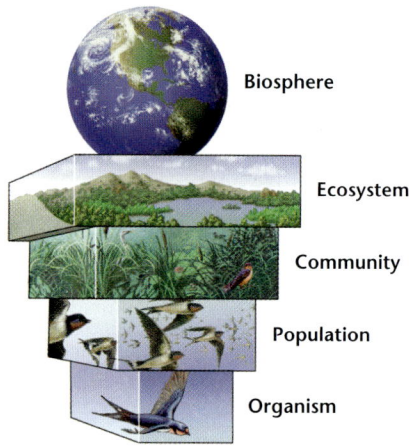

17.1.1 *The environment is organized into five levels.*

Similarly, a body is made of many organ systems, which are made up of many organs, which are made up of tissues, which are made up of cells. The biosphere can be divided into biomes, which can be divided into ecosystems, which contain communities, which are made up of populations, which are made up of individual organisms.

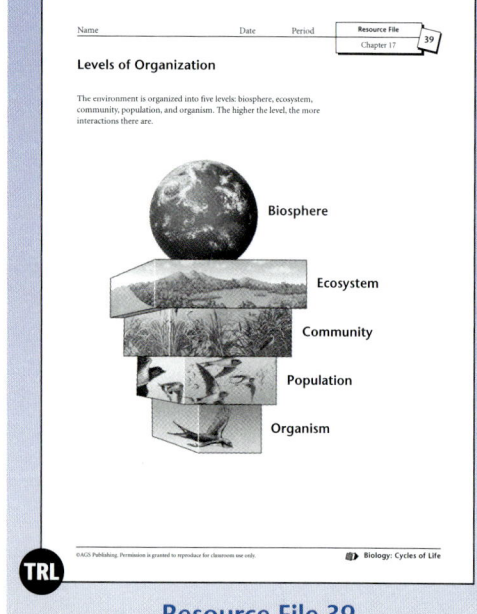

Resource File 39

Biome
A large area of the earth that has similar ecosystems and weather

The biosphere is all the areas of the earth where life can exist. These areas are the air, land, and water. All organisms are found in the biosphere.

Ecologists divide the biosphere into large areas called **biomes.** Biomes are areas of land or water that have similar weather conditions. Some biomes are oceans, forests, grasslands, wetlands, and deserts. Different biomes are found in different climates. You will learn more about the different biomes in Chapter 18.

Biomes are made of smaller units called ecosystems. Recall from Chapter 1 that an ecosystem is all the living and nonliving things found in a particular area. Ecosystems occur on land, in the water, and in the air. The interactions that occur in a pond make up an ecosystem. So do the interactions in a river or lake.

The third level of organization is the community. All organisms in an ecosystem are its community. Populations of different species that live in the same area make up a community.

Populations in a community interact with each another in many ways. In a forest, trees provide food and shelter for animals. Deer eat tree bark. Squirrels live in the trees. Squirrels eat the nuts from some trees. They also bury nuts, which then grow into new trees.

The next level of organization is a population. All the members of one species in an ecosystem are a population. The individual members of a population interact with each other. They interact when they mate or when they compete for food and water.

Notice that the lowest level of organization in Figure 17.1.1 is an individual organism. The place where an organism lives is its habitat. Every organism is adapted to live in its habitat.

> **Link to >>>**
>
> **Language Arts**
>
> The word *ecology* comes from the Greek word *oikos,* which means "house." The word *biosphere* comes from the Greek words *bios,* which means "life," and *sphaira,* which means "globe."

Warm-Up Activity

Show students a photograph of the sun, a raindrop, a fish, a tree, and a rabbit. For each photograph, ask students: Is this a living or a nonliving thing? *(Sun and raindrop, nonliving; fish, tree, and rabbit, living)* Then have students identify which of these objects could be considered part of the following categories: biome, ecosystem, community, and population. *(All are part of a biome or an ecosystem. Only the living things can be part of a community or a population.)*

Teaching the Lesson

Help students to understand the organization of the environment by comparing it to a classification system that is more familiar, such as the classification of students at school. In this analogy, the school can be considered the highest level of organization. The student body is the next level of organization, and grade level is the next. A grade level may be divided into classes. Finally, the lowest level of organization is the individual student.

Reinforce and Extend

CAREER CONNECTION

Have students research the career of an ecologist. If possible, have them interview an ecologist about the type of research he or she does and report their findings to the class. Encourage students to ask questions about the person's education, the types of ecosystems he or she studies, and the applications of his or her field of study.

Link to

Language Arts. Have students read the Link to Language Arts feature. Encourage students to look up the meaning of other words that are derived from the Greek word *oikos*. For example, other life science words with the root word *eco-* include *ecosystem* and *ecosphere*. Non-science words include *economy, economical,* and *economics*. Have students relate the meanings for the words *economy* and *ecology* to the word *house*.

ELL/ESL Strategy

Language Objective: *To use visuals*

Have students form groups. Have each group create six drawings that represent the biosphere, a biome, an ecosystem, a community, a population, and an organism. Have students use the drawings to plan a visual presentation explaining the different levels of organization of life. Be sure that they show how the lowest levels of organization are represented in the drawings for the higher levels of organization. Then have a student from each group use both sets of drawings to explain how the number of organisms of a species in the entire world is usually different from the population of that species within a single community.

Global Connection

Have students determine the average human population density of the world. They can use a world almanac or other reference tool to find current figures for the number of people in the world and the surface land area. To calculate population density, students can divide the number of people by the number of square kilometers. The total number of people in the world in 2000 was about 6 billion, or 6,000,000,000.
The number of square kilometers of land is about 150,000,000. The average population density in 2000 was thus about 40 people per square kilometer of land. Students may also want to calculate and compare the average population densities of various countries.

Population density
The number of individuals in a population in a particular area

Sample
A part that represents an entire population

Learning About Populations

Populations are made of members of one species that live in a particular place. A population is also the smallest unit that can evolve. Ecologists study how well a particular population survives in an ecosystem. They look at factors that affect a population's survival. Based on these data, ecologists can then determine the factors that cause a population or an entire species to evolve.

The number of individuals in a population is the size of that population. Size is an important property of population. Ecologists may be able to count a small population. However, the size of a large population can be difficult to measure. There may be too many individuals. Or, individuals may move around quickly, as with many species of insects and birds.

To measure size, ecologists often use **population density.** Population density measures how crowded a population is. It is the number of individual organisms of a particular species in a particular area of an ecosystem.

To measure population density, ecologists take **samples** of a population. A sample is a part that represents the entire population. Ecologists use samples to estimate the size of the population. To get a sample, ecologists count the number of organisms in a small area. Then they watch for changes in this number.

Technology and Society

Scientists know that wild relatives of food crops, such as corn and wheat, have valuable genetic diversity. People need to preserve these wild relatives. Consumers value some varieties of corn for consistent size, yield, and quality. This consistency may increase the chance of disease. Saving older species of corn can preserve valuable genetic diversity for future food crops.

Technology and Society

Have students read the Technology and Society feature. Explain that one benefit of genetic diversity is potential resistance to newly evolved or introduced diseases. A variety of corn that has always resisted common diseases might be vulnerable to a new mutant version of a disease. Preserving wild varieties of corn means that scientists and agriculture specialists could potentially find or develop a substitute crop that has disease-resistant genes.

Stability
The ability of a community to resist change

Learning About Communities

Communities are made of all of the populations that live in a certain area. Ecologists study communities to determine how populations of different organisms interact with each other. Every species has a niche, or a particular ecological role. The relationships between different species and their niches give each community its special properties.

For example, an ecologist counts 500 individuals in an area. This area is one-tenth of the area of an ecosystem. The ecologist then multiplies 500 by 10 to get an estimate of 5,000 individuals. In other words, 5,000 individuals make up the population in a certain ecosystem.

Ecologists study these relationships to understand common properties of communities. Two properties are the diversity of species and the interactions of these species. Diversity is the number of different species in a community. A third property is the **stability** of the community. The stability of a community shows how much it can resist change.

> **Link to >>>**
> **Math**
> Ecologists usually cannot measure all the variables in an ecosystem. They often use mathematical models to better understand the structure and function of an ecosystem. Ecologists base their models on data obtained from observations.

LEARNING STYLES

Auditory/Verbal
Have students work in small groups to write new lyrics about the different levels of organization of the environment for the tune "There Was an Old Lady Who Swallowed a Fly." Be sure students include each level shown in Figure 17.1.1 on page 536. Students may wish to use other tunes from children's songs, current popular music, or folk songs.

LEARNING STYLES

Logical/Mathematical
Explain that in chemistry, density is mass per unit volume. To determine the density of a substance, you can divide its mass in grams by its volume in milliliters. The result is a number with the units *grams per milliliter* (g/mL). Have students brainstorm possible units of population density. For example, for the population density of birds in a forest, the unit might be birds per square foot. In general, population density is given in number of individuals per unit of area.

Link to

Math. Have students read the Link to Math feature. Have students use math to predict the population density of a single organism in an area, such as their backyard, the schoolyard, or a local park. To do this, have them count the number of individuals of one species in one square foot or one square meter of that area. Then have them multiply that number by the total number of square feet or square meters in the area.

Lesson 1 Review Answers

1. community 2. niche 3. diversity 4. C
5. C 6. B 7. Rain forests and deserts are considered to be different biomes because they have different weather and ecosystems. 8. A population is all of the members of one species in a particular ecosystem. A community is all of the living species in an ecosystem. 9. Answers will vary. For example, students could describe squirrels, birds, insects, plants, etc., in a local park. 10. From lowest to highest, the order is organism, population, community, ecosystem, and biosphere.

Portfolio Assessment

Sample items include:
- Interview questions from Career Connection
- Drawings from ELL/ESL Strategy
- Measurements and calculations from Link to Math
- Measurements and calculations from Global Connection
- Song lyrics from Learning Styles Auditory/Verbal
- Lesson 1 Review answers

LAB ACTIVITIES

Chapter 17 has Investigation and Discovery Investigation lab activities. Two additional lab activities for Chapter 17 appear in the Biology: Cycles of Life Lab Manual and on the Teacher's Resource Library CD-ROM.

Lesson 1 REVIEW

Word Bank
community
diversity
niche

On a sheet of paper, write the word from the Word Bank that completes each sentence correctly.

1. All of the organisms of a particular species found in a certain area form a _____.
2. A _____ describes the role played by a species in an community.
3. In a community, _____ refers to the number of different species present.

On a sheet of paper, write the letter of the answer that completes each sentence correctly.

4. A scientist who studies the interactions of organisms with their environments is a(n) _____.
   A biologist   B zoologist   C ecologist   D botanist

5. Population density is a measure of the _____ of organisms in an area.
   A diversity   B health   C number   D niche

6. The smallest number of living things is found in the _____ level of ecological organization.
   A community   B population   C ecosystem   D biosphere

Critical Thinking
On a sheet of paper, answer the following questions. Use complete sentences.

7. Why are rain forests and deserts different biomes?
8. What is the difference between a population and a community?
9. Describe an ecological community in your area.
10. Order the following levels of organization from lowest to highest: community, organism, ecosystem, biosphere, population.

540 Chapter 17 Populations and Communities

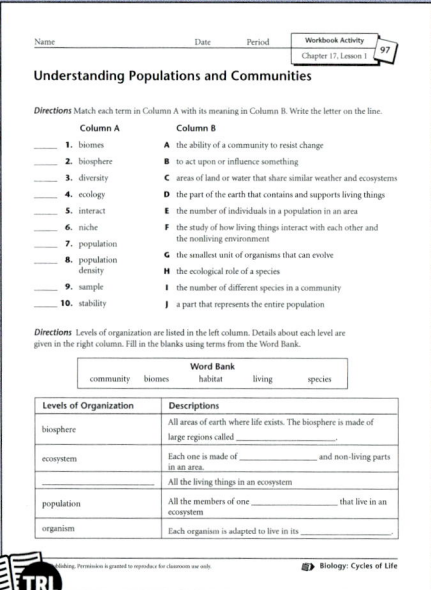

Workbook Activity 97

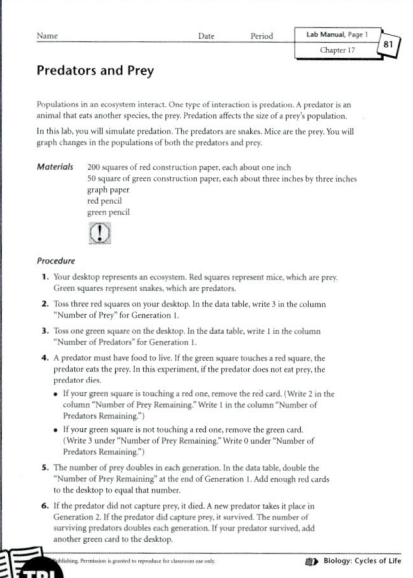

Lab Manual 81, pages 1–3

Lesson 2: Populations and Their Activities

Objectives

After reading this lesson, you should be able to
- identify factors affecting population growth
- describe population distribution patterns

Growth rate
The amount by which a population's size changes in a given time

Carrying capacity
The largest density an ecosystem can support for a particular population

As you know, populations are made of organisms of the same species. These organisms have similar structures and functions. They behave in similar ways.

When ecologists study populations, they study characteristics that arise through adaptation. These characteristics may help the entire population to survive. Ecologists also study the characteristics of the ecosystems that populations live in.

Limits on Population Density

Recall from Lesson 1 that ecologists can estimate a population's size by measuring its density. Density increases if a population is surviving well in an ecosystem. This means more organisms are being born than are dying. Density decreases if a population is not surviving well.

If a population has all the resources needed for survival, density should increase forever. However, these resources are not always available. A population's ability to grow is limited by food and water supplies, disease, shelter, and other factors in the environment.

Factors Affecting Population Growth

Many factors affect the **growth rate** of a population. The growth rate is the amount by which a population's size changes in a given time. Factors that limit how much a population can grow are found in all ecosystems. Some factors, such as food and water supplies, are common among all populations. Other factors are unique to certain populations.

An ecosystem and its factors will not support population growth forever. At some point, a population reaches its **carrying capacity** for its ecosystem. The carrying capacity is the largest density an ecosystem can support for a particular population. At carrying capacity, the number of organisms being born equals the number of organisms dying.

Lesson at a Glance

Chapter 17 Lesson 2

Overview In this lesson, students learn about population growth and distribution patterns.

Objectives
- To identify factors affecting population growth
- To describe population distribution patterns

Student Pages 541–547

Teacher's Resource Library
Workbook Activity 98
Alternative Workbook Activity 98
Lab Manual 82–83

Vocabulary

boom-bust cycle	emigrate
carrying capacity	growth rate
clumped	immigrate
competition	random
density-dependent factor	uniform
density-independent factor	

Have students use a dictionary to find the common meanings of the words *emigrate* and *immigrate*. Then have students compare these common meanings to their definitions in the text.

Background Information

The distribution of a population often depends on environmental or social factors. If resources in the environment are distributed in clumps, then the organisms that rely on those resources may have a clumped distribution. For example, plants may grow only where the soil is best, and animals may live only where there are plants. Uniform population distribution is often the result of competition. King penguins are generally distributed uniformly because they compete for space in breeding territories, and some species of desert plants are distributed uniformly because they compete for water. Random distribution occurs when these sorts of environmental and social factors are absent or insignificant.

1 Warm-Up Activity

Have students read and perform the Express Lab on page 544. Have students hypothesize why they used the roll of a die to choose their sample. Explain that the random choice ensures that they are not biased in their choice of sample.

Express Lab Answers

1. Answers will vary. It is unlikely that the sample contains one-sixth of the organisms unless they are distributed in a uniform pattern. **2.** Sampling of a clumped or random distribution pattern may not accurately reflect true population size. **3.** Increasing the number of samples will more accurately show the true population size.

2 Teaching the Lesson

Explain carrying capacity by making an analogy to party planning. If you have only 12 cupcakes, you can feed only 12 people at the party. A party population of 10 people can be supported by 12 cupcakes, but a party population of 14 people cannot. The carrying capacity of the party is therefore 12 people. Extend the analogy for a dynamic population, one that continually changes as a result of births and deaths. If people arrive and leave depending on the availability of cupcakes, then the number of people at the party at any one time depends on the number of cupcakes available. If you can produce cupcakes only in batches of 12, then the dynamic population of party guests remains 12.

3 Reinforce and Extend

TEACHER ALERT

 Point out that coevolution is distinct from convergent evolution. Coevolution involves the adaptations of two different species as a result of their influence on each other. Convergent evolution is the evolution of two different species that develop similar structures even though they are not closely related (do not share a recent common ancestor).

Competition
When organisms try to use the same resources

Density-dependent factor
A factor related to the density of a population that affects population size

Different populations share the same resources, such as food and water. Plant populations are the main food for many animal populations. Both plant and animal populations need water and space. Organisms in the same population also share resources with each other.

Organisms are in **competition** for the same resources. Some organisms get more resources than others. As populations grow, competition for resources becomes greater. **Density-dependent factors** are resources that affect population growth. Density-dependent factors include food, water, and habitat. When the number of organisms increases in an ecosystem, the amount of available resources usually stays the same. This means organisms have access to fewer resources.

Achievements in Science

Coevolution

Evolution shapes populations. If two species live together, the evolution of one species can influence the evolution of another species. Biologists call this coevolution. Coevolution means "evolving together." An example of coevolution is plants and the animals that pollinate them.

American biologists Paul Ehrlich and Peter Raven founded the study of coevolution in the early 1960s. Ehrlich and Raven worked together to study butterflies and their food plants. They observed that monarch butterfly larvae, or caterpillars, feed only on plants of the milkweed family. These plants produce bitter, poisonous chemicals. Insects do not eat milkweeds.

Monarch butterflies are different. Monarch butterflies have evolved to make a special enzyme. This enzyme lets caterpillars eat milkweed plants without being poisoned.

The poisonous chemicals give milkweeds an evolutionary advantage. Most insects do not eat them. However, monarch butterflies developed a method to overcome this advantage. The milkweed family and monarchs influenced each other's evolution, or coevolution.

Achievements in Science

Have students read the Achievements in Science feature about Ehrlich and Raven's work studying coevolution. Have students discuss how coevolution might account for different adaptations in flowering plants and nectar-collecting insects, such as butterflies. Explain that a butterfly has a long, tonguelike structure called a proboscis that allows it to reach into a flower and suck up the sweet nectar for food. Butterflies have good vision (unlike bees, they can see red) but a weak sense of smell. Colorful, odorless flowers attract butterflies, which sometimes unintentionally brush against the pollen of one flower and carry it to the next. The transfer of pollen from one flower to the next allows the flower to reproduce. Ask students: How might each organism have influenced the evolution of the other? *(Color and nectar are adaptations that help the flower attract butterflies. Color vision and the proboscis are adaptations that help the butterfly find the flower and get nectar from it.)*

Density-independent factor
A factor that affects population size, but does not depend on population density

Immigrate
To move into a population

Emigrate
To leave a population

Boom-bust cycle
A period in which the densities of populations increase or decrease at the same time

Uniform
When a population spreads out evenly through an ecosystem

Clumped
When a population spreads out in small groups through an ecosystem

Random
When a population has no order as to how it is distributed through an ecosystem

Density-independent factors do not depend on population density. These factors affect the same percentage of the population regardless of its density. Examples of density-independent factors are fires, freezes, droughts, and floods. Density-independent factors often are important in regulating the growth of a population. Both density-dependent factors and density-independent factors affect population size.

Other factors also affect population growth. Organisms **immigrate**, or move into a population. Organisms **emigrate**, or leave a population.

Some populations have **boom-bust cycles**. In these cycles, populations rely on other populations for survival. Their densities affect each other. As one population grows, the other population also grows. This is a boom period. As one population decreases, another population also decreases. This is a bust period. There are many causes of boom-bust cycles.

Boom-bust cycles respond to various factors. One factor is the changes in predator and prey populations. Other factors are the quality and amount of the prey's food.

Population Distribution

Factors that affect population growth also affect how organisms in a population distribute themselves throughout an ecosystem. Organisms in the same population spread out in three patterns: **uniform, clumped,** and **random.**

Science Myth

Myth: Experiments are the only way to gain scientific knowledge.

Fact: In addition to experiments, scientists can learn much from observations. Experimentation is not always possible in some fields of sciences such as ecology. Ecologists may not be able to control some variables like weather, for example. Ecologists often use observation and analysis to learn about populations.

At Home

Have students grow radish plants or bean plants at home and design an experiment to determine how plant spacing affects plant size. Have them plant a thin layer of seeds in a designated place in the garden or inside in a tray that holds 2 or 3 inches of soil. They should place the tray on a sunny windowsill. Be sure they mist the seeds daily with water. As the seedlings emerge, have them remove all but a few seedlings from one-half of the tray or garden patch and leave the others alone (not thinned). After a few weeks of growth, have students compare the sizes of the overcrowded radishes and the radishes that have plenty of space to grow. Have students share their observations with the class. Explain that space to live and grow is one important factor in determining population size.

Teacher Alert

Be sure that students understand that density-dependent factors and density-independent factors both place limits on population growth. Food supply can limit population growth. A limited food supply is depleted only after the population density increases beyond a certain point; that is, the food supply is density-dependent. Temperature is another factor that can limit population growth. For example, if a plant species has little tolerance for extremes of temperature, a heat wave or a cold wave might kill half the individuals of that species. Temperature is density-independent because the heat wave or cold wave may kill the same proportion of the population regardless of whether there are many plants of that species in the area or just a few.

Science Myth

Have students read the Science Myth feature. Remind students that scientists are not always able to control variables and therefore cannot always gather information through experimentation. Have students brainstorm different reasons why a scientist might use observation rather than experimentation to gather scientific knowledge. For example, it is difficult and often impossible to observe trends in evolution of species with long life spans. Some types of experiments are prohibitively expensive. Also, there are many ethical reasons to avoid experiments that might harm test subjects. Have students discuss how observation or modeling would be a better choice than experimentation in such cases.

ELL/ESL Strategy

Language Objective:
To explain by using a model

Have students form pairs composed of a student learning English and a student with strong English skills. Have students explain to each other the meanings of the terms *population density*, *density-dependent factor*, and *density-independent factor*. Encourage them to use visual aids to explain each term. For example, they can illustrate and compare models of low population density and high population density. Then they can determine the kind of effect certain factors, such as a fire or a limited amount of water, would have on each population. Explain that factors such as a limited amount of water will cause a larger population to decrease and will have little effect on a very small population. Therefore, water is a density-dependent factor. A fire will decrease both large and small populations and so is a density-independent factor.

Science Journal

Have students write descriptions of different situations in which a group of people would be distributed in three different patterns: uniform, clumped, and random. For example, people at a party might show clumped distribution because small groups of people would talk to one another. People in a crowd might show random distribution because they would all be headed in different directions toward different places. People in a classroom might show uniform distribution because they would be seated at desks arranged a certain distance apart.

544 Chapter 17

UNIFORM

CLUMPED

RANDOM

Figure 17.2.1
Population distribution patterns are uniform (top), clumped (center), or random (bottom).

Study Figure 17.2.1. In a uniform pattern, organisms spread evenly through their ecosystem. A clumped pattern is when organisms of the same population form small groups through the ecosystem. In a random pattern, organisms of a population are distributed in no particular way.

Express Lab 17

Materials
- 6 index cards
- six-sided number cube
- 30 buttons

Procedure
1. With a pen, label the index cards from 1 to 6.
2. Make a rectangle with two rows of index cards. In row 1, lay out index cards 1 to 3. In row 2, lay out index cards 4 to 6. The rectangle represents an ecosystem.
3. Each button represents one organism in a population. Select a distribution pattern: uniform, clumped, or random.
4. Put the buttons on the rectangle to show the distribution pattern you selected.
5. Roll the number cube. Find the card with that number. The organisms on this index card represent your sample.

Analysis
1. Does your sample contain one-sixth of the organisms in your ecosystem? Explain your answer.
2. How do distribution patterns affect sampling?
3. Which pattern will give the best estimate of true population size?

544 Chapter 17 Populations and Communities

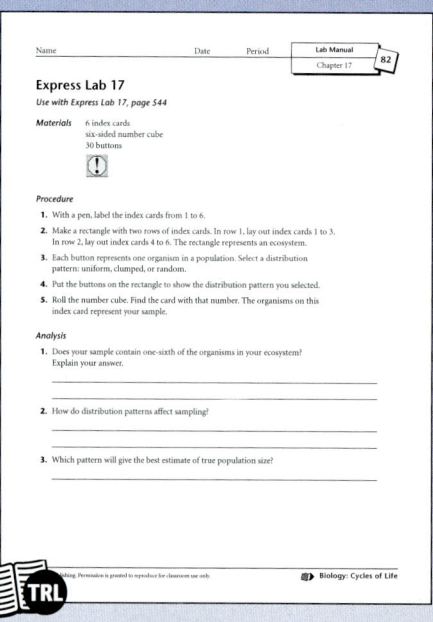

Lab Manual 82

Lesson 2 REVIEW

Word Bank
- density-independent
- immigrating
- increases
- more

On a sheet of paper, write the word or words from the Word Bank that complete each sentence correctly.

1. Organisms that are _____ are entering a population.
2. As populations grow, competition _____ and resources become _____ scarce.
3. Fires and lack of rainfall are examples of _____ factors.

On a sheet of paper, write the letter of the answer that completes each sentence correctly.

4. When a population reaches its carrying capacity, _____.
   - **A** the ecosystem cannot support more growth
   - **B** diversity increases
   - **C** organisms form random distribution patterns
   - **D** new individuals will immigrate

5. A population that is evenly distributed forms a(n) _____ pattern through an ecosystem.
   - **A** clumped **B** random **C** grouped **D** uniform

6. An example of a density-dependent factor is a _____.
   - **A** freezes
   - **B** droughts
   - **C** food supply
   - **D** fire

Critical Thinking

On a sheet of paper, answer the following questions. Use complete sentences.

7. Explain the role of competition in the use of density-dependent resources.
8. Wolves live in groups within their ecosystem. What kind of distribution pattern is this? Explain your answer.
9. How do immigration and emigration affect population density?
10. Compare density-dependent and density-independent factors.

Populations and Communities Chapter 17 545

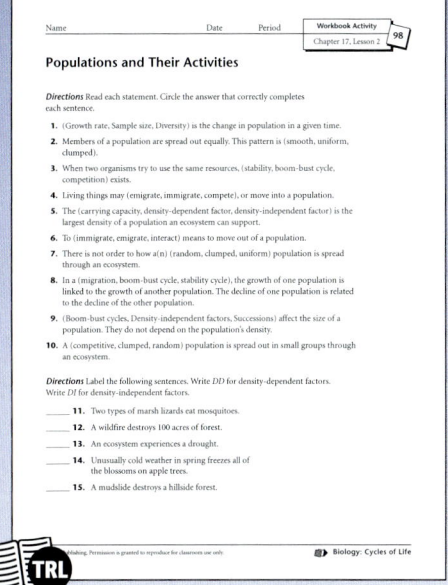

Workbook Activity 98

Lesson 2 Review Answers

1. immigrating 2. increases; more
3. density-independent 4. A
5. D 6. C 7. Organisms within an ecosystem that use the same density-dependent resources, such as food and habitat, have to compete harder for those resources as the number of organisms in an ecosystem increases. 8. It is a clumped distribution pattern because the wolves live within the ecosystem in groups rather than spread out evenly or randomly throughout the ecosystem.
9. Immigration increases population density. Emigration decreases population density. 10. Density-dependent factors, such as food, are influenced by population density. Density-independent factors, such as weather, are not. Both kinds of factors affect population growth.

Portfolio Assessment

Sample items include:
- Write-up from the Express Lab
- Observations from At Home
- Description from Science Journal
- Lesson 2 Review answers

Populations and Communities 545

Investigation 17

Encourage students to read the Investigation steps. Discuss questions they may have before beginning the investigation.

Objectives
- To list the characteristics of a population
- To estimate population size

Skills
Communicating, following written directions, observing, recording, applying information, comparing and contrasting, interpreting visuals, understanding concepts, making inferences, analyzing data, drawing conclusions

Background
Scientists frequently use the mark-recapture method of estimating population size in ecological studies of wild animals. Scientists mark captured animals with tags, bands, collars, or spots of dye, and then release the animals. The estimate of population size assumes that there have been no births, deaths, emigration, or immigration after the marking and release of the animals.

Time Frame
30 minutes

Procedure
- Have students work together in small groups to complete the activity.
- Provide each group with a small paper bag containing 50 white navy beans.
- You may want to supply some groups with a bag containing 100 navy beans instead of 50. These groups will find that their estimates of population size are less accurate because their populations are larger.
- You may want to review some sample math problems, using the formula in Analysis question 3.

INVESTIGATION 17

Materials
- small paper bag containing dried navy beans
- red wax pencil

Estimating Population Size

To study a population, ecologists must determine its size. Ecologists usually cannot count all the members of a population. Instead, they use sampling methods to estimate the size of a population. In this investigation, you will use the mark-recapture sampling method to estimate the size of a population of navy beans. Ecologists often use the mark-recapture method to estimate the size of animal populations.

Procedure

1. Remove 10 beans from the bag. Use the red wax pencil to put a large dot on each of the 10 navy beans. **Safety Alert: Do not put the navy beans in or near your mouth.**

2. Return the marked navy beans to the paper bag. Close the bag. Shake the bag gently.

546   Chapter 17   Populations and Communities

SAFETY ALERT
- Remind students not to put the navy beans in or near their mouths.

3. Remove 20 navy beans from the bag. This is your sample. Count the number of navy beans with red dots. The navy beans with red dots are your marked recaptures. Record this number.

4. Return the navy beans with red dots to the bag.

5. Count the total number of navy beans in the bag. This is the actual population size. Record this number.

Analysis

1. What does each navy bean represent?

2. What does the bag represent?

3. Use the following equation to estimate the population size, N:

$$N = \frac{M \times S}{R}$$

Where M = number marked
       S = total number in the sample
       R = number of marked recaptured

How close was your estimate of the population size to the total number of navy beans in the bag?

Conclusions

1. The mark-recapture method assumes that each marked individual has the same chance of being recaptured as each unmarked individual. What problems do you see with this assumption?

2. In a real population, what are some events or factors that could affect the accuracy of the mark-recapture method?

3. Write a new question about estimating population size that you could explore in another investigation.

Explore Further

Use a similar procedure to explore the effect of sample size on estimating population size.

Populations and Communities Chapter 17 **547**

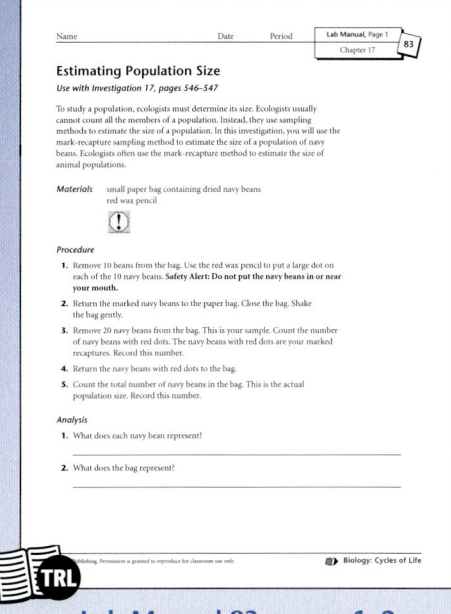

Lab Manual 83, pages 1–2

Cleanup/Disposal

Instruct students in proper cleanup and disposal of materials.

Results

Students will find that the mark-recapture equation will enable them to estimate population size. For example, if a student finds that 4 out of the 20 sample navy beans are marked, then the estimated population size will be 50 navy beans:

$$50 \text{ navy beans} = \frac{10 \text{ navy beans marked} \times 20 \text{ navy beans in the sample}}{4 \text{ marked recaptures}} = \frac{200}{4}$$

Analysis Answers

1. Each navy bean represents an individual in a population.

2. The bag represents the area being sampled.

3. Answers will vary depending on the number of marked navy beans recaptured.

Conclusions Answers

1. This assumption may not be correct. An animal that has been trapped earlier may be too wary of the trap to be recaptured.

2. Population events such as births, deaths, immigration, or emigration could reduce the accuracy of the mark-recapture method.

3. Students may wish to explore the effect of multiple-sampling events on estimating population size.

Explore Further Answers

Encourage students to explore the effect of sample size on estimating population size. The estimation of population size generally becomes more accurate as sample size increases. Point out to students that larger sample sizes require more time and money in ecological studies.

Assessment

You might include the following items from this investigation in student portfolios:

• Answers to Analysis and Conclusions

• Student proposal for additional work in Explore Further

Populations and Communities **547**

Lesson at a Glance

Chapter 17 Lesson 3

Overview In this lesson, students learn about diversity, niches, and interactions among organisms in communities.

Objectives

- To identify the major properties of communities
- To describe a niche
- To describe different interactions among organisms in communities

Student Pages 548–554

Teacher's Resource Library

Workbook Activity 99

Alternative Workbook Activity 99

Lab Manual 84

Vocabulary

camouflage	parasitism
canopy	predation
commensalism	symbiosis
host	trophic structure
interdependent	vegetation
mutualism	

Have students construct a diagram that organizes the terms *host*, *parasitism*, and *predation*. Have them use the diagram to compare and contrast the roles of parasites and predators and the roles of hosts and prey.

Background Information

Biologists often represent trophic structure in food chains and food webs. A food chain shows relationships between a producer and a consumer and one or more predator-prey relationships. The food chain below shows interactions of species in a land ecosystem. The arrows go from the organism that is eaten (the prey or producer) to the organism that consumes it (the predator or consumer).

grass → grasshopper → field mouse → rattlesnake → hawk

Lesson 3 — Relationships in Communities

Objectives

After reading this lesson, you should be able to

- identify the major properties of communities
- describe a niche
- describe different interactions among organisms in communities

Interdependent
Having to rely on each other

Recall from Lesson 1 that the populations in an ecosystem make up the community of the ecosystem. A community is all the living members of an ecosystem. This includes animals, plants, bacteria, and fungi.

The organisms in a community are **interdependent.** The organisms rely on each other for survival. For example, some animals eat plants. Plants rely on bacteria to break down dead trees on the forest floor. The nutrients from the dead trees enrich the soil so that plants can grow. Bacteria live on or inside other organisms. Fungi use plants and trees as places to grow.

Community Diversity

When ecologists study communities in ecosystems, they observe and measure properties for each community. A property common to all communities is diversity. Diversity is the number of different species in a community. Diversity is also the number of individuals in each population. The more diverse a community is, the more types of organisms it has.

Species Interactions

The members of species in a community interact with each other. For example, bears eat honey made by bees. Bees collect pollen from flowers. Some animals eat flowering plants. Every species in a community uses living and nonliving resources. Every species also provides resources. All of these activities make up the niche of a species. Every niche is unique.

Species in a community must interact to live and survive. Different types of interaction exist among species, including competition, predation, parasitism, mutualism, and commensalism. These interactions determine the makeup of a community.

548   Chapter 17   Populations and Communities

Because many predators prey on more than one type of organism, a food chain does not show the full complexity of trophic structure within a community. Food webs are used to show more complex interactions among many different species.

Competition

One type of interaction among species is competition. Members of a species compete with each other and with other species. They compete for food and water, for example.

Competition happens constantly in communities. Different species must share some resources. If two species had identical niches, they would compete for the same resources. Over time, one species would force the other species out of the ecosystem. Both species could stay if one species changed its niche.

> **Trophic structure**
> The feeding relationships between species in a community

Trophic Structure

The feeding relationships among the species of a community are called the **trophic structure.** In an ecosystem, all organisms that eat the same kinds of food are in the same trophic level. Look at Figure 17.3.1.

Figure 17.3.1 *How many trophic levels are in this ecosystem?*

Warm-Up Activity

Have students observe the schoolyard, a local park, or their own backyard and list the organisms that make up the community there. Have students observe whether any of these organisms interact with one another. For example, have them identify which organisms eat other organisms, which organisms are eaten, and which organisms produce their own food. Have students identify whether any of the organisms depend on other organisms for shelter, such as an insect depending on a plant.

Teaching the Lesson

Relate a stable ecosystem to an aquarium. It is nearly impossible to create a self-sufficient aquarium, because there are too many factors in a stable ecosystem. The many different interactions of species in a stable ecosystem contribute to the survival of the organisms. An aquarium has a limited number of species and organisms. An aquarium with only one or two organisms requires more maintenance than one with fish, plants, and snails. Each organism in the aquarium has a niche. If the aquarium contains only fish and no plants, someone must aerate the water so the fish can get oxygen. If enough plants are added, it is no longer necessary to aerate the tank artificially, because the plants will provide oxygen. Adding snails or bottom-feeding fish will help keep the aquarium clean, because these organisms feed on the detritus of the fish; without such organisms, the aquarium needs to be cleaned more often.

> **PRONUNCIATION GUIDE**
> Use the pronunciation shown here to help students pronounce difficult words in this lesson. Refer to the pronunciation key on the Chapter Planning Guide for the sounds of the symbols.
> allelopathy (ə lē´lə pa´thē)
> juglone (ju glōn´)

3 Reinforce and Extend

ELL/ESL Strategy

Language Objective:
To use visuals

Have each student draw a make-believe predator in a make-believe environment. Then have them exchange drawings. Have each student draw a second animal on the partner's drawing. The new animal should have one or more adaptations or mechanisms to help protect it from the first animal. *(examples: camouflage, mimicry, protective shelter)* Then have students explain to their partners how the animals they have drawn avoid predators.

Learning Styles

Body/Kinesthetic

Provide each pair of students with a stopwatch and equal numbers of red toothpicks and green toothpicks. Go outside and have one student in each pair dump all of the toothpicks on a patch of grass, making sure to spread them out evenly over an area of a few square feet. Have this student time the other student to see how many toothpicks he or she can pick up in 30 seconds. As a class, compare the relative numbers of green toothpicks and red toothpicks that were gathered in 30 seconds. Ask students: Why might you have found more red than green toothpicks? *(The green toothpicks are camouflaged to blend in with the grass.)* Guide students to make the analogy with camouflage that helps protect animals from predators.

Predation
A relationship in which one species eats another species

Camouflage
The colors or patterns on animals that help them hide in their surroundings

Symbiosis
A relationship in which two different species live in close association

Parasitism
A symbiotic relationship in which one organism feeds off of another organism

Host
An organism that is food for a parasite

Mutualism
A symbiotic relationship in which both organisms benefit

Commensalism
A symbiotic relationship in which one organism benefits and the other is not affected

Predation

Another type of interaction is **predation.** Predation is when one species eats another species. Recall from Chapter 16 that a predator eats an organism called the prey. There are many predator-prey relationships in any community. Deer are predators of grass. Snakes are predators of mice. Snakes are the prey of hawks. Species in predator-prey relationships often evolve different predator and defense, or prey, methods. Many big cats, such as lions and tigers, have long claws to catch prey. They can run fast, so they do not become prey. Mint plants use their strong flavor to defend themselves. Many animals dislike the taste of mint.

Many animals use defense methods against predators. As you learned in Chapter 16, some defend themselves by using warning coloration. Their bright colors and patterns scare off predators. Other organisms have colors or patterns that help them blend in and hide in their surroundings. Predators have difficulty seeing them. This is called **camouflage.** Another defense method is mimicry. In mimicry, one species looks like another poisonous or dangerous species. This causes predators to stay away.

Symbiotic Relationships

Other community interactions involve **symbiosis.** Symbiosis is the relationship between different species that live in close association with one another. **Parasitism** is a symbiotic relationship. In parasitism, one organism, the parasite, feeds off of another organism, the **host.** Fleas are parasites that feed off dogs and cats.

Mutualism is a symbiotic relationship in which two different organisms benefit from living together. Birds live on the backs of rhinoceros. The birds eat biting insects off of the skin of the rhinoceros. The birds get food, and the rhinoceros does not itch.

In **commensalism,** one organism benefits, and the other organism is not affected. Barnacles live on whales. Whales carry the barnacles around, which helps the barnacles feed. The barnacles do not hurt the whales.

Vegetation
The plant life in an area

Canopy
The tops of the forest trees

Science Myth

Myth: An organism at the top of the trophic structure preys on all the organisms below it.

Fact: In predator-prey relationships, a predator only consumes prey. Some species may feed at more than one trophic level. However, an organism does not prey on all organisms in the trophic levels below it.

Plant Life and Communities

Plant life, or **vegetation,** is a property of communities on land. Plants provide food for organisms. They also determine the structure of an ecosystem. Forest ecosystems have many tall plants such as trees. Trees provide homes for species such as birds and insects. Forest ecosystems have species that live in the **canopy,** or the tops of trees. These species are different than species living on the forest floor.

A desert ecosystem may have only a few plants, like cactus. A desert ecosystem may not support many species. The plant life in a community determines what other species can survive there.

Science at Work

Demographer

Demographers study the size, growth, density, and distribution of human populations. They collect and analyze data on births, marriages, deaths, and diseases. Demographers examine population trends due to changes in birth rate, death rate, emigration, and immigration. They predict how changes in population will affect public services such as health care, housing, and education.

Demographers need training in statistics. Statistics is the collecting of and using numerical facts about people, business, health, and so on. Jobs in demography may also require training in geography, economics, public health, medicine, or marketing. Many demographers work for federal, state, or local governments. Some work for state colleges and universities. Others work for private companies.

A demographer must be observant, orderly, and accurate. Demographers need good analytical and communication skills. They analyze and interpret data and work as a member of a team.

LEARNING STYLES

Interpersonal/Group Learning

Have groups of students perform skits in which they act out different interactions of species, such as competition, predation, parasitism, mutualism, and commensalism. In their skits, students may wish to demonstrate human interactions that are analogous to each type of interaction. Have students guess which interaction is being demonstrated by each skit.

TEACHER ALERT

Be sure that students understand the distinction between predation and parasitism. Unlike a parasite and its host, the predator and its prey do not live in close association with each other. Their relationship is not symbiotic. Also, two species in a parasitic relationship can live together for a very long time, with only the parasite benefiting. However, a predator must kill its prey in order to feed. The two do not coexist for very long.

Science at Work

Have students read the Science at Work feature about the work of demographers. Have students research and write a report about how the data that demographers collect could be applied to government and social policies, marketing, or medicine. For example, have them find out how the information gathered during Census 2000 might be used to determine the budgets for health benefits programs for older people.

Science Myth

Have students read the Science Myth feature. A familiar example of an organism at the top of the food chain that does not eat all the organisms below it is a human. Humans who eat chicken do not also eat the bugs and worms that the chicken may eat. The same is true of any carnivore that does not also eat plants. Its prey may be herbivores, which eat only plants.

Lesson 3 Review Answers

1. vegetation **2.** parasitism **3.** camouflage
4. C **5.** A **6.** A **7.** If two species have identical niches, they will compete for resources. Eventually, one of the species will change niches or be forced out of the ecosystem. **8.** All organisms in a community are considered interdependent because they rely on one another for survival. **9.** Some animals use warning coloration (bright patterns and colors) to discourage predators. Others use camouflage to blend in with their surroundings. Some animals use mimicry, resembling a different species that is dangerous and thus deters predators. **10.** In a predator-prey relationship, the relationship is short-lived because the prey dies when it is eaten. A parasite-host relationship, however, is an ongoing relationship. The parasite has a long-term need for the host, so there is no benefit if the host dies. Both kinds of relationships harm one partner for the benefit of the other.

Portfolio Assessment

Sample items include:
- Written observations from Warm-Up Activity
- Drawings from ELL/ESL Strategy
- Report from Science at Work
- Lesson 3 Review answers

Link to

Chemistry. Have students read the Link to Chemistry feature. Have students discuss why it is advantageous for the black walnut to produce a chemical that causes other plants to wilt and die. Have them explain how this adaptation might promote the success of the tree's offspring. *(There are fewer plants to compete with black walnut seedlings for resources such as sunlight, water, or nutrients in the soil.)*

Lesson 3 REVIEW

Word Bank
- camouflage
- parasitism
- vegetation

On a sheet of paper, write the word from the Word Bank that completes each sentence correctly.

1. The plant life in an area is the _____.
2. A symbiotic relationship in which one organism feeds off another organism is _____.
3. Animals with _____ have colors or patterns that help them hide from predators.

On a sheet of paper, write the letter of the answer that completes each sentence correctly.

4. A species that eats another species is _____.
   - **A** competition
   - **B** mutualism
   - **C** predation
   - **D** mimicry

5. Commensalism is a symbiotic relationship in which _____.
   - **A** one organism benefits and the other is not affected
   - **B** one organism captures and eats another
   - **C** one organism feeds off of another organism
   - **D** both organisms benefit

6. The trophic structure of a community describes its _____ relationships.
   - **A** feeding **B** mating **C** symbiotic **D** niche

Critical Thinking

On a sheet of paper, answer the following questions. Use complete sentences.

7. What will happen if two species have identical niches?
8. Why are all organisms in a community interdependent?
9. Describe three methods animals use to reduce the risk of being eaten.
10. How does a predator-prey relationship differ from a parasite-host relationship? How is it similar?

Link to ▶▶▶
Chemistry

Allelopathy is the natural secretion of harmful chemicals by certain plants. These chemicals discourage the growth of competitor plants of the same or another species. The black walnut tree is an allelopathic species. The buds, roots, and nut hulls of black walnut contain a poisonous chemical called juglone. Juglone causes many plants to wilt and die.

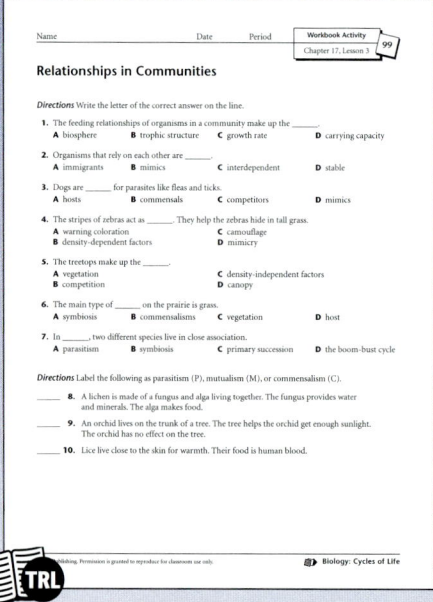

Workbook Activity 99

DISCOVERY INVESTIGATION 17

Materials
- heavy gloves
- meterstick
- 4 wood stakes
- string
- green, blue, brown, black, orange pencils or markers

Surveying an Ecological Community

An ecological community is made of all the biotic, or living, species in an ecosystem. Ecology is the study of the interactions among living things and the nonliving things in an environment. Living things are the biotic factors in the environment. Abiotic factors are nonliving things, such as air, temperature, light, and water. In this investigation, you will survey an ecological community in your area.

Procedure

1. Put on heavy gloves.
2. Using a meterstick, measure a 5 meter by 5 meter site. Put a stake at each corner of the site. **Safety Alert: Wear heavy gloves to push the stake into the ground. Stay only in the area as directed by your teacher.**

SAFETY ALERT

- Be sure student sites are located a safe distance from vehicular traffic.
- Be sure students have read and understood all safety rules for this investigation.
- Caution students not to collect or destroy anything in their site.
- Be sure students are able to recognize any poisonous plants, such as poison ivy, that they may encounter in their sites.

Discovery Investigation 17

This investigation is less structured that the first investigation in this chapter. It offers students more challenge and requires more teacher facilitation. Encourage students to read the Discovery Investigation steps. Discuss questions they may have before beginning the investigation.

Objectives

- To understand the structures of populations and communities
- To compare the roles of different organisms in the trophic structure of a community
- To describe the forces that affect population growth in communities
- To recognize the relationships among organisms in communities

Skills

Collecting information, formulating hypotheses, measuring, observing, recording, applying information, comparing and contrasting, drawing conclusions, making inferences, understanding concepts

Background

Students are often unaware of the ecological communities that are all around them. In this investigation, students will select outdoor study sites and analyze the communities within the sites.

Time Frame

One class period

Procedure

- Have students work together in groups to complete this activity.
- This investigation can be done almost anywhere outdoors. For example, students could study communities of living things at the edge of a parking lot or along a sidewalk.
- You may wish to provide students with hand lenses so that they can observe plants and animals more closely.

Continued on page 554

Continued from page 553

- You may wish to select sites in different kinds of areas to provide variety. For example, sites in frequently disturbed areas such as parking lots, sidewalks, or high-traffic grassy walkways are more likely to show signs of primary succession than those in secluded forest understory.
- Provide access to field guides to assist those students who wish to identify plants and animals.

Cleanup/Disposal

Instruct students in proper cleanup and disposal of materials.

Results

Students will discover a wide variety of living things in their sites. They should be able to identify organisms as producers, consumers, or decomposers. Remind students that many of the most important decomposers—bacteria—are too small to be seen.

Answers to Analysis, Conclusions, and Explore Further begin on page 670 of this Teacher's Edition.

Assessment

You might include the following items from this investigation in student portfolios:

- Student hypothesis and proposed procedure
- Answers to Analysis and Conclusions
- Student proposal for Explore Further

3. Make a border around the site by looping string around the first stake. Continue looping string around each stake until you have formed a border around the site.

4. To map your site, draw a 15 centimeter by 15 centimeter square on a sheet of paper. Draw the physical features of your site on your map.

5. Use a green pencil or marker to draw the plants in your site. Use blue to draw the animals. Use brown to represent evidence of animals, such as egg cases, animal tracks, or burrows. Use black to show dead organisms or parts of organisms, such as fallen leaves or twigs. Use orange to show decomposers.

6. Write a hypothesis, Safety Alerts, and procedure describing how to determine which organism in your site has the greatest population density.

7. Have your hypothesis, Safety Alerts, and procedure approved by your teacher. Carry out your experiment.

Analysis

1. List the abiotic and biotic features of your site.
2. Describe a distribution pattern—uniform, clumped, or random—for one organism in your site.
3. Which organisms at your site are producers? Which organisms are consumers?
4. Describe evidence of primary succession at your site.

Conclusions

1. Was your hypothesis supported by the results of your investigation?
2. Are consumers or producers found in the greatest number at your site?
3. What density-dependent and density-independent factors are likely to affect the organisms at your site?

Explore Further

What relationships exist among two or more different kinds of organisms at your site? Suggest a procedure to answer this question.

554   Chapter 17   *Populations and Communities*

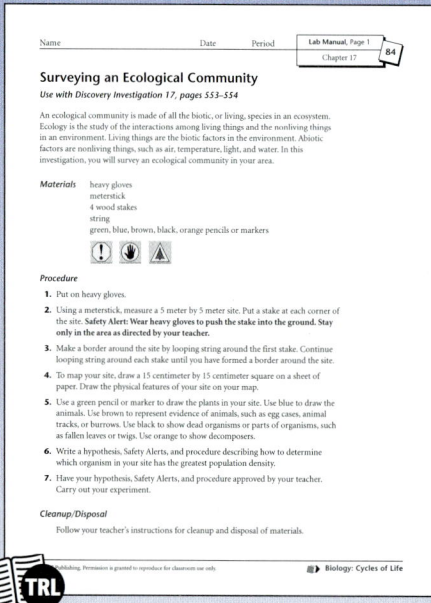

Lab Manual 84, pages 1–2

554   Chapter 17

Lesson 4: How Do Communities Start and Survive?

Objectives
After reading this lesson, you should be able to
- give examples of community disturbances
- define succession
- identify two types of succession
- describe the organisms found in successions

Disturbance
A large change in a community

Toxic
Poisonous

Succession
The process of ecological change in a community

Communities tend to be in a constant state of change. Natural **disturbances** such as fires, blizzards, freezes, floods, droughts, and storms affect communities. A disturbance is a major change in a community. Human disturbances such as **toxic**, or poisonous, spills also affect communities. For example, hurricanes and toxic spills can disturb marine communities. Disturbances destroy organisms. They also change the resources available to organisms that survive.

Stability

Ecologists study a community property called stability. Recall from Lesson 1 that stability is a community's ability to resist changes. Many disturbances happen regularly. Many large disturbances are density-independent factors that regulate populations and communities. Recall from Lesson 2 that a density-independent factor affects population or community size, but does not depend on population density.

Succession

A stable community can recover from some disturbances in a few years. Other communities may have to start over after a disturbance. A community that experiences major changes undergoes **succession.** Succession is the process of ecological change in a community.

Change is not necessarily bad for a community. Disturbances may remove some species and bring in new species. Sometimes, species struggling to survive are given a new chance. Major changes can open new niches and resources for them. For example, a fire destroys many trees in a forest. However, seeds of some plant species need high temperatures to sprout.

Communities that experience succession may take thousands or millions of years to become stable. However, disturbances continue to happen. Most communities never become completely stable.

Lesson at a Glance

Chapter 17 Lesson 4

Overview In this lesson, students learn about disturbances and succession in communities.

Objectives
- To give examples of community disturbances
- To define *succession*
- To identify two types of succession
- To describe the organisms found in successions

Student Pages 555–559

Teacher's Resource Library

Workbook Activity 100–101

Alternative Workbook Activity 100–101

Lab Manual 85

Resource File 40

Vocabulary

disturbance   succession
primary succession   toxic
secondary succession

Have students use a dictionary to look up the common meanings of the words *succeed, success, successor,* and *succession.* Then have them relate these common words to the vocabulary terms *succession, primary succession,* and *secondary succession.*

Background Information

Primary succession and secondary succession can be distinguished by the starting conditions of the community. In primary succession, there is little or no organic matter to provide nutrients for living things. Organisms called pioneer species must populate an area before other organisms can survive. Most of the needs of pioneer species can be met from inorganic resources such as water, air, sunlight, and minerals. Secondary succession requires starting conditions in which organic materials are present in the form of soil or dead or living organisms.

Resource File 40

Warm-Up Activity

Have students use the Internet or the library to find images of forests just after a forest fire, several months after a forest fire, and years after a forest fire. Have them identify ways that various organisms in the forest were negatively affected, unaffected, and positively affected by the fire. Then have them predict how the short-term effects of the fire might differ from the long-term effects.

 ## Teaching the Lesson

Compare primary succession and secondary succession to building a house. Building a house is like primary succession. The builders must bring in building materials and construct each part of the house. Refurbishing an old house and making it like new is like secondary succession. The builders can take parts of the old house and reuse them, such as taking bricks from a broken-down wall and stacking them again. Both processes result in a functional house. The processes differ in the condition of the lot and the materials available at the site.

 ## Reinforce and Extend

IN THE COMMUNITY

 Plan a field trip to a vacant lot or a natural area that has recently been torn up by construction. Have students observe the types of organisms that live at the site. For example, allow them to examine any soil that has been deposited there and identify the kinds of plants or animals that live in the soil. They are likely to find grasses and other plants that are grown from wind-blown seeds. They might find insects or earthworms that can live in uncultured soil. Have students compare these organisms to ones that they do not see, such as trees or large mammals. Ask what type of succession they see. *(In a paved lot, they might see the beginnings of primary succession. In a lot or site with soil, they might see secondary succession.)* Have students write their observations in a report.

Primary succession
The changes in a lifeless environment that create a community

Secondary succession
The changes in a community as it recovers from the effects of a disturbance

Link to ▶▶▶
Earth Science
The volcanic eruption of Mount St. Helens on May 18, 1980, created a natural outdoor laboratory. Mount St. Helens is in the state of Washington. Ecologists observed a succession following a major disturbance. They found that most early plant species thrived in nutrient-poor, disturbed areas. These areas had very little water.

Primary Succession

Communities can go through two types of succession. The first type is **primary succession.** Communities start in an area that had no life. These areas are usually made of nonliving rock and land. They are usually uncovered by melting glaciers or created by new rock from volcanic eruptions. For life to exist, the soil must build up nutrients that organisms need.

Primary succession begins with microorganisms, such as mosses and lichens. These small organisms perform photosynthesis. As these species take over the area, other plant species move into the area. As more plants move in, animals also start to move in. A diverse community has now formed. Primary succession creates a new community over a long period of time.

Secondary Succession

Secondary succession happens after disturbances have destroyed many populations in a community. Secondary succession often happens after a forest fire, or a human activity such as logging or mining. Secondary succession is more common than primary succession.

In secondary succession, soil nutrients remain in an area. Since vegetation supports all other organisms in a community, plants are the first species to appear. Plants include grass species and small, woody shrubs. These species make way for larger plants, including several species of trees. Eventually, the community grows into a large forest. As vegetation grows, the kinds and numbers of animal species also grow depending on the biome.

Figure 17.4.1 *A forest fire causes cones of Jack Pine trees to open and release seeds.*

556 Chapter 17 Populations and Communities

Link to
Earth Science. Have students read the Link to Earth Science feature. Explain that it might take many years for plants and animals similar to those present before the eruption to repopulate the areas devastated by the eruption. Plants that require nutrient-rich soil would not survive in areas that experienced a significant change in soil chemistry. Animals that require the shelter of large trees would not survive in areas that lost all trees. These organisms might eventually return after other plants contributed enough nutrients to the soil to support a variety of plants and trees.

Many communities remain stable. However, small areas are disturbed. These small areas experience secondary succession. A community can have several small areas undergoing secondary succession at one time. Like land communities, marine communities also experience disturbances and go through succession.

Biology in Your Life

The Environment: Choosing Native Plants

The next time you notice flowering garden plants for sale, take a closer look. You will see trays of healthy plants covered with colorful flowers. People buy them, plant them in their outdoor gardens, and then hope to enjoy months of flowers.

However, some garden plants fail to thrive. Why does this happen? In most parts of the United States, many flowering plants are non-native species. Non-native species are species originally from a different area. The ideal conditions for a non-native plant may be very different from those in an outdoor garden.

Flowering garden plants that die may be in an ecosystem that differs from their native ecosystem. Many gardeners choose favorite plant species. These species may be poorly suited for the local temperature, rainfall, and soil type.

Adding native plants to a garden boosts the chances of success. Because they occur naturally in the area, native plants are ideally suited for local conditions. In drier parts of the United States, many native plants are xeriscapic. The word *xeriscapic* comes from the Greek word *xeros*, meaning "dry." Xeriscapic plants do well in dry areas. They do not require extra watering. This is an advantage in areas where rainfall is scarce.

1. What are non-native plants?
2. Tony has just moved from Texas to Vermont. His family buys flowering garden plants like the ones they had in Texas. The plants soon die. Why?
3. A neighbor who has just moved into your area is planning a new garden. What gardening advice could you offer your new neighbor?

Biology in Your Life

Have students read the Biology in Your Life feature about native plants. Have students research the types of plants native to their area. Have them make a brochure that describes the native plants that are available at local plant stores and how to plant and care for them.

Biology in Your Life Answers

1. Non-native plants are plants that originally grew in a different region. Because they do not naturally occur in the area, non-native plants may not be suited for local conditions. **2.** The flowering garden plants are poorly suited for the local soils and climate. **3.** Learn about local native plants; visit local garden stores that stock native plants and ask questions about which plants will thrive in the area.

PRONUNCIATION GUIDE

Use the pronunciation shown here to help students pronounce a difficult word in this lesson. Refer to the pronunciation key on the Chapter Planning Guide for the sounds of the symbols.

xeriscapic (zir´i skăp´ik)

ELL/ESL STRATEGY

Language Objective: *To explain difficult concepts*

Have students form pairs composed of a student learning English and a student with strong English skills. Have students in each pair take turns reading the paragraphs on pages 556–557 and explaining the content of the paragraphs to their partner. Students may wish to use simple diagrams or storyboards to illustrate the different stages of primary and secondary succession. Encourage students to provide a helpful critique of their partner's explanation by pointing out any details they may have left out. As a class, make a list of the important points discussed in the text. Have students save these notes to use for studying for tests and quizzes.

LEARNING STYLES

Visual/Spatial

Allow students to examine a rock or piece of bark covered with moss and a small, potted houseplant. Have them compare the two types of plants in terms of how they obtain nutrients. *(Both make carbohydrates, using sunlight, carbon dioxide, and water.)* Ask students: Why are plants such as mosses part of primary succession, while plants such as this houseplant are not? *(The moss does not need soil and can grow on bare rock.)*

Lesson 4 Review Answers

1. stability **2.** succession **3.** primary succession **4.** D **5.** B **6.** D **7.** Secondary succession is more frequent because periodic disturbances in areas with existing life are far more common than new locations without any life. **8.** Mosses and lichens are among the first organisms to appear during primary succession. These microorganisms perform photosynthesis and then other plant species move into the area. **9.** Primary succession takes longer than secondary succession because it occurs in areas where no life has previously existed. **10.** If primary succession did not occur, many areas would remain without plants, soil, and animals.

Portfolio Assessment

Sample items include:
- Written report from In the Community
- Brochure from Biology in Your Life
- Report, presentation, or poster from Research and Write
- Notes from ELL/ESL Strategy
- Lesson 4 Review answers

Research and Write

Explain that Surtsey, off the coast of Iceland, is a volcanic island that did not exist before November 1963. Ecologists have studied Surtsey to find out more about primary succession. Have students share their research with the class in a written report, an oral presentation using visual aids, or an informative poster.

Lesson 4 REVIEW

Word Bank
primary succession
stability
succession

On a sheet of paper, write the word or words from the Word Bank that completes each sentence correctly.

1. A property called _____ is a community's ability to resist change brought on by disturbances.
2. When a community experiences major changes, it undergoes _____.
3. A process known as _____ takes place when communities start in an area that has no life at all.

On a sheet of paper, write the letter of the answer that completes each sentence correctly.

4. Organisms such as _____ are among the first to appear during primary succession.
   A trees   B wildflowers   C shrubs   D mosses
5. After _____, secondary succession will occur.
   A a volcanic eruption produces a new island
   B a forest fire takes place
   C a parking lot is paved
   D a melting glacier uncovers new earth
6. A _____ is a likely location for primary succession.
   A forest floor   C mowed field
   B grassy hillside   D large boulder

Critical Thinking

On a sheet of paper, answer the following questions. Use complete sentences.

7. Is primary or secondary succession more frequent? Why?
8. What kinds of organisms first appear during primary succession? Explain your answer.
9. Which takes longer: primary or secondary succession? Why?
10. What might happen if primary succession did not occur?

Research and Write

With a partner, use Internet and print resources to write a report on Surtsey. Surtsey is a volcanic island off the coast of Iceland. Describe how organisms began to grow on this island.

558 Chapter 17 Populations and Communities

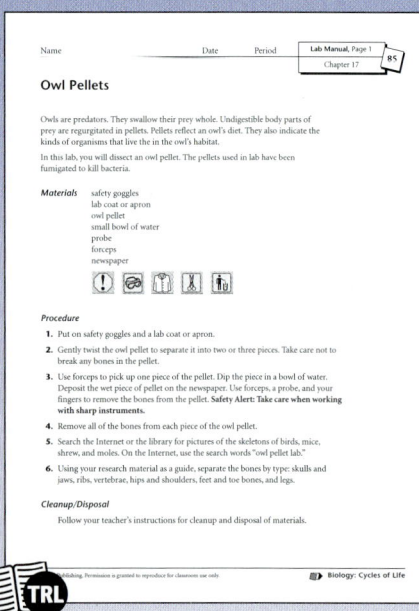

Workbook Activity 100   Lab Manual 85, pages 1–2

BIOLOGY IN THE WORLD

Friendly Predators

The insect in the photograph is a praying mantis. Its name comes from how it looks when it eats. The praying mantis uses its front legs to hold an insect as it eats. It looks like it is praying. Sometimes, this insect is called a "preying" mantis because it is a predator.

The praying mantis looks fearsome. However, it is harmless to people and it is very helpful. It eats small insects such as spiders and mosquitoes. It also eats beetles and aphids that attack garden plants. Gardeners and farmers sometimes find their tomato, rose, and other plant leaves full of holes. Insect pests eat these leaves.

To fight insect pests, some people use chemicals. Others use a natural method. They use natural predators of insect pests. For example, they plant praying mantis egg cases in their garden. The egg cases are small brown masses of eggs. Many garden supply stores and catalogs sell the egg cases.

Where do the egg cases come from? In autumn, a female praying mantis lays a mass of eggs. Then she dies. The eggs live over the winter because they are surrounded by protective material. In the spring, hundreds of tiny praying mantises hatch from the eggs. They gobble up harmful insects.

Using predators to kill harmful prey is called biological pest control. Other insect predators, such as ladybugs and lacewings, also control harmful insect populations.

1. Name two garden pests that are prey to praying mantises.
2. Why might a gardener use praying mantises to control pests rather than spraying plants with chemicals?

BIOLOGY IN THE WORLD

Have students read the Biology in the World feature about predators that are helpful to people. Have students answer the questions at the bottom of the page. Aphids are insect pests that eat young plants and can cause them to die before they produce fruit. Besides praying mantises, other insects that eat aphids include lacewings and ladybugs. Lacewings are brown or green insects that feed on flower nectar. They are helpful in the garden because their larvae eat aphids. Ladybugs are small, red and black beetles that are very helpful in vegetable gardening. Gardeners can purchase live ladybugs at gardening stores.

Biology in the World Answers

1. Aphids and beetles are eaten by praying mantises. 2. Chemicals can be harmful to humans. People might not want to spray their food products with chemicals.

SCIENCE JOURNAL

 Have students write an editorial essay or a letter to the editor describing their opinions about the need to protect biodiversity in an area. They may choose to address the advantages or disadvantages of preserving biodiversity in certain areas at the expense of local industry, agriculture, or other human livelihood.

ONLINE CONNECTION

 This site allows students to observe interactions among organisms in a forest ecosystem: www.cloudforestalive.org.

Have students visit www.census.gov for demographic data from the U. S. Census Bureau.

Students can read about human population growth issues by visiting www.prb.org.

This site teaches students about underwater predators belonging to the cephalopod class: www.cephschool.utmb.edu/cephschool/CSStudents Corner.cfm.

IN THE ENVIRONMENT

 Many forest rangers recommend prescribed burns, or the practice of intentionally setting controlled fires in a forest to remove excess dead leaves and brush whose buildup might lead to larger, more dangerous fires. Have students find out more about the benefits and drawbacks of prescribed burns. Have them identify the type of succession that would occur after a prescribed burn and compare it with that after a larger forest fire.

Chapter 17 Summary

Have volunteers read aloud each summary item on page 560. Ask volunteers to explain the meaning of each item. Direct students' attention to the Vocabulary box on the bottom of page 560. Have them read and review each term and its definition.

Graphic Organizer

As students read Chapter 17, have them finish completing the chart on Graphic Organizer 17: Populations and Communities. Encourage students to read each lesson of the chapter and then have them fill in the portion of the chart that pertains to the lesson. When they have completed the chart, ask them to answer the questions.

Chapter 17 SUMMARY

- Ecology focuses on the interactions of organisms with their environments.
- Ecologists organize the environment into five levels: the biosphere, ecosystems, communities, populations, and individual organism.
- All the organisms of the same species in a community form a population. A community is all the species in an ecosystem. Each organism has a role, or a niche, in its ecosystem.
- Population size is the total number of organisms of a particular species in an ecosystem. Population density is the number of individuals in a population in a particular area.
- Diversity and stability are properties of a community.
- Population growth is influenced by density-dependent factors, such as food and water. These factors are affected by density of the population.
- Population growth is also influenced by density-independent factors, such as fires, freezes, and floods. These factors are not affected by population density.
- Organisms in a community are interdependent. They rely on each other for survival.
- Species compete for resources. In predation, the predator eats an organism of a different species. Warning coloration, camouflage, and mimicry have evolved to reduce the chance of some species becoming prey.
- Symbiosis is the relationship between organisms living in close association. Parasitism, mutualism, and commensalism are three types of symbiotic relationships.
- Natural and human disturbances cause a community to change. Succession is the process of ecological change in a community. Primary and secondary succession occurs after different types of disturbances.

Vocabulary

biome, 537
biosphere, 536
boom-bust cycle, 543
camouflage, 550
canopy, 551
carrying capacity, 541
clumped, 543
commensalism, 550
competition, 542
density-dependent factor, 542
density-independent factor, 543
disturbance, 555
emigrate, 543
growth rate, 541
host, 550
immigrate, 543
interact, 536
interdependent, 548
mutualism, 550
parasitism, 550
population density, 538
predation, 550
primary succession, 556
random, 543
sample, 538
secondary succession, 556
stability, 539
succession, 555
symbiosis, 550
toxic, 555
trophic structure, 549
uniform, 543
vegetation, 551

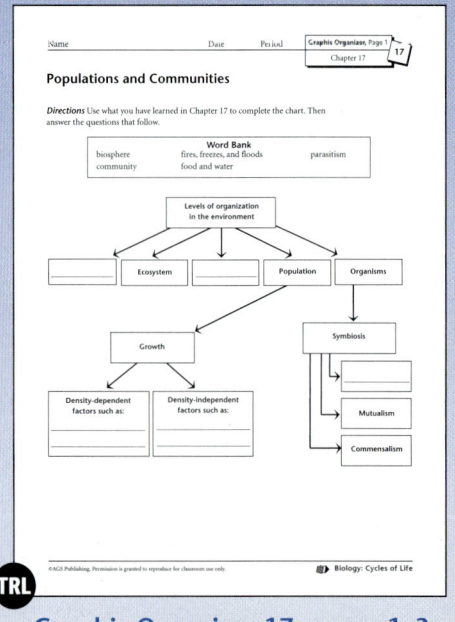

Graphic Organizer 17, pages 1–3

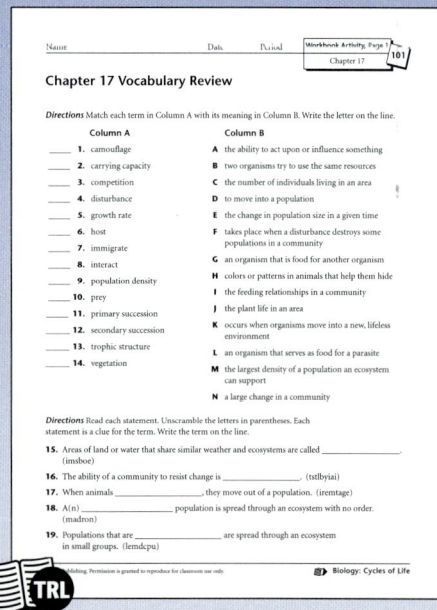

Workbook Activity 101, pages 1–2

Chapter 17 REVIEW

Word Bank
biome
biosphere
camouflage
carrying capacity
commensalism
competition
density-dependent factor
density-independent factor
growth rate
mutualism
parasitism
population density
primary succession
secondary succession
stability
succession
symbiosis
trophic structure

Vocabulary Review

On a sheet of paper, write the word or words from the Word Bank that best complete each sentence.

1. Organisms begin to grow in a lifeless area during _____.

2. Organisms reappear after a disturbance has destroyed many populations during _____.

3. A growth factor not influenced by how many organisms are in a population is a _____.

4. A species that uses _____ has colors or patterns that help it hide in its surroundings.

5. The ability of a community to resist change is _____.

6. The total area of the earth that contains and supports life the _____.

7. The number of individuals of a particular species in a small area of an ecosystem is measured by a _____.

8. The largest number of individuals that an ecosystem can support is its _____.

9. Both organisms benefit from living together in a relationship called _____.

10. One organism feeds off of another organism in a relationship called _____.

11. One organism benefits while the other is not affected in a relationship called _____.

12. When resources such as food and water are in short supply, _____ occurs between species and organisms.

13. The amount by which a populations size changes in a given time is the _____.

Review continued on next page

Populations and Communities   Chapter 17   561

Review Answers

14. trophic structure **15.** density-dependent factors **16.** biome **17.** symbiosis **18.** succession

TEACHER ALERT

In the Chapter Review, the Vocabulary Review activity includes a sample of the chapter's vocabulary terms. The activity will help determine students' understanding of key vocabulary terms and concepts presented in the chapter. Other vocabulary terms used in the chapter are listed below.

boom-bust cycle	interdependent
canopy	predation
clumped	random
disturbance	sample
emigrate	toxic
host	uniform
immigrate	vegetation
interact	

Concept Review

19. B **20.** B **21.** D

Critical Thinking

22. Density-dependent factors such as food and water affect population growth based upon the number of other organisms that exist in the population. As population size increases, these resources become scarcer. This scarceness causes organisms to compete harder for these resources. **23.** When a population exceeds the carrying capacity for its environment, organisms will begin to die or leave the environment because the environment cannot support any more population growth. **24.** Primary succession is an ecological change where a community starts in an area that had no life. Microorganisms start this process by taking over an area such as the one left by a melting glacier. Secondary succession can happen after a forest fire where vegetation has died but soil nutrients still remain. Small plants are the first species to appear in secondary succession.

Chapter 17 REVIEW - continued

14. The feeding relationships among the species of a community make up its _____.

15. A force that influences population growth and is affected by the number of individuals in the population is a _____.

16. A large area of land or water that has similar weather conditions is _____.

17. A close association between organisms of two different species is _____.

18. The process of ecological change in a community is _____.

Concept Review

On a sheet of paper, write the letter of the answer that completes each sentence correctly.

19. The regrowth of plants and trees after a forest fire is an example of _____.

- **A** competition
- **B** succession
- **C** emigration
- **D** parasitism

20. A community high in diversity _____.

- **A** has a uniform population distribution
- **B** contains many organisms
- **C** has few species
- **D** has few predators

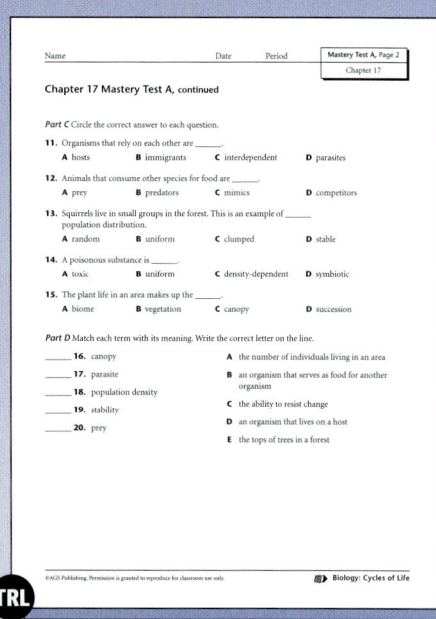

Chapter 17 Mastery Test A, pages 1–3

21. A _____ is a density-dependent factor.

- **A** fire
- **B** drought
- **C** freeze
- **D** food supply

Critical Thinking

Write the answer to each of the following questions.

22. Both density-dependent and density-independent factors affect population size. Which factor involves competition? Explain your answer.

23. What happens when a population exceeds the carrying capacity of its ecosystem?

24. Compare primary succession and secondary succession. Give one example of each.

25. Compare parasitism, commensalism, and mutualism.

Research and Write

Write a report on the warblers observed by ecologist Robert H. MacArthur. Explain how the warblers he observed shared resources and reduced competition. Use both Internet and print resources for your report.

Test-Taking Tip If a word on a test is new to you, take the word apart. Compare the parts to other words you know.

Populations and Communities Chapter 17 563

---

25. In parasitism, one organism, the parasite, feeds on another organism, the host. The parasite is helped and the host is harmed. In commensalism, one organism benefits while the other organism is unaffected. In mutualism, two organisms benefit from living together.

Research and Write

Have students use the library or Internet to find out more about the warblers observed by Robert MacArthur. Students may wish to do this research individually, in pairs, or in small groups. Suggest that students share their research with the class in a written report, an oral presentation, or a bulletin board display.

Alternative Assessment

Alternative Assessment items correlate to the student Goals for Learning at the beginning of this chapter.

- Have students draw a Venn diagram that shows the different levels of organization of the environment.
- Provide students with colored beads or colored modeling clay. Have them use the beads or clay to demonstrate the difference between a community and a population.
- Have students draw cartoons that illustrate uniform, clumped, and random population distributions. Have students predict and explain how well sampling would provide reliable data about population density in each case.
- Display the following terms on the board: *competition, predation, parasitism, mutualism,* and *commensalism.* Have students describe each term orally and give an example of each type of species interaction.
- Have students perform a skit that represents primary or secondary succession.

Chapter 18

Planning Guide
Ecosystems

	Student Pages	Vocabulary	Lesson Review	Critical-Thinking Questions
Lesson 1 How Does Energy Flow Through Ecosystems?	566–572	✔	✔	✔
Lesson 2 The Cycling of Chemicals in an Ecosystem	573–579	✔	✔	✔
Lesson 3 Biomes	580–585	✔	✔	✔

(Columns under heading: Student Text Lesson)

Chapter Activities

Teacher's Resource Library
Community Connection 18:
  Ecosystems and Conservation Biology
Graphic Organizer 18:
  Ecosystems and Conservation Biology

Teacher's Edition
Opener Activity

Assessment Options

Student Text
Chapter 18 Review

Teacher's Resource Library
Chapter 18 Mastery Tests A and B

Teacher's Edition
Chapter 18 Alternative Assessment

	Student Text Features							Teaching Strategies					Learning Styles				Teacher's Resource Library			
Achievements in Science	Science at Work	Biology in Your Life	Investigation/Discovery	Biology in the World	Express Lab	Link to	Research and Write	Technology and Society	ELL/ESL Strategy	Background Information	Science Journal	Applications (Home, Career, Community, Global, Environment)	Online Connection	Teacher Alert	Auditory/Verbal	Body/Kinesthetic	Interpersonal/Group Learning	Logical/Mathematical	Visual/Spatial	Workbook Activities	Alternative Workbook Activities	Lab Manual	Self-Study Guide
			571		570	✔	567		568	566		568		569	567	569	568	569		102	102	86–87	✔
576			578			✔			575	573	576	576		575					575	103	103	88	✔
		584	583		585	✔	589	581	582	580	583	581–583	585	582						104–105	104–105	89–90	✔

Pronunciation Key

a	hat	e	let	ī	ice	ô	order	ù	put	sh	she		a	in about
ā	age	ē	equal	o	hot	oi	oil	ü	rule	th	thin		e	in taken
ä	far	ėr	term	ō	open	ou	out	ch	child	ᵺ	then	ə {	i	in pencil
â	care	i	it	ȯ	saw	u	cup	ng	long	zh	measure		o	in lemon
													u	in circus

Alternative Workbook Activities

The Teacher's Resource Library (TRL) contains a set of lower-level worksheets called Alternative Workbook Activities. These worksheets cover the same content as the regular Workbook Activities but are written at a second-grade reading level.

Skill Track Online

Use Skill Track Online for *Biology: Cycles of Life* to monitor student progress and meet the demands of adequate yearly progress (AYP). Make informed instructional decisions with individual student and class reports of online lesson and chapter assessments. With immediate and ongoing feedback, students will also see what they have learned and where they need more reinforcement and practice.

Chapter at a Glance

Chapter 18: Ecosystems
pages 564–589

Lessons

1. How Does Energy Flow Through Ecosystems? pages 566–572

   Investigation 18 pages 571–572

2. The Cycling of Chemicals in an Ecosystem pages 573–579

   Discovery Investigation 18 pages 578–579

3. Biomes pages 580–585

   Biology in the World page 585

Chapter 18 Summary page 586

Chapter 18 Review pages 587–589

Audio CD

Skill Track Online for Biology: Cycles of Life

Teacher's Resource Library (TRL)

   Workbook Activities 102–105

   Alternative Workbook Activities 102–105

   Lab Manual 86–90

   Community Connection 18

   Graphic Organizer 18

   Resource File 41–42

   Chapter 18 Self-Study Guide

   Chapter 18 Mastery Tests A and B

(Answer Keys for the Teacher's Resource Library begin on page 675 of the Teacher's Edition. The Materials List for the Lab Manual activities begins on page 720.)

Opener Activity

Show students pictures from various ecosystems. Have them identify the living and nonliving parts of each ecosystem. Ask them to discuss where each living thing gets the energy and nutrients it needs to survive. Explain that in this chapter, they will be discussing how this energy and matter can cycle through an entire ecosystem.

Chapter 18 Ecosystems

The stream in this photograph is home to many living things. The stream is rich in nutrients released by the organisms that break down dead organic matter. The stream is rich in oxygen that dissolves in the water. The living things in and around the stream depend on the health of the stream, which is maintained by natural cycles. In Chapter 18, you will learn how living things exchange energy and materials with ecosystems.

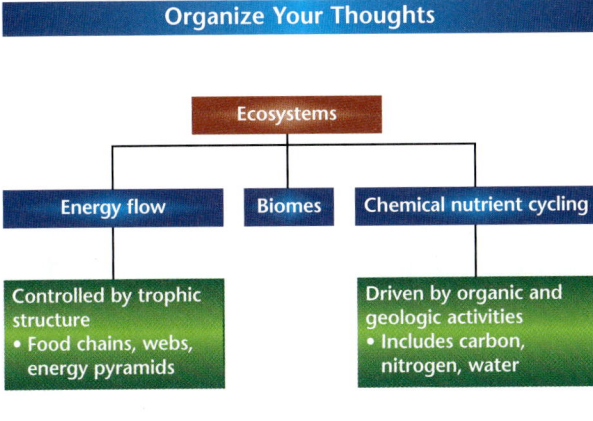

Goals for Learning

- ◆ To describe feeding relationships in ecosystems
- ◆ To describe how energy flows through ecosystems
- ◆ To identify major nutrients and describe how they cycle through ecosystems
- ◆ To identify major biomes in the world

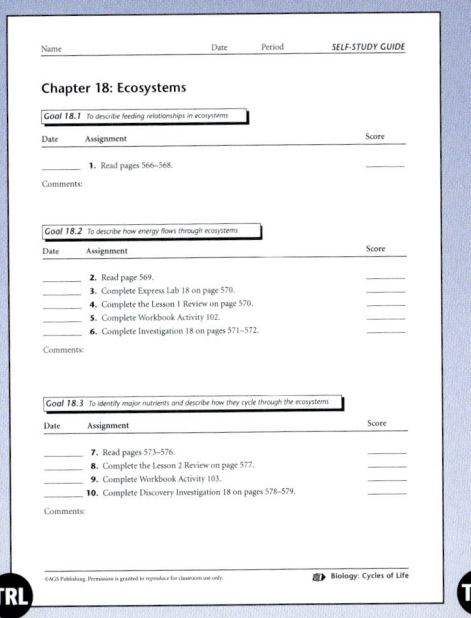

Chapter 18 Self-Study Guide

Introducing the Chapter

Have students examine the photograph of the rushing stream and trees. Then read the introduction aloud. Discuss the Organize Your Thoughts chart and the ways that energy and chemicals flow through an ecosystem. Encourage students to recall what they already know about the flow of energy in ecosystems. Review the concepts of photosynthesis and cellular respiration. Ask students: What are the reactants and products in photosynthesis and respiration? *(oxygen, carbon dioxide, glucose, and water)*

Have students read the Goals for Learning. Help them write questions about what they want to find out about ecosystems and conservation biology. For example, students might ask "Where do I fit in a food chain?" or "In which ecosystem do I live?" or "How do chemicals flow through an ecosystem?" Students can use their questions to help set a purpose for reading.

Notes and Math Tips

Ask volunteers to read the notes and math tips that appear in the margins throughout the chapter. Then discuss them with the class.

TEACHER'S RESOURCE

The AGS Publishing Teaching Strategies in Science Transparencies may be used with this chapter. The transparencies add an interactive dimension to expand and enhance the *Biology: Cycles of Life* program content.

CAREER INTEREST INVENTORY

The AGS Publishing Harrington-O'Shea Career Decision-Making System-Revised (CDM) may be used with this chapter. Students can use the CDM to explore their interests and identify careers. The CDM defines career areas that are indicated by students' responses on the inventory.

Lesson at a Glance

Chapter 18 Lesson 1

Overview In this lesson, students learn about how energy flows through an ecosystem.

Objectives
- To name the different ways organisms get energy
- To explain the feeding relationships in ecosystems
- To identify the different roles in a food chain or web
- To describe an ecosystem, using an energy pyramid

Student Pages 566–572

Teacher's Resource Library

Workbook Activity 102
Alternative Workbook Activity 102
Lab Manual 86–87
Resource File 41–42

Vocabulary

aquatic	organic matter
chemotroph	phototroph
consumer	plankton
decomposer	primary
energy pyramid	productivity
food chain	producer
food web	solar

Have students use a dictionary to find the meaning of the prefixes *photo-* and *chemo-* and the root *troph*. Review with students the definition for the term *trophic structure* from the previous chapter. Discuss how the terms *trophic structure*, *phototroph*, and *chemotroph* are related in meaning.

Background Information

Almost all energy on Earth ultimately comes from the sun. However, some specialized communities survive at the bottom of deep-ocean trenches where no sunlight reaches. Volcanic hydrothermal vents spew minerals that bacteria can convert into sustainable nutrients for themselves and their consumers. These bacteria are classified as part of a larger group of organisms that use either light or chemicals as a source of energy. This group is called *autotrophs*, which are self-feeders. In this system of classification, consumers are called *heterotrophs*, organisms that feed off others.

Lesson 1 — How Does Energy Flow Through Ecosystems?

Objectives
After reading this lesson, you should be able to
- name the different ways organisms get energy
- explain the feeding relationships in ecosystems
- identify the different roles in a food chain or web
- describe an ecosystem using an energy pyramid

Phototroph
An organism that gets its energy by capturing sunlight

Chemotroph
An organism that gets its energy from chemicals in food

Solar
Of or from the sun

In Chapter 17, you learned about lower levels of organization in ecology. The lower levels together form one of the largest and most important levels, the ecosystem. An ecosystem includes all the living and nonliving matter in an area. This matter includes organisms of different species and also nonliving things like rocks and rivers.

Ecologists study ecosystems to understand how living things interact with their surroundings and with each other. When ecologists look at an ecosystem, they examine how two major factors keep the ecosystem going. These factors are the flow of energy and the cycling of chemicals. In this lesson, you will focus on the flow of energy from the sun through different organisms in an ecosystem. In Lesson 2, you will look at how chemicals cycle through an ecosystem.

Phototrophs and Chemotrophs

Recall from Chapter 1 that the sun is the ultimate source of energy for the earth and all its ecosystems. The energy from the sun is transformed into food energy through photosynthesis. Ecologists label organisms based on how they get their energy. Plants and photosynthetic organisms get their energy directly from the sun. They are called **phototrophs**. *Photo* means "light." *Troph* means "the process of feeding."

Other organisms, such as animals and insects, get their energy from chemicals in food, like glucose. These organisms, which include humans, are called **chemotrophs**. *Chemo* means "chemicals."

Food Chains

The way organisms feed determines how they get their energy and chemicals. Recall from Chapter 17 that the feeding relationships in an ecosystem are called the trophic structure. Ecologists study the trophic structures of ecosystems to determine how **solar** energy is transferred to organisms.

566 Chapter 18 Ecosystems

Food chain
The feeding order of organisms in a community

Producer
An organism that makes its own food

Consumer
An organism that feeds on other organisms

Decomposer
An organism at the end of a food chain that feeds by breaking down dead organisms

Research and Write

Write a report on deep-sea vent communities found near volcanic vents on the ocean floor. Describe how organisms in these communities obtain energy in the absence of sunlight.

To describe the trophic structure, ecologists create diagrams to represent different feeding relationships. A **food chain** arranges organisms that feed on each other in a sequence, or series. Look at Figure 18.1.1. Food chains are arranged in trophic levels. The first trophic level in every food chain is the **producer.** Producers are plants and other photosynthetic organisms that produce food that all other organisms eventually eat.

After the producers are the **consumers.** Consumers are chemotrophs that eat other organisms. Consumers that eat the producers are primary consumers. A primary consumer is eaten by a secondary consumer. There can also be tertiary (third) and quaternary (fourth) consumers. Every food chain ends with **decomposers.** Decomposers are organisms, usually bacteria and fungi, that feed by breaking down dead organisms. As they break down dead organisms, they return nonliving elements, like carbon and nitrogen, to the ecosystem.

Humans are consumers in food chains. Depending on what you eat, you can be at two or more consumer levels in just one meal. For example, if you eat a steak and a salad meal, you are both a primary and secondary consumer. Eating the salad makes you a primary consumer because you are eating producers. The steak comes from cows that were already primary consumers. This makes you a secondary consumer.

A Food Chain

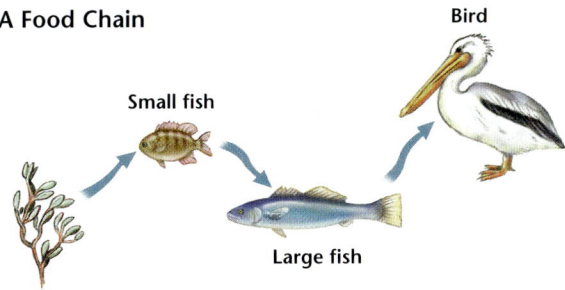

Figure 18.1.1 *A food chain shows the sequence of organisms that feed on each other.*

Ecosystems Chapter 18 **567**

1 Warm-Up Activity

Have students read and perform the Express Lab on page 570. Extend the lab by having students make multiple consumer index cards and arranging the cards in a food chain. Have students explain why a food chain can have several consumers but only one producer.

Express Lab Answers

1. Answers will vary. Students should recognize that photosynthetic organisms are producers, animals are consumers, and fungi and bacteria are decomposers.
2. Each trophic level is necessary in an ecosystem because each level plays a specific role in keeping the ecosystem going. Producers transform sunlight energy into food for other organisms. Consumers eat other organisms. Decomposers break down dead organisms and recycle chemical elements.

2 Teaching the Lesson

Help students identify food chains that they may see in their backyards, at a park, or in the schoolyard. For example, in a vegetable garden, they may be able to identify organisms that make up a complete food chain. Tomato plants (producers) are eaten by worms (consumers), which are eaten by birds (consumers). When the birds die, their remains are broken down by bacteria (decomposers).

3 Reinforce and Extend

Research and Write

Have students read the feature about deep-sea vents. Explain that there are entire food chains in these areas. Ask students: How does the producer obtain energy? Tell students to include a detailed description of this process in their reports. Encourage students to share their research with the class in the form of a written report, an oral presentation, or as part of an informative poster.

LEARNING STYLES

Auditory/Verbal

Have students draw a food chain based on the lyrics to the tune *There Was an Old Lady Who Swallowed a Fly*. You can obtain the lyrics online at www.niehs.nih.gov/kids/lyrics/oldlady.htm. Ask a volunteer to read the lyrics aloud. Ask students: What type of trophic level is represented in the song? Are there any producers or decomposers in this food chain?

AT HOME

Have students identify producers, consumers, and decomposers in or near their homes. For example, their homes may include a vegetable garden filled with producers, people and pets that are consumers, and leftover food that has mold, a decomposer. Discuss the idea that there are few visible food chains within a home because it is not a natural ecosystem.

ELL/ESL STRATEGY

Language Objective: *To explain the parts of a food chain*

Divide the class into groups. Point out that the term *food chain* is related to its two common words: *food* and *chain*. Have each group illustrate how this trophic structure resembles a chain. Tell them to also include examples of foods for each trophic level. Then have them describe what happens when one part of a chain is missing. *(If this gap is not filled by another organism, then the organisms reliant on the missing link will also die off.)*

LEARNING STYLES

Interpersonal/Group Learning

Have students work in pairs. Tell them to take turns identifying food chains in the food web shown. Encourage pairs to identify as many complete food chains as possible.

Aquatic
Growing or living in water

Plankton
Small organisms found in the ocean; usually at the beginning of a food chain

Food web
All the food chains in a community that are linked to one another

Organic matter
A compound that contains carbon

Every ecosystem is made up of many food chains at any one time. Food chains can be found on land and in water. Many **aquatic** food chains start with small organisms called **plankton.** Some plankton perform photosynthesis. Other plankton and larger organisms, like fish and whales, eat photosynthetic plankton. Ecologists studying a certain ecosystem work to define all of the food chains in that ecosystem. Many organisms are part of two or more food chains.

Food Webs

To better understand food chains, ecologists combine an ecosystem's food chains into a **food web.** Study the food web in Figure 18.1.2. A food web shows all the trophic levels that organisms are part of in an ecosystem. A food web can show that an organism can be a primary consumer in one food chain. It can also be a tertiary consumer in a different food chain.

After ecologists identify the feeding relationships in an ecosystem, they can understand how energy flows through that ecosystem. Recall that all energy in an ecosystem ultimately comes from the sun. Phototrophs capture that light energy. Through photosynthesis, they store it in **organic matter.** Organic matter is made up of compounds containing carbon. Phototrophs make enough organic matter, like sugars and proteins, to feed the rest of the ecosystem.

Figure 18.1.2 *A food web shows all the trophic levels that organisms are part of in an ecosystem.*

Primary productivity
The speed at which photosynthetic organisms produce organic matter in an ecosystem

Energy pyramid
A diagram that compares the amounts of energy available to the populations at different levels of a food chain

Science Myth

Myth: Bacteria are bad and useless.
Fact: Bacteria play an important role as decomposers. Decomposers break down dead organisms and recycle chemical nutrients.

Ecologists study how fast these phototrophs make organic matter. This is called **primary productivity**. How much organic matter is produced determines how much energy is available for the ecosystem. Energy in an ecosystem moves through different organisms and trophic levels according to feeding relationships.

Energy Pyramids

How much energy gets transferred during each feeding activity? As energy moves through the trophic levels, much of it is lost. Much of the chemical energy in food gets transformed into heat. Heat is the most random form of energy. It cannot be used for work or to do work. About 10 percent of the energy in one trophic level is transferred through to the next trophic level. Phototrophs must produce a lot of organic matter to support an ecosystem.

Look at Figure 18.1.3. Ecologists create diagrams called **energy pyramids** to represent the transfer of energy through trophic levels. The bottom of an energy pyramid is very large due to the large number of photosynthetic producers. Only a small amount of energy passes to each higher level. Because of this, the top of an energy pyramid is very small.

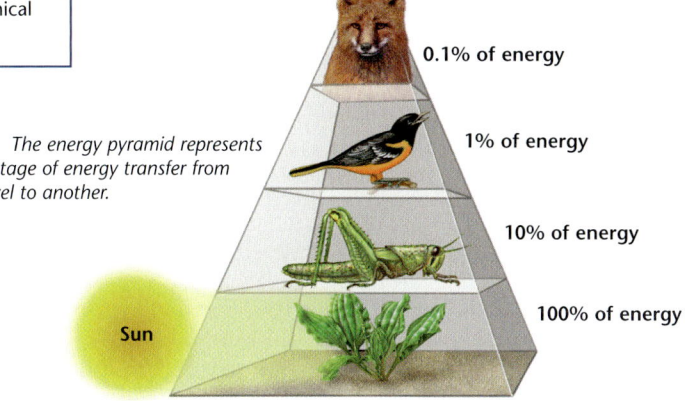

Figure 18.1.3 The energy pyramid represents the low percentage of energy transfer from one trophic level to another.

Ecosystems Chapter 18 **569**

Science Myth

Have students read the Science Myth feature. Explain that bacteria play several roles in an ecosystem as well as in our bodies. Though some bacteria do cause disease, many bacteria are helpful. For example, bacteria in our guts help break down food and aid in digestion. Other bacteria, decomposers, are useful in breaking down organic wastes in the environment. Some oil-eating bacteria can be used to clean up oil spills.

LEARNING STYLES

Logical/Mathematical
Have students calculate the amount of energy stored in the consumers at the fourth level of this energy pyramid given that the producers in the first level contain 2,000 joules of energy in their molecules. Remind them that only 10 percent of the energy in the food is stored in the molecules of the consumer. (*second level: 2,000 J × 0.10 = 200 J; third level: 200 J × 0.10 = 20 J; fourth level: 20 J × 0.10 = 2 J*)

LEARNING STYLES

Body/Kinesthetic
Students may wonder how so much energy is transformed into heat in an energy pyramid. To demonstrate how body activities can generate heat, have students vigorously rub their palms together. They will notice that their hands are significantly warmer. Explain that the friction between the two moving surfaces causes energy to be transformed into heat.

TEACHER ALERT

Point out that the energy that is "lost" between trophic levels is not necessarily wasted energy. Some of it goes into fueling an organism's metabolic functions. Much of it is given off as heat. Sometimes this heat is useful in helping an organism maintain a constant body temperature or warming an organism whose temperature relies on environmental conditions.

Lesson 1 Review Answers

1. secondary **2.** decomposers **3.** bottom
4. Phototrophs are organisms that get their energy directly from the sun. Chemotrophs are organisms that get their energy from chemicals in food. **5.** A food chain is a linear sequence of feeding relationships between organisms. A food web is made up of all of the food chains for an ecosystem.

Portfolio Assessment

Sample items include:
- Report from Research and Write
- Pictures from ELL/ESL Strategy
- Lesson 1 Review answers

Link to

Home and Career. Have students read this feature about capturing solar energy. Have students design a solar collector, solar oven, or solar-powered device. Students may wish to use store-bought solar cells to run their devices. Or they may wish to design devices that can heat water, food, air, or other materials in a useful way. Encourage students to design devices that they can construct and share with the class.

LAB ACTIVITIES

Chapter 18 has Investigation and Discovery Investigation lab activities. Two additional lab activities for Chapter 18 appear in the Biology: Cycles of Life Lab Manual and on the Teacher's Resource Library CD-ROM.

Lesson 1 REVIEW

Word Bank
bottom
decomposers
secondary

On a sheet of paper, write the word from the Word Bank that completes each sentence correctly.

1. When people eat meat, they are _____ consumers in an ecosystem.
2. Every food chain ends with _____.
3. The _____ is the largest part of an energy pyramid.

Link to ▶▶▶

Home and Career

Solar energy is radiation from the sun. Collection devices capture solar energy. Captured solar energy can then be converted to heat or electricity for home use. Some solar collectors contain a black metal plate. When sunlight strikes the plate, heat is transferred to air or water behind the plate and stored for later use.

Critical Thinking

On a sheet of paper, write the answers to the following questions. Use complete sentences.

4. Compare and contrast phototrophs and chemotrophs.
5. How does a food web differ from a food chain?

Express Lab 18

Materials
- 3 index cards
- marker
- photographs of organisms

Procedure
1. Label one index card "P" for producer. Label a second index card "C" for consumer. Label a third index card "D" for decomposers.
2. Put the cards in a row. Put each photograph under the correct index card to show the role the organism plays in its ecosystem. Some organisms may play more than one role.

Analysis
1. Which organisms are producers? Which are consumers? Which are decomposers?
2. Why is each trophic level necessary in an ecosystem?

570 Chapter 18 Ecosystems

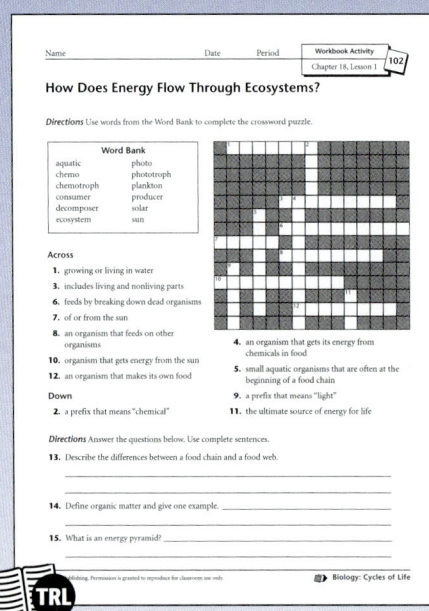

Workbook Activity 102

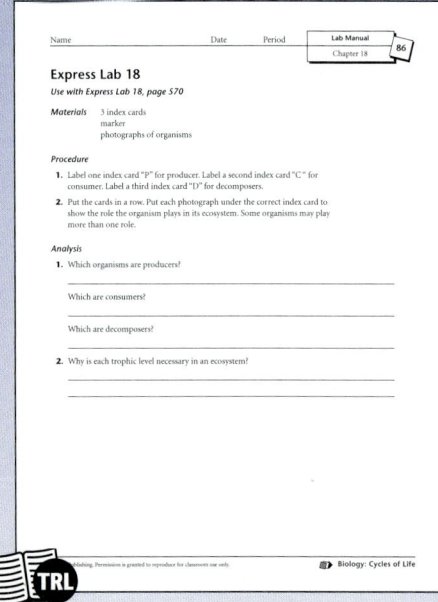

Lab Manual 86

INVESTIGATION 18

Materials
- organism cards

Building a Food Web

Ecologists observe the feeding relationships among organisms to study how energy moves through an ecosystem. In this investigation, you will build a food chain. The food chain will show a sequence, or series, of feeding relationships. You will then combine your food chain with other food chains to build a food web.

Procedure

1. Your teacher will give you a set of organism cards. Separate the cards into three groups to represent each trophic level: producers, consumers, and decomposers.

2. Begin your food chain by putting a producer card at the lower edge of your desktop.

Set 6: clover—butterfly—rabbit—fox—fungus

- You may wish to provide access to reference books or to the Internet if students need additional help to sequence their cards.

- You may create customized organism card sets to match your geographic area.

- Tell students that some living things may provide food for more than one organism. For example, clover provides nourishment for butterflies and rabbits.

Continued on page 572

Investigation 18

Encourage students to read the investigation steps. Discuss questions they may have before beginning the investigation.

Objectives

- To sequence organisms in a food chain
- To predict the pathway of energy through an ecosystem
- To distinguish between a food web and a food chain

Skills

Observing, recording, applying information, comparing and contrasting, understanding concepts, making inferences, drawing conclusions

Background

Animals depend on plants and one another for food. A food chain is a series of animals that eat plants and other animals. Food webs show the more complex interrelationships among two or more food chains.

Time Frame

30 minutes

Procedure

- Have students work together in groups.
- Provide each team with organism cards for a particular ecosystem. Use index cards to create the organism cards students will use. On each index card, write the name of the organism. Make an equal number of producer, consumer, and decomposer cards. The number of cards per ecosystem may vary. Each ecosystem must include at least one producer, one consumer, and one decomposer. Some sample organism card sets are shown below:

   Set 1: grass—plant-eating insect—mouse—king snake—falcon—fungus

   Set 2: tree—aphid—mouse—ladybug—bird—bacteria

   Set 3: grass—quail—mouse—rabbit—hawk—fungus

   Set 4: plant—rabbit—opossum—coyote—bacteria

   Set 5: plant—leaf-eating beetle—spider—bird—fox—bacteria

Continued from page 571

Results

Students will be able to arrange their cards to form a producer-consumer(s)-decomposer sequence. Some card sets may have more than one consumer. As students construct food webs, note that there may be several logical arrangements of producer, consumer, and decomposer.

Analysis Answers

1. Each food chain begins with a producer, contains one or more consumers, and ends with one or more decomposers. The number of organisms may differ from one food chain to the next.

2. A food chain is a linear sequence of organisms that feed on each other. A food web combines all of the food chains that are part of an ecosystem.

Conclusions Answers

1. If sunlight no longer existed, photosynthetic producers would die and consumers would no longer have the energy to survive.

2. Answers will vary. For example, students may wish to explore what would happen to each trophic level if the level(s) above and below it disappeared.

Explore Further Answers

Encourage students to consider the number of individuals in each trophic level. In most ecosystems, producers are present in greater numbers than are consumers. Since energy is lost as it travels from one trophic level to the next, producers outnumber consumers. Similarly, primary consumers outnumber secondary consumers.

Assessment

You might include the following items from this investigation in student portfolios:

- Answers to Analysis and Conclusions questions
- Student proposal for additional work for Explore Further

3. Put a consumer card just above the producer card. A consumer eats a producer. Put the other consumer cards on your desktop in the correct sequence.

4. Add one or more decomposer cards to complete your food chain. Copy your food chain on a sheet of paper.

5. Combine your food chain cards with a classmate's cards. Use your knowledge of trophic structure to arrange the cards into a food web. On a sheet of paper, copy your food chain.

Analysis

1. How was your food chain similar to your classmate's? How was it different?

2. What is the difference between a food chain and a food web?

Conclusions

1. What would happen to your food chain if sunlight no longer existed? Explain your answer.

2. Write a new question about the role of each trophic level you could explore in another investigation.

Explore Further

Use the procedure above to discuss the differences in the numbers of individuals at each trophic level.

Lab Manual 87, pages 1–2

Lesson 2: The Cycling of Chemicals in an Ecosystem

Objectives

After reading this lesson, you should be able to
- describe how energy and chemicals travel together in an ecosystem
- discuss different ways chemicals cycle through an ecosystem
- relate chemical cycling to geological processes
- trace the cycles of carbon, nitrogen, and water

Phosphorous
An element that cycles through an ecosystem and is used by organisms to make ATP

Atmosphere
The air that surrounds the earth

Ecologists study ecosystems to understand how energy and nutrients are used by different groups of organisms. Energy travels through ecosystems as it is passed to different trophic levels. But energy does not make this journey by itself. Energy gets transferred through food. Food also moves another major ecosystem factor, chemical nutrients. As you know, chemical nutrients are substances that organisms need to live.

Cycles of Nutrients

You have probably heard of the importance of nutrients, like vitamins and minerals, in foods you eat. When ecologists study nutrients, they look at molecules like water and carbon compounds. Organisms need water to survive. Organisms also need carbon to build molecules. Plants need carbon to make sugars that other organisms eat. As food is broken down and used, chemicals are rearranged into new molecules. These new molecules are returned to the ecosystem and can be used again.

Nutrients move through the living parts of an ecosystem. They also journey through the nonliving parts of an ecosystem. Water is an ecosystem nutrient. It is in organisms, rivers, and rain. Nutrients such as water and carbon move through ecosystems in different ways.

Some nutrients, like the element **phosphorous,** cycle within a single ecosystem. Phosphorous is found in soil and rocks. Phosphorous can also be dissolved in water and then transferred back to land. Land and some water sources stay in a particular area. Because of this, phosphorous used by organisms usually comes from their local ecosystem.

Other nutrients are available in the form of gases. These gases are found in the **atmosphere.** The atmosphere is the air that surrounds the earth.

Ecosystems Chapter 18 573

Lesson at a Glance

Chapter 18 Lesson 2

Overview In this lesson, students learn how energy and chemicals cycle through an ecosystem.

Objectives
- To compare how energy and chemicals travel together in an ecosystem
- To discuss different ways chemicals cycle through an ecosystem
- To relate chemical cycling to geological processes
- To trace the cycles of carbon, nitrogen, and water

Student Pages 573–579

Teacher's Resource Library
Workbook Activity 103
Alternative Workbook Activity 103
Lab Manual 88

Vocabulary

ammonium	nitrifying bacteria
atmosphere	nitrogen-fixer
evaporation	phosphorus
geological	precipitation
nitrate	

Have students use a chemistry book to look up the chemical formulas for ammonia and ammonium. (NH_3 and NH_4^+) Point out that both substances contain nitrogen. Have students identify all of the vocabulary terms that have to do with the element nitrogen. *(ammonium, nitrate, nitrogen-fixer, nitrifying bacteria)*

Background Information

Nitrogen-fixing bacteria can change atmospheric nitrogen into ammonium, which is used by other bacteria to make nitrates that plants can use. However, nitrogen can be fixed by nonliving processes as well. When lightning energizes molecules of nitrogen and oxygen in the atmosphere, they can react, forming nitrates. Other bacteria in soil can change nitrates back into nitrogen gas through a process called *denitrification*.

Ecosystems 573

Warm-Up Activity

Review the following equations for photosynthesis and cellular respiration. Have students write these on a sheet of paper:

photosynthesis: $6CO_2 + H_2O + energy \rightarrow C_6H_{12}O_6 + 6O_2$

cellular respiration: $C_6H_{12}O_6 + 6O_2 \rightarrow 6CO_2 + H_2O + energy$

Instruct students to highlight the carbon atoms in each substance. Then have students identify where each type of reaction takes place. Have students use markers to indicate with arrows where each substance comes from and where the products go. For example, they might draw an arrow to indicate that the carbon dioxide used for photosynthesis comes from cellular respiration and the atmosphere. Explain that this diagram represents part of the carbon cycle.

Teaching the Lesson

Have students revisit the chapter that discusses biological molecules. Have them identify elements that make up these molecules and which cycles would be important for providing these elements to humans. For example, DNA contains phosphate groups, nitrogenous bases, and sugar groups (containing carbon). Thus, our bodies rely on the phosphate cycle, nitrogen cycle, and carbon cycle to make DNA.

Have students create a chart for this lesson. Tell them to use the following as column headings: *Carbon Cycle, Nitrogen Cycle,* and *Water Cycle.* As students read the lesson, have them write facts about each topic under the correct heading.

Reinforce and Extend

Science Myth

Have students read the Science Myth feature. Explain that mineral nutrients such as phosphorus and nitrogen are needed for plants to survive. However, they are not considered food, because they do not provide the plant with energy. Some products are called "plant food," but they are really fertilizers. Fertilizers often contain nitrates and phosphates. Soil that is lacking in mineral nutrients can be improved by adding fertilizers.

574 Chapter 18

Geological
Having to do with the solid parts of the earth

Science Myth

Myth: Mineral nutrients in the soil, such as phosphorus and nitrogen, serve as food for plants.

Fact: Mineral nutrients are not food for plants. The term *plant food* is not accurate. A more accurate term is *plant fertilizer*.

Link to >>>
Earth Science

When precipitation sinks into the earth's surface, it fills spaces between rock particles. This water is called groundwater. An aquifer is an underground body of rock in which groundwater is stored. Aquifers supply drinking water for many communities.

Nutrients in gases can travel from one ecosystem to another. Because ecosystems share these nutrients, all ecosystems are connected. They rely on each other. Nutrients found in the atmosphere include carbon, nitrogen, and water. Water and the nutrients dissolved in it are also cycled through different ecosystems by the movement of rivers and oceans.

The Importance of Geological Processes

Chemical nutrients cycle through the living and nonliving parts of an ecosystem. **Geological** processes control the nonliving parts of an ecosystem. Geological processes have to do with different parts of the earth, like land and water. Any process that changes the earth affects the nutrient sources available to ecosystems. Geological processes include volcanoes, ocean currents, and weather. Weather moves gases in the atmosphere.

Another geological nutrient source is fossil fuels such as coal, oil, and natural gas. Recall that fossil fuels are made over millions of years. They are made from the breakdown of skeletons and organic waste deep inside the earth. Fossil fuels provide chemical nutrients such as carbon and nitrogen to ecosystems. When people burn fossil fuels, carbon dioxide gas is released into the atmosphere.

The Carbon Cycle

Now we will look at the cycles of three nutrients. Carbon cycling is very important to any ecosystem. Carbon is a main element in organic matter. The main source of carbon in any ecosystem is the atmosphere. Photosynthesis is the process that changes carbon dioxide into organic molecules. These molecules are used to build cells and tissue and to provide energy for organisms.

Organic molecules pass through different levels in a food chain, including decomposers that eat dead organisms. Eventually, cellular respiration breaks down organic molecules. Recall that cellular respiration produces carbon dioxide, which cycles back into the atmosphere.

574 Chapter 18 Ecosystems

Link to

Earth Science. Have students read the Link to Earth Science feature. Help students understand what an aquifer is by comparing it to a flavored snow cone. The shaved ice is like porous rock. The liquid flavoring is like groundwater, because it fills the spaces in between the pieces of shaved ice. A well is like a straw placed in the snow cone. If you suck the flavoring through the straw, it will leave the spaces in between the shaved ice. The deeper you place the straw, the more flavoring you have access to. When a well runs dry, it is because the groundwater level has lowered to below the depth of the well.

The Nitrogen Cycle

Another main nutrient cycle involves nitrogen. Study Figure 18.2.1. Animals need nitrogen to build proteins and nucleic acids. Ecosystems use the atmosphere as a source for nitrogen. Most gas in the atmosphere is nitrogen gas. Organisms cannot use this form of nitrogen. To use nitrogen gas, it must be changed into **ammonium** or **nitrates**.

Bacteria in the soil, called **nitrogen-fixers**, take in nitrogen gas and change it to ammonium. The ammonium is changed to nitrates by other bacteria called **nitrifying bacteria**. Nitrates dissolve in water in the soil, where they can be absorbed through the roots of plants. Plants use nitrates to build amino acids and nucleotides.

Nitrogen-containing molecules cycle through the food chains in an ecosystem. Decomposers return nitrogen to the soil in the form of ammonium. Once nitrogen is cycled into an ecosystem, it usually stays there without returning to the atmosphere.

Ammonium
A nitrogen-containing compound used to cycle nitrogen into an ecosystem

Nitrate
A nitrogen-containing compound used directly by plants

Nitrogen-fixer
Bacteria that convert nitrogen gas into ammonium

Nitrifying bacteria
Bacteria that convert ammonium into usable nitrates

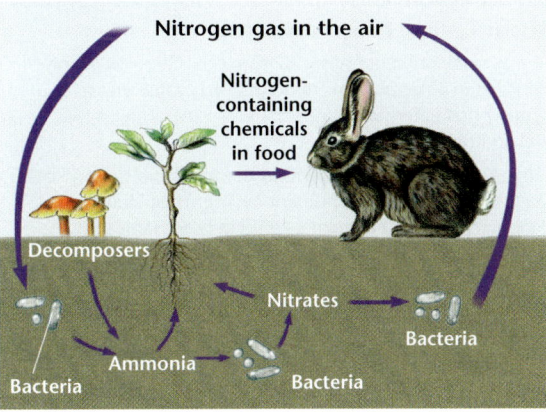

Figure 18.2.1 Nitrogen is a main nutrient in ecosystems.

The Water Cycle

A nutrient necessary for life is water. Water is involved in most metabolic reactions. As a human, you need to drink a certain amount of water every day to stay healthy. Water is in lakes, rivers, and oceans. Water is also in the atmosphere and underground. The water cycle depends on energy from the sun.

TEACHER ALERT

Point out that oxygen plays a major role in the carbon cycle. In fact, this matter and energy cycle is often called the "carbon-oxygen cycle."

ELL/ESL STRATEGY

Language Objective:
To compare and contrast

Pair students so that an English language learner is with a student with strong English skills. Have students use molecular models or colored marshmallows and toothpicks to compare nitrogen gas (N_2), nitrates (NO_3), and ammonium (NH_4). Then have students write the following terms on index cards: *nitrogen fixers, nitrifying bacteria, plants,* and *decomposers*. Have pairs use the molecular models and the index cards together to model the nitrogen cycle.

LEARNING STYLES

Visual/Spatial
Demonstrate for students a model of the water cycle by heating a glass of water in a microwave oven (or a beaker of water on a hot plate). Be careful when removing the hot item. Place a small, clear glass plate (or a watchglass) over the glass. Students should observe water vapor condensing on the underside of the glass plate and dripping back into the glass. To speed up the process, you can place an ice cube on top of the glass plate. Explain that this is a simple model of how water evaporates and condenses in the water cycle. Have students identify which part of the model represents the clouds in the atmosphere. *(the cooled glass plate)*

SCIENCE JOURNAL

Have students write a story from the point of view of a carbon atom, a nitrogen atom, or a water molecule as it goes through the carbon cycle, nitrogen cycle, or water cycle. Be sure they address each part of the cycle in their stories. Encourage them to illustrate their stories with one or more cartoons.

IN THE COMMUNITY

Ask an environmental lobbyist or environmental lawyer to visit the class and talk about his or her work. Ask the visitor to describe what he or she needs to know about cycles in ecosystems. Have students prepare questions to ask the visitor. Have them write a report based on the answers to their questions.

Achievements in Science

Have students read the Achievements in Science feature. Then ask them to research and find more information about the experiments of Bormann and Likens. Have students report their findings to the class.

PRONUNCIATION GUIDE

Use the pronunciation shown here to help students pronounce difficult words in this lesson. Refer to the pronunciation key on the Chapter Planning Guide for the sounds of the symbols.

Bormann (Bôr´man)

Likens (Lī´kənz)

Evaporation
The process of liquid water changing into gas due to heating

Precipitation
The moisture that falls to the earth from the atmosphere

Link to ▸▸▸
Chemistry

A hybrid car is a cross between a gasoline-powered car and an electric car. Hybrid vehicles offer greater fuel efficiency and reduced pollution. In a parallel hybrid, batteries supply power to an electric motor. Both the gasoline engine and the electric motor can turn the transmission, which then turns the wheels. In a series hybrid, the gasoline engine turns a generator. The generator charges the batteries or powers an electric motor that drives the transmission.

As solar energy warms bodies of water, **evaporation** occurs. During evaporation, water molecules become water vapor, a gas. As water vapors build up in the atmosphere, they form clouds. Clouds move through the atmosphere, constantly gaining more water. Eventually, clouds carry too many water molecules. These molecules return to their liquid form. Then clouds release **precipitation** as rain or snow. Rain and snow returns the water to the land and aquatic ecosystems. The weather that ecosystems experience is greatly influenced by the water cycle.

Cycles in Ecosystems

As you have seen, the different cycles in an ecosystem are linked to one another. Scientists sometimes study one cycle at a time. This makes it easier to understand that cycle. However, each cycle is a small part of a system of cycles in ecosystems. These cycles interact with one another.

Achievements in Science

Nutrient Cycling in an Ecosystem

Ecologists study nutrient cycling to learn how chemical elements are recycled in an ecosystem. To do this, they must measure everything that enters and leaves the ecosystem. How is this possible outdoors?

In 1963, American ecologists Herbert Bormann and Gene Likens began a long-term study of nutrient cycling. Their study was at the Hubbard Brook Experimental Forest in New Hampshire. A layer of bedrock, or solid rock, lies under the forest's shallow soil. Water cannot seep through the bedrock. A creek drains each valley within the forest. All water leaving the Hubbard Brook ecosystem exits through these creeks.

To measure the loss of water and nutrients from the ecosystem, the ecologists built a dam at the bottom of each creek. They found that most mineral nutrients cycled within the forest ecosystem. In one valley, the researchers cut down all trees and plants. They let the dead materials remain in place. Large amounts of water and minerals were lost. Bormann and Likens concluded that plants keep nutrients within an ecosystem.

576 Chapter 18 *Ecosystems*

Link to

Chemistry. Have a volunteer read aloud the Link to Chemistry feature. Ask students: What other benefits do hybrid cars offer? Are there any long-term advantages or disadvantages? Then ask students if they know about any other types of cars not powered by gasoline. Discuss the chemistry involved to power these other types of cars.

Lesson 2 REVIEW

Word Bank
carbon
carbon dioxide
precipitation

On a sheet of paper, write the word or words from the Word Bank that complete each sentence correctly.

1. Rain and snow are examples of _____ in an ecosystem.
2. Cellular respiration produces _____, which cycles back into the ecosystem.
3. A main element in organic matter is _____.

On a sheet of paper, write the letter of the answer that completes each sentence correctly.

4. The process of liquid water changing into gas due to heating is _____.
   A precipitation   C evaporation
   B nitrogen-fixing   D carbon cycling

5. Bacteria changes _____ from the atmosphere into a form that plants can use.
   A oxygen gas   C carbon dioxide
   B phosphorus   D nitrogen gas

6. Nutrients found in the atmosphere include all of the following except _____.
   A carbon   C phosphorus
   B nitrogen   D water

Critical Thinking

On a sheet of paper, write the answer to each question. Use complete sentences.

7. Describe how carbon cycles through an ecosystem.
8. How do plants obtain nitrogen?
9. Describe how phosphorus cycles through an ecosystem.
10. What is produced when fossil fuels are burned?

Ecosystems Chapter 18 577

Lesson 2 Review Answers

1. precipitation 2. carbon dioxide 3. carbon 4. C 5. D 6. C 7. Photosynthesis uses carbon dioxide and changes it into organic molecules. Then these molecules pass through a food chain as different organisms use them. Eventually, the organic molecules get broken down during cellular respiration and released back into the atmosphere. 8. Plants obtain nitrogen as nitrates dissolved in water in the soil. 9. Phosphorus can be found in soil, rocks, and water sources. It is used by plants and other organisms and then returned to the local ecosystem. 10. Energy in the form of heat and carbon dioxide are produced when fossil fuels are used.

Portfolio Assessment

Sample items include:
- Illustration from Warm-Up Activity
- Story from Science Journal
- Written report from In the Community
- Lesson 2 Review answers

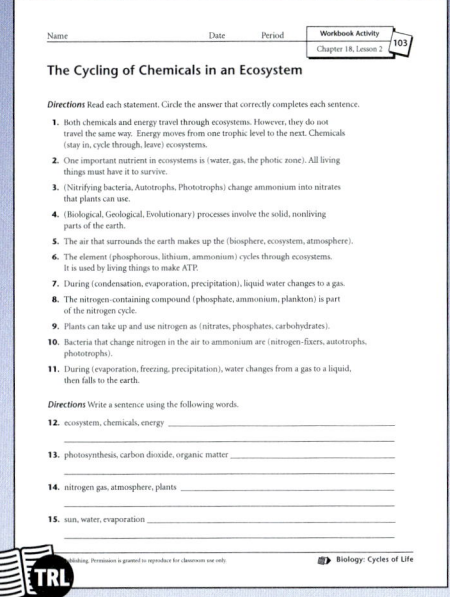

Workbook Activity 103

Discovery Investigation 18

This investigation is less structured than the first investigation in this chapter. It offers students more challenge and requires more teacher facilitation. Encourage students to read the Discovery Investigation steps. Discuss questions they may have before beginning the investigation.

Objectives

- To understand the cycling of phosphorus in an ecosystem
- To recognize the role of phosphates as pollutants
- To distinguish between independent and dependent variables

Skills

Applying information, performing experiments, comparing and contrasting, drawing conclusions, making inferences, predicting outcomes, recognizing cause and effect

Background

Phosphates were once added to many soaps and detergents to help them break down and reduce foaming in waterways and water-treatment plants. However, fertilizing abilities of phosphates can cause algae to grow rapidly, leading to eutrophication of ponds and lakes.

Time Frame

One class period

Procedure

- Have students work together in groups.
- If pond water is unavailable, use tap water that has been dechlorinated or allowed to stand in open containers for several days to allow any chlorine to evaporate. Aquarium water may also be used.
- *Elodea* and other pond plants and *Daphnia* may be found in local ponds or purchased in pet stores.
- To make the high phosphate detergent solution, use automatic dishwasher detergent or tri-sodium phosphate (sold in hardware stores). Mix $\frac{1}{2}$ cup of detergent with approximately 500 mL of tap water to create a detergent solution.

DISCOVERY INVESTIGATION 18

Materials
- safety goggles
- lab coat or apron
- gallon glass jar
- pond water
- pond plants, such as *Elodea*
- pond animals, such as protozoa or *Daphnia*
- four 250 mL beakers
- high-phosphate detergent solution
- eyedropper

Phosphate in Aquatic Ecosystems

Phosphorus is an element needed by organisms. In most ecosystems, phosphorus occurs in the form of phosphate, which can be found in soil and rocks. Too little phosphate can limit plant growth.

Procedure

1. Put on safety goggles and a lab coat or apron.
2. Fill the glass jar half-full with pond water.
3. Add the pond plants and animals to the water.
4. Put the glass jar on a sunny windowsill for several days.

SAFETY ALERT

- Be sure that students wear safety goggles and a lab coat or apron.
- Be sure students wash their hands immediately after handling the plants, animals, and pond water.

5. When the water in the glass jar has begun to turn green, divide the pond water and plants equally among the four beakers. Each beaker will represent an aquatic ecosystem. **Safety Alert: Be sure to wash your hands immediately after handling the pond water.**

6. Write a hypothesis and procedure describing how you can determine the effects of phosphate on aquatic ecosystems.

7. Have your hypothesis, procedure, and Safety Alerts approved by your teacher.

8. Set up your experiment. Observe and record your results after several days.

Analysis

1. Describe the appearance of each beaker after several days.

2. List the control group and the experimental group in your experiment. What is the variable?

Conclusions

1. What is the effect of adding phosphate to aquatic ecosystems?

2. Why do you think many states have banned phosphates from household laundry detergents?

Explore Further

What will eventually happen to the plants and animals in an aquatic ecosystem that contains a lot of phosphate? Suggest a procedure to answer this question.

Results

Student hypotheses should propose testing varying amounts of detergent solution (for example, 10 drops, 20 drops, 40 drops, and none) in the four respective beakers while keeping all other conditions constant. Student proposals must include one beaker that does not receive detergent to serve as a control.

The beaker with the largest amount of detergent solution will show the greatest extent of algal growth. If the phosphate concentration is high enough, the growth of the algae may consume so much oxygen that the pond plants and pond animals can no longer survive.

Answers to Analysis, Conclusions, and Explore Further begin on page 670 of this Teacher's Edition.

Assessment

You might include the following items from this investigation in student portfolios:

- Student hypothesis and proposed procedure
- Answers to Analysis and Conclusions questions
- Student proposal to investigate for Explore Further

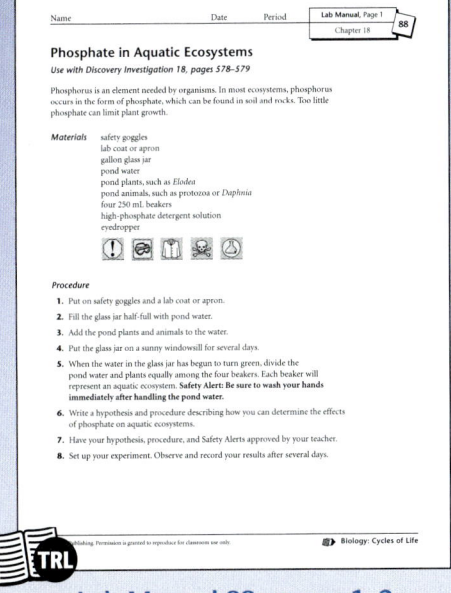

Lab Manual 88, pages 1–2

Lesson at a Glance

Chapter 18 Lesson 3

Overview In this lesson, students learn about the characteristics of different biomes.

Objectives
- To discuss how solar energy and weather influence ecosystems
- To give examples of different land biomes
- To identify different aquatic biomes

Student Pages 580–585

Teacher's Resource Library

Workbook Activity 104–105

Alternative Workbook Activity 104–105

Lab Manual 89–90

Vocabulary

aphotic zone	permafrost
benthic zone	photic zone
chaparral	savanna
climate	temperate
coniferous forest	deciduous forest
desert	temperate grassland
estuary	
freshwater	terrestrial
intertidal zone	tropical forest
marine	tundra

Remind students that the prefix *photo-* means "light." Explain that the prefix *a-* can mean "without." Have students use this information to predict the meaning of the terms *photic zone* and *aphotic zone*. Provide a hint that both terms have to do with ocean ecosystems.

Background Information

The types of organisms that thrive in a biome are determined by the physical factors that characterize the biome. When humans change the physical environment, biomes can recede or grow in size. For example, harvesting wood from trees can cause forest biomes to decrease in size, in a process called deforestation. Also, herding and overfarming of delicate ecosystems can cause deserts to increase in size, in a process called desertification.

580 Chapter 18

Lesson 3 Biomes

Objectives

After reading this lesson, you should be able to
- discuss how solar energy and weather influence ecosystems
- give examples of different land biomes
- identify different aquatic biomes

Climate
The average weather of a region over a long period of time

Terrestrial
Having to do with land

Weather influences ecosystems by driving the water cycle. The weather in an area also determines the overall **climate** of that area. Climate is the average weather conditions for a region over a long period of time. This includes temperature and precipitation. Climate also determines what kind of organisms, especially plants, can exist in an area. The type of plants in an area influence the community found in an ecosystem.

Factors that Control Weather and Climate

What controls weather and climate? One factor is land features. The weather on one side of a mountain can be very different from the other side. One side of a mountain often gets more rain and wind than the other side.

Weather and the water cycle move together. Both are driven by energy from the sun. Each area of the earth does not get the same amount of solar energy. This is due to the curve of the earth's surface and the tilt of the earth's axis. For example, areas near the equator are physically closer to the sun than areas farther north or south. These areas receive more sunlight. They stay warmer than areas closer to the poles of the earth. The larger amount of sunlight also means more solar energy is being used to drive the weather.

These differences in sunlight cause different weather and water cycles. Different cycles create different climates. This leads to different types of ecosystems.

Ecosystems that experience the same climate conditions are grouped together into larger regions called biomes. Recall from Chapter 17 that a biome is a large area of the earth that has similar ecosystems and weather. Ecosystems in the same biome share some of the same kinds of organisms. They may also share some of the same kinds of species.

The rest of this lesson will describe the different kinds of land and aquatic biomes found on the earth. Climate and typical communities are discussed for each **terrestrial**, or land, biome.

580 Chapter 18 Ecosystems

 Warm-Up Activity

Show students various pictures that represent biomes. Have them identify each biome as warm, cool, wet, or dry. Then have them guess which biome each image represents and identify where on a map it might be located.

Tropical forest
A terrestrial biome with many trees and organisms

Savanna
A terrestrial biome with grasses and grazing animals

Desert
A very dry terrestrial biome

Chaparral
A terrestrial biome with many shrubs

Temperate grassland
A terrestrial biome with fertile soil and tall grasses

Terrestrial Biomes

Tropical forests are the main type of biome near the equator. Temperatures are high here. Some tropical forests receive large amounts of rain. They typically have many species of plants. Many of these plants are large trees and other species that grow on them. Other tropical rainforests have less rainfall and more shrubs mixed in with trees. Tropical forests often have very diverse communities with many different species.

Savanna biomes are usually large areas of land that have many grass species with trees scattered throughout. The grass in these areas can grow tall. Some grasses grow taller than three feet. The climate in savannas includes a rainy season and a very dry season. Animals in these biomes are usually large, grazing animals and their predators, like zebras and lions.

Deserts are another biome caused by low rainfall. Temperatures in deserts can be very hot, mild, or very cold. Plants and animals live in many deserts. One key feature of these organisms is their ability to save water. To survive in this biome, organisms must use water carefully.

Chaparrals are biomes with rainy winters and long, dry summers. Instead of grasses, these areas have many shrubs along with a few pine and oak trees. Fires often control the ecosystems in this biome.

Temperate grasslands are biomes with large areas of grass species. Grazing animals and seasons of drought prevent larger plants from growing there. These biomes have fertile soil. People have converted many temperate grasslands into farmland.

Science Myth

Myth: Decay is an event caused by nonbiological processes.

Fact: Decomposing agents, such as bacteria and fungi, perform decay.

Technology and Society

Aquaculture, or fish farming, is the commercial raising of fish. People grow fish in freshwater or marine environments. The fish are raised in artificial ponds. They are given food and protected from predators. For example, aquaculture is used to produce fish such as catfish for the commercial market. Government agencies use aquaculture to raise sport fishes for restocking lakes and rivers.

2. Teaching the Lesson

Ask volunteers to read aloud the first page of this lesson. Then have students collect and record local weather information for a week. Students may wish to gather data by using rain gauges and thermometers, or they may get data from weather reports. Have students discuss whether they think this week is a normal week for the area in terms of weather. Have them classify the region as warm, cool, wet, or dry compared to other regions they have visited, read about, or seen on television. Ask students: How do you think plants and animals might respond to this week's weather?

3. Reinforce and Extend

CAREER CONNECTION

Have students research the career of a climatologist. If possible, have them interview a climatologist and report their findings to the class. Encourage students to find out what type of education climatologists need, the kinds of data they collect, and the types of climates they study.

Science Myth

Have a volunteer read aloud the Science Myth feature. Explain to students that decomposition is sometimes different from decay. Decomposition is the breakdown of materials or substances. Some kinds of decomposition are part of organic decay processes, while other kinds of decomposition are purely chemical. For example, in chemistry, a decomposition reaction is any reaction that involves the breakup of a substance into two or more simpler substances. Some decomposition reactions are carried out by decomposers. In nature, organic matter is broken down by decomposers, such as bacteria or fungi, through decay.

Technology and Society

Have students read the Technology and Society feature. Have students research the benefits and drawbacks of aquaculture. For example, aquaculture can help lessen the effects of overfishing. However, like agriculture, it can negatively affect the environment through water pollution and unwanted interbreeding of wild and farm-raised varieties. Have students present their research in the form of an editorial letter describing why a new fish farm should or should not be allowed to develop in a local body of water.

Lab Manual 89, pages 1–2

GLOBAL CONNECTION

Have students find out more about the importance of preserving tropical forests. Have them research important resources that tropical forests provide in current times and what they have provided in the past, such as rare woods, fruits, medicines, decorative plants, and natural rubber. Encourage students to read about how modern and historical cultures harvested resources from tropical forests. Have them present their findings in a mock newscast or documentary format.

ELL/ESL STRATEGY

Language Objective:
To describe an aquatic biome

Divide students into six groups. Have each group make a poster for one of the following aquatic biomes: freshwater, estuary, intertidal, photic, aphotic, and benthic. Be sure that they indicate where each type of biome is located and how that affects the nonliving resources available to resident organisms. Then have students use the Internet or library to find examples of plants and animals that live in each type of aquatic biome. Have them draw pictures or cut out photographs of representative organisms and glue them onto their posters. They may wish to include labels. Have each group use their poster to describe their biome to the class.

582   Chapter 18

Temperate deciduous forest
A terrestrial biome with wet forests that change activity during winter

Coniferous forest
A dry, cold terrestrial biome with cone-bearing trees

Tundra
A cold, dry terrestrial biome with shrubs and small trees

Permafrost
Permanently frozen soil

Freshwater
An area of water with no salt

Marine
An area of water that has salt

Intertidal zone
An area where an ocean meets land

Estuary
A marine biome where freshwater meets saltwater

Photic zone
An area in aquatic biomes that receives solar energy

Aphotic zone
An area in an aquatic biome that does not receive solar energy

Benthic zone
The floor of an aquatic biome

Temperate deciduous forests are biomes that experience hot summers and cold winters. These areas also receive a lot of rainfall. This allows for many different animal species to live in these forests. During fall and winter, deciduous trees shed their leaves. Mammals hibernate for the cold season.

Coniferous forests are biomes found in northern parts of the world. They have only a few kinds of cone-bearing trees. They experience heavy snowfall during the winter. The climate is drier and colder than the other biomes. Trees are the main plants in this land. Large mammals, such as moose, live in these forests.

Tundras are the coldest and driest biomes. They are also the furthest north biome on the earth. No trees grow in tundras because much of the soil is frozen. This permanently frozen soil is called **permafrost.** The vegetation is typically shrubs and small trees. Some animals migrate here during the summer, when water and vegetation become available.

Aquatic Biomes

Aquatic biomes include rivers and lakes. These are examples of **freshwater** biomes, meaning that the water does not contain salt. Aquatic biomes in oceans are called **marine** biomes. The area where an ocean meets land is called an **intertidal zone.** Another biome is formed where freshwater meets saltwater. It is called an **estuary.** Estuaries support a diverse group of organisms. These areas are often subjects of concern because of their unique communities.

All aquatic biomes are divided into three zones based on light exposure. The tops of these aquatic biomes receive the most solar energy. This area is called the **photic zone.** Photosynthesis takes place in the photic zone. The area under this zone does not receive sunlight. It is called the **aphotic zone.** The floor of an aquatic biome is called the **benthic zone.** Each zone has a unique collection of organisms.

582   Chapter 18   Ecosystems

TEACHER ALERT

Students may wonder how some plants can grow in the permafrost soil while others cannot. With permafrost, the topmost layer of soil is not always frozen, while the layer of soil that is an inch or so deeper remains frozen year-round. Plants that have deep roots and require deep soil, such as larger plants and trees, cannot grow in shallow soil. Grasses and shrubs do not send roots as deep and therefore can survive in the tundra.

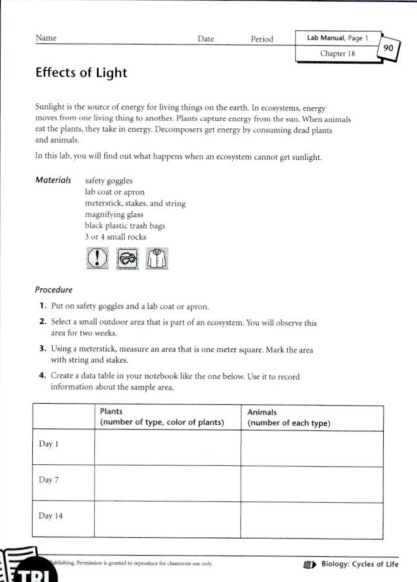

Lab Manual 90, pages 1–2

Biology in Your Life

Environment: Organic Farming

Organic farming is a unique form of agriculture. Unlike conventional farming, organic farming does not use synthetic (man-made) fertilizers or pesticides. These chemicals can hurt the environment. Instead, organic farmers use natural methods to grow plants and control insects. They add compost to soil instead of synthetic fertilizer. Compost is decayed organic material. Compost improves the soil and nourishes plants. As a result, the soil produces stronger plants that resist insects and disease.

To control weeds, organic farmers use tilling, mulching (covering the soil surface with organic materials), and hand weeding. To control insect pests, they use traps, stop insect mating, or introduce insect predators. Organic farmers also rotate crops. They switch the kinds of plants grown in a field from year to year. Crop rotation changes the ecology of a field and controls weeds and insects.

Organic products are grown and harvested without artificial chemicals, irradiation, or genetically engineered ingredients. Organic farms and processing facilities are regularly inspected to ensure that foods are grown and processed without artificial ingredients. Organic farms must be separated from nearby conventional farms by buffer zones. This prevents contamination from synthetic fertilizers or pesticides.

1. How does organically grown food differ from conventionally grown food?
2. How do organic farmers control insects?
3. Why might you prefer organic food instead of conventionally grown food?

Ecosystems Chapter 18 **583**

Science Journal

Have students write a persuasive essay or letter encouraging others to buy and consume organic foods.

IN THE ENVIRONMENT

Have students research the types of products that are grown organically in their area. Have them visit an organic farmer's market or farm to learn more about organic farming practices. Encourage them to research and discuss the potential health benefits, environmental benefits, economical benefits, or societal benefits of organic farming and organic produce consumption.

Biology in Your Life

Have students read the Biology in Your Life feature about organic farming. Explain that one result of overuse of fertilizers is water pollution. When runoff from fertilized areas flows into ponds and lakes, the excess nutrients can cause algal blooms in these freshwater ecosystems. When the algae die, bacteria decompose the organic matter. Bacteria use oxygen during the decomposition process. The excess organic matter from the algal bloom leads to a depletion of oxygen from the water as the dead algae are decomposed. Fish may die from lack of oxygen. Also, excess nutrients and algal growth can cause the water to become cloudy. Ask students: Why do you think cloudy water would be harmful? *(Cloudy water decreases the amount of sunlight that reaches deeper water.)*

Biology in Your Life Answers

1. Unlike conventionally grown food, organically grown food is raised without artificial pesticides or fertilizers.
2. Organic farmers control insect pests by using traps, disrupting insect mating, introducing insect predators, or rotating crops. **3.** Answers will vary. Consumers might prefer organic products instead of conventionally grown products because they wish to avoid any traces of pesticides in food items, or because they wish to support agricultural practices that benefit the soil and do not use unnatural pesticides and fertilizers.

Ecosystems **583**

Lesson 3 Review Answers

1. tropical forests 2. deserts 3. coniferous forests 4. Desert plants and animals can use very little water and are able to save water. 5. Differences in the amount of energy received from the sun cause different weather and water cycles. This affects the type of plants and organisms that can survive in a particular ecosystem.

Portfolio Assessment

Sample items include:
- Posters from ELL/ESL Strategy
- Lesson 3 Review answers

Link to

Health. Have students read the Link to Health feature. Discuss ways that cities attempt to reduce smog. For example, some cities have laws that encourage carpooling, provide subsidized transportation, or control vehicle emissions.

Science at Work

Have students read the Science at Work feature about the work of soil scientists. Explain that one aspect of their work is testing pH or nitrate levels. Allow students to use a soil test kit to determine the pH or nitrate levels in various soil samples around the school, in potted plants, or around their homes. Or they may wish to test the nitrate and pH levels of aquarium water, using test kits available at pet stores. Have them research how the pH or nitrate levels affect the organisms that live in the soil or water they are testing.

Lesson 3 REVIEW

Word Bank
coniferous forests
deserts
tropical forests

On a sheet of paper, write the word or words from the Word Bank that complete each sentence correctly.

1. Near the equator, _____ are the main biome.
2. Biomes that have little or no rainfall are _____.
3. Found in the north are biomes known as _____.

Link to
Health

Weather conditions in very populated cities may be affected by smog. *Smog* comes from the words *smoke* and *fog*. Brown colored smog forms when vehicles release nitrogen oxides and hydrocarbon vapors. These gases react with sunlight to produce ozone, a toxic gas. Smog irritates the eyes and can cause respiratory problems.

Critical Thinking

On a sheet of paper, write the answers to the following questions. Use complete sentences.

4. What key features do desert plants and animals share?
5. Why does differences in sunlight lead to different ecosystems?

Science at Work

Soil Scientist

Soil scientists study the composition of soils. They research the response of soils to fertilizers, crop rotation, and other farming practices. Soil scientists also help farmers and landowners find solutions to soil-related problems.

Many soil scientists work for federal, state, or university research stations. They may conduct soil surveys to classify and map soils in different areas. Soil scientists work with others to ensure environmental quality and effective land use. They may work with researchers who study the growth of plants in natural ecosystems. Soil scientists may work with ecologists to help them better understand how nutrients cycle within an area.

Soil scientists must be patient and observant. They must work well with others in project teams or research groups.

Workbook Activity 104

BIOLOGY IN THE WORLD

Water: Conserving a Scarce Resource

How much water does your household use every day? The average single-family home in the United States uses 350–400 gallons of water daily. Are you surprised at this amount? More than half of this water is used for watering lawns and gardens. Indoors, toilets are responsible for a fourth of this amount. Think about the water you use for drinking, cooking, showering, and washing dishes and clothes. It all adds up.

Most of us take water for granted. But if you live in an area where rainfall is scarce, you are aware of the need to conserve water. The fastest growing states in the United States are Nevada, Arizona, Colorado, Utah, and Idaho. Many cities in these states have very low rainfall.

As new residents move to these areas, population growth can strain the local water supplies. In many cities, ground water is pumped to the surface from deep within the bedrock. Lakes, springs, and wetlands may dry up if groundwater is removed faster than it is replaced.

Many communities provide rebate programs that pay homeowners who reduce water use. Some cities offer rebates for adding timers to sprinkler systems. They may also offer rebates for installing toilets, washing machines, and dishwashers that use low amounts of water. Other programs reward people for planting a certain percentage of their yard with desert plants that need little or no extra water. Local laws often do not allow outdoor watering during the hottest times of the day. That is when water evaporates most easily.

The city of Albuquerque in New Mexico has used programs like these to reduce water use. In the last 10 years, this city reduced its overall water use by 27 percent.

1. How can timers on sprinkler systems save water?
2. Suggest three ways that people can reduce indoor water use.

BIOLOGY IN THE WORLD

Have students read the Biology in the World feature about conserving water and answer the questions at the bottom of the page. Have students estimate the amount of water they use each day by keeping a journal of how often they use water in one 24-hour period. Ask them to record how many times they flush the toilet, how much water they use for cooking and drinking, how long they take a shower, and how long they run the faucet when washing their hands or brushing their teeth. They may need to use a stopwatch to make some of their measurements. Have the class pool their data to see how each student's water use compares.

Biology in the World Answers

1. Timers can help sprinkler systems save water by automatically turning the sprinklers off at a set time. 2. Indoor water use can be reduced by installing low water-use toilets, washing machines, or dishwashers.

ONLINE CONNECTION

The article "Ocean Color From Space: The Global Carbon Cycle" explains the relationship between human activities and the changing carbon cycle: http://daac.gsfc.nasa.gov.

Have students visit this site to find out more about how scientists are tracking the effects of humans on ocean environments: www.pbs.org/odyssey/index.html.

This online textbook provides lots of information about desert ecosystems: http://pubs.usgs.gov/gip/deserts.

Chapter 18 Summary

Chapter 18 Summary

Have volunteers read aloud each summary item on page 586. Ask volunteers to explain the meaning of each item. Direct students' attention to the Vocabulary box on the bottom of page 586. Have them read and review each term and its definition.

Graphic Organizer TRL

As students read Chapter 18, have them finish completing the chart on Graphic Organizer 18: Ecosystems. Encourage students to read each lesson of the chapter and then have them fill in the portion of the chart that pertains to the lesson. When they have completed the chart, ask them to answer the questions.

Chapter 18 SUMMARY

- The sun is the ultimate source of energy for the earth and all of its ecosystems.

- Phototrophs capture sunlight energy and store it as chemical energy. Chemotrophs get energy from the chemicals in food.

- The trophic structure of an ecosystem describes the flow of energy within the ecosystem. An ecosystem has producers, consumers, and decomposers.

- Producers are phototrophs. Consumers and decomposers are chemotrophs.

- Food chains and food webs show the feeding relationships within an ecosystem. Energy pyramids show the flow of energy from one trophic level to the next.

- Nutrients such as carbon, nitrogen, water, and phosphorus move through the living and nonliving parts of an ecosystem. Carbon compounds, nitrogen, and water are found in the atmosphere as gases. Phosphorus is found in soil and water. The carbon cycle, nitrogen cycle, and water cycle move these nutrients within and between ecosystems.

- Ecosystems with the same climate conditions are grouped together to form biomes. Each biome has characteristic plants and animals.

- There are several terrestrial biomes around the world. Aquatic biomes are freshwater or marine. Aquatic biomes are divided into zones based on the amount of light each zone receives.

Vocabulary

ammonium, 575
aphotic zone, 582
aquatic, 568
atmosphere, 573
benthic zone, 582
chaparral, 581
chemotroph, 566
climate, 580
coniferous forest, 582
consumer, 567
decomposer, 567
desert, 581
energy pyramid, 569
estuary, 582
evaporation, 576
food chain, 567
food web, 568
freshwater, 582
geological, 574
intertidal zone, 582
marine, 582
nitrate, 575
nitrifying bacteria, 575
nitrogen-fixer, 575
organic matter, 568
permafrost, 582
phosphorous, 573
photic zone, 582
phototroph, 566
plankton, 568
precipitation, 576
primary productivity, 569
producer, 567
savanna, 581
solar, 566
temperate deciduous forest, 582
temperate grassland, 581
terrestrial, 580
tropical forest, 581
tundra, 582

586 Chapter 18 Ecosystems

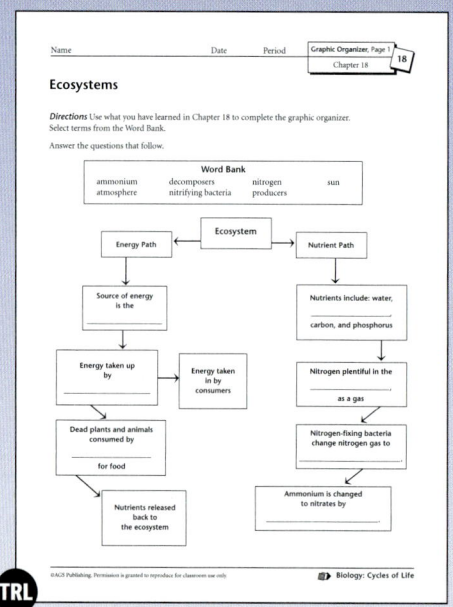

Graphic Organizer 18, pages 1–3

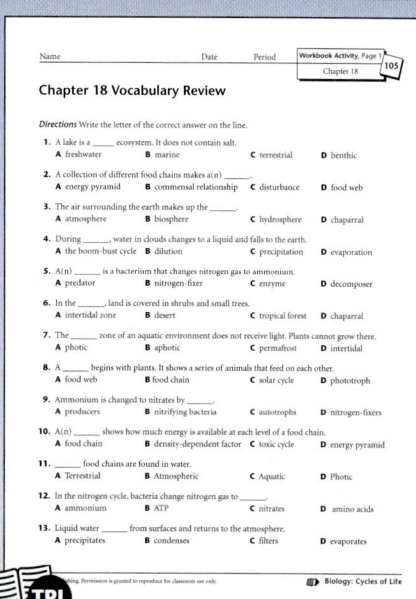

Workbook Activity 105, pages 1–3

Chapter 18 REVIEW

Word Bank
atmosphere
chemotroph
climate
consumer
decomposer
energy pyramid
estuary
evaporation
food web
freshwater
intertidal zone
marine
nitrogen-fixer
permafrost
phototroph
plankton
precipitation
primary productivity
producer
terrestrial

Vocabulary Review

On a sheet of paper, write the word or words from the Word Bank that best complete each sentence.

1. An organism that gets its energy by capturing light energy is known as a(n) _____. A(n) _____ is an organism that gets its energy from chemicals in food.

2. All of an ecosystem's food chains can be combined to form a(n) _____.

3. The _____ is the average weather an area experiences over a long period of time.

4. The first trophic level in a food chain is the _____.

5. Permanently frozen soil is _____.

6. In a food chain, an organism called a(n) _____ gets energy by eating other organisms.

7. An organism that breaks down dead organisms is called a(n) _____.

8. Water vapor that becomes concentrated and changes back into liquid as snow or rain is _____.

9. In an aquatic ecosystem, _____ are at the beginning of food chains.

10. Ecologists use a(n) _____ to show the movement of energy through trophic levels.

11. A bacterium that is a(n) _____ can change nitrogen into ammonium.

12. Biomes found on land are called _____ biomes.

13. The air that surrounds the earth is the _____.

14. A(n) _____ is a biome found where freshwater meets saltwater.

Review continued on next page

Review Answers

15. evaporation 16. freshwater, marine
17. primary productivity 18. intertidal zone

Teacher Alert

In the Chapter Review, the Vocabulary Review activity includes a sample of the chapter's vocabulary terms. The activity will help determine students' understanding of key vocabulary terms and concepts presented in the chapter. Other vocabulary terms used in the chapter are listed below.

ammonium	organic matter
aphotic zone	phosphorus
aquatic	photic zone
benthic zone	savanna
chaparral	solar
coniferous forest	temperate deciduous forest
desert	
food chain	temperate grassland
geological	tropical forest
nitrate	tundra
nitrifying bacteria	

Concept Review

19. B 20. D 21. C

Critical Thinking

22. Producers capture energy from sunlight and use it to make chemicals that provide energy for consumers. Decomposers break down dead producers and consumers, recycling the chemical nutrients that they contain. 23. An energy pyramid represents the flow of energy through an ecosystem, beginning with producers and ending with the top consumer. It is shaped like a pyramid with a wide base and a narrow top because energy is lost (as heat) from one trophic level up to the next.

Chapter 18 REVIEW - continued

15. When the sun heats bodies of water, molecules of water escape their liquid form to become water vapor during _____.

16. Aquatic biomes lacking salt are _____ biomes. Oceans contain salt and are examples of _____ biomes.

17. The production of organic matter by phototrophs is _____.

18. The ocean meets the land in the _____.

Concept Review

On a sheet of paper, write the letter of the answer that completes each sentence correctly.

19. A(n) _____ is an example of a phototroph.
    A elephant   B tree   C hawk   D fungus

20. The burning of oil and coal produces _____.
    A nitrogen gas
    B phosphorous
    C water
    D carbon dioxide

21. A very dry terrestrial biome with low rainfall is a _____.
    A chaparral
    B savanna
    C desert
    D temperate grassland

Chapter 18 Mastery Test A, pages 1–3

Critical Thinking

Write the answer to each of the following questions. Use complete sentences.

22. Explain the relationships among producers, consumers, and decomposers.
23. What does an energy pyramid represent? Explain why it is shaped like a pyramid.
24. Describe how carbon cycles through an ecosystem.
25. Which biome has the largest number of species? Explain your answer.

Research and Write

Write a report on plant fertilizers. Include information on the three main chemical nutrients found in most plant fertilizers.

Test-Taking Tip If you know you will have to define certain terms on a test, write each term on one side of an index card. Write its definition on the other side. Use the cards to test yourself, or use them with a partner.

Ecosystems   Chapter 18   589

---

24. Photosynthesis captures carbon in the form of CO_2 and changes it into organic molecules. These organic molecules provide food energy for other organisms.
25. The tropical forest biome has the largest number of species. This biome has a large amount of rain and many different plant species, which provide a large variety of habitats for many other kinds of organisms.

Research and Write

Ask a volunteer to read aloud the Research and Write feature. Have students use the library or Internet to find out more about the ingredients in commercially available varieties of plant fertilizers. Suggest that students share their research with the class in the form of a written report, an oral presentation, or an informative poster or display.

ALTERNATIVE ASSESSMENT

Alternative Assessment items correlate to the student Goals for Learning at the beginning of this chapter.

- Have students draw cartoons that explain what ecosystems, energy, and chemical nutrients are.
- Write the following words on the board: *rabbit, grass, bacteria,* and *wolf.* Have students describe how energy is transferred between these organisms.
- Have students do research on different biomes to construct a food chain and a food web that are not found in the chapter.
- Provide students with colored beads. Have them use the beads to demonstrate how nutrients are cycled through an ecosystem in the nitrogen, carbon, or water cycle.
- Have students choose a biome and make a travel brochure that describes where the biome is located, the type of organisms found in the biome, and the types of outdoor activities one can participate in while visiting.

Chapter 18 Mastery Test B, pages 1–3

Ecosystems   589

Chapter 19

Planning Guide
Human Impact and Technology

	Student Pages	Student Text Lesson Vocabulary	Lesson Review	Critical-Thinking Questions
Lesson 1 What Impact Do Humans Have on Ecosystems?	592–600	✔	✔	✔
Lesson 2 Conservation Biology	601–606	✔	✔	✔
Lesson 3 Science and Technology	607–613	✔	✔	✔

Chapter Activities

Teacher's Resource Library
Community Connection 19:
 Local Recycling
Graphic Organizer 19:
 Human Impact and Technology

Teacher's Edition
Opener Activity

Assessment Options

Student Text
Chapter 19 Review

Teacher's Resource Library
Chapter 19 Mastery Tests A and B
Chapters 1–19 Final Mastery Test

Teacher's Edition
Chapter 19 Alternative Assessment

Student Text Features									Teaching Strategies						Learning Styles					Teacher's Resource Library			
Achievements in Science	Science at Work	Biology in Your Life	Investigation/Discovery	Biology in the World	Express Lab	Link to	Research and Write	Technology and Society	ELL/ESL Strategy	Background Information	Science Journal	Applications Home, Career, Community, Global, Environment	Online Connection	Teacher Alert	Auditory/Verbal	Body/Kinesthetic	Interpersonal/Group Learning	Logical/Mathematical	Visual/Spatial	Workbook Activities	Alternative Workbook Activities	Lab Manual	Self-Study Guide
598	593		599		597	✔			595	592		594, 596, 597		595				593	595	106	106	91–92	✔
		605				✔	603		604	601	605	602, 603		603	604					107	107	93	✔
			611	613		✔	617	608	610	607	609		613	609		613	609			108–109	108–109	94–95	✔

Pronunciation Key

a	hat	e	let	ī	ice	ô	order	ů	put	sh	she
ā	age	ē	equal	o	hot	oi	oil	ü	rule	th	thin
ä	far	ėr	term	ō	open	ou	out	ch	child	ᴛʜ	then
â	care	i	it	ȯ	saw	u	cup	ng	long	zh	measure

ə { a in about, e in taken, i in pencil, o in lemon, u in circus }

Alternative Workbook Activities

The Teacher's Resource Library (TRL) contains a set of lower-level worksheets called Alternative Workbook Activities. These worksheets cover the same content as the regular Workbook Activities but are written at a second-grade reading level.

Skill Track Online

Use Skill Track Online for *Biology: Cycles of Life* to monitor student progress and meet the demands of adequate yearly progress (AYP). Make informed instructional decisions with individual student and class reports of online lesson and chapter assessments. With immediate and ongoing feedback, students will also see what they have learned and where they need more reinforcement and practice.

Chapter at a Glance

Chapter 19: Human Impact and Technology
pages 590–617

Lessons

1. **What Impact Do Humans Have on Ecosystems?** pages 592–600

   Investigation 19 pages 599–600

2. **Conservation Biology**
   pages 601–606

3. **Science and Technology**
   pages 607–613

   Discovery Investigation 19
   pages 611–612

   Biology in the World page 613

Chapter 19 Summary page 614

Chapter 19 Review pages 615–617

Audio CD 🎧

Skill Track Online
for Biology: Cycles of Life

Teacher's Resource Library TRL

Workbook Activities 106–109

Alternative Workbook Activities 106–109

Lab Manual 91–95

Community Connection 19

Graphic Organizer 19

Resource File 43–44

Chapter 19 Self-Study Guide

Chapter 19 Mastery Tests A and B

Chapters 1–19 Final Mastery Test

(Answer Keys for the Teacher's Resource Library begin on page 675 of the Teacher's Edition. The Materials List for the Lab Manual activities begins on page 720.)

Opener Activity

Have each student make a chart with the headings *Know*, *Want to Know*, and *Learned* for the topics in this chapter. Have students fill in what they know about the topics of human impact on ecosystems and the environment, actions being taken to reduce the impact and the relation between science and technology. Then have students fill in what they would like to learn about these topics. Guide an informal discussion in which students share what they know and would like to learn. After students complete the chapter, have them fill in what they have learned.

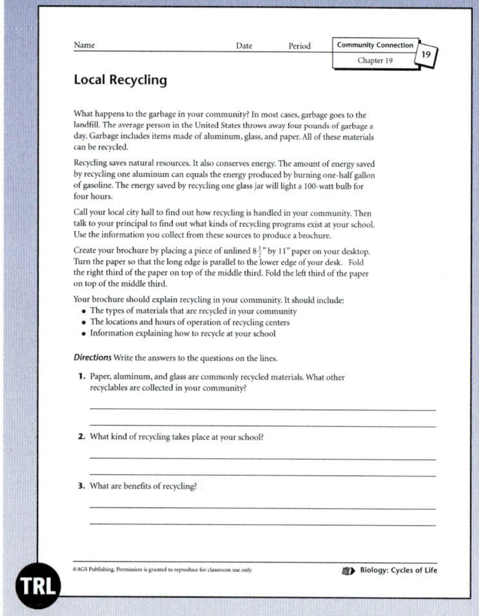

Community Connection 19

Chapter 19

Human Impact and Technology

In some parts of the United States, fields of wind turbines, or wind farms, produce electricity. Electricity made by wind farms is clean energy. The process releases no pollutants, but it has some drawbacks. Turbines can slightly alter the local climate. Scientists look for ways to obtain resources while protecting the environment. In Chapter 19, you will learn how people affect ecosystems. You will also learn how technology can help us keep the earth's ecosystems healthy and productive.

Goals for Learning

- To recognize that some human activities damage some ecosystems
- To discuss how changing human activities can help the environment
- To describe conservation efforts to reduce damage
- To describe how technology helps people and to understand how science and technology work together

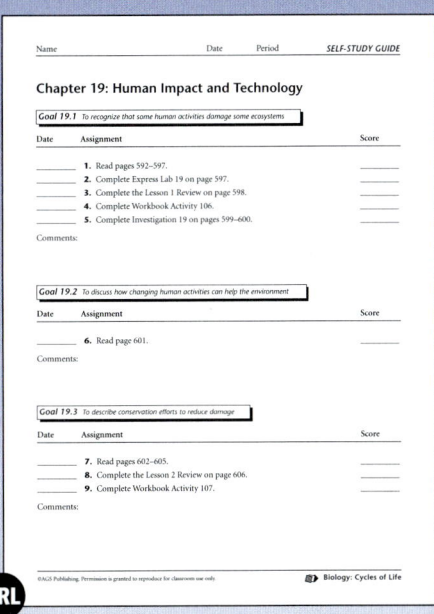
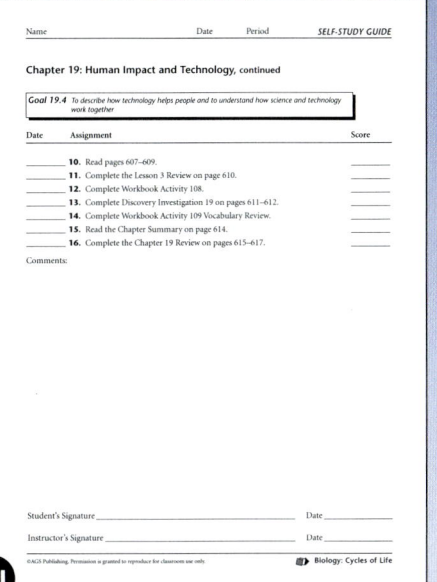

Chapter 19 Self-Study Guide

Introducing the Chapter

Have students study the photograph of the wind turbines on page 590. Remind students that as the wind turns the blades on the turbine, electricity is generated. Have students think about the wind conditions in the local area. Would using wind energy be possible? Why or why not? Is wind energy already being used locally? What are some advantages and disadvantages associated with the use of wind energy? *(advantages: using wind energy does not cause pollution; disadvantages: wind does not blow consistently, turbines can alter the local climate)*

Have students study the Organize Your Thoughts diagram. Growing human populations cause pollution, habitat destruction, and species extinction. Have students discuss solutions. *(recycling and reducing waste, stopping deforestation, creating reserves, protecting endangered species)*

Notes and Math Tips

Ask volunteers to read the notes and math tips that appear in the margins throughout the chapter. Then discuss them with the class.

TEACHER'S RESOURCE

The AGS Publishing Teaching Strategies in Science Transparencies may be used with this chapter. The transparencies add an interactive dimension to expand and enhance the *Biology: Cycles of Life* program content.

CAREER INTEREST INVENTORY

The AGS Publishing Harrington-O'Shea Career Decision-Making System-Revised (CDM) may be used with this chapter. Students can use the CDM to explore their interests and identify careers. The CDM defines career areas that are indicated by students' responses on the inventory.

Lesson at a Glance

Chapter 19 Lesson 1

Overview In this lesson, students learn about the impact of human activities on the environment.

Objectives

- To describe the growth of the human population
- To explain how human activities can harm ecosystems
- To describe the greenhouse effect
- To describe introduced species and their effects

Student Pages 592–600

Teacher's Resource Library TRL

Workbook Activity 106
Alternative Workbook Activity 106
Lab Manual 91–92
Resource File 43–44

Vocabulary

acid rain
chemical runoff
deforestation
eutrophication
greenhouse effect
introduced species
land development
ozone
pollution

Have students write a short fictional story that uses at least five of the vocabulary words in context. Encourage students to create a setting and characters for the story. The plot may include changes happening to the ecosystem in which the characters live.

Background Information

The United States Census Bureau maintains a POPClock, or population clock, which projects the population of the United States. The clock uses the following statistics:

One birth every 8 seconds

One death every 13 seconds

One international migrant every 26 seconds

Net gain of one person every 12 seconds

Have students visit the POPClock Web site at www.census.gov/population/www/popclockus.html to check the most recent projection.

Lesson 1: What Impact Do Humans Have on Ecosystems?

Objectives

After reading this lesson, you should be able to

- describe the growth of the human population
- explain how human activities can harm ecosystems
- describe the greenhouse effect
- describe introduced species and their effects

Humans are one species of organisms. Humans coexist with many different species in many different places in the world. Humans affect every ecosystem in the world. This is true even though they are not part of every ecosystem. Like other organisms, humans have basic needs that must be met, such as having food, water, and space. These resources usually limit how large a population of organisms can grow. However, this is not true for humans.

Growth of Human Population

Most populations eventually reach carrying capacity for their ecosystem. Recall from Chapter 17 that the carrying capacity is the largest density an ecosystem can support for a particular population. At carrying capacity, populations are using all of the limited resources that are shared with other populations. Populations usually stay at carrying capacity unless a major disturbance happens.

Humans do not follow this pattern. Scientists do not know the carrying capacity for the human population. Human populations use their knowledge to find ways to expand their carrying capacity. When food runs short, humans find other food sources. Humans find more space or build more in the space they have when space becomes limited. When resources become limited, humans find solutions for their needs.

Today, the world population is more than 6,000,000,000 people. The human population adds about 100 people every minute of the day. More than 70 million people are added to the population every year. The activities of this growing population of humans affect the ecosystems in which they live. Natural resources are limited. To get more resources, humans often harm other organisms in their ecosystems. Humans change ecosystems every day, in many different ways.

592 Chapter 19 Human Impact and Technology

Impact of Trash

Humans damage many ecosystems by destroying habitats. Remember that a habitat is an area where an organism naturally lives. Many habitats make up an ecosystem. Many factors cause habitats to be destroyed. As humans go through their daily lives, they produce a large amount of trash and waste. These waste products are often disposed of in certain areas that were once habitats. Humans do not use some of these areas. Instead, they litter the land and water around them. This trash can harm or kill other organisms.

Science at Work

Park Ranger

Every day is different for a park ranger. A ranger may work for a local, state, or national park system. The tasks of a park ranger can include supervising or performing conservation work and protecting forests. Park rangers may also watch for and fight fires. Rangers may work with the public by demonstrating outdoor skills, preparing exhibits, and promoting safety and conservation. They may lead nature walks, enforce laws, and operate campgrounds.

Park rangers must be able to work independently. A love of nature is important for this job because much of the work is outdoors. Rangers must be able to think clearly in emergencies. They may rescue lost hikers and mountain climbers or provide first aid.

Most park ranger jobs require a bachelor's degree in park and recreation management or a natural science, plus on-the-job training. Other positions allow people with work experience or a combination of work experience and college courses to qualify for jobs. Completion of police academy or peace officer training could be helpful, because some park rangers are also peace officers.

---

1 Warm-Up Activity

Have students read and conduct the Express Lab on page 597. Then have students read the Science Myth on page 594. Acid rain is produced when sulfur dioxide and nitrogen oxides are released into the air and dissolve in water vapor. Both sulfur dioxide and nitrogen oxides are by-products of burning fossil fuels such as coal. Natural causes also contribute slightly to making rain acidic.

Express Lab Answers

1. The pH of distilled water should be close to 7. **2.** Answers will vary. Normal pH of rainwater is between 5.2 and 6. If the pH of the sample is below 5.2, your area is experiencing acid rain.

2 Teaching the Lesson

Have students make a table to help organize the material presented in the lesson, with these column headings: *Definition, Air, Water, Land,* and *Ecosystem*. Row headings should be *Runoff, Waste Gases, Land Development,* and *Introduced Species*. Have students complete each row by giving a definition and examples of each type of pollution and how it affects air, water, and/or land. In the last column, *Ecosystem*, have students provide an example of how each type of pollution can lead to a change in an ecosystem.

3 Reinforce and Extend

Science at Work

Have students read the Science at Work feature. Invite a park ranger from a local park to be a guest speaker in your classroom. Have students write out questions they may have for the ranger prior to the visit.

LEARNING STYLES

Logical/Mathematical

Have students use the statistic given on page 592 to calculate how many people are added to the human population each day. *(100 people per minute × 60 minutes per hour × 24 hours per day = 144,000 people per day)*

IN THE ENVIRONMENT

Eutrophication is a natural process in the succession of lakes and estuaries. However, human activities can accelerate the process, leading to a decrease in biodiversity. Have students research how eutrophication has affected local bodies of water and what steps individuals can take to reduce the nutrients they add to ecosystems. Students may want to visit the U.S. Environmental Protection Agency's Web site about eutrophication at www.epa.gov/maia/html/eutroph.html. Have students present the results of their research to the class in an oral report.

Link to

Earth Science. Have students read the Link to Earth Science feature. Ask students: Have you ever been in a greenhouse? Have a volunteer tell the class about his or her experience and describe the temperature in the greenhouse. Explain that the greenhouse walls let in sunlight and act as a trap for the sun's heat. Earth's atmosphere acts like the greenhouse walls by letting sunlight pass through and trapping the heat from the sun near Earth's surface. Many students may be familiar with a similar phenomenon inside a car on a sunny day. Heat is trapped inside the car as the car sits in the sunlight.

Pollution
Anything added to the environment that is harmful to living things

Chemical runoff
The chemical waste produced on land that enters water sources

Eutrophication
A process in which chemical runoff causes algae growth that chokes out other organisms in a water ecosystem

Acid rain
Rain that is caused by pollution and is harmful to organisms because it is acidic

Greenhouse effect
The warming of the atmosphere because of trapped heat energy from the sun

Impact of Pollution

Pollution also destroys habitats. Pollution is anything added to the environment that is harmful to living things. Factories, cars, trucks, boats, and many other machines that burn fuels give off chemicals as waste. These chemicals move into the air, land, or water. There they can build up to levels poisonous to many organisms.

Chemical runoff is liquid chemical waste from factories and other sources that enter into water sources. Chemical runoff usually contains high concentrations of nitrogen compounds. These chemicals cause fast growth of algae. Remember from Chapter 15 that algae are water plants. The algae soon take over and force other organisms out of that ecosystem. This process is called **eutrophication.**

Waste gases enter the atmosphere and cause pollution in many ways. Sulfur dioxide dissolves in water vapor in the air. The water vapor falls to land as rain, carrying those chemicals with it. This polluted rain is called **acid rain.** It can damage ecosystems and poison many organisms, especially plants.

Machines that burn fuels give off carbon dioxide gas. This is the same gas humans breathe out. Plants remove carbon dioxide from the atmosphere during photosynthesis.

However, humans and industry are giving off carbon dioxide faster than plants can use it. The extra carbon dioxide traps solar energy in the atmosphere. As this energy gets trapped, it causes the temperature to rise around the world. This warming of the atmosphere is called the **greenhouse effect.**

Link to ▶▶▶

Earth Science

The greenhouse effect is a natural process that warms the earth. Radiant energy from the sun is absorbed by the earth's surface. The warmed surface gives off heat. Most of the heat radiates back into space. Some is trapped in the earth's atmosphere by gases such as carbon dioxide. This trapped heat maintains the earth's temperature and makes life on the earth possible.

Ozone
A form of oxygen

Land development
The changes people make to natural land so it becomes land for farming or living space

The earth is also being harmed by another gas, **ozone.** Ozone is a form of oxygen. Look at Figure 19.1.1. Ozone makes up a tiny but important part of the atmosphere. A thin layer of ozone high in the atmosphere absorbs ultraviolet radiation from the sun. The ozone layer prevents most of the ultraviolet radiation from reaching the earth. Ultraviolet radiation can cause sunburn and skin cancer.

Humans have damaged this protective ozone layer. For example, certain gases released from spray cans drift high into the atmosphere and break down ozone. Holes have appeared in the ozone layer over Antarctica.

Ozone is also an ingredient in smog. This hazy mixture of gases damages the lungs and can worsen heart disease. Ozone collects at ground level because vehicle exhaust releases ozone. Factories make and use ozone for cleaning flour, oil, fabrics, and water.

Impact of Land Development

The growing human population must have space and food. These needs drive **land development.** Land development is when humans change natural land to land used for farming or living space. This change disrupts and sometimes destroys ecosystems.

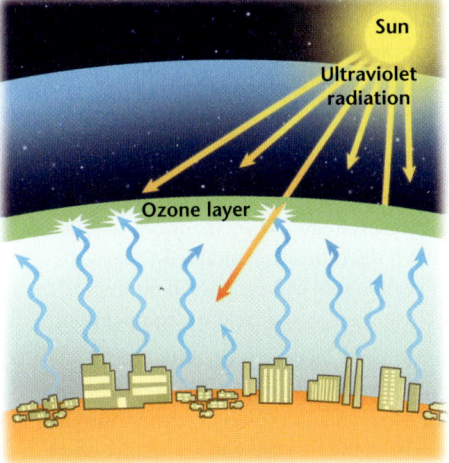

Figure 19.1.1 *The ozone layer prevents most ultraviolet radiation from reaching the earth.*

TEACHER ALERT

Explain to students the different roles that ozone plays in Earth's atmosphere. Ozone high in the atmosphere (in the stratosphere), helps humans because it absorbs harmful ultraviolet radiation from the sun, preventing it from reaching Earth's surface. However, when ozone forms in the lowest layer of the atmosphere (the troposphere), it contributes to air pollution and can cause health problems for humans.

ELL/ESL STRATEGY

Language Objective:
To learn vocabulary

Have students who are learning English make a collage to become familiar with the vocabulary terms in this lesson. Have students cut out pictures from magazines that show examples of each of the vocabulary terms. As they arrange their collage, students should label each picture with a vocabulary term and write a caption explaining how the picture is related to the term.

LEARNING STYLES

Visual/Spatial

Have students keep a journal, recording the trash and litter they see every day for five days. Have them record the type and quantity of trash and where they see it. Ask students: How do you feel about seeing trash and litter in your surroundings? What actions in relation to trash and litter could improve the appearance of your surroundings?

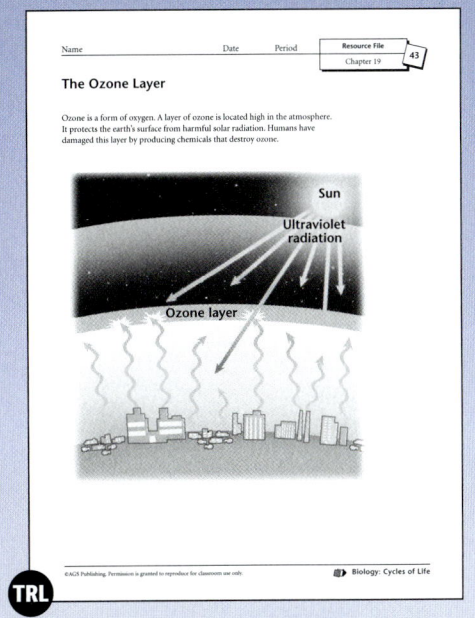

Resource File 43

GLOBAL CONNECTION

Have students research a situation in which an introduced species has caused changes to an ecosystem and threatened a native species. From which part of the world does the introduced species originate? Into which part of the world was it introduced? How was the species introduced? What changes to the ecosystem resulted? What steps, if any, are being taken to reduce the impact of the introduced species on the ecosystem? Have students share the results of their research with the class.

PRONUNCIATION GUIDE

Use the pronunciation shown here to help students pronounce a difficult word in this lesson. Refer to the pronunciation key on the Chapter Planning Guide for the sounds of the symbols.

kudzu (kŭd′zü)

Science Myth

Have students read the Science Myth feature. The more acidic water is, the lower its pH. Slight acidity is natural in rainwater as a result of volcanoes and other factors. Rain that is more acid than the natural range can lower the pH of streams and lakes significantly, causing stress to organisms that live in these habitats. Most species of fish eggs cannot hatch if the pH of the water is below 5. At lower pH levels, adult fish may die. Even if a species can live in water with a lower pH, its food source may not be able to. For example, frogs may be able to tolerate the lower pH levels, but mayflies, a source of food for frogs, cannot. Thus, the frogs are affected indirectly by acid rain through the loss of a food source.

596 Chapter 19

Deforestation
The removal of forest ecosystems for land development

Introduced species
A species taken from its natural ecosystem and placed in another ecosystem

Science Myth

Myth: The typical pH of rainwater is 7. Rainwater is neither acidic nor basic.

Fact: Rainwater usually has a pH between 5.2 and 6, with an average of 5.6. The slight acidity is due to natural acids dissolved in rainwater. Acid rain is rainwater with a pH below 5.2.

For example, **deforestation** clears out forested areas to make room for buildings or farmland. Land development in deforested areas can greatly harm the natural ecosystem. New buildings may give off waste and pollute the environment. Humans removed most or all of the trees and plants in the area. Fewer trees and plants are available to remove carbon dioxide from the atmosphere. Farmers may overwork the land and remove important nutrients from the soil. Topsoil may be lost because of construction or bad farming practices.

To make room for humans, natural ecosystems and their many different organisms are removed. The original organisms may not have other ecosystems to go to. They often die. Species then become extinct. Remember that extinction is when all the members of a species are dead. Almost 100 species become extinct every day around the world.

Impact of Introduced Species

Extinction is caused by another damaging human activity, **introduced species.** Introduced species are species that are introduced into new ecosystems. When an introduced species enters an ecosystem, it disturbs the natural food chains. Its members hunt and eat natural consumers and producers. An introduced species usually does not have any competition.

Because of this, the introduced species can take over an ecosystem. It may eventually destroy the ecosystem. Introduced species usually come from humans carrying them from their natural environments. Many governments have strict laws to stop the spread of introduced species.

An example of an introduced species is kudzu, a vine. It grows quickly, up a to foot a day. Kudzu was introduced into the United States from Japan in 1876. Farmers in the South planted kudzu to reduce the loss of topsoil. In 1972, the United States Department of Agriculture declared kudzu a weed.

596 Chapter 19 Human Impact and Technology

Link to ›››
Health

Smog is a type of air pollution found mostly in cities. The exhaust from vehicles and factories react chemically in sunlight to form ozone. Because ozone is a pollutant, breathing smoggy air can harm people. It can damage the lungs and cause lung diseases such as emphysema and bronchitis. Smog can also make it harder for people to resist lung infections.

Today, kudzu is common throughout much of the southeastern United States and some northern states. Kudzu can destroy valuable forests by preventing trees from getting sunlight. Scientists are developing chemicals to stop its growth.

Summing Up

The human population continues to grow. This growth is taking resources away from other species and ecosystems. However, not all human activities hurt the environment. By understanding ecology and the environment, humans are also performing activities to help ecosystems. You will learn more about these activities in Lesson 2.

Express Lab 19

Materials
- rainwater sample
- small jar with lid
- forceps
- 2 pieces of pH paper
- 2 eyedroppers
- pH chart
- distilled water

Procedure

1. In a small jar, collect a small sample of rainwater from a clean puddle or directly from the air. Put the lid on the jar and bring it to class.
2. Put on safety goggles and a lab coat or apron.
3. Use the forceps to pick up a piece of pH paper. Use an eyedropper to put a drop of distilled water onto the pH paper.
4. Compare the color of the wet pH paper to the pH chart. Record your observations.
5. Using a new eyedropper, repeat Steps 3 and 4 with a drop of rainwater.
6. When you are finished, wash your hands well.

Analysis

1. What is the pH of distilled water?
2. What is the pH of the rainwater? Is this acid rain?

Link to

Health. Have students read the Link to Health feature. Ozone is the primary component of smog. Ask students: How could you find out how much ozone is in the air you breathe? A good source of quantitative information about the air quality in the local area is to check a local newspaper for the Air Quality Index (AQI) reading each day. The AQI assigns a value to air quality based on the amount of ozone and several other air pollutants in the air on a given day in a given location. If ozone levels are high, people with respiratory illness may be cautioned not to exert themselves physically outdoors. Bring newspapers for students to check the AQI values for a few days.

IN THE ENVIRONMENT

 Have students research how deforestation of the rain forest affects other aspects of the environment such as the carbon cycle and global warming, or how it affects other ecosystems such as nearby rivers and oceans and the organisms in those habitats. Have students present a report on their research to the class.

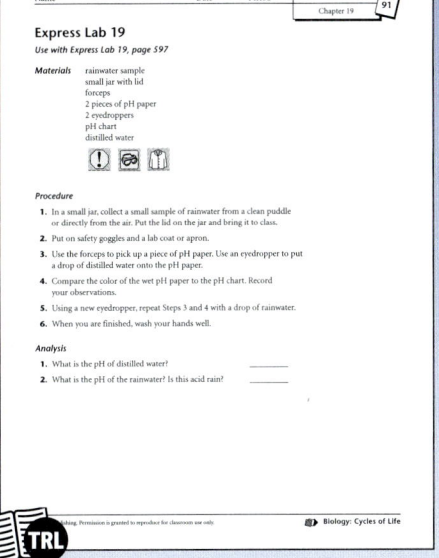

Resource File 44

Lab Manual 91

Lesson 1 Review Answers

1. greenhouse effect **2.** eutrophication **3.** chemical runoff **4.** Waste gases enter the atmosphere when factories, cars, trucks, and boats burn fuel. Carbon dioxide is one of the main types of waste gases that can cause problems when there is too much of it. Carbon dioxide can cause solar energy to get trapped in the earth's atmosphere, making temperatures rise around the world. **5.** Humans are able to use their knowledge and their inventiveness to find solutions to problems that might limit their growth rate.

Portfolio Assessment

Sample items include:
- Express Lab answers
- Data from Learning Styles Visual/Spatial
- Lesson 1 Review answers

Achievements in Science

Have students read the Achievements in Science feature. One of the most well-publicized projects of the International Crane Foundation (ICF) has been its contribution to the Whooping Crane Recovery Team, which has been working since 1999 to establish a new migratory population of whooping cranes. Baby chicks are imprinted using an ultralight aircraft, which they follow along a new autumn migration route from Wisconsin to Florida. For more information on work that the ICF is doing, visit www.savingcranes.org.

Lab Activities

Chapter 19 has Investigation and Discovery Investigation lab activities. Two additional lab activities for Chapter 19 appear in the Biology: Cycles of Life Lab Manual and on the Teacher's Resource Library CD-ROM.

Lesson 1 REVIEW

Word Bank
eutrophication
greenhouse effect
chemical runoff

On a sheet of paper, write the word or words from the Word Bank that complete each sentence correctly.

1. The warming of the atmosphere caused by trapped solar energy is the _____.
2. A process in which algae growth chokes out other water ecosystems is _____.
3. The chemical waste produced on land that enters water sources is _____.

Critical Thinking

On a sheet of paper, write the answers to the following questions. Use complete sentences.

4. How do waste gases enter the atmosphere and cause problems?
5. Human populations do not have a carrying capacity for their ecosystems. Explain why.

Achievements in Science

Bringing Back the Whooping Crane

About 1,500 whooping cranes once lived in the North American wetlands. As people drained the wetlands, the number of these great white birds decreased. By the 1940s, the worldwide population was only 14. Members of other crane species were also decreasing. Thanks to a unique conservation effort, there are 320 whooping cranes in the world today.

In 1973, two graduate students, George Archibald and Ron Sauey, realized cranes were nearly extinct. They founded the International Crane Foundation near Baraboo, Wisconsin. There they developed methods to breed and raise the 15 crane species.

Whooping cranes are bred at the International Crane Foundation. When the chicks hatch, they first see puppets that look like cranes. The chicks are raised by volunteers who wear crane costumes. This is done so the chicks form social attachments to other cranes. This is important for releasing them into the wild.

Workbook Activity 106

INVESTIGATION 19

Measuring Particulates in the Air

Materials
- safety goggles
- lab coat or apron
- 2 microscope slides
- 2 petri dishes
- marker
- petroleum jelly
- 2 petri dish lids
- microscope

Particulates are a form of air pollution. They are tiny particles suspended in the air you breathe. Particulates come from fires, tobacco smoke, vehicle exhaust, plants, and animals. In this investigation, you will collect two air samples and count the particulates in each sample. Where do you think you will find the most particulates?

Procedure

1. Put on safety goggles and a lab coat or apron.
2. Make a data table like the one shown below.
3. Get two microscope slides and two petri dishes with lids. Using a marker, label a corner of one slide A. Label a corner of the other slide B. **Safety Alert: Handle glass microscope slides with care. Dispose of broken glass properly.**
4. Choose two locations to test for particulates. Using a marker, label the bottom of a petri dish A. Write its location. Label the bottom of the other petri dish B. Write its location.

	Slide A	Slide B
Location		
Number of particulates—first field of view		
Second field of view		
Third field of view		
Fourth field of view		
Fifth field of view		
Total number of particulates		

Human Impact and Technology Chapter 19 **599**

Investigation 19

Encourage students to read the investigation steps. Discuss questions they may have before beginning the investigation.

Objectives
- To prepare slides for collecting particulates in two air samples
- To use a microscope to count the number of particulates in two air samples
- To graph the data from the investigation

Skills
Observing, collecting data, organizing, comparing and contrasting, making and using graphs, analyzing data, drawing conclusions

Background
Dust, soot, ash, smoke, plant pollen, and lint are particulates, the most visible form of air pollution. Emissions from diesel engines and smoke from burning wood are the largest sources of particulates. Particulates are harmful to human health because they cause respiratory symptoms and lung damage. Students may not realize that particulates are a form of harmful pollution because the particles cannot be seen without a microscope.

Time Frame
20 minutes to set up the experiment, then 45–50 minutes about 24 hours later to collect data

Procedure
- This investigation can be done by students working in pairs. Each student can collect data from one slide.
- Parking lots, busy street corners, inside homes, and parks or backyards are possible locations for collecting air samples.
- If students choose locations in public areas, have them get prior permission to place the petri dishes there. An area can be set aside so that petri dishes will not be disturbed.
- Students can collect an air sample directly from a car's tailpipe as follows: Have students put a coated slide on a small surface about 6 inches from the end of the tailpipe of a car parked in an open area. Have an adult start the car engine and let the car idle for about 30 seconds. The student should wait until the engine is turned off before collecting the slide. Warn students not to touch the tailpipe.
- Review with students the correct way to carry, use, and store the microscope.
- Data from the entire class can be plotted on one large bar graph to compare all locations that were sampled.

Continued on page 600

SAFETY ALERT

- Be sure that students have read and understood all safety rules for working in the lab. Discuss the Safety Alert with students.
- Remind students not to press down on the slide when spreading the petroleum jelly.

Human Impact and Technology **599**

Continued from page 599

Results

Students may see some larger particles under low power. Under high power, they will see many particles. The smallest particles cannot be seen with a light microscope. If no particles are observed, the jelly coating might not have been sticky enough to trap particles.

Analysis Answers

1. The petroleum jelly traps the particles and holds them on the slide.
2. A bar graph is best for comparing two samples. Students should label the *y*-axis *Total number of particles*.

Conclusions Answers

1. Parking lots and car emissions will have large numbers of particulates.
2. Students will most likely suggest car and truck emissions and cigarette smoke.
3. Students may want to explore different ways particulates could be reduced using filters or scrubbers.

Explore Further Answers

Students may be surprised at the number of particulates in the air of a smoker's home. Have students research the dangers of secondhand smoke, which are largely due to particulates.

Assessment

Monitor students as they use microscopes to ensure that they follow correct procedures. Check to make sure that students have correctly recorded their data in their data tables. Check student graphs. You may need to review graph-making procedures with them.

You might include the following items from this investigation in student portfolios:

- Data table
- Student graphs
- Answers to Analysis and Conclusions questions
- Student performance of additional work in Explore Further

600 Chapter 19

5. Use petroleum jelly to lightly coat the unlabeled side of each slide. Put the slide, with the petroleum jelly side up, in the petri dish with the same letter. Wash your hands well.
6. Put the uncovered petri dishes containing the slides in the chosen locations. Do not disturb them for 24 hours.
7. Cover the petri dishes with the lids.
8. Use a microscope to observe slide A. Use low power and then high power. Count the number of particulates in each of 5 different high-power fields of view. Record your data. Find the total number of particulates counted for slide A.
9. Repeat Step 8 for slide B.

Cleanup/Disposal
When you are finished, wash the slides and petri dishes thoroughly with detergent and warm water. Wash your hands well.

Analysis
1. What is the purpose of the petroleum jelly?
2. Make a graph comparing the total number of particulates counted from your two locations. What kind of graph would best compare your data?

Conclusions
1. Which location had the largest number of particulates?
2. Where do you think the particulates in your locations came from?
3. Write a new question about particulates that you could explore in another investigation.

Explore Further
If you know someone who smokes, repeat the investigation by placing a slide in his or her home. Place a slide in the home of a nonsmoker for comparison.

600   Chapter 19   Human Impact and Technology

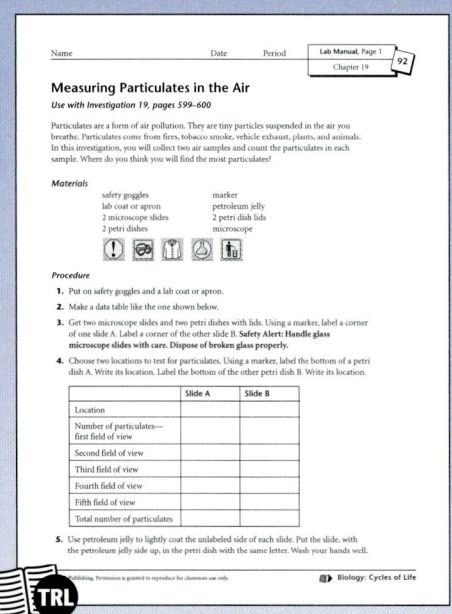

Lab Manual 92, pages 1–2

Lesson 2 Conservation Biology

Objectives

After reading this lesson, you should be able to
- define conservation biology
- describe how people are reducing air and water pollution
- discuss how people are protecting threatened and endangered habitats

Conservation biology
The science of using ecological information to help reduce damage to the environment

Landfill
An area where trash is collected and stored

As you learned in Lesson 1, humans can cause major problems in ecosystems. The human population is threatening the lives of many organisms.

People Helping the Environment

Today, many people work to help threatened organisms. Recall that a threatened species is a species that has many fewer members today than in the past. Many people are trying to correct or limit factors that harm these species.

Some people belong to organizations that fight pollution and ecological damage. Government agencies also help by passing laws to reduce pollution and habitat destruction. Government agencies and environmental organizations rely on scientific knowledge to make their decisions.

This knowledge comes from a branch of biology called **conservation biology.** Conservation biology uses ecological information to understand how to rescue and restore damaged ecosystems. Conservation efforts are targeted in several areas. These include controlling pollution, limiting habitat destruction, and protecting species.

Controlling Pollution

Efforts to control pollution are aimed at reducing the amount of waste people produce. People produce large amounts of trash that must be placed somewhere. Local governments usually collect trash in areas called **landfills.** However, landfills are becoming full.

In modern landfills, garbage is deposited in shallow layers, then covered with six inches of soil. This process is carried out every day. This seals in the garbage and prevents the spread of insects, mice, rats, and other rodents. Rodents carry diseases.

Human Impact and Technology Chapter 19 601

Lesson at a Glance

Chapter 19 Lesson 2

Overview In this lesson, students learn about actions that help reduce the impact of human activities on ecosystems.

Objectives
- To define *conservation biology*
- To describe how people are reducing air and water pollution
- To discuss how people are protecting threatened and endangered habitats

Student Pages 601–606

Teacher's Resource Library
Workbook Activity 107
Alternative Workbook Activity 107
Lab Manual 93

Vocabulary

biodiversity	landscape ecology
conservation biology	recovery plan
	recycling
emission	reserve
landfill	

Write sentences on the board in which the vocabulary terms are used in context. Leave a blank where each vocabulary term should be. Have students complete the sentences using vocabulary terms from this lesson.

Background Information

Methane gas is an example of an emission. Large amounts of methane gas are released from landfills. In the United States, about 34 percent of all human-related methane gas emissions come from landfills. The gas is a by-product of the decomposition of solid waste. In some areas of the United States, the methane gas from landfills is captured and used to generate electricity. This helps reduce the amount of methane gas released into the atmosphere and replaces the need for fossil fuels to generate electricity.

---

1 Warm-Up Activity

Guide a discussion about recycling. Ask students: How many of you participate in recycling programs of any type? Does our school provide any opportunities for students to recycle? Do you recycle at home? What are some objects that can be recycled? *(Sample answers: aluminum cans, plastic water or soft-drink bottles, glass bottles, newspapers, cereal boxes)*

Bring in plastic containers that have the recycling number in the triangle on the bottom. These might include shampoo bottles, empty bottles of pain relievers, lotion bottles, and bottles of contact lens solution. The numbers range from 1 to 7. Check with your local recycling center beforehand to determine what types of plastics they will take; some centers will not take all seven numbers. Ask students: How can you tell whether a plastic item can be recycled? Have students examine the plastic containers you have displayed. Based on the information you got from the recycling center, tell students which numbers are accepted for recycling in their area. Ask students: Which of these containers can be recycled locally?

Human Impact and Technology 601

2 Teaching the Lesson

To help students organize the material presented in this lesson, have them make a two-column chart. Have them label the first column *Problem* and the second column *Solutions*. In the first column, have students list each of the problems discussed in the lesson. *(for example, landfills, emissions, deforestation, water pollution, ecosystems disrupted, threatened species, endangered species)* Have them fill in the second column with solutions for each problem.

3 Reinforce and Extend

CAREER CONNECTION

Encourage students to research the career of conservation biologist. A conservation biologist is someone who studies not only species in danger of extinction, but also the ecosystem in which organisms of that species live. Conservation biologists monitor global and regional species diversity and possible species extinction. A conservation biologist may work for a government agency or a nonprofit organization. Course study for conservation biology includes biology, ecology, botany, and environmental science. Have students report their research results to the class.

Link to

Chemistry. Have students read the Link to Chemistry feature. There are more than 10,000 different types of plastic. Plastic is made from petroleum or natural gas. Different types of plastic are made by adding other elements such as chlorine and oxygen. Review with students the meaning of the word *decompose*. Ask students: Why is it important to recycle plastics instead of throwing them away? *(Trash is taken to a landfill; plastics will fill up the landfill because they will not decompose.)*

Recycling
Using waste products to create new products

Emission
A chemical waste given off as gas

Link to ▶▶▶
Chemistry

Plastics are made from very large molecules called polymers. A polymer contains thousands of repeating units bonded together in a long chain. Most polymers have a backbone of carbon atoms with hydrogen atoms attached. Some polymers, such as polyvinylchloride (PVC), contain other atoms. Plastics are very stable and do not decompose in landfills. Be sure to recycle plastics instead of throwing them away.

Trash is often made of substances that do not naturally break down quickly. To reduce trash in landfills, people are **recycling**. Recycling is a process of using certain kinds of trash to make new products. Most trash made of paper, plastic, or metal can be recycled. Many local governments have public recycling programs. Does your community have a recycling program? If not, maybe you could help start one.

Another source of pollution is chemical waste. Chemical waste has many forms, including chemical runoff and smoke from factories. Vehicles give off carbon monoxide and carbon dioxide. Carbon monoxide is poisonous. Both waste gases contribute to the greenhouse effect. Waste gases released in the environment are called **emissions**. Many countries have laws that limit the amounts of emissions and chemical runoff that factories can produce. Companies that break the laws pay fines. They also must fix the problem quickly.

Many governments have emissions standards for vehicles. If a vehicle does not meet these standards, the vehicle cannot be driven. The owner must fix the vehicle before driving it.

Limiting Habitat Destruction

Efforts to reduce pollution also help reduce habitat destruction. Deforestation makes more space for people. It also provides materials for making paper. By recycling paper products, companies can make more paper products without cutting down trees. You can help by buying paper products that are made of recycled paper.

Organisms in water ecosystems threatened by chemical runoff and litter must move to clean water. These areas also supply clean water for people. Reducing the amount of water people use helps these ecosystems survive. You can help by not wasting water. Turn the faucet off while you brush your teeth. Use water only when you need it. Do not throw trash on the ground or in a stream. Use a trash can. Recycle trash.

602 Chapter 19 Human Impact and Technology

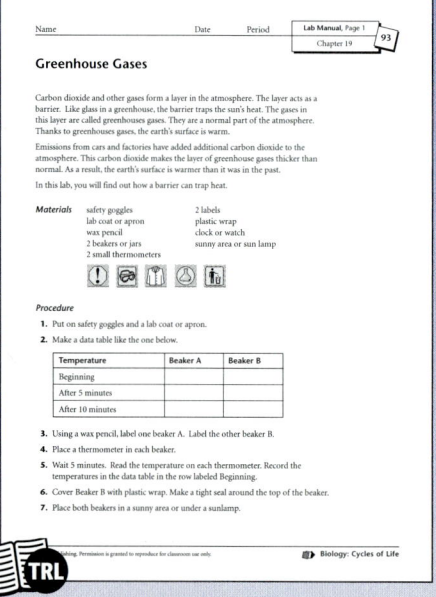

Lab Manual 93, pages 1–2

Reserve
A protected area that cannot be used for building or growth

Landscape ecology
Using ecological information to help balance human and environmental needs

Research and Write

Use both Internet and print resources to research and write a report about how paper is made. Trace the path from a tree to a sheet of paper. If you wish, make a poster showing the process. Label each step on your poster.

Creating Reserves

Ecosystems in danger get help in other ways. Governments create natural areas called **reserves.** These areas are left in their natural state. Their ecosystems are not disturbed. Many reserves have unique species. Companies and people are not allowed to use these areas for building or growth. Many of these areas are used as parks. Parks allow people to see plants and animals in their natural environments.

Most local governments require that builders be mindful of local ecosystems. Many governments do not allow companies to build in an area if it threatens a natural ecosystem. Builders often rely on **landscape ecology** to help them balance their needs with an ecosystem's needs.

Landscape ecology uses scientific knowledge to help develop land and design buildings without damaging natural ecosystems. This knowledge is also used to change existing buildings so they have less impact on their surroundings. Landscape ecology can also be used to identify and create more reserves.

Protecting Threatened Species

Protecting unique ecosystems helps protect the species that live in them. However, some threatened species do not live in protected areas. These organisms are being threatened in several ways. People hunt some species to use their skins for clothes or their bones for jewelry. Other threatened species are hunted for food, like many fish species. However, they are being hunted too much. As a result, populations cannot reproduce fast enough.

Governments help by creating hunting seasons. These seasons are the only times when certain animals can be hunted or fished. People who hunt out of season may pay fines. They may also go to jail.

At Home

Encourage students to start recycling at home. They can sit down with their families and discuss a recycling plan. If they are already recycling, have them decide if there are ways they can do more. Is everything that could be recycled going into a recycling bin? Have students go through their home, especially the kitchen and bathroom, and check for items that can be recycled.

Teacher Alert

Explain to students the difference between the terms *threatened species* and *endangered species*. An endangered species is a species that is in danger of extinction throughout all or part of its range. A threatened species is a species that is likely to become endangered in the foreseeable future.

In the Community

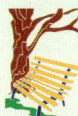

Have students research information about any reserves that are in their area. What ecosystems are preserved? What organisms live in the reserve? What is the history of the reserve? How was it determined to be a reserve? Have students share the results of their research with the class.

Research and Write

Have students use the library and the Internet to find out more about the process of making paper. Students may wish to do this research individually, in pairs, or in small groups. Suggest that students share their research with the class.

Science Myth

Have students read the Science Myth feature. Reinforce the idea that extinction is a natural process and that extinctions occurred long before humans populated Earth. However, the rate of extinction is increasing. According to calculations made based on the fossil record, before humans, extinction rates ranged from 10 to 100 species per year. Today, as many as 27,000 species are becoming extinct each year. Human activities that result in habitat destruction for other organisms contribute to the high rate of extinction today.

ELL/ESL STRATEGY

Language Objective: *To build on prior word knowledge*

Students learning English may be familiar with some of the vocabulary terms in this lesson. Students may have heard or used terms such as *recycling, reserve,* and *recovery* (recovery plan) outside of science class. Have students look up other definitions of these words in a dictionary. Have them write sentences using the words in both a science and a nonscience context.

LEARNING STYLES

Auditory/Verbal
The conservation of biodiversity is a leading issue in science today. Guide a class discussion about the importance of preserving and conserving habitats worldwide. Encourage students to use the vocabulary terms from the chapter as they express their views.

Recovery plan
A plan using scientific knowledge to help bring endangered species back from possible extinction

Biodiversity
The total of all life on the earth

Science Myth

Myth: Humans cause all extinctions.

Fact: Dinosaurs and other organisms became extinct long before humans existed. Extinctions are natural processes of evolution. They are often the result of a species not adapting to a changing environment.

Protecting Endangered Species

Some populations of species become so small that they are considered endangered. Endangered species have only a small number of individuals. These species are nearly extinct. Many governments have laws that do not allow anyone to harm these species.

The United Nations has created a list of endangered species. The United Nations is a world government body with representatives from many countries. Most countries have laws that protect the species on this list. People who break these laws are fined and may be put into jail.

Areas where endangered species live are often turned into reserves. Conservation biologists help the population of these species grow. Ecologists study the factors causing the greatest harm to these species. They also identify what these species need to better survive. Using this information, **recovery plans** are designed to restore endangered species and prevent extinction.

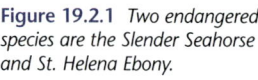

Figure 19.2.1 *Two endangered species are the Slender Seahorse and St. Helena Ebony.*

Protecting Biodiversity

Conservation biology's main goal is to help protect the **biodiversity** threatened by human growth. Biodiversity is all the different types and systems of life that exist, from organisms to ecosystems. People can protect the earth's biodiversity by changing or stopping destructive activities. People can use scientific knowledge to help improve their lives and the environment.

Biology in Your Life

Technology: Municipal Water Treatment

The water that comes out of your kitchen or bathroom faucet is from rivers, lakes, or reservoirs. A reservoir is a place where water is collected and stored for use. Many water sources have been exposed to pollutants. How is water made safe for drinking and cooking?

Municipal (city) water treatment plants purify the water supply to make it safe for human use. Water treatment often occurs in five steps: coarse filtration, sedimentation, sand filtration, aeration, and sterilization. First, water passes through a screen that removes large pieces of solids. This is coarse filtration. The water then flows into a settling tank. Medium-sized particles settle out. This step is sedimentation. Chemicals are added to cause the smallest particles to clump together and settle out. After settling, the water passes through a sand filter. This step, called sand filtration, removes any remaining particles.

The filtered water is then sprayed into the air. This is aeration. During this step, oxygen from the air is added to the water. Oxygen combines with certain pollutants and changes them into harmless substances. Finally, chlorine is added to the water for sterilization. Chlorine kills disease-causing bacteria. The water is now safe to use.

1. Why are chemicals needed to remove the smallest particles?
2. If water looks clean after filtration, why are aeration and sterilization needed?
3. Treatment processes can vary. What are the processes used for your household water?

Biology in Your Life

Have students read the Biology in Your Life feature. Some water treatment plants may use ozone to disinfect water. Ozone is effective in killing bacteria and viruses that may be present in water. Another alternative for disinfecting water is to pass it under lamps producing ultraviolet (UV) radiation. UV radiation is also effective at killing microorganisms in water. Ask students: Why it is important that drinking water be free of pollution and harmful microorganisms? *(because they can cause illness)*

Biology in Your Life Answers

1. Small particles will not settle out by themselves because they are too light. By adding chemicals that clump together the small particles, larger and heavier particles are formed. These can settle out by gravity. 2. Although the water looks clean after filtration, it still contains dissolved pollutants and bacteria that cannot be seen. The water is not safe for human use. 3. Answers will vary. Most treatment processes follow the same five steps.

SCIENCE JOURNAL

Have students write a paragraph about how their daily life would be affected if they did not have clean, safe water coming from a faucet in their homes. What if there was no treated water available? What would they have to do to get clean water? How would this affect their daily activities? Tell students that some areas of the world do not have water treatment and sewage systems in place and that people must face this situation on a daily basis.

PRONUNCIATION GUIDE

Use the pronunciation shown here to help students pronounce a difficult word in this lesson. Refer to the pronunciation key on the Chapter Planning Guide for the sounds of the symbols.

municipal (myù ni′sə pəl)

Lesson 2 Review Answers

1. biodiversity 2. conservation biology
3. recovery plan 4. emissions 5. landfill
6. recycling 7. Students may say that many kinds of trash do not break down quickly or that the increasing human population is generating more trash.
8. The amount of trash in landfills can be reduced by recycling as much as possible.
9. Students may mention creating reserves, reducing pollution, passing laws to protect species and to prevent overhunting and over-fishing, and the development of recovery plans.
10. Answers will vary. Three ways that a water ecosystem can be protected are by preventing chemical runoff, not littering, and conserving water.

Portfolio Assessment

Sample items include:
- Chart from Teaching the Lesson
- Paragraph from Science Journal
- Lesson 2 Review answers

Lesson 2 REVIEW

Word Bank
biodiversity
conservation biology
recovery plan

On a sheet of paper, write the word or words from the Word Bank that complete each sentence correctly.

1. All the types of life that exist is _____.
2. The science that uses ecological information to reduce damage to the environment is _____.
3. A _____ is designed to bring species back from possible extinction.

On a sheet of paper, write the word in Column B that best matches the phrase in Column A.

Column A

4. waste gases
5. where trash is collected
6. reduces the amount of trash

Column B

emissions

landfill

recycling

Critical Thinking

On a sheet of paper, answer the following questions. Use complete sentences.

7. Why are landfills becoming full?
8. How can the amount of trash in landfills be reduced?
9. Describe two ways governments are protecting species.
10. Describe three ways people can protect water, land, or species.

606 Chapter 19 Human Impact and Technology

Lesson 3: Science and Technology

Objectives

After reading this lesson, you should be able to
- define technology
- discuss how technology supports science, and vice versa
- compare the goals of science and technology
- give examples of science and technology

Geology
The study of the nonliving parts of the earth

Biogeology
The study of the interaction between living and nonliving parts of the environment

Engineering
The use of math and science to create methods and machines to help solve problems or make life better

Engineer
A person who works in engineering

Scientists try to understand the world. They want to make it a better place to live for humans and other organisms. To do this, scientists use historical and current information about the world. This information is based on scientific evidence gathered by conducting investigations. Scientific knowledge influences the design and understanding of investigations.

Science is made up of many different areas, including biology, **geology,** chemistry, ecology, genetics, and more. These different areas focus on different pieces of the world. For example, biology focuses on the living parts of the earth. Geology focuses on the nonliving parts of the earth. To understand the world better, scientists from these different areas bring their information together. As they combine their knowledge sometimes new areas of science are created, like **biogeology.** Biogeology is the study of the interaction between living and nonliving parts of the environment.

Engineering and Technology

An important area of science that uses knowledge from many other areas is **engineering.** Engineering is the use of math and science to create methods and machines to help solve problems or make life better. **Engineers** are people who work in engineering. Engineers use the resources of matter and energy to design solutions to problems.

The products of engineering designs are called **technology.** Technology is any device, machine, or method designed to solve a problem or improve a situation. People use technology constantly in their daily lives. You may have used technology to get to school. Did you use a bus, bicycle, car, or other vehicle? You probably use telephone technology. You use both computer and Internet technology to browse the Internet.

Technology helps people live. Doctors use special machines and methods to help people who are sick. **Medical technology** is designed to solve medical problems.

Lesson at a Glance

Chapter 19 Lesson 3

Overview In this lesson, students learn about the relationship between science and technology.

Objectives
- To define *technology*
- To discuss how technology supports science, and vice versa
- To compare the goals of science and technology
- To give examples of science and technology

Student Pages 607–613

Teacher's Resource Library

Workbook Activity 108–109

Alternative Workbook Activity 108–109

Lab Manual 94–95

Vocabulary

biogeology	medical technology
engineer	patent
engineering	scientific journal
geology	technology

Have students use each vocabulary term in a sentence. Encourage them to make the sentence include an example that helps to illustrate the meaning of the term.

Background Information

One of the newest areas of technology that is influencing science is nanotechnology. Nanotechnology involves working at the atomic or molecular level on a scale of a nanometer (10^{-9} m). In medicine, potential uses for nanotechnology include real-time imaging of body processes at the molecular and cellular level. It may also offer new drug delivery methods. Currently, the National Cancer Institute is researching the use of nanotechnology to deliver cancer-fighting drugs to targeted areas of the body. This could possibly reduce the side effects of the toxic drugs on the whole body.

Warm-Up Activity

Have students repeat the same activity, once without the use of technology and once with some form of technology. For example, give students three long division problems to solve (each with a decimal in the answer). Have them time themselves while solving the problems on their own. Then have them time themselves while using a calculator to solve the same problems. Have them compare the times and the answers for each part of the activity. Ask students: How did technology make the activity easier? Did technology allow you to complete the activity more quickly? How did technology affect the accuracy of results?

Teaching the Lesson

Have students make an outline of the material presented in the lesson. Students should use the main headings in the lesson as the headings for their outlines.

Reinforce and Extend

Technology and Society

Have students read the Technology and Society feature. One of the ultimate goals of using robotic surgery is to be able to perform surgery on the heart without opening the chest. In traditional open-heart surgery, the chest of the patient is opened and the sternum is split in two in order to reach the heart. With the use of robotic surgery, heart surgery could be performed by making only three small incisions in the chest, keeping it closed.

Technology
Any device, machine, or method designed to solve a human problem or question

Medical technology
Any technology designed to solve a medical problem

Engineers do performance testing on new technology. Performance testing determines how well or, how fast a system process, or product performs. For example, software engineers performance test the system design of new software. To test performance, engineers sometimes use models, computer simulations, or similar systems.

To solve a problem, someone has to understand the problem. Medical knowledge helps doctors and engineers understand the causes of medical problems. Once the causes are known, engineers can design technology to stop or limit the causes. Designing new medical technology often results in the discovery of new scientific knowledge.

The Relationship Between Science and Technology

The relationship between science and technology is important. They rely on and influence each other. One could not exist by itself. As scientists try to understand life better, they become limited by the tools they can use to explore it. When scientists cannot explore further with these tools, engineers then design new technology. This new technology drives more scientific exploration. This leads to new scientific discoveries. Sometimes, these discoveries open new fields of science and technology.

As science and technology develop, they follow some of the same steps. Recall from Chapter 1 that the scientific method begins by observation and questioning. Technology development uses the same steps. Engineers observe current technology. They also observe people's problems, needs, and desires. Then they ask how a new technology might solve a problem or meet a need or desire. Scientists design and create experiments to answer questions. Engineers imagine and design new technology to help answer these questions. Both scientists and engineers rely on success that can be repeated with experiments or inventions. Scientists and engineers must be creative and work from a good knowledge base.

Technology and Society

Many hospital operating rooms have surgical robots. They cannot operate without human guidance. However, robots offer many advantages. Surgeons located far away from their patients can perform surgery by remote control. Robotic surgery is precise. A robotic arm can make smaller cuts than those made by surgeons. Smaller cuts means a patient recovers faster, with less pain.

Patent
A government notice of ownership for a piece of technology

Scientific journal
A scientific magazine

In 1980, the United States Supreme Court ruled that Dr. Ananda Chakrabarty could patent a unique bacterium. This was an oil-decomposing bacterium he created using genetic engineering methods. Since then, thousands of genetically modified organisms have been patented.

The Goals of Technology and Science

Although science and technology work together, the goals of each are different. The main goal of engineers designing technology is to make people's lives better, solve their problems, and meet their needs and desires. Since people are the focus, people are often affected more directly by technology than science.

People usually accept new technology since it benefits them. Some technology is only necessary because people desire it, such as improved televisions. Sometimes technology is not free to the public. Businesses use technology to make money. Many businesses get **patents** for new technologies they develop. A patent is a government notice of ownership for a piece of technology.

The main goal of scientists is to understand the natural world. People are not always the focus of scientific questions. They are not always affected by scientific discovery. People do not always accept new scientific information.

Scientific information is usually shared freely with the public. Scientists publish their findings in magazines called **scientific journals.** They hold meetings to tell other people about their findings. Funds for science research come from federal government agencies, industry, and private foundations. These funds often influence the areas of scientific research and discovery.

Science and Technology Working Together

Sometimes technology can be harmful to the environment while helping people. For example, factories make products and pollution. Ecologists are beginning to understand the damage that technology causes. Engineers use this scientific knowledge to design better technology. These activities have created factories and machines that produce less waste and less pollution.

In this way, science and technology work together in a cycle. Solving technical problems often results in new scientific knowledge. New technologies often extend current scientific understanding and open new research areas.

Human Impact and Technology Chapter 19 **609**

TEACHER ALERT

Remind students that although advances in science and technology have benefited humans, some advances have harmed the environment and the quality of life of some plant and animal species. Some advances also lead to controversy concerning ethical issues. Cloning and stem cell research are two achievements that have received a high level of public attention in terms of ethical issues.

SCIENCE JOURNAL

Have students think of an example of a technology that has helped humans while harming the environment. Have them write a paragraph about the example and how they feel about its effects. Do they feel the use of the technology should be changed? How?

LEARNING STYLES

Interpersonal/Group Learning

Have students hold a mock science conference. They can use the opportunity to share the results of any research they have done during the course. Encourage students to appoint a conference manager to record the topic of each individual or group report. Have another student make an agenda for the conference that shows the order of the presentations, who is presenting, and the topic. Have students make a poster that shows the name of the conference and some of the "scientists" who will be presenting topics.

PRONUNCIATION GUIDE

Use the pronunciation shown here to help students pronounce a difficult word in this lesson. Refer to the pronunciation key on the Chapter Planning Guide for the sounds of the symbols.

Chakrabarty (Chaʹkrə bärʹtē)

Lesson 3 Review Answers

1. patent **2.** engineering **3.** technology **4.** C **5.** A **6.** B **7.** Answers will vary. One example is a factory or machine that produces a helpful product but harms the environment by producing pollutants. **8.** Engineers must understand the science of a problem before they can design technology to solve the problem. Scientists need new technology to further scientific exploration. **9.** It is any technology, such as a special machine or a medical procedure, that helps solve medical problems. **10.** The goals of both science and technology are to answer a particular question or solve a particular problem. For science, this goal is to understand the natural world. For technology, this goal is to find a way to better meet society's needs or desires.

Portfolio Assessment

Sample items include:
- Outline from Teaching the Lesson
- Paragraph from Science Journal
- Lesson 3 Review answers

Link to

Social Studies. Have students read the Link to Social Studies feature. An inventor may apply for a patent through the U. S. Patent and Trademark Office. There are different types of patents. A design patent protects the design of an item from being copied. Certain types of plants can even be patented if the plant variety has been newly developed by an individual or a company. Certain types of corn and tomato plants are patented. Students can find out more about the process of applying for a patent at the U.S. Patent and Trademark Office Web site for kids at www.uspto.gov/go/kids/.

ELL/ESL Strategy

Language Objective: *To practice writing skills*

Have students learning English write a paragraph that explains how science and technology work together.

610 Chapter 19

Lesson 3   R E V I E W

Word Bank
- engineering
- patent
- technology

Link to >>>
Social Studies

Some people think a patent gives its owner the right to use, make, or sell an invention. This is not true. A patent only excludes other people from using, making, or selling the invention. To patent an invention, it must be useful. It also must be something that no one has created before.

On a sheet of paper, write the word that completes each sentence correctly.

1. Inventors protect their ownership of a technology by getting a(n) _____.
2. An area of science that creates methods and machines to solve problems is _____.
3. A machine or method designed to solve a human problem is _____.

On a sheet of paper, write the letter of the answer that completes each sentence correctly.

4. All of the following are examples of technology except _____.
   - **A** bicycles
   - **B** the Internet
   - **C** rocks
   - **D** computers
5. The goal of _____ is to understand the natural world.
   - **A** science
   - **B** technology
   - **C** engineering
   - **D** engineers
6. Any device, machine, or method designed to help a situation is _____.
   - **A** science
   - **B** technology
   - **C** a patent
   - **D** a factory

Critical Thinking

Write the answers to the following questions. Use complete sentences.

7. Give an example of technology that is harmful.
8. How are science and technology related?
9. What is medical technology?
10. How are the main goals of science and technology alike? How are they different?

610   Chapter 19   Human Impact and Technology

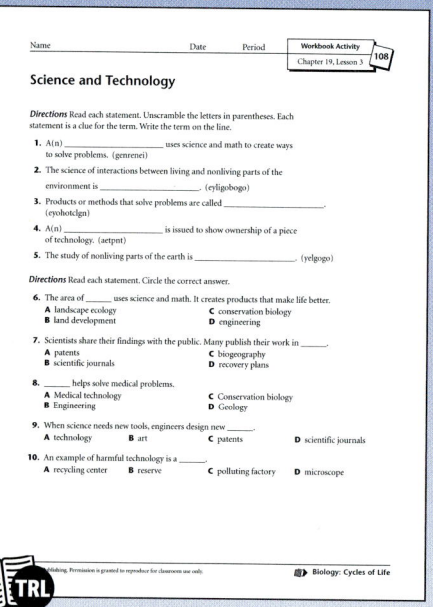

Workbook Activity 108

DISCOVERY INVESTIGATION 19

Materials
- 2 small aluminum pans, each with 6 holes punched in one end
- garden soil
- large aluminum pan
- turf to fit in a small aluminum pan
- watering can
- graduated cylinder or metric measuring cup
- water
- 2 or 3 books or wooden boards to raise end of pan

Conservation of Soil

One of the most important natural resources is soil. Soil provides nutrients to plants. Plants are the base of almost all food chains on the earth. In this investigation, you will compare the effect of running water on the soil of a bare slope and on a slope planted with grass. What causes soil erosion? What happens to a bare slope and a grassy slope during a rainstorm? How can soil be conserved? You will investigate these questions.

Procedure

1. Discuss the questions in the first paragraph with your group. Write a hypothesis to answer this question: How does planting a slope with grass affect the amount of soil erosion caused by a rainstorm? The hypothesis should be one you can test.

Human Impact and Technology   Chapter 19   611

SAFETY ALERT
- Be sure students wear safety goggles and a lab coat or apron.
- Remind students to avoid placing their hands near their mouth and eyes when working with plants and soil. They should wash their hands thoroughly with soap and water after handling soil.

Discovery Investigation 19

This investigation is less structured than the first investigation in this chapter. It offers students more challenge and requires more teacher facilitation. Encourage students to read the Discovery Investigation steps. Discuss questions they may have before beginning the investigation.

Objectives
- To make a model of soil erosion by running water
- To make a hypothesis about how planting a slope with grass affects the amount of soil erosion from a rainstorm
- To design an experiment to test a hypothesis

Skills
Observing, comparing and contrasting, making a model, measuring, recognizing cause and effect, hypothesizing

Background
The erosion of soil is a natural process. Whenever water runs over the surface of land, it removes soil from the upper areas and deposits it in lower areas. Slope, soil texture (proportions of sand, silt, and clay), and the amount of ground cover are factors that determine how much erosion will take place.

Time Frame
One class period

Procedure
- Have students work in groups of three or four.
- For this investigation, ordinary garden soil works better than potting soil from a bag.
- Before class, prepare the small aluminum pans. Punch six holes in each small pan, using scissors, an awl, or a compass point. Holes should be on the end near the bottom of the pan. Pans can be reused, but the soil should be returned to its source.

Continued on page 612

Human Impact and Technology **611**

Continued from page 612

- A piece of turf can be purchased in a garden center or dug up from a lawn area. Alternatively, grass seed can be planted directly into soil in the pans at least three weeks before the lab.
- To prevent introducing another variable, the amount of soil in both pans should be equal. The amount of water poured over both pans must be equal. Water must be poured at the same rate and from the same height over both pans.
- Students should measure both the volume of water they pour over the small pan (between 200 mL and 300 mL works well) and the volume of water that runs off into the large pan. Data tables should reflect this procedure.
- Ask students where the eroded soil ends up. Discuss the process of sedimentation and silting of rivers and streams.
- Discuss the root systems of plants and how roots hold soil in place.
- Ask students to discuss what problems they had in performing the experiment. Ask them which part(s) of the procedure they would change for the experiment to be more successful.

Results

Less water will drain into the large pan from the small pan that is planted with grass. The roots of the grass plants hold back the soil and prevent it from being washed away.

Answers to Analysis, Conclusions, and Explore Further begin on page 670 of this Teacher's Edition.

Assessment

You might include the following items from this investigation in student portfolios:

- Student's hypothesis, data table, and experimental procedure
- Answers to Analysis and Conclusions
- Student experimental design for Explore Further

2. Design an experiment to test your hypothesis. Make a table for the data you will collect. **Safety Alert: Be sure to include any Safety Alerts such as protecting your clothing and not touching your mouth or eyes with your hands.**
3. Have your hypothesis, Safety Alerts, experimental design, and data table approved by your teacher.
4. Carry out your experiment.

Cleanup/Disposal
When you are finished, clean up your materials and wash your hands with warm, soapy water.

Analysis
1. How much water ran off the bare slope? What did the water look like?
2. How much water ran off the slope with turf? What did the water look like?

Conclusions
1. Was your hypothesis supported by the results of your experiment?
2. How does this experiment model soil erosion?
3. How could a farmer practice soil conservation?

Explore Further
Design an experiment to determine how the steepness of a slope affects erosion. Carry out the experiment. Record your results.

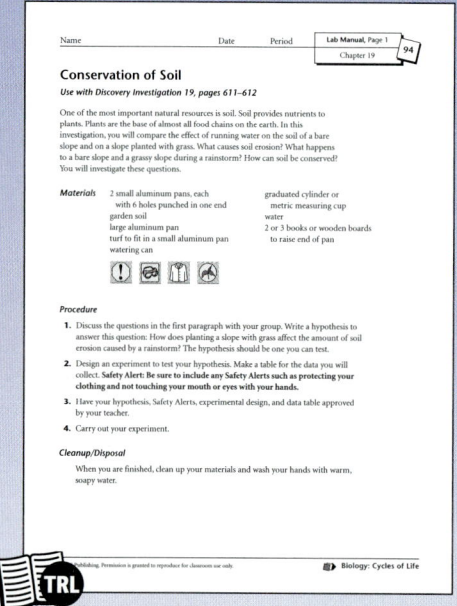

Lab Manual 94, pages 1–2

BIOLOGY IN THE WORLD

Restoring the Prairies

Prairies once covered most of the North American Midwest. Tall grasses and beautiful wildflowers grew on the flat and gently rolling land. Not many trees grew in this area. Prairies were once home to huge numbers of bison, prairie dogs, deer, and wolves. As settlers came to this area after the Civil War, they plowed the prairie for farmland. The grasses and wildflowers began to disappear. Cities grew where animals once roamed.

Today, only one percent of the prairie exists. Many species of prairie animals are endangered or extinct.

Natural fires once played an important role in prairie life. Fires caused by lightning burned the grasses and prevented trees from taking over. Although fire destroyed the upper parts of the grasses, it did not harm their roots. The ashes added nutrients to the soil. New grasses soon sprouted. However, the settlers put out natural fires to protect their homes. As a result, trees took over parts of the prairies.

Today, people are beginning to appreciate the value of prairie ecosystems. Many former prairie areas in the United States and Canada are being restored. To do this, workers cut down trees. Then they plant the seeds of native prairie plants. To keep the restored prairies healthy, controlled fires are set every few years. The fires kill trees and nonnative plants growing in the prairie. Without fire, dead plant material piles up and gradually chokes out new growth. Prairie plants need sunlight to grow. Shade from trees stops their growth.

Americans probably will never again see the "sea of grass" that the pioneers saw. However, people are preserving and restoring small prairie areas and their unique plants and animals.

1. Why did prairie plants disappear?
2. Why do you think prairie animals disappeared?
3. Why must restored prairies be set on fire? How often are the fires set?

ONLINE CONNECTION

One Web site students may find interesting after completing Chapter 19 is the United States Environmental Protection Agency at www.epa.gov. This site has information on environmental issues such as water pollution, air pollution, ozone, and acid rain, as well as their effects on human health. The site also provides information on how to reduce the negative impact of human activity on the environment.

Chapter 19 Summary

Have volunteers read aloud each summary item on page 614. Ask volunteers to explain the meaning of each item. Direct students' attention to the Vocabulary box on the bottom of page 614. Have them read and review each term and its definition.

Graphic Organizer

As students read Chapter 19, have them finish completing the chart on Graphic Organizer 19: Human Impact and Technology. Encourage students to read each lesson of the chapter and then have them fill in the portion of the chart that pertains to the lesson. When they have completed the chart, ask them to answer the questions.

Chapter 19 SUMMARY

- Like all organisms, humans have basic needs. The carrying capacity of human populations is unknown. The human population is growing rapidly.

- Expanding human populations harm ecosystems. They destroy the habitats of other organisms and pollute the environment.

- Chemical runoff is liquid pollution that damages ecosystems. It can result in eutrophication.

- Air pollution by waste gases causes acid rain. Buildup of carbon dioxide from emissions causes global warming. Pollution harms the ozone layer.

- Deforestation results when a forest is cut down. This results in habitat loss.

- Species may become threatened, endangered, or extinct if their habitats are destroyed and they cannot move away. Introduced species disrupt food chains and threaten native species.

- Conservation efforts to reduce pollution include recycling and preventing chemical runoff and emissions from cars and factories.

- Conservation efforts such as creating reserves limit habitat destruction and protect species. Recovery plans restore endangered species.

- Conservation biology protects biodiversity. People can help by changing some destructive activities.

- Engineers use math and science to create methods that solve problems or make life better.

- Patents provide ownership of technology. Some technologies create pollution. Solving technical problems often results in new scientific knowledge. New technologies open new areas of scientific research.

Vocabulary

acid rain, 594
biodiversity, 604
biogeology, 607
chemical runoff, 594
conservation biology, 601
deforestation, 596

emission, 602
engineer, 607
engineering, 607
eutrophication, 594
geology, 607
greenhouse effect, 594
introduced species, 596

land development, 595
landfill, 601
landscape ecology, 603
medical technology, 608
ozone, 595
patent, 609
pollution, 594

recovery plan, 604
recycling, 602
reserve, 603
scientific journal, 609
technology, 608

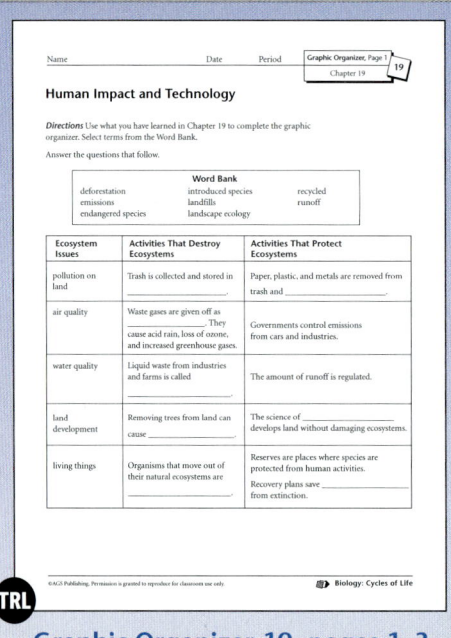

Graphic Organizer 19, pages 1–3

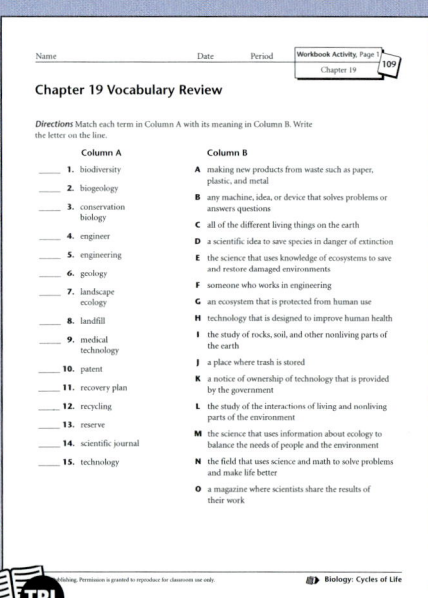

Workbook Activity 109, pages 1–2

Chapter 19 REVIEW

Word Bank
acid rain
biodiversity
chemical runoff
conservation biology
deforestation
emission
engineering
greenhouse effect
landfill
landscape ecology
medical technology
ozone
patent
recovery plan
recycling
reserve
technology

Vocabulary Review

On a sheet of paper, write the word or words from the Word Bank that complete each sentence correctly.

1. The warming of the earth by trapped solar energy is the _____.
2. Most trash is collected and stored in a(n) _____.
3. The science that uses ecological information to prevent or reduce damage to the environment is _____.
4. Water sources can be polluted by _____ that contains nitrogen compounds.
5. The process of cutting down trees to make room for buildings and farms is _____.
6. The _____ of plastics and paper can slow the growth of landfills.
7. A thin layer of _____ prevents most ultraviolet radiation from reaching the earth.
8. Precipitation that is polluted is known as _____.
9. Human activity is not allowed in a(n) _____ to protect the land and the organisms in it.
10. Any technology designed to help human medical problems is _____.
11. A waste gas produced by cars and factories is a(n) _____.
12. A government notice of ownership for a piece of technology is a(n) _____.
13. The total of all the living things on the earth is _____.
14. When people talk on a telephone or ride in a car, they are using _____.

Review continued on next page

Human Impact and Technology Chapter 19 615

Chapter 19 Review

Use the Chapter Review to prepare students for tests and to reteach content from the chapter.

Chapter 19 Mastery Test

The Teacher's Resource Library includes two forms of the Chapter 19 Mastery Test. Each test addresses the chapter Goals for Learning. An optional third page of additional critical-thinking items is included for each test. The difficulty level of the two forms is equivalent.

The Teacher's Resource Library includes the Final Mastery Test. This test is pictured on pages 668–669 of this Teacher's Edition. The Final Mastery Test assesses the major learning objectives of this text, with emphasis on Chapters 11–19.

Review Answers

Vocabulary Review

1. greenhouse effect 2. landfill
3. conservation biology 4. chemical runoff 5. deforestation 6. recycling
7. ozone 8. acid rain 9. reserve
10. medical technology 11. emission
12. patent 13. biodiversity 14. technology

Human Impact and Technology 615

Review Answers

15. engineering **16.** landscape ecology
17. recovery plan

Teacher Alert

In the Chapter Review, the Vocabulary Review activity includes a sample of the chapter's vocabulary terms. The activity will help determine students' understanding of key vocabulary terms and concepts presented in the chapter. Other vocabulary terms used in the chapter are listed below.

biogeology	land development
engineer	pollution
eutrophication	scientific journal
geology	
introduced species	

Concept Review

18. D **19.** B **20.** C **21.** B **22.** B

Chapter 19 REVIEW - continued

15. The use of math and science to create methods and machines to solve problems or make life better is _____.

16. A builder may use _____ to balance people's needs with the needs of the environment.

17. An idea that uses scientific knowledge to bring species back from possible extinction is a(n) _____.

Concept Review

On a sheet of paper, write the letter of the answer that completes each sentence correctly.

18. Conservation practices include _____.

   A reducing pollution

   B limiting habitat destruction

   C protecting species

   D all of the above

19. Science often advances when _____ design new technology.

   A eutrophication   **C** engineers

   B introduced species   **D** scientists

20. All of the following are good conservation practices except _____.

   A turning off the water when brushing your teeth

   B recycling glass jars and bottles

   C buying products with a lot of packaging

   D walking short distances instead of riding in a vehicle

Chapter 19 Mastery Test A, pages 1–3

21. Many governments have _____ standards for vehicles.

 A reserve **C** science

 B emissions **D** habitat

22. Eutrophication occurs in a pond when rapidly growing algae _____.

 A use up all the water in the pond

 B force other organisms out of the pond

 C use up all the nutrients in the pond

 D all of the above

Critical Thinking

On a sheet of paper, answer the following questions. Use complete sentences.

23. A scientist wants to study the structures of organelles in a cell. How can technology help the scientist?

24. Explain how introducing a new kind of fish into a lake might damage the lake's ecosystem.

25. How does the United Nations protect endangered species?

Research and Write

People do not agree on whether to reintroduce wolves into the environment. Research both sides of this issue. Organize your information. Choose one side of the argument. Pair up with classmates who have chosen the other side. Conduct a debate for the rest of the class.

Test-Taking Tip When choosing answers from a Word Bank, complete the items you know first. Then study the remaining answers to complete the items you are not sure about.

Human Impact and Technology Chapter 19 **617**

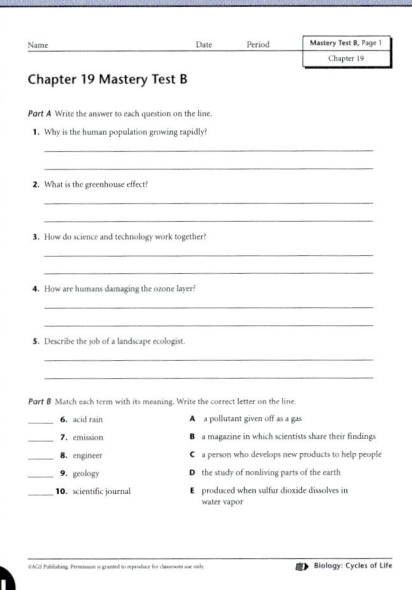

Chapter 19 Mastery Test B, pages 1–3

Critical Thinking

23. Sample answers include the development of more powerful microscopes, more precise tools for handling cells, new techniques for disrupting cells to make the organelles accessible, and new microscopes that allow scientists to examine cells under different conditions. **24.** The newly introduced fish might eat the native fish or eat the food that the native fish need to survive. They could also eat the native fishes' young. **25.** The United Nations maintains a list of current animals that need protection. This list makes people aware of endangered species that are protected by laws in most countries.

Research and Write

A Web site students may find helpful is www.nps.gov/olym/issues/isswolf.htm. It has a question-and-answer fact sheet about the reintroduction of wolves on the Olympic Peninsula in Washington. Another site that may be helpful is that of the International Wolf Center at www.wolf.org.

ALTERNATIVE ASSESSMENT

Alternative Assessment items correlate to the student Goals for Learning at the beginning of this chapter.

- Have students list different ways human activities have negatively impacted ecosystems. Have students pick one example from their list and explain it in detail.
- Have students explain one action they can take as individuals to reduce the impact of human activities on the environment and how that action will help.
- Have students list different conservation efforts and explain how those efforts can reduce damage.
- Have students list several different ways technology has affected their lives, both positively and negatively.

Human Impact and Technology **617**

Appendix A: The Periodic Table of Elements

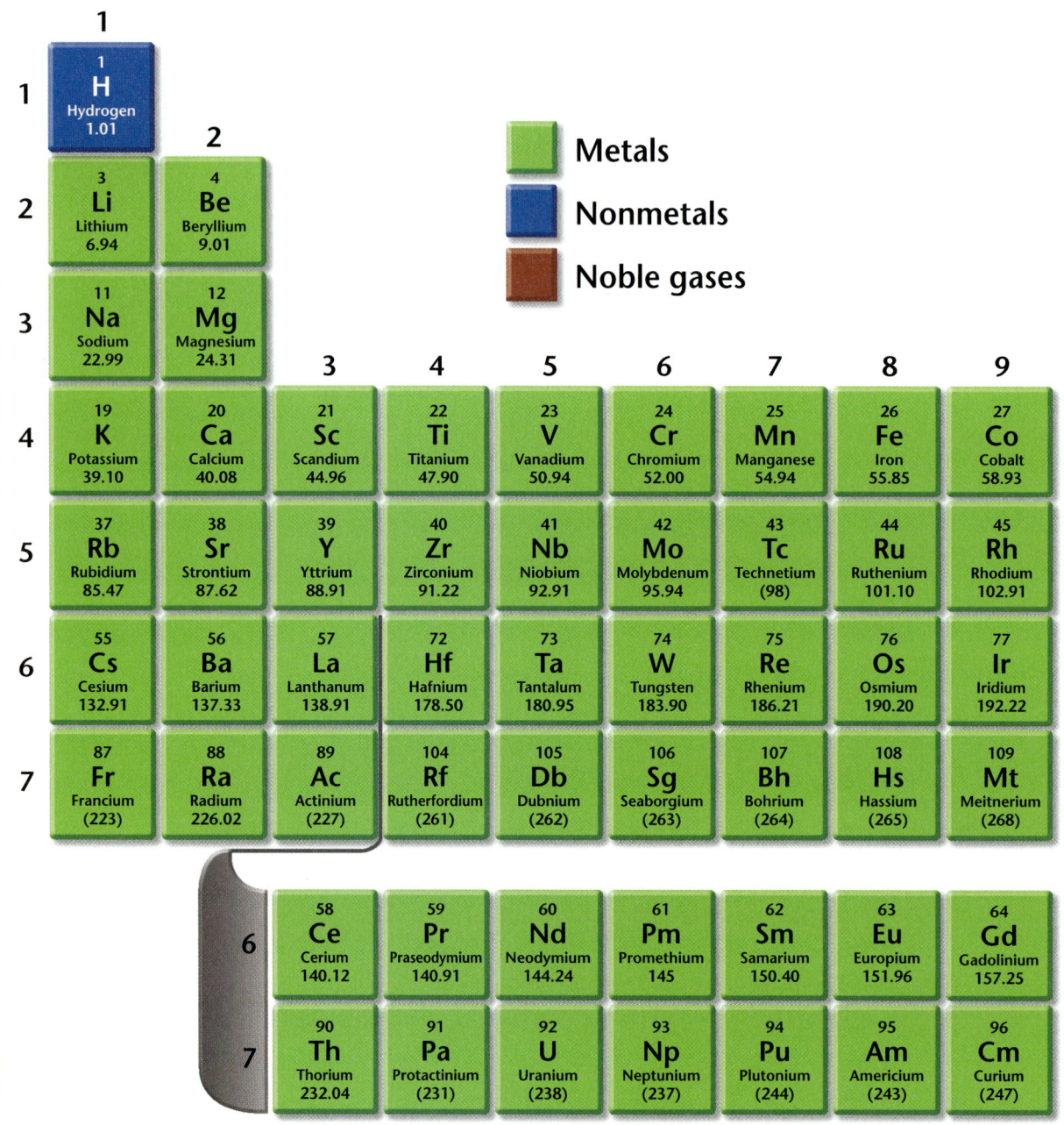

			13	14	15	16	17	18
								2 **He** Helium 4.00
			5 **B** Boron 10.81	6 **C** Carbon 12.01	7 **N** Nitrogen 14.01	8 **O** Oxygen 16.00	9 **F** Fluorine 19.00	10 **Ne** Neon 20.18
10	11	12	13 **Al** Aluminum 26.98	14 **Si** Silicon 28.09	15 **P** Phosphorus 30.97	16 **S** Sulfur 32.07	17 **Cl** Chlorine 35.45	18 **Ar** Argon 39.95
28 **Ni** Nickel 58.70	29 **Cu** Copper 63.55	30 **Zn** Zinc 65.39	31 **Ga** Gallium 69.72	32 **Ge** Germanium 72.59	33 **As** Arsenic 74.92	34 **Se** Selenium 78.96	35 **Br** Bromine 79.90	36 **Kr** Krypton 83.80
46 **Pd** Palladium 106.42	47 **Ag** Silver 107.90	48 **Cd** Cadmium 112.41	49 **In** Indium 114.82	50 **Sn** Tin 118.69	51 **Sb** Antimony 121.75	52 **Te** Tellurium 127.60	53 **I** Iodine 126.90	54 **Xe** Xenon 131.30
78 **Pt** Platinum 195.09	79 **Au** Gold 196.97	80 **Hg** Mercury 200.59	81 **Tl** Thallium 204.40	82 **Pb** Lead 207.20	83 **Bi** Bismuth 208.98	84 **Po** Polonium 209	85 **At** Astatine (210)	86 **Rn** Radon (222)
110 **Uun** Ununnilium (269)	111 **Uuu** Unununium (272)	112 **Uub** Ununbium (277)		114 **Uuq** Ununquadium (289)		116 **Uuh** Ununhexium (289)		

65 **Tb** Terbium 158.93	66 **Dy** Dysprosium 162.50	67 **Ho** Holmium 164.93	68 **Er** Erbium 167.26	69 **Tm** Thulium 168.93	70 **Yb** Ytterbium 173.04	71 **Lu** Lutetium 174.97
97 **Bk** Berkelium (247)	98 **Cf** Californium (249)	99 **Es** Einsteinium (254)	100 **Fm** Fermium (257)	101 **Md** Mendelevium (258)	102 **No** Nobelium (259)	103 **Lr** Lawrencium (260)

Note: *The atomic masses listed in the table reflect current measurements. The atomic masses listed in parentheses are those of the element's most stable or most common isotope.*

Appendix B: Body Systems

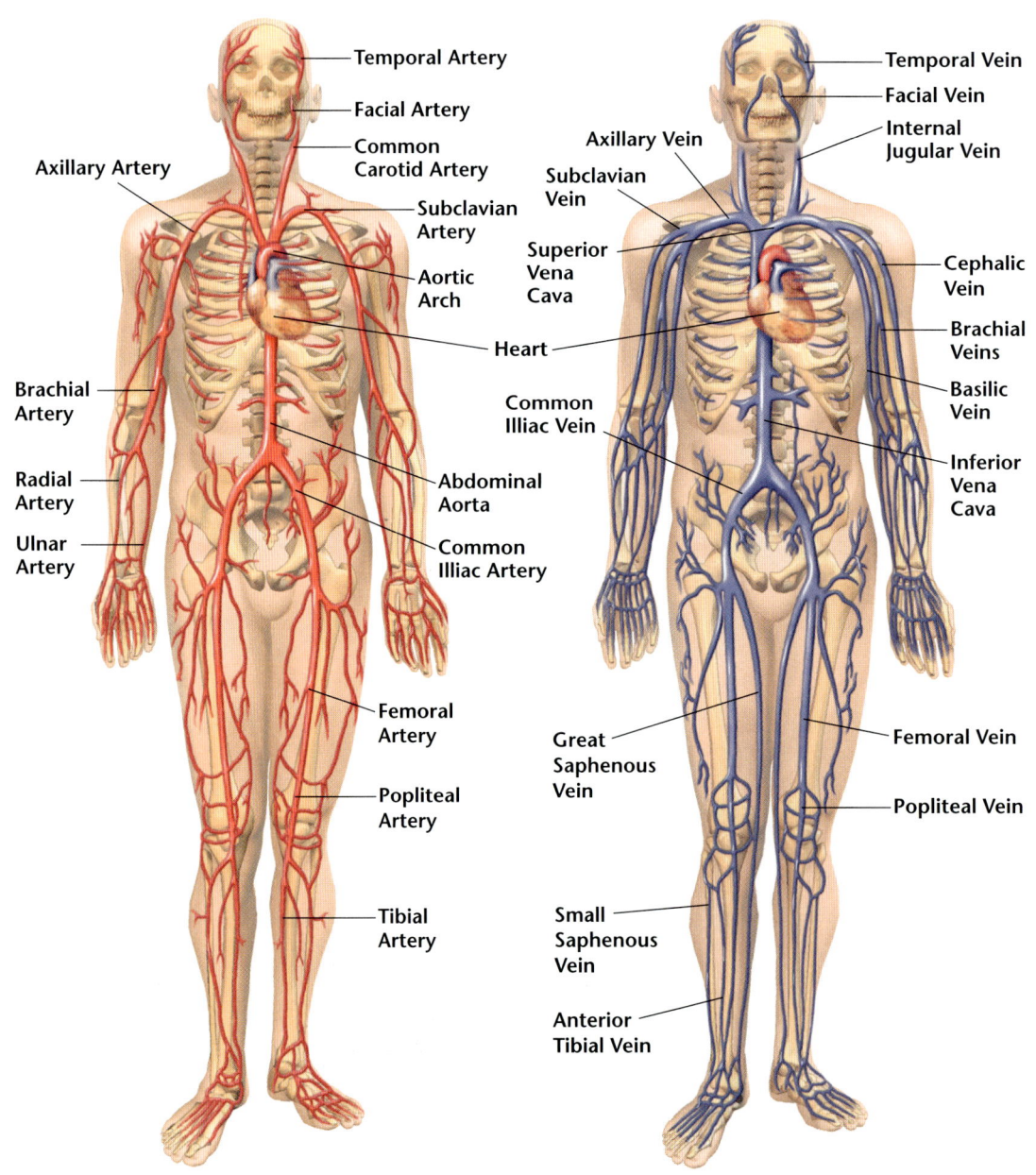

The Circulatory System

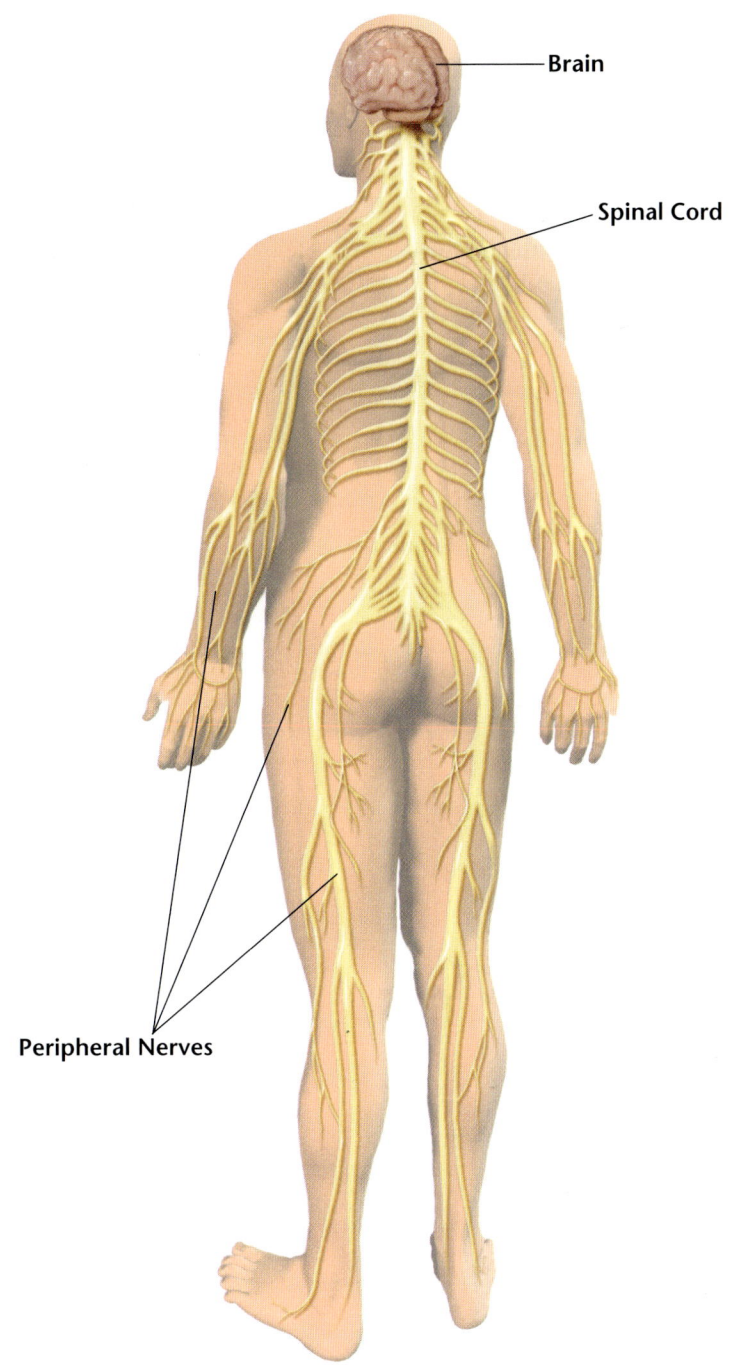

The Nervous System

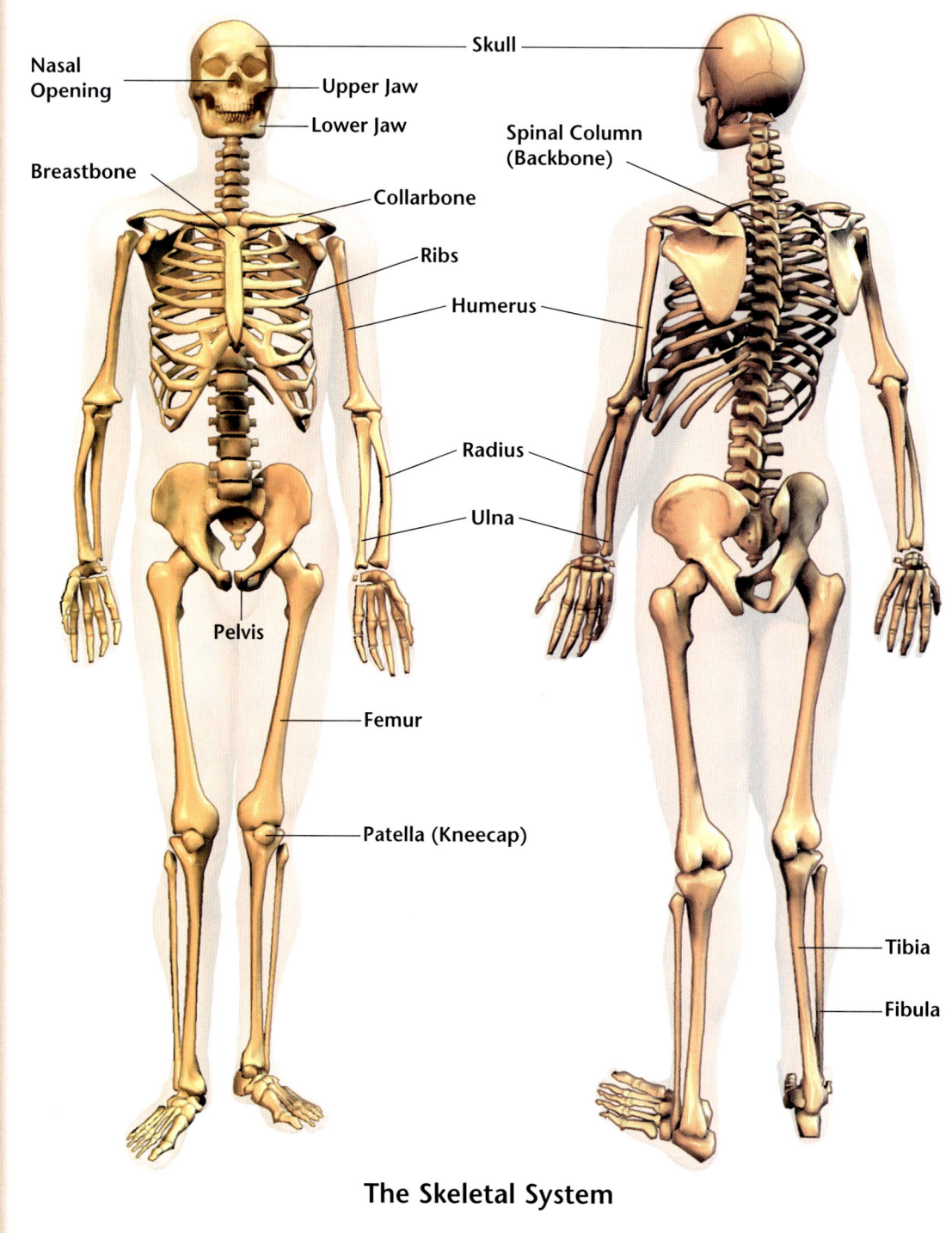

The Skeletal System

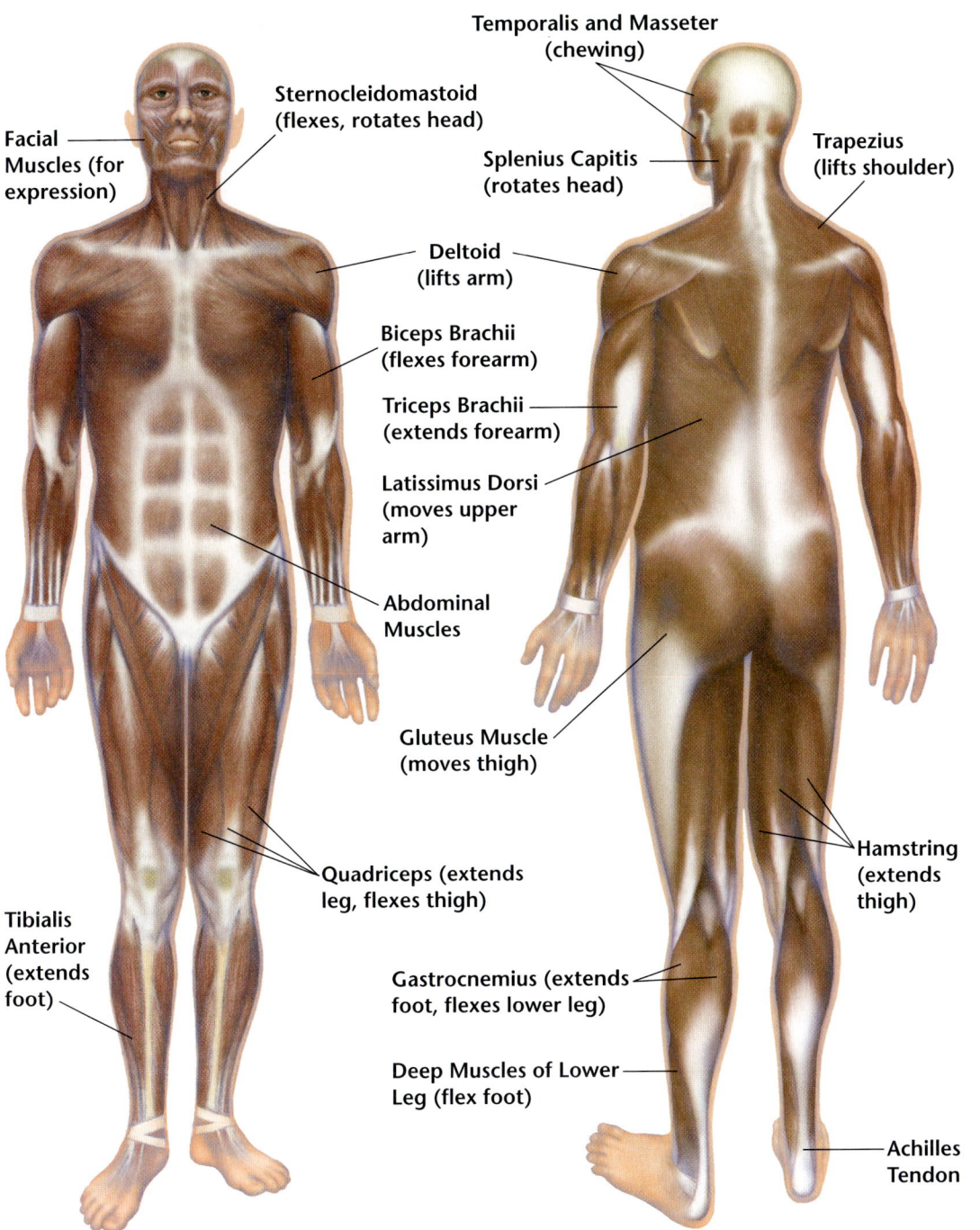

The Muscular System

Appendix C: Measurement Conversion Factors

Metric Measures

Length
1,000 meters (m) = 1 kilometer (km)
100 centimeters (cm) = 1 m
10 decimeters (dm) = 1 m
1,000 millimeters (mm) = 1 m
10 cm = 1 decimeter (dm)
10 mm = 1 cm

Area
100 square millimeters (mm^2) = 1 square centimeter (cm^2)
10,000 cm^2 = 1 square meter (m^2)
10,000 m^2 = 1 hectare (ha)

Volume
1,000 cubic meters (m^3) = 1 cubic centimeter (cm^3)
1,000 cubic centimeters (cm^3) = 1 liter (L)
1 cubic centimeter (cm^3) = 1 milliliter (mL)
100 cm^3 = 1 cubic decimeter (dm^3)
1,000,000 cm^3 = 1 cubic meter (m^3)

Capacity
1,000 milliliters (mL) = 1 liter (L)
1,000 L = 1 kiloliter (kL)

Mass
100 grams (g) = 1 centigram (cg)
1,000 kilograms (kg) = 1 metric ton (t)
1,000 grams (g) = 1 kg
1,000 milligrams (mg) = 1 g

Temperature Degrees Celsius (°C)
0°C = freezing point of water
37°C = normal body temperature
100°C = boiling point of water

Time
60 seconds (sec) = 1 minute (min)
60 min = 1 hour (hr)
24 hr = 1 day

Customary Measures

Length
12 inches (in.) = 1 foot (ft)
3 ft = 1 yard (yd)
36 in. = 1 yd
5,280 ft = 1 mile (mi)
1,760 yd = 1 mi
6,076 feet = 1 nautical mile

Area
144 square inches (sq in.) = 1 square foot (sq ft)
9 sq ft = 1 square yard (sq yd)
43,560 sq ft = 1 acre (A)

Volume
1,728 cubic inches (cu in.) = 1 cubic foot (cu ft)
27 cu ft = 1 cubic yard (cu yard)

Capacity
8 fluid ounces (fl oz) = 1 cup (c)
2 c = 1 pint (pt)
2 pt = 1 quart (qt)
4 qt = 1 gallon (gal)

Weight
16 ounces (oz) = 1 pound (lb)
2,000 lb = 1 ton (T)

Temperature Degrees Fahrenheit (°F)
32°F = freezing point of water
98.6°F = normal body temperature
212°F = boiling point of water

To change	To	Multiply by	To change	To	Multiply by
centimeters	inches	0.3937	meters	feet	3.2808
centimeters	feet	0.03281	meters	miles	0.0006214
cubic feet	cubic meters	0.0283	meters	yards	1.0936
cubic meters	cubic feet	35.3145	metric tons	tons (long)	0.9842
cubic meters	cubic yards	1.3079	metric tons	tons (short)	1.1023
cubic yards	cubic meters	0.7646	miles	kilometers	1.6093
feet	meters	0.3048	miles	feet	5,280
feet	miles (nautical)	0.0001645	miles (statute)	miles (nautical)	0.8684
feet	miles (statute)	0.0001894	miles/hour	feet/minute	88
feet/second	miles/hour	0.6818	millimeters	inches	0.0394
gallons (U.S.)	liters	3.7853	ounces avdp	grams	28.3495
grams	ounces avdp	0.0353	ounces	pounds	0.0625
grams	pounds	0.002205	pecks	liters	8.8096
hours	days	0.04167	pints (dry)	liters	0.5506
inches	millimeters	25.4000	pints (liquid)	liters	0.4732
inches	centimeters	2.5400	pounds advp	kilograms	0.4536
kilograms	pounds avdp	2.2046	pounds	ounces	16
kilometers	miles	0.6214	quarts (dry)	liters	1.1012
liters	gallons (U.S.)	0.2642	quarts (liquid)	liters	0.9463
liters	pecks	0.1135	square feet	square meters	0.0929
liters	pints (dry)	1.8162	square meters	square feet	10.7639
liters	pints (liquid)	2.1134	square meters	square yards	1.1960
liters	quarts (dry)	0.9081	square yards	square meters	0.8361
liters	quarts (liquid)	1.0567	yards	meters	0.9144

Appendix D: Geologic Time Scale

Era	Period	Epoch	Years Before the Present (approximate)		Forms of Life	Physical Events
			Began	Ended		
Cenozoic	Quaternary	Recent	11,000		Humans dominate	West Coast uplift continues in U.S.; Great Lakes form
		Pleistocene	2,000,000	11,000	Primitive humans appear; mammoths	Ice age
	Tertiary	Pliocene	7,000,000	2,000,000	Modern horse, camel, elephant develop	North America joined to South America
		Miocene	23,000,000	7,000,000	Grasses; grazing animals thrive	North America joined to Asia; Columbia Plateau
		Oligocene	38,000,000	23,000,000	Mammals progress; elephants in Africa	Himalayas start forming; Alps continue rising
		Eocene	53,000,000	38,000,000	Ancestors of modern horse, other mammals	Coal forming in western U.S.
		Paleocene	65,000,000	53,000,000	Many new mammals appear	Uplift in western U.S. continues; Alps rising
Mesozoic	Cretaceous		145,000,000	65,000,000	Dinosaurs die out; flowering plants	Uplift of Rockies and Colorado Plateau begins
	Jurassic		208,000,000	145,000,000	First birds appear; giant dinosaurs	Rise of Sierra Nevadas and Coast Ranges
	Triassic		245,000,000	208,000,000	First dinosaurs and mammals appear	Palisades of Hudson River form
Paleozoic	Permian		280,000,000	245,000,000	Trilobites die out	Ice age in South America; deserts in western U.S.
	Pennsylvanian		310,000,000	280,000,000	First reptiles, giant insects; ferns, conifers	Coal-forming swamps in North America and Europe
	Mississippian		345,000,000	310,000,000	Early insects	Limestone formation
	Devonian		395,000,000	345,000,000	First amphibians appear	Mountain building in New England
	Silurian		435,000,000	395,000,000	First land animals (spiders, scorpions)	Deserts in eastern U.S.
	Ordovician		500,000,000	435,000,000	First vertebrates (fish)	Half of North America submerged
	Cambrian		540,000,000	500,000,000	Trilobites, snails; seaweed	Extensive deposition of sediment in inland seas
Precambrian			4,600,000,000	540,000,000	First jellyfish, bacteria, algae	Great volcanic activity, lava flows, metamorphism of rocks; evolution of crust, mantle, core

Appendix E: World Map

Appendix F: Alternative Energy Sources

Fossil Fuels

We fly through the air in planes. We roll down highways in cars. On the coldest days, our homes are warm. Our stores are full of products to satisfy our needs and wants.

The power that runs our lives comes from fossil fuels. A fossil is the remains of ancient life. Fossil fuels formed from the remains of dead matter—animals and plants. Over millions of years, forests of plants died, fell, and became buried in the earth. Over time, the layers of ancient, dead matter changed. The carbon in the animals and plants turned into a material we now use as fuel. Fossil fuels include coal, oil, natural gas, and gasoline.

Fossil fuels power our lives and our society. In the United States, electricity comes mainly from power plants that burn coal. Industries use electricity to run machines. In our homes, we use electricity to power lightbulbs, TVs, and everything else electric. Heat and hot water for many homes come from natural gas or oil, or from fuels that come from oil.

Of course, cars and trucks run on gasoline, which is also made from oil. Powering our society with fossil fuels has made our lives more comfortable. Yet our need for fossil fuels has caused problems. Fossil fuels are a nonrenewable source of energy. That means that there is a limited supply of these fuels. At some point, fossil fuels will become scarce. Their cost will increase. And one day the supply of fossil fuels will run out. We need to find ways now to depend less and less on fossil fuels.

Fossil fuels cause pollution. The pollution comes from burning them. It is like the exhaust from a car. The pollution enters the air and causes disease. It harms the environment. One serious effect of burning fossil fuels is global warming. Carbon dioxide comes from the burning of fossil fuels. When a large amount of this gas enters the air, it warms the earth's climate. Scientists believe that warming of the climate will cause serious problems.

Renewable Energy

Many people believe that we should use renewable fuels as sources of energy. Renewable fuels never run out. They last forever.

What kinds of fuels last forever? The energy from the sun. The energy in the wind. The energy in oceans and rivers. We can use these forms of energy to power our lives. Then we will never run out of fuel. We will cut down on pollution and climate warming. Using renewable energy is not a dream for the future. It is happening right now—right here—today.

Energy from the Sun

As long as the sun keeps shining, the earth will get energy from sunlight. Energy from the sun is called solar energy. It is the energy in light. When you lie in the sun, your skin becomes hot. The heat comes from the energy in sunlight. Sunlight is a form of renewable energy we can use forever.

We use solar energy to make electricity. The electricity can power homes and businesses. Turning solar energy into electricity is called photovoltaics, or PV for short. Here's how PV works.

Flat solar panels are put near a building or on its roof. The panels face the direction that gets the most sunlight. The panels contain many PV cells. The cells are made from silicon—a material that absorbs light. When sunlight strikes the cells, some of the light energy is absorbed. The energy knocks some electrons loose in the silicon. The electrons begin to flow. The electron flow is controlled. An electric current is produced. Pieces of metal at the top and bottom of each cell make a path for electrons. The path leads the electric current away from the solar panel. The electric current flows through wires to a battery. The battery stores the electrical energy. The electrical wiring in a building is connected to the battery. All the electricity used in the building comes from the battery.

Today, PV use is 500 times greater than it was 20 years ago. And PV use is growing about 20 percent per year. Yet solar energy systems are still not perfect. PV cells do not absorb all the sunlight that strikes them, so some energy is lost. Solar energy systems also are not cheap. Still, every year, PV systems are improved. The cost of PV electricity has decreased. The amount of sunlight PV cells absorb has increased.

On a sunny day, every square meter of the earth receives 1,000 watts of energy from sunlight. Someday, when PV systems are able to use all this energy, our energy problems may be solved.

Energy from the Wind

Sunlight warms different parts of the earth differently. The North Pole gets little sunlight, so it is cold. Areas near the equator get lots of sunlight, so they are warm. The uneven warming of the earth by the sun creates the wind. As the earth turns, the wind moves, or blows. The blowing wind can be used to make electricity. This is wind energy. Because the earth's winds will blow forever, the wind is a renewable source of energy.

Wind energy is not new. Hundreds of years ago, windmills created energy. The wind turned the large fins on a windmill. As the fins spun around, they turned huge stones inside the mill. The stones ground grain into flour.

Modern windmills are tall, metal towers with spinning blades, called wind turbines. Each wind turbine has three main parts. It has blades that are turned by blowing wind. The turning blades are attached to a shaft that runs the length of the tower. The turning blades spin the shaft. The spinning shaft is connected to a generator.

Biology: Cycles of Life   Appendix F

A generator changes the energy from movement into electrical energy. It feeds the electricity into wires, which carry it to homes and factories.

Wind turbines are placed in areas where strong winds blow. A single house may have one small wind turbine near it to produce its electricity. The electricity produced by the wind turbine is stored in batteries. Many wind turbines may be linked together to produce electricity for an entire town. In these systems, the electricity moves from the generator to the electric company's wires. The wires carry the electricity to homes and businesses.

Studies show that 34 of the 50 United States have good wind conditions. These states could use wind to meet up to 20 percent of their electric power needs. Canada's wind conditions could produce up to 20 percent of its energy from wind, too. Alberta already produces a lot of energy from wind, and the amount is expected to increase.

Energy from Inside the Earth

Deep inside the earth, the rocks are burning hot. Beneath them it is even hotter. There, rocks melt into liquid. The earth's inner heat rises to the surface in some places. Today, people have developed ways to use this heat to create energy. Because the inside of the earth will always be very hot, this energy is renewable. It is called geothermal energy (*geo* means earth; *thermal* means heat).

Geothermal energy is used where hot water or steam from deep inside the earth moves near the surface. These areas are called "hot spots." At hot spots, we can use geothermal energy directly. Pumps raise the hot water, and pipes carry it to buildings. The water is used to heat the space in the buildings or to heat water.

Geothermal energy may also be used indirectly to make electricity. A power plant is built near a hot spot. Wells are drilled deep into the hot spot. The wells carry hot water or steam into the power plant. There, it is used to boil more water. The boiling water makes steam. The steam turns the blades of a turbine. This energy is carried to a generator, which turns it into electricity. The electricity moves through the electric company's wires to homes and factories.

Everywhere on the earth, several miles beneath the surface, there is hot material. Scientists are improving ways of tapping the earth's inner heat. Some day, this renewable, pollution-free source of energy may be available everywhere.

Energy from Trash

We can use the leftover products that come from plants to make electricity. For example, we can use the stalks from corn or wheat to make fuel. Many leftover products from crops and lumber can fuel power plants. Because this fuel comes from living plants, it is called bioenergy (*bio* means life or living). The plant waste itself is called biomass.

People have used bioenergy for thousands of years. Burning wood in a fireplace is a form of bioenergy. That's because wood comes from trees. Bioenergy is renewable, because people will always grow crops. There will always be crop waste we can burn as fuel.

Some power plants burn biomass to heat water. The steam from the boiling water turns turbines. The turbines create electricity. In other power plants, biomass is changed into a gas. The gas is used as fuel to boil water, which turns the turbine.

Biomass can also be made into a fuel for cars and trucks. Scientists use a special process to turn biomass into fuels, such as ethanol. Car makers are designing cars that can run on these fuels. Cars that use these fuels produce far less pollution than cars that run on gas.

Bioenergy can help solve our garbage problem. Many cities are having trouble finding places to dump all their trash. There would be fewer garbage dumps if we burned some trash to make electricity.

Bioenergy is a renewable energy. But it is not a perfect solution to our energy problems. Burning biomass creates air pollution.

Energy from the Ocean

Have you ever been knocked over by a small wave while wading in the ocean? If so, you know how much power ocean water has. The motion of ocean waves can be a source of energy. So can the rise and fall of ocean tides. There are several systems that use the energy in ocean waves and tides. All of them are very new and still being developed.

In one system, ocean waves enter a funnel. The water flows into a reservoir, an area behind a dam where water is stored. When the dam opens, water flows out of the reservoir. This powers a turbine, which creates electricity. Another system uses the waves' motion to operate water pumps, which run an electric generator. There is also a system that uses the rise and fall of ocean waves. The waves compress air in a container. During high tide, large amounts of ocean water enter the container. The air in the container is under great pressure. When the high-pressure air in the container is released, it drives a turbine. This creates electricity.

Energy can also come from the rise and fall of ocean tides. A dam is built across a tidal basin. This is an area where land surrounds the sea on three sides. At high tide, ocean water is allowed to flow through the dam. The water flow turns turbines, which generate electricity. There is one serious problem with tidal energy. It damages the environment of the tidal basin and can harm animals that live there.

The oceans also contain a great deal of thermal (heat) energy. The sun heats the surface of the oceans more than it heats deep ocean water. In one day, ocean surfaces absorb solar energy equal to 250 billion barrels of oil! Deep ocean water, which gets no sunlight, is much colder than the surface.

Scientists are developing ways to use this temperature difference to create energy. The systems they are currently designing are complicated and expensive.

Energy from Rivers and Dams

Dams built across rivers also produce electricity. When the dam is open, the flowing water turns turbines, which make electricity. This is called hydroelectric power (*hydro* means water). The United States gets 7 percent of its electricity from hydroelectric power. Canada gets up to 60 percent of its electricity from hydroelectric plants built across its many rivers.

Hydroelectric power is a nonpolluting and renewable form of energy—in a way. There will always be fresh water. However, more and more people are taking water from rivers for different uses. These uses include drinking, watering crops, and supplying industry. Some rivers are becoming smaller and weaker because of the water taken from them. Also, in many places dams built across rivers hurt the environment. The land behind the dam is "drowned." Once the dam is built, fish may not be able swim up or down the river. In northwestern states, salmon have completely disappeared from many rivers that have dams.

Energy from Hydrogen Fuel

Hydrogen is a gas that is abundant everywhere on the earth. It's in the air. It is a part of water. Because there is so much hydrogen, it is a renewable energy source. And hydrogen can produce energy without any pollution.

The most likely source of hydrogen fuel is water. Water is made up of hydrogen and oxygen. A special process separates these elements in water. The process produces oxygen gas and hydrogen gas. The hydrogen gas is changed into a liquid or solid. This hydrogen fuel is used to produce energy in a fuel cell.

Look at the diagram on page 377. Hydrogen fuel (H_2) is fed into one part of the fuel cell. It is then stripped of its electrons. The free electrons create an electric current (e). The electric current powers a lightbulb or whatever is connected to the fuel cell.

Meanwhile, oxygen (O_2) from the air enters another part of the fuel cell. The stripped hydrogen (H+) bonds with the oxygen, forming water (H_2O). So a car powered by a fuel cell has pure water leaving its tailpipe. There is no exhaust to pollute the air.

When a regular battery's power is used up,

the battery dies. A fuel cell never runs down as long as it gets hydrogen fuel.

A single fuel cell produces little electricity. To make more electricity, fuel cells come in "stacks" of many fuel cells packaged together. Stacked fuel cells are used to power cars and buses. Soon, they may provide electric power to homes and factories.

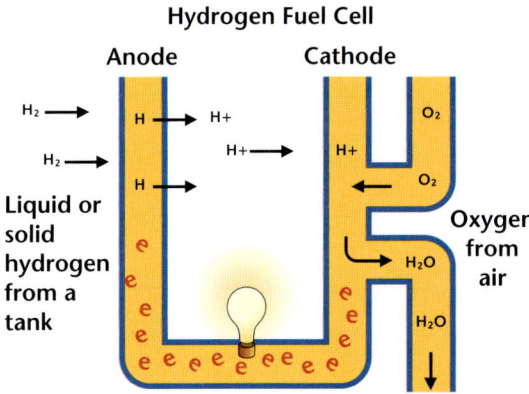

Hydrogen fuel shows great promise, but it still has problems. First, hydrogen fuel is difficult to store and distribute. Today's gas stations would have to be changed into hydrogen-fuel stations. Homes and factories would need safe ways to store solid hydrogen.

Second, producing hydrogen fuel by separating water is expensive. It is cheaper to make hydrogen fuel from oil. But that would create pollution and use nonrenewable resources. Scientists continue to look for solutions to these problems.

Energy from Atoms

Our sun gets its energy—its heat and light—from fusion. Fusion is the joining together of parts of atoms. Fusion produces enormous amounts of energy. But conditions like those on the sun are needed for fusion to occur. Fusion requires incredibly high temperatures.

In the next few decades, scientists may find ways to fuse atoms at lower temperatures. When this happens, we may be able to use fusion for energy. Fusion is a renewable form of energy because it uses hydrogen atoms. It also produces no pollution. And it produces no dangerous radiation. Using fusion to produce power is a long way off. But if the technology can be developed, fusion could provide us with renewable, clean energy.

Today's nuclear power plants produce energy by splitting atoms. This creates no air pollution. But nuclear energy has other problems. Nuclear energy is fueled by a substance we get from mines called uranium. There is only a limited amount of uranium in the earth. So it is not renewable. And uranium produces dangerous radiation, which can harm or kill living things if it escapes the power plant. Used uranium must be thrown out, even though it is radioactive and dangerous. In 1999, the United States produced nearly 41 tons of radioactive waste from nuclear power plants. However, less uranium is being mined. No new nuclear power plants have been built. The amount of energy produced from nuclear power is expected to fall. People are turning toward less harmful, renewable energy sources: the sun, wind, underground heat, biomass, water, and hydrogen fuel.

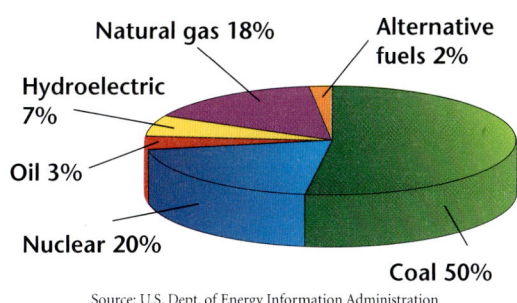

Appendix G: Plant Kingdom

Spore Plants

Group	Description	Examples
Bryophyte *Division**	Nonvascular (no tubes for carrying materials in plant); live in moist places	liverwort, hornwort, moss
Club Moss *Division*	Spores in cones at end of stems; simple leaves	club moss
Horsetail *Division*	Spores in cones at end of stems; hollow, jointed stem	horsetail
Fern *Division*	Spores in sori; fronds	fern

Seed Plants

Group	Description	Examples
Palmlike *Division*	Naked seeds in cones; gymnosperm (nonflowering seed plant); male and female cones on different trees; palm-shaped leaves	cycad, sago palm
Ginkgo *Division*	Naked seeds in conelike structures; gymnosperm; male and female cones on different trees; fan-shaped leaves; only one known species	ginkgo
Conifer *Division*	Naked seeds in cones; gymnosperm; male and female cones; most are evergreen; needlelike or scalelike leaves	pine, fir, spruce, yew
Angiosperm *Division*	Produce flowers; seeds protected by ovary that ripens into a fruit; organs of both sexes often in same flower	
Monocot *Class*	One cotyledon; parallel veins; flower parts in multiples of three	grass, palm, corn, lily
Dicot *Class*	Two cotyledons; branching veins; flower parts in multiples of four or five	cactus, maple, rose, daisy

*For plants, biologists use *Division* instead of *Phylum*.

Glossary

A

Absorb (ab sôrb´) to retain (p. 230)

Acetic acid (ə sē´ tik as´ id) a sharp-smelling, colorless acid formed from the breakdown of pyruvic acid (p. 201)

Acetyl CoA (ə sē´ tl kō ā) a compound made from the bonding of coenzyme A and acetic acid (p. 201)

Acid (as´ id) a substance that can donate a proton (H^+) or accept an electron pair (p. 59)

Acid rain (as´ id rān) rain that is caused by pollution and is harmful to organisms because it is acidic (p. 594)

Acquired trait (ə kwir´ d trāt) a trait that comes from an organism's behavior (p. 389)

Actin (ak´ tən) a ball-shaped protein used to make microfilaments (p. 154)

Activation energy (acti va´ tion en´ ər jè) the amount of energy needed to start a chemical reaction (p. 184)

Active site (ak´ tiv sīt) the area on an enzyme where the substrate fits in shape and chemistry (p. 185)

Active transport (ak´ tiv trans pôrt´) the movement of molecules across a membrane when the movement requires energy (p. 138)

Adapt (ə dapt´) to change genetically over generations to become more suited to the environment (p. 390)

Adaptation (ad ap tā´ shən) an adjustment to environmental conditions (p. 10)

Adenine (ad´ n ēn) a nitrogen-containing compound found in ATP, DNA, and RNA (p. 170)

Adolescence (ad l es´ ns) the teenage years of a human (p. 266)

ADP (ā dē pē) adenosine diphosphate; a molecule converted to ATP by the addition of a phosphate (p. 174)

Aerobic (âr ō´ biks) requiring oxygen (p. 208)

Aggressive behavior (ə gres´ iv bi hā´ vyər) a behavior that warns predators not to approach (p. 514)

Agonistic interaction (ag nos´ tik in ter ak´ shən) a type of social behavior in which individuals have contests and show aggressive behavior (p. 521)

Algae (al´ jē) a protist that makes its own food and usually lives in water (p. 464)

Allele (ə lēl´) one form of a gene (p. 279)

Allopatric speciation (a lə pa´ trik spē shē ā´ shən) when similar organisms do not interbreed due to physical barriers (p. 431)

Alternation of generations (ol tər nā´ shən ov jen ə ra´ shən) a life cycle of mosses, algae, and some protists that alternates between a haploid phase and a diploid phase (p. 473)

Alveolus (al vē´ ə ləs) a tiny air sac at the end of each bronchiole that holds air (plural is alveoli) (p. 349)

Amino acid (ə mē´ no as´ id) a molecule that makes up proteins (p. 72)

Ammonium (ə mō´ nē əm) a nitrogen-containing compound used to cycle nitrogen into an ecosystem (p. 575)

Amniotic egg (am nē ot´ ik eg) the egg of a vertebrate that lives on land (p. 491)

Amoeba (ə mē´ ba) a protozoan that moves by pushing out parts of its cell (p. 465)

Amphibian (am fib´ ē ən) a vertebrate that lives at first in water and then on land (p. 398)

Anaerobic (an ə rō´ bik) not requiring oxygen (p. 208)

Analysis (ə nal´ ə sis) making sense of the results of an experiment; also the fifth step of the scientific method (p. 20)

Anatomy (ə nat´ ə mē) the structure of an organism (p. 394)

Angiosperm (an´ j ə spėrm) a flowering seed plant (p. 472)

Anticodon (an ti kō´ don) a three-base sequence complementary to the codon, found in tRNA (p. 318)

Antidiuretic hormone (ADH) (an ti dī yu re´ tik hôr´ mōn) a hormone that controls the absorption of water back into the body (p. 360)

Antigen (an´ tə jən) a foreign molecule that activates the immune system (p. 334)

Aorta (ā ôr´ tə) a large vessel through which the left ventricle sends blood to the body (p. 353)

Aphotic zone (ā fō´ tik zōn) an area in aquatic biomes that does not receive solar energy (p. 582)

Aquatic (ə kwat´ ik) growing or living in water (p. 568)

Arachnid (a rak´ nid) a class of arthropods that includes spiders, scorpions, mites, and ticks (p. 484)

Archaea (är kē´ ə) the domain of prokaryotic organisms that are not bacteria (p. 436)

a	hat	e	let	ī	ice	ȯ	order	u̇	put	sh	she	ə {	a in about
ā	age	ē	equal	o	hot	oi	oil	ü	rule	th	thin		e in taken
ä	far	ėr	term	ō	open	ou	out	ch	child	ᴛH	then		i in pencil
â	care	i	it	ȯ	saw	u	cup	ng	long	zh	measure		o in lemon
													u in circus

Artery (är´ tər ē) a blood vessel that carries blood away from the heart (plural is arteries) (p. 353)

Arthropod (är´ thrə pod) a member of the largest group of invertebrates; this group includes insects (p. 484)

Artificial selection (är tə fish´ əl si lek´ shən) a process of changing a species by people who select the breeding of certain traits (p. 410)

Asexual reproduction (ā sek´ shü əl rē prə duk´ shən) reproduction that involves one parent and no egg or sperm (p. 431)

Asthma (az´ mə) a condition that narrows or blocks the airways and makes breathing difficult (p. 350)

Atherosclerosis (ath ər ō sklə rō´ sis) a disease that harms the arteries by narrowing them (p. 355)

Atmosphere (at´ mə sfir) the air that surrounds the earth (p. 573)

Atom (at´ əm) the basic unit of matter (p. 32)

Atomic mass (ə tom´ ik mas) the average mass of the atom of an element (p. 40)

Atomic number (ə tom´ ik num´ bər) the number of protons in the nucleus of an atom (p. 39)

ATP (ā tē pē) adenosine triphosphate; a molecule in all living cells that acts as fuel (p. 105)

ATP synthase (ā tē pē sin´ thās) an enzyme at the end of the electron transport chain that helps drive the bonding of a phosphate to ADP to create ATP (p. 203)

Atrium (ā´ trē əm) a heart chamber that receives blood returning to the heart (plural is atria) (p. 353)

Auditory nerve (o´ də tôr ē nėrv) a bundle of nerves that carry impulses from the ear to the brain (p. 369)

Autosome (o´ tə sōm) a chromosome other than a sex chromosome (p. 292)

Autotroph (o´ tə trof) a self-nourishing organism that makes its own food (p. 224)

Axon (ak´ son) a long extension of the nerve cell that carries information to other cells (p. 364)

B

Bacteria (bak tir´ ē ə) the simplest single cells that carry out all basic life activities (p. 33)

Bacteriophage (bak tir´ ē ə) a virus that infects bacteria (p. 310)

Base (bās) a substance that can accept a proton (H$^+$), release OH$^-$, or donate an electron pair; an alkali (p. 59)

Behavior (bi hā´ vyər) the way an organism acts (p. 506)

Behavioral biology (bi hā´ vyər əl bi ol´ ə jē) the study of the behavior of living things (p. 506)

Benign tumor (bi nin´ tü´ mər) a tumor that is only in the area where it began (p. 252)

Benthic zone (ben´ thik zōn) the floor of an aquatic biome (p. 582)

Bilateral symmetry (bi lat´ ər əl sim´ ə trē) a body made of left and right halves that are the same (p. 483)

Bilayer (bī´ lā ər) two layers (p. 134)

Bile (bīl) a substance made in the liver that breaks down fats (p. 345)

Binary compound (bi´ nər ē kom´ pound) a compound that contains two elements (p. 45)

Binary fission (bi´ nər ē fish´ ən) reproduction in which a bacterial cell divides into two cells that look the same as the original cell (p. 117)

Biochemistry (bi´ ō kem´ ə strē) chemistry that deals with the chemical compounds and processes in organisms (p. 429)

Biodiversity (bi ō di vėr´ sə tē) the total of all life on the earth (p. 604)

Biogeography (bī ō jē og´ rə fē) the study of the geographical distribution of fossils and living organisms (p. 393)

Biogeology (bī ō jē ol´ ə jē) the study of the interaction between living and nonliving parts of the environment (p. 607)

Biological evolution (bī ə loj´ ə kəl ev ə lü´ shən) the change in the gene pool of a population over time (p. 388)

Biological species concept (bī ə loj´ ə kəl spē´ shēz kon´ sept) a principle that defines a species as populations that can interbreed and produce offspring (p. 430)

Biologist (bi ol´ o jist) a person who studies life (p. 2)

Biology (bi ol´ ə jē) the study of life (p. 2)

Biome (bī´ ōm) a large area of the earth that has similar ecosystems and weather (p. 537)

Biosphere (bī´ ə sfir) the total area of the earth that contains and supports life (p. 536)

Biotechnologist (bī o tek nol´ ə jist) a scientist who studies biotechnology (p. 325)

Biotechnology (bī ō tek nol´ ə jē) the use of organisms and their genetics in industry to make products (p. 325)

Bipedal locomotion (bi ped´ əl lō kə mō´ shən) the ability to walk upright on two feet (p. 497)

Blastula (blas´ chə lə) a hollow ball of cells formed by cell divisions of a zygote (p. 479)

B lymphocyte (bē lim´ fə sit) a white blood cell that produces antibodies (p. 333)

Boom-bust cycle (büm bust sī´ kəl) a period in which the densities of populations increase or decrease at the same time (p. 543)

Brain stem (brān stem) the part of the brain that controls automatic activities and connects the brain and the spinal cord (p. 362)

Bronchiole (brong´ kē əl) a tube that branches off the bronchus (p. 349)

Bronchitis (brong ki´ tis) an inflammation of the bronchial tubes (p. 350)

Bronchus (brong′ kəs) a tube that connects the trachea to a lung (plural is bronchi) (p. 349)
Buffer (buf′ ər) a solution that can receive moderate amounts of either acid or base without significant change in its pH (p. 61)

C

Calorie (kal′ ər ē) a unit used to measure the amount of energy food contains (p. 171)
Calvin-Benson cycle (kal′ vən ben′ sun sī′ kəl) a process in photosynthesis that produces sugar (p. 233)
CAM plant (kam plant) a plant that takes in CO_2 only during the night (p. 239)
Camouflage (kam′ ə fläzh) the colors or patterns on animals that help them hide in their surroundings (p. 550)
Cancer (kan′ sər) a condition in which a cell grows without control and divides too much (p. 252)
Canopy (kan′ ə pe) the tops of the forest trees (p. 551)
Capillary (kap′ ə ler ē) a blood vessel through which oxygen and food molecules pass to body cells (p. 348)
Capsid (kap′ səd) the protein shell of a virus (p. 321)
Carbohydrate (kär bō hi′ drāt) a sugar or starch that living things use for energy (p. 72)
Cardiac (kär′ dē ak) relating to the heart (p. 352)
Cardiovascular disease (kär dē ō vas′ kyə lər də zēz′) a disease of the heart and blood vessels (p. 355)
Carotenoid (kər ot′ n oid) any yellow, orange, or red pigment found widely in plants and animals (p. 232)
Carrier (kar′ ē ər) an organism that carries an allele but does not show the effects of the allele (p. 294)
Carrying capacity (kar′ ē ing kə pas′ ə tē) the largest density an ecosystem can support for a particular population (p. 541)
Cartilage (kär′ tlij) a soft material found in vertebrae skeletons (p. 489)
Catalyst (kat′ l ist) a chemical that helps in a chemical reaction, but is not consumed or changed in the reaction (p. 180)
Cell (sel) the basic unit of life (p. 7)
Cell cycle (sel sī′ kəl) the life cycle of a cell from its beginning until it divides (p. 248)
Cell theory (sel thē′ ər ē) a theory that all living things are made of cells, that cells are the basic units of structure and function in living things, and that cells only come from already present cells (p. 107)
Cellular respiration (sel′ yə lər res pə rā′ shən) the process in which cells break down food to release energy (p. 147)

Cellulose (sel′ yə lōs) a woody polymer of glucose (p. 78)
Cell wall (sel wȯl) the rigid layer of cellulose outside the plasma membrane of plant cells (p. 159)
Central vacuole (sen′ tral vak′ yü ol) a large membrane sac in the center of a plant cell used for water storage (p. 159)
Centromere (sen′ trə mir) the area where two sister chromatids are tightly joined together (p. 249)
Cephalaspidomorphi (sef ə las pə də môr′ fi) a class of fish with a cartilage skeleton and no jaws or scales; lampreys (p. 490)
Cerebellum (ser ə bel′ əm) the part of the brain that controls balance (p. 362)
Cerebral cortex (sə rē′ brəl kôr′ tex) the part of the brain in which most of the high-level functions take place (p. 362)
Cervix (sėr′ viks) an opening that connects a female's uterus and vagina (p. 265)
C_4 plant (sē fôr plant) a plant that photosynthesizes in hot, dry weather (p. 239)
Chaparral (shap ə ral′) a terrestrial biome with mostly shrubs (p. 581)
Chemical bond (kem′ ə kəl bond) the force holding atoms together in a compound or molecule (p. 34)
Chemical formula (kem′ ə kəl fôr′ myə lə) a set of symbols and subscripts that tell the kinds of atoms and how many of each kind are in a compound (p. 42)
Chemical process (kem′ ə kəl pros′ es) a rearrangement of atoms or molecules to produce one or more new substances with new properties (p. 33)
Chemical property (kem′ ə kəl prop′ ər tē) a characteristic that describes how a substance changes into a different substance (p. 34)
Chemical reaction (kem′ ə kəl rē ak′ shən) a chemical change in which elements are combined or rearranged (p. 34)
Chemical runoff (kem′ ə kəl run ȯf) the chemical waste produced on land that enters water sources (p. 594)
Chemistry (kem′ ə strē) the study of matter and how it changes (p. 33)
Chemotroph (ki′ mō trof) an organism that gets its energy from chemicals in food (p. 566)
Chlorophyll (klôr′ ə fil) a molecule in chloroplasts that traps energy from the sunlight (p. 146)
Chloroplast (klôr′ ə plast) an energy organelle in plants that harvests energy from the sun (p. 146)
Chondrichthyes (kän drik′ thē əz) a class of fish with a flexible skeleton made of cartilage (p. 490)

a	hat	e	let	ī	ice	ȯ	order	ů	put	sh	she	ə {	a	in about
ā	age	ē	equal	o	hot	oi	oil	ü	rule	th	thin		e	in taken
ä	far	ėr	term	ō	open	ou	out	ch	child	ᴛʜ	then		i	in pencil
â	care	i	it	ȯ	saw	u	cup	ng	long	zh	measure		o	in lemon
													u	in circus

Biology: Cycles of Life　　Glossary　　**637**

Chordate (kôr´ dāt) an animal that, in its embryo stage, has a dorsal nerve cord, a notochord, pharyngeal slits, and a tail that goes past the anus (p. 489)

Chromosome (krō´ mə sōm) a structure in the nucleus made of individual DNA molecules folded and coiled together with proteins (p. 143)

Chyme (kīm) the liquid food in the digestive tract that is partially digested (p. 345)

Cilia (sil´ ē ə) small, hair-like structures made of microtubules; found on the outside of some cells to aid in movement (p. 155)

Circulatory system (sėr´ kyə lə tôr ē sis´ təm) a collection of organs, including the heart, which moves blood and gases throughout the body (p. 124)

Classify (klas´ ə fī) to group (p. 428)

Cleavage furrow (klē´ vig fur´ row) a structure that is formed when fibers pinch in the membrane of a dividing cell (p. 250)

Climate (klī´ mit) the average weather of a region over a long period of time (p. 580)

Clumped (klumpt) when a population spreads out in small groups throughout an ecosystem (p. 543)

Cnidarian (nī da´ rē ən) a group of invertebrates, including jellyfish, corals, and hydras (p. 482)

Co-adaptation (kō ad ap tā´ shən) one species becoming dependent on another species (p. 448)

Cochlea (kok´ lē ə) the organ in the ear that sends impulses to the auditory nerve (p. 369)

Codominance (kō do´ mə nəns) two different alleles come together and produce both trait forms (p. 286)

Codon (kō´ don) a specific sequence of three consecutive nucleotides that is part of a gene (p. 90)

Coenzyme A (kō en´ zīm ā) an organic molecule that helps move the products of glycolysis into mitochondria (p. 201)

Cognition (kog nish´ ən) knowledge (p. 524)

Cold-blooded (kōld blud´ əd) having a body temperature that changes with the temperature of the surroundings (p. 491)

Commensalism (kə men´ sə liz əm) a symbiotic relationship in which one organism benefits and the other is not affected (p. 550)

Common descent (kom´ ən di sent´) a theory that present organisms descend from past organisms (p. 389)

Communication (ka myü nə ka shən) sending information (p. 520)

Community (kə myü´ nə tē) a group of different populations that live in the same area (p. 447)

Comparative anatomy (kəm par´ ə tiv ə nat´ ə mē) the study of the anatomy of different species (p. 394)

Competition (kom pə tish´ ən) when organisms try to use the same resources (p. 542)

Competitor (kəm pet´ ə tər) an animal that tries to get the same resources as another animal (p. 521)

Complement protein (kəm plēt prō´ tēn) a protein that breaks the membranes of pathogens (p. 333)

Complementary base pairing (kom plə men´ tər ē bās pâir´ ing) the pairing of the nitrogenous bases adenine to thymine and cytosine to guanine in DNA strands (p. 308)

Complete metamorphosis (kəm plēt´ met ə môr´ fə sis) the changes in form during development in which earlier stages do not look like the adult (p. 485)

Complete protein (kom plə ment´ prōtēn) a protein source that provides the body with the essential amino acids (p. 91)

Compound (kom´ pound) a substance that is formed when atoms of two or more elements join together (p. 38)

Concentration (kon sən trā´ shən) a measurement of the amount of dissolved substance in a fixed amount of solvent (p. 112)

Concentration gradient (kon sən trā´ shən grā´ dē ənt) a difference in the concentration of a substance across a distance (p. 113)

Conifer (kon´ ə fər) a cone-bearing gymnosperm (p. 475)

Coniferous forest (kō nif´ ər əs fôr´ ist) a dry, cold terrestrial biome with cone-bearing trees (p. 582)

Connective tissue (kə nek´ tiv tish´ ü) the supporting framework of the body and its organs (p. 354)

Conservation biology (kon sər vā´ shən bī ol´ ə jē) the science of using ecological information to help reduce damage to the environment (p. 601)

Consumer (kən sü´ mər) an organism that feeds on other organisms (p. 567)

Continental drift (kon tə nen´ tl drift) a theory that the major landmasses of the earth move (p. 399)

Contractile (kən trak´ təl) able to become shorter or longer (p. 89)

Control group (kən trōl grüp) the setup in an experiment that has no factor, or variable, changed (p. 19)

Cooperation (kō op ə rā´ shən) a type of social behavior in which two or more individuals work or act together (p. 521)

Coordinated stasis (kō ôrd´ n ə tid stā təs) a pattern where most species appear at about the same time (p. 442)

Cornea (kôr´ nē ə) a clear layer of the eye that light passes through (p. 368)

Courtship behavior (kôrt´ ship bi hā´ vyər) a behavior that helps attract a mate (p. 513)

Covalent bond (kō vā´ lənt bond) a bond resulting from the sharing of one or more pairs of electrons between two atoms (p. 49)

Cristae (kris´ tē) the folded layers of the inner membrane inside mitochondria (p. 148)

Cross-fertilization (krȯs fėr tl ə zā′ shən) a process in which pollen from one type of plant fertilizes the eggs in a flower of a different plant (p. 278)

Crossing over (krȯ′ sing ō′ vər) the process of homologous chromosomes in a tetrad trading pieces of similar DNA (p. 257)

Crust (krust) the outer layer of the earth (p. 400)

Crustacean (krus tā′ shən) a class of arthropods that includes crabs, lobsters, crayfish, and pill bugs (p. 484)

Crystalline (kris′ tl ən) a substance with a regularly repeating arrangement of its atoms (p. 55)

Culture (kul′ chər) the languages, religions, customs, arts, and dress of a people (p. 497)

Cycle (sī′ kəl) a course or series of events or operations that repeats (p. 3)

Cynobacterium (sī nə bak tī′ rē um) a blue-green algae (p. 469)

Cytokinesis (sī tō kə nē′ səs) the process of dividing the cytoplasm of a cell into two (p. 250)

Cytoplasm (sī′ tə plaz əm) the area inside a cell; contains organelles and cytosol (p. 136)

Cytosine (C) (sī′ tə sēn) a single-ringed nitrogenous base found in DNA and RNA (p. 307)

Cytoskeleton (sī′ tə skel′ ə tən) a group of fibers running throughout the inside of a cell that supports the cell and helps the cell move (p. 154)

Cytosol (sī tə sol) the fluid base of the cytoplasm; contains molecules used and made by the cell (p. 136)

Cytotoxic T cell (sī tə tok′ sin t sel) a lymphocyte that scans for antigens and then destroys infected cells (p. 334)

D

Data (dā′ tə) information collected from experiments (p. 20)

Decomposer (dē kəm pō′ zər) an organism at the end of a food chain that feeds by breaking down dead organisms (p. 567)

Defensive behavior (di fen siv bi hā′ vyər) a behavior to avoid or protect against predators (p. 514)

Deforestation (dē fôr ist ā′ shən) the removal of forest ecosystems for land development (p. 596)

Dehydration synthesis (dē hi drā′ shən sin′ thə sis) the process of joining monomers by removing a molecule of water (p. 73)

Deletion (di lē′ shən) a mutation in which one or more nucleotide bases are removed from a DNA sequence (p. 319)

Dendrite (den′ drit) a thin branch out of the cell body that receives information from other cells (p. 364)

Density-dependent factor (den′ sə tē di pen′ dənt fak′ tər) a factor related to the density of a population that affects population size (p. 542)

Density-independent factor (den′ sə tē in di pen′ dənt fak′ tər) a factor that affects population size, but does not depend on population density (p. 543)

Deoxyribose (dē ok sə rī bōs) the five-carbon sugar in DNA (p. 95)

Dermis (dėr′ mis) the thick layer of cells below the epidermis (p. 360)

Descent with modification (di sent′ with mod ə fə kā′ shən) the theory that more recent species of organisms are changed descendants of earlier species (p. 389)

Desert (dez′ ərt) a very dry terrestrial biome (p. 581)

Diabetes (di ə bē′ tis) a genetic disease in which a person has too much sugar in his or her blood (p. 181)

Diencephalon (dī ən se′ fə lon) the front part of the brain (p. 362)

Differential reproduction (dif ə ren′ shal rē prə duk′ shən) when individuals leave more offspring than other individuals (p. 418)

Diffusion (di fyü′ zhən) the movement of molecules from an area of high concentration to an area of low concentration (p. 112)

Dihybrid cross (dī hī′ brid kros) a cross between two plants that differ in two traits (p. 280)

Dipeptide (di pep′ tīd) two amino acids joined by a peptide bond (p. 90)

Diploid (dip′ loid) having two copies of each kind of chromosome (p. 256)

Disaccharide (dī sak′ ə rīd) a sugar formed from two monosaccharide molecules (p. 77)

Disturbance (dis tėr′ bəns) a large change in a community (p. 555)

Diversity (də vėr′ sə tē) differing from one another (p. 33)

DNA (dē ēn ā) deoxyribonucleic acid; a chemical in an organism that contains the instructions for life (p. 7)

DNA ligase (dē ēn ā lī gās) an enzyme that bonds all pieces of newly made DNA to make one strand (p. 312)

DNA polymerase (dē ēn ā pol′ ə mə rās) an enzyme that adds new nucleotide bases to a new strand during DNA replication (p. 311)

Dominant (dom′ ə nāt) having the most influence or control (p. 521)

a	hat	e	let	ī	ice	ȯ	order	u̇	put	sh	she	ə	a in about
ā	age	ē	equal	o	hot	oi	oil	ü	rule	th	thin		e in taken
ä	far	ėr	term	ō	open	ou	out	ch	child	₮H	then		i in pencil
â	care	i	it	ȯ	saw	u	cup	ng	long	zh	measure		o in lemon
													u in circus

Biology: Cycles of Life Glossary **639**

Dominant gene (dom′ ə nāt jēn) a gene that shows up in an organism (p. 279)
Dorsal (dôr′ səl) the back part of an animal (p. 489)
Downs syndrome (dounz sin′ drōm) a medical condition caused by cells having an extra chromosome 21 (p. 327)
Dysentery (dis′ n ter ē) a disease of the intestines (p. 465)

E

Eardrum (ir′ drum) a thin tissue in the middle ear that vibrates when sound waves strike it (p. 369)
Ecological species concept (ē kə loj′ ə kəl spē′ shēz kon′ sept) a principle that defines species as populations that can interbreed and produce offspring based on their niche (p. 431)
Ecologist (ē kol′ ə jist) a person who studies ecology (p. 12)
Ecology (ē kōl′ ə jē) the study of interactions among living things and the nonliving things in their environment (p. 12)
Ecosystem (e′ kō sis təm) all of the living and nonliving things found in any particular area (p. 12)
Ectotherm (ek′ tə thərm) an animal whose main source of body heat is its environment (p. 491)
Effector cell (ə fek′ tōr sel) a muscle or gland cell that carries out the body's responses to stimuli (p. 357)
Egg (eg) the female gamete (p. 256)
Ejaculation (i jak yə lā′ shən) the release of semen from the penis (p. 261)
Electromagnetic radiation (i lek trō mag net′ ik rā dē ā′ shən) radiation that is made up of electric and magnetic waves (p. 230)
Electromagnetic spectrum (i lek trō mag net′ ik spek′ trəm) the range of wavelengths of electromagnetic radiation (p. 231)
Electron (i lek′ tron) a tiny particle in an atom that moves around the nucleus; it has a negative electrical charge (p. 39)
Electron carrier (i lek′ tron kar′ ē ər) a molecule that carries electrons from one set of reactions to another (p. 198)
Electron cloud (i lek′ tron kloud) the space effectively occupied by electrons in an atom (p. 39)
Electron shell (i lek′ tron shel) a specific energy level in which electrons orbit the nucleus (p. 48)
Electron transport chain (i lek′ tron tran spôrt′ chān) the third stage of cellular respiration (p. 202)
Element (el′ ə mənt) a substance that cannot be separated into other kinds of substances (p. 34)
Element symbol (el′ ə mənt sim′ bəl) one, two, or three letters that represent the name of an element (p. 38)
Embryo (em′ brē ō) an early stage in the development of an organism (p. 263)
Emigrate (em′ ə grāt) to leave a population (p. 543)

Emission (i mish′ ən) a chemical waste given off as gas (p. 602)
Empirical formula (em pir′ ə kəl fôr′ myə lə) the simplest formula for a compound (p. 42)
Endangered (en dān′ jərd) a condition in which there are almost no members of a certain species left (p. 407)
Endocytosis (en′ dō sī tō səs) a process in which a cell surrounds and encloses a substance to bring the substance into the cell (p. 139)
Endomembrane system (en′ dō mem brān sis′ təm) a group of organelles that help a cell make and use different molecules (p. 150)
Endoplasmic reticulum (ER) (en dō′ plaz mik ri′ ti kyə ləm) an organelle that makes different molecules (p. 150)
Endoskeleton (en′ dō skel′ ə tən) an internal skeleton (p. 487)
Endotherm (en′ dō thėrm) an animal that creates its own body heat through metabolism (p. 492)
Energy (en′ ər jē) the ability to do work; found in many different forms (p. 5)
Energy pyramid (en′ ər jē pir′ ə mid) a diagram that compares the amounts of energy available to the populations at different levels of a food chain (p. 569)
Engineer (en jə nir′) a person who works in engineering (p. 607)
Engineering (en jə nir′ ing) the use of math and science to create methods and machines to help solve problems or make life better (p. 607)
Environment (en vī′ rən mənt) an organism's natural and man-made surroundings (p. 11)
Enzyme (en′ zīm) a protein that brings about a chemical reaction in an organism (p. 89)
Epidermis (ep ə dėr′ mis) the thin outer layer of skin (p. 360)
Epithelial cell (ep ə thē′ lēəl sel) a skin cell (p. 123)
Epithelium (ep ə thē′ lēəm) a thin layer of cells forming a tissue that covers body surfaces and lines some organs (p. 348)
Equilibrium (ē kwə lib′ rē əm) a state where concentrations are equal in all parts of an area (p. 114)
Estrogen (es′ trə jən) the female sex hormone (p. 262)
Estuary (es′ chü ər ē) a marine biome where freshwater meets saltwater (p. 582)
Ethologist (i thol′ ə jist) a scientist who studies the behaviors of animals (p. 506)
Ethyl alcohol (eth′ əl al′ kəhol) a colorless liquid waste produced by anaerobic fermentation (p. 209)
Euglena (yü glē′ nə) a protist that makes its own food (p. 464)
Eukarya (yü kar′ ē ə) the domain of eukaryotic organisms (p. 436)

Eukaryote (yü kar´ ē ōt) a cell with several internal structures, including the nucleus, that are surrounded by membranes (p. 117)

Eutrophication (yü trə fə kā´ shən) a process in which chemical runoff causes algae growth that chokes out other organisms in a water ecosystem (p. 594)

Evaporation (i vap ərā´ shən) the process of liquid water changing into gas due to heating (p. 576)

Evolution (ev ə lü´ shən) the changes in a population over time (p. 10)

Evolutionary (ev ə lü´ shə ner´ē) of or relating to evolution (p. 440)

Evolutionary biology (ev ə lü´ shə nerē bī ol´ ə jē) the study of genetic changes within and among populations of organisms (p. 419)

Evolve (i volv´) to change biologically (p. 321)

Exocytosis (ek´ sō sī tō səs) a process in which a substance is released from a cell trough a pouch that transports the substance to the cell surface (p. 139)

Exon (ek´ sän) a part of mRNA that has protein-making instructions (p. 317)

Exoskeleton (ek sō skel´ ə tən) an external skeleton (p. 484)

Experimental group (ek sper ə men´ tl grüp) the same group as the control group, except for one factor, or variable, to be tested (p. 19)

External stimulus (ek stėr´ nl stim´ yə ləs) a stimulus that occurs outside of an organism (p. 506)

Extinct (ek stingkt´) when no members of a species are alive (p. 10)

Extinction (ek stingk´ shən) the death of all members of a species (p. 407)

Extracellular matrix (ek strə sel´ yə lər mā´ triks) a sticky coating outside the plasma membrane of animal cells that joins cells together (p. 136)

F

Facilitated diffusion (fə sil´ ə tā td di fyü´ zhən) passive transport that involves membrane proteins (p. 138)

FADH$_2$ (fad āch tü) an electron carrier produced by the Krebs cycle (p. 201)

Fallopian tube (fə lō´ pē ən tüb) a tube through which eggs pass from an ovary to the uterus (p. 262)

Fat (fat) a chemical that stores large amounts of energy (p. 73)

Fatty acid (fat´ ē as´ id) a long hydrocarbon with a carboxyl group at the end (p. 73)

Fatty layer (fat´ ē lā´ ər) the layer of skin that protects organs and keeps in heat (p. 360)

Feces (fē´ sēz) the solid waste material remaining in the large intestine after digestion (p. 346)

Feedback inhibition (fēd´ bak in hi bish´ ən) a process used by cells to control metabolic pathways (p. 214)

Fermentation (fėr men tā´ shən) an anaerobic process for making ATP (p. 208)

Fern (fėrn) a seedless vascular plant (p. 472)

Fertile (fėr´ tl) capable of producing offspring (p. 429)

Fertilization (fėr tl ə zā´ shən) the joining of male and female gametes to create a new organism (p. 257)

Fetus (fē´ təs) an embryo after eight weeks of development in the uterus (p. 266)

Fibrinogen (fi brin´ ə jen) a protein in the platelets that forms into threads, creating a clot (p. 355)

Fixed action pattern behavior (fiksd ak´ shən pat´ ərn bi hā´ vyər) a behavior that always occurs the same way (p. 507)

Flagella (flə jel´ ə) long, tail-like structures made of microtubules; found on the outside of some cells to aid in movement (p. 155)

Flatworm (flat´ wėrm) a simple worm that is flat and thin (p. 483)

Fluid mosaic model (flü´ id mō zā´ ik mod´ l) a plasma membrane model where proteins float freely through the phospholipid bilayer (p. 136)

Follicle (fol´ ə kəl) a ball of cells with a growing oocyte found inside (p. 262)

F$_1$ generation (ef wun jen ə rā´ shən) the offspring that result when two different kinds of pure plants are cross-pollinated (p. 279)

Food chain (füd chān) the feeding order of organisms in a community (p. 567)

Food web (füd web) all the food chains in a community that are linked to one another (p. 568)

Fossil (fos´ əl) the remains or impressions of an organism that lived in the past (p. 388)

Fossil fuel (fos´ əl fyü´ əl) the fuel formed millions of years ago from the remains of plants and animals (p. 475)

Fossil record (fos´ əl rek´ ərd) the history of life on the earth, based on fossils that have been discovered (p. 392)

Frequency (frē´ kwən sē) the rate of occurrence (p. 416)

Freshwater (fresh´ wot ər) an area of water with no salt (p. 582)

Frond (frond) a large, feathery leaf of a fern (p. 475)

a	hat	e	let	ī	ice	ȯ	order	u̇	put	sh	she	ə {	a in about
ā	age	ē	equal	o	hot	oi	oil	ü	rule	th	thin		e in taken
ä	far	ėr	term	ō	open	ou	out	ch	child	ᵺ	then		i in pencil
â	care	i	it	ȯ	saw	u	cup	ng	long	zh	measure		o in lemon
													u in circus

Fructose (fruk′ tōs) a form of sugar found in fruit and honey (p. 77)

F₂ generation (ef tü jen ə rā′ shən) the offspring that result when two hybrid plants are crossed (p. 279)

Functional group (fungk′ shə nəl grüp) a group of atoms within a molecule that causes the molecule to react in a specific way (p. 71)

G

Gallbladder (gôl′ blad ər) the digestive organ that stores bile (p. 345)

Gamete (gam′ ēt) a sex cell, such as sperm or egg (p. 256)

Gametophyte (ga mē′ tō fīt) in alternation of generations, the phase in which gametes are formed; a haploid individual that produces gametes (p. 474)

Gap junction (gap jungk′ shən) connections between cells made for support and communication (p. 140)

Gene (jēn) the information about a trait that a parent passes to its offspring; a section of DNA (p. 90); a section of DNA that carries instructions to make a specific protein (p. 143)

Gene flow (jēn flō) the movement of genes into or out of a population (p. 406)

Gene pool (jēn pül) the genes found within a population (p. 388)

Genetically modified food (jə net′ ī kal ē mod′ ə fīd füd) a food product with genes that have been changed (p. 327)

Genetic code (jə net′ ik kōd) a specific code used to translate base sequences in RNA into amino acid sequences in proteins (p. 317)

Genetic drift (jə net′ ik drift) the random changes in the gene pool of a small population (p. 407)

Genetics (jə net′ iks) the study of heredity (p. 284)

Genome (jē′ nōm) the entire DNA found in a cell (p. 143)

Genotype (jen′ ə tīp) an organism's combination of genes for a trait (p. 284)

Genus (jē′ nəs) a group of similar species (p. 434)

Geological (jē ə loj′ ə kəl) having to do with the solid parts of the earth (p. 574)

Geologic time (jē ə loj′ ik tīm) all the time that has passed since the earth formed (p. 397)

Geologic time scale (jē ə loj′ ik tīm skāl) a table that divides the earth's history into time periods (p. 398)

Geology (jē ol′ ə jē) the study of the nonliving parts of the earth (p. 607)

Germinate (jėr′ mə nāt) to start to grow into a new plant (p. 477)

Gestation time (je stā′ shən tīm) the period of development of a mammal, from fertilization until birth (p. 265)

Gill (gil) a structure used by some animals to breathe in water (p. 490)

Glomerulus (glə mer′ yə ləs) a group of capillaries that make up a tiny tube in nephrons (p. 360)

Glottis (glot′ is) the opening to the windpipe (p. 348)

Glucose (glü′ kōs) a monosaccharide used as a source of energy in animals and plants (p. 77)

Glycerol (glis′ ə rol) a sweet, syrupy alcohol with three hydroxyl groups (OH) (p. 73)

Glycogen (glī′ kə jən) the main storage form of glucose found in animal cells (p. 78)

Glycolysis (glī kol′ ə sis) the first stage of cellular respiration in which glucose is first split (p. 200)

Golgi apparatus (gol′ jē apə rat′ əs) an organelle made of stacked membrane sacs that makes final changes to and packages molecules made in the cell (p. 151)

Gonad (gō′ nad) an organ that makes gametes (p. 260)

Grana (grä′ na) stacks of thylakoids inside chloroplasts (p. 147)

Greenhouse effect (grēn′ hous ə fekt′) the warming of the atmosphere because of trapped heat energy from the sun (p. 594)

Growth factor (grōth fak′ tər) a protein that helps control the growth and division of cells (p. 327)

Growth rate (grōth rāt) the amount by which a population's size changes in a given time (p. 541)

G3P (jē thrē pē) a sugar molecule (p. 233)

Guanine (gwä′ nēn) a double-ringed nitrogenous base found in DNA and RNA (p. 306)

Gymnosperm (jim′ nə spėrm) a nonflowering seed plant (p. 472)

H

Habitat (hab′ ə tat) the place where an organism lives (p. 408)

Haploid (hap′ loid) having one copy of each kind of chromosome (p. 257)

Heat (hēt) a form of energy resulting from the motion of particles in matter (p. 6)

Helix (hē′ liks) a twisted shape like a spiral staircase (p. 94)

Helper T cell (hel′ pər tē sel) a lymphocyte that scans for antigens (p. 335)

Hemoglobin (hē mə glō′ bən) an iron-containing protein in red blood cells that carries oxygen (p. 89)

Hemophilia (hē mə fil′ ē ə) a genetic disease in which a person's blood fails to clot (p. 293)

Heredity (hə red′ ə tē) the passing of traits from parents to offspring (p. 278)

Heterotroph (het′ ər ə trof) an organism that cannot make its own food (p. 479)

Heterozygous (het ər ə zī′ gəs) having chromosomes that contain an identical pair of genes that do not code for the same trait form (p. 280)

Homeostasis (hō mē ə stā′ sis) the ability of organisms to maintain their internal conditions (p. 111)

Homologous chromosome (hō mol′ ə gəs krō′ mə sōm) one of a matching pair of chromosomes that comes from each parent (p. 256)

Homologous structure (hō mol′ ə gəs struk′ chər) the body parts that are similar in related animals (p. 394)

Homozygous (hō mə zī′ gəs) having chromosomes that contain an identical pair of genes for a particular trait (p. 280)

Hormone (hôr′ mōn) a chemical signal used to control body function (p. 105)

Host (hōst) an organism that is food for a parasite (p. 550)

Host cell (hōst sel) a cell infected and used by a virus (p. 322)

Hybrid (hī′ brid) the offspring of two different true-breeding plants (p. 279)

Hydrocarbon (hī drō kär′ bən) a molecule that contains carbon and hydrogen (p. 72)

Hydrogen bond (hī′ drə jən bond) a weak electrical attraction between the slight positive charge on a hydrogen atom and a slight negative charge on another atom (p. 54)

Hydrolysis (hī drol′ ə sis) a chemical process in which a molecule is separated into two parts by adding a molecule of water (p. 73)

Hydrophilic (hī drə fil′ ik) water-loving; polar molecules are hydrophilic (p. 55)

Hydrophobic (hī drə fō′ bik) water-hating; nonpolar molecules are hydrophobic (p. 55)

Hypertension (hī per ten′ shən) high blood pressure (p. 355)

Hypertonic (hī pər ton′ ik) a solution whose solute concentration is higher than the solute concentration of another solution (p. 114)

Hyphae (hī′ fā) threadlike fibers containing membranes and cytoplasm (p. 468)

Hypothalamus (hī pō thal′ ə məs) a part of the brain that regulates hormones, the pituitary gland, body temperature, and other activities (p. 363)

Hypothesis (hī poth′ ə sis) an educated guess; also the third step of the scientific method (p. 19)

Hypotonic (hī pə ton′ ik) a solution whose solute concentration is lower than the solute concentration of another solution (p. 114)

I

Immigrate (im′ ə grāt) to move into a population (p. 543)

Immune system (i myün′ sis′ təm) the body's most important defense against diseases (p. 323)

Immunity (i myü′ nə tē) the ability of the body to fight off a specific pathogen (p. 335)

Imprinting (im prin′ ting) learning in which an animal bonds with the first object it sees (p. 515)

Incomplete dominance (in kəm plēt′ dom′ ə nəns) two different alleles that come together and produce a trait that is neither dominant nor recessive (p. 286)

Incomplete metamorphosis (in kəm plēt′ met ə môr′ fə sis) the changes in form during development in which earlier stages look like the adult (p. 486)

Infect (in fekt′) to cause disease or an unhealthy condition by introducing germs and viruses (p. 322)

Infectious disease (in fek′ shəs də zēz′) an illness that can pass from person to person (p. 332)

Inferior vena cava (in fēr′ ēər vēnə kā′ və) a large vein that carries blood from the trunk and legs to the heart (p. 353)

Inflammatory response (in flam′ ə tôr ē ri spons′) an increase in blood flow to infected body tissue (p. 333)

Ingestion (in jes′ chən) the intake of food; the first stage of digestion (p. 344)

Innate behavior (i nāt′ bi hā′ vyər) a behavior that is present at birth (p. 507)

Insertion (in sėr′ shən) a mutation in which one or more nucleotide bases are added to a DNA sequence (p. 319)

Insoluble (in sol′ yə bəl) not able to dissolve in water (p. 92)

Instantaneous speciation (in stən tā′ nēəs spē shē ā′ shən) a new species formed in one to several generations (p. 448)

Instinct (in′ stingkt′) a pattern of innate behavior (p. 514)

Interact (in tər akt′) to act upon or influence something (p. 536)

Interbreed (in tər brēd′) to breed together (p. 429)

Interdependent (in tər di pen′ dənt) having to rely on each other (p. 548)

Intermediate filament (in tər mē′ dēit fil′ ə mənt) a rod-like cytoskeleton fiber used to strengthen the cell's shape; organelles anchor themselves to these rods (p. 154)

Internal stimulus (in tėr′ nl stim′ yə ləs) a stimulus that occurs inside of an organism (p. 506)

Interphase (in′ tər fāz) the phase of a cell cycle in which a cell grows to mature size and carries out typical activities (p. 248)

a	hat	e	let	ī	ice	ȯ	order	u̇	put	sh	she	ə {	a in about
ā	age	ē	equal	o	hot	oi	oil	ü	rule	th	thin		e in taken
ä	far	ėr	term	ō	open	ou	out	ch	child	ᴛʜ	then		i in pencil
â	care	i	it	ȯ	saw	u	cup	ng	long	zh	measure		o in lemon
													u in circus

Interstitial fluid (in ter stish´ əl flü´ id) a fluid that fills the space around cells and exchanges nutrients and wastes with blood (p. 353)

Intertidal zone (in tər tī´ dl zōn) an area where an ocean meets land (p. 582)

Introduced species (in´ trə düsd spē´ shēz) a species taken from its natural ecosystem and placed in another ecosystem (p. 596)

Intron (in´ tron) a part of mRNA that does not have protein-making instructions (p. 317)

Invertebrate (in vėr´ tə brit) an animal that does not have a backbone (p. 398)

Involuntary muscle (in vol´ ən ter ē mus´ əl) a muscle that a person cannot control (p. 377)

Ion (ī´ ən) an atom that has either a positive or a negative charge (p. 42)

Ionic bond (ī on´ ik bond) a type of bonding in which ions are held together by the strong attraction of their opposite charges (p. 50)

Ionic compound (ī on´ ik kom´ pound) two or more ions held next to each other by electrical attraction (p. 42)

Iris (ī´ ris) the part of the eye that controls the amount of light that enters (p. 368)

Isomer (ī´ sə mər) one of two or more compounds with the same molecular formula but different structures (p. 78)

Isotonic(ī sə ton´ ik) a solution whose solute concentration is equal to the solute concentration of another solution (p. 114)

Isotope (ī´ sə tōp) one of a group of atoms of an element with the same number of protons and electrons but different numbers of neutrons (p. 40)

K

Kinetic energy (ki net´ ik en ər jē) energy of motion (p. 170)

Kingdom (king´ dəm) a group of similar phyla or divisions (p. 434)

Krebs cycle (krebz sī´ kəl) the second stage of cellular respiration (p. 201)

L

Lactic acid (lak´ tik as´ id) an organic waste produced by anaerobic fermentation (p. 209)

Lagging strand (lag´ ging strand) the side of the replication fork where the newly made DNA is in several small pieces (p. 312)

Land development (land di vel´ əp mənt) the changes people make to natural land so it becomes land for farming or living space (p. 595)

Landfill (land´ fil) an area where trash is collected and stored (p. 601)

Landmark (land´ märk) an object used to mark a location or position (p. 515)

Landscape ecology (land´ skāp ē kol´ əjē) using ecological information to help balance human and environmental needs (p. 603)

Larva (lär´ və) the immature form of an animal that looks different from the adult form (p. 491)

Larynx (lar´ ingks) the voice box (p. 348)

Law of conservation of energy (lô ov kon´ sər vā shən ov en´ ər jē) energy cannot be created or destroyed (p. 6)

Law of independent assortment (lô ov in di pen´ dənt ə sôrt´ mənt) a law that states that each pair of chromosomes separates independently of other pairs of chromosomes in meiosis (p. 280)

Law of segregation (lô ov seg rə gā´ shən) a law that states that the pairs of homologous chromosomes separate in meiosis and each gamete receives one gene of a pair (p. 280)

Leading strand (lē´ ding strand) the side of the replication fork where the newly made DNA is in one piece (p. 312)

Learned behavior (lėrnd bi hā´ vyər) a behavior that results from experience (p. 507)

Lichen (lī´ kən) an organism that is made up of a fungus, a green alga, and cynobacterium (p. 469)

Life span (līf span) the number of years an individual lives (p. 497)

Ligament (lig´ ə mənt) a strong tissue that connects bone to bone (p. 376)

Limbic system (lim´ bik sis´ təm) the part of the brain that registers feelings (p. 362)

Linkage map (ling´ kij map) a map that shows distances between linked genes on a chromosome (p. 287)

Linked gene (lingkt jēn) a gene close to another gene on a chromosome, causing their alleles to be inherited together (p. 287)

Lipid (lip´ id) a macromolecule that is not soluble in water (p. 72)

Lipid bilayer (lip´ id bī lā´ ər) two layers of phospholipids (p. 84)

Lymphocyte (lim´ fə sīt) a white blood cell that has receptor proteins that recognize antigens (p. 333)

Lymph system (limf sis´ təm) a human organ system that transports hormones and human immune cells throughout the body (p. 332)

Lysogenic cycle (lī sə jen´ ik sī´ kəl) a cycle in which a virus hides its genetic information in the host cell until it switches to the lytic cycle (p. 323)

Lysosome (lī´ sə sōm) a membrane sac with special enzymes used to break down large molecules (p. 152)

Lytic cycle (lit´ ik sī´ kəl) a cycle in which a virus uses a host cell to make more virus particles until the host cell is destroyed (p. 322)

M

Macroevolution (mak rō ev ə lü′ shən) the large-scale changes in a population over long periods of time (p. 416)

Macromolecule (mak rō mol′ ə kyül) a molecule composed of a very large number of atoms (p. 72)

Macrophage (mak′ rō fāj) a large white blood cell that eats pathogens and cellular waste (p. 335)

Magma (mag′ mə) hot, liquid rock inside the earth (p. 400)

Malaria (mə ler′ ē ə) a disease that causes bouts of chills and fever (p. 411)

Malignant tumor (mə lig′ nənt tü′ mər) a tumor that has spread from its original site to other body areas (p. 252)

Mammary gland (mam′ ərē gland) a milk-producing structure on a mammal (p. 428)

Marine (mə rēn′) an area of water that has salt (p. 582)

Marker (mär′ kər) a material, such as an atom, used to mark an item (p. 310)

Marsupial (mär sü′ pē əl) a mammal with a pouch (p. 493)

Mass (mas) the amount of material an object has (p. 32)

Mass extinction (mas ek stingk′ shən) the dying out of large numbers of species in a short period of time (p. 447)

Matched submission (macht səb mish′ ən) a type of social behavior in which a threatened animal yields to a dominant animal (p. 521)

Matrix (mā′ triks) a thick fluid inside mitochondria (p. 147)

Matter (mat′ ər) anything that has mass and takes up space (p. 32)

Medical technology (med′ əkəl tek nol′ ə jē) any technology designed to help human medical problems (p. 608)

Meiosis (mī ō′ sis) a process that results in sex cells (p. 257)

Membrane (mem′ brān) a wall made of different molecules that separate a cell from its surroundings (p. 79)

Memory cell (mem′ ər ē sel) a lymphocyte that is activated if an antigen causes a second infection (p. 335)

Menopause (men′ ə pôz) the period when menstruation naturally stops; usually occurs between the ages of 45 and 55 (p. 263)

Menstruation (men strü ā′ shən) the process during which an unfertilized egg, blood, and pieces of the lining of the uterus exit the female body (p. 263)

Mesophyll (mes′ əfil) the green tissue inside a leaf (p. 225)

Messenger RNA (mRNA) (mes′ n jər är en ā) an RNA molecule that carries instructions for the order of amino acids in a protein (p. 316)

Metabolism (mə tab′ ə liz əm) the collection of the chemical reactions that occur in the cell (p. 170)

Metacommunication (met ə kə myü nə kā′ shən) a signal that changes the meaning of the next set of signals (p. 522)

Metamorphosis (met ə môr′ fə sis) a major change in form that occurs as some animals develop into adults (p. 485)

Metaphase plate (met′ ə fāz plāt) the middle of a cell where chromosomes line up during metaphase (p. 249)

Metastasis (mə tas′ tə sis) the process of cancer cells spreading from one body area to another (p. 252)

Microevolution (mī krō evə lü′ shən) the minor changes in a population's allele-frequencies from generation to generation (p. 416)

Microfilament (mī krō fil′ ə mənt) a long cytoskeleton fiber used to move the cell (p. 154)

Microscope (mī krō skōp) an instrument used to magnify things (p. 106)

Microtubule (mī krō tü′ byül) a tube-like cytoskeleton fiber used by organelles to move around (p. 155)

Mimicry (mim′ i krē) a method of defense in which a species looks like another poisonous or dangerous species (p. 514)

Mitochondrion (mī tə kon′ drē ən) an energy organelle that converts energy from bonds in glucose into ATP (plural is mitochondria) (p. 146)

Mitosis (mī tō′ sis) the process of dividing a cell's nucleus to make two identical nuclei (p. 249)

Modern synthesis (mod′ ərn sin′ thəsis) a theory that states evolution involves changes in a population's gene pool over time (p. 390)

Mold (mōld) a fungus that grows quickly on a surface (p. 468)

Molecular (mə lek′ yə lər) related to molecules (p. 33)

Molecular biology (mə lek′ yə lər bī ol′ ə jē) the study of the biochemical and molecular processes within cells (p. 395)

Molecule (mol′ ə kyül) the smallest particle of a substance that has all the properties of the substance (p. 32)

Mollusk (mol′ əsk) an invertebrate that has three body parts (p. 483)

Molting (mōlt ing) the process by which an arthropod sheds its exoskeleton (p. 484)

Monohybrid cross (mon ə hī′ brid kros) a cross between two plants that differ in only one trait (p. 279)

Monomer (mon′ ə mər) a small molecular structure that can chemically bond to other monomers to form a polymer (p. 72)

Monosaccharide (mon ə sak′ ə rīd) a carbohydrate made of one sugar (p. 72)

a	hat	e	let	ī	ice	ò	order	ù	put	sh	she	ə	a in about
ā	age	ē	equal	o	hot	oi	oil	ü	rule	th	thin		e in taken
ä	far	ėr	term	ō	open	ou	out	ch	child	ᴛʜ	then		i in pencil
â	care	i	it	ȯ	saw	u	cup	ng	long	zh	measure		o in lemon
													u in circus

Morphology (môr fol´ ə jē) the study of differences in body forms of organs (p. 428)

Moss (mos) a nonvascular plant that has simple parts (p. 472)

Multicellular (multi sel´ yə lər) made up of many cells (p. 479)

Multiple allele (mul´ tə pəl ə lēl´) one of more than two forms of a gene (p. 285)

Mutagen (myü tā´ jən) a physical or chemical material that causes changes in DNA (p. 319)

Mutation (myü tā´ shən) a change in the sequence of DNA (p. 319)

Mutualism (myü´ chü ə liz əm) a symbiotic relationship in which both organisms benefit (p. 550)

Mycelium (mī sē´ lē əm) the underground feeding network of a fungus (p. 468)

Mycorrhiza (mī´ kə rī zə) a closeness in which a fungus and the roods of a plant live together and help each other (p. 473)

Myxini (mik´ sī nē) a class of fish with a cartilage skeleton and no jaws or scales; hagfish (p. 490)

N

NADH (en ā dē āch) nicotinamide adenine dinucleotide; the main electron carrier involved in cellular respiration (p. 198)

Natural selection (nach´ ər əl si lek´ shən) the process by which organisms best suited to the environment survive, reproduce, and pass their genes to the next generation (p. 389)

Nectar (nek´ tər) a sweet liquid that many flowers produce (p. 477)

Nephron (nef´ ron) a small tubule that is the excretory unit of the kidney (p. 360)

Nervous tissue (nèr´ vəs tish´ ü) nerves made from a collection of nerve cells (p. 123)

Neuron (nùr´ on) a nerve cell (p. 364)

Neurotransmitter (nùr ō tran smit´ ər) a substance that transmits nerve impulses across a synapse (p. 364)

Neutral solution (nü´ trəl sə lü´ shən) a solution that has a pH of 7; it is neither an acid nor a base (p. 60)

Neutron (nü´ tron) a tiny particle in the nucleus of an atom; it has the same mass as the proton and no electrical charge (p. 39)

Niche (nich) the way of life of a species (p. 431)

Nitrate (nī´ trāt) a nitrogen-containing compound used directly by plants (p. 575)

Nitrifying bacteria (nī´ trə fī ing bak tir´ ē ə) bacteria that convert ammonium into usable nitrates (p. 575)

Nitrogen-fixer (nī trə jən fiks´ ėr) bacteria that convert nitrogen gas into ammonium (p. 575)

Nitrogenous base (nī troj´ ə nəs bās) a nitrogen-containing molecule attached to a nucleotide (p. 306)

Nondisjunction (non dis jungk´ shən) chromosomes that do not separate during anaphase, resulting in extra chromosomes in some cells (p. 327)

Nonspecific defense (non spi sif´ ik di´ fens) the use of a skin barrier, complement proteins, and the inflammatory response to defend against pathogens (p. 333)

Nonvascular plant (non vas´ kyə lər plant) a plant that does not have tubelike cells (p. 473)

Notochord (nō´ tə kôrd) a rod found in the back of embryo chordate (p. 490)

Nuclear envelope (nü´ klē ər en´ və lōp) the membrane surrounding the nucleus of a cell (p. 142)

Nucleic acid (nü´ klē ik as´ id) a large macromolecule that stores important information in a cell (p. 72)

Nucleolus (nü klē´ ə ləs) a ball of fibers in the nucleus that makes ribosomes (p. 142)

Nucleotide (nu´ klē ə tīd) the repeating monomer in nucleic acid; consists of a nitrogen base, a sugar, and a phosphate group (p. 73)

Nucleus (nü´ klē əs) an atom's center; made of protons and neutrons (p. 39)

O

Obesity (ō bē´ sə tē) a condition of being greatly overweight (p. 181)

Observational learning (ob zər vā´ shə nəl lėr´ ning) learning by watching or listening to another animal (p. 515)

Oocyte (ō´ ə sīt) an early egg cell that has not finished meiosis (p. 262)

Oogenesis (ō ə jen´ ə ləs) the process of creating an egg cell (p. 262)

Operculus (ō pėr´ kyə ləs) a protective flap over gills that allows a fish to breathe without swimming (p. 491)

Optic nerve (op´ tik nėrv) a bundle of nerves that carry impulses from the eye to the brain (p. 369)

Organ (ôr´ gən) a group of different tissues that work together to perform specific functions (p. 124)

Organelle (ôr gə nel´) a tiny membrane-bound structure inside a cell (p. 117)

Organic compound (ôr gan´ ik kom´ pound) a compound that contains carbon (except carbon dioxide, carbon monoxide, and carbonates) (p. 70)

Organic matter (ôr gan´ ik mat´ ər) a compound that contains carbon (p. 568)

Organism (ôr´ gə niz əm) a living thing; one of many different forms of life (p. 2)

Organization (ôr´ gə nə zā´ shən) the arrangement of parts into a whole (p. 33)

Organ system (ôr′ gən sis′ təm) a group of organs that work together to perform specific connected tasks (p. 124)

Origin of replication (ôr′ ə jin ov rep lə kā′ shən) a site where DNA replication begins (p. 311)

Osmosis (oz mō′ sis) the movement of water through a cell membrane (p. 113)

Osteichthyes (os tē ik′ thē ēz) a class of bony fish with jaws and scales (p. 490)

Osteoporosis (os tē ō pə rō sis) a disease in which bones become lighter and break easily (p. 375)

Ovary (ō′ vərē) the female organ that makes egg cells (p. 262)

Overproduction (ō vər prə duk′ shən) when organisms produce more offspring than can survive (p. 418)

Ovulation (ov′ yə lā shən) the process of releasing an egg from an ovary (p. 262)

Oxidation (ok sə dā shən) a chemical reaction that results in a loss of electrons (p. 197)

Ozone (ō′ zōn) a form of oxygen (p. 595)

P

Paleontologist (pā lē on tol′ ə jist) a scientist who studies fossils (p. 397)

Parasite (par′ ə sīt) an organism that absorbs food from a living organism and harms it (p. 321)

Parasitism (par′ ə sī tiz əm) a symbiotic relationship in which one organism feeds off another organism (p. 550)

Parental care behavior (pə ren′ tl cār bi hā′ vyer) the caring for offspring by a parent (p. 513)

Passive transport (pas′ iv tran spôrt′) the movement of molecules across a membrane when the movement requires no energy (p. 138)

Patent (pat′ nt) a government notice of ownership for a piece of technology (p. 609)

Pathogen (path′ ə jən) a germ (p. 332)

Penis (pē′ nis) the male organ that delivers sperm to the female body (p. 261)

Pepsin (pep′ sən) an enzyme produced in the stomach for digestion (p. 182)

Peptide (pep′ tīd) a compound made up of two or more amino acids; peptides combine to make proteins (p. 90)

Peptide bond (pep′ tīd bond) a covalent bond between two amino acids (p. 90)

Peristalsis (per ə stôl′ sis) the movement of digestive organs that pushes food through the digestive tract (p. 345)

Permafrost (pėr′ mə frôst) permanently frozen soil (p. 582)

Perspiration (pėr spə rā′ shən) a liquid waste made of heat, water, and salt released through skin (p. 360)

PGA (pē jē ā) phosphoglycerate; a three-carbon molecule formed in the first step of the Calvin-Benson cycle (p. 238)

P generation (pē jen ə rā′ shən) parental generation; the first two individuals that mate in a genetic cross (p. 279)

pH (pē āch) a number that tells whether a substance is an acid or a base (p. 59)

Phagocyte (fag′ ə sīt) a cell that eats infected cells and pathogens (p. 333)

Pharyngeal slit (fə rin′ jē əl slit) an opening in the wall of the pharynx of a chordate embryo (p. 490)

Pharynx (far′ ingks) the passageway between the mouth and the esophagus for air and food (p. 345)

Phenotype (fē′ nə tīp) an organism's appearance as a result of its combination of genes (p. 284)

Pheromone (fer′ ə mōn) a chemical signal produced by an animal (p. 524)

Phloem (flō′ em) the vascular tissue in plants that carries food from leaves to other parts of the plant (p. 473)

Phospholipid (fos′ fə lip id) a lipid with two fatty acid molecules joined by a molecule of glycerol (p. 82)

Phosphorous (fos′ fər əs) an element that cycles through an ecosystem and is used by organisms to make ATP (p. 573).

Phosphorylation (fos fôr ə lā′ shən) the addition of a phosphate group to a molecule (p. 174)

Photic zone (fō′ tik zōn) an area in aquatic biomes that receives solar energy (p. 582)

Photon (fō′ ton) the smallest unit of light (p. 230)

Photosynthesis (fō tō sin′ thə sis) a process that chloroplasts use to convert energy from the sun into chemical energy stored in glucose (p. 146)

Photosystem (fō tō sis′ təm) an assembly of proteins and pigments through which electrons are transferred to reaction centers (p. 234)

Phototroph (fō′ tō trof) an organism that gets its energy by capturing light energy (p. 566)

Phylogeny (fī loj′ ə nē) the origin and evolution of a species (p. 482)

Phylum (fī′ ləm) a subdivision of a kingdom (plural is phyla) (p. 434).

Physical property (fiz′ ə kəl prop′ ərtē) a characteristic of a substance or an object that can be observed without changing the substance into a different substance (p. 33)

Pistil (pis′ tl) the female organ of reproduction in a flower (p. 477)

a	hat	e	let	ī	ice	ô	order	u̇	put	sh	she	ə	a in about
ā	age	ē	equal	o	hot	oi	oil	ü	rule	th	thin		e in taken
ä	far	ėr	term	ō	open	ou	out	ch	child	ᵺ	then		i in pencil
â	care	i	it	ȯ	saw	u	cup	ng	long	zh	measure		o in lemon
													u in circus

Pituitary gland (pə tü′ ə ter ē gland) a gland in the brain that produces secretions that regulate basic body functions (p. 363)

Placenta (plə sen′ tə) a tissue that provides the embryo with food and oxygen from its mother's body (p. 266).

Plankton (plangk′ tən) small organisms found in the ocean; usually at the beginning of a food chain (p. 568)

Plasma (plaz′ mə) the liquid part of blood (p. 354)

Plasma membrane (plaz′ mə mem′ brən) the membrane that surrounds a cell and separates it from the environment (p. 135)

Plasmid (plaz′ mid) a small, circular piece of DNA, usually found in bacteria (p. 325)

Plasmodesmata (plaz mə dez′ mətə) openings in the cell wall used for communication and transport of molecules (p. 159).

Plastid (plas′ tid) a small, special part of a plant cell (p. 79)

Plate (plāt) a large section of the earth's crust that moves (p. 400)

Platelet (plāt′ lit) a tiny piece of cell that helps form clots (p. 354)

Plate tectonics (plāt tek ton′ iks) a theory that the earth's surface is made of large sections of crust that move (p. 399)

Pleiotropy (plī o′ trə pē) one gene that affects many traits (p. 286)

Polar molecule (pō′ lər mol′ ə kyül) a molecule with an uneven distribution of electron density (p. 54)

Pollen (pol′ ən) tiny grains containing sperm; the male plant gamete (p. 278)

Pollination (pol ə nā′ shən) the process by which pollen is transferred from the stamen to the pistil (p. 477)

Pollution (pə lü′ shən) anything added to the environment that is harmful to living things (p. 594)

Polygenic trait (polē jē′ nik trāt) a trait controlled by two or more genes (p. 287)

Polymer (pol′ ə mər) a very large molecule made from simple units (p. 72)

Polypeptide (pol ē pep′ tīd) several amino acids joined to form a chain (p. 90)

Polysaccharide (pol ē′ sak′ ə rīd) a carbohydrate that can be broken down by hydrolysis into two or more monosaccharides (p. 73)

Polyunsaturated fatty acid (pol ē un sach′ ə rā tid fat′ ē as′ id) a fatty acid containing many double or triple bonds (p. 83)

Population (pop yə lā′ shən) a group of organisms of the same species that live in the same area (p. 388)

Population density (pop yə lā′ shən den′ sətē) the number of individuals in a population in a particular area (p. 538)

Pore (pôr) a hole in the nuclear envelope used to send and receive messages (p. 142)

Potential energy (pə ten′ shəl en′ ər jē) stored energy (p. 170)

Precipitation (pri sip ə tā′ shən) the moisture that falls to earth from the atmosphere (p. 576)

Predation (prē dā′ shən) a relationship in which one species eats another species (p. 549)

Predator (pred′ ə tər) an organism that eats another organism (p. 514).

Pregnancy (preg′ nən sē) the development of a fertilized egg into a baby inside a female's body (p. 265).

Prey (prā) an organism that is eaten by another organism (p. 514)

Primary productivity (prī mer′ ē prō duk tiv′ ətē) the speed at which photosynthetic organisms produce organic matter in an ecosystem (p. 569)

Primary succession (prī mer′ ē sək sesh′ ən) the changes in a lifeless environment that create a community (p. 556)

Producer (prə dü′ sər) an organism that makes its own food (p. 567)

Product (prod′ əkt) a substance that is formed in a chemical reaction (p. 51)

Prokaryote (prō kar′ ē ōt) a cell with only one outside membrane and no nucleus or other internal structures (p. 116)

Promoter (prə mō′ tər) the sequence of DNA at the beginning of genes (p. 317)

Protein (prō′ tēn) a chemical used by cells to grow and work (p. 8)

Proton (prō′ ton) a tiny particle in the nucleus of an atom; it has a positive electrical charge (p. 39)

Protozoan (prō tə zō ən) protists that ingest food and usually live in water (plural is protozoa) (p. 464)

Pseudopod (sü′ də pod) a part of some one-celled organisms that sticks out like a foot and moves the cell along (p. 465)

Punctuated equilibrium (pungk′ chü āt əd ē kwə lib′ rē əm) a theory that states species stay the same for a long time, then new species evolve suddenly due to global changes and mass extinctions (p. 441)

Punnett square (pun′ it skwer) a model used to represent crosses between organisms (p. 281)

Pupil (pyü′ pəl) the black circle in the center of the iris (p. 368)

Pyruvic acid (pī rü′ vik as′ id) a major product of glycolysis (p. 200)

R

Radial symmetry (rā′ dē əl sim′ ə trē) an arrangement of body parts that resembles the spokes on a wheel (p. 482)

Radical (rad′ ə kəl) a group of two or more atoms that acts like one atom (p. 43)

Radioactive (rā dē ō ak′ tiv) the property of some elements (such as uranium) or isotopes (such as carbon-14) to give off energy as they change to another substance over time (p. 40)

Radioactive element (rā dē ō ak′ tiv el′ əmənt) an element that decays to form another element (p. 398)

Radioisotope (rā dē ō ī′ sə tōp) a radioactive isotope (p. 40)

Radula (raj′ ù lə) a tonguelike organ covered with teeth that is used for feeding (p. 484)

Random (ran′ dəm) when a population has no order as to how it is distributed through an ecosystem (p. 543)

Reactant (rē ak′ tənt) a substance that is altered in a chemical reaction (p. 51)

Reaction center (rē ak′ tənt sen′ tər) a special molecule of chlorophyll a in which electron transfer occurs (p. 233)

Recessive gene (ri ses′ iv jēn) a gene that is hidden by a dominant gene (p. 279)

Recombination (rē kom bə nā′ shən) the creation of new combinations of alleles in offspring (p. 405)

Recovery plan (ri kuv′ ər ē plan) a plan using scientific knowledge to help bring endangered species back from possible extinction (p. 604)

Rectum (rek′ təm) the lower part of the large intestine where feces are stored (p. 346)

Recycling (rē sī′ kəl ing) using waste products to create new products (p. 602)

Red marrow (red mar′ ō) the spongy material in bones that makes blood cells (p. 375)

Redox reaction (rē′ doks rē ak′ shən) a chemical reaction in which electrons are transferred between atoms (p. 197)

Reduction (ri duk′ shən) a chemical reaction that results in a gain of electrons (p. 197)

Reflex (rē′ fleks) an automatic response (p. 344)

Releaser (rē lēs′ ər) a stimulus that brings out a certain behavior in another animal (p. 515)

Replication (rep lə kā′ shən) the process DNA uses to copy itself (p. 310)

Replication bubble (rep lə kā′ shən bub′ əl) an area in which DNA replication is occurring with both strands unwound and being used as templates (p. 311)

Replication fork (rep lə kā′ shən fôrk) the end of a replication bubble in which DNA polymerase is actively adding nucleotide bases to a new strand (p. 311)

Reproduction (rē prə duk′ shən) the process of making new life (p. 7)

Reproductively isolated (rē prə duk′ tiv lē īsə lāt əd) a division between populations that once mated, but can no longer mate and produce fertile offspring (p. 429)

Reptile (rep′ tīl) an egg-laying vertebrate that breathes with lungs (p. 398)

Reserve (ri zėrv′) a protected area that cannot be used for building or growth (p. 603)

Respiration (res pə rā′ shən) the process by which living things release energy from food (p. 196)

Restriction endonuclease (ri strik′ shən en dō nü′ klē ās) an enzyme that cuts DNA molecules at specific sequences (p. 326)

Retina (ret′ nə) the back part of the eye where light rays are focused (p. 369)

Rhizoid (rī′ zoid) a tiny rootlike thread of a moss plant (p. 473)

Ribose (rī′ bōs) the five-carbon sugar in RNA (p. 95)

Ribosomal RNA (rRNA) (rī bə sō məl är en ā) an RNA molecule found in ribosomes that positions mRNA during translation (p. 317)

Ribosome (rī′ bə sōm) an information organelle that uses the instructions in DNA to make a protein (p. 142)

RNA (är en ā) a molecule that works together with DNA to make proteins (p. 94)

RNA polymerase (är en ā pol′ ə mə rās) an enzyme that adds RNA nucleotides to a new RNA molecule (p. 316)

RNA splicing (är en ā splīs′ ing) the removal of introns from an mRNA (p. 317)

Roundworm (round′ wėrm) a worm with a smooth, round body and pointed ends (p. 483)

RuBP (rü bē pē) ribulose bisphosphate; a five-carbon carbohydrate that combines with CO_2 in the first step of the Calvin-Benson cycle (p. 238)

S

Saccharide (sak′ ə rīd) a simple sugar (p. 77)

Saliva (sə lī′ və) a liquid produced by glands in the mouth that helps in chewing and starts digestion (p. 182)

Sample (sam′ pəl) a part that represents an entire population (p. 538)

a hat	e let	ī ice	ȯ order	ù put	sh she	ə { a in about
ā age	ē equal	o hot	oi oil	ü rule	th thin	e in taken
ä far	ėr term	ō open	ou out	ch child	ᵺ then	i in pencil
â care	i it	ȯ saw	u cup	ng long	zh measure	o in lemon, u in circus

Saturated fatty acid (sach´ ə rā tid fat´ ē as´ id) a fatty acid containing no double carbon bonds and the maximum number of hydrogen atoms (p. 82)

Savanna (sə van´ ə) a terrestrial biome with grasses and grazing animals (p. 581)

Scent (sent) having a smell or odor (p. 521)

Scientific journal (sī ən tif´ ik jėr´ nl) a scientific magazine (p. 609)

Scientific method (sī ən tif´ ik meth´ əd) a series of steps used to test possible answers to scientific questions (p. 17)

Scrotum (scrō´ təm) a sac that holds the testes (p. 260)

Secondary succession (sek´ ən der ē sək sesh´ ən) the changes in a community as it recovers from the effects of a disturbance (p. 556)

Secrete (si krēt´) to make and then give off (p. 151)

Sedimentary rock (sed ə men´ tərē rok) the rock formed from pieces of other rock and organic matter that have been pressed and cemented together (p. 392)

Seed (sēd) a plant part that contains a beginning plant and stored food (p. 472)

Segmented worm (seg´ mentəd wėrm) a worm whose body is divided into sections (p. 483)

Selectively permeable membrane (sə lek´ tiv lē pėr´ mē ə bəl mem´ brān) a membrane that allows some molecules to pass but blocks other molecules from coming through (p. 113)

Semen (sē´ mən) a mixture of fluid and sperm cells (p. 261)

Semi-conservative replication (sem´ ē kən sėr´ va tiv rep lə kā´ shən) a model of DNA replication in which an old strand of DNA is used to make a new strand of DNA (p. 310)

Seminiferous tubule (sem ə nif´ ər əs tü´ byül) the tissue in the testes where spermatogenesis happens (p. 261)

Sensory receptor (sen´ sər ē ri sep´ tər) a specialized neuron that detects sensory stimuli, then converts them to nerve impulses that go to the brain (p. 367)

Sequence (sē´ kqəns) a continuous or connected series (p. 90)

Sex chromosome (seks krō´ mə sōm) a chromosome that determines the sex of an organism (p. 292)

Sex-linked inheritance (seks lingkt in her´ ə təns) the passing on of traits with genes located on the X chromosome (p. 295)

Sex-linked trait (seks lingkt trāt) a trait determined by an organism's sex chromosomes (p. 293)

Sickle-cell disease (sik´ əl sel də zē´) a genetic disease in which a person's red blood cells have a sickle shape (p. 286)

Signal (sig´ nəl) a behavior that causes a change in the behavior of another animal (p. 521)

Simple dominance (sim´ pəl dom´ ə nəns) one allele is dominant to a recessive allele (p. 284)

Simulate (sim´ yə lāt) to make the same conditions as the natural or original conditions (p. 513)

Sister chromatid (sis´ tər krō´ mə tid) one of a pair of identical chromosomes created before a cell divides (p. 249)

Skeletal system (skel´ ə təl sis´ təm) the network of bones in the body (p. 375)

Sleep apnea (slēp ap´ nē ə) a condition in which short periods of not breathing occur during sleep (p. 350)

Slime mold (slīm mōld) a protist that lives as an individual cell, then joins other slime mold cells to form a community that produces spores (p. 466)

Social behavior (sō´ shəl bi hā´ vyər) the interaction between two or more animals (p. 520)

Sociobiologist (sō sē ō bī ol´ ə jist) a scientist who studies how animals communicate and interact with each other (p. 520)

Solar (sō´ lər) of or from the sun (p. 566)

Solute (sol´ yüt) a dissolved substance (p. 114)

Solvent (sol´ vənt) a substance capable of dissolving one or more other substances (p. 55)

Somatic cell (sō mat´ ik sel) a non-sex cell (p. 256)

Sori (sôr´ ē) the clusters of reproductive cells on the underside of a frond (p. 475)

Spatial learning (spā´ shəl lėr´ ning) learning by recognizing features (p. 515)

Speciation (spē shē ā´ shən) the process of making a new species (p. 10)

Species (spē´ shēz) a group of organisms that can reproduce with each other (p. 10)

Specific defense (spi sif´ ik di fens´) the use of lymphocytes to recognize antigens and attack infected cells based on antigens (p. 333)

Specimen (spes´ ə mən) a sample; an individual item or part considered typical of a group or whole (p. 17)

Sperm (spėrm) the male gamete (p. 256)

Spermatogenesis (spėr ma tō jen´ ə sis) the process of making a sperm cell (p. 260)

Spermatogonia (spėr ma tō gō´ nēa) early gamete cells that have not grown into sperm (p. 261)

Spindle (spin´ dl) a network of fibers that move chromosomes during mitosis (p. 249)

Spore (spôr) a reproductive cell of some organisms (p. 466)

Sporophyte (spôr´ ə fit) in alternation of generations, the diploid individual or generation that produces haploid spores (p. 474)

Stability (stə bil´ ə tē) the ability of a community to resist change (p. 539)

Stamen (stā´ mən) the male organ of reproduction in a flower, which includes the anther and filament (p. 476)

Starch (stärch) a polymer of glucose found in plants (p. 78)

Stasis (stā´ sis) showing little change over time (p. 441)

Steroid (ster´ oid) a lipid containing four attached carbon rings (p. 82)

Stigma (stig´ ma) the upper part of the pistil on the tip of the style (p. 477)

Stimulus (stim´ yə ləs) anything to which an organism reacts (p. 12)

Stoma (stō´ mə) an opening on the underside of a leaf for gas exchange (plural is stomata) (p. 225)

Stroma (strō´ mə) a thick fluid inside chloroplasts (p. 147)

Subatomic particle (sub e tom´ ik pär´ tə kəl) a proton, neutron, electron, or other particle smaller than the atom (p. 39)

Subpopulation (sub pä pyə lā´ shən) a division of a population (p. 432)

Subspecies (sub´ spē shēz) a division of a species (p. 431)

Substitution (sub stə tü´ shən) a mutation in which one nucleotide base is replaced with another (p. 319)

Substrate (sub´ strāt) a reactant molecule; the molecule on which an enzyme reacts (p. 185)

Succession (sək sesh´ ən) the process of ecological change in a community (p. 555)

Sugar-phosphate backbone (shüg´ ər fos´ fāt bak´ bōn) the negatively charged backbone of a nucleic acid molecule (p. 306)

Superior vena cava (sə pir´ ē ər vē´ nə kā´ və) a large vein that carries blood from the head, neck, and arms to the heart (p. 353)

Swim bladder (swim blad´ ər) a gas-filled organ that allows a bony fish to move up and down in water (p. 491)

Symbiosis (sim bē ō sis) a relationship in which two different species live in close association (p. 550)

Sympatric speciation (sim pa´ trik spē shē ā´ shən) when similar organisms live nearby, but do not interbreed due to behavioral differences (p. 431)

Synapse (si naps´) a tiny gap between neurons (p. 364)

Synthesize (sin´ thə sīz) to make into a whole substance (p. 91)

T

Taxonomist (tak so´ nə mist) a scientist who classifies and assigns scientific names to organisms (p. 458)

Taxonomy (tak son´ ə mē) the science of classifying organisms based on the features they share (p. 458)

Technology (tek nol´ ə jē) any device, machine, or method created to solve a human problem or question (p. 608)

Temperate deciduous forest (tem´ pər it di sij´ ü əs fôr´ ist) a terrestrial biome with wet forests that change activity during winter (p. 582)

Temperate grassland (tem´ pər it gras´ land) a terrestrial biome with fertile soil and tall grasses (p. 581)

Template (tem´ plit) a pattern used for copying (p. 311)

Tendon (ten´ dən) a tough tissue that attaches muscles to bones (p. 377)

Tentacle (ten´ tə kəl) an armlike body part of cnidarians that is used to capture food (p. 482)

Terminator (tėr´ mə nā tər) the sequence of DNA that signals the end of transcription (p. 317)

Terrestrial (tə res´ trē əl) having to do with land (p. 580)

Territorial behavior (ter´ ə tôr´ ē əl bi hā´ vyər) a behavior that claims and defends an area (p. 515)

Testcross (test´ kros) a test that determines an unknown genotype of an organism by crossing it with a homozygous recessive organism (p. 285)

Testis (tes´ tis) the male sex organ that produces sperm cells (plural is testes) (p. 260)

Testosterone (te stos´ tə rōn) a male sex hormone (p. 260)

Tetrad (tet´ rad) a pair of homologous chromosomes joined together (p. 257)

Thalamus (thal´ ə məs) a part of the brain that directs sensory messages (p. 363)

Theory (thē´ ə rē) a well-tested explanation that makes sense of a great variety of scientific observations (p. 21)

Three-domain system (thrē dō mān sis´ təm) a system that classifies all living things into three broad groups (p. 436)

Thrombus (throm´ bəs) a clot of blood formed within a blood vessel (p. 354)

Thylakoid (thī´ lə koid) membrane sac that contains chlorophyll (p. 147)

Thymine (T) (thī´ mēn) a single-ringed nitrogenous base found in DNA (p. 307)

Tissue (tish ü) a group of cells that are similar and work together (p. 123)

T lymphocyte (tē lim´ fa sit) a specific defense cell that signals and destroys infected cells (p. 333)

Toxic (tok´ sik) poisonous (p. 555)

Trachea (trā kē ə) the tube that carries air to the bronchi (p. 349)

Trait (trāt) a characteristic of an organism (p. 278)

Transcription (tran skrip´ shən) the creation of an RNA molecule using the bases in a DNA molecule as a template (p. 316)

a	hat	e	let	ī	ice	ô	order	u̇	put	sh	she	ə {	a in about
ā	age	ē	equal	o	hot	oi	oil	ü	rule	th	thin		e in taken
ä	far	ėr	term	ō	open	ou	out	ch	child	ŦH	then		i in pencil
â	care	i	it	ȯ	saw	u	cup	ng	long	zh	measure		o in lemon
													u in circus

Trans fat (tranz fat) an unsaturated fat that has been changed to a saturated fat (p. 83)

Transfer RNA (tRNA) (tran sfėr är en ā) an RNA molecule that brings in amino acids during translation (p. 317)

Transform (tran sfôrm´) to change form or makeup (p. 5)

Transformation (tran sfər mā´ shən) the process of adding foreign DNA to a bacterial cell (p. 326)

Translation (tran slā´ shən) the creation of a protein using the bases in an RNA molecule as a template (p. 316)

Transport (tran spôrt´) to move molecules from one side of a membrane to the other (p. 112)

Transport protein (tran spôrt´ prō´ tēn) a protein in the plasma membrane that helps move molecules across the membrane (p. 136)

Triglyceride (trī glis´ ə rīd) a lipid made of three fatty acids and one molecule of glycerol (p. 82)

Trophic structure (trō´ fik strək´ chər) the feeding relationships between species in a community (p. 549)

Tropical forest (trop´ ə kəl fôr´ ist) a terrestrial biome with many trees and organisms (p. 581)

Truncate (trung´ kāt) to shorten (p. 91)

Tube foot (tūb fùt) a small structure used by echinoderms for attachment and movement (p. 486)

Tubulin (tü´ byə lən) a ball-shaped protein used to make the hollow tube structure of microtubules (p. 155)

Tumor (tü mər) a ball of cells made from the extra divisions of a cancer cell (p. 252)

Tundra (tun´ drə) a cold, dry terrestrial biome with shrubs and small trees (p. 582)

U

Umbilical cord (um bil ə kəl kôrd) the cord that connects an embryo to the placenta (p. 266)

Uniform (yü nə fôrm) when a population spreads out evenly through an ecosystem (p. 543)

Unsaturated fatty acid (un sach ə rā tid fat´ ē as´ id) a fatty acid containing double or triple bonds and less than the maximum number of hydrogen atoms (p. 83)

Uracil (U) (yú´ r ə səl) a single-ringed nitrogenous base found only in RNA (p. 307)

Ureter (yù rē´ tər) a tube that carries urine from the kidney to the urinary bladder (p. 359)

Urethra (yü rē´ thrə) the tube that carries urine and semen out of the body (p. 261)

Urine (yùr´ ən) liquid waste formed in the kidneys (p. 359)

Uterus (yü tər əs) an organ in most female mammals that holds and protects an embryo (p. 262)

V

Vaccine (vak´ sēn) a material that causes the body to make antibodies against a specific pathogen (p. 323)

Vacuole (vak´ yü ol) a membrane sac that transports and stores molecules (p. 151)

Vagina (və jī´ nə) the tube-like canal in the female body through which sperm enter the body (p. 265)

Variable (ver´ ēə bəl) the factor that is tested in an experiment (p. 19)

Vascular bundle (vas´ kyə lər bun´ dl) a vein in a leaf that transports water and food (p. 225)

Vascular plant (vas´ kyə lər plant) a plant that has tubelike cells (p. 473)

Vascular tissue (vas´ ky ə lər tish´ ü) a group of plant cells that form tubes through which food and water move (p. 473)

Vas deferens (vas def ər enz) the tubes that connect the testes to the urethra (p. 261)

Vegetation (vej ə tā´ shən) the plant life in an area (p. 551)

Ventricle (ven´ trə kəl) a heart chamber that pumps blood out of the heart (p. 353)

Vertebra (vėr te bra) one of the bones or blocks of cartilage that make up a backbone (plural is vertebrae) (p. 489)

Vertebrate (vėr´ tə brit) an animal that has a backbone (p. 398)

Villi (vil´ ī) the tiny, fingerlike structures in the small intestine through which food molecules enter the blood (p. 345)

Virus (vī´ rəs) a type of germ that is not living (p. 310)

Voluntary muscle (vol´ ən ter ē mus´ əl) a muscle that a person can control (p. 377)

W

Warm-blooded (wôrm blud´ id) having a body temperature that stays the same (p. 492)

Warning coloration (wôr´ ning kul ə rā´ shən) the bright colors or patterns on animals that scare off predators (p. 514)

Wavelength (wāv´ lengkth) the distance between repeating units of a wave pattern (p. 230)

White blood cell (wit blud sel) a cell of the immune system (p. 333)

X

Xylem (zī´ lem) the vascular tissue in plants that carries minerals from roots to stems and leaves (p. 473)

Z

Zygote (zī´ gōt) a fertilized cell (p. 257)

Index

A

Absorb defined, 230
Accessory pigments in photosynthesis, 232
Acetic acid defined, 201
Acetyl CoA defined, 201
Achievements in Science
 animal behavior research, 518
 atomic ideas, early, 52
 biochemical pathways, discovering, 205
 cancer, 268
 cells, lab culture, 118
 classification systems, history of, 466
 coevolution, 542
 diabetes, 186
 ecosystems, nutrient cycling in, 576
 finding HIV, 334
 genes for genetic disorders, discovering, 296
 human ancestors, discovering, 436
 infectious disease, preventing, 21
 medical advances, 365
 photosynthesis, discovering, 239
 plant disease, 148
 protein structure, 89
 whooping crane recovery, 598
 Y chromosome, 409
Acid-base chemistry, 59–61
Acidosis described, 63
Acid rain defined, 23, 594, 614
Acids
 vs. bases, 60
 defined, 59, 62
Acquired trait defined, 389
Actin defined, 154
Activation energy defined, 184
Active site defined, 185
Active transport defined, 138

Adaptation defined, 10, 27
 See also Biological evolution
Adapt defined, 390
Adenine defined, 170, 306, 309, 311, 338
Adolescence defined, 266
ADP (adenosine diphosphate)
 converting, 177, 190
 defined, 174
Adrenal gland, function of, 372
Aerobic defined, 208
African clawed frogs and ecosystem disruption, 13
Aggressive behavior defined, 514, 530
Agnostic interaction defined, 520, 521
Agriculture and biotechnology, 326
AIDS (acquired immunodeficiency syndrome), 334
Algae
 defined, 464, 465
 and eutrophication, 594
Alkali. *See* Bases
Alkalosis described, 63
Alleles
 blood type, tracking, 414–15
 creation of, 319, 405
 defined, 279, 405
 frequency, measuring, 407
 multiple defined, 285, 300
 relationships among, 284–86
 Science Myths, 281, 405
 See also DNA (deoxyribonucleic acid); Genes
Allopatric speciation defined, 431, 441, 452
Alternation of generations defined, 473
Altitude and respiration, 350, 351

Alveolus defined, 349
American Cancer Society, 259
Amino acids
 defined, 72
 essential, list of, 91
 in proteins, 88
Amino group described, 71
Ammonium defined, 575
Amniotic egg defined, 491
Amobezoa described, 466
Amoeba defined, 464, 465
Amphibia, 491, 493, 494
Amphibian defined, 398, 514
Amylase, function of, 181
Amylotrophic lateral sclerosis (ALS), 365
Anaerobic defined, 208
Analysis
 defined, 19
 scientific method, 20
Anatomy
 comparative and biological evolution, 394, 396
 defined, 394
Angiosperm defined, 472, 476–77, 478, 634
Animalia, 479–81
Animals
 behavior in, 513–19
 behavior research, 518
 breeding, 421
 cellular ATP, production of, 175–76
 See also Organisms
Annelids, 483, 487
Anthophyta, 476–77, 500
Antibacterial products, 140
Antibiotics described, 140, 322, 326, 438
Antibodies as cellular defense, 338
Anticodon defined, 318
Antidiuretic hormone (ADH) defined, 360
Antigen defined, 334
Aorta defined, 353
Aphotic zone defined, 582

Aquatic
 biomes, 582, 586, 587
 defined, 568
 ecosystems, 578–79, 602
Arachnid defined, 484, 485
Archaea defined, 436, 459
Artery defined, 353
Arthropoda, 484–86, 487
Arthropod defined, 484
Artificial selection defined, 410
Asbestos and cancer, 267
Asexual reproduction defined, 431
Association neurons defined, 365
Asthma defined, 350
Atherosclerosis defined, 355, 356
Atomic mass defined, 40
Atomic number defined, 39
Atoms
 bonding in, 49, 70
 defined, 32
 energy levels in, 50
 ideas, early, 52
 structure, 39–40, 47, 64
ATP (adenosine triphosphate)
 in Archaea, 459
 defined, 105, 170, 190
 functions of, 172, 173
 production of, 171, 174–76, 190, 200
 anaerobic, 212–13
 in cellular respiration, 204, 218, 242
 phosphorylation and, 190, 234
 plant cells, 175–76, 184
ATP synthase defined, 203
Atrium defined, 353
Auditory nerve defined, 369
Autosome defined, 292, 300
Autotroph defined, 224
Aves, 492, 493, 494
 See also Birds
Axon defined, 364

B

Bacteria
　anaerobic, 221
　in biotechnology, 325, 326
　defined, 25, 33
　domain overview, 458–59
　evolution of, 398, 438–39
　functions of, 116
　and photosynthesis, 226, 459
　Science Myths, 569
Bacteriophage defined, 310, 313
Ball and socket joint described, 376, 379
Barium nitrite described, 44
Bases
　vs. acids, 60
　defined, 59, 62, 316
　pairing in DNA, 94, 308, 312, 338
Behavior
　aggressive defined, 514, 530
　in animals, 511–12, 513–19
　courtship, 513, 521, 533
　defensive, 514
　defined, 505, 506
　evolution of, 508–9, 530
　and heredity, 507
　innate, 507
　learned, 507–8
　social, 520, 530
　territorial, 515
　twins, studies of, 529
　types of, 513–19, 530
　wasp, 515–16
　See also Communication
Behavioral biology defined, 506, 525, 530
Benign tumor defined, 252
Benthic zone defined, 582
Bilateral symmetry defined, 483
Bilayer defined, 134
Bile defined, 345
Binary compounds, 45–46
Binary fission defined, 117
Biochemical pathways, discovering, 205
Biochemistry defined, 429
Biodiversity defined, 604
Bioenergy, 631

Biogeography defined, 392, 393, 396
Biogeology defined, 607
Biological cycles
　carbon, 574
　nitrogen, 575
　water, 575–76, 581
　See also Human body systems
Biological evolution
　defined, 388, 404, 408, 417
　evidence of, 392–96, 422
　overview, 388–91
　patterns of, 442–43
　processes in, 404–9
　rates of, 397–401
　study of, 419, 433
Biological pest control, 559
Biological species concept defined, 430, 452
Biologists
　described, 2, 27
　and the scientific method, 17
Biology defined, 2, 4, 26
Biology in the World
　animal breeding, 421
　biological pest control, 559
　blood and pH, 63
　blood donations, 381
　catalytic converters, 189
　cellular respiration, boosting, 217
　dinosaurs and birds, 499
　Human Genome Project, 337
　karyotyping, 299
　life without DNA, 271
　mad cow disease, 25
　mitochondrial DNA, 163
　photosynthesis, worldwide, 241
　prairies, restoring, 613
　species, discovery of, 451
　stem cells, 127
　twins, behavior studies of, 529
　Vitamin A and blindness, 97
　water: conserving, 585
Biology In Your Life
　antibacterial products, 140

　artificial blood technology, 125
　blood pressure, 356
　carbon monoxide detectors, 215
　the environment, 13
　environment and cancer, 267
　environment and dog evolution, 432
　enzyme products, 181
　genetic testing, 288
　grow lights for plants, 227
　municipal water treatment, 605
　native plants, 557
　Nature's recycling system, 470
　organic farming, 583
　technology and plastic, 41
　vaccine delivery, 336
　vegetarian diets, 91
　wireless communications, 525
　X-rays, 412
Biomes
　defined, 537, 587
　overview, 580–84, 586
Biosphere defined, 536, 537
Biotechnologist defined, 325
Biotechnology
　agriculture and, 326
　bacteria in, 325, 326
　defined, 325, 338
　enzymes in, 325, 329
　and genetic makeup, 325–28
　See also Technology
Bipedal locomotion defined, 497
Birds
　bonding in, 517
　overview, 492, 493, 494
　songs, learning, 517–18
　territorial behavior in, 515
Blastula defined, 479
Blindness and Vitamin A, 97
Blood
　artificial blood technology, 125
　cells
　　described, 354–55, 356
　　synthesis of, 375, 378
　circulation of, 348, 353–54

　donations, 381
　and pH, 63
　pressure, 356
　transfusion, 365
　types, determination of, 285–86
B lymphocyte defined, 333
Body processes. *See* Human body systems
Bonding. *See* Chemical bonds
Bones described, 375–76
Boom-bust cycle defined, 543
Brain described, 362–63, 366
Brain stem defined, 362
Breathing, 349–50
Bronchiole defined, 348, 349
Bronchitis defined, 350
Bronchus defined, 349
Brown algae described, 465
Bryophyta, 473–74, 500, 634
Buffer defined, 61, 63
Butterflies, 486

C

Calorie
　defined, 171, 173
　in food, 172
Calvin-Benson cycle
　defined, 233, 242
　overview, 238–39
Cambrian period, 398, 401
Camouflage defined, 550
CAM plants in photosynthesis, 239
Cancer
　Achievements in Science, 268
　asbestos and, 267
　chemotherapy in, 252
　defined, 252, 272
　and environment, 267
　genetic testing for, 288
　hormones and breast cancer, 268
　lung, 349
　skin, 252, 404
　smoking and, 267, 268
　See also Tumors
Canopy defined, 551
Capillary defined, 348, 354
Capsid defined, 321

Carbohydrates
  defined, 72, 95
  function of, 105, 130
  and health, 79–80
  overview, 77–80
  sources of, 79
Carbon
  bonding in, 70–71
  cycle, 574
Carbon dioxide in respiration, 196, 349–50
Carbon monoxide detectors, 215
Carbonyl group described, 71
Carcinogens, 267, 268
Cardiac defined, 352, 377
Cardiovascular disease defined, 355
Careers. See Science at Work
Carotenoid defined, 232
Carrier defined, 294, 300
Carrying capacity defined, 541, 545, 592, 614
Cartilage defined, 376, 489
Catalyst defined, 180
  See also Enzymes
Catalytic converters, 189
Cells
  activities, regulating, 144, 177
  blood
    described, 354–55, 356
    synthesis of, 375, 378
  cycle defined, 248, 272
  defined, 7, 27, 104
  energy production in, 105, 148, 190, 215, 218
  environment, effects of on, 114
  eukaryotic (See Eukaryotic cells)
  hydrolysis in, 73
  inflammatory response in, 333
  Investigations, 109–10, 157–58
  lab culturing of, 118
  membranes
    function of, 135–36
    structure of, 134, 164
  and microscopes, 106–7, 128
  osmosis in, 121–22
  plant, comparing, 161–62
  plants vs. animal cells, 157–58
  prokaryotic (See Prokaryotic cells)
  reproduction in (See Meiosis; Mitosis)
  sperm/egg, 264
  structure/functions of, 104–6, 111–15, 128 (See also Behavior)
  See also DNA (deoxyribonucleic acid); Human body systems; Organelles
Cell theory defined, 107, 128
Cellular respiration
  ATP production in, 204, 218, 242
  boosting, 217
  carbon dioxide in, 196, 349–50
  defined, 147, 172, 196–97
  enzymes in, 214
  glucose in, 196–98, 218
  in mitochondria, 201, 218
  plants and, 198
  products of, 206–7
  regulating, 214–15
  stages of, 200–204, 577
Cellulose defined, 78, 79
Cell wall defined, 159
Centipedes, 485
Central vacuole defined, 159
Centromere defined, 248, 249
Cephalaspidomorphi defined, 490, 493
Cerebellum defined, 362
Cerebral cortex defined, 363
Cervix defined, 265
Chaparral defined, 581
Chapter study tips, xi
Chargraff, Erwin, 307
Chase, Martha, 310, 313
Chemical balances, maintaining, 59
Chemical bonds
  atoms, 49, 70
  in carbon, 70–71
  defined, 34
  and molecules, 48–51
  in salt, 50
  in water, 49
  See also Covalent bonds; Hydrogen bonds; Ionic bonds
Chemical formulas
  configuration of, 44, 47
  defined, 42
  overview, 42–46, 64
Chemical processes defined, 33
Chemical property defined, 34
Chemical reactions
  defined, 34
  and enzymes, 180
  overview, 51
Chemical runoff defined, 594, 614
Chemical waste in ecosystems, 602
Chemistry, 31–34
Chemoreceptor described, 367, 368
Chemotherapy in cancer treatment, 252
Chemotroph defined, 566, 586
Chlorophyll
  defined, 146
  in photosynthesis, 225
Chlorophyll *a* in photosynthesis, 231, 242
Chlorophyll *b* in photosynthesis, 232
Chloroplasts
  defined, 146
  function of, 164
  in photosynthesis, 225, 233
  structure of, 146–47
Choice. See Consumer choices
Cholesterol described, 84
Chondrichthys defined, 490–91, 493
Chordata, 489–93
Chordate defined, 489
Chromosomes
  crossover in, 257
  defined, 143, 269, 277
  karyotyping, 299
  Math Tips, 144
  movement of, modeling, 269–70
  recombination in, 405
  replication of, 311
  sex, 292–96, 300, 409
  See also Genes; Heredity
Chyme defined, 345
Cilia defined, 155, 348
Circle diagrams, using, xviii
Circulatory system, 124, 348, 350, 352–56, 365, 382, 621
Classification
  of animals, 500
  levels of, 428, 431, 452, 458–61, 500
  of plants, 477
  of species, 434–37, 443
  systems, history of, 466
  See also Taxonomy
Classify defined, 428
Cleavage furrow defined, 249, 250
Climate defined, 580, 586
  See also Ecosystems; Weather
Clot. See Thrombus defined
Clumped pattern of population distribution defined, 543, 544
Cnidarian defined, 482, 487
Co-adaptation defined, 448
Coal. See Energy; Fossil fuels
Cochlea defined, 369
Cocoa butter, 83
Codominance defined, 286, 289, 300
Codon defined, 90, 93, 317
Coenzyme A defined, 201
Coevolution, 542
Cognition defined, 524
Cold-blooded defined, 491
Collagen described, 89
Column charts, using, xvii
Commensalism defined, 550, 552
Common descent theory defined, 389, 424
Communication
  defined, 520
  forms of, 520–26
  in the scientific method, 20, 22
  wireless, 525
  See also Behavior; Cells, structure/functions of
Communities
  defined, 447, 560
  diversity in, 548, 560
  dynamics of, 555–58
  ecological, surveying, 553–54
  organization of, 536–39

Biology: Cycles of Life   Index   655

properties of, 560
relationships in, 548–52
succession in, 555–56
trophic structure of, 549, 552, 566–67, 586
See also Ecosystems; Populations
Comparative anatomy defined, 394
Competition
in communities, 549
defined, 542
Competitor defined, 521
Complement protein defined, 332, 333
Complete metamorphosis defined, 485, 486
Complete protein defined, 91
Complementary base pairing defined, 308, 309, 310
Composting defined, 470
Compounds
defined, 38
naming, 45–46
and radicals, 43–45
See also Chemical bonds; Chemical reactions
Concentration defined, 112
Concentration gradient defined, 113, 203
Concept maps, using, xvi–xvii
Conifer defined, 475, 476, 634
Coniferophyta, 475–76, 500
Coniferous forest defined, 582
Connective tissue defined, 354
Conservation biology, 601–6, 614
Conservation practices, 611–12, 614, 615
Consumer choices
antibacterial products, 140
blood pressure, 356
enzyme products, 181
vegetarian diets, 91
Consumer defined, 567, 586
Continental drift defined, 399, 400, 422
Contractile defined, 89

Control group defined, 19, 27
Conversion factors, 624–25
Cooperation defined, 521, 530
Coordinated stasis defined, 442
Cornea defined, 368
Courtship behavior defined, 513, 521, 533
Covalent bonds
defined, 49, 52, 56, 64
overview, 49–50
C_4 plants in photosynthesis, 239
Creutzfeldt-Jakob disease, 25
Crick, Francis, 307–8
Cristae defined, 148
Cross-fertilization defined, 278
Crossing over defined, 257
Crustacean defined, 484, 485
Crust defined, 400
Crystalline defined, 55
Culture defined, 497
Cyanobacteria, 171, 469
Cycles
defined, 3, 4, 27
groups of, 3, 26
See also Biological cycles
Cystic fibrosis defined, 288
Cytokinesis defined, 249, 250, 254, 258
Cytoplasm defined, 136
Cytosine defined, 307, 311, 338
Cytoskeleton
defined, 154
structure/function of, 154–55, 156, 164
Cytosol defined, 136
Cytotoxic T cell defined, 334

D
Darwin, Charles
evolutionary theories of, 389–90, 393, 418
on speciation, 422, 428–29, 440
Data defined, 19
Decomposer defined, 567, 569, 586
Decomposition defined, 470
Defensive behavior defined, 514

Deforestation defined, 596, 614
Dehydration synthesis defined, 73
Deletion defined, 319
Dendrite defined, 364
Density-dependent factor defined, 542, 560
Density-independent factor defined, 543, 560
Deoxyribose defined, 95
Dermis defined, 360
Descent with modification theory defined, 389
Desert defined, 581
Desert ecosystems, 551
Diabetes, 186
and biotechnology, 326
defined, 181
Diaphragm described, 349
Diatoms described, 466
Diencephalon defined, 362
Diet
beta-carotene in, 245
heart disease and, 101
vegetarian, 91
See also Nutrients, cycling in ecosystems
Differential reproduction defined, 418
Differentiation defined, 124
Diffusion defined, 112, 128
See also Osmosis; Passive transport defined
Digestion, 92, 344–47, 382
Dihybrid cross defined, 280
Dinosaurs, 491
and birds, 499
extinction of, 448, 449
humans and, 449
Dipeptide defined, 90
Diploid defined, 256
Disaccharides defined, 77, 78
Discovery Investigations
anaerobic ATP production, 212–13
blood type alleles, tracking, 414–15
dichotomous keys, 495–96
ecological communities, surveying, 553–54
a faulty protein, 330–31
human communication, exploring, 527–28

human joints, models of, 379–80
light and photosynthesis, 236–37
modeling chromosome movement, 269–70
osmosis in cells, 121–22
pedigrees, interpreting, 297–98
pH and enzyme activity, 187–88
phosphate in aquatic ecosystems, 578–79
plant cells, comparing, 161–62
plant evolution, 445–46
soil conservation, 611–12
testing for lipids, 86–87
using the scientific method, 23–24
water, properties of, 57–58
Disease
defenses against, natural, 332–35
genetics of, 327
heart, 355
immunity from, 335
infectious disease, preventing, 21
respiratory, 350
Disturbance defined, 555, 558
Diversity
in communities, 548, 560
defined, 33
See also Heredity; Organisms; Species
Division defined, 434
DNA (deoxyribonucleic acid)
bacterial, 325, 329
base pairing in, 94, 308, 312, 338
defined, 7, 26, 143, 277, 309
discovery of, 307–8
life without, 271
mitochondrial, 163
modeling, 307, 314–15
mutations, 143
organization of, 269
radiation and, 267
replication in, 310–12, 316–19, 338

656   Index   Biology: Cycles of Life

sequences in evolution, 395, 396
structure of, 306–9, 338
synthesis, 95, 180
vs. RNA, 95
DNA ligase defined, 312
DNA polymerase defined, 311, 312
Dobzhansky, Theodore, 441
Domains. *See individual domain by name, ie Bacteria, Eukarya*
Dominant defined, 521
Dominant gene defined, 279
Dorsal defined, 489
Down syndrome defined, 327, 329
Dysentery defined, 464, 465

E

Eardrum defined, 369
Ears described, 369, 371
Echinodermata, 486, 487
Ecological species concept defined, 431, 452
Ecologist described, 12
Ecology
  communities, surveying, 553–54
  defined, 12, 26, 536, 553, 560
  landscape, 603
  species concept defined, 431, 452
Ecosystems
  aquatic, 578–79, 602
  carrying capacity of, 541, 545, 592, 614
  chemical waste in, 602
  cycles in, 12, 573–77
  defined, 12, 14, 26, 537, 551
  disruption of, 13
  energy flow in, 566–70, 586
  feeding relationships in (*See* Food chains; Food webs)
  human impacts on, 592–98, 614, 631
  mathematical models of, 539
  nutrient cycling in, 573–77, 586
  population growth in, 541
  succession in, 555–56
  trophic structure of, 549, 552, 566–67, 586
  See also Adaptation; Communities; Energy pyramid; Environment; Populations
Ectotherm defined, 491
Effector cell defined, 367
Egg defined, 256
Ejaculation defined, 261
Electromagnetic radiation defined, 230
Electromagnetic spectrum defined, 231
Electron carrier defined, 198
Electron cloud defined, 39
Electrons
  defined, 39
  energy levels in, 48
Electron shell defined, 48
Electron transport chain
  defined, 202
  overview, 202–4
  in photosynthesis, 234
Elements
  defined, 34, 64
  radioactive defined, 398
  symbol defined, 38
  See also Periodic Table of Elements
Elimination
  and circulation, 353
  and digestion, 346
  See also Excretory system
Embden-Meyerhoff pathway. *See* Krebs cycle
Embryo defined, 263, 265
Emigrate defined, 543
Emission defined, 602
Empirical formulas defined, 42
Endangered species
  defined, 406
  protecting, 604
Endocrine system, 372–74, 382
Endocytosis defined, 139
Endomembrane system
  defined, 150
  functions of, 152
Endoplasmic reticulum, 150–51
Endoskeleton defined, 486
Endotherm defined, 492
Energy
  cellular, obtaining, 105, 148, 190, 215, 218
  cycles, 5–6, 33–34
  defined, 5, 26, 81
  ecosystems, flow in, 566–70, 586
  and heat, 569
  levels, 48, 50, 51
  of motion, 173
  organelles, 146–48
  in organisms, 184, 215
  overview, 170–72
  in plant cells, 190
  sources, alternative, 628–31
  transfer of, 51
Energy pyramid defined, 569, 586
  See also Ecosystems
Engineer defined, 607, 614
Engineering and technology, 607–8
Engineering defined, 607
Environment
  Biology In Your Life, 13
  and cancer, 267
  defined, 11, 27
  and dog evolution, 432
  effects of on cells, 114
  factors in, 553
  genetics and, 287
  and native plants, 557
  and natural selection, 411, 413
  organization of, 536–37, 560
  recycling in, 470
  and technology, 609
  See also Adaptation; Biology In Your Life; Ecosystems; Link to Environmental Science; Technology and Society
Enzymes
  in biotechnology, 325, 329
  in cellular respiration, 214
  defined, 89, 98, 106, 180, 190
  in digestion, 345
  and disease, 333
  and DNA replication, 311, 313
  function of, 92, 180–82, 183, 184–85, 190
  products of, 181
Epithelial cell defined, 123, 126
Epithelium defined, 348
Equilibrium defined, 114
Erythrocytes, function of, 354
Erythropoietin and blood cell production, 217
Estrogen
  defined, 262
  production of, 372, 374
Estuary defined, 582
Ethnologist defined, 506
Ethyl alcohol
  defined, 209
  fermentation, 209–10, 218
Euglenia defined, 464, 465
Eukarya defined, 436, 459–60
Eukaryotic cells
  defined, 117, 128
  overview, 117–19
  reproduction in, 119, 248–50, 256–59
  structures in, 120, 164
Eutrophication defined, 594, 614
Evaporation defined, 575, 576
Evolution
  defined, 10, 26, 321
  See also Biological evolution
Evolutionary biology defined, 419, 420
Evolutionary cycles, 10–11
  See also Biological evolution
Excretory system, 359–61, 382
  See also Elimination
Exercise and heart disease, 355
Exocytosis defined, 139
Exon defined, 317
Exoskeleton defined, 484
Experimental group defined, 19, 27

Experiments in the scientific method, 18–19, 22
See also Discovery Investigations; Investigations
Express Lab, 5, 33, 74, 107, 135, 172, 198, 226, 250, 283, 308, 346, 393, 433, 460, 509, 544, 570, 597
External stimulus defined, 506
Extinct defined, 10, 14
Extinction defined, 406
Extracellular matrix defined, 136
Eyes described, 368–69

F

Facilitated diffusion defined, 138, 164
$FADH_2$ defined, 201
Fallopian tube defined, 262, 263
Farming, organic, 583
Fat
　defined, 73 (*See also* Lipids)
　and heart disease, 101
Fatty acids
　defined, 73
　overview, 82–83
　See also Lipids
Fatty layer defined, 360
Feces defined, 346
Feedback inhibition defined, 214, 216, 218
Feedback loop defined, 373
Fermentation
　in ATP production, 208, 209, 212–13
　defined, 208, 218
　overview, 208–10
Fern defined, 472, 475
Fertile defined, 429
Fertilization defined, 256, 257
Fetus defined, 265, 266
Fever
　and heart rate, 354
　inflammatory response in, 333
F_1 generation defined, 278, 279
F_2 generation defined, 279

Fibrinogen defined, 355
Fixed action pattern behavior defined, 507
Flagella defined, 155
Flagellate described, 465
Flatworm defined, 482, 483, 488
Flowcharts, using, xvii
Fluid mosaic model defined, 136, 137
Follicle defined, 262
Food
　macromolecules described, 72–73, 190
　and potential energy, 171–72
Food chains
　defined, 567
　overview, 566–68, 586
　See also Ecosystems
Food Guide Pyramid described, 80
Food webs, 568–69, 586
Forest ecosystems, 551
Fossil fuels
　defined, 475
　overview, 628
　See also Energy
Fossil record defined, 392, 397, 450
Fossils
　dating, 398, 401, 422, 424
　defined, 388, 397, 442, 628
Franklin, Rosalind, 307
Frequency defined, 416
Freshwater defined, 582
Frond defined, 475
Fructose defined, 77, 79, 81
Functional group defined, 71
Fungi, 468–71, 500

G

Galapagos Island finches, 429
Gallbladder defined, 345
Gamete defined, 256, 259, 264, 272
　See also Genes; Heredity; Reproduction
Gametophyte defined, 474
Gap junction defined, 140
Gas exchange defined, 351
Gene flow defined, 406
Gene pool defined, 388

Genes
　and alleles, 405
　changes in (*See* Mutations; Natural Selection; Recombination)
　defined, 90, 93, 94, 98, 143, 316
　exchange among species, 430
　function of, 390
　for genetic disorders, discovering, 7, 282, 296
　sex-linked, 294–95, 296
　transfer of (*See* Transcription; Translation)
　variation, loss of, 406
Genetically modified food defined, 327
Genetics
　biotechnology and, 325–28
　code, 317
　defined, 284
　drift, 406, 408
　and environment, 287
　testing, 288
Genome
　defined, 143
　digital chips and, 328
Genotype
　defined, 284, 300
　determining, 285
Genus defined, 434
Geological defined, 574
Geological processes in nutrient cycling, 574
Geologic time
　defined, 397
　overview, 397–400
　scale, 626
　scale defined, 398
Geology defined, 607
Geothermal energy, 630
Germinate defined, 477
Gestation time defined, 265
Gill defined, 490
Global warming described, 628
Glomerulus defined, 360
Glottis defined, 348

Glucose
　in cellular respiration, 196–98, 218
　defined, 77
　in photosynthesis, 224, 242
　storage of, 346
Glycerol defined, 73
Glycogen defined, 78, 81, 346
Glycolysis
　defined, 200
　overview, 200–201
Golgi apparatus defined, 151
Gonad defined, 260
Gonads, function of, 372
G3P defined, 233
Grana defined, 147
Graphic organizers, using, xvi–xviii
Graphs, using, xviii
Greenhouse effect defined, 594, 595, 614
Growth cycles, 7–8
Growth factor defined, 327
Growth rate defined, 541
Guanine defined, 306, 309, 311, 338
Gymnosperm
　defined, 472, 475
　reproduction in, 476

H

Habitat
　defined, 406, 447, 593 (*See also* Ecosystems; Environment)
　destruction, limiting, 602
　human impact on, 593, 614
Haploid cells defined, 256, 257
Hardy-Weinberg equilibrium defined, 407
Health
　carbohydrates and, 79–80
　and enzymes, 181–82
　and proteins, 90–92
Hearing, sense of, 369
Heart
　blood circulation in, 348, 353–54
　described, 124, 352–53, 377, 382

disease and lipid
  deposits, 83
 rate, measuring, 357
 transplantation, 365
 valves, 354
Heat
 capacity in water, 54
 as energy form, 569
Helium described, 39
Helix defined, 94
Helper T cell defined, 335
Hemoglobin
 defined, 89, 327
 function of, 354
 in sickle cell disease, 328
Hemophilia
 defined, 293, 355
 inheritance of, 293–94
Heredity
 and behavior, 507
 defined, 278
 sex-linked, 294–95
 See also Biological
  evolution; DNA
  (deoxyribonucleic
  acid); Genes
Hershey, Alfred, 310, 313
Heterotroph defined, 479
Heterozygous defined, 280
High fructose corn syrup
 (HFCS) described, 78
Hinge joint described, 376,
 379
Homeostasis
 defined, 111, 128
 maintaining, 190
Homologous chromosome
 defined, 256
Homologous structure
 defined, 394
Homozygous defined, 280
Hormones
 and breast cancer, 268
 defined, 105
 and heart rate, 354
 in human reproduction,
  262, 264
 and metabolism, 346,
  347, 382
Host cell defined, 322
Host defined, 550
How to study tips, x
Human body systems
 circulatory, 124, 350,
  352–56, 365, 382, 621

digestive, 344–47, 382
endocrine, 372–74, 382
excretory, 359–61, 382
immune system,
  332–36, 338
muscular, 377–78, 382,
  623
nervous, 362–66, 382, 620
reproductive, 260–64, 272
respiratory, 348–51, 382
sensory, 367–71, 382
skeletal, 375–76, 382, 622
Human Genome Project,
  337, 395
Humans
 aggressive behavior in,
  516
 ancestors, discovering,
  436
 babies, birth statistic of,
  266
 and bacteria, 458
 body systems (*See*
  Human body
  systems)
 carrying capacity, 592, 614
 communication,
  exploring, 527–28
 development of, 265–66
 and dinosaurs, 449
 ecosystems, impacts on,
  592–98, 614
 and extinction, 604
 fluid requirements of, 54
 in the food chain, 567
 joints, models of, 379–80
 overview, 497, 498, 500
 populations, growth of,
  592
 reproduction in,
  260–64, 272
Hybrid defined, 279
Hydrocarbon defined, 72
Hydrogenation described, 84
Hydrogen bonds
 defined, 54
 in DNA structure, 308
 notes, 55
Hydrolysis defined, 73
Hydrophilic defined, 55,
  84, 134
Hydrophobic defined, 55,
  84, 134
Hydroxide ion, properties
 of, 59

Hydroxyl group described,
  71
Hypertension defined, 355
Hypertonic defined, 114
Hyphae defined, 468
Hypothalamus, function
 of, 372
Hypothalamus defined,
  362, 363
Hypothesis defined, 19, 22,
  27
Hypotonic defined, 114

I

Immigrate defined, 543
Immune system
 defined, 323, 338
 overview, 332–36
Immunity defined, 335, 338
Imprinting defined, 515, 530
Impulses defined, 364
Incomplete dominance
 defined, 286, 300
Incomplete metamorphosis
 defined, 486
Infect defined, 322
Infectious disease defined,
  332
Inferior vena cava defined,
  353
Inflammatory response
 defined, 333
Ingestion defined, 344
Inheritance. *See* Heredity
Innate behavior defined, 507
Insects described, 430,
  485–86, 488
Insertion defined, 319
Insoluble defined, 92
Instantaneous speciation
 defined, 448
Instinct defined, 514
Insulin and diabetes, 186,
  326
Interact defined, 536
Interbreed defined, 429
Interdependent defined,
  548, 560
Intermediate filament
 defined, 154
Internal stimulus defined,
  506
Interphase defined, 248, 272
Interstitial fluid defined, 353
Intertidal zone defined, 582

Introduced species
 defined, 596
Intron defined, 317, 320
Invertebrate
 defined, 398, 480, 500
 overview, 482–88
Investigations
 air particulates,
  measuring, 599–600
 amino acids and
  proteins, 75–76
 animal behavior, 511–12
 bacteria, natural
  selection in, 438–39
 cellular respiration,
  products of, 206–7
 comparing plant and
  animal cells, 157–58
 enzymes in saliva, 178–79
 exercise and heart rate,
  357–58
 food web, building,
  571–72
 living cells, 109–10
 modeling DNA, 314–15
 natural selection in
  action, 402–3
 observing cell cycle
  phases, 254–55
 organisms, classifying,
  462–63
 oxygen production during
  photosynthesis,
  228–29
 physical and chemical
  properties, 36–37
 population size,
  estimating, 546–47
 Punnett squares, 290–91
 What is Life?, 15–16
Involuntary muscle
 defined, 377
Ion defined, 42
Ionic bonds
 defined, 50, 64
 overview, 50–51
Ionic compound defined,
  42, 64
Iris defined, 368
Irish potato famine, 469
Isomer defined, 78
Isotonic defined, 114
Isotope defined, 40, 52, 64

J

Joints described, 376

K

Karyotyping, 299
Kidneys described, 359–60, 361, 382
Kinetic energy defined, 170–71
Kingdom defined, 434
  See also individual kingdom by name, ie Protista
Knee described, 376
Krebs cycle
  defined, 201, 205
  overview, 201–2, 218

L

Lactic acid
  defined, 209
  fermentation, 209, 218
Lactose described, 78
Lagging strand defined, 312
Lamarck, Jean Baptiste de, 389
Lampreys, 490
Land development
  defined, 595
  impact of on ecosystems, 595–96
Landfill defined, 601
Landmark defined, 515
Landscape ecology defined, 603
Larva defined, 491
Larynx defined, 348
Law of Conservation of Energy defined, 6, 27
Law of Independent Assortment defined, 280, 281, 300
Law of Segregation defined, 280, 300
Leading strand defined, 312
Learned behavior defined, 507–8
Leaves
  color changes in, 226
  photosynthesis in, 225–26
  structure of, 225
Lesson study tips, xiii–xiv
Lichen defined, 469

Life, studying, 3
  See also Animals; Organisms; Plants
Life span defined, 497
Light
  energy of, 231–33
  visible spectrum of, 231, 242
Light reaction of photosynthesis, 230–34, 242
Limbic system defined, 362, 366
Linkage map defined, 287
Linked gene defined, 287
Link to Chemistry, 78, 106, 148, 197, 250, 282, 320, 354, 395, 508, 552, 576, 602
Link to Cultures, 523
Link to Earth Science, 3, 59, 171, 204, 226, 400, 449, 556, 574, 596
Link to Environmental Science, 11, 146, 285, 318, 346, 475
Link to Health, 18, 54, 79, 152, 174, 185, 252, 418, 460, 584, 597
Link to Home and career, 51, 183, 216, 377, 570
Link to Language arts, 233, 279, 324, 435, 465, 476, 491, 497, 522, 537
Link to Math, 144, 539
Link to Physics, 39, 231, 264
Link to Social Studies, 112, 209, 234, 259, 293, 327, 365, 390, 440, 469, 516
Linnaeus, Carolus, 434
Linnaeus Classification System, 434–35, 452
Lipase, function of, 181
Lipid bilayer defined, 84
Lipids
  defined, 72, 98
  function of, 105
  overview, 82–84
  See also Fatty acids
Liver and digestion, 345
Lorenz, Konrad, 515, 517
Lou Gehrig's disease, 365
Lung cancer, 349
Lungs described, 348
Lymph nodes in disease, 332

Lymphocyte defined, 333
Lymph system defined, 332
Lysogenic cycle defined, 323
Lysosomes defined, 152
Lytic cycle defined, 322

M

Macroevolution defined, 416, 420
Macromolecule
  defined, 72, 96
  functions of, 128
  overview, 72–73
  See also Carbohydrates; DNA (deoxyribonucleic acid); Food; Lipids; Proteins; RNA (ribonucleic acid)
Macrophage defined, 332, 335, 354, 480
Mad cow disease, 25
Magma defined, 400
Malaria defined, 411
Malignant tumor defined, 252
Maltose described, 78
Mammalia, 492, 493
Mammary gland defined, 428
Marine defined, 582
Marker defined, 310
Mark-recapture sampling method, 546–47
Marsupial defined, 493
Mass defined, 32
Mass extinction defined, 447
Matched submission defined, 521
Math Tips, 40, 144, 283
Matrix defined, 147
Matter
  in chemical reactions, 51
  defined, 32, 33, 64
Mayr, Ernst, 441
Measurement conversion factors, 624–25
Mechanoreceptor described, 367, 368
Medical advances, 365
Medical technology defined, 608
Meiosis
  defined, 257, 272
  errors during, 293

  in mosses, 473
  overview, 256–59, 405
  vs. mitosis, 258
Membranes
  cells
    function of, 135–36
    structure of, 134, 164
  defined, 79
  plasma
    defined, 135
    function of, 138, 164
    structure of, 136
    selectively permeable, 113, 128, 135
  tympanic, 369
Memory, brain areas for, 363
Memory cell defined, 335
Mendel, Gregor, 278–82, 300, 422
Menopause defined, 263
Menstruation defined, 263
Meselson, Matthew, 310
Mesophyll defined, 225
Metabolism
  defined, 170
  hormones and, 346, 347
Metacommunication defined, 522
Metamorphosis defined, 485
Metaphase plate defined, 249
Metastasis defined, 252
Meteorites defined, 397
Methane, properties of, 72
Microevolution defined, 416, 420, 422
Microfilament defined, 154, 156
Microorganisms. *See* Amoeba; Bacteria; Euglenia; Fungi; Paramecium
Microscopes
  cells and, 106–7, 128
  defined, 106
Microtubule defined, 155, 156
Millipedes, 485
Mimicry defined, 514
Mitochondria
  cellular respiration in, 201, 218
  defined, 146
  electron transport chain in, 202
  overview, 147–48

Mitochondrial DNA, 163
Mitosis
  defined, 249, 251, 254, 272
  overview, 248–50
  vs. meiosis, 258
Models
  chromosomes, movement of, 269–70
  DNA, 307, 314–15
  ecosystems, mathematical, 539
  fluid mosaic defined, 136, 137
  human joints, 379–80
Modern synthesis defined, 390
Mold defined, 468
Molecular biology defined, 395
Molecular defined, 33
Molecules
  chemical bonds in, 48–51
  defined, 32
  diffusion within, 138
  motion of, 112
  structure of, 39–40, 47
Mollusca, 483–84, 487, 488
Mollusk defined, 483
Molting defined, 484
Monohybrid cross defined, 279
Monomer defined, 72
Monosaccharides
  defined, 72
  overview, 77–78
Morgan, Thomas, 294
Morphology defined, 428
Moss
  defined, 472, 473
  reproduction in, 474
  water, obtaining, 472, 478
Moths *(Biston betularia)*, 416–17
Motor neurons defined, 365
mRNA (messenger RNA)
  defined, 316, 318
Mucus and disease, 332
Multicellular defined, 479
Multiple allele defined, 285, 300
Municipal water treatment, 605
Muscles, growth of, 80

Muscular system, 377–78, 382, 623
Mushrooms, function of, 468
Mutagen defined, 319, 320
Mutations
  defined, 319, 330
  and disease, 327
  DNA, 143
  evolution and, 402, 404–5, 416, 422
  Science Myths, 319
  See also Chromosomes; DNA (deoxyribonucleic acid); Genes; Heredity
Mutualism defined, 550
Mycelium defined, 468
Mycorhizza defined, 472, 473
Myxini defined, 490, 493

N

NADH defined, 198
Native plants, choosing, 557
Natural selection
  in bacteria, 438–39
  and behavior evolution, 508–9, 530
  environment and, 411, 413
  and gene mutation, 405
  overview, 402–3, 410–13, 418
  theory defined, 389, 408, 422
  See also Biological evolution
Nature's recycling system, 470
Nectar defined, 477
Nematoda, 483, 487
Nephron defined, 360
Nerves
  defined, 123, 369
  function of, 367
  nervous system, 362–66, 382, 620
  See also Neurons
Nervous system, 362–66, 382, 620
  See also Behavior
Nervous tissue defined, 123
Neurons
  defined, 364

  overview, 364–65
  See also Nerves, function of; Nervous system
Neurotransmitter defined, 364
Neutral solution defined, 60
Neutron defined, 39
Niche defined, 431
Nitrate defined, 575
Nitrifying bacteria defined, 575
Nitrogen cycle, 575
Nitrogen-fixer defined, 575
Nitrogenous base defined, 306, 307
Nitroglycerin described, 44–45
Nondisjunction defined, 327
Nonspecific defense defined, 332–33
Nonvascular plant defined, 473
Notes
  algae, 465
  Armillaria ostoyae, 468
  atoms, energy levels in, 50
  atoms and valence, 49
  blue whale, 492
  breathing, 350
  chemical processes, 34
  chlorophyll, 147
  collagen, 89
  the Dead Sea, 459
  dinosaur extinction, 448
  DNA, 143
  DNA models, 307
  endocrine system, 372
  fluoride, 45
  Galapagos Island finches, 429
  genetically modified organisms, 609
  human baby, birth statistic of, 266
  humans and bacteria, 458
  hydrogen bonds, 55
  insects, 430
  Lorenz and Tinbergen, 517
  lung cancer, 349
  molecules, 46
  nephrons, 360
  oocytes, 262
  performance testing, 608

  rocks, oldest known, 398
  scientific method, 20
  seawater, 114
  sickle-cell allele, 411
  theories, 21
  toothpaste, 60
  ulcers, 345
Notochord defined, 489, 490
Nuclear envelope defined, 142
Nucleic acids
  defined, 72, 98
  overview, 94–95
  See also DNA (deoxyribonucleic acid); RNA (ribonucleic acid)
Nucleolus defined, 142
Nucleotide defined, 73, 98, 306, 309, 314, 338
Nucleus
  defined, 39, 164
  functions of, 144
  See also Cells
Nutrients, cycling in ecosystems, 573–77, 586

O

Obesity
  defined, 181
  and heart disease, 355
Observational learning defined, 515
Observation in the scientific method, 18
Ocean energy, 631
Oceans and photosynthesis, 241
Oocyte defined, 262
Oogenesis defined, 262
Operculum defined, 491
Optic nerve defined, 369
Organ defined, 124
Organelles
  defined, 117, 120
  development of, 167
  energy, 146–48
  functions of, 136
  information, 142–44
Organic matter defined, 568
Organic molecules
  defined, 70, 98
  overview, 70–73
  properties of, 71–72

Organisms
    activation energy in, 184
    alleles in, 279
    ATP, production of, 175–76
    behavior of, 13
    classifying (*See* Classification; Taxonomy)
    defined, 2, 4, 120
    diversity and evolution, 397, 404, 422
    energy storage in, 215
    and environment, 287
    identifying, 495–96
    organization, levels of, 125, 128
    sex, determining, 292–93, 296
    transport within, 155
    water in, 53, 56, 59
    See also Behavior; Reproduction
Organization defined, 33
Organ system defined, 124, 128
    See also Human body systems
Origin of replication defined, 311
Osmosis
    defined, 113, 128
    overview, 113–14
    See also Diffusion defined
Osteichthys defined, 490–91, 493
Osteoporosis defined, 375
Ovary defined, 262
Overproduction defined, 418
Ovulation defined, 262, 263
Oxidation, 197
Oxygen
    in photosynthesis, 228–29
    in respiration, 348–50
Ozone defined, 595

P

Pain receptors described, 367
Paleontologist defined, 397, 442
Pancreas, function of, 372, 374
Paramecium described, 464, 465
Parasite defined, 321
Parasitism defined, 550
Parental care behavior defined, 513
Passive transport defined, 138, 164
Patent defined, 609
Pathogen
    defined, 332
    reproduction of, 333
    See also Bacteria; Disease; Fungi
Pedigree defined, 297
Penicillin, mechanism of action, 184, 469
Penis defined, 261
Pepsin defined, 182
Peptide bond defined, 90
Peptides defined, 90
Periodic Table of Elements, 67, 618–19
Peristalsis defined, 345, 377
Permafrost defined, 582
Perspiration defined, 360
PET (Polyethylene terephthalate) described, 41
PGA (phosphoglycerte) defined, 238
P generation defined, 278, 279
pH
    blood and, 63
    defined, 59, 64
    and enzyme activity, 187–88
    overview, 60–61
    and protein structure, 92
    of rainwater, 594
Phagocyte defined, 333, 334
Pharyngeal slit defined, 489, 490
Pharynx defined, 345
Phenotype
    defined, 284, 289, 300, 418
    and evolution, 419
Phenylketonuria (PKU), 282
Pheromone defined, 524, 526
Phloem defined, 472, 473
Phospholipids
    in cell membranes, 164
    defined, 82
    overview, 83
Phosphorus in ATP production, 174, 578
Phosphorylation
    in ATP production, 190, 234
    defined, 174, 177
    in photosynthesis, 234
Photic zone defined, 582
Photon defined, 230
Photoreceptor described, 367, 368
Photosynthesis
    in bacteria, 226, 459
    dark reaction (*See* Calvin-Benson cycle)
    defined, 146, 164, 184, 190, 574
    discovering, 239
    glucose in, 224, 242
    light and, 236–37
    light reaction of, 230–34
    Links to, 146, 148, 233
    overview, 224–26, 242
    oxygen production during, 228–29
    phytoplankton and, 241
    processes of, 232–34
    Science Myths, 225, 239
    sunlight and, 224
    worldwide, 241
Photosystem defined, 234
Photosystem I defined, 234
Photosystem II defined, 234
Phototroph defined, 566, 586, 587
Photovoltaic cells, 629
Phylogeny defined, 482
Phylum defined, 434
Physical property defined, 33
Phytophthora infestans, 469
Phytoplankton and photosynthesis, 241
Pineal gland, function of, 372
Pistil defined, 477
Pituitary gland
    defined, 362, 363
    function of, 372
Pivot joint described, 376, 379
Placenta defined, 265
Plankton defined, 568
Plant kingdom (Plantae), 472–78, 500, 634
Plants
    and air pollution, 475
    vs. animal cells, 157–58
    cells
        ATP, production of, 175–76, 184
        comparing, 161–62
        overview, 159, 164
    and cellular respiration, 198
    classification of, 477
    disease, 148
    evolution of, 445–46
    fertilizers, 587
    grow lights for, 227
    native, choosing, 557
    soil pH and health, 59
Plasma defined, 354
Plasma membrane
    defined, 135
    function of, 138, 164
    structure of, 136
Plasmid defined, 325
Plasmodesmata defined, 159
Plastids defined, 78, 79
Plate defined, 400
Platelet defined, 354, 355
Plate tectonics defined, 399, 400, 401
Platyhelminthes, 482, 487, 488
Pleiotropy defined, 286
Pneumonia defined, 334
Polar molecule defined, 54, 64
Pollen defined, 278
Pollination defined, 477
Pollution
    controlling, 601–2, 628
    defined, 594
    impact on ecosystems, 594–95, 614
    trash, impact on ecosystems, 593, 631
Polygenic trait defined, 287
Polymer defined, 72
Polypeptide defined, 90
Polypodiophyta, 475, 500
Polysaccharides defined, 73, 78, 98
Polyunsaturated fatty acid defined, 82, 83
Population density
    defined, 538, 540, 560
    limits on, 541

Populations
  allele frequency, measuring, 407
  defined, 388, 404, 432, 560
  distribution of, 543–44
  genetic drift in, 406, 408, 422
  growth of, 541–43, 560, 592
  organization of, 536–39
  size, estimating, 546–47
  See also Communities; Ecosystems
Pore defined, 142
Porifera, 482, 487
Potential energy defined, 170–71
Prairies, restoring, 613
Precipitation defined, 575, 576
Predation defined, 550, 560
Predator defined, 514, 550
Pregnancy, 265–66
Prey defined, 514
Primary productivity defined, 569
Primary succession defined, 556, 558, 560
Prions defined, 25
Producer defined, 567, 586
Product defined, 50
Prokaryotic cells
  defined, 116, 128
  fermentation in, 208, 218
  overview, 116–17
  reproduction, 117, 120
Promoter defined, 316, 317
Protease, function of, 181
Proteins
  amino acids and, 75–76, 88
  complement, 332, 333
  complete, 91
  defined, 8, 25, 27
  digestion of, 92
  faulty, 330–31
  function of, 89, 106
  and health, 90–92
  overview, 88–92
  structure, 89, 92
  synthesis of, 90, 164
  transport, 136, 138
Protista, 464–67, 500
Proton defined, 39

Protozoa defined, 464–65
Pseudopod defined, 464, 465
Punctuated equilibrium defined, 441–42
Punnett square
  defined, 281, 290
  overview, 281–82
Pupil defined, 368
Pyruvic acid
  defined, 200
  in glycolysis, 201

Q
Questions in the scientific method, 18

R
Radial symmetry defined, 482
Radiation
  in cancer treatment, 252
  and DNA, 267
Radicals
  and compounds, 43–45
  defined, 43, 47, 64
  list of, 43
Radioactive defined, 40
Radioactive element defined, 398
Radio frequency identification chips, 525
Radioisotope defined, 40
Radula defined, 484
Random pattern of population distribution defined, 543, 544
Reactant defined, 50
Reaction center defined, 233
Recessive gene defined, 279
Recombination defined, 405
Recovery plan defined, 604
Rectum defined, 346
Recycling defined, 602, 614
Red marrow defined, 375
Redox reaction defined, 197
Reduction defined, 197
Reflex defined, 344, 365
Releaser defined, 515
Renal artery, function of, 360
Renewable energy, 628
Replication bubble defined, 311, 312
Replication defined, 310
Replication fork defined, 311

Reproduction
  defined, 7, 27, 248, 431
  eukaryotic, 119, 248–50, 256–59
  in gymnosperms, 476
  in humans, 260–64, 272
  prokaryotic, 117, 120
Reproductively isolated defined, 429
Reptile defined, 398
Reptilia, 491, 493
Research and Write, 29, 67, 84, 101, 131, 143, 167, 193, 221, 245, 275, 289, 303, 307, 341, 385, 425, 455, 503, 533, 558, 563, 567, 587, 603, 617
Reserves defined, 603
Reservoir defined, 605
Respiration
  altitude and, 350, 351
  cellular (*See* Cellular respiration)
  defined, 196
  oxygen in, 348–50
Respiratory system, 348–51, 382
Restriction endonucleases defined, 325, 326
Retina defined, 369
Reviews, tips for using, xv
Rhizoid defined, 473
Ribose defined, 95, 170
Ribosomes
  defined, 142
  functions of, 144, 151, 317–18
  overview, 143–44
RNA polymerase defined, 316
RNA (ribonucleic acid)
  defined, 94, 306, 316–18
  and protein synthesis, 164
  splicing, 316–17
  structure of, 309
  synthesis of, 180, 316–17, 320, 338
  vs. DNA, 95
  See also DNA (deoxyribonucleic acid); Genes; Heredity
RNA splicing defined, 317
Roundworm defined, 483

rRNA (ribosomal RNA) defined, 317
RuBP (ribulose bisphosphate) defined, 238

S
Saccharide defined, 77
Safety rules and symbols, list of, xix–xxi
Saliva defined, 182, 344
Salivary amylase defined, 344
Salt, bonding in, 50
Sample defined, 538
Saturated fatty acid defined, 82
Savanna defined, 581
Scent defined, 521
Science and technology, 607–10, 614
Science at Work
  agricultural plant scientist, 240
  biochemist, 81
  certified athletic trainer, 210
  demographer, 551
  developmental biologist, 124
  environmental engineer, 11
  food chemist, 35
  forensic technician, 373
  genetic counselor, 294
  laboratory technician, 261
  museum guide, 474
  paleontology technician, 408
  park ranger, 593
  pharmaceutical researcher, 318
  pharmacy technician, 176
  plant pathologist, 150
  scientific illustrator, 442
  social worker, 524
  soil scientist, 584
Science Myths
  acids, 60
  alleles, 281
  antibiotics, 322
  bacteria, 569
  birds and human language, 517

blood, 355
cells in living things, 105
cellular activity, 258
dark reaction of photosynthesis, 239
decay, 581
dietary supplements, 80
enzymes and heat, 182
fluids, replacing, 113
genes and alleles, 405
humans and dinosaurs, 449
humans and extinction, 604
mineral nutrients, 574
mutations, 319
pH of rainwater, 594
photosynthesis, 225
plant cells, 160
plants and cellular respiration, 198
plant tissues, 473
predator-prey relationships, 551
probability, 287
scientific knowledge, 543
theory *vs.* hypothesis, 21
Scientific journal defined, 609
Scientific method
 defined, 17, 26, 608
 overview, 17–21
Scientific name defined, 434, 452
Scrotum defined, 260
Secondary succession defined, 556–57, 558, 560
Secrete defined, 151
Sedimentary rock defined, 392, 396
Seed defined, 472
Segmented worm defined, 483
Selection. *See* Artificial selection defined; Natural selection
Selectively permeable membrane defined, 113, 128, 135
Semen defined, 261
Semi-conservative replication defined, 310
Seminiferous tubule defined, 261

Sensory neurons defined, 365
Sensory receptor defined, 367
Sensory system, 367–71, 382
Sequence defined, 90
Sex chromosome defined, 292, 300, 409
Sex-linked trait defined, 293, 300
Sharks, 490
Sickle cell disease defined, 286, 327, 328, 411
Sight, sense of, 368–69
Signal defined, 521
Simple dominance defined, 284, 289, 300
Simulate defined, 513
Sister chromatid defined, 248, 249
Size and population, 538
Skeletal systems, 375–76, 382, 622
Skin
 as defense against disease, 332
 described, 360, 361
 and touch, 370
Skin cancer, 252, 404
Sleep apnea defined, 350
Slime mold defined, 466
Small intestine described, 345, 347
Smell, sense of, 370
Smog, effects of, 584, 595, 596
Smoking and cancer, 267, 268
Social behavior defined, 520, 530
Sociobiologist defined, 520
Soil pH and plant health, 59
Solar defined, 566
Solar energy, 629
Solute defined, 114
Solvent defined, 55
Somatic cell defined, 256
Sori defined, 475
Spatial learning defined, 515
Speciation
 causes of, 429
 Darwin's theories, 428–29
 defined, 10, 14, 26, 428, 452

 mechanisms of, 431–32, 440–44
 rates of, 440–41
Species
 classification of, 434–37, 443
 community interactions, 548
 concepts defining, 430–31
 defined, 10, 27, 452
 discovery of, 451
 introduced, impact on ecosystems, 596–97
 protection of, 614
 survival of, 447–50
Specific defense defined, 333
Specimen defined, 17
Sperm, production of, 372, 374
Spermatogenesis defined, 260, 264
Spermatogonia defined, 261
Sperm defined, 256, 264
Spinal cord described, 363
Spindle defined, 248, 249
Sponges, 482
Spore defined, 466
Sporophyte defined, 473, 474
Stability defined, 539, 560
Stahl, Franklin, 310
Stamen defined, 476
Starch defined, 78, 79
Stasis defined, 441
Stem cells, 127
Steroids, 82, 84
Stigma defined, 477
Stimulus defined, 12
Stoma defined, 225
Stress response, 373
Stroma defined, 146, 147
Subatomic particle defined, 39
Subpopulation defined, 432
Subspecies defined, 431
Substitution defined, 319
Substrate defined, 185
Succession defined, 555, 560
Succession in communities, 555–56
Sucrose described, 78
Sugar-phosphate backbone defined, 306
Sugars. *See* Carbohydrates

Summaries, using, xv
Sunlight and photosynthesis, 224
Superior vena cava defined, 353
Surface tension in water, 54–55
Survival. *See* Adaptation; Biological evolution; Mutations; Natural selection
Swim bladder defined, 491
Symbiosis defined, 550, 552, 560
Sympatric speciation defined, 431, 448, 452
Synapse defined, 364
Synthesize defined, 91
Systems. *See* Ecosystems; Human body systems; Organelles

T

Taste, sense of, 370
Taxonomist defined, 458
Taxonomy
 defined, 458
 See also Classification; Organisms
Tay-Sachs disease defined, 288
Technology
 artificial blood, 125
 defined, 608
 and environment, 609
 and plastic, 41
 science and, 607–10, 614
 See also Technology and Society
Technology and Society
 aquaculture, 581
 bioreactions, 182
 carbon dioxide generators, 231
 communication, 522
 digital chips and genome information, 328
 electron microscopes, 143
 food crops and genetic diversity, 538
 gene chips, 253
 genetic disorders, 7
 hemophilia, 287

high-tech medications, 151
hydrogenation, 84
industrial fermentation, 208
LASIK surgery, 370
organisms, classification of, 484
organisms, discovery of, 437
physiological saline, 115
radon, 40
skin cancer, 404
surgical robots, 608
Temperate deciduous forest defined, 582
Temperate grassland defined, 581
Temperature and heart rate, 354
Template defined, 311
Tendon defined, 377
Tentacle defined, 482
Terminator defined, 316, 317
Terrestrial biome defined, 580, 586
Territorial behavior defined, 515
Testcross defined, 285, 289
Testis defined, 260
Testosterone defined, 260
Tests, preparing for, xv
Tetrad defined, 257, 259
Thalamus defined, 362, 363
Theory defined, 21, 27
Thermoreceptors described, 368, 371
Threatened species
 defined, 601
 protecting, 603
Three-domain system of species classification defined, 436, 458
Thrombus defined, 355
Thylakoid defined, 147, 225
Thymine defined, 307, 311, 338
Thymus gland, function of, 372
Thyroid gland, function of, 372
Tinbergen, Niko, 515–16, 517
Tissue culture described, 118
Tissue defined, 123, 128, 480
T lymphocyte defined, 333, 334
Touch, sense of, 370
Toxic defined, 555
Tracers. *See* Radioisotope defined
Trachea defined, 349
Traits
 defined, 278
 inheritance, sex-linked, 293
 See also Heredity
Transcription, 316–17, 319, 320, 338
Trans fat defined, 83
Transformation defined, 5, 325, 326
Translation
 defined, 316
 overview, 317–18, 319
Transport
 active, 138
 defined, 112
 within organisms, 155
 passive, 138, 164
 proteins, 136, 138
Transport protein defined, 136, 138
Trash, impact of on ecosystems, 593, 631
 See also Pollution
Triclosan described, 140
Triglyceride defined, 82, 98
tRNA (transfer RNA) defined, 317, 318
Trophic structure defined, 549, 552, 566–67, 586
Tropical forest defined, 581
Truncate defined, 91
Tube foot defined, 486
Tubulin defined, 155
Tumors
 defined, 252, 253
 removing, 252
 See also Cancer
Tundra defined, 582
Twins, behavior studies of, 529
Tympanic membrane defined, 369

U

Umbilical cord defined, 265, 266
Uniform pattern of population distribution defined, 543, 544
United Nations described, 604
Unsaturated fatty acid defined, 82, 83
Uracil defined, 307, 338
Ureter defined, 359
Urethra defined, 261
Urine defined, 359
Uterus defined, 262, 263

V

Vaccines
 defined, 323
 delivery, 336
 polio, 341
Vacuole defined, 151
Vagina defined, 265
Variable defined, 19, 27
Vascular bundle defined, 225
Vascular plant defined, 472
Vascular tissue defined, 472, 473
Vas deferens defined, 261
Vegetarian diets, 91
Vegetation defined, 551
Venn diagrams, using, xviii
Ventricle defined, 353
Vertebra defined, 489
Vertebrates
 defined, 398, 480, 500
 overview, 489–94
Villi defined, 345
Viruses
 classification of, 460
 defined, 25, 310, 324, 338
 infection, mechanism of action, 322–23
 structure of, 321–22, 324
Vitamin A and blindness, 97
Voluntary muscle defined, 377

W

Warm-blooded defined, 492
Warning coloration defined, 514
Wasp behavior, 515–16
Water
 absorption of, 360
 balance, regulating, 359
 chemical bonds in, 49
 conserving, 585
 cycle, 575–76, 581
 heat capacity of, 54
 in organisms, 53, 56, 59
 properties of, 53–55, 56
 surface tension in, 54–55
Watson, James, 307308
Wavelength defined, 230
Weather, factors affecting, 580
Wegener, Alfred, 399–400
White blood cells. *See* Macrophage defined
Whooping crane recovery, 598
Wind energy, 629–30
Windmills described, 629
Wireless communications, 525
World map, 627

X

X-rays, 412
Xylem defined, 472, 473

Y

Y chromosome, 409
Yeasts and sugar fermentation, 210

Z

Zygote defined, 256, 257

Photo and Illustration Credits

Cover photos: background, © Royalty-free/Corbis; left inset, © P. Robinson/Robert Harding Picture Library; middle inset, © P. Robinson/Robert Harding Picture Library; right inset, © Jonathan Plant/Alamy Images; p. xxii, © Gray Hardel/Corbis; p. 2, © Douglas Faulkner/Photo Researchers, Inc.; p. 8, © Richard Hutchings/PhotoEdit; p. 10 (left), © Erwin & Peggy Bauer/Animals Animals; p. 10 (right), © Shane Moore/Animals Animals; p. 11, © Nicholas Secor/Phototake; p. 13, © Studio Carlo Dani/Animals Animals; p. 25, © Larry Lefever/Grant Heilman Photography; p. 30, © Steve Allen/Brand X Pictures; p. 32, © Jon Nash/ImageState; p. 34, © Charles D. Winters/Timeframe Photography Inc./Photo Researchers, Inc.; p. 35, © Robin Laurance/Photo Researchers, Inc.; p. 55, © E.R. Degginger/Color-Pic Inc.; p. 63, © Spencer Grant/PhotoEdit; p. 68, © Rick Gayle/Corbis; p. 79, © Matthew Klein/Photo Researchers, Inc.; p. 81, © Jean-Paul Chassenet/Photo Researchers, Inc.; p. 83, © Michael Newman/PhotoEdit; p. 88, © Dwight Kuhn/Dwight R. Kuhn Photography; p. 92 (left), © Arthur Beck/Corbis; p. 92 (right), © Color-Pic Inc.; p. 97, © Alain Evrard/Photo Researchers, Inc.; p. 102, © Dr. Gopal Murti/Visuals Unlimited; p. 116, © Dr. Dennis Kunkel/Visuals Unlimited; p. 119, © David Madison/David Madison Sports Images, Inc.; p. 123, © Robb Kendrick/Aurora Photos; p. 124, © Gary Hansen/Phototake; p. 125, © Custom Medical Stock Photo; p. 127, © Andy Sacks/Stone/Getty Images; p. 132, © David Becker/Photo Researchers, Inc.; p. 142, © Dennis Kunkel Microscopy, Inc.; p. 144, © Dennis Kunkel Microscopy, Inc.; p. 150, © Maximilian Stock LTD/Phototake; p. 163, © Richard T. Nowitz/Corbis; p. 168, © Jeff J. Daly/Fundamental Photographs, NYC; p. 176, © Jose Luis Pelaez, Inc./Corbis; p. 189, © PhotoDisc by Getty Images; p. 194, © Gilles Martin-Raget/MTP Network; p. 210 (top), © David Young-Wolff/PhotoEdit; p. 210 (bottom), © Myrleen Ferguson Cate/PhotoEdit; p. 215, © RDF/Visuals Unlimited; p. 217, © Reuters/Corbis; p. 222, © Doc White/Ardea.com; p. 227, © Galen Rowell/Corbis; p. 240, © Michael Rosenfeld/Stone/Getty Images; p. 241, © Carolina Biological Supply Company/ Phototake; p. 246, © ISM/Phototake; p. 255, © Carolina Biological/Visuals Unlimited; p. 261, © Susan Van Etten/PhotoEdit; p. 271, © Martin Hanczyc/Martin Hanczyc; p. 276, © Dr. Daon Fawcett/Visuals Unlimited; p. 286, © Eye of Science/Photo Researchers, Inc.; p. 288, © Dana White/PhotoEdit; p. 294, © Robin Nelson/PhotoEdit; p. 299, © Science VU/Visuals Unlimited; p. 304, © TEK Image/Photo Researchers, Inc.; p. 318, © Tom & Dee Ann McCarthy/Corbis; p. 321, © Dr. Gopal Murti/Visuals Unlimited; p. 326, © Robert Ginn/PhotoEdit; p. 337, © PhotoDisc by Getty Images; p. 342, © Dennis O'Clair/Photographer's Choice/Getty Images; p. 356, © PhotoDisc by Getty Images; p. 373, © Dwayne Newton/PhotoEdit; p. 381, © Yoav Levy/Phototake; p. 386, © William Lampas/Omni Photo Communications; p. 406, © Ablestock/Alamy Images; p. 408, © Kenneth Garrett/National Geographic Image Collection; p. 410, © Tom McHugh/Photo Researchers, Inc.; p. 421, © Juniors Bildarchiv/Alamy Images; p. 426, © Gerald & Buff Corsi/Visuals Unlimited; p. 432, © Lynn Stone/Animals Animals; p.442, © Jonathan Blair/Corbis; p. 443, © Sharna Balfour; Gallo Images/Corbis; p. 451, © Daniel Harder, Ph.D./Arboretum at the University of California, Santa Cruz; p. 456, © Jacques Jangoux/Visuals Unlimited; p. 469, © Darlyne A. Murawski/Peter Arnold, Inc./Alamy Images; p. 474, © Kelly-Mooney Photography/Corbis; p. 499, © Jonathan Blair/Corbis; p. 504, © Tom Walker/ImageState/Alamy Images; p. 508, © Mitssuaki Iwago/Minden Pictures; p. 523, © Susan Van Etten/PhotoEdit; p. 524, © Bill Aron/PhotoEdit; p. 529, © Jose Luis Pelaez, Inc./Corbis; p. 534, © Stephen Frink/Corbis; p. 551, © Bob Daemmrich/The Image Works, Inc.; p. 556, © Douglas Faulkner/Corbis; p. 559, © Bill Beatty/Visuals Unlimited; p. 564, © Aaron Horowitz/Corbis; p. 584, © Comstock Production Department/Comstock Images/Alamy Images; p. 585, © Andy Sotiriou/PhotoDisc; p. 590, © PhotoDisc by Getty Images; p. 593, © Lowell Georgia/Corbis; p. 613, © Richard Hamilton Smith/Corbis; p. 628, © Royalty-free/Corbis; p. 629, © PhotoDisc by Getty Images; p. 630 (left), © Royalty-free/Corbis; p. 630 (right), © PhotoDisc by Getty Images; p. 631, © Royalty-free/Corbis; p. 632, © PhotoDisc by Getty Images; illustrations: John Edwards Illustration

Midterm Mastery Test

Chapter 1–10 Midterm Mastery Test

Part A Circle the correct answer to each question.

1. ATP is manufactured during the process of _____.
   A cellular respiration   C digestion
   B photosynthesis   D reproduction

2. _____ is the green pigment in plants that can capture sunlight.
   A Cellulose   B Chlorophyll   C Photosynthesis   D Glucose

3. The smallest unit of a living thing is a(n) _____.
   A molecule   B compound   C atom   D cell

4. One end of a water molecule has a slightly positive charge. The other end has a slightly negative charge. For this reason, water is a(n) _____ molecule.
   A hydrophilic   B balanced   C polar   D ionic

5. ATP is made of ribose, adenine, and _____.
   A one phosphate group   C three phosphate groups
   B two phosphate groups   D a fatty acid

6. Birds and bats have _____, an adaptation for flying.
   A wings   B clawed feet   C sharp beaks   D good eyesight

7. A chemical _____ shows the number and kinds of atoms in a compound.
   A formula   B molecule   C compound   D equation

8. Cells depend on the monosaccharide _____ for energy.
   A starch   B cellulose   C sucrose   D glucose

9. Cell membranes are made of phospholipids molecules. Each molecule has two ends. The _____ end interacts with the watery environment.
   A hydrophobic   B hydrophilic   C fatty acid   D ionic

10. The ability to do work is _____.
    A heat   B energy   C reproduction   D DNA

Chapter 1–10 Midterm Mastery Test, continued

11. A(n) _____ is a substance formed during a chemical reaction.
    A equation   B molecule   C reactant   D product

12. Water molecules move into and out of cells by a type of passive transport called _____.
    A exocytosis   B osmosis   C endocytosis   D facilitated diffusion

13. All of the chemical processes in a cell are known as _____.
    A digestion   B phosphorylation   C hydrolysis   D metabolism

14. Male gonads are _____.
    A gametes   B sperm   C testes   D eggs

15. A species can undergo changes or _____ that help it survive.
    A growth cycles   B cell divisions   C migrations   D adaptations

Part B On the line, write the answer to complete each sentence.

16. During _____, the unfertilized egg, blood, and tissue pass out of a female's body.

17. The study of heredity is _____.

18. Chemicals that can change the rates of chemical reactions in living systems are called _____.

19. _____ are orange or gold accessory pigments found in some leaves.

20. _____ is a condition in which cells divide too much.

21. A(n) _____ process, like cellular respiration, is one that involves oxygen.

22. New cells for growth are produced in a type of cell division called _____.

23. Cells can store energy as _____ molecules. These molecules are not soluble in water.

24. The full range of the energy radiated by the sun is the _____. It includes visible light.

25. A cell's contents are separated from the environment by the _____.

Chapter 1–10 Midterm Mastery Test, continued

Part C Write the answer to each question on the line.

26. How does feedback inhibition in cells control the rate of energy production?

27. What two molecules contain and translate instructions for making proteins in cells?

28. What happens in meiosis during the event called crossing over?

29. Why does a cell in a very salty solution lose water?

30. Hydrogen has an atomic number of 1 and a mass number of 1. How many protons, neutrons, and electrons can be found in one hydrogen atom?

Part D Match each term with its meaning. Write the correct letter on the line.

_____ 31. coenzyme A   A results from the split of a glucose molecule
_____ 32. homeostasis   B organelle that converts glucose to energy of ATP
_____ 33. hormone   C a group of lipids that include hormones
_____ 34. mitochondrion   D helps acetic acid cross the membranes of mitochondria
_____ 35. phenotype   E describes how an organism looks
_____ 36. photosynthesis   F a storage structure in a cell
_____ 37. pyruvic acid   G a balance of internal conditions in cells
_____ 38. steroids   H the process that captures sunlight and uses the energy to make food
_____ 39. vacuole   I male sex chromosomes
_____ 40. XY   J a chemical signal sent from one part of the body to another

Chapter 1–10 Midterm Mastery Test, continued

Part E Write your answer to each question. Use complete sentences. Support each answer with facts and examples from the textbook.

41. Compare and contrast prokaryotic cells and eukaryotic cells. (2 points)

42. Describe the structure and function of DNA. (2 points)

Part F Write a paragraph for each topic. Include a topic sentence, body, and conclusion in the paragraph. Support your answers with facts and examples from the textbook.

43. What is the scientific method? Explain how you could use the steps of the scientific method to find whether cup A or cup B is the best at keeping a liquid warm. (3 points)

44. Explain the roles of photosynthesis and cellular respiration in plant cells. What is the relationship between these two processes? (3 points)

Final Mastery Test

Page 1

Final Mastery Test

Part A Match each term with its meaning. Write the correct letter on the line.

_____ 1. fibrinogen
_____ 2. binary fission
_____ 3. heterotroph
_____ 4. niche
_____ 5. nitrogenous base
_____ 6. recycle
_____ 7. ribosome
_____ 8. urine
_____ 9. vascular tissue
_____ 10. virus

A a nonliving piece of DNA or RNA that can infect a cell
B an organism's way of life
C create new products from wastes
D an organelle that helps assemble amino acids into proteins
E a blood clotting protein
F part of a plant that carries food and water
G any organism that cannot make its own food
H a waste product made in the kidneys
I part of a nucleotide
J asexual reproduction in a one-celled organism

Part B Circle the correct answer to each question.

11. Three bases on a strand of DNA make a(n) _____.
    A anticodon B codon C gene D mutation

12. The theory of _____ says that today's organisms evolved from those of the past.
    A plate tectonics C common descent
    B continental drift D recombination

13. Animals show _____ when they work together.
    A competition B predation C cooperation D cognition

14. The gamete made in the female reproductive system is a(n) _____.
    A ovary B uterus C follicle D egg

15. ATP is manufactured during the process of _____.
    A cellular respiration C the immune response
    B digestion D photosynthesis

Page 2

Final Mastery Test, continued

16. The study of life is _____.
    A oceanography B chemistry C biology D economics

17. The layer of skin on the outside of the body is the _____.
    A epidermis B dermis C fatty layer D photic zone

18. Cellular respiration produces _____.
    A pyruvic acid B alcohol C energy D glycolysis

19. The smallest particle of glucose with all the properties of glucose is one _____.
    A atom B molecule C electron D ion

20. Cells use the energy of carbohydrates in the form of _____.
    A DNA B RNA C ATP D peptides

21. The brain and _____ make up the central nervous system.
    A hormones B peripheral nerves C spinal cord D motor nerves

22. Asexual reproduction involves _____.
    A crossing over C two parents
    B gene pooling D one parent

23. The _____ of an ecosystem is made up of plant life.
    A biome B vegetation C intertidal zone D succession

24. Chromosome are made of _____.
    A microtubules B microfilaments C DNA D bilayers

25. Several _____ link to make a food web.
    A populations B trophic structures C energy pyramids D food chains

26. The _____ system's first line of defense is nonspecific.
    A circulatory C nervous
    B immune D respiratory

27. Pollution can be defined as _____.
    A trash C anything harmful added to the environment
    B eutrophication D ozone

Page 3

Final Mastery Test, continued

28. A _____ includes an organism's genus and species names.
    A title C scientific name
    B kingdom D common name

29. _____ is a type of cell division that produces gametes.
    A Meiosis B Binary fission C Mitosis D Gestation

30. _____ are plants that have vascular tissue and reproduce without seeds.
    A Mosses B Ferns C Grasses D Lichens

31. Light exists in particles known as _____.
    A photons B waves C wavelengths D electromagnetic radiation

32. One job of a(n) _____ is to create products that help people.
    A biogeologist B engineer C geologist D conservation biologist

33. Animals like jellyfish have stinging cells on their tentacles. Jellyfish are examples of _____.
    A flatworms B myxini C cnidarians D crustaceans

34. One of the body's waste products is _____. It is a salty liquid produced by the skin.
    A feces B carbon dioxide C perspiration D urine

35. All parts of the earth that support living things make up the _____.
    A biosphere B ecosystem C environment D population

Part C On the line, write the answer to complete each sentence.

36. One animal needs the same resources as another animal. These two animals are _____.

37. The trophic structure of an ecosystem explains how _____ flows through it.

38. Some animals blend in with the environment. They have colors or patterns that act as _____ and help them hide.

39. The time that has passed from the earth's beginning to now is known as _____.

40. A(n) _____ is an organism that kills and eats other organisms.

41. _____ is a form of oxygen that blocks some of the sun's radiation.

42. A layer of air called the _____ surrounds the earth.

Page 4

Final Mastery Test, continued

43. Water-hating, or _____, molecules do not mix with water.

44. A(n) _____ is an idea or plan that can save an endangered species.

45. The genetic code travels from the nucleus to a ribosome. The code makes this trip on a strand of _____.

46. A(n) _____ is a foreign molecule that activates the immune system.

47. Energy is needed to add a phosphate group to a molecule of _____. The result is a molecule of ATP.

48. An ecosystem cannot support unlimited population growth. The number of individuals an ecosystem can support depends on its _____.

49. Animals with backbones, like humans and birds, are classified as _____.

50. Hemophilia is a sex-linked. It is carried on the _____ chromosome.

Part D Write the answer to each question on the line.

51. What is a biome?

52. Why do living things need energy?

53. How are fermentation and cellular respiration similar?

54. State the products of photosynthesis.

55. What is the fossil record?

56. State the theory of natural selection.

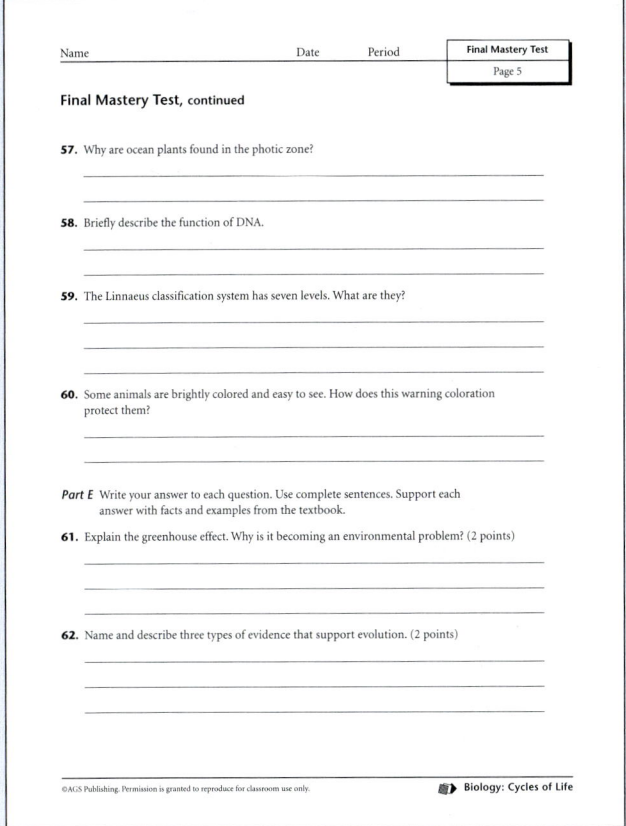

Final Mastery Test Page 5

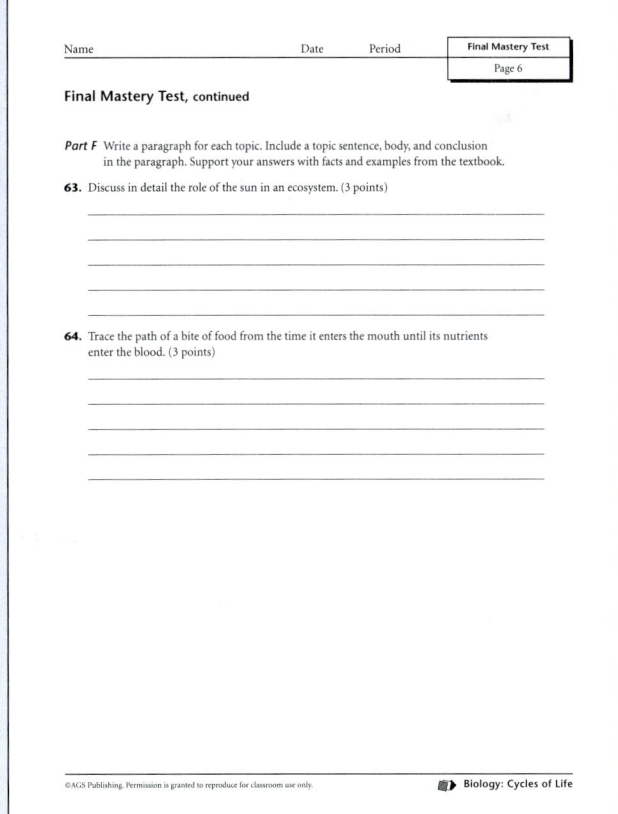

Final Mastery Test Page 6

The lists below show how items from the Midterm and Final correlate to the chapters in the student edition.

Midterm Mastery Test

Chapter 1: 3, 6, 10, 15
Chapter 2: 4, 7, 11, 30
Chapter 3: 8, 23, 27, 39
Chapter 4: 29, 32, 33
Chapter 5: 9, 12, 25, 34, 35
Chapter 6: 5, 13, 18
Chapter 7: 1, 21, 26, 31, 38
Chapter 8: 2, 16, 19, 24, 37
Chapter 9: 14, 20, 22, 28
Chapter 10: 17, 36, 40

Critical Thinking Items:

41. Chapter 4 (prokaryotic and eukaryaotic cells)
42. Chapter 3 (structure and function of DNA)
43. Chapter 1 (scientific method)
44. Chapters 7 and 8 (cellular respiration and photosynthesis)

Final Mastery Test

Chapter 1: 16, 52
Chapter 2: 19, 43
Chapter 3: 45, 58
Chapter 4: 2, 20
Chapter 5: 7, 24
Chapter 6: 15, 47
Chapter 7: 18, 53
Chapter 8: 31, 54
Chapter 9: 14
Chapter 10: 29, 50
Chapter 11: 5, 10, 11, 26, 46
Chapter 12: 1, 8, 17, 21, 34
Chapter 13: 12, 39, 55, 56
Chapter 14: 4, 22, 28, 59
Chapter 15: 3, 9, 30, 33, 49
Chapter 16: 13, 36, 40, 60
Chapter 17: 23, 35, 38, 48, 51
Chapter 18: 25, 37, 42, 57
Chapter 19: 6, 27, 32, 41, 44

Critical Thinking Items:

61. Chapter 19 (the greenhouse effect)
62. Chapter 13 (evidence of evolution)
63. Chapters 1, 8, and 18 (role of the sun in ecosystems)
64. Chapter 12 (structure and function of the digestive system)

Discovery Investigation Answers

Discovery Investigation 1, page 24

Analysis Answers

1. The substance used to "water" the plant was the variable that was changed.
2. Answers may vary. After Day 4, those watered with water should have sprouted. The sprouts should be more visible after Day 8. A few seeds "watered" with vinegar may sprout.

Conclusions Answers

1. Answers will vary depending on students' hypotheses and results. Students should indicate whether the hypothesis was supported, not whether it was correct.
2. Answers will vary. Students should note the problems that occurred during the investigation and include any modifications they would make to the procedure.
3. An experiment that does not support a hypothesis is not a failure because the information allows more accurate hypotheses to be made.
4. Acid rain prevents seeds from sprouting and plants from growing.

Explore Further Answers

Encourage students to ask questions about what a plant needs to grow. Have student groups pick one question to investigate. Then help them shape their question into a process that uses the scientific method. Students should propose a testable hypothesis and then create an experiment that tests this hypothesis.

Discovery Investigation 2, page 58

Analysis Answers

1. Student groups should present their data to the class. They should explain the results clearly and be able to answer questions about the procedure.
2. If problems developed during the procedure, be sure students evaluate the problems. Have students write a new procedure to correct the problem.

Conclusions Answers

1. Answers will vary depending on the property that groups choose to investigate.
2. Answers will vary. Students should offer explanations about the consequences for life forms about the property they chose.
3. The hydrogen bonds that form as part of the water molecule are responsible for the unique properties of water.

Explore Further Answers

Have students write a procedure to test another property of water. As an alternative to choosing another property, students could trade their procedure with another group who chose a different property. If time allows, have each group read through the procedure and perform it. If more than one group performs the procedure, have them compare their results.

Discovery Investigation 3, page 87

Analysis Answers

1. In Test Tube 1, the Sudan III forms a layer on top of the water and does not mix with it. In Test Tube 2, the Sudan III mixes with the vegetable oil.
2. Sudan III mixes with oil, but not with water. Methylene blue mixes with water, but not with oil.

Conclusions Answers

1. Answers will vary depending on students' hypotheses and results. Students should indicate whether the hypothesis was supported, not whether it was correct.
2. The tails of the fatty acid chains are hydrophobic (water-hating) or nonpolar, which results in fatty acids not mixing with water. Carbohydrates such as glucose are polar and mix with water.

Explore Further Answers

Encourage students to ask questions about basic observations they have made. Some examples could include: Why does the Sudan III/oil layer float on top of the water? What other liquids can we test? Help students shape their observations into a process that uses the scientific method. Students should propose a testable hypothesis and then create an experiment that tests this hypothesis.

Discovery Investigation 4, page 122

Analysis Answers

1. Distilled water is a hypotonic environment for *Elodea*.
2. If *Elodea* cells were surrounded by salt water, water would exit the cells.

Conclusions Answers

1. Answers will vary depending on students' hypotheses and results. For example, students may wish to prepare a second slide with *Elodea* mounted in a drop of 10% NaCl solution instead of distilled water. Students should indicate whether the hypothesis was supported, not whether it was correct.
2. Too much plant fertilizer will cause water to leave the plant cells, causing wilting and possible death.

Explore Further Answers

Encourage students to predict possible outcomes based upon observations they have made. For example, if a salt solution is surrounding a plant cell, what might happen when the plant takes up more water after a rainstorm? Help students to shape these observations into a process that uses the scientific method. Students could propose a testable hypothesis and then create an experiment that tests this hypothesis.

Discovery Investigation 5, page 162

Analysis Answers

1. Students should see chloroplasts, vascular cells, and cell walls of various forms.
2. Students should see large groups of chloroplasts in the leaves. Stem cells should contain vascular cells with very thick cell walls for support. Root cells should have thinner walls organized for massive division and elongation. Root cells can also be seen in various stages of maturation as they mature away from the tip.

Conclusions Answers

1. Answers will vary. Students should gain a better understanding of the roles that the cell wall, nucleus, and chloroplasts play in a plant cell. Have them review and discuss any misconceptions.
2. Encourage students to consider different types of plants, such as a cactus, tree, grass plant, and various fruit and flower structures. Have students share their predictions.

Explore Further Answers

Potato: root (sweet potato), stem (white potato); thorn: leaf; celery stalk: stem; lettuce: leaf; onion bulb: root. Answers will vary, but should reflect some of the knowledge about plant cells that students have learned from this investigation and the plant structure they researched. For example, the cells of a lettuce leaf would contain chloroplasts.

Discovery Investigation 6, page 188

Analysis Answers

1. Students' data tables should reflect that the egg whites break down faster in the acidic solutions.
2. Generally, a pH of 1 to 3 is optimal.

Conclusions Answers

1. The stomach creates and needs to maintain an acidic environment to allow pepsin to digest proteins.
2. The test tubes were placed in warm water to simulate the warm environment inside the human body. In addition to pH, pepsin works best in a warmer environment.

Explore Further Answers

People take antacids to ease stomach pain. However, changing the pH in the stomach can cause problems with digestion by deactivating key enzymes. Some studies show that the stomachs of people who regularly take antacids produce even larger amounts of acid to compensate for the medicine.

Optional: Students may wish to create a chart from their data to illustrate how pH affects digestion.

Discovery Investigation 7, page 213

Analysis Answers

1. Yeast cells use fermentation to make ATP.
2. Yes, fermentation is occurring. The production of bubbles indicates that a gas is being produced. The lowering of the pH in the bromothymol blue solution suggests the presence of carbonic acid, which is produced when carbon dioxide gas dissolves in water.

Conclusions Answers

1. Answers will vary depending on students' hypotheses and results. Students should indicate whether the hypothesis was supported, not whether it was correct.
2. Yes, temperature affects the rate of fermentation. Students may wish to replace the warm water in the beaker with ice water or hot water. Students could then count the number of bubbles per minute and compare this number to the number of bubbles per minute produced at the warm temperature.

Explore Further Answers

Encourage students to predict possible outcomes based on observations they have made. For example, if bread dough typically rises in an hour at $38°$ to $43°C$, what happens when it is placed in the refrigerator instead? *(It rises slowly over several hours.)* Help students shape their observations into a process that uses the scientific method. Students should propose a testable hypothesis and then create an experiment that tests this hypothesis.

Discovery Investigation 8, page 237

Analysis Answers

1. The water in the flask absorbs heat. By changing the water before each time trial, heat is eliminated as a factor in this experiment.
2. Answers will vary. Photosynthesis is usually greatest at the smallest distance from the light.

Conclusions Answers

1. Answers will vary depending on students' hypotheses and results. Students should indicate whether the hypothesis was supported, not whether it was correct.
2. Yes, temperature affects the rate of photosynthesis. Answers will vary. For example, students could vary the water temperature in the flasks while keeping the distance to the lamp constant. Students could then count the number of bubbles per minute and compare the rate of photosynthesis at various temperatures.

Explore Further Answers

Encourage students to suggest possible experiments for finding out the effects of different colors of light on photosynthesis. For example, students may wish to heat or cool the water in the flasks. Ask students to propose a testable hypothesis and then create an experiment that tests the hypothesis.

Discovery Investigation 9, page 270

Analysis Answers

1. Students should discover a variety of differences. In the crossing over model, they may see that different chromosomes will have crossed over, different segments, different sizes, and so on. In the meiosis II model, they will see different combinations that will have occurred between groups.

2. The most obvious difference will be haploid products versus diploid products. Products in meiosis I will have segments changed from crossing over. In meiosis II, products will be changed because of redistribution.

Conclusions Answers

1. Genes on the ends of the arms of chromosomes are more likely to be crossed over than genes near the center. The size and location of the genes crossed over can vary.
2. As happens in real life, using products from meiosis I would contribute to the diversity by starting with chromosome pairs that were mixed from crossing over.

Explore Further Answers

This increases diversity the most. Combining genes from two separate sources brings together gametes from entirely different sets of chromosomes to create new combinations.

Discovery Investigation 10, page 298

Analysis Answers

1. Persons in Step 2:
   I-1 Type AB; AB
   I-2 Type O; OO
   I-3 Free earlobes; Ff
   I-4 Free earlobes; Ff
   II-1 Type O; OO
   II-2 Type AB; AB
   II-3 Type A; AO
   II-4 Type B; BO, Attached earlobes; ff
   II-5 Attached earlobes; ff
   II-6 Attached earlobes; ff
   II-7 Free earlobes; Ff
2. The first son II-1 (type O) and the first daughter II-2 (type AB) are adopted. They cannot be the biological children of two parents with the blood types AB and O. This is because these two parents can have only type A or type B offspring.

Conclusions Answers

1. The traits are not sex-linked. Both traits are inherited regardless of the individual's sex. Attached earlobes (ff) cannot be sex-linked because two parents with free earlobes (Ff) can produce a boy or a girl with attached earlobes. If this was a sex-linked trait, the father with free earlobes would pass his one copy of this dominant allele to every daughter.
2. For Generation III, since the parents (II-4 and II-5) have attached earlobes, their genotype must be ff. This means all of the Generation III individuals will have attached earlobes (ff). Since the father, II-4, is type B and has a parent, I-2, who is type O, his genotype is BO. The Generation III individuals could be type O (if the mother, II-5, is type O), type B (if the mother, II-5, is type B or type AB), or type AB (if the mother, II-5, is type A or type AB).

Explore Further Answers

Encourage students to research hereditary diseases and prepare sample pedigrees. Have students include a description of the risks of inheriting the diseases to accompany their pedigrees.

Discovery Investigation 11, page 331

Analysis Answers

1. The corresponding mRNA sequence is ACUCCUGAGGAG. This sequence contains four codons.
2. This mRNA sequence will produce the amino acids threonine, proline, glutamic acid, and glutamic acid.
3. The corresponding mRNA sequence for the DNA shown in Step 4 is ACUCCUGUGGAG. This mRNA sequence will produce the amino acids threonine, proline, valine, and glutamic acid.

Conclusions Answers

1. Transcription is occurring in Step 2.
2. Translation is occurring in Step 3.
3. In Step 4, the third trio of DNA nucleotides reads CAC instead of CTC. This is an example of a substitution.

Explore Further Answers

Students should recognize that a gene mutation will fail to affect a protein if the resultant mRNA codon codes for the same amino acid. For example, if the nucleotide trio TGA in the DNA sequence in Step 1 changes to TGG, it will ultimately still produce the amino acid threonine.

Discovery Investigation 12, page 380

Analysis Answers

1. Possible answers include the movement of the joint, how the joint is connected, the type of hardware available, and how the available materials are conducive to creating different types of joints.
2. Be sure students understand how their joint works. If possible, have them demonstrate the joint in their body next to their model.
3. Answers will vary. For example, the hinge joint moves only in one direction.

Conclusions Answers

1. Most joints constructed from the hardware materials will not be as flexible as body joints. Most hardware models will be stronger than the body joints they represent.
2. Some hardware materials available may not be sufficient to create some of the joints studied.
3. The body constantly maintains its joints. Unlike hardware joints, body joints are constantly being repaired. As the body ages or undergoes extraordinary stress, the joints may break down or fracture.

Explore Further Answers

Students can often create an impressive working model of a human joint. Students should point out that by using a motor or pulley, they have added the muscle to the joint and connected the two with ligaments.

Discovery Investigation 13, page 415

Analysis Answers

1. The children of Child W and Spouse W can have any blood type because they can inherit a combination of any kind of allele.
2. The children of Child W and Spouse W must be blood type B. They can only inherit a B allele from Spouse W. Although they can inherit either a B allele or an O allele from Child W, the O allele will not affect the resulting blood type.
3. The A allele has been eliminated.

Conclusions Answers

1. The O allele is recessive, and one O allele cannot determine a blood type. Only by grouping two O alleles together can an O blood type result.
2. Using a coin flip to randomly decide which gene gets passed on is appropriate, since alleles are passed on randomly to offspring.
3. The children of Grandchild X or Grandchild Y could receive an A allele if either parent reproduces with an individual who has at least one A allele.

Explore Further Answers

Explain the Rh factor to students. Tell them that if a person receives two positive alleles, he or she will have a positive blood type. If a person receives two negative alleles, he or she will have a negative blood type. If a person receives one positive and one negative allele, he or she will have a positive blood type. Have students go through the exercise in a similar way that they determined blood types. They can use a coin flip again to determine which allele is passed on. Have them start with different Rh types and see how the dominant (+) allele moves and affects blood types as it is passed on or is absent.

Discovery Investigation 14, page 446

Analysis Answers

1. Moss grows on the surface of wet or damp ground. It has no stems to grow upright. This is a disadvantage because it restricts moss to wet areas.
2. The moss and fern reproduce from spores. The conifer and flowering plant create seeds.
3. Answers will vary. A possible answer is that coniferous and flowering plants are adapted to living in drier environments than mosses and ferns.
4. The flowering plant creates a flower that turns into a seed after being pollinated. Flowers attract animals and use animals as pollinators. Animals also can carry the seeds far from the parent plant. This means that flowering plants spread over a large area.

Conclusions Answers

The sequence should be moss → fern → conifer → flowering plant.

Explore Further Answers

Although blue-green algae are not plants, they are thought to be the organism from which plants came.

Discovery Investigation 15, page 496

Analysis Answers

1. Students should describe some characteristics that were helpful in identifying their specimen.
2. Physical characteristics that differentiate the appearance of different organisms are used in dichotomous keys.
3. Things such as DNA and living activities are usually not included.

Conclusions Answers

1. An effective key will include information on all organisms that could be identified. A dichotomous key is unreliable if organisms are left out. However, organisms that would not normally be considered, such as trees in a key that identifies mushrooms, are unnecessary.
2. Using a key saves time. Instead of reading descriptions of each possible organism, the key allows a person to quickly narrow down the possible identities.

Explore Further Answers

Students should use the information they learned in using the keys to create their own valid key.

Discovery Investigation 16, page 528

Analysis Answers

1. Students should describe some of the observations they made during the investigation.
2. Emotions often play a key role in human communication. Emotions are often evident as part of facial expressions, voice tone, or body language.

Conclusions Answers

1. Answers will vary depending on students' observations.
2. Students should realize that many of the gestures, tones, and body language that they have observed in the investigation are also a part of normal verbal communication between humans. Examples can include the aggressive body language that is used when someone is angry, or the gestures and body language that are used between two humans who are cooperating on some activity.

Explore Further Answers

Students should create a simple investigation to examine the types of behavior that accompany being untruthful. Have them make notes on some of the behavior that they believe someone uses when being truthful and untruthful. Classic signs of being untruthful are looking away, fidgeting, and speaking quickly.

Discovery Investigation 17, page 554

Analysis Answers

1. Abiotic (nonliving) features include water, soil, rocks, temperature, light, and nutrients. Biotic (living) features may include any of the living things found at the site: animals, vascular plants, lichens, mosses, molds and other fungi, and bacteria.
2. The most common distribution pattern is clumped, with individuals grouped in patches where soil and/or moisture conditions are ideal for growth. Insects may also be clumped due to social behaviors.
3. Photosynthetic plants and algae are producers. Animals are consumers.
4. Students may describe the growth of mosses, lichens, or small plants in previously barren areas such as rocks or pavement.

Conclusions Answers

1. Answers will vary depending on students' hypotheses. Proposed student procedures may suggest counting individual organisms to support or disprove a hypothesis. In many study sites, plants will have the greatest population density. In other areas, animals may have the greatest density (for example, pill bugs beneath rotting logs).
2. At most sites, producers will be found in greatest number. Remind students that decomposers such as bacteria are present in large numbers, but cannot be seen in a field study such as this one.
3. Density-dependent factors include food, water, and soil nutrients. Density-independent factors may include temperature, fires, and severe weather conditions such as drought or flooding.

Explore Further Answers

Students should recognize that organisms might exhibit predator-prey relationships or symbiotic relationships such as parasitism, mutualism, or commensalism. Student procedures may suggest additional field observation and/or research to learn more about possible relationships among local species.

Discovery Investigation 18, page 578

Analysis Answers

1. Answers will vary. The jars with the largest amounts of detergent will have the greenest color and the strongest odor. If eutrophication occurs, the odor of decay may be present.
2. The control group is the setup that had no phosphate solution added. The experimental group is the setup or setups that had various amounts of phosphate solution added. The variable is the amount of phosphate solution.

Conclusions Answers

1. Phosphorus fuels the growth of algae in aquatic ecosystems.
2. Phosphates were banned from household laundry detergents to reduce excessive algal growth in polluted ponds, lakes, and streams.

Explore Further Answers

Student responses will vary, but students should recognize that too much phosphorus could cause excessive algal growth, which results in too little oxygen to sustain aquatic plants and animals.

Discovery Investigation 19, page 612

Analysis Answers

1. Answer will depend on how much water was poured over the soil. Most of the water poured over the bare soil will be collected. The water will be muddy with suspended soil.
2. Very little water will be collected from the pan containing grass. The water will contain very little suspended soil.

Conclusions Answers

1. Answers will vary depending on students' hypotheses and results. Students should indicate whether or not the hypothesis was supported, not whether or not it was correct.
2. Pouring water over the soil models a rainstorm. Collecting the runoff that contains suspended soil is a measure of the amount of erosion.
3. A farmer could plant a cover crop on unused fields before the bare soil washes away.

Explore Further Answers

Encourage students to predict possible outcomes to this experiment based on everyday observations they may have made. For example, they probably have observed rainwater running in gutters during a storm. They may have observed that the water runs faster downhill than on level ground. Help students to use these observations in making a hypothesis. They can then design an experiment that tests this hypothesis.

Teacher's Resource Library Answer Key

Workbook Activities

Workbook Activity 1—What Is Biology?
1. L 2. NL 3. L 4. L 5. NL 6. B 7. NB 8. NB 9. B 10. B 11. C
12. B 13. E 14. D 15. A

Workbook Activity 2—Energy and Growth Cycles
1. law of conservation of energy 2. energy 3. sun 4. cycles 5. heat
6. C 7. A 8. B 9. A 10. B

Workbook Activity 3—Evolutionary and Ecological Cycles
1. evolution 2. extinct 3. environment 4. adaptation 5. species
6. ecosystem 7. stimulus 8. speciation 9. A light-colored mouse. It blends in with the desert sand and is difficult for a predator to see.
10. Students answers will vary. Answers could include thick fur, fat under the skin, warm-blooded, and a high rate of metabolism.

Workbook Activity 4—The Scientific Method
1. scientific method 2. experimental 3. data 4. theory
5. experiment 6. observation 7. hypothesis 8. experiment
9. analyzed 10. communicated 11. hypothesis 12. experiment
13. data 14. observed 15. communicate

Workbook Activity 5—Chapter 1 Vocabulary Review
1. E 2. N 3. J 4. M 5. I 6. D 7. K 8. G 9. H 10. F 11. C 12. A
13. O 14. L 15. B 16. hypothesis 17. theory 18. variable
19. control group 20. experimental group 21. energy 22. biology
23. protein 24. heat 25. biologist 26. law of conservation of energy
27. speciation 28. reproduction 29. extinct 30. species
31. specimen

Workbook Activity 6—Matter, Energy, and Chemical Processes of Life
1. P 2. C 3. P 4. C 5. P 6. P 7. C 8. C 9. P 10. C 11. M 12. M
13. NM 14. M 15. NM

Workbook Activity 7—Atoms and Molecules

	Symbol	Atomic Number	Atomic Mass	Number of Protons	Number of Neutrons	Number of Electrons
carbon	C	6	12	6	6	6
hydrogen	H	1	1	1	0	1
oxygen	O	8	16	8	8	8
nitrogen	N	7	14	7	7	7

1. The 3 isotopes differ in their number of neutrons. C-12 has 6 neutrons, C-13 has 7 neutrons, and C-14 has 8 neutrons.
2. Radioisotopes can be used to trace the movement of elements in the body or to determine the age of fossils. 3. Student answers will vary. Three compounds are water, salt (sodium chloride), and DNA.
4. An element's atomic number tells the number of protons in the nucleus on one atom of that element. 5. An element's atomic mass tells the total mass of protons, neutrons, and electrons, although the electrons have almost no mass.

Workbook Activity 8—Chemical Formulas
1. A chemical formula tells the kind and number of each type of atom present in a compound. 2. Water is made up of hydrogen and oxygen. 3. There are three atoms in one molecule of water. 4. The 2 indicates two hydrogen atoms. 5. The absence of a subscript indicates that one atom of oxygen is present. 6. An ion is an atom or particle with a positive or negative charge. 7. Student answers will vary. One example of an ionic compound is sodium chloride. 8. An empirical formula is the simplest formula for a compound. 9. A radical is a group of two or more atoms that act like one atom.
10. To indicate two radicals, the radical is enclosed in parentheses and followed by the subscript 2.

Formula	Name of Compound
LiBr	lithium bromide
H_2S	hydrogen sulfide
ZnI_2	zinc iodide
$Ba(NO_3)_2$	barium nitrate
$CuSO_4$	copper sulfate

Workbook Activity 9—Bonding Patterns
1. A 2. D 3. A 4. C 5. D 6. D 7. C 8. An atom fills its outer orbits to gain stability. 9. An ionic bond forms when one atom gives up electrons, and another accepts them, to fill its outer orbits. The atom that gives up electrons becomes a positive ion. The atom that accepts electrons becomes a negative ion. The two ions attract each other, forming a bond. 10. Five atoms of hydrogen will be found in the products.

Workbook Activity 10—Properties of Water
1. solvent 2. polar molecule 3. hydrophilic 4. crystalline
5. hydrogen bonds 6. hydrophobic 7. six 8. two 9. one 10. two

Workbook Activity 11—Acids, Bases, and pH
1. C 2. E 3. A 4. D 5. B 6. electron pair 7. neutral 8. pH scale
9. buffer 10. hydroxide ions

Workbook Activity 12—Chapter 2 Vocabulary Review
1. physical property 2. chemical bond 3. chemical property
4. electron 5. atomic mass 6. atom 7. covalent bond 8. proton
9. acid 10. neutral solution 11. atomic number 12. chemical formula 13. chemical reaction 14. neutron 15. ionic bond
16. base 17. hydrogen bond 18. buffer 19. pH 20. diversity
21. isotope 22. electron cloud 23. organization 24. bacteria
25. molecule

Across: 3. molecular 5. ion 8. chemistry 10. product 11. atom
13. solvent 14. subatomic particle 18. hydrophobic 20. shell
21. radioisotope 22. molecule 23. radioactive

Down: 1. empirical 2. radical 4. reactant 6. crystalline 7. chemical reaction 9. nucleus 10. polar 12. hydrophilic 15. ionic compound
16. compound 17. proton 19. matter

Workbook Activity 13—What Are Organic Molecules?
1. monomer 2. functional group 3. proteins 4. dehydration synthesis 5. nucleic acids 6. hydrocarbon 7. hydrolysis
8. lipid 9. organic compounds 10. polymer 11. The majority of a cell is made up of water. 12. The four types of organic compounds found in cells are proteins, carbohydrates, lipids, and nucleic acids.
13. Dehydration synthesis means to put together by removing water.
14. Proteins, polysaccharides, and nucleotides are made of repeating units. 15. Shape plays a role in the way carbon molecules interact and function.

Workbook Activity 14—Carbohydrates
1. D 2. A 3. C 4. B 5. A 6. D 7. C 8. D 9. C 10. A

Workbook Activity 15—Lipids
1. sulfur 2. information storage 3. carbohydrate 4. olive oil
5. proteins 6. Cholesterol is part of cell membranes and many hormones are made from it. 7. A saturated fat contains no double bonds. An unsaturated fat contains some double and triple bonds.
8. A phospholipid molecule has a phosphate group on one end and fatty acids on the other end. 9. Transfats are made by adding hydrogen to unsaturated fats. 10. Saturated fats may contribute to heart disease because lipids build up in the walls of blood vessels and reduce the flow of blood to the heart. 11. Three types of lipids are fats, phospholipids, and steroids. 12. Animal fats are saturated fats and the carbon chains can stack closely together, creating solids.
13. Unlike most plant oils, cocoa butter is made of saturated fats.
14. A phospholipid has a polar end that interacts with water (hydrophilic) and a nonpolar end that interacts with fats (hydrophobic). 15. A triglyceride is made of three fatty acids and one molecule of glycerol.

Workbook Activity 16—Proteins
1. synthesize 2. R group 3. insoluble 4. gene 5. contractile
6. enzymes 7. amino acids 8. polypeptide 9. codon
10. hemoglobin 11. Four atoms or groups of atoms are the amino group, carboxyl group, hydrogen, and R group. 12. Some animal structures and compounds made of protein include spider webs, hair, feathers, ligaments, contractile proteins, hemoglobin, and enzymes. 13. A dipeptide forms when two peptides join by removing a water molecule to form a bond. 14. A complete protein is a food that provides the body with all nine essential amino acids.
15. Foods that contain proteins include meat, beans, and eggs.

Workbook Activity 17—Nucleic Acids
1. DNA 2. bases 3. helix 4. RNA 5. sugar-phosphate bond
6. DNA and RNA are both nucleic acids made of chains of nucleotides. DNA is a double chain and RNA a single chain. DNA contains the base thymine and RNA contains uracil. DNA contains the sugar deoxyribose and RNA contains ribose. 7. The three parts of a nucleotide include a base, sugar, and phosphate group.
8. The bases make up the rungs of the ladder. 9. DNA is made of a chain of nucleotides, which are the monomers of the DNA polymer.
10. Genes are series of nucleotides and they are located on DNA molecules.

Workbook Activity 18—Chapter 3 Vocabulary Review
1. I 2. C 3. Y 4. R 5. F 6. O 7. W 8. T 9. N 10. V 11. M 12. B
13. D 14. L 15. P 16. U 17. J 18. G 19. S 20. X 21. E 22. H
23. Q 24. K 25. AA 26. BB 27. A 28. Z 29. F 30. C 31. F 32. C
33. P 34. F 35. P 36. N 37. F 38. P

Across: 1. nucleic acid 6. insoluble 7. membrane 8. isomer
11. helix 12. unsaturated fatty acid 14. hydrolysis 15. gene
16. truncate 17. organic compound 18. complete protein

Down: 2. lipid bilayer 3. monomer 4. macromolecule 5. plastid
9. transfat 10. functional group 13. contractile

Workbook Activity 19—What Is a Cell?
1. cell 2. molecules 3. carbohydrates 4. lipids 5. microscope
6. cork 7. cells 8. plants 9. animals 10. cells 11. Cell functions include producing energy, taking in oxygen, producing water, and carrying the instructions for life. 12. Carbohydrates, lipids, proteins, and nucleic acids four kinds of organic molecules found in cells.
13. Cells store the energy of carbohydrates in molecules of ATP.
14. The cell theory states that living things are made of cells, cells are the basic units of structure and function, and cells come from already existing cells 15. Robert Hooke saw cork cells under the microscope in 1665, then Anton von Leeuwenhoek saw living cells in 1675.

Workbook Activity 20—Cellular Structure and Function
1. F 2. D 3. C 4. B 5. A 6. G 7. E

Environment	Solute Concentration in the Environment Is	Prefix Means
isotonic solution	(lower than, higher than, the same as) inside the cell	equal
hypertonic solution	(lower than, higher than, the same as) inside the cell	higher
hypotonic solution	(lower than, higher than, the same as) inside the cell	lower

Workbook Activity 21—What Kind of Cell Is It?
1. B 2. D 3. A 4. B 5. C

Cell Features	Prokaryotic Cell	Eukaryotic Cell
has a nucleus		X
membranes surround internal structures		X
includes bacteria	X	
includes human cells		X
reproduces by binary fission	X	
possesses organelles		X

Workbook Activity 22—After the Cell
1. B 2. C 3. D 4. B 5. B 6. B 7. eukaryotes 8. tissue 9. organ
10. organ system

Workbook Activity 23—Chapter 4 Vocabulary Review
1. C 2. N 3. D 4. V 5. H 6. W 7. T 8. J 9. K 10. E 11. A 12. M
13. I 14. L 15. B 16. O 17. R 18. Q 19. U 20. X 21. G 22. S
23. P 24. F 25. OS 26. T 27. C

Workbook Activity 24—What Are Cell Membranes?

Part of Molecule	Phosphate	Glycerol and 2 Fatty Acids	Negative Charge	No Charge	Nonpolar	Polar	Hydrophilic	Hydrophobic
head	X		X			X	X	
tail		X		X	X			X

1. G 2. B 3. I 4. E 5. D 6. H 7. F 8. A 9. J 10. C

Workbook Activity 25—What Do Membranes Do?

Type of Transport	Energy Requirements	Process
passive	does not require energy	osmosis, diffusion, facilitated diffusion
active	requires energy	transport proteins, endocytosis, exocytosis

1. C 2. B 3. D 4. A 5. D

Workbook Activity 26—Information Organelles
1. nucleus 2. Ribosomes 3. genome 4. nucleolus 5. chromosomes
6. RNA 7. nuclear envelope 8. genome 9. amino acids 10. pores
11. Both the nuclear envelope and the plasma membrane are made of a lipid bilayer. 12. A cell's DNA makes several separated molecules or chromosomes. Within each chromosome, DNA is folded with proteins. 13. Ribosomes assemble proteins from a strand of RNA which is made from the cell's DNA. 14. Chromosomes contain DNA and proteins. 15. RNA and proteins make up ribosomes.

Workbook Activity 27—Energy Organelles

Organelle	Held within a Membrane	Located in Cytoplasm	Found in Plant Cells	Found in Animal Cells	Harvests Energy	Uses Energy	Contains Grana and Stroma	Contains Cristae and Matrix
mitochondrion	X	X	X	X		X		X
chloroplast	X	X	X		X		X	

1. Chloroplasts 2. photosynthesis 3. stroma 4. mitochondria
5. thylakoids 6. The job of chlorophyll in a cell is to capture the sun's energy. 7. The mitochondria break down glucose and convert it to ATP. 8. Thylakoids are sacs that are stacked in piles called grana and surrounded by a liquid, the stroma. 9. It is filled with a folded membrane called the cristae which is surrounded by a liquid matrix. 10. The cristae are highly folded to increase the surface area and therefore increase the space for chemical processes of respiration.

Workbook Activity 28—The Endomembrane System
1. F 2. E 3. C 4. H 5. G 6. I 7. D 8. A 9. J 10. B 11. The endoplasmic reticulum makes molecules and the Golgi apparatus packages them. 12. Organelles in the nucleus include the endoplasmic reticulum, Golgi apparatus, vacuoles, and lysosomes. 13. Proteins are produced in the rough endoplasmic reticulum. 14. Lipids and carbohydrates are produced in the smooth endoplasmic reticulum. 15. A vacuole ships molecules inside or outside of the cell.

Workbook Activity 29—The Cytoskeleton
1. B 2. B 3. D 4. C 5. D 6. The cytoskeleton gives the cell shape and support, anchors organelles, provides tracks along which organelles move, and helps the cell move. 7. Organelles slide along fibers as if they are tracks. 8. Cytoskeleton fibers add fiber molecules to one moving end and remove fiber molecules from the other end of a cell. 9. Cilia are short, hair-like structures on the outsides of mobile cells or on cells that move substances; flagella are long, tail-like structures. 10. Microfilaments, intermediate filaments, and microtubules are three types of fibers in the cytoskeleton.

Workbook Activity 30—Plant Cells
1. C 2. B 3. A 4. D 5. E 6. Student answers may vary and could include cell wall, chloroplast, large central vacuole, and plasmodesmata. 7. Student answers may vary and could include Golgi apparatus, endoplasmic reticulum, lysosomes, ribosomes, nucleus, nucleolus, and plasma membrane. 8. Plants wilt when they lose some of the water in their central vacuole. 9. Plasmodesmata enable adjacent cells to communicate. 10. Plant leaves receive sunlight and roots do not.

Workbook Activity 31—Chapter 5 Vocabulary Review
1. N 2. S 3. L 4. U 5. X 6. V 7. H 8. G 9. M 10. I 11. D 12. F 13. B 14. J 15. K 16. O 17. Q 18. P 19. R 20. W 21. E 22. T 23. A 24. Y 25. C

Down: 1. cilia 3. cytosol 5. cristae 6. bilayer 8. nucleolus 10. chromosome 12. thylakoid 13. mitochondrion 15. chlorophyll 16. lysosome 19. secrete

Across: 2. vacuole 4. tubulin 7. actin 9. stroma 11. cytoplasm 14. cytoskeleton 17. chloroplast 18. ribosome 20. pore 21. photosynthesis 22. grana 23. matrix 24. flagella

Workbook Activity 32—What Is Energy?
1. B 2. A 3. C 4. C 5. B 6. C 7. A 8. Fats contain 9 calories of energy per gram. Carbohydrates and proteins have 4 calories of energy per gram. 9. The parts of an ATP molecule include adenine, 3 phosphate groups, and ribose. 10. The human body stays at 98.6°F because of the heat released during metabolism.

Workbook Activity 33—Making ATP

Type of Molecule	Contains 3 Phosphate Groups	Contains 2 Phosphate Groups	A High-Energy Molecule	A Low-Energy Molecule	Called Adenosine-triphosphate	Called Adenosine-diphosphate
ADP		X		X		X
ATP	X		X		X	

1. Energy is used to add a phosphate group to the ADP molecule.
2. Like a battery, ADP can be energized and put back to work.
3. ATP is manufactured in mitochondria. 4. Energy is stored when a bond is formed in a macromolecule. 5. The energy to make glucose, which is converted to ATP, comes from the sun.

Workbook Activity 34—Enzymes and Energy Flow
1. catalyst 2. enzymes 3. saliva 4. pepsin 5. diabetes 6. proteins
7. Obesity 8. amount of energy 9. released 10. very specific to that reaction

Type of Molecule	Found in Nonliving Systems	Found in Living Systems	Lowers the Energy Needed to Start a Reaction	Made of Protein	Is Not Consumed by the Reaction	Can Speed Up Chemical Reaction	Can Stop Chemical Reaction
enzyme		X	X	X	X	X	X
catalyst	X		X		X	X	X

Workbook Activity 35—More About Enzymes
1. catalyst 2. enzyme 3. activation energy 4. activation energy
5. food 6. heat 7. Student answers will vary, but could include: yeast causes bread dough to rise; bacteria produce enzymes that break down cellulose, animals, and plants; and fungi use enzymes in many life processes. 8. Plants use carbon dioxide, water, and energy to make sugar during photosynthesis. 9. Reactants are substances that are changed during a reaction. Products are substances created during a reaction. 10. For a chemical reaction to occur, the chemical bonds of a reactant must be broken.

Workbook Activity 36—Chapter 6 Vocabulary Review
1. J 2. L 3. A 4. O 5. D 6. F 7. N 8. B 9. C 10. E 11. I 12. G 13. M 14. H 15. K

Workbook Activity 37—What Is Cellular Respiration?
1. D 2. A 3. B 4. C 5. E 6. C 7. A 8. B 9. C 10. A

Workbook Activity 38—The Stages of Cellular Respiration
1. glycolysis 2. cytoplasm 3. mitochondria 4. glucose 5. membrane 6. electron carriers 7. electron transport chain 8. electron transport chain 9. convert glucose to ATP 10. cyclic

Stages of Cellular Respiration	Products That Result from this Stage			Location of this Stage		
	Pyruvic Acid	ATP	NADH & FADH$_2$	Cytoplasm	Matrix	Membrane of Mitochondria
glycolysis	X			X		
Krebs cycle			X		X	
electron transport chain		X				X

Workbook Activity 39—Fermentation
1. aerobic 2. oxygen 3. fermentation 4. glycolysis 5. energy 6. products 7. yeast 8. carbon dioxide 9. cellular respiration 10. lactic acid 11. Two types of fermentation are alcoholic fermentation and lactic acid fermentation. 12. Lactic acid gives milk a sour taste. 13. Aerobic respiration requires oxygen and anaerobic respiration does not. 14. A jogger might use up all of the oxygen in his/her tissues. 15. Prokaryotes produce energy in the cytoplasm.

Workbook Activity 40—Controlling Cellular Respiration
1. feedback inhibition 2. cellular respiration 3. fermentation 4. fat 5. energy 6. energy 7. enzymes 8. metabolic pathway 9. energy 10. fat 11. The products of one step may stop or slow another step. 12. Cells can use lipids and proteins for energy. 13. Cells have different energy needs on different days. 14. Cells carry out cellular respiration to produce ATP. 15. When energy is plentiful, cells can store it as fat.

Workbook Activity 41—Chapter 7 Vocabulary Review
1. N 2. A 3. H 4. L 5. O 6. G 7. P 8. E 9. Q 10. M 11. J 12. C 13. O 14. K 15. F 16. I 17. B 18. NADH 19. the Krebs cycle 20. the electron transport chain 21. glycolysis

Workbook Activity 42—What Is Photosynthesis?
1. A 2. E 3. D 4. B 5. C 6. X 7. X 10. X 11. X 12. X 14. X 15. X

Workbook Activity 43—Light Reactions
1. A 2. B 3. C 4. A 5. D 6. B 7. A 8. Krebs cycle; The Krebs cycle is part of respiration and the other two are part of the photosynthesis process. 9. electron; An electron is a subatomic particle and the other two are sugars. 10. electromagnetic spectrum; The electromagnetic spectrum is a form of energy and the other two are gases involved in photosynthesis.

Workbook Activity 44—The Dark Reaction: The Calvin-Benson Cycle
1. carbon dioxide 2. light reaction 3. stomata 4. cellular respiration 5. stroma 6. glucose 7. photosynthesis 8. carbohydrate 9. dark reaction 10. crabgrass 11. CAM plants 12. C$_4$ plants 13. photosynthesis 14. RuBP 15. PGA

Workbook Activity 45—Chapter 8 Vocabulary Review
1. stoma 2. vascular bundle 3. mesophyll 4. autotroph 5. electromagnetic radiation 6. photon 7. absorb 8. wavelengths 9. spectrum 10. carotenoids 11. Calvin-Benson cycle 12. G3P 13. reaction center 14. photosystems 15. photophosphorylation 16. C$_4$ plants 17. RuBP 18. crabgrass 19. PGA 20. CAM plants

Workbook Activity 46—The Cell Cycle and Mitosis
1. sister chromatids 2. mitosis 3. growth and repair 4. prophase 5. metaphase 6. anaphase 7. telophase 8. Prokaryotic cells reproduce by binary fission. 9. The purpose of mitosis in eukaryotic cells is to produce new cells for growth and repair. 10. The phases of interphase include: G$_1$, a period of growth; S, the time when DNA is copied and sister chromatids are formed; and G$_2$, when the cell copies its organelles and continues to grow.

Workbook Activity 47—What Is Cancer?
1. G 2. J 3. E 4. A 5. H 6. C 7. D 8. I 9. F 10. B 11. Three cancer treatments include chemotherapy, using drugs to kill cancerous cells; radiation therapy, using a beam of radiation to kill cancerous cells; and surgery, removing cancerous cells. 12. A malignant tumor is one that can or has spread throughout the body. A benign tumor is one that does not spread. 13. During metastasis, cancerous cells spread throughout the body. 14. Cancer is a condition in which cells divide and grow too much. 15. A tumor is a ball of cells caused by too many cell divisions.

Workbook Activity 48—Meiosis: The Life Cycle of Sex Cells
1. D 2. B 3. C 4. A 5. metaphase I 6. prophase I 7. anaphase I 8. metaphase II 9. anaphase II 10. telophase II

Workbook Activity 49—The Human Reproductive System
1. testes 2. testosterone 3. spermatogonia 4. vas deferens 5. seminiferous tubules 6. semen 7. urethra 8. scrotum 9. ejaculation 10. penis 11. menstruation 12. follicle 13. estrogen 14. fallopian tube 15. uterus

Workbook Activity 50—Human Development
1. pregnancy 2. fetus 3. vagina 4. embryo 5. placenta 6. adolescence 7. cervix 8. gestation time 9. vagina 10. umbilical cord 11. Humans are born helpless and mature slowly, through the teenage years. 12. A three-week-old embryo is a ball made of three cell layers. A four-week-old embryo has a heartbeat and its blood vessels have begun to form. 13. An embryo is called a fetus after nine weeks. 14. A fetus can suck its thumb by the end of the third month of development. 15. Muscles in the uterus and vagina squeeze together, pushing the fetus and the placenta out of the uterus.

Workbook Activity 51—Chapter 9 Vocabulary Review
1. adolescence 2. cancer 3. centromere 4. cytokinesis 5. ejaculation 6. estrogen 7. fertilization 8. follicle 9. haploid 10. meiosis 11. metastasis 12. menstruation 13. oogenesis 14. ovulation 15. placenta 16. pregnancy 17. reproduction 18. spermatogenesis 19. spindle 20. testosterone 21. C 22. C 23. A 24. D 25. C 26. A 27. D 28. C 29. C 30. B 31. A 32. A 33. C 34. D 35. B 36. A 37. A 38. A 39. C 40. C 41. C 42. A 43. C 44. D 45. B 46. D 47. F 48. K 49. J 50. M 51. I 52. H 53. C 54. L 55. B 56. E 57. A 58. G

Workbook Activity 52—What Did Mendel Discover?
1. A They are generations of organisms in genetic studies. **B** F_1 is the first generation and F_2 is the second generation. **2. A** Dominant and recessive genes are alleles. **B** A dominant gene shows its form of a trait. A recessive gene does not show its form of a trait because it is hidden by the dominant gene. **3. A** Monohybrid and dihybrid crosses are genetic crosses used to study traits. **B** A monohybrid cross looks at one pair of traits and a dihybrid cross examines two pairs of traits. **4. A** True-breeding plants and hybrids are types of organisms used in genetic crosses. **B** A true-breeding plant comes from parents that are the same true-breeding plants. A hybrid comes from two different true-breeding plants. **5. A** Both laws explain what happens to chromosomes during cell division. **B** The law of segregation says that homologous chromosomes separate during meiosis, providing one gene for each gamete. The law of independent assortment states that each pair of chromosomes separates on its own during meiosis, resulting in as many as four allele pairings.

	T	T			T	t			T	T
t	Tt	Tt	T	**7.** TT	Tt	T	**9.** TT	TT
6. t	Tt	Tt	t	**8.** Tt	tt	t	Tt	**10.** Tt

Workbook Activity 53—Different Ways Alleles Cooperate
1. A **2.** C **3.** C **4.** D **5.** C **6.** B **7.** C **8.** In simple dominance, a plant with a genotype of Tt is tall. **9.** In incomplete dominance, a plant with genes Tt is mid-sized (combination of tall and short). **10.** Blood type has three alleles, A, B, and O. A and B are codominant.

Workbook Activity 54—The Importance of Sex Chromosomes
1. B **2.** E **3.** D **4.** I **5.** H **6.** C **7.** A **8.** F **9.** G **10.** J **11.** fruit flies **12.** red **13.** red **14.** half had red eyes and half had white eyes **15.** X

Workbook Activity 55—Chapter 10 Vocabulary Review
1. C **2.** C **3.** C **4.** B **5.** A **6.** B **7.** C **8.** A **9.** B **10.** A **11.** C **12.** B **13.** C **14.** dominant **15.** P generation **16.** trait **17.** monohybrid cross **18.** heredity **19.** hybrid **20.** recessive gene **21.** cross fertilization **22.** law of independent assortment **23.** F_1 generation **24.** genetics **25.** genotype **26.** testcross **27.** pleiotropy **28.** linkage map **29.** hemophilia **30.** polygenic traits **31.** sex-linked inheritance **32.** sex-linked trait **33.** autosomes **34.** linked gene **35.** sex chromosomes **36.** carrier **37.** sickle cell disease

Workbook Activity 56—How Are Molecules of Life Involved in Heredity?
1. complimentary base pairing **2.** nitrogenous base **3.** sugar-phosphate backbone **4.** phosphate group **5.** cytosine **6.** uracil **7.** hydrogen **8.** Chargraff **9.** Wilkins and Franklin **10.** Watson and Crick

Molecule	Contains a Phosphate Group	Contains Sugar		Contains Nitrogenous Bases			
		Deoxy-ribose	Ribose	Adenine	Thymine	Uracil	Cytosine	Guanine
DNA	X	X		X	X		X	X
RNA	X		X	X		X	X	X

Workbook Activity 57—DNA Replication
1. D **2.** B **3.** G **4.** A **5.** C **6.** J **7.** H **8.** F **9.** E **10.** I **11.** C **12.** B **13.** D **14.** A **15.** A

Workbook Activity 58—The Path of Genetic Information
1. X **2.** X **4.** X **5.** X **6.** X **8.** X **9.** mRNA **10.** codon **11.** mutation **12.** promoter **13.** exon **14.** deletion **15.** mutagen

Workbook Activity 59—What Are Viruses?
1. Answers will vary. One possible answer: A virus is a parasite that uses a host cell to copy its own DNA. **2.** Answers will vary. One possible answer: A virus can infect a host cell and produce new virus particles in the lytic cycle. **3.** Answer will vary. One possible answer: In the host cell, a virus can switch from the lysogenic cycle to the lytic cycle. **4.** viruses **5.** lysogenic cycle **6.** capsid **7.** evolve **8.** vaccine **9.** immune system **10.** host cell **11.** lytic cycle **12.** parasite **13.** infect **14.** lytic cycle **15.** vaccine

Workbook Activity 60—Using the Path of Genetic Information
1. biotechnology **2.** biotechnologist **3.** bacteria **4.** plasmids **5.** restriction endonuclease **6.** DNA ligase **7.** transformation **8.** genetically modified food **9.** C **10.** B **11.** F **12.** E **13.** A **14.** G **15.** D

Workbook Activity 61—Natural Defenses Against Disease
1. D **2.** E **3.** A **4.** C **5.** B

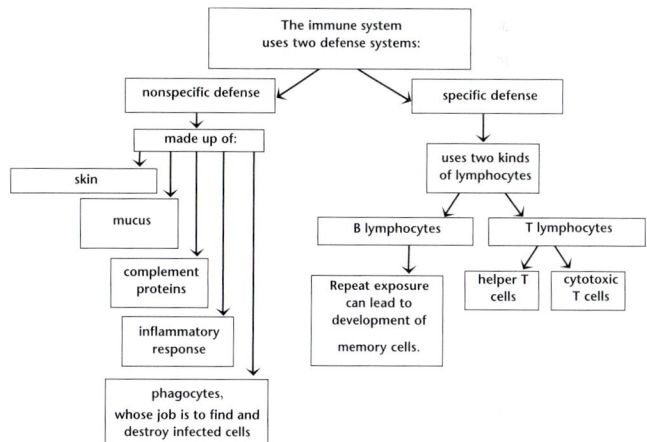

Workbook Activity 62—Chapter 11 Vocabulary Review
1. nitrogenous base **2.** Guanine **3.** complementary base pairing **4.** replication **5.** template **6.** leading strand **7.** mRNA **8.** promoter **9.** Introns **10.** exon **11.** tRNA **12.** Ribosomal RNA **13.** deletion **14.** host cell **15.** uracil **16.** immune system **17.** lytic cycle **18.** thymine **19.** parasite **20.** insertion **21.** Adenine **22.** nondisjunction **23.** cytosine **24.** Down syndrome **25.** semi-conservative replication **26.** bacteriophage **27.** virus **28.** genetic code **29.** capsid **30.** evolve **31.** lysogenic cycle **32.** biotechnologist **33.** lymph system **34.** specific defense **35.** white blood cells **36.** infectious disease **37.** pathogens **38.** nonspecific defense **39.** inflammatory response **40.** complement proteins **41.** T lymphocyte **42.** immunity **43.** B lymphocytes **44.** memory cells **45.** antigen **46.** phagocyte **47.** helper T cell **48.** phosphate backbone **49.** DNA polymerase **50.** Both terms refer to the process of making a new strand of DNA. The origin of replication is the place where replication begins. The replication bubble is the entire area of replication. **51.** Transcription and translation are steps in the production of a protein. Transcription is copying the DNA sequences onto a strand of mRNA. Translation is converting the message on mRNA into a protein.

52. Both are enzymes. RNA polymerase binds new nucleotides to a growing RNA strand. DNA ligase binds together pieces of newly made DNA. **53.** Both are sequences of nucleotides on DNA. The promoter sequence indicates the place where replication begins. The terminator sequence indicates the place where it ends. **54.** Both are areas of newly made DNA. The leading strand is a long piece of new DNA and the lagging strand is made up of several small pieces that have to be connected with DNA ligase. **55.** Hershey and Chase placed different markers on the DNA and proteins in bacteriophages. They found that the markers that had been placed on DNA were transferred to offspring. Markers on proteins were not passed to offspring. **56.** A replication fork is an area at the end of the replication bubble. It is the place where nucleotides are being added to a new strand of DNA. **57.** A terminator signals the stop of DNA replication. **58.** During a mutation, DNA changes. **59.** "Infect" means to cause disease or unhealthy conditions by introducing a germ. **60.** A vaccine introduces a harmless piece of a germ. It stimulates the immune system to make antibodies. These protect the person if they are exposed to the actual germ. **61.** A plasmid is a ring of DNA. It is found in bacteria. **62.** A substitution is a mutation in which one nucleotide base is replaced with another. It can change the codon structure on mRNA and lead to the production of an incorrect protein. **63.** A genetically modified food is one that has been genetically changed through biotechnology. **64.** The phosphate group of one nucleotide forms a covalent bond with the sugar group of another nucleotide. The repeating pattern of bonded nucleotides forms a sugar-phosphate backbone.
65. anticodon **66.** restriction endonuclease **67.** transformation **68.** growth factor **69.** cytotoxic **70.** lymphocyte **71.** markers **72.** RNA splicing

Workbook Activity 63—The Digestive System

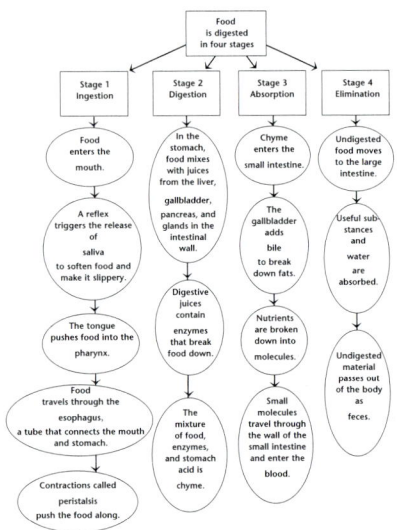

Workbook Activity 64—The Respiratory System
1. D **2.** B **3.** A **4.** B **5.** D **6.** C **7.** A **8.** Muscle around the lungs and diaphragm contract. The rib cage expands and lung volume increases. Air rushes into the lungs. **9.** The respiratory system brings oxygen into the body and the circulatory system transports it to body cells. The circulatory system picks up carbon dioxide at cells and carries it to the lungs, which exhale the gas. **10.** The path of oxygen begins at the nose then proceeds to the pharynx, glottis, trachea, bronchus, bronchiole, alveolus, and finally the capillary.

Workbook Activity 65—The Circulatory System
1. cardiac **2.** Veins **3.** connective **4.** plasma **5.** platelets **6.** fibrinogen **7.** Hemophilia **8.** hypertension **9.** thrombus **10.** cardiovascular disease **11.** aorta **12.** arteries **13.** veins **14.** atrium **15.** ventricle

Workbook Activity 66—The Excretory System
1. water **2.** kidney **3.** urine **4.** ureter **5.** nephrons **6.** perspiration **7.** antidiuretic **8.** kidneys **9.** glomerulus **10.** dermis **11.** Water from cells is picked up by blood. Blood flows into the kidneys through the renal artery and enters the capillaries of the glomerulus. Water filters into the nephrons, then into collecting ducts. Fluid travels down a ureter to the bladder, to the urethra, then to the outside environment. **12.** The excretory system includes the kidneys, ureters, bladder, urethra, liver, lungs, and skin. **13.** Three layers of skin are the topmost epidermis, middle dermis, and deep fatty layer, which contain blood vessels and nerves. **14.** When the blood contains too much water, ADH levels in the blood drop and the kidneys remove more water. **15.** Urine is made from water and solutes in the blood. When blood flows into the capillaries around the glomerulus, pressure forces water and solutes out of the blood and into the nephron.

Workbook Activity 67—The Nervous System

Area of the Brain	Subdivision of That Area	Function(s)
brain stem		controls these functions: heart rate, digestion, and breathing
cerebellum		controls balance and helps muscles work together
limbic system		registers feelings like anger and pleasure
diencephelon	thalamus	directs incoming sensory information
	hypothalamus	regulates pituitary gland and other hormones and body temperature
cerebral cortex	frontal lobe parietal lobe temporal lobe occipital lobe	involved in body functions like vision, hearing, thinking and memory

1. C **2.** B **3.** D **4.** B **5.** D

Workbook Activity 68—The Sensory System
1. Photoreceptors are located on the retina. **2.** Pain receptors can be found in the skin. **3.** Chemorecptors detect chemicals in food and in the air. **4.** Mechanoreceptors detect pressure. **5.** The brain needs input from chemoreceptors in the nose and mouth to interpret taste.
6. E **7.** F **8.** H **9.** C **10.** D **11.** B **12.** A **13.** J **14.** G **15.** I

Workbook Activity 69—The Endocrine System
1. pituitary gland **2.** thymus gland **3.** gonads **4.** hormones **5.** feedback loop **6.** adrenaline **7.** glucose **8.** calcium **9.** hypothalamus **10.** adrenal glands **11.** The endocrine system produces hormones that regulate body functions. **12.** The major glands of the endocrine system include hypothalamus, pituitary, thyroid, pancreas, adrenal, and thymus glands and the gonads. **13.** After hormones reach their targets, cells send back chemical signals that let the gland know whether to stop or continue secreting hormones. **14.** Stress causes the release of adrenaline, which speeds up heart rate, breathing, and other metabolic activities. **15.** Stress of performing well in a race is an example of good stress.

Workbook Activity 70—The Skeletal and Muscular System

1. voluntary muscle. Joint, red marrow, and skeleton are parts of the skeletal system; voluntary muscle is not. 2. osteoporosis. Cardiac muscle, skeletal muscle, and tendon are part of the muscular system; osteoporosis is not. 3. muscles in face. Muscles in arteries, stomach, and heart are involuntary muscles. Muscles in the face are voluntary. 4. skeletal system 5. involuntary muscles 6. pivot joint 7. tendons 8. ball and socket joints 9. voluntary muscles 10. hinge joint

Workbook Activity 71—Chapter 12 Vocabulary Review

1. C 2. B 3. A 4. C 5. B 6. A 7. C 8. C 9. B 10. D 11. C 12. B 13. B 14. D 15. C 16. A 17. C 18. B 19. C 20. C 21. E 22. T 23. G 24. D 25. L 26. N 27. R 28. J 29. C 30. B 31. I 32. P 33. A 34. V 35. M 36. X 37. U 38. K 39. Q 40. H 41. S 42. F 43. W 44. O 45. Both axons and dendrites are extensions of neurons. Dendrites receive information and axons send out information. 46. The dermis and epidermis are both layers of the skin. The epidermis is the topmost layer and the dermis is beneath it. 47. The retina and pupil are parts of the eye. The retina is the region where light strikes photoreceptors. The pupil is the opening through which light travels. 48. The ureter and urine are part of the excretory system. The ureter is a tube that carries urine from the kidney to the bladder. Urine is the waste product made in the excretory system. 49. The cochlea and eardrum are parts of the ear. The eardrum is a membrane that vibrates when hit by sound waves. The cochlea is a fluid-filled organ of the middle ear. 50. reflex 51. pharynx 52. chime 53. villi 54. bile 55. feces 56. rectum 57. glottis 58. trachea 59. cardiac 60. aorta 61. platelets 62. thrombus 63. atherosclerosis 64. nephrons 65. neuron 66. synapse 67. iris 68. adrenaline

Workbook Activity 72—What Is Biological Evolution?

1. F 2. B 3. J 4. G 5. E 6. A 7. D 8. I 9. H 10. C 11. Lamarck stated that organisms acquired traits as they adjusted to changes in the environment. 12. The theory of common descent says that present day organisms descended from organisms that lived in the past. 13. Descent with modification suggests that recent species are changed descendants of earlier species. 14. Natural selection is a process in which the organisms that are best suited for the environment survive and reproduce. 15. Modern synthesis states that a population's gene pool changes over time.

Workbook Activity 73—Evidence of Evolution

1. fossil record 2. Sedimentary rock 3. homologous structures 4. biogeography 5. Comparative anatomy 6. molecular biology 7. DNA 8. Fossils 9. natural selection 10. more closely related 11. evolution 12. ancestor 13. nucleotides 14. anatomy 15. fossils

Workbook Activity 74—Rates of Evolutionary Change

1. B 2. C 3. C 4. D 5. B 6. C 7. C 8. As plates spread apart, the organisms on them were separated. The fossils of these organisms now appear in different parts of the world. 9. Radioactive elements decay at a constant rate. Paleontologists can compare the amounts of different elements in a sample of rock or fossil. 10. Plates are pushed apart by magma that comes to the surface.

Workbook Activity 75—Processes in Evolution

1. extinct 2. Recombination 3. gene flow 4. mutation 5. genetic drift 6. habitat 7. natural selection 8. Gene flow 9. alleles 10. endangered

Mechanism	Mutation	Recombination	Gene Flow	Genetic Drift	Natural Selection
can bring genes into a population	X	X	X		
can take genes out of a population				X	X

Workbook Activity 76—Natural Selection

1. Malaria is a disease that causes recurring chills and fever. 2. People who have one gene for sickle cell anemia are less likely than the general population to get malaria. 3. Artificial selection is a process of changing a species by people who select the breeding of certain traits. Examples may vary, but could include breeding pigeons or dogs for certain physical characteristics. 4. The purpose of natural selection is to keep life going even as environmental conditions change. 5. Both are processes that choose for certain traits or adaptations. Natural selection is controlled by the environment and artificial selection is controlled by people.

Description	Natural Selection	Artificial Selection
Cattle are bred to create offspring that produce a lot of milk.		X
After a flood, all of the lizards that cannot swim die. Only lizards that swim live to reproduce.	X	
A farmer crosses silver kernel corn with gold kernel corn. The offspring produce pale gold kernels.		X
Two male wild turkeys fight. The weaker one is killed. The winner mates with all the females.	X	
People with one sickle-cell allele are not likely to get malaria.	X	

Workbook Activity 77—Microevolution and Macroevolution

Description	Microevolution	Macroevolution
Moth populations changed from mostly light colored to mostly dark colored in the 1800s.	X	
Populations can change over a long period of time.		X
Minor changes can occur over a few generations. The changes produce variations in a population.	X	
Over millions of years, birds developed as a species.		X
A population of squirrels lives in a forest. In 1900, most had bushy tails and a few had smooth tails. All of the bushy-tailed squirrels were killed in an earthquake in 1940. Most of the smooth-tailed squirrels also died. In 1965, a small group of smooth-tailed squirrels were found living in the forest.	X	

1. Evolutionary biology is the study of genetic changes within and among populations of organisms. 2. Overproduction is the production of more offspring than can survive. 3. A Organisms produce more offspring than can survive. B Individuals in a population vary. C Individuals with traits best suited to the environment survive. D Individuals that survive can produce offspring. 4. Two factors that affect a population's phenotype are genes and environment. 5. An example in change of phenotype without change in genotype: people have gotten larger because of better nutrition.

Workbook Activity 78—Chapter 13 Vocabulary Review
1. A Both refer to changes in groups of organisms over time. B Macroevolution has to do with changes at the species level over long periods. Microevolution is related to smaller change over generations. **2.** A Both deal with changes in the gene pools. B Artificial selection is controlled by people. Natural selection is controlled by the environment. **3.** A Both theories refer to changes that occur in the crust. B Continental drift is a theory that suggests that crustal plates move. Plate tectonics is a theory that says the crust is made of large plates. **4.** A Both are branches of science used in the study of evolution. B Anatomy examines body structures and molecular biology refers to the molecules that make up organisms. **5.** A Both are related to changes in gene pools. B Gene flow is the movement of genes into or out of a gene pool, and can be due to a number of factors. Genetic drift refers to changes in the genes of a small population. **6.** fossil **7.** common descent **8.** modern synthesis **9.** acquired trait **10.** comparative anatomy **11.** population **12.** biogeography **13.** plates **14.** crust **15.** paleontologist **16.** habitat **17.** malaria **18.** magma **19.** B **20.** B **21.** C **22.** A **23.** D **24.** A **25.** A **26.** C **27.** A **28.** A **29.** K **30.** I **31.** C **32.** G **33.** A **34.** E **35.** L **36.** H **37.** D **38.** F **39.** J **40.** B

Workbook Activity 79—What Is Speciation?
1. subpopulation **2.** classify **3.** niche **4.** fertile **5.** biochemistry **6.** subspecies **7.** morphology **8.** interbreed **9.** D **10.** A **11.** C **12.** E **13.** F **14.** G **15.** B

Workbook Activity 80—Classifying Species
1. B **2.** C **3.** D **4.** D **5.** C **6.** A **7.** C **8.** B **9.** Scientists used characteristics such as DNA, biochemistry, and morphology to group organisms. **10.** Yes. All organisms in the same class are also in the same phylum.

Workbook Activity 81—Conditions for Speciation to Occur
1. speciation **2.** geography **3.** evolutionary **4.** environment **5.** stasis **6.** punctuated equilibrium **7.** In coordinated stasis, several new species develop about the same time. An example is the development of new species after the African environment changed from wet forest to dry grassland 2.8 million years ago. **8.** A change in the environment could change the geography. Organisms could die if they could not live with the changes that occur. Some may become extinct. **9.** Examples can vary, but could include global warming or a meteor strike. **10.** Allopatric speciation occurs in members if a species are separated by a geographical barrier.

Workbook Activity 82—Conditions That Affect Species Survival
1. E **2.** D **3.** A **4.** B **5.** C **6.** Mass extinction can occur if there is a change in the environment and organisms cannot adapt. **7.** After a community develops, rapid evolution can lead to speciation if populations become isolated. **8.** Harmful genes that influence the genetic health of a species occur more often in a small population than a large one. **9.** Much of the extinction that occurs today results from the way people change the environment. **10.** Species that interact regularly may undergo co-adaptation and evolve to be dependent on each other.

Workbook Activity 83—Chapter 14 Vocabulary Review
1. Scientists use genus and species names to create scientific names. **2.** The levels of the Linneaus classification system are: Kingdom, phylum, class, order, family, genus, and species. **3.** Speciation is the creation of a new species from an existing species. It most often occurs because populations in a species separate, evolve, and are no longer able to interbreed. **4.** Reproductive isolation is a division between organisms that once mated so that they no longer mate. One example of reproductive isolation is a population separated by a geographical barrier. **5.** The three-domain system classifies all living things into three large groups. The major divisions are Bacteria; Archaea, prokaryotes that are not bacteria; and Eukarya, eukaryotic organisms. **6.** morphology **7.** biochemistry **8.** fertile **9.** domain **10.** stasis **11.** mass extinction **12.** co-adaptation **13.** classify **14.** mammary glands **15.** community **16.** coordinated stasis **17.** punctuated equilibrium **18.** instantaneous speciation **19.** phylum **20.** asexual **21.** niche **22.** subspecies **23.** interbreed **24.** Archaea **25.** genus **26.** kingdom **27.** subpopulation **28.** Eukarya **29.** Both the biological species concept and the ecological species concept define species as populations that can interbreed and produce fertile offspring. In the ecological species concept, this ability is due to niche. **30.** Both allopatric and sympatric speciation refer to mechanisms of speciation. In allopatric speciation, organisms cannot interbreed because of physical barriers. In sympatric speciation, they cannot interbreed because of behavioral differences.

Workbook Activity 84—How Do Scientists Classify Living Things?
1. B **2.** C **3.** A **4.** C **5.** A **6.** D **7.** C **8.** Helpful bacteria digest food and produce vitamins in the body. Harmful bacteria cause disease. **9.** Bacteria and Archaea are similar in that they are both prokaryotes. Archaea have genes that make it possible to live in extreme environments. **10.** Eukarya cells are large and have nuclei and organelles. Many can move using flagella or cilia. Eukarya cells divide by mitosis and in sexual reproduction by meiosis.

Workbook Activity 85—The Kingdom Protista
1. J **2.** H **3.** I **4.** B **5.** F **6.** C **7.** A **8.** E **9.** D **10.** G **11.** The four kingdoms of Eukarya include Protista, Fungi, Plantae, and Animalia. **12.** The ciliates have hair-like structures that help them move. The amoebae move by pseudopods. The flagellates have whip-like flagella that propel them. **13.** Slime molds have amoeba-like cells that digest food. **14.** Seaweeds are algae, and they do not have the same structures as plants. They lack roots, stems, and leaves. **15.** When food and water are scarce, single cells of slime molds gather together and form one structure. As a structure, they move to a new source of food and water. At the new location, they form reproductive cells, spores. Spores mature into new slime mold cells.

Workbook Activity 86—The Kingdom Fungi
1. mycelium **2.** cyanobacteria **3.** mold **4.** lichen **5.** hyphae **6.** fungi **7.** yeast **8.** spores **9.** photosynthesis **10.** dead organisms **11.** enzymes **12.** penicillin **13.** cheese **14.** bread rise **15.** potato

Workbook Activity 87—The Kingdom Plantae
Down: 1. cones **3.** gymnosperm **4.** moss **6.** frond **7.** stigma **8.** gametophyte **10.** seed **11.** stamen **12.** rhizoid **15.** phloem **16.** sori

Across: 2. pollen **5.** sporophyte **9.** pollination **13.** nectar **14.** angiosperm **17.** pistil **18.** germinate **19.** fern **20.** xylem

Workbook Activity 88—The Kingdom Animalia

Features of Animals	Description
Animals are heterotrophs.	Animals cannot make their own food. They must consume food to get energy to carry out life functions.
Animals have coordinated movement.	Animals can move because they have muscle cells. The actions of muscle cells are controlled by nerve cells.
Animals are multicellular.	Animals are made of more than one cell.
Animals cells are diploid.	They have two copies of each chromosome. In animals, sex cells are haploid. They have one set of chromosomes.
Animals reproduce sexually.	Female reproductive cells are eggs. Male reproductive cells are sperm.
Animal zygotes form blastulae.	A fertilized egg develops into a hollow ball of cells. The hollow ball forms three layers. These develop into different body parts.
Animal cells do not have cell walls.	These structures are rigid and prevent movement.
Animal cells are organized into tissues.	These are a group of cells that work together, such as muscle.

1. vertebrate **2.** haploid **3.** heterotrophs **4.** eggs **5.** invertebrate

Workbook Activity 89—Invertebrates
1. roundworms **2.** tentacles **3.** metamorphosis **4.** endoskeleton **5.** arachnid **6.** radulae **7.** molting **8.** phylogeny **9.** mollusk **10.** cnidarians **11.** radial symmetry **12.** segmented worm **13.** crustaceans **14.** incomplete metamorphosis **15.** exoskeleton

Workbook Activity 90—Vertebrates

Description	Myxinis and Cephalaspido-morphi	Osteichthyes	Amphibians	Reptiles	Birds	Mammals
Skeleton made of cartilage	X					
Skeleton made of bone		X	X	X	X	X
Amniotic eggs				X	X	X
Breathe with gills	X	X	X			
Breathe with lungs			X	X	X	X
Cold-blooded	X	X	X	X		
Warm-blooded					X	X

1. B **2.** D **3.** B **4.** A **5.** B

Workbook Activity 91—Humans
1. Humans, or *Homo sapiens,* are unique because they have culture. **2.** The life span of humans is increasing because of medicine and technology. **3.** There are about 6.5 billion humans on Earth, most of which live in the Asian regions. **4.** Humans are unique from other species in their intelligence, language, and culture. **5.** Bipedal locomotion is the ability to walk upright on two feet. Answers will vary. Students might suggest that humans would not have their hands free if they did not have bipedal locomotion.

Worksheet Activity 92—Chapter 15 Vocabulary Review
1. archaea **2.** flatworm **3.** blastula **4.** algae **5.** marsupial **6.** dysentery **7.** hyphae **8.** germinate **9.** pistil **10.** notochord **11.** spore **12.** stigma **13.** reptile **14.** vertebra **15.** cyanobacteria **16.** taxonomy **17.** eukarya **18.** protozoan **19.** pseudopod **20.** mycelium **21.** lichen **22.** moss **23.** frond **24.** stamen **25.** nectar **26.** heterotroph **27.** invertebrate **28.** tentacles **29.** roundworm **30.** crustacean **31.** molting **32.** metamorphosis **33.** tube feet **34.** chordate **35.** gills **36.** C **37.** A **38.** C **39.** A **40.** D **41.** B **42.** C **43.** B **44.** C **45.** D **46.** D **47.** C **48.** B **49.** B **50.** D **51.** B **52.** A **53.** D **54.** A **55.** A **56.** B **57.** A **58.** C **59.** D **60.** C **61.** B **62.** B **63.** A **64.** D **65.** C **66.** A **67.** A **68.** A **69.** D **70.** C **71.** C **72.** B **73.** C **74.** D **75.** B **76.** A

Workbook Activity 93—What Is Behavioral Biology?
1. B **2.** G **3.** E **4.** C **5.** D **6.** A **7.** H **8.** F **9.** Innate behavior includes a spider spinning a web, a fish swimming toward food, and a dog playing. **10.** External stimuli that might cause one to eat include other people eating, food that looks good, or an established meal time. **11.** This is innate behavior because the baby birds did not learn to do it. **12.** Behaviors evolve that ensure reproductive success of a species. **13.** A learned behavior in monkeys is food washing. **14.** Ethologists observe behaviors in natural situations such as bird flocking or fish schooling. **15.** Birds that mate in the spring have plenty of food available to feed their offspring.

Workbook Activity 94—Types of Behavior
1. A **2.** D **3.** A **4.** D **5.** C **6.** C **7.** D **8.** B **9.** C **10.** B

Workbook Activity 95—Forms of Communication
1. dominant **2.** competitor **3.** communication **4.** pheromones **5.** cognition **6.** signal **7.** scent **8.** cooperation **9.** sociobiologist **10.** agonistic interaction **11.** matched submission **12.** social biology **13.** metacommunication **14.** cooperation **15.** communication

Workbook Activity 96—Chapter 16 Vocabulary Review
1. behavior **2.** ethologists **3.** simulate **4.** internal stimulus **5.** external stimulus **6.** innate behavior **7.** courtship behavior **8.** learned behavior **9.** spatial learning **10.** behavioral biology **11.** fixed action pattern behavior **12.** mimicry **13.** pheromone **14.** metacommunication **15.** dominant **16.** imprint **17.** Defensive behavior **18.** prey **19.** territorial behavior **20.** agonistic interaction **21.** D **22.** O **23.** H **24.** N **25.** K **26.** F **27.** L **28.** G **29.** A **30.** B **31.** E **32.** P **33.** M **34.** J **35.** I **36.** C

Workbook Activity 97—Understanding Populations and Communities
1. C **2.** D **3.** I **4.** F **5.** B **6.** H **7.** G **8.** E **9.** J **10.** A

Levels of Organization	Descriptions
biosphere	All areas of earth where life exists. The biosphere is made of large regions called biomes.
ecosystem	Each one is made of living and non-living parts in an area.
community	All the living things in an ecosystem
population	All the members of one species that live in an ecosystem
organism	Each organism is adapted to live in its habitat.

Workbook Activity 98—Populations and Their Activities
1. Growth rate **2.** uniform **3.** competition **4.** immigrate **5.** carrying capacity **6.** migrate **7.** random **8.** boom-bust cycle **9.** Density-independent factors **10.** clumped **11.** DD **12.** DI **13.** DD **14.** DI **15.** DI

Workbook Activity 99—Relationships in Communities
1. B **2.** C **3.** A **4.** C **5.** D **6.** C **7.** B **8.** M **9.** C **10.** P

Workbook Activity 100—How Do Communities Start and Survive?
1. Succession is the process of ecological change in a community.
2. Primary succession takes place on a new, lifeless environment. Secondary succession occurs after a disturbance destroys some population in a community. **3.** A disturbance is a large change in a community. Disturbances include natural events like fires, flood, and volcanoes and man-caused events such as toxic spills and land clearing. **4.** Toxic substances are poisonous. They can destroy organisms. **5.** SS **6.** PS **7.** SS **8.** SS **9.** SS **10.** PS **11.** succession **12.** lichens **13.** plants **14.** disturbance **15.** toxic

Workbook Activity 101—Chapter 17 Vocabulary Review
1. H **2.** M **3.** B **4.** N **5.** E **6.** L **7.** D **8.** A **9.** C **10.** G **11.** K **12.** F **13.** I **14.** J **15.** biomes **16.** stability **17.** migrate **18.** random **19.** clumped **20.** host **21.** canopy **22.** parasite **23.** toxic **24.** succession **25.** M **26.** P **27.** C **28.** B **29.** C **30.** D **31.** B **32.** C **33.** A **34.** B

Workbook Activity 102—How Does Energy Flow Through Ecosystems?
Across: 1. aquatic **3.** ecosystem **6.** decomposers **7.** solar **8.** consumer **10.** phototroph **12.** producer
Down: 2. chemo **4.** chemotroph **5.** plankton **9.** photo **11.** sun
13. A food chain is a series of steps showing a producer and the consumers that depend directly on that producer. A food web shows the relationships between several food chains. **14.** Organic matter is carbon-containing material. An example is decaying plant matter. **15.** An energy pyramid shows how energy is lost as it moves through a food chain.

Workbook Activity 103—The Cycling of Chemicals in an Ecosystem
1. cycle through **2.** water **3.** Nitrifying bacteria **4.** Geological **5.** atmosphere **6.** phosphorous **7.** evaporation **8.** ammonium **9.** nitrates **10.** nitrogen-fixers **11.** precipitation **12.** Energy and chemicals travel through an ecosystem. **13.** Photosynthesis changes the carbon in carbon dioxide into organic matter. **14.** Plants cannot take up and use nitrogen gas in the atmosphere. **15.** The sun drives the water cycle by powering evaporation.

Workbook Activity 104—Biomes
1. G **2.** C **3.** A **4.** D **5.** F **6.** B **7.** H **8.** E **9.** permafrost **10.** terrestrial **11.** estuary **12.** photic **13.** freshwater **14.** climate **15.** marine

Workbook Activity 105—Chapter 18 Vocabulary Review
1. A **2.** D **3.** A **4.** C **5.** B **6.** D **7.** B **8.** B **9.** B **10.** D **11.** C **12.** A **13.** D **14.** A **15.** B **16.** tundra **17.** organic matter **18.** phosphorous **19.** coniferous forest **20.** marine **21.** temperate forest **22.** plankton **23.** geological **24.** desert **25.** terrestrial **26.** primary productivity **27.** benthic zone **28.** solar **29.** photic zone **30.** permafrost **31.** estuary **32.** nitrates **33.** climate **34.** Temperate grasslands and savannas are two biomes where grasses are the primary plants. Savannas may contain some scattered trees whereas grasslands are dominated by different varieties of grasses. **35.** The three trophic levels of an ecosystem are producer, consumer, and decomposer. Producers use the sun's energy to make their own food. Consumers eat other organisms. Decomposers break down dead organisms.
36. Phototrophs use the sun's energy to get their energy, and plants are examples. Chemotrophs get their energy by feeding on other living things. Decomposers and animals are examples.

Workbook Activity 106—What Impact Do Humans Have on Ecosystems?
1. pollution **2.** runoff **3.** eutrophication **4.** acid rain **5.** greenhouse effect **6.** ozone **7.** land development **8.** deforestation **9.** Kudzu is an introduced species that uses space and sunlight that trees would normally use. **10.** Land development destroys habitats of organisms.

Workbook Activity 107—Conservation Biology
1. H **2.** C **3.** F **4.** G **5.** A **6.** D **7.** B **8.** E **9.** A reserve is a place where natural ecosystems and their organisms are left undisturbed. **10.** Answers will vary. One way to reduce pollution is to recycle paper, plastic, and metal.

Workbook Activity 108—Science and Technology
1. engineer **2.** biogeology **3.** technology **4.** patent **5.** geology **6.** D **7.** B **8.** A **9.** A **10.** C

Workbook Activity 109—Chapter 19 Vocabulary Review
1. C **2.** L **3.** E **4.** F **5.** N **6.** I **7.** M **8.** J **9.** H **10.** K **11.** D **12.** A **13.** G **14.** O **15.** B **16.** chemical runoff **17.** emission **18.** ozone **19.** pollution **20.** eutrophication **21.** deforestation **22.** The greenhouse effect is the warming of the earth's surface by a layer of gases in the atmosphere. Carbon dioxide is one of the primary greenhouse gases. Carbon dioxide emissions are increasing because of industry and cars. **23.** Introduced species take up space and use resources ordinarily used by native species. **24.** Land development can damage or remove habitats such as forests. **25.** Acid rain is produced when emissions such as sulfur dioxide dissolve in water vapor and fall to the earth. Acidic rain can damage organisms directly as well as harm their habitats.

Alternative Workbook Activities

Alternative Workbook Activity 1—What Is Biology?
1. L **2.** NL **3.** L **4.** NL **5.** B **6.** NB **7.** NB **8.** B **9.** C **10.** B **11.** E **12.** D **13.** A

Alternative Workbook Activity 2—Energy and Growth Cycles
1. A **2.** C **3.** C **4.** C **5.** A **6.** B **7.** B **8.** A

Alternative Workbook Activity 3—Evolutionary and Ecological Cycles
1. evolution **2.** extinct **3.** environment **4.** adaptation **5.** species **6.** ecosystem **7.** stimulus **8.** speciation

Alternative Workbook Activity 4—The Scientific Method
1. analyzed **2.** data **3.** control **4.** theory **5.** hypothesis **6.** question **7.** experiment **8.** communicated **9.** scientific method **10.** observations **11.** specimen **12.** variable

Alternative Workbook Activity 5—Chapter 1 Vocabulary Review
1. E **2.** F **3.** J **4.** I **5.** D **6.** G **7.** H **8.** C **9.** A **10.** B **11.** hypothesis **12.** theory **13.** variable **14.** control group **15.** experimental group

Alternative Workbook Activity 6—Matter, Energy, and Chemical Processes of Life
1. P 2. C 3. C 4. P 5. P 6. C 7. C 8. C 9. M 10. M 11. NM 12. NM

Alternative Workbook Activity 7—Atoms and Molecules

Table	Symbol	Atomic Number	Atomic Mass	Number of Protons	Number of Neutrons	Number of Electrons
carbon	C	6	12	6	6	6
hydrogen	H	1	1	1	0	1
oxygen	O	8	16	8	8	8
nitrogen	N	7	4	7	7	7

1. atoms 2. neutron 3. radioisotopes 4. atomic mass 5. atomic number

Alternative Workbook Activity 8—Chemical Formulas
1. two 2. three 3. one 4. one 5. four

Formula	Name of Compound
LiBr	lithium bromide
H_2S	hydrogen sulfide
ZnI_2	zinc iodide
$Ba(NO_3)_2$	barium nitrate
$CuSO_4$	copper sulfate

Alternative Workbook Activity 9—Bonding Patterns
1. B 2. A 3. D 4. A 5. C 6. D 7. A 8. D

Alternative Workbook Activity 10—Properties of Water
1. hydrophobic 2. hydrogen bonds 3. solvent 4. hydrophilic 5. heat 6. perspiration 7. surface tension 8. hydrogen bond

Alternative Workbook Activity 11—Acids, Bases, and pH
1. C 2. E 3. A 4. D 5. B 6. electron 7. neutral 8. pH scale

Alternative Workbook Activity 12—Chapter 2 Vocabulary Review
1. hydrophilic 2. chemical property 3. atomic mass 4. atom 5. proton 6. neutral solution 7. chemical formula 8. buffer 9. diversity 10. acid 11. chemistry 12. chemical bond 13. hydrophobic 14. ion 15. electron shell

Alternative Workbook Activity 13—What Are Organic Molecules?
1. dehydration synthesis 2. monomers 3. hydrocarbon 4. nucleic acids 5. proteins 6. hydrolysis 7. lipid 8. Water is the molecule that makes up most of the cell. 9. Dehydration synthesis is the creation of a long chain of amino acids by removing water molecules. 10. Nucleic acids, carbohydrates, and proteins are macromolecules made up of repeating units.

Alternative Workbook Activity 14—Carbohydrates
1. C 2. A 3. B 4. A 5. D 6. C 7. D 8. A

Alternative Workbook Activity 15—Lipids
1. sulfur 2. information storage 3. carbohydrate 4. olive oil 5. proteins 6. cholesterol 7. solids 8. water 9. trans fats 10. liquid

Alternative Workbook Activity 16—Proteins
1. R group 2. gene 3. amino acids 4. polypeptide 5. codon 6. ion 7. fat 8. water 9. vegetable oil 10. shape

Alternative Workbook Activity 17—Nucleic Acids
1. DNA 2. sugar-phosphate backbone 3. helix 4. RNA 5. bases 6. RNA 7. phosphate group, sugar, and base 8. bases

Alternative Workbook Activity 18—Chapter 3 Vocabulary Review
1. C 2. I 3. G 4. H 5. A 6. D 7. B 8. F 9. J 10. E 11. F 12. C 13. F 14. C 15. P 16. F 17. P 18. N 19. F 20. P

Alternative Workbook Activity 19—What Is a Cell?
1. lipids 2. molecules 3. carbohydrates 4. cell 5. microscope 6. cell theory 7. hormones 8. B 9. D 10. C 11. A 12. E

Alternative Workbook Activity 20—Cellular Structure and Function
1. C 2. B 3. A 4. E 5. D

Environment	Solute Concentration in the Environment Is	Prefix Means
hypotonic solution	(lower than,) higher than, the same as) inside the cell	lower
hypertonic solution	(lower than, (higher than), the same as) inside the cell	higher
isotonic solution	(lower than, higher than, (the same as) inside the cell	equal

Alternative Workbook Activity 21—What Kind of Cell Is It?
1. B 2. D 3. A 4. B 5. C

Cell Features	Prokaryotic Cell	Eukaryotic Cell
has a nucleus		X
membranes surround internal structures		X
includes bacteria	X	
includes human cells		X
possesses organelles		X

Alternative Workbook Activity 22—After the Cell
1. B 2. C 3. B 4. C 5. muscle 6. heart 7. organ system 8. circulatory

Alternative Workbook Activity 23—Chapter 4 Vocabulary Review
1. C 2. G 3. D 4. J 5. A 6. E 7. F 8. B 9. H 10. I 11. OS 12. O 13. T 14. T 15. C

Alternative Workbook Activity 24—What Are Cell Membranes?
1. E 2. D 3. H 4. I 5. B 6. F 7. C 8. J 9. G 10. A 11. phospholipids 12. fibers

Alternative Workbook Activity 25—What Do Membranes Do?
1. C 2. B 3. D 4. A 5. D 6. B 7. A 8. D

Alternative Workbook Activity 26—Information Organelles
1. ribosomes 2. nucleus 3. genome 4. nucleolus 5. chromosomes 6. RNA 7. nuclear envelope 8. genes 9. amino acids 10. pores 11. ribosomes 12. RNA

Alternative Workbook Activity 27—Energy Organelles

Organelle	Held in a Membrane	Located in Cytoplasm	Found in Plant Cells	Found in Animal Cells
mitochondrion	X	X	X	X
chloroplast	X	X	X	

1. Chloroplasts **2.** photosynthesis **3.** stroma **4.** mitochondria **5.** thylakoids

Alternative Workbook Activity 28—The Endomembrane System

1. F **2.** I **3.** H **4.** A **5.** D **6.** E **7.** G **8.** J **9.** B **10.** C **11.** Organelles in the endomembrane system help cells make, adjust, package, ship, and receive many different molecules. **12.** Smooth endoplasmic reticulum makes lipids and carbohydrates.

Alternative Workbook Activity 29—The Cytoskeleton

1. cytoskeleton **2.** flagella **3.** microfilament **4.** cilia **5.** protein **6.** B **7.** B **8.** A

Alternative Workbook Activity 30—Plant Cells

1. D **2.** B **3.** A **4.** C **5.** cell membrane **6.** loses water **7.** communicate **8.** leaves receive more sunlight than roots

Alternative Workbook Activity 31—Chapter 5 Vocabulary Review

1. N **2.** L **3.** H **4.** G **5.** M **6.** I **7.** D **8.** F **9.** B **10.** J **11.** K **12.** O **13.** E **14.** A **15.** C

Alternative Workbook Activity 32—What Is Energy?

1. C **2.** B **3.** C **4.** fat **5.** adenine, ribose **6.** kilocalorie **7.** cellular respiration **8.** metabolism

Alternative Workbook Activity 33—Making ATP

1. ADP **2.** energy **3.** ATP **4.** sun

Type of Molecule	Contains 3 Phosphate Groups	Contains 2 Phosphate Groups	Called Adenosine-triphosphate	Called Adenosine-diphosphate
ADP		X		X
ATP	X		X	

Alternative Workbook Activity 34—Enzymes and Energy Flow

1. catalyst **2.** enzymes **3.** saliva **4.** pepsin **5.** proteins **6.** diabetes **7.** amount of energy **8.** released

Alternative Workbook Activity 35—More About Enzymes

1. active site **2.** substrate **3.** catalyst **4.** enzyme **5.** activation energy **6.** food **7.** Student answers will vary, but could include: yeast causes bread dough to rise; bacteria produce enzymes that break down cellulose; and animals, plants, and fungi use enzymes in many life processes. **8.** The enzyme and substrate fit together at the active site. The active site changes shape and causes the reaction.

Alternative Workbook Activity 36—Chapter 6 Vocabulary Review

1. M **2.** I **3.** K **4.** O **5.** A **6.** G **7.** B **8.** C **9.** D **10.** F **11.** J **12.** H **13.** N **14.** E **15.** L

Alternative Workbook Activity 37—What Is Cellular Respiration?

glucose + oxygen ➔ carbon dioxide + water + energy
1. C **2.** A **3.** B **4.** A **5.** A

Alternative Workbook Activity 38—The Stages of Cellular Respiration

1. glycolysis **2.** cytoplasm **3.** glucose **4.** electron carriers **5.** mitochondria **6.** ATP

Stages of Cellular Respiration	Products That Result from this Stage			Location of this Stage		
	Pyruvic Acid	ATP	NADH & FADH$_2$	Cytoplasm	Matrix	Membrane of Mitochondria
glycolysis	X			X		
Krebs cycle			X		X	
electron transport chain		X				X

Alternative Workbook Activity 39—Fermentation

1. aerobic **2.** fermentation **3.** oxygen **4.** glycolysis **5.** energy **6.** products **7.** yeast **8.** carbon dioxide **9.** anaerobic **10.** lactic acid **11.** ethyl alcohol **12.** anaerobic

Alternative Workbook Activity 40—Controlling Cellular Respiration

1. metabolic pathway **2.** energy **3.** cellular respiration **4.** fat **5.** energy **6.** energy **7.** enzymes **8.** lipids and protein **9.** energy **10.** fat **11.** feedback inhibition **12.** cellular respiration

Alternative Workbook Activity 41—Chapter 7 Vocabulary Review

1. H **2.** G **3.** A **4.** E **5.** D **6.** I **7.** C **8.** J **9.** F **10.** B **11.** NADH **12.** pyruvic acid **13.** Kreb's cycle **14.** cytoplasm **15.** electron transport chain

Alternative Workbook Activity 42—What Is Photosynthesis?

1. D **2.** A **3.** C **4.** B **5.** X **7.** X **8.** X **9.** X **10.** X **12.** X

Alternative Workbook Activity 43—Light Reactions

1. B **2.** C **3.** A **4.** caretenoid **5.** absorb **6.** spectrum **7.** Calvin-Benson cycle **8.** photophosphorylation

Alternative Workbook Activity 44—The Dark Reaction: The Calvin-Benson Cycle

1. stroma **2.** glucose **3.** carbon dioxide **4.** light reaction **5.** stomata **6.** CAM plants **7.** C4 plant **8.** photosynthesis **9.** RuBP **10.** PGA

Alternative Workbook Activity 45—Chapter 8 Vocabulary Review

1. photosynthesis **2.** mesophyll **3.** autotroph **4.** photon **5.** absorb **6.** spectrum **7.** Calvin-Benson cycle **8.** reaction center **9.** vascular bundle **10.** crabgrass

Alternative Workbook Activity 46—The Cell Cycle and Mitosis

1. eukaryotes **2.** growth and repair **3.** interphase **4.** mitosis **5.** prophase **6.** anaphase **7.** telophase **8.** metaphase

Alternative Workbook Activity 47—What Is Cancer?
1. B 2. D 3. E 4. C 5. A 6. surgery 7. benign 8. metastasis
9. Cancer 10. tumor 11. Cancer is a condition in which cells grow too much and divide without control. 12. A tumor is a ball of cells made from divisions of cancerous cells.

Alternative Workbook Activity 48—Meiosis: The Life Cycle of Sex Cells
1. D 2. B 3. D 4. A 5. metaphase II 6. anaphase II 7. prophase II 8. telophase II

Alternative Workbook Activity 49—The Human Reproductive System
1. testes 2. testosterone 3. scrotum 4. urethra 5. penis
6. seminiferous tubules 7. semen 8. ovary 9. uterus 10. oogenesis
11. ovulation 12. estrogen

Alternative Workbook Activity 50—Human Development
1. Adolescence 2. pregnancy 3. fetus 4. vagina 5. embryo 6. placenta
7. cervix 8. gestation time 9. vagina 10. umbilical cord
11. Adolescence is a period of rapid growth and physical changes when humans learn about become adults. 12. Answer will vary. A three week old embryo has three layers that will develop into different parts of the body. A four week embryo has a heart and blood vessels.

Alternative Workbook Activity 51—Chapter 9 Vocabulary Review
1. C 2. C 3. A 4. D 5. C 6. C 7. C 8. B 9. A 10. A 11. A 12. A

Alternative Workbook Activity 52—What Did Mendel Discover?
1. trait 2. heredity 3. pollen 4. pea plants 5. hybrid 6. alleles
7. homozygous 8. recessive 9. Tt 10. TT

Alternative Workbook Activity 53—Different Ways Alleles Cooperate
1. D 2. C 3. A 4. B 5. testcross 6. linked 7. linkage map
8. polygenic

Alternative Workbook Activity 54—The Importance of Sex Chromosomes
1. autosome 2. carrier 3. hemophilia 4. sex-linked inheritance
5. sex-linked trait 6. C 7. B 8. D 9. A 10. red 11. X 12. Males

Alternative Workbook Activity 55—Chapter 10 Vocabulary Review
1. recessive 2. Punnett square 3. homozygous 4. phenotype
5. genotype 6. codominance 7. multiple alleles 8. heredity
9. hybrid 10. testcross 11. hemophilia

Alternative Workbook Activity 56—How Are Molecules of Life Involved in Heredity?
1. complementary base pairing 2. nitrogenous base 3. sugar-phosphate backbone 4. guanine 5. uracil

Molecule	Contains a Phosphate Group	Contains Sugar		Contains Bases	
		Deoxyribose	Ribose	Uracil	Thymine
DNA	X	X			X
RNA	X		X	X	

Alternative Workbook Activity 57—DNA Replication
1. B 2. A 3. F 4. G 5. E 6. C 7. D 8. C 9. B 10. A 11. A 12. D

Alternative Workbook Activity 58—The Path of Genetic Information
1. X 2. X 3. X 6. X 7. X 8. X 9. mRNA 10. codon 11. RNA polymerase 12. promoter

Alternative Workbook Activity 59—What Are Viruses?
1. DNA 2. virus 3. lysogenic cycle 4. evolve 5. immune system
6. host cell 7. parasite 8. infect 9. lytic cycle 10. vaccine 12. capsids
11. vaccine

Alternative Workbook Activity 60—Using the Path of Genetic Information
1. biotechnology 2. biotechnologist 3. bacteria 4. restriction endonuclease 5. transformation 6. B 7. G 8. E 9. C 10. D 11. A 12. F

Alternative Workbook Activity 61—Natural Defenses Against Disease
1. pathogen 2. Cytotoxic T cells 3. complement 4. immunity
5. infectious disease 6. lymph 7. nonspecific defense 8. white blood cells

Alternative Workbook Activity 62—Chapter 11 Vocabulary Review
1. Guanine 2. template 3. mRNA 4. Exons 5. tRNA 6. host cell
7. immune system 8. DNA polymerase 9. virus 10. pathogens
11. lymph system 12. antigen 13. B lymphocytes 14. infectious disease

Alternative Workbook Activity 63—The Digestive System
1. saliva 2. chime 3. peristalsis 4. anus 5. villi 6. bile 7. glucose
8. water 9. feces 10. reflex 11. ingestion 12. absorption

Alternative Workbook Activity 64—The Respiratory System
1. A 2. B 3. D 4. B 5. D 6. A 7. B 8. C

Alternative Workbook Activity 65—The Circulatory System
1. thrombus 2. connective 3. Interstitial fluid 4. Arthrosclerosis
5. platelets 6. fibrinogen 7. plasma 8. cardiac 9. Veins
10. hypertension 11. ventricle 12. Arteries

Alternative Workbook Activity 66—The Excretory System
1. ureter 2. nephron 3. glomerulus 4. antidiuretic 5. perspiration
6. water 7. kidney 8. urine 9. dermis 10. fatty layer 11. The three layers of the skin are the epidermis, dermis, and fatty layer. 12. The excretory system includes the kidneys, ureters, bladder, urethra, liver, lungs, and skin.

Alternative Workbook Activity 67—The Nervous System

Area of the Brain	Subdivision of That Area	Function(s)
brain stem		controls these functions: heart rate, digestion, and breathing
cerebellum		controls balance and helps muscles work together
limbic system		affects feelings like anger and pleasure
diencephalon	thalamus	directs incoming sensory information
	hypothalamus	regulates the pituitary and other glands
cerebral cortex	frontal lobe parietal lobe temporal lobe occipital lobe	involved in body functions like vision, hearing, thinking and memory

1. synapse 2. dendrites 3. spinal cord 4. brain stem 5. neurons

Alternative Workbook Activity 68—The Sensory System
1. E 2. F 3. H 4. C 5. D 6. B 7. A 8. J 9. G 10. I 11. The eye is one type of sensory receptor. 12. Pain receptors, located in the epidermis, respond to high temperature, heavy pressure, or specific chemicals.

Alternative Workbook Activity 69—The Endocrine System
1. feedback loop 2. adrenaline 3. pituitary gland 4. thymus gland 5. glucose 6. calcium 7. hypothalamus 8. adrenal glands 9. gonads 10. hormones 11. Answers will vary, but could include: adrenal, hypothalamus, pancreas, gonads, pineal, pituitary, thymus, and thyroid. 12. Answers will vary, based on the gland chosen.

Alternative Workbook Activity 70—The Skeletal and Muscular System

Type of Joint	What the Joint Does
ball and socket	allows arms and legs to rotate
hinge	allows movement in one direction
pivot	allows rotation

1. ligaments 2. tendons 3. calcium 4. red marrow 5. skeletal system

Alternative Workbook Activity 71—Chapter 12 Vocabulary Review
1. C 2. B 3. C 4. A 5. C 6. D 7. C 8. B 9. A 10. D 11. F 12. E

Alternative Workbook Activity 72—What Is Biological Evolution?
1. C 2. H 3. D 4. G 5. B 6. E 7. A 8. F

Description	Darwin's Idea	Lamarck's Idea
Giraffes stretch their necks. Their offspring have long necks.		X
Horses and zebras are similar. They have a common ancestor.	X	
Wolves eat most of the rabbits in a field. A few smart rabbits find hiding places. They survive and reproduce.	X	
A mouse loses its tail in a fight. Its offspring will not have tails.		X

Alternative Workbook Activity 73—Evidence of Evolution
1. lemur 2. sedimentary rock 3. fossil record 4. homologous structures 5. Fossils 6. natural selection 7. comparative anatomy 8. evolution 9. ancestor 10. nucleotides 11. anatomy 12. biogeography

Alternative Workbook Activity 74—Rates of Evolutionary Change
1. D 2. B 3. C 4. C 5. D 6. B 7. C 8. A 9. C 10. D

Alternative Workbook Activity 75—Processes in Evolution
1. gene flow 2. genetic drift 3. extinct 4. Recombination 5. gene flow 6. mutation 7. habitat 8. natural selection 9. alleles 10. endangered

Alternative Workbook Activity 76—Natural Selection
1. malaria 2. natural selection 3. artificial selection 4. sickle cell disease 5. natural selection

Description	Natural Selection	Artificial Selection
A flood drowns most of the lizards in an area. Only lizards that can swim live to reproduce.	X	
A farmer crosses two kinds of corn. He produces a new, better tasting type of corn.		X
Two male wild turkeys fight. The weaker one is killed. The winner mates with all the females.	X	

Alternative Workbook Activity 77—Microevolution and Macroevolution
1. evolutionary biology 2. vary 3. struggle 4. reproduce

	Microevolution	Macroevolution
In the 1800s moth populations were mostly light colored. In a few years, they changed to mostly dark colored.	X	
A population can change over thousands of years.		X
Small changes in a population can happen over a few generations.	X	
At one time dinosaurs lived on the earth. Today they are extinct.		X

Alternative Workbook Activity 78—Chapter 13 Vocabulary Review
1. B 2. D 3. C 4. B 5. B 6. A 7. A 8. D 9. A 10. D

Alternative Workbook Activity 79—What Is Speciation?
1. morphology 2. interbreed 3. subpopulation 4. classify 5. niche 6. fertile 7. subspecies 8. C 9. D 10. E 11. B 12. A

Alternative Workbook Activity 80—Classifying Species
1. B 2. C 3. D 4. A 5. B 6. phylum 7. plant 8. Archaea

Alternative Workbook Activity 81—Conditions for Speciation to Occur
1. evolutionary 2. speciation 3. geography 4. stasis 5. environment 6. extinct 7. stable 8. fossils

Alternative Workbook Activity 82—Conditions That Affect Species Survival
1. D 2. C 3. A 4. B 5. D 6. A 7. C 8. D

Alternative Workbook Activity 83—Chapter 14 Vocabulary Review
1. mammary glands 2. community 3. coordinated stasis 4. punctuated equilibrium 5. morphology 6. fertile 7. domain 8. stasis 9. genus 10. subspecies 11. speciation 12. interbreed

Alternative Workbook Activity 84—How Do Scientists Classify Living Things?
1. A 2. A 3. C 4. D 5. C 6. B 7. C 8. B 9. E 10. A 11. E 12. B

Alternative Workbook Activity 85—The Kingdom Protista
1. F 2. A 3. D 4. C 5. B 6. E 7. fungi 8. Ciliates 9. Algae 10. spores 11. flagellates 12. Amoebae

Alternative Workbook Activity 86—The Kingdom Fungi
1. mycelium 2. Lichens 3. cyanobacteria 4. mold 5. fungi 6. spores 7. dead organisms 8. hyphae 9. enzymes 10. penicillin 11. cheese 12. potato

Alternative Workbook Activity 87—The Kingdom Plantae
Down: 1. pistil 2. conifer 3. sori 5. nectar
Across: 4. rhizoid 6. phloem 7. fern 8. moss 9. xylem 10. stamen

Alternative Workbook Activity 88—The Kingdom Animalia

Features of Animals	Description
Animals are heterotrophs.	Animals cannot make their own food. They must consume food.
Animals have coordinated movements.	Animals can move because they have muscle cells. These cells are controlled by nerve cells.
Animals are multicellular.	Animals are made of more than one cell.
Animals reproduce sexually.	Female reproductive cells are eggs. Male reproductive cells are sperm.
Animal cells are organized into tissues.	These are groups of cells that work together, such as muscle.

1. invertebrate 2. heterotroph 3. eggs 4. vertebrate 5. blastula

Alternative Workbook Activity 89—Invertebrates
1. endoskeleton 2. arachnid 3. mollusk 4. cnidarians 5. radula
6. tentacles 7. metamorphosis 8. phylogeny 9. crustaceans
10. incomplete metamorphosis 11. exoskeletons 12. radial symmetry

Alternative Workbook Activity 90—Vertebrates

Description	Fish	Amphibians	Reptiles	Birds and Mammals
Breathe with gills	X	X		
Breathe with lungs		X	X	X
Cold-blooded	X	X	X	
Warm-blooded				X

1. B 2. A 3. C

Alternative Workbook Activity 91—Humans
1. animal 2. culture 3. bipedal locomotion 4. brain
5. environment 6. B 7. C 8. C 9. D 10. C 11. A 12. A

Alternative Workbook Activity 92—Chapter 15 Vocabulary Review
1. pseudopod 2. mycelium 3. frond 4. stamen 5. heterotroph
6. tentacles 7. molting 8. flatworm 9. pistil 10. notochord
11. marsupial 12. archaea 13. spore 14. blastula 15. algae

Alternative Workbook Activity 93—What Is Behavioral Biology?
1. D 2. C 3. A 4. B 5. E 6. B 7. H 8. F 9. G 10. D 11. C 12. A

Alternative Workbook Activity 94—Types of Behavior
1. B 2. A 3. D 4. A 5. D 6. B 7. C 8. B 9. C 10. D

Alternative Workbook Activity 95—Forms of Communication
1. pheromones 2. cognition 3. cooperation 4. dominant
5. metacommunication 6. scent 7. competitor 8. communication
9. social biology 10. signal 11. matched submission
12. sociobiologist

Alternative Workbook Activity 96—Chapter 16 Vocabulary Review
1. metacommunication 2. dominant 3. imprint on 4. behavioral biology 5. fixed action pattern behavior 6. D 7. B 8. C 9. E 10. A
11. G 12. H 13. J 14. F 15. I

Alternative Workbook Activity 97—Understanding Populations and Communities
1. E 2. F 3. H 4. D 5. B 6. A 7. G 8. C

Levels of Organization	Descriptions
biosphere	Made of large areas called biomes
ecosystem	Made up of living and nonliving things
community	All the living things in an ecosystem
population	All the members of one species that live in an ecosystem
organism	Each organism is adapted to live in its habitat.

Alternative Workbook Activity 98—Populations and Their Activities
1. Carrying capacity 2. emigrate 3. Density-independent factors
4. clumped 5. Growth rate 6. random 7. uniform 8. competition
9. immigrate 10. DI 11. DD 12. DI

Alternative Workbook Activity 99—Relationships in Communities
1. A 2. C 3. D 4. A 5. C 6. B 7. B 8. C 9. A 10. P 11. C 12. M

Alternative Workbook Activity 100—How Do Communities Start and Survive?
1. SS 2. PS 3. SS 4. SS 5. SS 6. PS 7. primary succession
8. succession 9. lichens 10. disturbance 11. stability 12. toxic

Alternative Workbook Activity 101—Chapter 17 Vocabulary Review
1. E 2. C 3. F 4. B 5. D 6. A 7. parasite 8. toxic 9. canopy 10. B
11. B 12. C

Alternative Workbook Activity 102—How Does Energy Flow Through Ecosystems?
Down: 1. plankton 2. aquatic 3. producer 4. decomposer
5. chemotroph

Across: 5. consumer 6. solar 7. phototroph 8. food chain
9. Organic compounds 10. energy pyramid 11. Primary productivity

Alternative Workbook Activity 103—The Cycling of Chemicals in an Ecosystem
1. Phosphorous 2. evaporation 3. ammonium 4. nitrates
5. nitrogen-fixers 6. precipitation 7. Nitrifying bacteria
8. Geological 9. atmosphere 10. energy 11. carbon 12. nitrogen

Alternative Workbook Activity 104—Biomes
1. climate 2. marine 3. photic 4. permafrost 5. terrestrial
6. estuary 7. B 8. A 9. F 10. E 11. D 12. C

Alternative Workbook Activity 105—Chapter 18 Vocabulary Review
1. photic zone 2. permafrost 3. estuary 4. coniferous forest 5. temperate forest 6. plankton 7. C 8. B 9. A 10. B 11. A 12. D

Alternative Workbook Activity 106—What Impact Do Humans Have on Ecosystems?
1. pollution **2.** runoff **3.** eutrophication **4.** acid rain **5.** greenhouse effect **6.** ozone **7.** land development **8.** deforestation **9.** introduced species **10.** Pollution can damage an ecosystem and harm living things. **11.** A hole in the ozone layer above Antarctica lets in harmful radiation. **12.** Kudzu is an introduced species that takes the space and light used by trees.

Alternative Workbook Activity 107—Conservation Biology
1. C **2.** G **3.** B **4.** F **5.** D **6.** H **7.** E **8.** A **9.** People can protect threatened habitats by creating reserves. **10.** Answers will vary. One way to reduce air pollution is have car emissions checked. **11.** Plastic, paper, and metal can be recycled. **12.** Pollution reduces the number of living things in an ecosystem.

Alternative Workbook Activity 108—Science and Technology
1. patent **2.** geology **3.** engineering **4.** engineer **5.** biogeology **6.** technology **7.** D **8.** D **9.** B **10.** A

Alternative Workbook Activity 109—Chapter 19 Vocabulary Review
1. pollution **2.** eutrophication **3.** deforestation **4.** runoff **5.** emission **6.** E **7.** I **8.** J **9.** C **10.** G **11.** B **12.** H **13.** F **14.** D **15.** A

Lab Manual

Lab Manual 1—Express Lab 1
1. the sun **2.** The source of energy, the sun, was blocked. **3.** Solar energy from the sun was transformed into electrical energy in the solar cells. The electrical energy was transformed into mechanical energy of the motor.

Lab Manual 2—Cycles of Energy
Analysis 1. Worms ate the dead plant matter (leaves, soft stems and roots, fruit). **2.** The living things include worms and radish seeds; the nonliving substances are soil and water. **3.** Students' answers will vary. The seeds sprouted into small plants and the worms created tunnels through the soil. **Conclusions 1.** Organisms live and grow within their ecosystems, where they interact with nonliving parts of the environment. **2.** Grass in the field or pasture absorbs the sun's energy to make food. Cows eat the grass and take in the energy themselves. Cows are used as a source of meat for hamburgers. When you eat the hamburger, you take in some of that energy. The grain that is used to make bread also depends on the sun. **Explore Further** Nutrient cycling is similar in pond and terrestrial mini-ecosystems. Animals living in the pond eat plant matter.

Lab Manual 3—What Is Life? (Investigation 1)
Analysis 1. Students should easily classify the plant, sprout, seeds, insect, bacteria, and mushroom as living. The rock and flashlight are nonliving. **2.** The flashlight shows a cycle that is common with living samples. (energy cycle) The flashlight transforms energy. A rock may break apart into smaller rocks, but does not reproduce itself. **Conclusions 1.** Energy takes many forms. Energy is converted from the sun into sugars by plants. Plant material serves as an energy source for the insect, mushroom, and bacteria. Dead organisms ultimately serve as energy sources for the bacteria and mushroom. **2.** The plant is part of the insect's cycle. The plant provides energy (food) for the insect. The seeds and sprout represent stages in the growth cycle of the plant's life. **Explore Further** If students are having trouble getting started, encourage them to skim through the text. Various illustrations and photographs may prompt their thinking. Examples include birds flying south for the winter and returning in the spring, and a dinosaur species arising and then becoming extinct. Suggest that students use arrows in the diagram to help them visualize and communicate the cyclic nature of the processes involved.

Lab Manual 4—No More Music

Steps of the Scientific Method	Your Data
1. observation	The CD will not play. Jody uses the CD player a lot.
2. question	Answers could include a statement that the CD player batteries no longer work.
3. hypothesis	The CD player needs new batteries.
4. experiment	Replace the batteries and see what happens.
5. analysis	The CD player works when the batteries are replaced.
6. communication	Tell other people what happened in the experiment.

Analysis 1. Answers will vary. The original batteries could have been restored, and a new CD tested in the CD player. **2.** Scientists need to communicate to share their ideas and findings with other scientists. **3.** Jody can let other people know what happened to her CD player in case they have the same problem. **Conclusions 1.** The scientific method uses a logical, systematic approach to problem solving. **2.** Answers will vary, but could include students, teachers, mechanics, doctors, and lawyers. **Explore Further** Answers will vary. To compare mileage from gasoline X and gasoline Y, a person could put 10 gallons of gasoline X in their tank and write down the mileage. When gasoline X was gone, they could calculate the number of miles per gallon the gasoline yielded. The same procedure could be followed with gasoline Y. The two mileages could be analyzed to determine which gasoline is the best.

Lab Manual 5—Using the Scientific Method (Discovery Investigation 1)
Analysis 1. The substance used to "water" the plant was the variable that was changed. **2.** Answers may vary. After Day 4, those watered with water should have sprouted. The sprouts should be more visible after Day 8. A few seeds "watered" with vinegar may sprout. **Conclusions 1.** Answers will vary depending on students' hypotheses and results. Students should indicate whether the hypothesis was supported, not whether it was correct. **2.** Answers will vary. Students should note the problems that occurred during the investigation and include any modifications they would make to the procedure. **3.** An experiment that does not support a hypothesis is not a failure because the information allows more accurate hypotheses to be made. **4.** Acid rain prevents seeds from sprouting and plants from growing. **Explore Further** Encourage students to ask questions about what a plant needs to grow. Have student groups pick one question to investigate. Then help them shape their question into a process that uses the scientific method. Students should propose a testable hypothesis and then create an experiment that tests this hypothesis.

Lab Manual 6—Express Lab 2
1. In the cup with water, the baking soda dissolved in the water. In the cup with vinegar, fizzing occurred. **2.** in the cup with vinegar

Lab Manual 7—Physical and Chemical Properties (Investigation 2)
Analysis 1. The water changed state from liquid to gas. Energy from the hot plate caused the water molecules to move rapidly and change state. This is a physical change. **2.** The nail rusts because it reacts chemically with oxygen and water. This is a chemical change. **3.** In Step 4, a physical change took place. The iron is magnetized due to rearrangements of its molecules. **4.** The mass of the ashes should be more than the mass of the strip. **5.** When magnesium burns, it reacts chemically with oxygen. This is a chemical change.
Conclusions 1. Students should summarize what they observed and label each activity as a chemical or physical change. They can present their data in a table like the one below or in short paragraphs.

Object	Observations
boiling water	physical change
rusty nail and non-rusty nail	chemical change
paper clips	physical change
mass of crucible and magnesium	physical change or chemical change
mass of crucible and magnesium ashes	chemical change

2. The magnesium reacted with the oxygen to create a new substance—magnesium oxide. The oxygen gas became solid and added mass to the magnesium. When something burns, a chemical change takes place because burning is a chemical reaction with oxygen. **Explore Further** Answers may vary. Some examples of chemical changes in daily life might be cooking food, using hair products, or eating.

Lab Manual 8—Atomic Model
Analysis

Atoms	Atomic Mass	Atomic Number	Number of Protons	Number of Neutrons	Number of Electrons
hydrogen (H)	1	1	1	0	1
lithium (Li)	7	3	3	4	3
nitrogen (N)	14	7	7	7	7
sodium (Na)	23	11	11	12	11

Conclusions 1. True. Since all matter is made up of atoms, it is also made up of the parts of atoms. **2.** Moving from the left to the right side of the Periodic Table, models increase in size because atoms have increasingly larger numbers of subatomic particles. **Explore Further** A model of an O_2 molecule would show two oxygen atoms side-by-side sharing four electrons.

Lab Manual 9—The Properties of Water (Discovery Investigation 2)
Analysis 1. Student groups should present their data to the class. They should explain the results clearly and be able to answer questions about the procedure. **2.** If problems developed during the procedure, be sure students evaluate the problems. Have students write a new procedure to correct the problem. **Conclusions 1.** Answers will vary depending on the property that groups choose to investigate. **2.** Answers will vary. Students should offer explanations about the consequences for life forms about the property they chose. **3.** The hydrogen bonds that form as part of the water molecule are responsible for the unique properties of water. **Explore Further** Have students write a procedure to test another property of water. As an alternative to choosing another property, students could trade their procedure with another group who chose a different property. If time allows, have each group read through the procedure and perform it. If more than one group performs the procedure, have them compare their results.

Lab Manual 10—Acids and Bases

Household Item	Amount of pH	Household Item	Amount of pH
window cleaner	11	vinegar	4
shampoo	7	lemon juice	4
cola	2.5	antacid	8
coffee	2–5	baking soda	8

Analysis 1. 4, 4 (or 3, if shampoo is neutral) **2.** in the kitchen **3.** Answers will vary: bath soap (slightly less basic than shampoo), laundry detergent (slightly less basic than window cleaner), oven cleaner (extremely basic), apple juice (slightly less acidic than orange juice), a cup of hot tea (slightly less acidic than coffee). **Conclusions 1.** Most acids are found in the kitchen because many foods are slightly acidic. Bases are used to make cleaners such as laundry detergent, soap, and glass cleaner. **2.** Student answers will vary. Food would all taste very neutral, without any tart flavors. Cleaners would be no more effective than water. **Explore Further** Answers will vary. Chalk in water is slightly basic. Most commercial cleaners are bases. Foods are neutral or slightly acidic.

Lab Manual 11—Studying Dehydration Synthesis
Analysis 1. one **2.** two **Conclusions 1.** Each time a glucose molecule is added to the chain, a water molecule is removed. **2.** Yes. To add a glucose molecule, one water molecule would have to be removed. **3.** Put the water molecules back on the glucose molecules. **Explore Further** The two molecules have different kinds of bonds between the individual units of glucose.

Lab Manual 12—Express Lab 3
1. sugars, dietary fiber **2.** Answers will vary depending on the food but should be determined by dividing the number of calories from fat by the total number of calories.

Lab Manual 13—Amino Acids and Proteins (Investigation 3)
Analysis 1. Test Tubes 2 and 3 contain a protein. **2.** When a protein is present, the liquid in the tube turns pink or purple. **3.** Test Tube 1 is the control. Students should explain why they were or were not surprised by the results. **Conclusions 1.** All proteins are made of amino acids linked together. Substances that are not proteins do not produce a color change because they do not contain amino acids. **2.** Test Tube 1 contained distilled water because it was the control. Distilled water will not react with the other solutions used in the experiment. A control is always included to ensure that results are due only to the factor being tested or examined in the experiment. In this experiment, the control tube is identical to the other tubes except for one factor: It does not contain a substance to be tested. **3.** Answers will vary. For example, students may suggest comparing different methods of preparing food samples for testing, or examining the effects of temperature on the testing. **Explore Further** Results will vary depending on the foods selected by students. Students will need to prepare dilute suspensions of foods they want to test. If students need help choosing another food, suggest a 1% solution of powdered gelatin. Gelatin is a soluble mixture of polypeptides, and it will produce a purple color.

Lab Manual 14—Testing for Starches
Analysis 1. Answers will vary depending on lab materials. Foods of animal origin include milk, eggs, and meat. **2.** Answers will vary depending on lab materials. Foods of plant origin include lettuce, potato, and corn. **Conclusions 1.** Chemical change. The production of a new material represents a chemical reaction in which the material is chemically changed. **2.** Answers will vary, but might include meals with pasta, bread, cereals, or potatoes. **3.** People who load trucks because they use more energy so they need more energy supplies. **Explore Further** The two chains of macromolecules differ in the way they are linked.

Lab Manual 15—Testing for Lipids (Discovery Investigation 3)
Analysis 1. In Test Tube 1, the Sudan III forms a layer on top of the water and does not mix with it. In Test Tube 2, the Sudan III mixes with the vegetable oil. **2.** Sudan III mixes with oil, but not with water. Methylene blue mixes with water, but not with oil. **Conclusions 1.** Answers will vary depending on students' hypotheses and results. Students should indicate whether the hypothesis was supported, not whether it was correct. **2.** The tails of the fatty acid chains are hydrophobic (water-hating) or nonpolar, which results in fatty acids not mixing with water. Carbohydrates such as glucose are polar and mix with water. **Explore Further** Encourage students to ask questions about basic observations they have made. Some examples could include: Why does the Sudan III/oil layer float on top of the water? What other liquids can we test? Help students shape their observations into a process that uses the scientific method. Students should propose a testable hypothesis and then create an experiment that tests this hypothesis.

Lab Manual 16—Express Lab 4
1. Answers will vary. Students may see algae, ciliates, flagellates, and diatoms. They may also see large bacteria if magnification is sufficient. **2.** Answers will vary.

Lab Manual 17—Cork Cells
Analysis 1. Answers will vary. **2.** Answers will vary; a regularly shaped structure is visible. **Conclusions 1.** Cell wall **2.** Answers will vary. Cork cells are dead, so the cytoplasm is absent. **3.** Answers will vary. **Explore Further** Bamboo cells are longer and thinner than cork cells. The shape of bamboo cells is cylindrical while cork cells are more rounded. Both types of cells have easy-to-see cell walls and there is no cytoplasm in either. In some species of bamboo, the cell walls are decidedly thicker than the cell walls of cork.

Lab Manual 18—Living Cells (Investigation 4)
Analysis 1. Sucrose is the energy source for the yeast cells. **2.** A cell membrane surrounds each yeast cell. **Conclusions 1.** The cell membrane acts as a barrier for the cell, separating it from the surrounding environment. **2.** Students may suggest comparing different carbohydrates (such as sucrose, lactose, and fructose) to learn which carbohydrate provides the most energy for yeast. **Explore Further** Students could examine the effects of a variety of temperatures (cool, room temperature, warm, hot) on the ability of living yeast cells to grow. Yeast requires warm temperatures (38°C to 43°C) to grow. Temperatures that are too cool or too hot will prevent growth.

Lab Manual 19—Diffusion
Analysis 1. in the place where the drop was added to the water **2.** Students' answers will vary; the blue color begins to diffuse in the water. **Conclusions 1.** diffusion **2.** Answers will vary; the blue dye diffuses evenly throughout the water. **3.** Tea diffuses into the water. **Explore Further** Students should record their results of this comparison. Diffusion occurs faster in warm water than in cold water.

Lab Manual 20—Osmosis in Cells (Discovery Investigation 4)
Analysis 1. Distilled water is a hypotonic environment for *Elodea*. **2.** If *Elodea* cells were surrounded by saltwater, water would exit the cells. **Conclusions 1.** Answers will vary depending on students' hypotheses and results. For example, students may wish to prepare a second slide with *Elodea* mounted in a drop of 10 percent NaCl solution instead of distilled water. Students should indicate whether the hypothesis was supported, not whether it was correct. **2.** Too much plant fertilizer will cause water to leave the plant cells, resulting in wilting and possible death. **Explore Further** Encourage students to predict possible outcomes based upon observations they have made. For example, if a salt solution is surrounding a plant cell, what might happen when the plant takes up more water after a rainstorm? Help students to shape these observations into a process that uses the scientific method. Students could propose a testable hypothesis and then create an experiment that tests this hypothesis.

Lab Manual 21—Express Lab 5
1. The water is similar to the polar head, and the vegetable oil is similar to the nonpolar tail. **2.** The layers stay separated no matter what motion occurs. This accurately represents the fluid mosaic model of the plasma membrane, which allows motion and shifting while still maintaining the layers.

Lab Manual 22—A Day in the Life of a Protein
Analysis 1. Vacuoles move materials around the cell. **2.** Lysosomes break down materials. **Conclusions 1.** Answers will vary. Possible answer: Proteins are made on ribosomes in the endoplasmic reticulum. They are carried to the Golgi apparatus for modification. Vacuoles then transport them to the cell membrane for export. **2.** Answers will vary. Possible answer: The modifications tell the molecules where to go next. The modifications label the molecules so that other molecules can recognize them. **Explore Further** To simulate protein production on a plant cell, students could edge their desktops with stiff cardboard. They might include a very large central vacuole filled with water in their model.

Lab Manual 23—Cells Made of Gelatin
Analysis 1. The plastic bag represents the cell membrane. Gelatin represents the cytoplasm. **2.** Answers will vary. Possible answer: Cytoplasm, ribosomes, nucleus, and Golgi apparatus were visible. No. A cut in a different place would reveal different cell structures. **3.** Animal cell. There is no cell wall or chloroplast. **Conclusions 1.** Answers will vary. Student could tape their baggies together and connect their "cytoplasms" by creating holes in the baggies that represent gap junction. **2.** Answers will vary. By studying a living cell, a scientist could see organelles at all levels.

By cutting a dead cell in half, a scientist could closely study the organelles in one region. **Explore Further** Student should create their gelatin mixture in a dish or pan using the same kinds of fruits, vegetables, and noodles to represent cell parts. A plant cell will also need a large central vacuole, which can be represented with a water-filled balloon. The sides of the pan represent the stiff cell wall.

Lab Manual 24—Comparing Plant and Animal Cells (Investigation 5)

Analysis 1. Answers will vary. Students should be able to identify the nucleus and cytoplasm in both cells. In the onion cell, students should be able to identify the cell wall and probably the central vacuole. **2.** Students should note the shape and structure of the plant cell because of the presence of a cell wall. Some students may identify the central vacuole, which helps give the plant cell its rigidity. **Conclusions 1.** Students probably will not find the smaller organelles, such as mitochondria, nucleolus, and the parts of the endomembrane system. These organelles are generally too small to be found, even under high resolution. Students will not find chloroplasts in the onion cell because the onion bulb is not photosynthetic. **2.** The onion plant requires a cell wall to remain rigid and function under different environmental conditions. Animal cells in the cheek do not need this structure and instead are much more fluid. **Explore Further** There will be some slight variation in the shape of the onion cells and the position of organelles within the cells, but generally, the cells will be similar.

Lab Manual 25—Comparing Plant Cells (Discovery Investigation 5)

Analysis 1. Students should see chloroplasts, vascular cells, and cell walls of various forms. **2.** Students should see large groups of chloroplasts in the leaves. Stem cells should contain vascular cells with very thick cell walls for support. Root cells should have thinner walls organized for massive division and elongation. Root cells can also be seen in various stages of maturation as they mature away from the tip. **Conclusions 1.** Answers will vary. Students should gain a better understanding of the roles that the cell wall, nucleus, and chloroplasts play in a plant cell. Have them review and discuss any misconceptions. **2.** Encourage students to consider different types of plants, such as a cactus, tree, grass plant, and various fruit and flower structures. Have students share their predictions. **Explore Further** Potato: root (sweet potato), stem (white potato); thorn: leaf; celery stalk: stem; lettuce: leaf; onion bulb: root. Answers will vary, but should reflect some of the knowledge about plant cells that students have learned from this investigation and the plant structure they researched. For example, the cells of a lettuce leaf would contain chloroplasts.

Lab Manual 26—Express Lab 6

1. The ball dropped from the shelf or the high place had the most potential energy. **2.** The ball on the ground had the least potential energy. **3.** Energy was transferred by pushing the balls off objects and allowing gravity to take over. **4.** The bounce height corresponds to the amount of kinetic energy, which is directly proportional to the amount of potential energy due to the balls' position above the ground. The greater the potential energy, the greater is the kinetic energy.

Lab Manual 27—The Structure of ATP

Analysis 1. ATP **2.** ADP **3.** The prefix "di" stands for two and "tri" stands for three. **Conclusions 1.** Energy is used to attach a phosphate group to ADP. **2.** When a phosphate group is removed from ATP to form ADP, a water molecule is formed. **Explore Further** ATP $\rightarrow$ ADP + H_2O + Energy

Lab Manual 28—Enzymes in Saliva (Investigation 6)

Analysis 1. Amylase broke down the starch into simple sugars. **2.** Test Tube 1 (maltose solution) and Test Tube 2 (starch solution with amylase) give a positive test for sugars with the Benedict's reagent. Test Tube 2 may give a positive test for starch with the iodine if the amylase has not broken down the entire sample. Test Tube 3 (starch control) tests negative for sugars and positive for starch. **Conclusions 1.** The maltose was a control to compare a known positive result with the experimental test tube (amylase 1 starch). **2.** Amylase works to break down the starchy foods you eat. This process takes place in your mouth as you chew. **3.** Chewing your food well gives amylase a chance to digest the food properly before it goes to your stomach. **Explore Further** Encourage students to use small amounts of food and chop them into small pieces for easier digestion. You may need to add more enzyme to break down the food particles. Be sure to point out that the physical breakdown of food—chewing—influences the rate of digestion by enzymes by increasing the surface area of the food.

Lab Manual 29—The Action of an Enzyme

Analysis 1. A **2.** Boiling stopped the production of bubbles. Cooling slowed bubble production. **Conclusions 1.** At body temperature (98.6°C) **2.** Heat stopped the enzyme. Cold slowed the enzyme activity. **3.** Peroxidase in the blood speeds up the breakdown of hydrogen peroxide into oxygen gas and water. **Explore Further** Answers will vary. One possible answer: Manganese dioxide causes as much bubbling as peroxidase. Therefore, manganese dioxide is as good at breaking down hydrogen peroxide as the enzyme.

Lab Manual 30—How Does pH Affect Stomach Enzymes? (Discovery Investigation 6)

Analysis 1. Students' data tables should reflect that the egg whites break down faster in the acidic solutions. **2.** Generally, a pH of 1 to 3 is optimal. **Conclusions 1.** The stomach creates and needs to maintain an acidic environment to allow pepsin to digest proteins. **2.** The test tubes were placed in warm water to simulate the warm environment inside the human body. In addition to pH, pepsin works best in a warmer environment. **Explore Further** People take antacids to ease stomach pain. However, changing the pH in the stomach can cause problems with digestion by deactivating key enzymes. Some studies show that the stomachs of people who regularly take antacids produce even larger amounts of acid to compensate for the medicine. Optional: Students may wish to create a chart from their data to illustrate how pH affects digestion.

Lab Manual 31—Express Lab 7

1. Answers will vary depending on the labels selected. For example, granola and granola bars often contain several forms of sugar. **2.** Answers will vary depending on the labels selected. Sweetened breakfast cereals, cookies, and cakes are high in sugar.

Lab Manual 32—Products of Cellular Respiration (Investigation 7)
Analysis 1. It becomes green, then yellow. **2.** The exhaled air contains carbon dioxide, which dissolves in the bromthymol blue solution to form carbonic acid. The carbonic acid changes the bromthymol blue to a yellow color. **3.** Glucose is the source of the carbon atoms in the CO_2 released during cellular respiration. **Conclusions 1.** Carbon dioxide causes the bromthymol blue solution to turn yellow. **2.** Exercise increases the rate of cellular respiration. As exercise occurs, cells need more oxygen and break down more glucose, so more carbon dioxide is released. **Explore Further** Encourage students to propose different methods to test the effects of exercise on cellular respiration. For example, students may want to examine the effect of exercise, such as bench-stepping or running in place, just prior to blowing into the bromthymol blue. Be sure that proposed methods will be respectful of those students who are less physically fit and students with physical disabilities.

Lab Manual 33—Cabbage Fermentation
Analysis 1. The pH dropped over time. **2.** As time passed, the balloon accumulated more gas each day. **Conclusions 1.** Bacteria changed the color and texture of the bacteria. **2.** Bacteria made the mixture more acidic. **3.** carbon dioxide gas and acid **Explore Further** Students could try fermenting lettuce, broccoli, beans, or onion. Be sure to follow the directions for using saltwater in the fermenting process to prevent the growth of undesirable bacteria.

Lab Manual 34—Making ATP Without Oxygen (Discovery Investigation 7)
Analysis 1. Yeast cells use fermentation to make ATP. **2.** Yes, fermentation is occurring. The production of bubbles indicates that a gas is being produced. The lowering of the pH in the bromthymol blue solution suggests the presence of carbonic acid, which is produced when carbon dioxide gas dissolves in water. **Conclusions 1.** Answers will vary depending on students' hypotheses and results. Students should indicate whether the hypothesis was supported, not whether it was correct. **2.** Yes, temperature affects the rate of fermentation. Students may wish to replace the warm water in the beaker with ice water or hot water. Students could then count the number of bubbles per minute and compare this number to the number of bubbles per minute produced at the warm temperature. **Explore Further** Encourage students to predict possible outcomes based on observations they have made. For example, if bread dough typically rises in an hour at 38° to 43°C, what happens when it is placed in the refrigerator instead? (It rises slowly over several hours.) Help students shape their observations into a process that uses the scientific method. Students should propose a testable hypothesis and then create an experiment that tests this hypothesis.

Lab Manual 35—Cellular Respiration in Plants
Analysis 1. blue; green **2.** blue; blue **Conclusions 1.** Yes. Carbon dioxide released by germinating seeds changed the color of bromthymol blue. **2.** No. The color of bromthymol blue in Test Tube B did not change. **3.** In Test Tube A, the change in color would be faster or more dramatic. In Test Tube B, the color would not change. **Explore Further** Students might compare respiration rates of radish, corn, bean, and grass seeds.

Lab Manual 36—Express Lab 8
1. After 7 days, the bean seedlings raised in the light are green. The bean seedlings raised in the dark are pale white with elongated stems. After 14 days, the stems may be slightly longer than before but will eventually stop growing. **2.** The elongated stems of the seedlings raised in darkness help the growing seedling reach the light sooner.

Lab Manual 37—Oxygen Production During Photosynthesis (Investigation 8)
Analysis 1. Bubbles appeared in Test Tube 1, containing sodium bicarbonate ($NaHCO_3$) solution, at the cut surface of the *Elodea* stem. **2.** The bubbles contain oxygen. **Conclusions 1.** Sodium bicarbonate serves as a source of the carbon dioxide needed for photosynthesis. **2.** Bubbles do not appear at the cut surface of the *Elodea* stem in Test Tube 2 containing cooled, boiled distilled water. This is because boiling has driven away the CO_2 dissolved in the water, so photosynthesis cannot take place. **Explore Further** Encourage students to propose different methods to test the effects of light on photosynthesis.

Lab Manual 38—Light and Photosynthesis (Discovery Investigation 8)
Analysis 1. The water in the flask absorbs heat. By changing the water before each time trial, heat is eliminated as a factor in this experiment. **2.** Answers will vary. Photosynthesis is usually greatest at the smallest distance from the light. **Conclusions 1.** Answers will vary depending on students' hypotheses and results. Students should indicate whether the hypothesis was supported, not whether it was correct. **2.** Yes, temperature affects the rate of photosynthesis. Answers will vary. For example, students could vary the water temperature in the flasks while keeping the distance to the lamp constant. Students could then count the number of bubbles per minute and compare the rate of photosynthesis at various temperatures. **Explore Further** Encourage students to suggest possible experiments for finding out the effects of different colors of light on photosynthesis. For example, students may wish to heat or cool the water in the flasks. Ask students to propose a testable hypothesis and then create an experiment that tests the hypothesis.

Lab Manual 39—Leaf Cross Section
Analysis 1. Answers may vary. The mesophyll is spongy and filled with air spaces. **2.** green **Conclusions 1.** Answers may vary. Photosynthesis primarily occurs in the mesophyll. This is the greenest area of the plant, and the region where chloroplasts are concentrated. **2.** Answers may vary. The mesophyll is a loose, open region with plenty of space for air circulation. **3.** Answers may vary. The outermost layers of cells (the upper and lower epidermis) and the waxy layer protect the mesophyll. **Explore Further** Privet is an example of a dicotyledonous leaf. If privet is not available, any divot leaf sample will work as well. To compare privet leaves to structures in CAM leaves, you might order prepared slides or make your own. Sections of CAM structures will show more water-filled tissue than dicotyledon leaves and the stomata will be distributed differently.

Lab Manual 40—Chlorophyll Chromatography
Analysis 1. Answers will vary. Bands may be yellow, green, blue-green, or red. **2.** Answers will vary. Alcohol moves further up the filter paper than the pigments. **Conclusions 1.** Answers will vary. Spinach contains several pigments including carotenoids and

chlorophylls. **2.** Dark green. Answers will vary, but might include chlorophyll *a,* chlorophyll *b,* and carotenoid. **3.** Answers will vary. Lightweight pigments traveled further up the paper strip than heavy pigments. **Explore Further** Plants that are rich in yellow and red pigments may also contain small amounts of green or blue-green pigment. Most of the bands produced on the filter paper will be in shades of yellow and red.

Lab Manual 41—Express Lab 9
1. The sister chromatid was created by making an exact copy of the chromosome, using the same colored beads in the same sequence. **2.** The beads represent the genes on the chromosome. The twist tie represents a centromere. **3.** The sister chromatid is created in the S phase of mitosis.

Lab Manual 42—Whitefish Mitosis
Analysis 1. Chromatids look like dark, thick cords. **2.** In interphase, chromatids are not visible and the nucleus is intact. **3.** The cell undergoes cytokinesis. **Conclusions 1.** In whitefish, there is no metaphase plate between newly forming cells. There is a metaphase plate in plants. **2.** Animal and plant cells go through the same phases of mitosis. **Explore Further** Since cells in the whitefish blastula are actively undergoing mitosis, their chromosomes are thick and visible. Not many of the cells scraped from the human cheek are mitotic, so the chromosomes in them are not thick and visible. The nuclei of cheek cells appear as dark areas within the cells.

Lab Manual 43—Observing Cell Cycle Phases (Investigation 9)
Analysis 1. Students should be able to identify the nucleus (when present) and chromosomes during mitosis. They should notice that the nucleus has broken down during mitosis. **2.** Students will likely not be able to identify spindle fibers. In addition, they may not be able to identify DNA during interphase or cytokinesis. **Conclusions 1.** Students should recognize that the nucleus is intact in interphase. **2.** Students should identify and recognize the state and position of chromosomes in the cell during the different phases and the activity that is occurring. **3.** Students may be able to witness the cell wall being built to separate two new cells as part of cytokinesis. **Explore Further** Students can count and identify that most cells are in interphase. They should infer that a cell spends most of its life cycle in interphase. They may also notice more cells in mitosis around the tip of the root than in the middle because of the active growth of the root.

Lab Manual 44—Stages of Mitosis Flip Chart
Analysis 1. prophase, metaphase, anaphase, telophase **2.** interphase **3.** Cells make sister chromatids so that each new cell will have a full set of chromosomes. **Conclusions 1.** In the tips of shoots and roots because that is where plants are growing. **2.** In embryos because embryonic development is a time of rapid growth in animals. **3.** The function of mitosis is to create new cells that are just like the parent cell. Mitosis creates cells for growth and repair. **Explore Further** A flip chart of meiosis would show and describe the phases of meiosis I and meiosis II.

Lab Manual 45—Modeling the Movement of Chromosomes (Discovery Investigation 9)
Analysis 1. Students should discover a variety of differences. In the crossing over model, they may see that different chromosomes will have crossed over, different segments, different sizes, and so on. In the meiosis II model, they will see different combinations that will have occurred between groups. **2.** The most obvious difference will be haploid products versus diploid products. Products in meiosis I will have segments changed from crossing over. In meiosis II, products will be changed because of redistribution. **Conclusions 1.** Genes on the ends of the chromosomes' "arms" are more likely to be crossed over than genes near the center. The size and location of the genes crossed over can vary. **2.** As happens in real life, using products from meiosis I would contribute to the diversity by starting with chromosome pairs that were mixed from crossing over. **Explore Further** This increases diversity the most. Combining genes from two separate sources brings together gametes from entirely different sets of chromosomes to create new combinations.

Lab Manual 46—Express Lab 10
1. Alleles are different versions of the same gene. For example, the gene for height in pea plants had two alleles: tall and short. Each coin toss also has two possibilities: heads or tails. **2.** In the Punnett square, write the probability of each possible outcome along the top and side: $\frac{1}{2}$ heads, $\frac{1}{2}$ tails. The square will show a typical genotypic ratio of $\frac{1}{4}$ heads-heads, $\frac{2}{4}$ heads and tails, $\frac{1}{4}$ tails-tails.

Lab Manual 47—Using Punnett Squares (Investigation 10)
Analysis 1. All F_1 individuals resulting from this cross are purple-flowering pea plant flowers. All F_1 individuals have the allele combination Pp. **2.** The allele combinations PP, Pp, and pp appear in the F_2 pea plants. These allele combinations are found in a ratio of 1 PP: 2 Pp: 1pp in the F_2 pea plants. The F_2 pea plants have purple or white flowers. These colors appear in a 3 purple: 1 white ratio. **Conclusions 1.** For each trait that he studied, Mendel used true-breeding pea plants for each parental cross. He knew these plants would always produce only pea plants with the same form of that trait. **2.** Answers will vary depending on students' questions. For example, students may want to prepare Punnett squares showing the inheritance of Mendel's factors for height in pea plants. **Explore Further** Encourage students to draw a Punnett square to show the offspring of a dihybrid cross. Students could follow the inheritance of flower color and height, two traits described in Lesson 1. For example, students could prepare a 16-box dihybrid Punnett square to show a cross between two heterozygous, purple-flowering, tall plants.

Lab Manual 48—Probability of Gender

Analysis 1. Answers will vary, but should be near 50 percent for each. **2.** Answers will vary, but should be near 50 percent for each. **Conclusions 1.** Their chances of having a boy are 50 percent. Each baby has a 50:50 chance of being male. The number of babies in the family does not affect this probability. **2.** The probability of reaching 50 percent is greater in the 50 coin tosses. Large samples give more reliable results than small ones.
3. Sample:

	X	Y
X	XX	XY
X	XX	XY

The Punnett square indicates that each child has a 50:50 chance of being male or female. **Explore Further** Because 100 coin tosses provides a greater sample size than 50 coin tosses, it is more likely to reflect a 50-50 percentage

Lab Manual 49—Traits Depend on Chromosomes

Sample:

	First Drawing:	Second Drawing:	Third Drawing:	Fourth Drawing:
Father's gene	B	B	B	B
Mother's gene	b	b	b	b
Eye color of offspring with these genes	brown	brown	brown	brown

Analysis 1. The Father is homozygous for brown eyes. **2.** bb. The Mother's phenotype is blue eyes. **Conclusions 1.** The offspring have brown eyes. **2.** In the second cross, 75 percent have brown eyes, 25 percent have blue eyes. **3.** Mendel crossed individual pea plants to study the way their traits were passed to their offspring. **Explore Further** To perform dihybrid crosses, students will need to create two bags of pipe-cleaners for each parent. For example, brown and blue pipe cleaners could represent eye color. Black and white pipe cleaners could represent height.

Lab Manual 50—Interpreting Pedigrees (Discovery Investigation 10)

Analysis 1. Persons in Step 2:

I-1	Type AB; AB
I-2	Type O; OO
I-3	Free earlobes; Ff
I-4	Free earlobes; Ff
II-1	Type O; OO
II-2	Type AB; AB
II-3	Type A; AO
II-4	Type B; BO, Attached earlobes; ff
II-5	Attached earlobes; ff
II-6	Attached earlobes; ff
II-7	Free earlobes; Ff

2. The adopted persons cannot be identified from their genotypes, since the genotypes of the parents make all the offspring's genotypes possible. **Conclusions 1.** The traits are not sex-linked. Both traits are inherited regardless of the individual's sex. Attached earlobes (ff) cannot be sex-linked because two parents with free earlobes (Ff) can produce a boy or a girl with attached earlobes. If this was a sex-linked trait, the father with free earlobes would pass his one copy of this dominant allele to every daughter. **2.** For Generation III, since the parents (II-4 and II-5) have attached earlobes, their genotype must be ff. This means all of the Generation III individuals will have attached earlobes (ff). Since the father, II-4, is type B and has a parent, I-2, who is type O, his genotype is BO. The Generation III individuals could be type O (if the mother, II-5, is type O), type B (if the mother, II-5, is type B or type AB), or type AB (if the mother, II-5, is type A or type AB). **Explore Further** Encourage students to research hereditary diseases and prepare sample pedigrees. Have students include a description of the risks of inheriting the diseases to accompany their pedigrees.

Lab Manual 51—Express Lab 11

1. Cytosine and thymine are single-ringed bases. Adenine and guanine are double-ringed bases. **2.** The proportions vary slightly among different living things, but A and T, and also G and C, are always present in the same relative amounts. This suggests that DNA has the same fundamental structure in all living things

Lab Manual 52—Modeling DNA (Investigation 11)

Analysis 1. Both sets of base pairs are approximately equal in width. This is because a double-ring base can pair only with a single-ring base. **2.** Adenine and thymine are always paired together. Guanine and cytosine are always paired together. **Conclusions 1.** Complementary base pairing ensures that a DNA double helix is the same width throughout, since a double-ring base always pairs with a single-ring base. **2.** Answers will vary. Students may wish to explore the relationship between DNA structure and proteins, which would set the stage for Lesson 3. **Explore Further** Encourage students to join their base pairs with those of another group to lengthen the DNA molecule. Make sure that both groups follow the rules of complementary base pairing.

Lab Manual 53—Extracting DNA

Analysis 1. Answers will vary. Students could use split peas, onion, spinach, chicken liver, calf thymus, or wheat germ. **2.** DNA is located in the nucleus of cells. **3.** Cell membranes and nuclear membranes must be opened to release the DNA. **Conclusions 1.** DNA carries information by encoding it within the sequences of nucleotides. **2.** A strand of DNA is made up nucleotides (bases, sugar, and phosphates) that are assembled in strands. Two strand of DNA make a double stranded molecule that is twisted in the shape of a helix. **Explore Further** Some sources provide better DNA samples than others. The DNA extract from all materials has the same white, stringy texture.

Lab Manual 54—Crime Scene DNA

Crime Scene	Suspect 1
TATTCGAA CCCCATATAGAGGT TTTAATAGGGGCACGGGCC	AA AAAGCCCATAGGGGC CATATTTTTTGAGAGAAAAGGGG
Suspect 2	**Suspect 3**
TATTCGAA CCCCATATAGAGGT TTTAATAGGGGCACGGGCC	CCCCAATTTAGCCAAAGAGAT GGCTTAACCTTAACCCCACACACAGGGGTTT

Analysis 1. Yes. Suspect #2. **2.** To cut strands of DNA **Conclusions 1.** Answers will vary, but could include blood, a scraped elbow, or saliva on a drinking glass. **2.** A restriction enzyme cuts big pieces of DNA into smaller pieces that can be analyzed. **3.** If the DNA of a suspect is like DNA found at a crime scene, it acts as evidence against the suspect. **Explore Further** Any type of DNA can be run on gel electrophoresis. Samples prepared by biological supply houses

are "cleaner" than those made in most school labs and produce more distinct banding patterns. Suppliers also provide restriction endonucleases for cutting DNA samples.

Lab Manual 55—A Faulty Protein (Discovery Investigation 11)
Analysis 1. The corresponding mRNA sequence is ACUCCUGAGGAG. This sequence contains four codons. **2.** This mRNA sequence will produce the amino acids threonine, proline, glutamic acid, and glutamic acid. **3.** The corresponding mRNA sequence for the DNA shown in Step 4 is ACUCCUGUGGAG. This mRNA sequence will produce the amino acids threonine, proline, valine, and glutamic acid. **Conclusions 1.** Transcription is occurring in Step 2. **2.** Translation is occurring in Step 3. 3. In Step 4, the third trio of DNA nucleotides reads "CAC" instead of "CTC." This is an example of a substitution. **Explore Further** Students should recognize that a gene mutation will fail to affect a protein if the resultant mRNA codon codes for the same amino acid. For example, if the nucleotide trio "TGA" in the DNA sequence in Step 1 changes to "TGG," it will ultimately still produce the amino acid threonine.

Lab Manual 56—Express Lab 12
1. Cellulose is a type of dietary fiber. Cellulose and all other types of fiber are not digested by the digestive system. They pass right through. **2.** It is recommended that adults have about 24 grams of dietary fiber each day. **3.** Fiber helps keep the digestive system working properly and eliminates waste.

Lab Manual 57—Blood Cells
Analysis 1. red blood cells **2.** yes; no **Conclusions 1.** no **2.** Red blood cells do not have nuclei and are small. White blood cells are large and have nuclei. **3.** Red blood cells carry oxygen. White blood cells are part of the immune system. Platelets help blood clot. **Explore Further** Like human blood, frog blood contains red and white blood cells in a liquid matrix. Frog white blood cells are similar to those of humans. Unlike humans, the red blood cells of frogs have nuclei. Frog blood has no platelets.

Lab Manual 58—How Exercise Affects Heart Rate (Investigation 12)
Analysis 1. As the level of exercise increases, the heart rate increases. **2.** After the exercise has stopped and the person begins to rest, his or her heart rate begins to drop to the resting rate. **Conclusions 1.** The heart responds to the need for more oxygen by the cells in the body. As exercise increases, energy is used and oxygen is required. **2.** Heart rate responds to the intensity of the exercise. As you increase intensity, the heart rate also increases. As you rest, your heart rate drops back down. **Explore Further** Have students show the link between heart rate, respiration rate, and activity.

Lab Manual 59—Examining the Body Systems of a Grasshopper
Analysis 1. head, thorax and abdomen **2.** The external surface protects the organs and muscles and provides support. **3.** simple eyes, compound eyes, antennae, tympanum **Conclusions 1.** Grasshoppers have some of the same body systems as humans. **2.** The grasshopper lacks an internal skeleton; its skeletal structure is external. There are no lungs in the respiratory system. The heart is just a bulge in the aorta. Malphighian tubules rather than kidneys take care of excretion. The digestive system includes parts not found in humans. **Explore Further** Under the dissecting microscope, both external and internal structures will be visible that are difficult to see with the naked eye. Encourage students to examine the structure of the wings, the legs, the mouth parts, and the compound eyes. Internally, the salivary glands, Malphighian tubules, and spiracles can be seen.

Lab Manual 60—Constructing Models of Human Joints (Discovery Investigation 12)
Analysis 1. Possible answers include the movement of the joint, how the joint is connected, the type of hardware available, and how the available materials are conducive to creating different types of joints. **2.** Be sure students understood how their joint works. If possible, have them demonstrate the joint in their body next to their model. **3.** Answers will vary. For example, the hinge joint moves only in one direction. **Conclusions 1.** Most joints constructed from the hardware materials will not be as flexible as body joints. Most hardware models will be stronger than the body joints they represent. **2.** Some hardware materials available may not be sufficient to create some of the joints studied. **3.** The body constantly maintains its joints. Unlike hardware joints, body joints are constantly being repaired. As the body ages or undergoes extraordinary stress, the joints may break down or fracture. **Explore Further** Students can often create an impressive working model of a human joint. Students should point out that by using a motor or pulley, they have added the muscle to the joint and connected the two with ligaments.

Lab Manual 61—Express Lab 13
1. The oldest fossil is in the bottom rock layer (sponge). **2.** As the sponges folded, the order of fossils changed. A fossil that was on top may have ended up in the middle or on the bottom. **3.** The scientist needs to know whether the rock has been folded greatly or overturned.

Lab Manual 62—Dinosaur Tracks
Analysis 1. Dinosaur A tracks are closest together. **2.** Answers may vary; Dinosaur A tracks or Dinosaur B tracks may be the most shallow. **Conclusions 1.** Dinosaur 2 may have walked across the area first. Its tracks are underneath those of Dinosaur 3. **2.** No. Dinosaur 1 is largest and Dinosaur 4 is smallest. **3.** Answers will vary. Dinosaurs 3 and 4 are similar in size. They might be the same type as Dinosaur 1, perhaps an adult and two babies. Dinosaur 3 is walking parallel to Dinosaur 1, while Dinosaur 4 is moving is an irregular path. The strides of Dinosaur 4 are longer than those of Dinosaur 3, indicating that it might be moving faster or have longer legs. **Explore Further** Students may create scenarios such as a meeting, a fight, or a chase for others to interpret.

Lab Manual 63—Radioactive Dating
Analysis 1. The water in the cup was ice at one time. It was produced by the "decay" of ice. **2.** Answers will vary. **Conclusions 1.** Over time, a radioactive element decays to form a different element. **2.** Like a radioactive element, ice changes into a different material. **3.** Scientists find out how much radioactive material and how much of the breakdown product are in a fossil. Since the decay occurs at a constant rate, scientists can then determine the age of the fossil. **Explore Further** Give students glasses or beakers containing partially melted ice and have them determine how long the ice has been melting.

Lab Manual 64—Natural Selection in Action (Investigation 13)

Analysis 1. The population of normal-range organisms dropped due to the cold environment. **2.** The cold-tolerant organisms reproduced at an increasingly greater rate as normal-range organisms were selected out. **Conclusions 1.** The population will slowly be replaced by cold-tolerant organisms. **2.** The change would stabilize. Normal-range organisms would no longer be selected out of the population and would begin to reproduce at the same rate as the cold-tolerant organisms. However, if the warm weather was detrimental to the cold-tolerant organisms, the trend could reverse entirely. **3. Sample answers: 1.** Reproduction could combine the genes from cold-tolerant organisms with normal-range organisms. **2.** Natural death should occur within the cold-tolerant organisms, although this death would be applied to both organisms at the same rate in addition to the deaths caused by selection. **Explore Further** Encourage students to add a natural death percentage into the exercise or to somehow determine a method for recombining the genes.

Lab Manual 65—Tracking Blood Type Alleles (Discovery Investigation 13)

Analysis 1. The children of Child W and Spouse W can have any blood type because they can inherit a combination of any kind of allele. **2.** The children of Child W and Spouse W must be blood type B. They can only inherit a B allele from Spouse W. Although they can inherit either a B allele or an O allele from Child W, the O allele will not affect the resulting blood type. **3.** The A allele has been eliminated. **Conclusions 1.** The O allele is recessive, and one O allele cannot determine a blood type. Only by grouping two O alleles together can an O blood type result. **2.** Using a coin flip to randomly decide which gene gets passed on is appropriate, since alleles are passed on randomly to offspring. **3.** The children of Grandchild L or Grandchild M could receive an A allele if either parent reproduces with an individual who has at least one A allele. **Explore Further** Explain the Rh factor to students. Tell them that if a person receives two positive alleles, he or she will have a positive blood type. If a person receives two negative alleles, he or she will have a negative blood type. If a person receives one positive and one negative allele, he or she will have a positive blood type. Have students go through the exercise in a similar manner to the way they determined blood types. They can use a coin flip again to determine which allele is passed on. Have them start with different Rh types and see how the dominant (+) allele moves and affects blood types as it is passed on or is absent.

Lab Manual 66—Express Lab 14

1. Answers will vary. **2.** Answers will vary, but should include a reasonable explanation of how the objects are related. **3.** Answers will vary.

Lab Manual 67—Magnetobacteria

Analysis 1. Bacteria moved toward the north pole of the magnet. **2.** Bacteria did not respond to the south pole of the magnet. **Conclusions 1.** Student answers will vary. The ability to move along the magnetic field helps the bacteria move back into the sediments. **2.** No. Without the ability to move, bacteria could not orient themselves toward the north. **3.** The ability to detect north could help these birds fly quickly to their mating and nesting grounds.

Explore Further Most magnetotrophic bacteria are anaerobic, so most likely will not be found in the top layer of soil. They are more common under the surface of water or in water-logged soil.

Lab Manual 68—Natural Selection in Bacteria (Investigation 14)

Analysis 1. The antibiotic disks should suppress the growth of bacteria. **2.** Some bacteria will be more successful growing than other populations. This is likely because of genetic differences in the populations, as well as some environmental differences between the dishes and techniques of different students. **Conclusions 1.** The antibiotic suppressed the growth of the bacteria on petri dish A to different degrees. **2.** The bacteria that do not have resistance to the antibiotic are being killed or not reproducing. The bacteria with resistance are surviving and reproducing. The resistant bacteria are increasing as a percentage of the bacterial population. **3.** If antibiotics are used frequently, the general population of bacteria that cause illness in humans becomes more resistant to antibiotics. If this trend continues, it becomes increasingly likely that people will become sick due to bacteria that cannot be treated with antibiotics. **Explore Further** Students may notice that their second bacteria culture is more resistant to the antibiotics. They have selected for a population that is more resistant than the first. Look at students' notes to be sure they are making observations about the growth on their Petri dishes.

Lab Manual 69—Plant Evolution (Discovery Investigation 14)

Analysis 1. Moss grows on the surface of wet or damp ground. It has no stems to grow upright. This is a disadvantage because it restricts moss to wet areas. **2.** The moss and fern reproduce from spores. The conifer and flowering plant create seeds. **3.** Answers will vary. A possible answer is that coniferous and flowering plants are adapted to living in drier environments than mosses and ferns. **4.** The flowering plant creates a flower that turns into a seed after being pollinated. Flowers attract animals and use animals as pollinators. Animals also can carry the seeds far from the parent plant. This means that flowering plants spread over a large area. **Conclusions** The sequence should be moss › fern › conifer › flowering plant. **Explore Further** Although blue-green algae are not plants, they are thought to be the organism from which plants came.

Lab Manual 70—Bird Adaptations

Analysis 1. Answers will vary, depending on type of seed and abilities of students to manipulate tools. **2.** Answers will vary, depending on type of seed and abilities of students to manipulate tools. **Conclusions 1.** Animals that are not well-adapted do not survive to produce offspring. **2.** The environment determines what kinds of beaks will be most successful at gathering food. **3.** Student answers will vary, but might include a long, straw-shaped beak. **Explore Further** Answers will vary, depending on instruments available. Some possibilities include tweezers, scissors, wire snips, and toothpicks.

Lab Manual 71—Express Lab 15
1. Students may consider such things as color, size, number of legs, amount of hair, what the pet eats, etc. **2.** Both the students' and scientists' classification systems are based on physical observations about the organisms. The students' classification system is limited to very basic observations, while a biological classification system uses more in-depth information such as chemical composition, DNA analysis, and evolutionary relationships.

Lab Manual 72—Classifying Organisms (Investigation 15)
Analysis 1. Students should notice that organisms in domains Archaea and Bacteria are small and single-celled, while organisms in domain Eukarya are mostly larger and multicelled. **2.** Bacteria are found almost everywhere, although they are too small to be seen without a microscope. Eukaryans inhabit a variety of environments. Archaeans are found in extreme conditions, such as very hot, very cold, or extremely salty environments. **Conclusions 1.** Scientists use information about the cells that make up an organism to classify the organisms into the domains. **2.** Answers will vary. Students should make general observations about some kingdoms, such as that the organisms in kingdom Plantae are green and photosynthetic. **Explore Further** Students can create and interpret the key characteristics that allow classification with their organisms.

Lab Manual 73—Lichens Up Close
Analysis 1. algae **2.** fungi **Conclusions 1.** Lichens differ in shape and color. **2.** No. Lichens are made up of different combinations of algae and fungi. **3.** The fungi absorb and hold moisture around the algal cells. **Explore Further** Under the compound light microscope, individual hyphae and green algal cells are visible.

Lab Manual 74—Earthworm Dissection
Analysis 1. The earthworm's brain is connected to the rest of its body by a long dorsal nerve cord. **2.** Nephridia are organs of excretion. Each segment holds a pair of thin, white nephrida. **3.** 5; The worm has five arches or swollen places that act as blood pumps. The human circulatory system has one large pump. **Conclusions 1.** Setae are located on each segment. Setae help the worm crawl over and burrow into soil. **2.** Exchanging sperm and eggs lets worms exchange genetic material. Animals that exchange genetic material have offspring that show variety in their traits. This improves the group's chances of survival. **Explore Further** By taking out the digestive tract, students can slice it open and examine the contents in the crop, gizzard, and intestine.

Lab Manual 75—Using a Dichotomous Key (Discovery Investigation 15)
Analysis 1. Students should describe some characteristics that were helpful in identifying their specimen. **2.** Physical characteristics that differentiate the appearance of different organisms are used in dichotomous keys. **3.** Things such as DNA and life activities are usually not included. **Conclusions 1.** An effective key will include information on all organisms that could be identified. A dichotomous key is unreliable if organisms are left out. However, organisms that would not normally be considered, such as trees in a key that identifies mushrooms, are unnecessary. **2.** Using a key saves time. Instead of reading descriptions of each possible organism, the key allows a person to quickly narrow down the possible identities. **Explore Further** Students should use the information they learned in using the keys to create their own valid key.

Lab Manual 76—Express Lab 16
1. The second time should be shorter than the first time. The student learned from the first attempt and was able to do the maze faster. **2.** Answers may vary. The second student's time may be faster than the first student's first time but slower than that student's second attempt. The second student learned from watching the first student complete the maze, but may not be as proficient as someone who has already completed the maze. **3.** This is learned. The students are responding to stimuli (the maze) and learning how to solve it faster.

Lab Manual 77—Investigating Animal Behavior (Investigation 16)
Analysis 1. Students should observe that most or all of the sow bugs move into the dark environment. **2.** The stimulus in this investigation is the light. Sow bugs react to light by moving away from it. **Conclusions 1.** Sow bugs prefer a dark environment. **2.** The behavior of the sow bugs is innate. Sow bugs naturally move into darker environments. **3.** Sow bugs have evolved to prefer darker environments for many reasons. Some of the most likely reasons are to avoid predators and to avoid drying out. **Explore Further** Students can create an additional investigation that shows that the sow bugs will seek out a moist environment.

Lab Manual 78—Planarian Behavior
Analysis 1. Student answers will vary. **2.** Answers among groups will differ. Reasons for differences include: students used different planarians, the distance from planarian to syringe varied from one group to another, and the depth of water in the petri dish varied from one group to another. **Conclusions 1.** This is innate behavior. Planarians knew how to do it without being taught. Avoiding a stimulus like a puff of air may help the animals avoid predators. **2.** In most experiments, accuracy increases as the number of trials increase. **3.** Error could come from several sources, such as lack of a control, small number of trials, math errors, and variability in subjects (worms). **Explore Further** Planarians can be trained to turn quickly to avoid air puffs. Initially, a planarian may require several puffs before it will change its course. Over time, it will change course with one puff.

Lab Manual 79—Exploring Human Communication (Discovery Investigation 16)
Analysis 1. Students should describe some of the observations they made during the investigation. **2.** Emotions often play a key role in human communication. Emotions are often evident as part of facial expressions, voice tone, or body language. **Conclusions 1.** Answers will vary depending on students' observations. **2.** Students should realize that many of the gestures, tones, and body language that they have observed in the investigation are also a part of normal verbal communication between humans. Examples can include the aggressive body language that is used when someone is angry, or the gestures and body language that is used between two humans who are cooperating on some activity. **Explore Further** Students should create a simple investigation to examine the types of behavior that accompany being untruthful. Have them make notes on some of the behavior that they believe someone uses when being truthful and untruthful. Classic signs of being untruthful are looking away, fidgeting, and speaking quickly.

Lab Manual 80—Crickets Are Territorial
Analysis 1. Crickets chase or attack intruders. **2.** Student answers may vary. A subordinate male might avoid a confrontation. **3.** Student answers may vary because individual crickets vary. If the resident male is aggressive, interactions occur near the intruder's corner. Interactions will be closer to the resident's corner if the intruder is aggressive. **Conclusions 1.** In most cases, the resident cricket is dominant. It displays aggressive behavior toward the intruder. **2.** In nature, resident crickets chase away intruders. **Explore Further** When roles are swapped, the new resident may take on the role of aggressive defender of the territory.

Lab Manual 81—Predators and Prey
Analysis 1. increase **2.** The snake population would decrease. **3.** The mouse population would grow rapidly. Eventually there would be more mice than the community could support. **Conclusions 1.** If the numbers of prey increase, so do the numbers of predators. If the numbers of prey decrease, so do the numbers of predators. **2.** Owls in the community would reduce the numbers of mice and snakes. Over time, the three populations would find a balance. **Explore Further** To add owls, make 25 blue cards that are three inches by three inches. Since owls can prey on both snakes and mice, their populations increase dramatically.

Lab Manual 82—Express Lab 17
1. Answers will vary. It is unlikely that the sample contains one-sixth of the organisms unless they are distributed in a uniform pattern. **2.** Sampling of a clumped or random distribution pattern may not accurately reflect true population size. **3.** Increasing the number of samples will more accurately show the true population size, or if the distribution pattern is uniform.

Lab Manual 83—Estimating Population Size (Investigation 17)
Analysis 1. Each navy bean represents an individual in a population. **2.** The bag represents the area being sampled. **3.** Answers will vary depending on the number of marked navy beans recaptured. **Conclusions 1.** This assumption may not be correct. An animal that has been trapped earlier may be too wary of the trap to be recaptured. **2.** Population events such as births, deaths, immigration, or emigration could reduce the accuracy of the mark-recapture method. **3.** Students may wish to explore the effect of multiple-sampling events on estimating population size. **Explore Further** Encourage students to explore the effect of sample size on estimating population size. The estimation of population size generally becomes more accurate as sample size increases. Point out to students that larger sample sizes require more time and money in ecological studies.

Lab Manual 84—Surveying an Ecological Community (Discovery Investigation 17)
Analysis 1. Abiotic (nonliving) features include water, soil, rocks, temperature, light, and nutrients. Biotic (living) features may include any of the living things found at the site: animals, vascular plants, lichens, mosses, molds and other fungi, and bacteria. **2.** The most common distribution pattern is clumped, with individuals grouped in patches where soil and/or moisture conditions are ideal for growth. Insects may also be clumped due to social behaviors. **3.** Photosynthetic plants and algae are producers. Animals are consumers. **4.** Students may describe the growth of mosses, lichens, or small plants in previously barren areas such as rocks or pavement. **Conclusions 1.** Answers will vary depending on students' hypotheses. Proposed student procedures may suggest counting individual organisms to support or disprove a hypothesis. In many study sites, plants will have the greatest population density. In other areas, animals may have the greatest density (for example, pill bugs beneath rotting logs). **2.** At most sites, producers will be found in greatest number. Remind students that decomposers such as bacteria are present in large numbers, but cannot be seen in a field study such as this one. **3.** Density-dependent factors include food, water, and soil nutrients. Density-independent factors may include temperature, fires, and severe weather conditions such as drought or flooding. **Explore Further** Students should recognize that organisms might exhibit predator-prey relationships or symbiotic relationships such as parasitism, mutualism, or commensalism. Student procedures may suggest additional field observation and/or research to learn more about possible relationships among local species.

Lab Manual 85—Owl Pellets
Analysis 1. Student answers will vary. Pellets will contain one to four skeletons. Students can determine the number of skeletons by counting the skulls. **2.** Student answers will vary. Owls dine on a variety of small animals including mice, moles, shrew, and birds. **Conclusions 1.** Students answers will vary. To find the total number of animals eaten, students multiply the number of animals in one pellet by 365. **2.** Without owls, populations of prey would increase dramatically. **3.** Owls are not able to digest bones, fur, and feathers. **Explore Further** To assemble the skeleton of a mole, shrew, mouse, or bird, use research material as a reference. Bones can be glued to sheets of paper to create two-dimensional models.

Lab Manual 86—Express Lab 18
1. Answers will vary. Students should recognize that photosynthetic organisms are producers, animals are consumers, and fungi and bacteria are decomposers. **2.** Each trophic level is necessary in an ecosystem because each level plays a specific role in keeping the ecosystem going. Producers transform sunlight energy into food for other organisms. Consumers eat other organisms. Decomposers break down dead organisms and recycle chemical elements.

Lab Manual 87—Building a Food Web (Investigation 18)
Analysis 1. Each food chain begins with a producer, contains one or more consumers, and ends with one or more decomposers. The number of organisms may differ from one food chain to the next. **2.** A food chain is a linear sequence of organisms that feed on each other. A food web combines all of the food chains that are part of an ecosystem. **Conclusions 1.** If sunlight no longer existed, photosynthetic producers would die and consumers would no longer have the energy to survive. **2.** Answers will vary. For example, students may wish to explore what would happen to each trophic level if the level(s) above and below it disappeared. **Explore Further** Encourage students to consider the number of individuals in each trophic level. In most ecosystems, producers are present in greater numbers than are consumers. Since energy is lost as it travels from one trophic level to the next, producers outnumber consumers. Similarly, primary consumers outnumber secondary consumers.

Lab Manual 88—Phosphate in Aquatic Ecosystems (Discovery Investigation 18)

Analysis 1. Answers will vary. The jars with the largest amounts of detergent will have the greenest color and the strongest odor. If eutrophication occurs, the odor of decay may be present. **2.** The control group is the setup that had no phosphate solution added. The experimental group is the setup or setups that had various amounts of phosphate solution added. The variable is the amount of phosphate solution. **Conclusions 1.** Phosphorus fuels the growth of algae in aquatic ecosystems. **2.** Phosphates were banned from household laundry detergents to reduce excessive algal growth in polluted ponds, lakes, and streams. **Explore Further** Student responses will vary, but students should recognize that too much phosphorus could cause excessive algal growth, which results in too little oxygen to sustain aquatic plants and animals.

Lab Manual 89—Mini Ecosystem

Analysis 1. Answers will vary depending on the locale, but could include grasses, wildflowers, ferns, and mosses. **2.** Answers will vary depending on the locale, but could include crickets, worms, lizards, and insects. **Conclusions 1.** Answers will vary but could include the death of plants or animals or the growth of plants. **2.** The plants capture the sun's energy and use it to make food. They release oxygen in the process. Without plants, other living things in an ecosystem would die. **3.** Answers will vary. Students might suggest an enclosed ecosystem that contains plants, animals, and decomposers like bacteria and fungi. **Explore Further** Different kinds of ecosystems will contain different plants and animals.

Lab Manual 90—Effects of Light

Analysis 1. Answers will vary, but could include grass, moss, dandelions, or ferns. **2.** Answers will vary, but could include insects, worms, and spiders. **Conclusions 1.** Over a two-week period, the plants became yellow due to loss of their chlorophyll. **2.** During the experimental period, some animals may have moved out of the ecosystem. Animals that prefer dark places to live may have moved in. **3.** The sun is the source of energy for every ecosystem. **Explore Further** In mini-ecosystems, the plant results would be similar. Since animals could not move into or out of the ecosystem, some may die.

Lab Manual 91—Express Lab 19

1. The pH of distilled water should be close to 7. **2.** Answers will vary. Normal pH of rainwater is between 5.2 and 6. If the pH of the sample is below 5.2, your area is experiencing acid rain.

Lab Manual 92—Measuring Particulates in the Air (Investigation 19)

Analysis 1. The petroleum jelly traps the particles and holds them on the slide. **2.** A bar graph is best for comparing two samples. Students should label the *y*-axis "Total number of particles." **Conclusions 1.** Parking lots and car emissions will have large numbers of particulates. **2.** Students will most likely suggest car and truck emissions and cigarette smoke. **3.** Students may want to explore different ways particulates could be reduced using filters or scrubbers. **Explore Further** Students may be surprised at the number of particulates in the air of a smoker's home. Have students research the dangers of secondhand smoke, which are largely due to particulates.

Lab Manual 93—Greenhouse Gases

Analysis 1. Answers will vary, but the temperature change in Beaker A will be small. The temperature change in Beaker B will be greater than in Beaker A. **2.** The plastic wrap represents greenhouse gases. **Conclusions 1.** Plastic wrap on the beaker traps heat and causes temperature to increase. **2.** Greenhouse gases trap heat and causes temperature to increase. **3.** Excess greenhouse gases are heating the earth's surface more than usual. **Explore Further** Temperatures do not rise as dramatically on cloudy days.

Lab Manual 94—Conservation of Soil (Discovery Investigation 19)

Analysis 1. Answer will depend on how much water was poured over the soil. Most of the water poured over the bare soil will be collected. The water will be muddy with suspended soil. **2.** Very little water will be collected from the pan containing grass. The water will contain very little suspended soil. **Conclusions 1.** Answers will vary depending on students' hypotheses and results. Students should indicate whether or not the hypothesis was supported, not whether or not it was correct. **2.** Pouring water over the soil models a rainstorm. Collecting the runoff that contains suspended soil is a measure of the amount of erosion. **3.** A farmer could plant a cover crop on unused fields before the bare soil washes away. **Explore Further** Encourage students to predict possible outcomes to this experiment based on everyday observations they may have made. For example, they probably have observed rainwater running in gutters during a storm. They may have observed that the water runs faster downhill than on level ground. Help students to use these observations in making a hypothesis. They can then design an experiment that tests this hypothesis.

Lab Manual 95—Overpackaging

Sample:

	Large Bag	Single-Serving Bag
Number of potato chips in package	120	20
Area of packaging	112 square inches	24 square inches
Chips per square inch of packaging	1.1 chips/square inch	0.83 chips/square inches

Analysis 1. In the large bag, 1.1 chips. In the small bag, 0.83 chips. **2.** The large package used the least material per chip. **Conclusions 1.** Empty potato chip bags are thrown in the trash and often taken to a landfill. **2.** Answer will vary, but might include cookies and candy. **3.** A shopper could reduce trash by buying products in large quantities instead of single-serving sizes. **Explore Further** Students might include their experimental results in their letters.

Graphic Organizer

A clean copy of each Graphic Organizer appears on the Biology: Cycles of Life TRL CD-ROM.

Graphic Organizer 1—Cycles of Life

Cycles	Definitions	More Facts About the Cycles
Energy	Energy is the ability to do work.	• The primary source of energy is the sun. • Energy cannot be created or destroyed. • Energy can change forms, or transform.
Growth	Cells are the basic units of life.	• Cells make proteins, chemicals that have special jobs in cells. • Cells reproduce, the process of making new life.
Evolutionary	Evolution can lead to making new species. New species adjust or have adaptations. Can lead to extinction, when no members of the species exist.	• Evolutionary changes are caused by changes in DNA, cells, and the environment. • Life grows and changes over time in a process called evolution.
Ecological	Living things respond to stimuli, anything to which organisms react. Behavior may run in cycles, which means that many life activities repeat themselves.	• Ecosystems include living things and nonliving things in the environment.

1. transformed **2.** DNA **3.** energy **4.** stimulus **5.** speciation

Graphic Organizer 2—Matter, Energy, and Chemical Processes of Life

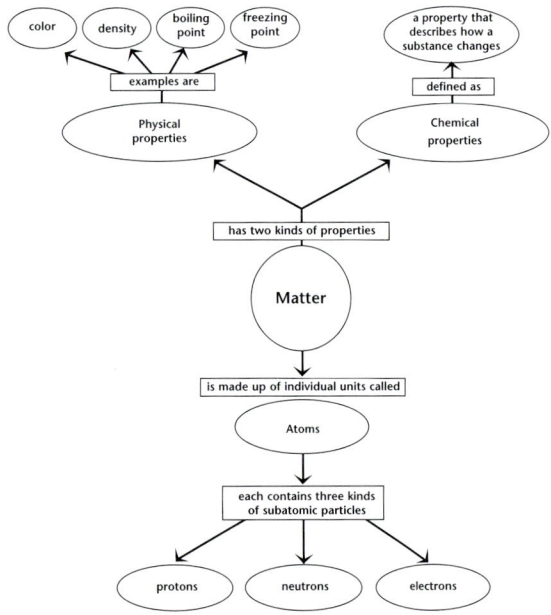

1. Matter is anything that has mass and takes up space. **2.** Student answers will vary, but could include red or green color and smooth skin. **3.** P, C, P, P, P

Graphic Organizer 3—Organic Molecules

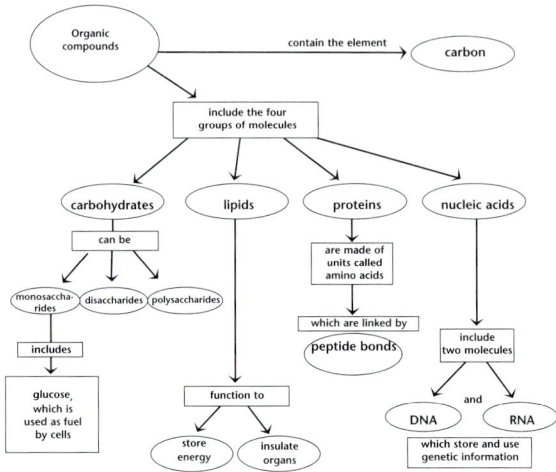

1. A monosaccharide is one unit of sugar. A disaccharide is two units. **2.** carbohydrates **3.** saturated fatty acid **4.** amino acids **5.** nucleic acids

Graphic Organizer 4—Cells: The Basic Units of Life

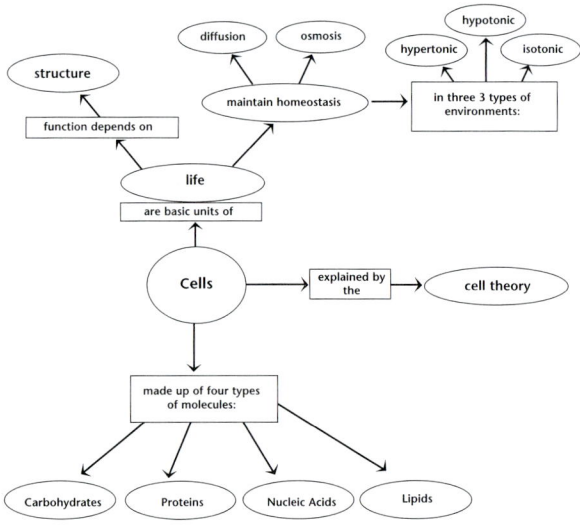

1. osmosis **2.** ATP **3.** plasma membrane **4.** homeostasis **5.** hypertonic

Graphic Organizer 5—Traits of Plant and Animal Cells

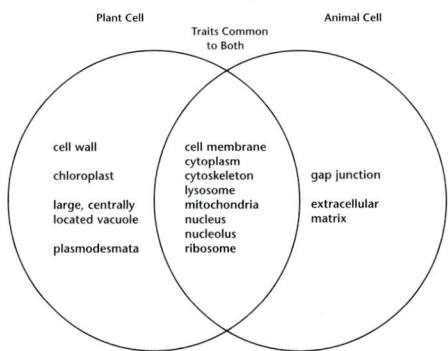

1. Plant cells are designed to capture the sun's energy and change that energy to glucose. Animal cells are not designed to capture energy. Since animals move, many of their cells are modified for movement. **2.** If animal cells had cell walls, animals would not be able to move. **3.** Chloroplasts in plant cells gather sunlight.

Graphic Organizer 6—Cells Use Energy

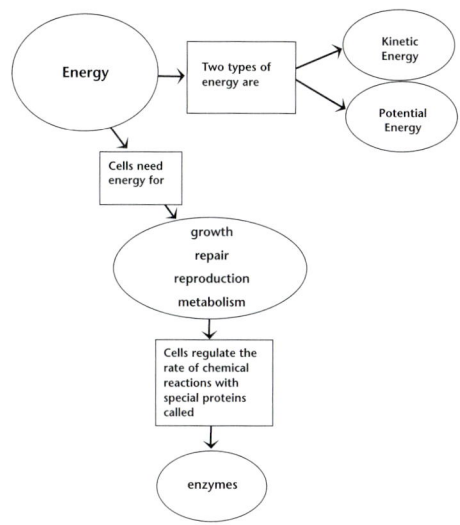

1. Kinetic and potential energy are two types of energy. 2. Cells need energy to carry out the functions of life. 3. The sun is the source of energy for life on the earth. 4. Cells regulate the rate of their chemical reactions with enzymes. 5. Answers will vary and can include diabetes, albinism, and cystic fibrosis.

Graphic Organizer 7—Cellular Respiration

Analysis of Cellular Respiration			
Stages of Cellular Respiration	Reactants	Products	Location in Cell
glycolysis	glucose + ATP	pyruvic acid, NADH, ATP	cytoplasm
Krebs cycle	acetic acid	NADH, FADH$_2$, CO$_2$, ATP	mitochondria in the matrix
electron transport chain	NADH and FADH$_2$	ATP	mitochondrial membrane

1. Acetic acid binds to coenzyme A to make acetyl CoA. 2. Four ATP molecules are produced in glycolysis. 3. In the electron transport chain, 34 ATP molecules are produced. 4. Glucose is oxidized during cellular respiration. 5. The purpose of cellular respiration is to produce ATP.

Graphic Organizer 8—Respiration and Photosynthesis

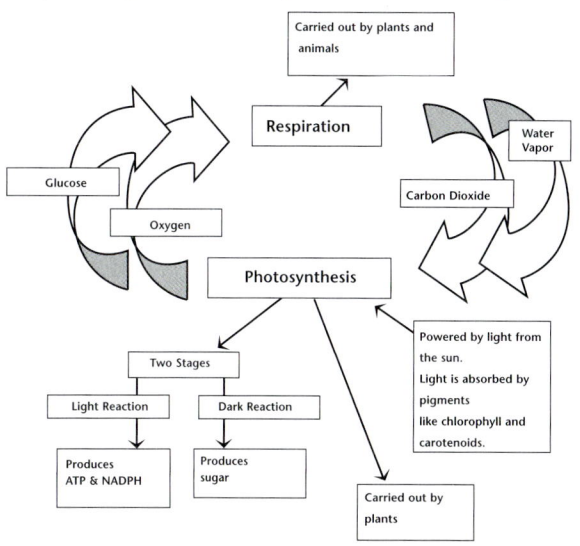

1. The light reaction and the dark reaction are the two stages of photosynthesis. 2. The source of carbon in glucose is carbon dioxide. 3. In the reaction center, electrons excited by light enter an electron transport chain. 4. During phosphorylation, the energy of electrons is used to make ATP. 5. During the light reaction of photosynthesis, energy from the sun is changed into ATP and NADPH. Oxygen is released. During the dark reaction, the energy of ATP and NADPH are used to make sugar.

Graphic Organizer 9—Mitosis and Meiosis

Cell Event	Happens During Mitosis	Happens During Meiosis
1. Homologous chromosomes pair.		X
2. Two divisions take place.		X
3. Four daughter cells are produced.		X
4. Type of cell division associated with growth, repair and asexual reproduction.	X	
5. One division of chromosomes occurs.	X	
6. Two daughter cells are produced.	X	
7. The number of chromosomes is halved.		X
8. Chromosomes cross over.		X
9. The daughter cells are just like the parent cells.	X	

1. The purpose of meiosis is to produce gametes. 2. A haploid cell has one copy of each chromosome. A diploid cell has two copies of each chromosome (homologous chromosomes). 3. If crossing over did not occur, there would be less variety. 4. There are 46 chromosomes in each human somatic cell and 23 in each human gamete. 5. Interphase is a period of growth, organelle reproduction, and DNA replication.

Graphic Organizer 10—Mendel's Work

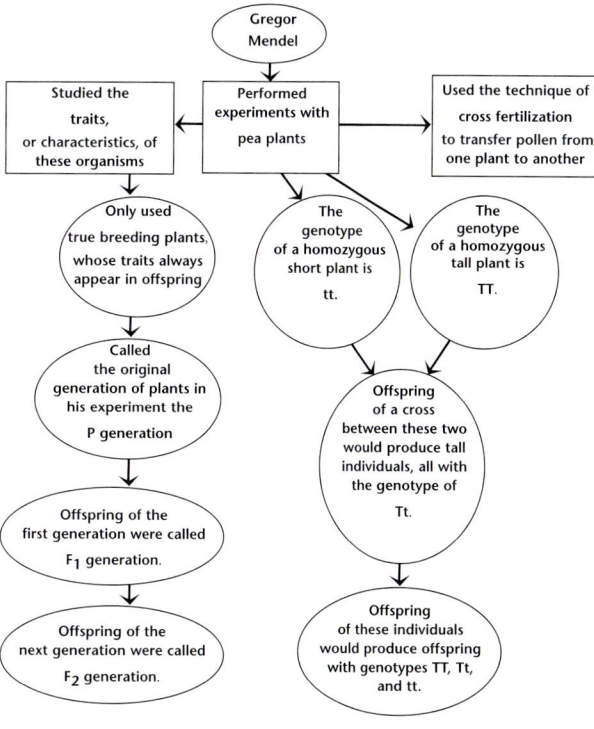

1. The law of independent assortment explains this genotype.
2. The flowers in the F₂ generation will be red and white. 3. The F₂ generation plants are hybrids. Each of the parents is a true-breeding organism. When two true-breeding organisms mate, the offspring are hybrids. 4. Plants with the genotype TTRr are tall and red.
5. Answers will vary. One example of a monohybrid cross is with a tall pea plant and a short pea plant. An example of a dihybrid cross is between a tall pea plant with wrinkled seeds and a short pea plant with smooth seeds.

Graphic Organizer 11—DNA Structure

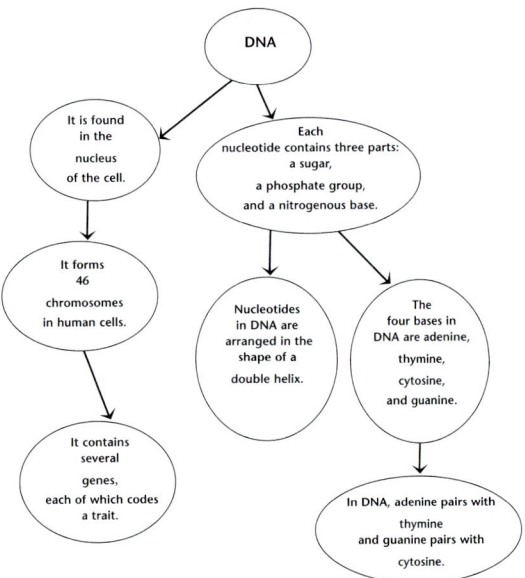

1. DNA polymerase helps a strand of DNA untwists and opens at the origin of replication. Each old strand acts as a template for the production of a new strand, forming a replication bubble. Nucleotides base pair to nucleotides on the two exposed strands of DNA with the aid of DNA ligase. One new strand is made as a long piece, the leading strand, and the other as several small pieces, the lagging strand. 2. Enzymes unwind DNA and open the strand, and they attach the growing strand of nucleotides. 3. DNA opens and RNA nucleotides use it as a template to form a strand of mRNA. mRNA travels from the nucleus to the ribosome. 4. A codon is a sequence of three nucleotides on mRNA. 5. The anticodon to UCG is AGC.

Graphic Organizer 12—Comparing Body Systems

Body Systems	Function of the Body System	Body System Made Up of
Skeletal	Supports the body and protects organs	Bones, cartilage
Endocrine	Sends messages to organs and tissues	Glands and hormones
Excretory	Gets rid of wastes	Kidneys, ureters, bladder, urethra, skin, lungs
Digestive	Takes in food and breaks it down into nutrients	Mouth, esophagus, stomach, liver, intestines
Respiratory	Takes in oxygen and releases carbon dioxide	Lungs, bronchi, trachea, nose, mouth
Circulatory	Carries food and oxygen to cells	Blood vessels, blood, heart
Muscular	Moves the body	Muscles and tendons

1. Bile produced in the liver is stored in the gallbladder until needed. Its job is to break down fats. 2. During an inhalation the lungs expand, the diaphragm drops, and air rushes into the lungs. 3. As blood travels through nephrons, excess water and waste products are left in the nephrons. The mixture drains into the bladder for storage.
4. Answers will vary. Each body system requires all of the others to maintain it. For example, the respiratory system brings in oxygen for cells in all other systems. 5. The nervous and endocrine systems respond to stimuli from both the internal and external environments. Both are involved in coordinating the activities of different parts of the body.

Graphic Organizer 13—Evolution and Natural Selection

Aspects of Evolution	Definitions	More Facts About These Aspects
Theory	The theory of modern synthesis says that evolution involves changes in a population's gene pool over time.	Modern synthesis is based on the work of Darwin. His theory of natural selection states that organisms best suited for the environment survive, reproduce, and pass their genes to the next generation.
Evidence	Four types of evidence that support evolution are: 1. the fossil record 2. biogeography 3. comparative anatomy 4. molecular biology	• Fossils are usually found in sedimentary rocks. • Examples of homologous structures are arms of humans, wings of birds, and forelimbs of reptiles. • Comparing DNA can show whether two organisms are closely related.
Processes	Five processes that allow evolution to take place are: 1. mutation 2. recombination 3. gene flow 4. genetic drift 5. natural selection	• In the process of recombination, new combinations of alleles occur. • Gene flow is the movement of genes in and out of a population. • Genetic drift is the random changes in the gene pool of a small population.
Scale	Microevolution is the minor changes from one generation to the next. Macroevolution is major changes over geologic time.	• An example of microevolution occurred in England in the 1800s when the frequency of dark-colored alleles increased in moths. • Scientists use the fossil record to explain the process of macroevolution.

1. In artificial selection, people change a species by selecting to breed for certain traits. 2. In natural selection, the environment determines the traits that are beneficial. 3. a. Organisms produce more offspring than can survive. b. Individuals in a population vary. c. Individuals with alleles best suited to the environment are more likely to survive. d. Individuals with alleles best suited to the environment leave more offspring. 4. Mendel explained how traits are passed from parents to offspring through a population.

Graphic Organizer 14—Speciation and Punctuated Equilibrium

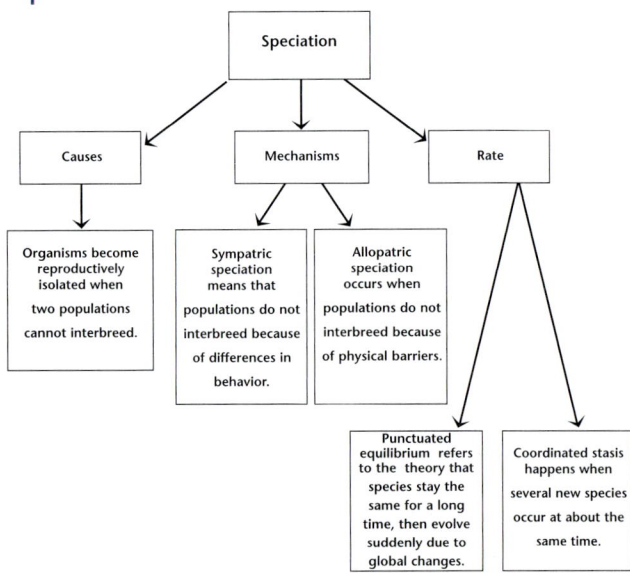

704 Answer Key

1. The concept of a biological species states that a species is made up of groups of sexually reproducing, interbreeding populations that produce fertile offspring. The ecological species concept refers to asexual organisms that interbreed based on their niche. 2. Linnaeus classified living things on seven levels, the largest being the kingdom and the smallest the species. 3. Scientists use morphology, biochemistry, body functions, and behavior to classify organisms. 4. The three primary groups of the three domain system are Bacteria, Archaea, and Eukarya. 5. Species are disappearing quickly because people are changing the environment.

Graphic Organizer 15—Phylogenies and Classifying Diversity

Kingdom	Groups	More Information
Protista	Includes protozoans and slime molds, which can be single-celled or a community of cells	Three types of protozoans are: amoebas, ciliates, and flagellates.
Fungi	Includes yeast, molds, and fungi	
Plantae	Two large groups are vascular and nonvascular plants.	Vascular plants include ferns, seed plants, and conifers.
		An example of a nonvascular plant is moss.
Animals	Two large groups are invertebrates and vertebrates.	Invertebrates include porifera, cnidaria, platyhelminthes, nematode, annelida, mollusca, arthropoda, and echinodermata.
		Vertebrates include fish, amphibians, reptiles, aves, and mammals.

1. Taxonomy is the science of classifying organisms based on the features they share. 2. Archaea includes prokaryotes that live in extreme conditions and are not bacteria, Bacteria include prokaryotes that are classified as bacteria, and Eukarya includes all eukaryotes. 3. The four kingdoms of Eukarya are Protista, Fungi, Plantae, and Animalia.

Graphic Organizer 16—Behavioral Biology

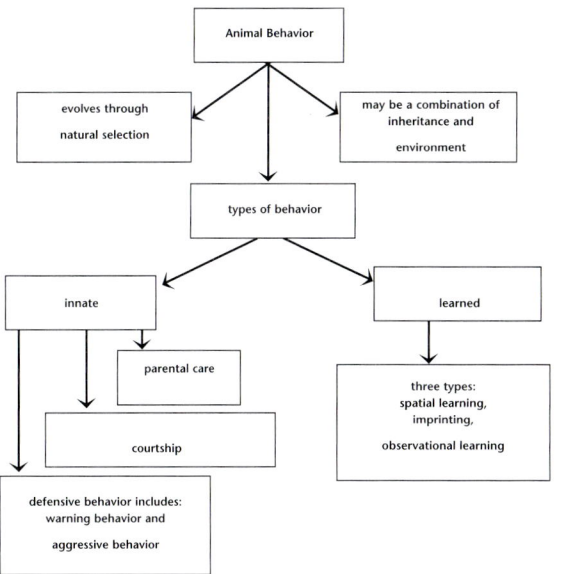

1. Social behavior refers to the interactions of animals, and can include aggression, courtship, and cooperation. 2. Animals communicate in a variety of ways, including sounds, scents, and behaviors. 3. Animals communicate to warn of danger, signal the location of food, or identify members of the community.

Graphic Organizer 17—Populations and Communities

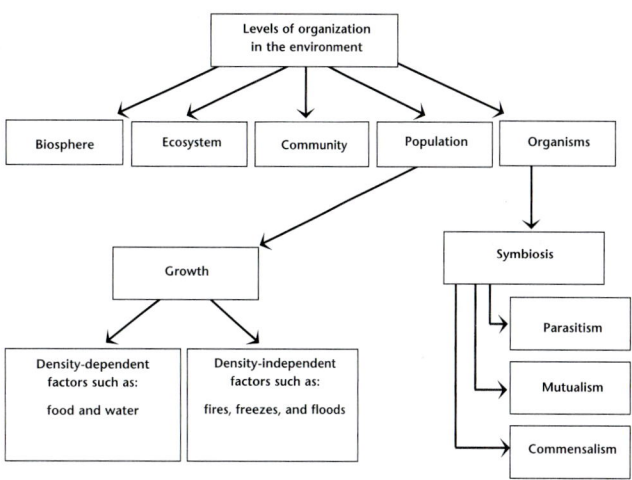

1. The focus of ecology is on the interactions of organisms with their environments. 2. A community is made up of several populations. 3. Ecologists take samples of populations to measure them. 4. Adaptations that help reduce the chances of becoming prey include warning coloration, camouflage, and mimicry. 5. An ecosystem might experience primary or secondary succession.

Graphic Organizer 18—Ecosystems

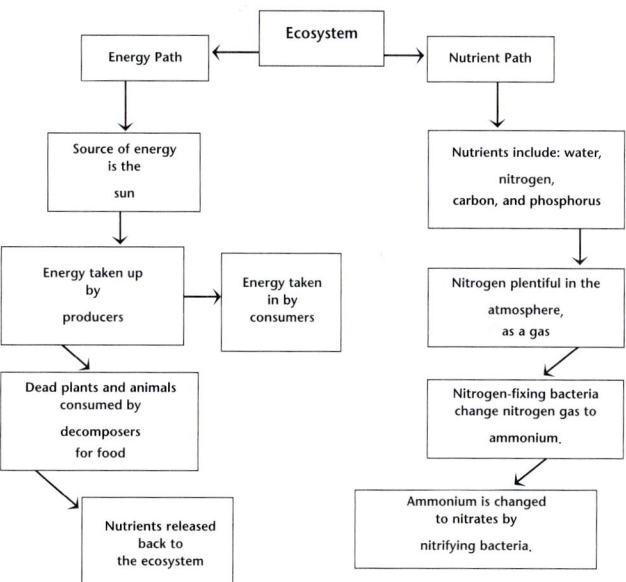

1. The trophic structure of an ecosystem describes the energy flow through that system. 2. Chemotrophs are organisms like animals and fungi that get their energy from food. Phototrophs are green organisms, like plants, that make their own food from the sun's energy. 3. Water cycles through the living and nonliving parts of the ecosystem. Water falls from the atmosphere to earth as precipitation. Water can be taken up by living things or fall on the earth. Water evaporates from surfaces and bodies of water to return to the atmosphere. 4. Biomes are large groups of ecosystems with the same climates and similar organisms. Two examples of terrestrial biomes are the desert and the tundra. 5. Two types of aquatic biomes are freshwater and saltwater biomes.

Graphic Organizer 19—Human Impact and Technology

Ecosystem Issues	Activities That Destroy Ecosystems	Activities That Protect Ecosystems
pollution on land	Trash is collected and stored in landfills.	Paper, plastic, and metals are removed from trash and recycled.
air quality	Waste gases are given off as emissions. They cause acid rain, loss of ozone, and increased greenhouse gases.	Governments control emissions from cars and industries.
water quality	Liquid waste from industries and farms is called runoff.	The amount of runoff is regulated.
land development	Removing trees from land can cause deforestation.	The science of landscape ecology develops land without damaging ecosystems.
living things	Organisms that move out of their natural ecosystems are introduced species.	Reserves are places where species are protected from human activities. Recovery plans save endangered species from extinction.

1. Loss of the ozone layer lets more dangerous radiation strike organisms on the earth. **2.** As human populations expand, they destroy and pollute habitats. **3.** Alien species can use the resources of native species.

Community Connection

Completed activities will vary for each student. Community Connection activities are real-life activities that students complete outside the classroom. These activities give students practical learning and practice of the concepts taught in *Biology: Cycles of Life*. Check completed activities to see that students have followed directions, completed each step, filled in all charts and blanks, provided reasonable answers to questions, written legibly, and used appropriate science terms and proper grammar.

Self-Study Guides

Self-Study Guides outline suggested sections from the text and workbook. These assignment guides provide flexibility for individualized instruction or independent study.

Mastery Tests

See page 717 for the Scoring Rubric for Short-Response Items in Part E and Essay Items in Part F of the Chapter Mastery Tests. See page 719 for the Scoring Rubric for Short-Response Items in Part E and Essay Items in Part F of the Midterm and Final Mastery Tests.

Chapter 1 Mastery Test A

Part A 1. B **2.** C **3.** D **4.** C **5.** A **Part B 6.** Energy is the ability to do work. Answers may vary. One type of energy is heat. **7.** All growth cycles, including reproduction, require energy. **8.** Answers may vary. A fish's scales help keep water out of its body, fins enable it to maneuver, and the tail propels the fish forward. **9.** DNA carries the instructions that tell a cell what to do during reproduction. **10.** Answers may vary. A forest ecosystem might contain living things such as trees, shrubs, birds, and squirrels and nonliving things such as water and soil. **Part C 11.** C **12.** E **13.** A **14.** D **15.** B **Part D 16.** reproduction **17.** cycle **18.** species **19.** DNA **20.** proteins **Part E 21.** Answers will vary, but should include some of these facts: Biology is the study of life. Life includes activities such as eating, drinking, and cleaning yourself. A biologist studies life, and might investigate plants or animals. Some biologists specialize in the study of birds, snakes, or the organisms in pond water. **22.** Answers will vary but should include some of these facts: Extinction is the loss of a species. An extinct species never appears again. Extinction can be caused by earthquakes, floods, and other natural disasters. When one species becomes extinct, it makes room for a new species. New species may develop from those that were left. **Part F 23.** Answers will vary, but students' paragraphs should include some of these facts: Growth occurs at many levels. One part of all growth cycles is reproduction. DNA, or deoxyribonucleic acid, controls reproduction. Energy makes it possible for cells to use their DNA reproduce and grow. As organisms reproduce they start new cycles. The cycle of growth eventually ends in death. **24.** Answers will vary, but students' paragraphs should include some of these facts: Observation—You read an advertisement claiming that Super Fine flour produces taller biscuits than Old Mill flour. Question—You ask the question: Does Super Fine flour produce taller biscuits than Old Mill flour? Hypothesis—You state a hypothesis: Biscuits made with Super Fine flour are taller than biscuits made with Old Mill flour. Experiment—You use your favorite recipe to bake one batch of biscuits with Super Fine flour and another batch of biscuits with Old Mill flour. Other than varying the type of flour, you use the same ingredients and techniques each time. Analysis—You measure biscuits from both batches and decided which type of flour produced the tallest ones. Communication—You share your results with all of your friends who enjoy baking.

Chapter 1 Mastery Test B

Part A 1. E **2.** C **3.** B **4.** D **5.** A **Part B 6.** B **7.** A **8.** B **9.** C **10.** C **Part C 11.** Answers will vary. Some of the living things in a desert ecosystem are cactus and birds. Some of the nonliving things are sand and rock . **12.** Answers will vary. A biologist might study plants, animals, and disease transmission. **13.** Living things need energy to carry out the work in cells **14.** Answers will vary. A polar bear has thick, white fur and a lot of body fat to keep it warm. **15.** The scientific method is a logical way of solving problems that uses facts and evidence. **Part D 16.** Communication **17.** experiment **18.** analysis **19.** observation **20.** hypothesis **Part E 21.** Answers will vary, but should include some of these facts: Energy is the ability to do work. Energy can change forms depending on how it is used, but energy never runs out. Energy is used in many ways. Examples include humans using energy to chew, lift a box, and run a marathon. **22.** Answers will vary, but should include some of these facts: Energy is the ability to do work, and the work of all forms of life is to grow. Growth is found on many levels. Without energy, DNA could not make instructions for life processes like division. **Part F 23.** Answers will vary, but students' paragraphs should include some of these facts: Biology is the study of life. Biology helps explain living things, like plants and animals, as well as how these organisms live in the world. Biology is part of every person's life. Some activities of organisms include eating, drinking, and cleaning themselves. **24.** Answers will vary, but students' paragraphs should include some of these facts: Speciation is a process in which new species are created over time. Extinctions can lead to the loss of existing species and make room for new species. The new species have adaptations that make them better able to live in a new area. Speciation can occur in bursts after some natural disaster like an earthquake or flood.

Chapter 2 Mastery Test A
Part A 1. polar **2.** hydrophobic **3.** crystalline **4.** pH **5.** buffer
Part B 6. B **7.** B **8.** A **9.** C **10.** D **Part C 11.** C **12.** A **13.** D **14.** E **15.** B **Part D 16.** When water gains heat, some is used to break the hydrogen bonds between water molecules. **17.** Hydrogen bonds cause water molecules to stick together. **18.** C-13 has one more neutron than C-12. **19.** The energy in compounds is stored in chemical bonds. **20.** acetic acid, water, soap **Part E 21.** Answers will vary, but should include some of these facts: Atoms are made up of protons, neutrons, and electrons. Protons are positively charged particles that have mass. Neutrons are neutral particles that have mass. Electrons are negatively charged particles that have a negligible amount of mass. Protons and neutrons are located in the nucleus, and electrons orbit the nucleus in energy shells. **22.** Answers will vary, but should include some of these facts: The formula H_2O_2 shows that this compound contains two atoms of hydrogen and two atoms of oxygen. **Part F 23.** Answers will vary, but students' paragraphs should include some of these facts: Burning is a chemical reaction. During this reaction, atoms are rearranged into new substances. The reactants (fuel) create new products (ash and gas). As the chemical bonds of the reactants are broken, heat is released. **24.** Answers will vary, but students' paragraphs should include some of these facts: Both ionic and covalent compounds hold atoms together to form molecules. These types of bonds differ in that ionic compounds are formed by the mutual attraction of oppositely charged ions. In covalent compounds, atoms share electrons.

Chapter 2 Mastery Test B
Part A 1. C **2.** A **3.** C **4.** C **5.** A **Part B 6.** B **7.** D **8.** A **9.** E **10.** C **Part C 11.** hydrogen bonds **12.** bonds **13.** isotope **14.** surface tension **15.** nitric acid **Part D 16.** The reactants are hydrogen and chlorine. **17.** Fats and oils are described as hydrophobic because they do not mix with water. **18.** Potential hydrogen, or pH, is a measure of hydrogen ion concentration. **19.** Buffers are substances that moderate the affects of acids and bases. **20.** A crystalline substance has a regularly repeating internal atomic structure. **Part E 21.** Answers will vary, but should include some of these facts: Water is a unique molecule with some unusual properties. Because water molecules form hydrogen bonds, the compound has high surface tension, a large heat capacity, and acts as an excellent solvent. **22.** Answers will vary, but should include some of these facts: The formula for sulfuric acid, H_2SO_4, indicates that the compound contains two atoms of hydrogen, one atom of sulfur, and four atoms of oxygen. **Part F 23.** Answers will vary, but students' paragraphs should include some of these facts: Atomic mass indicates the number of protons and neutrons in an atom. The atomic number tells how many protons an atom contains. Hydrogen has an atomic mass of one, which means that there is only one particle in its nucleus, a proton. If hydrogen had any neutrons, they would be in the nucleus, also. Hydrogen's one electron orbits the nucleus in an electron shell. **24.** Answers will vary, but students' paragraphs should include some of these facts: Water is a polar molecule. When a water molecule forms, the oxygen atom pulls electrons toward it more strongly than the two hydrogen atoms. As a result, the electrons spend more time near the oxygen end of the molecule than near the hydrogen ends. For this reason, the hydrogen ends tend to have a slightly positive charge and the oxygen end a slightly negative charge.

Chapter 3 Mastery Test A
Part A 1. B **2.** D **3.** E **4.** C **5.** A **Part B 6.** C **7.** C **8.** A **9.** C **10.** B **Part C 11.** Lipids **12.** glycerol **13.** fructose **14.** plastids **15.** Membranes **Part D 16.** Three examples of steroids are hormones, vitamin D, and cholesterol. **17.** When one amino acid loses an H and the other an OH, water is formed and the amino acids combine. **18.** A disaccharide is made of two monosaccharides joined together. Examples include sucrose, lactose, and maltose. **19.** Two polysaccharides are cellulose and starch. Cellulose is a structural component and starch stores glucose molecules. **20.** A phospholipid is a molecule that is hydrophobic on one end and hydrophilic on the other. **Part E 21.** Answers will vary, but should include some of these facts: DNA and RNA are both nucleic acids. DNA is the molecule that stores genetic information. It is a double molecule shaped as a helix. RNA helps translate that genetic information to produce proteins. RNA is a single molecule. **22.** Answers will vary, but should include some of these facts: A well-balanced meal, with each type of food, includes all food groups: carbohydrates, proteins, and fats. An example of such a meal is steak, potatoes, and salad. **Part F 23.** Answers will vary, but students' paragraphs should include some of these facts: Lipids have several functions in living things. As fats, they store energy and provide insulation. Lipids carry fat-soluble vitamins and essential fatty acids. They are also important components of cell membranes. **24.** Answers will vary, but students' paragraphs should include some of these facts: Proteins and carbohydrates share some similarities in their structures. Both are long polymers and organic molecules. However, the two types of molecules are not identical. Proteins are made of units called amino acids and carbohydrates are made of units called monosaccharides.

Chapter 3 Mastery Test B
Part A 1. organic molecules **2.** RNA **3.** monomers **4.** glucose **5.** enzymes **Part B 6.** D **7.** A **8.** B **9.** E **10.** C **Part C 11.** B **12.** D **13.** A **14.** D **15.** B **Part D 16.** RNA translates the genetic information in the nucleus into proteins. **17.** A polysaccharide is a long molecule made of monomers of monosaccharides. Starch and cellulose are two polysaccharides. **18.** During hydrolysis, water is added to proteins or polypeptides as they separate from individual amino acids. **19.** Carbohydrates and proteins are both organic compounds that are made of polymers. **20.** Saturated fat in the diet may lead to deposits of lipids in the walls of blood vessels, which can reduce the flow of blood. **Part E 21.** Answers will vary, but should include some of these facts: Four types of organic molecules in all living things are carbohydrates, lipids, proteins, and nucleic acids. Carbohydrates contain carbon, hydrogen, and oxygen, and function to provide the cell with energy. Lipids are insoluble in water and function to store energy, carry fat-soluble vitamins, and serve as insulation. Proteins are made of chains of amino acids and they include structural components as well as molecules like enzymes. Nucleic acids are made of chains of nucleotides and include RNA and DNA. **22.** Answers will vary, but should include some of these facts: Glucose is a monosaccharide, a simple sugar. Glucose plays an important role in cells as a source of energy. **Part F 23.** Answers will vary, but students' paragraphs should include some of these facts: DNA and RNA are classified as nucleic acids. Both molecules are polymers constructed of nucleotides of sugar, phosphate, and a base. The job of DNA is to store genetic information, while that of RNA is to carry that stored information to the cytoplasm. DNA is a double

molecule and RNA is a single stranded molecule. The bases on the two molecules are not the same: DNA is made of adenine, thymine, cytosine, and guanine. Instead of thymine, RNA contains uracil. The sugar in a DNA nucleotide is deoxyribose; in RNA it is ribose. **24.** Answers will vary, but students' paragraphs should include some of these facts: Proteins, carbohydrates, and fats are essential components of a balanced diet. Proteins provide the body with amino acids, which are used to build new proteins. Carbohydrates are a source of energy. Fats provide energy and also make cell structures like membranes.

Chapter 4 Mastery Test A
Part A 1. homeostasis **2.** hypertonic **3.** diffusion **4.** water molecules **5.** selectively permeable **Part B 6.** D **7.** C **8.** B **9.** A **10.** A **Part C 11.** B **12.** A **13.** D **14.** E **15.** C **Part D 16.** The levels of organization in living things are: cells, tissues, organs, and organ systems. **17.** A tissue is a group of similar cells working together. Examples of tissues include blood, skin, nerves, and muscles. **18.** During binary fission, a prokaryotic cell copies its DNA then divides in two. **19.** Answers could include the circulatory or digestive systems. **20.** Answers could include plants, animals, or fungi. **Part E 21.** Answers will vary, but should include some of these facts: Four types of molecules in cells are: carbohydrates, lipids, proteins, and nucleic acids. Carbohydrates are used for immediate energy. Lipids provide long term energy. Proteins have roles in structure and as enzymes. Nucleic acids contain the cell's information. **22.** Answers will vary, but should include some of these facts: A cell's structure determines its function. Each cell's DNA carries instructions for making specific proteins, which in turn determine what jobs the cells can perform. **Part F 23.** Answers will vary, but students' paragraphs should include some of these facts: Cells maintain homeostasis, or balance. They constantly move water molecules in and out through the process of osmosis. Other important molecules, such as simple sugars, move in and out of the cell through diffusion. **24.** Answers will vary, but students' paragraphs should include some of these facts: Prokaryotic and eukaryotic cells differ in structure. Prokaryotes are simple cells with cell structures floating feely. The only membrane in a prokaryote is the cell membrane. The DNA is not contained in a nucleus, so it floats freely. Eukaryotic cells are larger and more complex than prokaryotic cells. The cells of eukaryotes have organelles contained in membranes, including the nucleus.

Chapter 4 Mastery Test B
Part A 1. C **2.** A **3.** D **4.** C **5.** B **Part B 6.** A **7.** C **8.** E **9.** B **10.** D **Part C 11.** binary fission **12.** tissue **13.** organ system **14.** cell **15.** Eukaryotic **Part D 16.** A selectively permeable membrane lets some molecules into the cell but blocks others. **17.** Homeostasis is a state of balance inside the cell. **18.** During diffusion, molecules move from an area of high concentration to an area of low concentration. **19.** Diffusion is the movement of any type of cell from an area of high concentration to an area of low concentration. Osmosis is the diffusion of water molecules. **20.** In a salty solution, cells lose water. **Part E 21.** Answers will vary, but should include some of these facts: Osmosis and diffusion play important roles in cell homeostasis. Water enters and leaves cells through osmosis to maintain the correct cellular balance. Other types of molecules enter and leave cells through diffusion, the movement of molecules from an area of high concentration to one of low concentration.

22. Answers will vary, but should include some of these facts: Prokaryotic and eukaryotic cells differ in structure. Prokaryotes are simple cells with cell structures that float feely. The only membrane in a prokaryote is the cell membrane. The DNA is not contained in a nucleus, so it floats freely. Eukaryotic cells are larger and more complex than prokaryotic cells. The cells of eukaryotes have organelles contained in membranes, including the nucleus.
Part F 23. Answers will vary, but students' paragraphs should include some of these facts: Carbohydrates form molecules involved in cell recognition, as well as glycogen in animals and starch and cellulose in plants. Lipids are components of cell membranes. Proteins form several structures, including some that keep the structure of the cell steady, and enzymes. Nucleic acids form DNA and RNA. **24.** Answers will vary, but students' paragraphs should include some of these facts: Different kinds of cells carry out different functions. The function of a cell is determined by the proteins it produces. The information for the production of proteins is coded in each cell's DNA.

Chapter 5 Mastery Test A
Part A 1. A **2.** C **3.** C **4.** A **5.** C **Part B 6.** bilayer **7.** facilitated diffusion **8.** gap junctions **9.** nucleolus **10.** DNA **Part C 11.** C **12.** E **13.** A **14.** B **15.** D **Part D 16.** Rough endoplasmic reticulum is covered with ribosomes; smooth ER is not. **17.** Answers could include two of the following: The cytoskeleton gives cells shape and support, helps anchor organelles, and helps cells move. **18.** Flagella and cilia are both made of microtubules. **19.** When a plant wilts, the cellulose cell walls support the tissues. **20.** DNA controls a cell's activities by dictating the proteins it produces. **Part E 21.** Answers will vary, but should include some of these facts: The fluid mosaic model explains the positions of molecules in the cell membrane. According to this model, the cell membrane is made of a bilayer of phospholipid molecules. Proteins and other components of the cell membrane float among these phospholipid molecules. **22.** Answers will vary, but should include some of these facts: The two energy organelles in plant and animal cells are the mitochondrion and chloroplast. The job of the chloroplast is to gather light energy and use it to make glucose. The mitochondrion converts that glucose into ATP. **Part F 23.** Answers will vary, but students' paragraphs should include some of these facts: Microtubules and microfilaments are both parts of the cytoskeleton. Both types of fibers are made of proteins. Microtubules are made of tubulin, and they function to move organelles around the cell. Microfibers are made of actin, and they move the entire cell. **24.** Answers will vary, but students' paragraphs should include some of these facts: Plant and animal cells have many similarities, and a few differences that support their specific functions. Both cells are eukaryotic and have basic cell parts such as nucleus and other organelles. Plant cells differ from animal cells in that they are surrounded by rigid walls of cellulose. In addition, plant cells contain chloroplasts for gathering light. A large central vacuole in plant cells enables them to store water. Plasmodesmata between plant cells enable them to communicate. Many animal cells are surrounded by an extracellular matrix that holds them together. They communicate through gap junctions.

Chapter 5 Mastery Test B

Part A 1. C **2.** C **3.** A **4.** D **5.** C **Part B 6.** extracellular matrix **7.** osmosis **8.** plasma membrane **9.** phosphate or head **Part C 10.** E **11.** A **12.** D **13.** B **14.** C **Part D 15.** The fatty acid or tail end of a phospholipid molecule is neutral. **16.** The cytoskeleton supports the cell's structure, holds organelles in place, enables the cell to move, and helps move organelles. **17.** Plasmodesmata are found in the cell walls of plant cells. Their function is to provide communication. **18.** Passive transport does not require energy. Active transport requires energy. **19.** Once manufactured, a lipid molecule is processed in the Golgi apparatus then shipped out of the cell. **20.** Folds in the inner membranes of mitochondria and chloroplast increase surface area of those molecules. **Part E 21.** Answers will vary, but should include some of these facts: Phospholipid molecules are lipids with a head and a tail. The head, a phosphate group, is joined to a glycerol molecule. The phosphate group has a negative charge and interacts with water. The glycerol molecule is neutral and interacts with fats. The molecules form a bilayer with their glycerol ends together and their phosphate ends exposed to the watery environment. This allows them to form a barrier to the outside environment that controls what enters and leaves the cell. **22.** Answers will vary, but should include some of these facts: Mitochondria and chloroplasts are both organelles that work with energy in cells. Chloroplasts capture the sun's energy and use it to make glucose. Mitochondria change the energy of glucose to ATP. **Part F 23.** Answers will vary, but students' paragraphs should include some of these facts: The three types of cytoskeletal fibers in cells include microtubules, intermediate fibers, and microfilaments. Microtubules are hollow tubes made of the protein tubulin that help organelles move. Intermediate filaments are long and string-like structures that help the cell keep its shape. Microfilaments are long strings of actin that help the cell move. **24.** Answers will vary, but students' paragraphs should include some of these facts: Plant and animal cells are different because they have different functions. Plant cells have a cellulose cell wall for support, a large central vacuole for water storage, plasmodesmata between cells for communication, and chloroplasts that capture the sun's energy. Plant cells are able to make their own food. Animal cells are not able to make their own food. Many animal cells produce an extracellular matrix that helps the cells stick together. Channels of communication between animal cells are called gap junctions.

Chapter 6 Mastery Test A

Part A 1. C **2.** C **3.** A **4.** A **5.** C **Part B 6.** ADP **7.** catalysts **8.** pepsin **9.** glucose (sugar) **10.** activation energy **Part C 11.** C **12.** D **13.** A **14.** E **15.** B **Part D 16.** Kinetic energy is related to motion and potential energy to position or configuration. **17.** Metabolism is the sum total of a cell's chemical reactions. **18.** Enzymes are not changed by chemical reactions. **19.** No. Enzymes are specific and cannot be used for different tasks. **20.** The potential energy of food is stored in the bonds of food molecules. **Part E 21.** Answers will vary, but should include some of these facts: Cells use energy for a variety of cellular processes. Cells reproduce, make proteins and other products, remove wastes, and take in needed materials. All of the activities of life require energy. **22.** Answers will vary, but should include some of these facts: ATP is an energy-carrying molecule that is made up of a five-carbon sugar, a nitrogen base, and three phosphate groups. ATP is made by adding a phosphate group to a molecule of ADP. When the phosphate group is released, energy is released for cellular use. **Part F 23.** Answers will vary, but students' paragraphs should include some of these facts: Energy harvested from glucose is used to connect a phosphate group to a molecule of ADP. In this way, energy is stored in the bonds of ATP molecules. When the cell needs energy, one of the phosphate groups breaks off and energy is released. The molecule that results from this reaction is ADP. ADP is a low-energy molecule that can be changed back into ATP by the addition of a phosphate group, a reaction that requires energy. **24.** Answers will vary, but students' paragraphs should include some of these facts: Enzymes are proteins that regulate the rates of chemical reactions in living things. Enzymes recognize specific reactant molecules and bind to their active sites. By bringing the substrate molecules in contact with one another, enzymes lower the reaction energy needed to get a reaction going.

Chapter 6 Mastery Test B

Part A 1. C **2.** D **3.** B **4.** A **5.** C **Part B 6.** ATP **7.** calories **8.** ADP **9.** Obesity **10.** substrate **Part C 11.** C **12.** D **13.** E **14.** B **15.** A **Part D 16.** Energy is used to add a phosphate group to ADP. **17.** Some of the health problems that result from lack of enzymes include albinism, cystic fibrosis, and diabetes. **18.** During hydrolysis of ATP, a phosphate group is removed, energy is released, and a water molecule is added to ATP. **19.** Enzymes speed up chemical reactions by lowering the activation energy needed to get the reaction started. **20.** A catalyst works in nonliving systems, and an enzyme works in living systems. **Part E 21.** Answers will vary, but should include some of these facts: Enzymes make it possible for chemical reactions in living things to occur quickly enough to support life. Without enzymes, most of the reactions in cells would not occur. **22.** Answers will vary, but should include some of these facts: A cell that runs out of ATP cannot carry out any life functions. As a result, the cell would die. ATP is the source of energy needed to support life. **Part F 23.** Answers will vary, but students' paragraphs should include some of these facts: Cells function on the energy they gather from the sun. The sun's energy is taken in by plants, converted to glucose during photosynthesis, and stored in the chemical bonds of glucose. When glucose is broken down in the mitochondrion, the energy in its bonds is transferred to ATP. **24.** Answers will vary, but students' paragraphs should include some of these facts: ATP is stored in the cell and released as needed. When energy is needed, ATP releases energy. In the process, the ATP molecule loses a phosphate group and is changed into ADP. When energy is available in the cell, it is used to add a phosphate group to a molecule of ADP, forming ATP once again.

Chapter 7 Mastery Test A

Part A 1. Feedback inhibition is the control mechanism used in cells. **2.** ATP synthase is an enzyme that helps make ATP. **3.** Lactic acid can accumulate in tissues when oxygen is low and cells are making energy anaerobically. **4.** Electron carriers in the cell include NADH and $FADH_2$. **5.** Redox reactions involve the transfer of electrons. **Part B 6.** C **7.** A **8.** C **9.** A **10.** D **Part C 11.** ethyl alcohol **12.** electron transport chain **13.** glycolysis **14.** aerobic **15.** fermentation **Part D 16.** E **17.** C **18.** D **19.** A **20.** B **Part E 21.** Answers will vary, but should include some of these facts: Cellular respiration takes place in three stages. During glycolysis, glucose is broken down into smaller molecules of pyruvic acid. In the Krebs cycle, electron carriers are generated. During the electron

Answer Key 709

transport chain, the electron carriers use the electrons to make ATP. **22.** Answers will vary, but should include some of these facts: Bacteria that live in mud cannot carry out cellular respiration because they live in an oxygen-free environment. As a result, they produce energy through anaerobic methods. **Part F 23.** Answers will vary, but students' paragraphs should include some of these facts: Fermentation and cellular respiration have some similarities. Both processes are used by cells to produce ATP. Of the two mechanisms, cellular respiration produces the most energy, so is used most of the time in eukaryotes. Cellular respiration is an aerobic process and fermentation is an anaerobic process. **24.** Answers will vary, but students' paragraphs should include some of these facts: Mitochondria are organelles associated with production of energy, so all cells have them. However, cells that produce large amounts of energy have more. Two of the places where mitochondria are dense are the muscle cells of the thigh and in cardiac cells.

Chapter 7 Mastery Test B
Part A 1. Acetic acid is the sharp-smelling product made when pyruvic acid breaks down. **2.** Acetyl CoA is made of acetic acid plus coenzyme A. **3.** The purpose of cellular respiration is to produce ATP. **4.** During oxidation, a molecule loses electrons. **5.** Glucose is the source of energy used to make ATP. **Part B 6.** C **7.** B **8.** B **9.** B **10.** A **Part C 11.** E **12.** C **13.** D **14.** B **15.** A **Part D 16.** cellular respiration **17.** mitochondria **18.** oxidation **19.** pyruvic acid **20.** electron transport chain **Part E 21.** Answers will vary, but should include some of these facts: Cellular respiration is an aerobic process that produces a lot of ATP. The cells of humans carry out cellular respiration. Fermentation is an anaerobic process that produces a small amount of ATP. Some anaerobic bacteria produce energy by fermentation. **22.** Answers will vary, but should include some of these facts: Reduction is a chemical reaction in which a substance gains electrons. Oxidation is a chemical reaction in which a substance loses electrons. Oxidation occurs when glucose gains electrons during cellular respiration. **Part F 23.** Answers will vary, but students' paragraphs should include some of these facts: The three stages of cellular respiration include glycolysis, the Krebs cycle, and the electron transport chain. Glycolysis, which occurs in the cytoplasm, converts a molecule of glucose into pyruvic acid then acetic acid. Acetic acid binds to coenzyme A and moves into the mitochondria. Inside the matrix of the mitochondria, the Krebs cycle produces molecules that are electron carriers. In the electron transport chain, which occurs on mitochondrial membranes, the electron carriers transport electrons generated by the breakdown of glucose along a chain of molecules. The energy in these electrons is released and used to make ATP. **24.** Answers will vary, but students' paragraphs should include some of these facts: Cells do not carry out fermentation or cellular respiration at a constant rate. Feedback inhibition is a mechanism for slowing or stopping a reaction. The enzymes produced during these chemical reactions can be used to control their speed. When the products of the reaction become concentrated, they can cause the enzymes that run the reaction to slow down or stop.

Chapter 8 Mastery Test A
Part A 1. D **2.** B **3.** B **4.** C **5.** A **Part B 6.** An accessory pigment captures wavelengths of light missed by chlorophyll *b*. **7.** Plants release oxygen during photosynthesis. **8.** A chloroplast holds chlorophyll which captures the sun's energy. **9.** The two stages of photosynthesis are the light reaction and dark reaction. **10.** The photosystem transfers electrons to the reaction center. **Part C 11.** D **12.** B **13.** A **14.** E **15.** C **Part D 16.** C4 **17.** Calvin-Benson cycle **18.** mesophyll **19.** vascular bundle **20.** autotrophs **Part E 21.** Answers will vary, but should include some of these facts: The light reaction must come before the dark reaction because it provides the energy that fuels the dark reaction. Energy of sunlight creates molecules of ATP and NADPH which drive the production of sugar. **22.** Answers will vary, but should include some of these facts: The products of respiration are carbon dioxide and water. These are the raw materials of photosynthesis. The products of photosynthesis are oxygen and glucose. They are the raw materials of respiration. **Part F 23.** Answers will vary, but students' paragraphs should include some of these facts: Animals do not contain chlorophyll. However, they depend on the process of photosynthesis for food, and the process of photosynthesis is powered by sunlight. Many animals eat plants directly. Others eat animals that eat plants. Without plants, animals could not exist. **24.** Answers will vary, but students' paragraphs should include some of these facts: Photosynthesis occurs in two stages, the light reaction and the dark reaction. The purpose of the dark reaction in photosynthesis is to convert carbon dioxide to sugar. Molecules of NADPH and ATP produced in the light reaction fuel this reaction.

Chapter 8 Mastery Test B
Part A 1. B **2.** C **3.** A **4.** B **5.** A **Part B 6.** photosynthesis **7.** light **8.** chlorophyll *b* **9.** electromagnetic radiation (energy) **10.** stomata **Part C 11.** light reaction **12.** dark reaction **13.** visible light **14.** Carotenoids **15.** sugar **Part D 16.** C **17.** D **18.** E **19.** B **20.** A **Part E 21.** Answers will vary, but should include some of these facts: During the light reaction, the sun's energy is changed to ATP and NADPH. Water is split and oxygen released. **22.** Answers will vary, but should include some of these facts: During the dark reaction, ATP and NADPH produced in the light reaction capture the carbon in carbon dioxide to make G3P, an energy-rich sugar. G3P is used by cells to make glucose. **Part F 23.** Answers will vary, but students' paragraphs should include some of these facts: Photosynthesis provides food for almost every living thing. It captures the sun's energy and changes it into the energy of glucose. This glucose nourishes plants. It also indirectly feeds many organisms that eat plant-eating organisms. **24.** Answers will vary, but students' paragraphs should include some of these facts: When light strikes chlorophyll, some of the electrons in it become excited. These electrons are transferred through a series of reactions that result in the creation of high-energy molecules. The high energy molecules are then used to form short-chain sugar molecules, which are assembled into molecules like glucose.

Chapter 9 Mastery Test A
Part A 1. D **2.** B **3.** D **4.** D **5.** A **Part B 6.** interphase **7.** sister chromatids **8.** centromere **9.** embryo **10.** ovulation **Part C 11.** C **12.** E **13.** A **14.** D **15.** B **Part D 16.** During crossing over, homologous chromosomes trade pieces of DNA. **17.** Haploid cells contain one set of chromosomes and diploid cells contain two

sets. **18.** The end result of meiosis I is two cells, each of which contains two copies of the same chromosomes. **19.** The end result of meiosis II is four cells, each of which contains one copy of the same chromosomes. **20.** Both the male and female reproductive systems contain gametes and are regulated by hormones.
Part E 21. Answers will vary but should include some of these facts: After an egg is fertilized, it begins undergoing mitotic cell divisions. Through the process of mitosis, the fertilized egg develops into a zygote which continues to form a fully developed human.
22. Answers will vary but should include some of these facts: Male gametes are formed by meiosis. In males, the process is called spermatogenesis. Spermatogonia, which are diploid cells, produce haploid sperm. **Part F 23.** Answers will vary, but students' paragraphs should include some of these facts: Mitosis and meiosis are two forms of cell division. Somatic cells undergo mitosis to create two new cells that are exactly like the parent. Cells made in mitosis are diploid and are created for growth and repair. The only cells that undergo meiosis are cells that form gametes, the egg and sperm. The diploid cells that become gametes are oocytes and spermatogonia. **24.** Answers will vary, but students' paragraphs should include some of these facts: The stages of mitosis include interphase, prophase, metaphase, anaphase, and telophase. During interphase, a cell grows and makes copies of its DNA. During prophase, spindle fibers develop that will move chromosomes. In metaphase, chromosomes line up in the center of the cell. In anaphase, chromosomes are pulled toward opposite ends of the dividing cell. In telophase, chromosomes reach their destinations and nuclear membranes form around them to create two new cells.

Chapter 9 Mastery Test B
Part A 1. C **2.** D **3.** A **4.** E **5.** B **Part B 6.** In interphase, the cell grows and makes copies of the chromosomes. **7.** The phases of mitosis are interphase, prophase, metaphase, anaphase, and telophase. **8.** During metaphase, chromosomes line up in the middle of the cell. **9.** Cells that result from mitosis are diploid. Before cell division, chromosomes make copies. **10.** Homologous chromosomes trade pieces of DNA. **Part C 11.** B **12.** C **13.** D **14.** C **15.** D **Part D 16.** cytokinesis **17.** ovulation **18.** tetrad **19.** menstruation **20.** spindle **Part E 21.** Answers will vary but, should include some of these facts: The purpose of mitosis is to produce cells for growth and repair. Somatic cells such as skin and muscle can undergo mitosis. For example, skin cells are continuously shed. Replacement skin cells are made by mitosis.
22. Answers will vary, but should include some of these facts: The purpose of meiosis is to produce gametes for production. Oocytes in females undergo meiosis to result in eggs. Spermatogonia in males undergo meiosis to produce sperm. **Part F 23.** Answers will vary, but students' paragraphs should include some of these facts: A male gamete forms in the testes. Spermatogonia in the testes undergo meiosis, also called spermatogenesis. The sperm develop in the seminiferous tubules, then travel down the vas deferens to the urethra. The penis delivers sperm into the female's vagina during ejaculation. Sperm fuse with the egg in the process of fertilization.
24. Answers will vary, but students' paragraphs should include some of these facts: Egg and sperm combine in fertilization to produce a zygote. The zygote undergoes cell divisions and forms a hollow ball called an embryo. By nine weeks, the embryo has developed into a fetus. The fetus develops in the female's body over a period of nine months. When the fetus reaches full size, it and the placenta are pushed out of the body by contractions of the uterus and vagina.

Chapter 10 Mastery Test A
Part A 1. tt **2.** tall **3.** homozygous **4.** medium height **5.** TT **Part B 6.** D **7.** C **8.** A **9.** E **10.** B **Part C 11.** F_1 generation **12.** law of segregation **13.** dominant trait **14.** Y **15.** X **Part D 16.** B **17.** C **18.** B **19.** C **20.** D **Part E 21.** Answers will vary, but should include some of these facts: A dominant gene is one that masks the effects of a recessive gene. It always shows up. A recessive gene will only show if the dominant gene is not present. **22.** Answers will vary, but should include some of these facts: Hemophilia is considered to be sex linked because it is carried on the X chromosome. Because of its location on the X chromosome, males only receive one gene for blood clotting. If they receive the recessive gene, they show the disease hemophilia. **Part F 23.** Answers will vary, but students' paragraphs should include some of these facts: Mendel's work helped explain the way traits are inherited. He showed how traits that disappeared in one generation showed up in the next generation. He also explained dominant and recessive genes and wrote the laws of segregation and independent assortment to explain how traits are distributed as they pass from one generation to another. **24.** Answers will vary, but students' paragraphs should include some of these facts: Chromosomes are the materials on which traits are inherited. Traits are the expression of genes, and genes are portions of long DNA molecules. Individual DNA molecules contain hundreds of traits. In the cell, a DNA molecule makes up a chromosome.

Chapter 10 Mastery Test B
Part A 1. The Y chromosome determines the sex of an offspring. The Y chromosome produces chemicals found in males.
2. Mendel studied pea plants to understand how traits are passed from one generation to the next. **3.** In simple dominance, a dominant trait hides the presence of a recessive trait. In codominance, both traits are expressed. **4.** The law of segregation says that pairs of homologous chromosomes pull apart in meiosis. An organism has two genes for each trait, one inherited from each parent. **5.** Hemophilia is carried on the X chromosome.
Part B 6. black **7.** bb **8.** white **9.** black **10.** gray **Part C 11.** D **12.** B **13.** A **14.** B **15.** A **Part D 16.** B **17.** D **18.** E **19.** A **20.** C **Part E 21.** Answers will vary, but should include some of these facts: Most sex-linked traits are recessive traits carried on the X chromosome. Since females have two X chromosomes, one usually carries the dominant trait. Males only have one X chromosome. If that chromosome carries the recessive trait, it will be expressed.
22. Answers will vary, but should include some of these facts: Blood type is inherited as a multiple allele. Alleles A and B are codominant, so if they are present both will be expressed. Allele O is recessive so is only expressed if A and B are not present. **Part F 23.** Answers will vary, but students' paragraphs should include some of these facts: Mendel experimented with pea plants to learn how traits are passed from parent to offspring. He crossed pure-breeding plants, such as tall plants and short plants, and analyzed their offspring for at least two generations. From this work he concluded that an organism has two genes for each trait, one from each parent, and that the genes assort independently. **24.** Answers will vary, but students' paragraphs should include some of these facts: Phenotype is dependent on genotype. Genotype refers to the actual genes of an organism, the combination of traits on the DNA. The expression of those genes is the phenotype. A change in genotype would result in a change in phenotype.

Chapter 11 Mastery Test A
Part A 1. D **2.** C **3.** B **4.** E **5.** A **Part B 6.** bacteriophage **7.** B lymphocytes **8.** antigen **9.** mRNA **10.** biotechnologist
Part C 11. C **12.** B **13.** C **14.** B **15.** D **Part D 16.** Transfer RNA carries amino acids to the ribosome. It places the amino acid in the right position by matching to a codon on mRNA. **17.** DNA polymerase adds new nucleotides to a growing strand of DNA. **18.** A virus is made of a nucleic acid and a protein capsid. **19.** Nondisjunction of chromosomes 21 results in Downs syndrome. **20.** A mutation is a change in DNA. **Part E 21.** Answers will vary, but should include some of these facts: During transcription, a double strand of DNA opens. A strand of mRNA is made from one side of the DNA. The mRNA leaves the nucleus and enters the cytoplasm. This mechanism moves information stored on DNA into the cytoplasm where it can be used to manufacture proteins. **22.** Answers will vary, but should include some of these facts: DNA is a double-stranded molecule in the shape of a double helix. The long, connecting sides of the strand are made of chains of negatively-charged sugar and phosphate. The middle portion of the molecule is made of paired nitrogenous bases.
Part F 23. Answers will vary but, students' paragraphs should include some of these facts: The skin and mucus membrane help keep it from entering the body. If the pathogen does enter the body, the nonspecific defense system attacks the it first. Phagocytes come to the site of infection and consume infected cells. Compliment proteins break up the infected cells. The specific defense system creates T cells and B cells to further fight the infection. B cells produce antibodies to the specific antigen on the pathogen. T cells help destroy infected cells. **24.** Answers will vary, but students' paragraphs should include some of these facts: When a virus enters a host cell, it can go into the lytic or lysogenic cycle. In the lytic cycle, the virus uses the host cell to make new viral parts. Eventually the host cell is destroyed and the viral parts released. In the lysogenic cycle, the virus hides in the host's DNA.

Chapter 11 Mastery Test B
Part A 1. D **2.** C **3.** B **4.** B **5.** B **Part B 6.** memory cells **7.** template **8.** specific defense **9.** DNA ligase **10.** compliment proteins
Part C 11. C **12.** D **13.** A **14.** E **15.** B **Part D 16.** A mutation is a change in DNA. **17.** A virus is made up of a nucleic acid inside a protein capsid. **18.** Transfer RNAs carry amino acids to ribosomes. **19.** Downs syndrome is caused by nondisjunction of chromosome 21 during meiosis. **20.** DNA polymerase adds new nucleotides to a growing strand of DNA. **Part E 21.** Answers will vary, but should include some of these facts: DNA carries instructions for making proteins. In this way, DNA controls the cell's activities. For example, one protein produced by some cells is insulin. DNA carries the instructions for making insulin. **22.** Answers will vary, but should include some of these facts: A change in DNA can result in a change in the protein product. The changed product may not be functional. If the protein does not function properly, it may cause problems for the body. **Part F 23.** Answers will vary, but students' paragraphs should include some of these facts: Transcription and translation are two steps in protein production. During transcription, a strand of mRNA is made from DNA. The strand travels to a ribosome. tRNAs carry amino acids to the strand and assemble them in a specific order. The growing chain of amino acids forms a protein. **24.** Answers will vary, but students' paragraphs should include some of these facts: The nonspecific immune system attacks all invading particles and reduces the number of antigens that are able to activate the specific immune system. The nonspecific defense includes the skin and mucus membranes, which keep particles out of the body. If these are breached, compliment proteins punch holes in pathogens and phagocytes surround and destroy them.

Chapter 12 Mastery Test A
Part A 1. C **2.** D **3.** E **4.** A **5.** B **Part B 6.** C **7.** B **8.** A **9.** C **10.** C
Part C 11. axon **12.** pituitary gland **13.** optic nerve **14.** eardrum **15.** adrenaline **Part D 16.** The presence of hormone sends a signal to the gland to stop production. **17.** Voluntary muscle can be controlled by conscious thought, but involuntary muscle cannot. **18.** Cardiovascular diseases are conditions of the heart and circulatory system. **19.** Red blood cells are made in red bone marrow. **20.** The brain stem controls automatic functions like heart rate and breathing. **Part E 21.** Answers will vary but should include some of these facts: When an impulse reaches the end of a neuron, it cannot travel directly to the next neuron. There is a gap between the two. The neuron releases a chemical called a neurotransmitter. The impulse travels across the gap on the chemical. **22.** Answers will vary but should include some of these facts: The liver produces bile, which is stored in the gallbladder. During digestion, the gallbladder releases bile into the small intestine. The liver also takes up glucose from the blood when it is abundant and stores it as glycogen. When the blood is low in glucose, the liver releases it. **Part F 23.** Answers will vary, but students' paragraphs should include some of these facts: Food begins its trip through the digestive system when it is ingested. Food travels from the mouth to the pharynx, down the esophagus, to the stomach, to the small intestine. The small intestine is covered with tiny protrusions called villi. Nutrients from food are absorbed through the villi and enter directly into the bloodstream. **24.** Answers will vary, but students' paragraphs should include some of these facts: The eight body systems include the circulatory system, respiratory system, nervous system, digestive system, reproductive system, endocrine system, skeletal and muscular system, and excretory system. The circulatory system transports food and oxygen to cells and takes away wastes and carbon dioxide. The respiratory system takes in oxygen and expels carbon dioxide. The nervous system controls and coordinates the behavior of other systems. The digestive system takes in and breaks down food into nutrients. The reproductive system makes gametes, and in females it provides a place for development. The endocrine system makes hormones that help control the functions of cells and organs. The skeletal and muscular systems support and protect organs and provide movement. The excretory system removes wastes from the body.

Chapter 12 Mastery Test B
Part A 1. C **2.** B **3.** D **4.** C **5.** A **Part B 6.** C **7.** A **8.** D **9.** E **10.** B
Part C 11. The nose warms, humidifies, and cleans air before it enters the rest of the respiratory system. **12.** Oxygen diffuses across the walls of the alveolus and capillary to enter the blood. **13.** Urine is a liquid waste produced by the kidneys. **14.** Fibrinogen is a protein that helps blood clot. **15.** Plasma is the liquid part of blood.
Part D 16. perspiration **17.** epidermis **18.** chime **19.** spinal cord **20.** antidiuretic hormone **Part E 21.** Answers will vary, but should include some of these facts: Blood leaves the right ventricle of the heart through arteries. The aorta and other arteries carry blood that is high in oxygen to the body. Blood travels through capillaries where it delivers oxygen and food to interstitial fluid. Capillaries join

to form veins, which carry blood back to the heart. Two large veins are the superior and inferior vena cavae. The blood enters the right atrium and is pumped into the right ventricle. It leaves the ventricle and travels to the lung where it picks up oxygen. Oxygenated blood travels into the left atrium, then the left ventricle. From there it is pumped to the body again. **22.** Answers will vary, but should include some of these facts: The reproductive system is dependent on all other body systems. Other body systems remove waste products and supply food, oxygen, and hormones. The nervous system enables the reproductive system to communicate with the rest of the body. Without all of the other body systems, the reproductive system could not function. **Part F 23.** Answers will vary, but students' paragraphs should include some of these facts: Nutrients in food reach cells through the combined work of the digestive and circulatory systems. Food enters the mouth and travels through the digestive system where it is broken down into nutrients. Nutrients diffuse across villi into the blood stream, which carries them to cells. **24.** Answers will vary, but students' paragraphs should include some of these facts: The nervous system and endocrine systems control the body. The nervous system takes in information from the body and the environment. After processing the information, the nervous system responds appropriately by sending out impulses. Much of the nervous system's work is to coordinate body functions. The endocrine system also responds to the body, but instead of impulses it sends out hormones. Hormones travel in the blood to target cells or organs where they cause something to happen.

Chapter 13 Mastery Test A
Part A 1. C **2.** D **3.** E **4.** A **5.** B **Part B 6.** A **7.** C **8.** D **9.** A **10.** B **Part C 11.** Microevolution is the minor change in allele frequencies in a population over a few generations. **12.** The fossil record is a history or diary of life on the earth based on fossils in sedimentary rocks. **13.** Descent with modification states that more recent species are changed descendants of earlier species. **14.** Evolutionary biology is the study of genetic changes within and among populations of organisms. **15.** A gene pool is made up of all of the genes found in a population. **Part D 16.** geologic time **17.** vertebrates **18.** extinction **19.** recombination **20.** artificial selection **Part E 21.** Answers will vary, but should include some of these facts: New species come from old species that become reproductively isolated form one another. **22.** Answers will vary, but should include some of these facts: Evidence that supports evolution includes fossils, anatomy, molecular biology, and biogeography. Fossils are usually found in sedimentary rock. By examining fossils, scientists can see how organisms have changed over time. The anatomy of many organisms is similar, suggesting a common ancestor. The molecular biology of closely related organisms is similar. Biogeography helps explain the distribution of present day organisms and their ancestors. **Part F 23.** Answers will vary, but students' paragraphs should include some of these facts: The theory of natural selection states that individuals in a populations with traits best suited for the environment survive and increase in number. These individuals pass their traits on to offspring. As the population acquires more traits that help it survive, it adapts to the environment. **24.** Answers will vary, but students' paragraphs should include some of these facts: Mendel showed how characteristics are passed from parent to offspring. The work of Mendel made it possible for Darwin to show that the genes passed down could change over periods of time, depending on the environmental conditions.

Chapter 13 Mastery Test B
Part A 1. descent with modification **2.** radioisotope **3.** microevolution **4.** extinction **5.** fossils **Part B 6.** D **7.** A **8.** E **9.** C **10.** B **Part C 11.** A **12.** C **13.** A **14.** D **15.** B **Part D 16.** An acquired trait is a trait caused by the behavior of an organism. **17.** New species develop when populations within the species are reproductively isolated. **18.** The theory of natural selection states that individuals best suited for the environment survive and produce offspring. **19.** During recombination, alleles on genes exchange places or shuffle so that every sperm and egg contains a unique mixture of genes. **20.** According to the theory of common descent, species that exist today are descendants of earlier species. **Part E 21.** Answers will vary, but should include some of these facts: Homologous structures are body parts of different animals that are similar in structure. The function of the limb differs in each animal. However, the similar structure suggests that the animals may have had a common ancestor. **22.** Answers will vary, but should include some of these facts: The theory of plate tectonics says that the earth's crust is made of several, moveable plates. The plates move slowly, over millions of years. The study of plate tectonics lead to the theory of continental drift. In 1912, Wegener stated that at one time all of the continents were one big land mass. The continents have been slowly separating for millions of years. **Part F 23.** Answers will vary, but students' paragraphs should include some of these facts: Changes in genes pools occur through mutation and genetic drift. Mutations are random changes in DNA. They provide new genetic variation in a species. A mutation can be helpful or harmful. Helpful mutations improve the chances of survival and are passed on to offspring. Genetic drift refers to the random changes that occur in the gene pool of a small population. These changes can result in the loss of gene variety. Genetic drift may be pronounced after a disaster that removes alleles from the population. **24.** Answers will vary, but students' paragraphs should include some of these facts: Fossils provide scientists with evidence for evolution in several ways. The location of fossils in sedimentary rock can be used for relative dating. Fossil in older rocks lived before fossils in younger rocks. Radioisotopes in the rock help with absolute dating. Radioisotopes are unstable elements that break apart to form new elements at a precise rate. By comparing fossils to living organisms, scientists can find similarities and differences that give clues about ancestry.

Chapter 14 Mastery Test A
Part A 1. C **2.** B **3.** C **4.** A **5.** D **Part B 6.** D **7.** C **8.** A **9.** B **10.** E **Part C 11.** Yes. Organisms in the same class are in the same phylum since a phylum is a broader classification than a class. **12.** The most common cause of extinction today is loss of habitat. **13.** The seven levels of the Linnaeus classification system are kingdom, phylum, class, order, family, genus, and species. **14.** Organisms that are reproductively isolated were once able to mate, but now cannot do so. **15.** Speciation is the development of a new species from an existing species. **Part D 16.** morphology **17.** genus **18.** community **19.** mammary glands **20.** punctuated equilibrium **Part E 21.** Answers will vary, but should include some of these facts: Punctuated equilibrium is a theory that states species stay the same for long periods of time, then new species evolve suddenly due to global changes and mass extinctions. Examples may vary, but could include the four periods of global warming in the earth's past. **22.** Answers will vary, but should include some of these facts: A dramatic environmental change, such as global warming or the

impact of a comet, could alter the environment so much that organisms can no longer survive. Comets may have hit the earth 250 million years ago and again 65 million years ago. The comets caused the crust to move and volcanoes to erupt. Gases and dust in the air blocked sunlight. Plants and animals died. **Part F 23.** Answers will vary, but students' paragraphs should include some of these facts: Sympatric and allopatric speciation are two mechanisms of speciation. Allopatric speciation means that similar organisms cannot interbreed because of a physical barrier that separates them. The barrier could be a river, canyon, or some other geography. Sympatric speciation occurs when a subpopulation can no longer interbreed with the main population because of differences in behavior. **24.** Answers will vary, but students' paragraphs should include some of these facts: When the size of a population gets very small, the genetic health of the group suffers. In a population of less than 100, harmful mutations show up more often than they do in larger populations. Death can result. A population of less than 50 is in danger of suffering from poor genetic health. A healthy population includes 500 individuals or more.

Chapter 14 Mastery Test B

Part A 1. C **2.** A **3.** D **4.** E **5.** B **Part B 6.** C **7.** A **8.** C **9.** A **10.** D **Part C 11.** kingdom **12.** interbreed **13.** reproductively isolated **14.** speciation **15.** species **Part D 16.** Coordinated stasis is a pattern where most species appear at about the same time. **17.** Punctuated equilibrium is a theory that species stay the same for a long time, then new species evolve suddenly due to global changes and mass extinctions. **18.** The three domain system classifies all living things into three broad groups. **19.** Loss of habitat is the most common cause of extinction today. **20.** The biological species concept defines a species as populations that can interbreed and have offspring. **Part E 21.** Answers will vary, but should include some of these facts: Speciation occurs when members of a species become isolated from one another. Allopatric speciation occurs when organisms are separated by physical barriers. Sympatric speciation happens when interbreeding cannot occur because of differences in behavior. **22.** Answers will vary, but should include some of these facts: Linnaeus divided organisms into groups based on physical characteristics. The broadest level is divided into increasing smaller subgroups. The groups in Linnaeus' system include kingdom, phylum, class, order, family, genus, and species. **Part F 23.** Answers will vary, but students' paragraphs should include some of these facts: Instantaneous speciation takes place if a new species forms in a few generations. In one generation, a plant can produce offspring that cannot interbreed with the parental generation. Sympatric speciation can also produce new species in a short time. Fruit flies that breed on one kind of plant cannot interbreed with flies that breed on another kind of plant. **24.** Answers will vary, but students' paragraphs should include some of these facts: In a mass extinction, large numbers of species are killed or die, and the species does not appear again on Earth. A mass extinction can occur after a dramatic change in the environment. One mass extinction took place after a comet hit the earth. The comet caused the earth's crust to move and volcanoes erupted. Sunlight was blocked for years and plants and animals died.

Chapter 15 Mastery Test A

Part A 1. C **2.** E **3.** D **4.** B **5.** A **Part B 6.** D **7.** B **8.** C **9.** A **10.** C **Part C 11.** A chordate embryo has pharyngeal slits, notochord, dorsal nerve, and a tail that goes past the anus. **12.** Fungi are heterotrophs that do not move. They get food by secreting enzymes on dead matter, then absorbing it. **13.** Domain Archaea includes the prokaryotes that are not bacteria, domain Bacteria includes the prokaryotes that are bacteria, and domain Eukarya includes all eukaryotes. **14.** A gymnosperm is a vascular plant that produces seeds but does not have flowers. **15.** A fish's swim bladder helps it move up and down in the water column. **Part D 16.** flagellates **17.** mosses **18.** pollination **19.** vertebrates **20.** slime mold **Part E 21.** Answers will vary, but should include some of these facts: Complete metamorphosis is a process in which an organism changes from a form that does not resemble the adult into the adult form. Frogs undergo complete metamorphosis. A female frog lays eggs that develop into larvae that swim and breathe with gills. Swimming larvae go through stages of development and change into air-breathing, walking adults. **22.** Answers will vary, but should include some of these facts: A cold-blooded animal's body temperature depends on the temperature of the environment. For example, on a cold day, the body temperature of a fish or turtle will be cool. A warm-blooded animal maintains a constant body temperature through metabolism. On a cold day, a warm-blooded animal, such as a dog or bird, will have the same internal temperature that it has on a warm day. **Part F 23.** Answers will vary, but students' paragraphs should include some of these facts: Animals that show radial symmetry are round, and their bodies resemble the spokes of a wheel. A jellyfish or hydra is has radial symmetry. The bodies of animals with bilateral symmetry are the same on the left and right halves. Examples include worms, mollusks, crustaceans, insects, and all vertebrates. **24.** Answers will vary, but students' paragraphs should include some of these facts: Vascular and nonvascular plants have some similarities as well as differences. Nonvascular plants do not have tissue designed to carry food and water, so they are small. Their method of reproduction is spores. Moss is a nonvascular plant. Vascular plants have tube-like vascular tissue that carries food and water. The plants are larger. Some reproduce with spores (ferns) while others reproduce with seeds (angiosperms, gymnosperms).

Chapter 15 Mastery Test B

Part A 1. heterotroph **2.** mycelium **3.** taxonomy **4.** molting **5.** metamorphosis **Part B 6.** B **7.** C **8.** E **9.** A **10.** D **Part C 11.** In complete metamorphosis, the young animal does not look like the parent. In incomplete metamorphosis, the young animal resembles the parent, but is smaller. **12.** Warm-blooded animals include any birds and mammals. They maintain their body temperature with the heat of their metabolism **13.** Human have larger brains to body mass, have developed culture, and show bipedal locomotion. **14.** Taxonomists classify organisms by how they are alike and their evolutionary features. **15.** The four groups of eukarya are protists, fungi, plants, and animals. **Part D 16.** A **17.** A **18.** C **19.** B **20.** D **Part E 21.** Answers will vary, but should include some of these facts: Nonvascular plants lack vascular tissue, so they cannot move food and water through their systems. They are usually small plants that reproduce with spores. Vascular plants do have tissue for transporting food and water, so they grow larger. Some reproduce with spores and others reproduce with seeds.

22. Answers will vary, but should include some of these facts: The highest level of classification is the domain. The three domains are bacteria, archaea, and eukarya. Bacteria are small prokaryotes, like those in soil. Archaea are small prokaryotes that live in extreme conditions. Eukarya are eukaryotic cells, and include all other organisms. **Part F 23.** Answers will vary, but students' paragraphs should include some of these facts: The two types of vascular tissue in plants are xylem and phloem. Both are tube-shaped tissues that transport materials. After leaves manufacture food, phloem carries the food to all other parts of the plant. Xylem carries the water and minerals taken up by roots to the rest of the plant. **24.** Answers will vary, but students' paragraphs should include some of these facts: Plants have male and female reproductive structures. The male structure, the stamen, includes the pollen-making anther and filament. The female structure, the pistil, includes the stigma. Fertilization occurs during pollination, when pollen on the anther is transferred to the stigma.

Chapter 16 Mastery Test A
Part A 1. B **2.** A **3.** C **4.** A **5.** D **Part B 6.** fixed action pattern **7.** mimicry **8.** agonistic interaction **9.** prey **10.** metacommunication **Part C 11.** D **12.** B **13.** A **14.** E **15.** C **Part D 16.** Warning coloration is bright colors or patterns that warn predators of danger. **17.** Dogs show matched submission when a submissive dog turns its stomach up to a dominant one. **18.** Bird song involves learned and innate behaviors. **19.** Pheromones are used in communication. **20.** Territorial behavior helps an animal defend an area. **Part E 21.** Answers will vary, but should include some of these facts: Innate behavior is inherited and does not have to be learned. Animals are born with innate behavior. Learned behavior is gained through observing and learning. Animals both invent and learn new ways to behave. **22.** Answers will vary, but should include some of these facts: The hatchling chicks would imprint on the turkey, and follow it everywhere. Imprinting is a type of learned behavior that increases the chances of survival of young birds. **Part F 23.** Answers will vary, but students' paragraphs should include some of these facts: Parental care behavior, courtship behavior, and defensive behavior are all innate animal behaviors. Parental care behavior ensures that young animals will survive. One type of parental care is feeding. Courtship behavior is designed to attract mates and ensure that animals mate with members of their own species. Defensive behaviors are strategies for avoiding or defending against predators. They can be aggressive acts. **24.** Answers will vary, but students' paragraphs should include some of these facts: Communication is sending information. Animals communicate through actions, smells, and sounds when they interact or exhibit social behavior. Actions include agonistic interaction and matched submission. Smells can be pheromones, chemicals produced in scent glands. Sounds include warnings and mating calls.

Chapter 16 Mastery Test B
Part A 1. cognition **2.** cooperation **3.** competitor **4.** social biologist **5.** predator **Part B 6.** B **7.** A **8.** C **9.** D **10.** A **Part C 11.** An internal stimulus comes from within an animal, such as a feeling of hunger. **12.** One example of spatial learning is the ability of wasps to remember the locations of their nests. **13.** Behavior is the way an organism acts. **14.** Warning coloration tells predators to stay away. **15.** An ethologist studies the behaviors of animals. **Part D 16.** C **17.** D **18.** A **19.** E **20.** B **Part E 21.** Answers will vary, but should include some of these facts: In imprinting, an animal bonds with the first thing it sees. Newly hatched chicks imprint on their mother and follow her. **22.** Answers will vary, but should include some of these facts: Social behavior refers to the interactions among animals. Examples could include cooperation, aggression, agonistic interaction, and matched submission. **Part F 23.** Answers will vary, but students' paragraphs should include some of these facts: Animals communicate in several ways: actions, smells, and sounds. Examples could include showing teeth, producing pheromones, and barking. Signals may be used to change the way another animal is acting. Birds give signals through songs to tell competitors to stay away. Offspring give begging signals to parents to be fed. Honeybees perform dances to show the way to food. Alarm signals tell other members of the group to hide. Metacommunication signals change the meaning of following signals. **24.** Answers will vary, but students' paragraphs should include some of these facts: Courtship behavior and territorial behavior are two forms on innate behavior. Both help animals survive and reproduce. The purpose of courtship behavior is to find a mate of the correct species. The purpose of territorial behavior is to defend an area where an animal plans to search for food, mate, and raise young.

Chapter 17 Mastery Test A
Part A 1. camouflage **2.** interact **3.** biomes **4.** boom-bust cycle **5.** biosphere **Part B 6.** A trophic structure refers to the feeding relationships in a community. **7.** During emigration, organisms leave a population. In immigration, organisms move into a population. **8.** Parasitism occurs when one organism feeds on another organism. **9.** Organisms that need the same resources are in competition. **10.** The carrying capacity is the largest density of a population that an ecosystem can support. **Part C 11.** C **12.** B **13.** C **14.** A **15.** B **Part D 16.** E **17.** D **18.** A **19.** C **20.** B **Part E 21.** Answers will vary, but should include some of these facts: Density-dependent factors are resources like food and water that can limit population growth. Large populations have access to fewer density-dependent factors than small ones. Density-independent factors affect population size, but do not depend on the number of organisms in the population. Fires, freezes, and floods are examples. **22.** Answers will vary, but should include some of these facts: A disturbance is a large change in a community. Examples of disturbances include natural disasters like hurricanes or flooding and man-made disasters like toxic spills. **Part F 23.** Answers will vary, but students' paragraphs should include some of these facts: Both primary and secondary succession are processes of change in communities. Changes may be good or bad. Some destroy all habitats, but others open new niches and resources. Primary succession occurs when organisms move into a lifeless environment and change it. For example, a new island created by a volcanic eruption will show bacteria, lichens, and fungi on its surface after a few months. Secondary succession occurs after a change in a population of an established community. An example is a forest fire that removes populations of trees. Shortly after the fire, new plants will appear. **24.** Answers will vary, but students' paragraphs should include some of these facts: Symbiosis is a close relationship between two organisms. Symbiotic relationships include parasitism, mutualism, and commensalism. In parasitism, one organism lives on another and damages it. A flea and dog have a parasitic relationship. In mutualism, two organisms living together help each other. A clown fish and sea anemone have a mutualistic relationship. In commensalism, one organism is helped and the other is neither helped nor harmed. Mistletoe on a tree is an example of commensalism.

Chapter 17 Mastery Test B

Part A 1. Camouflage is colors and patterns that help an animal blend in. An example is the stripes of a zebra. **2.** Symbiosis is a close relationship between organisms. The parasitic relationship of a deer and tick is a close one. **3.** Their relationship is mutualism. Each organism helps and supports the other. **4.** A natural disturbance might be a hurricane, flood, or fire. A man-made disturbance could be a toxic spill or digging. **5.** A predator is an organism that eats another species. A lion is an example of a predator. **Part B 6.** C **7.** A **8.** D **9.** E **10.** B **Part C 11.** immigration **12.** biomes **13.** carrying capacity **14.** population density **15.** biosphere **Part D 16.** D **17.** B **18.** C **19.** A **20.** D **Part E 21.** Answers will vary, but should include some of these facts: Density-dependent factors include those things that are affected by the population size, such as food and water. Density-independent factors are not affected by population size. Examples include fire, flood, and earthquake. **22.** Answers will vary, but should include some of these facts: Parasitism, mutualism, and commensalism are examples of symbiosis, or close relationships between individuals. They are different in that in parasitism, one organism is helped and the other harmed. In mutualism, both organisms are helped. In commensalism, one is helped and the other is neither helped nor harmed. **Part F 23.** Answers will vary, but students' paragraphs should include some of these facts: The five levels of organization in the environment are biosphere, ecosystem, community, population, and organism. The biosphere is all parts of the earth that support living things. An ecosystem is made up of living and nonliving parts of the environment in an area. A community is a group of different populations in an area. A population is a group of the same species in an area. **24.** Answers will vary, but students' paragraphs should include some of these facts: Two types of succession in communities are primary succession and secondary succession. Primary succession takes place when organisms move into an area that has not been inhabited, like cooled volcanic rock or soil exposed by a glacier. In secondary succession, one or more populations are wiped out in a community. Their departure makes it possible for different organisms to move in. A fire might take out all of the trees in a forest, but leave room for shrubs and grasses.

Chapter 18 Mastery Test A

Part A 1. D **2.** E **3.** A **4.** B **5.** C **Part B 6.** B **7.** D **8.** A **9.** D **10.** C **Part C 11.** Marine **12.** atmosphere **13.** energy **14.** estuary **15.** primary productivity **Part D 16.** The sun's energy is captured by phototrophs and passed on to chemotrophs. **17.** Two types of aquatic biomes are lakes and estuaries. **18.** Answers may vary, but should include three of the following: nitrogen, phosphorous, carbon, and water. **19.** Plant-like plankton are phototrophs that capture the sun's energy. **20.** There is no light in the aphotic zone, so plants cannot carry out photosynthesis there. **Part E 21.** Answers will vary, but should include some of these facts: Terrestrial ecosystems are located on land and contain living and nonliving parts. Terrestrial ecosystems can be found among forests, grasslands, deserts, and other ecosystems. **22.** Answers will vary, but should include some of these facts: Energy cycles through an ecosystem. It travels from phototrophs, or producers, to chemotrophs, or consumers, then on to decomposers. Nutrients cycle between the living and nonliving parts of the ecosystem. **Part F 23.** Answers will vary, but students' paragraphs should include some of these facts: Ecosystems contain at least three trophic levels: producers, consumers, and decomposers. Producers are green organisms that can capture the sun's energy. Consumers cannot capture energy, so they get the energy they need by eating producers or other consumers. Decomposers break down the molecules in decaying matter. **24.** Answers will vary, but students' paragraphs should include some of these facts: Water travels in a cycle through the living and nonliving parts of an ecosystem. Living things consume water. The sun's energy evaporates water from the soil, bodies of water, and living things. In the air, water condenses and falls to the earth as precipitation. The cycle repeats.

Chapter 18 Mastery Test B

Part A 1. A terrestrial biome is one associated with the land. **2.** Permafrost is permanently frozen soil. It is found in the tundra. **3.** The trophic structure of an ecosystem shows the feeding relationships of producers and consumers. **4.** Plants do not grow in the aphotic zone because it is an area where there is no light. **5.** The primary productivity shows the activity level of producers in an ecosystem. **Part B 6.** coniferous forest **7.** temperate forest **8.** tropical forest **9.** desert **10.** tundra **Part C 11.** E **12.** D **13.** A **14.** B **15.** C **Part D 16.** C **17.** A **18.** B **19.** D **20.** B
Part E 21. Answers will vary, but should include some of these facts: Producers capture the sun's energy and use it for themselves. Consumers get the energy in plants by eating them or consumers that eat plants. Decomposers get energy by breaking down plants and consumers when they die. **22.** Answers will vary, but should include some of these facts: A food chain shows the producers, consumers, and decomposers in an ecosystem. It also indicates what consumers eat, and what eats them. **Part F 23.** Answers will vary, but students' paragraphs should include some of these facts: Nitrogen is a nutrient that moves between the living and nonliving parts of the environment. Nitrogen gas is found in the atmosphere. Nitrogen-fixing bacteria convert nitrogen gas to ammonium. Nitrifying bacteria then change ammonium into nitrogen that plants can take up. Animals get this nitrogen when they eat plants. Decomposers take it up when they break down plants and animals. During decomposition, nitrogen gas is released back into the atmosphere. **24.** Answers will vary, but students' paragraphs should include some of these facts: Plants and animals would die. Plants would be affected first, since they depend directly on the sun for energy. After all of the plants are gone, animals, which consume plants and other organisms, would begin to die. Eventually, without a source of food, all living things would die.

Chapter 19 Mastery Test A

Part A 1. C **2.** B **3.** D **4.** A **5.** D **Part B 6.** recovery plan **7.** conservation biology **8.** runoff **9.** ozone **10.** reserves **Part C 11.** E **12.** C **13.** A **14.** B **15.** D **Part D 16.** One way scientists share their findings is by publishing them in scientific journals. **17.** Biodiversity refers to all of the different living things on the earth. **18.** Ecological landscaping helps meet the needs of humans and those of the environment. **19.** Eutrophication, the rapid growth of algae, interferes with the growth of other living things. **20.** Humans are able to find ways to meet their needs. **Part E 21.** Answers will vary, but should include some of these facts: Science and technology are closely related. Science leads to the production of new technology. Technology makes it possible for science to advance. **22.** Answers will vary, but should include some of these facts: Acid rain is formed when sulfur dioxide and other

emission dissolve in water vapor in the air. When it falls on living things, the acidic rain can harm them. **Part F 23.** Answers will vary, but students' paragraphs should include some of these facts: Humans damage the environment in several ways. They create pollutants such as trash that can reduce the quality and quantity of space available to organisms. Some human activities generate emissions which reduce air quality, contribute to acid rain, and damage the ozone layer. Human activities that create runoff cause erosion of soil and loss of vital nutrients. Habitats are lost through such human practices as deforestation and the introduction of alien species.
24. Answers will vary, but students' paragraphs should include some of these facts: Clams and other organisms that expand beyond their natural borders can cause problems for native species. Invasive clams may out-compete the bay species for both food and space. They use the same resources that native species rely on and in some cases can cause the extinction of native organisms.

Chapter 19 Mastery Test B

Part A 1. The human population is growing rapidly because it has an infinite carrying capacity. **2.** The greenhouse effect is the warming of the earth's surface because of heat energy from the sun trapped by a layer of gases. **3.** Science develops the need for new technology. Technology makes it possible for science to make new discoveries. **4.** Products made by humans are destroying the ozone layer. **5.** In construction projects, a landscape ecologist helps blend the needs of humans and those of the environment. **Part B 6.** E
7. A **8.** C **9.** D **10.** B **Part C 11.** ozone **12.** deforestation
13. reserves **14.** medical technology **15.** biodiversity **Part D 16.** B
17. B **18.** B **19.** A **20.** D **Part E 21.** Answers will vary, but should include some of these facts: Fast growing, non-native species can out-compete the native species for food and space. By doing so, the non-natives crowd out the native species. **22.** Answers will vary, but should include some of these facts: Levels of carbon dioxide produced by factories and cars are greater than the earth can handle. These "greenhouse" gases build up to form a layer that heats the surface of the earth. **Part F 23.** Answers will vary, but students' paragraphs should include some of these facts: Humans have created several types of programs to conserve ecosystems, including establishing reserves, creating recovery plans, recycling, and reducing emissions. Reserves are areas that are set aside for non-human use where ecosystems can develop naturally. Recovery plans are strategies for saving endangered organisms. Recycling helps reduce energy consumption and save natural resources and the land in which those resources are located. By reducing emissions, the amount of ecosystem-damaging acid rain is reduced.
24. Answers will vary, but students' paragraphs should include some of these facts: Humans cause pollution in a variety of ways: trash, emissions, chemical runoff, and other air pollutants. Three types of air pollution cause major damage: carbon dioxide production, which that leads to the greenhouse effect; loss of ozone, which filters out harmful radiation from the sun; and production of sulfur dioxide, which combines with water vapor to produce acid rain.

Scoring Rubric for Short-Response Items in Part E of Chapter Mastery Tests

2 points—The student demonstrates a solid understanding of the content by providing:
- a complete set of accurate facts that support the answer
- a clearly stated answer to the question

1 point—The student demonstrates a partial understanding of the content by providing *one* of the following:
- a complete set of accurate facts that support the answer
- a clearly stated answer to the question

0 points—The student fails to demonstrate understanding of the content by doing *one* of the following:
- includes no facts or incorrect facts, and fails to provide a clearly stated answer
- provides no answer at all

Scoring Rubric for Essay Items in Part F of Chapter Mastery Tests

3 points—The student demonstrates a solid understanding of the content by providing:
- a complete set of accurate facts that support the answer
- a clearly stated answer to the essay's primary question
- a standard essay response (topic sentence, body, conclusion)

2 points—The student demonstrates a good understanding of the content by providing *two* of the following:
- a complete set of accurate facts that support the answer
- a clearly stated answer to the essay's primary question
- a standard essay response (topic sentence, body, conclusion)

1 point—The student demonstrates a partial understanding of the content by providing *one* of the following:
- a complete set of accurate facts that support the answer
- a clearly stated answer to the essay's primary question
- a standard essay response (topic sentence, body, conclusion)

0 points—The student fails to demonstrate understanding of the content by doing *one* of the following:
- includes no facts or incorrect facts, fails to answer the essay's primary question, and fails to include a standard essay response (topic sentence, body, conclusion)
- provides no answer at all

Chapters 1–10 Midterm Mastery Test
Part A 1. A 2. B 3. D 4. C 5. D 6. A 7. A 8. D 9. B 10. B 11. D 12. B 13. D 14. C 15. D **Part B** 16. menstruation 17. genetics 18. enzymes 19. Carotenoids 20. Cancer 21. aerobic 22. mitosis 23. lipid 24. electromagnetic spectrum 25. plasma membrane **Part C** 26. When the products of energy production build up, they cause the reaction to slow down or stop. 27. Two nucleic acids, DNA and RNA, contain and translate the information for making protein in cells. 28. During crossing over, two homologous chromosomes exchange pieces of DNA. 29. Water molecules always move from an area of high concentration to one of low concentration. Compared to a salt water environment, there is more water in a cell than in the environment. As a result, water moves out of the cell. 30. Hydrogen contains one proton, one electron, and no neutrons. **Part D** 31. D 32. G 33. J 34. B 35. E 36. H 37. A 38. C 39. F 40. I **Part E 41.** Answers will vary, but should include some of these facts: Prokaryotic cells and eukaryotic cells are similar in many ways. Both contain molecules necessary for the cell to carry out chemical processes within a plasma membrane. In addition, prokaryotic and eukaryotic cells are equipped with DNA and are able to reproduce by mitosis. Of the two, prokaryotic cells are smaller and simpler. Cells of prokaryotes, like bacteria, do no have membranes surrounding their DNA or their organelles. Eukaryotic cells, like those found in humans, have membrane-bound structures. **42.** Answers will vary, but should include some of these facts: DNA is a polymer made of repeating monomers of nucleotides. Each nucleotide contains a nitrogen base, a sugar, and a phosphate group. Strands of DNA are arranged as double helixes. A group of three nitrogen bases forms a codon, which codes for a particular amino acid. The arrangement of codons on DNA determines the proteins that the cell will produce. **Part F 43.** Answers will vary, but students' paragraphs should include some of these facts: The scientific method is a logical way of solving problems. It involves six basic steps: observation, question, hypothesis, experiment, analysis, and communication. The following is one way in which the scientific method could be used to determine whether cup A or cup B is best at keeping a liquid warm: Observation—Fill both cups with hot water and notice that the water in cup A seems to stay warm the longest. Question—Ask the question: Does water in cup A stay warm longer than water in cup B? Hypothesis—State a hypothesis: Water in cup A stays warm longer than water in cup B. Experiment—Pour hot water in both cups and insert thermometers in each. Record the temperature every five minutes for one hour. Analysis—Analyze the data on temperature to decide which cup stays warm for the longest period of time. Communication—Share your results with all of your friends who enjoy warm drinks. **44.** Answers will vary, but students' paragraphs should include some of the following facts: Plant cells carry out cellular respiration and photosynthesis. During photosynthesis, chlorophyll in cells captures the sun's energy, which the plant uses to make glucose. In cellular respiration, the product of photosynthesis (glucose) is broken down through a series of steps to yield ATP. ATP drives all of the activities in the plant cell, including photosynthesis. The products of respiration (carbon dioxide and water vapor) are the raw materials used in photosynthesis.

Final Mastery Test
Part A 1. E 2. J 3. G 4. B 5. I 6. C 7. D 8. H 9. F 10. A **Part B** 11. B 12. C 13. C 14. D 15. A 16. C 17. A 18. C 19. B 20. C 21. C 22. D 23. B 24. C 25. D 26. B 27. C 28. C 29. A 30. B 31. A 32. B 33. C 34. C 35. A **Part C** 36. competitors 37. energy 38. camouflage 39. geologic time 40. predator 41. Ozone 42. atmosphere 43. hydrophobic 44. recovery plan 45. RNA or mRNA 46. antigen 47. ADP 48. carrying capacity 49. vertebrates 50. X **Part D 51.** A biome is a large section of the earth with similar ecosystems and weather. **52.** Living things need energy to carry out life processes. **53.** Fermentation and cellular respiration are two methods of energy production in cells. **54.** The products of photosynthesis are glucose and oxygen. **55.** The fossil record is a history or diary of life on the earth based on fossils in sedimentary rocks. **56.** The theory of natural selection states that the individuals in a population who have traits best suited for the environment are most likely to survive and pass on their traits to offspring. **57.** Ocean plants are found in the photic zone because they need sunlight to carry out photosynthesis. **58.** DNA stores genetic information and instructions for making proteins. **59.** The seven levels of the Linnaeus classification system are kingdom, phylum, class, order, family, genus, and species. **60.** Organisms that are toxic to predators are brightly colored to warn them away. **Part E 61.** Answers will vary, but should include some of the following facts: The greenhouse effect is the warming of the earth's surface caused by a layer of gases trapping heat in the atmosphere. The most common greenhouse gas is carbon dioxide. As the numbers of carbon dioxide-emitting industries and automobiles increase, so does the thickness of the layer of greenhouse gases. Over the last few years, these gases have been trapping more than the usual amount of heat near the earth's surface. **62.** Answers will vary, but should include some of the following facts: Evidence that supports evolution includes fossils, comparative anatomy, molecular biology, and biogeography. Fossils are remains or impressions of organisms that have lived in the past. Many fossils are different from present-day organisms. The anatomy of some organisms, like the wings of birds and flippers of whales, suggests a common ancestor. The molecular biology of closely-related organisms is more similar than of less closely-related organisms. Fossils and living specimens of similar organisms are found on different continents, suggesting similar ancestry before continental drift separated the land masses. **Part F 63.** Answers will vary, but students' paragraphs should include some of the following facts: The sun is the source of energy for all living things in an ecosystem. Energy is taken in by plants, which contain chlorophyll. Through the process of photosynthesis, plants convert the sun's energy into carbohydrates. Living things convert the energy in carbohydrates to ATP, which they use for life processes. Organisms that do not contain chlorophyll must consume other organisms to get energy. When living things die, decomposers break them down and get energy from them. **64.** Answers will vary, but students' paragraphs should include some of the following facts: Food is made of complex molecules that must be broken down into simple nutrients for use by cells. In the mouth, food is broken apart and mixed with saliva. It travels down the esophagus by peristalsis and enters the stomach. In the stomach, acid, digestive enzymes, and muscle contractions further break up the food and form a mixture called chyme. Chyme travels to the small intestine, where it is further digested by enzymes and absorbed into the blood stream.

Scoring Rubric for Short-Response Items in Part E of Midterm and Final Mastery Tests

2 points—The student demonstrates a solid understanding of the content by providing:
- a complete set of accurate facts that support the answer
- a clearly stated answer to the question

1 point—The student demonstrates a partial understanding of the content by providing *one* of the following:
- a complete set of accurate facts that support the answer
- a clearly stated answer to the question

0 points—The student fails to demonstrate understanding of the content by doing *one* of the following:
- includes no facts or incorrect facts, and fails to provide a clearly stated answer
- provides no answer at all

Scoring Rubric for Essay Items in Part F of Midterm and Final Mastery Tests

3 points—The student demonstrates a solid understanding of the content by providing:
- a complete set of accurate facts that support the answer
- a clearly stated answer to the essay's primary question
- a standard essay response (topic sentence, body, conclusion)

2 points—The student demonstrates a good understanding of the content by providing *two* of the following:
- a complete set of accurate facts that support the answer
- a clearly stated answer to the essay's primary question
- a standard essay response (topic sentence, body, conclusion)

1 point—The student demonstrates a partial understanding of the content by providing *one* of the following:
- a complete set of accurate facts that support the answer
- a clearly stated answer to the essay's primary question
- a standard essay response (topic sentence, body, conclusion)

0 points—The student fails to demonstrate understanding of the content by doing *one* of the following:
- includes no facts or incorrect facts, fails to answer the essay's primary question, and fails to include a standard essay response (topic sentence, body, conclusion)
- provides no answer at all

Materials List for Biology: Cycles of Life Lab Manual

This section lists the materials for all the labs that appear in the Biology: Cycles of Life Lab Manual. The quantities of materials listed are enough for one student. Students can do some of these activities in pairs or groups. The Lab Manual worksheets for the Express Labs, Investigations, and Discovery Investigations in the Student Edition are identified in this list.

Chapter 1

Lab Manual 1: Express Lab 1
Express Lab 1
safety goggles; solar cell with small connecting motor

Lab Manual 2: Cycles of Energy
safety goggles; lab coat or apron; one 1-gallon or 2-gallon fish bowl; 4 cups of garden soil (from a garden supply store); 1 sheet of notebook paper; 3–5 earthworms (from a bait and tackle shop); 1 dead plant or dead plant parts (soft plant parts like leaves or fruits instead of stems); $\frac{1}{4}$ cup of water

Lab Manual 3: What Is Life?
Investigation 1
safety goggles; lab coat or apron; houseplant; insect in a jar; mushroom in a plastic bag; petri dish with bacteria culture; plant seeds; plant sprout; rock; flashlight

Lab Manual 4: No More Music
pencil; science notebook

Lab Manual 5: Using the Scientific Method
Discovery Investigation 1
safety goggles; lab coat or apron; 2 plastic cups; 20 corn seeds; water; vinegar; paper towels; eyedropper

Chapter 2

Lab Manual 6: Express Lab 2
Express Lab 2
safety goggles; lab coat or apron; 2 clear plastic cups; plastic spoon; baking soda; water; measuring cup; vinegar

Lab Manual 7: Physical and Chemical Properties
Investigation 2
safety goggles; lab coat or apron; flask; water; hot plate; rusty nail; non-rusty nail; 2 paper clips; hammer; magnet; balance; crucible; magnesium strip

Lab Manual 8: Atomic Model
safety goggles; lab coat or apron; gum drops (in a variety of colors); small marshmallows (in a variety of colors); clay or Playdough (in a variety of colors); paper plates; toothpicks; skewers; glue; tape; scissors

Lab Manual 9: The Properties of Water
Discovery Investigation 2
safety goggles; lab coat or apron; clear plastic cups; sand; water; sugar; salt; spoon; thermometers; heat lamp; eyedropper; pipette; vegetable oil; plastic water bottle; freezer; hot plate; paper towels

Lab Manual 10: Acids and Bases
safety goggles; lab coat or apron; 8 pieces of hydronium test paper; color chart of changes to hydronium test paper; cotton swabs or small pipettes; paper towels; window cleaner (a few drops); shampoo; cola; coffee; vinegar; lemon juice; antacid dissolved in $\frac{1}{4}$ cup water; baking soda dissolved in $\frac{1}{4}$ cup water; sheet of notebook paper; tape

Chapter 3

Lab Manual 11: Studying Dehydration Synthesis
safety goggles; lab coat or apron; Figure A; scissors; tape; notebook paper

Lab Manual 12: Express Lab 3
Express Lab 3
food labels with Nutrition Facts

Lab Manual 13: Amino Acids and Proteins
Investigation 3
safety goggles; lab coat or apron; wax pencil; test tubes; test tube rack; graduated cylinder; distilled water; egg albumin solution; 5% milk solution; 5% starch solution; dropper bottle of biuret solution

Lab Manual 14: Testing for Starches
safety goggles; lab coat or apron; 10 or more small samples of food (such as cheese, bread, raw potato, cooked pasta, luncheon meat, mayonnaise, lettuce, tomato, apple, onion, radish, cucumber, milk); pipette; small bottle of iodine; paper towel

Lab Manual 15: Testing for Lipids
Discovery Investigation 3
safety goggles; lab coat or apron; wax pencil; test tubes; test tube rack; water; vegetable oil; unknown liquid; Sudan III dye solution; methylene blue dye solution

Chapter 4

Lab Manual 16: Express Lab 4
Express Lab 4
safety goggles; lab coat or apron; eyedropper; pond water or hay infusion; microscope slide; coverslip; microscope

Lab Manual 17: Cork Cells
safety goggles; lab coat or apron; microscope; microscope slide; coverslip; razor or scalpel; small piece of cork; eyedropper; water; pen or pencil; paper

Lab Manual 18: Living Cells
Investigation 4
safety goggles; lab coat or apron; 100 mL beaker; sucrose; warm water (38°C to 43°C); glass rod; 1 envelope active dry yeast; eyedropper; microscope slide; dropper bottle of iodine solution; coverslip; microscope

Lab Manual 19: Diffusion
safety goggles; lab coat or apron; 200 mL beaker; dropper bottle of ink or blue dye; water; pen or pencil; paper; watch or clock with a second hand

Lab Manual 20: Osmosis in Cells
Discovery Investigation 4
safety goggles; lab coat or apron; microscope slide; forceps; *Elodea* leaf; dropper bottle of distilled water; coverslip; microscope; dropper bottle of 10% NaCl solution

Chapter 5

Lab Manual 21: Express Lab 5
Express Lab 5
safety goggles; lab coat or apron; medium-sized beaker; warm tap water; vegetable oil

Lab Manual 22: A Day in the Life of a Protein
construction paper; markers or crayons; scissors; modeling clay (about the size of a golf ball); 10–12 thumbtacks

Lab Manual 23: Cells Made of Gelatin
safety goggles; lab coat or apron; 1 self-sealing plastic bag (pint size); 1 envelope of unflavored gelatin; small saucepan; hot pads; measuring cup; spoon; knife; $1\frac{1}{2}$ cups water; hot plate; variety of small fruits or vegetables, dried peas and beans, and uncooked noodles (to represent organelles)

Lab Manual 24: Comparing Plant and Animal Cells
Investigation 5
safety goggles; lab coat or apron; tweezers; onion; glass slide; dropper bottle of iodine solution; coverslip; microscope; prepared slide of human cheek cells

Lab Manual 25: Comparing Plant Cells
Discovery Investigation 5
Elodea plant; safety goggles; lab coat or apron; tweezers; eyedropper; distilled water; glass slide; coverslip; microscope; prepared slide of onion root tip (longitudinal section); prepared slide of corn stem (cross section)

Materials List for Biology: Cycles of Life Lab Manual

Chapter 6
Lab Manual 26: Express Lab 6
Express Lab 6
3 tennis balls; meterstick
Lab Manual 27: The Structure of ATP
patterns in Figure C; scissors; tape
Lab Manual 28: Enzymes in Saliva
Investigation 6
safety goggles; lab coat or apron; wax pencil; 6 test tubes; test tube rack; maltose solution; starch solution; 1% amylase solution; 250 mL beaker; warm water; eyedropper; iodine solution; Benedict's reagent
Lab Manual 29: The Action of an Enzyme
safety goggles; lab coat or apron; piece of liver (about the size of a quarter); 3 test tubes; test tube rack; scalpel or knife; tape or labels; hydrogen peroxide; forceps; hot pads; hot water (200 mL beaker of water warmed on a hot plate); $\frac{1}{2}$ cup of crushed ice; polystyrene cup; timer or clock
Lab Manual 30: How Does pH Affect Stomach Enzymes?
Discovery Investigation 6
safety goggles; lab coat or apron; 6 test tubes; test tube rack; 2% pepsin solution; cool tap water; diluted sodium hydroxide; diluted hydrochloric acid; wax pencil; pieces of boiled egg whites; eyedropper; large beaker; warm water

Chapter 7
Lab Manual 31: Express Lab 7
Express Lab 7
ingredients list from a food label; dictionary or encyclopedia
Lab Manual 32: Products of Cellular Respiration
Investigation 7
safety goggles; lab coat or apron; small beaker; ruler; bromthymol blue; plastic wrap; soda straw
Lab Manual 33: Cabbage Fermentation
safety goggles; lab coat or apron; test tube; test tube rack; $\frac{1}{4}$ cup of shredded cabbage; 100 mL salt (NaCl) solution; pH paper; balloon (to fit over test tube); graph paper
Lab Manual 34: Making ATP Without Oxygen
Discovery Investigation 7
safety goggles; lab coat or apron; large beaker; warm water (38°C to 43°C); large test tube; solution of yeast and sucrose; one-hole rubber stopper with gas delivery tube; small beaker; tap water; limewater
Lab Manual 35: Cellular Respiration in Plants
safety goggles; lab coat or apron; 20 mL bromthymol blue; 5 germinating seeds; 5 boiled seeds; 2 test tubes; 2 stoppers; test tube rack; labels

Chapter 8
Lab Manual 36: Express Lab 8
Express Lab 8
lab coat or apron; 8 paper towels; tap water; 10 bean seeds; 2 containers, such as plastic cups or self-sealing plastic bags
Lab Manual 37: Oxygen Production During Photosynthesis
Investigation 8
safety goggles; lab coat or apron; scissors; 2 *Elodea* sprigs; heavy-duty thread; 2 glass rods; 2 large test tubes; wax pencil; 0.25% sodium bicarbonate (NaHCO$_3$) solution; cooled, boiled distilled water; test tube rack; lamp
Lab Manual 38: Light and Photosynthesis
Discovery Investigation 8
safety goggles; lab coat or apron; large flask; cool tap water; scissors; *Elodea* sprig; heavy-duty thread; glass rod; large test tube; 0.25% sodium bicarbonate (NaHCO$_3$) solution; meterstick; lamp; stopwatch
Lab Manual 39: Leaf Cross Section
prepared slide of leaf cross section; compound microscope

Lab Manual 40: Chlorophyll Chromatography
safety goggles; lab coat or apron; 1 piece of coffee filter paper (or chromatography paper); 5–10 fresh spinach leaves; 15 mL 95% ethanol; pinch of sand; 2 toothpicks; tape; mortar and pestle; 50 mL Erlenmeyer flask and stopper (or small jar with lid); test tube; test tube rack; plastic wrap (enough to cover test tube); ruler; pencil; scissors

Chapter 9
Lab Manual 41: Express Lab 9
Express Lab 9
20 different colored beads; 2 pieces of string or twine; twist tie
Lab Manual 42: Whitefish Mitosis
safety goggles; lab coat or apron; prepared slides of whitefish blastula in mitosis; microscope
Lab Manual 43: Observing Cell Cycle Phases
Investigation 9
safety goggles; lab coat or apron; prepared slide of onion root; microscope
Lab Manual 44: Stages of Mitosis Flip Chart
3 sheets of paper; pen or pencil; markers, paints, or crayons; stapler
Lab Manual 45: Modeling the Movement of Chromosomes
Discovery Investigation 9
lab coat or apron; modeling clay in different colors

Chapter 10
Lab Manual 46: Express Lab 10
Express Lab 10
safety goggles; 2 coins
Lab Manual 47: Using Punnett Squares
Investigation 10
paper; pencil
Lab Manual 48: Probability of Gender
safety goggles; lab coat or apron; notebook; pen or pencil; 2 pennies; masking tape; calculator
Lab Manual 49: Traits Depend on Chromosomes
safety goggles; lab coat or apron; 4 brown pipe cleaners; 4 blue pipe cleaners; 2 small paper bags
Lab Manual 50: Interpreting Pedigrees
Discovery Investigation 10
paper; pencil

Chapter 11
Lab Manual 51: Express Lab 11
Express Lab 11
paper; pen
Lab Manual 52: Modeling DNA
Investigation 11
safety goggles; lab coat or apron; paper models for sugar, phosphate group, cytosine (C), thymine (T), adenine (A), guanine (G); large sheet of paper; tape; wooden craft sticks; ruler
Lab Manual 53: Extracting DNA
safety goggles; lab coat or apron; DNA source ($\frac{1}{2}$ cup of the following: split peas, onion, spinach, chicken liver, calf thymus, or wheat germ); 2 cups ice cold water; pinch of salt (less than $\frac{1}{4}$ teaspoon); pinch of meat tenderizer (less than $\frac{1}{8}$ teaspoon); 2 tablespoons liquid dish washing detergent; 10 mL ice cold 95% ethyl alcohol; blender; teaspoon; tablespoon; measuring cup; test tube; graduated cylinder; 200 mL beaker; strainer; stirring rod; wooden stick (about the size of a stirring rod) or swab
Lab Manual 54: Crime Scene DNA
Figure A; scissors; 2 sheets of $8\frac{1}{2}'' \times 11''$ paper
Lab Manual 55: A Faulty Protein
Discovery Investigation 11
paper; pencil

Materials List for Biology: Cycles of Life Lab Manual

Chapter 12

Lab Manual 56: Express Lab 12
Express Lab 12
food products with nutrition labels

Lab Manual 57: Blood Cells
prepared slide of human blood; microscope

Lab Manual 58: How Exercise Affects Heart Rate
Investigation 12
clock with a second hand; graph paper

Lab Manual 59: Examining the Body Systems of a Grasshopper
safety goggles; lab coat or apron; gloves; preserved grasshopper; dissecting tray; scissors; probe; forceps; eyedropper; small beaker of water

Lab Manual 60: Constructing Models of Human Joints
Discovery Investigation 12
safety goggles; lab coat or apron; assorted materials to model joints such as screws, washers, hinges, ball-like lollipops, bottle caps, craft sticks, pipe cleaners, modeling clay, push pins, glue

Chapter 13

Lab Manual 61: Express Lab 13
Express Lab 13
marker; 3 flat sponges

Lab Manual 62: Dinosaur Tracks
safety goggles; lab coat or apron; outdoor area of sand or soft soil; yardstick; rake; Figure A

Lab Manual 63: Radioactive Dating
safety goggles; lab coat or apron; 10 ice cubes; 2 large paper cups; funnel; graduated cylinder; clock or watch

Lab Manual 64: Natural Selection in Action
Investigation 13
about 50 blue plastic chips; about 50 white plastic chips; blue pencil; red pencil

Lab Manual 65: Tracking Blood Type Alleles
Discovery Investigation 13
Blood Type Allele Chart; coin

Chapter 14

Lab Manual 66: Express Lab 14
Express Lab 14
buttons or other objects

Lab Manual 67: Magnetobacteria
safety goggles; lab coat or apron; about 1 cup of water and sediment from a bay, marsh, lake, or pond; compound microscope; eyedropper; bar magnet; $\frac{1}{2}$ inch rubber O-ring; glass slide; coverslip; petroleum jelly

Lab Manual 68: Natural Selection in Bacteria
Investigation 14
safety goggles; lab coat or apron; gloves; wax pencil; 2 nutrient agar petri dishes; Bunsen burner; inoculation loop; bacteria culture; forceps; antibiotic disk

Lab Manual 69: Plant Evolution
Discovery Investigation 14
safety goggles; lab coat or apron; moss plant; fern plant; coniferous tree branch; flowering tree branch

Lab Manual 70: Bird Adaptations
safety goggles; lab coat or apron; chopsticks (1 set); tongs; straw; plastic fork; stopwatch or clock with a second hand; $\frac{1}{2}$ cup of birdseed; aluminum pie pan; 5 paper cups

Chapter 15

Lab Manual 71: Express Lab 15
Express Lab 15
pictures of pets

Lab Manual 72: Classifying Organisms
Investigation 15
pictures of different organisms

Lab Manual 73: Lichens Up Close
safety goggles; lab coat or apron; scissors; samples of several different kinds of lichens; forceps; slide; eyedropper; water; notebook; dissecting microscope; colored pencils

Lab Manual 74: Earthworm Dissection
safety goggles; lab coat or apron; gloves; preserved earthworm; dissection tray; dissecting needle; dissecting pins; forceps; scalpel; scissors; probe; hand lens

Lab Manual 75: Using a Dichotomous Key
Discovery Investigation 15
dichotomous key; specimens or photos of several insects

Chapter 16

Lab Manual 76: Express Lab 16
Express Lab 16
3 copies of a maze puzzle; stopwatch or clock with a second hand

Lab Manual 77: Investigating Animal Behavior
Investigation 16
safety goggles; lab coat or apron; shoebox and lid; scissors; 6 paper towels; tap water; 10 sow bugs; small lamp

Lab Manual 78: Planarian Behavior
safety goggles; lab coat or apron; stopwatch; 20 cc syringe (without a needle); petri dish; spring or pond water to fill petri dish; planarian; small paint brush

Lab Manual 79: Exploring Human Communication
Discovery Investigation 16
index cards

Lab Manual 80: Crickets Are Territorial
safety goggles; lab coat or apron; 2 adult male crickets; 2 plastic cups; 2 small pieces of aluminum foil; 10 gallon aquarium; clock or watch; pencil

Chapter 17

Lab Manual 81: Predators and Prey
200 squares of red construction paper, each about one inch; 50 squares of green construction paper, each about three inches by three inches; graph paper; red pencil; green pencil

Lab Manual 82: Express Lab 17
Express Lab 17
6 index cards; six-sided number cube; 30 buttons

Lab Manual 83: Estimating Population Size
Investigation 17
small paper bag containing dried navy beans; red wax pencil

Lab Manual 84: Surveying an Ecological Community
Discovery Investigation 17
heavy gloves; meterstick; 4 wood stakes; string; green, blue, brown, black, orange pencils or markers

Lab Manual 85: Owl Pellets
safety goggles; lab coat or apron; owl pellet; small bowl of water; probe; forceps; newspaper

Chapter 18

Lab Manual 86: Express Lab 18
Express Lab 18
3 index cards; marker; photographs of organisms

Lab Manual 87: Building a Food Web
Investigation 18
organism cards

Lab Manual 88: Phosphate in Aquatic Ecosystems
Discovery Investigation 18
safety goggles; lab coat or apron; gallon glass jar; pond water; pond plants, such as *Elodea*; pond animals, such as protozoa or *Daphnia*; four 250 mL beakers; high-phosphate detergent solution; eyedropper

Materials List for Biology: Cycles of Life Lab Manual

Lab Manual 89: Mini Ecosystem
safety goggles; lab coat or apron; 10 gallon aquarium with a perforated cover or a wide-mouth, glass gallon jar with a perforated lid; 2 cups gravel; 4 cups soil from a local ecosystem; a few small plants from a local ecosystem; $\frac{1}{2}$ cup water; small beaker or cup; a few small animals from a local ecosystem such as worms or crickets; tap water; ruler

Lab Manual 90: Effects of Light
safety goggles; lab coat or apron; meterstick, stakes, and string; magnifying glass; black plastic trash bags; 3 or 4 small rocks

Chapter 19
Lab Manual 91: Express Lab 19
Express Lab 19
rainwater sample; small jar with lid; forceps; 2 pieces of pH paper; 2 eyedroppers; pH chart; distilled water

Lab Manual 92: Measuring Particulates in the Air
Investigation 19
safety goggles; lab coat or apron; 2 microscope slides; 2 petri dishes; marker; petroleum jelly; 2 petri dish lids; microscope

Lab Manual 93: Greenhouse Gases
safety goggles; lab coat or apron; wax pencil; 2 beakers or jars; 2 small thermometers; 2 labels; plastic wrap; clock or watch; sunny area or sun lamp

Lab Manual 94: Conservation of Soil
Discovery Investigation 19
2 small aluminum pans, each with 6 holes punched in one end; garden soil; large aluminum pan; turf to fit in a small aluminum pan; watering can; graduated cylinder or metric measuring cup; water; 2 or 3 books or wooden boards to raise end of pan

Lab Manual 95: Overpackaging
safety goggles; lab coat or apron; scissors; large bowl; calculator; single serving bag of potato chips; ruler; large bag of potato chips; small bowl

Some Suppliers of Science Education Materials

Carolina Biological Supply Company
2700 York Road
Burlington, NC 27215
800-334-5551
Fax: 800-222-7112
www.carolina.com

Fisher Science Education
4500 Turnberry Drive
Hanover Park, IL 60133
800-955-1177
Fax: 800-955-0740
www.fisheredu.com

NASCO
901 Janesville Avenue
Fort Atkinson, WI 53538
800-558-9595
Fax: 920-563-8296
www.nascofa.com

Sargent-Welch
P.O. Box 5229
Buffalo Grove, IL 60089-5229
800-727-4368
Fax: 800-676-2540
www.sargentwelch.com

Science Kit & Boreal Laboratories
777 E. Park Drive
P. O. Box 5003
Tonawanda, NY 14150
800-828-7777
Fax: 800-828-3299
www.sciencekit.com

Ward's Natural Science Establishment, Inc.
5100 West Henrietta Road
Rochester, NY 14692
800-962-2660
Fax: 800-635-8439
www.wardsci.com